LET'S GO:
FRANCE

is the best book for anyone traveling on a budget. Here's why:

No other guidebook has as many budget listings.

In Paris we list dozens of hotels and hostels for less than $17 a night. In the countryside we found hundreds more. We tell you how to get there the cheapest way, whether by bus, plane, or thumb, and where to get an inexpensive and satisfying meal once you've arrived. There are hundreds of money-saving tips for everyone plus lots of information on student discounts.

LET'S GO researchers have to make it on their own.

Our Harvard-Radcliffe researchers travel on budgets as tight as your own—no expense accounts, no free hotel rooms.

LET'S GO is completely revised every year.

We don't just update the prices, we go back to the places. If a charming café has become an overpriced tourist trap, we'll replace the listing with a new and better one.

No other budget guidebook includes all this:

Coverage of both the cities and the countryside; directions, addresses, phone numbers, and hours to get you there and back; in-depth information on culture, history, and the people; listings on transportation between and within regions and cities; tips on work, study, sights, nightlife, and special splurges; city and regional maps; and much, much more.

LET'S GO is for anyone who wants to see France on a budget.

LET'S GO:

The Budget Guide to

FRANCE

1991

Jennifer L. Schuessler
Editor

Rebecca E. Zorach
Assistant Editor

Written by Harvard Student Agencies, Inc.

PAN BOOKS
London, Sydney and Auckland

Helping Let's Go

If you have suggestions or corrections, or just want to share your discoveries, drop us a line. We read every piece of correspondence, whether a 10-page letter, a postcard, or, as in one case, a collage. All suggestions are passed along to our researcher/writers. Please note that mail received after June 1, 1991 will probably be too late for the 1992 book, but will be retained for the following edition. Address mail to: *Let's Go: France;* Harvard Student Agencies, Inc.; Thayer Hall-B; Harvard University; Cambridge, MA 02138; USA.

In addition to the invaluable travel advice our readers share with us, many are kind enough to offer their services as researchers or editors. Unfortunately, the charter of Harvard Student Agencies, Inc. enables us to employ only currently enrolled Harvard students.

Published in Great Britain 1991 by Pan Books Ltd
Cavaye Place, London SW10 9PG
9 8 7 6 5 4 3 2 1

Published in the United States of America
by St. Martin's Press, Inc.

ISBN: 0 330 31706 7

Let's Go: France is written by Harvard Student Agencies, Inc., Harvard University, Thayer Hall-B, Cambridge, Mass. 02138, USA.

ACKNOWLEDGMENTS

Now that the smoke has cleared, revealing the wreckage of what was once a desk, there seems to be nothing left to do but sincerely thank those coworkers without whom this book never would have been put together and sundry others who helped make this summer the most pleasant nightmare I have ever had.

First, thanks and congratulations are in order for the six indefatigable researchers who poked their collective noses into every corner of France, sending back a few thousand pages of handwritten copy and enough tacky postcards to wallpaper a mid-sized tattoo and massage parlor. Christy Cannon bushwhacked through Brittany, the Loire Valley, and Poitou-Charentes, enduring endless crowds and *crêpes* with unflagging energy and dedication. With a little help from her lovely assistant Theresa, Christy tackled a huge and often inaccessible expanse of territory while missing precious few of those minute details that make editors all warm and mushy inside. Undaunted by the amorous advances of a stray Alpine bull, Brenda Coughlin continued on to Franche-Comté, Burgundy, the Massif Central, and Perigord-Quercy. The *joie de vivre* and humor that shone through in her copy were a great antidote to early morning editorial sluggishness. Becca Dillingham didn't let her difficult Corsica itinerary keep her from 5am boar hunts and feasts of local chestnut pie. Once on the mainland, Rebecca used her considerable knowledge of southwestern France to send back the most comprehensive coverage of Languedoc-Rousillon, Gascony, and the Basque Country ever. When we were looking for a researcher who could handle the wild outbacks of the Channel Islands, Normandy, the North, Champagne, and Alsace-Lorraine and still look elegant in a raincoat and bulky sweater, only Mary Louise Kelly seemed up to the job. Her research was as thorough and her evaluations as carefully considered as her handwriting was legible— and *boy*, was it legible. Veteran researcher Joel Kurtzberg tap-danced his way into every hotel room, campground, museum, nightclub, and petting zoo along the Côte d'Azur before heading inland to the Rhône Valley, Lyon, and Auvergne. When preparing the most thorough copy batches ever to pass an editor's desk, Joel asked every bank for its telephone number, queried after every laundromat's zodiacal sign, and even hitched a ride with some Parisian babes. Debbie Levi, the official *Let's Go* Parisian babe, returned to the City of Lights for the second time, swearing up and down that the copy she laid in place two years ago was perfect but somehow managing to make it better anyway. Although this current Emory grad student (don't bother looking—her number is unlisted) won't be writing for us again, rumor has it that she'll be returning to Paris next summer as the Moulin Rouge's resident feminist theorist.

I never believed those authors and editors who gave their alleged "assistants" the lion's share of the credit until I worked with Rebecca Zorach. With all the fury of a reincarnated Simon de Montfort and considerably more humor than Jerry Lewis, Rebecca hunted down 12th-century Protestants, a 300-year-old Christopher Columbus, variously misplaced Romantics, and countless circon flexes piggybacking the wrong vowels. Those seasoned Francophiles who looked forward to another summer of hooting at our historical gaffes have Rebecca to thank for spoiling their fun, just as I can't thank her enough for generating a lot of mine. Managing editor and housemate Ravi Desai found time between poetasting, eating thatch, chomping cigars, and defending capitalism against flame-throwing barbarians from Illinois to make helpful suggestions and wry comments.

The other editors relegated to the corner of the office without so much as a consoling duncecap—Zan, Ian, Darcy, Liane, Andrew—deserve thanks for the welcome distractions. I am grateful to Jessica Avery for her 11th-hour help, hospitality, and sympathy, as well as her legendary quiet ebullience. Housemates Ben and Gil kept things interesting with countertop-and-colon-corroding salsa and stand up comedy spelled out on the refrigerator each morning. Thanks also to my family, who forgave my infrequent phone calls, and to Katie, Stephanie, Mallay, Marcey, Lisa, Julie, Seth, and anyone else who managed to change the subject when I did call. Finally, a hearty "yo" to the New Kids on the Block, the official *Let's Go* band, who showed us that there are even more ridiculous ways to make a living than working for a travel guide.

—JLS

I am thrilled to have had the opportunity to work with Jenny Schuessler; the unflagging style and wit of her editing made even late-night typing enjoyable. Thanks are due to Ravi Desai for his confidence in us and for his apocalyptic vision, which I hope we have managed to live up to. Without Chris Cowell's patience, good humor, patience, and technical expertise (and patience) this book would not exist. I appreciate the good humor of all of my roommates and *Let's Go*-mates (especially the lucky few at the intersection of those sets!!!); you all made the job easier in lots of big and little ways I wish I had room to mention. Thanks also to the typists and proofreaders who helped out at the last minute. I don't think I would have made it through the summer without Debbie Fass, who shouldered *Advocate* responsibilities and dutifully showed up at the office for ice cream breaks. John H. gave me roses, "particle man," and puzzlement. Greetings to my friends from the Collège Cévenol. Finally, it seems trite in these situations to thank one's parents, but since I so rarely have this opportunity, and since I never thank them enough, well . . . you know what I'm trying to say.

—RZ

About Let's Go

In 1960, Harvard Student Agencies, a three-year-old nonprofit corporation established to provide employment opportunities to Harvard and Radcliffe students, was doing a booming business selling charter flights to Europe. One of the extras HSA offered passengers on these flights was a 20-page mimeographed pamphlet entitled *1960 European Guide,* a collection of tips on continental travel compiled by the staff at HSA. The following year, students traveling to Europe researched the first full-fledged edition of *Let's Go: Europe,* a pocket-sized book with a smattering of tips on budget accommodations, irreverent write-ups of sights, and a decidedly youthful slant. The first editions proclaimed themselves to be the companions of the "adventurous and often impecunious student."

Throughout the 60s, the series reflected its era: a section of the 1968 *Let's Go: Europe* was entitled "Street Singing in Europe on No Dollars a Day;" the 1969 guide to America led off with a feature on drug-ridden Haight-Ashbury. During the 70s, *Let's Go* gradually became a large-scale operation, adding regional European guides and expanding coverage into North Africa and Asia. In 1981, *Let's Go: USA* returned after an eight-year hiatus, and in the next year HSA joined forces with its current publisher, St. Martin's Press. Now in its 31st year, *Let's Go* publishes 13 titles covering more than 40 countries.

Each spring, over 150 Harvard-Radcliffe students compete for some 70 positions as *Let's Go* researcher/writers. Those hired possess a rare combination of budget travel sense, writing ability, stamina, and courage. Each researcher/writer travels on a shoestring budget for seven weeks, researching seven days per week, and overcoming countless obstacles in the quest for better bargains.

Back in a basement in Harvard Yard, an editorial staff of 25, a management team of five, and countless typists and proofreaders—all students—spend four months poring over more than 50,000 pages of manuscript as they push the copy through 12 stages of intensive editing. In September the efforts of summer are converted from computer diskettes to nine-track tapes and delivered to Com Com in Allentown, Pennsylvania, where their computerized typesetting equipment turns them into books in record time. And even before the books hit the stands, next year's editions are well underway.

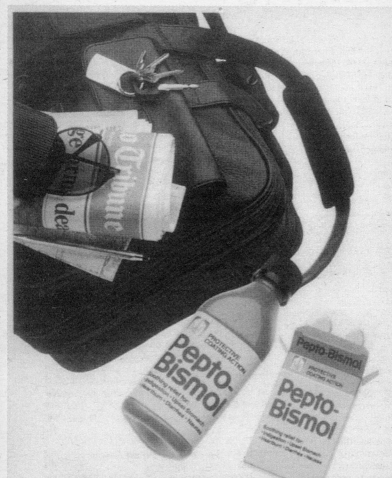

CARRY-ON RELIEF.

CONTENTS

LIST OF MAPS

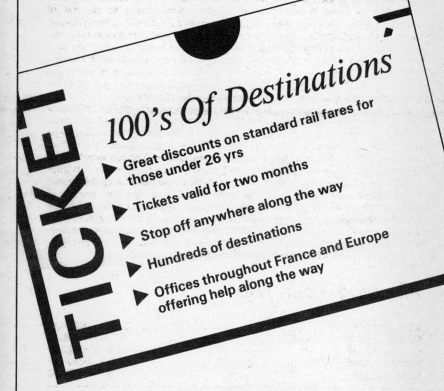

LET'S GO: FRANCE

General Introduction

Monolith of culture, cuisine, fashion, and snobbery to some, France is actually a mosaic of tiny villages, walled medieval cities, seamy ports, and sophisticated Paris. The elusive "real France" lurks in Mediterranean horizons and majestic Alps, the Massif Central's volcanic spires and tangled Breton forests, the vineyards and open fields of Burgundy and Champagne and the caves of the Dordogne. Each region has not only its own geographic personality but also its own culture, its own architectural flourishes, its own *patois* (dialect). Most French people can define themselves as being in some sort of minority with respect to the rest of France—whether they belong to a deeply entrenched traditional culture (Basque, German, Occitan, Breton, Corsican), a religion with an uneasy history in traditionally Catholic France (Protestantism, Judaism, or Islam) or more recent urban infusions of African, Asian, or *Maghrébin* (French North African) culture. France has dozens of vocal political parties and hundreds of kinds of cheese. As you travel in France, be aware that the regions and peoples that make up the Hexagon (so called for the country's rough outline) are by no means homogeneous.

Every so often a book appears that promises to solve the "mystery" of the French and resolve the love-hate relationship that English speakers have had with them for centuries. But perhaps the best way to unravel the mystery is to take advice from fellow Anglophones with a grain of salt and experience France the way its natives do. Budget travelers have a distinct advantage here. You can bicycle down back roads, stay in *foyers* and hostels with French workers and students, buy your bread in local *boulangeries,* and see the sights without constantly being shepherded by an English-speaking guide. *Let's Go* helps you plan your trip with coverage of the formalities of travel, parking, health information, and special concerns. We fill you in on the history, language, literature, and cuisine of France so you can put what you see in context. Our researchers travel on a shoestring; they have been there before you and give you inside information on how to get there, where to stay, how to eat cheaply, and which sights are most worth your time and money.

Planning Your Trip

US$1 = 5.26F	1F = US$0.19
CDN$1 = 4.61F	1F = CDN$0.22
UK£1 = 10.13F	1F = UK£0.10
AUS$1 = 4.28F	1F = AUS$0.23
NZ$1 = 3.29F	1F = NZ$0.30

A Note on Prices and Currency

The information in this book was researched in the summer of 1990. Since then, inflation will have raised most prices at least 10%. The exchange rates listed were compiled on September 1, 1990. Since rates fluctuate considerably, confirm them before you go by checking a national newspaper.

For a successful trip, plan ahead. Research places you'd like to visit, ways to get there, and what to do along the way. Travel is a large industry in France; you will be surprised by how much information is available. Write to the organizations listed in *Let's Go* and request specific information.

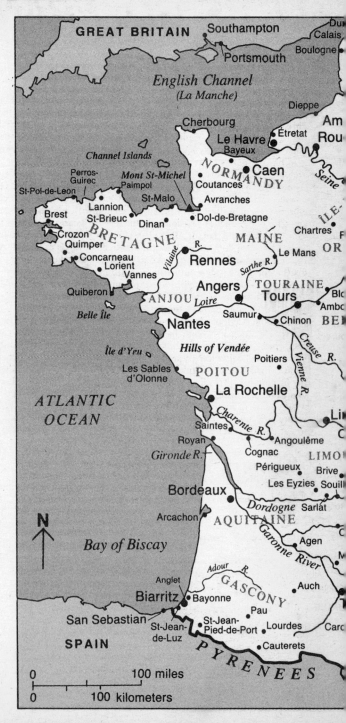

No matter how you do it, remember that traveling shouldn't be a chore. When every city seems to have 1001 points of historical interest, and none of your trains connect with one another, it's easy to forget that a trip is supposed to be *fun*. Avoid letting cathedrals and museums blur into boredom—take a break from the routine of traveling. Go running on the backroads, have a picnic in the park, watch street artists, or spend the afternoon sipping a *citron pressé* while trying to decipher the local newspaper.

Remember that traveling during the off-season cuts costs. Fall wine harvests, skiing in the Alps, and springtime in Paris are some of the enticements of non-summer travel. Airfares are lower, and flying standby is simple (except around major holidays). You also don't have to compete with hordes of summer tourists flocking to establishments and driving up prices. Off-season travel does, however, have its drawbacks. Winters in France are usually mild, but the frequent rain and overcast skies can dampen more than just your spirits. Many hostels and some hotels close down, and museums and tourist offices keep shorter hours. If you do travel in summer, remember that France goes on vacation in July and August. Getting anywhere during peak weekends is difficult. You should reserve seats on trains and try to book accommodations in advance.

Useful Organizations and Publications

Research your trip early. The government and private agencies listed below will provide useful information.

Tourist Offices

All large cities in France have an **Office de Tourisme.** Smaller French towns that attract a significant number of visitors have a tax-supported office called the **Syndicat d'Initiative** to provide information on the town and the surrounding area. Since these offices have the same purpose and France is in the process of merging these bureaucratically different offices, *Let's Go* lists both as "Tourist Offices." Write to the French Government Tourist Office for information on tourism, culture, lodging, and activities particular to specific areas.

Cultural Services of the French Embassy, 972 Fifth Ave., New York, NY 10021 (tel. (212) 439-1400). General information about France including culture, student employment, and educational possibilities.

French Government Tourist Office: U.S., 610 Fifth Ave., New York, NY 10020-2452; 645 N. Michigan Ave., #630, Chicago, IL 60611; 9454 Wilshire Blvd. #303, Beverly Hills, CA 90212-2967 (tel. nationwide (900) 420-2003). **Canada,** 1981 av. McGill College, #490, Montreal, Que. H3A 2W9 (tel. (514) 288-4264); 1 Dundas St. W., #2405 Box 8, Toronto, Ont. M5G 1Z3 (tel. (416) 593-4717). **Australia,** c/o UTA, Kindersley House, 33 Bligh St., Sydney NSW 2000 (tel. (612) 233 32 77). **U.K.,** 178 Piccadilly, London W1V OAL (tel. (1) 629 12 72). Write for information on any region of France, festival dates, and tips for disabled travelers.

Consulates

U.S., 3 Commonwealth Ave., Boston, MA 02116 (tel. (617) 266-1680); Visa Section, 20 Park Plaza, Statler Bldg., 6th floor, Boston, MA 02116 (tel. (617) 451-6755); 540 Bush St., San Francisco, CA 94108 (tel. (415) 397-4330); 934 Fifth Ave., New York, NY 10021 (tel. (212) 606-3688). There are also consulates in Detroit, Honolulu, Houston, Los Angeles, and Miami.

Canada, 2 Elysée Pl., Bonaventura, Montreal B.P. 202, Que. H5A 1B1 (tel. (514) 878-4381).

U.K., 21 Cromwell Rd., London SW7 2DQ (tel. 581 5292). **Visa Section,** 6A Cromwell Pl., London SW7 2JN (tel. 823 9555).

Australia, 291 George St., Sydney NSW 2000 (tel. 29 47 78 or 29 47 79).

Travel Services

Council on International Educational Exchange (CIEE)/Council Travel, 205 E. 42nd St., New York, NY 10017 (tel. (212) 661-1414; charter flights (800) 223-7402, in NY (212) 661-

1450). Write, call, or visit for information on low-cost travel, educational, volunteer, and work opportunities. Sells the Eurailpass/Youthpass and hostel cards. Discount fares on major airlines. Issues ISIC and International Youth Card (for non-students under 26). They also publish *Work Abroad* (free), *Work, Study, Travel Abroad: The Whole World Handbook* (US$10.95, postage $1), *Volunteer! The Comprehensive Guide to Voluntary Service in the U.S. and Abroad* (US$6.95, postage $1), and *Emplois d'Eté en France* (US$12.95, postage $1). Branch offices throughout the U.S.

Educational Travel Center (ETC), 438 N. Frances St., Madison, WI 53703 (tel. (608) 256-5551). Flight information, IYHF (AYH) membership cards, railpasses. Write or call for a free copy of their travel newspaper *Taking Off.*

Let's Go Travel Services, Harvard Student Agencies, Inc., Thayer Hall-B, Harvard University, Cambridge, MA 02138 (tel. (617) 495-9649). Sells Railpasses, American Youth Hostel memberships (valid at all IYHF youth hostels), International Student and Teacher ID cards, YIEE cards for nonstudents, travel guides and maps (including the *Let's Go* series), discount airfares and a complete line of budget travel gear. All items are available by mail; call or write for a catalog.

Société Nationale de Chemins de Fer (SNCF), 610 Fifth Ave., New York, NY 10020 (tel. (212) 582-2816). French national railway. Stocks schedules and maps of train routes throughout France and Europe. Information on railpasses. Hard-to-reach **FrenchRail**, an agent for the SNCF in the U.S., stocks information on railpasses and travel in France and neighboring regions. 226-230 Westchester Ave., White Plains, NY (tel. (800) 848-7245).

Travel CUTS (Canadian Universities Travel Service), 187 College St., Toronto, Ont. M5T 1P7 (tel. (416) 979-2406). Offices throughout Canada; in London, 295-A Regent St. (tel. (071) 255 1944). Sells discounted transatlantic flights, the ISIC, International Youth Card, and also runs the Canadian Work Abroad Programme. Sells the Eurailpass/Youthpass. Arranges adventure tours and work abroad. Their newspaper, *The Canadian Student Traveler,* is free at all offices and on campuses across Canada.

International Student Exchange Flights (ISE Flights), 5010 E. Shea Blvd., #A104, Scottsdale, AZ 85254 (tel. (602) 951-1177). Budget student flights on major regularly scheduled airlines. International Student Exchange ID cards and railpasses.

International Student Travel Conference (ISTC), Weimbergerstrasse 31, CH-8006 Zurich, Switzerland (tel. (411) 262 29 96). In the US, they are represented by CIEE. In Canada: Travel CUTS (see address above). In the UK: London Student Travel, 52 Grosvenor Gardens, London WC1 England (tel. (071) 730 34 02). In Australia: STA/SSA, 222 Faraday St., Melbourne, Victoria 3053, Australia (tel. (03) 347 69 11). In New Zealand: Student Travel, 2nd Floor, Courtenay Chambers, 15 Courtenay, Wellington (tel. (04) 85 05 61). Issues ISICs.

STA Travel, a worldwide youth travel organization, offers bargain flights, railpasses, accommodations, tours, insurance, and ISICs. 10 offices in the U.S. including 17 E. 45th St., #805, New York, NY 10017 (tel. (212) 986-9470 or (800) 777-0112) and 7202 Melrose Ave., Los Angeles, CA 90046 (tel. (213) 934-8722). In the UK, STA's main office is at 74 and 86 Old Brompton Rd., London SW7 3LQ England (tel. (071) 937 99 21 for European travel; (01) 937 99 71 for North American.

Publications

Forsyth Travel Library, 9154 W. 57th St., P.O. Box 2975, Shawnee Mission, KS 66201 (tel. (913) 384-3440 or (800) FORSYTH (367-7984)). A mail-order service that stocks a wide range of city, area, and country maps, as well as guides for rail and ferry travel in Europe. Sole North American distributor of the Thomas Cook *European Timetable* for trains, a guide covering all of Europe and Britain which Eurailpass holders may find essential (US$19.95, postage $3). Write for free catalog and newsletter.

John Muir Publications, P.O. Box 613, Sante Fe, NM 87504 (tel. (505) 982-4078) or (800) 888-7504. Publishes 3 books by veteran traveler Rick Steves. *Europe through the Back Door,* revised spring 1990 (US$14.95), offers good advice, especially on traveling light and avoiding tourist traps. *Europe in 22 Days* (US$7.95) provides a 3-week itinerary for those who want to see the essential Europe. *Europe 101: History, Art and Culture for the Traveler* (US$12.95) is excessively simplistic.

Press and Information Division of the French Embassy, 4101 Reservoir Rd. NW, Washington, DC 20007 (tel. (202) 944-6060). Write for information about employment and political, social, and economic life.

Superintendent of Documents, U.S. Government Printing Office, Washington, DC 20402 (tel. (202) 783-3238). Publishes helpful booklets including *Your Trip Abroad* (US$1), *Safe Trip Abroad* (US$1), and *Health Information for International Travel* (US$4.75).

Wide World Books & Maps, 1911 N. 45th St., Seattle, WA 98105 (tel. (206) 634-3453). Useful, free catalog listing the most recent guidebooks to every part of the world.

Documents and Formalities

Remember to file all applications several weeks or even months before your planned departure date. A backlog at any agency could spoil even the best-laid plans.

Passports

You need a valid passport to enter France and to re-enter your own country. Apply well in advance. Most offices suggest that you apply in the winter off-season for speedy service.

U.S. citizens over age 17 may apply for a 10-year U.S. passport at one of the several thousand Federal courts or U.S. post offices that accept passport applications, or at any one of the 13 Passport Agencies, which are located in Boston, Chicago, Honolulu, Houston, Los Angeles, Miami, New Orleans, New York, Philadelphia, San Francisco, Seattle, Stamford, and Washington, DC. Those under 18 can obtain a five-year passport. Parents must apply in person for children under age 13. If this is your first U.S. passport, if you are under 18, or if your current passport is more than 12 years old or was issued before your 16th birthday, you must apply in person. Otherwise, you can renew by mail for US$35.

For a U.S. passport you must submit the following documents: (1) a completed application form; (2) proof of U.S. citizenship, which can be your original birth certificate or a certified copy, naturalization papers, or a previous passport issued no more than 12 years ago; (3) identification bearing your signature and either your photo or personal description, e.g., an unexpired driver's license or passport; and (4) two identical, recent, passport-sized photographs. If you are renewing by mail, your old passport will serve as both (2) and (3); do not forget to enclose it with your application. To obtain or renew a passport when ineligible for application by mail, bring items (1-4) and US$42 (ages under 18 US$27) in the form of a check (cashier's, traveler's, certified, or personal) or money order. Passport agencies will accept cash in the exact amount, but post offices and courts may not. The Passport Service also requests that you write your birth date on your check.

Processing usually takes two to three weeks (longer through a court or post office), but it's best to apply several months early. If you are leaving within five working days, the passport office can provide express service while you wait, but you must have valid proof of your departure date (e.g., an airline ticket) and arrive early at the office. For more details, call the U.S. Passport Information's 24-hour recording (tel. (202) 647-0518) or write to the Washington Passport Agency, 1425 K St. NW, Washington, DC 20522-1705 (tel. (202) 326-6060).

Canadian citizens must present their passport application in person at one of the 21 regional offices (addresses are in the telephone directory) or mail it to the Passport Office, Department of External Affairs, Ottawa, Ont. K1A 0G3. Passport applications are available from passport offices, post offices, and travel agencies. Passport requirements include (1) a completed application; (2) original documentary evidence of Canadian citizenship; (3) two identical photographs, both signed by the holder, and one certified by a "guarantor," of an approved profession (e.g., lawyer, mayor, medical doctor, notary public, *Let's Go* editor) who has known you for at least two years; and (4) proof of identity in the form of a Canadian passport, certificate of identity, or refugee travel document in which the name of the applicant appears. Children may be included on a parent's passport; they also need proof of Canadian citizenship. The fee is CDN$25 and may be paid in cash, money order, certified check, or bank draft. Passports normally require three to five working days at a regional office; mailed applications require two weeks from the day the application is received. There is no rush service. A Canadian passport is valid for five years. For more information, consult the booklet *Bon Voyage, But . . .* , available free from the Passport Office and at Canadian airports. Canadian citizens residing in the U.S. should apply at a Canadian consulate.

There are two types of **British** passport. The **Visitor's Passport** is available over-the-counter at main post offices; you must bring two photos and identification. It is valid for travel to Western Europe for one year and costs £7.50. For a **Full British Passport**, you may apply by mail or at any one of the passport offices in London, Liverpool, Newport, Peterborough, Glasgow, and Belfast. You need a completed application, your birth certificate and marriage certificate (if applicable), and two identical copies of recent photos signed by a guarantor. The fee is £15 for a 10-year adult passport (5 years if under age 16). A spouse who does not have a separate passport, and children under 16, may be included on one person's passport. The application process averages four weeks.

Australian citizens must apply in person at a local post office or a passport office (usually located in the provincial capital). You need an application, two passport-sized photos signed by a guarantor, proof of citizenship, and proof of identity. The fee (changed four times a year) is AUS$76, and the passport is valid for 10 years. Those under 18 can get a five-year passport for AUS$31. Consult the local post office for more information. Before leaving Australia you must buy an AUS$10 Departure Tax Stamp at a post office or airport (children under 12 exempt). For more information, call toll-free (in Australia) (008) 02 6022.

New Zealanders must contact their local passport office or consulate for an application which may be filed in person or by mail. Evidence of identity and New Zealand citizenship and two passport-sized photos signed by a friend must accompany your application. The fee for a 10-year passport (5 years if under age 18, though children may be included on parents' passports up to age 16) is NZ$50. The application process normally requires three weeks, but the office will speed up processing in an emergency. For more information, write to Department of Internal Affairs (Passports Head Office), Private Bag, Wellington (tel. 738 699).

Be sure to record your passport number in a separate, safe place, and photocopy the pages with your photograph and visas in case of loss or theft. These precautions will help prove your citizenship and facilitate the issuing of a new passport if needed. Notify the nearest embassy or consulate and the local police immediately if your passport is lost or stolen. Registering with the nearest embassy or consulate is wise if you intend an extended stay in France. The U.S. consulate can usually issue new passports, given proof of citizenship, within two hours. In an emergency, ask for an immediate temporary passport.

Bring two extra pieces of identification when traveling abroad. A second proof of citizenship can be anything from your birth certificate to a driver's license. Keep these items separate from your passport. A few extra passport-type photos can also come in handy if you lose your passport or decide to apply for a visa. For a complete list of all U.S. embassies, consulates, consulates general, and missions abroad, write or call the Superintendent of Documents (see above) for the pamphlet *Key Officers of Foreign Serving Posts* (updated 3 times per year, US$5 per year or $1.75 for a single copy).

Visas

Visas are currently required of all visitors to France, except those from the U.S., Canada, Western Europe, and South Korea. A visa is an endorsement or stamp placed in your passport by a foreign government allowing you to visit that country for a specified purpose and period of time. For more details write to Consumer Information Center, Department 455W, Pueblo, CO 81009, for *Foreign Visa Requirements* (US50¢).

Requirements for a long-stay visa vary with the nature of the stay: work, study, or *au pair*. Apply to the nearest French Consulate at least three months in advance. For a **student visa** you must present a passport valid at least 60 days after the date you plan to leave France, an application with references, a passport photo, a letter

of admission from a French university or a study abroad program, a notarized guarantee of financial support, and a fee which fluctuates according to the exchange rate (currently US$9). To obtain a **work visa,** you must first obtain a work permit. After getting a job and a work contract from your French employer, your employer will obtain this permit for you and will forward it with a copy of your work contract to the Consulate nearest you. After a medical checkup and completion of the application, the visa will be issued on your valid passport. Note, however, that it is illegal for foreign students to work during the school year, although they can receive permission from their local *Direction départementale du travail et de la main-d'oeuvre étrangère* to work in summer. An **au pair's visa** can be obtained within two weeks by submission of a valid passport, two completed application forms, two passport photos, US$15, a medical exam, the original copy of the *au pair*'s work contract signed by the *au pair,* and proof of admission to a language school or university program.

Those staying longer than 90 days in France must obtain a **carte de séjour** (residency permit). You must present a valid passport, six application forms completed in French, six passport photos, a letter of financial guarantee, and, if you're under 18, proof of parental authorization; you must also undergo a medical exam. To obtain the *carte de séjour,* report to the local *préfecture* (district office) immediately after arrival, and be prepared to wait in line repeatedly.

Student and Youth Identification

The **International Student Identity Card (ISIC)** (US$10) is an internationally recognized proof of student status. If you have a student ID from a school in France or from your home country, it will usually qualify you for the same discounts on train and theater tickets and on admission to museums, historical sites, and festivals. The ISIC offers other benefits including lower fares on many forms of transportation, local and international—it's essential if you plan to use student charter flights or clubs. The card incorporates the International Union of Students card. If you purchase the card in the U.S., it also provides you with US$3000 medical/accident insurance and US$100 per day for up to 60 days in case of in-hospital illness.

To apply, submit the following: (1) current, dated proof of student status (a photocopy of your school ID showing this year's date, a letter on school stationery signed and sealed by the registrar, or a photocopied grade report); (2) a 1½ × 2-inch photo with your name printed in pencil on the back; (3) proof of your birthdate and nationality. The card is valid from September 1 through December 31 of the next year. If you are about to graduate, you can still get a card by proving student status during the same calendar year. You cannot purchase a new card in January unless you were in school during the fall semester.

If you will be studying at a French university, you will be given a **carte d'étudiant** (student card) by the enrollment office at your school upon presentation of a receipt for your university fees and your residency permit.

If you're not a student but are under age 26, inquire about other youth discounts. The **Federation of International Youth Travel Organizations (FIYTO)** issues the **International Youth Card** to anyone under age 26. The card is internationally recognized and gives you access to over 8000 discounts on international and intra-European transport, accommodations, restaurants, cultural activities, and tours. Applications must include a passport number, proof of age, a passport-sized photo and a certified check or money order for US$14. For further information and an application, write to FIYTO, Islands Brygge 81, DK-2300 Copenhagen S, Denmark (tel. (31) 54 60 80). CIEE offices, Travel CUTS, STA, and agencies all over Europe issue the FIYTO card.

International Driver's License

An International Driving Permit (essentially a translation of your driver's license into 9 languages) is not usually required to drive in France, but is recommended if you don't speak French. Most rental agencies will not ask to see the permit but will want to see a valid driver's license. The permit is available at any branch of

DISCOUNTS
Aren't Just For Students Anymore!

The International Youth Card

If you are under 26, you're eligible for the International Youth Card. So even though you are not a student, you can get:

- Low-priced youth airfares
- Sickness and accident insurance
- Discounts on travel, museum admissions, accommodations, and more
- 24-hour international toll-free hotline for help in medical, legal, and financial emergencies

You must be under 26 years of age to be eligible for the International Youth Card, which is valid from January 1, 1991 to December 31, 1991.

FREE GUIDE!

With your Card you will receive a free guide with more information: discounts around the world on airfares, accommodations, museums, theaters, and rail, bus, and boat tickets.

For more information and an application, call any of 31 Council Travel offices across the U.S. (see our ad in this section), or contact one of our regional offices:

Council on International Educational Exchange
CIEE-ISS Dept. 205 E. 42nd Street, New York, NY 10017 (212) 661-1414

Council Travel Regional Offices

729 Boylston St. #201	2000 Guadalupe St.	1153 N. Dearborn St.	919 Irving St. #102
Boston, MA 02116	Austin, TX 78705	Chicago, IL 60610	San Francisco, CA 94122
(617) 266-1926	(512) 472-4931	(312) 951-0585	(415) 566-6222

the **American Automobile Association** or at the main office, AAA Travel Agency Services, 1000 AAA Drive, Heathrow, FL 32746-5063 (tel. (407) 444-7000 or (800) 556-1166). It is also available from the **Canadian Automobile Association (CAA)**, 2 Carlton St., Toronto, Ont. M5B 1K4 (tel. (416) 964-3170). You will need a completed application, two recent passport-sized photos, a valid U.S. (or Canadian) driver's license (which must always accompany the International Driving Permit), and US$10. You must be over 18 to apply.

If you are going to drive, buy, or borrow a car that is not insured, you will need an **International Insurance Certificate,** or **green card,** to prove you have liability insurance. If you are renting or leasing, you must get the green card (and the coverage too, if your insurance does not apply abroad) from the rental agency or dealer.

Customs

Customs often evoke more alarm than they should. Visitors have an allowance of what they can bring into the country. Anything exceeding the allowance is charged a duty. Upon reentering your own country, you must declare all articles acquired abroad. Keep receipts from all your purchases. If you are bringing into France more than 200 cigarettes, 2ℓ of wine, 1ℓ of alcohol over 38.8 proof, or 50g of perfume, you must declare such items.

Before leaving, **U.S. citizens** should record the serial numbers of expensive (especially foreign-made) items that will accompany you abroad. Have this list stamped by the Customs Office before you leave. U.S. citizens may bring in US$400 worth of goods duty-free but must pay a 10% duty on the next US$1000 worth, and variable rates above that. The duty-free goods must be for personal or household use and cannot include more than 100 cigars or 200 cigarettes (1 carton) and 1ℓ of wine or liquor. You must be 21 or older to bring liquor into the U.S. These items may not be shipped. Exemptions of persons traveling together may be combined.

Non-prescription drugs and narcotics, many foods, plant and animal products, and other harmful items, including pornography and lottery tickets, may not be imported into the U.S. Similar restrictions apply in many other countries. Write for the U.S. Customs Service's brochure, *Know Before You Go* (free), U.S. Customs Service, 1301 Constitution Ave., Washington, DC 20229 (tel. (202) 566-8195). To avoid problems when carrying prescription drugs, make sure the bottles are clearly marked, and have the prescription ready to show the customs officer. *Travelers' Tips on Bringing Food, Plant, and Animal Products into the United States* is available from the Animal and Plant Health Inspection Service, U.S. Department of Agriculture, Attn: ¬ublic Information, Washington, DC 20250. They also provide information on restrictions in the wildlife trade.

While in Europe, you can mail unsolicited gifts back to the U.S. duty-free if they're worth less than US$50. Mark the package "unsolicited gift" and indicate the nature of the gift and its retail value. Again, you may not mail liquor, tobacco, or perfume into the U.S. If you send back a parcel worth over US$50, the Postal Service will collect the duty plus a handling charge when it is delivered. If you mail home personal goods of U.S. origin, mark the package "American goods returned."

Before departure, **Canadian citizens** should identify or list the serial numbers of all valuables on a Y-38 form at the Customs Office or point of departure; these goods can then be reimported duty-free. Once every year after seven days' absence, you can bring in goods up to a value of CDN$300. After any two-day absence, you can bring in goods up to a value of CDN$100. These two allowances may not be claimed on the same trip. Duty-free goods may not include more than 50 cigars, 200 cigarettes, 1kg of tobacco, or 1.1 ℓ of alcohol. The minimum age to import tobacco is 16; the age for liquor varies by province. Anything above the duty-free allowance is charged a 20% tax. Shipped items will be taxed at a higher rate and may not include alcohol or tobacco products. You can send gifts up to a value of CDN$40 duty-free, but again, you cannot mail alcohol or tobacco. Canadians traveling to or from Europe via the U.S. should also note that pain-killers containing codeine—available over-the-counter in Canada—are illegal in the U.S. For more information, get the pamphlet *I Declare,* available from the Revenue Canada Customs and Excise Department, Communications Branch, Mackenzie Ave., Ottawa, Ont. K1A 0L5.

Americans and Canadians must declare any items bought at **duty-free shops** abroad with your other purchases. "Duty-free" means only that you didn't pay taxes in the country of purchase. When you return from abroad, you may also run into trouble with clothing or jewelry of foreign make that you originally purchased in North America. You must be able to prove their origin with purchase receipts or identifying marks.

Returning **British citizens** are allowed an exemption of up to £32 of goods. This includes not more than 100 cigarettes; 100 cigarillos; 50 cigars; 250g tobacco; and 2 ℓ of still table wine plus 1 ℓ of alcohol over 22% by volume, or 2 ℓ of alcohol not over 22% by volume. Allowances are about 50% higher for goods obtained tax- and duty-paid in the European Community. You must be 18 or over to import liquor or tobacco.

If you are an **Australian citizen,** your allowance upon returning home is 250g of tobacco (equivalent to 250 cigarettes) and 1 ℓ of alcohol. Customs Form B263 allows you to reimport your own valuables duty-free. The duty-free allowance is AUS$400 (under 18 AUS$200). Goods above the limit will be taxed and may not include tobacco, alcohol, or furs and must be carried into the country with you. You may not export more than AUS$5000 in cash without permission from the Reserve Bank of Australia. You may mail back personal property; mark it "Australian goods returned" to avoid duty. For additional information, consult the brochure *Customs Information for All Travellers,* available at an Australian Consulate or offices of the Collector of Customs.

New Zealand citizens list goods they're taking with them on a Certificate of Export. The duty-free allowance is NZ$500 (children included). Those over age 16 may bring in 200 cigarettes, 250g of tobacco, or 50 cigars, or a combination of the three not weighing more than 250g; 4.5 ℓ of wine or beer; and 1.125 ℓ of spirits or liqueur. You may not, however, import raw egg, azaleas, birds' nests or homemade noodles. There are no restrictions on the amount of New Zealand currency

More Than One Million Students Get It... Shouldn't You?

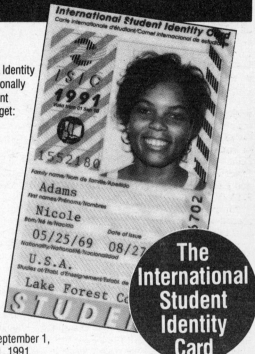

Beware of imitations!
The International Student Identity Card is the ONLY internationally recognized proof of student status. With the card you get:

- Low student airfares
- Sickness and accident insurance
- Discounts on travel, museum admissions, accommodations, and more
- 24-hour international toll-free hotline for help in medical, legal, and financial emergencies

Students 12 years of age and over are eligible for the Card, which is valid from September 1, 1990 through December 31, 1991.

The International Student Identity Card

——— FREE GUIDE! ———

With your Card you will receive a free guide with more information: discounts around the world on airfares, accommodations, museums, theaters, and rail, bus, and boat tickets.

For more information and an application, call any of 31 Council Travel offices across the U.S. (see our ad in this section), or contact one of our regional offices:

Council on International Educational Exchange
CIEE-ISS Dept. 205 E. 42nd Street, New York, NY 10017 (212) 661-1414

——— Council Travel Regional Offices ———

729 Boylston St. #201 Boston, MA 02116 (617) 266-1926	2000 Guadalupe St. Austin, TX 78705 (512) 472-4931	1153 N. Dearborn St. Chicago, IL 60610 (312) 951-0585	919 Irving St. #102 San Francisco, CA 94122 (415) 566-6222

that may be brought into or taken out of New Zealand. For more information, contact the New Zealand Customs Department for the *New Zealand Customs Guide for Travellers.*

Money

Currency and Exchange

The basic unit of currency in France is the franc, also divided into 100 centimes, and issued in both coins and paper notes. The smallest unit of French currency is the five-centime piece. The new franc, equal to 100 old francs, was issued in 1960. Old habits die hard, though, especially in the provinces, so if an elderly waiter or waitress demands "mille (1000) francs" for two cups of coffee, relax—10F should cover it.

When changing money, it pays to compare rates. Banks often offer the best rates, but usually charge a commission which can be as much as US$3. Large, local banks or national ones, such as **Crédit Agricole** or **Crédit Lyonnais,** have competitive rates and charge the smallest commission. Avoid exchanging money at hotels, airports, train stations, or restaurants; their convenient hours and locations allow them to offer less favorable exchange rates. To minimize losses, exchange fairly large sums at one time, though never more than is safe to carry around. Be sure to procure enough cash to carry you through weekends, holidays, and side trips in isolated areas. Before leaving home, convert US$50 or so into French bills; this will save you time at the airport.

Traveler's Checks

Toting about large amounts of cash, even in a moneybelt, is risky. Traveler's checks are the safest and least troublesome means of carrying funds. Several agencies and many banks sell them, usually for face value plus a 1-2% commission. American Express checks are perhaps the most widely recognized, though other major checks are sold, exchanged, cashed, and refunded with almost equal ease. Each agency provides refunds if your checks are lost or stolen, and many provide additional services. (Note that you may need a police report verifying the loss or theft.) Inquire about toll-free refund hotlines, emergency message relay services, and stolen credit card assistance when you purchase your checks.

You should expect a fair amount of red tape and delay in the event of theft or loss. To expedite the refund process, separate your check receipts and keep them in a safe place. To help identify which checks are missing, record check numbers when you cash them and leave a list of check numbers with someone at home. When you buy your checks, ask for a list of refund centers. American Express and Bank of America have over 40,000 centers worldwide. Most importantly, keep a separate supply of cash or traveler's checks for emergencies.

Buy most of your checks in large denominations (US$50 or US$100) to avoid spending too much time in line at banks. A few checks in small denominations (US$10 or US$20) will minimize losses when you must settle for unfavorable exchange rates.

Finally, consider purchasing traveler's checks in francs. While U.S. citizens can easily exchange dollars for francs in France, New Zealanders and Australians may have difficulty exchanging their currencies. Dealing with double exchange rates (such as Canadian to U.S. dollars and then U.S. dollars to francs) can be expensive. If you buy traveler's checks in French francs at a favorable exchange rate, you don't have to worry as much later about where to exchange money (though you may still be charged commissions); however, if you buy them at an unfavorable rate, you're stuck with it.

American Express (tel. in the U.S. and Canada (800) 221-7282, collect from elsewhere (44 27) 357 16 00; in France, (1905) 90 86 00). Available in 7 currencies. Many offices will cash personal checks up to US$1000, assist in replacing missing travel documents, arrange temporary IDs, and help make airline, hotel, and car rental reservations. 1% commission. AAA

Don't forget to write.

If your American Express® Travelers Cheques are lost or stolen, we can hand-deliver a refund virtually anywhere you travel. Just give us a call. You'll find it's a lot less embarrassing than calling home.

offers AmEx traveler's checks to members without commission. AmEx maintains a Global Assist hotline for travel emergencies ((800) 554-AMEX or collect (202) 783-7474).

Bank of America (tel. in the U.S. (800) 227-3460, collect from elsewhere (415) 624-5400). Checks available in U.S. dollars only. Normally charges a 1% commission. A free booklet lists over 40,000 refund offices worldwide. Checkholders get access to a Travel Assistance hotline (tel. in the U.S. (800) 368-7878, collect from elsewhere (202) 347-7113). Hotline offers services including free legal and medical assistance, urgent message relay, lost document services, translator/interpreter referral, and up to US$1000 advance to a medical facility to ensure prompt treatment.

Visa (tel. in the U.S. and Canada (800) 227-6811, collect from the U.K. (01) 937 80 91, collect from elsewhere (415) 574-7111). Checks available in U.S. and Canadian dollars and 11 other currencies. 1% commission. The many banks issuing Visa traveler's checks include **Barclays Bank** (tel. in the U.S. and Canada during business hours (800) 221-2426; for lost or stolen traveler's checks (800) 227-6811 in the U.S., U.S. possessions and Canada; collect from the U.K. (01) 937 80 91; collect from elsewhere (415) 574-7111 or (212) 406-4200). Checks available in U.S. and Canadian dollars and British pounds. Many locations, including branches in the British Airways terminals at Kennedy and Heathrow Airports. For other locations write to Barclays, 54 Lombard St., London EC3P 3AH; or P.O. Box 2853, Church St. Station, New York, NY 10008.

Citicorp (tel. in the U.S. (800) 645-6556, collect from elsewhere (813) 623-1709). Checks available in U.S. dollars, British pounds, deutschmarks, and Japanese yen at banks throughout the U.S. 1% commission. Checkholders are automatically enrolled for 45 days in Travel Assist Hotline (tel. (800) 523-1199), a slightly abridged version of Europ Assistance Worldwide's Travel Assist program.

MasterCard International (tel. in the U.S. (800) 223-7373, collect from elsewhere (212) 974-5696). Traveler's checks available in 11 currencies at many banks and from **Thomas Cook** (tel. same as Mastercard). Checks available in U.S. and Canadian dollars, British pounds, and 8 other currencies at Thomas Cook offices and at banks displaying the MasterCard sign. 1% commission.

Credit Cards

Although many low-cost establishments don't accept plastic, credit cards can be invaluable in an emergency. With major credit cards, you can obtain an instant cash advance in local currency as large as your remaining credit line from banks honoring the card. This is a real boon, especially if your traveler's checks or cash are lost or stolen, and it may be your only source of cash, as many traveler's check vendors will not cash personal checks and transatlantic money cables take at least 48 hours. Visa has increased its number of foreign offices; its cards are accepted at over 6000 automated teller machines throughout Europe. You can withdraw up to US$300 per day in the local currency until you reach your cash advance limit.

American Express Travel Service (tel. (800) 221-7282) has offices in 120 countries and will cash personal checks up to US$1000 every seven days (US$200 in cash and the rest in traveler's checks) and up to US$5000 for gold card holders. In addition, American Express operates 19,000 automated teller machines worldwide, where cardmembers can get up to US$1000 (US$500 in cash and US$500 in traveler's checks); call (800) CASH NOW (227-4669) for more information. It takes about two weeks to enroll and receive a PIN number in order to withdraw money from international ATMs.

The card also allows you to use American Express offices as mailing addresses for free; otherwise you may have to pay (or show your Amex traveler's checks) to pick up your mail. American Express offices abroad will also wire the U.S. to replace cards that have been lost or stolen. The *Traveler's Companion,* a list of full-service offices worldwide, is available from American Express, 65 Broadway, New York, NY 10006.

If a family member already has a card it's easy to get joint-account cards. American Express will issue an extra green card for US$30 per year or an extra gold card for US$35 (bills go to your loved ones). Fees for Visa and MasterCard joint-account cards vary from bank to bank. You might not have to pay extra, but you may be given a very low credit limit.

When looking for places in France that will accept your card, remember that MasterCard is often called Eurocard, and Visa the Carte Bleue. Look for the familiar cheery logos rather than the names.

Sending Money

Sending money overseas is costly and often frustrating. Do your best to avoid it. Carry a credit card or a separate stash of traveler's checks for emergencies.

The quickest and cheapest way to have money sent is to tell your home bank, by mail or telegram, the amount you need in what currency and the name and address of the bank to which it should be cabled (preferably the office of a large French bank with many regional branches). This service takes about 24 hours, a bit longer in small cities, and costs US$15-80. It is possible to arrange to have your home bank send you money at specified periods, but the procedure is cumbersome and confusing, and most banks are reluctant to do it.

Sending money through a company such as **American Express** costs about as much as sending it through a bank. Normally, the sender must have an American Express card, but certain offices will waive this requirement for a commission. The money is guaranteed to arrive within 72 hours at the designated overseas office, where it will be held. It costs US$45 to send US$500 and US$70 to send US$1000, with a US$10,000 limit. The money will be disbursed in traveler's checks. This service operates only between American Express offices proper, not their representatives; call (800) 543-4080.

Western Union offers a convenient service for cabling money abroad, though it covers only 20 or so cities in France. In the U.S., call Western Union any time at (800) 325-6000 to cable up to US$3000 with your **Visa** or **MasterCard.** No money orders are accepted. It costs US$59 to send US$500 and $69 for $1000. The money will arrive at the target city's central telegram office and can be retrieved with proper identification. The cabled money is handled by Citibank in France and should arrive in francs within two to five business days. It is generally held 14 days after which it will be returned to the sender minus the fee.

In emergencies, U.S. citizens can have money sent via the **Citizen's Emergency Center,** Department of State, 2201 C St. NW, #4811, Washington, DC 20520 (tel. (202) 647-5225; at night and on Sundays and holidays, (202) 647-4000). The center serves only Americans in the direst of straits abroad, and prefers not to send sums greater than US$500. The quickest way to have the money sent is to cable the State Department through Western Union or to leave cash, a certified check, a bank draft, or a money order at the department itself.

Value-Added Tax

Value-Added Tax (in France, abbreviated T.V.A.) is a varying sales tax levied especially in the European Economic Community. The French rate is 18.6% on all goods except books, food, and medicine. There is a 33% luxury tax on such items as video cassettes, watches, jewelry, and cameras.

If you spend more than 1200F in a particular store, you can participate in a complex over-the-counter export program for foreign shoppers that exempts you from paying T.V.A. Ask the store for a duplicate pink sales invoice (*facture*) and a stamped envelope. At the border, show the invoices and your purchases to the French customs officials, who will stamp the invoices. On a train, be sure to find an official (they won't find you) or get off at a station close to the border. Then send a copy back to the vendor. With this official T.V.A.-exempt proof, they will refund the agreed amount. The refunds are usually sent to your bank account and not your address. You must take the goods out of the country with you within three months of purchase.

Keeping in Touch

Mail

Between major cities in France and the east coast of the U.S., air mail takes five to 10 days and is fairly dependable. Send mail from the largest post office in the area. Surface (*par eau* or *par terre*) mail is considerably cheaper, but takes one to three months to arrive. It's adequate for getting rid of books or clothing you no longer need. If you send a parcel air mail (*par avion* or *poste aérienne*), you must complete a green customs form for any package over 1kg (2kg for letter-post rate).

When writing to organizations in France, enclose an International Reply Coupon (available at post offices for US$1) for a response by surface mail; send two for airmail.

Air-mailing a 25g (about an ounce) letter from France to the U.S. or Canada costs 9.60F. *Aérogrammes* are 4.20F and post cards (*cartes postales*) 3.50F when mailed to the U.S. Special delivery is called *avec recommandation,* and express mail *exprès postaux.*

You can also receive mail through the **Poste Restante** system. In major cities, the central post office handling Poste Restante is open long hours and on weekends. Almost all post offices function as Postes Restantes. To specify a particular post office, you must know its postal code—*Let's Go* lists postal codes for the central post office in the Practical Information section of every city. To ensure the safe arrival of your letter, address it: LAST NAME (in capitals), first name; Poste Restante; city name, R. P. (*Recette Principale*); Postal code, FRANCE. You will have to show your passport as identification and pay a few francs for every letter received. You can forward mail from most post offices to other French Postes Restantes. **American Express** also receives and holds mail for up to 30 days, after which they return it to the sender. The envelope should be addressed with your name in capital letters, and "Client's Mail" should be written below your name. Most big-city American Express offices will hold mail free of charge if you have their traveler's checks, but some require that you be an AmEx cardholder. The free pamphlet *Directory of Travel Service Offices* contains the addresses of American Express offices worldwide, and can be obtained from any American Express office or by calling customer service at (800) 528-4800 (allow 6-8 weeks for delivery).

The post office is also the place to send or receive money orders, and to change *postcheques.* In more than 150 post offices in major towns, you can also exchange foreign currency; look for the *CHANGE* sticker. If you have a Visa or AmEx card, or a Eurocheque guarantee card issued by your bank, you can withdraw money at any of 780 post offices indicated by the sticker *CB/VISA ou EC.*

Post offices are often open weekdays until 7pm (they stop changing money at 6pm) and on Saturday mornings. Banks are open weekdays only. Avoid long lines by purchasing stamps at local *tabacs* or from the yellow coin-operated vending machines outside major post offices.

Telephones and Telegraph

Almost all French pay phones accept only **télécartes;** in outlying districts and cafés and bars, some phones are still coin-operated. You may purchase the card in two denominations: 40F for 50 *unités,* and 96F for 120 *unités,* each worth anywhere from six to 18 minutes of conversation, depending on the rate schedule. The *télécarte* is available at post offices, railway ticket counters, and some *tabacs.*

The best places to call from are phone booths and post offices. If you phone from a café, hotel, or restaurant, you risk paying up to 30% more.

You can make **intercontinental calls** from any pay phone or post office. The clerk will assign you to a phone from which you can usually dial direct, and will collect your money when you complete your call. In many towns, you can dial directly overseas from a corner phone booth.

A brief directory:

Operator (*Téléphoniste*), tel. 10.

International Operator, tel. 19 33 11.

Directory information (*Renseignements téléphoniques*), tel. 12.

International information, 19 + 33 + 12 + country code (Australia 61; Ireland 353; New Zealand 64; U.K. 44; U.S. and Canada 1).

Direct long-distance calls within France, in the Paris region dial 16 1 + the number, elsewhere dial the number only.

Direct international calls, tel. 19 + country code + the number.

AT&T operator, 19 00 11.

Fire: 18.

SAMU (Ambulance): 15.

Police Emergency: 17.

A brief glossary: A call is *un coup de téléphone* or *un appel;* to dial is *composer;* a collect call is made *en PCV* (pay-say-vay); a person-to-person call is *avec préavis.*

Remember that you must have a card (or coin) to initiate even an emergency or collect call. Rates are reduced Monday through Friday 9:30pm-8am, Saturday 2pm-8am, and Sunday all day for calls to the Common Market and Switzerland; Monday through Friday noon-2pm and 8pm-2am, and Sunday afternoon to the U.S. and Canada; Monday through Saturday 9:30pm-8am and Sunday all day to Israel.

Telegrams can be sent from any post office and can sometimes be called in if you have a local address.

If your itinerary is unplanned and you don't want to be constrained by mailstops or the expense of phone calls, you might also consider **Overseas Access,** a telephone checkpoint service offered by EurAide. In its Munich office, an American staff relays messages to and from family, business, or other travelers. As a member, you can call the Munich office for news from home (US$15 initial registration, US$15 per week or US$40 per month). If you buy a Eurailpass from them, the initial registration fee is waived and the monthly rate is US$35. In the U.S., contact EurAide, Inc., P.O. Box 2375, Naperville, IL 60567 (tel. (708) 420-2343). In Germany, contact Bahnhofplatz 2, 8000 München 2 (tel. (089) 59 38 89).

Packing

Pack light. Lay out everything you think you'll need, pack only half of it, and take more money. Remember that you can buy almost anything you'll need in Europe, and that the more luggage you carry, the more alien you'll feel.

Decide what kind of luggage is best suited to your trip. A **backpack** is ideal if you plan to cover a lot of ground and want to hike or camp often. If you intend to stay mainly in cities and towns, consider a light **suitcase.** For unobtrusive travel, choose a large **shoulder bag** that zips or closes securely. This may also be the best choice for hitchhikers because it's less intimidating to drivers than a large backpack. Whenever you can, store your luggage in secure lockers while you see the sights; bring a small **daypack** to carry your *Let's Go,* lunch, map, rain poncho, and camera.

Pack solid, dark-colored clothes that won't show the wear they'll eventually receive. If they're loose and wearable in layers, they will be more versatile. Dress neatly and conservatively—you'll fare better when dealing with hotel owners. Sturdy cotton-blend pants or a skirt are cooler for summer and look more polished than jeans. French women rarely wear short shorts; avoid wearing them outside of beach and camping areas, and especially in cities and towns. Also remember that you should dress neatly when visiting any house of worship, whether or not services are being held. Taking clothes that you can wash in a sink and that dry quickly and wrinkle-free will save you laundromat visits.

France is generally warm in the summer with temperatures in the 70s (around 25°C) in the north, 80s (30°C) in Paris, and 90s (35°C) in the south. Winters are mild, averaging about 40°F (5°C) during the day, though some regions (predictably, mountainous areas and Picardie) are considerably colder. Lightweight cottons or blends are a must in summer, with a sweater for cool evenings. Light wool clothing is good for autumn and will carry you through winter as well except in the north and in the mountains. You'll need **rainwear** in all seasons, and if you plan to camp, it's worth paying a little more for a lightweight poncho that unbuttons to form a groundcloth.

Avoid taking electrical appliances, but if you must, remember that electricity in most European countries is 220 volts AC, twice as much as in North America and enough to fry any of your appliances. If you can't or don't want to run on batteries, you'll need an **adapter.** In France, as in most of Europe, sockets accommodate mainly two-pin round plugs, but some places may have three-pin plugs. If your rotary nose-hair clipper is not dual voltage, you'll also need a **converter** (US$15-18). But remember that you can use these converters only in areas with AC current. You can buy adapters and converters when you get to Europe, or order them in advance from the **Franzus Company,** Murtha Industrial Park, P.O. Box 142, Railroad Ave., Beacon Falls, CT 06403 (tel. (212) 463-9393). The company also distributes a pamphlet called *Foreign Electricity Is No Deep Dark Secret.*

The following is a checklist of items you should definitely squeeze in the corners of your pack: needle and thread, string, a pocket knife, a plastic water bottle, earplugs, safety pins, rubber bands, a small flashlight, a cold-water soap (Dr. Bronner's Castile Soap, available in camping stores, claims to work as everything from clothes detergent to toothpaste), a bath towel, ziplock bags (for damp clothing, soap, or messy foods), a notebook and pens or pencils, a pocket French-English dictionary or phrasebook, and a travel alarm clock. Waterproof matches and English-language maps might be useful as well. If you take expensive **cameras** or equipment abroad, it's best to register everything with customs at the airport before departure. Buy a supply of film before you leave; it's more expensive in France.

Security

A few precautions will see you safely through your travels more effectively than constant paranoia. Keep all valuables with you whenever you leave your room, even if it has a lock, as others may have a passkey. At night, sleep with valuables on your person; laying your pack alongside the bed won't deter thieves.

Checking luggage on trains is risky, especially if you are transferring. Avoid overnight trains—sleeping compartments have been known to be gassed and burgled. If you do sleep in a train berth in summer, keep the window ajar. Keep your money, passport, and other important documents with you in a pouch or **moneybelt** at all times. **Neck pouches** worn under the shirt prove the most theft-resistant. Look for packs that have zippers designed to accept combination locks. If you plan to sleep outside, or simply can't carry everything with you, store your gear in sturdy lockers or at the baggage check of a bus or train station. Yet since these lockers are sometimes broken into, always carry essential documents with you. Be aware that most lockers have time limits of a few days and are cleared out regularly; you may have to pay extra to reclaim your belongings.

Pickpockets are fast, practiced, and professional. Pros can unzip a bag in just a few seconds, so wear yours with the opening against your body. Threading a safety pin or keyring through both zippers on a pack makes it difficult to open quickly and prevents it from slipping open accidentally. Thieves often work in pairs, one providing a distraction and the other grabbing your wallet or purse. Some street children will do anything to distract you, even pretend that they are being molested. In busy areas, walk quickly and purposefully. Thieves in Métro stations may try to grab your bag as you board, just before the doors close.

Photocopy all important documents such as your passport, identification, credit cards, and traveler's checks serial numbers. Keep one set of copies in a separate, secure place in your luggage, and leave another set at home. Although copies can seldom substitute for originals, at least you'll have the relevant information. If you are robbed, check your surroundings carefully. Thieves may throw away your wallet after taking the cash, and you might be able to retrieve non-cash items such as credit cards. Report the theft to the police station in the area where it occurred. Be insistent; a police report may be necessary to claim stolen traveler's checks.

Traveling Alone

Traveling with other people can be emotionally taxing; at one time or another you may want to strike out on your own. There are many possible rewards, including a sense of adventure, freedom to go where and when you want, and the chance to reflect on your experiences without the stress of another person. The following safety precautions apply to all travelers, but people traveling alone should be particularly attentive.

Be sure that someone knows your itinerary, and check in with that person reasonably often. Steer clear of empty train compartments, and avoid bus and train stations and public parks after dark. When on foot, stick to busy, well-lit streets. Ask the managers of your hotel, hostel or campground for advice on specific areas, and consider staying in places with a curfew or night attendant.

Some cheap accommodations may entail more risks than savings. Forego dives and city outskirts in favor of university accommodations, youth hostels, and *foyers,* and remember that centrally located accommodations are usually safest. Never say that you're traveling alone.

If you are female, you may want to consider staying in *foyers* or religious organizations that offer rooms for women only. Foreign women in France are frequently beset by unwanted and tenacious followers. Try to exercise reasonable caution without falling prey to the notion that all French men are best avoided. Remember that hitching is *not* safe for lone women. Cultural sensitivity can often short-circuit threatening situations. To better escape unwanted attention, follow the example of local women. In the more rural provinces, the more skin you cover, the less obtrusive you'll be. If you spend time in cities, you may be harassed no matter how you're dressed. Look as if you know where you're going, and ask women or couples for directions if you're lost or if you feel uncomfortable. Your best answer to verbal harassment is no answer at all. In crowds, you may be pinched, squeezed, or otherwise molested. Wearing a walkman or a conspicuous wedding band may help prevent such incidents. If you are propositioned directly, a loud *"Non!"* or *"Laissez-moi tranquille!"* (leh-say mwah trahn-keel; "leave me alone") is best, with no further explanation. Seek out a police officer or a female passerby before a crisis erupts, and don't hesitate to scream for help ("Au secours": oh suh-coor). *Always* carry a *télécarte* and change for the phone (emergency numbers are free, but you need a card or coin to initiate any call) and enough extra money for a bus or taxi. Women may want to consult *The Handbook for Women Travellers* (£4.95) published by Judy Piatkus Publishers, 5 Windmill St., London W1, England.

Insurance

Beware of unnecessary insurance coverage. Your current **medical insurance** policy may cover costs incurred abroad. University term-time medical plans often include insurance for summer travel. Medicare's foreign travel coverage is limited and is valid only in Canada and Mexico. Canadians are protected by their home province's health insurance plan; check with the provincial Ministry of Health or Health Plan Headquarters. Your **homeowners' insurance** (or your family's coverage) often covers theft during travel. Homeowners are generally covered against loss of travel documents (passport, plane ticket, railpass, etc.) up to about US$500.

Claims can only be filed to your home medical or homeowner's insurance upon return to the U.S. or Canada and must be accompanied by the proper documents (i.e., police reports and/or doctor's statements) written in English if possible, and all relevant receipts. Note that some of the plans listed below offer cash advances or guaranteed transferrals, so it is not always necessary to use your own vacation cash to pay doctor bills. Full payment in cash before check-out (and sometimes even before treatment) is virtually the rule at most European hospitals. If your coverage doesn't include on-the-spot payments or cash transferrals, budget for emergencies.

When purchased in the U.S., the **ISIC** will provide you with US$3000 worth of accident insurance plus US$100 per day for up to 60 days of in-hospital sickness coverage as long as the card is valid. CIEE offers an inexpensive Trip-Safe package that extends coverage of medical treatment and hospitalization, accidents, and even charter flights missed due to illness. ISIC also provides a 24-hour traveler's assistance line for legal and financial aid. American Express cardmembers receive automatic car-rental and flight insurance on purchases made with the card.

The following agencies offer insurance against theft, loss of luggage, trip cancellation/interruption, and medical emergencies; rates average around US$6 per $100 of coverage. You can buy a policy directly from insurance agencies or from some travel agencies.

Access America, Inc., 600 Third Ave., P.O. Box 807, New York, NY 10163 (tel. (800) 851-2800). Their travel insurance covers nearly everything: luggage damage or loss, trip cancellation/interruption, stolen passports, bail money, emergency medical evacuation, and on-the-spot hospital and doctor payments. 24-hr. hotline.

ARM Coverage, Inc., P.O. Box 310, 120 Mineola Blvd., Mineola, NY 11501 (tel. (800) 626-3149 or (516) 294-0220). Offers comprehensive Carefree Travel Insurance. 24-hr. hotline. Underwritten by Hartford Insurance.

Edmund A. Cocco Agency, 220 Broadway, #201, Lynnfield, MA 01940 (tel. (800) 821-2488, in MA (617) 595-0262). Accident, sickness, medical evacuation, and trip cancellation/interruption coverage, and for payment of medical expenses "on-the-spot" worldwide. Protection against bankruptcy or default of airlines, cruise lines, or charter companies. Group rates available. 24-hr. hotline.

Travel Assistance International, 1133 15th St. NW, #400, Washington, DC 20005 (tel. (800) 821-2828). Travel packages include medical and travel insurance, medical and financial assistance, medical and legal referrals, and lost passport and visa assistance. A year-long policy (US$120, $200 for families) covers all trips under 90 days. Package prices vary with trip length.

WorldCare Travel Assistance Association, Inc., 605 Market St., #1300, San Francisco, CA 94105 (tel. (800) 666-4993). Annual membership US$162; short-term policies also available. Also offers a Scholarcare program for students and faculty spending a semester or year abroad. 24-hr. emergency medical hotline.

Drugs

Possession of drugs in France can end your stay immediately. Never bring anything across any border, since drug laws and the severity with which they are enforced vary considerably among different countries (e.g., between Holland and France). In France, police may legally stop and search anyone on the street. It is not uncommon for a pusher to increase profits by first selling drugs to a tourist and then turning that person in to the authorities for a reward. If you are arrested, your home country's consulate can visit you, provide a list of attorneys, inform family and friends, and tell you bedtime stories, but they cannot get you out of jail. You're virtually on your own if you become involved, however innocently, in illegal drug trafficking. Write the Bureau of Consular Affairs, CA/PA #5807, Department of State, Washington, DC 20520 (tel. (202) 647-1488) for more information and the pamphlet *Travel Warning on Drugs Abroad.*

Health

The simplest prescription for health while traveling is to eat well, keep clean, and avoid excessive exertion. All food, including seafood, dairy products, and fresh produce, is normally safe in France. The water is chlorinated and also safe, but in parts of the country, the bacteria differ from those found in North American water and may cause diarrhea. Relying on bottled mineral water during the first couple of weeks is a sensible precaution. When traveling in the summer, especially in the south, take precautions against **heatstroke** and **sunburn**: drink lots of liquids, wear a hat and sunscreen, and stay inside in the middle of the day. To minimize the effects of jet lag, try to get on the schedule of your destination as soon as possible: even before you go, you can gradually shift mealtimes and bedtimes.

Although no special immunizations are necessary for travel to France, be sure that your **inoculations** are up-to-date. Typhoid shots remain good for three years, tetanus for 10. *Health Information for International Travel* (US$5) provides U.S. Public Health recommendations and other hints; write the Superintendent of Documents (address above).

Depending on your plans, you may wish to bring a few of the following items: mild antiseptic soap, aspirin, a decongestant, an antihistamine, diarrhea medicine, motion sickness medicine, earplugs, a thermometer, bandages, contraceptives (remember time zone changes when taking the Pill), mosquito repellent, and a small Swiss army knife with tweezers.

Travelers with corrective lenses should bring an extra pair, or at least a copy of their prescription. Since the pressurized atmosphere of an airplane can dehydrate soft lenses, clean them just before leaving, and don't drink coffee or alcohol or read for long periods of time while on the plane. Bring along adequate supplies of your cleaning solutions, and don't let them get overheated in luggage. Foreign brands with familiar names may have different formulations than your brand. For heat disinfection you'll need outlet and low-watt voltage adapters.

Travelers with a chronic medical condition requiring regular treatment should consult their doctors before leaving. Diabetics, for example, may need advice on adapting insulin levels for flights across multiple time zones. Carry an ample supply of all medicines, since matching your prescription with a foreign equivalent may be difficult. Always carry up-to-date prescriptions (in legible, preferably typewritten form, including the medication's trade name, manufacturer, chemical name, and dosage) and/or a statement from your doctor, especially if you use insulin, syringes, or any narcotic drug. Keep all medicines and syringes in your carry-on luggage.

If you have a medical condition that cannot be easily recognized (e.g., diabetes, allergies to antibiotics, epilepsy, heart conditions), you should obtain a **Medic Alert identification tag.** This internationally recognized tag indicates the nature of the condition, and provides the number of Medic Alert's 24-hour hotline, through which medical personnel can obtain information about the member's medical history. Lifetime membership, which includes the price of the tag, costs US$25; contact Medic Alert Foundation International, P.O. Box 1009, Turlock, CA 95381-1009 (tel. (800) ID-ALERT (432-5378), emergency (209) 634-4917).

At night and on Sundays, the local *commissariat de police* will supply the address of the nearest open *pharmacie* (drugstore) and that of a doctor on duty. The *pharmacie de garde* is also noted in newspapers and on the doors of pharmacies in town. For an ambulance to the *hôpital,* look in the phone book under *ambulances municipales.*

Few areas of France are so isolated that you will have to worry about finding competent medical attention. Before you go, obtain a directory of English-speaking physicians worldwide from the **International Association for Medical Assistance to Travelers (IAMAT),** 417 Center St., Lewiston, NY 14092 (tel. (716) 754-4883); in Canada, 40 Regal St., Guelph, Ont. N1K 1B5 (tel. (519) 836-0102). They also publish the pamphlets *How to Avoid Traveler's Diarrhea, How to Adjust to the Heat,* and *How to Adapt to Altitude.* Membership to IAMAT is free (although a donation is requested), and doctors are always on call for members. American, Canadian, and British embassies and consulates, and American Express offices can also help you find English-speaking doctors. You may also be able to find a good doctor in the emergency room of a university hospital. As a last resort, go to the largest city nearby and hope that someone at the hospital speaks English.

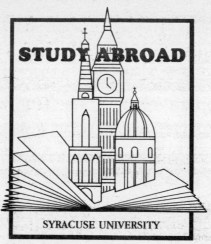

Alternatives to Tourism

Useful Publications

The Council on International Educational Exchange (see address above) publishes a wide variety of books on work and study abroad. Their offerings include the free pamphlets *Student Travel Catalog* and *Work Abroad (US$9.95),* and also *The Teenager's Guide to Study, Travel, and Adventure Abroad* (US$11.95) and *Work, Study, Travel Abroad: The Whole World Handbook* (US$10.95).

The Institute of International Education (IIE), 809 UN Plaza, New York, NY 10017 (tel. (212) 883-8200). Publishes a number of useful books, including *Basic Facts on Foreign Study* (free), and the annual, very thorough *Academic Year Abroad* (US$29.95), *Vacation Study Abroad* (US$24.95), and *Teaching Abroad* (US$21.95). When ordering, send $1 for postage. You can call or write IIE for information, or visit their reference library (open by appointment). IIE administers the very competitive **Fulbright** fellowships and other grants which provide money for study, teaching, and work in the creative arts abroad. Write to IIE for more information. They also distribute several books published by the **Central Bureau for Educational Visits and Exchanges** in the UK, including *Study Holidays* (US$18.95) and *Working Holidays* (US$18.95). In the UK, write to the Central Bureau directly at Seymour Mews House, Seymour Mews, London W1H 9PE, England (tel. (071) 486 51 01).

Vacation Work Publications, 9 Park End St., Oxford OX1 1HJ, England (tel. (0865) 241 978)). Distributes books on work and volunteer opportunities, including *Directory of Summer Jobs Abroad* (£6.95), *Work Your Way Around the World* (£7.95), *The Au Pair and Nanny's Guide to Working Abroad* (£5.95) and *International Directory of Voluntary Work* (£6.95). Add £1 for postage in the UK, £2 for international orders.

Study

If you choose your program well, study in France can be one of the best ways to get acquainted with the country and its people. A good place to begin investigating study abroad programs is CIEE's *Work, Study, Travel Abroad: The Whole World Handbook. Basic Facts on Foreign Study,* put out by the **Institute of International Education (IIE)** and **CIEE,** is a free brochure that covers the nitty-gritty—from visas to tax returns. **UNESCO** publishes *Study Abroad* (US$18.50, postage US$2.50), available from Unipub Co., 4611-F Assembly Dr., Lanham, MD 20706 (tel. (800) 274-4888). For free pamphlets on various fields of study in France, contact the **Cultural Services of the French Embassy.** The **American Center for Students and Artists** is a student advisory service that provides information on both housing and education. Contact the Student Advisory Service, American Cathedral, 23, av. Georges V, 75008 Paris (open Sept.-June).

Language instruction is a booming business in France; programs are run by American universities, independent international or local organizations, and divisions of French universities. The **tourist office** in Paris maintains a list of member language schools.

Alliance Française, Ecole Internationale de Langue et de Civilisation Française, 101, bd. Raspail, 75270 Paris Cédex 06 (tel. 45 44 38 28; Métro Notre-Dame-des-Champs, St-Placide, or Rennes). Offers language courses at various levels, a business course, teacher training, and refresher courses.

Institut Catholique de Paris, 21, rue d'Assas, 75270 Paris Cédex 06 (tel. 42 22 41 80; Métro St-Placide). Semester-long and summer classes at all levels, including business French and courses for teachers of French.

Cours de Civilisation Française, 47, rue des Ecoles, 75005 Paris (tel. 40 46 22 11). The **Sorbonne** has been giving its French civilization course since 1919. Academic year course which can be taken by the semester; four-, six-, and eight-week summer programs with civilization lectures and language classes at various levels; and a special course in commercial French. You can also take the Cours de Civilisation through the **American Institute for Foreign Study (AIFS),** 102 Greenwich Ave., Greenwich, CT 06830 (tel. (203) 863-9090 or (800) 727-2437). AIFS also arranges accommodations and meals in Paris for its students.

Eurocentres, another of the many hats worn by CIEE. Long and short intensive courses, holiday courses, and teacher refresher courses at centers in Paris (13, passage Dauphine, 75006 Paris, tel. (1) 43 25 81 40); La Rochelle (10ter rue Amelot, 17000 La Rochelle, tel. 46 50 57 33); and Amboise (9 Mail Saint-Thomas, BP 214, 37402 Amboise-Cédex, tel. 47 23 10 60). Call or write the nearest CIEE office for information on centers worldwide.

While it is tempting (and comforting) to meet and talk to other Americans, you may regret it later. An academic program in a French university may be more rewarding than a language class filled with English-speakers. The French educational system is structured to prepare students for a consecutive series of standard examinations that must be passed to earn degrees. However, there is often more flexibility for foreign students, and tuition is low by U.S. standards. Most French universities require at least a *baccalauréat* degree or its putative equivalents (British A-levels or a year of college in the United States) for admission. For details on application procedures, contact the cultural services office at the nearest French consulate or embassy.

As a student registered in a French university, you will be given a student card (*carte d'étudiant*) by your school upon presentation of your residency permit and a receipt for your university fees. In addition to the card's student benefits, many benefits are administered by the **Centre Régional des Oeuvres Universitaires et Scolaires (CROUS).** Founded in 1955 to improve the living and working conditions of its members, this division of the Oeuvres Universitaires welcomes foreign students. A student card entitles you to subsidized rates at restaurants, accommodations, and various social and cultural services. In Paris, the regional center is at 39, av. Georges-Bernanos, 75231 (tel. 40 51 36 00). The CROUS center for foreign students is also at this address. The Paris office of CROUS also publishes an annual brochure, *Guide Infos Etudiants,* listing addresses and information on every aspect of student life. Pick up the helpful guidebook *Je vais en France* (free), available in French or English, from any French embassy or consulate.

Work

Finding work in France is extremely difficult. Because of high unemployment, the French government has become wary of hiring foreigners. Before you can obtain a work permit through normal channels, your employer must convince the Ministry of Labor that there is no French citizen capable of filling your position. Even when a foreigner is considered, Common Market country members have priority. Long-term employment is difficult to secure unless you have skills in high-demand areas such as medicine, computer programming, or teaching. If you have the appropriate skills or educational background, you might investigate positions with US firms, government agencies, or non-profit organizations which hire Americans for work abroad.

With the exception of *au pair* jobs, it is illegal for foreign students to hold full-time jobs during the school year. Students registered at French universities may get work permits for the summer with a valid visa, a student card from a French university, and proof of a job. If you are not a student in a French university, check the fact sheet *Employment in France,* put out by **Cultural Services of the French Embassy,** which provides basic information about work in France and also lists the government-approved organizations through which foreign students must secure their jobs. **CIEE** operates a reciprocal work program with France and is the only U.S. organization so approved. If you are a permanent degree-seeking college or university student, a resident U.S. citizen, and have an intermediate level knowledge of French (at least 2 years of college French), CIEE will issue you a three-month work permit for US$96. Under this system, you do not need a job prior to obtaining a work permit. CIEE will provide information on accommodations and job-hunting but will not place you in a job. Jobs available are mostly short-term, unskilled work in hotels, shops, restaurants, farms, and factories. Wages should cover food, lodging, and basic living expenses. Complete information and application are enclosed in their *Student Travel Catalog.*

CIEE's *Work, Study, Travel Abroad: The Whole World Handbook* (US$10.95, postage US$1), available in bookstores or from a CIEE office, is a comprehensive guide to overseas opportunities which includes a work-abroad section with listings by country. The handbook also includes a section on long-term employment. For more detail, consult *Emplois d'Eté en France* (US$12.95, postage US$1), also available from CIEE and from Vacation Work Publications. *The 1991 Directory of Over-*

seas Summer Jobs (US$10.95), available from Writer's Digest Books, 1507 Dana Ave., Cincinnati, OH 45207 (tel. (800) 543-4644, in OH (800) 551-0884), lists 50,000 openings worldwide, volunteer and paid. The **World Trade Academy Press** (50 E. 42nd St., New York, NY 10017; tel. (212) 697-4999) publishes a *Directory of American Firms Operating in Foreign Countries* (look at it in the library—it costs an awe-inspiring US$175), and the more manageable *Looking for Employment in Foreign Countries* (US$16.50). Another general guide, *International Jobs: Where They Are, How To Get Them* (US$12.45) is available from **Addison Wesley,** 1 Jacob Way, reading, MA 01867 (tel. (800) 447-2226). When writing to a French employer, you should send two International Reply Coupons (available at the post office) to guarantee a rapid reply by airmail.

A good place to start your job search in France is the **American Chamber of Commerce,** 21, av. George V, 75008 Paris (tel. 47 23 80 26). The *Membership Directory of the French-American Chamber of Commerce* is available from its office at 509 Madison Ave., #1900, New York, NY 10022 (tel. (212) 371-4466). It is quite expensive, so go through the directory at the office. The **Agence Nationale Pour l'Emploi,** 4, rue Galilés, 93198 Noisy-le-Grand Cedex (tel. 49 31 24 00) has specific information on job opportunities. Check help-wanted columns in newspapers, especially *Le Monde, Le Figaro,* and the English-language *International Herald Tribune.* You can also check job listings at the **American Cathedral,** 23, av. Georges V, 75008 Paris (tel. 47 20 17 92) and *The American Church,* 65 quai d'Orsay, 75007, Paris.

A number of programs offer practical experience to people with technical and business skills. The **International Association for the Exchange of Students for Technical Experience (IAESTE)** program, a division of the Association for International Practical Training (AIPT), is an internship exchange program for science, architecture, engineering, agriculture and math students who have completed two years at an accredited four-year institution. There is a non-refundable US$75 fee. Apply to the IAESTE Trainee Program, c/o AIPT, 10 Corporate Ctr., Suite 250, Columbia, MD 21044 (tel. (301) 997-2200). Applications are due in December for summer placement.

Summer positions as tour group leaders are available with **American Youth Hostels (AYH)**, P.O. Box 37613, Washington, DC 20013-7613 (tel. (202) 783-6161). You must be over age 20 and are required to take a week-long leadership course (US$250, room and board included; in Washington, DC US$350). You must lead a group in the U.S. before taking one to Europe. The **Experiment in International Living (EIL)**, Kipling Rd., Brattleboro, VT 05301 (tel. (802) 257-7751), requires leadership ability and extensive overseas experience (minimum age 24). Applications are due in late November for summer positions. CIEE also has group leader positions available; contact its International Voluntary Projects division.

Volunteering

Volunteering is a great way to meet people (who're guaranteed to be less uptight than the average Parisian) and you may even get room and board in exchange for your work. *Volunteer! The Comprehensive Guide to Voluntary Service in the U.S. and Abroad* is co-published by CIEE and the Commission on Voluntary Service and Action. It offers advice on choosing a voluntary service program and lists over 170 organizations in fields ranging from health care and social work to construction. Write to CIEE (US$6.95, postage US$1).

CIEE also offers placement in international **workcamps** in the U.S. and Europe each summer. Volunteers from throughout the world live and work together on a two- to four-week community project. A working knowledge of French is required for projects in France, and participants must be at least 16. The camp provides room and board; the application fee is US$125. Write to CIEE International Voluntary Projects (address above).

Volunteers for Peace, a workcamp organization, publishes an annual *International Workcamp Directory* to workcamps in 29 countries, primarily in Europe (US$10, postage included). They also publish a free newsletter. Write to VFP, 43 Tiffany Rd., Belmont, VT 05730 (tel. (802) 259-2759). Placement is quick; volunteer reservations are generally confirmed within a week. There is a $90 registration fee for camps in Western Europe. **Service Civil International** runs workcamps through-out France that aim to advance international peace. Contact them at 129, rue du Faubourg Poissonière, F-75009 Paris (tel. 48 74 60 15). In the U.S., contact S.C.I., Innisfree Village, Rte. 2, Box 506, Crozet, VA 22932 (tel. (804) 823-1826). Apply well in advance. Registration fees for placement in camps are US$25-80. Many French organizations run *vacances en chantier,* workcamps involving building and restoration. You should know some French before embarking on a project run by a French organization. Write to **Club du Vieux Manoir,** 10, rue de la Cossonnerie, 75001 Paris (tel. 45 08 80 40), which works to protect the environment and restore churches, castles, fortresses, and other historical French monuments. The club of-fers summer- and year-long programs. Anyone 15 or over (14 for some programs) is eligible, and the application fee is 60F. If you are 17 or over and work during the off-season, your room and board are free after a 15-day trial period. **Compagnons Bâtisseurs,** 5, rue des Immeubles Industriels, 75011 Paris (tel. 43 73 70 63), an inter-national volunteer association, renovates and converts local buildings into facilities for the mentally, economically, and physically underprivileged. Work includes heavy physical labor, but extensive experience is not necessary. Terms run two to three weeks, June to October. Volunteers prepare their own food (cooking facilities provided) and sleep in provided tents or barracks. Apply two months in advance. **Etudes et Chantiers,** AAC BP 01-15300 Murat (tel. 71 20 04 51, fax 71 20 03 85) organizes international work camps throughout France for ages 13 and up. Two-to three-week programs run 480F-2300F, everything included. **REMPART,** 1, rue des Guillemites, 75004 Paris, organizes similar projects, mostly for participants 18 and over. Programs cost anywhere from nothing to 90F per day.

If working on an archaeological dig interests you, the **Archaeological Institute of America** publishes a *Fieldwork Opportunities Bulletin,* listing international field-work projects, in January. Contact the AIA at 675 Commonwealth Ave., Boston, MA 02215 (tel. (617) 353-9361). Also contact the Cultural Services of the French Embassy for possible positions in France as **camp counselors.**

There are a variety of resources available to those interested in teaching English in a foreign school. The U.S. State Department **Office of Overseas Schools** (Rm. 245 SA-29, Washington, DC 20522-2902, tel. (202) 875-7800) maintains a list of schools abroad and agencies which arrange placement. One such agency is **Teachers of English as a Second Language (TESL)** which runs a recruiting service to hire teachers for European schools. Send a letter and resume to TESL Recruiting Serv-ice, Rte. 6 Box 174, New Orleans, LA 70129.

International Schools Services, P.O. Box 5910, 15 Roszel Rd., Princeton, NJ 08543 (tel. (609) 452-0990) publishes a free newsletter, *NewsLinks;* call or write to get on the mailing list. Their Educational Staffing Department, which coordinates placement of teachers in foreign schools, publishes the free brochure *Your Passport to Teaching and Administrative Opportunities Abroad.* The *ISS Directory of Overseas Schools* (US$29.95 plus $5.75 domestic postage, $10 international) is distributed by **Petersen's, Inc.** (P.O. Box 2123, Princeton, NJ 08543-2123, tel. (800) EDU-DATA (338-3282)).

Au Pair Positions

And then there is the old standby—*au pair* work. Positions are reserved primarily for single women aged 18 to 30 with some knowledge of French; a few men are also employed. The *au pair* cares for the children of a French family and does light housework five or six hours each day (1 day off per week) while taking courses at a school for foreign students or a French university. Talking with children can be a great way to improve your French, but looking after them may be extremely stren-uous. Make sure you know in advance what the family expects of you. *Au pair* posi-tions usually last six to 18 months; during the summer the contract can be as short as one to three months, but you may not be able to take courses. You'll receive room, board, and a small monthly stipend (around 1300F). Be sure to acquire a visa *long séjour* before arriving in France.

The Cultural Services of the French Embassy offers a detailed information sheet on *au pair* jobs. Organizations offering placement include **L'Accueil Familial des Jeunes Etrangers**, 23, rue du Cherche-Midi, 75006 Paris (tel. 42 22 50 34 or 42 22 13 34) and **L'A.R.C.H.E.**, 7, rue Bargue, 75015 Paris (tel. 42 73 34 39).

Additional Concerns

Senior Travelers

Senior citizens enjoy an assortment of discounts on transportation, tours, admission to museums, and more. Write the Superintendent of Documents for a copy of *Travel Tips for Older Americans* (US$1). The following organizations offer information, assistance, and discounts to seniors.

American Association of Retired Persons, Special Services Department, 1909 K St. NW, Washington, DC 20049 (tel. (800) 227-7737; for travel information, (202) 662-4850). For an annual membership fee of $5, anyone 50 or over and their spouses can receive benefits from AARP Travel Services and get discounts on hotels, motels, car rental, and sightseeing companies.

Elderhostel, 80 Boylston St., #400, Boston, MA 02116 (tel. (617) 426-7788). Weeklong educational workshops in over 30 countries in the Americas and Europe cover a variety of subjects. US$1500-5000 fee for 2-4 weeks includes room, board, tuition, and extracurricular activities. You must be 60 or over to enroll; companions must be 50 or over.

National Council of Senior Citizens, 925 15th St. NW, Washington, DC 20005 (tel. (202) 347-8800). Information on discounts and travel abroad.

Pilot Industries, Inc., 103 Cooper St., Babylon, NY 11702 (tel. (516) 422-2225). Publishes *The International Health Guide for Senior Citizen Travelers* (US$4.95, postage US$1) and *Senior Citizen's Guide to Budget Travel in Europe* (US$4.95, postage US$1).

Disabled Travelers

The French Tourist Board supplies disabled travelers with free handbooks and access guides, but these directories can be misleading since they are not compiled by disabled travelers. Accurate information about ramps, the width of doors, the dimensions of elevators, and so on, remains difficult to secure. The best method is directly to ask restaurants, hotels, railways, and airlines about their facilities.

All TGV high-speed trains can accommodate wheelchairs, and guide dogs are transported free. Other trains have a special compartment and an escalator for boarding. It is worth writing to the train station at your destination to alert the conductor of your needs. In Paris, travel by Métro is facilitated by wider seats reserved for the disabled, although many stations have stairs rather than escalators or elevators. The new RER network, which complements the Métro coverage of Paris, operates a number of stations with lift access and others with flat/ramped access.

If you bring a seeing-eye dog into France, you must carry a vaccination certificate for rabies issued in your home country or a certificate showing there have been no cases of rabies in your country for over three years.

The American Foundation for the Blind, 15 W. 16th St., New York, NY 10011 (tel. (800) 232-5463, in NY (212) 620-2147). Information, travel books, and ID cards (US$6) for the blind. Write for an application.

L'Association des Paralysés de France, Délégation de Paris, 22, rue du Père Guérion, 75013 Paris (tel. 40 38 28 96). Publishes *Où ferons-nous étape?* (70F), which lists French hotels and motels accessible to the disabled.

Le Comité National Français de Liaison pour la Réadaption des Handicapés (CNFLRH), 38, bd. Raspail, 75007 Paris (tel. 45 48 90 13). Information service to help the disabled visitor. Offers *Touristes quand même! promenades en France pour voyageurs handicapés,* updated in 1984.

Disability Press, Ltd., Applemarket House, 17 Union St., Kingston-upon-Thames, Surrey KT1 1RP, England. Publishes the *Disabled Traveler's International Phrasebook* (£1.75), listing useful phrases in 8 languages, including French.

The Guided Tour, 555 Ashbourne Rd., Elkins Park, PA 19117 (tel. (215) 782-1370). Year-round full-time travel program for developmentally and learning-disabled adults as well as separate trips for those with physical disabilities.

Federation of the Handicapped, 211 W. 14th St., New York, NY 10011 (tel. (212) 206-4200). Leads tours as well as an annual summer trip for its members. Annual membership US$4.

Mobility International, USA (MIUSA), P.O. Box 3551, Eugene, OR 97403 (tel. (503) 343-1284, voice and TDD). MIUSA has information on travel and exchange programs, accommodations, and organized tours. They also publish *A World of Options: A Guide to International Educational Exchange and Community Service and Travel for Persons with Disabilities.* In the U.K., contact Mobility International, 228 Burough High St., London SE1 1JX.

Travel Information Service, Moss Rehabilitation Hospital, 1200 W. Tabor Rd., Philadelphia, PA 19141-3099 (tel. (215) 456-9603). Distributes free fact sheets on travel for the physically disabled. Send US$5 for more specific information on up to three destinations.

Pauline Hephaistos Survey Projects Group, 39 Bradley Gardens, West Ealing, London W13 8HE. *Access Guides* to Paris, Jersey, and the Channel Ports, detailing ease of access to hotels and points of interest (£4 each). The guides are researched by disabled people.

Wings on Wheels, c/o Evergreen Travel Service, 19505L 44th Ave. W., Lynnwood, WA 98036 (tel. (800) 435-2288 or (206) 776-1184, in WA (800) 562-9298). Provides services for disabled travelers. Charters buses with on-board wheelchair-accessible facilities and runs White Cane Tours for the blind as well as tours for deaf travelers and slow walkers.

Gay and Lesbian Travelers

In general, the French public is unperturbed by gay people living openly, especially in the capital. Gay life continues to be rather discreet outside Paris, with more openness in Nice, Lyon, Marseille, Toulouse, and Nantes.

Paris has a weekly journal *Gai Pied Hebdo,* which is distributed nationally. The best of the gay and lesbian monthly magazines are *Gay International, Gay Men,* and *Lesbia. Illico* is available free in bars and other gay meeting places. Well-regarded Parisian **bookstores** include Les Mots à la Bouche, 6, rue Ste-Croix de la Bretonnerie, 75004 Paris (tel. 42 78 88 30); Librairie Des Femmes, 74, rue de Seine, 75006 Paris (tel. 43 29 50 75); and Librairie Pluriel, 3, rue Keller, 75011 Paris (tel. 48 06 30 53). There is a feminist information and meeting center for women only at La Maison des Femmes, 8, Cité Prost, 75011 Paris (tel. 43 48 24 91). The **Centre du Christ Liberateur, Sexual Minorities,** at 3bis, rue Clairaut, 75017 Paris (tel. 46 27 49 36; Métro La Fourche), provides legal, medical, pastoral, and psychological help to various sexual minorities. They also operate the gay switchboard, **SOS Homosexualité.** The multilingual staff can also help locate inexpensive housing.

Gaia's Guide, an excellent "international guide for traveling women," lists local lesbian, feminist, and gay information numbers, publications, womens and cultural centers and resources, bookstores, restaurants, hotels, and meeting places. The book, revised annually, is available in local bookstores or by mail (US$12.50, postage included). In the U.S. and Canada, write to Giovanni's Room, 345 S. 12th St., Philadelphia, PA 19107; in Britain or Ireland, contact Gaia's Guide, 9-11 Kensington High St., London W8; in Australia or New Zealand, contact Open Leaves, 71 Cardigan St., Carlton, Victoria 3053, Australia.

The *Spartacus Guide for Gay Men* provides similar information (US$24.95, £12.50). Write c/o Bruno Gmunder, Lützowstr. 106, P.O. Box 30 13 45, D-1000 Berlin 30, West Germany.

Traveling with Children

A car is almost indispensable when traveling with children. In the culinary domain, don't fight the siren song of *le hot dog* or *le croque monsieur* (a grilled ham-and-cheese sandwich) if your kids don't take to the subtleties of *haute cuisine.*

France also offers great ice cream (if you don't buy it in supermarkets), and older children may enjoy a *demi-panaché* (shandy) made half-and-half with beer and an otherwise uninspiring carbonated lemonade (*limonade;* for true mix-it-yourself lemonade, ask for *citron pressé*). Not all restaurants have highchairs, but French servers are generally less put out by children than their North American counterparts. Young diners are especially welcome in informal cafeterias, *café-restaurants* and *brasseries.* The French habit of family roadside picnics is another convenience you'll enjoy.

Paris is blessed with many delights, and traveling with your kids gives you a chance to enjoy them too. **The Jardins du Luxembourg** have a *guignol* (Punch-and-Judy show), pony rides, go-carts, a carousel, boats to rent and sail on the ornamental ponds, and swings with attendants who, for a tip, will push the swings while you vanish into a café. The gardens also maintain some of the few lawns in Paris that children may play on. In the summer, there is an amusement park in the **Tuileries.** **Les Invalides** will fascinate older kids with its full-scale dioramas of Napoleon's battles. The **Jardin des Plantes** and the Paris **Zoo** are also fun, and even the most clichéed sights, such as the Eiffel Tower and the *bateaux mouches* (tour boats on the Seine), are made new when you see them with children.

Outside Paris, watch for village *fêtes,* which usually have a few rides. Châteaux (in the Loire Valley and elsewhere) and medieval walled towns like **Carcassonne** and **Avignon** are a child's fairytale dreams realized in stone. Children may also enjoy exploring crypts and catacombs, if you don't mind getting the creeps.

For bedtime stories before or during your trip, follow the 12 little girls around the sights of Paris in Hugo Bemelmans's *Madeline* picture books. *Crin blanc* and *Le ballon rouge,* both by Albert LaMorisse, are two poignant stories that exemplify a peculiarly French sentimentality regarding early childhood; Antoine de St-Exupéry's books, especially *Le petit prince,* are in the same vein. The well-known *Tintin* and *Astérix* comics appeal to a wide range of ages, and the hardbound copies are both travel- and child-proof (well, almost).

If you plan to camp with very young children, consult *Backpacking with Babies and Small Children* (US$8.95) and *Sharing Nature with Children* (US$6.95), both published by Wilderness Press, 2440 Bancroft Way, Berkeley, CA 94704 (tel. (800) 443-7227).

Specific Diets

While you should have little trouble finding tastefully prepared vegetables in France, they are often cooked with salt, butter, or sugar. Vegetarians will have trouble eating cheaply in restaurants, since *menus à prix fixe* almost always feature meat or fish. Ordering a salad may prove cheaper (if you don't eat eggs, be careful of green salads with eggs in them). *Viande* refers only to red meat. If you don't eat pork, chicken, fish, eggs, or dairy products, you should clearly state this to the server. Although the natural foods movement began in Europe, American-style health food merchandising has not caught on outside of large cities, and you may have to search long and hard for tofu and tahini. Health food stores are *diététiques* or *maisons de régime.* Health food products are sometimes referred to as *produits à santé.*

American Diabetes Association, 1660 Duke St., Alexandria, VA 22314 (tel. (800) 232-3472). Write for a reprint of the article "Ticket to Safe Travel," which provides travel tips (about US50¢). Also request an ID card (US15¢) that comes with an information sheet listing ways to request help and state that you have diabetes in several languages.

North American Vegetarian Society, P.O. Box 72, Dolgeville, NY 13329 (tel. (518) 568-7970). Sells *The International Vegetarian Travel Guide Handbook* (US$8.95, postage US$2). In the U.K., order direct (£3.99) from the **Vegetarian Society of the U.K., Parkdale, Dunham Rd., Altrincham, Cheshire WA14 4QG (tel (061) 928 07 93).**

Sephor-Herman Press, Inc., 1265 46th St., Brooklyn, NY 11219 (tel. (718) 972-9010). Sells *The Jewish Travel Guide* (US$10.75), which lists kosher restaurants, synagogues, and other Jewish institutions in over 80 countries. In the U.K., it is sold by Jewish Chronicle Publications, London EC4A IJT, England.

EUROPE BY YOURSELF

WITH THE YOUTH & STUDENT TRAVEL SPECIALIST

FROM PARIS TO

ONE WAY	✈	🚂
Athens	FFR 1200	660
Copenhagen	FFR 1460	665
Istanbul	FFR 2000	813
Marakech	FFR 1820	750
Londra	FFR 640	262
New York	FFR 2200	-
Rome	FFR -	415
Tunisi	FFR 1940	-
Venice	FFR -	357

FROM ROME TO

ONE WAY	✈	🚂
Amsterdam	$ 117	96
Athens	$ 112	75
Berlin	$ 146	94

FROM LONDON TO

ONE WAY	✈	🚂
Athens	£ 99	206
Rome	£ 95	146
Venice	£ 120	135

ACCOMODATION

WORLDWIDE	🛏
Paris	$ 13
London	$ 23
Amsterdam	$ 23
Athens	$ 12
Florence	$ 16
Munich	$ 21
Rome	$ 24
Venice	$ 20

Prices are valid in autumn '90

 **YOUTH & STUDENT TRAVEL CENTRE**

PARIS V°	20, Rue des Carmes - Tel. (00331)/ 43250076
	Metro Maubert Mutualité
LONDON	W1P 1HH - 33, Windmill Street - Metro Goodge street
	Tel.(071)EUROPE 5804554 - USA 3235130 - LONG HAUL 3235180
ROME	16, Via Genova - Tel. (06):46791
	297, Corso Vittorio Emanuele II - Tel. (06)6547883/6872560
FLORENCE	11 R, Via dei Ginori - Tel. (055)292150
MILAN	2, Via S. Antonio - Tel. (02)/72001121
NAPLES	25, Via Mezzocannone - Tel. (081)/264800
VENICE	3252, Dorso Duro Cà Foscari - Tel. (041)/5205660

CARTAVERDE OFFERS DISCOUNT ON ITALIAN RAIL FARES

If you are under 26 years you can buy CARTAVERDE at all CTS offices in Italy. It costs about $7, is valid for a year and offers you up to 30% discount on domestic rail fares.

Getting There

From North America

It's difficult to generalize about flights to Europe or to offer exact fares because prices and market conditions can fluctuate significantly from one week to the next. The best advice is to have patience and begin looking for a flight as soon as possible.

Flexibility is the best strategy because prices for direct, regularly scheduled flights are ordinarily beyond the resources of any budget traveler. Consider leaving from a travel hub; flights from certain cities—e.g., New York, Chicago, Los Angeles, San Francisco, Seattle, Vancouver, Toronto, and Montreal—are generally cheaper than flights from smaller cities. The savings on international flights from these cities may more than pay for the connecting flight or the gasoline you'll spend getting to the travel hub.

It also pays to be flexible in terms of destination. Fares to cities only 100km apart may differ by as many dollars. London and Brussels have remained consistently cheap travel targets. Cities such as Paris, Amsterdam, and especially London are popular intra-European budget flight destinations.

You may be able to arrange an "open jaw" itinerary, in which you arrive at one European city and leave from another, cutting down on travel costs within Europe. Cheaper return flights are sometimes available in Europe. You may want to be daring and wait until you're over there to buy your ticket home, though this plan could backfire and leave you temporarily stranded. European cities with consistently inexpensive transatlantic fares include London, Paris, Amsterdam, and Athens. Contact **CIEE** in France, 31, rue St. Augustin, 75002 Paris (tel. 42 66 34 73; Métro Opéra). In England, visit **STA Travel**, 74 & 86 Old Brompton Rd., London SW7 3LQ (tel. (071) 937 99 21 for European travel, 937 99 62 for the rest of the world) or **Travel CUTS**, 295-A Regent St., W1R 7YA London (tel. (071) 255 19 44). Most major airlines maintain a fare structure that reaches its peak between mid-June and early September. Of course, off-season travel is usually cheaper. If you know well in advance that you will be traveling in the summer, talk to a travel agent right away; there may be special fares available for those who book in February or March.

Finally, shop around. Have a knowledgeable travel agent guide you through the morass of travel options. It's best to inquire at several places. In addition, check the Sunday travel sections of major newspapers for bargain fares. Student travel organizations such as CIEE in the U.S. or Travel CUTS in Canada are excellent sources of information; they specialize in budget travel and offer deals of which regular travel agents may be unaware.

A **charter** flight is the most consistently economical option. You can book charters up until the last minute although most summer flights fill up several months in advance. Charter flights allow you to stay abroad up to one or two years. You must choose your return dates when you book your flight, and if you cancel your ticket within 14 or 21 days of your departure, you will lose some or all of your money. Few travel insurance policies will cover your cancellation unless it's caused by serious unforeseen illness, death, or natural disaster.

Although charter flights are less expensive, they can also be less reliable. Charter companies reserve the right to cancel flights up to 48 hours before departure. They will do their best to find you another flight, but your delay could be days, not just hours. To avoid last-minute problems, pick up your ticket in advance of the departure date. In the summer of 1990, charter flights from the East Coast of the US to Paris started around US$289 one way.

CIEE was among the first on the charter scene and offers flights to destinations worldwide. Their subsidiary, **Council Travel,** offers extremely popular flights, so reserve early. Call (800) 223-7402, in NY (212) 661-1450, or write them at the address listed above. Their special student fares from the East Coast to Europe were about US$195-295 one way in summer 1990. Other charter companies include **DER Tours,** 11933 Wilshire Blvd., Los Angeles, CA 90025 (tel. (800) 937-1234); **Travel Avenue,** 641 W. Lake St., #1104, Chicago, IL 60606 (tel. (800) 333-3335 or (312) 876-1116); and **Canadian Holidays,** 3507 Frontage Rd., #220, Tampa, FL 33607

(tel. (800) 237-0314). In Canada, try **Travel CUTS,** 187 College St., Toronto, Ont. M5T 1P7 (tel. (416) 979-2406).

If you decide to make your transatlantic crossing with a commercial airline, you'll be purchasing greater flexibility, reliability, and comfort. Look into smaller carriers such as Icelandair, Virgin Atlantic, and Martinair Holland which may undercut the fares of large airlines. **Advanced Purchase Excursion (APEX) fares** provide you with confirmed reservations, a benefit for those with a relatively fixed itinerary. **Super APEX** fares are available to those who plan to stay between 7 and 21 days and book at least 30 days in advance. Non-refundable, round-trip fares from the East Coast to Paris were about US$498-730 in 1990. Regular APEX fares allow you to stay up to three months, are partially refundable, and require purchase at least 21 days ahead; in 1990 round trip fares ranged from around US$622 for low season to $886 for high. To change an APEX reservation, you must pay a US$50 to $100 penalty, and to change a return flight you must pay a US$100 penalty or upgrade your ticket, which will cost well over US$100. For summer travel, book APEX fares early—by June you may have difficulty getting the departure date you want.

Another option is to fly **standby.** It's flexible; you can come and go as you please. The disadvantage is that flying standby during the peak season can be uncertain. Few major airlines offer standby fares; call individual carriers for more information.

And then there's **Airhitch,** 2970 Broadway, #100, New York, NY 10025 (tel. (212) 864-2000). You choose a date range in which to travel and several possible destinations, and they place you with 99% certainty in a vacant spot on a flight in your date range to one of your destinations. Your flexibility pays off; one way flights to Europe from the East Coast have cost US$160 for years.

In recent years last-minute discount clubs have sprung up, making available unsold seats on scheduled flights, cruises, and tours. Members save on European travel, including charter flights and tour packages. (Annual dues US$30-50.) Check with the following companies for details: **UniTravel,** P.O. Box 12485, St. Louis, MO 63132 (tel. (800) 325-2222 or (314) 569-0900); **Access International,** 101 W. 31st St., #1104, New York, NY 10001 (tel. (800) TAKE OFF (825-3633) or (212) 333-7280); **Worldwide Discount Travel Club,** 1674 Meridian Ave., Miami Beach, FL 33139 (tel. (305) 534-2082); **Discount Travel International,** Ives Bldg., #205, Narberth, PA 19072 (tel. (800) 543-0110 for travel informaion, (305) 726-0062 for membership information, in PA (215) 668-2182); and **Traveler's Advantage,** 49 Music Sq. W., Nashville, TN 37203 (tel. (800) 548-1116). The **Last Minute Travel Club** recently waived its membership fee; it is located at 132 Brookline Ave., Boston, MA 02215 (tel. (800) 527-8646, in Boston (617) 267-9800). Ask about any restrictions that might affect your travel plans when buying a charter ticket.

Enterprising travelers who can travel light might consider flying to Europe as a **courier.** A company hiring you as a courier will use your checked-luggage space for freight; you're left with only the carry-on allowance. You must make one- to three-month advance reservations and also turn your luggage receipts over to a company representative upon arrival. In return, the company pays the lion's share of your fare. You can fly from New York to Paris and back as a courier for **NOW Voyager,** 74 Varick St., #307. New York, NY 10013 (tel. (212) 432-1616). NOW Voyager also arranges flights from New York to London, Madrid, and Frankfurt; you can easily get to France from any of these cities. Another courier company is **Halbert Express,** 147-05 176th St., Jamaica, NY 11434 (tel. (718) 656-8189). *Courier Air Travel Handbook,* by Mark Field, explains procedures for traveling as a courier; for a copy (US$9.95) write to Courier Air Travel, 3661 N. Campbell Ave. #342, Tucson, AZ 85719.

From Europe

By Plane

If charters to your ultimate destination are booked and commercial flights are too expensive, you can always fly to London and connect with an intra-European flight. **Council Travel** offers rates of around US$55-89 between London or Amsterdam and Paris. In London, check newspapers, travel agencies, and student travel organizations for bargain charter flights. The **Air Travel Advisory Bureau,** Morley House, Regent St., London W1R 5AB (tel. (071) 636 50 00) puts travelers in touch with the cheapest carriers for free. Also contact **STA Travel** or a **CIEE** office for information about inexpensive flights throughout Europe.

You may also want to consider special student fares offered within Europe, which can be competitive with ferry ticket prices. See a student travel organization such as CIEE about this option. Finally, check on special deals offered by national airlines if you fly with them across the Atlantic. For continental travel, some of the lowest fares can be found on Eastern European airlines. Note that baggage limitations for intra-European flights are lower than those for flights to and from North America (20kg as opposed to 70 lbs).

By Train

You can get to France from nearly anywhere on the continent by train. **BIJ** tickets remain one of the cheapest options for travelers under 26. They cut up to 50% off regular second-class rail fares on international routes and are valid on the vast majority of trains. When you buy a BIJ ticket, you specify both your destination and route and have the option of stopping anywhere along that route for up to two months.

You can buy BIJ tickets in the U.K. or on the continent. They are available from **Eurotrain** outlets as well as other student travel agencies. Eurotrain consists of nine student organizations in Europe; in England, it is located at 52 Grosvenor Gardens, London SW1W OAG (tel. (071) 730 85 18).

By Bus

Miracle Bus and **Grey-Green Coaches** are two other reasonable coach services running between major cities. For information on Miracle Bus routes, contact their office at 408 The Strand, London WC2 (tel. (01) 379 60 55). Contact Grey-Green Coaches at 53 Stamford Hill, London N16 5DT (tel. (01) 800 80 10). **Eurolines** and **Europabus,** run by European Railways, both serve major European cities. In England, tickets are sold by National Express offices and at stations. For more information, contact Eurolines/Via in France, 3-5, av. de la Porte de la Villette, 75019 Paris (tel. (1) 40 38 93 93); Europabus *c/o* German Rail, 747 Third Ave., 33rd Floor, New York, NY 10017 (tel. (800) 223-6063; in NY (212) 308-6447); or Europabus/Deutsche Touring, Mannheimerstr. #4, 6000 Frankfurt (tel. (069) 23 07 35).

By Ferry

Many ferries link France with England and Ireland. **Sealink British Ferries** and **P&O European Ferries** offer extensive service across the English Channel. Sealink ferries leave from Dover, take about one and a half hours, and are the most frequent (at peak times every 75 min.). Seven miles away at the Folkestone port, ships leave for Boulogne daily (6 per day). Standard foot passenger fare on the Dover and Folkestone routes is £17.50, with savings up to 50% on certain return packages. Alternate routes between England and France include Portsmouth (4¾ hr., night service 6 hr.) or Weymouth (3 hr. 55 min., night service 6 hr.) to Cherbourg, and Newhaven to Dieppe (4 per day, 4 hr.). **P&O European Ferries** operates the fastest crossing by ship—just 75 minutes from Dover to Calais. Other convenient channel crossings include Portsmouth to Le Havre and Cherbourg, and Dover to Oostende and Zeebrugge in Belgium (3¾-4¼ hr.). Le Havre has the fastest road connections to Paris, and Cherbourg is ideal for a scenic route through Normandy to Brittany. **Brittany Ferries** run from Plymouth to Santander/Roscoff, and Portsmouth and St-Malo/Caen. Standard foot passenger fare from all Dover routes is £17.50, with substantial savings available on fixed-period returns. **Irish Continental Lines** offers ferry service to Cherbourg or Le Havre from Rosslare in Ireland, and to Le Havre from Cork. Irish Continental is rather expensive, but covered by Eurail and Inter-Rail passes.

Traveling by hovercraft is quicker (35 min.), but one should book in advance. **Hoverspeed** hovercrafts depart for Calais or Boulogne from Dover. Service is suspended in rough weather, so you may find yourself waiting for a ferry instead. Hoverspeed also offers combination rail/bus and hovercraft service to and from London, Paris, Brussels, Amsterdam, and points in southwestern France. Hoverspeed operates a new summer service to and from London, Lourdes, and Andorra. Students under 26 travel at youth rates. For information, write **Travelloyd,** 8 Berkeley Sq., London W1, or the British Travel Centre, 12 Lower Regent St., London SW1.

Once There

Transportation

Plane

Two main airlines serve major French cities and resorts: **Air France** and **Air Inter. U.T.A.** (Union des Transports Aériens) offers limited service within France. Although Air Inter and U.T.A. offer a wide range of discounts, domestic air travel in Europe is rarely an inexpensive option.

Train

Most European trains are fast, punctual, and convenient. France has a vast rail network, and its national rail company, the **Société Nationale de Chemins de Fer (SNCF),** is frighteningly efficient. Trains go almost everywhere. Off the main lines between cities and large towns, however, service is both less frequent and less convenient. Consequently, be prepared for long waits and obscure timetables. Buses fill in shorter gaps in the system, and recently a few unprofitable SNCF train routes have been replaced with SNCF buses, which also honor railpasses.

Overnight trains will save you money on accommodations but are a prime target for thieves. Spend a few extra dollars for a berth in a *couchette* (bunkbed) car. Keep the window open while you sleep, as compartments have been known to be gassed and then burgled. Bring your own food and drink—it's expensive (and often indigestible) in the restaurant cars, and the water from the bathroom faucets is not suitable for drinking. If you'll be traveling during a peak (red) period and don't want to risk standing for hours, you should reserve a seat in advance. Train discounts apply during the off-peak blue and white periods.

Every major railroad station in France carries schedules, and you can purchase the complete SNCF timetable at newsstands in the stations. SNCF representatives in the U.S. provide material on France Railpasses and Eurailpasses, as well as a booklet of French and European fares. Thomas Cook publishes the incredibly useful *European Timetable,* available from Forsyth Travel Library. Every major train station provides train information at computer tellers, via various representatives at the station, or most commonly, on poster timetables.

If you purchase your ticket in France, always remember to validate it in one of the orange ticket punches (with signs marked "compostez votre billet") at the entrance to the platforms. If the ticket is purchased in the U.S. or Canada, these requirements are waived. Eurailpass, Eurail Youthpass, or France Railpass holders *must* validate their passes before boarding their first train; otherwise, they may be heavily fined. A railroad ticket counter (not a regular ticket window) can validate your pass. If you break your journey, you must validate your ticket again after the stopover. Always keep your ticket with you, as you may have to present it during your trip and when you finally leave the train.

Reservations are recommended for longer trips on all international trains, though you can usually find a seat on shorter journeys. The TGV (*train à grande vitesse*) serves major cities and is faster and more comfortable than normal express trains ("express" or "rapide"); it always requires a reservation fee even if you have a railpass. The TGV is also more expensive than other trains, and during peak periods you may have to pay a supplementary fee.

With a **France Railpass** (formerly the France Vacances Special pass), travelers can travel for four days within a 15-day period (US$149 1st class, US$99 2nd class) or nine days within a 30-day period (US$249 1st class, US$175 2nd class). The days of use need not be consecutive. The pass includes a pass for the Paris Métro, covering the city's buses, subways, and RER trains for one day. You also get free transfer from Orly or Roissy Airports to Paris and back, and you are exempted from the supplement on TGV trains (though you still must pay the reservation fee). Other bonuses include a discount on car rentals at over 200 rail stations. You can buy the railpasses in North America at offices of the French National Railroad or from travel agents.

The **Carte Vermeille** entitles travelers over 60 to 50% off first- or second-class tickets for trips in the blue period. It can be obtained at the larger rail stations (valid for 1 yr.). Travelers under 26 may take advantage of the **Carte Jeune.** For 150F, you get a card valid all over France from June 1 to September 30, good for reductions of up to 50% on all blue period train routes except those in Paris and its suburbs. The card also gets you a 50% discount on one round-trip ferry ride and bargains at campgrounds, hotels, restaurants, theaters, museums, and discos. The card is available at all major train stations throughout France. Bring a passport-type photo and ID. The **Carré Jeune,** like the Carte Jeune, gets discounts of up to 50% on blue period trips and is valid for one year. Unlike the Carte Jeune, it is valid only for four train rides, so make sure the combined savings are more than the Carré Jeune itself. SNCF also offers family discounts of up to 50% during "blue" periods, but you must provide proof of marriage and bring ID photos.

Once in Europe, those under 26 may also purchase **BIJ tickets,** available at Eurotrain and Wasteels offices, which cut up to 50% off regular second-class rail fares on international runs. In Paris, Eurotrain is are located at 3, bd. des Capucines,

75002 (tel. 42 66 00 90), and at the Student Travel Center (STC), 20, rue des Carmes, 75005 (tel. 43 25 00 76). Most major cities have have Eurotrain or Wasteels offices. Check at STC's Travel Services Desk or at any office in Europe for addresses and information.

If you plan to travel a great deal during your trip, look into purchasing a railpass. The **Eurailpass** is valid for unlimited rail travel in Western European countries, including the Republic of Ireland, but not Great Britain or Northern Ireland. You can travel first class for periods ranging from 15 days (US$340) to three months (US$930). If you're under 26, you qualify for the **Eurail Youthpass**, good for one month (US$380) or two months (US$500) of second-class travel. With the **Eurail Saverpass,** three or more people may travel together for 15 days, valid to the end of the year, for US$240 per person. Two people traveling together may take advantage of this Saverpass October to March. The **Flexipass** allows you to travel on specific days during a longer period: five days within a 15-day period for US$198, or 14 days in a month-long period for US$458. You must get your Eurailpass or Eurail Youthpass in North America; you *cannot* buy these tickets in Europe. Purchase them from a travel agent, CIEE, the Educational Travel Center, or Let's Go Travel Services.

The **InterRail** pass is an alternative for travelers under 26 who plan to travel in countries not covered by the Eurailpass. The pass allows for one month of unlimited second-class travel in all countries covered by Eurail, plus Great Britain, Morocco, Yugoslavia, Romania, and Hungary. You may purchase the pass only if you can prove (or convince a clerk) that you have been a European resident for six months. The pass gives you only a 50% reduction in the country where you buy it, so you should try to purchase it outside France if that is where you will do most of your traveling. Major rail stations sell the pass (about US$240).

Bus

In France, buses usually serve tour groups or fill in gaps in train service. When buses and trains cover the same routes, the bus is usually slightly cheaper and slower. For routes and fares, check at the local tourist office or bus station (*gare routière,* usually next to the railway station). **Europabus, Eurolines,** and **Miracle Bus** offer inexpensive transport to major cities in Europe and beyond.

Car

If you are traveling with a companion or in a group, renting or leasing a car may be the most enjoyable way to see France. Renting is expensive, though; you can expect to pay at least US$175-200 per week for a four-seater, excluding taxes (28%) and deposit. Parking in cities can be expensive.

If you want a car for longer than three weeks, leasing becomes more economical than renting. Beware, though, that along with the economy of leasing come several potential pitfalls, such as hidden servicing expenses. Some tourists have found that a purchase/resale plan is cheaper than renting for long vacations. You must arrange the deal before you go; contact the AAA or the CAA for advice.

Most car-rental companies require renters to be over age 20 and have a major credit card. Several U.S. firms offer rental and leasing plans in France. Send for their catalogs. Compare prices carefully; they vary substantially between firms. Also, make sure that rental prices include the T.V.A. tax. Some companies are **Auto-Europe,** P.O. Box 1097, Camden, ME 04843 (tel. (800) 223-5555; in Canada (800) 458-9503); **Europe by Car, Inc.,** 1 Rockefeller Plaza, New York, NY 10020 (tel. (800) 223-1516); and **Kemwel Group,** 106 Calvert St., Harrison, NY 10528-3199 (tel. (800) 678-0678). **France Auto Vacances,** 420 Lexington Ave., New York, NY 10170 (tel. (800) 234-1426) has a three-week minimum and offers a $50 rebate for students; CIEE also offers discounted rental and leasing plans to students and faculty members.

If you know before you go that you will need to rent a car, it's a good idea to make arrangements in advance to ensure availability; making arrangements once in France is also relatively simple. **Avis, Hertz, Solvet, Budget,** and **Europcar** oper-

ate agencies all over the world, the last two generally being the least expensive. **Europcar** has an office at 145 av. Malekoff, 75016 Paris (tel. 45 00 08 06). The **French National Railroad (SNCF)** offers a train-plus-car rental package available in about 200 cities. Many firms in the U.S. and France rent campers (sometimes called "motor caravans"), which can also be practical when the cost is split among several people.

Buying a used car in Europe is another option. *How to Buy and Sell a Used Car in Europe* (US$4.95 plus 75¢ postage) contains useful tips; write to Gil Friedman, 226 Redmonde Rd., Eureka, CA 95501 (tel. (707) 444-8474). If you can afford a new car, contact **Nemet Auto International,** 153-12 Hillside Ave., Jamaica, NY 11432 (tel. (800) 221-0177), a major firm dealing with European car purchase plans and overseas delivery. Send for their catalog of prices and shipping rates. The **Kemwel Group** also has a European car purchase plan. The **National Highway Traffic Safety Administration,** U.S. Department of Transportation, Office of Vehicle Safety Compliance, 400 7th St. SW, #6113, Mailbox NES-32, Washington, DC 20590 (tel. (202) 366-2830), will provide you with information on safety requirements for imported cars.

Once you have a car, you'll have to adjust to the French road system. The speed limit on *autoroutes* is 130kph, or 80mph. Somewhat slower are the *Routes Nationales* that run through towns. For a synopsis of French driving regulations, write to the French Government Tourist Office. Cars drive on the right side of the road in France. You should be especially aware of the *priorité à droite:* cars approaching from the right have the right of way, no matter what the relative size of the roads. Although you do not need an international driving permit to drive in France, it can aid in smoothing over difficulties with police officers, and provides you with an additional piece of identification.

Michelin makes good road maps, available in book stores and kiosks. The large map #989 is especially useful. The suggested roads, drawn in yellow, supposedly bypass congested areas.

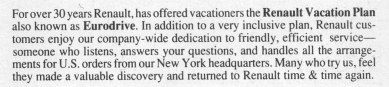

Bicycle

Cycling is an excellent way to see the countryside, and French roads, with a wealth of well-paved minor routes, are generally fine. Ride in the morning or evening when it's cool and you'll have the road to yourself. Michelin maps, available in most bookstores, mark the main roads in red, secondary roads in yellow, and local roads in white. Cyclists should avoid major *autoroutes* (marked in red with a dotted line), and heed the round road sign bordered in red with a diagram of a bike; this means bikes are forbidden. Bikers may also want the larger-scale, more expensive maps (21-52F) from the **Institut Géographique National (IGN)**, 107, rue la Boétie, 75008 Paris (tel. 42 25 87 90; Métro St-Philippe du Roule or Franklin D. Roosevelt). Experienced cyclists recommend a front bag with a transparent pocket for maps, as well as panniers, which can hold a sleeping bag. At about US$35-66, the best bike helmets are cheaper and more pleasant than critical head surgery or a well-appointed funeral. Check the helmet ratings in the May 1990 *Consumer Reports* for details.

When purchasing a bike, mail-order items will probably be cheapest, but you may want to check a local biking club or store for advice. A good mail-order outfit is **Bike Nashbar**, 4111 Simon Rd., Youngstown, OH 44512 (tel. (800) 627-4227). French treads and rim sizes differ from English sizes, but spare parts in English sizes have become available in many towns. Even so, if you plan a long ride, carry one or two extra inner tubes (*chambres à l'air*), a spare tire, a few spokes taped to the body, and a pump. You can also buy an excellent bicycle in France and have it shipped back home, but make sure you get one fitted for export. French parts are even harder to find in the U.S. than American ones are in France.

Outstanding touring regions include the Loire Valley (especially the route west of Tours to Villandry and Ussé), Normandy, Brittany, Provence, the Vosges, the Massif Central, and the somewhat mountainous Jura. In the Pyrenees and the Alps, you (and your bicycle) can catch a lift up the mountain on a train and then cycle down. For touring information, first consult the tourist bureau annexed to most French embassies. The **Fédération Française de Cyclotourisme,** 8, rue Jean-Marie Jégo, 75013 Paris (tel. 45 80 30 21; Métro Corvisart), is a non-profit, member-supported liaison between 2000 cycle-touring clubs. Although they are not a travel agency or tourist information bureau, they are friendly and will advise foreign cyclists on a limited basis. (Include 3 reply coupons for an airmail response.)

Most airlines will accept a boxed bike as one of your two pieces of luggage, provided that the total baggage weight does not exceed the given limit (70 lbs. for flights to and from North America, 20kg for intra-European flights). You can also count a bicycle as an extra piece of luggage on transatlantic flights; it will cost about US$30-50 each way, even if you have a round-trip ticket. Some airlines supply bike boxes; you can also obtain one at a bike shop, which often give away old cartons. Carry a wrench to the airport and know how to make adjustments on the spot if necessary.

Bikers will find it convenient to fly into Orly, since you can assemble your bike in the airport and ride it into Paris on the *piste cyclable,* a bike path that avoids heavy traffic the first few miles. If you arrive at the Roissy-Charles de Gaulle airport, you can take the Roissy Rail commuter train into Paris. Bikes are not allowed on the métro, though this may not be rigorously enforced.

Once in France, you can easily combine biking with train travel. For information in advance, write to SNCF for the brochure *Guide du train et du vélo.* Regardless of how far you go, it will cost about 42F to register a bicycle as baggage for transport. The SNCF provides cartons (about 15F) to protect the bike in transit. Bicycles are easily damaged in transit, so all removable parts, such as headlights, should be taken off the frame or padded and taped. Look for the SNCF advertisements that say "*Dans certains trains votre vélo peut voyager avec vous, gratuitement.*" On trains thus advertised (sometimes called *trains omnibus*), your bike travels with you, and you save the registration fee. On other trains, your bike may arrive up to 48 hours after you.

You can also rent bicycles in many of the larger towns, and it is usually possible to get a serviceable 10-speed model. Try Bicyclub S.A., 8, pl. de la Porte Champerret, 75017 Paris (tel. 42 27 28 82; Métro Porte Champerret). Bicyclub also organizes tours for individuals or small groups in different areas of France and Europe. The SNCF rents bicycles at most train stations for about 50F per day with a 500F deposit.

Thumb

> *Let's Go* strongly urges you to seriously consider the risks before you choose to hitch. We do not recommend hitching as a means of travel.

Hitching in France takes patience, as the country ranks among the worst in Europe for hitchhikers. If you chose to hitch, you'll have better luck in regions such as Brittany, with lots of French vacationers and relatively few foreign tourists. Getting out of big cities such as Lyon or traveling along the Riviera can be almost impossible.

The system of primary roads consists of *Autoroutes* (designated by A) and the *Routes Nationales* (the N roads). Hitchhikers find the *autoroutes* best for long-distances, but it is illegal to stand on the *autoroute* itself—hitchhikers often stand on entrance ramps.

Hitchhikers will have more luck if they try to look neat and respectable, if they stand rather than sit, if they carry a destination sign, and if they travel light. Service stations and the stopping areas near toll booths are places where drivers can stop and get back on the road safely. Truckers may offer long rides, but find gas stations, weigh stations, and roadside restaurants easier to stop at than on the roadside. It is illegal for truckers to pick up more than two passengers at one time.

It is not safe to hitch alone in France. Women should always hitch in pairs. Two men may have difficulty securing a ride. Always refuse rides in the back of a two-door car. Don't lock the door, and keep your luggage handy—don't put it in the trunk if you can avoid it. In an emergency try opening the car door; this may surprise the driver enough to make them slow down. If you feel uneasy about the ride for any reason, get out at the first opportunity or firmly demand to be let out.

You may be able to find rides (or hitching companions) by checking message boards in student travel offices or in student gathering places. **ALLOSTOP**, 84, passage Brady, 75010 Paris (tel. 47 70 02 01, departures from Paris 42 46 00 66), with offices in many major cities, brings together drivers and riders to share expenses. Telephone or write a few days in advance if you can. For passengers, it costs 200F for eight trips within a two-year period. Check with ALLOSTOP about prices for other packages.

Boat

France has more than 7000 miles of navigable rivers, canals, lakes, and sea coast. To float through the countryside or take better advantage of your time at the seaside, contact the **Syndicat National des Loueurs de Bateaux de Plaisance**, Port de la Bourdonnais, 75007 Paris (tel. 45 55 10 49). They'll set you up in whatever region and boat that interests you, from dinghies and canoes to yachts. For information on waterways suitable for canoeing, contact the **Fédération Française de Canoe-Kayak**, BP 58-94340 Joinville Le Pont (tel. 48 89 39 89).

Foot

If you have more time than money and prefer countryside to cityscape, try hiking France's extensive network of long-distance footpaths. The **Fédération Française de la Randonnée Pédestre**, 8, av. Marceau (*entrée* 9, av. George V), 75008 Paris (tel. 47 23 62 32), provides topographical maps (*topo-guides*) with itineraries for 40,000km of footpaths. Huts or mountain hostels, which usually serve meals, are located along many of the suggested routes. The member organizations of the federation organize group trips through the countryside.

Proper **hiking gear** is essential. Lightweight non-leather hiking boots are lighter, more comfortable, less expensive, and just as rugged as the old-fashioned thick leather ones. You will also need a sweater, water-proof poncho, change of socks, long pants, shorts, and a comfortable pack with a hip belt. You may also want to carry a light butane or white gas stove and a mess kit. Remember that high altitudes and hot sun make mid-day trekking unsafe; bring sunscreen, a hat, and plenty of water.

For more information about hiking, contact the **Club Alpin Français**, 9, rue la Boëtie, 75008 Paris (tel. 47 42 38 46). The club runs several centers in the Alps that provide instruction in Alpine technique. The following books may also help you plan your journey: *Walking in the Alps* (Hunter, US$9.95); *Hiking and Walking Guide to Europe* (Passport Books, US$7.95); and *Walking in France* (Oxford Illustrated Press, US$9.95).

Accommodations

Hostels

The **International Youth Hostel Federation (IYHF)**, 9 Guessens Rd., Welwyn Garden City, Herts, AL8 6GW, England (tel. (0707) 33 24 87) offers IYHF cards, hostel handbooks, information on budget travel, and summer positions as tour group leaders. It distributes the *International Youth Hostel Handbook, Vol. 1: Europe and the Mediterranean* (US$10.95, postage included). To stay in an IYHF hostel, you must be a member. The **IYHF** card costs US$25 (ages over 54 US$15, under 18 US$10, family US$35).

The **Fédération Unie des Auberges de Jeunesse (FUAJ)**, the French branch of the **International Youth Hostel Federation (IYHF)**, runs more than 200 youth hos-

5,300 hostels in 68 countries on 6 continents.

One card.

With the American Youth Hostels Membership Card,

you can stay at 5,300 hostels around the world.

Hostels are great places to make new friends.

And the prices are incredibly low,

just 35¢ to $20 a night for a dorm-style room.

For an application, call 202-783-6161.

Or write: American Youth Hostels,

Dept. 801, P.O. Box 37613, Washington, DC 20013-7613.

INTERNATIONAL YOUTH HOSTEL FEDERATION
American Youth Hostels

tels in France. **American Youth Hostels,** the U.S. affiliate of IYHF, dispenses the cards in most major cities. Write them at AYH, Inc., P.O. Box 37613, Washington, DC 20013-7613 (tel. (202) 783-6161). In Canada, write to the **Canadian Hostelling Association,** 1600 James Maysmyth Dr., 6th Floor, Gloucester, Ottawa, Ont. K1B 5N4 (tel. (613) 748-5638). **Youth Hostels Association of England and Wales (YHA),** 14 Southampton St., Covent Gardens, London WC2E 7HY (tel. (071) 836 10 36); also at Trevalyn House, 8 St. Stephen's Hill, St. Alban's, Herts AL 1 2DY (tel. (07) 275 52 15). **Australian Youth Hostels Association (AYHA),** 60 Mary St., Surry Hills, Sydney, New South Wales 2010, Australia (tel. (02) 212 11 51). **Youth Hostels Association of New Zealand,** P.O. Box 436, cnr. Manchester and Gloucester St., Christchurch, 1, New Zealand (tel. 79 99 70). Let's Go Travel Services, the Educational Travel Center, and Travel CUTS dispense the cards as well. IYHF cards are also available in France at the Paris office or at any hostel; according to international agreement, though, you should buy a membership in your home country. Membership purchased in France costs about 100F, but if you've lived there for a year, it costs 70F. The *International Youth Hostel Handbook,* volume one (US$10.95), details the locations of many hostels in Europe and includes a basic map. For a more detailed list of hostels in France, contact the FUAJ, 27, rue Pajol, 75018 Paris (tel. 42 41 59 00; Métro La Chapelle).

A night in an *auberge de jeunesse* costs roughly half the price of a hotel stay—prices average 24 to 70F, with breakfast (usually not obligatory) averaging an additional 12 to 15F. Accommodations usually consist of bunk beds in single-sex dormitories, and most hostels either serve evening meals or have kitchen facilities you can use. Quality varies widely; some hostels are extremely well-kept and well-situated; others are in run-down barracks far from the center of town.

Hostel life has its drawbacks: an early curfew (usually 10-11pm, in Paris midnight-2am), lack of privacy, prohibitions against smoking and drinking, a 10am-5pm lockout, a three-day limit to your stay, hordes of vacationing school-children, and (sometimes) required household chores. But the prices compensate for these inconveniences, and many hostels fill quickly in July and August. Lockout and curfew times are often flexible—many hostels leave a back door open most of the night. Some hostels accept reservations—it's worth calling ahead—but always arrive early if you can.

Many hostels require **sheet sleeping sacks,** which they rent or sell. Some hostels will let you use your sleeping bag instead. You can make one by folding a sheet lengthwise and sewing the long side and one end. You can also get a sleeping sack before you go for an extravagant US$14-16.

In many cities and towns, rooms are available in **Foyers de Jeunes Travailleurs et de Jeunes Travailleuses,** residence halls founded for young workers with jobs in cities far from home. They are usually single-sex dorms with single rooms and a bathroom in the hall. They accept foreign travelers if there's space available, and offer the advantages of hostels without the disadvantages (lockout, curfew). The *foyers* offer a fairly good deal to the single traveler, and they almost always have room because tourists don't know about them.

Hotels

French hotels can be a bargain. The French government publishes a comprehensive guide that classifies hotels with a star system: 4L (luxury), 4, 3, 2, 1. Most hotels in *Let's Go* are one-star or unclassified establishments, though two-star establishments offering inexpensive rooms are sometimes included. As a rule, French hotels charge by the room and not by the number of people staying in it, so two traveling together can sleep more inexpensively than one. Most rooms come with double beds. Expect to pay at least 65-90F for singles. If your room has no shower, you'll have to pay extra (12-25F) or, especially in small hotels, go without. When looking at hotels, remember that the French call the ground floor the *rez-de-chaussée,* and start numbering with the first floor *above* the ground floor (*premier étage*).

Many hotels serve a *petit déjeuner obligatoire* (obligatory breakfast), which costs 12-20F. Since local cafés often serve croissants and coffee for less, you may want to opt out of breakfast if you can. Beware of hotels, usually in heavily touristed areas, that require *demi-pension* (one obligatory meal with each night's stay).

If you plan to visit a popular tourist area, especially during a festival, it is advisable to write ahead for reservations. Most hotels will confirm reservations only upon receipt of a check—not a credit card number—for the first night's rent. Include an International Reply Coupon for a prompt reply.

Student Accommodations

Short-term student housing is available in summer in the dormitories of most French universities. Contact the **Centre Régional des Oeuvres Universitaires (CROUS)** (address above). Travelers interested in summer housing and students interested in year-long accommodations can also contact the **Cité Internationale Universitaire de Paris,** 19, bd. Jourdan, 75690 Paris Cédex 14 (tel. 45 89 68 52). *Foyers* (youth residence halls) are a good bet in Paris. These single-sex dormitories require a three-day minimum stay. You can also find a bed through the **Accueil des Jeunes en France (AJF),** a central booking organization for youth accommodations in Paris. AJF has 8000 beds at its disposal year-round and more than 11,000 beds during the summer. The following are AJF's offices in Paris.

AJF Beaubourg, 119, rue St-Martin, 75004 Paris (tel. 42 77 87 80; Métro Rambuteau/Hôtel de Ville/Châtelet-Les-Halles), opposite the Centre Georges Pompidou. Open Mon.-Sat. 9:30am-7pm.

AJF Gare du Nord (tel. 42 85 86 19; Métro Gare du Nord), facing platform 19 in the arrival hall. Open June-Sept. 8am-10pm; March-May and Oct. 9:30am-6:30pm.

AJF Marais (Hôtel de Ville), 16, rue du Pont Louis Philippe, 75004 Paris (tel. 42 78 04 82; Métro Hôtel de Ville/Pont Marie). Open June-September Mon.-Sat. 9:30am-6:30pm.

AJF Quartier Latin, 139, bd. St-Michel, 75005 Paris (tel. 43 54 95 86; Métro Port Royal). Open Mon.-Fri. 9:30am-6:30pm.

These offices guarantee every young traveler an immediate reservation for decent, low-cost lodging. Prices average 77-95F per night for bed and breakfast. Avoid buying AJF vouchers from travel agents, who sometimes charge high commissions; deal directly with the offices listed above. AJF also provides train and bus tickets at reduced prices and runs a youth center in Paris near pl. de la Bastille, **Résidence Bastille,** 151, av. Ledru Rollin, 75011 Paris (tel. 43 79 53 86; Métro Voltaire/Ledru Rollin/Bastille). Singles cost 150F, and rooms with two, three, or four beds are 80F per person.

Camping

Camping liberates you from hostel regulations and drab hotels. There are campgrounds all over France, many of which are by lakes, rivers, or the ocean. However, be aware that the vacationing French often arrive at campgrounds with their trailers, radios, and a great deal of cooking paraphernalia, and there usually isn't much space between sites. In August you might have to arrive well before 11am to ensure yourself a spot.

French campgrounds, like hotels and restaurants, are classified by a star system. Three- and four-star sites are usually large, grassy campgrounds with hot showers, bathrooms, a restaurant or store, and often a lake or swimming pool nearby. Occasional student discounts are offered. Some campsites will ask for your passport, but resist giving it to them, and try to substitute a less vital piece of identification. The **International Camping Carnet** (membership card) is one highly acceptable substitute, and will save you a lot of time and money if you intend to do much camping (see below).

Purchase your equipment before you leave. American packs are generally more durable and comfortable, and less expensive, than European ones. As a rule, prices go down in the fall as old merchandise is cleaned out. **Backpacks** come with either an external frame or an internal X- or A-shaped frame. If your load is not extraordinarily heavy and you plan to use the pack mainly as a suitcase, choose an internal-frame model. It's more manageable on crowded trains and when hitching, and it's less likely to be mangled by rough handling. A good pack costs US$100-300.

Your **sleeping bag** need not be down; a good synthetic fiber is almost as warm and dries much more quickly. A sleeping bag is rated according to the lowest temperature in which it can be used. A three-season bag (spring, summer, fall) is good in temperatures ranging from 5° to 30° and will cost at least US$110 for synthetic or US$135 for down. A bag for more casual use, however, will cost about US$40. At about US$10-15, an **ensolite pad** (much warmer than foam rubber) is a real bargain, providing crucial protection from cold, damp, and often rocky ground. Therm-A-Rest (US$40) is a hybrid ensolite pad and air mattress which virtually inflates itself, and regular air mattresses start at US$50. Good **tents** are expensive (at least US$95 for a 2-person), but are a sound investment. Often you can find a model from the previous year at a drastically reduced price. A **tarpaulin** rigged between two trees will keep you from getting completely soaked in a downpour, but only experienced campers should rough it with just a tarp. The following organizations provide camping information or supplies.

Campor, 810 Rte. 17N, P.O. Box 997-P, Paramus, NJ 07653-0997 (tel. (800) 526-4784). Offers name-brand equipment at attractive prices.

L.L. Bean, 1 Casco St., Freeport, ME 04033 (tel. (800) 221-4221, customer service (800) 341-4341). A well-established firm that sells camping equipment and outdoor clothes. Publishes a quarterly catalog. Always open.

National Campers and Hikers Association, Inc., 4804 Transit Rd., Bldg. 2, Depew, NY 14043 (tel. (716) 668-6242). Issues the **International Camping Carnet,** required by some European campgrounds. The US$23 fee includes membership in the association. Short bibliography of travel guides for campers and a list of camping stores in major European cities.

Recreational Equipment, Inc. (REI), Commercial Sales, P.O. Box C-88126, Seattle, WA 98188 (tel. (800) 426-4840). Long-time outdoor equipment cooperative favorite. Lifetime membership (not required) US$10. Sells *Europa Camping and Caravanning* (US$13), an ency-clopedic catalog of campsites in Europe.

A good general book is *Camp Europe by Train* (US$13), available from the Forsyth Travel Library. If you plan to camp extensively, you should buy the *Guide Officiel Camping/Caravaning*. The book provides good maps and lists both ordinary campsites (including those available to caravans only—no tents), and *terrains à la ferme* (farm sites). It is available from the **Fédération Française de Camping et de Caravaning,** 78, rue de Rivoli, 75004 Paris (tel. 42 72 84 08). Michelin publishes a similar, but much less comprehensive guide, *Camping Caravaning,* geared to car-camping and designed to accompany the Michelin 1:200,000 scale maps. If you choose to camp unofficially, leave the site just as spotless as you found it. Within sight of a farmhouse, you should ask permission.

Alternative Accommodations

For a more pastoral experience, look for **logis** and **auberges de France,** hotels and restaurants roughly comparable to country inns. They serve excellent food and charge reasonable prices for comfortable rooms, although they usually charge more than the cheapest hotel. A list of them is available by writing **La Fédération Nationale des Logis de France,** 25, rue Jean Mermosz, 75008 Paris (tel. 43 59 86 67).

Gîtes de Frances offer furnished lodgings in farmhouses, cottages, and even camp-sites that meet fixed standards of comfort and price. Intended for stays of two weeks or longer and located in areas where you might hike, sail, or ski, they range from fully-equipped houses to campgrounds near working farms. **Gîtes d'étape** are designed for cyclists, hikers, and other ramblers. For further information, contact the **Fédération Nationale des Gîtes de France,** 35, rue Godot-de-Mauroy, 75009 Paris (tel. 47 42 25 43). *Gîtes et refuges en France* lists over 1600 places to stay for hikers, climbers, cross-country and downhill skiers, and mountaineers. Order from Editions Créer, rue Jean Amariton, 63340 Nonette.

Servas is an international host organization devoted to promoting peace and understanding among different cultures. Members may stay in host members' homes in 90 different countries. You are asked to be genuinely interested in sharing with your hosts, to contact them in advance, and to conform to the household routine. Stays are limited to two nights unless you are invited to stay longer. Prospective members are interviewed and asked to contribute US$45 plus a US$15 deposit for the host lists. To apply, write U.S. Servas Committee, Inc., 11 John St., #706, New York, NY 10038 (tel. (212) 267-0252).

Also try **Amicale Culturelle Internationale,** a non-profit organization that offers placements to visitors as paying guests in French families everywhere in France on a full-board basis, and in Paris and its suburbs on a half-board basis. Write them at 27, rue Godot-de-Mauroy, 75009 Paris (tel. 47 42 94 21). **Accueil France Famille** is a similar organization; its address is 5, rue François Coppée, F-75015 Paris (tel. 45 54 22 39).

Monasteries are ideal for those seeking a few days of peaceful contemplation. Reservations must be made well in advance. For a list of monasteries, *Repertoire de l'Hospitalité Monastique en France* (80F), write to **La Procure,** 3, rue de Mézières, 75006 Paris (tel. 45 48 20 25). For peace and quiet, **L'Accueil des Pèlerins de Chartres,** 9km from Chartres at 8, rue du Fossé-Bourg, JOUY, 28300 Mainvilliers (tel. 37 22 24 44), may be just the place. Light chores are expected and smoking is prohibited, but the five-day maximum stay comes with nightly slide presentations on Chartres and its previous pilgrims. Rooms cost 35F per night, dormitory beds 15F, and camping 5F, and meals are available. The obligatory member card is 5F.

Life and Times

History and Politics

Little is known about the early inhabitants of France who left haunting cave paintings, carved implements and statues, and huge standing stones. The first tribe whose existence is recorded by contemporaries were a Celtic tribe the Romans called "Gauls" who arrived in the region around 1000 BC. In the 6th century BC, the Greeks founded colonies in southern France, among them Massilia (Marseille). The Romans ventured into the same area in the 2nd century BC and gave it the name "Provincia" (now Provence). In 52 BC, **Julius Caesar** defeated the Celtic leader **Vercingétorix** at the battle of Alésia, and the Romans gained control most of what is now France. Gaul's relative stability under Roman rule began to crumble in the 3rd century AD with invasions by the Franks (who gave their name to the country and its people), Alamans, Goths, Visigoths, Invisigoths and other tribes, completing the melting pot of Celts, Romans, and Germanic peoples. As Roman political power in the West waned, the once-persecuted Christian church began its 1500-year ascendance.

In 481 AD, 15-year-old **Clovis** (whose name is an early form of that most frequent of royal monikers, Louis) acceded to the Frankish throne. He united the barbarian tribes, conquered Gaul, established Paris as the capital, and converted to Christianity, making France's conversion official. Under his rule, the infamous Salic Laws, which forbade women to rule in Frankish lands, were compiled. After his death, Clovis's four sons split the kingdom. With no central authority, the Merovingian dynasty declined into incompetence, until Pepin II, the "mayor" of the royal palace, took control and unified the Merovingian lands in 687. After succeeding his father in 714, **Charles Martel** turned back Muslim invaders at Poitiers in 732, securing the French borders. His son **Pepin III**, also known as Pepin the Short, helped Rome fight off the invading Lombards from northern Italy, and, having convinced the Pope to condone his appropriation of the Frankish crown, began the Carolingian dynasty.

Pepin's son, **Charlemagne,** extended Frankish control and was crowned Holy Emperor of the Romans by Pope Leo III on Christmas Day 800. His patronage of the arts and letters brought about the "Carolingian Renaissance," a rebirth of Latin culture, which lasted from Charlemagne's accession in 768 to the death of Charles the Bald in 877. Viking raids and the splintering of the empire after Charlemagne's death put an end to the leisure necessary to sustain a flowering of learning.

When **Hugh Capet** became King of France in 987, he wielded power only in his own domain, the Ile-de-France (the greater Parisian region). He founded the Capetian line, which lasted until 1328. The 11th and 12th centuries were a period of political consolidation and expansion and of the evolution of the feudal economy, a decentralized, complex system of hierarchical agricultural dependance. **William the Conqueror,** Duke of Normandy, brought his province under firm central government, rivaling the king of France in military power, and conquered England in 1066. in 1095, Pope Urban II preached the first crusade to "liberate" the Holy Sepulchre in Jerusalem from the Muslims; many crusades followed, most bloody and unsuccessful, but the contact with other cultures brought new ideas. Eleanor of Aquitaine, wed first to Louis VII of France and then to Henry Plantagenet of England, was a patron of arts and a principal figure in the development of courtly ideals in the 12th century. **Philip II Auguste** was chiefly responsible for France's unification. During his 43-year reign, Philip married his way into the Artois, Valois, and Vermandois families and conquered Normandy and Anjou. His pious grandson **Louis IX** led two Crusades and was canonized after his death. Back in France, the Sorbonne was founded in 1253 and church schools flourished. Though in a position of relative security, the Catholic Church persecuted religious minorities—Jews, Muslims, and heretics—as a prelude to the 16th-and-17th-century Inquisition, witch hunts, and wars of religion. The bloody Albigensian crusade not only suppressed the Cathar heresy, but subordinated the culture of southern France to that of the north.

During the troubled reign of **Philip the Fair** (1285-1314), political turmoil in Rome drove Pope Clement VII to Avignon, where French popes reigned in "Babylonian captivity," while a separate line continued to sit in Rome until 1377. But Philip the Fair's troubles were minor compared to those of his successors. **Philip VI Valois**'s reign was afflicted with famine, the Black Death of 1348, and the outbreak of the Hundred Years' War, which began as a dispute over Edward III of England's right to the French throne. The French like to attribute their salvation from these threats to a peasant girl from Lorraine, **Jeanne d'Arc** (Joan of Arc). Her career began with a vision instructing her to don armor and deliver France from the English. She led the French to victory at Orléans and had **Charles VII** crowned King at Reims. Although Jeanne was tried and burned as a heretic by the English in Rouen, she bolstered France's morale, ultimately tipping the balance against the English.

The spread of Protestantism in the mid-16th century engendered new kinds of religious hostilities; many nobles were converted to the rebellious new form of devotion. In 1572, **Catherine de Medici,** regent for her son Charles IX, persuaded him to order an attack which turned into the St. Bartholomew's Day Massacre. The Paris mob ran wild and slaughtered some 2,000 Parisian Huguenots—an event that made reconciliation between the Protestant and Catholic communities a rather remote possibility. In 1589 Henri III, who had succeeded Charles IX, was assassinated and the Protestant **Henry IV** (of the Bourbon family) acceded. He reduced tensions by converting to Catholicism, reportedly saying upon conversion, *"Paris vaut bien une messe"* (Paris is well worth a mass). Issuing the Edict of Nantes in 1598, he guaranteed the religious and political rights of the Protestant community. The edict remained in effect for nearly 100 years, until 1685 when Louis XIV revoked it.

Henri's successor, **Louis XIII,** and his minister **Cardinal Richelieu,** ushered in absolutist and Catholic conservatism. The Estates General (medieval parliament) was recessed until 1789. Richelieu's reputation as a cunning statesman rested on his foreign policy and his strategies for suppressing aristocratic power. When both the Cardinal and Louis died in 1642, **Louis XIV** was five years old. During his 72-year reign, the Sun King continued Richelieu's work of constructing an absolute monarchy. He assembled the nobility around him at his magnificent and costly château Versailles and engaged them in an assortment of elaborate court rituals, keeping them busy and out of mischief. A patron of artists and playwrights (among them Corneille, Racine, and Molière), Louis XIV glittered while his people starved. His death in 1715 again left a five-year-old heir, his great-grandson Louis XV. The aging Louis XV's prophetic words, *"Après moi, le déluge"* (After me, the deluge), ushered in the ill-starred reign of Louis XVI. As the financial situation of the overextended monarchy grew worse, an attempt was made to reform national finances with an Assembly of Notables called in 1787. The group suggested that an Estates General be called to try to solve the crisis. The first Estates General since 1614 was convened at Versailles with all three estates present: the nobility, the clergy, and the bourgeoisie (who together represented a tiny fraction of French society).

After several months spent struggling for more representative government, the Third Estate dramatically declared itself the National Assembly. When the lower clergy, led by Talleyrand, joined them, the French Revolution began. Fearing a royal reactionary coup, the Paris mob seized the city and stormed the Bastille prison on July 14, 1789. On August 4, the assembly voted away all peasant feudal obligations and rents and abolished hereditary privilege. Three weeks later it adopted the Declaration of the Rights of Man. A new constitution was presented to Louis XVI on the first anniversary of Bastille Day.

Following internecine strife among revolutionary factions, the radical Jacobins were victorious, and in January 1793, Louis XVI was executed. The First Republic was scarred by the Reign of Terror. **Maximilien Robespierre** and his radical followers guillotined the perceived enemies of the state, including the widely hated Marie

Antoinette. Robespierre too was toppled from power and guillotined, and soon thereafter, most of the original revolutionaries went the way of their victims. The subsequent power vacuum was filled by the Directorate, a corrupt oligarchy. **Napoleon Bonaparte,** then a young Corsican artillery officer, used his prestige as a military strategist and dashing young general to snatch power from the Directorate in 1799. Napoleon swiftly named himself First Consul and then Emperor, drew up a new constitution, strengthened central bureaucracy, collected taxes, and instituted a draft. Taking advantage of new revenues and a strong military, Napoleon began a series of military campaigns, as remarkable for their daring as for their heaps of corpses. By 1809, Napoleon ruled all Europe west of Prussia, but the imperial adventure screeched to a halt when Napoleon confronted a foe no amount of French blood could conquer, the Russian winter. He abdicated in October 1814 and was exiled to the island of Elba, off Italy. While Talleyrand and Louis XVIII (the late king's brother) were negotiating a peace, Napoleon tried hitchhiking to southern France. In the strange footnote to his career known as the Hundred Days, he marched on Paris with an increasingly large army. The British General Wellington met and defeated Napoleon at Waterloo in Belgium in June 1815. The Emperor was then sent to the even smaller island of St-Helena, and the Congress of Vienna met and legislated an attempt to turn back time. The Bourbon dynasty was restored, and the borders of France were set as they had been in 1792.

In 1830 people revolted against conservative King Charles X. While the Revolution of 1830 could hardly be called a change of regime, the new "citizen king" **Louis-Philippe** extended suffrage and adopted a self-consciously bourgeois lifestyle. In 1848 Louis-Philippe was overthrown by a moderate Republic, which crushed a more radical workers' uprising a few months later. The first president of the Second Republic, elected by an overwhelming majority, was **Louis Napoleon,** nephew of the emperor.

Louis Napoleon outmaneuvered parliament, won over the army, found financial backing, and seized the government before the election of 1851. A year later he was proclaimed Emperor Napoleon III by national plebiscite. Industrialization sped ahead under Napoleon III. In foreign affairs, he was himself outmaneuvered by the wilier and even more cynical Bismarck. Prussia's defeat of Napoleon in 1871 sent him into exile, and the Third Republic was born. The Republican regime received its first challenge from the Paris Commune of 1871. Angry at the government for signing a humiliating peace with Germany in which Alsace and Lorraine were lost, Parisians rioted and set up a communal government. Government forces regained control by pitilessly exterminating the Communards. This was but one of the difficulties which plagued the Third Republic. A parade of politicians presided over financial crashes, blundering imperialist tactics, and the Dreyfus affair, in which the nation was polarized by the false conviction of a Jewish army officer for treason. France still lives with the legacy of the faltering Third Republic.

France, everybody's favorite battleground, emerged from the ravages of deeply entrenched warfare with Germany in **World War I** with the help of British and American forces. During the inter-war years, the country suffered from financial problems stemming from war debt and the international depression of the 1930s. Although England began to rearm heavily in the 30s, France relied on the Maginot Line, a series of fortifications on the northeastern frontier begun in 1927. In the face of Hitler's expansionism, France and England declared war on Germany in September 1939. French military leaders were unprepared to meet the German military machine that simply marched *around* the Maginot Line in May 1940. Fighting ended after a month, and a collaborationist government was set up at Vichy under aging WW I hero **Marshal Pétain.** French officials cooperated with Nazi roundups of French Jews while much of the public averted its eyes and principled individuals did what they could. The Resistance, led by **Charles de Gaulle,** again needed the help of the Allied powers to shake off the German yoke. In 1944 de Gaulle became the first president of the Fourth Republic; in the next year French women won the vote. While holding France's diverse political factions together, de Gaulle sought and eventually obtained greater powers for the presidency. In 1946 he resigned, partially to show how indispensable he was. After a series of unstable coalition governments, war in Vietnam and a revolt of the army and French settlers in Algeria in 1958, de Gaulle returned and inaugurated the Fifth Republic, which has lasted to this day.

Under the 1958 Constitution, legislative power is held by Parliament, comprised of a 317-member Senate and a 491-member National Assembly. These representatives are directly elected by universal suffrage. Executive power is held by the president, who is elected by popular vote for a term of seven years. The president appoints a Council of Ministers, headed by the Prime Minister, which manages the country and is responsible to Parliament. In January 1959, when de Gaulle became the Fifth Republic's first president, the newly formed Gaullist party swept the National Assembly elections. De Gaulle favored an aggressive foreign policy, and U.S. NATO forces were ejected from the country. After much bloodshed, the Algerian crisis came to an uneasy conclusion with the granting of independence to the former colony in 1962.

In May 1968, Paris exploded with internal unrest. For two weeks, students fought to alter the authoritarian French university system. Demonstrations led to riots, and students occupied the Sorbonne and the Odéon. The students were joined by several million workers in a general strike against low wages and lack of social reform which brought French industry to a halt and effectively paralyzed the country. The National Assembly was immediately dissolved, yet in the next general election, the Gaullist party received its greatest majority ever.

In April 1969, de Gaulle resigned (again) after staking his presidency on the outcome of a national referendum on some constitutional amendments. His successor, **Georges Pompidou,** tried to combine Gaullist foreign policy with conservative domestic policy. The continuation of Gaullism and authoritarian policies was threatened, however, by the Union of the Left—an alliance of the Socialist (*Parti Socialiste,* PS) and Communist (*Parti Communiste,* PC) parties. When Pompidou died in 1974, the Gaullists were split. A large segment refused to back the official party candidates and instead supported **Valéry Giscard d'Estaing,** nominee of the business-oriented Républicains Indépendants, who defeated the leftist candidate Mitterrand by a narrow margin. Giscard's term started with significant reforms (the voting age was reduced to 18 and abortion legalized), but gradually adopted a more conservative tone. Only the collapse of the Socialist-Communist coalition in 1977 saved Giscard's party from a major defeat in the 1978 elections. Unemployment dogged him during the 1981 presidential campaign, but the major issue was Giscard's personal style. To Europe's surprise, **François Mitterrand** was elected president by a comfortable majority, and the socialists swept 60% of the seats in the National Assembly.

Within his first two months of office, Mitterrand raised the minimum wage and instituted a mandatory fifth week of annual vacation. In March 1982, he passed a law beginning the transfer of administrative and financial power from government-appointed prefects to locally-elected departmental assemblies and regional councils, thus dismantling the strongly centralized political system that had dominated France since the time of Napoleon. As a result of this decentralization, Corsica was made a *collectivité territoriale* with its own directly elected 61-seat assembly. Much of current politics has to do with debate over the future of other territorial holdings, notably New Caledonia. Mitterand nationalized 36 banks, five key industrial groups, and two financial holding companies in the largest government takeover of private industry since World War II.

Although social benefits and working conditions have substantially improved under Mitterand, he has met with serious opposition. An economic recession in 1983 led to the adoption of deflationary policies, including reductions in public expenditures. Efforts to control inflation through wage freezes have caused a number of union strikes. The decreased support for Mitterrand's government was reflected in the poor performance of Socialists in countrywide municipal elections. Right-wing parties gained a majority in the National Assembly as well. In the June 1984 elections of the European Parliament, Socialists again suffered serious setbacks, taking only 20 of the 81 seats allocated to France. The united Rassemblement pour la République (RPR) and Union pour la Démocratie Française (UDF) opposition, headed by Simone Veil, won 41 seats.

The real test of strength for the governing institutions came after the March 1986 legislative elections, the beginning of the two-year experiment in *cohabitation*. The opposition became the majority in the legislature, but with the same president. Mitterand was thus obliged to choose a member of the new majority to be prime minister, and he appointed **Jacques Chirac,** the mayor of Paris. Chirac moved quickly to reprivatize much of the industry earlier nationalized by Mitterand. In the same elections, the National Front (FN), a racist, ultra-rightist, ultra-nationalist party headed by **Jean-Marie Le Pen,** won more than 10% of the vote, under the slogan "La France pour les Français" (France for the French, with a very narrow interpretation of "French"). Though the FN's one representative in the National Assembly was expelled from her party in 1989 for holding slightly less reactionary views, Le Pen and several other members are among France's delegation to the European Parliament.

In May 1988, Mitterand was reelected president. He promptly chose fellow socialist **Michel Rocard** to be prime minister and dissolved the National Assembly, hoping that voters would choose a Socialist Party majority. In June 1988, the right lost seats and the Socialist Party gained some. No party secured a majority, but the period of cohabitation was ended. In 1989, elections to the European Parliament gave the ecological party (*Les Verts*) its first seats. Because of the government's inefficacy in dealing with a series of strikes (*grèves*: be prepared for this fact of life in modern France), Chirac's opposition coalition attempted a motion to censure the government in 1989. The motion narrowly failed. On Mitterand's current agenda are extension of minimum wage to immigrants and the democratization of higher education's last bastion of elitism, the Grandes Ecoles. France anxiously awaits the economic consequences of the impending unification of Germany and the solidification of the European community in 1992.

To keep abreast of the latest in the circus that is French politics, pick up one of the excellent daily papers. Most are more frankly partisan and more open with their dissent than American newspapers. *Le Figaro* leans to the right, *Le Monde* is on the left, *La Libération* is liberal and trendy, *Le Canard Enchaîné* is a witty parody, and there is no shortage of others.

Literature

Your trip is likely to afford you plenty of opportunities for reading: long train rides, waiting for buses, rainy days, and the flight there and back. The following is a slightly eccentric list of books that mixes masterpieces and less-acclaimed works. Most of the books mentioned are available in English translation and in paperback. The French department of any university or a librarian should be able to give you further guidance.

Narratives in the French vernacular (as opposed to Latin, the dominant medieval literary language) began to appear in the 11th century. The *chansons de geste* were tales of battle that retained the rhythms of oral storytelling; the most famous, the *Chanson de Roland* (*Song of Roland*) is a tale of heroism and betrayal in the battle of Roncesvalles between the Franks, under Charlemagne, and the Spanish Muslims. Stories of the travails of adulterous lovers, one of the grand themes of French literature, appear in the 12th century with a phenomenon that later scholars dubbed "courtly love." The story of *Tristan et Iseult* is one of the earliest. The story of King Arthur and the knights of the Round Table were first put into sophisticated literary form by Chrétien de Troyes, a court poet of Champagne and one of the founders of the romance genre. In southern France, the troubadours created a new genre of vernacular lyric poetry. Their complex lyrics, written in the Southern dialect of Provençal, are tinged with eroticism and mystical religion. In the fourteenth century, Christine de Pisan wrote love poetry and allegorical works such as *La Cité des Dames* (*The City of Ladies*) in which she refuted male misogynists. In *Gargan-*

tua, Pantagruel, and several continuations, François Rabelais expressed the carnivalesque vitality of the Renaissance with comic, scatological stories of giants and their adventures in a partly real, partly imaginary geography. All these medieval and Renaissance works are available both in modernized French editions and in English translation.

The mainstays of French theater are still the classical works of 17th-century playwrights Corneille, Racine and Molière. Tragedies like Corneille's *Le Cid* and Racine's *Phèdre* draw on historical and mythological sources; Moliere's comedies, among them *Le Misanthrope, Les Femmes Savantes (The Learned Ladies),* and *Le Docteur malgré lui (The Doctor in Spite of Himself),* satirize the *mœurs* (habits) of his day and draw on comic material from popular literature and folklore. Works by these three dramatists are frequently performed; read before you go to enhance your viewing pleasure. For a vivid portrayal of everyday life among the 17th-century elite, read Mme de Sévigné's *Lettres,* which comment on everything from kitchen recipes to palace intrigues. Fictional letters in Choderlos de Laclos's *Les Liaisons Dangereuses* sustain and finally undo a complex network of seductions. Jean de la Fontaine's *Fables* and Charles Perrault's *Contes* (fairy tales) are familiar stories enhanced by 17th-century morals and wit.

The 18th century, age of Enlightenment *(les Lumières)* and revolution, celebrated an ideal of the well-rounded man (yes, *man*) of letters who was philosopher, encyclopedist, dramatist, essayist, novelist, critic of established institutions, and prominent personality, all wrapped into one. Montesquieu's *Les lettres persannes* is a thinly veiled critique of Parisian political and cultural life as seen through the "naive" eyes of two Persian newcomers. Denis Diderot's *Jacques le fataliste et son maître* and Voltaire's *Candide* are unconventional tales of adventure laced with philosophy. While Enlightenment philosophers maintained an attitude of cynicism toward the world as it is, they had great faith in the power of reason to sort everything out. The aftermath of the French Revolution was a blow to this faith, and the 19th century opened with deep uncertainties. Though Jean-Jacques Rousseau is considered a philosopher of the Enlightenment, the sentimentality and introspection of his reflections usher in French Romanticism. A subjective view of nature and profound distress over the ills of the modern world (the so-called *mal du siecle*) are hallmarks of the works of poets Musset, Vigny, Lamartine, and Chateaubriand.

Romantic poet Victor Hugo also distinguished himself in politics and in prose. His panoramic work *Les Miserables* (available in abridged editions) traces the fortunes and complex social interrelationships of the high and low of Paris and the provinces around the time of the failed revolution of 1834. Honoré de Balzac's *La Comédie Humaine,* with some ninety volumes, and Emile Zola's 20-volume Rougon-Macquart saga, continue the tradition of portraying the high and low of French society on a grand scale. Paris looms large on the literary horizon of 19th-century France. The industrial revolution and the transformation of the city into a modern metropolis, with concomitant urban ills, is the subject of horror, disgust and wonderment in the works of these and other writers.

Poets Gerard de Nerval and Charles Baudelaire lie somewhere between Romanticism and the later Symbolist movement. Nerval's peregrinations around Paris with a lobster on a leash provided inspiration for his dreamy prose and poetry, in which he obsesses over the women in his life and creates a patchwork mythology out of world religions. Baudelaire celebrates the seductions of the senses and expresses the anguish ("spleen") of Paris and its various vices in his *Les Fleurs du Mal (The Flowers of Evil),* banned for immorality in 1857, the same year as Flaubert's classic *Madame Bovary.* Baudelaire's translation of Edgar Allen Poe accounts for the enthusiasm of the French for this American (putting him in the dubious company of Jerry Lewis).

At the end of the 19th century, Decadent and Symbolist poets Verlaine, Rimbaud and Mallarmé, all influenced by the work of Baudelaire, broke from conventions of poetic form and created lyrical webs of symbols and associations, emphasizing nature and the senses. Shot by Verlaine after a lovers' spat, Rimbaud gave up poetry for commercial adventurism at the age of nineteen; the whiny, angst-ridden letters he wrote to his mother from Ethiopia resemble a bad existentialist novel. In the 20th century, the more political Surrealists (André Breton, Paul Eluard) went further in their destruction of traditional form and the search for bizarre images.

The novels of Colette offer a woman's perspective on the sexual politics of her time; among her best-known are *Cheri, La Vagabonde,* and *La Chatte.* Alain-Fournier's *Le Grand Meaulnes,* a classic young adult novel about a boy and his mysteriously driven friend, evokes a dreamy childhood view of Loire valley countryside. Marcel Proust's monumental *A la recherche du temps perdu* is a masterly evocation of upper-class life during the *belle époque,* though its deeper subject is the experience of time and memory and the exploration of narrative methods for rendering them. André Gide wrote novels, including *L'Immoraliste* and *Les Faux-Monnayeurs,* which shocked contemporary readers with their portrayal of repressed sexuality and their disregard for fictional conventions.

Simone de Beauvoir's *Mémoires d'une jeune fille rangée* deals with her upbringing in a narrowly bourgeois family whose values she rejects. In the novel *Les Mandarins,* Beauvoir writes of the temporary bewilderment of Parisian intellectuals after World War II. Existentialist thinker Jean-Paul Sartre, de Beauvoir's lifetime companion, is a national obsession among students; his works (among them *La Nausée* and *Huis Clos*) can be puzzling or dogmatic, but are certainly worth reading.

Experimental writing in France in the 50s and 60s produced the *Nouveau Roman* (the New Novel), works which challenge the reader by abandonning conventional narrative techniques and embracing subject matter previously considered too trivial and mundane. Among its best known exponents are Alain Robbe-Grillet and Nathalie Sarraute. As a collection of reactions against the conventions of the novel, the Nouveau Roman could only go so far, and much recent fiction in France has exchanged its techniques for accessibility. In the 20th century, Francophone writers from Africa and the Caribbean (among them Aimé Césaire and Léopold Sédar Senghor) and Quebecois writers (Hubert Aquin and Anne Hebert) have enriched the literary canon of the Hexagon. A recent best-seller in France is Moroccan writer Tahar Ben Jelloun's *La Nuit Sacrée.* Well-known writers of the later 20th century include Françoise Sagan, Marguerite Duras, Michel Tournier, Nobel laureate Claude Simon, and Marguerite Yourcenar (the first woman elected to the elite Académie Française). If you're interested in the latest French writing (in French), check the lists of best-sellers in the weekly magazine *Livre* or look for reviews in the literary section (usually weekly) of a national newspaper.

Art and Architecture

Art and architecture in France spans thousands of years, from disappearing cave paintings of Lascaux to controversial postmodern building projects. Remains from the Roman period include monumental aqueducts, ruined fortifications, and bronze statues. Scattered all over the country, medieval churches attest to religion's pervasive influence on life in the Middle Ages. During the Carolingian Renaissance, builders rediscovered Roman construction techniques and turned to fire-proof stone instead of wood. Some buildings from this period or before survive, but most extant churches date from the second millenium, when building techniques were further perfected.

The round arches and blunt, heavy walls of **Romanesque** churches resemble ancient Roman fortifications. The extreme regularity and grand-scale precision of this architectural style are evident in the **Basilique St-Sernin** in Toulouse. Designed to accommodate large crowds of worshippers, the church maps out a Latin Cross, and the vaulted nave adds grandeur. But while St-Sernin's thick walls and barrel vaults provide ample space, they do not let in much light.

This problem was solved in the **Gothic** style, with its pointed arches and flying buttresses, which appeared in the late 12th century. Gothic architecture, which has nothing to do with the Goths, owes its name to the same Renaissance snobs who gave us "the Dark Ages." While the barrel-vaulted roofs in Romanesque structures rest on fortified pillars, Gothic structures utilize a system of arches that distribute weight outward rather than straight down. Flying buttresses counterbalance the pressure of the ribbed vaulting, relieving the walls of the roof's weight and allowing for the installation of more windows. As a result, the walls of Gothic churches seem to soar weightlessly, and light streams in through enormous windows.

The rebuilt **Church of St-Denis** in Ile-de-France is one of the earliest examples of Gothic style. Its circular string of chapels, luminous glass, and ribbed vaults proclaimed a new era. The windows here were enlarged from holes cut in thick walls to translucent walls in themselves. The outward pressure of the vaults is absorbed by heavy buttresses jutting out between chapels, so the bulk of the masonry is visible only from the outside. Other notable Gothic cathedrals are Amiens Cathedral, Nôtre-Dame de Paris, Nôtre-Dame de Chartres, and Nôtre-Dame de Reims. The architecture of castles remained almost purely functional until the Renaissance; early ones sit in strategic locations and have thick walls and tiny windows.

Less immediately visible are the other arts of the Middle Ages—manuscript illumination, tapestry weaving, and decorative arts—on view in various museum collections, notably the Musée Cluny in Paris. Medieval art is concerned with conveying feeling and narrative meaning; rather than exact representation of what is seen, it seeks to express what cannot be seen. The importance of story-telling derives from the use of art as "Bible for the illiterate." Manuscript illumination accounts for some of the most important and innovative art of the later Middle Ages. In the 13th-14th centuries, illustrated Books of Hours, intended for private devotion and popular among the nobility and bourgeoisie, brought this art to a wider audience. The International Courtly Gothic style, which swept the continent around the year 1400, used a combination of realistic detail and standard decorative motifs to create a luxurious interiors and exteriors. The Limbourg Brothers' "Très Riches Heures du Duc de Berry," created for a brother of Charles V and now housed in the Musée Condé in Chantilly, is a magnificent example.

Caught between the two centers of Renaissance art (Italy and the Netherlands), France did not develop an indigenous tradition to rival them. French artists took cues from both the Italian return to the classical past and the novelty of Flemish art. Gothic architecture continued to develop, eventually becoming "Flamboyant Gothic." François I attempted unsuccessfully to woo Italian artists to his court, but managed at least to commission such buildings as the Château de Chambord and the Louvre, which combine French Gothic motifs with Italianate design. In 1528 he hired Italian artists to improve the original hunting lodge of **Fontainebleau.** The resulting Renaissance palace shows few traces of its medieval origins.

In the 17th century, the center of art in Europe shifted decisively from Rome to Paris. Georges de la Tour and the Le Nain brothers chose simple subjects for their paintings and made striking use of light and shadow. In sharp contrast, the grandiose Baroque manner reached its pinnacle in the triumphs of conspicuous consumption that are Versailles and the Château of Vaux-le-Vicomte. Nicolas Poussin elaborated the theory of the "grand manner," with its huge canvases and panoramic subjects taken from mythology and history. His precepts regarding appropriate subjects and techniques dictated academic French tastes for centuries to come. Claude Lorrain focused on natural scenes and developed similarly durable conventions for landscape painting. In the early 18th century, Watteau painted aristocrats prancing around in peasant garb. The sugary creations of Fragonard, another **Rococo** painter, are still more elaborate.

After the fluffy extravagance of the Baroque and Rococo periods, **neoclassicism,** the official academic style of the Napoleonic era, was austere and dignified, with pure, clean lines and colors. Caught up in the dawn of an empire, France turned to ancient Rome for inspiration. Jacques-Louis David, chief painter of the period, painted such revolutionary subjects as the death of Marat and the coronation of Napoleon. His *Oath of the Horatii* uses an ancient subject—the swearing of an oath to defend Rome—to express contemporary nationalistic values. Jean-Auguste-Dominique Ingres, a student of David, was a conservative force in the 19th century whose work nevertheless had a great influence on later, more experimental painters. While maintaining the emphasis on purity of outline and form, Ingres dressed his subjects in opulent materials while drawing attention to the sensual surface of his canvases.

The **Romantics** relied on vivid color and expressive brush strokes to create an emotional and subjective visual experience. Artists like Théodore Gericault (1791-1824) and Eugène Delacroix reacted against the austerity of the neoclassical movement, while retaining some of the dictates of academic painting—grand sizes and subjects. They nevertheless asserted the right of individual sensibility over traditional rules. Delacroix's dramatic *Liberty on the Barricades* is an emotional and triumphant scene of revolution. Delacroix also took subjects from medieval and Renaissance literature and from the Middle East and North Africa. In Gericault's *Raft of the Medusa,* the starving survivors of a shipwreck are given the muscular contours of Greek athletes, rendering their suffering majestically unrealistic.

Mid-19th century landscape painters Corot and Théodore Rousseau depicted landscape and rural subjects from direct observation. Their attention to light and atmosphere creates a blithely idyllic feeling. 19th-century Realism involved looking closely at the "humble" aspects of life. Gustave Courbet's *Burial at Ornans* (1850) uses the grand scale of history painting for a simple village scene; many of his works enigmatically combine realism and allegory, notably the work entitled "A Real Allegory." Courbet's somewhat abrasive personality did not help his work get accepted in salons; when his paintings were refused by the Universal Exposition of 1855, he set up his own Pavilion of Realism right outside. Fellow Realist Jean Millet invested peasants with grandeur through the value of their work; Honoré Daumier, best known for his lithographed caricatures, also painted vivid social commentaries.

The Impressionist movement in the later 19th century changed art forever through its approach to artistic subjects and visual experience. Treating color as an inherent property not of objects but of light, Edouard Manet, Claude Monet, and their followers painted outside, endeavoring to capture a moment of vision involving movement and the changing effects of light. Manet's *Déjeuner sur l'herbe* (with a naked women and two men in contemporary clothing) and *Olympie* (a portrait of a prostitute in her boudoir gazing coolly at the viewer) revolutionized the possibilities of subject matter and revolted his contemporaries. Lighter and airier than Manet's, Monet's works include views of water and waterlilies (*nymphéas*), Rouen's cathedral, haystacks, and Norman seashores. His painting *Impression: Soleil levant* (*Impression: Sunrise*), gave the movement its name. The Impressionists, once relegated to a "Salon des Réfusés," became a huge collective success and paved the way for all of 20th century Western art. Other important impressionists include Berthe Morisot, Camille Pissarro, Pierre Auguste Renoir, and Edgar Degas.

The inheritors of the Impressionist tradition share the label of Post-Impressionism, though they largely went their separate ways. Paul Cézanne worked in Aix-en-Provence and created geometric landscapes (among them his *Mont Ste-Victoire*) with planes of orange, gold and green, and still lifes that anticipate cubism. Georges Seurat's *pointillisme* takes Impressionism a step further, using even tinier dots and further simplifying forms. Using large flat blocks of intense color, Gauguin painted scenes from Brittany and Arles in the same primitive style he used to depict Tahiti and Martinique. In his own words, Vincent van Gogh "tried to express the terrible passions of humanity by means of red and green." His wavy strokes of color create an individual and deeply expressive view of the world.

Matisse, Dérain, and Braque exchanged the pale Impressionist palette for intensely bright colors; critics dubbed them "Fauves," meaning "wild beasts." Georges Braque went on to create the sharply geometric abstractions of the Cubist style along with Pablo Picasso, probably the 20th century's greatest artist. Picasso's career, spanning many decades and many movements, is chronicled at the Musée Picasso in Paris and, a bit less spectacularly, at an older Musée Picasso in Antibes.

For up-to-the-minute information on art in France, check out the numerous good art magazines or the galleries around Les Halles, Bastille, or bd. St- Germain in Paris. Paintings no longer seem to shock the French, but contemporary architecture in highly visible places continues to cause uproar. The Centre Pompidou, hated by some and adored by others, was built in 1970 in the Marais, the heart of "le vieux

Paris." Its innards (heating and plumbing pipes, electrical wires, and escalators) on the outside, the vast interior space houses a cultural center and modern art museum. The less controversial Musée d'Orsay displays 19th-century masterpieces in a beautifully restored train station. I.M. Pei's glass pyramid, planted smack in the middle of the Louvre courtyard, was blocked for months while the conservative Finance Ministry took its time moving out of offices in the surrounding buildings. Towering urban architecture, except for the Montparnasse tower stayed out of Paris proper. Instead, skyscrapers cluster in the business and industrial suburb of La Défense, home to the new Grande Arche, a giant, hollowed-out Rubik's cube aligned with the Arc de Triomphe and the smaller arch in the Tuileries.

Food

> The French will only be united under the threat of danger. No one can simply bring together a country that has 265 kinds of cheese.
>
> —Charles de Gaulle

De Gaulle, in fact, underestimated France's culinary diversity (it produces over 400 kinds of cheese). The aristocratic tradition of extreme richness and elaborate presentation known as *haute cuisine* originated in the 12-hour feasts of Louis XIV at Versailles and is preserved today in a few expensive restaurants such as the Tour d'Argent in Paris. In their work and writings, great 19th-century chefs made fine food an essential art of civilized life. To learn about the skills involved, leaf through the *Larousse Gastronomique,* a standard reference for chefs first compiled in the 19th century. The style made famous in the U.S. by Julia Child is *cuisine bourgeoise,* high quality French home-cooking. A glance through her books, *Mastering the Art of French Cooking I & II,* should give you a long list of dishes to try while in France.

Both *haute cuisine* and *cuisine bourgeoise* rely heavily on the *cuisine des provinces* (provincial cooking, also called *cuisine campagnarde*), which create hearty peasant dishes using refined methods. The richness of these styles is derived from butter, and the freshness from the ideal climate and efficient inland transport.

The trendy *nouvelle cuisine,* consisting of tiny portions of delicately cooked, artfully arranged ingredients with light sauces, became popular in the seventies; since then, its techniques have been integrated with heartier provincial fare. Though *le fast-food* and *le self-service* have hit France with a vengeance, most French people still shop daily and make the effort to create fine meals and take the time to enjoy them.

The French breakfast (*petit déjeuner*) is usually light, consisting of bread (*pain*) and sometimes *croissants* or *brioches* (buttery breads almost like pastries) and *café au lait* (espresso with hot milk) or hot chocolate (*chocolat*). Many people still eat the largest meal of the day (*déjeuner*) between noon and 2pm. Most shops and businesses close for two hours during this time; even Paris has four rush hours—morning, evening, and two in the middle of the day as people hurry home and back. Dinner (*dîner*) begins quite late.

Most restaurants offer a *menu à prix fixe* (fixed-price meal) that costs less than ordering *à la carte* and includes appetizer or soup, an *entrée* such as *pâté, crudités* (raw vegetables), or *jambon* (ham); and a main course (*plat principal*). Chicken (*poulet*), duck (*canard*), veal (*veau*), lamb (*agneau*), and pork (*porc*) are generally the best-prepared meats. Cheese (*fromage*) and/or dessert may also be included.

Bread is served with every meal. It is perfectly polite to use a piece of bread to wipe your plate (in extraordinarily refined circles, French diners may push their bread around their plates with a fork). French etiquette dictates keeping one's hands above the table, not in one's laps, even if this means resting one's elbows on the table. Mineral water is ubiquitous; order sparkling water (*eau pétillante* or *gazeuse*) or flat mineral water (*eau plate*). Ice cubes (*glaçons*) are rare.

Salad may be served either before or (more traditionally) after the *plat.* It generally consists of lettuce with a mustard vinaigrette. Finish the meal with espresso, which comes in lethal little cups. You will often see the words *"service compris"* (service included), which means the tip will be automatically added to the check (*l'addition*). Otherwise you should tip 15%.

For an occasional US$12-20 spree you can have a marvelous meal, but you needn't pay dearly to eat well. It's easy to find satisfying dinners for under 50F or to assemble inexpensive meals yourself with staples such as cheese, wine, and bread. The government controls the prices of bread, so you can afford to indulge with every meal, as do the French.

When in France, do as the French do: go from one specialty shop to another to assemble a picnic, or find an outdoor market or *marché.* A *charcuterie,* the French version of the delicatessen, offers cooked meats, *pâtés,* and sausages. You can also find delicious prepared dishes here, though they sometimes cost as much as restaurant fare. *Crémeries* sell dairy products, and a street-corner *crémerie* will stock over 100 kinds of cheese. A *boulangerie* sells breads, including the *baguette* (the long, crisp, archetypal French loaf), its larger cousin the *pain parisien,* round, soft, wholewheat *pain de campagne,* or rye bread (*pain de seigle*), as well as an assortment of pastries. A *pâtisserie* offers pastry and candy, and a *confiserie* stocks candy and ice cream (though the borders between these two kinds of stores are fluid). You can buy your fruits and vegetables at a *primeur.* For the adventurous carnivore, a *boucherie chevaline* sells horse-meat (look for the gilded horse-head over the door); the timid can stick to steaks and roasts from a regular *boucherie.*

Like most things American, the *supermarché* has invaded France. Look for the small foodstore chains such as **Casino, Prisunic** and **Félix Potin.** *Epiceries* (grocery stores) also carry staples, wine, produce, and a bit of everything else. The open-air markets, held at least once a week in every town and village, remain the best places to buy fresh fruit, vegetables, fish, and meat. Competition here is fierce, and prices low.

Each region has its specialties. In Brittany, eat *Camembert, Pont L'Evêque,* and *chèvre* (goat) cheese, drink cider, and sample local *fruits de la mer* ("fruits of the sea," or seafood). In addition, the infamous crêpe was first folded in Brittany. Wine-based dishes are best in Burgundy (home of *boeuf bourguignon*), as are *escargots* (snails) and *grenouilles* (frogs). Look for local *pâtés* in Dordogne, and head for Alsace-Lorraine for heavier German-style foods. Hallmarks of Provençal fare are garlic, olive oil and tomatoes; specialties include *ratatouille* and dishes made with the pungent basil and garlic sauce *pistou,* as well as seafood specialties such as *bouillabaisse,* a saffron-flavored fish stew. A Spanish menu prevails in the southwest and includes *cassoulet* and paella. Alpine cuisine makes use of local cheese in its *raclette* and *fondue.* In cities, you can find cuisine from all over the world; especially promising are the Spanish, Italian and North African restaurants, supported by large immigrant populations.

Cafés in France, as in most of southern Europe, figure pleasantly in the daily routine. When choosing a café, remember that you pay for its location. Those on a major boulevard can be much more expensive than smaller establishments a few steps down a side street. Prices in cafés are two-tiered, cheaper at the counter (*comptoir*) than in the seating area (*salle*). Both these prices should be posted. Coffee, beer, *Pernod* (a licorice-flavored cordial often served with mineral water or orange juice), and (in the south) the anise-flavored *pastis,* are the staple drinks; *citron pressé* (lemonade—*limonade* is a soda) and *diabolo menthe* (peppermint soda) are popular non-alcoholic choices. Cafés also offer Coke, but be prepared to pay twice what you would in the U.S. If you order "café," you'll get espresso; for coffee with milk, ask for "café au lait" (cah-fay oh lay). If you order a *demi* or a *pression* of beer, you'll get a pale lager on tap (often Kronenbourg or 33 Export). You can also order bottled imported beer: Heineken is popular in Paris, and Pelforth, a dark beer, is the southern choice. A glass of red is the cheapest wine in a café (4-6F), with white costing about twice as much; southerners prefer rosé to white. Tips expected in cafés are small—usually only a few francs.

Cafés are not suited to cheap eating. A *croque monsieur* (grilled ham-and-cheese sandwich), a *croque madame* (the same with a fried egg), and assorted omelettes cost about 15F and rarely make a filling meal. Only occasionally is the food good and reasonably priced. Since the menu is always posted outside, check before you go inside. Avoid places billed as *brasseries*—they often specialize in tough, minimal portions of steak or unspectacular chicken with fries.

In addition to serving drinks and food, many cafés provide two other essential services: telephones and toilets. The toilets are usually free and sometimes very dirty. In the fancier cafés, an attendant sits outside and expects a 1-2F tip. A red, diamond-shaped sign outside a café signifies that it is also a *tabac* and sells cigars, cigarettes, matches, stamps, and a selection of other useful items such as batteries, razor blades, and Métro and lottery tickets.

Wine

Wine is an institution in France and is served at almost every occasion. The character and quality of a wine depend upon the climate, soil, and variety of grape from which it is made. Long, hot, and fairly dry summers with cool, humid nights create the ideal climate. Soil is so much a determining factor that identical grapes planted in different regions yield very different wines. **White wines** are produced by the fermentation of white grapes; **rosés** from the white-wine-style vinification of black grapes; and **reds** by the fermentation of the juice, skins, and sometimes stems of black grapes.

The major wine-producing regions are distributed throughout the country. The Loire Valley produces a number of whites, with the major vineyards at Angers, Anjou, Touraine, Tours, Pouilly Sancerre, and Quincy Reuilly. Normandy produces Calvados, an apple brandy distilled from cider, in the area near Caen. Cognac, farther south on the Atlantic coast, is famous for the double-distilled and blended spirit of the same name. Centered on the Dordogne and Garonne rivers, Bordeaux produces both the reds and white wines of Médoc, Graves, and the sweet Sauternes. Armagnac, similar to cognac, comes from Gascony (in the area around Auch), while Jurançon wines come from vineyards higher up the slopes of the Pyrenees. Southern wines include those of Languedoc and Roussillon on the coast and Limoux and Gaillac inland. The vineyards of Provence on the coast near Toulon are famous for their rosés. The Côtes du Rhône from Valence to Avignon in the Rhône Valley are home to some of the most celebrated wines of France. Burgundy is famous for both whites and reds, from the wines of Chablis and the Côte d'Or in the north, to the Mâconnais and Beaujolais in the south. There are also vineyards in the Jura and in Alsace. Many areas produce sparkling white wine; the only *true* bubbly is bottled in a region of Champagne centered around Reims.

France passed the first comprehensive wine legislation in 1935, and since then the Appellation d'Origine Controlée regulations (AOC or "controlled place of origin" laws) have ensured the quality and fine reputation of French wines. All wines are categorized according to place of origin, alcohol content, and wine-making practices; only about 16% of French wines are deemed worthy of the top classification. Categories include *Vins Délimités de Qualité Supérieure* (VDQS or "restricted wines of superior quality") and *Vins de Pays* (country wines).

One way to discriminate among the bewildering range of wines in France is to examine the varieties of grapes that go into their production. Burgundies are made from *Pinot Noir* and other grapes, while Bordeaux wines come from different mixtures of four varieties of grape, with *Cabernet-sauvignon* the dominant variety. Whites are usually made from *Chardonnay* or *Chenin Blanc* grapes.

When shopping for a fairly expensive wine, study the label carefully. The majority of wines are matured by shippers who buy young wines from the growers and mix them to achieve the desired blend. In general, the label will indicate a product's region but not its specific grower. Look for the term *mis en bouteille au domaine* (or *au château*) to ensure the wine was estate-bottled.

In the wine country of Bordeaux, Burgundy, or Champagne, small local wine-makers sell their product from *caves* (sometimes literally caves) and offer *dégustations* (tastings) to those who tour their establishments. These brands tend to be cheaper and often enjoy little fame only because they do not travel well. In many regions of France, you can fill a bottle from the kegs of wine in *épiceries* and *supermarchés*. These local wines are often both very cheap and of fine quality. Labels have little meaning for ordinary French table wines (*vins de table*), which are often artificially matured and adulterated with sugar and colorings. The real mongrels, such as *beaujolais villages* (blends of various bottlers' leftovers) or those made from the grapes of "various Common Market countries," cost as little as 6F per bottle and will give you memorable headaches. Seek out a decent little regional vintage for around 24F to quaff with your *baguette* and *brie*.

Sports, Recreation, and Holidays

The French are crazy about tennis (the French Open is in early June), skiing, sailing, windsurfing, and many other sports. The whole populace cheers on the rugby and soccer teams, among the world's best. If you're in France in May or June, be prepared to discuss the fortunes of the *footballers* in the World Cup. Le Mans is a 24-hour car race on the second weekend of June. The Tour de France, a three-week bicycle race in July, traverses most of France. Check the itinerary to see if the participants will cycle past one of your stopovers.

The French are serious vacationers; government-mandated vacation time is upwards of a month, not counting national holidays. Recreational activities are likely to be readily available in even the smallest French town.

France blossoms with festivals throughout the year. In summer, almost every town celebrates a local *fête* that may include carnivals, markets, and folk dancing. The Cannes Film Festival, the Nice Jazz Parade, the Avignon Drama Festival, and the festivities in Aix-en-Provence occur in May, June, July, and August, respectively. In addition, there are at least 100 smaller events every year, such as the Paris Festival du Marais from mid-June to early July.

For a comprehensive listing by region of all festivals (music, dance, film, jazz, folklore, puppetry, *son et lumière*, theater, and literature) write for the catalog *Nouvelles de France*, available from the Ministère du Commerce, de l'Artisanat et du Tourisme, Direction du Tourisme, 17, rue de l'Ingénieur-Keller, 75740 Paris (tel. 45 75 62 16). The detailed catalog publishes a special summer issue in March (actually covering March-Nov.). The same ministry publishes *France in a holiday mood*, a highly condensed version of the catalog in English. For a list of music festivals, write to the French Tourist Office and request *Festivals en France 91*. For every other kind of festival, request *Festivals* from the European Association of Music Festivals, 122, rue de Lausanne, 211 Geneva 21, Switzerland (tel. (22) 732 28 03). In Paris, **AlloConcerts** maintains a 24-hour hotline that provides information (in French) on free open-air concerts in the parks (tel. 42 76 50 00). **FNAC,** the Fédération Nationale d'Achat des Cadres, is the main agency for buying tickets to anything in Paris. Their main office is at 136, rue de Rennes, 75006 Paris (tel. 45 44 39 12; Métro Montparnasse-Bienvenue).

Try to be somewhere special for **Bastille Day** on July 14 (the founding of the First Republic); it's the one day each year when Parisians indulge in berserk but semi-harmless pyromania. May 1, **La Fête du Travail** (French Labor Day), marks a socialist celebration all over the country. For **Jeanne d'Arc Day** (the 2nd Sun. in May), Orléans has a commemorative celebration. The **Feux de St-Jean** is a rural bonfire holiday combining John the Baptist's Day (June 24) with the ancient Celtic summer solstice observance. Brittany has become famous for its *pardons,* festivals held to honor a parish's patron saint.

Banks, museums, and other public buildings close on the following public holidays: January 1, Easter Monday, May 1 (Labor Day), May 8 (Victory in Europe Day), Ascension Day (the 40th Thurs. after Easter), Whit Monday (the 7th Mon. after Easter), July 14 (Bastille Day), August 15 (Assumption Day), November 1

(All Saints' Day), November 11 (Armistice Day), and December 25 (Christmas). When a holiday falls on a Tuesday or Thursday, the French often also take off the Monday or Friday, a practice known as *faire le pont* (to make a bridge). Note that banks close at noon on the day, or the nearest working day, before a public holiday.

Also keep in mind that most food stores close on Monday, though they remain open on Sunday mornings. Smaller stores (including groceries, shops, and even some banks) often close for lunch between noon and 2pm. Some stores and smaller businesses also close for a few weeks in July or August; they will post on their doors the names of similar stores open in the area. Almost all museums close on Tuesday.

Climate

The following information is drawn from the International Association for Medical Assistance to Travelers (IAMAT)'s *World Climate Charts*. In each monthly listing, the first two numbers are the average daily maximum and minimum temperatures in degrees Celsius; the numbers in parentheses represent the same data in degrees Fahrenheit.

		Jan.		April		July		Oct.
Bastia	11/6	(52/42)	18/11	(65/52)	28/19	(82/60)	20/11	(68/52)
Bordeaux	9/2	(48/36)	17/6	(63/43)	25/14	(77/57)	18/8	(64/46)
Boulogne-sur-Mer	6/2	(43/36)	12/6	(54/43)	20/14	(68/57)	14/10	(57/50)
Brest	9/4	(48/39)	13/6	(55/43)	19/12	(66/54)	15/9	(59/48)
Lourdes	10/1	(50/33)	17/6	(63/42)	25/14	(77/57)	18/8	(65/46)
Lyon	5/−1	(41/30)	16/6	(61/43)	27/15	(81/59)	16/7	(61/45)
Nantes	8/2	(46/36)	15/6	(59/43)	24/14	(75/57)	16/8	(61/46)
Nice	13/4	(55/39)	17/9	(63/48)	27/18	(81/64)	21/12	(70/54)
Paris	6/1	(43/34)	16/6	(61/43)	25/15	(77/59)	16/8	(61/46)
Strasbourg	3/−2	(37/28)	16/5	(61/41)	25/13	(77/55)	14/6	(57/43)

Weights and Measures

1 millimeter (mm) = 0.04 inch   1 inch = 25mm
1 meter (m) = 1.09 yards   1 yard = 0.92m
1 kilometer (km) = 0.62 mile   1 mile = 1.61km
1 gram (g) = 0.04 ounce   1 ounce = 25g
1 liter (ℓ) = 1.06 quarts   1 quart = 0.94ℓ

Language

> If they would speak slowly and distinctly I might understand them well enough, being perfectly familiar with the written language, and knowing the principles of its pronunciation; but, in their customary rapid utterance, it sounds like a string of gabble.
> —Nathaniel Hawthorne

The imposition of the northern *langue d'oïl*, the dialect that evolved into modern French, was critical in forging the political unity of the nation and in creating the image of a monolithic national culture that still persists. However, France is not a country of one language. Breton (a Celtic tongue) in Brittany, Flemish in Flanders, Alsatian in Alsace, Occitan in Languedoc, Catalan in Roussillon, Corsican in Corsica, and Basque in the Pyrenees are all spoken and are the source of a fierce regional pride that has recently begun to challenge the hegemony of French in the public school system. As France gradually adapts to an ever-increasing number of tourists, you will find more and more multi-lingual signs in airports, train stations, and major tourist sites. In most towns, the tourist office staff speaks passable English, and at sites where the guided tours are in French, there is often a printed English translation available. In large cities and heavily touristed areas, hotelkeepers and waiters know enough English for essential transactions.

Glossary

Here you will find an compilation of most of the French terms *Let's Go* has use, plus a few useful terms. The gender of the noun is either indicated in parentheses or by the article (*la,* feminine; *le,* masculine). The glossary is followed by an addendum listing phrases you may find helpful during your stay in France.

l'allée (f.)	lane, avenue
l'arc (m.)	arch
les arènes (f.)	arena
l'auberge (f.)	inn, tavern
la banlieue	suburbs
la basse ville	lower town
la bastide	walled town
le beffroi	bell tower
la bibliothèque	library
le billet	ticket
le billet d'aller et retour	round-trip ticket
le bois	forest
la calanque	creek; cove
le cap	cape, foreland
la cave	(wine) cellar
le centre ville	downtown, town center
la chambre	room
la chambre d'hôte	rural bed and breakfast (B&B)
la chapelle	chapel
la chartreuse	charterhouse (Carthusian monastery)
le château	castle
le cimetière	cemetery
la cité	city; housing development
le cloître	cloister
le col	pass
la corniche	cliff road, coastal road; cornice
la côte	coast
le couvent	convent
la croix	cross
le cru	wineyard; vintage
la dégustation	wine tasting
la douane	customs
l'école (f.)	school
l'église (f.)	church
l'escalier (m.)	stairway
l'evêché (m.)	bishop's palace; bishopric
la falaise	cliff
le faubourg	quarter
la foire	fair
la fontaine	fountain
la forêt	forest
la gare	train station
la gare routière	bus station
le gîte d'étape	rural lodging for non-drivers
le gîte rural	rural bed and breakfast (B&B)
la gorge	gorge; pass

le gouffre	gulf, pit
la halle	market hall, covered market
la haute ville	upper town
l'horloge (f.)	clock
l'hôtel (particulier) (m.)	mansion (town house)
l'hôtel de ville (m.)	town hall
l'île (f.)	island
le logis	lodging, dwelling
la mairie	town hall
le marché	market
la mosquée	mosque
le mur	wall
le pic	peak
le pilier	pillar
la place	square
la plage	beach
la pointe	headland, promontory
le pont	bridge
la porte	gate; mountain pass
la randonnée	run, hike
la rencontre	meeting
la roche	boulder
le rocher	rock; crag
la rue	street
le salon	drawing or living room
le sentier	path, lane
le tabac	store selling cigarettes, stamps, etc.
la tapisserie	tapestry
le téléphérique	suspended cable car
les thermes (m.)	hot springs
le thon	tuna
la tour	tower
le trésor	treasure
la vendange	grape harvest; vintage season
la vieille ville	old town

Helpful Phrases

thank you	*merci*
hello	*bonjour*
good evening	*bonsoir*
How are you?	*Comment allez-vous? Comment ça va?*
I am well.	*Je vais bien.*
goodbye	*au revoir*
Excuse me.	*Excusez-moi.*
Do you speak English?	*Parlez-vous anglais?*
I need . . .	*J'ai besoin de . . .*
I would like . . .	*Je voudrais . . .*
I want . . .	*Je veux . . .*
I don't want . . .	*Je ne veux pas . . .*
The bill, please.	*L'addition, s'il vous plaît.*
Where is/are . . .	*Où est/sont . . . ?*
. . . the bathroom?	*. . . le w.c.? (vay say)*
. . . the police?	*. . . la police?*
to the right	*à droite*
to the left	*à gauche*
straight ahead	*tout droit*
Fiddlesticks!	*Bah! Quelle blague!*

a room	*une chambre*
double room	*pour deux*
single room	*pour une personne*
a shower	*une douche*
breakfast	*le petit déjeuner*
lunch	*le déjeuner*
dinner	*le dîner*
with	*avec*
without	*sans*
shower included	*douche comprise*
breakfast included	*petit déjeuner compris*
service included	*service compris*

Paris

Paris is a metaphor, a slogan, a shrine, a fantasy before it is anything so mundane as the hometown of three million people. Because so many dream about Paris before actually strolling through its streets, no one is at a loss for words to speak about it. Few, however, have anything original to say. The city seems haunted by the writers, artists, and thinkers who have tried to describe—or change—its façade and social milieux. In addition to the annual flood of tourists, the city witnesses a neverending influx of foreign expatriates in search of the Paris of Hemingway, Gertrude Stein, James Joyce, and Janet Flanner. Those who fail to find this heavily mythologized Paris may experience an intense nostalgia for things never known, and even those who come with less specific expectations can find their first visit to Paris a sort of uncanny homecoming. There is the Eiffel Tower, looming above the Champs de Mars, and Notre-Dame, its towers seeming to await the arrival of Hugo's Quasimodo. Crowded with bespectacled students in biker jackets, psychoanalysts in cashmere turtlenecks, and other citizens of bohemia, the Latin Quarter's remaining medieval streets still tie themselves in almost unnavigable knots. Focal point of the 19th-century urban planning aimed at untying such knots, Napoleon's Arc de Triomphe rises above the place Charles de Gaulle, ready to receive the triumphant batallions of cars that surge down the twelve radiating avenues each day.

Originally home to the Parisii on the Seine, the city was named Lutetia (Lutèce) by the conquering Romans in 52 BC. In 987, when Hugh Capet, count of Paris, became King of France, he brought prestige to the tiny medieval town by naming it his capital. King Phillipe Auguste (1180-1223) consolidated the crown's possessions and established the basic segregation of functions that still characterizes the city: political and ecclesiastical institutions on the Ile de la Cité, academia on the Left Bank, and commerce on the Right Bank. Over the centuries, the city expanded outward in concentric ovals, swallowing up whole villages.

Baron Haussmann's redesign of the city in the mid-19th century was intended to facilitate movement and social interaction among the rising bourgeoisie, but the persistance of winding passages and small districts with specialized reputations seems to combat the alienation one expects in an immense, modern city. This does not mean that the city has not experienced its share of discontent. Though Parisians believe that *la politesse* keeps life civilized, they also believe in their right to say and do what they want behind closed doors and, on a number of occassions throughout the centuries, in the streets. Paris saw Europe's first mass revolution in 1789 and has since witnessed the violent comings and goings of two empires, a monarchy, four republics, and two military occupations, not to mention the furious civil riots of 1968 and the more recent student protests of 1986 and 1987.

In addition to a cultural hothouse, Paris has also served as a European political center. The city is a frequent choice for international conferences, and President Mitterand has been among the staunchest supporters of European unification. As the Seine splits the city, the city itself marks a divide between northern and southern Europe. The winters here testify that Paris is a northern city, but the presence of southern European, Latin American, and African rhythms, fashions, language, and cuisine reminds visitors of the multiethnic background of its residents. In the last decade, the city has experienced an influx of Vietnamese and Chinese immigrants, and interest in Asian culture and cuisine remains is strong. However, the popular candidacy (for everything from mayor to chairman of the European Parliament) of Jean-Marie Le Pen—proponent of expelling all immigrants and their offspring—and persistent rumors of Arab, African, and Jewish conspiracy suggest a continuing racism.

Many a visitor from abroad or even from the French provinces has returned with stories of the Parisians' xenophobia and snobbery. As elsewhere, courtesy is the key to maintaining harmony here. Tall tales of Parisian rudeness may come true if you

Paris

1 Accueil Central de France
   127 Champs Elysées
2 Transalpino: 16, rue La Fayette
3 American Express: 11, rue Scribe
4 Post Office: 52, rue du Louvre

5   Sainte Chapelle and Palais de Justice
6   Notre Dame
7   Place des Vosges
8   Musée Carnavalet
9   Centre National d'Art et Culture
    Georges Pompidou
10 Musée and Palais de Louvre
11 Palais Royal
12 Comedie Française
13 Place Vendôme
14 Musée du Jeu de Paume
15 Orangerie
16 Petit Palais
17 Grand Palais
18 Opéra
19 Musée Rodin
20 Les Invalides
21 St-Germain-des-Prés
22 St-Severin
23 Musée de Cluny
24 Sorbonne
25 Panthéon
26 Palais du Luxembourg
27 Cité Internationale de l'Université de Paris
28 Sacré-Coeur
29 Tour Eiffel
30 Musée d'Orsay

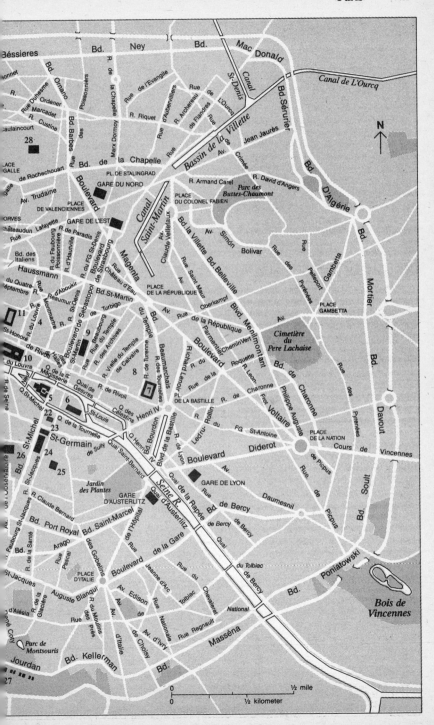

address people in English without the prefatory *"Parlez-vous anglais, Madame/Monsieur?"* Although some Parisians have the somewhat annoying habit of answering all queries in English, even the simplest of efforts to speak French are appreciated. Be lavish with your *Monsieurs, Madames,* and *Mademoiselles,* and greet everyone with a friendly *bonjour* or *bonsoir.* When you do encounter surly locals, consider their point of view. Every summer, tourists more than double the city's population. Many do not speak French and are unwilling to accept the challenge of dealing with people who do not understand them. Be patient with Parisians, whom Emerson found "terribly derisive of all absurd pretensions—but "their" own." In addition to fumbling along in French, avoid short shorts and other skimpy or loud sportswear, especially in houses of worship or in restaurants. Most importantly, don't let intimidation keep you from doing and seeing what you want. A surrender to Paris can be the sweetest of defeats.

Practical Information

Note: In Paris addresses "Mo." indicates the nearest Métro stop.

Getting There

By Plane

Most transatlantic flights land at the Roissy-Charles de Gaulle Airport, 23km northeast of Paris (tel. 48 62 22 80 or 48 62 12 12; open 24 hrs.). As a general rule, Terminal 2 serves Air France, and most other carriers operate from Terminal 1. Airport d'Orly (tel. 49 75 15 15), 12km south of the city, is used by charters and many intracontinental flights. Paris's third airport, Le Bourget (tel. 48 62 22 80) handles only private flights within France. Signs in all three airports warn that packages or luggage left unattended may be destroyed by the police for fear of bombs.

The cheapest and fastest way to get into the city from Roissy-Charles de Gaulle is the **Roissy Rail** (tel. 42 82 50 50) bus-train combination. Take the free shuttle bus from Aérogare 1 arrival level gate 28, Aérogare 2A gate 5, Aérogare 2B gate 6, or Aérogare 2D gate 6 to the Roissy train station. From there the **RER** (one of the Parisian Métro systems) will transport you to the Gare du Nord and other places in central Paris. Once inside the city, you can transfer to any of the Métro lines for free (35 min., 27.50F).

Alternatively, **Air France Buses** (tel. 42 99 20 18) run to the Arc de Triomphe (every 12 min., 40 min., 37F), **Bus #35D** to Gare du Nord and Gare de l'Est (50 min., 30F), and **Bus #351** to pl. de la Nation (40 min., 30F). Unless your hotel is near one of these terminals, you'll wind up having to take the Métro anyway. Taxis cost around 150F during the day, 200F at night.

From Orly Sud gate H or Orly Ouest arrival level gate F, you can take the shuttle bus (5:40am-11:15pm every 15 min.) to the **Orly Rail Station** (tel. 42 61 50 50), where you can board the **RER** for a number of destinations in Paris. Buy 21F tickets from machines inside the airport at Orly Sud gate H or Orly Ouest arrival gate F. **Air France Buses** (tel. 43 23 97 10, 30 min., 30F), **Orly Bus** (25 min., 17.50F) and **Jet Bus** (15 min., 14F) run to Invalides, pl. Denfert-Rochereau, and Villejuif, respectively. The problems with the Roissy buses apply to the Orly buses as well. Finally, taxis to the airport cost about 100F during the day and more at night.

If you happen to land in Paris at Le Bourget, take bus #350 (6:10am-11:52pm every 15 min., 2 Métro tickets) to Gare du Nord or Gare de l'Est. Bus #152 also makes these stops, and, for the same price, will take you to Porte de la Villette, where you can catch the Métro or a bus.

By Train and Bus

Each of Paris's six train stations is a veritable community of its own, with resident street people and police, cafés, restaurants, *tabacs,* and banks. Locate the ticket counters *(guichets)*, the platforms *(quais)*, and the tracks *(voies)* and you will be ready to roll. Each terminal has two divisions: the *banlieue* and the *grandes lignes*. Trains to the **banlieue** serve the suburbs of Paris and make frequent stops. **Grandes lignes** depart for and arrive from distant cities and other countries. Each division has its own ticket counters, information booths, and timetables; distinguishing between the two before you get in line will save you hours of frustration. All train stations are reached by at least two Métro lines, and the Métro station bears the name of the train station. For train information, call 45 82 50 50; for reservations, call 45 65 60 60 (both open daily 8am-9pm). An English-speaking staff member is always available. There is a free telephone with direct lines to the stations on the right-hand side of the Champs-Elysées tourist office.

A word on safety: though full of atmosphere, each terminal is also full of thieves and worse. Gare du Nord, for example, is safe during the day but becomes rough at night, when drugs and prostitution take over. As in all big cities, beware the characters in and around the stations; the unsuspecting may be invited out for a drink only to be doped up and ripped off. Above all, **do not** change cash or buy anything from these con artists. Any money you hand over will never be seen again.

Gare du Nord: Trains to northern France, Belgium, the Netherlands, Scandinavia, the USSR, and northern Germany.

Gare de l'Est: To eastern France (Champagne, Alsace, Lorraine), Luxembourg, parts of Switzerland (Basel, Zürich, Lucerne), southern Germany, Austria, and Hungary.

Gare de Lyon: To southern and southeastern France (Riviera, Provence), parts of Switzerland (Geneva, Lausanne, Bern), Italy, Greece, and points east.

Gare d'Austerlitz: To the Loire Valley, southwestern France (Bordeaux, Pyrenees), Spain, and Portugal.

Gare St-Lazare: To Normandy.

Gare de Montparnasse: To Brittany.

Most buses into Paris arrive at **Gare Routière Internationale,** 3, av. Porte de la Villette, 19ème (tel. 40 38 93 93; Mo. Porte de la Villette). Other buses have more bizarre ports of call. The Terminal City Sprint bus (tel. 42 85 44 55) that operates in conjunction with Hoverspeed from England, for example, drops its passengers in front of the Hoverspeed offices, 3 blocks from Gare du Nord. Find the nearest Métro stop, and the extensive maps will direct you from there. For information about buses to other European countries, call **International Express Eurolines Coach Station** at 40 38 93 93.

By Thumb

If you treasure your safety and sanity more than money, you'll take a train or bus out of Paris. Competition for rides is fierce. You might hear stories of three-day waits, and even if they're not true, you'll begin to believe them after the first few hours. Don't wait at a *porte* (city exit); traffic is too heavy for cars to stop safely. Those who insist on hitching out of Paris (presumably to be able to boast of it, not because you're looking for a convenient and safe means of transport) should figure out which *autoroute* leads to their destination, then trace the local train or bus line until it approaches this highway—the spot where they should start hitching.

Toward the east: Metz, Strasbourg, Munich. Take the Métro to Porte de Charenton and walk along bd. Massena, where you can catch the *Autoroute de l'est* A4. (This is the worst highway to hitch on.)

Toward the north: Lille, Brussels, Cologne, Hamburg, Berlin, Scandinavia. Catch the Métro to Porte de la Chapelle, which is next to the *Autoroute du nord* A1.

Toward the west: Rouen, Caen, Cherbourg, Mont St-Michel, St-Malo. Take the Métro to Porte de St-Cloud and walk up bd. Murat toward pl. de la Porte d'Auteuil, where *Autoroute de Normandie* A13 begins.

Toward the south: Take the Métro to Porte d'Orléans, walk down av. de la Porte d'Orléans, and turn left. You can get on to a number of *autoroutes* from Porte d'Orléans. **Southeast** A6: Lyon, Marseille, Cannes, Nice, Monaco, Switzerland, Italy, Barcelona. **Southwest** A10: Orléans, Bordeaux, Madrid, Galicia, Portugal. A11 branches off A10 toward Brittany: Chartres, Le Mans, Rennes.

As always, the more original and inventive the method of reaching an entrance to an *autoroute* outside of Paris, the fewer hitchhikers there will be to compete for rides. A sign clearly stating the destination, ornamented by the letters "S.V.P." *(s'il vous plaît)* helps ingratiate hitchhikers. Hitchhikers also sometimes ask customers at gas stations or truck stops if they are going their way. It is not safe for women to hitchhike alone.

If you have a little money and want to save some time, try **Allostop-Provoya,** 84, passage Brady, 10*ème* (tel. 42 46 00 66; Mo. Strasbourg-St-Denis). They will try to match you with a driver going your way. The cost is 45-150F, depending on distance. If you plan to use this service more than two or three times, it pays to spend the 120F for sixth months or 200F for a year's worth of rides. You can pay 30F more for **Eurostop International** membership, valid in 76 cities in Switzerland, Germany, Spain, France, Hungary, Italy, Holland, Belgium, and Canada. If your home country is one of the nine listed above, you must purchase your card there. At Allostop-Provoya, you can also buy train, bus, and camel tickets to points throughout Europe. They sell BIJ/Eurotrain tickets and arrange special weekend tours in Europe. Several offices operate in other cities throughout France, including Bordeaux, Lyon, Strasbourg, and Toulouse. To find their addresses, check the respective city's practical information section or call 47 70 48 71. (Open Mon.-Fri. 9am-7:30pm, Sat. 9am-1pm and 2-6pm.)

Getting Around

Walking is an excellent way to get around in this compact city. A stroll from the Arc de Triomphe to pl. de la Bastille passes all the major monuments and only takes about two hours.

Paris is divided into *arrondissements* (districts) that spiral clockwise from the Louvre (1*er*) to Porte de Vincennes (20*ème*). Paris addresses usually include the number and street, *arrondissement,* and nearest Métro stop. The postal code of Paris addresses is formed by affixing the two-digit *arrondissement* number to 750. Thus, the postal code of an address in the 8*ème* (eighth) is 75008.

Perhaps the broadest division between wealthy and bohemian Paris is that between the *Rive Droite* (Right Bank), north of the Seine, and the *Rive Gauche* (Left Bank), south of the river. The former is, for the most part, more elegant and affluent than the left bank, but the student population on the latter has made it the more intimate half of Paris. However, broad generalizations about the banks become impossible as old neighborhoods are increasingly converted into homes for BCBGs (*bon chic bon genre,* the fashionable and wealthy).

Maps

By far the best guide to Paris is a *Plan de Paris par Arrondissements,* which includes a detailed map of each *arrondissement,* all the bus lines, a wealth of miscellany, and an essential index of streets and their nearest Métro stop. It costs 34-100F, depending on how elaborate an edition you buy. The 45F guide should suffice unless you plan to drive in Paris. Most bookstores, *papeteries* (stationery stores), and kiosks sell a wide variety. Unfortunately, the Métro map in these guides is out of date. Instead, pick up a free updated one in any Métro station. As well as showing all the Métro lines, this map includes bus lines and the RER suburban system.

Métro

Safe and efficient, the Paris Métro can take you within walking distance of almost any spot in the city. All trains run frequently, and connections *(correspondances)* are easy. A disabled Métro train is a rare sight. The first trains start running at

Paris Arrondissements

■ Train stations (Gares)

▨ Parks, gardens, or cemeteries

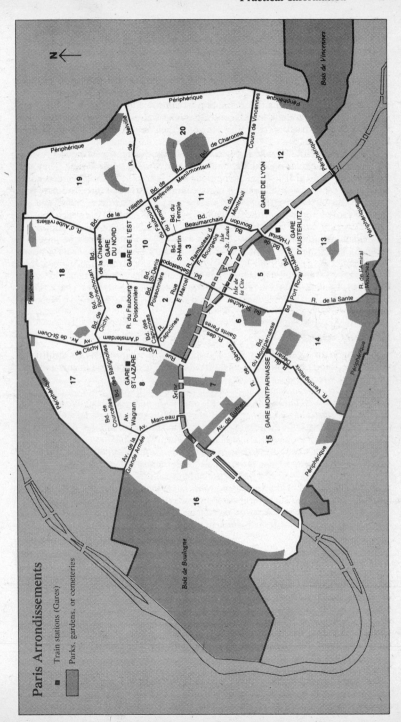

5am; the last leave the stations at the *"portes de Paris"* (i.e., Porte d'Orléans, Porte de Clignancourt, etc.) for the center at about 12:15am. The exceptions are trains leaving from Porte de Balard, which do not go through to Porte Charentou but stop at République. In the other direction, however, they go through the center to Balard. For the exact departure times of the last trains from the *portes,* check the poster in the center of each station called *"Principes de Tarification"* (Rate Guidelines).

The entire subway and bus system is under the direction of RATP (Régie Aùtonome des Transports Parisiens). In addition to the Métro (short for Métropolitain), RATP also runs the RER (Réseau Express Régional), the local suburban system. For information on the services of RATP, contact their main office at 53ter, quai des Grands-Augustins, 6ème (tel. 43 46 14 14; Mo. St-Michel; open daily 6am-9pm). You can also stop by at **Bureau de Tourisme RATP,** pl. de la Madeleine, 8ème (tel. 43 46 14 14; Mo. Madeleine; open Mon.-Sat. 7:30am-7pm, Sun. and holidays 6:30am-6pm). An English-speaking representative is usually available at both offices. RATP can also be reached round the clock through Minitel: 3615 RATP. (See Communications.)

All the train lines are well traveled at night, and Parisian women often travel alone. Although violent crime on the Métro is relatively uncommon, use common sense. Avoid empty cars, even if they are first class. At night, many people choose to ride in the first car, where the conductor is only a door away. Stay away from the most dangerous stations (Barbès-Rochechouart, Pigalle, and Anvers) and be careful in the long, empty corridors of larger stations.

Free Métro maps are available at most stations. The display maps posted in all stations have a *plan du quartier,* a detailed map of the surrounding neighborhood. Connections to other lines are indicated by orange *"correspondance"* signs, and the exits by blue *"sortie"* signs. All Métro lines are numbered but are referred to by their final destination. Transfers to other lines are free if made in the same station.

Each trip on the Métro costs one ticket. Tickets can be bought individually (2nd class 5F, 1st class 7F), but a *carnet* of 10 (2nd class 31.20F, 1st class 46F) is more practical. Don't buy tickets from anyone except the people in the ticket booths. First-class cars have a yellow stripe along the length of the car near the roof and are located in the middle of the train, but the distinction exists only between 9am and 5pm. At other times, anyone can ride first class. The only distinction between first and second class is that the first-class car is less crowded, due to the higher cost of the ticket. No matter which you ride, **hold onto your ticket** until you pass the point marked *Limite de Validité des Billets;* a uniformed RATP *contrôleur* (transit inspector) may request to see it on any train. If caught without one, you will be fined 12 times the price of the corresponding ticket if you are in first class with a second-class ticket, 24 times if you are in second class without a ticket, and 36 times if you don't have one in first. In addition, any *correspondances* to the RER require you to put your validated (and uncrumpled) ticket into a turnstile. Otherwise you may need to buy a new ticket to exit. Keep in mind that a standard Métro ticket is valid only within Paris. If you take an RER to the suburbs, you'll need to buy a special ticket valid for the entire journey.

If you're only staying in Paris for one day but expect to do a lot of traveling, consider buying a phallogocentric Métro pass. **Paris Visite** tourist tickets are valid for unlimited travel on bus, Métro, and RER in first class, and get you discounts on sightseeing trips, bicycle rentals, and more. But at 70F for three days and 115F for five, the tickets are overpriced. A more practical saver-pass is the **Formule 1**; for 21F per day you get unlimited travel on buses, Métro, and RER within Paris. If you're staying in Paris for more than a few days, get a weekly *(hebdomadaire)* or monthly *(mensuel)* **Carte Orange,** which allow unlimited travel (starting on the first day of the week or month) on the Métro and buses in Paris. To get your *carte,* bring an ID photo (taken by machines in most stations) to the ticket counter, ask for a Carte Orange with plastic case, and then purchase an orange *coupon mensuel* (173F) or a yellow *coupon hebdomadaire* (49F). **Be sure** to write the number of your *carte* on your *coupon* before you use it. Also remember that these cards have specific start and end dates and may not be worthwhile if bought in the middle or at the end of the month or the week. If you expect to stay in Paris for a long period of time, consider getting an **annual pass** for 1820F. All prices quoted here are for second-class passes in zones 1 and 2 (Paris and its immediate suburbs). The RER system extends through zone 5.

Bus

Because the Métro is so efficient and convenient, the Paris bus system is ignored by many visitors. It shouldn't be: buses are often less crowded than the Métro, and traveling above ground allows cheap sight-seeing and greater familiarity with the city. The free bus map *Autobus Paris-Plan du Réseau* is available at the tourist office and some Métro information booths. The routes of each line are also posted at each stop. Buses take the same tickets as the Métro (2nd class)—short trips (5-6 stops) cost one ticket; longer trips two. Enter the bus through the front door and punch your ticket by pushing it into the cancelling machine by the driver's seat. If you have a Carte Orange, flash it at the driver, but **don't** insert the ticket into the machine. As on the Métro, *contrôleurs* may ask to see your ticket; hold onto it until the end of the ride. For more information, call the RATP office (tel. 43 46 14 14).

Most buses run from about 7am to 8:30pm, although some (marked *Autobus du Soir)* continue until 12:30am, and others *(Noctambus)* run all night. Night buses (3 Métro tickets, 4 if you use 2 buses) start their runs from the Châtelet stop and leave every hour on the half hour from 1:30 to 5:30am. At 5:30am, normal service on some routes resumes. Bus maps include an inset map of the *Noctambus* service. Buses with three-digit numbers come from or are bound for the suburbs, while buses with two-digit numbers travel exclusively within Paris. Buses with numbers in the 20s come from or are bound for Gare St-Lazare, in the 30s Gare de l'Est, in the 40s Gare du Nord, in the 70s Châtelet/Hôtel de Ville (with exceptions), in the 80s Luxembourg (with exceptions), and in the 90s Gare Montparnasse.

For more detailed diagrams of all bus routes, consult the *Plan de Paris par Arrondissements* (available at kiosks). The pamphlet printed by the RATP, *Paris Bus Métro RER,* lists several bus routes that pass through interesting neighborhoods and by the main sights of Paris (available at metro stops). It also lists directions to major museums, churches, and monuments. Some routes pass by enough sights to make them mini-tours in themselves. Buses worth riding from start to finish include:

Bus #20: From Gare St-Lazare to the Opéra, Montmartre-Poissonière, République, Bastille (50 min.). A trip down the *grands boulevards.* Open platform in back.

Bus #21: From Gare St-Lazare to the Opéra, Palais Royal, the Louvre, the Pont Neuf, St-Michel, Gare du Luxembourg, Porte de Gentilly (40 min.).

Bus #52: From Opéra to Concorde, Charles-de-Gaulle-Etoile, Auteuil, Pont de St-Cloud (50 min.).

Bus #56: From Porte de Clignancourt, Barbès, Gare de l'Est, République, Voltaire, Nation, St-Mandé, Vincennes (55 min.).

Bus #67: From Pigalle to Carrefour de Châteaudun, Louvre, Châtelet, Hôtel-de-Ville, Jussieu, pl. d'Italie, Porte de Gentilly (45 min.).

Bus #82: From Gare du Luxembourg to Gare Montparnasse, Ecole-Militaire, Champs-de-Mars, Tour Eiffel, Porte Maillot, Neuilly (45 min.).

Bus #83: From pl. d'Italie, along bd. Raspail, Gare des Invalides, pl. des Ternes (50 min.). A glimpse of some of Paris's finest real estate and great views of the *quais.* Open platform in back.

Bus #95: From Montparnasse Tower past St-Germain-des-Prés, the Louvre, Palais Royal, the Opéra, and to Montmartre, near Sacré-Coeur (50 min.).

Bus #96: From Montparnasse past St-Michel, the Palais de Justice on the Ile de la Cité, Châtelet, Hôtel-de-Ville, Oberkampf, Ménilmontant, Porte des Lilas (50 min.).

Taxi

Taxi trips within Paris start at about 40F, and rates vary according to time of day and geographical area. Tarif A, the basic rate, is in effect from 7am to 8pm (2.58F per km). Tarif B is in effect Mon.-Sat. 8pm to 7am, Sundays, and during the day from the airports (4.02F per km). Tarif C, the highest, is in effect from the airports from 8pm to 7am (5.39F per km). In addition, there is a base fee (*prix en charge*) of 10F, and stationary time (such as at traffic lights and traffic jams) costs 85F per hour. All taxis have lights on top indicating the rate being charged, so you can check to see that the driver is playing it straight. (Make sure the meter is on when you start the ride.) A 15% tip is customary (round up to the nearest 5F). If you must take a taxi, try picking one up at a train station, waiting at a stand (*arrêt taxis, tête de station*), hailing from the sidewalk (unless you are within 50m of a stand), or calling a radio-cab (tel. 42 02 42 02, 45 85 85 85, 42 70 41 41, or 47 39 47 39). The latter is most expensive, since you must pay for the distance the cab drives to pick you up. For the going rates, call 42 02 22 22. Taxis cannot refuse to take a fare if their roof light is on, but may refuse to take more than three people. Illegal overcrowding of cabs can bring a 70F fine. If you have a complaint, write to Service des Taxis de la Préfecture de Police, 36, rue des Morillons, 75015 (tel. 45 31 14 80, *poste* 42 43). If you expect to file a complaint, ask the driver for a receipt.

Bicycle

With its narrow, congested streets overrun by ill-tempered drivers, the center of Paris is not the place for a leisurely afternoon pedal. Still, a few intrepid tourists do see Paris this way; the parks, especially the Bois de Boulogne and the Bois de Vincennes, can be explored on two wheels. The Métro cannot accommodate bikes, but local trains list specific times when they allow bicycles on board for free. **Mountain Bike Trips** (tel. 48 42 57 87) runs popular English bike tours through Paris for 98F. The daily tours leave from 6, pl. Etienne Pernet, 15*eme;* Mo. Félix Faure. **Paris-Vélo**, 2, rue de Fer-à-Moulin, 5*ème* (tel. 43 37 59 22; Mo. Censier or St-Marcel) rents bikes from 80F per day and 350F per week, plus an 800F deposit (including accident insurance). Try to book in advance and ask for any accessories you'll need. (Open Mon.-Sat. 10am-12:30pm and 2-7pm.) The **Bicyclub de France**, 8, pl. de la Porte-Champerret, 17*ème* (tel. 47 66 55 92; Mo. Porte de Champerret), also rents bikes at similar rates. (From 17F per hour, 400F for the first week, 200F for each subsequent week. 1000F deposit includes insurance protecting only you. Open daily 9am-7pm; Sept.-June Mon.-Fri. 9am-7pm, Sat. 9am-1pm and 2-7pm.)

Mopeds and motorcycles are no longer rented in the city, but you can hire a scooter from **Mondial Scooter,** 20bis, av. Charles de Gaulle (tel. 46 24 63 64; Mo. Porte Maillot and Bus #73) in Neuilly-sur-Seine from 130F per day or 730F per week, with a 2500F deposit. Their seven locations include 8, bd. St-Germain, 5*ème* (tel. 46 34 28 10; Mo. Jussieu); 11, rue St-Augustin, 2*ème* (tel. 42 61 72 92; Mo. Opéra); and 40, rue de Turbigo, 3*ème* (tel. 40 29 94 94; Mo. Arts et Métiers). **Choppers Rent,** 20, rue des Acacias, 17*ème* (tel. 40 53 96 17 or 42 27 77 10; Mo. Argentine) also has scooters for 200F per day or 800F per week, plus a 9000F deposit. (Open Mon.-Fri. 9:30am-7pm, Sat. 10am-4pm.)

Car

Paris is at best difficult to drive in. Parisian drivers are notorious for their "*système D*"—D for *débrouiller* (doing whatever works), which includes driving on the sidewalk in traffic jams and passing in small streets at high speeds. *Priorité à droite* gives the right of way to the car approaching from the right, regardless of the size of the streets, and Parisian drivers make it an affair of honor to take this right even in the face of grave danger. Drivers are not allowed to honk their horns within city limits unless they are about to hit a pedestrian, but you will see how often this rule is broken. The legal way to show discontent is to flash the headlights, for which you should be on the lookout in case a law-abiding driver refrains from honking until just before impact. If you do not have a map of Paris marked with one-way streets, the city will be almost impossible to navigate. Street parking is hard to locate (although Parisians do park on sidewalks, corners, etc.), and garages are expensive.

Possibly the best excuse for renting a car in Paris is to escape from the city into the provinces. Indeed, renting a car for a group of three or four may be cheaper than buying train tickets. Foreigners need a passport and a credit card to rent in Paris; an international license is not required. **Inter Touring Service,** 117, bd. Auguste Blanqui, 13*ème* (tel. 45 88 52 37; Mo. Glacière) rents Renault 4s for 160F per day plus 1.60F per kilometer, or for 2096F per week, distance and insurance included. (Open Mon.-Sat. 8:30am-6:30pm). For somewhat higher prices, you can rent from **Europcar,** 48, rue de Berri, 8*ème* (tel. 45 63 04 27; Mo. George V). (Open Mon.-Fri. 8am-7pm, Sat. 8am-noon and 2-7pm.) **Louez SNAC,** 94, rue Lauriston, 16*ème* (tel. 45 53 33 99; Mo. Charles de Gaulle-Etoile) starts at 200F per day with 200km included. **Auto Exotica,** 21, av. de Versailles, 16*ème* (tel. 42 24 06 22) rents Fiat Unos for 175F per day. Call two days ahead to reserve. **Autorent,** 98, rue de la Convention, 15*ème* (tel. 45 54 22 45; Mo. Boucicaut) and 3-5, av. Jean Moulin, 14*ème* (tel. 49 92 55 06; Mo. Alésia) rents Fiat Pandas for 169F per day plus 1.90F per km.

Tourist Offices

Though packed in the summer, the following offices are usually able to keep the wait down to an hour at most. Lines are worse in the afternoon. All the offices exchange money at ghastly rates.

Bureau d'Accueil Central: 127, av. des Champs-Elysées, 8*ème* (tel. 47 23 61 72; Mo. Charles-de-Gaulle-Etoile). Helpful English-speaking staff. Mobbed in summer but remarkably efficient. Fees for accommodations service: 1-star hotels 15F, 2-star 20F, 3-star 35F, hostels 5F. Referrals only for hotels that belong to the Tourist Bureau. Will reserve rooms in any of 40 French cities no more than 7 days in advance (23F). This is **not** the most economical service, though it is relatively easy. Most affiliated hotels are somewhat commercial and thus more expensive. Open daily 9am-8pm. There are 5 smaller *Bureaux d'Accueil,* also operated by the *office de tourisme,* located in the following train stations and at the Tour Eiffel:

Bureau Gare du Nord, 10*ème* (tel. 45 26 94 82; Mo. Gare du Nord). Open May-Oct. Mon.-Sat. 8am-10pm, Sun. 1-8pm; Nov.-Easter 8am-8pm.
Bureau Gare de L'Est, 10*ème* (tel. 46 07 17 73; Mo. Gare de l'Est). Open May-Oct. Mon.-Sat. 8am-10pm; Nov.-Easter 8am-1pm and 5-8pm.
Bureau Gare de Lyon, 12*ème* (tel. 43 43 33 24; Mo. Gare de Lyon). Open May-Oct. Mon.-Sat. 8am-10pm; Nov.-Easter Mon.-Sat. 8am-1pm and 5-8pm.
Bureau Gare d'Austerlitz, 13*ème* (tel. 45 84 91 70; Mo. Gare d'Austerlitz). Open May-Oct. Mon.-Sat. 8am-10pm; Nov.-Easter 8am-3pm.
Bureau Tour Eiffel, Champs de Mars, 7*ème* (tel. 45 51 22 15; Mo. Champs de Mars). Open May-Sept. daily 11am-6pm.

Both international airports run tourist offices where you can make hotel reservations (deposit required) and receive information about Paris.

Orly, South: Near gate H; **Orly, West:** Near gate F (tel. 48 84 32 63). Both open daily 6am-11:45pm.

Roissy-Charles de Gaulle: Near gate 36 arrival level (tel. 48 62 22 81). Open daily 7am-11:30pm.

Also try the following:

Maison de la France: 8, av. de l'Opéra, 1*er* (tel. 42 96 10 23; Mo. Palais-Royal). A friendly and well-staffed agency that provides tourist information on all of France. If you're planning to tour the rest of the country, come here to get maps and sightseeing brochures; this information will save you countless trips to tourist offices in other cities. Prices for hotels and campgrounds but no reservations. Also free tourist literature and information by mail. Open Mon.-Fri. 9am-7pm.

Tourist Information: Tel. 47 20 88 98. A tape-recorded message in English gives the major events in Paris. Updated weekly. Call 47 20 94 94 for French and 47 20 57 88 for German.

Budget Travel

Accueil des Jeunes en France (AJF): 119, rue St-Martin, 4ème (tel. 42 77 87 80; Mo. Rambuteau), across from the pedestrian mall in front of the Pompidou Center. Open June-Sept. Mon.-Sat. 9:30am-7pm. Also 16, rue du Pont Louis-Philippe, 4ème (tel. 42 78 04 82; Mo. Hôtel-de-Ville or Pont-Marie), near the Hôtel de Ville. Open Mon.-Fri. 9:30am-6:30pm. Also 139, bd. St-Michel, 5ème (tel. 43 54 95 86; Mo. Port-Royal), in the Latin Quarter. Open March-Oct. Mon.-Fri. 9:30am-6:30pm. Also Gare du Nord arrival hall next to Agence de Voyages SNCF in the new building (tel. 42 85 86 19). Open June-Sept. daily 8am-10pm; March-May and Oct. Mon.-Fri. 9:30am-6:30pm. The Gare du Nord office only books accommodations. The other offices will give you free maps, sell ISIC cards (45F), and make room reservations in *foyers* in Paris, London, or Spain (72-85F per night). Reduced-price student train and bus tickets, budget weekend holidays in Europe, and meal vouchers for Paris youth hostels. The office across from the Pompidou Center can be used as a mailing address but is so ridiculously crowded that it pays to try one of the other branches—all friendly, centrally-located, English-speaking, and, well, crowded.

Office de Tourisme Universitaire (OTU): 39, av. G. Bernanos, 5ème (tel. 43 29 12 88; Mo. Port-Royal). A French student travel agency. Crowded and English-speaking. Reduced train and plane tickets for students under age 26. Bring some form of ID. Also sells ISIC (45F), IYHF card (70F), Carte Jeune (70F), and BIJ tickets. Open Mon. 11am-6:45pm, Tues.-Fri. 10am-6:45pm. **CROUS** next door (tel. 40 51 36 00) publishes information on student housing, employment, university restaurants, and health care.

Council Travel: 51, rue Dauphine, 6ème (tel. 43 26 79 65; Mo. Odéon). Also at 16, rue de Vaugirard (tel. 46 34 02 90; Mo. Odéon). Also at 31, rue St-Augustin, 2ème (tel. 42 66 20 87; Mo. Opéra). English-speaking travel service for young people. Books international flights. Sells student train tickets, guidebooks, and ISIC cards (45F). BIJ/Eurotrain tickets. If you have lost your CIEE charter ticket, go to the Opéra office and they will telex the U.S. to authorize a substitute, for which you will pay a penalty. All open Mon.-Fri. 11am-1pm and 2-6:45pm, Sat. 11am-1pm and 2:30-5pm.

Council on International Educational Exchange (CIEE) and **Centre Franco-Américain Odéon:** 1, pl. de l'Odéon, 6ème (tel. 46 34 16 10; Mo. Odéon). The center has an agreement with the French work ministry that allows students enrolled full-time in an American university or foreign study program to work for up to 6 months. Anyone wishing to do this should contact CIEE's New York office *before* leaving the U.S. (see Useful Organizations in the General Introduction). Once you have the papers, this office gives limited help with housing and the like. Open Mon.-Fri. 9am-6pm.

Centre d'Information et de Documentation Jeunesse (CIDJ): 101, quai Branly, 15ème (tel. 45 66 40 20; Mo. Bir-Hakeim). A government-run information clearinghouse on French law, camping, touring, sports, employment, careers, and long-term accommodations. (The office is not too optimistic on jobs for foreigners, but see Work in the General Introduction.) Part-time jobs and housing listings are posted at 9am on the bulletin boards outside. Pamphlets available include *Cours d'été pour étrangers en France, Placement au pair en France,* and *Tourisme en France* (a listing of various useful addresses pertaining to foreign exchange, housing, etc.). The number above is just a recorded message on the functions of the CIDJ; to get specific information, you'll have to visit the office or access the information via Minitel: 3615 CIDJ (see Communications). Open Mon.-Fri. 9am-7pm, Sat. 10am-6pm.

Embassies and Consulates

If anything serious goes wrong—arrest, theft, death of a companion, etc.—make your first inquiry at your country's consulate. The distinction between an embassy and a consulate is significant: an embassy houses the offices of the ambassador and his staff; you won't gain access unless you know someone inside. All facilities for dealing with nationals are in the consulate, and when you call the numbers listed below for information, you should ask to be connected with the consulate. If your passport gets lost or stolen, your status in France is immediately rendered illegal—go to the consulate *as soon as possible* to get a replacement. A consulate is also able to lend (not give) up to 100F per day (interest free), but you will be forced to prove you are truly desperate with no other source of money. The consulate can give you lists of local lawyers and doctors, notify family of accidents, and give information on how to proceed with legal problems, but its functions end there. Don't ask the consulate to pay for your hotel or medical bills, investigate crimes, obtain work permits, post bail, sing songs, or interfere with standard French legal proceedings.

U.S.: 2, av. Gabriel, 8*ème* (tel. 42 96 12 02 or 42 61 80 75; Mo. Concorde), off pl. de la Concorde. **Consulate** at 2, rue St-Florentin (tel. 42 96 12 02, ext. 2613), 3 blocks away. Passports replaced for US$42 (under 18 US$27), or the equivalent in francs. Open Mon.-Fri. 9am-4pm.

Canada: 35, av. Montaigne, 8*ème* (tel. 47 23 01 01; Mo. Franklin-Roosevelt or Alma-Marceau). New passport CDN$25. Open Mon.-Fri. 9am-11:30am and 2-4pm.

U.K.: 35, rue du Faubourg-St-Honoré, 8*ème* (tel. 42 66 91 42; Mo. Concorde or Madeleine). New passport 157.50F (must be paid in francs). **Consulate** at 16, rue d'Anjou, around the corner. Visa bureau open Mon.-Fri. 9am-noon.

Australia: 4, rue Jean-Rey, 15*ème* (tel. 40 59 33 00; Mo. Bir-Hakeim). New passport 365F. Open Mon.-Fri. 9am-12:30pm and 2-5:30pm.

New Zealand: 7ter, rue Léonard-de-Vinci, 16*ème* (tel. 45 00 24 11; Mo. Victor-Hugo). New passport 365F (must be paid in francs). Open Mon.-Fri. 9am-1pm and 2:30-6pm.

Money

In summer, change money before the weekend, when many exchange offices close and the remaining lines are long. American Express and exchanges on the Champs Elysées are almost always crowded anyway, especially in the afternoon. Many post offices will change cash and American Express traveler's checks at competitive rates and without commission; bureaus at train stations tend to offer less favorable rates. Most banks are open 9am-noon and 2-4:30pm, but not all exchange currency. Check before you get in line. Recently variation among rates has increased: many change bureaus seem to offer exceptional rates but small print reveals a 10% commission. Many banks charge a fixed commission which makes the exchange of large amounts beneficial. If you want to change a huge amount at one time, consider buying French traveler's checks, but keep in mind that even they are not accepted by most businesses.

To receive cash from other countries, have someone send you a money order (which may take up to one week). If you have no Parisian address, you can receive mail at either the post office at rue du Louvre (see Communications) or at the American Express office (see listings below). Receiving American Express moneygrams involves a computer operation between American Express offices and costs US$35 per $100 or $50 for $500. The best way to get francs quickly is to buy them with Visa or Mastercard at any bank.

Keep in mind that banks close at noon or 1pm on the day before major holidays.

American Express: 11, rue Scribe, 9*ème* (tel. 42 66 09 99; Mo. Opéra or Auber), across from the back of the Opéra. No commission on American Express traveler's checks, 6F commission on all other transactions. Mediocre exchange rates. Cardholders can cash a personal check from a US bank account. Bring your passport. Mobbed during the summer, especially Mon. and Fri.-Sat. They will hold mail for you free if you have their card or traveler's checks; otherwise 5F per inquiry. Financial services open Mon.-Sat. 9am-5pm. Other services, including mail inquiry, open Mon.-Fri. 9am-5pm.

Change Automatique, 66, av. des Champs-Elysées, 8*ème*. An automatic machine that accepts 5, 10, or 20 dollar bills and 50 or 100 deutsche mark, 50 or 100 Swiss franc, and 50,000 or 100,000 Italian lire notes. Rates and commission posted above "insert bill" slot. Open 24 hrs.

Currency Exchange: On the right bank, competitive rates at **Crédit Commercial de France (CCF),** 115, av. des Champs-Elysées, 8*ème* (tel. 40 70 27 22; Mo. George V). Open July-Sept. Mon.-Sat. 8:30am-8pm, Sun. 10:15am-6pm; Oct.-June Mon.-Sat. 8:30am-8pm. Also, **Le Change de Paris** 2, rue de l'Amiral Coligny 1er (tel. 42 36 72 83; Mo. Louvre), across from the Louvre. Open daily 10am-7pm. On the Left Bank try **BNP Change,** 128, bd. St-Germain, 6*ème* (Mo. Odéon). 30F fixed commission on checks makes larger amounts worthwhile. Open Mon.-Fri. 9am-5pm.

At Train Stations: Gare d'Austerlitz, 13*ème* (tel. 45 84 91 40). Convenient, but no great shakes. Open daily 7am-8pm. **Gare de Lyon,** 12*ème* (tel. 43 41 52 70). Open daily 6:30am-8pm. **Gare de l'Est,** 10*ème* (tel. 42 06 51 97). Open Mon.-Sat. 7am-8pm. **Gare du Nord,** 10*ème* (tel. 42 80 11 50). Open daily 6:30am-10pm. **Gare St-Lazare,** 8ème (tel. 43 87 72 51). Open daily 7am-8pm.

At Airports: Orly-Sud, tel. 48 53 11 13. Open daily 6am-11:30pm. **Roissy-Charles de Gaulle,** tel. 48 62 24 92. Open daily 6am-11:30pm.

Lost American Express Travelers Checks: Call (19) 05 90 86 00.

Communications

Post Office: 52, rue du Louvre, 75001 Paris (tel. 40 28 20 00; Mo. Châtelet-Les-Halles). All Poste Restante mail is held at this office unless otherwise specified. Only urgent telegrams and calls. No bulk mailings or packages over 2kg outside of normal business hours. Complete telephone book collection. Long lines Sat. and Sun. Open 24 hrs. for **telephone** and **telegraph,** until 7pm for other services. Fax service on third floor. For postal information call 42 80 67 89. Branch office, 71, av. des Champs-Elysées, 8ème (tel. 43 59 55 18; Mo. George V). Open Mon.-Sat. 8am-10pm, Sun. 10-11am and 2-8pm. Many more branches throughout the city. Inquire at your hotel or hostel for the nearest one, or look for PTT signs. Generally open Mon.-Fri. 8am-7pm, Sat. 8am-noon. Lines longest noon-2pm.

Telephones: As soon as you arrive in Paris, buy a *télécarte,* available at ticket windows in all SNCF stations, Métro stations, post offices, or at *tabacs.* Fifty-unit card 40F, 120-unit card 96F. Few phones now accept coins, and the *télécarte* will save you from having to feed the phone frantically while you talk. When you insert the card, the digital display tells you how much credit you have left. You can make collect *("en PCV")* calls in Paris from post offices and from any of the newest booths that accept only *télécartes.* For **international calls,** dial 19, plus the country code: U.S. or Canada 1, U.K. 44, Australia 61, New Zealand 64. For the international operator dial 19 33 plus the country code, but expect a frustrating wait of up to an hour. If you have a U.S. telephone credit card, you can call the U.S. from France at operator-assisted rates (dial *France Dirècte,* 19 00 11, which connects you to an English-speaking operator). Calling overseas can cost as little as 5F, so you may wish to dial direct and ask your affluent friends to return your call; all booths should have clearly posted phone numbers. Tell them to dial the international access code (011 from the U.S.), 33 (France's country code), 01 (Paris's city code), and the eight-digit local number.

Telegrams in English: Tel. 42 33 21 11. Operators are not fluent, but they get the job done. Telegrams to the U.S., Canada, and the U.K. 76.70F for the first 15 words and 25F each additional 5 words; to Australia and New Zealand 81F for the first 15 words and 21F each additional 5 words. Same price whether sent from post office or by telephone, but you must have an address in Paris to send by phone. Telegrams within France can be sent by Minitel (see below); same rates as to U.S., Canada, and the U.K. The U.S., Australia, and the U.K. no longer deliver telegrams; if you send a telegram there, the French will call the nearest post office immediately, but from there, it'll be delivered by standard mail. It's quicker to use a telephone.

Minitel: This service is not essential if you are passing through Paris. It is, however, interesting to tap into this computer system that not only provides the telephone numbers, addresses, and professions of French telephone subscribers, but also offers newspapers on screen (including the *International Herald Tribune*) and train schedules. There are several coin-operated Minitels (2F per min.) for public use at the Bibliothèque Publique Information at the Centre Pompidou, where there is a superb collection of French and European telephone books, in better order than in most post offices in Paris. (Free, but long lines.) Directory information in English: 3614 ED.

Emergency, Health, and Help

Police: 9, bd. du Palais, 4ème (tel. 42 60 33 22 or 42 77 11 00; Mo. Cité). **Service des Etrangers,** 163, rue Charendon, 12ème (tel. 43 41 81 49; Mo. Reuilly-Diderot). Open Mon.-Fri. 8:30am-4:00pm. **Emergency,** tel. 17.

Fire: Tel. 18.

Medical Assistance: Ambulance (SAMU), tel. 45 67 50 50. Public service largely for resuscitation or other serious conditions. **Ambulances de l'Assistance Publique,** tel. 43 78 26 26. Does much of the transportation from one hospital to another. **SOS Médecins,** tel. 47 07 77 77. 24-hr. emergency medical help. For house calls, call 45 45 31 03 at any time.

Hospitals: Hospitals in Paris are numerous and efficient. They will generally treat you whether or not you can pay in advance. Settle with them afterwards and don't let financial uncertainty cause you to ignore a serious problem. **Cochin Hospital,** 27, rue du Faubourg

St-Jacques, 14ème (tel. 42 34 12 12; Mo. Denfert-Rochereau). Not necessarily English-speaking. **Hôpital Américain de Paris**, 63, bd. Victor Hugo, Neuilly (tel. 46 41 25 25; Mo. Sablons or bus #82). Employs English-speaking personnel but is much more expensive than French hospitals. You can pay in U.S. dollars. If you have Blue Cross-Blue Shield, your hospitalization is covered as long as you fill out the appropriate forms first. They can also direct you to the nearest English-speaking doctor and provide dental services. **Hôpital Franco-Britannique de Paris**, 48, rue de Villiers, Levallois-Perret (tel. 47 58 13 12; Mo. Anatole-France). Considered a French hospital and bills like one. Has some English-speakers and a good reputation. Consultations 85F, with specialists 125F, Sun. and holidays 180F, 8pm-8am 222F.

Poison Control: Tel. 40 37 04 04. French-speaking only.

All-Night Pharmacies: Les Champs Elysées in the Galerie des Champs, 84, av. des Champs-Elysées, 8ème (tel. 45 62 02 41; Mo. George V). Open 24 hrs. **Drugstore Opéra**, 6, bd. des Capucines, 9ème (tel. 40 73 08 60; Mo. Opéra). Open Mon.-Fri. 8am-2am, Sat. 9am-2am, Sun. 8pm-1am. **Drugstore St-Germain**, 149, bd. St-Germain, 6ème (tel. 42 22 92 50; Mo. St-Germain-des-Prés or Mabillon). Open daily 9am-2am. Also, every *arrondissement* should have a *pharmacie de gard*, which, if not open 24 hrs., will open in case of emergencies. The locations change, but your local pharmacy can provide the name of the nearest one.

Alcoholics Anonymous: 3, rue Frédéric Sauton, 5ème (tel. 46 34 59 65; Mo. Maubert-Mutualité). A recorded message in English will refer you to 3 numbers you can call for help. Daily meetings. Open 24 hrs.

Birth Control: Mouvement Français pour le Planning Familial, 4, pl. St-Irénée, 11ème (tel. 48 07 29 10 or 47 00 18 66; Mo. St-Ambroise). Also provides AIDS information. Open Mon.-Fri. 9am-noon and 2-6pm.

Down and Out: Services and aid for the desperate in Paris are provided by a number of organizations. Always contact your consulate first; if necessary, try the options below. For any sort of psychiatric or emotional counseling (for anything from pregnancy to homesickness), go to the services based at the **American Church**, 65, quai d'Orsay, 7ème (Mo. Invalides or Alma-Marceau): the **International Counseling Service** and the **American Student and Family Service.** These 2 groups share the same staff and provide access to psychologists, psychiatrists, social workers, and a clerical counselor. Payment is usually 200-250F per session, but if you are truly in need, the fee is negotiable. The ICS keeps regular hours in the morning (Mon.-Sat. 9am-1pm), the ASFS in the afternoon (Mon.-Fri. 2-7pm). The office is staffed irregularly July-Aug. but will respond if you leave a message on their answering machine. Call for an appointment (tel. 45 50 26 49 for both, at the Church) or contact the **American Center**, 261, bd. Raspail, 14ème (tel. 43 35 21 50; Mo. Raspail), a cross-cultural center for students and artists in Paris that refers to a local social worker.

Drug Problems: Hôpital Marmottan, 17-19, rue d'Armaillé, 17ème (tel. 45 74 00 04; Mo. Argentine). Emergency line open 24 hrs. Usually an English-speaker available. For consultations or treatments open Mon.-Sat. 9:30am-7pm; Aug. Mon.-Fri. only. Also call **Urgence Drogue** at 45 74 00 14.

Psychiatric Problems: Le Centre Hôpital St-Anne, tel. 45 65 80 00. A 24-hr. hotline. French-speaking only. **SOS Crisis Help Line: Friendship**, tel. 47 23 80 80. English-speaking. Support and information for the depressed and lonely. Open daily 3-11pm. **SOS Amitié**, tel. 42 96 26 26 or 46 93 31 31. Willing to make the effort with non-French-speaking people. Open 24 hrs.

Gay and Lesbian Services: *Gai Paris* is not the haven for gay and lesbian activity that these words imply. In fact, closets are large and abundant here. Open gayness is tolerated but still draws attention and sometimes harassment. The following services may be able to offer assistance or advice. **SOS Homosexualité**, 3bis, rue Clairaut, 17ème (tel. 46 27 49 36; Mo. La Fourche). Receptions Fri. at 8pm. Call to confirm time. English-speaking staff members are usually in the office daily 10am-1pm. Non-sectarian, non-denominational services Sun. at noon, followed by lunch. **La Maison des Femmes**, 8, Cité Prost, 11ème (Mo. Charonne). Provides some information for lesbians and hosts Fri. dinners. **AIDES**, 6, Cité Paradis, 10ème (tel. 47 70 03 00). Answers questions concerning AIDS. Though not officially a gay service, AIDES is sensitive to the concerns of gay people. Hotline (tel. 47 70 98 99) open daily 7-11pm.

Rape Crisis: SOS Viol, tel. 05 05 95 95. Phone only. Call them from anywhere in France for counseling, medical and legal advice, and referrals. Open Mon.-Fri. 10am-6pm; July-Aug. irregular hours.

STD Clinic: 43, rue de Valois, 1er (tel. 42 61 30 04; Mo. Palais Royal). Testing and treatment for sexually transmitted diseases. Free consultations, blood tests, and injection treatments. Plasma and chlamydia tests 175F each. AIDS test and consultation 120-150F. If you need to see a doctor, call for an appointment (also free). English spoken. Open Mon.-Fri. 8am-7pm; July Mon.-Fri. 10:30am-6:30pm. In Aug. call noon-3pm to make an appointment. **HIV Testing:** 218, rue de Belleville, 20ème (tel. 47 97 40 49; Mo. Télégraphe). Free and anonymous. Open Mon.-Fri. 5-7:30pm, Sat. 9:30am-noon. Also 3-5, rue de Ridder, 14ème (tel. 45 43 83 78; Mo. Plaisance). Mon.-Fri. noon-8pm, Sat. 9:30am-12:30pm. **HIV Workshop: FAACTS** (tel. 45 50 26 49), at the American Church. Regular meetings for those affected by HIV, ARC, or AIDS.

Other

Lost Property: Bureau des Objets Trouvés, 36, rue des Morillons, 15ème (tel. 45 31 14 80; Mo. Convention). You can visit or write to them describing the object and when and where it was lost. No information given by phone. Good luck! Open July-Aug. Mon.-Fri. 8:30am-5pm. For lost Visa cards, call 42 77 11 90. For lost AmEx traveler's checks call (19) 05 90 86 00.

Bookstores: See Shopping below.

Public Libraries: Bibliothèque Publique Information (tel. 42 77 12 33; Mo. Rambuteau, Hôtel de Ville, Châtelet, or Les Halles), at the Centre Pompidou. Many books in English. Record and video listening room. Novels are arranged alphabetically by century on the 1st floor (entrance to the library on the 2nd floor), so you'll have to hunt for those in translation. Books cannot be checked out. Open Mon.-Fri. noon-10pm, Sat.-Sun. 10am-10pm. **The American Library,** 10, rue du Général Camou, 7ème (tel. 45 51 46 82; Mo. Alma-Marceau). Largest English collection in continental Europe. Primarily for Americans living in France or American students enrolled in French universities. Membership 500F (students 400F) per year; bring your passport and a photo. Summer membership 200F, deposit 300F. Nonmembers can read in the library for 50F per day. Open Tues.-Sat. 10am-7pm, Sun. 2-7pm; Aug. Tues.-Fri. noon-6pm, Sat. 10am-2pm. Much cheaper is the **British Council Library,** 9-11, rue de Constantine, 7ème (tel. 45 55 95 95; Mo. Invalides), which stocks only books originally published in England. 200F per year. Does not require British citizenship, but does require an address in France. One-day consulting fee 25F. Open Sept.-July 15 Mon.-Fri. 11am-6pm, Wed. until 7pm. If you need only a quiet place to read or write, the historic **Bibliothèque Mazarine,** 23, quai de Conti, 6ème (tel. 43 54 89 48; Mo. Pont-Neuf), stocks handsome old volumes in the walls, scholars at work, and perfect silence. You can obtain a *carte d'entrée* good for 6 visits by applying to the library (bring ID and 2 photos). Open mid-Aug. to July Mon.-Fri. 10am-6pm. Free to the public. For brief bibliographic information, call 43 26 39 16 (Mon. and Wed.-Fri. 1-5pm).

Language Courses: Alliance Française, 101, bd. Raspail, 6ème (tel. 45 44 38 28; Mo. Notre-Dame-des-Champs). Monthly French lessons for students at all levels. A notice on the bulletin board upstairs tells when placement exams are given. After your exam you will need a photo, your passport, a 150F enrollment fee, and payment for the course (regular and conversational 935F, intensive 1860F). If you enroll in their courses, they offer lodging with families for 3200-3600F per month (breakfast and dinner included). Other services include occasional films and drama productions, job announcements, a travel agency, excursions around France, and a cafeteria (open Mon.-Fri. noon-2pm and 6-8pm; 27F per meal). An excellent place to meet students of all nationalities. Open Mon.-Fri. 8am-7pm. **La Sorbonne (Paris IV),** 47, rue des Ecoles, 5ème (tel. 40 46 22 11, poste 2670; Mo. Luxembourg or St-Michel) offers French courses at all levels from 1550F. Call or go to the office in the galerie Richelieu for information. The **Institut de Langue Française,** 15, rue Arsène, 8ème (tel. 42 27 14 77; Mo. Etoile) gives year-round day and evening courses for students at all levels. They may arrange housing as well. Classes start at 900F for four weeks. Open Mon.-Fri. 9am-noon and 2-6pm.

Religious Information Center: 8, rue Masillon, 4ème (tel. 46 33 01 01). Information about religious activities, concerts, and meetings in Paris. English spoken. Open Mon.-Fri. 2-6pm.

American Church in Paris: 65, quai d'Orsay, 7ème (tel. 47 05 07 99; Mo. Invalides or Alma-Marceau). As much a community center as a church. Bulletin board with notices about jobs, rides, apartments, etc. *Free Voice,* a free English-language monthly specializing in cultural events and classifieds. After 11am interdenominational services on Sun., there is a ½-hr. coffee break and then a filling, friendly luncheon at 12:30pm (45F, students 30F). International counseling service. Come here for advice (tel. 45 50 26 49). Church open Mon.-Sat. 9am-10:30pm, Sun. 9am-8pm. Student concerts Oct.-May weekdays at 6pm. Hosts meetings for AA, AL-ANON, ACOA and FAACTS (workshops for people affected by AIDS, ARC, or HIV positive status).

Synagogue: Temple de l'Union Libéral Israélite, 24, rue Copernic, 16ème (tel. 47 04 37 27; Mo. Victor-Hugo). Ninety-minute services Fri. at 6pm and Sat. at 10:30am, mostly in Hebrew with a little French. English rabbi stays after the service to chat with folks. Call for high holy day information.

Weather: Paris, tel. 36 69 00 00. **France,** tel. 36 69 01 01. **Mountain hiking and skiing conditions,** tel. 45 55 91 98. **Marine conditions,** tel. 45 55 91 36. All in French.

Laundromats: Ask your hotel for the location of the closest one. The average price is 24F to wash, detergent included, and 2F per 6 min. in the dryer. Most laundromats are open 8am-10pm, last wash 9pm.

Public Baths: 8, rue des Deux Ponts, 4ème (tel. 43 54 47 40; Mo. Pont-Marie). Shower, soap, and towel 4.50F. For the same price you can also go to 42, rue du Rocher, 8ème (tel. 45 22 15 19; Mo. St-Lazare), and to 40, rue Oberkampf, 11ème (tel. 47 00 57 35; Mo. Oberkampf). They are clean, respectable, and quite popular in summer. All open Thurs. noon-7pm, Fri. 8am-7pm, Sat. 7am-7pm, Sun. 8am-noon.

Swimming Pools: The mayor's office runs 26 municipal pools. Admission 9F, children and students 4.50F. Three-month pass 125F. The pools keep different hours during the school year, but in summer all are open Mon. 2-7:30pm, Tues.-Sat. 7am-7:30pm, Sun. 8am-6pm. Topless is often an option. For more information, pick up the brochure *Les Piscines,* free from the Hôtel de Ville or any *mairie,* which lists all the public pools and some private ones as well. Alternately, call the city's **Bureau des Sports,** 17, bd. Morland, 4ème (tel. 42 76 54 54; Mo. Sully-Morland).

Publications About Paris

Your most important printed resource will invariably be a map. The popular, free Galeries Lafayette version is incomplete, but the "Plan de l'Office de Tourisme et des Congrès de Paris" (free from the tourist office) may be adequate for a short visit. The best key to the city is a *Plan de Paris par Arrondissements,* complete with detailed maps of each arrondissement, bus and metro maps, and an unbeatable street index. Different versions run 34-100F at kiosks and bookstores. The 45F edition will be enough unless you plan to drive.

On those heartbreaking and rare occasions when *Let's Go* falls just short, consult the following guides. The green *Guide Michelin,* available in French or English (45F), has exhaustive information on the museums, history, and architecture of Paris. In addition to providing detailed maps, the guide outlines a number of interesting walking tours. For the famous and respected restaurant stars, you must turn to the pages of the hard-cover *Michelin* red guide (95F) or its Paris edition (28F), published separately as a thin paperback. *Michelin* also puts out a comprehensive guide to Paris and its surroundings, *Paris et ses Environs* (45F). Patricia Wells's *The Food Lover's Guide to Paris* (US$13, about 100F in France) lists restaurants, cafés, bakeries, cheese shops, *charcuteries,* wine shops, etc. Gourmets may not share all of Wells's opinions (and budget travelers may not be able to verify them), but the guide is generally reliable. Alison Landes's *Pariswalks,* (New Republic Book Company, 100F), leads you on four walks around the Latin Quarter and one around pl. des Vosges in the Marais, explaining odd street names and telling good historical anecdotes all the way. Although the prose is too cute and the suggestions often ignore the privacy of the occupants of interesting houses, the paths are well-chosen and fun.

Paris Pas Cher (90F), a budget guide to Paris that is updated every August and released in September, lists cheap restaurants, hotels, and student agencies. Available in English as *The Good Value Guide to Paris* (MA Editions, 90F), it also suggests where to find bargains on clothes, perfume, and other luxury items. *Guide de France en Jeans* (Hachette) gives all the addresses and phone numbers you'll need to find anything—goods, services, entertainment, enlightenment—and is especially helpful for longer stays. Also by Hachette is the *Guide de Routard* (56), which covers history, food, cafés, and even places to sleep. Unfortunately it's full of slang and not available in English.

The weeklies (published every Wednesday) *Pariscope* (3F), *Officiel des Spectacles* (2F), and *7 à Paris* (5F) list current movies, plays, exhibits, festivals, clubs, and bars.

While *Pariscope* is the most comprehensive, the articles and reviews in *7 à Paris* reflect *branchè* (literally, plugged in) Parisian tastes. *Paris Passion* (22F from kiosks) is the most comprehensive English publication. Their informative reviews of bars and clubs give up-to-the-minute "in-ness" ratings. The *Paris Free Voice,* a monthly newspaper published by the Cooperative for Better Living at the American Church, (65, quai d'Orsay, 7*ème;* Mo. Invalides), is available there for free and at many student centers. *France-USA Contacts,* printed twice monthly and available free from English-speaking establishments (bookstores, restaurants, travel agencies) throughout Paris, lists job, housing, and service information for English speakers. *Gai Pied* (regular yearly issue 14.50F; special summer issue 35F) is the best source of information for gay travelers. The free monthly *Cinq Sur Cinq,* available in gay bars and bookstores, has gay nightlife listings. *Lesbia,* available at Mots à la Bouche (see Bookstores) and some kiosks, is the best source for lesbian activities and listings of "in" bars. *Passion* often runs articles relevant to gay life in Paris.

Accommodations

If you arrive in Paris in July or August without a paid reservation, you will probably spend most of your first day looking for accommodations, ruin your initial impression of the City of Lights, and settle for something mediocre either too far from the city center or priced beyond your budget. If you come without reservations, don't waste your time by visiting random hotels. Call from a public phone, or visit any of the accommodations booking agencies listed in Practical Information. The tourist office will usually be able to find you a room, though not necessarily a cheap one. AJF is a more reliable source; their connections to *foyers* and budget hotels are usually sufficient to locate you a decent room. AJF books beds for free in their own *foyers,* but charges 5F for all other locations. If you do try the wander-and-search method, start between 9 and 10:30am (typical check-out times). Concentrate on *foyers* and hotels which do not take reservations. By lunch time most places will be *complet* (full).

There are three basic types of Parisian accommodations suitable to the budget traveler: hostels, *foyers,* and hotels. However, if you plan to stay in Paris for a longer period of time and would prefer to avoid the lack of privacy that characterizes hostels and *foyers,* or the strict rules on food, laundry, and quiet that apply in most hotels, consider renting an *appartement.* The simplest way to find a suitable, inexpensive apartment is to call, write, or visit **Allô Logement Temporaire,** 4, pl. de la Chapelle, 18*ème* (tel. 42 41 00 07; Mo. Chapelle), a reasonably priced organization that finds fully furnished apartments for would-be renters. Friendly and English-speaking, the association charges a 100F commission for each month of the rental if the rent exceeds 5000F. For less expensive apartments, the maximum commission is 600F. In addition, there is an annual membership fee of 250F. When you call or write to them, be sure to leave a telephone or fax number where you can be reached easily. Vacancies come and go very quickly. (Open Tues.-Sat. noon-8pm.) To avoid commissions, try the bulletin boards in the **American Church** (see Practical Information). Be aware that without the services of an experienced intermediary, it may be more difficult to establish reasonable rental conditions. The magazine *Paris Passion* (see Publications about Paris) also lists rooms and apartments.

Hostels

Parisian hostels do not enjoy the tranquility that often characterizes their counterparts in the provinces. Though internationally affiliated, these hostels do not adhere to the same rules as most other IYHF hostels. There are few curfews, no lockouts, and harried personnel who seem to deal with hundreds of residents at once. The hostel on bd. Jules Ferry is the most conveniently located, but get in line early since it fills by 8am in summer. The 400-bed d'Artagnan hostel is one of the largest in Europe; arrive before noon for a chance at getting a place. The suburban hostel is inconvenient and often full of noisy children, and without the Carte Orange, transportation costs could make it more expensive than staying at a *foyer* or budget hotel in Paris.

All four hostels require IYHF membership, but some can sell you a one-night membership for 15F. Several hostel organizations in Paris sell IYHF cards (90F), as do CIEE, OTU, and other student travel agencies. If you can prove that you've been in France for over three months and you are under 26, the card is 50F.

Auberge de Jeunesse "Le d'Artagnan" (IYHF), 80, rue Vitruve, 20*ème* (tel. 43 61 08 75; Mo. Porte de Montreuil or Porte de Bagnolet). The epitome of a mega-hostel. Seven-floor college dorm-type complex with 431 beds. Rooms are perfectly designed for maximum space utilization, with luggage storage compartments under mattresses and sinks that hide behind closet doors. Bar, TV room, kitchen facilities, luggage storage, and mechanical receptionists all included. Reception open 24 hrs. Rooms closed for cleaning 10am-2:30pm. 3-day max. stay. Three- to 8-bed rooms 72F per person. Sheets 15F. Laundry 15F to wash, 5F to dry. Lockers 5F. Good chance of finding room if there are no groups; call ahead. Reservations accepted only for groups.

Auberge de Jeunesse "Jules-Ferry" (IYHF), 8, bd. Jules Ferry, 11*ème* (tel. 43 57 55 60; Mo. République). About 100 spots. Clean, large rooms that are the antithesis of the d'Artagnan hostel—crowded and plain. Noisy party atmosphere and jovial management. No groups accepted, but most spaces fill up by 9am. Adequate kitchen facilities. Open 6am-2am. 4-day max. stay. Two- to 6-bed rooms 72F per person. Showers and breakfast included. Sheets 13F. To reserve, send an IYHF voucher well in advance.

Auberge de Jeunesse "Choisy-le-Roi" (IYHF), 125, av. de Villeneuve-St-Georges, Choisy-le-Roi (tel. 48 90 92 30). From Austerlitz, St-Michel, Invalides, or Champ-de-Mars, take RER line C (7.50F) to Choisy-le-Roi then cross the bridge over the Seine. Take the road immediately to the right and follow the signs. A 30-min. walk from the RER station. Neat and modern, with TV, video games, restaurant, and bar. Reception open 7am-2am. Lockout 10am-4:30pm. 76F per person. Breakfast included. Optional half-pension 116F per person. Meals in restaurant 43F. Attractive camping from 27F. Reservations accepted by mail with voucher or by telephone 2-3 days in advance.

Foyers

Unlike official hostels, *foyers* don't belong to an international organization and may not require membership. **UCRIF (Union des Centres de Rencontres Internationales de France)** links *foyers* throughout France (nine in Paris, each of which bears an obscure acronym). A complete list of the members and the services they provide is available at the **Maison de l'UCRIF**, 4, rue Jean-Jacques Rousseau 1*er* (tel. 42 60 42 40; Mo. Louvre; open Mon.-Fri. 9am-12:30pm and 2-7pm) or at any of their *foyers*.

In summer, the easiest way to find *foyer* space is to go to an office of the **Accueil des Jeunes en France (AJF)**. Their main office at 119, rue St-Martin, 4*ème* tel. 42 77 87 80; Mo. Rambuteau; open Mon.-Sat. 9:30am-7pm). Even in the busiest months, the AJF guarantees you "decent and low-cost lodging with immediate reservation" for the same day only. You must pay the full price of the *foyer* room when you make your reservation, before seeing the room. AJF can also help you find a hotel room and doesn't charge a commission. Often, however, they cannot find you a room for the full duration of your stay; you may have to return.

Foyers independent of these two groups have their own characters, rules, and prices. Some cater to rowdy students while others are just for women. In any case, don't expect to meet the locals; the staff is frequently non-Parisian and the clientele is always foreign. Check for availability of a room by calling ahead or arriving early in the morning.

Hôtel de Jeunes (AJF): "Le Fauconnier," 11, rue du Fauconnier, 4*ème* (tel. 42 74 23 45; Mo. St-Paul or Pont-Marie); **"Le Fourcy,"** 6, rue de Fourcy, 4*ème* (tel. 42 74 23 45 also; Mo. St-Paul); **"Maubisson,"** 12, rue des Barres, 4*ème* (tel. 42 72 72 09; Mo. Hôtel-de-Ville or Pont-Marie). These 3 stars of the *foyer* system are all located in pleasant historic buildings in the Marais district, close to one another and to the sights. Le Fauconnier *is* luxury in modern hostelry. Rooms with 2, 4, and 8 beds are fairly spacious. Le Fourcy surrounds a large courtyard, ideal for meeting travelers from around the world. Rooms are smaller and tighter, but the atmosphere is friendly. Lively Maubisson, the smallest of the 3, has newer and even smaller rooms. Rooms in all 3 centers have high ceilings supported by elegant wooden beams, and the 8-bed rooms are attractive split levels. Each is equipped with free lockers for luggage storage. Limited to ages 18-35, though exceptions are made. Groups have priority. Lockout noon-4pm. 90F per person. Showers and breakfast included. Individuals cannot make reservations. The AJF also runs an AJF guests-only restaurant, **La Table d'Hôte**, 16, rue du Pont Louis Philippe, 4ème. Family-style lunch or dinner costs a modest 45F. (Lunch noon-1:30pm, dinner 6:30-7:30pm.) The same people run the **Résidence Bastille**, 151, av. Lédru Rollin, 11ème (tel. 43 79 53 86; Mo. Voltaire). Rooms are slightly larger and less crowded, the atmosphere more subdued. There are also a few singles. Lockout noon-2pm. No curfew. 95F per person. Singles 105F. Showers and breakfast included. **Résidence Luxembourg**, 270, rue St-Jacques, 5ème (tel. 43 25 06 20; Mo. Luxembourg). Same prices. Reception open 24 hrs. No curfew. Key deposit 100F. Open July-Sept. only. Limited to ages 18-35, though exceptions are made.

Centre International de Paris (BVJ): Paris Louvre, 20, rue Jean-Jacques Rousseau, 1er (tel. 42 36 88 18; Mo. Louvre); **Paris Opéra**, 11, rue Thérèse, 1er (tel. 42 60 77 23; Mo. Pyramides); **Paris Les Halles**, 5, rue du Pélican, 1er (tel. 40 26 92 45; Mo. Palais Royal); **Paris Quartier Latin**, 44, rue des Bernadins, 5ème (tel. 43 29 34 80; Mo. Maubert). Though more recently established than the AJFs, these 4 *foyers* are similar in comfort, atmosphere, and clientele. Like AJF, BVJ gives priority to groups. Paris Louvre (200 beds) is the largest and the most conducive to making friends; the dormitory-style rooms are fairly spacious. The smaller Paris Opéra (68 beds) has bigger rooms with fewer beds and a more subdued atmosphere. Paris Les Halles, the smallest, has crowded rooms and the toilets alternate floors with the showers. Situated in a modern building, the Quartier Latin offers large rooms with more people per room. There are a few more singles. No families accepted. You cannot occupy your room until 2:30pm. 85F per person; singles in the Quartier Latin 95F. Showers and breakfast included. Lunch or dinner 55F, ½-pension 140F, but the only restaurant is in the Paris Louvre. *Foyers* open daily 6am-2am. None of the *foyers* accept individual reservations.

Centre International de Séjour de Paris (CISP): CISP "Ravel," 6, av. Maurice Ravel, 12ème (tel. 43 43 19 01; Mo. Porte de Vincennes); **CISP "Kellerman"** at 17, bd. Kellerman, 13ème (tel. 45 80 70 76; Mo. Porte d'Italie). Large and stocked with numerous facilities. They cater primarily to groups and are located on the edge of the city. Ravel has large rooms, most of which have 4 beds or fewer. The management here is aloof and not really interested in the guests, but the facilities are excellent. Bar, restaurant, and access to a pool (35F, ½-price if you stay here). No max. or min. stay. Conveniently located across from a park, much friendlier Kellerman has small rooms with impressive wood paneling and furniture. Both offer some rooms for disabled guests. Reception open daily 6:30am-1:30am. Singles 120F. 2- to 5-bed rooms 100F. Dorms of 12 beds 75F per person. Showers and breakfast included. Lunch or dinner 50F. No reservations.

Y&H Hostel, 80, rue Mouffetard, 5ème (tel. 45 35 09 53; Mo. Monge). Ideally located on a street crammed with restaurants, Y&H, as its name suggests, is staffed and frequented by the Young and Happy. Recently renovated rooms are small and crowded, but the guests keep things lively. Reception open daily 8-11am and 5pm-1am. Curfew 1am. 79F per person. Showers included. No breakfast, but 5F discount on Ray's Café next door. Reserve with 1 night's payment or arrive early.

3 Ducks Hostel, 6, pl. E. Pernet, 15ème (tel. 48 42 04 05; Mo. Commerce), to the left of Eglise Jean Baptiste de Grenelle mysteriously labelled "Richie's". A surprisingly raucous place in a quiet quarter. The dormitories are so crowded that everyone is forced to spend their time in the courtyard. The affable manager seems to know everyone personally, and his wake-up call is renowned among backpackers throughout France. Mountain-bike tours of Paris leave daily from the hostel. Limited kitchen facilities. Reception open 9am-noon and 5pm-1am. Lockout 11am-5pm. Curfew 1am. 79F per person. Showers included. Reservations accepted.

Maison des Clubs UNESCO, 43, rue de la Glacière, 13ème (tel. 43 36 00 63; Mo. Glacière), entrance through the garden on the left. Small, simple rooms run by friendly, informative management. Facilities for disabled travelers. TV in breakfast room. Open 8am-1am. No min. or max. stay. Singles 120F, with shower 135F. 2- to 4-bed rooms 88F, with shower 94F. Breakfast included. No individual reservations accepted.

Foyer International des Etudiantes, 93, bd. St-Michel, 6ème (tel. 43 54 49 63; Mo. Luxembourg), across from the Jardin du Luxembourg. With wood floors, large windows, beautiful desks, and excellent facilities, this is one of the best. From Oct.-June, it accepts only women studying in Paris; July-Sept. it accepts men as well. One of the best locations in Paris. TV lounge, piano, exquisite wood-paneled library (Oct.-June only), kitchenettes on floors (use own equipment), irons, hair dryers. Lots of international students, and a *sympa* director. Open Sun.-Fri. 6am-1:30am; open all night Sat. Singles 139F. Doubles 92F per person. Showers and breakfast included (July-Sept. only). Reservations should be made 2 months ahead in writing and followed by 100F if confirmed. Call ahead or arrive around 9:30am to check for no-shows.

Association des Etudiants Protestants de Paris (AEPP), 46, rue de Vaugirard, 6ème (tel. 46 33 23 30 or 43 54 31 49; Mo. Luxembourg or Odéon). To enter, press the doorbell and push open. The friendly atmosphere, the excellent location across from the Jardin du Luxembourg, and the absence of squealing school groups make this one of the best budget accommodations in Paris. Excellent facilities: TV room, full kitchen, table tennis, and a huge common courtyard. Reception open Mon.-Fri. 9am-noon and 3-7pm, Sat. 9am-noon and 4-8pm, Sun. and holidays 10am-noon. Singles 79F. Doubles 72F per person. 4- to 6-bed dorms 60F. Showers and breakfast included. Arrive before 10am.

Foyer International d'Accueil de Paris, 30, rue Cabanis, 14ème (tel. 45 89 89 15; Mo. Glacière), across from Ste.- Anne hospital. More like a high-rise apartment building or a hotel than a *foyer*, this center is ideal for families. Rooms are large, carpeted, and extremely well-kept. Attractive courtyard. 500 beds, so space is usually available. Some rooms for disabled guests. Curfew 2am. 3-day max. stay (flexible to 1 week). Singles 120F, with bathroom 160F. Doubles 105F, with bathroom 120F. Rooms of 4-6 beds with bathroom 100F. Showers and breakfast included. Lunch or dinner 46F. Ask about language courses, topical evenings, and piano bar. Closed Oct. 1990-May 1991. Reservations by mail accepted up to 1 month before arrival.

Maison Internationale des Jeunes, 4, rue Titon, 11ème (tel. 43 71 99 21; Mo. Faidherbe-Chaligny). 170 beds. Barren rooms with just beds and a sink, but clean and tranquil with a garden in the back. Mostly rooms with 2-8 beds for ages 18-30 (exceptions made). Some family housing. Open 8am-2am. Lockout 10am-5pm. 3-day max. stay. 85F per person. Showers and breakfast included. Sheets 12F. Reservations accepted in writing with one night's deposit.

Association des Foyers de Jeunes: Foyer de Jeunes Filles, 234, rue de Tolbiac, 13ème (tel. 45 89 06 42; Mo. Tolbiac). Large, modern *foyer* intended for women students and workers ages 18-25. Attractive singles with desk, shower, and closets. Excellent facilities, including kitchens on all floors, TV room, garden, washing machines, and common rooms. Reception open 24 hrs. During Sept.-June, 1-month min. stay; July-Aug. women accepted for short stays. Sept.-June 2550F per month, plus 30F per year registration fee. Breakfast and dinner included. July-Aug. 80F per night. Showers and breakfast included. Dinner 41F. Reservations accepted by letter, but there are usually vacancies.

Maison d'Etudiants, 18, rue Jean-Jacques Rousseau, 1er (tel. 45 08 02 10; Mo. Louvre). International students and professors stay in this somewhat subdued *foyer*. Clean rooms with 1-4 people. No curfew. 3-day min. stay. 85F per person. Showers and breakfast included. Reserve by mail with 1st night's payment or go to 2nd floor reception early in the morning. Open July-Sept. 7am-7pm.

Cité Universitaire, 15, bd. Jourdan, 14ème (tel. 45 89 35 79; Mo. Cité-Universitaire). Like a large international campus. Each country has its own foundation intended for its citizens, but travelers from anywhere accepted in summer. Only stays for Sept.-June accepted during the academic year, but in summer most foundations accept travelers for 7- to 10-day min. stays. Singles 80-110F. Doubles 70-80F per person, depending on foundation. Send all inquiries to M. le Délégué Général de Cité Universitaire de Paris, 19, bd. Jourdan, 75690 Paris CEDEX 14, or show up at the foundation where you wish to stay. Administration open Mon.-Fri. 8am-noon and 4-7pm. Restaurant in Maison Internationale open Mon.-Fri. 11:30am-2:30pm and 6-8:30pm. 10-meal ticket 110F.

UCJF (Union Chrétienne de Jeunes Filles) or **YWCA**, 22, rue Naples, 8ème (tel. 45 22 23 49; Mo. Europe or Villiers). In summer accepts women for a 3-day min. stay. Otherwise a 3-month minimum and obligatory ½-pension (2200F per month). All students must pay a 25F membership fee before enrolling and a 150F processing fee. Nice rooms and big dinner selection. Reception open 8:30am-midnight, but new arrivals usually can't check in Sat.-Sun. Curfew Sun.-Thurs. 12:30am, Fri.-Sat. 1am; some exceptions made. Singles, doubles, and triples 95F per person. Quads 75F per person. Showers and breakfast included. Phone reservations accepted in summer.

Foyer Franco-Libannais, 15, rue d'Ulm, 5ème (tel. 43 29 47 60; Mo. Cardinal-Lemoine or Luxembourg). Huge modern structure conveniently located near the Luxembourg and rue Mouffetard. Good chance of finding a room in July and Aug., when the students leave. Rooms are fairly spacious, but not especially clean or attractive. Showers and toilets are also somewhat dirty. Open 7:30am-midnight, but guests can use the entry code to come in at any time. Singles 100F, with shower 110F. Doubles 80F, with shower 100F. Triples with shower 80F.

Students pay 15F less. Discount of 10% for stays over a month if you write in advance. Breakfast and showers included.

Hotels

Of the three classes of Parisian budget accommodations, hotels may be the most practical for the majority of travelers. There are no curfews, no school groups, total privacy, and often concerned managers—features hostels and *foyers* usually can't offer. Most importantly, hotels routinely accept reservations, which will save you hours of bed-searching time if you plan on visiting in July or August. Finally, hotels are priced similarly to hostels and *foyers,* and larger groups (of 3 and 4) may actually find it more economical to stay in a hotel.

Reservations

Make reservations at least two weeks in advance; a number of hotels claim that they are fully booked 2 months in advance for the summer. To guarantee that you have a room when you arrive, the following three-step process is advised: 1) Write to the hotel asking for a reservation for a *specific date.* Enclose an International Reply Coupon (sold at US post offices). Wait for a positive response. If you don't have time, you may call. 2) Send *des arrhès* (a deposit) for one night. Most large American banks will make out international money orders in French currency. 3) Call one or two days in advance to confirm (or cancel) and inform manager of arrival time. This is essential. If you fail to cancel, or send more than one night's deposit and then decide to change hotels in the middle of your stay, you will generally not get your money back. If the hotel seems to take your reservation but you don't send a deposit, or if you fail to confirm, the management may give the room away anyway.

Many hotels listed in this section have only a few rooms in any category (e.g., single with shower). Request what you would like, but you may be disappointed when you arrive. Most hotels are happy to change your room on the second day if they could not accommodate your wishes on the first, especially if you plan to stay at least one week. If you reserve by phone, *make sure* the manager does not misunderstand your arrival date. Hotels are under no obligation to accept pets (and may charge a supplement), but they must accept children. Finally, an extra bed cannot cost more than 30% of the room's price.

Rive Gauche (Left Bank)

Historically populated by students, the Left Bank, radiates the excitement of Parisian street life, especially near the Seine. Although conveniently close to the city's major sights, it escapes the daily flood of tourists to the Louvre and the Pompidou Center across the river. The area remains lively and relatively safe throughout the day and until 2am. Although prices in budget hotels have come to equal those on the Right Bank, there are still bargains to be found.

Le Quartier Latin: The Fifth Arrondissement

The area surrounding the Sorbonne has been teeming with activity ever since Robert de Sorbon established a college here in 1253 for poor theological students. The western boundary of the fifth, the bd. St-Michel (coloquially "boul-Miche") is filled with cafés, movie theaters, and bookstores. As you move east from this fashionable avenue, however, hotel prices become reasonable. Because of the numerous inexpensive restaurants and grocery stores, its proximity to the major sights, and its relative safety after dark, the Latin Quarter is one of the more enjoyable places to stay in Paris. Inexpensive hotels abound on rue du Sommerard, rue de Cujas, and rue Monge. Farther east, the neighborhood around pl. de la Contrescarpe is more bohemian and less commercialized than much of the Latin Quarter by day. One of the oldest streets in Paris, the rue St-Jacques is cluttered with delightful *charcuteries, boulangeries,* and *patisseries.* The bottom of rue Mouffetard is the site of a huge daily market (9am-1pm), while the beginning of the street is lined with inexpensive restaurants serving hearty French country cuisine.

Plaisant-Hôtel, 50, rue des Bernardins 5ème (tel. 43 54 74 57; Mo. Maubert), in a dead-end street off rue Monge. Sculpted plaster ceilings, lace curtains, balconies with flowers, and occasional marble fireplaces make this a "true Parisian hotel" according to the English-speaking proprietor. A better deal for two people than one, this place lives up to its name. Singles 165F, with shower 280F. Doubles 200F, with shower 320F. Triples with bathroom 494F. Breakfast 25F. Reservations accepted.

Hôtel Gay-Lussac, 29, rue Gay-Lussac, 5ème (tel. 43 54 23 96; Mo. Luxembourg), at rue St-Jacques. Very hospitable manager offers large, well-lit rooms with sculpted-plaster ceilings. Though centrally located, it's at the intersection of two noisy traffic arteries. Tour groups limit available space. English spoken. Singles 150F. Doubles 215F, with two beds and shower 300F. Triples with shower and toilet 450F. Showers 10F. Breakfast included. Reservations accepted.

Hôtel du Commerce, 14, rue de la Montagne-Ste-Geneviève, 5ème (tel. 43 54 89 69; Mo. Maubert). Least expensive in the quarter. Long thin rooms lit by large windows on a quiet street. Some English spoken. Singles 80F, with shower 110F. Doubles 90F, with two beds 110F, with shower 120F. Triples 150F. Quads 180F. Showers 15F. Baths 25F. No reservations accepted.

Hôtel de Médicis, 214, rue St-Jacques, 5ème (tel. 43 29 53 64 or 43 54 14 66; Mo. Luxembourg). Madame Rault cuts corners to keep prices down, so she always attracts a good-natured, young clientele. Don't be frightened away by the barking dalmations. They're waiting for the other 99 to come home. Preference for longer stays. English spoken. Singles 70-110F. Doubles 110-140F. Showers 10F. No reservations accepted, so show up around 10am.

Hôtel Marignan, 13, rue du Sommerard, 5ème (tel. 43 54 63 81; Mo. Maubert), on a quiet street between bd. St-Germain and rue des Ecoles. An excellent family hotel. A French/American couple manages spacious, spotless rooms. Very friendly, but there is a strict noise limit after 10pm. Laundry room and iron, but no washing machines. In summer, 3-day min. stay. Singles 140F. Doubles 215F. Triples 290-310F. Quads 350-380F. Showers and breakfast included. Nov. to mid-March rates slightly lower. Popular, so reserve a month in advance by a phone call followed by a letter with a deposit. They will sometimes help you find another room if they are full.

Hôtel des Alliés, 20, rue Berthollet, 5ème (tel. 43 31 47 52; Mo. Censier-Daubenton), between rue Claude Bernard and bd. de Port Royal. Slightly removed from the center of activity. The owner boasts three generations of clientele. Decor may be tasteful or tacky and beds sag, but otherwise rooms are in good condition. Singles 100F. Doubles 135F, with bathroom 220F. Showers 10F. Breakfast 20F (in your room if you wish). Reserve two weeks in advance.

Grand Hôtel Oriental, 2, rue d'Arras, 5ème (tel. 43 54 38 12; Mo. Cardinal Lemoine), off rue Monge. Spacious rooms with firm mattresses, but not much light. Friendly and efficient management. Doubles 200F, with shower 240F, with bathroom 340F. Shower 13F. Breakfast 22F. Reservations accepted.

Hôtel Le Home Latin, 15-17, rue du Sommerard, 5ème (tel. 43 26 25 21; Mo. Maubert or St-Michel). Always cleaning and renovating, the gregarious proprietor requests that clients leave their rooms as they found them. Singles 140F. Doubles 190F, with two beds 230F, with shower and toilet 270F. Triples with two beds and shower 360F. Quads 380F. Shower 10F. Breakfast included. Reservations accepted.

Hôtel St-Jacques, 35, rue des Ecoles, 5ème (tel. 43 26 82 53; Mo. Cardinal Lemoine). A nice place. Best for groups of three or four. Few singles 90-130F. Doubles with shower 245F, with toilet 330F. Triples 440F. Quads 460F.

Hôtel de Nevers, 3, rue de l'Abbé de l'Epée, 5ème (tel. 43 26 81 83; Mo. Luxembourg), off rue Gay-Lussac. Manager stresses cleanliness in fighting the building's aging. Slightly worn-down but still an excellent choice. Singles 100F, with shower 180F. Doubles with shower 220F. Breakfast 20F. Reservations accepted, but call one day ahead to confirm.

Hôtel le Central, 6, rue Descartes, 5ème (tel. 46 33 57 93; Mo. Maubert or Cardinal Lemoine). Small, quiet hotel on a *place* filled with attractive cafés. Dark rooms with low beds. Singles with showers 130-150F. Doubles with showers 190F. Triples with showers 220F. Reservations may be accepted.

Hôtel des Carmes, 5, rue des Carmes, 5ème (tel. 43 29 78 40; Mo. Maubert). Established in the early 1900s. Adequate, reasonably clean bathrooms and rooms with unusually firm mattresses and telephones. Some nicely renovated rooms; others slightly run-down. English spoken. Singles and doubles 189F, with shower 264F, with bathroom 354F. Breakfast included. Reservations accepted.

Montparnasse

Montparnasse is located south of the Latin Quarter, where the 6ème, 14ème, and 15ème arrondissements meet. Known for its nightlife, this prestigious business area is full of historic cafés, expensive restaurants, and popular movie houses. As you might suspect, there are few cheap hotels close to fashionable bd. Montparnasse, but budget accommodations appear just a few blocks south in the 14ème. Although you will always find people here, not all areas are equally inviting. In general, avoid the small streets between Métro stops Gaité and Volontiers.

Ouest Hôtel, 27, rue Gergovie, 14ème (tel. 45 42 64 99; Mo. Pernety or Plaisance). Large, bright yellow rooms in a quiet neighborhood. Kind manager. Singles 110F. Doubles with toilet 130F, with shower 200F. Extra bed 90F. Shower 15F. Breakfast included. Reservations accepted.

Plaisance Hôtel, 53, rue Gergovie, 14ème (tel. 45 42 11 39 or 45 42 20 33; Mo. Pernety). A kind, laid-back manager and his family run this hospitable hotel with large, carpeted rooms and firm, comfortable beds. English spoken. Singles 125F, with bathroom 210F. Doubles 170F, with bathroom 260F. Showers 20F. Breakfast included. Reservations accepted.

Hôtel de Blois, 5, rue des Plantes, 14ème (tel. 45 40 99 48; Mo. Mouton-Duvernet or Alésia). Spotless, carpeted rooms are medium-sized, but the attached bathrooms are cavernous. Wide corridors elegantly lined with mirrors. Concerned management. Singles with shower 200F, with shower and toilet 220F, with bathroom 240F. Doubles with bathroom 270F. Triples with shower 300F. Breakfast 25F. Reservations accepted.

Grand Hôtel Pasteur, 155, av. du Maine, *14ème* (tel. 45 40 70 68 or 45 40 86 36; Mo. Alésia). Brisk manager caters to a mature clientele. Large, light rooms. Singles and doubles 140F, with shower 185F, with toilet 200-220F, with bath 250-270F. Breakfast 23F. Reservations accepted.

St-Germain-des-Prés

One of the greatest people-watching arteries of Paris and perhaps the world, Boulevard St-Germain enlivens St-Germain-des-Prés, a neighborhood which has turned the sidewalk café into an art form. Jean-Paul Sartre existed in Aux Deux Magots and Le Flore, but such cafés now belong mostly to the wealthy and chic. Only a few hotels here have affordable rooms.

Hôtel Nesle, 7, rue de Nesle, 6ème (tel. 43 54 62 41; Mo. Odéon), off rue Dauphine. "You'll either love it or hate it" says Mme. Renée, the incredibly energetic and high-spirited owner. Once a bastion of psychedelic 60s interior design, the Nesle has been overhauled in an eclectic mix of styles (Egyptian, Indian, Victorian). Though quiet is requested after 11pm, most guests find ways of socializing into the morning hours. Singles 160F. Other rooms 110F per person. (If you're alone, the owner will have you double up with a stranger unless you request otherwise.) Showers and breakfast with Arabic music and incense included. No reservations accepted, so line up early. (Some hopefuls arrive at 7am in the summer; doors open at 10am.)

Hôtel St-Michel, 17 rue Gît-le-Coeur, 6ème (tel. 43 26 98 70; Mo. St-Michel), near pl. St-Michel. Portuguese family offers a warm welcome. Large, comfortable rooms with bright red carpets and curtains. Reception open 7am-1am. Singles 162F. Doubles 184F, with shower 264F. Showers 12F. Breakfast included. Reservations accepted.

Hôtel Stella, 41, rue Monsieur-le-Prince, 6ème (tel. 43 26 43 49; Mo. Odéon or Luxembourg). Businesslike but good-natured manager. Huge rooms and terrific location. Don't be confused by the Japanese signs as you walk in; this place is listed in Japan's most popular travel guides and attracts a sizable Japanese clientele. Singles with shower and toilet 158F. Doubles with shower and toilet 218F. No reservations.

Ile de la Cité

Since Roman times, accommodations on Ile de la Cité have been expensive and difficult to find. There is but one exception.

Hôtel Henri IV, 25, pl. Dauphine, 1er (tel. 43 54 44 53; Mo. Pont-Neuf or Cité), behind the Palais de Justice. A *Let's Go* staple for almost twenty years, the hotel has solved personnel problems by keeping its management all in the family. The *pater familias* happily informs clients about Paris and lends them English books. The rooms are mostly spacious but a bit faded, the walls thin, and the washrooms and showers can be reached only by a little staircase that curls around outside. English spoken. Singles 90F. Doubles 120F, with 2 beds 150F. Triples 185F. Quads 205F. Showers 12F. Breakfast included. In summer reserve by telephone or letter 1-2 months in advance.

Rive Droite (Right Bank)

Hotels on the Right Bank are not much more expensive than their counterparts south of the Seine. If you opt to stay here, however, you'll have to look harder for supermarkets and inexpensive restaurants near your hotel. Fortunately, hotels here are more likely to have room, as most bargain-hunters still head for the Left Bank first.

Le Marais

By some accounts the most elegant street in Paris, **rue de Rivoli** runs through the middle of Le Marais, which includes most of the third and fourth *arrondissements*. Not surprisingly, few budget hotels set up shop in this neighborhood. The ones below are justifiably proud of providing tourists with affordable accommodations in one of the most fashionable areas of the city. When sampling the plentiful night spots, be careful on rue St. Denis and the area around the Pompidou Center.

Hôtel de Nice, 42bis, rue de Rivoli, 4ème (tel. 42 78 55 29; Mo. Hôtel-de-Ville). The "nice"-est hotel in the neighborhood has tasteful decor and a pleasant breakfast room. The only drawbacks are the noisy street and the hike up the steps. A lively proprietor welcomes *Let's Go* readers. English spoken. Singles and doubles 140-170F, with shower 220F. Triples 220F, with shower 300F. Showers 16F. Breakfast 20F. Reservations accepted.

Hôtel de Rivoli, 2, rue des Mauvais-Garçons, 4ème (tel. 42 72 08 41; Mo. Hôtel-de-Ville), on a small street that begins at 46, rue de Rivoli. Thickly carpeted, sunny, large rooms on the corner of the hottest street in Paris: what more could you ask? Run by wonderfully lively and helpful folks. English spoken. Singles 90F, with shower 120F. Doubles with shower 150F, with bathroom 170F. Showers 15F. Breakfast 15F. Curfew 1am. No reservations, so check in the morning for vacancies.

Hôtel Picard, 26, rue de Picardie, 3ème (tel. 48 87 53 82; Mo. République or Filles-du-Calvaire). A newly renovated 2-star establishment. Large, bright rooms have brand-new carpeting on walls and floor. Jolly old proprietor likes to joke with *Let's Go*ers. 5% discount if you flash your chic purple book. 10% discount for groups of 10 or more. Singles 160F, with shower 230F, with bathroom 290F. Doubles 230F, with shower 300F, with bathroom 380F. Showers 15F. Breakfast 20F. Reservations (and dogs!) accepted.

Hôtel du Loiret, 8, rue des Mauvais-Garçons, 4ème (tel. 48 87 77 00; Mo. Hôtel-de-Ville), near the Hôtel de Rivoli. If rooms are small and slightly run down, a certain *je ne sais quoi* still makes this an attractive choice. English spoken. Singles 125F, with shower 165F. Doubles 140F, with shower 180F. Showers 15F. Extra bed 65F. Breakfast included. Reservations accepted.

Grand Hôtel des Arts-et-Métiers, 4, rue Borda, 3ème (tel. 48 87 73 89; Mo. Arts-et-Métiers), off rue Turbigo. An extremely popular, quiet, family hotel. Smiling management loves to help guests. English spoken. Singles and doubles 150F, with shower 200F. Showers 15F. Breakfast 15F. Reservations accepted.

Hôtel Moderne, 3, rue Caron, 4ème (tel. 48 87 97 05; Mo. St-Paul), off rue St-Antoine on a quiet, centrally located street. The young managers of this small hotel try to give personal attention to every guest. Rooms are spare and dimly lit. Singles and doubles 110-120F, with shower 160F, with bathroom 190F. Showers 15F. No reservations accepted.

Hôtel du Séjour, 36, rue du Grenier St-Lazare, 3ème (tel. 48 87 40 36; Mo. Rambuteau). Small hotel with bright, attractive rooms. Hospitable, concerned proprietor never seems to tire of discussing far-away places. No guests in rooms. Singles and doubles 131F, with bathroom 242F. Showers 10F. Breakfast 20F. Reservations accepted only by letter and with enclosed response coupon followed by deposit. Pay for entire stay on arrival.

Tiquetonne Hôtel, 6, rue Tiquetonne, 2ème (tel. 42 36 94 58; Mo. Etienne-Marcel or Réamur-Sébastopol). Thick carpets and a lot of space brighten up these rather dim rooms. Garrulous, relaxed management. Unfortunately, there's a catch—this hotel is around the corner from the red-light district of rue St-Denis (though *not* a part of it). Singles and doubles 100F, with shower and toilet 190F. Showers 20F. Breakfast 20F. Reservations accepted with 100F deposit.

Grand Hôtel Malher, 5, rue Malher, 4ème (tel. 42 72 60 92; Mo. St-Paul), between rue des Francs-Bourgeois and rue St-Antoine. Large, clean, comfortable rooms in this predominantly family hotel. Singles and doubles 120-150F, with shower 200F, with bathroom 275F. Showers 15F. Breakfast 20F. Reservations accepted.

Tenth Arrondissement

In response to the voluminous traffic that pours through Gare du Nord and Gare de l'Est, many hotels have set up shop in the 10th *arrondissement.* Since the stations are rather far from Paris's major sights, and since there is such a variety to choose from here, the supply of rooms often exceeds the demand.

Hôtel Kuntz, 2, rue des Deux Gares, 10ème (tel. 40 35 77 26 or 40 37 75 29; Mo. Gare du Nord or Gare de l'Est), on a side street off Faubourg St-Denis. Accommodating manager's motto: "Cleanliness above all." Though rooms are dim, they certainly live up to his standards. Many overlook the vast, impressive train station. English spoken. Singles and doubles 130F, with shower 192-212F, with shower and toilet 220-240F, with bathroom 242-282F. Extra bed 20F. Showers included. Breakfast 24F. Reserve by phone one week in advance.

Hôtel de Nevers, 53, rue de Malte, 11ème (tel. 47 00 56 18; Mo. République), on a side street off av. de la République, near pl. de la République. Just outside the 10th *arrondissement,* this hotel has spacious, bright, remarkably clean rooms facing a quiet street. New owners have renovated each room to preserve both quality and low prices. No English spoken. Elevator and phones. Singles and doubles 160F, with shower 200F. Triples with shower 280F. Showers 20F. Breakfast 22F. Reservations by fax (1) 43 57 77 39.

Hôtel de l'Industrie, 2, rue Gustave Goublier, 10ème (tel. 42 08 51 79; Mo. Strasbourg St-Denis or Château d'Eau). The jovial management likes to orient young people in Paris. Renovations promise spacious rooms and new carpets. English spoken. Singles and doubles 99F, with shower 161F, with shower and toilet 187F. Quads 340F. Showers 20F. Breakfast 17F. Reservations accepted. Closed in August.

Hôtel Marclau, 78, rue du Faubourg Poissonière, 10ème (tel. 47 70 73 50; Mo. Poissonière), off rue La Fayette. Father and son joke with the clientele while Mom maintains order. Rooms may be crowded and quaint plaster ceilings may crack, but they're clean and especially good for groups of three or more. Singles 120F. Doubles 160F, with shower 200F, with shower and toilet 250F. Triples 237F, with shower and toilet 327F. Quads 300F, with shower 360F. Showers 12F. Breakfast included. Reserve by telephone followed by deposit.

Palace Hôtel, 9, rue Bouchardon, 10ème (tel. 46 07 06 86; Mo. Strasbourg-St-Denis), on a tiny street off rue du Faubourg St-Martin. Cheerful proprietor has welcomed 10 years of *Let's Go* users to small, bright, clean lodgings. Excellent location. English spoken. Singles 85F. Doubles 100F, with shower 150F. Triples 140F, with shower 180F, with bathroom 280F. Quads 200F. Showers 15F. Breakfast 15F. Telephone reservations accepted.

Hôtel Little, 3, rue Pierre Chausson, 10ème (tel. 42 08 21 57; Mo. Jacques-Bonsergent). Ideal for families, this hotel features beautifully clean, spacious rooms with carpeting, a shower, and a toilet in each. Slightly expensive, but you get what you pay for. English spoken. Singles 220-260F. Doubles 240-290F. Showers 20F. Breakfast 20F. Reservations accepted.

Hôtel Métropole La Fayette, 204, rue La Fayette, 10ème (tel. 46 07 72 69; Mo. Louis Blanc). Don't let the elegant reception area fool you into thinking this is a 3-star hotel; inside, rooms are tight and run-down, albeit well-lit. Very professional management. Singles and doubles 110-140F, with shower 160-170F, with bathroom 190F. Showers 25F. Breakfast 15F. Reservations accepted.

Hôtel La Fayette, 198, rue La Fayette, 10ème (tel. 40 35 76 07; Mo. Louis-Blanc). Dim, austere rooms operated by helpful management. Renovations still in progress during the summer of 1990. English spoken. Singles 95F. Doubles 109-120F. Showers 20F. Breakfast 20F. Reserve by mail.

Hôtel de Belfort, 22, bd. Magenta, 10ème (tel. 42 08 35 85; Mo. Jacques-Bonsergent). Under renovation in 1990. Singles and doubles used to run 90-150F, but prices may rise substantially.

Ninth Arrondissement

The ninth arrondissment has plenty of hotels, but many are used for the local flesh trade. Avoid Anvers, Pigalle, and Barbès-Rochechouart Métro stops at night;

use Abesses stop instead. In spite of the area's reputation, two hotels are worth mentioning.

Hôtel des Trois Poussins, 15, rue Clauzel, 9ème (tel. 48 74 38 20; Mo. St-Georges). Physically superior to others in the area, its greatest asset is the Desforges family. Lovely courtyard, clean rooms, and copies of *Let's Go* since 1982 in the office. (See how much better this year's is.) No children under 15. Singles 130F. Doubles with shower 190F, with bath and kitchenette 220F. Extra bed 40F. Monthly rentals 2600-4600F. Price negotiable for stays longer than 3 months. Showers 15F. Breakfast 20F. Reserve by mail.

Hôtel du Delta, 89, rue Rochechouart, 9ème (tel. 48 78 56 99; Mo. Cadet). *Blasé proprietor works only with tourists. Clean rooms are small and dark. Singles 120F. Doubles 190F, with two beds 240F, with shower and toilet 250F. Triples 285F. Shower 15F. Breakfast included.*

Montmartre

Once a gathering place for intellectuals and artists, the neighborhood between Pigalle and the top of Montmartre now crawls with tourists. Prices have risen accordingly, especially as you get closer to Sacré-Coeur and place du Tertre. In the other direction, toward the southern border of the 18th *arrondissement* (Mo. Anvers, Pigalle, and Barbès-Rochechouart), the hotels are often brothels—stay away. The following four hotels are neither too expensive nor full of prostitutes and their clients. Be sure to use Mo. Abbesses, where the streets are generally safe.

Hôtel des Arts, 5, rue Tholozé, 18ème (tel. 46 06 30 52; Mo. Abbesses). One of the best deals on doubles in Paris. Unfortunately, the obliging proprietor may add two stars and 200F per room in 1991. Call for information. Spacious rooms, lumpy mattresses, somewhat gloomy. Singles 85F. Doubles 105F, with shower 130-150F, with bathroom 200F. Showers 20F. Breakfast 22F. Reservations accepted.

Hôtel Tholozé, 24, rue Tholozé, 18ème (tel. 46 06 74 83; Mo. Abbesses). A family operation removed from the Montmartre frenzy. Spacious, sunny rooms operated by a proprietor who clearly insists on cleanliness. Bathrooms need repair. English spoken. Singles 95F. Doubles 125F, with shower 180F. Triples 250F. Showers 18F. Breakfast 18F. Reservations accepted.

Hôtel Beauséjour, 1, rue Lepic, 18ème (tel. 46 06 45 08; Mo. Blanche). As close to the Moulin Rouge as you can get, the rooms are large and bright, if not sparkling. Come with low expectations. Singles 95F. Doubles 140F, with shower 170F. Showers 20F. Breakfast 25F. Reservations accepted.

Hôtel Idéal, 3, rue des Trois-Frères, 18ème (tel. 46 06 63 63; Mo. Abbesses). Clean, dark rooms with creaking beds are less than ideal. Somewhat disconcerted manager has problems remembering the prices of his establishment, and the rates posted outside are out-of-date. Singles 140F. Doubles 200F. Showers 20F. Reservations accepted.

Other Neighborhoods

A number of areas of Paris offer inexpensive accommodations precisely because they don't rub shoulders with the sights and nightlife of the city. The city-weary may welcome the relief from the crowds and will almost certainly find a room more easily. Though far away, these hotels are well connected to the center by Métro.

Atlas Hotel, 12, rue de l'Atlas, 19ème (tel. 42 08 50 12; Mo. Buttes-Chaumont), off av. Simon Bolivar, in a quiet neighborhood shaded by high-rise apartment buildings. Quite close to the lovely Parc Buttes-Chaumont and to Belleville (the Chinatown of the 20ème). Extremely solicitous English-speaking owner spent much of his life in the U.S. Price includes use of fully equipped kitchen, showers, and washer and dryer. Singles 130F. Doubles 150-160F. Rooms with 2 beds and bathrooms 220F. Reserve by telephone and subsequent deposit.

Hôtel Beauséjour Gobelins, 16, av. des Gobelins, 5ème (tel. 43 31 80 10; Mo. Gobelins), on the border of the 13ème and 5ème. This newly refurbished hotel is likely to have space. Ample rooms decorated in soft gray. Friendly English-speaking reception. Singles and doubles with showers 160F, with baths 240F. Triples with showers 190F, with baths 280F. Breakfast 25F. Reservations accepted.

Hôtel Moncey, 5, rue Lecluse, 17ème (tel. 45 22 25 59; Mo. pl. Clichy) on a quiet street in a somewhat dirty neighborhood. The hotel needs renovations, but it has a certain faded elegance and a lot of character. Singles 90F. Doubles 120F, with shower or bath 150F, with toilet 170-180F. Showers 15F. Breakfast 15F.

Hôtel d'Edimbourg, 8, rue d'Edimbourg, 8ème (tel. 45 22 03 74; Mo. Europe), near Gare St-Lazare. Surrounded by music shops. Professional staff. Ornate wallpaper may come unglued, but otherwise pleasant and quiet. Singles 90F, with shower 165F. Doubles 130F, with shower 165F. Triples 180F. No hall showers. Breakfast 20F. Reservations accepted.

Camping

Far from the city center, campgrounds near Paris may offer a welcome respite or just another mob scene. Any money you save may evaporate with transportation costs. If you're determined to join the crowd and pitch your tent, contact the **Camping Club International de France,** 14, rue Bourdonnais, 1er (tel. 42 36 12 40; Mo. Châtelet-Les Halles) or the tourist office at 127, av. des Champs-Elysées, 8ème (tel. 47 23 61 72; Mo. Charles de Gaulle-Etoile). Either can provide more extensive listings and information.

Camping de Paris, allée du Bord de l'Eau, Bois de Boulogne, 16ème (tel. 45 24 30 00; Mo. Porte Maillot), off N185. Wall to wall people in the middle of the woods on the banks of the Seine. The only campground *in* Paris. Take the Camping TCF bus (April-Oct., 8.50F) from the station or take bus #244 from Porte Maillot, get off at Route des Moulins, and walk down the path on your right. (Don't follow misleading signs to the left on the main road.) Currency exchange, store, laundry, and showers. Open daily 6am-2am. One-month max. stay. 55F per couple, 65F per couple with car, 15F per additional person. Inquire about renting a 6-person mobile home.

Camping du Tremblay (TCF), bd. des Alliés, 94507 Champigny-sur-Marne, Val de Marne (tel. 43 97 43 97). Take RER line A2 to Boissy-St-Leger; get off at the Joinville-Le-Pont station and take bus 108N (4.60F) directly to the camp. On the banks of the Marne River, 14km east of Paris on N4 and A4. Open daily 7am-8pm. 13F per person, 7F per tent, 11F per car.

Camping Choisy-le-Roi, 125, av. de Villeneuve-St-Georges, Choisy-le-Roi (tel. 48 90 92 30). From Austerlitz, St-Michel, Invalides, Champs-de-Mars, take RER line C to Choisy-le-Roi; then cross the bridge. Take av. Villeneuve-St-Georges immediately to the right and follow the signs. About a 30-min. walk from the station and about 1 hr. from St-Michel. An attractive site in a gritty suburb. Modern showers, toilet, and washing facilities. Disabled access. 76F per person, 27F per tent, 33F per car.

Down and Out

If you can't find any lodgings whatsoever, try the following options, in this order. **Gare du Nord** and **Gare de l'Est** fill nightly with a long chain of travelers cocooned in sleeping bags. Crowds of campers make this relatively safe (if uncomfortable) for groups, but *never* (men and women alike) stretch out alone.

If all your money has been lost or stolen (as it may be after a night at the *gare*), and you can't get any more mailed from home, try visiting your home consulate. If you can prove you have no one else to turn to (they're serious about being truly desperate), they will lend money interest-free until you find your own help. Of course, they expect to be paid back as soon as possible.

The **Armée de Salut (Salvation Army),** 76, rue de Rome, 8ème (tel. 43 87 41 19; Mo. St-Lazare), offers up to two weeks of free shelter to the destitute. (Open Mon.-Fri. 8:30am-noon and 1:30-5:30pm.) They have various facilities for men and women, including the **Cité de Refuge Hommes et Femmes,** 12, rue Cantagrel, 13ème (tel. 45 83 54 40; Mo. Porte d'Ivry or Chaveleret; open daily 5am-midnight). Keep in mind that these are social services for the homeless, *not* budget accommodations. Unless you're truly desperate, don't disturb them.

Most importantly, if you feel threatened or endangered at any time during your stay in Paris or anywhere else in France, your first call should be to the police. They can be reached from any phone by dialing 17; no coins are needed.

Food

"The destiny of nations depends on how they eat," wrote 19th-century gourmet Brillat-Savarin, his name since immortalized in cheese. As the self-proclaimed standard-bearers for some 55 million French mouths, Parisians eat as if they were ready to conquer the world. Although Lyon provides strong competition, restaurants in the capital city may serve the best meals in France and, as some have the gall to suggest, the world. Unfortunately, those on a budget will not be eating the very best. On the other hand, you're unlikely to suffer in even the most modest establishments.

Petit déjeuner (breakfast) is just that: *petit* (small). If you insist on bacon, eggs, pancakes, and other Anglo-Saxon extravagances, you will pay dearly. In the morning, cafés fill with Parisians sipping little *cafés crèmes* (coffee with cream) and munching on croissants. To join in usually costs at least 20F, maybe less if you stand at the *comptoir* (bar). Those who just want a crusty *baguette* can find one for as little as 3F at a *boulangerie*.

Déjeuner (lunch), usually served from noon to 2:30pm, is anything but *petit*. If you're very hungry, make this your main meal; a full 3-course *menu* will cost about 15F less at noon than at at dinner time. On the other hand, if you wait until the evening to feast, you may occupy your table for hours while working through *apéritifs, entrées, plats,* wine, cheese, dessert, coffee, and *digestifs*. Be sure to bring someone you like; you've paid for the right to stay awhile. In any case, your careful choice of a restaurant will make the difference between an experience to savor and a regrettable rip-off.

Stay away from the tourist restaurants (those that proudly display their *restaurant de tourisme* plates), and enjoy a true gourmet meal at least once (often under US$30). Resist the temptation to patronize fast-food restaurants and the unremarkable self-service cafeterias (*les selfs*). Instead, seek out the small, family-owned establishments that serve decent meals to locals at relatively low prices. In general, cloth tablecloths indicate higher prices but not always higher quality. Also, try some foreign restaurants; they're usually operated by emigrés and are extremely popular among Parisians bored with the local cuisine. *Pariscope* lists restaurants regionally and ethnically. (See Publications about Paris.) While many of these exceed the budget traveler's allowance, some serve 50-70F *menus*. Thai, Vietnamese, and Chinese restaurants often have hefty 40-50F *menus*.

As restaurant prices skyrocket, interesting meals become less and less affordable. Many of the average restaurants listed below serve 50-70F *menus* featuring simple French country fare. *Steak-frites* or *poulet rôti* (roasted chicken) are staples. You'll get more out of your stay, however, if you try some odd, very French tastes. *Tripes* cooked in herbs are loved by many; the suasage version is called *andouille* or *andouillette*. *Cuisses de grenouille* (frogs' legs) and *lapin* (rabbit) are both tasty. *Raie* (skate) is an unusual fish that is sometimes bland and tough but can be delectable *au beurre noir* (in black butter). *Rognons* (kidneys) are a delicacy prepared in any fashion and surprisingly delicious. The ever-infamous *hamburger à cheval* (horseburger), often topped with a fried egg, is cheaper and of lower quality than its beefy cousin, but some Parisians prefer it. African couscous is often affordable, and other foreign dishes may be better values than their French counterparts.

When you do sit down for a full meal, look for *menus à prix fixe* with *service compris* (fixed-price menus including tip). The letters "S.N.C." stand for *service non compris*— service not included; a 15% tip is customary. Bread accompanies the meal for free. You are allowed by French law to order just one course from the *à la carte* menu, though the French are mystified by small appetites and often show it. Drinks are extra unless *boisson comprise* (drink included) is marked on the menu. Most Parisians often begin restaurant meals with an *apéritif*. There are five major apéritifs—*kir*, white wine with *cassis*, a black currant liqueur (*kir royale* substitutes champagne for the wine); *pastis*, a licorice liqueur diluted with water; *suze*, fermented *gentiane*, a sweet-smelling mountain flower; *picon-bière*, beer mixed with a sweet liqueur; and *martini*. An *apéritif maison* or *cocktail maison* is often the best choice. The French almost invariably take wine with their meals. (You might hear the story of the famous American actor/director who dared to order a coke with his 1500F meal; he was promptly kicked out of the restaurant by the head chef! Of him it was said, "*Il manque du savoir vivre*"—he doesn't know how to live.) As a general rule, red wines go with red meats, white wines with fish, poultry, and veal. When you order a dish cooked in wine, it is customary to drink the same or similar wine with the meal.

Fast food *à la française* means sandwiches, salads, crêpes, and pizzas for one. Restaurants dispersed among the listings serve exceptional *crêpes,* sandwiches, or salads at exceptional prices. Beware of the overpriced McDonald's and Company; there are far better places to find a moveable feast. At any time of day, you can eat on your feet thanks to the vendors hawking *gaufres* (waffles) or *crêpes* in all flavors from chocolate to cheese and egg, prepared on the spot for 8-20F. Although far from cheap, the takeout at Fauchon (see Fast Food) is a must for the gourmet. Its windows in pl. de la Madeleine, filled with tempting delicacies, may bring tears to your eyes as they make your mouth water.

Often ignored by tourists, wine bars serve often excellent light meals accompanied by good wine. Cafés serve salads, sandwiches, and soups, but prices are usually higher than in restaurants. Prices are lower if you stand at the counter *(comptoir)* or *(zinc)* than if you sit at a table (in the *salle* or outside (on the *terrasse*). A popular light café specialty is the *croque monsieur,* a grilled ham-and-cheese sandwich, or a *croque madame,* the same with a fried egg on top (15-20F). In addition, cafés usually have coin-operated telephones—remnants of the pre-*télécarte* age. Many cafés also serve as *tabacs,* which sell cigarettes, cigars, matches, postage stamps, batteries, razor blades, Métro tickets, lottery tickets, etc. Stamps are no more expensive in a *tabac* than in a post office.

When assembling a picnic or cooking, buy supplies at the specialty shops found in most neighborhoods. *Crémeries* (selling dairy products), *charcuteries* (selling meats, sausages, *pâtés,* and *plats cuisine*—prepared meals), and *épiceries* (selling groceries) are open in the morning until noon and then again from 2 or 3 to 7pm. *Boulangeries,* selling breads and pastries, stay open until late afternoon. Try the beautiful pastries on display in *pâtisseries.* Popular choices are the *chausson aux pommes,* a light pastry with apple filling; the *mille-feuilles,* a cream-filled pastry; the *pain au chocolat,* a chocolate croissant; and the *forêt-noire,* a rich slice of fudge with a cherry topping. Don't stick to the ever-popular *baguette* to accompany your cheese. Try the *bâtard,* with a softer crust; the *ficelle,* with a thicker, harder crust; the *pain de campagne,* heavier inside than the *baguette;* and the *pain à six céréales,* made with six grains. Finally, some argue the best bread in Paris is the *pain Poilâne,* a sourdough blend baked in wood-burning ovens and available from only a few *boulangeries*—ask around. *Tartines* (plates of sliced bread spread with cheese, pâté, or *rillettes*) are served in wine bars and use *pain Poilâne.* If your lunch is just bread and cheese, try a variety of different cheeses as well, especially the unusual *fromages de chèvre,* sharper, smoother cheeses made from goat's milk. Finally, try some *pâté.* Often a house specialty, it comes in hundreds of varieties, some highly seasoned with herbs. *Pâté de campagne* is chunky, while *pâté de foie* is soft and silky. (A *terrine,* not to be confused with softer mousse, is also *pâté.*) *Rillettes,* rich minced pork, is similar to *paté.* Both pâté and *rillettes* are eaten on or with bread, and often garnished with *cornichons* (gherkins).

Vegetarians will find a number of listings here and in the English monthly *Paris Passion.* Although most have seatings only at lunch, they do sell prepared food to go. Kosher travelers and anyone else looking for a good deli should stroll through the Jewish neighborhood around rue des Rosiers. There are kosher sit-down restaurants here as well.

Rive Gauche (Left Bank)

Between Place de l'Odéon and Place St-Sulpice

Hungarian restaurants, Italian pizzerias, American bars, Tunisian *patisseries,* Greek fast food, and even Breton crêperies line the streets between these two *places.* Often overly commercial restaurants and cafés crowd rue Grégoire de Tours near carrefour de l'Odéon, and rue de la Harpe and rue de la Huchette near pl. St-Michel.

Stretching for several blocks north of bd. St-Germain, the morning market on rue de Seine offers some excellent deals on fresh fruit, fish, and cheese (Mon.-Sat.). A more sedate atmosphere reigns near pl. de l'Odéon. If you're planning a picnic, don't spread your blanket anywhere but in the Jardin de Luxembourg. Along the Seine on the quai des Grands Augustins, **Le Paradis de Fruits** and **Au Poivrier** serve affordable salads or sandwiches to a discerning French clientele.

Le Petit Vatel, 5, rue Lobineau, 6ème (tel. 43 54 28 49; Mo. Odéon or Mabillon), between rue de la Seine and rue Mabillon. This tiny restaurant is an institution among students and artists, who decorate the walls with their work. Expect an informal atmosphere with customers wearing shorts and waiters chatting casually with everyone. No menu, but dishes like *lapin au vin blanc* (rabbit in white wine) and curried rice (42F) are quite filling. A different vegetarian dish each night (30F). Open Mon.-Sat. noon-3pm and 7pm-midnight, Sun. 7pm-midnight. Closed 1 week in Aug.

Così, 54, rue de Seine, 6ème (tel. 46 33 35 36; Mo. Odéon). Homemade pita bread stuffed with delicious cheese or meat salads elevates the sandwich to gourmet status. Try the blue cheese with *crème fraîche* and celery (24F). Apple "grumble" (18F) and "Gat choc" (almost fudge; 26F) are addictive. Operas of the day are posted. Open Tues.-Sat. 11am-11pm, Sun. 3-11pm.

Crêperie St-Germain, 35, rue St. André des Arts, 6ème (Mo. St. Michel). Funky interior features neon lights on every table, graffiti on the walls, and booming music. Equally funky *galettes* (22-29F), dessert *crêpes* (25F) and cider (13F). Open daily noon-1am.

Restaurant des Arts, 73, rue de Seine, 6ème (Mo. Odéon). Behind closed curtains, a mother/daughter team serves hearty homestyle food at low prices. 67F *menu*.

Restaurant des Beaux-Arts, 11, rue Bonaparte, 6ème (tel. 43 26 92 64; Mo. St-Germain-des-Prés), across from the Ecole des Beaux-Arts and around the corner from where Oscar Wilde died and Jorge Luis Borges lived. Extremely crowded place where delicious French specialties and prompt service are a long-standing tradition. The 60F *menu* includes some eccentric choices like *maquereau aux pommes à l'huile* (mackerel with apples in oil) and a daily vegetarian dish. Open daily noon-2:15pm and 8pm-1am.

Guenmaï, 6, rue Cardinale, 6ème (tel. 43 26 03 24; Mo. St-Germain-des-Prés). Natural, vegetarian food that is popular enough to inspire customers to stand and munch when the few tables are full. *Plat du jours* such as tofu ravioli (50F). Open Mon.-Fri. noon-3:30pm. Store sells health food Mon.-Fri. 9am-8:30pm.

La Petite Hostellerie, 35, rue de la Harpe, 5ème (tel. 43 54 47 12; Mo. St-Michel). Well-known for regional dishes from all over France. Tucked cozily into a psychedelic cave, the two floors are engulfed by the smells of regional cuisine from Corsica, Flanders, and everywhere in between. The 57F and 72F *menus* are both excellent deals. Open daily 11:30am-2:30pm and 7pm-12:30am.

La Citrouille, 10, rue Gregoire-de-Tours, 6ème (tel. 43 29 90 41; Mo. Odéon). Affectionately named "The Pumpkin," this restaurant presents some juicy dishes. The 69F lunch *menu* and 75F dinner *menus* (*boisson comprise*) include choices such as *foie de veau à la Lyonnaise* (Lyon-style veal liver). The clientele is almost as attractive as the hanging plants. Open daily 11:45am-2:30pm and 6:30-11:45pm.

Near Place de la Contrescarpe

Southwest of the Sorbonne, rue Mouffetard, rue Descartes, rue Pot de Fer and rue de la Montagne-Ste-Geneviève are jammed with promising restaurants. The market at the base of rue Mouffetard (Mon.-Sat. 9am-1pm and 4-7pm) supplies the French, Greek, East Asian, North African, and Latin American places which line the surrounding streets. As elsewhere in Paris, the Chinese and Vietnamese restaurants may be the most affordable, but the French establishments are competitive and friendly. Center of it all, pl. de la Contrescarpe fills nightly with good street performers and large audiences.

Le Tire Bouchon, 47, rue Descartes, 5ème (tel. 43 26 39 11; Mo. Cardinal-Lemoine). Delicious, filling French cuisine. 58F and 72F *menus* (*boisson comprise* at lunch) are both great deals. Expect meat and potatoes. Prompt and friendly service. Open daily noon-3pm and 6pm-1am.

X **Le Gratte Pied,** 45, rue Descartes, 5ème (tel. 43 54 69 78; Mo. Cardinal Lemoine). Enjoy French country fare in a dining room above three levels of 12th century caves. If you ask nicely, the proprietor may show you the site of a true knight's table inaugurated by King Philippe Auguste. Piano music nightly. 69F and 89F *menus* until 9pm. Open daily noon-2pm and 7pm-midnight.

Ray's Café and Restaurant, 80, rue Mouffetard, 5ème (tel. 47 07 47 07; Mo. Monge). Boister-ous student crowd, kosher-style pastrami, and discounts for residents of Y & H or Three Ducks hostels. Scrambled eggs with hashed browns and toast (28F), sandwiches (15-28F), generous salads (18-25F), and brownies with whipped cream (15F). Open daily 8:30am-10:30pm.

Restaurant Perraudin, 157, rue St-Jacques, 5ème (tel. 46 33 15 75; Mo. Luxembourg). The new owners of this old restaurant attempt to preserve the bistro atmosphere (and prices) of a bygone era. Home cooking and a large selection of country wines. Regional specialties such as *la caille aux raisins* (quail with grapes, 48F). Professional but courteous service. 59F lunch *menu.* Appetizers 20F, main dishes 45-55F, desserts 15-20F. Open Mon.-Fri. noon-2:30pm and 7:30-10:30pm. If you enjoy this place, try their new restaurant, **Bistro d'André,** 232, rue St. Charles, 15ème (tel. 45 57 89 14; Mo. Place Balard) near the old Citroën factory. 49F lunch *menu.* Open Mon.-Fri. noon-2:30pm and 7:30-10:30pm, Sat. 7:30-10:30pm.

Savannah Café, 27, rue Descartes, 5ème (tel. 43 29 45 77; Mo. Cardinal-Lemoine). "The only international restaurant in Paris," claims the exaggerating Richard as he presents Peruvian, Italian, French and Lebanese cuisine. Relax for the evening with a hip international crowd. Hummos and tabouli (34F) not to be missed. 70F and 80F lunch *menus.* Pastas 60F. Open Mon. noon-2:30pm, Tues.-Sat. noon-2:30pm and 7-11:30pm.

Randy and Jay's American Barbecue, 14, rue Thouin, 5ème (tel. 43 26 37 09; Mo. Monge). Genuine charcoal-grilled barbecue in a meeting place for Anglophones. Randy calls it "a place where people can get centered when they're blue in Paris." Chase those blues with chicken or ribs, coleslaw, potato salad, beans and pecan pie (90F). Open Tues.-Sun. 6pm-2am.

Au Bistro de la Sorbonne, 4, rue Toullier, 5ème (tel. 43 54 41 49; Mo. Luxembourg). An orange sign with a large #4 marks the spot on a street off rue Soufflot. Non-English-speaking host gives foreigners a warm welcome to this popular, attractive restaurant. Plenty of locals enjoy excellent food under Toulouse-Lautrec-style posters. *A la carte* dishes 38-80F. The salad and hors d'oeuvres bar is included in the 65F (lunch) and 90F (dinner) *menus.* Open Mon.-Sat. noon-2pm and 6:30pm-midnight.

Crêperie Cousin Cousine, 36, rue Mouffetard, 5ème (tel. 47 07 73 83; Mo. Monge). Whether it's for the posters of foreign movies or for the delicious *crêpes* (10-21F) and *galettes* (15-30F), customers keep coming back to this perpetually crowded restaurant. Open 11am-3pm and 6:30pm-1am.

Restaurant Chez Léna et Mimille, 32, rue Tournefort, 5ème (Mo. Censier Daubenton). Truly elegant, overlooking a pretty tree-lined *place.* Soak up French *joie de vivre* when the festive sing-along begins. *Menu* including *apéritif,* wine, appetizer, main dish, dessert, and coffee (170F). In the summer, sit on the terrace for lunch (88F *menu*). Open Tues.-Fri. noon-2pm and 7-11pm, Mon. and Sat. 7-11pm.

Au Jardin des Pâtes, 4, rue Lacépède, 5ème (tel. 43 31 50 71; Mo. Jussieu). Gourmet pasta made from organically grown grains. Main courses 40-60F. Open Tues.-Sun. noon-2:30pm and 7-10:30pm. Fills up fast so get there early.

La Petite Légume, 36, rue des Boulangers (Mo. Jussieu), near the intersection with rue Linne. Vegetarian and macrobiotic dishes 15-30F. Open Mon.-Fri. noon-2:30pm and 7-9:30pm.

La Mosquée, 39, rue Geoffroy-St-Hilaire, 5ème (tel. 43 31 18 14; Mo. Censier-Daubenton). An institution since the 1920s. Behind the high white walls are a real mosque, Turkish baths, and an exquisite courtyard. 80F *menu* served Mon.-Fri. includes *crudités, brik* (a thin dough with a fried egg inside), and a huge helping of chicken *couscous* (the best in Paris, according to expatriate Algerians). Huge 90F *menu* served Sat.-Sun. offers more choice, more courses, and lamb *couscous.* No alcohol. End your meal with mint tea. Tea room open Sept.-July 11am-9pm. Restaurant open daily 7-11pm.

Au Pot de Fer, 12, rue Pot de Fer, 5ème (tel. 45 35 83 69; Mo. Monge). Always crowded with locals, this restaurant offers a 45F lunch *menu* and 75F dinner *menu* with lots of choices. Also **La Chaumière** next door. Both places serve traditional food at identical prices. Slightly expensive, but worth it. Both open daily noon-2pm and 7-11pm. **Pizza Vino** across the street is open slightly later. All run by same management.

Montparnasse, the Thirteenth, Fourteenth and Fifteenth Arrondissements

These three adjoining *arrondissements* feature entirely different types of restaurants. The 13th is home to many Asian émigrés, and French seems to be the second language. Inexpensive East Asian restaurants line the streets around av. de Choisy and rue de Tolbiac. The 15th contains comparatively few restaurants. Boulevard Montparnasse, running along the northern borders of the 14th and 15th is dominated by chic movie theaters and exorbitantly priced restaurants and historic cafés. ⁊

Chez Wadja, 10, rue de la Grande Chaumière, *6ème* (tel. 43 25 66 10; Mo. Vavin). Family-style dining and unbeatable prices. No decor, but loving service. Appetizers 10F; pork chops and other entrees 30-50F. Wine 20F per bottle. Open Mon.-Sat. noon-2:30pm and 7-9:30pm.

Colorado Cookie Company, 27, rue Vavin, *6ème* (tel. 43 54 38 66; Mo. Vavin). Incredible sandwiches include PB&J (14F) or BLT with guacamole (24F). Recent expatriate Heather's baking rivals Mrs. Field's. No smoking inside. Open Mon.-Sat. 11am-9pm.

Sampieru Corsu, 12, rue de l'Amiral-Roussin, *15ème* (tel. 43 06 62 14; Mo. Cambronne). Run by a Corsican separatist and Marxist family which claims that the purpose of work isn't to make money, but to be useful to society. As evidence, they display statistics for the restaurant indicating that although they ask for 31F for each meal, it costs them 31.10F to cook it. You are expected to pay according to your means. Simple 3-course *menu*. On some nights there is entertainment, and you should add about 10F for the artist. Open Mon.-Fri. 11:45am-1:45pm and 7-9:30pm.

Café du Commerce, 51, rue du Commerce, *15ème* (tel. 45 75 03 27; Mo. La Motte-Picquet). An excellent choice if you have some time to spare. The service is somewhat slow, but the changing 80F *menu* (*boisson comprise*) has a wide variety of good selections like *côtes d'agneau grillées aux herbes* (lamb grilled with herbs). A traditional atmosphere and a balcony add to the appeal. Open daily noon-midnight.

Le Petit Parnasse, 138, rue de Vaugirard, *15ème* (tel. 47 83 29 52; Mo. Falguière). It takes a terrific restaurant like this one to keep impecunious students coming back for 63F (lunch only), 81F, and 115F *menus.* Start with the assorted appetizers (they will leave the whole tray at your table) and finish with hot apple pie, fresh from the oven. Open Sept.-July Mon.-Fri. noon-2:30pm and 7-10:30pm. Closed Christmas-New Year's day.

Théâtre de l'Arlequin, 13, passage du Moulinet, *13ème* (tel. 45 89 43 22; Mo. Tolbiac), off rue Tolbiac. A young, artsy crowd patronizes this restaurant, affiliated with a local semi-professional theater. The 49.50F lunch and 59.50F dinner *menus* feature dishes like *bisque de homard* (lobster bisque). Open for meals Tues.-Sat. noon-2pm and 7pm-midnight. At other times, it's a popular student café with 12F beers and 7F wine. Tickets to offbeat and classical productions in the tiny theater 60F, students 40F.

Mikado, 125, rue de Tolbiac, *13ème* (tel. 45 86 59 79; Mo. Tolbiac). An elegant Japanese restaurant with an excellent sushi bar, frequented by a local Japanese clientele. Sushi or skewers 30F. Open Mon.-Sat. 11:30am-3pm and 6:30-11pm.

Cap-Saint-Jacques, 129, av. de Choisy, *13ème* (tel. 45 83 61 15; Mo. Tolbiac). Solicitous host offers filling Vietnamese fare (22-30F). Warmer than many of the big factory-like establishments in the area. Open daily 11:45am-2:30pm and 7pm-midnight.

Hawai, 87, av. d'Ivry, *13ème* (tel. 45 86 91 90; Mo. Tolbiac). Photographs on the menu show you exactly what you will eat. Despite the misplaced (and misspelled) name, there may be a line of French people waiting for the famous chow. Large portions 25-40F. Open Mon.-Fri. 11am-3pm and 6-11:30pm, Sat. 6-11:30pm.

Palais de Cristal, 70, rue Baudricourt, *13ème* (tel. 45 84 81 56; Mo. Tolbiac). East Asian food popular with families. Huge helpings of chop suey (25F) and soup (25F). Open Thurs.-Tues. 11am-3pm and 6:15-11pm.

Rive Droite (Right Bank)

Les Halles and Le Marais

The streets surrounding the Centre Pompidou attract the kind of diner who enters a restaurant because it looks elegant, not because it's cheap. As a result, most places in this neighborhood feature beautiful decor and tuxedo-clad waiters serving *menus* that start at around 70F. You'll have to look hard to find affordable food that's better than McDonald's or the indigenous Quick. Try the small side-streets where the food may be served in a less remarkable setting but the prices fit your budget. In the Jewish neighborhood around **Rue des Rosiers,** you'll find superb kosher delicatessens and excellent Middle Eastern *pâtisseries*. Even here, the prices aren't terribly low.

Chez Suzy, 41, rue Berger, 1er (tel. 40 26 52 09; Mo. Halles or Louvre). After passing the exorbitantly priced restaurants along this street, your first impulse might be to think that the prices posted on the windows are a joke; they're not. Excellent French cuisine for unbelievable prices in a highly fashionable area. Not surprisingly, it's always crowded; come early for the largest selection. All main dishes, including fish and rabbit specialties, are 29F. First courses 8F. Desserts 8F. The service is quick and courteous and the food is *fantastique*. Open for lunch daily 12:30-3:30pm. Bar open 8am-6pm.

La Dame Tartine, 2, rue Brismarche, 4ème (tel. 42 77 32 22; Mo. Châtelet), near the Pompidou Center. Facing Niki de St-Phalle's fountain full of mechanical sculptures. *Incroyable* sandwiches only 15-30F. Desserts to be savored (15-20F). Open daily noon-11pm.

Joe's Dough, 168, rue St-Martin, 3ème (tel. 42 77 68 02; Mo. Rambuteau). "We make short salad, tall salad, fat salad, long salad, but never ever . . . skimpy salad." Choose your own mix of ingredients and dressing from a delicious selection. Generous salads 35-45F. Open daily 10am-midnight.

La Feuillade, 2, rue de la Petite Truanderie, 1er (Mo. Les Halles), in a relatively quiet square. The owner swears by his fresh ingredients. Tasty French fare includes *flan de poireaux à la crème de ciboulette* (leek flan with chive cream sauce). Main dishes 42F, salads 34F. Open daily 12:30-2:30pm and 8pm-midnight.

Bistro Rousse, 31, rue Vieille du Temple, 4ème (tel. 42 71 08 39; Mo. St. Paul), at rue Sainte Croix de la Bretonnerie. Russian dolls stare in envy as you guzzle filling borscht (24F) or blinis (22-34F). The smell alone will make you a fan of Russian cuisine. Open Mon.-Sat. noon-1:30pm and 8-11pm.

La Canaille, 4, rue Crillon, 4ème (tel. 42 78 09 71; Mo. Sully-Morland or Bastille), on a street parallel to bd. Bourdou. This place serves remarkable food to a French business crowd. 60F *menu* (55F at lunch) includes items like a mind-expanding *sorbet aux trois legumes* or *coquelet à la crème de carotte et d'estragon* (chicken in an addictive tarragon carrot purée). Abrupt but theatrical management asks you to write down your order. Open Sept.-July Mon.-Fri. 11:45am-2:15pm and 7:30-11:30pm, Sat.-Sun. 11:45am-2:15pm.

Chez Marianne, 2, rue des Hospitaliers St-Gervais, 4ème (tel. 42 72 18 86; Mo. St-Paul), at rue des Rosiers. Nearly every Israeli specialty served here. Popular and friendly, this restaurant is known for its felafel, blini, *pirogi*, and strudel. Pick a combination of 4, 5, or 6 specialties (50F, 60F, or 70F) such as chopped liver, fried eggplant, or hummos. Open Sun.-Thurs. 11am-10pm.

Le Kairouan, 55, bd. Sebastopol, 1er (Mo. Les Halles). A tiny restaurant that, because of its size, is able to give personalized attention to every serving. Many varieties of *couscous* 25-55F. Try one of the extraordinary Middle Eastern pastries (6-10F) with mint tea (4F). Open daily noon-midnight.

Aquarius, 54, rue Ste-Croix-de-la-Bretonnerie, 4ème (tel. 48 87 48 71; Mo. Hôtel-de-Ville). Small vegetarian restaurant. Organically grown vegetables (*légumes biologiques*). Salads 12-35F, vegetable tarts 24F, and other prepared dishes such as *quenelles de soja* (soybean patties). Harmony and understanding an extra 37F. 45F *menu* available noon-2pm and 7-10pm. No smoking and no alcohol. Open Sept.-July Mon.-Sat. noon-10pm. Similar *menu* at 40, rue de Gergovie, 14ème (tel. 45 41 36 88; Mo. Pernety). Open Mon.-Sat. noon-3pm and 7-10pm.

La Lézardière, 11, rue Mandar, 2ème (tel. 45 08 16 30; Mo. Sentier). Every imaginable *crêpe, galette,* and salad. Try the *galette* with chicken, mushrooms, eggs, tomatoes, and cheese (40F). Open Thurs.-Tues. noon-3pm and 7pm-12:30am.

La Tourelle, 2, rue de la Vrillière, 1er (tel. 42 61 35 41; Mo. Bourse), at rue Croix des Petits Champs. Quick service and large, delicious servings make this a popular choice among lunching businessfolk. The 59F *menu* includes excellent *terrine de saumon* (salmon pâté) and *bavette aux echalottes* (steak and fries). Open Mon.-Sat. 11:30am-2:30pm and 6-11pm.

Chez Jo Goldenberg, 7, rue des Rosiers, 4ème (tel. 48 87 20 16; Mo. St-Paul). Everyone's favorite kosher deli since 1920. Target of a 1985 terrorist attack that claimed the life of the owner's son, the restaurant seems to have recovered and is now filled daily with regulars who keep coming back for delicious meats (60F) and courteous service. Also a take-out counter where you can get home-cooked borscht, sauerkraut, pickles, pastries, and other traditional delights. Deli open daily 9am-1pm and 2:30-6pm. Tea room open 2:30-6pm. Closed on Yom Kippur.

The Front Page, 56-58, rue St-Denis, 1er (tel. 42 36 98 69; Mo. Châtelet-Les-Halles). Extremely popular among Americans living in (or just visiting) Paris, this expensive but lively restaurant offers warm memories of the New World. Menu declares "I must be suffering from a mental disease" to choose American over French cuisine. Hamburgers 42-55F, salads 35-44F, and every imaginable American cocktail 25-40F. Open daily noon-5am.

La Perla, 26, rue François Miron, 4ème (tel. 42 77 59 40; Mo. St. Paul). The offspring of Café Pacifico serves affordable Mexican enchiladas and burritos plus the widest selection of Mezcals and Tequilas in Europe. Informal, friendly owner. Open daily noon-2am.

La Patata, 25, bd. des Italiens, 2ème (tel. 42 68 16 66; Mo. Opéra). Plump potatoes with 19 different fillings. The overstuffed spuds run 38-76F. Open daily 11am-midnight.

Near Place de l'Opéra and Place Vendôme

Historically a residential neighborhood for French aristocracy, the streets between these two *places* are stocked with appropriately expensive restaurants. The four places below are exceptional values.

L'Incroyable, 26, rue de Richelieu, 1er (tel. 42 96 24 64; Mo. Palais-Royal). An excellent, intimate restaurant with a Parisian crowd. Most diners know each other just from coming back so frequently. Serves a changing *menu* of simple pleasures: pork chops, steak, and the like at an *incroyable* 45F, *boisson comprise.* Open Tues.-Fri. 11:45am-2:15pm and 6:30-8:30pm, Sat. and Mon. 11:45am-2:45pm, but squeeze in early for the most choices.

Country Life, 6, rue Daunou, 2ème (tel. 42 97 48 51; Mo. Opéra). Vegetarian *haute cuisine* in yet another health food store. Crowded 50F buffet includes soups and salads so complex you'll need a theoretical apparatus to dissect them. 140 seats. Mon.-Fri. 11:30am-2:30pm. Store open Mon.-Thurs. 10am-6:30pm, Fri. 10am-3pm.

Chez Morgane, 12, rue Chabanais, 2ème (Mo. Pyramides). Quiches (32F) and salads (36F) made with "craftsmanship and fresh ingredients." 52F *menu* includes 1 of each and a *tarte* for dessert. All the pink and white may prompt the question, "Am I inside a candy cane?" Open Mon.-Sat. 11:30am-5pm.

Ma Normandie, 11, rue Rameau, 2ème (tel. 42 96 87 17; Mo. Pyramides), down from the Bibliothèque Nationale on pl. Louvois. A crowded restaurant with a wonderfully cheerful atmosphere. Friendly service, excellent location, and a jovial clientele make this an excellent choice. 47F lunch *menu* promises *service rapide.* 96F dinner *menu* includes many traditional choices. Eat downstairs; only the most expensive *menu* is served upstairs. Open Mon.-Fri. 11:30am-2:30pm and 7pm-midnight.

Ninth Arrondissement

Heading north from Le Marais, the elegant mansions become less frequent and the number of affordable restaurants increases correspondingly. With fewer popular tourist sights, the ninth *arrondissement* hides some terrific deals that only locals know. Explore.

Verdeau, 25, passage Verdeau, 9ème (tel. 45 23 15 96; Mo. Montmartre), on a covered street off rue de la Grange Batelière. Home of *le spud.* Their huge baked potatoes, served with a wide variety of mouth-watering toppings, outdo anything from Idaho. Sweet and delicious, the least expensive (with tomato and hot chèvre, 32F) is a filling meal. So popular that some people reserve their tables. Potatoes 32-60F. Desserts, including a huge chocolate mousse, run 14-22F. Open for lunch only 11:30am-3pm.

Au Boeuf Bourguignon, 21, rue Douai, 9ème (tel. 42 82 08 79; Mo. Pigalle). The checked tablecloths and movie posters contribute to the *gai* atmosphere. Cheerful French family presents a 60F *menu,* including drinks and three courses. *Boeuf bourguignon, plat du jour,* and anything chocolate are recommended. Open Mon.-Sat. noon-3pm and 6:30-10:30pm, Sun. 7-10:30pm.

Le Chartier, 7, rue du Faubourg-Montmartre, 9ème (tel. 47 70 86 29; Mo. Montmartre), at bd. Montmartre. Don't flee when you notice the doormen dressed in formal attire; they're just facilitating the process of serving 2000 meals per day in a single restaurant. Housed in a beautiful, mirrored salon straight from the 18th century, Le Chartier offers a wide selection of delicious, traditional French delights at good prices. Favorites include the *terrine de lapin* (bunny pâté, 12F) as an appetizer, *tendron du veau grand-mère* (tender veal just like grandma used to make, 37F) as a main course, and *melba au framboises* (ice cream on raspberries with whipped cream, 12F) as a dessert. As much a sight as an excellent restaurant, this is worth going out of your way to experience. **Le Drouot,** 103, rue de Richelieu, *2ème* (tel. 42 96 68 23; Mo. Richelieu-Drouot), and **Le Commerce,** 51, rue de Commerce, *15ème* (tel. 45 75 03 27; Mo. La Motte-Picquet), are under the same management and serve the same food in a less glorious setting. All 3 are open daily 11am-3pm and 6-9:30pm.

Maison Champagne, 21, rue Joubert, *9ème* (Mo. Havre-Caumartin). Small restaurant run by a kind, concerned proprietor. *Habitués* (regulars) are working people hungry for French country fare. Changing *menu* (40-55F) features several choices. Open daily 11:30am-2:30pm and 6:30-8:30pm.

Casa Miguel, 48, rue St-Georges, *9ème* (tel. 42 81 09 61; Mo. St-Georges). Proudly displaying its *Guiness Book* certificate for being the cheapest restaurant in the western world, this restaurant offers a complete meal (entree, main dish, dessert, wine, bread, and service) for 5F (no joke!). However, you get you what pay for. This joint is worth a visit only to read the international articles on the 80-year-old owner Mme Lodina, an emigré from Franco's Spain who has been serving penniless customers for 40 years. Arrive early because there is 32-person max. per meal. Open Mon.-Sat. noon-1pm and 7-8pm, Sun. noon-1pm. Closed for 1 week late July-early Aug.

L'Omeletterie, 48, rue Condorcet, *9ème* (tel. 45 26 98 19; Mo. Anvers), at rue Rodier. Small, attractive restaurant that serves delicious omelettes (40-70F). The three-course 79F *menu* is a terrific deal. Featured are *chèvre chaud* (warm goat cheese) and a delightful kiwi *tarte.* Open Mon.-Sat. 7pm-midnight.

Montmartre

You pay for location in Montmartre more dearly than you do anywhere else in Paris. Restaurants around the Moulin Rouge and pl. du Tertre are ridiculously expensive and not particularly interesting. Between the tourist Scylla and Charybdis, however, inexpensive restaurants serve decent food to a local crowd. Place du Tertre is full of pricey options, but nightly music and dancing in the cafés may make it worth the expense. Eat in groups to ensure safety in the area at night.

La Poutre, 10, rue des Trois-Frères, *18ème* (tel. 42 57 45 04; Mo. Abbesses or Anvers). A lovely little establishment that specializes in Périgordin cuisine. Excellent 49F *menu* served until 10pm. Open daily noon-3pm and 6pm-1am.

Joy in Food, 2, rue Truffaut, *17ème* (tel. 43 87 96 79; Mo. Pl. de Clichy), slightly removed from the center. Chef/owner mentally purified by his guru, Sri Chinmoy. Food sanctioned by *Gault Millau*'s august writers. *Entrées* 22-27F, *plats du jour* 36F, transgressive chocolate cake (22F). Meditation on Wednesdays at 8pm. No smoking. Open Mon. and Wed.-Thurs. noon-2pm, Tues. and Fri.-Sat. noon-2pm and 7-9:30pm.

Au Grain Folie, 24, rue de la Vieuville, *18ème* (tel. 42 58 15 57; Mo. Abbesses), at the top of rue des Martyrs. A tiny vegetarian restaurant with excellent thin-crusted vegetable *tartes.* 69F *menu.* Get a *tarte garnie* (with salad, rice, and beans, 36-45F) or a salad (25-40F). More expensive but more convenient than Joy in Food. English-speaking host. Open Tues.-Sun. noon-2pm and 7-10:30pm, Mon. 7-10:30pm.

Refuge des Fondus, 19, rue des Trois-Frères, *18ème* (tel. 42 55 22 55; Mo. Abbesses). The food is not fantastic, but a goofy gimmick makes this restaurant overwhelmingly popular: customers are treated to a full baby bottle of wine with the *menu* (refills 5F). 70F *menu* includes cocktail or hors d'oeuvres, cheese or meat fondue, and pineapple in kirsch. Open daily 7pm-2am.

La Cantina, 4, rue des Trois Frères, *18ème* (tel. 42 23 02 78; Mo. Abbesses). One of the best and best-loved Mexican spots in Paris. Sing along to well-known Mexican tunes. Specialties are *poulet cacao* (chocolate chicken, 65F) and three varieties of enchiladas (from 43F). Filling portions served with beans and rice. Open Tues.-Sun. 7:30pm-1am.

Restaurant l'Esterel, 8, rue Tardieu, *18ème* (tel. 46 06 05 02; Mo. Abbesses). This extremely popular, barrel-strewn restaurant is the opposite of intimate. 46F *menu;* try the house specialty *roule de jambon "Esterel."* A good place to sample traditional dishes such as *lapin à la moutarde* (bunny in mustard sauce, 49F). Open daily noon-2:30pm and 7pm-1am.

Near the Arc de Triomphe

Whether or not you agree that the Champs-Elysées is the grandest thoroughfare in the world, there's no doubt that restaurants here are priced as though it is. As you move toward the river, restaurants become affordable and locals begin to outnumber tourists.

Chez Mélanie, 27, rue de Colisée, 8ème, 8ème (tel. 43 59 42 76; Mo. George V), through the courtyard and up 3 flights of stairs. You'll see both blue and white collars in this family-run restaurant. Fresh daily specialties. 50F menu. Open Mon.-Fri. 11:30am-3pm.

L'Epicerie Verte, 5, rue Saussier Leroy, 17ème (tel. 47 64 19 68; Mo. Etoile). One of the few vegetarian restaurants that serves dinner. Delicious smells may lure flesh eaters onto the green bandwagon. Salads 27-32F. Specialties 35-42F. Open Sept.-July Mon.-Fri. 12:15-2:15pm and 7:15-9:30pm.

The Chicago Pizza Pie Factory, 5, rue de Berri, 8ème (tel. 45 62 50 23; Mo. George V). Strictly for those craving huge American pizzas (116-221F) in a huge commercial restaurant. Garlic bread 16F. Call 25 minutes ahead for take out. Open daily 11:45am-1am.

Tenth Arrondissement

With two of Paris's busiest railway stations looming above, the 10th arrondissement's restaurants are the sort that appeal to departing and arriving travelers: fast and cheap. You'll find African, Middle Eastern, Asian, and other foreign restaurants here.

Paris-Dakar, 95, rue Faubourg St-Martin, 10ème (tel. 42 08 16 64; Mo. Gare de l'Est). Run by a Senegalese family, this place is extremely popular among Parisians who keep coming back to what is advertised as "the most African of all African restaurants." Main dishes 68-86F. Try the délice africain, wonderful coconut ice cream served in a coconut shell. Open daily noon-4pm and 7pm-midnight.

Restaurant Sizin, 36, rue Faubourg du Temple, 10ème (tel. 48 06 54 03; Mo. République), in an alley off a crowded street. Spicy individual Turkish pizzas 8F, salads 16-20F, main dishes 33-50F, and great baklava 15F. Open Mon.-Sat. noon-3pm and 7:30-11:30pm.

Wine Bars

Although wine bistros have existed since the early 19th century, the spiffier modern wine bar emerged only a few years ago with the invention of a machine that pumps nitrogen into the open bottle, thus preserving the wine indefinitely. Rare, expensive wines, exorbitant by the bottle, have become somewhat affordable by the glass. Any establishment (cafés included) that will sell you a glass of wine with a pâté can be classified as a "wine bar," but the term generally refers to those beautiful, expensive restaurants that specialize in the wine of a certain region (or regions). These are not places for pinching pennies. Expect to pay 20-40F for a glass of high-quality wine; your entire meal (and you should do more than drink a glass) will run about 150F. With restraint, lunch verges on affordable.

Enjoy your bottle or glass with a cooked dish or a tartine (cheese and/or charcuteries—the French equivalent of cold cuts—served on pain Poilâne or pain de campagne). Each place has its own flavor and specialty, whether Bordeaux or Vouvray or Côtes du Rhône. The all-important owners, who carefully select the wines in their caves (cellars), set the tone for their establishments. Over 100-strong, the wine shops in the **Nicolas** chain are reputed for having the world's most inexpensive cellars, while Nicolas himself owns the fashionable and expensive wine bar **Jeroboam,** 8, rue Monsigny, 2ème (tel. 42 61 21 71; Mo. Opéra).

Willi's Wine Bar, 13, rue des Petits-Champs, 1er (tel. 42 61 05 09; Mo. Bourse). Named for one of Colette's husbands. Owners Tim Johnston and Mark Williamson specialize in Côtes-du-Rhône. His wine menu includes the best and the oldest from that region. Even if you're not a wine expert, the 145F menu is a treat. The least expensive wines (14F per glass, 75F per bottle) deserve consideration. Reserve for lunch. Open Mon.-Fri. noon-11pm.

Juveniles, 47, rue Richelieu, 1er (tel. 42 97 46 49; Mo. Bourse) around the corner from Willi's. Under the same ownership as its neighbor, Juveniles serves lighter food in a lighter atmosphere. Sherries, malts, and Côtes du Rhône (12-50F per glass) served with tapas (small Spanish *hors-d'oevres,* 15-30F). 159F *menu* for two includes wine. English spoken. Open Mon.-Sat. noon-11pm.

Jacques Mélac, 42, rue Léon-Frot, 11*ème* (tel. 43 70 59 27; Mo. Charonne). A handlebar moustache, transcribed from Mélac's face, marks the label of the house wine. Crowd is friendly, especially in September when Mélac harvests his own vines and convinces some women to crush them with their feet. (Call for exact date.) *Tartines* from 14F, wine from 12F per glass. Open Aug. 15-July 15 Mon.-Fri. 9am-midnight.

Taverne Henri IV, 13, pl. du Pont Neuf, 1*er* (tel. 43 54 27 90; Mo. Pont-Neuf). Robert Cointepas's traditional and friendly oak tavern, long known for its extensive wine list and delicious *charcuteries* with *Poilâne* bread, served quickly but *à la française.* Though still immensely popular among Parisians, this wine bar is now falling prey to camera-toting tour groups. *Tartines* 20-25F; wine 20-30F per glass. Open mid-Sept. to mid-Aug. Mon.-Fri. noon-midnight.

Le Pain et le Vin, 1, rue d'Armaillé, 17*ème* (tel. 47 63 88 29; Mo. Argentine). Founded by 4 renowned chefs famous for having invented the "Toques Gourmandes" cuisine, this wine bar features unusual food-and-wine combinations unique to the establishment. *Plat du jour* 63F, *tartines* 26-39F, wine 12-40F per glass. Open daily 11:30am-12:30am.

L'Ecluse, rue Mondétour, 1*er* (tel. 47 03 30 73; Mo. Les Halles). Possibly the most famous Parisian wine bar. The food is prepared not in a kitchen but in a "laboratory." Says Bernard Ginestet, the owner, "Our clientele is modern, *chic, sympa;* they drink little, well, and slightly expensively." Various dishes 40-90F. Bordeaux specialties start at 20F per glass. Four other locations: 15, quai des Grands-Augustins, 6*ème* (Mo. St-Michel); rue Mondétour, 1*er* (Mo. Etienne Marcel); 15, pl. de la Madeleine, 8*ème* (Mo. Madeleine); 4, rue Halévy, 9*ème* (Mo. Opéra). Open daily noon-2am.

University Restaurants

Institutional food is poor even in France, but at least it's inexpensive. Anyone can buy meal tickets at each restaurant from 11:30am to 1:30pm and from 6 to 8pm. (Tickets 19.20F, with Carte Jeune 15.40F. Student book of 10 96F.) For a complete list of university restaurants, stop in at **CROUS,** 39, av. Georges Bernanos, 5*ème* (tel. 40 51 36 00; Mo. Port-Royal). All restaurants generally serve meals Monday through Friday 11:30am-1:30pm and 6-8pm. On weekends and in summers, they open on a rotating schedule; check at CROUS to see which are in operation. The following university restaurants are the most convenient, but the list is far from exhaustive. All the restaurants listed, except Citeaux, Grand Palais, and C.H.U. Necker, are also *brasseries,* open between lunch and dinner for sandwiches and drinks.

Bullier, 39, av. Georges Bernanos, 5*ème* (Mo. Port-Royal).

Censier, 31, rue Geoffroy St-Hilaire, 5*ème* (Mo. Censier Daubenton).

Chatelet, 10, rue Jean Calvin, 5*ème* (Mo. Censier Daubenton).

Assas, 92, rue d'Assas, 6*ème* (Mo. Port-Royal or Notre-Dame-des-Champs).

Mabillon, 3, rue Mabillon, 6*ème* (Mo. Mabillon).

Grand Palais, cours de la Reine, 8*ème* (Mo. Champs-Elysées).

Citeaux, 45, bd. Diderot, 12*ème* (Mo. Gare de Lyon).

C.H.U. Pitié-Salpe-Triere, 105, bd. de l'Hôpital, 13*ème* (Mo. St-Marcel).

Dareau, 13-17, rue Dareau, 14*ème* (Mo. St-Jacques).

C.H.U. Necker, 156, rue de Vaugirard, 15*ème* (Mo. Pasteur).

Dauphine, av. de Pologne, 16*ème* (Mo. Porte Dauphine).

Fast Food

If you don't feel like sitting down to two meals per day, but don't want to stand in the street clutching your *baguette* and brie, try French fast food restaurants. These are not hamburger joints, but places where you can consume real French food while standing up or sitting down only briefly. Self-service cafeterias are extremely popular among businesspeople who only have a few minutes to eat. **La Brioche Dorée, Tout Chaud,** and **La Croissanterie** are big chains that are ideal for light pastries and drinks. **McDonald's** and **Burger King** are oppressively common, but they're more expensive and not as quite as popular as their French spin-offs, **Quick** and **Free-Time.** When the French use the American expression "Fast Food," they mean any meals that are served quickly—price is clearly a secondary consideration.

> **Fauchon,** 30, pl. de la Madeleine, 8*ème* (tel. 47 42 60 11; Mo. Madeleine), behind Eglise de la Madeleine. A shrine for the worship of good food for years and a must for window shoppers seeking the height of visual gluttony. In other words, this is more a sight than a genuine eatery. Nothing is cheap, but everything is delicious and authentically French. Head for the cafeteria downstairs, not the outrageous restaurant upstairs. *Plat du jour* (50-70F) served 11am-2pm. Pastries 16F. Open Mon.-Sat. 8:15am-7pm.

> **Feri's,** 76, rue Mazarine, 6*ème* (tel. 43 26 77 35; Mo. Odéon). A variety of sandwiches (15-30F), croissants (5-10F), and salads (10-25F) to take out. One of the few restaurants in Paris open all night. Open daily 11am-6am.

> **Cafétéria Monte Carlo,** 9, av. de Wagram, 17*ème* (tel. 43 80 02 21; Mo. Etoile). This snazzy *self* (cafeteria) features well-prepared food at reasonable prices. Beautiful presentation and a French crowd. Long lines at lunch. Daily *menu* 18-46F. Open daily 11am-10pm.

> **Mélodine,** 42, rue Rambuteau, 3*ème* (Mo. Rambuteau) across the street from the Pompidou center. Again, impressive presentation of average cafeteria fare. 3-4 daily specials, but salads and desserts are tastier. Full meals from 50F. Open daily 11am-11pm.

Hanging Out

Hanging out in cafés, *salons de thé,* and bars is the first step to becoming *branché* ("connected," or hip). Correct etiquette is essential. Learning to nurse a tiny coffee for hours, to stare at passers-by without lowering your eyes if they stare back, or to buy round after round of beer as a lively conversation spins off into the night will combine to make you feel in step in this often intimidating and overwhelming city. Cafés, tea salons, and bars are all designed so that anyone can perfect these skills at any time in the day. While some people try to identify general qualitative differences between these establishments (for example tea salons serve dessert or bars are just for drinking), no rule is unhobbled by frequent exceptions. Some claim that closing times distinguish them. Cafés serve breakfast, salads, and light meals, but must close at 2am. *Salons de thé* operate in the afternoon (at tea time). Bars can serve a greater variety of alcohol and stay open until 4am, 5am, or all night.

Cafés

Since the days when Voltaire drank 40 cups of coffee daily in Le Procope (Paris's first café, founded in 1686), cafés have been an integral part of Parisian social life. Ideal for light meals, they can provide the inexpensive high ground from which to watch the Parisian tide surge by. Cafés situated on fashionable thoroughfares, such as the Champs-Elysées, bd. St-Germain, or rue de la Paix, charge exorbitant prices (coffee 11-16F), but an intriguing crowd usually passes their sidewalk tables. Cafés near monuments charge monumental prices for minimal atmosphere. In such lively places as pl. St-André-des-Arts, the Forum des Halles, pl. de la Sorbonne, and Montparnasse, you can get coffee for about 8F. Indigenous crowds frequent the more dilapidated, hidden spots where coffee is only 4F and the use of *argot* (slang) makes eavesdropping an educational challenge. Make sure the prices posted outside correspond to your budget, and be picky before you relax. Prices are as much as halved if you stand at the bar (*comptoir* or *zinc*) rather than sitting down.

> **Café Mouffetard,** 116, rue Mouffetard, 5*ème* (tel. 43 31 42 50; Mo. Censier Daubenton). Behind this average exterior lies a marvelous breakfast treat. Gather with Parisian executives and laborers for fresh *croissants, brioches,* and *pain au chocolat.* A *café au lait* with croissant

will set you back only 13F. Keep track of your intake or you'll rack up quite a bill. Open Sept.-July Tues.-Sat. 7am-9pm, Sun. 7am-3pm.

La Palette, 43, rue de Seine, 6ème (tel. 43 26 68 15; Mo. Mabillon). An artsy bunch gathers here in the late afternoon. Prices more reasonable than at the cafés on nearby bd. St. Germain. Open Sept.-July Mon.-Sat. 8am-2am.

Café Costes, 4-6, rue Berger, pl. des Innocents, 1er (tel. 45 08 54 39; Mo. Les Halles). Opened only in 1985, Philippe Starck's absurdly modern café has quickly grown into the most fashionable people-watching spot in Paris. Starck even designed the coffee cups. *Café* 14F. Sandwiches 22-34F. Open daily 8am-2am.

Café Beaubourg, 100, rue St-Martin, 4ème (tel. 48 87 63 96; Mo. Les Halles). Owned by Costes and his brother, Jean-Louis. Widely acknowledged to have the most elegant bathrooms of any French café. Upstairs, rest your elbows on tables displaying original artworks under glass. Newspapers in several languages downstairs. Open daily 8am-2am.

Les Deux Magots, 6, pl. St-Germain-des-Prés, 6ème (tel. 45 48 55 25; Mo. St-Germain-des-Prés). It was here, in his favorite hangout, that Jean-Paul Sartre composed *L'être et le néant* (*Being and Nothingness*). Open daily 7:30am-2am.

Le Flore, 172, bd. St-Germain, 6ème (tel. 45 48 55 26), next door to Les Deux Magots. Sartre's second choice and Apollinaire's first. De Beauvoir, Picasso, and André Breton also sipped here. A traditionally light and happy atmosphere prevails here. Gay men claim this is a good place to start cruising. Cashes in on its auspicious past with 20F cups o' Joe. Open daily 7:30am-1:30am.

La Coupole, 102, bd. du Montparnasse, 14ème (tel. 43 27 09 22; Mo. Vavin) and **Le Séléct,** 99, bd. du Montparnasse, 6ème (tel. 45 48 38 24; Mo. Vavin). Two of the most famous cafés in Paris; discussion is more conspicuous than consumption. Cited by many authors, they have served political exiles (Lenin and Trotsky), musicians (Stravinsky and Satie), writers (Hemingway, Breton, Cocteau, and artists (Picasso and Eisenstein). *Café* 9F. Both open daily 8am-2am.

Closerie des Lilas, 171, bd. de Montparnasse, 6ème (tel. 43 26 70 50; Mo. Vavin). Once graced by Paul Verlaine and André Gide, this café currently plays host to France's most popular philosopher, Jean-Edern Hallier, and his incomprehensible disciples. Exquisite decor and a *terrasse* in summer. Dress well. Open daily 10:30am-2am.

Le Fouquet's, 99, av. des Champs-Elysées, 8ème (tel. 47 23 70 60; Mo. George V). Located in the shadow of the Arc de Triomphe, this is the favorite gathering place for Parisian *vedettes* of radio, television, and cinema. Tourists, oblivious to the celebrities drinking inside, bask on the *terrasse.* Here James Joyce ate with relish the inner organs of beasts and fowl. Bank-breaking coffee 32F. Open daily 9am-2am.

Le Procope, 13, rue de l'Ancienne Comédie, 6ème (tel. 43 26 99 20; Mo. Odéon). The first café in Paris, founded in 1686 when coffee was still a novelty. Diderot conceived his *Encyclopédie* here, and Voltaire entertained Marat, Danton, and other revolutionaries. Although fame and popularity have sent prices through the roof, this, shall we say, *splurge* is definitely worth it. The 289F dinner *menu,* however, is not. Light meals served 11am-8pm. Open daily 7am-1am.

Salons de Thé

Perfectly delightful at tea time, the following three choices are quiet places to relax with a sweet.

La Mosquée, 39, rue Geoffroy-St-Hilaire, 5 ème (tel. 43 31 18 14; Mo. Censier-Daubenton). An institution since the 1920s. Behind the high white walls are a real mosque, turkish bath, and exquisite courtyard. The tea room inside is reminiscent of Casablanca. Sweet mint tea (8F) and fabulous Arabic pastries (8F) served on a silver platter. No alcohol. 90F and 100F *menus* served nightly (7-9:30pm). Tea room open Sept.-July 11am-9pm.

Under Hemingways, 72, rue du Cardinal Lemoine, 5 ème (Mo. Cardinal Lemoine). Hemingway lived upstairs. Take books off the shelf to read while sipping tea or coffee (8.50F). Occasional art shows. Often delicious *plat du jour* 40F. Open daily noon-1am.

Maison du Chocolat, 52, rue François Ier, 9ème (tel. 47 23 38 25; Mo. George V). No tea, just chocolate. The mere smell may prove orgasmic. Large, ambrosial chocolate with whipped cream and a glass of water (32F). No smoking, to protect the delicate chocolate. Open Sept.-June Mon.-Sat. 9:30am-6:30pm, July-Aug. Mon.-Fri. only.

The Village Voice, 6, rue Princesse, 6ème (tel. 46 33 36 47; Mo. Mabillon). A crowded English bookstore with a tearoom in back. Open Mon. 2-8pm, Tues.-Sat. 11am-8pm.

Bars

Sometimes totally abandoned and characterless during the day, bars draw colorful crowds after sunset. Depending on the crowd, revelry often lasts until dawn. Law dictates a price increase after 9pm.

Le Violon Dingue, 46, rue de la Montagne Ste-Géneviève. Always like a frat party, especially on toga nights. American baseball on the TV. The bar organizes a soccer team. Dos Equis 20F. Drinks 15F-40F. Open daily 6pm-1:30am.

Polly Magoos, 13, rue St-Jacques, 5ème (tel. 46 33 33 64; Mo. St-Michel). When the Violon Dingue closes at 1:30, Polly's gets going. Friendly, international crowd can get seriously weird, and often bubbles over into the street. Backgammon and chess in the afternoon. Beer 8-15F before 9pm, 15-25F after. Open noon-4am.

Pub St-Germain-des-Prés, 17, rue de l'Ancienne Comédie, 6ème (tel. 43 29 38 70; Mo. Odéon). Perhaps the largest pub in Europe with 7 rooms, 100 types of whisky, 450 different types of bottled beer, and 24 on tap. Three underground rooms look like opium dens and are the most fun. Contemporary pop music and 40s tunes play to a packed-in Parisian crowd. Most beers 40F per bottle. Specials of the month are 33F per pint. A great selection of mixed drinks from 30F. Open 24 hrs.

Café Pacifico, 50, bd. de Montparnasse, 6ème (tel. 45 48 63 87; Mo. Montparnasse-Bienvenue). Rambunctious young whippersnappers and lots of Americans. You may have to stand to drink. Mexican dishes around 70F, *service non compris.* Brunch (noon-4pm) 80F and 100F. During the week (until 3pm) you get a free buck fizz (champagne and orange juice). Wide variety of cocktails from 29.50F. Tequilas from 27F, margaritas 40F (pitcher 325F), sangria 30F (pitcher 125F). Snacks and drinks are half-price during Heureux Hour (daily 6-7pm). Open Tues.-Sun. noon-2am, Mon. 3pm-2am. Owned by the same people, **Café Perla,** 26, rue François Miron, 4ème (tel. 42 77 59 40; Mo. St. Paul) is less crowded, but equally appealing.

City Rock Café, 13, rue de Berri, 8ème (tel. 43 59 52 09; Mo. George V). Paris's answer to the Hard Rock Café is a museum of Americana. The entrance alone contains a Pink Cadillac, Michael Jackson's glove, a lifesize Marilyn Monroe, and a welcoming Statue of Liberty. Slightly expensive: beer 32F, cocktails 52F. Music downstairs nightly. Open daily noon-2am.

The Mayflower, 49, rue Descartes, 5ème (tel. 43 54 56 47; Mo. Cardinal Lemoine). English-style place with wood paneling and brass gleam. American license plates on the walls. French atmosphere with reasonable prices (for Paris). Wide range of beers, including excellent Alsatians (25F) and Guinness on tap (½-pint 22F). *Pain Poîlane* sandwiches 20-29F. Open daily until 2am.

Sights

Before turning your attention to individual monuments and museums, consider Paris's overall design, largely the product of Napoleon III's prefect, Baron Georges-Eugène Haussmann. Charged with making the city both more accessible and more resistant to popular rebellion, Haussmann widened the major avenues to facilitate movement of both residents and the military. But he did more, transforming Paris from an intimate medieval city to a modern metropolis which accommodated the rising bourgeoisie at its center and banished workers to the periphery. His "assaults" on the city included leveling hills (there were seven before Haussmann; now only Montmartre and Parc des Buttes-Chaumont remain), improving railroad access, expanding the system of sewers, enlarging existing streets, and replacing 20,000 medieval buildings with 40,000 new structures. Most importantly, he built new thoroughfares to both untangle traffic and create the monumental vistas that define Paris today. Haussmann's major triumphs are the city's primary axes, emanating from the Châtelet: boulevard St-Michel on the Left Bank extending to boulevard Sebastopol on the Right Bank, boulevard St-Germain, and rue de Rivoli. To appreciate the city's metamorphosis, consider that before 1850, the widest residential street in Paris measured 12m from building to building.

Probably the biggest mistake you can make while sightseeing around Paris is to forget to look out from under your tour books and maps. Your strongest memories will come from discoveries you made on your own; not just in the Louvre or the Panthéon, but also at a street market, on the *quais* of the Seine, or from a curbside seat at a café. At least once during your visit to Paris (even if you only stay for a couple of days), you should leave your *Let's Go* and your map at home and engage in the fine art of *la flânerie* (aimless strolling). Don't stick to the major avenues, but wander through the tiny, twisting passages. (If you get totally lost, you can always ask for the nearest Métro stop and take the train back home.) Keep in mind that Paris was built for Parisians, not for 20th-century tourists and their photo albums.

Try to look at the Arc de Triomphe as a memorial to Napoleon's Grande Armée, at the Eiffel Tower as a showpiece of a 19th-century world's fair, and at museums as storehouses for France's artistic heritage. Be sensitive to the fact that Parisian churches (even Notre-Dame) are places of worship; many Parisians attend services, and those who don't expect to find quiet places for contemplation. When visiting, be as quiet as possible at all times (especially during a service or mass), respect areas that are cordoned off for prayer, and dress appropriately (no shorts, low necklines, or bare shoulders).

The parks of Paris are an integral part of the city and are used extensively by young and old, by students and street people—and by dogs. Each park has its *habitués* (regulars) who come to play *boules* or *pétanque* (two versions of a shuffleboardesque sport with metal balls), to feed their feathered friends, or to cogitate. Though walking is free, sitting down sometimes costs. The unauthorized chair franchise is run by tough old women who may extort about 1F per seat. Benches are generally free.

Museums and Galleries

Paris is not a museum, but you could certainly spend all your time going from one to the next. Every institution, ethnic group, and custom seems to have a museum devoted to its history, art and memorabilia. For listings of the often excellent temporary exhibits, consult the bimonthly *Le Bulletin des Musées et Monuments Historiques,* available at the tourist office and the Hôtel Sully (see Marais sights). *Musées et Monuments, Paris,* published by the tourist office, provides not only phone numbers, addresses, and hours, but also describes the museums and indexes them by theme and *arrondissement. Pariscope, 7 à Paris,* and *L'Officiel des spectacles* also list museums with hours and temporary exhibits.

Frequent museum-goers, especially those ineligible for ticket discounts, may want to invest in a Carte 60, which grants entry into 60 Parisian museums as well as monuments in the suburbs and environs. The card is available at all major museums and Métro stations (1 day 50F, 3 days 100F, 5 days 150F). Do not even dream of trying to see 60 museums in five days; a few well-chosen selections will leave fonder memories.

Not as well-known among tourists as the museums, **galleries** are extremely popular among Parisians. These far more intimate spots generally feature only one or two showrooms, so they can be easily enjoyed in a half-hour or so. Most of the city's 200 galleries specialize in one type of art, such as *naïf* painting, modern sculpture, or drawings of Parisian scenes. The highest concentration is in the Marais; in a casual stroll through the third and fourth *arrondissements,* you're sure to pass by dozens. St-Germain-des-Prés's galleries are small and enticing. For a complete list, pick up a free poster in any gallery.

Ile de la Cité and Ile St-Louis

Although pre-Celtic peoples may have settled in this area as early as the third millenium BC, the existing city wasn't founded until the third century BC when the Parisii, a tribe of hunters, sailors, and fishing folk, built huts on the Ile de la

Cité and began collecting tolls. Although Paris has expanded considerably over the past 23 centuries, the Ile de la Cité and neighboring Ile St-Louis remain at its physical and sentimental heart. (Interestingly, these are only two of the eight islands the Parisii initially populated; the other six were destroyed by Henry IV, Paris's first city planner.) In 1163, Pope Alexander III laid the cornerstone for the **Cathédrale de Notre-Dame** (tel. 43 26 07 39; Mo. Cité) over the remains of a Roman temple to Jupiter. Completed in 1361, this Gothic marvel briefly reverted to a paganism of sorts during the Revolution, when it was rededicated to the Cult of Reason. The cathedral found a patron in the Citizen King, Louis-Philippe, and an able restorer in Viollet-le-Duc, whose controversial work (he added a spire, 1844-64) changed—but saved—the cathedral. The rose windows inside are widely considered the most exquisite in the world. Guided tours leave from the back of the church by the main portals. (Mon.-Fri. at noon, Sat. at 2:30pm, Sun. at 2pm. Free.) For a view of Paris made famous by Victor Hugo's *Notre-Dame de Paris* (*The Hunchback of Notre-Dame*), climb the worn and winding stairs to the bell tower. (Open Aug. daily 10am-6:30pm; April-July and Sept. 10am-5:30pm; Oct.-March 10am-4:30pm. Admission 27F, students 15F, ages under 17 5F.) The cathedral's treasury includes relics from the church's history—primarily religious icons and old prayer books. (Open Mon.-Sat. 10am-6pm, Sun. 2-6pm. Admission 12F.) The cathedral's archaeological crypt (tel. 43 29 83 51) was unearthed during excavation in the 1960s; those interested in the early history of Paris should find the ruins well worth the admission fee. The pamphlet (available in English) is detailed and interesting. (Open daily 10am-5:30pm. Admission 23F, students 12.50F. Combined tickets to tower and crypt 36F.) Open daily 8am to 7pm, the cathedral is packed with tourists all day in summer. Outside the west door in the courtyard, a star marks the spot from which all distances from the provinces to Paris are measured.

Behind the cathedral, across from pl. Jean XXIII and down a narrow flight of steps, is the **Mémorial de la Déportation,** an abstract and hauntingly moving memorial erected in remembrance of the 200,000 French victims of Nazi concentration camps. Two hundred thousand flickering lights represent the dead, and an eternal flame burns over the tomb of an unknown victim. "Pardonne; N'Oublie Pas"(Forgive; Do Not Forget) is engraved over the exit.

The **Palais de Justice,** at the other end of Ile de la Cité, contains the district courts for Paris. All trials are open to the general public, but don't expect an extraordinary display. *Chambre 1* of the *Cour D'Appel* (up *escalier* K) witnessed Pétain's conviction after WW II. Unless your French is up to legal jargon, not even the thrill of antique legal costumes will make the short trials interesting. (Trials Mon.-Fri. 1:30pm until the day's agenda is completed—around 5pm.) Criminal cases are the most interesting; ask for the location of the criminal courtrooms (Mon.-Fri. 1:30-4pm). A small church inside the courtyard of the Palais de Justice, **Ste-Chapelle,** bd. du Palais, 4*ème* (tel. 43 54 30 09; Mo. Cité), is one of the oldest buildings in the city. Begun in 1246 to house Christ's Crown of Thorns, Jesus' swaddling clothes, and a bottle of the Virgin's milk (all "authentic" relics St-Louis brought back from the Holy Land) this stunning structure, perhaps the supreme achievement of Gothic architecture, was completed in an unbelievable 33 months. (The Crown—minus the thorns St-Louis gave away as political favors—now rests in Notre-Dame.) Check the weekly publications for occasional concerts here. (Open daily 9:30am-6pm; Oct.-March 10am-4:30pm. Admission 23F, ages 18-25 and over 60 12F, ages 7-18 5F. Combined ticket for the chapel and the Conciergerie (see below) available. Check posted schedule of irregular guided tours in French (see signs at entrace.)

The fortified, turreted edifice at 1, quai de l'Horloge, is the **Conciergerie** (tel. 43 54 30 06; Mo. Cité), where the famous prisoners of the Revolution—Marie Antoinette, Danton, and Robespierre—were allowed their last sip of brandy before execution. A guillotine gleams in the chapel where prisoners went before their execution; also on display is a facsimile of Marie Antoinette's last letter, written in pinpricks and addressed to her sister-in-law. Especially interesting is the room where Marie Antoinette spent her final days and the chamber where Robespierre uttered his final words: "*Je vous laisse ma mémoire. Elle vous sera chère, et vous la defendrez.*" (I leave you my memory. It will be dear to you, and you will defend it.) The Concierge-rie is still used as a temporary prison for those awaiting trial in the Palais de Justice. (Open daily 9:30am-7pm; Oct.-March 10am-6pm. Admission (including guided tour in French) 23F, students 12F, ages under 17 5F. Last tickets sold 30 min. before closing. Tours according to demand. Combined tickets for the Conciergerie and Ste-Chapelle 36F.)

At the western tip of the island, **place Dauphine,** a peaceful shaded area behind the Palais de Justice and the Conciergerie, is surrounded by early 17th-century houses. Intended by Henry IV to be as uniform as those in place des Vosges, these buildings were altered by the merchants, bankers, and goldsmiths who moved into them. The **Pont Neuf** (New Bridge) is actually the oldest in Paris. Built in the late 16th century to connect the Ile de la Cité to both the Right and Left Banks, this other pet project of Henry IV was the first bridge in Paris without houses on it.

Upstream, the residential **Ile St-Louis** has always lived in the shadow of the grand, public buildings of Ile de la Cité. Constantly ignored, the inhabitants grew tired of the lack of press and whimsically proclaimed the island an independent re-public in the 1930s. The charming streets hide the houses in which such luminaries as Voltaire, Mme. de Châtelet, Daumier, Ingres, Baudelaire, and Cézanne resided. More solid citizens like the Rothschilds and Pompidou's widow now call this scrap of land home. Although the Ile St-Louis does not contain the tourist attractions of the Cité, the *hôtels particuliers* (aristocratic mansions) along quai d'Anjou are particularly beautiful. Furthermore, Paris's best ice cream (to Parisians who haven't visited Boston that means the world's best ice cream) is scopped at **Berthillon,** 31, rue St-Louis-en-l'Ile, 4*ème* (tel. 43 54 31 61; Mo. Pont-Marie). (Open Sept.-July Wed.-Sun. 10am-8pm.) If their main store is closed, try the smaller branches at 88, rue St-Louis-en-l'Ile or 17, rue des Deux Ponts. Take a *cornet pâtissier* (waffle cone, rather than the edible styrofoam version) full of pear, passion fruit, or white choco-late to the Seine (3 cruelly small scoops 16-18F). *This* is it: *joie de vivre.*

Rive Droite (Right Bank)

Le Marais

The district stretching from the rue du Temple to place de la Bastille and from the Seine to rue Pastourelle was swampland until the 13th century, when Parisians drained it to provide land for convents and monasteries. In the 17th century, Henri IV commissioned the building of pl. Royale (now pl. des Vosges) on the site of an old horse market. After Henry auctioned the formerly identical buildings to nobles and wealthy merchants, the *place* became the center of activity for this fashionable district. The elegant *hôtels particuliers,* the townhouses for which the area is famous, were erected during this period. Madame de Sévigné and other residents invited La Fontaine, Boileau, Molière and other prominent figures to their *salons,* drawing cultural life away from the traditionally bohemian Latin Quarter to the Marais. With the fall of the Bastille, however, the aristocracy fled, and members of the in-dustrial working class moved into the area's dilapidated mansions. Writers and art-ists returned to their cafés in the Latin Quarter, quickly restoring that area's reputa-tion. Largely untouched by Haussmann and beautifully restored as part of a 1962 preservation plan, the Marais bears traces of the past that has all but disappeared from the rest of Paris. (Look for the stretch of the late 12th-century city rampart along rue des Jardins, its back to a neighborhood playground.) The restoration proj-ect has made the Marais fashionable again in the past few years. In addition to the wealthy households, some excellent museums have been set up in the vacated man-sions. Few other areas of the city are as suited to a leisurely stroll.

One of Paris's least-visited museums, the interesting **Musée de l'Histoire de France,** 60, rue des Francs-Bourgeois, 3*ème* (tel. 40 27 60 96; Mo. Rambuteau), traces the country's history through some of its most influential documents. Housed in the elegant Hôtel de Soubise, the museum exhibits items such as Louis XIV's and Napoleon's wills; Henry IV's Edict of Nantes, which granted religious freedom to Protestants, and its repeal by Louis XIV; and Marie Antoinette's last letter. (Open Wed.-Mon. 1:45-5:45pm. Admission 12F, students and seniors 8F.) Nature-lovers might enjoy the **Musée de la Chasse et de la Nature,** 60, rue des Archives, *3ème* (tel. 42 72 83 86; Mo. Rambuteau), in the Hôtel Guénégaud, but even the most dedicated hunters will wonder, "Were the 15F worth it?" (Open Wed.-Mon. 10am-12:30pm and 1:30-5:30pm. Admission 15F. No discounts.) The **Musée Car-navalet,** 23, rue de Sévigné, *3ème* (tel. 42 72 21 13; Mo. St-Paul), is housed in a building wher famous letter-writer Madame de Sévigné, born in the place des Vosges, lived from the 1670s to the 1690s. This museum of the history of Paris pres-ents five centuries of paintings, objects, and letters in unusually accessible exhibits. (Open Tues.-Sun. 10am-5:40pm. Admission 15F, students 8.50F, free Sun. Prices vary with temporary exhibits.)

An impressive young upstart on the Paris museum scene, the **Musée Picasso,** in the Hôtel Salé at 5, rue de Thorigny, *3ème* (tel. 42 71 25 21; Mo. Chemin-Vert or St-Paul), contains 203 paintings, 158 sculptures, 88 ceramics, 1500 drawings, and the artist's collection of primitive art, all given to the government in lieu of inheritance taxes. The museum thoroughly traces the development of the artist's style; each room is dedicated to a certain stage in Picasso's career, and the character-istic aspects are described (in French and English) on wall panels. Even those am-bivalent toward Picasso will be seduced by this exceptional museum. (Open Thurs.-Mon. 9:15am-5:15pm, Wed. 9:15am-10pm. Last admission 30 min. before closing. Admission 28F, ages 18-25 and over 60 16F. Sun. and holidays 16F. Tours in French Mon., Thurs., and Sat. at 2pm; price depends on exhibits covered.)

After the inauguration of Haussmann's urban renewal plans, the Marais was ig-nored by the upper class and subsequently became a home to immigrants, Jews in particular. **Rue des Rosiers,** near the Musée Carnavalet, is still the center of the Jewish community in Paris and is lined with kosher restaurants, butcher shops, *bou-langeries,* and synagogues. Across rue de Rivoli, the solemn 1956 **Mémorial du Mar-tyr Juif Inconnu** (Memorial to the Unknown Jewish Martyr) at 17, rue Geoffrey l'Asnier (tel. 42 72 44 72; Mo. St-Paul), commemorates the Parisian Jews who died at the hands of the Nazis and their French collaborators. Founded by Isaac Schneer-son (a Bolshevik firebrand and veteran of the French resistance in WW II), the mu-seum recalls the conditions of the concentration camps; an eternal flame burns in memory of those who died. Note the bullet holes in the glass surrounding the flame; though caused by terrorist gunfire back in 1983, the museum has not covered them up as evidence that discrimination against Jews has not ended. Though the monu-ment met strong opposition in the Jewish community from 1951-56, it has since become a gathering place for demonstrators opposing anti-Semitism and racism. Upstairs, the **Centre de Documentation Juive Contemporaine (C.D.J.C.)** (Jewish Contemporary Documentation Center) attests to the atrocities of the Holocaust with over 600,000 documents and an ever-expanding collection of articles on the condition of Jews in Europe. Researchers are welcome. (Open Sun.-Fri. 10am-noon and 2-5pm, Sept.-June Mon.-Fri. 10am-noon and 2-5pm. Admission 12F.)

One of the oldest remaining buildings in Paris to have served as a private resi-dence, the **Hôtel de Sens,** 1, rue du Figuier, *4ème* (tel. 42 78 14 60; Mo. St-Paul), is one of Paris's two showcases of medieval residential architecture. (The other is Hôtel de Cluny in the Latin Quarter.) Built from 1474 to 1519, Hôtel de Sens has a beautiful garden and an impressive façade. The *hôtel* now houses a fine arts library and a collection of 250,000 postcards. (Open Tues.-Fri. 1:30-8:30pm, Sat. 10am-8:30pm. Library pass available at front desk with ID. Tours every second Thurs. of the month. Call 48 87 24 17 for tour information.) Another impressive *hôtel par-ticulier,* the **Hôtel de Sully,** 62, rue St-Antoine, *4ème* (tel. 42 74 22 22; Mo. St-Paul) built in 1624, now houses the national office of historical monuments and sights. (Court and gardens open daily 10am-7pm. French tours of the interior on Sat. and Sun.; 30F. Call ahead for tour hours.)

In 1605, Henri IV became frustrated with the lack of any public place for walks and celebrations and decided to build Paris's first grand square, the **place des Vosges.** Unfortunately, Henri never got to see the completion of his plans, as he was killed in a duel in 1610. Place Royale, as it was first called, was completed in 1612 and inaugurated with the marriage of Louis XIII and Anne d'Autriche, which drew ten thousand spectators. A masterpiece of 17th-century secular architecture, place des Vosges derives part of its charm from its grassy enclosure. Madame de Sévigné lived at 1bis, Cardinal Richelieu at #21. A favorite is the **Maison de Victor Hugo** at #6 (tel. 42 72 16 65; Mo. Chemin Vert), Hugo's home from 1832 to 1848. The collection includes photographs, manuscripts, letters, furniture designed by Hugo, and even his geometry notebook. One entire exhibit is devoted to 19th-century advertisements using Hugo's face: "Victor Hugo Clothes for Men," "Victor Hugo Stationer's," and so on. (Open Tues.-Sun. 10am-5:40pm. Admission 12F, students 6.50F, Sun. free.) *Les Miz* fans shouldn't miss the original drawing of Cosette which became the musical's logo. Today, pl. des Vosges is home to Jack Lang, France's Minister of Culture, whom French youth revere for his socialist wardrobe and adorable smile.

On July 14, 1789, rioters in the nearby **place de la Bastille** (Mo. Bastille) freed from the infamous prison some 400 social misfits and petty criminals who were actually living like kings compared to their comrades behind bars elsewhere. The event quickly escalated to tremendous symbolic significance, perhaps culminating in 1989's outrageous bicentennial hoopla. By October 1792, revolutionaries had completely demolished the prison that once housed such notables as Voltaire and the Marquis de Sade. Some of its stones are now interred in Pont de la Concorde, which spans the river near place de la Concorde. A certain citizen Palloy used the other stones to construct 83 models of the prison, which he sent to the provinces outside Paris to remind them of "*l'horreur du despotisme*" (the horror of despotism). Only the ground plan of the prison remains, marked by a line of stones. President Mitterand, whose 1981 triumph was celebrated here with great fanfare, commissioned Canadian architect Carlos Ott to build a modern opera house on the *place*. Appropriately enough, the **Bastille Opéra** saw its first performance on July 14, 1989, the bicentennial of the French Revolution. With two concert halls, an amphitheater, and a studio, this upstart will host all Paris opera, thus leaving the old Opéra Garnier with only ballet. (Hourly tours in French July-Sept. 11am-5pm. Call 40 01 19 70 for tour information. For recorded schedule information, call 43 43 96 96.)

Les Halles

In the second half of the 19th century, Emile Zola, father of French literary naturalism, proclaimed the old market neighborhood of Les Halles "le ventre dc Paris" (Paris's belly). Since 1135, when King Louis VI built two wooden buildings here to house a bazaar, Les Halles has been the site of the largest market in Paris. In 1969, after 850 years of hawking chicken, carrots, and cabbages, vendors were shunted off to the less visible suburbs of Rungis, near Orly, and space-age architecture soon replaced their humble stalls. The Forum des Halles and the Centre Pompidou have infused the district with new spirit, although not without stirring up exemplary controversy.

After the demolition of the old market, politicians and city planners debated how to fill *le trou des Halles* (the hole of Les Halles), 106 open acres which presented Paris with the largest urban redesign opportunity since Haussmann's time. In 1977, the city and state compromised and built the

Forum des Halles (Mo. Les Halles or Châtelet), a mostly subterranean shopping mall with hundreds of stores and numerous fast-food joints, plus the RER and Métro station Châtelet-Les-Halles (the largest underground station in the world). Parisians descend into the belly of the beast to get fairly good deals on just about anything you can imagine. Computerized maps (in 4 languages) are scattered throughout the four-story complex. Inside át level -1, a branch of the **Musée Grevin** (tel. 40 26 28 50) presents a fascinating spectacle on the "Belle Epoque," Paris at the turn of the century. A terrific sound and light show features a history of Paris in 1900 displayed through wax figures of Hugo, Verne, Debussy, Degas, Renoir, Pasteau, Eiffel, and many others. It's well worth the cost. (Continuous shows in French or English last 35 min. Open Mon.-Sat. 10:30am-6:45pm, Sun. 1-7:15pm.

Admission 36F, children 22F.) Also in the Forum, the **Musée de l'Holographie** (tel. 42 96 96 83) displays a small, mostly unimpressive collection of holograms. (Open Mon.-Sat. 10am-7pm, Sun. 1-7pm. Admission 28F, students and seniors 22F.) Popular student bars, old restaurants, cafés, and clothing stores pack the streets surrounding Les Halles. Be careful in this area at night. The recognized hangout of drug addicts, it is carefully patrolled by police with large-fanged dogs.

The disparity between the painfully modern design of the Forum and its Gothic and Renaissance neighborhood is most evident in a comparison of the Forum and **Eglise St-Eustache** (tel. 42 36 31 05), a cavernous, ramshackle beauty of a Gothic church begun in 1532. A Rubens painting of 1611, *The Pilgrim of Emmaüs,* hangs in the 11th north chapel. In the chapel next to the tremendous organ lies the body of Jean-Baptiste Colbert, minister to Louis XIV. (Open daily 8:30am-7pm, but no tourists allowed during mass. Organ music during masses on Sundays at 11am and 6pm. Guided tours in French Sun. at 3pm.)

The **Centre National d'Art et de Culture Georges-Pompidou,** plateau Beaubourg, is commonly known as **Beaubourg.** (Tel. 42 77 12 33, recorded information in French on the week's events 42 77 11 12; Mo. Rambuteau, Hôtel-de-Ville, Châtelet, or Les Halles.) Chosen from 681 designs, Richard Rogers's and Renzo Piano's building turned inside-out has been a magnet for controversy since its opening in 1977. Piping and ventilation ducts in various colors run up, down, and sideways along the outside (blue for air, green for water, yellow for electricity, red for heating), while escalators scoot up amidst this appealing mess. Inside, the repository of finished art and workshop for international artists in all media attracts more visitors annually than the Louvre and the Eiffel Tower combined. From the fifth floor on clear days, the view is as panoramic as that from the Tour Eiffel. The masses assemble on the vast stone place between Pompidou and rue St-Martin to watch fire-eaters, jugglers, fortune-tellers, and caricaturists do their thing.

Invest in a pass which admits you to all areas of the center. (Daily pass 50F, students and seniors 45F. Yearly pass 180F, students and seniors 138F.) The **Musée National d'Art Moderne** houses the center's main permanent collection, a rich selection of 20th-century art, from Fauves and Cubists to Pop and conceptual art. Practically all the great names are represented, including Matisse, Picasso, Magritte, Braque, Kandinsky, Klee, Chagall, Miró, Pollock, Warhol, and Stella. Call ahead for information on current expositions. (Open Mon. and Wed.-Fri. noon-10pm, Sat.-Sun. 10am-10pm. Admission 24F, students and seniors 18F, Sun. 10am-2pm free.) The numerous temporary exhibits downstairs all charge separate admission fees. Your ticket to the modern art museum also admits you to the **Atelier Brancusi** on rue Rambuteau at pl. Georges Pompidou. Constantin Brancusi donated his sculptures to the center under the condition that his 1917 *atelier* located at 8, impasse Ronsin, be reproduced exactly. Although quite small, the museum showcases the Romanian sculptor's main works and his tools. As funds for hiring security guards have been limited, the *atelier* may close without notice on certain days. (Supposedly open Mon. and Thurs. noon-2:30pm, Sat. 10:30am-6pm). Most visitors don't realize that the art galleries form only one of the three primary functions of the Centre Pompidou. Also available to the general public is the **Bibliothèque Publique d'Information** (tel. 42 77 12 33), a free noncirculating library, with open stacks and a large selection of English books. It also has a computer room, a sitting room with the latest international newspapers, a stereo center, and a language lab. (Library open Mon. and Wed.-Fri. noon-10pm, Sat.-Sun. 10am-10pm.) The third permanent department of the center, the **Centre de Création Industrielle (CCI),** focuses on the relations between humanity and the environment. (Open Mon. and Wed.-Fri. 2-6pm. Tours in French Wed.-Mon. 3:30pm; admission 35F, students under 25 28F.)

Between the Pompidou Center and Eglise St-Merri, **place Igor Stravinsky** honors the Russian composer, with the playful mobile fountains Jean Tinguely and Niki de St-Phalle designed to illustrate the composer's famous pieces. **Eglise St-Merri** conceals some impressive Renaissance painted glass windows behind its pure Flamboyant façade. Seriously vandalized during the Revolution, this church was known as the "Temple of Commerce" from 1796-1801, a sly reference to the flesh trade which has dominated this area since the 14th century. Note the hermaphroditic demon atop the central portal.

Tour St-Jacques, the 16th-century Flamboyant Gothic tower on rue de Rivoli, originally surmounted a church destroyed during the Revolution. It was one of the starting points for the pilgrimage to Santiago de Compostela in Spain. Paris's impressive **Hôtel de Ville** (City Hall) was built after its predecessor went up in smoke during the Commune. Note the staircase by Delorme and the murals by Puvis de Chavannes. (Visits Mon. 10:30am only.) Drop by their information office, 29, rue de Rivoli, 4ème (tel. 42 76 40 40; Mo. Hôtel-de-Ville), where exhibits are sometimes held. (Open Mon.-Fri. 9am-5:15pm.) Place de l'Hôtel de Ville, with refreshing fountains and Victorian lampposts, offers a great view across the Seine of Notre-Dame and the Left Bank beyond.

Palais-Royal and Opéra

Just north of the Louvre, in the first, second, and ninth *arrondissements,* some of France's greatest cultural institutions (and remarkably few churches) endure amid a fast-paced business quarter. The **Palais-Royal** (Mo. Palais-Royal) is a sedate collection of buildings, columns, and galleries opening onto a garden of roses and fountains. (The roses and fountains lie just beyond the garden of striped concrete stumps which Daniel Buren planted in the Palais's former parking lot in 1986.) Constructed in 1639 as Cardinal Richelieu's *Palais Cardinal,* it became a *Palais Royal* when Anne of Austria, regent for Louis XIV, set up house here. Bawdy cafés and traveling sideshows invaded the garden soon after it was opened to the public in 1784 by a young Philippe d'Orléans eager to pay his debts by renting out the surrounding buildings. It was in this meeting place for thieves, con artists, and prostitutes that Camille Desmoulins urged his fellow citizens to arm themselves on July 13, 1789—the eve of the storming of the Bastille. On the southwestern corner of the Palais-Royal is the **Comédie Française,** home to France's leading dramatic group. A monument to Molière, the company's founder, rises up not far from here on rue Molière at rue Richelieu. Continuing along the latter, you'll come to the **Bibliothèque Nationale,** 58, rue Richelieu, 2ème (tel. 46 03 81 26). Competing with the British Museum for the title of largest library in Western Europe, this leviathan contains seven million volumes, including two Gutenberg Bibles and countless first editions of famous French authors from the 15th century to the present. To get inside the stacks, you'll have to prove you're doing research which calls for publications not available elsewhere in Paris; this is not an easy task. If you can get a letter from a university, publisher, or publication, call 47 03 81 02 for approval. (Office open Mon.-Fri. 9am-4pm.) The library's **Musée des Medailles** displays a wide mix of coins and medallions that have been in circulation during various stages in French history. This museum, however, is far outdone by the Musée de la Monnaie de Paris (see St-Germain-des-Prés sights). (Open daily 1-4pm. Admission 20F, students and seniors 12F.) Call for information on temporary exhibits of the library's inventory.

Charles Garnier's **Opéra** (tel. 42 66 50 22; Mo. Opéra) epitomizes the excessive Napoleon style. The unknown Garnier's design got the nod in an 1861 competition, outshining even the design of the imperial family's favorite grimthorper, Viollet-le-Duc. The interior is graced with Gobelin tapestries, gilded mosaics, a 1964 Chagall ceiling, and a six ton chandelier that fell onto the audience in 1896. Since the opening of the new Opéra de la Bastille, only ballet takes the stage here. (Open daily 11am-5pm. Admission 20F, ages 10-16 10F. Tickets go on sale two weeks in advance (30-300F).)

The **Musée Grévin,** 10, bd. Montmartre (tel. 42 61 28 50; Mo. Montmartre), features mainly wax figures in historical scenes (Marie Antoinette in jail, for example) indulges in such lunacy as an outer-space rendezvous between George Bush, Mikhail Gorbachev, Helmut Kohl, Margaret Thatcher, and Deng Xiaoping. Appropriately, Woody Allen served as impresario for this big event. Although the figures don't look much like their models, the place is fun, especially for the kids who come by the busload. (Open 10am-7pm, Oct.-June 1-7pm. Admission 42F, ages 6-14 28F.) Connecting bd. Montmartre with rue du Faubourg Montmartre are *passages* Jouffroy and Verdeau, two 19th-century shopping arcades full of antique book, print, and jewelry shops. Rue Richer, an old Jewish quarter lined with kosher butchers and good stores, cuts through Faubourg Montmartre.

In the center of Paris's primary business quarter stands the **Bourse,** rue du 4 Septembre (tel. 42 33 99 83 or 40 41 10 00; Mo. Bourse) at rue Vivienne. Although subdued in comparison to the stock exchanges of New York and London, Napoleon's 1808 "Temple of Money" seems to have weathered the storm of Mitterand's socialism. The 90-minute tours (in French) include several presentations on the role of the stock exchange in the international economy and finish with entry into the visitors' gallery, from which you can watch stockbrokers playing chess. (Open Mon.-Fri. 11am-1pm.)

Place Vendôme and Place de la Concorde

The majesty of French urban planning becomes evident in the squares and buildings that dominate this area. Beautiful **Place Vendôme,** with its uniformly dignified structures, was constructed between 1687 and 1720 according to plans by Jules Hardouin-Mansart, who convinced Louis XIV add a group of five financiers to invest in the ensemble of private mansions and public institutions. To commemorate his 1805 victory at Austerlitz, Napoleon erected a central column modeled after Trajan's column in Rome and constructed of melted Austrian and Russian cannons captured during the battle. Toppled during the Commune, the column was restored at the expense of artist Gustave Courbet, who was though to have organized the vandalism. The entire square shimmers with opulence. Chopin died at #12, and the rich and famous still take less permanent naps at #15 (the Ritz). Here are well-known bankers, perfumers, jewellers, and the Paris branch of IBM. Supposedly, Rothschild, instead of lending his friends money, would simply allow them to stroll with him around pl. Vendôme for a few minutes. The next morning the fortunate souls would be certain of credit at the most prestigious banks.

Geometry prevails over nature in the **Jardin des Tuileries,** probably the most famous of Paris's parks. Catherine de Medici missed the public promenades of her native Italy and so had the gardens built in 1564; a century later André le Nôtre (designer of the gardens at Versailles) gave them their present aspect. Rodin sculptures dot the manicured park, which has more gravel than greenery. Site of an annual summer carnival, this garden is known to have a seamy side after dark.

At the far end of the gardens, the **Musée de l'Orangerie** (tel. 42 97 48 16; Mo. Concorde) displays the *Collection Jean Walter et Paul Guillaume.* Mme Guillaume, who married both of these private art collectors (at different times), donated to the French government a series of paintings that range in style from impressionism to surrealism. The museum's prize is Monet's series *Les Nymphéas* (*The Water Lilies*), located on the ground floor of the museum; you'll have to cross the gallery on the upper floor and descend the staircase in the middle. Renoirs, Matisses, Picassos, and Monets line the walls upstairs, making this one of the most precious, if little known, collections in Paris. (Open Wed.-Mon. 9:45am-5:15pm. Admission 23F, students 12F, Sun. 12F. Last admission 15 min. before closing.)

Connecting the Tuileries with the Champs Elysées is Paris's largest and most infamous public square, the **place de la Concorde** (Mo. Concorde). Constructed between 1757 and 1777 as monument to Louis XV, the vast area soon became known as place de la Révolution, site of the guillotine which severed the heads from 1343 bodies. Louis XVI, Marie Antoinette, Charlotte Corday (Marat's assassin), Lavoisier, Robespierre, and other celebrated heads rolled on this grand scrap of pavement, optimistically renamed place de la Concorde after the Reign of Terror. Although the area's architectural grandeur is somewhat obscured by a flood of traffic as deadly as any guillotine, a marvelous fireworks display recalls its history each July 14.

Construction of a church to be called **La Madeleine** began in 1764 at the end of rue Royale. The slow construction was halted during the Revolution, when the Cult of Reason proposed making it into a bank, a theater, or a courthouse. In 1806,

Napoleon decided to consecrate the partially completed building as a Temple of Glory, dedicated to his Grande Armée. He had the monument completed in a design reminiscent of a Greek temple. Completed in 1842 as a church, the building is distinguished by its gold detail work and four ceiling domes. (Open 8:30am-7pm. Occasional organ concerts.) A picturesque flower market fills the east side of the square, Emile Zola wrote *J'accuse* in the old Café Durand at #2, pl. de la Madeleine, a spot of earth long since usurped by Thomas Cook. Marcel Prouse spent most of his childhood at 9, bd. Malesherbes, which runs northwest from the square.

Palais du Louvre

The **Palais du Louvre** (tel. 40 20 50 50, *poste* 49 25 or 49 38; Mo. Palais-Royal/Musée du Louvre) has been drawing huge crowds since the Revolution opened its doors to the public in 1793. As early as 1214, a fortress was built here to defend the city's west side. François I transformed the utilitarian building into a splendid Renaissance palace in 1546, and Catherine de Medici, Henry IV, Louis XIII, Louis XIV, and Napoleon III all tacked on additions to their heart's content. Not until 1871 did the palace assume its present aspect. In the garden between the Pavillon de Marsan and the Pavillon de Flore stands the **Arc de Triomphe du Carrousel,** inspired by the Arch of Septimus Severus in Rome and built in 1806-08 to commemorate Napoleon's victories of 1805. The four bronze horses from St-Mark's in Venice, "borrowed" when Napoleon conquered the Veneto, once graced this little arch. The colorful, bloody history of the palace has included some six centuries of monarchs; consider taking the 90-minute tour (23F). Call for times.

The debate on exactly which of the world's museums is actually the richest is not likely to be resolved in the near future, but few will dispute that the **Musée du Louvre** is a strong contender. Although unfortunate, a gang of thieves' 1990 absquatulation with a small Rembrandt and several other works hardly made a dent in the collection. Don't try to cover the entire museum in two hours; the most satisfaction you're likely to derive is the pride in saying you saw the *Mona Lisa* through a forest of golf hats. Spending a full day in the museum is more likely to dull your powers of perception than to increase your appreciation of the art. Try to take in a few galleries over the course of several days. The extra admission charges are a small price to pay for the satisfaction.

Not built for the purpose of housing a major art collection, the Louvre was once upon a time one of the most poorly equipped museums in the world. In order to travel between the Louvre's two long wings, visitors had to make a 30-minute trek through the palace's eastern bridge. As a result, the northern wing was not used to display any of the museum's collections. The previous entrances, ill-equipped for handling crowds, were hobbled by an extremely inefficient welcoming service. The government hired I.M. Pei, designer of the National Gallery of Art in Washington, to make the Louvre museum more accessible.

Pei's remarkable proposal, though met with gross disapproval at first, is now acknowledged to be nothing short of brilliant. The architect proposed moving the main entrance to the center of the Cour Napoléon (courtyard), but since the great space would have to remain unspoiled, the only possibility was to excavate. An enlarged reception area has solved the problem of an unstructured welcoming service, and newly installed escalators provide ready access into any of the palace's wings. A pyramid tops the entrance, providing sufficient light and beautifully reflecting both the sky and the newly added fountains. Since the new entrance's opening in March 1989, visiting the Louvre is easier than ever before. The construction, however, continues. Since the conservative ministers of finance (fearful of losing their prestigious address and unwilling to cooperate with the socialists' plan) have evacuated the Richelieu (North) wing is being renovated to provide museum space and a parking lot is being built under the palace. The expected date of completion for the "Grand Louvre" project is 1995. An exhibit in the North Wing details its progress. (Open Wed.-Mon. 11am-7pm. Free.)

Unlike every other museum in Paris, the Louvre has no overarching theme. Whereas the Musée d'Orsay presents an exhaustive history of art in the second half of the 19th century, relatively few of its contents are as historically important or as well known as the *Mona Lisa, Venus of Milo, Slaves* by Michelangelo, or *Winged Victory of Samothrace.* Frequent tours (in French and English) or a rented cassette recorder can give an excellent introduction to the museum, but the exploring and the appreciating are up to you. (Museum open Thurs.-Mon. 9am-5:15pm and Wed. 9am-9:15pm. Pyramid open Wed.-Mon. 9am-10pm. Principal entrance through the pyramid, but students and seniors can skip the long line by entering through the gate opposite the Métro station. Admission 27F, ages 18-25 and over 60 14F, under 18 free. Frequent guided tours 23F. Recorded tours 22F.)

Within the Palais, the **Musée des Arts Décoratifs,** Pavillon de Marsan, 107, rue de Rivoli, 1er (tel. 42 60 32 14; Mo. Palais-Royal), features furniture, objets d'art, china, and household items from the Middle Ages to the present, including an art-deco apartment, an exhibition room from the 1900 art-nouveau exposition, and art-nouveau jewelry. (Open Wed.-Sat. 12:30-6pm, Sun. 11am-6pm. Admission 20F, students 14F plus special exhibit price.) The **Musée des Arts de la Mode,** 109, rue de Rivoli, 1er (tel. 42 60 32 14; Mo. Palais-Royal), displays 8000 complete costumes and more than 30,000 accessories. The free opening presentation highlights the collections. (Open Wed.-Sat. 12:30-6pm, Sun. 11am-6pm. Admission 25F, students 18F.) Not far from the Louvre, the **Musée de la Publicité,** 107, rue de Rivoli, 1èr (tel. 42 60 32 14; Mo. Louvre), celebrates the art of the poster in a turn-of-the-century crockery shop. Though the permanent collections are rather small and insignificant, past temporary exhibits have included prints and posters by such giants as Toulouse-Lautrec, Magritte, and Daumier. (Open Wed.-Mon. noon-6pm. Last admission 5:30pm. Admission 18F, students and seniors 10F.)

Champs-Elysées and l'Arc de Triomphe

Ever since Le Nôtre planted trees in 1667 to extend the Tuileries vista (and renamed it Elysian Fields because of its shade), the **avenue des Champs-Elysées** has been one of Paris's biggest attractions. Crowded with tourists seeking entertainment in summer, this 10-land wonder becomes a popular place for rallies and demonstrations in winter. (The march celebrating Général de Gaulle was held here in 1970.) The **Grand Palais** (tel. 42 89 54 10) and **Petit Palais** (tel. 42 65 12 73; Mo. Champs-Elysées-Clemenceau), facing one another on av. Winston Churchill, were both built for the 1900 World's Fair. The Grand Palais houses temporary exhibitions and occasional summer concerts on the courtyard. The Petit Palais displays an excellent collection of Flemish and French art, including many Courbets, Cézannes, and Gauguins. (Grand Palais open Thurs.-Mon. 10am-8pm, Wed. 10am-10pm. Petit Palais open Tues.-Sun. 10am-5:40pm. Admission 28F, students and seniors 18F. Price varies.) The wing of the Grand Palais facing av. de Franklin D. Roosevelt has become the **Palais de la Découverte** (tel. 43 59 16 65; Mo. Champs-Elysées-Clemenceau), an extensive science museum emphasizing visitor participation. Turn wheels, pull levers, and push buttons to verify the scientific principles described. Different demonstrations take place throughout the day. (Open Tues.-Sun. 10am-6pm. Admission 20F, students and seniors 10F. With planetarium 33F, students and seniors 19F.) The guards pacing around the house at the corner of avenue de Marigny and rue Faubourg St-Honoré are protecting the home of the French president, the **Palais de l'Elysée** (classified tel.; Mo. Champs-Elysées-Clemenceau).

You would have to be made of stone not to be moved by your first glimpse of the Arc de Triomphe looming gloriously above the Champs-Elysées in place Charles de Gaulle (tel. 43 80 31 31; Mo. Charles-de-Gaulle/Etoile). The world's largest triumphal arch and an internationally recognized symbol of France, its construction was ordered by Napoleon to honor his Grande Armée and was completed in 1836 (21 years after the humiliating defeat of this same army). In 1810 the architect had to stretch a full-scale canvas mockup over scaffolding for Napoleon's grand entrance to the city with his new bride, Marie-Louise of Austria. As no one could agree on what to put on top of the arch after its completion, it has kept its simple unfinished form. Since 1920 it has contained the Tomb of the Unknown Soldier. The eternal flame is rekindled every evening at 6:30pm, when veterans and small children lay wreaths decorated with blue, white, and red. The most famous of the allegorical sculpture groups depicting the history of France is Rude's *La Marseillaise,* to the right on the Champs-Elysées side. Rather than risk an early death by crossing the Etoilé's busy traffic circle to reach the Arc, use the underpasses on the even-numbered side of both the Champs-Elysées and av. de la Grande-Armée. The top of the Arc provides a terrific view of the main east-west axis and of all of Paris. (Open daily 10am-5:30pm. Admission 27F, students and seniors 15F.)

Of the twelve perfectly symmetrical avenues radiating from **place Charles de Gaulle,** the most handsome is shady **avenue Foch,** a Haussmann masterpiece which runs west through the 16th *arrondissement* to the Bois de Boulogne. The little dogs proudly parading along its tree-bordered sidewalks call the wealthiest households in Paris home. Probably the only building here to which you can gain entrance is the **Musée d'Ennery,** 59, av. Foch, 16*ème* (tel. 45 53 57 96; Mo. Porte Dauphine), a small collection of Japanese and Chinese art in Ennery's 19th-century residence. (Open Sept.-July Thurs. and Sun. 2-5pm. Free.)

Parc de Monceau

One of the most exclusive quarters of the French capital, Monceau is the place to find France's affluent youth jogging and relaxing. The small park in the 8*ème* (Mo. Monceau), designed by the painter Carmontelle for the Duc d'Orléans, contains some picturesque Roman ruins. (Open 7am-9:30pm.) The French aristocracy still inhabits the mansions surrounding the park. Some, however, have been willed to the state or to service organizations and now function as museums.

The **Musée Nissim de Camondo,** 63, rue de Monceau, 8*ème* (tel. 45 63 26 32; Mo. Villiers) was inspired by the Petit Trianon in Versailles. If you can't get to the real thing, come here to get a hint of palatial grandeur. The last descendant of the Camondo family (the one-time Rothschilds of the East), Moïse de Camondo dedicated this museum of 18th-century art and antiques to his son Nissim, who was killed in 1917. (Open Wed.-Sun. 10am-noon and 2-5pm. Admission 15F, students and seniors 10F. Recorded tours in English, French, and Japanese.) Largely supported by the personal funds of Dr. Armand Hammer of baking soda fame, the **Musée Jacquemart-André,** 158, bd. Haussemann, 8*ème* (tel. 45 62 39 94; Mo. Miromesnil), contains a small but important collection of works gathered by 19th-century tycoon Edouard André. (Open Wed.-Sun. 1:30-5:30pm. Admission 10F.) The **Musée Cernuschi,** 7, av. Vélasquez, 8*ème* (tel. 45 63 50 75; Mo. Villiers), in a villa just east of the park, displays a fairly extensive collection of ancient Chinese art. (Open Tues.-Sun. 10am-5:40pm. Admission 12F, students and seniors 6F. Frequent temporary exhibits additional.)

In the days of pre-revolutionary Russia, many Russian aristocrats owned vacation houses in France. Nice and Paris still retain a sizable Russian community. Though not as magnificent as the multicolored version in Nice, Paris's onion-domed **Eglise Russe,** 12, rue Daru, 8*ème* (tel. 42 27 57 34; Mo. Termes), built in 1860, is an attractive church that continues to serve the area's Russian inhabitants. (Open 10am-7pm.)

Sixteenth Arrondissement and Bois de Boulogne

Some of Paris's most diverse museums are scattered among the handsome residences of affluent BCBGs (*bon chic, bon genre,*) just east of the immense Bois de Boulogne. Across the river from the Tour Eiffel are the **Jardins du Trocadéro** and the **Palais de Chaillot** (Mo. Trocadéro), both built for the 1939 International Exposition. The Palais now contains several museums. The **Musée de l'Homme** (tel. 45 53 70 60) captivates visitors with its educational display of archaeological finds. The museum, which highlights the past and present societies of many peoples, functions as an excellent introduction to non-Western culture. (Open Wed.-Mon. 9:45am-5:15pm. Admission 16F, students 8F.) Next door, the **Musée de la Marine** (tel. 45 53 31 70), established by Charles X in 1827 to display the royal collection of model ships depicts the history of maritime travel. (Open Wed.-Mon. 10am-6pm. Admission 22F, students 10F.) **Musée du Cinéma,** salle du Palais de Chaillot (tel. 45 53

74 39), traces the history of sound and light in film, starting with magic lanterns and shadow theaters. (Open Wed.-Mon. for guided 1½ hr. tour in French only at 10am, 11am, 2pm, 3pm, and 4pm. Tours cancelled if fewer than 8 people. Admission 22F.) The most unusual museum in the Palais de Chaillot is the **Musée des Monument Français** (tel. 47 27 35 74), which presents a collection of replicas of the most important monuments in France. (Open Wed.-Mon. 9am-6pm. Admission 16F, students and seniors 8F.)

Although not as flashy from the outside as its counterpart at the Centre Pompidou, the **Musée d'Art Moderne de la Ville de Paris,** 11, av. du Président Wilson, 16ème (tel. 47 23 61 27; Mo. Iéna), owns a well-lit collection of modern art of comparable wealth. The permanent exhibits include works by Matisse, Picasso, and Magritte. Temporary exhibits display very recent, very bizarre works. Its organization by style rather than artist may confuse or amuse the neophyte. (Open Tues. and Thurs.-Sun. 10am-5:30pm, Wed. 10am-8:30pm. Admission depends on temporary expositions, which usually charge 20-35F.) Next door, the **Palais de Tokyo** (tel. 47 23 36 53), built for the 1937 World's Fair, now displays temporary photography exhibits. (Open Wed.-Mon. 9:45am-5pm. Admission 25F, students and seniors 12F.) Across the street, the **Palais Galliera** now functions as the **Musée de la Mode et du Costume** (tel. 47 20 85 23) and displays temporary exhibitions of dress through the centuries. Enter on av. Pierre 1er de la Serbie. (Open Tues.-Sun. 10am-5:40pm. Admission 28F, students and seniors 18F.) The **Musée Guimet,** 6, pl. d'Iéna, 16ème (tel. 47 23 61 65; Mo. Iéna), exhibits one of the most extensive collections of Asian art in the Western world. Its huge library and photographic documents are also open to the public. (Both open Wed.-Mon. 9:45am-5:15pm. Admission 15F, students and seniors 8F, Sun. 8F.) Fans of Balzac's novels will enjoy the **Maison de Balzac,** 47, rue Raynouard, 16ème (tel. 42 24 56 38; Mo. Passy), full of interesting memorabilia from the life and work of Honoré de Balzac, who penned the last part of *La comédie humaine* here (1840-1847). (Open Tues.-Sun. 10am-5:40pm. Admission 12F, students 6.50F.)

As Paris's third Impressionism specialist, the **Musée Marmottan,** 2, rue Louis-Boilly, 16ème (tel. 42 24 07 02; Mo. La Muette), does its best to keep up with the Orsay and the Orangerie. Set inside the erstwhile *hôtel* of art historian Marmottan, the collection includes a fair display of Italian Renaissance painting and a tremendous group of Monet's flower paintings. Marmottan inherited most of the latter from Michel Monet, son of Claude. It was from here in 1986 that Impressionism's namesake, Monet's *Impression: Soleil Levant,* was stolen. (Open Tues.-Sun. 10am-5:30pm. Admission 25F, students and seniors 10F.) The **Musée du Vin,** rue des Eaux, 16ème (tel. 45 25 63 26; Mo. Passy), is in Abbey Passy's vaulted *caves,* dating from the 13th and 14th centuries. A must for all lovers of civilization's oldest and favorite beverage, the museum explains the process of fabricating wine and presents exhibits on distinguishing between different types. Yes, there's a free tasting at the exit. (Open Tues.-Sun. noon-6pm. Admission 26F, students 19F, seniors 23F.)

Unfairly condemned by Carlyle as a "dirty, scrubby place," the vast **Bois de Boulogne,** which spreads its leafy umbrella just beyond the 16ème *arrondissement,* is as Parisian as late-night onion soup (Mo. Porte Maillot, Sablons, Pont de Neuilly, Porte Dauphine, or Porte d'Auteuil). If you come here seeking late-night anything, however, you're quite likely to be turned into *au gratin.* Safe during the day, the park becomes extremely dangerous for both men and women after dark. This former royal hunting ground contains lakes, restaurants, horse and bicycle races—even a baseball diamond in the corner of the Bagatelle soccer and rugby fields. The stroll along **Lac Inférieur** (lower lake), down route de Suresnes from porte Dauphine (Mo. Porte Dauphine), is quite pleasant. The manicured islands in the middle of the lake can be reached by rowboats rented by the hour (42F, deposit 100F) or by ferry (every 10 min. round-trip 5F). Across from the rowboat dock you can also rent a bike (14F per hr., 60F per 4 hr., deposit ID). West of Lac Inférieur is the picture-perfect **Pré Catelan.** The **Jardin Shakespeare,** in the center of the Pré Catelan, contains every plant ever mentioned by the Bard, patterned here to reproduce scenes from *As You Like It, Hamlet, A Midsummer Night's Dream, Macbeth,* and *The*

Tempest. In addition, the **Theater Shakespeare** (tel. 42 27 39 54; Mo. Porte Maillot, then bus 244, stop "Bagatelle-Pré Catalan") produces a Shakespeare play every year. (Garden open Mon.-Sat. 10am-7pm. Admission 80F, students 40F.) The **Bagatelle** (tel. 40 67 97 00), once a private estate within the Bois, now nourishes a well-preserved flower garden famous for its water lilies and June rose exhibition. (Occasional concerts. Open daily 8:30am-8pm. Admission 5F.)

In the north end of the Bois, the **Jardin d'Acclimatation** (tel. 40 67 90 82; Mo. Sablons) has a small zoo and amusement park that includes a small train, brook that babbles in French, and temporary children's exhibits. (Open daily 10am-6pm. Admission 6F.) Finally, be sure to visit the nearby **Musée National des Arts et Traditions Populaires,** 6, route du Mahatma-Gandhi (tel. 40 67 90 00; Mo. Sablons), one of Paris's newest, most innovative museums. Geared towards French speakers, the excellent exhibits of tools and everyday artifacts illustrate rural French life before the industrial revolution. (Open Wed.-Mon. 9:45am-5pm. Audio-visual presentation daily. Admission 16F, ages under 25 and over 60 8F, Sun. 8F.)

Rive Gauche (Left Bank)

Quartier Latin (Latin Quarter)

Erstwhile home to Villon, Pascal, and other giants of French intellectual history, the Latin Quarter looms so large in the imagination that many visitors confuse it with the whole Rive Gauche. The university quarter (which Rabelais christened "le quartier latin" after the academic tongue of choice), is really a small area bounded by the Seine to the north, the Jardin des Plantes to the east, rue Mouffetard to the south, and **boulevard St-Michel** to the west. One of Haussmann's few intrusions into this area, Boul-Miche soon replaced rue St-Jacques (the old Roman road to Orléans) as the Latin Quarter's main thoroughfare. Untouched medieval streets remain tangled between the bookstores and cafés of bd. St-Michel and the equally riotous rue St-Jacques. (Mitterand is reputed to frequent his second apartment just on rue de Bièvre, just off bd. St-Germain, but the only sign of him may be the police officers who guide the street.)**Square Réné Viviani,** just east of rue St-Jacques, boasts both the oldest tree in Paris (a false acacia dating from 1693) and one of the best views of Notre-Dame.

Just south of bd. St-Germain and west of rue St-Jacques is the **Musée de Cluny,** 6, pl. Paul-Painlevé (tel. 43 25 62 00; Mo. St-Michel), Paris's museum of medievalia. The most famous of its treasures is the tapestry *La Dame à la Licorne* (*The Lady with the Unicorn*); five of its six wall-length panels allegorically represent the five senses. Recently unearthed and exhibited here is *La Galerie des Rois de Judas,* a set of kingly statues of which were sheltered above Notre-Dame's portals until the revolutionaries of 1793 shattered them in their battle against all Gothic and classical representation. One half of the museum is in a late Gothic *hôtel,* the other in the remains of the baths of the Roman city of Lutetia. (Open Wed.-Mon. 9:45am-12:30pm and 2-5pm. Admission 15F, students and Sun. 8F.) Inside the headquarters of the Parisian police is the **Musée des Collections Historiques de la Préfecture de la Police,** 1bis, rue des Carmes, *5ème* (tel. 43 29 21 57, 336; Mo. Maubert-Mutualité), on the second floor of the building. Tourists are welcome despite forbidding signs and inquiring looks. Non-historians and non-French speakers will enjoy the exhibits detailing the developments of crime and punishment since the Middle Ages. Don't miss the torture devices near the end of the exhibit. (Open Mon.-Thurs. 9am-5pm, Fri. 9am-4:30pm. If locked, ask across the hall in room 201 to be let in. Free.)

South of rue des Ecoles, the medieval maze gives way to the 19th-century buildings of the **Sorbonne,** the longtime intellectual hothouse whose insignia and name have been taken in vain by sweatshirt manufacturers around the world. Founded in 1208 as a theological center bent on defending orthodoxy, the university contests with Bologna the title of the oldest university in Europe. All of the present buildings (except for the church of Ste-Ursule) were rebuilt between 1885 and 1901. Following student riots of May 1968, the old University of Paris was broken up into 13 autonomous campuses scattered across Paris. The Sorbonne presently comprises Paris III and Paris IV. Tourists are welcome only in the chapel, which hosts occasional art exhibits (Open Mon.-Fri. 9am-5pm.) If you're really bent on getting inside the rest of the Sorbonne, ask about language and civilization courses at office number 9 in the Galerie Richelieu. Otherwise, gawk at the Sorbonne's students and leading scholars at **Librairie J. Vrin**, 6, pl. Sorbonne (tel. 43 54 03 47), France's premier bookstore for philosophical texts and dissertations.(Don't look for feminist philosophy here; "those books" are published and sold elsewhere.) Behind the Sorbonne is the considerably less exclusive **Collège de France**, an institution created by François I in 1530 to contest the university's supreme authority. The outstanding morning and evening courses given over the years by the likes of Henri Bergson, Paul Valéry, and Milan Kundera are free and open to all. Check the schedules that appear by the door in September. (Courses run Sept.-May. For more information, call 43 29 12 11.)

Visible from almost everywhere in the Latin Quarter, the huge dome of the **Panthéon** (tel. 43 54 34 51; Mo. Luxembourg) towers over the highest (65m) and most central point of the Left Bank. Originally a church, the Panthéon was constructed by Louis XV to fulfill a vow he made when ill that if he recovered, he would replace the fallen Abbey of St-Généviève with such a building. In 1791, the Constituent Assembly started the practice of honoring the greatest figures in France by granting them burial in the former church. The crypt of the Panthéon houses the heart of Léon Gambetta (in an urn) and the tombs of Victor Hugo, Voltaire, Rousseau, Louis Braille, Emile Zola, and Sadi Carnot. The dome of the neoclassical building is decorated with 19th-century paintings of mythical scenes from Paris's early history, the most famous of which is by Puvis de Chavannes. Beyond that is a *terrasse* with a view of Paris as impressive as that from the Eiffel Tower or the Tour Montparnasse, but for less than half the price. Do not be dissuaded by the signs alerting tourists to the renovations in progress. (Open 10am-6pm. Last admission 30 min. before closing. Admission 23F, students 12F.)

St-Germain-des-Prés and the Jardin du Luxembourg

Rival to the Latin Quarter in both popularity and bohemian theatrics, this area of the 6*ème arrondissement* between the Seine and the Jardin du Luxembourg fills day and night with tourists, artists, and poseurs. On the streets radiating from **Carrefour de Buci** and the **boulevard St-Germain**, would-be F. Scotts and Zeldas linger in Le Flore, Aux Deux Magots, La Coupole, and other historic cafés. Just on the edge of this fashionable frenzy, at the intersection of bd. St-Germain and rue de Rennes, **Eglise St-Germain-des-Prés** is Paris's oldest church and one of the few Romanesque structures remaining in the area. Founded in 558 and rebuilt in the 11th century, the church merits special attention for its 11th-century nave, early Gothic choir, and (in the second chapel on the right) a stone marking the interred heart of Descartes. The **Musée Eugène Delacroix**, 6, pl. de Furstenberg, 6*ème* (tel. 43 54 04 87; Mo. Saint-German-des Prés), commemorates the 19th-century Romantic painter. Preserved by a Delacroix society anxious to protect memories of the artist, the house in which he worked and died now displays busts of the painter, works by his friends, and a fascinating set of captioned illustrations of Shakespeare's plays. (Open Wed.-Mon. 9:45am-12:30pm and 2-5:15pm. Admission 11F, students under 26 6F.)

The streets around nearby rue de Seine are full of expensive art galleries—the struggling artists of the past have given way to wealthier individuals. To see what Parisian art students are doing, walk around the **Ecole des Beaux-Arts**, 14, rue Bonaparte at quai Malaquais, 6*ème* (tel. 42 60 34 57; Mo. St-Germain-des-Prés). France's best-known art school presents periodic exhibits of student work (admission around 20F). Check Parisian publications for exhibit information. Just east in pl. de l'Institut, the **Palais de l'Institut de France** stares out from under its elegant dome at the Louvre, which stretches along the opposite band of the Seine. The most famous of the *institut's* five learned societies, the **Académie Française**, has since its founding by Richelieu in 1635 carried out its task of purifying the French language and compiling its official dictionary. Already having registered its adamant disapproval of *l'hamburger, le leadership,* and other "Franglais" nonsense, the academicians are gearing up for a fight with those government-sponsored heretics who want to eliminate the circon flex, the pointed hat of an accent found on words like *tête* and *crêpe.* So difficult is it to become elected to this arcane society that Molière and Proust never made it, and only in 1981 was a woman (the late Marguerite Yourcenar) granted membership.

Musée de la Monnaie de Paris, 11, quai de Conti, 6*ème* (tel. 43 29 12 48; Mo. Pont-Neuf), makes the most of its money through an impressive display of coins and medals reflecting French artistic styles and political conditions from the 9th century to the present. Collectors can buy the newest items here. (Open Tues. and Thurs.-Sat. 1-6pm, Wed. 1-9pm. Admission 15F. Students 18-25 10F.) The oldest theater in Paris, the **Théâtre de l'Odéon,** pl. de l'Odéon, was constructed in 1770 to house the national group *la Comédie Française.* Reconstructed several times, **Eglise St-Sulpice** towers over the neighborhood. Don't miss the organ loft by Chalgrin (generally regarded as the most beautiful in the country) or the extravagant fountain outside in pl. St-Sulpice.

An 11th-century crop farm later manicured by Marie de Medici, the **Jardin du Luxembourg** is immensely popular with Parisians of all ages. Flowers and trees—including some palms—are interspersed with statues of such poets as Baudelaire and Hérédia, modern sculpture, and even a miniature Statue of Liberty. Sail a toy boat on the pond for 9F per hour, or attend the *Grand Guignol,* a puppet show given daily at 4pm (tel. 43 50 25 00; admission 15F). Pony rides, tennis, basketball, and *pétanque* round out the possible activities. Inside the park is the **Palais du Luxembourg,** commissioned by Marie de Medici in 1615 as a reminder of her birthplace, the Pitti Palace in Florence. An interesting architectural mix of French and Tuscan styles, the palace now houses the largely powerless French Senate. The president of the Senate lives in **Petit-Luxembourg,** a gift from Marie de Medici to her nemesis, Cardinal Richelieu. The **Musée de Luxembourg** (tel. 42 34 20 00), next to the palace on rue Vaugirard, displays temporary exhibitions of art from around the world.

The Seventh Arrondissement: Musée d'Orsay and La Tour Eiffel

The staid seventh *arrondissement* has been an exclusive enclave since the early 18th century, when the aristocrats of the Marais traded one swampy quarter for another and built new *hôtels particuliers* near the city's new southwestern border. In the **Faubourg St-Germain,** an area lying roughly between the Les Invalides and rue des Sts-Pères, many of the elegant *hôtels* now house embassies and ministries. Removed from the intellectual hyperactivity of the neighboring Latin Quarter, this area is a good place for a quiet stroll. One of the most magnificent but lesser-known landmarks of the seventh is the massive **Palais-Bourbon** (33, quai d'Orsay, 7*ème,* Mo. Chambre des Députés), a rather somber affair commissioned by Napoleon in 1803. Now the seat of the French National Assembly, it displays Delacroix paintings in its library (tel. 40 63 60 00; open Sat. 10am-2pm). The sessions of the French National Assembly are open to the public Monday through Thursday at 3pm. West of the Palais on rue de Litle, the **Musée National de la Légion d'Honneur et des Ordres de Chevalerie,** 2, rue de Bellechasse, 7*ème* (tel. 45 55 95 16; Mo. Solférino), occupies the handsome Hôtel de Salm. The collection of medals, plaques, ribbons, and other decorations is devoted to France's Legion of Honor and to foreign orders of chivalry. (Open Tues.-Sun. 2-5pm. Admission 10F.)

Looming just across the street, the **Musée d'Orsay** is much more than a museum of Impressionist paintings (1, rue de Bellechasse, 7*ème;* tel. 40 49 48 14; RER Musée d'Orsay; Mo. Solférino). In addition to housing all the old favorites from the Jeu de Paume, this 1986 addition to the Parisian museum firmament captures the artistic ideals of the second half of the 19th century in the Western hemisphere. The Orsay's collection was chosen not to display merely the greatest works between 1850 and 1905, but to trace the development of contrasting artistic styles throughout the second half of the 19th and the early years of the 20th centuries. The museum is in the old Gare d'Orsay, one of Paris's first rail stations (completed in 1840) and once considered as bold an expression of modernity as the Eiffel Tower. To emphasize the contrast between mid-19th century works (such as those by Ingres and Delacroix) and later works (such as those by Monet and Manet), the Orsay museographers placed the traditional works on the right side of the ground floor in the central hall and the early modern works on the left. The Impressionist masterpieces are on the north side of the third floor. Dig in by ascending the staircase at the end of the first floor gallery opposite the entrance. (Open Tues.-Wed. and Fri.-Sat. 10am-6pm, Thurs. 10am-9:45pm, Sun. 9am-6pm. Last admission ¾-hr. before closing. Exhibits close ½-hr. before general closing. Admission 27F, ages under 25 and over 60 and Sun. 14F. Tours in English Tues.-Fri. at 11:30am and 2:30pm; tours in French Tues.-Sat. at 11am and 1pm. Thurs. at 7pm. Tours 27F.)

Dwarfed by the d'Orsay, the more manageable **Musée Auguste Rodin** at the Hôtel Biron, 77, rue de Varenne, *7ème* (tel. 47 05 01 34; Mo. Varenne), is considered by many to be the top attraction of the Faubourg St-Germain. Displayed in this elegant 18th-century *hôtel* are the works of August Rodin (1840-1918), generally acknowledged to be France's greatest sculptor. Rodin's tortured interpretation of Dante's *Inferno* welcomes visitors to the otherwise tranquil garden. *Le Penseur* (Dante contemplating his work) guards the entrance and faces *La Porte d'Enfer* (The Gates of Hell). The *Burghers of Calais,* commemorated here for heroism in the Hundred Year's War, wander nearby. Inside the *hôtel, Le Baiser* (The Kiss) *La Main de Dieu* (the Hand of God) and other famous small works display the talents of the master. Fans of horror may enjoy the room of pain on the second floor which displays *La Douleur* (Suffering), *Le Cri* (the Shriek), *La Pleureuse* (the Weeper) and *Le Desespoir* (Despair). Devotées of Camille Claudel will be happy to find her works, including the famed *L'Abandon,* exhibited with the sculptures for which she modeled. Lesser-known Rodin sculptures fill the rose garden. Although the Métro is cheaper, buses connect this Rodin museum with the smaller one in Meudon. (Museum open Tues.-Sun. 10am-5:15pm. Admission 20F, ages 18-25, over 60 and everyone on Sun. 8F.)

No building better exemplifies monumental architecture than the **Hôtel des Invalides,** 2, av. de Tourville, *7ème* (tel. 45 55 92 30; Mo. St-François Xavier or La Tour-Maubourg). Constructed by Louis XIV as a shelter for war veterans, this behemoth clutches Napoleon's remains in what may well be the most pretentious coffin ever created. (Open daily 10am-7pm. Admission 25F, students 13F.) The ticket also includes the enormous **Musée de l'Armée** (tel. 45 55 92 30, *poste* 33936), which bloats one wing of the Invalides. The museum's four floors seem to contain only two exhibits, possibly entitled "Variations on a Uniform" and "Variations on a Sword." (Open daily 10am-6pm; Oct.-March 10am-5pm.) Southwest of the Invalides along av. de la Motte Picquet is the **Ecole Militaire** (Mo. Ecole-Militaire), an intriguing example of 18th century entury military-mindedness that counts the Little Corporal himself among its alums. Its antithesis, **UNESCO House** (tel. 45 68 10 00; Mo. Cambronne), is across the street on pl. du Fontenoy. One of Paris's most famous modern buildings, it counts works by Miró, Picasso, Calder, and Giacometti among its treasures. (Open daily 9:30am-12:30pm and 2-6pm. Free.) You might enjoy the smokes at **Musée Seita,** 12, rue Surcouf, *7ème* (tel. 45 56 61 50; Mo. Invalides), at rue de l'Université. The beautifully hung exhibit on the history of tobacco displays Native American ceremonial pipes, Middle Eastern hookahs, and more. Temporary exhibits usually have nothing whatsoever to do with the weed. (Open Mon.-Sat. 11am-6pm. Free.)

Upon completion of his impressive iron monument, Gustave Eiffel proudly declared in 1889 that "France will be the only country in the world with a 300m flagpole." Today, the **Tour Eiffel** (tel. 45 50 34 56; Mo. Bir Hakeim) continues to symbolize Paris to much of the world. Although avant-garde artists and writers rallied around this symbol of modernity, most Parisians loathed the darn thing. Slated to meet the wrecking ball in 1909, the tower was spared only after the French army discovered that it would make an excellent communications station. Loving centennial renovations have made the tower look sparkling-new, the result being an even greater onslaught of tourism. You can climb the staircase only as far as the second level; an elevator hauls visitors to the third. Don't miss the free *Cinemax* documentary about the tower's history. (Open daily 9:30am-midnight. Shows 9:30am-11pm. Admission 1st level by foot 8F, by elevator 16F; 2nd level by foot 8F, by elevator 30F; 3rd level from 2nd level (if you've walked the 1st 2 flights) 17F, from ground 47F.) The **Champ de Mars** lies in the tower's shadow, forever doomed to serve as its doormat. This 18th-century parade ground now hosts puppet shows Wednesday, Saturday, and Sunday at 4:15pm.

As Victor Hugo wrote in *Les Misérables,* "Paris has beneath it another Paris, a Paris of sewers, which has its streets, squares, lanes, arteries, and circulation, which is mud, with the human form at least." Over 2100km of **Les Egouts de Paris** are accessible at pl. de la Résistance, 7*ème* (tel. 47 05 10 29; Mo. Alma-Marceau). The new museum details the fascinating history of these subterranean avenues traveled by Hugo's Jean Valjean and many a lower life form. *Egotiers* (sewer workers) guide you along through the exhibit and are delighted to answer any questions. It's not as gross as it sounds, but it does smell. (Open Sat.-Wed.. 11am-4pm. Admission 20F, 18-25 years 10F.)

Montparnasse

At the turn of the century, artists, writers, and sundry hangers-on disillusioned with Montmartre decamped to Montparnasse. Picasso, Gauguin, Whistler, and others set up *ateliers* here, and an equally august set of writers held forth in the local cafés. Although the memory of Henry Miller picking fleas off himself and Mona in the Closerie des Lilas has receded along with Mitterand's hairline, **boulevard Montparnasse** remains devoted to people-watching. Around this chic thoroughfare, the meeting place of the 6th, 14th, and 15th *arrondissements* has beome one of the capital's most modern business quarters. The 58-story **Tour Montparnasse** (tel. 45 38 52 56; Mo. Montparnasse-Bienvenue) breaks the city's polished surface, providing a view from the 56th-story observatory that is as spectacular as it is expensive. The open-air terrace on the 58th is the highest in Paris. (Open daily 9:30am-11pm; in off-season 10am-10pm. Admission to observatory 26.50F, students 18F. Admission to terrace 33.50F, students 25F.)

Fifty-eight stories and six feet below, Baudelaire, Guy de Maupassant, Saint-Saëns, Charles Garnier, Henri Poincaré, Jean-Paul Sartre, Simone de Beauvoir, Samuel Beckett, Alfred Dreyfus, and others slumber in the **Cimetière Montparnasse,** bd. Edgar Quinet, 14*ème* (tel. 43 20 68 52; Mo. Edgar-Quinet or Raspail). Ask for an *Index des Célébrités* at the main entrance. (Open Mon.-Fri. 7:30am-6pm, Sat. 8:30am-6pm, Sun. 9am-6pm. Free.) Five to six million lesser Parisians are jumbled together in **Les Catacombes,** 1, pl. Denfert-Rochereau, 14*ème* (tel. 43 22 47 63; Mo. Denfert-Rochereau), an 18th-century mass grave built after the smells emanating from cemeteries around Paris became unbearable. During World War II the Resistance set up its headquarters among the old bones. (Open Tues.-Fri. 2-4pm, Sat.-Sun. 9-11am and 2-4pm. Admission 15F, students 10F. Flashlight recommended.)

The **Musée de la Poste,** 34, bd. Vaugirard, 15*ème* (tel. 43 20 15 30; Mo. Montparnasse-Bienvenue), leaves its stamp on exhibits of postal history, the modern post, and a complete collection of French stamps. Start on the fifth floor with the Middle Ages and descend toward the present of airmail and Oedipa Maas. (Open Mon.-Sat. 10am-4:45pm. Admission 12F, ages 18-25 7F.) Farther south and almost undiscovered by tourists, **Parc Montsouris,** 14*ème* (Mo. Cité-Universitaire), contributes an attractive, peaceful, hilly landscape to the neighborhood of the Cité Universitaire across the street. The old and young gather to feed the ducks, walk their dogs, and blow their tuneless post horns.

Arènes de Lutèce and Jardin des Plantes

The spirit of the Latin Quarter spills eastward into this neighborhood of bookstores and inexpensive restaurants. In a small park just south of the Faculté des

Sciences, the **Arènes de Lutèce** is a restored Roman arena that still bears the original Roman appellation for Paris. The **Jardin des Plantes,** main entrance at 57, rue Cuvier, 5ème (tel. 40 79 30 00; Mo. Jussieu), contains a park, the National Museum of Natural History, botanical gardens, and a small zoo. Here, post-Impressionist Henri Rousseau found inspiration for his jungle fantasies. The **museum** displays a large collection of gems, minerals, and seashells. Next door, the **zoology museum** presents changing exhibits on the history of science and medicine. (Both open Wed.-Mon. 10am-5pm. Admission 25F, students 15F. At the **zoo** don't miss the vivarium, which houses the axolotls, aquatic creatures which bear an uncanny resemblance to Julio Cortazar and other human beings. (Zoo open daily 9am-6pm, Oct.-June 9am-5pm. Park open daily 7:30am-7pm.)

Outside the botanical gardens on quai St-Bernard lies the sculpture-filled **Jardin Tino Rossi.** The new **Institut du Monde Arabe** (Mo. Sully-Morland), also at quai St-Bernard, ia an architectural wonder featuring rotating exhibits. (Open Tues.-Sun. 1-8pm.) The **Mosquée,** 39, rue Geoffroy-St-Hilaire, 5ème (tel. 45 35 97 33; Mo. Monge), is Paris's Muslim mosque. The Alhambra in Granada, Spain partially inspired this impressive Hispano-Moorish edifice with carved wooden ceilings, mosaics, and hidden gardens. Enjoy a *hamam* (Turkish bath) for 60F. (Men on Fri. 11am-8pm and Sun. 10am-1pm; women Mon. noon-7pm, Wed. 11am-7pm, Thurs. 11am-9pm, Sat. 10am-7pm. Mosque open for guided tours Sat.-Thurs. 10am-noon and 2-6pm. Admission 10F, students 6F.) The **Manufacture Nationale des Gobelins,** 42, av. des Gobelins, 13ème (tel. 48 87 24 14; Mo. Gobelins), produces tapestries using methods which have not changed since Louis XIV's time. Accountable only to the President of the Republic, the *manufacture* still functions as a village isolated from its urban surroundings. Apprentices learn the art of transcribing paintings onto tapestry, a process which may take several artists over five years. A laboratory measures dyes to the one-thousandth of a gram so that they resist age for 100 years. Infrequent tours are well worth the trip. (Open for tours Tues.-Thurs. 2 and 3pm. Admission 23F, ages 18-25 12F.)

The Periphery

Montmartre

Mont des Martyrs, or Montmartre, takes its name from the three saints beheaded here in 272: Rusticus, Eleutherius, and St-Denis (Paris's first bishop). The last promptly picked up his head, washed it off in a nearby fountain, and walked off. According to legend, he ultimately expired 7km away on the spot where Basilique St-Denis stands today. For centuries a village of monks, vintners, and stonecutters, the Butte de Montmartre became a part of Paris proper as the city expanded in the 19th century. The Paris Commune first assembled here on January 28, 1871. The *communards* gathered 170 cannons on the hill to hold off both the Prussian invaders and the armies of the conservative French National Assembly, which was trying to punish the rebellious city from its refuge in Versailles. The French army seized the cannons on March 18 but was unable to move them, as the *communards* captured and killed its generals, held elections, and on March 28 set up the Commune at the Hôtel de Ville. This radical government lasted until May 23, when the *communards* lost a battle among the graves in Père-Lachaise cemetery in eastern Paris. Although the Impressionists made their debut in Montmartre, giving it a reputation as distinguished as the Latin Quarter's, Montmartre today is anything but a refuge for radical and Bohemian Paris. Most of the painters who sell their work here cater slavishly to tourists. Still, the views and famous cabarets are worth an afternoon.

The celebrated hill rears up in the 18th *arrondissement,* just north of Métro stations Blanche, Abbesses, and Anvers. (Mo. Abbesses is the safest, especially at night.) A funicular runs from the end of rue Steinkerque (Mo. Anvers) to the base of Sacré-Coeur (fare one Métro ticket), the stairs offer a great view of the receding metropolis below. At the summit, Montmartre's **tourist office,** 21, pl. du Tertre,

18ème (tel. 42 62 21 21), distributes free annotated maps and gives guided tours of the area three times daily. (English and French. 50F, ages 6-14 30F. Open daily 10am-10pm; Oct.-March daily 10am-7pm.)

Place du Tertre, west of Sacré-Coeur, is full of overpriced cafés, tourists, tourists, spontaneous musicians, tourists, on-the-spot portrait artists, and tourists. Don't have your portrait drawn unless you're willing to fork over more than a few francs. The **Musée du Vieux Montmartre,** 12, rue Cortot, 18ème (tel. 46 06 61 11; Mo. Lamarck-Caulaincourt), is located on a side street behind Tertre in the old home of Rose of Rosimond, the actor who replaced Molière at the head of his troupe after the playwright's death. The museum overdoes its idolatry but does contain some fascinating photographs the butte in its heyday, as well as the original sign of the old (and now revived) folk club **Au Lapin Agile.** (Open Tues.-Sat. 2:30-5:30pm and Sun. 11am-5:30pm. Admission 20F, students 10F.)

Basilique du Sacré-Coeur, 35, rue du Cheval de la Barre, 18ème (tel. 42 51 17 02; Mo. Château Rouge), the most visible landmark of the Montmartre area, is an impressive Romanesque-Byzantine pastiche constricted after the Franco-Prussian War of 1870-71. Climb the 112m bell tower for yet another view of Paris far below. (Church and dome open daily 9am-6pm. Dome 15F, students 8F. Crypt 15F, students 8F.) **Cimetière Montmartre,** 20, av. Rachel, 18ème (tel. 43 87 64 24; Mo. pl. Clichy), on the north side of the butte, is the final resting place of Dumas *fils,* Stendhal, Berlioz, Zola, Offenbach, and Nijinsky. (Open Mon.-Fri. 8am-5:30pm, Sat. 8:30am-5:30pm, Sun. 9am-5:30pm.)

Throughout the past century, the picturesque bohemian lifestyle of **Pigalle** attracted and inspired artists and writers such as Toulouse-Lautrec, Nerval, and Heine. When the artistic navel moved to Montparnasse, however, the area's character changed radically. Today, the famous red light district along bd. Clichy is overrun with strange men who murmur "have good peep here" to random passersby. Fortunately, the sheer number of tourists that constantly stroll between here and Sacré-Cœur makes the area less than lethal during the tourist season. At the western end of bd. de Clichy, just past the red light district, stands the **Moulin Rouge** of Toulouse-Lautrec and *Can-Can* fame (see Cabarets in Entertainment).Aficionados of 19th-century symbolist painting will enjoy the **Atelier of Gustave Moreau,** 14, rue de la Rochefoucauld, 9ème (tel. 48 74 38 50; Mo. Trinité), off rue Pigalle. Pay a visit to the studio of the man who taught Matisse, Roualt, and many other wild beasts, er, *fauves.* (Open Wed.-Mon. 10am-12:30pm and 2-5pm. Admission 15F, ages under 25 and over 60 and Sun. 8F.)

Northeastern and Eastern Paris

With no famous towers or churches to record on film, the 10th, 12th, 19th, and 20th *arrondissements* draw relatively few tourists.Attractions here cater to a native crowd hiding out from the activity of the *centre ville.* Some of these neighborhoods are inhabited by the *économiquement faibles*—a French euphemism translated as "financially weak" and equivalent to American "low-income groups." **Belleville,** in the 20ème, has become one of Paris' Chinatowns, though gentrification threatens to squeeze it out.

One of the capital's best non-Western museums, the **Musée d'Arts Africains et Océaniens,** 293, av. Daumesnil, 12ème (tel. 43 43 14 54; Mo. Porte Dorée) houses a terrific collection of several millenia of African and Pacific art. Exhibits include native masks, costumes, jewelry, pottery, sculpture, and armor from prehistoric times to the present. Don't skip the beautiful aquarium downstairs. (Open Mon. and Wed.-Fri. 10am-noon and 1:30-5:30pm, Sat.-Sun. aquarium 9:45am-6pm, museum 12:30-6pm.)

The **Parc des Buttes-Chaumont,** 19ème (Mo. Buttes-Chaumont or Botzaris), combines scenery and seclusion, with little gullies skipping merrily down the hill and high cliffs overlooking the lake. Eighteenth-century Paris was built on seven hills like this one, but Baron Haussmann had five of them leveled; Montmartre and Parc des Buttes-Chaumont occupy the city's only remaining high ground. If you walk along the upper periphery, you'll see old men playing *pétanque* on your left and a great view of Paris and the park on your right. (Open April-Sept. 7am-11pm, Oct.-March 7am-9pm.)

North of the Buttes-Chaumont, sliced by the canals St-Denis and de l'Ourcq, **Parc de la Villette** (tel. 42 78 70 00, Mo. Porte de la Villette) covers a 150-acre expanse and is still expanding. Product of architectural collaboration and presidential charter, the park's design became Philippe Starck's responsibility in 1985 after an international competition. Four major sights are worth the trip. Once a cattle slaughterhouse, **La Grande Halle** (tel. 42 40 27 28) is a huge, converted 19th-century iron-and-glass construction now used for concerts, art exhibits, and boxing matches. (Open Wed.-Mon. 10am-5:50pm.) Behind the hall sits **La Géode** (tel. 46 42 13 13), a state-of-the-art cinema where documentaries with spectacular special effects are projected on a hemispherical screen and accompanied by face-slapping sound. (Admission 40F, students 30F. See *Pariscope* for more info.) Although the **Cité des Sciences et de l'Industrie** (tel. 40 05 70 00 or 40 05 72 72) doesn't perform any incredible demonstrations like the Palais de la Découverte, its sheer size and quantity of displays make it the best science museum in the country. Most of the well-presented exhibits are explained in several languages. (Open Tues.-Fri. 10am-6pm, Sat.-Sun. noon-8pm. Admission 35F, students 25F. Planetarium 15F, students 12F. Géode and Cité together 60F, students 50F.) You may also want to check out *Argonaute,* a beached submarine-turned-museum opened in December 1990.

The **Cité de la Musique** (tel. 42 40 27 28) includes a huge concert hall, a conservatory, and the **Musée de la Musique**, which which exhibits four Stradivarius violins, a harpsichord made for Marie de Medicis, and other western musical instruments played throughout the past eight centuries. Besides its most important collections, including four Stradivarius violins and a harpsichord made for Marie de Medici, the museum is only able to exhibit a small fraction of the 4000 instruments in its inventory. (Museum open Wed.-Sat. 2-6pm. Call for admission prices. Free recitals.)

Cimetière Père-Lachaise, main entrance at 16, rue Repos, 20*ème* (tel. 43 70 70 33; Mo. Père-Lachaise), is the grandfather of Paris's cemeteries and one of the city's most moving memorials to its rich past. The crowded cemetery is the final resting place of Balzac, Colette, Danton, Delacroix, Haussmann, Molière, Piaf, Proust, and Seurat. Foreigners buried here include Chopin, Oscar Wilde, and Gertrude Stein. The most frequently visited grave in the cemetery is, appallingly enough, that of James Douglas Morrison. Enter through the main door and follow the graffiti arrows labeled "Jim" to his grave in the sixth division. The last members of the 1871 Paris Commune were killed in the northeast corner of Père Lachaise, against the **Mur des Fédérés,** and are buried beneath it. The guards distribute useful maps marked with the famous graves (10F). (Open 7:30am-6pm; Nov.-March 8am-5pm.)

Although less famous and less posh than the Bois de Boulogne, the **Bois de Vincennes,** 12*ème* (Mo. Porte Dorée or Château-de-Vincennes), is more interesting in many ways. In the **Vincennes Zoo** (tel. 43 43 84 95; Mo. Porte Dorée), considered the best in France, uncaged animals wander in relatively natural surroundings. In the center, wild goats make their homes on a 72-meter artificial rock. (Open daily 9am-6pm. Admission 30F, students 15F.) Rows of sunbathers bake along the shores of peaceful **Lac Daumesnil** in the middle of the park. A magnificent if seldom visited monument, the **Château de Vincennes** (Mo. Château de Vincennes) is known as "The Versailles of the Middle Ages." Though the Louvre Palace was their principal home, every French monarch from Charles V to Henri IV whiled away at least part of their time at Vincennes. Frequent tours of the 13th-century château and the royal chapel are only in French, but the guide has the keys. Even if you can't understand, it's worth following along to revel in the medieval architecture. (Open 9:30am-7pm; Oct.-April 10am-5pm. Tours 23F, students and seniors 12F.) To reach the horticultural displays of the **Parc Floral de Paris,** esplanade du Château (tel. 43 43 92 95), walk from the château down rue de la Pyramide. Children—but no dogs—are allowed. (Open daily 9:30am-8pm. Admission 8F.)

Banlieue (Suburbs)

One of the most important historical monuments in France lies in **St-Denis** (Mo. St-Denis Basilique), 10km north of Paris. Built on the spot where St-Denis had asked to be buried, the **Basilique St-Denis** (tel. 48 09 83 54) now houses the remains of nearly every French monarch. Remnants of the original 8th-century church as well as Gallo-Roman tombs have been uncovered in the crypt. St-Denis slumberes here, surrounded by the mausoleums of French kings, queens, and their children. The remains of the ill-fated Bourbons, though placed here initially, were thrown into an anonymous pit during the Revolution and are now kept (but are they the right bones?) in an ossuary at one end of the chapel. Recorded tours, included with the entrance fee, offer excellent histories and descriptions of the funerary sculpture. Guided tours are given at 10:30am and 3pm. (Open Mon.-Sat. 10am-6:30pm, Sun. noon-6:30pm. Admission 23F, students and seniors 12F. Sun. organ concerts 11:15am-noon.)

St-Germain-en-Laye (RER: St-Germain-en-Laye) might have been known merely as the birthplace of Claude Debussy were it not for the magnificent 11th-century castle that served as the birthplace of Louis XIV, who returned here while Versailles was being built. The château now houses the outstanding **Musée des Antiquités Nationales** (tel. 34 51 53 65), which displays French artifacts from 1 million BC. Don't miss the *Dame de Brassempouy,* a fairly ornate ivory bust that has remained perfectly preserved since 22,000 BC (Open Wed.-Mon. 9:45am-noon and 1:30-5:15pm. Admission 15F, students and Sun. 8F.) Also in St-Germain-en-Laye is the **Musée Départemental du Prieuré,** 2bis, rue Maurice-Denis (tel. 39 73 77 87; RER: St-Germain-en-Laye), the former home of symbolist painter Maurice Denis and now a museum displaying his mediocre work. (Open Wed.-Fri. 10am-5:30pm, Sat.-Sun. 10am-6:30pm. Admission 20F, ages under 25 and over 60 10F.)

The peaceful suburb of **Sceaux** (RER: Sceaux), 10km south of Paris, is the site of the estate of Colbert (Louis XIV's finance minister) and includes the Château Perrault, built for him in the mid-1600s. Although part of the château was destroyed in 1798, the park remains in all of its splendor. The more recent **Château de Sceaux** (RER: Bourg-la-Reine) houses the **Musée de l'Ile de France** (tel. 46 61 06 71), dedicated to the *haute culture* and *traditions folkloriques* of the region surrounding Paris. (Open Mon. and Fri. 2-6pm, Wed.-Thurs. 10am-noon and 2-6pm, Sat.-Sun. 10am-noon and 2-7pm; in off-season until 5pm. Park open daily 6:45am-9:30pm. Admission 8F, students and seniors 4.50F.)

In addition to their more permanent homes at Versailles and Fontainebleau, Napoleon and Josephine played house in the **Château de Malmaison,** 1, av. du Château, Rueil-Malmaison (tel. 47 49 20 07; RER: La Défense, bus 158A: Château or Malmaison). Although Napoleon divorced his first wife, a native of Martinique, he never evicted her. The madatory guided tours leave on demand. (Open Wed.-Mon. 10:30am-12:30pm and 2-5:30pm. Last tours at noon and 5pm. Admission 23F, students and Sun. 10F.)

St-Cloud (bus #72 from Hôtel de Ville or #52 from Madeleine; Mo. Boulogne-Pont de St-Cloud; RER: Gare de St-Cloud), 3km southwest of Paris proper, was the scene of the assassination of Henri III in 1589 and the coup d'état of 18 Brumaire in 1799, among other notable occurrences. Nothing remains but Le Nôtre's magnificent park, which includes fountains, statues, arbors, and an English garden. The museum shows a short film on the château's history. (Park open daily 7am-10pm; March-April and Sept. 7am-9pm; Oct.-Feb. 7am-8pm. Museum open Wed., Sat., and Sun. 2-5:30pm. Free.)

François Mitterand's reputation as the "Builder President" is already established, but the French head of state continues to develop new projects. The most recent is the **Arche de la Défense** (RER: La Défense), a 35-story hollowed out cube. This bizarre office building is the latest addition to the Champs-Elysées axis, which includes the Louvre Pyramid, the Arc de Triomphe du Carrousel, pl. de la Concorde's obelisk, and the Arc de Triomphe. (Open daily 9am-6pm. Admission 30F, students and ages over 65 20F.)

Parc Astérix, (tel. 44 60 60 00) creates a fantasy world around France's premier comic hero. Near Plailly, 38km from Paris, the park boasts 1,343,563 visitors, 95,000 plants, 1000 employees, international and historically varied towns, the river Styx, a dolphin show, and the whole amusement park shebang. It's better than *Cats.* Trust us. Take the bus from Mo. Fort d'Aubervilliers between 9:30am and 2:30pm. (Open May-Oct. Sun.-Fri. 10am-6pm, Sat. 10am-10pm. Admission 120F, ages under 12 90F.

If the Musée Rodin in Paris made you an addict of the master's sculpture, visit the smaller **Musée Rodin,** 19, av. Auguste Rodin (tel. 45 34 13 09), in **Meudon** (RER: Meudon-Val Fleury). The house where Auguste Rodin spent the final years of his life now contains most of his minor works and the plaster models for *Le Penseur, Les Portes d'Enfer, Les Bourgeois de Calais,* and his other major bronze casts. In the garden, *Le Penseur* (the thinker) sits contemplatively above the tomb of Rodin and his wife, Rose Beuret.(Open April-Sept. Thurs.-Sun. 1:30-6:30pm. Admission 8F.) Convenient buses shuttle visitors here from the Rodin museum at 77, rue de Varenne (Sat.-Sun. only, 22F), but the Métro is cheaper.The gardens surrounding Meudon's **Observatoire** provide a magnificent hilltop view of Paris. The telescope and laboratories are closed to the public. (Open daily 9am-7:30pm; in off-season 9am-5pm.)

Entertainment

Paris after dark—you've heard a lot about it. The city does have plenty to offer, but don't sit back and expect the offerings to swirl around you. The hottest spots in town are usually hard to find and frequented by a moderately exclusive crowd that will not go out of the way to accommodate newcomers. Meeting a local may be your only chance to become absorbed in a highly private culture that loves to disappear behind unbreathably smoky air and stomp, clap, sing, or mellow out until dawn. Although nightclubs, jazz *caves,* theater, even opera don't have to cost an arm and a leg, you usually have to sacrifice a few digits to have fun indoors. The most popular places are expensive to, to say the least.

Fortunately, the most fulfilling Parisian entertainment—*la flânerie*—is free. Stroll along the banks of the Seine or weave your way through the Latin Quarter—and join the many Parisians doing so already. The area around Beaubourg (the Pompidou Center) fills with people watching fire-eaters, sword-swallowers, old men strumming the songs of Jacques Brel or Georges Brassens. Around pl. St-Germain, you'll find throngs of people parading by in the latest fashions and a few bars where one drink comes with unlimited jazz. If you want to see a movie or linger in the more fashionable cafés, wander around Montparnasse, the touristy Champs-Elysées, and the streets radiating from bd. St-Michel, bd. St-Germain, and bd. Sebastopol.

Several sections of Paris have developed an entertainment business of a different sort. The areas around Pigalle, Gare St-Lazare, the Bastille, and Beaubourg fill nightly with prostitutes and drug dealers. The Bois de Boulogne is especially dangerous after dark and should be avoided.

Plays and concerts are often quite expensive, but numerous discounts exist for most events. The student organization **COPAR,** whose ticket agency (Service des Activités Culturelles) is at 39, av. Georges Bernanos, 5*ème* (tel. 43 29 12 43; Mo. Port-Royal), sells discounted tickets and publishes a monthly list of plays for which these tickets may be obtained. The agency also sells reduced-priced concert tickets, even in summer. They accept any student ID. (Open Sept.-July Mon.-Tues. and Thurs.-Fri. 9am-4:30pm, Wed. 9am-noon and 1-4:30pm.) Another useful service is **Alpha FNAC: Spectacles** at 136, rue de Rennes, 6*ème* (tel. 45 44 39 12; Mo. Montparnasse-Bienvenue); 26, av. de Wagram, 8*ème* (tel. 47 66 52 50; Mo. Charles de Gaulle-Etoile); and Forum des Halles, 1-7, rue Pierre Lescot, 1*er* (tel. 42 61 81 18; Mo. Châtelet-Les Halles). They sell tickets for theater and a variety of concerts and festivals. Their Carte Alpha (50F for 1 year) or Carte FNAC (100F for 3 yrs., students 50F) entitles you to discounts of up to 40% on all classical music and theater tickets. (Open Tues.-Sat. 10am-7pm.) Many theaters sell discounted student tickets 45 minutes before showtime.

Cinema

In addition to the latest European and American big-budget features, Paris's cinemas screen classics from all countries, avant-garde and political films, and little-known or forgotten works. Ever since the New Wave crested, French interest in American movies has been nothing short of phenomenal; in fact, many American films play here that have not been shown in U.S. cinemas for years. First-run, big-studio films are screened in the sumptuous, expensive behemoths on the Champs-Elysées and bd. du Montparnasse. Artsier flicks play in the little theaters on the side streets of the Left Bank.

The three entertainment weeklies list showtimes and theaters. Film festivals are listed separately. The notation "V.O." (for *version originale*) after a non-French movie listing means that the film is being shown in its original language with French subtitles; "V.F." (for *version française*) means that it is dubbed. During the peak tourist season, French movies are sometimes shown with English subtitles. Almost all cinemas grant students a 10F discount off their regular 30-45F admission on weekdays and sometimes before 5pm. Many cinemas lower their prices by several francs on Mondays. France's three major film producers, *Gaumont, Pathé,* and *UGC* operate the majority of Paris's cinemas and screen the most popular current films. Most cinemas have disabled access. The movie houses listed below, some of the best known in Paris, show more unusual films.

Cinémathèque Française, at the Musée de Cinéma in the Palais de Chaillot, on av. Albert de Mun at av. Président Wilson, 16*ème* (tel. 47 04 24 24; Mo. Trocadéro). Answering machine lists all shows. A must for serious film buffs. This government-supported theater shows 3-5 films per day, many of them classics, near-classics, or soon-to-be classics. Foreign films almost always shown with French subtitles. Expect long lines. Open Tues.-Sun. Last show 9pm. Admission 20F.

Le Grand Rex, 1, bd. Poissonière, 2*ème* (tel. 42 36 83 93; Mo. Bonne-Nouvelle). This immense 2800-seat theater (the largest in Paris) shows primarily first-runs in a unique atmosphere. Last showing around 9:30pm. Admission 40F, students 30F.

La Géode, 26, av. Corentin-Coriou, 19*ème* (tel. 46 42 13 13; Mo. Corentin-Coriou), in La Villette. Mostly documentaries on this huge hemispherical screen. Shows hourly Tues.-Sun. 10am-9pm. Admission 45F, students 35F Mon.-Fri.

La Pagode, 57bis, rue de Babylone, 7*ème* (tel. 47 05 12 15; Mo. St-François-Xavier). No tremendous screen, and not even Dolby sound, but the intimate *salon de thé* and the orientalist architecture make this one of the city's most charming cinemas. Current films in the original language. Open daily 2pm-midnight. Admission 39F, students 29F.

Le Cosmos, 76, rue de Rennes, 6*ème* (tel. 45 44 28 80; Mo. St-Sulpice). Only Soviet films—Russian, Armenian, Georgian, etc.—in the original version. Open 2pm-midnight. Admission 35F, students 25F.

L'Entrepôt, 7-9, rue Francis-de-Pressensé, 14*ème* (tel. 45 43 41 63; Mo. Pernety). Organizes festivals which run for about a week. The Marx Brothers and Richard Gere are favorites. Two branches: the **Les Trois Luxembourg,** 67, rue Monsieur-le-Prince, 6*ème* (tel. 46 33 97 77; Mo. Odéon), with 3 cinemas; and **Le St-Germain-des-Prés,** pl. St-Germain-des-Prés, 6*ème* (tel. 42 22 87 23; Mo. St-Germain-des-Prés), with a big, beautiful theater. Both screen high-quality independent, classic, and foreign films. Open noon-midnight. Admission 32F, students 24F.

Action Ecoles, 23, rue des Ecoles, 5*ème* (tel. 43 25 72 07; Mo. Maubert); **Action Rive Gauche,** 5, rue des Ecoles, 5*ème* (tel. 43 29 44 40; Mo. Maubert), both on a large street parallel to bd. St-Germain; and **Action Christine,** 4, rue Christine, 6*ème* (tel. 43 29 11 30; Mo. Odéon), off rue Dauphine. Excellent festivals, from Marilyn Monroe to Marx Brothers. Showings 2-10pm. Admission 36F, students 26F.

Theater

Theater in Paris is not limited to Molière, Corneille, and Racine. The classics are there if you want them, but so are Broadway-type comedies and musicals, experimental plays, and political satires. The lucky may catch a *commedia dell' arte* in the courtyard of the Bibliothèque Nationale, harlequin costumes glittering in the twilight. Aside from the intimate *café-théâtres, cafés chansonniers,* and the Las Vegas-style *revues,* theater in Paris takes three main forms: the national theaters, such as the Comédie Française; the private theaters, which concentrate more on newer works; and the surburban theaters, which have taken hold of Paris's avant-garde scene. René González's **Maison de la Culture 39** in Bobigny, the **Théâtre Gérard-Philippe** in St-Denis (tel. 42 43 00 59), and **Théâtre de Boulogne-Billancourt** in Boulogne-Billancourt (tel. 46 03 60 44) have all made news. The most acclaimed, however, is the **Théâtre des Amandiers de Nanterre** in Nanterre (tel. 47 21 18 81), whose renowned director Patrice Chereau brought American avant-gardist Robert Wilson back to Paris in the fall of 1987 for collaboration on an event called *Hamlet Machine.* In 1988, *A Chorus Line* became international here, and *Cats* was added to the list in 1989. In 1990, the **Comédie Française** grabbed the most attention with a new production of Molière's *Médecin Volant* and *Le Médecin Malgré Lui,* which dazzled Parisians with acrobatics. The company's stark presentation of *No Exit* marked its first encounter with Sartre's work. Although intended for children, the famous *guignol* (traditional puppet show) may offer the most comprehensible text for Anglophones.

Theater tickets typically start at 130F, but there are usually a few 17-60F tickets. Some theaters sell rush tickets to student standby tickets a half an hour before the performance. Most theaters and close for August, if not longer. *Pariscope* has complete listings of current shows.

National Theaters

Supported by the French government, these are the stars of Parisian theater. With the benefit of giant auditoriums, superb acoustics, veteran actors, and, in some cases, several centuries of history, these companies stage superlative and extremely popular productions. Although modern pieces appear occasionally, expect Molière, Racine, Goethe, and Shakespeare (all in French). Don't worry about your shaky or non-existent French; excellent articulation and unmistakable gestures are usually sufficient.

La Comédie Française, 2, rue de Richelieu, 1*er* (tel. 40 15 00 15; Mo. Palais Royal). Founded by Molière, this is the grandfather of all French theaters. The repertory company hosts different directors. 892 seats. Open Sept. 15-July. Box office open daily 11am-6pm. Admission 40-180F.

Théâtre National de Chaillot, in the Palais de Chaillot, pl. du Trocadéro, 16*ème* (tel. 47 27 81 15; Mo. Trocadéro). Occasional musicals. 1000 seats. Box office open Mon.-Sat. 11am-7pm, Sun. 11am-5pm. Admission 130F, ages under 25 and over 60 90F. Student standby tickets 60F.

Théâtre National de la Colline, 15, rue Malte-Brun, 20*ème* (tel. 43 66 43 60; Mo. Gambetta). 760 seats. Also **Petit Théâtre,** 200 seats. Open Sept.-July. Box office open daily 11am-7pm. Admission 110F, ages under 25 and over 60 75F.

Théâtre de l'Odéon, 1, pl. Paul-Claudel, 6*ème* (tel. 43 25 70 32; Mo. Odéon). 1042 seats. Also **Petit Odéon,** 82 seats. Open Sept.-July. Box office open daily 11am-6:30pm. Admission 28-140F, Petit Odéon 40F.

Private Theaters

Although these theaters don't carry the reputations or historical baggage of the national theaters, some stage outstanding productions. Poor showings are much more common than in the national theaters; check the reviews before investing in a seat. All the following are well-respected.

Athénée-Louis Jouvet, sq. de l'Opéra, 9ème (tel. 47 42 67 27; Mo. Auber or Havre-Caumartin). 687 seats. A hard-to-find and unremarkable exterior, but a magnificent 18th-century interior and outstanding classical productions. Box office open Mon.-Sat. 11:30am-6pm. Admission 65-90F.

Mogador, 25, rue Mogador, 9ème (tel. 48 78 75 00; Mo. Trinité). At 1792 seats, one of the biggest theaters in Paris. Grandiose comedies and musicals on a huge stage. Box office open daily 11am-7pm. Admission 80-240F.

Théâtre de la Ville, 2, pl. Châtelet, 1er (tel. 42 74 22 77; Mo. Châtelet). 1000 seats. Excellent productions of all sorts. Box office open Tues.-Sat. 11am-8pm, Sun.-Mon. 11am-6pm. Admission 60-110F.

Théâtre Renaud-Barrault, 2bis, av. Franklin D. Roosevelt, 8ème (tel. 42 56 60 70; Mo. Franklin D. Roosevelt). 920 seats. Also **Petite Salle** (tel. 42 56 08 80), 150 seats. Large stage allows for some outlandish musicals and comedies. Open Sept.-July. Box office open Tues.-Sat. 11am-6pm, Sun. noon-5pm. Admission 120-200F, students and seniors 80F.

Théâtre de la Huchette, 23, rue de la Huchette, 5ème (tel. 43 26 38 99; Mo. St-Michel). 100 seats. Tiny theater whose productions of Ionesco's *La Cantatrice Chauve,* (*The Bald Soprano*) and *La Leçon* (*The Lesson*) are still popular—after 33 years. Shows Mon.-Sat. Box office open Mon.-Sat. 5-10pm. Admission 80F, students 60F; for both shows 120F, students 80F. No discounts Sat.

Jardin Shakespeare du Pré Catelan, at the end of the Bois de Boulogne (tel. 42 72 00 33). Take bus #244 from Porte Maillot. In Summertime Shakespeare in French. Tickets at the door or at FNAC. Shows start 8:45pm. Buses won't be running after the show. Admission 80-120F.

The Sweeney, 18, rue Laplace, 5ème (tel. 46 33 28 12; Mo. Maubert Mutualité). This Irish pub hosts the Gare St-Lazare players, a Chicago-based theater company under the direction of Bob Mayer. One-hour productions Sun. and Mon. at 8pm. Admission 25F. Call for more information.

Experimental Theater Wing Studio, 14, rue Letelier, 15ème (Mo. Emile-Zola). Four-year-old extension of New York University's theater program. Productions in English.

Café-Théâtres

Continuing the European showtime tradition, *café-théâtres* deliver caustic, often political, satire through skits and short plays. Puns and double-entendres abound; those who aren't up on French slang and politics might miss a lot of the fun. Despite the name, not all *café-théâtres* have tables with waiter service.

Au Bec Fin, 6, rue Thérèse, 1er (tel. 42 96 29 35; Mo. Palais Royal). Usually 2 different shows a night in this tiny place (60 seats). Dinner and 1 show 200F. Dinner and 2 shows 250F. Auditions sometimes open to the public (20F). Admission 70F, students (except Sat.) 55F. Two shows 115F.

Blancs Manteaux, 15, rue des Blancs-Manteaux, 4ème (tel. 48 87 15 84; Mo. Hôtel-de-Ville or Rambuteau). Three different shows per night. Reservations after 5pm. Open Mon.-Sat. Admission 65F, Mon. 45F, ages 25 and under Tues.-Thurs. 50F. Two shows (except Sat. and holidays) 100F.

Le Café d'Edgar, 58, bd. Edgar-Quinet, 14ème (tel. 42 79 97 97; Mo. Edgar-Quinet or Montparnasse). 80 seats. Three different shows per night. Reserve by phone 2:30-7:30pm. Admission 70F, students Sun.-Fri. 55F. Two shows 110F. Open Mon.-Wed. 11:30am-7:30pm, Sat. 11:30am-6:30pm.

Le Point Virgule; 7; rue Sainte-Croix-de-la-Bretonnerie; 4ème (tel. 42 78 67 03; Mo. Hôtel-de-Ville); often features gay subject matter; admission 75F; students 50F; disabled access; reserve 3pm-midnight.

Théâtre de l'Arlequin, 13, passage du Moulinet, 13ème (tel. 45 89 43 22; Mo. Tolbiac). Experimental and classic works—and much uncanned laughter. Shows Tues.-Sat. at 8:30pm. Admission 40-60F.

Chansonniers

In a *chansonnier,* the musical cousin of the *café-théâtre,* you'll discover the old-style Paris that seems (and is) all but extinct. The audience is invited to sing along to French folk songs. Again, the better your French, the better you'll follow the proceedings. Admission usually includes one drink.

Au Lapin Agile, 22, rue des Saules, 18ème (tel. 46 06 85 87; Mo. Lamarck-Coulaincourt). Picasso and his friends, among others, used to hang out here when Montmartre was Montmartre. Get here before 7pm for a good seat. Usually crowded with tourists. Shows at 9pm. Open Tues.-Sun. until 2am. Admission and 1st drink 90F, students 70F. Subsequent drinks 25F.

Caveau de la République, 1, bd. St-Martin, 3ème (tel. 42 78 44 45; Mo. République). A more Parisian crowd fills the 100 seats. Tickets sold 6 days in advance from 11am. Shows daily at 9pm. Admission 130F, students 75F.

Guignols

These renowned traditional puppet shows entertain adults as much as children. Almost all parks have *guignols*, but the **Guignol du Parc de Choisy,** 149, av. de Choisy, 13ème (tel. 43 66 72 39; Mo. Tolbiac or pl. d'Italie), is the classic with life-sized puppets. Unless it rains, there are shows on Wednesday, Saturday, and Sunday at 3:30pm (9F). Check *Pariscope* for other *guignols*.

Cabarets

Contrary to popular tourist belief, Parisian cabarets (officially called *revues*) are not exclusively for foreigners. The big names—the Moulin Rouge and the Folies Bergère—are frequented by as many cameras as people, but some of the less-publicized cabarets often lure Parisians. Crowds of well-hoofed locals and the odd emir unwind at the Crazy Horse after work. Though the complete dinner package is forbiddingly expensive, you might be able to watch from the bar while hanging on to your cash. You'll have to dull your feminist sensibilities to endure the shows at any of these establishments.

Le Bal du Moulin Rouge, pl. Blanche, 9ème (tel. 46 06 00 19; Mo. Blanche). This *revue* celebrated its 100th anniversary in 1989. Unfortunately, tourists have replaced Toulouse-Lautrec and his leering disciples, who carefully selected their models from the women on stage. Shows daily at 10pm. Reserve by phone 10am-7pm. Dinner and show 570F. Champagne and show 395F.

Crazy Horse Saloon, 12, av. George V, 8ème (tel. 47 23 32 32; Mo. Alma-Marceau). More Parisians, fewer tourists; more flesh, less glamour. Shows Sun.-Thurs. at 9pm and 11:35pm, Fri.-Sat. at 8pm, 10:30pm, and 12:50am. Reserve by phone 11am-6pm. Admission, including 2 drinks, 540F. Bar stool 190F.

Les Folies Bergère, 32, rue Richer, 9ème (tel. 42 46 77 11; Mo. Cadet or rue Montmartre). Reserve by phone 11am-6:30pm. Show Tues.-Sun. at 9pm. Turned 100 in 1987. Manet painted the waitress behind the bar. Table and dinner 570F; you can stand at the bar (1st drink included) for 92F.

Classical Music, Opera, and Dance

Classical music, opera, and dance are as alive in Paris as in Vienna, Berlin, or New York, but since the musicians aren't as well-known as in these cities, few visitors attend performances here. There are numerous free concerts at all levels, and even the most prestigious orchestras and ballet and opera companies are within the means of the budget traveler.

The internationally renowned **Orchestre de Paris,** playing in the Salle Pleyel, 252, rue du Faubourg St-Honoré, 8ème (tel. 45 63 07 40; Mo. Ternes), delivers first-class performances under the baton of music director Semyon Bychkov. Their season runs September through May; call or stop by for the concert calendar. (Admission 50-250F.) Guest orchestras and ballet companies normally perform in the acoustically superb 2300-seat **Théâtre Musical de Paris,** pl. du Châtelet, 1er (tel. 42 33 00 00; Mo. Châtelet). Tickets run 50-300F; call for a recorded schedule.

The first season (1990-91) at the new **Opéra,** pl. de la Bastille (tel. 43 43 96 96; Mo. Bastille) will include Puccini's *Manon Lescaut,* Saint-Saëns's *Samson and Delilah,* Mozart's *Magic Flute,* and Janacek's *Katia Kabanova.* Meanwhile the old

Opéra Garnier, pl. de l'Opéra (tel. 47 42 53 71; Mo. Opéra), will host only the Ballet de l'Opera de Paris. In July 1991, the American Ballet Company will take the stage. (Box office open Mon.-Sat. 11am-7pm. Tickets 30-300F.)

Free concerts are often given in churches and parks, especially when summer festivals scatter music throughout the city. Such concerts are *extremely* popular; get there early if you want a place to breathe. Check any of the three Alpha FNAC offices (see Entertainment introduction) and the entertainment weeklies for concert notices. The **American Church,** 65, quai d'Orsay, 7ème (tel. 47 05 07 89; Mo. Invalides or Alma-Marceau), sponsors free concerts (Oct.-June Sun. at 6pm). The **Eglise St-Merri** is also known for its free concerts; contact Accueil Musical St-Merri, 76, rue de la Verrerie, 3ème (tel. 42 76 93 93, Mo. Châtelet or Hôtel-de-Ville). Other churches, such as **Eglise St-Germain-des-Prés,** 3, pl. St-Germain-des-Prés, 6ème (Mo. St-Germain-des-Prés); **Eglise St-Eustache,** rue du Jour, 1er (Mo. Les Halles); and **Eglise St-Louis-en-l'Ile,** 19, rue St-Louis-en-l'Ile, 4ème (Mo. Pont-Marie), stage concerts that are either free or reasonably priced. For information about all church concerts, call 43 29 68 68. **Ste-Chapelle** hosts concerts a few times per week in summer (sometimes free on Sun.). Contact the box office at 4, bd. du Palais, 1er (tel. 43 40 55 17; Mo. Cité; open daily 1:30-5:30pm; admission 110F, students 65F). Weather permitting, Sunday concerts are held in the bandshell of the **Jardin Luxembourg** (tel. 42 37 20 00, *poste* 2023). For recorded information about free outdoor concerts, call 42 76 50 00. Infrequent concerts in the Musée d'Orsay are free with museum ticket.

Jazz

Some critics mourn that Paris is no longer the jazz center it once was. True, the big names find it more profitable to play the huge summer festivals in southern France and in Switzerland, and the small club scene has partly moved north to Copenhagen and Oslo. Paris, however, still has plenty of clubs worth visiting 'round midnight. Not only do many fine, lesser-known American musicians play here, but the variety of music—including African, Antillean, Brazilian—is fantastic. For the most complete listings, pick up a copy of the monthly *Jazz Magazine* or one of the three entertainment weeklies.

New Morning, 7-9, rue des Petites-Ecuries, 10ème (tel. 45 23 51 41; Mo. Château d'Eau). 500 seats in a former printing plant. All the greats have played here. Open Sept.-July from 9:30pm (times vary). Admission around 110F.

Le Petit Opportune, 15, rue des Lavandières-St-Opportune, 1er (tel. 42 36 01 36; Mo. Châtelet). This hopelessly small club (60 seats) is so popular that even if it had 500 seats, it would probably be just as crowded. 200 plaques in the entrance hall commemorate an internationally renowned artist who blew, strummed, or tickled the ivories here. Mostly modern jazz. First drink 100F, 50F thereafter. Jazz concerts daily 11pm-2am. Bar open until 7am. May be closed in July.

Le Petit Journal St-Michel, 71, bd. St-Michel, 5ème (tel. 43 26 28 59; Mo. Luxembourg). A crowded, intimate establishment. New Orleans bands and first-class performers play in this Parisian center of the Old Style. Music Sept.-July Mon.-Sat. 10pm-2:30am. Obligatory 1st drink 85F, 40F thereafter.

Les Bouchons, 19, rue des Halles, 1er (tel. 42 33 28 73; Mo. Les Halles). This chic tri-level club presents young jazz and rock talents. Expensive restaurant upstairs. Open daily noon-2am. *Le jazz* starts at 10:30pm. Drinks 80F.

Slow Club, 130, rue de Rivoli, 1er (tel. 42 33 84 30; Mo. Châtelet). Miles Davis' favorite Paris jazz club. Big bands, traditional jazz, and Dixieland in a setting that hasn't changed in years. Expect dancing and a crowd in their 30s. Open Tues.-Thurs. 9:30pm-2:30am, Fri. until 3:30am, Sat. until 4am. Cover 55F, weekends 65F. Women and students 5F less during the week. Drinks from 18F.

Caveau de la Huchette, 5, rue de la Huchette, 5ème (tel. 43 26 65 05; Mo. St-Michel). The one-time tribunal, prison, and execution rooms here were used by Danton, Marat, St-Juste, and Robespierre during the Revolution. Now a traditional jazz hotspot. Maxim Saury often whistles dixie. Moving and breathing difficult on weekends. Open Sun.-Thurs. 9:30pm-

2:30am, Fri. until 3am, Sat. until 4am. Must be over 18. Cover Sun.-Thurs. 50F, students 45F; Fri.-Sat. 60F. Drinks from 20F.

Les Trois Mailletz, 56, rue Galande, 5ème (tel. 43 54 00 79; Mo. Maubert Mutualité). Crazy fun until the *oui* hours of the morning. Rock and rollers get the crowd roaring to classic American tunes sung with French accents. Sing, shout and clap Wed.-Sun. 5pm-5am, but arrive late. Admission 60F. Drinks 40F.

Distrito, 49, rue Berger, 1er (tel. 40 26 91 00; Mo. Châtelet-Les Halles). Live rhythm and blues or rock shakes the downstairs *cave*. Bar upstairs open 7pm-2am. Music Tues.-Sat. 11pm-3am. Drinks from 30F.

Jazz Club Lionel Hampton of Le Méridien, 81, bd. Gouvion-St-Cyr, 17ème (tel. 46 68 34 34; Mo. Porte Maillot) in a luxury hotel. Classic jazz in a cozy atmosphere. Lots of foreign businesspeople. Sunday brunch at 11am with the big band of Claude Bolling (300F). Music daily from 11pm. Cover with 1st drink 95F. Cocktails 50F.

Théâtre Dunois, 28, rue Dunois, 13ème (tel. 45 84 72 00; Mo. Nationale). American avant-garde jazz. Extremely popular among French youth. Resembles a New York hideaway from the 70s. Jazz daily from 10:30pm. Cover 80F, 1st drink 50F, 15-30F thereafter.

Le Nouveau Furstemberg, 27, rue de Buci, 6ème (tel. 43 54 79 51; Mo. St-Germain-des-Prés). Large international audience. Come early. Open daily 6pm-3am with New Orleans jazz from 11pm. A/C and comfortable leather booths. Drinks 60-80F.

L'Escale, 15, rue Monsieur-le-Prince, 6ème (tel. 43 54 63 47; Mo. Odéon). Live Latin American music—upstairs in spirited sing-along, downstairs with a dance band. Open daily 11pm-dawn. No cover. Drinks 80F.

Jazz O' Brazil, 38, rue Mouffetard, 5ème (tel. 45 87 36 09; Mo. Monge). Excellent samba guitarists and new groups. Try the house drink *caitirissa* (lime juice and vodka). Open daily 9:30pm-2am. No cover. Drinks 50F.

Chica, 71, rue St-Martin, 4ème (tel. 48 87 73 57; Mo. Châtelet). Primarily an excellent Brazilian restaurant (first courses 45F, main dishes 90F). Devoted clients reserve tables downstairs in the *cave* for late night samba. Live bands tune up at midnight. *Vachement sympa*. Fruit drinks 35F. Open Tues.-Thurs. and Sun. 8pm-2am, Fri.-Sat. 8pm-4:30am.

Discos and Rock Clubs

The discos that are "in" (or even in business) change drastically from year to year, though a few have been popular since the 60s. *Paris Passion* is the best guide to the current scene (see Publications). Many Parisian clubs are officially private, which means they have the right to pick and choose their clientele. The management can judge prospective customers through peepholes in the handle-less front doors. Many of the smaller places in the Latin Quarter admit almost anyone who is sufficiently decked out. Parisians tend to dress up more than Americans for a night on the town; haggard backpackers might be wise to try a bar instead. To gain entry into one of the more exclusive places you must be accompanied by a regular. Many clubs reserve the dubious right to refuse entry to unaccompanied men. Women often get a discount or get in free, but don't go alone if you feel shy of French men. (Don't assume that you're safe if you're married.) Private clubs are expensive—admission and a drink can cost more than 75F. Some of the following clubs take pride in the fact that they play no disco music. The French dance any way they please and often alone. Weekdays are cheaper and less crowded so you'll have a better chance of moving then, but most of the action (by force of inevitable body contact) happens on weekends.

Les Bains, 7, rue de Bourg l'Abbée, 3ème (tel. 48 87 01 80; Mo. Les Halles or Réaumur-Sébastopol). Ultraselective and ultraexpensive, but worth it. Prince played a free concert here once upon a time. You may see famous artists, models, or literary theorists. If the swimming pool is open, the sweaty may rip off their clothes to jump in. A turn-of-the-century façade conceals the remains of municipal baths where Proust used to shower. Open Tues.-Sun. midnight-5am. First drink 120F, 2nd drink 100F.

La Locomotive, 90, bd. Clichy, 18ème (tel. 42 57 37 37; Mo. Blanche). Shaped like a huge locomotive, this was "the place" in summer 1990. Major physical contact: a pick-up scene.

Open Tues.-Sun. 11pm-5am. Tues.-Thurs. and Sun. first drink 60F, Fri.-Sat. 100F. Second drink 50F.

Zed Club, 2, rue des Anglais, 5*ème* (tel. 43 54 93 78; Mo. Maubert-Mutualité). Occasional live bands. Brazilian samba, bebop, 60s music, and jazz. Wednesday evening and Sun. afternoon rock only. Thursday rock and java. Open Sept.-July Wed.-Thurs. 10:30pm-4am, Fri.-Sat. 10:30pm-5am, Sun. '4-8pm. Cover Wed. and Sun. afternoons 50F. Obligatory 1st drink 90F, 40F thereafter.

Le Palace, 8, Faubourg Montmartre, 9*ème* (tel. 42 46 10 87; Mo. Montmartre). The funkiest disco in Paris. 2000 people a night on multi-level dance floors, shaken by an awesome sound system. American cocktails. Tea dances and rollerskating afternoons. Occassional rock concerts. Expensive restaurant. Open Tues.-Thurs. and Sun. 11pm-6am., Fri.-Sat. 11pm-10am. Cover Tues.-Thurs. 100F, Fri.-Sat. 130F, Sun. 130F for men, women free. Subsequent drinks 85F. The British owners also run **Le Central,** 102, av. des Champs-Elysées, Mo. George V. Same prices.

Scala de Paris, 188bis, rue de Rivoli, 1er (tel. 42 60 45 64 or 42 61 64 00; Mo. Palais-Royal). Three balconies, a dance floor, small *salons,* and video rooms. Open daily 10:30pm-dawn. Cover Sun.-Thurs. 80F; Fri. 80F, women 60F; Sat. 80F for all. Sat.-Sun. 2:30-7pm ages 13-18 only (no alcohol served), 40F.

Le Balajo, 9, rue de Lappe, 11*ème* (tel. 47 00 07 87; Mo. Bastille). Formerly the favorite stage of Edith Piaf, Le Balajo has retained her popularity, if not her style of music. Jammed with a youthful crowd faintly sniffing of danger. Open Thurs.-Mon. 10pm-dawn. Cover and first drink 100F.

Also popular in France are clubs specializing in Brazilian samba and African music:

Chez Félix, 23, rue Mouffetard, 5*ème* (tel. 47 07 68 78; Mo. Monge). Eat on the top level; sway to the excellent Brazilian beat in the *caves.* Open Sept.-July Tues.-Sat 8pm-5am. Music 11pm-dawn. Tues.-Thurs. obligatory first drink 80F, 50F thereafter; Fri.-Sat. 1st 2 drinks 100F each, 50F thereafter. Tues. and Thurs. no cover for women.

La Plantation, 45, rue Montpensier, 1er (tel. 42 97 46 17; Mo. Palais-Royal). A friendly place playing mostly African, Antillean, and salsa music. Dress well. M. Yaffa, the owner, is dedicated to improving race relations. Open Tues.-Sun. 11pm-dawn. Doesn't pick up until 2am. Cover and 1st drink 80F, 2nd drink 50F.

Le Tchatch au Tango, 13, rue au Maire, 3*ème* (Mo. Arts et Métiers). Crowd boogies to Antillean, African, Salsa, and Zouk music. Regulars all know each other. Wed. is lambada night. Prince spaghetti night has been moved to Thurs. Open Wed.-Sat. 11pm-4am. Cover Wed.-Thurs. 40F, Fri. 50F, Sat. 60F. Drinks 25-35F.

Gay and Lesbian Entertainment

Separation of the sexes is a general rule, and men have many more options than women. Despite the growing epidemic, AIDS education has not, unfortunately, caught on here; always be careful. Between the Métro stops Rambuteau and Hôtel-de-Ville, flourishing gay restaurants, cafés, and bars fill nightly. The gay discós scattered throughout Paris change more rapidly than *hétéro* spots, so check *Gay Pied* (summer guide 50F from kiosks) for up-to-date information and an English introduction. *Lesbia*'s ads are a good gauge of what's hot, or at least, what's open (22F from kiosks). In the summer of 1990, three lesbian discos were closed for renovation or for good, leaving lamentably slim pickins. *Paris Passion* also has some listings (22F from kiosks). Le Palace and La Locomotive (see Discos) hold men's tea dances on Sundays from 5-10pm.

Club 18, 18, rue du Beaujolais, 1er (tel. 42 97 52 13; Mo. Bourse). A happy, hopping place with a mirrored dance floor. Mostly men, but friendly to women as well. Open daily 11pm-dawn. Cover 40-50F.

The Broad, 3, rue de la Ferronnerie, 1er (tel. 42 33 93 08; Mo. Châtelet). Huge place with dancing. Downstairs *cave* with intimate corners. No women allowed. Cover 45F, free Mon.-Fri. Drinks 30-40F. Open Tues.-Sun. 11pm-dawn. Café next door has more space (open 5pm-4am).

La Champmeslé, 4, rue Chabanais, 2ème (tel. 42 96 85 20; Mo. Opéra). Intimate women's bar with comfortable couches, dim lighting, and varied music. Few men. Beer 15F, after 10pm 20F. Open Oct.-Aug. Mon.-Sat. 6pm-2am. Expansion in 1991 may permit opening at noon.

Le Boy, 6, rue Caumartin, 9ème (tel. 47 42 68 05; Mo. Havre-Caumartin). Young crowd parties to old and new dance music. Open 11pm-dawn. 50F cover includes one drink.

Le Bar Central, 33, rue Vieille du Temple, 4ème (tel. 42 78 11 42; Mo. Hôtel-de-Ville). Small and crowded, but friendly and in the middle of things. Mostly men. Drinks 15-30F. Open Mon.-Sun. 4pm-2am.

Le Swing, 42, rue Vieille du Temple, 4ème (tel. 42 72 16 94; Mo. Hôtel de Ville). Bar with 50s decor and happy hour 9-11pm. Cocktails 45F. Open Mon.-Sat. noon-2am, Sun. 2pm-2am.

Le New Monocle, 60, bd. Edgar Quinet, 14ème (tel. 43 20 81 12; Mo. Edgar Quinet). Renovated in 1990. *Sympa.* Cover 60F. Open 11pm-dawn.

Le Piano Zinc, 49, rue des Blancs Manteaux, 4ème (tel. 42 74 32 42; Mo. Rambuteau). Upstairs it's crowded, but the downstairs piano bar with Liza Minnelli/Judy Garland style decor is, well, also crowded. Mostly men. Open 6pm-2am. Drinks 12-50F; after 10pm 30-60F.

Le Petit Prince, 12, rue de Lanneau, 5ème (tel. 43 54 77 26; Mo. Maubert-Mutalité). A mixed crowd enjoys some superb food. Light and tasty *quenelles* (baked fish mousse) included in the 69F and 92F *menus.* Delicious white-chocolate mousse 15F. Make reservations. Open daily 7:30pm-12:30am.

Au Petit Cabanon, 7, rue Sainte-Appolline, 3ème (tel. 48 87 66 53; Mo. Strasbourg St-Denis). Classic French cuisine for women. 120F *menu.* Open daily noon-2pm and Thurs.-Sat. 8pm-midnight.

Other Entertainment

Every evening after sunset and until midnight (1am on Sat.), Paris lives up to its reputation as the City of Lights. The Arc de Triomphe (Mo. Etoile), Notre-Dame (Mo. St-Michel), the Tour Eiffel (Mo. Bir-Hakeim), pl. de la Concorde (Mo. Concorde), the Hôtel de Ville (Mo. Hôtel-de-Ville), and the Panthéon (Mo. Luxembourg) are illuminated and truly dazzling sights. In summer, the historic buildings of Le Marais (Mo. St-Paul) and some of the buildings and gardens of Montmartre (Mo. Abbesses) are lit up as well. The French have developed a new art form: take an impressive building, add a light show, superimpose a recorded message about the glorious history of the building, or the region, or the country, *et voilà:* **son et lumière.** It's as tacky as it sounds, but that's half the fun. Check the three entertainment weeklies for listings.

A ride on the **bateaux-mouches** (tel. 42 25 96 10) may seem like goofy fun until you actually get on the boat. The high embankments on both sides of the river obscure everything but the tops of the highest buildings. If that doesn't deter you, imagine one and a half hours of continuous commentary on what you see in five languages and dozens of tourists straining their necks to see beyond the next person. Convinced? (If not, boats leave on the ½ hr. 10am-11:30pm from the right bank pier near pont d'Alma. 30F, ages under 14 15F.) The **Canauxrama** (tel. 42 39 15 00) boat tours of Paris get much better reviews. The shortest (3 hr.) tour leaves at 9:15am from Bassin de la Villette, 9bis quai de la Loire, 19ème (Mo. Jaurès) and at 2:30pm from Port de l'Arsenal facing 50, quai de la Bastille, 12ème (Mo. Bastille). (Admission 70F, students 60F, children under 12 45F.) Day-long trips to the countryside leave the Bassin de la Villette at 8:30am Thursday through Tuesday. Reserve ahead (190F). The **Batobus** (tel. 47 05 50 00) makes frequent stops along both sides of the river from April to September. A spin on this ridiculous form of transportation costs 10F. (Day pass 50F.) Buy tickets on board.

Festivals and Other Seasonal Events

The French love of celebration is most evident in Paris, where the slightest provocation brings masses of people into the streets to drink, dance, and generally lose themselves in the spirit of the *fête* (festival) or *foire* (fair). Expect crowds in the hundreds of thousands. The gatherings in Washington on July 4, or in Times Square on New Year's Eve, pale in comparison to the assemblages of humanity on hand for Bastille Day fireworks, the coming of the New Year, or political demonstrations. The **tourist office,** 127, av. des Champs-Elysées, 8*ème,* (tel. 47 23 61 72; Mo. Etoile), has a booklet in English that lists all the celebrations that take place in Paris each month. The English information number (tel. 47 20 88 98) will give you the low-down each week on current festivals. *Pariscope* lists *fêtes populaires* for the coming week. You can also get a listing of festivals from the **French National Tourist Office** in New York at 610 Fifth Ave., New York, NY 10020 (tel. (212) 757-1125), or from any French Consulate.

March and April

> **Foire du Trône,** Neuilly Lawn of the Bois de Vincennes (Mo. Porte Dorée). A gigantic amuse-ment park with roller coasters, pony rides, fortune-tellers, funhouses, and enough caramel apples, cotton candy (*barbe à papa*), doughnuts, and waffles to keep the most gluttonous junk-food junkie happy for days. Jammed on warm weekends. End of March-May. Open 2pm-midnight.

May

> **Festival de Versailles** (tel. 30 21 20 20, *poste* 234). Ballet, operas, concerts, and theater. Prices vary radically from one event to another. Late May-late June.

> **Festival de Musique de St-Denis** (tel. 42 43 72 72). Music in the Basilique. Late May to late June.

> **Festival de Paris,** 38, rue des Blancs-Manteaux, 4*ème* (tel. 40 26 45 34). A harmonic conver-gence of some of the greatest orchestras and choruses. Mid-May to late June. Admission 50-500F.

> **Foire du Trône** continues.

June

> **Fête de la Musique.** June 21 is perhaps the most fun. Major concerts in all the big *places.* Latin Quarter fills with anyone who can blow a horn, carry a tune, or watch others do so. Dancing all night. Free and obvious to anyone who goes out.

> **Fête de Cinéma,** June 28. One movie ticket allows you to go from theater to theater until your head spins from *too many* movies.

> **Fête de la Moissons,** 24 June. In 1991, expect a repeat performance of 1990's first-ever wheat harvest on the Champs-Elysées.

> **Festival du Marais,** 68, rue François Minon, 4*ème* (tel. 45 23 18 25; Mo. St-Paul). Classical and jazz music, theater, and exhibits. Many of the events are outside, in courtyards, or in renovated Renaissance buildings in Le Marais. The classical concerts tend to be expensive, but other events are free. Early June-early July.

> **Festival Foire St-Germain** (tel. 43 29 12 78). Antique fair in pl. St-Sulpice, concerts in the Mairie du 6*ème,* sports events in the Jardin du Luxembourg. All events free. Two weeks in mid-June.

> **Musique en Sorbonne,** at the Sorbonne Grand Amphithéâtre, 47, rue des Ecoles, 5*ème* (tel. 42 62 71 71). Everything in classical music from chamber groups to grand operas. Late June to early July. Admission 60-140F.

> **Fêtes du Pont Neuf** (tel. 42 77 92 26; Mo. Pont-Neuf). The bridge is closed to traffic and opened for dancing, music, street artists, and minstrels. A weekend in late June.

> **Festival de la Butte Montmartre,** 14bis, rue Ste-Isaure, 18*ème* (tel. 42 62 46 22). Experimental drama, dance, and jazz performances. Master classes in jazz and acting. Mid-June to mid-July.

> **Foire du Trône, Festival de Musique de St-Denis, Festival de Paris,** and **Festival de Versailles** continue.

July

July 14 is Bastille Day. Big-time celebrations nationwide. *Vive la République* and pass the champagne. The day starts with the army parading down the Champs-Elysées and ends with fireworks at Montmartre, the Parc Montsouris, and the Palais de Chaillot. Traditional street dances are held on the eve of Bastille Day at the tip of the Ile St-Louis (the Communist Party always throws its gala there), the Hôtel de Ville, pl. de la Contrescarpe, and of course, pl. de la Bastille, where it all started. Dancing continues the next night. Unfortunately, the entire city also becomes a nightmarish war zone of leering men cunningly tossing firecrackers (sometimes ignited inside bottles) under the feet of unsuspecting bystanders (and into the Métro). Check the newspapers a few days before to see where the main *bals* will take place.

End of the Tour de France (a few days after Bastille Day). Thousands of spectators turn out along the Champs-Elysées to watch the finish of the month-long bicycle race, which attracts as much attention in France as the World Series does in the U.S. Get there early and bring something to stand on (and something to read as well).

Festival Estival, 20, rue Geoffroy-l'Asnier, 4*ème* (tel. 48 04 98 01). Opera, chamber music, and recitals in churches, palaces, and concert halls throughout the city. Early July to mid-Sept. Admission 25-40F.

Festival de l'Orangerie de Sceaux. In the Orangerie of the Château de Sceaux (tel. 46 60 07 79). A mixture of chamber music, popular music, and piano recitals. Performances late July-early Oct. Sat.-Sun. at 5:30pm. Admission 60-110F.

Versailles Display (tel. 39 50 71 81) Spectacular fountain effects every Sun. starting the 1st Sun. in July at 4pm. Runs through Aug.

Festival du Marais, Musique en Sorbonne, and **Festival de la Butte Montmartre** continue.

August

Festival Estival, Festival de Musique de Sceaux, and **Versailles Display** continue.

September

Festival d'Automne (tel. 42 96 12 27), in the Pompidou Center and other museums and churches. Drama, ballet, expositions, and chamber music concerts. Late Sept.-Dec.

Fête de l'Humanité, parc de la Courneuve (Mo. Porte de la Villette, then special buses). The annual fair of the French Communist Party—like nothing you've ever seen. A million people show up to hear debates, ride roller-coasters, and collect Marxist-Leninist leaflets. (*Humanité* is the newspaper of the French CP, which which is known—rather anachronistically—as the PC.) Communist parties from all over the world distribute literature and sell their native food and drink. Entertainers in recent years have included Charles Mingus, Marcel Marceau, the Bolshoi Ballet, and radical theater troupes. newspaper.) A cross between the Illinois state fair, the Republican Convention, and Woodstock; you don't have to be a Communist to enjoy it. Second or 3rd week of Sept.

Festival de l'Ile-de-France (tel. 47 39 28 26). Concerts in churches and monuments in the area. Late Sept.-late Dec.

Festival Estival, Festival de Sceaux and **Festival de Montmartre** continue.

October

Festival de Jazz de Paris, 5, rue Bellart, 15*ème* (tel. 47 83 33 58). There's so much jazz in Paris that this is hardly necessary, but it makes things official. Everybody on the European circuit (Nice, Antibes, Montreux, etc.) should be here. At the Théâtre Musical de Paris and the Théâtre de la Ville. Late Oct.-early Nov.

Fête des Vendanges à Montmartre, rue Saules, 18*ème* (Mo. Lamarck-Caulaincourt). The celebration of the harvest of the vineyards on Montmartre. Though not France's best-known wine-producing region, Montmartre still bottles enough wine to warrant setting aside a day for celebrating its accomplishment. The 1st Sat. in Oct.

Festival d'Art Sacré, 4, rue Jules Cousin, 4*ème* (tel. 42 77 92 26). Sacred music at churches around Paris (including Notre-Dame) by the Radio France philharmonic orchestra and the Choir of Cologne. Early Oct.-Dec.

Festival d'Automne and **Festival de Sceaux** continue.

November

Armistice Day (Nov. 11). Military parade from the Arc de Triomphe to the Hôtel des Invalides.

Festival Internationale de la Guitarre (tel. 45 23 18 25). Concerts in many Parisian churches. Mid-Nov. until mid-Dec.

Concours international de danse de Paris (tel. 45 22 28 74). Weeklong dance competition in mid-Nov.

Festival d'Automne, Festival d'Art Sacré, Festival de Jazz de Paris, and **Festival de l'Ile-de-France** continue.

December

Christmas Eve. At midnight, with the celebration of the Christmas Eve Mass, Notre-Dame becomes what it only claims to be the rest of the year: the cathedral of the city of Paris. Thousands of people fill the church. Many of the neighboring cafés stay open late for those who want to start celebrating Christmas early. Children's entertainment continues until the end of school vacation.

New Year's Eve. When the clock strikes midnight, the Latin Quarter erupts: strangers embrace, motorists find people dancing on their hoods, and for an hour bd. St-Michel becomes a pedestrian mall, much to the dismay of the *agents de police* who are still attempting to direct traffic. A similar scene occurs on the Champs-Elysées.

Festival d'Automne continues.

Shopping

Whether or not you can afford to buy anything, Paris offers incomparable window shopping and, if you can muster the courage to face the salespeople staring down their long noses, even browsing. On place de la Concorde, where the guillotine stood during the Terror, polished windows display gleaming silverware, crystal, and leather goods. The mouthwatering windows of Fauchon, just north at 2, pl. de la Madeleine, display tarts, *pâtés,* and meats which not even the finest silverware is fit to touch. On rue du Faubourg St-Honoré, which runs northwest through the 8*ème,* gawk at the ridiculously expensive scarves and Grace Kelly bags at Hermès (#24). For quality perfume, watches, pens, clothing, and beauty products at a 30-40% discount, try **Honoré 316,** rue St-Honoré, 1*er* (tel. 45 26 13 10; Mo. Tuileries). Clients are treated well. (Open Mon.-Sat. 9:45am-6:45pm.) Also ask the staff at **Raoul et Curly,** 47, av. de l'Opéra, 2*ème* (tel. 47 42 50 10; Mo. Opéra) about foreigners' discounts—at least 20% off. (Open Mon.-Sat. 9am-6:30pm.) Running northwest from the Rond Point des Champs-Elysées, avenue de Montaigne and its side streets are lined with the houses of Dior, Chanel, Valentino, St-Laurent, and other *couturiers.* The windows in place Vendôme and along rue de la Paix, which runs north to the Opéra, glitter with the designs of Cartier, Van Cleef & Arpels, and other jewelers. The stretch of rue de Rivoli between pl. de la Concorde and bd. Sébastopol has decent souvenir shops, a few English bookstores, and big antique emporia selling Louis XIV dining sets and other big antiques. More good browsing awaits under the glass roofs of turn-of-the-century Galeries Vivienne and Colbert, just north of the Palais Royal and Bibliothèque Nationale. You'll find trendier, more eclectic boutiques in the Marais, which stretches between the Pompidou center and pl. de la Bastille. In general, the stores on the Left Bank may be a bit less intimidating. Bookstores, art galleries, and antique shops line the streets between the Seine and bd. St-Germain. A number of specialized bookstores cluster around pl. St-Germain-des-Prés, at the end of rue Bonaparte. A phalanx of clothes boutiques (including Sonia Rykiel, Kenzo, and Claude Montana) march down rue Bonaparte, rue du Four, rue de Grenelle, and the other streets just south of bd. St-Germain. Look on St-Germain, but buy on rue St-André-des-Arts, around rue de Seine, and the upper part of bd. St-Michel.

Good deals can be found just about anywhere during the major *soldes* (sales) in January and August. For clues on where to track down bargains at any time of year, pick up a copy of *Paris Pas Cher* (90F) at a kiosk. (Some bookstores may stock *The Good Value Guide to Paris*, an English translation.) This handy guide lists stores by type of merchandise and rates them—the foot symbol represents the lowest prices. The logo "Paris Pas Cher" indicates that you'll get a discount if you buy the book.

In all stores, non-Europeans can receive a rebate of 13% or 23% on large purchases of perfume, precious jewelry, cameras, and other items. To get this rebate, you must spend 1200F or more in the same store within a period of six months. Each time you make a purchase, tell the cashier to mark your sales slip for a *détaxe*, and save the sales slips. When you have made your last purchase, take your sales slips to the export discount desk. At this time you can also choose how you want your money (e.g., paid to you directly in francs or sent to a U.S. bank). You'll receive an export sales docket, and a stamped envelope to be presented to the French customs officials at the airport and then mailed back to the place of purchase. (Make sure you leave all the articles you have purchased near the top of your suitcase since the customs official might ask to see them). A *détaxe* savings may also be allowed when purchasing bicycles or cars, but the paperwork can be annoying. If your dealer is familiar with foreigners, you can get 17% back on bicycles purchased in France and 33% back on cars. Upon returning to the U.S., you must pay customs if purchases amount to over US$400, but often this is less than the rebate returned by French customs.

The large department stores, many of them clustered on the *grands boulevards* around the Opéra and the Gare St-Lazare, 9*ème* (Mo. Opéra or Havre-Caumartin), have *détaxe* desks that help demystify this process. **Galeries Lafayette** and **Printemps,** the Macy's and Gimbel's of Paris, stand across from each other on bd. Haussmann, 8*ème* and 9*ème* (Mo. Chausée-d'Antin). The British **Marks and Spencer** is across the street. (Open 10am-7pm.) Along the Seine, the four buildings of **la Samaritaine** (named for the large pumphouse that once stood there and supplied the Louvre and Tuileries with water; Mo. Pont-Neuf) and **Bazar de l'Hôtel de Ville** (Mo. Hôtel-de-Ville) carry everything you think you want and many things you know you don't (open 9:30am-7pm).

TATI, 4-30, bd. Rochechouart, 18*ème* (tel. 42 55 13 09; Mo. Anvers), is the cheapest department store in Paris, as the flood of humans spilling in and out of its doors will attest. (Open Mon.-Sat. 10am-7pm.) Next door, you'll find the best prices on fabrics in the city. In the same neighborhood, on rue de la Goutte d'Or, is the **Algerian market,** which looks like Middle-Eastern *suqs* and hides a few bargains. If you're looking for a five-and-dime complete with a supermarket, go to any of the **Monoprix** or **Prisunics** that litter the city. For bargains on books and records, as well as audio and video equipment and concert tickets, visit one of many FNAC locations (see Entertainment). FNAC at pl. de la Bastille (Mo. Bastille) also shows music videos.

Finding English books should not be a problem. The most famous English bookseller is **Shakespeare and Co.,** 37, rue de la Bûcherie, 5*ème* (Mo. St-Michel), across the Seine from Notre-Dame. Run by George Whitman (alleged great-grandson of Walt), this cozy shop seeks to reproduce the atmosphere of Sylvia Beach's original establishment (at 8, rue Dupuytren and, later, at 12, rue de l'Odéon), which published Joyce's *Ulysses* and hosted Hemingway before perishing, along with expatriate Paris, in 1945. Unfortunately, Whitman's new and used selection is quirky, and battered paperbacks can cost as much as 50F. Still, the profits support impoverished writers who live and work in this literary cooperative. The first *Let's Go* writer stayed at Shakespeare's; so did Allen Ginsberg and Lawrence Ferlinghetti. (Tea on Sunday at 4pm. Open daily noon-midnight.) For a better selection, especially American literature, and a large display of guidebooks, seek out **Brentano's,** 37, av. de l'Opéra, 2*ème* (tel. 42 61 52 50; Mo. Opéra; open Mon.-Sat. 10am-7pm). The **Village Voice,** 6, rue Princesse, 6*ème* (tel. 46 33 36 47; Mo. Mabillon), is an excellent place with a small café in the back and poetry readings and lectures throughout the year.

It has a decent feminist literary collection. (Open Mon. 2-8pm; Tues.-Sat. 11am-8pm.) **W.H. Smith,** 248, rue de Rivoli, 1er, (tel. 42 60 37 97; Mo. Concorde), has the best selection of magazines and British literature and a pleasant but pricey English tea room upstairs. *Let's Go* goes for 150F here. (Open Mon.-Sat. 9:30am-7pm.) For guidebooks (including *Let's Go,* 130F), travel literature, and paperback Penguins, go to **Nouveau Quartier Latin,** 78, bd. St-Michel, 6ème (tel. 43 26 42 70; Mo. Luxembourg; open daily 10am-7pm), or to **Calignani,** 224, rue de Rivoli, 1er (tel. 42 60 76 07; Mo. Tuileries), which also sells British hardbacks. (Open 9:30am-6:30pm; July-Aug. Tues.-Sat. 9:30am-5pm, Mon. 1:30-5pm.) **Gibert Jeune,** 51, bd. St-Michel near the Seine (Mo. St. Michel) is *the* bookstore on bd. St-Michel. It is also a good bet for French classics. **Les Mots à la Bouche,** 6, rue Ste-Croix-de-la-Bretonnerie, 4ème (tel. 42 78 88 30; Mo. Hôtel-de-Ville), is a serene bookstore with French and English titles, magazines, postcards, and newsletters of interest to both gay men and lesbians. The friendly English-speaking owner can be a fountain of information. (Open Mon.-Sat. 11am-8pm; Aug. Tues.-Sat. 11am-1pm and 2-7pm.) **Librairie des Femmes,** 74, rue de Seine, 6ème (tel. 43 29 50 75; Mo. Odéon), is a large, peaceful place to browse through the collection of women's literature. Don't come here with radical expectations. (Open 10am-7pm.)

Markets

Although the days when the eagle-eyed could spot Rembrandt's smudged signature in the corner of a 5F painting are long gone, you may find some quirky piece of junk with your name written all over it languishing in one of Paris's outdoor markets. Be aware that in any of these markets, more thieves than merchants have their eyes on your wallet. The **Marché aux Puces de St-Ouen,** 17ème (Mo. Porte de Clignancourt; Sat.-Mon. 8am-8pm) is the largest flea market in Paris and one of the largest in Europe. The hundreds of stalls cluttered with antiques, junk, old and new clothes, records, and food hold bargains only for those who are willing to haggle. If you can't get there by 9am, arrive late in the day when vendors are anxious to unload their stock. The Marché Biron section displays silver services and other big-ticket family heirloom-type items. The market can be extremely dangerous; organized bands of pickpockets can become violent while the police look the other way. You may be better off skipping it and heading for the cheaper, junkier **Marché de Montreuil** (Mo. Porte de Montreuil; Sat.-Mon.). Get here early or all the quality merchandise will be gone. Quality items are equally few and far between at the **Porte de Vanves** (Mo. Porte de Vanves; Sat.-Sun. 9am-7pm). Finally, the **Marché d'Aligre,** pl. d'Aligre near the Bastille, 12ème (Mo. Ledru Rollin), is the cheapest but least interesting of the flea markets (Tues.-Sun. until noon). The **Marché du Temple,** Carreau du Temple, 3ème (Mo. Hôtel-de-Ville), is not a flea market but a beautiful building where new clothes are sold at wholesale prices. Overstock from the large store is sometimes sold *al fresco.* (Open Tues.-Sat. 9am-noon and 2-7pm, Sun. 9am-1pm.)

Place Louis Lepine, on the Ile de la Cité, 4ème (Mo. Cité), blooms with color as the **Marché aux Fleurs** takes over the small square (Mon.-Sat. 8am-7pm). On Sunday from 9am to 7pm, the colors literally come alive as the plants are replaced by hundreds of birds for the **Marché aux Oiseaux.** Be careful, they bite. Every day, on quai Megisserie and quai des Gesvres, 1er (Mo. Pont Neuf), ferrets, chipmunks, wombats, and various other imprisoned animals wait to be picked out from the crowd. Plants and gardening equipment are also sold here.

Stamp and postcard collectors congregate every Thursday, Saturday, Sunday, and holidays from 10am to nightfall at the **Marché aux Timbres,** on av. Gabriel at av. Marigny, 8ème (Mo. Champs-Elysées-Clemenceau). If you're looking for **old books, prints,** or **posters,** check out the *bouquinistes'* stalls which line the quais of the Seine from the Louvre to the Hôtel de Ville and, on the Left Bank, from quai de Conti to quai de Montebello. You might come across a treasure among overpriced maps and postcards. For some real bargains and lots of free entertainment, stop by Paris's largest auction house, **Hôtel Drouot** 9, rue Drouot, 9ème (tel. 42

46 17 11; Mo. Richelieu-Drouot), where everything from collectors' pieces to odd lots of toilet plungers goes on the block almost every day. (Open Sept.-July Mon.-Sat. 11am-6pm.)

Each neighborhood has its own **street market** that convenes every day except Sunday afternoon and Monday. (Hours vary slightly, so ask a shop owner.) Early in the morning, merchants set up their stands with an attention to detail that extends far beyond cellophane wrapping. In the livelier markets (on rue Mouffetard, 5ème (Mo. Censier-Daubenton) and rue de Lévis, 17ème (Mo. Villiers)), some merchants make a show of crooning their prices and begging you to come and buy. Most stands stay open until 6 or 7pm. Prices go down just before they close, especially on Sunday. In August, most stores close but post the address of the nearest open *marché*. A covered food market, **Marché St-Martin,** 33, rue du Château d'Eau, 10ème, is known for excellent quality. (Open Tues.-Sat. 8:30am-1pm and 3:30-7:30pm, Sun. 8:30am-1pm.)

Near Paris

In the 10th century, the Capet kings began their expansion of the French domain from the **Ile-de-France.** It was also in this area around Paris that those things that seem most quintessentially French—the language, Gothic architecture—were born. Their history has left a rich concentration of spectacular châteaux, monuments, museums, and cathedrals within easy reach of the capital by train, bus, or car. *Pariscope* and other weeklies list the museums of the Ile-de-France, as does the free booklet on museums by the Hôtel de Sully (see Le Marais in Sights above). Although the listings below include the most popular tourist sights around Paris, try taking the RER to a random stop to experience the lifestyle of the rest of France. Even when the sights are not spectacular, the escape from the city is worthwhile. Parisian suburbs are ideal for light shopping, as stores normally charge less than their counterparts downtown. In addition, you're likely to find the people more relaxed and warmer toward foreigners. During the daily afternoon lull, *boulangers* and *charcutiers* will want to discuss your experiences in France, and even when giving directions, people will be friendlier and not so hurried as Parisians. Keep in mind that nearly every establishment outside of Paris closes for lunch (usually noon-2pm); to place telephone calls out of Paris, you must dial 16.

Versailles

"Well! and is this the great front of Versailles? What a huge heap of littleness!" a rather ill-tempered Thomas Gray exclaimed in 1754 upon seeing the magnificent palace Louis XIV had built for himself. While the Sun King surely would have fumed at Gray's reaction, he did intend Versailles as a place where more than a thousand of the petty nobles whose power struggles had disgusted him in his youth would be heaped together under his watchful eye. In addition to keeping them away from the more decentralized political life of Paris, Louis destroyed the financial independence of the nobility by forcing them to pay crippling taxes to support his lavish expenditures. The ostentatious rooms and endless gardens constitute the climax of the *Ancien Régime*'s economic drain on its citizens.

The guided tour of the interior of the **Château** leads through those apartments and halls that have been restored. These include the **Galerie des Glaces** (Hall of Mirrors), where the Treaty of Versailles was signed in 1919, ending World War I; the **Petits Appartements,** private royal chambers; **La Chapelle,** the setting for the marriage of the 16-year-old prince (future King Louis XVI) and Marie Antoinette in 1770; and **Les Grands Appartements du Roi et de la Reine,** the bedroom where Marie Antoinette spent her last night in luxury before attempting to escape the rising tide of revolution. Tours leave Tuesday through Friday at 2pm for the Apartments of the Dauphin and Dauphine (the royal children) and at 3:30pm for the private rooms of the Queen and the Dauphine. If you take only one tour, make it of the king's bedchamber and the gorgeous **Royal Opera.** (Tours 9:45am-4pm every 20 min., 51F. Check for times of English tours). The first performance at the opera took place after Louis XVI's marriage to Marie Antoinette. The prices may be high, but a tour will greatly enhance your visit to the château. Pierre Lemoine's guide (30F, available in 6 languages) is a worthwhile investment.

The park still has many of its original *bosquets* (groves), first planted in the 17th century. Designed by Le Nôtre, the endless gardens are sprinkled with mythological figures. The tourist office has a list of the times and dates of particularly spectacular water shows involving the elaborate fountains. Generally, *les grandes eaux,* as these displays are called, take place on Sunday afternoons from May through September; call the tourist office to confirm. The **Apollo Fountain** and the **Neptune Fountain,** with 99 independent jets, are the two most lavish. (Free with admission, 16F if you don't go into the château.) Mansart built the **Grand Trianon,** pink-and-white marble wings joined by a colonnade, as the royal guesthouse for Louis XIV. When she wasn't frolicking in the **Petit Trianon,** a play palace built under Louis XV, Marie Antoinette amused herself by pretending to lead a pastoral life in **Le Hameau.** (Château open Tues.-Sun. 9am-7pm. Admission 27F, ages under 26 and Sun. 14F. Grand Trianon open Tues.-Sun. 9:45am-12:30pm and 2-5pm. Admission 15F, ages under 26 and Sun. 8F. Petit Trianon open Tues.-Fri. 2-5pm. Admission 10F and 5F. Last admission 4:30pm. Combination tickets to both Trianons 18F, ages under 26 and Sun. 9F, under 18 free. Gardens open sunrise-sundown.) For more information, call the **Musée National du Château de Versailles** at 30 84 74 00 or 30 84 76 18.

Versailles also puts on a series of summer **Fêtes de Nuit** at the Neptune fountain. Fireworks, fountains, and lights combine for a fantastic show that serves the same purpose as a *son et lumière,* but on a scale to match the château. Derived from the Grandes Fêtes given in the park by Louis XIV, the 90-minute shows run regardless of weather on eight Saturdays. Tickets (45-150F) go on sale one month before each festival at the Versailles tourist office and at some ticket agencies in Paris. Call the tourist office (tel. 39 50 36 22) for information and reservations. Although the palace will almost certainly be mobbed by tourists, the edge of the river is usually a relatively calm place to spread your picnic blanket.

You can reach Versailles by RER Line C5 to the Versailles Rive Gauche station (every 15 min., 35 min., 20.80F). If you already have a metro ticket, take RER to bd. Victor, get off, and buy a 6F ticket there for the rest of the trip. You must take the train labeled Vick; all others turn off before Versailles. Alternately, take the Métro to Pont de Sèvres and transfer to bus #171. You can also catch the train at Gare St-Lazare and arrive a half-hour later at Versailles Rive Droite, where a special bus runs to the château. For more information on tours of the old section of Versailles, the town, and private tours of individual sections of the palace (15-30F), call the **tourist office,** 7, rue des Réservoirs (tel. 39 50 36 22), a five-minute walk from the palace. (Open daily 9am-noon and 2-6:15pm; Oct.-April Mon.-Sat. 9am-noon and 2-6:15pm.)

Chartres

Unforgettable **Cathédrale de Chartres,** spared by bureaucratic inefficiency after being condemned during the Revolution, survives today as one of the most sublime creations of the Middle Ages—worshipped by Henry Adams in print, Rodin in study, and by thousands of visitors in mute admiration. In the Middle Ages pilgrims came to admire a small cloth relic that legend says Mary wore while giving birth to Jesus. Today, most come to admire the dark vault's intricate stained glass, the statuary, and the outer buttressing.

Larger and more imposing cathedrals exist, but few reward time spent as generously as Chartres does. A masterpiece of finely crafted details—architecture, sculpture, and glass—the cathedral is a statement of profound unity (in spite of the asymmetrical towers, the shorter surviving from an earlier structure), as well as an extraordinary fusion of Romanesque and Gothic elements. Most of the glass is from the 13th century and was preserved through both world wars by the town authorities, who dismantled more than 3000 square meters piece by piece and stored them until the end of hostilities. Films on stained-glass production, stained-glass history, and Chartres in the Middle Ages are shown free on request in the **Galerie du Vitrail,** 17, rue du Cloître Notre-Dame (tel. 37 36 10 03; open Feb.-Dec. Tues.-Sat. 10am-6pm, Sun. 10:30am-1pm and 2-6pm).

The structure stands on the site of a Romanesque cathedral that was destroyed in 1194 by a huge fire. All that survived was the holy relic, and clerics took advantage of the miracle to solicit funds for rebuilding on a scale befitting the Virgin, dedicating the cathedral to Mary. (Shroud displayed in the Treasury Mon.-Sat. 10am-noon and 3-6pm, Sun. 2-6pm; Oct.-Dec. Mon.-Sat. 10am-noon and 2-6:30pm, Sun. 2-5pm; Feb.-April Mon.-Sat. 10am-noon and 2:30-5pm, Sun. 2:30-5pm. Free. Cathedral open daily 7:30am-7:30pm; Oct.-March 7:30am-7pm.) The largest in France, Chartres's **crypt** is thought to be the site of a Druidic sanctuary. (Open daily at 11am, 2:15pm, 3:30pm, and 4:30pm; in July-Aug. also at 5:15pm. Admission 7F.) The north **Tour Jehan-de-Beauce** rewards its climbers with a great you-know-what. (Open April-Sept. 9:30-11:30am and 2-5:30pm, Sun. 2-5:30pm; Oct.-Dec. and Feb.-Mar. 10-11:30am and 2-4:30pm, Sun. 2-4:30pm. Admission 16F, students 9F.) **Organ recitals** are given July through October Sunday at 5pm (free); **Samedis Musicaux** are not always on Saturday; call the tourist office for a schedule (admission 50F, ages under 26 40F).

No cathedral in the world has a tour guide quite like Malcolm Miller, Chartres's master of ceremonies who, for the last 33 years, has brought the cathedral to life for English-speaking visitors. An international authority on Gothic architecture, Miller composes each lecture individually to explain the symbolic detail in different parts of the cathedral's windows and sculptures. (Tours April-Jan. Mon.-Sat. at noon and 2:45pm; converts can catch both in 1 day. Pay what you can at the end.)

Secular Chartres possesses quite a bit of its own elegance. Though the town lies on wheat-growing plains, its narrow, hilly streets climb and dip enough to afford moving glimpses of the cathedral. The **Centre International du Vitrail,** 5, rue du Cardinal Pie (tel. 37 21 65 72), hosts temporary exhibits on stained glass. (Open Tues.-Sun. 10am-12:30pm and 1:30-6pm. Admission 28F, students 20F.) Also notable are the ancient collegiate **Eglise St-André,** a stately Romanesque structure by the Eure, and **Eglise St-Pierre,** a delicate Gothic masterpiece from the 13th century. (Both open daily 9am-7pm; Oct.-June 10am-5pm.) The Renaissance **Eglise St-Aignan,** reveals yet a third style in its colorful, well-preserved interior. (Open 8am-7pm.) The best views of the cathedral are from the residential part of town across the three rivers. Climb up rue St-Pierre to return to the *ville haute,* and spend some time here in the ancient city of Chartres. Tapes in English may be rented from the tourist office (35F, deposit 100F and passport, 1 hr.). A 40-minute minitrain tour of the old town leaves every 50 minutes from pl. de la Cathédrale. (Runs 10am-6:30pm. Tickets 25F, children 13F.)

Chartres is accessible by hourly **trains** from Gare Montparnasse (1 hr., round-trip 108F). Although getting out of Paris is a nuisance, some people bicycle or hitching. The friendly **tourist office** (tel. 37 21 50 00), opposite the cathedral's main entrance, will find you accommodations for 8F, plus a 50F deposit. Get information on Samedis Musicaux here. (Open Mon.-Sat. 9:30am-12:30pm and 2-6:15pm, Sun. 9:30am-12:30pm and 1:45-6:45pm; Nov.-April Mon.-Sat. 9:30am-12:30pm and 2-6:15pm.) Consider taking a brief respite from Paris and staying the night. The pleasant **Auberge de Jeunesse (IYHF),** 23, av. Neigre (tel. 37 34 27 64), is 2km north of the station. Follow the signs past the cathedral and over the river by Eglise St-André. Clean and comfortable six-bed rooms run 51F per person. (IYHF card required. Open daily 8-10am and 6-11pm; Oct.-June 8-10am and 6-10:30pm. No lockout, but belongings are not watched during the day. Curfew 10:30pm in winter, 11:30pm in summer. Breakfast included. Sheets 14F.) Two lefts from the station lead to the attractive **Hôtel St-Jean,** 6, rue de Faubourg St-Jean (tel. 37 21 35 69), where each clean, spacious room has a direct phone. (Closed Sun. 2-5pm, but ring bell anyway. Singles and doubles 90F, with shower 120F, with toilet 160F. Showers 10F. Parking lot.)

A 45-minute train ride from Chartres will take you to well-preserved **Illiers-Combray,** the childhood vacation home of Marcel Proust and setting for much of *Remembrance of Things Past.* The well-preserved town still looks much as it must have to Proust. The highlight of this literary pilgrimage, the **Maison de Tante Léonie,** 4, rue Docteur Léonie (tel. 37 24 30 97), displays mementos of Proust's life in the home of his favorite aunt. The jangling bell which figures so prominently in Marcel's ruminations on *le temps retrouvé* is still tied tight to the garden gate. (By tour only, Wed.-Mon. at 3 and 4pm.) A brochure available at the museum will direct you along Swann's Way and to Proust's other nearby haunts. To reach Illiers, take the *Micheline* (old train) from Gare de Chartres (tel. 37 28 50 50; 6 per day 8:49am-7:41pm, 19F).

Fontainebleau

Try to imagine what Louis XIV's château at Versailles would look like if it were not filled with mobs of tourists. Now go see the château at Fontainebleau. Though Versailles is symbolically more important, Fontainebleau's comparative obscurity may lead you to agree with the many travelers who consider it the more worthwhile day-trip.

Fontainebleau owes its existence to the royal passion for hunting. For eight centuries, this hunting lodge and royal residence was favored by some of France's most famous rulers, many of whom added to its grandeur by constructing extra rooms or entire wings. It is this eclectic blend of architecture that caused Napoleon to dub the château *La Maison des Siècles* (the house of centuries). The emperor and his wife Josephine lived here for much of his reign; cour des Adieux was so named after serving as the scene of his dramatic farewell in 1814.

As at Versailles, not all parts of the château are open to the public. The **Grands Appartements,** the standard visitors' circuit, include the main bedchambers as well as the state meeting rooms and the magnificent throne room. The same ticket admits you to the **Musée Napoléon,** which displays such trite memorabilia as His utensils, His field tent, and His gambling dice. The **Petits Appartements,** the private chambers of Empress Josephine, are accessible by guided tour only (limit 10 people). (Château open Wed.-Mon. 9am-12:30pm and 2-5pm; Sept.-June Mon. and Wed.-Sat. 9am-12:30pm and 2-5pm, Sun. 9am-12:30pm. Admission to Grands Appartements and museum 23F, students and seniors 12F, Sun. 12F. Morning ticket also valid in afternoon. Tour in French of the Petits Appartements at 2pm and 3pm. 11F, students and seniors 6F.) Though not as vast as the grounds at Versailles, Fontainebleau's gardens still make for a pleasant stroll. If you throw some bread into the **Etang des Carpes,** the hundreds of carp that live in this pond will battle for the last soggy crumb. The gardens also include the **Jardin Anglais** and the **Jardin de Diane,** where royal peacocks flaunt their feathers. (Gardens open daily sunrise-sunset.)

As splendid as the palace, **Forêt de Fontainebleau** is a thickly wooded 41,632-acre preserve with hiking trails and the famous sandstone rocks used for training alpine climbers. Fontainebleau's **tourist office,** 31,.pl. Napoléon (tel. 64 22 25 68), across from the **post office** and near the château, organizes tours of the surrounding village and can help you with accommodations. (Open Mon.-Sat. 9am-12:30pm and 1:45-6pm, Sun. 10am-12:30pm.) Hourly trains run to the town from Paris's Gare de Lyon (45 min., round-trip 59F). The château is a pleasant 2km walk or bus ride (take bus A, 7.20F) from the station. The train station (tel. 64 22 38 52) rents bikes for 30F per half-day with a 500F deposit.

Vaux-le-Vicomte

The **Château de Vaux-le-Vicomte** may seem like a hut when compared to Versailles or Fontainebleau, but its fascinating history makes it one of the most famous palaces in the country. A diminutive masterpiece designed by Le Vau, decorated by Le Brun, and landscaped by Le Nôtre, the château was built for Fouquet, the

Minister of Finance under Louis XIV, who decided he needed a home reflecting his wealth and stature. Unfortunately, the château's grandeur hastened its owner's downfall. Young King Louis, received here for a feast in 1661, became enraged at being outshone and stripped Fouquet of all his power, condemning him to life in prison. Astonished with the magnificence of Vaux, prototype of the classical style, the king appropriated Vaux-le-Vicomte's artists (and eventually some of its works) before beginning the construction of Versailles, where the style would reach full maturity.

While it may have inspired Versailles, Vaux-le-Vicomte itself remains unfinished. Many rooms exhibit overwhelming extravagance, but others have barren walls and only partially painted ceilings. Your ticket will also admit you to the **équipages,** former stables that now house a carriage museum. Whether the trek to the palace is worth the investment depends on your love of truly independent sightseeing. The crowds may be wonderfully sparse, but so is the information on the pamphlet. There are no guided tours. To reach the château, take a train from Paris's Gare de Lyon to Melun, 6km from the château (frequent departures, 45 min., round-trip 55.20F). From there, it's a 90-minute hike, a frustrating hitch, or an expensive taxi ride (90F from the station). Cabs are sometimes plentiful, but prepare to wait up to a ½-hour. Your persistence in getting here may be best rewarded on Saturday evenings from May to September, when the candlelit château seems private and homey. The fountain in Le Nôtre's abundant gardens are turned on every second and last Saturday of the month from 3 to 6pm. (Château open Mon.-Fri. 10am-12:30pm and 2-5:30pm, Sat. 8:30-11pm, Sun. 10am-5:30pm. *Equipages* open Mon.-Fri. 10am-6:30pm, Sat. 8:30-11pm, Sun. 10am-6:30pm. Gardens open Mon.-Fri. 10am-7pm, Sat. 8-11pm, Sun. 10am-7pm. Admission 42F, ages 18-25 34F. Saturday night 55F, ages 18-25 46F. Gardens 15F. No picnicking.)

Chantilly

Set in the magnificent gardens Le Nôtre sculpted from the surrounding forest, Chantilly floats over its ponds and canals like a meringued pear in a pool of *sabayon* sauce. Luxurious residences have occupied this choice site since a Roman citizen named Cantilius built his villa here. A succession of medieval lords constructed elaborate fortifications, but Chantilly did not come into its own until the Grand Condé, celebrated victor of Rocroi and cousin of Louis XIV, brought Le Nôtre to create the gardens and, eventually, commissioned the Grand Château. The dramatic Renaissance façade, the lush greenery, and the extravagant entrance hall whet your appetite for something truly remarkable. Unfortunately, the rest of the interior disappoints. The collection of elegant furnishings and classical paintings (Raphael, Delacroix, Corot) in the château's **Musée Condé** (tel. 44 57 08 00) hints at the luxurious lifestyle of the princes, but you have to be a real château-lover to think the 30F admission fee justified. You may be satisfied with a 12F wander through the gardens, which themselves are more than worth the trip. (Open Wed.-Mon. 10:30am-6pm; Nov.-March Mon.-Fri. 1-5pm and Sat.-Sun. 10:30am-5:30pm. Admission to park and museum 30F; to park alone 12F.)

As you approach the castle, you'll pass the **Grandes Ecuries,** enormous stables that housed 240 horses and hundreds of hunting dogs until the Revolution. They were constructed in 1719 to satisfy Louis-Henri Bourbon, who hoped to occupy them when reincarnated as a horse (of course). Called "the most beautiful stables in the world" by François the talking mule, they now house the **Musée Vivant du Cheval** (tel. 44 57 13 13), a huge museum dealing with all things equine: on display are dozens of saddles, horseshoes, merry-go-rounds, horse postcards, horse sculptures, and, of course, horses. Lower those expectations! You may not pet these rippling beasts. (Open Mon. and Wed.-Fri. 10:30am-6:30pm, Sat.-Sun. 10:30am-7pm; May-June Tues. 10:30am-5:30pm, July-Aug. Tues. 2-5:30pm. Horse-training demonstrations (in French only) April-Oct. daily at 11:30am, 3:30pm, and 5:15pm. Admission to museum and show 40F, students and seniors 35F. Special show Sun.

at 4pm; admission 1-4:30pm is 50F.) Two of France's premier horseraces are held here in June—the **Prix de Diane** and the **Prix du Jockey Club.**

The tourist office is stabled at 23, av. du Maréchal Joffre (tel. 44 57 08 58). (Open Wed.-Mon. 10am-12:30pm and 2-5:30pm., Sun. 9am-2pm.) Hourly **trains** run to Chantilly from Paris's Gare du Nord (every hr., 35 min., round-trip 62F). To reach the château from the station, walk down rue des Otages and turn left in front of the tourist office (2km). Rent **bikes** at Chantilly VTT (tel. 44 57 57 25), straight ahead and to the left of the station (30-40F per day; open Sat. 1-8pm and Sun. 11am-8pm).

Not far from Chantilly, tiny **Senlis** basks in the ineffable glory of being the quaintest and best-preserved village in the Ile-de-France. Its cobbled streets, friendly residents, and intimate atmosphere are the closest you'll get to traditional France this side of Brittany and Normandy. Senlis's **Cathédrale de Notre Dame,** begun in 1191, exposes the primitive underbelly of Gothic architecture. Especially remarkable is the Grand Portail consecrated to the Virgin Mary, later imitated in Chartres and Notre-Dame de Paris. **Eglise St-Frambourg,** founded around 900 by the merciful yet often touchy Queen Adélaïde, also deserves a look. Reconstructed in 1177 by Louis VII and then ransacked during the Revolution, this beauty found its most recent savior in the great pianist Girogy Cziffra, who restored the church as an international music center. Enter the park next to the tourist office to reach the **Château Royal,** a hunting lodge for kings from Charlemagne to Henri IV, now converted into a hunting museum. The remains of its Gallo-Roman fortifications, with 31 towers, still surround the town. (Open April-Sept. Thurs.-Mon. 10am-noon and 2-6pm, Wed. 2-6pm. Admission 11F, students 5F.) The old town is a network of medieval alleyways winding between several of the original gates. Senlis's **tourist office,** pl. du Parvis Notre-Dame (tel. (16) 44 53 06 40), has information on concerts, exhibitions, and the rest of the local brouhaha. (Open March-Nov. Mon. and Wed.-Fri. 2-6pm, Sat.-Sun. 10am-noon and 2-6pm.) SNCF buses meet most trains to Chantilly for the 25-minute ride to Senlis (one way 12F; railpasses valid).

Beauvais

Cathédrale St-Pierre in Beauvais boasts the tallest Gothic chancel in the world, the product of architectural ambition pushed beyond reason. Begun in 1225, the chancel was completed in 1272 only to collapse in 1284. Rebuilding began immediately and continued until 1578, when the chancel and transept were completed. In the 1560s, however, the appropriately named Jean Vast the Younger built an additional central spire above the intersection of transept and choir, again overburdening the supporting pillars and resulting in the disastrous collapse of 1573. So much time and money was then spent on rebuilding and strengthening the chancel again (see the complex of flying buttresses around it) that the construction of the nave never began; the opening from the transept has been bricked up for the last 400 years. Stand back from the cathedral and try to imagine its immense proportions—the largest of any Gothic church in the world—if the nave had been built.

Enter (if you dare) to examine the stained-glass windows, three centuries of tapestries, and the *Horloge Astronomique,* which Vérité built from 90,000 pieces in the 19th century. Don't miss the older (1302) and smaller *horloge,* less obviously placed. Both timepieces do their thing Tuesday through Saturday noon, 3pm, 4pm, and 5pm and on Sunday at 3pm, 4pm, and 5pm. To get there from the train station, follow bd. du Général de Gaulle past the garden on the left. At the first large intersection, turn left on rue de la Madeleine, or simply head toward the sound of the bells. (Open daily 9am-12:15pm and 2-6:15pm.)

The old bishop's palace is now the **Musée Départemental de l'Oise,** rue du Musée (tel. 44 84 37 37), home to a permanent collection on the paleontological history of the area, as well as wood-carving, ceramics, 14th- to 18th-century Beauvais stoneware, local artwork, and temporary exhibits. Whew! (Open Wed.-Mon. 10am-noon and 2-6pm. Admission 10F, students 5F.)

Fascinating **Eglise St-Etienne,** south of pl. de la Hachette, combines a sober Roman nave and a richly decorated Gothic choir with some beautiful stained glass. Note the great 16th-century windows and the magnificent *Arbre de Jessé*. (Church open only for masses, Sun. 11am, 5pm, Mon.-Sat. 7pm.)

In 1664, the only other branch of Paris's great **Gobelins Tapestry Factory** opened in Beauvais. The weavers in the country operation concerned themselves mainly with upholstering tapestry with pastoral rather than historical or mythological themes. Located next to the cathedral, the modern **Galerie Nationale de la Tapisserie** houses an interesting collection of tapestries from the ancient and historical to the contemporary and abstract. You are encouraged to interrogate (in French) the artists in the workshop. (Open Tues.-Sun. 9:30-11:30am and 2-6pm; Oct.-March 10-11:30am and 2:30-4:30pm. Admission 15F, students 9F. *Atelier de Demonstration* open the same hours but closed Sun. and holidays.)

On the last weekend in June, the **Festival de Jeanne Hachette** celebrates, with medieval costumes and processions through the streets, the gallantry of the women of Beauvais in resisting the onslaught of Charles the Bold's Burgundian army. Beauvais's **tourist office** (tel. 44 45 25 26) opposes the cathedral. (Open April-Sept. Tues.-Sat. 9am-noon and 2-6:30pm.) The branch at 6, rue Malherbe (tel. 44 45 08 18) keeps the same hours year-round. Fifteen daily **trains** run from Paris's Gare du Nord to Beauvais (90 min., round-trip 100F).

Meaux

Forty-five km east of Paris is the ancient town of Meaux, capital of northern Brie and known, appropriately, for its cheese. There are three types of Brie: *Brie de Meaux,* the classic; *Brie de Melun,* thicker in texture and stronger in taste; and *Brie de Coulommiers,* less fully fermented. Not surprisingly, Brie is astoundingly cheap in all the local stores, but the manufacturing *boutiques* (as they are called) are not open to the public. The *fromager* **Desroques** (tel. (16) 64 34 22 82), off bd. Raoult at the corner of rue Général Leclerc and rue L'Arbalète, is one of the finest shops. All stores are closed on Monday. You may notice locals making a stink about Meaux's excellent strong mustard.

Cathédrale St-Etienne, with its mixed Gothic façade, is the suitably grand final resting place of Marie de France, best known for her transcription of *lais* and French folktales. The stained glass dates from the 14th century. (Open 8-11:55am and 2-5:55pm.) The bishop's palace next door was the nest of Jacques-Bénigne Bossuet, nicknamed l'Aigle de Meaux (the eagle), who was Bishop of Meaux from 1681 to 1704. The **Musée Bossuet** (tel. 64 34 84 45) now fills the house with Bossuet's theological memorabilia and a fine collection of French painting from the Renaissance to the 19th century. (Open Wed.-Mon. 10:30am-noon and 2-6pm. Free.)

For information, call the **tourist office,** 2, rue Notre-Dame (tel. 64 33 02 26; open Tues.-Sat. 10am-noon and 2-6:30pm). Every Sunday at 3:30pm from June to September, guided tours leave from 8, rue de Vieux Moulins (22F, children 11F). Ask the tourist office for more information. Frequent trains run to Meaux from Paris's Gare de l'Est (every ½-hr., 40 min., round-trip 52F). Those on their own wheels should follow A4 and N36.

Normandy (Normandie)

The province of Normandy, whose jagged coastline, gently sloping valleys, and elaborate cathedrals provided inspiration for the Impressionists, has had a history separate from that of the rest of France. Seized by Vikings in the 9th century, Normandy was officially recognized as independent in 911, when the French king acknowledged the domination of the Norsemen (a name later corrupted to "Normans"). The great age of Norman independence, during which the Normans continued to expand their territory, lasted from the 10th to the 13th century. During this period, the Normans also created their greatest architectural monuments, a string of ornate cathedrals, each more impossible than the last.

During the Hundred Years' War, the English invaded and overpowered fierce Norman resistance. Led by the Duke of Bedford, the English troops succeeded in capturing Joan of Arc after a great victory on September 8, 1430. She was held in Rouen's Tour Jeanne d'Arc (which still stands today), charged with heresy and sorcery, and condemned to be burned at the stake on May 30, 1431 at the age of 19. When the British were finally overthrown, they left behind a deep imprint on the customs, crafts, and cuisine of the area. The British did not attempt another invasion until D-Day, June 6, 1944, when they returned with their American and Canadian allies to wrest Normandy from German occupation.

Accessible by ferry from England and Ireland and by hovercraft from England, the Norman ports of Le Havre, Dieppe, and Cherbourg greet travelers coming to France. Within Normandy, only the major towns are connected by rail, with smaller towns often connected by bus. SNCF buses are covered by railpass; STN (Société de Transport Nationale) buses are not. Since many of the most memorable spots lie off the main roads, a bike or car is helpful for extended touring. Cyclists should keep in mind that the roads are hilly and the coastal winds blow roughly west-to-east.

Flaubert once wrote, "All of us Normans have a drop of cider in our veins. It's a bitter, fermented drink which sometimes bursts the bung." The province's traditional *cidre* comes both hard (*brut*) and sweet (*doux*). *Calvados,* apple brandy aged 12 to 15 years, ranks with the finest, most lethal cognacs. In many places, you can buy from the farmers themselves. More famous for its produce and dairy products, Normandy supplies a large percentage of the nation's butter. Try the creamy, pungent *camembert* cheese, but be sure it's ripe (soft in the middle).

Rouen

Joan of Arc was burned here, and Emma Bovary was bored here—but don't let the bad press deter you from visiting Rouen.

From the 10th through the 12th century, Rouen (pop. 400,000) witnessed a flowering of Gothic architecture while enjoying great power and prestige as capital of the Norman empire, which controlled much of France and England. Victor Hugo dubbed Rouen the city of a hundred spires, and visitors today still admire the towers, dutifully leering gargoyles, and gables that embellish Rouen's skyline. Rouen's most famous legends revolve around the life and death of Joan of Arc. Held prisoner here by the English after her great campaign across France, she was interrogated and tried for heresy by the French clergy. Joan stood firm for three months and was sentenced to life imprisonment. Still not satisfied, the English pressed for a heavier punishment, and in May, 1431, Joan was burnt at the stake in Rouen's pl. du Vieux Marché, today a busy marketplace.

152

During World War II, Rouen was badly damaged by both German and American bombing. Nearly every church and dozens of medieval houses in Rouen are currently being reconstructed and renovated.

Orientation and Practical Information

The Seine River divides Rouen into two parts—the **Rive Droite** and the **Rive Gauche.** Most sights are located in the old city on the Rive Droite, while the Rive Gauche contains modern buildings along wide avenues.

Rouen is served frequently by trains from Paris's Gare St-Lazare (70 min., 86F). There are train stations on both Rives, but passenger trains stop only at the Rive Droite. To get to the center of town from that station, walk straight down rue Jeanne d'Arc for several blocks. A left on rue du Gros Horloge leads to pl. de la Cathédrale and the tourist office; a right leads to pl. du Vieux Marché. Continue straight on rue Jeanne d'Arc to a bridge crossing the Seine to the Rive Gauche.

Tourist Office: 25, pl. de la Cathédrale (tel. 35 71 41 77), opposite the cathedral. Accommodations service 11F. The free guide *Le P'tit Normand* covers the Rouen area (44F). English spoken. Open Mon.-Sat. 9am-7pm, Sun. 9:30am-12:30pm and 2:30-6pm; Oct.-March Mon.-Sat. 9am-12:30pm and 2-6:30pm.

Budget Travel: Voyage Wasteels, 111bis, rue Jeanne d'Arc (tel. 35 71 92 56). BIJ tickets. Youth railcards. Open Mon.-Fri. 9am-noon and 2-7pm, Sat. 9am-noon and 2-6pm.

Post Office: 45, rue Jeanne d'Arc (tel. 35 08 73 66). Poste Restante and **currency exchange.** Open Mon.-Fri. 8am-7pm, Sat. 8am-noon. **Postal Code:** 76000.

Trains: rue Jeanne d'Arc (tel. 35 98 50 50). To: Paris (at least 1 per hr., 70 min., 86F); Dieppe (every 1-2 hr., 40 min., 44F); Caen (every 1½-2½ hr., 2½ hr., 86F); Le Havre (1 per hr., 50 min., 57F). Lockers 12-25F. Information office open Mon.-Sat. 7:15am-7pm, Sun. 9am-noon and 2-7pm.

Buses: SATAR, rue des Charettes (tel. 35 71 81 71), by the river off rue Jeanne d'Arc. Expensive. Bus #163 to Dieppe (4 per day, 2 hr., 53F); #30a and 30b to Le Havre (every 1-2 hr., 3 hr., 66F); #261 to and from Fécamp (1 per day, 2¼ hr., 56F). Information office open Mon.-Fri. 5:30am-7:30pm.

Public Transportation: Rouen is working on a new system, but right now **buses** are the only way to get around town. **TCAR,** 79, rue Thiers (tel. 35 98 02 43). 4F per ticket, *carnet* of 10 30.30F. Information office open Mon.-Fri. 8-11:45am and 1:45-5:30pm.

Taxis 67, rue Thiers (tel. 35 88 50 50). Open 24 hrs.

Bike Rental: Rouen Cycles 45, rue St-Eloi (tel. 35 71 34 30). Bicycles 70F per day, 200F per week, deposit 200F. Scooters 120F per day, 320F per week, deposit 320F. Open Tues.-Sat.

Hitchhiking: If you chose to hitchhike to Paris and Caen, take bus #12 to the end of the line. For Dieppe, take bus #2 or 8 to Déville. For Le Havre, get on autoroute du Havre, which starts in the center of town. For destinations on the right bank of the Seine (Duclair, Jumièges, St-Wandrille), take bus #19 ("Mesnil-Esnard") to Cantelen, an easier hitch.

Laundromat: 79, rue Beauvoisine. Fairly central. Wash 14F, dry 2F per 7 min. Open daily 7am-9pm. Also on the Rive Gauche on rue Lafayette, off pl. St-Sever. Wash 12F, dry 2F per 7½ min. 2F and 5F pieces only.

Pharmacy: Grande Pharmacie du Centre, pl. de la Cathédrale (tel. 35 71 13 17). Open Tues.-Sun. 9am-7pm.

Hospital: Hôpital Charles Nicolle, 1, rue de Germont (tel. 35 08 81 81). Also **Hôtel Dieu,** 51, rue de Lecat (tel. 35 89 81 30).

Police: 7, rue Brisout de Barneville (tel. 35 63 81 17). **Emergency,** tel. 17.

Accommodations and Camping

Finding a room in Rouen is more difficult in the off-season than in the summer. As a number of Parisians commute to work here, accommodations are tight during

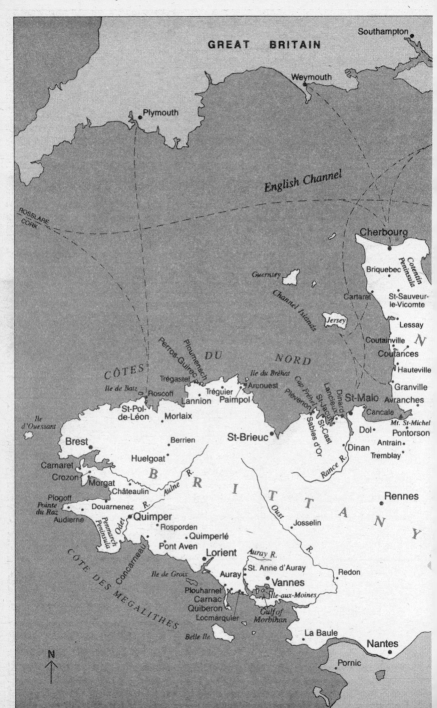

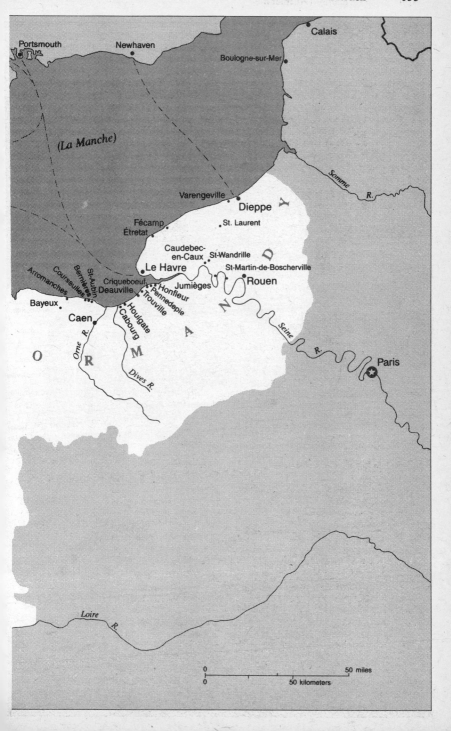

Portsmouth

Newhaven

Calais

Boulogne-sur-Mer

(La Manche)

Somme
R.

Varengeville

Dieppe

Y

Fécamp
Étretat

St. Laurent

Caudebec-
en-Caux

St-Wandrille

D

Le Havre

St-Martin-de-Boscherville

Arromanches
Courseulles
Bernières
St-Aubin

Criqueboeuf
Deauville

Honfleur
Pennedepie
Trouville

Jumièges

Rouen

N

Bayeux

Caen

Houlgate
Cabourg

A

Seine

O

Orne R.

R

M

Dives R.

R.

Paris

Loire

R

0   50 miles
0   50 kilometers

the week. The cheaper lodgings are on the quiet side streets, particularly those between the train station and the Hôtel de Ville.

Auberge de Jeunesse (IYHF), 17, rue Diderot (tel. 35 72 06 45), on the Rive Gauche 2km from the station. Take bus #12 from the station or from rue Jeanne d'Arc and ride to rue Diderot. Modern and chaotic; sleep among schoolchildren. Dining room open late for socializing. IYHF card required. Reception 7:30-10am, 5-11pm. Lockout 10am-5pm. Curfew 11pm. 50F includes breakfast and linen. Lunch and dinner 32-41F. Kitchen facilities.

University Housing, available through **CROUS,** 3, rue d'Herbouville (tel. 35 98 44 50). Call before hopping bus #10 from the town center. The Cité Universitaire is 3km from the center of town in Mont St-Aignan. You will need a student ID and an extra photo. 40F per person, reduced price for longer stays. Open June-Sept.

Hôtel Normandya, 32, rue du Cordier (tel. 35 71 46 15), between Tour Jeanne d'Arc and rue Beauvoisine. Attractive rooms with pretty lace curtains and wicker furniture. Singles and doubles 70-90F, with shower 120F. Breakfast 15F.

Hostellerie du Vieux Logis, 5, rue de Joyeuse (tel. 35 71 55 30), off rue Picard. Cozy rooms, faded Persian rugs, winding antique stairways, and funky-fresh flower arrangements. Great restaurant downstairs. Singles 60F. Doubles 70F.

Hôtel St-Ouen, 43, rue des Faulx (tel. 35 71 46 44), across from Eglise St-Ouen. Large, pleasant rooms. Singles and doubles 70-95F. Breakfast 16F.

Hôtel du Palais, 12, rue Tambour (tel. 35 71 41 40), centrally located off rue du Gros Horloge. Clean, carpeted, colorful rooms. Singles and doubles from 70F; with shower 115F.

Camping: Camping Municipal at Déville, rue Jules Ferry in Déville-les-Rouen (tel. 35 74 07 59), 4km from Rouen. Take bus #2 from the ironworks museum (3 per hr., last at 9pm) or bus #161/163 from the *gare routière* (1 per hr., last at 8pm). Attractive sites with squeaky clean bathrooms. Hot showers. Open March-Oct.

Food

Local specialties include duck *pâté, canard au sang* (pressed duck), *sole normande,* and *tripe à la normandaise.* A mouth-watering range of fish, cheese, and produce is available Tuesday through Sunday in and around pl. du Vieux Marché (8am-2pm); on Sunday, the vendors move to pl. St-Marc (8am-noon). **Monoprix,** 67, rue du Gros Horloge, has *calvados* (apple liqueur) at cheaper rates than specialty shops. (Open Tues.-Sat. 9am-7pm, Sun. 9:30am-12:30pm.)

Hostellerie du Vieux Logis, 5, rue de Joyeuse (tel. 35 71 55 30). Cozy place with overstuffed chairs, candlelight, and a garden view. Lots of French and Norman specialties and wine for only 55F. Make reservations for evening meals. Open noon-1:30pm and 7-8:30pm.

Café Leffe, 36, pl. des Carmes. A traditional neighborhood bar transformed into a glitzy, neon watering hole for *jeunes cadres* (yuppies). Simple sandwiches and salads. Open daily 7am-1am.

Pizzeria du Drugstore, 2, rue Beauvoisine. A romantic cave with a painted ceiling and vine-covered walls imprisoned beneath a drugstore. 49F *menu* includes pizza, dessert, drink, and coffee. Open Mon.-Sat. noon-11pm.

La Galette, 168, rue Beauvoisine. *Galettes* (whole-wheat *crêpes*): shrimp or mushroom 20F, salmon in cream sauce 40F. Open Sept.-July Mon.-Fri. 11am-2pm and 7pm-midnight, Sat. 7pm-midnight.

Les Flandres, 5, rue des Bons-Enfants (tel. 35 98 45 16). French favorites like *cordon bleu* and *pâté* de campagne served in a friendly, unpretentious atmosphere. Simple, filling *menu* 50F; *plats du jour* 35F. Open Mon.-Fri. noon-1:30pm and 7:30-9:15pm, Sat. noon-1:30pm.

Restaurant Le Lotus, 100, rue Ganterie. Vietnamese and French fare. 55F *menu.* Open Mon. 7-11pm, Tues.-Sun. noon-2:30pm and 7-11pm.

Natural Vital, 3, rue du Petit Salut. A well-stocked health food store. Deli has ready-made salad, quiche, and sandwiches. Open Mon.-Sat. 8am-7pm.

Sights and Entertainment

Many of Rouen's sights cluster around the **rue du Gros Horloge,** a crowded, noisy pedestrian zone off pl. du Vieux Marché that is crammed with shops and cafés. Built into a bridge halfway down the street, the **Gros Horloge** tells the time with speciously charming imprecision. Climb up the belfry for the obligatory stunning view. (Free.)

At the end of the rue du Gros Horloge lies the **Cathédrale de Notre Dame.** Built between the 12th and the 16th centuries, it incorporates nearly every intermediate style of Gothic architecture. The façade that fascinated Monet is now black with soot, but current renovations promise to eventually return it to a gleaming Impressionist hue. The disturbing asymmetry results from damage sustained early in World War II. The cathedral is illuminated nightly during July and August (Saturdays and Sundays only in the off-season).

Behind the cathedral stands flamboyant **Eglise St-Maclou.** Dating from the 15th century, its curved west front showcases one of the most monstrous collections of gables and sculpture of any Gothic church. Beyond the church, turn left into 186, rue de Martinville; a small passageway leads to the **Aitre St-Maclou,** the church's former charnel house, which saw much use during the great plagues of the later Middle Ages. Appropriately, its wooden beams bear a gory 15th-century frieze of the *danse macabre.* Today, in a happier incarnation, the building houses Rouen's Ecole des Beaux-Arts. (Open daily 9am-6pm. Free.)

Up rue Damiette and rue Boucheries, next to the Hôtel de Ville, is **Eglise St-Ouen** (begun in 1318), the purest expression of Gothic architecture in Rouen. Its towering vaults are second in height only to those of Beauvais. The entrance, somewhat difficult to find, is on the side, through the Marmouset Portal. (Open daily 10am-5pm. Free.)

The **Musée des Antiquités** in Cloître Ste-Marie, 198, rue Beauvoisine, houses a collection of Gallo-Roman, Merovingian, and Renaissance relics, mostly from local sources. (Open Fri.-Wed. 10am-noon and 2-5:30pm. Admission 4F, ages over 65 2F, students and teachers with ID free.) The **Tour Elvis d'Arc** on rue de Donjon is the last remaining tower of the château where Joan was imprisoned. The display inside contains material relating to the trial. (Open Fri.-Wed. 10am-noon and 2-5:30pm. 6F, students free.)

On rue Thiers is Rouen's superb **Musée des Beaux Arts.** The collection includes works by the usual suspects—Rubens, Dufy, Sisley and Monet (including one from his famous series on Rouen's cathedral). (Open Thurs.-Mon. 10am-noon and 2-6pm, Wed. 2-6pm. 11F, students and children free.) Next to the Musée des Beaux Arts on rue Jacques-Villon, the **Musée de Ferronnerie Le-Secq-des-Tournelles** (Ironworks Museum) fills a 15th-century church with an unusual collection of fancy grillwork, locks, keys, and other household objects, dating from the 3rd to the 19th century. (Open Thurs.-Mon. 10am-noon and 2-6pm, Wed. 2-6pm. 11F, students and children free.)

Walk along rue aux Juifs to find the elaborate **Palais de Justice.** Though the interior was restored after World War II, the façade, crawling with more of those darn gargoyles, still bears large pockmarks inflicted by heavy shelling. An 11th-century synagogue, known simply as the **Monument Juif,** was recently discovered during excavation around the Palais de Justice. Unfortunately, you must arrange at least three days in advance to take the tourist office's guided tour in French on Sunday at 11am. (Oct.-April. Sat. at 2pm; admission 24F, ages under 25 and over 60 20F.)

Rouen's most unusual church is **Eglise Jeanne d'Arc,** cattycorner to pl. du Vieux Marché, built on the site of her execution. Opened in 1979 by former president Giscard d'Estaing, this whimsical structure is commonly mistaken for a beached hydrofoil. (Open daily 10am-12:30pm, 2-6pm.) Avoid the slipshod Joan of Arc museum opposite the church.

Dramatist **Pierre Corneille's** home is at 4, rue de la Pie, off pl. du Vieux Marché. (Open Wed. afternoon-Mon. 10am-noon, 2-6pm. Admission 2F, students free.) Novelist **Gustave Flaubert** grew up at 51, rue de Lecat, next door to Hôtel-Dieu hospital (which bears the same address). Now the **Musée Flaubert et d'Histoire de la Médecine,** the building houses a collection of frighteningly archaic medical instruments and a few of Flaubert's possessions, including the stuffed parrot he supposedly borrowed from the Musée de Rouen when writing "Un Coeur simple." (Open Tues.-Sat. 10am-noon and 2-6pm. Free.) On a small bay of the Seine 15 minutes out of town, **Croisset,** where Flaubert wrote *Madame Bovary,* is of interest only to hardcore fans.

Share a cup or glass with your future lambada partner at **Café le Leffe,** pl. des Carmes (open 7am-1am) or **La Rotonde,** 61bis, rue St-Sever. The **Night-On,** 8, rue de l'Ancienne Prison (tel. 35 70 60 60) is a popular mainstream place to do the Hustle. (Open Fri.-Sat. 11pm-4am, 70F cover.) For a more sedentary evening, try **Le Scottish,** 21, rue Verte (tel. 35 71 46 22), which hosts a weekend jazz concert on an outdoor terrace (café open 10:30am-2am). Local students frequently make the trek to **Exo 7** (tel. 35 72 28 92), a disco/club 6km south of Rouen. Take bus #5, get off at pl. des Chartreux in Petit Quévilly, and stick out your thumb. To return, you're on your own, as bus service stops at 10pm. Call ahead if you're going to Exo 7 to confirm hours and prices, which vary depending on the evening's entertainment.

From the end of May through early July, Rouen celebrates the balmy days of summer in the **Festival d'Eté de Seine Maritime.** The impressive program offers an unusual range of events including classical and Baroque music, theater, and water ballet. For tickets and information, call 35 70 04 07, or write to Festival d'Eté, Hangar 23, Port Automne, bd. Emile Duchemin, 76000 Rouen.

Near Rouen

From Rouen to Le Havre, the Seine meanders through protected forests and apple orchards. In this undisturbed part of Normandy, Benedictine monks founded great abbeys in the 17th century. Today, many exceptional ruins as well as functional abbeys still dot the countryside. Only 15 minutes away on bus #3 is the shady **Forêt Verte,** a perfect picnic spot.

Bus #30a and b, leaving from the *gare routière* for Le Havre, will take you on the D982 along the Seine. Service is frequent but a bit expensive (18 per day, to Le Havre 3 hr., 66F). You can get off at any of the remote villages along the way and get back on the next bus.

Twelfth-century **Abbaye St-Georges** in St-Martin de Boscherville, with its rounded arches and pyramidal towers, remains a masterpiece of Romanesque architecture. The bus fare to St-Martin de Boscherville is 12.60F. The abbey is a mere 10-minute walk from the bus stop (follow the signs). (Open April-Sept. Wed.-Mon. 9:30am-noon and 2-7pm. Admission 10F, students 8F.) In **Jumièges,** about 4km off the D982, the gorgeous ruins of a once-majestic 11th-century Romanesque church, the **Ancienne Abbaye Notre Dame,** stand in a half-forgotten landscape. (Open 9am-6:30pm; April-June 15 and Sept. 15-Oct. Mon.-Fri. 9am-noon and 2-5pm, Sat.-Sun. 9am-12:30pm and 2-6pm; Nov.-March Mon.-Fri. 10am-noon and 2-4pm, Sat.-Sun. 10am-noon and 2-5pm. Whew! Admission 15F, ages 18-25 and over 60 9F.) You will probably have to walk the 4km from Yainville, the closest bus stop. The only bus serving this region (still #30a and b) goes all the way to Jumièges once per day (24.60F); the area is not served by train.

About 10km farther down D982 in the tiny village of St-Wandrille is the **Abbaye St-Wandrille** (tel. 35 96 23 11). The monks still live, work, and perform their devotions according to the 1200-year-old Benedictine rule. Mass is performed in Gregorian chant. (Mon.-Sat. at 9:30am, Sun. 10am; vespers Mon.-Wed. and Fri.-Sat. at 5:30pm, Thurs. 6:45pm, Sun. and holidays 5pm.) An amusing monk leads guided tours of the cloister and other buildings twice per day (10F). The bus fare to St-Wandrille is 31F.

Both Jumièges and St-Wandrille are located within the **Parc Naturel Régional de Brotonne,** a protected area of forests and hills perfectly suited for camping, fishing, and riding. A picturesque campground sits next to an outdoor recreational center at **Base de Plein Air et de Loisirs Jumièges-le-Mesnil** (tel. 35 37 93 84; open daily May-Aug). Jumièges **Camping Municipal** (tel. 35 37 24 15) is 3km down the hill on the main road from the ruins of the Abbaye. (Open May-Aug. daily.) For more information on activities and fishing licenses, contact Centre Administratif du Parc, 2, Rond-Point Marbec, 76580 Le Trait (tel. 35 37 23 16).

Caudebec-en-Caux is a few kilometers beyond St-Wandrille in the heart of the Parc de Brotonne, still on the #30a and b bus line (32F). A large network of long and short hiking trails penetrates the forested hills behind the rather ordinary town. The Caudebec **tourist office,** rue Thomas Basin (tel. 35 96 20 65), is up rue des Boucheries. (Open July-Aug. daily 10am-noon and 3-6:30pm; Easter-June and Sept. Sat. afternoon and Sun. only.) When it's closed, bring your inquiries to the *mairie* (tel. 35 96 11 12), a palatial building by the river and past the Romanesque miniature golf course. An adequate **campground** awaits 1km beyond the town hall by the riverside (tel. 35 96 26 38; open mid-April to Sept.). On the last Sunday in September, Caudebec hosts the **Festival du Cidre,** the region's largest folk festival.

Along the Seine south of Rouen lies <u>Giverny,</u> site of Claude Monet's pink and green painted home and flowery garden, where the notorious Impressionist lived from 1883 until his death in 1926, and where he painted his famous water lily series. The property was opened to the public as the **Musée Monet** (tel. 32 51 28 21) only five years ago. (Open April-Oct. Tues.-Sun. 10am-noon and 2-6pm.) The gardens themselves are open all day and are a great place for a picnic. Giverny lies across from Vernon on the Rouen-Paris St-Lazare train line, and is accessible only by the cabs which line up outside the station. Biking is a popular alternative. ✓ Bus

Near the intersection of N182 and N138 in the Risle Valley, 16km from Rouen, the religious community of **Notre-Dame du Bec-Hellouin** (tel. 32 44 86 09) boasts a 15th-century tower and Baderist cloister. The abbey is open to the public only during guided visits. (Open Wed.-Sat. and Mon. 10am-5:15pm, Sun. noon-6pm; Oct.-May Wed.-Sat. and Mon. 11am-4:30pm; Sun. noon-4pm.) Take the daily train from Paris to Evreux and catch a bus from there.

The countryside around Rouen is as ideal for admiring *pigeonniers* (pigeon towers), home to the nasty birds who conspire to dampen the soaring grandeur of Normandy's cathedrals with their insolent droppings. Before 1789 pigeon-keeping was a special privilege of the nobility and clergy and served as an indicator of an individual's wealth. **Château de Vascoeuil,** 22km east of Rouen on N31 (tel. 35 23 62 35) has a striking pigeon tower as well as public gardens and a permanent art exhibit. (Open 10:30am-12:30pm and 2:30-6:30pm; April-May and Sept.-Nov. 2:30-6:30pm. Admission 30F, students 15F.)

Coast: Upper Normandy

Overlooking both the white cliffs along the coast and the fertile interior, the road from Dieppe to Le Havre passes through some of the finest Norman countryside. Hitchhiking find the going easier inland on D925. Trains frequently connect the larger towns of Dieppe, Fécamp, and Le Havre, but do not stop at any other towns along the upper coast. Cycling is best for exploring, though the **CNA (Compagnie Normande d'Autobus)** and **Car Gris** bus services will shuttle you up and down the steep hills more easily. Buses run infrequently on Sunday.

Inaccessible by bus or train, **Varengeville** lies eight km south of Dieppe. Cyclists are in for some challenging slopes. A right off Varengeville's main road leads to **Parc Floral des Moutiers** (tel. 35 85 10 02), botanical gardens of unusual variety planted in 1900. (Open Easter-Nov. Wed.-Mon. 10am-noon and 2-7pm, Sun. 2-7pm. Admission 5F.) One km farther, a beautiful 12th-century Romanesque church surrounded by a 13th- to 15th-century **Maritime Cemetery** perches at the end of a rocky outcrop of coastal cliffs. Before he was buried in the church's cemetery, co-founder of cubism Georges Braque designed stained-glass windows to replace those destroyed in the war. Just outside the eastern edge of Varengeville lies the

Manoir d'Ango (tel. 35 85 12 08), a 16th-century château with a striking Byzantine-style pigeon tower. (Open late March to mid-Nov. Call ahead for hours and prices.)

A bit farther inland, toward Rouen, lies a tranquil beech forest. Guy de Maupassant was born August 5, 1850, in the nearby **Château de Miromesnil** (don't pronounce the "s"), which his mother rented for three years to ensure him a noble birth. Call ahead (tel. 35 04 40 30) and ask to be guided by Count Bertrand de Vogüe, the château's present inhabitant, who gives delightful tours in French or English. (Open May-Oct. 15 Wed.-Mon. 2-6pm. Admission 12F.)

Fécamp, two-thirds of the way to Le Havre from Dieppe, takes pride in being both an important deep-sea fishing port and a resort. Check out the impressive memorial to St-Rebecca, an 11th-century fishmonger who experienced visions after being struck by a falling tuna. The **bus station** on 8, av. Gambetta (tel. 35 28 16 04), behind Eglise St-Etienne, is served by two companies: **Auto-Car Gris,** which serves Le Havre via Goderville (8 per day, 34F) or via Etretat (8 per day, 21F), and **Compagnie Normande d'Autobus,** which runs to Rouen via Yvetot (3 per day) and to Dieppe via St-Valéry-en-Caux (4 per day). The **train station** on bd. de la République (tel. 35 28 24 82), down the steps from av. Gambetta, offers more frequent service. (Open Mon.-Fri. 5-6:30am and 8am-8pm, Sat. 8am-noon and 2-8:20pm.) Trains run from Dieppe (3 per day, 2 hr., 84F); Le Havre (6 per day, 1¼ hr., 33F); and Paris (7 per day, 21/3 hr., 123F). Fécamp's massive 11th-century **Abbatiale de la Trinité** boasts a nave that is as long as that of Notre Dame de Paris, and a tower at the transept crossing that rises some 70m. (Open May-Oct. Mon.-Sat. 11am-3pm, Sun. 11am-5pm.) To fully appreciate this "book in stone," consider taking one of the guided tours, which leave at 11am and 3pm daily from the front of the abbey (10F). The **tourist office,** pl. Bellet (tel. 35 28 20 51), across from the theater, provides free maps and a booking service. (Open daily 10am-12:30pm and 2:30-6:30pm; in off-season Mon.-Sat. 9:30am-noon and 2-6pm.) In summer, a branch office (tel. 35 29 16 34) keeps the same hours on quai Vicomte by the beach. Fécamp produces the celebrated Benedictine liqueur, distilled from aromatic plants that grow on the cliffs nearby. Guided tours of the factory, **Musée de la Bénédictine,** 110, rue Alexandre-le-Grand (tel. 35 28 00 06), last about 45 minutes and cost 23F, including a sample. (Open Easter-Nov. 11 daily 9:30-11:30am and 2-5:30pm. Without tasting ages 14-18 and over 65 10F, ages under 14 free.)

Fécamp's newly restored **Auberge de Jeunesse (IYHF),** above the town on rue du Commandant Roguigny (tel. 35 29 75 79), requires a short uphill climb from the station. (37F per person. IYHF card required. Camping 17F. Breakfast 13F. Sheets 12F. Kitchen facilities. Call ahead. Open May-Oct. 15.) They rent decent bikes for 50F per day. **Hôtel du Commerce** 28, pl. Bigot (tel. 35 28 19 28), behind the theater, has rooms for 75-85F and an 18F breakfast. The luxurious **Hôtel de la Poste,** 4, av. Gambetta (tel. 35 29 55 11) offers singles and doubles for 120F. Across town from the hostel, **Camping Château de Reneville** (tel. 35 28 20 97) is an adequate campground with hot water and a view of the beach. (9.90F per person, ages 4-7 4.95F. 3.30F per tent and per car.)

A much smaller coastal resort, **Etretat** stands guarded by its two famed portals of granite, the natural cliff arches of the **Falaise d'Amont** and the **Falaise d'Aval.** These cliffs inspired a dazzling Monet series and prove as impressive in life. A walk around the base of the Falaise d'Aval (possible only at low tide) reveals that the whole cliff has been honeycombed with block houses and gun-emplacements now plastered with seaweed and barnacles. In town, the luminous nave of the **Eglise de Notre-Dame** is worth a look. The steep hike up the cliffs from the beach brings panting visitors to the **Chapelle des Marins** (Sailors' Chapel). The view of the town and seashore will take away whatever breath you have left. The **tourist office,** pl. de la Mairie (tel. 35 27 05 21), provides free help with accommodations. Their tide table indicates the best times to explore the base of the cliffs. (Open daily 9:30am-12:30pm and 3-6pm, Sun. 10am-12:30pm; Sept. 15-June 15 Mon.-Fri. 10am-noon and 2-6pm.) **Hôtel de la Poste,** 6, av. Georges V (tel. 35 27 01 34), welcomes the weary with 100F singles (additional beds 35-55F, breakfast 25F). **Hôtel l'Escale,** pl. Maréchal Foch (tel. 35 27 03 69), offers rooms for 160F, with shower 240F, with bathtub 260F; breakfast is 25F. A better-than-average **campground** (tel. 35 27 07 67) with clean bathrooms and a playground lies 1km from town on rue Guy de Maupassant. (Adults 9F, children 4.70F, 9F per car and per tent. Gate closed 10pm-7:30am. Open March 15-Sept.)

Dieppe

In 1030 the Vicomte Gosselin d'Arques de Cigare traded the port of Dieppe, along with five salt marshes and five farm houses, to the Abbey of Mont Ste-Catherine-les-Rouen in exchange for five thousand smoked herrings each year. With its busy port, white chalk cliffs, and thriving pedestrian district, Dieppe is probably worth far more than five thousand fish today. Much smaller than Calais and Boulogne, Dieppe is connected to England only by **Sealink** ferries. Those arriving by boat should get their francs on board; there is no currency exchange in Dieppe on Sunday or Monday.

Orientation and Practical Information

Dieppe is accessible by train from Rouen or from Paris's Gare St-Lazare. Service is most frequent on Sundays, when SNCF reduces the round-trip fare. Sealink runs ferries from its terminal in the center of Dieppe and Newhaven. The Sealink terminal is conveniently close to the center of town. **Grande Rue,** across from the terminal, is the main commercial street. The beach is two blocks to your right as you walk down Grande Rue. To get to the main train station, walk along quai Duquesne away from the Sealink terminal and the beach. The tourist office is to the right down bd. Général de Gaulle. From the train station, take the footpath to the left of the building across the street and bear left through the gardens. When you get to bd. Général de Gaulle, turn right.

Tourist Office: bd. Général-de-Gaulle (tel. 35 84 11 77), in an annex of the Hôtel de Ville. Books rooms for 7F. Open Mon.-Sat. 9am-noon and 2-7pm; Sept. 16-April Mon.-Sat. 9am-noon and 2-6pm. **Annex,** Rotonde de la Plage (tel. 35 84 28 70), by the beach. Open July-Aug. only, 10am-1pm and 3-8pm.

Currency Exchange: Banks in Dieppe are open Tues.-Sat. 9am-noon and 2-5:30pm. Also at the **train station.** No Sun. or Mon. exchange anywhere.

Post Office: 2, bd. Maréchal Joffre (tel. 35 82 16 00). Open Mon.-Fri. 8am-6pm, Sat. 8am-noon. **Postal Code:** 76200.

Trains: bd. G. Clemenceau (tel. 35 98 50 50). To: Paris St-Lazare via Rouen (every 1-2 hr., 2½ hr., 97F); Rouen (every 1-2 hr., ¾-1¼ hr., 42F); Caen (change at Rouen, 123F); Le Havre (change at Rouen, 87F). Ticket office open daily 6am-8pm. Information office (tel. 35 84 23 32) open Mon.-Fri. 9am-7pm, Sat. 9am-noon and 2-6:15pm, Sun. 9am-noon and 3-6pm.

Buses: Compagnie Normande d'Autobus (tel. 35 84 21 97), next to the train station. To Rouen (4 per day, 1¾ hr., 53F) and Fécamp (1 per day, 2½ hr., 56F). Information office open Mon.-Sat. 9am-noon and 2-6pm.

Ferries: Sealink, quai Henri IV, *gare maritime* (tel. 35 84 22 60). To Newhaven (July-Sept. 4 per day, Jan.-June 3 per day; 4 hr.; one way 238F, 60 hr. return 238F, 5-day return 356F). Information office open daily 9:30am-2pm and 3-6pm.

Bike Rental: At the train station (tel. 35 84 20 71). 45F per ½-day, 50F per day, 285F per week, deposit 500F. Open daily 7am-7pm.

Laundromat: 46, rue de l'Epée (tel. 35 82 64 36), near the pedestrian district. 14F per load. Stock up on 10F and 2F coins.

Pharmacy: Pharmacie du Port, 29, quai Henri IV (tel. 35 84 22 80), across from the ferry terminal. Open Tues.-Sat. 9am-noon and 2-7pm.

Hospital: av. Pasteur.

Police: 68, quai Duquesne (tel. 35 84 87 32). **Emergency,** tel. 17.

Accommodations and Camping

Unless you have a reservation, it will be nearly impossible to find a room here in summer. Start early in the day, call two or three days ahead, or try the tourist office's booking service.

Auberge de Jeunesse (IYHF) (tel. 35 84 85 73), rue Louis Fromager. It's a long, uphill trek. Take bus #1 opposite the tourist office on bd. de Gaulle to "Javie" (every 20 min.). If you walk, turn left outside the station, turn right on rue de la République, then turn sharply left on rue Gambetta. Go up a hill, then right on av. Jean Jaurès, and left on rue Fromager. Cross through the parking lot; the hostel will be on the right (25 min.). A stopover for noisy English schoolchildren. Lumpy beds and cracking linoleum floors, but decent showers. No card needed. No lockout. Curfew 10:30pm. 49F. Showers and kitchen facilities.

Hôtel au Grand Duquesne, 15, pl. St-Jacques (tel. 35 84 21 51). Decent rooms and friendly proprietors. Singles 120F, with shower 150F. Breakfast 17F. Hearty, expensive meals available in their restaurant.

Hôtel de la Jetée, 5, rue de l'Asile Thomas (tel. 35 84 89 98), near the beach. Pleasant rooms, many with an ocean view. Exceptionally friendly management is, oddly enough, fond of *Let's Go.* Singles and doubles 105F, with bathroom 160F. Breakfast 21F.

Camping: The exceptional **Camping Vitamin** (tel. 35 82 11 11) lies on the coast a few kilometers from downtown Dieppe on chemin des Vertus. Take a bus from the train station. Showers, bar/café, swimming pool, tennis courts, bike rental. 22F per person, 45F per tent. Open April-Oct. **Camping Pré-St-Nicholas,** route de Pourville (tel. 35 84 11 39), is a more economical alternative. Atop a cliff 3km west of the city, it's a 25-min. climb from the station. 12F per person, 6F per tent. Primitive cold showers. Sells expensive hot food and groceries.

Food

Stay away from the neighborhood around the Sealink terminal, and look for the local fish specialties: *sole dieppoise, harengs marinés* (marinated herring), *soupe de poisson* (fish soup), and *marmite dieppoise* (a fish and shellfish chowder). There are several **supermarkets** on rue Duquesne and rue Gambetta, near the hostel. Unlike Calais and Boulogne, which bombard British visitors with *friteries,* Dieppe offers authentic fare at decent prices. If you prefer inauthentic fare, **Cafétéria le Viking,** near the hostel on rue Gambetta at rue Jaurès, will fill you up for 30-40F. (Open Tues.-Sun. noon-2pm and 7-9pm, Mon. noon-2pm). **Crêperie,** 22, rue de la Morinière, off Grande Rue, flips a mouth-watering selection of *galettes* for 20-38F *à la carte.* (Open Thurs.-Tues. 11:30am-2pm and 6-10pm.) **Bar-Pizzeria de L'Europe,** 57-61, rue d'Ecosse serves lasagne (34F), *couscous* (60F), *escargots* (25F), and, of course, pizza (25-38F). (Open daily noon-1:30pm and 7:30pm-12:30am.)

Sights

The German invasion of World War II is commemorated in the **Musée de Guerre,** tucked away in an underground radar base 3km southwest along route de Pourville, near Camping St-Nicolas. (Open July-Aug. daily 10am-noon and 2-6pm; Easter-June and Sept. Tues.-Sun. 10am-noon and 2-6pm. Admission 20F.) Those staying at the hostel should pay their respects at the **Canadian Cemetery** in nearby Hautot-Sur-Mer, where each identified gravestone bears an individual poem or inscription. Turn right out of the hostel, walk 15 minutes, and then turn right at the cross and sign.

Dieppe's major attraction is still its beach. On the cliffs west of the city stands the 15th-century **Château** (tel. 35 84 19 76), now the civic museum, with its celebrated ivory collection, sampling of Impressionist paintings, and permanent exhibit of George Braque's prints. (Open daily 10am-noon and 2-6pm; in off-season Wed.-Mon. Admission 10F, children 7F.)

Le Havre

Whether you approach Le Havre (pop. 200,000) by land or sea, the smog and glut of the refineries, warehouses and factories that line the docks of France's largest transatlantic port will overwhelm you. Most cruise ships from North America stop here, as do car ferries from Rosslare and Cork in Ireland and Portsmouth in England. Although he renamed the city "Bouville" ("Mudville") in his novel *La Nausée*, Jean-Paul Sartre thoroughly enjoyed pre-war Le Havre's pastel *vieille ville* and smoky port cafés.

Bombed to rubble during World War II, Le Havre has since become an experiment in French civic design. The rebuilding of the city was entrusted to architect Auguste Perret, the "magician of concrete," whose designs produced sprawling complexes, sharply geometric war monuments, and a spartan church—startling contrasts to the ornate detail found in the rest of Normandy. Perret's **Eglise St-Joseph,** with its somber interior and 107m steeple, particularly merits attention. The **Musée des Beaux Arts-André Malraux,** on bd. J. F. Kennedy (tel. 35 42 33 97), houses an airy, well-displayed collection of canvases by Ernest Boudin and the Norman Impressionists, as well as many works by Dufy, Pissarro, Monet, Sisley, and others. (Open Wed.-Mon. 10am-noon and 2-6pm. Free.) The huge white structure resembling an upside-down toilet in l'Espace Oscar Niemeyer, pl. Gambetta, is actually the newly opened **Maison de la Culture du Havre.** Whatever its shape may imply, it contains a state-of-the-art theater and cinema, which admits students into showings of classic and new films for only 20F. Unfortunately, the theater and cinema are closed mid-June through August. If postmodern architecture doesn't appeal to you, escape to the more sedate surroundings of the public park on av. Foch near the beach.

Orientation and Practical Information

Le Havre lies at the mouth of the Seine River, bordered by beach on one edge and port basins on the other. The large avenues of bd. de Strasbourg and rue de Paris intersect at **pl. de Hôtel de Ville.** Straight down av. Foch, across from bd. de Strasbourg, is the **beach.**

The train station lies east of the center of town and is an easy walk down bd. de Strasbourg. The P&O European ferry terminal lies on the southern side of town. To get to the tourist office from here, take bus #3 from Perrey or walk down rue de Paris for about 10 minutes. The Irish Ferries terminal lies much farther to the southeast. The long walk will take you through a bad neighborhood; ask at the terminal for directions to the St-Nicholas bus stop on pl. Marion (bus #4). Those arriving by ferry should change money on board. You must pay for the bus in francs, and there is no place to change money in the terminal.

Tourist Office: pl. de l'Hôtel de Ville (tel. 35 21 22 88). Turn left from the station onto bd. de Strasbourg, and walk for about 10 min., or take bus #1, 3, 4, 5, 6, or 12 from outside the train station. Accommodations service. English spoken. Open Mon.-Sat. 8:45am-12:15pm and 1:30-7pm; Nov.-Mar. 8:45am-12:15pm and 1:30-6:30pm.

American Express: 57, quai Georges V (tel. 35 42 59 11). Travel service will book anything from Eurotrain to theater tickets. Open Mon.-Fri. 8:45am-noon and 1:30-6pm.

Post Office: rue Jules-Siegfried. Poste Restante. **Currency Exchange.** Open Mon.-Fri. 8am-7pm, Sat. 8am-noon. **Postal Code:** 76600.

Trains: cours de la République (tel. 35 43 50 50). Information office open daily 7:30am-6pm. Ticket office open daily 7:30am-7pm. To: Paris (10 per day, 2 hr., 125F); Rouen (10 per day, 45 min., 56F); Fécamp (3 per day, 45 min., 35F). Baggage room open daily 5:15am-8:40pm (8F manual, 3F automatic).

Buses: bd. de Strasbourg (tel. 35 26 67 23), across from the train station. **CNA.** To: Rouen (9 per day, 106.40F) via St-Romain, Bolbec, Lillebonne, Caudebec, and Duclair. **Bus Verts** runs to Caen (3 per day, 98F), Deauville, and Honfleur via Pont Route de Tancarville. **Car**

Gris serves Fécamp (6 per day, 41F) via Etretat, Yport, or Goderville, and Etretat via Octeville. Information office open daily 8am-noon and 2-5:15pm.

Public Transportation: Buses, CGFTE, 115, rue Jules Lecesne (tel. 35 41 72 22), and at the kiosk, pl. de l'Hôtel de Ville, next to the tourist office. Fairly useful. 5F per trip; *carnet bleu* covers 10 trips (34F). All bus service stops around 9pm.

Ferries: P&O European Ferries, quai de Southampton (tel. 35 21 36 50). Bus #3 from the train station or the Hôtel de Ville. To Portsmouth, England (3 per day; 6 hr., 7 hr. at night; 280F, students 240F, children 145F, same fares for round-trip within 60 hr.). You can reserve cabins on both day and night ferries. Tickets available and information office open Mon.-Sat. 7am-noon and 2-11:30pm. **Irish Ferries,** quai du Môle Central (tel. 35 53 28 83). Take bus #4 from the Hôtel de Ville or the train station to stop Marceau. To Rosslare and Cork, Ireland (May-Sept. 4 per week; 705, students 670F, children 465F all departures; Oct.-April 3-4 per week; 565F, students 530F, children 135F.)

Laundromat: 23, rue Jean de la Fontaine. 16F per load, dry-cleaning 35F. Open daily 7am-9pm.

Pharmacy: Pharmacie Notre-Dame, 69, rue de Paris (tel. 35 41 33 41), open Mon. 2-7pm, Tues. and Thurs. 9am-noon and 2:30-7pm, and Sat. 9am-noon.

Hospital: Jacques Monat, Montvilliers (tel. 35 20 35 20).

Medical Emergency: SAMU, tel. 35 21 77 00.

Police: rue de la Victoire (tel. 35 21 11 00). **Emergency:** dial 17.

Accommodations, Camping, and Food

If you find yourself in Le Havre, avoid the questionable areas around the station and the port. The **Union Chrétienne des Jeunes Gens,** 153, bd. de Strasbourg (tel. 35 42 47 86; look for the triangular neon sign), is a centrally located YMCA *foyer* for French workers that usually has room. Decent and dormlike, it is run by a supportive staff. Their cafeteria serves breakfast and lunch Monday through Saturday (*plats du jour* 30-35F). Call ahead or show up at 5pm to book a room; they will not let you in earlier. (Open daily 7am-11pm. Singles 43F. Doubles 36F per person. Sheets 15F.) The pleasant **Hôtels St-Pierre and Jeanne d'Arc,** both at 91, rue Emile-Zola (tel. 35 41 26 83), off rue de Paris across the bridge from the tourist office, are also centrally located. (Singles and doubles with toilet 80F. Breakfast 15F.) Friendly **Hôtel France,** 85, rue Louis Brindeau (tel. 35 41 79 96) is on the other side of the river. (Open daily 7am-noon and 4:30pm-midnight. Singles 100F, with shower 130F, with bath 160F. Breakfast 20F.) **Hôtel Séjour Fleuri,** 71, rue Emile Zola (tel. 35 41 33 81), has comfortable rooms for 90-115F. (Showers 10F. Breakfast 18F.) To get to Le Havre's **Camping Municipal** (tel. 35 46 52 39) from the station, take bus #5 (last bus at 9:05pm) or bus #71 (last bus at 8:30pm) to Jenner and walk the last 20 minutes. Hot showers, ping-pong, and a nearby grocery make a stay more pleasant. (Gates closed 11pm-6:30am. 15F per person, ages 4-14 8F. 11F per tent, 11F per car. Open April through Sept.)

Good food lurks in the small streets between rue de Paris and quai Lamblardie. **Le Tilbury,** 39, rue Jean de la Fontaine, serves *à la carte* dishes (25-60F) and an elegant 68F *menu.* Their 50F luncheon *menu* is delicious but meager. (Open Tues. 7-10pm, Wed.-Sun. noon-1:30pm and 7-10pm.) On the same street at #17, the small **Crêperie Bretonne** serves *crêpes* for 6-16F in a comfortable atmosphere. (Open Tues.-Sat. noon-2pm and 7-11pm, Sun. noon-2pm.) At **Le P'tit Comptoir,** rue de la Fontaine and av. Faidherbe, by the port, business executives and sailors rub shoulders over the hearty 52F and 72F *menus.* The seafood is especially good. (Open daily 10am-2pm and 7-10pm.) Be sure to visit the **Maison des Jeunes et de la Culture,** 2, av. Foch (tel. 35 42 66 97), across from the beach and 10 minutes from the Hôtel de Ville. Take bus #1 from the Hôtel de Ville to **Porte Océane** (every 20 min., last bus at 8:30pm). This lively restaurant enjoys a great view of the ocean. (*Plat garni* 25F, children's *menu* 20F. Open Mon.-Fri. 11:30am-1:30pm, Sat. 11:30am-1pm.) The cafeteria on the first floor has daily newspapers (open Jan.-July and Sept.-Dec. Tues.-Sat. noon-8pm, Mon. noon-2pm), and a *cabaret de jazz* one Friday each month at 8:30pm. Call 35 42 61 90 for more information.

Coast: Lower Normandy

The **Corniche Normande** stretches from Honfleur to Trouville. The steep 14km road weaves through characteristically large Norman hedges, thatched-roof houses, and undisturbed green pastures that slope down to the water's edge. You should pick one of the smaller villages or nearby **Cabourg** as a touring base; the hotels in the larger resort towns charge exorbitant rates.

The best way to explore the seaside towns and the rural areas in between is by bike, but be aware that the hills are astoundingly steep. The terrain makes hitchhiking difficult and dangerous. **Bus Verts du Calvados** (tel. 31 44 77 44 in Caen, 31 89 28 41 in Honfleur, and 31 88 95 36 in Deauville) serves the entire region from Caen to Le Havre. Bus #20 runs along the coast. The fare varies with the number of zones crossed; one zone currently costs 3.90F. Tickets are sold for a minimum of two-zone travel (7.80F); a *carnet* of five tickets buys travel through ten zones at a reduced price (32F). Be sure to investigate youth reductions, and consider a *Carte Liberté* if you will be traveling extensively in the region (unlimited travel for 3 days, 100F). Three buses per day run the entire distance between Caen and Le Havre (incorporating 23 zones), but numerous buses run certain segments of the route, and you can connect almost every hour. Bus service on Sunday is less frequent.

Honfleur launched some of the great French voyages of discovery to America in the 16th and 17th centuries, including Samuel de Champlain's to Canada. Known as a *trésor des artistes* since the last century, the city drew numerous painters, who gathered around Eugène Boudin at the ferme St-Siméon. The **tourist office,** 33, cour des Fossés (tel. 31 89 23 30), by the bus station, has information on art exhibits and accommodations. (Open Mon.-Sat. 9am-noon and 2-6pm, Sun. 10am-noon; in off-season Mon.-Sat. 9am-noon and 2-6pm.)

A rich collection of pre-Impressionist and contemporary paintings from the St-Siméon school is housed at the **Eugène Boudin Museum,** rue de l'Homme du Bois (tel. 31 89 16 47). (Open March 15-Oct. 1 Wed.-Mon. 10am-noon and 2-6pm; Oct.-March 15 Mon. and Wed.-Fri. 2:30-5pm, Sat.-Sun. 10am-noon and 2:30-5pm. Admission 15F, students 12F.) Honfleur's dependence on the sea is evident in **Eglise Ste-Catherine,** unique in its use of wooden materials and parallel naves. The church was built by naval craftsmen schooled in shipbuilding techniques; its vaulted roof resembles a ship's overturned hull. (Open daily 9am-noon and 2-6pm. Free.)

Hotel prices in Honfleur are outrageous: currently the cheapest place to stay is **Hôtel Le Bras d'Or,** 55 rue de la République (tel. 31 98 81 80) which offers shabby rooms with peeling linoleum floors in a converted horse stable for 150F. Honfleur does, however, have the lovely **Le Phare campsite,** with a tiny store and restaurant about 300m from the center of town. (16.50F, children 9F, 20F per tent or car. Open April-Sept.) Honfleur's other campsite, **La Briquerie,** about 3km outside the center of nearby Equemauville (tel. 31 89 28 32), has fantastic facilities in a less convenient location (21F, children 11F, 21F per tent or car. Open May-Sept.).

Le Goéland, 21, rue de la Ville near the bus station, serves *galettes* and a delicious 65F *menu* including such house specialties as almond trout, marinated mussels, and escaloped duck. (Open Feb.-Nov. daily noon-10pm.) With reasonable prices and quick service, **La Saladerie,** in pl. Allais off bd. Charles V, tosses a huge selection of salads daily. Try the yummy *Salade au Noix,* with mixed nuts, Roquefort cheese, and potatoes (45F).

A few kilometers farther down the road are **Deauville** and **Trouville,** twin playgrounds of the 19th century's Beautiful People. Somewhat worn by the years, the two towns come alive in the summer when horse racing, casinos, and a thriving nightlife attract the flotsam and jetsam of the European elite. With wide treelined avenues and chic boutiques and restaurants, these cities are an aesthete's dream and a budgetarian's nightmare. You will probably have little use for the 350F purple umbrellas proffered by glittering shops, but both towns offer ample opportunities to stroll and people-watch. Hotels are exorbitant, but **Camping Hamel,** in Trouville (tel. 31 88 15 56), is an affordable site right on the beach (16F per person, 10F per tent or car).

The seaside resorts west of Deauville are less pretentious and more inviting. **Houlgate** has a casino right in the middle of town and a mile-long, sandy beach, perhaps the most attractive in the area. An hour's walk eastward along the beach between Houlgate and Deauville takes you to the **Vache Noire** cliffs, crumbling limestone hills that contain fossil deposits of ancient crustaceans. A tide chart is available at Houlgate's **tourist office** (tel. 31 91 33 09), next to the town hall on bd. des Belges. (Open daily 9am-1pm and 3-7pm; in off-season Tues.-Sat. only.) There is an annex just off the beach next to the casino (tel. 31 91 06 28; open in mid.-June to Aug. 9am-1pm and 3-7pm). If you wander in to Houlgate before mid-June, the town may seem as dead as the old crabs. In season, most of the hotels in town have typical coastal resort prices, leaving **Hôtel Mon Castel,** 1, bd. des Belges (tel. 31 91 34 75), as the only affordable choice. (Singles 100F. Doubles 115F, with bath 155F.) Overlooking Houlgate beach is **Camping de la Plage,** rue Henri Dobert (tel. 31 91 61 25), with hot showers. (Open daily April-Sept. Adults 14.50F, children 8.50F, 8.50F per tent, 7.50F per car.) **Club Oasis,** on the beach (tel. 31 24 41 96), rents windsurfers for 65F per hour. After a blistering day on the beach, settle down in the sedate restaurant of the **Hôtel Mon Castel** (see above), where 50F, 73F, 95F and 130F *menus* feature standard French fare such as chicken *cordon bleu* and *escargots.* (Open daily noon-2pm and 7:30-9:30pm.) Locals flock to **La Maison du Coquillage,** 37, rue des Bains, for its heaping platters of stuffed oysters and mussels (3-course seafood *menu* 85F).

Cabourg

Across the River Dives sits Cabourg, another faded 19th-century resort. Visit the impressive casino and the grand hotel facing the sea across promenade Marcel Proust, so named because the author frequently sojourned here. The town's street design follows an interesting semi-circular pattern; all roads converge on the grand hotel. Though Cabourg's beach may be its main attraction, a stroll down av. de la Mer provides an interesting glimpse of the commercial legacy of a summer boomtown. On the beach in front of the grand hotel, you can rent windsurfers for 80F per hour or 180F per day, no deposit required.

Cabourg is served by regular trains from Paris-St-Lazare; in the off-season, trains run only on Sunday. **Trains** go to Deauville (2 per day, 25F) and to Paris-St-Lazare via Deauville (2 per day, 130F). The train station (tel. 31 91 00 74) is across the Dives River from Cabourg. (Open Mon.-Sat. 9am-noon and 2-5:30pm, Sun. 10am-noon and 2:30-8:10pm.) **Bus Verts du Calvados** (tel. 31 44 77 44) has three stops in Cabourg and frequent service to Caen, Houlgate, Honfleur, Deauville, Trouville, and Le Havre. Check any convenient stop for exact times; there is no station. Buy a ticket from the driver. You'll find the **tourist office,** Jardins du Casino (tel. 31 91 01 09) in front of the grand hotel as you approach the beach. (Open Mon.-Sat. 9am-noon and 2-6:30pm, Sun. 10am-1pm and 3-6:30pm.) You can rent standard Peugeot 10-speed bicycles for 48F per day from the train station (open daily 8am-noon and 2-6pm; deposit 300F) or adult and children's bikes for 60F per day at the **Bureau de Bains,** facing the Grand Hôtel (tel. 31 91 27 00).

The most reasonable place to stay is the **Hôtel au Bon Coin,** 23, av. du Commandant Levillain (tel. 31 91 03 64), across from the 8 Mai bus stop. (Singles and doubles 100F, with bath 130F. Showers 10F. Breakfast 18F.) Expensive (and carcinogenic) but attractive **L'Oie qui Fume,** 18, av. de la Brèche-Buchot (tel. 31 91 27 79), off the end of av. Georges Clemenceau, has pleasant rooms with sagging mattresses for 135F. Obligatory breakfasts (20F) are served in a flower-filled dining room. **Camping Plage,** rue Charles de Gaulle (tel. 31 91 05 75), has prices to match its high rating. (Adults 24F, children 14F, 40F per tent or car. Tax 1F. Open April to mid-Nov.) You can also try the smaller **Oasis Camping,** rue Charles de Gaulle (tel. 31 91 10 62), farther down the road from Camping Plage. (Adults 15F, children 10F, 22F per tent or car. Open April to mid-Sept.) For a good meal after a day in the sun, try **Le Champagne,** pl. du Marché (tel. 31 91 02 29), with 3-course *menus* from 60F, *à la carte* 40-70F. (Open in summer daily noon-2pm and 7-9pm.) At **El Mamounia,** 33, rue de la Mer (tel. 31 24 13 63), the turbaned chef serves up heaping platters of *couscous* mixed with 7 Indian vegetables (48F). Recline, stuffed, on the red and green pillows scattered across the floor, and remind yourself that you're in Normandy. (Open daily 11:30am-3pm and 6:30-11pm.)

Caen

"One moment it was there; the next, the whole town—parks, churches, shops—dissolved into a pile of dust." So gasped an American soldier to reporters in 1944, but in the years since World War II, the capital of Lower Normandy has been neatly rebuilt with a feeling for its history; William the Conqueror's favorite town retains a charm unmatched by other reconstructed cities.

Caen (pop. 120,000) served as William's ducal seat from 1035 to 1087. The red flag with two gold lions that flies above the château was the standard of the Dukes of Normandy, later incorporated into the English flag by the Plantagenet kings. Today, Caen has visibly become a politically aware university town. Political posters and graffiti cover all wall space, and students crowd the many small cafés and bookstores around the château.

Orientation and Practical Information

Caen is served frequently by trains from Paris's Gare St-Lazare (2 hr., 133F). The station is far from the center of town and from the university. Walk to your right as you exit, and then take a right onto rue de la Gare, which continues as av. du 6 Juin. Any of the buses stopping every few minutes at the station (except #5) will take you to the center of town (5.50F); you will be let off a block from rue St-Pierre and the tourist office.

The center of Caen is neatly enclosed by a parallelogram: the station is outside the southern edge, and the château and Abbaye-aux-Hommes serve as adjacent northern corners. **Rue St-Pierre** and **rue de Strasbourg** flank the major pedestrian precincts and shopping centers.

Tourist Office: pl. St-Pierre (tel. 31 86 27 65), by the church. English-speaking staff will help you find accommodations for a 10F fee. Ask for regional information; they have itineraries covering all of Lower Normandy's "cheese-and-cider routes." From June through Sept., they also change money. Open Mon. 10am-7pm, Tues.-Sat. 8am-7pm, Sun. 10am-12:30pm and 3-6pm; Oct.-May Mon. 10am-noon and 2-7pm, Tues.-Sat. 9am-noon and 2-7pm.

Post Office: pl. Gambetta. Poste Restante. Open Mon.-Fri. 8am-7pm, Sat. 8am-noon. **Postal Code:** 14000.

Trains: pl. de la Gare (tel. 31 83 50 50). To: Paris (17 per day, 2 hr., 133F); Rouen (4 per day, 1½ hr., 96F); Cherbourg (5 per day, 1½ hr., 81F); Rennes (5 per day, 143F); Tours (5 per day, 148F). There are **baggage lockers** on the platforms (5-10F, 3-day max.); you can also store your bags in the office (9F per day). Information center open Mon.-Sat. 7:30am-7:30pm. Station open daily 5am-9:30pm.

Buses: Next to the train station (tel. 31 86 55 30). This is the central terminal for the **Bus Verts** covering the Calvados region from Le Havre to Carentan. Frequent service to Pont l'Eveque, Deauville, Bayeux, Corseulles, Falaise, Le Havre, and Carentan (5-10 daily). Open Mon. 6:40am-12:30pm and 1-7pm, Tues.-Fri. 7:30am-12:30pm and 1-7pm, Sat. 9am-12:30pm and 3-7pm.

Bike Rental: At the station. 40F per half-day, 50F per day, deposit 500F. Open daily 6am-8:30pm.

Laundromat: Lavomatique, 16, rue de Strasbourg. About 20F per load; accepts all coins. Open daily 7:30am-8pm.

Pharmacy: 56, rue St-Pierre (tel. 31 85 44 31). Open Mon.-Sat. 8:30am-12:30pm and 1:45-7:30pm.

Hospital: Hôpital Clemenceau, av. Côte de Nacre (tel. 31 44 81 12).

Police: rue Jean Romain (tel. 31 86 08 34). **Emergency,** tel. 17.

Accommodations and Camping

In addition to the youth hostel, there are plenty of pleasant, reasonable hotels and student accommodations in Caen. In summer, the inexpensive hostel and university housing fills quickly, so call ahead and reserve if possible.

Auberge de Jeunesse (IYHF), Foyer Robert Reme, 68bis, rue Restout (tel. 31 52 19 96). It's a long walk—about 30 minutes from the train station and 40 from the *centre ville*. Take bus #3 (*direction* "Grâce de Dieu") to Armand Marie. A clean and recently renovated hostel and workers' dormitory. Melvin, one of the directors, is an American baseball player and all-around cool guy. IYHF card preferred but not required. Reception open daily 5-10pm. Lockout 10am-5pm. 52F per person. Breakfast included. Filling lunch and dinner 35F. Open June-Sept.

Centre International de Séjour, la Cité (tel. 31 95 41 00), 5km north of town in Hérouville-St-Clair. Take bus #6 or 7 from the station. Spacious, carpeted singles 73F. IYHF members 62F per person. Triples available. Hot showers and breakfast included.

University Housing: CROUS, 23, av. de Bruxelles (tel. 31 94 73 37), north of the château. Student ID required. Office open Mon.-Fri. 9am-12:15pm and 1:45-4pm, Sat. 1:45-4pm. Call ahead; reserve in writing at least 2 weeks in advance if possible. No curfew. Adequate singles are a good value at 53F. Hot showers included. Breakfast about 5F at **Restaurant B,** east of the track. Dinner at 7:30pm with student's meal ticket about 10F. Open Feb.-Sept.

Hôtel de la Paix, 14, rue Neuve-St-Jean (tel. 31 86 18 99), off av. du 6 Juin. Comfortable establishment with a helpful proprietor. Singles and doubles 93F, with shower 128F. Breakfast 20F.

Hôtel Demolombe, 36, rue Demolombe (tel. 31 85 48 70), between pl. St-Pierre and the Abbaye-aux-Hommes. Acceptable, somewhat rundown rooms in excellent location. Singles 85-90F. Doubles 110F. Breakfast 18F.

Hôtel St-Jean, 20, rue des Martyrs (tel. 31 86 23 35), near pl. de la Résistance. Quiet location. Clean and modern place with a cathedral view. Private parking. Singles and doubles 110F, with shower 140F. Breakfast 16F.

Camping: Terrain Municipal, route de Louvigny (tel. 31 73 60 92). Take bus #13 ("Louvigny"). 6F per person, 3F per tent. Hot showers. Open June-Sept.

Food

There are several inexpensive *crêperies* and *brasseries* near the château around rue du Vaugueux and av. de la Libération. For the jaded travelers who find themselves incapable of facing another meal ending in "*-ette*," the area also has Indian, Spanish, Chinese and Italian restaurants. Fruit and vegetable sellers show off their wares Tuesday through Saturday mornings under the trees in pl. Courtonne. For large quantities, bargain.

Restaurant Kouba, 6, rue du Vaugueux. Hearty *couscous* from 46F. Tabouli 19F. Open daily noon-2pm and 7-11pm.

Le Ty-Coz, 13, rue Pierre Aimé Lair, off bd. de Strasbourg across from pl. de la République. A comfortable dinerlike *crêperie* serving basic *crêpes* (6-18F) and *galettes* (8-28F). Open Mon.-Sat. 11:30am-7pm.

La Petite Marmite, 43, rue des Jacobins, not far from the theater. Some fine cooking. Dress nicely—tuxedos have been spotted here. 88F and 138F *menus* include Norman specialties such as *soupe de pêcheur* and *faux filet grillé au poivre vert.* Open Mon.-Fri. and Sat. evening.

Sights and Entertainment

Because of Caen's great prosperity in the late 11th century, the contemporary city has inherited some of France's finest Romanesque architecture. William the Conqueror's reign coincided with a newly fervid acceptance of Christianity by Norman dukes and initiated the reopening of monasteries and the construction of new churches across the region. William and his incestuous bride Matilda founded both of Caen's great abbeys in 1066.

In the center of town lie the ruins of William's imposing **château** (open daily 6am-9:30pm; Oct.-April 6am-7:30pm). Within the walls, the modern **Musée des Beaux Arts** (tel. 31 85 28 63) contains a few paintings by Perugino, Rubens, Van Dyck, and Monet, as well as van der Weyden's outstanding *La Vièrge à l'Enfant* and a collection of modern works (Open Wed.-Mon. 10am-noon and 1:30-6pm; 6F, students 3F, Sun. free). The **Musée de Normandie** (tel. 31 86 06 24), across the way, traces Norman peasant life through the centuries, highlighting such local crafts as lace and candle making. (Open Wed.-Mon. 10am-noon and 2-6pm; Nov.-Feb. 10am-noon and 2-5pm. Admission 6F, students 3F, Sun. free. Combination ticket 7F.)

Caen boasts seven noteworthy churches scattered throughout the city. In the shadow of the château stands **Eglise St-Pierre,** whose famous bell tower and detailed exterior illustrate the evolution of the Gothic style from the 13th through the 16th centuries. (Open daily 9am-noon and 2-6pm.) Straight down rue St-Pierre at the west end of the city stands **Eglise St-Etienne,** which dates from the 11th to the 13th centuries. The church mixes the Romanesque and Gothic schools of architecture, its sober exterior façade hiding a beautifully intricate interior. (Open daily 8:15am-noon and 2-7:30pm.) The adjacent **Abbaye-aux-Hommes,** off rue Guillaume le Conquerant, was founded by William the Conqueror as atonement for the sin of marrying his cousin Matilda. Rebuilt in the 18th century, the abbey was used as a *lycée* and is now Caen's Hôtel de Ville. (Tours in French daily every hr. 9am-noon and 2-5pm. Admission 8F, groups 4F per person. Call ahead.) The smaller and less ornate **Eglise de la Trinité** of the **Abbaye-aux-Dames,** off rue des Chanoines (Matilda's penance for her part in the same sin), has a Romanesque interior and two 16th-century towers. To visit the crypt, enter through the low doorway in the south transept. (Open daily 9am-noon and 2-6pm. Free guided visits, in French only, daily 2:30 and 4pm.)

On the northern edge of town, the new **Mémorial: Un Musée pour la Paix** (tel. 31 06 06 44), is definitely worth a visit. Take bus #12 (every 15-20 min.) from the city center to the Memorial. Opened in July 1988, this modern museum uses high tech audiovisual aids as well as photos, sketches, newspapers, and armaments from WWII to make a serious plea for world peace. This unique museum covers the pre-war years in Europe as well as the Battle of Normandy and the liberation of France. The entire visit takes at least two hours, including an excellent hour-long series of films on the war and humanity's hopes for the future. (Open daily 9am-10pm; Sept.-May 9am-7pm. Admission 30F, students 15F.)

North of the château (left along the ramparts to rue du Gaillon) is Caen's **Université,** founded in 1432 by England's Henry VI. Unlike most French universities, all the buildings lie within a clearly defined campus. The iron phoenix at the entrance symbolizes the university's rebirth after its destruction in 1944. Although you can always meet students here, be aware that Americans take over in summer. Near the university, you can picnic or meditate in the expansive, bucolic **Jardin des Plantes** on pl. Blot (open 8am-sunset).

Caen puts up with a number of bars and discos, especially on the streets that wind around the château toward the university. At the £Pub Concorde, 7, rue Montoir Poissonnerie (tel. 31 93 61 29) a friendly crowd drinks 150 types of beer gathered from around the world. Mellow out with the locals over nightly jazz concerts at the **Retro Piano-Bar,** 9, rue Fresnel (tel. 31 44 09 19), or mingle with the livelier, younger crowd dancing to disco and house music at **Le Chic,** 19, pl. Courtonne (tel. 31 94 48 72).

Stop by the university housing office at CROUS, 23, av. de Bruxelles (tel. 31 94 73 37) for a free copy of *Le Mois à Caen,* which lists plays, concerts, and exhibitions for the month.

Bayeux

A beautifully preserved, ancient town, Bayeux (pop. 15,000) is famous for its tapestry, an 11th-century linen embroidery nearly a football field long that depicts the Norman invasion of Britain. In addition, Bayeux is home to a large museum commemorating the 1944 invasion of Normandy and a convenient base for exploring the D-Day beaches themselves by bicycle or bus. The first French city to be liberated by Allied troops during World War II, Bayeux suffered far less damage than its neighboring cities.

Orientation and Practical Information

Bayeux is on the Caen-Rennes and Paris-Cherbourg train lines. The station is about 10 minutes from the town center. Turn left onto the highway (bd. Sadi-Carnot) and then right, following the signs to the *centre ville.* Once there, continue up rue Larcher until it hits **rue St-Martin,** Bayeux's commercial boulevard. On your right, **rue St-Jean** marks the beginning of the pedestrian zone.

Tourist Office: 1, rue des Cuisiniers (tel. 31 92 16 26), in a 14th-century wooden building. From the cathedral, turn right onto rue Bienvenue, which becomes rue des Cuisiniers. English spoken. You can book a room for the cost of a phone call. Open Mon.-Sat. 9:30am-12:30pm and 2-6:30pm, Sun. 10am-12:30pm and 3-6:30pm; mid-Sept. to May Mon.-Sat. 9:30am-12:30pm and 2-6:30pm.

Currency Exchange: Banks open Tues.-Fri. 9:15am-5:30pm, Sat. 9:15am-4:30pm, and the 1st Monday of each month. Change money at the **tourist office** on Mon. when banks are closed.

Post Office: rue Larcher. Poste Restante. Open Mon.-Fri. 8am-7pm, Sat. 8am-noon. **Postal Code:** 14400.

Trains: pl. de la Gare (tel. 31 92 92 40), 10 min. from the center of town. To: Paris (2¼ hr., 8 per day, 143F); Lille (5 per day, 239F); Caen (12 per day, 24F). Open daily 6am-9pm, information office open daily 8am-8pm.

Buses: Bus Verts, pl. de la Gare (tel. 31 44 71 44), serves Port-en-Bessin and other points west as well as Le Havre and other towns east, via Caen. **STDC,** pl. de la Gare (tel. 31 92 02 92), provides a coach-hire service. No local bus transportation in Bayeux.

Taxis: Les Taxis du Bessin, tel. 31 92 92 40. Open 24 hrs. **Allo Taxi,** at the train station (tel. 31 92 04 10). Open 7am-9pm.

Bike Rental: At the station (tel. 31 92 80 50). 50F per day, 175F per week. Open daily 8am-8pm. **Family Home,** 39, rue Général de Dais (tel. 31 92 15 22). Rusty 3-speeds only. 50F per day. Deposit 100F. Open 7am-7pm. **Daniel Pitard,** 29, rue St-Jean (tel. 31 92 27 85). Decent 10-speeds. 40F per day.

Laundromat: 10, rue Maréchal Foch. Walk down the main street from the tourist office and turn left at the traffic light. About 16F per load; bring plenty of 2F coins.

Pharmacy: rue des Chanoines (tel. 31 92 03 97).

Hospital: rue de Nesmond (tel. 31 92 29 47), conveniently located next to the tapestry exhibit.

Police: av. Conseil (tel. 31 92 94 00). **Emergency,** tel. 17.

Accommodations, Camping, and Food

The Family Home in Bayeux is a rare find, both for food and lodging. Make reservations a day or two in advance or arrive in the morning.

Auberge de Jeunesse (IYHF)—Family Home, 39, rue Général de Dais (tel. 31 92 15 22). Follow the signs for the "Family Home" from the train station; the signs for "Auberge de Jeunesse" have no arrows. Not a traditional hostel, but a converted 16th-century abbey that has eclectic decor. The evening meal is wonderful and huge (55F)—do not stay overnight in Bayeux without eating here. If they have room at the table, you can eat without being an overnight guest; just call ahead. Camping facilities available in nearby field. Open daily 7am-11pm. 69F, nonmembers 75F. Showers and breakfast included. Bicycle rental 50F per day; deposit 100F. Reservations accepted and often necessary. Open year-round.

Centre d'Accueil, chemin de Boulogne (tel. 31 92 08 19), 10 min. from the town center. Walk left along bd. Sadi-Carnot, following it as it becomes bd. Leclerc; the center is near the Musée de la Bataille de Normandie. Big, modern, comfortable, and noisy. A good deal, but not as much fun as the Family Home. Groups welcome. Reception open 9-11:30am and 2:30-8pm. No lockout. Single rooms 65F, nonmembers 70F. Breakfast included. Kitchen facilities. Open year-round.

Hôtel de la Tour d'Argent, 31, rue Larcher (tel. 31 92 30 08), over a *brasserie* behind the cathedral. Decent singles and doubles 105F. Triples 150F. No showers. Breakfast 18F.

Hôtel Notre-Dame, 44, rue des Cuisiniers (tel. 31 92 87 24), next to the cathedral. A luxurious establishment with high prices. Singles and doubles 103F, with shower 180F. Fancy restaurant downstairs posts 75-165F *menus.*

La Poulinière (tel. 31 92 51 03), 6km from bayeux in Nonant. English-speaking Mme Simand offers Family Home-style bed and breakfast on the edge of her apple orchard. *Cidre* and calvados made on the premises. Doubles 80F per person. 4-course evening meal 80F, under 12 40F (not served on weekends).

Camping: Municipal Camping, bd. Eindhoven (tel. 31 92 08 43), within easy reach of the town center and right next to RN13. Follow the signs from the train station. Covered swimming pool. 8F per person, 5F per tent, 3.70F per car. Hot showers included. Open March-Oct.

Slide into the leather seats of **Les Arcades,** 10, rue Laitière, where 49F, 65F and 79F *menus* include typical French *pâtés,* chicken and veal dishes (open daily 11:30am-1:30pm, 7-9:30pm). **Ma Normandie,** 41, rue St-Patrice, has a good three course lunch *menu* for 50F, as does the **Hôtel Notre-Dame** (open daily 11:30am-1:30pm and 7:30-9:30pm). Two doors up the street, **Crêperie de la Notre Dame,** 8, rue de la Juridiction, folds surprisingly inexpensive *crêpes* (6-21F) and *galettes* (9-29F) to eat in or take out. (Open Mon.-Sun. noon-2pm and 7-9pm.) **Pizza Marsala,** 17, rue des Cuisiniers, serves good 'za and a fine variety of omelettes, plus spaghetti (26-42F) and *escalope bolognaise* (62F).

Sights

The **Tapisserie de Bayeux,** actually a linen embroidery, was probably commissioned by Odon de Conteville, bishop of Bayeux, to illustrate the Norman conquest of the English King Harold by his half-brother William at the Battle of Hastings in 1066. Despite the legend that Queen Matilda herself did the embroidery, experts now believe that the tapestry is the product of an English workshop. If you can't tell a long bow (Norman) from a crossbow (English), note that the English are depicted with moustaches and the Normans without. Seventy meters long but not quite two feet high, the tapestry was probably designed to hang in the cathedral. It is now preserved in a spacious, renovated seminary on rue de Nesmond (tel. 31 92 05 48). Viewing is preceded by a brilliant slide show and various (lengthy) exhibitions; the 5F cassette explanation is interesting. (Exhibitions and audio cassette in French and English. Open daily 9am-7pm; Oct.-March 15 9:30am-12:30pm and 2-6pm; March 16-May 9am-12:30pm and 2-6:30pm. Admission 20F, students 10F.)

If you plan to visit other museums in Bayeux as well, consider investing in a slightly discounted ticket good for admission to the **Musée Mémorial de la Bataille de Normandie, Musée Diocésain d'Art Religieux, Musée Baron Gérard,** and the Tapisserie de Bayeux. (44F, students and children 22F. Available at all museums.) A masterpiece of Norman design, Bayeux's impressive **Cathédrale** stands near the Tapisserie de Bayeux. Gothic spires top Romanesque towers, which squat on top of a small Roman church, now an underground crypt. Informal guided tours are given in summer. (Open daily 8am-7:30pm; Sept.-June 8am-noon and 2-7pm.) Across the street, the Musée Baron Gérard, pushes a rather inconsequential collection of porcelain, but does houses a few David canvases and some nice lacework. In front of the entrance to the museum stands an *arbre de la liberté* (liberty tree), planted in 1797. (Museum admission included in the ticket to the tapestry. Open same hours.) Nearby, the **Jessica Avery Museum of Commemorative Flatware** is unfortunately closed for renovations.

Near the Centre d'Accueil and the British war cemetery, the **Musée Memorial de la Bataille de Normandie—1944**, bd. Fabian Ware (tel. 31 92 93 41), recalls the Battle of Normandy through a large collection of uniforms, equipment, and photographs, and 100 life-size models and dioramas. The cost of admission includes an excellent, 40-minute film in English and French. (Open daily 9am-7pm; March-May and Sept.-Oct. daily 9:30am-12:30pm and 2-6:30pm; Nov.-Feb. Sat.-Sun. 10am-12:30pm and 2-6:30pm. Admission 18F, students 9F.)

The **Musée Diocésain d'Art Religieux**, 6, rue Lambert-Leforestier, at the Hôtel du Doyen, displays an unexciting collection of ecclesiastical dress, ceremonial banners, chalices, and ancient manuscripts. (Open daily 10:30am-12:30pm and 2-7pm; Sept. 18-March 18 Mon.-Sat. 10am-12:30pm and 2-7pm. 8F;, students 5F.)

The **Monastère St-Trinité**, 48, rue St-Loup (tel. 31 92 02 99) was founded in 1648 and is today home to about 35 aging Benedictine nuns who have dedicated their lives to reflection and prayer but are more than willing to chat with visitors in French. Although the central buildings are closed to the public, you can wander in the garden and attend a one-hour, incense-laden mass in the monastery. (Mass Mon.-Sat. 8am, Sun. 9:30am).

Near Bayeux: The D-Day Beaches

North of Bayeux are the British and Canadian D-Day landing beaches and, farther west, the American landing beaches of Omaha and Utah. Commemorative monuments, war cemeteries, and battle museums near the beaches pay homage to those who participated in military history's largest seaborne invasion. The drama began here at dawn on June 6, 1944, along a 50-mile stretch of coastline divided into lengths dubbed Utah, Omaha, Sword, Juno, and Gold. Operation "Overlord" dispersed over 16,000 troops of the American 82nd and 101st airborne divisions and the British 6th parachute brigade. The mission of the 82nd and 101st was to cut road and rail links between Paris and Cherbourg and to cover the Utah Beach landings; that of the 6th parachute brigade was to capture bridges over the Orne River and protect the eastern flank of the invasion.

Most of the paratroopers' objectives were successfully carried out. The town hall in Ste-Mère-Eglise displays the American flag that paratroopers of the 82nd division planted to mark the liberation of the village. The **Voie de la Liberté** (Liberty Highway) begins at kilometer "0" in front of the town hall; similar milestones indicate each kilometer of the U.S. Army's advance to Bastogne in Belgium. The **Musée C-47** houses the C-47 that spilled U.S. paratroops over the Ste-Mère-Eglise district. (Open daily June-Aug. 9am-7pm; Jan. 15-May and Sept.-Nov. 16 9am-noon and 2-7pm. Admission 12F, under 14 6F. For group tours call 38 41 41 35.)

At **Utah Beach,** near Isigny-sur-Mer, an exhibition on the landing is housed in a blockhouse near the American Commemorative Monument. A model of the operation shows how 836,000 soldiers, 220,000 vehicles, and 725,000 tons of equipment were brought ashore. (Open daily 9am-noon and 2-7pm; in off-season Sun. and bank holidays only. For group tours, call 33 42 04 03 or 33 42 05 36.)

Following D514 from Isigny to Port-en-Bessin, you will cross the landing point behind Omaha Beach. At **Colleville-St-Laurent,** 19km from Bayeux on the coast between Arromanches and Grandchamps, the American cemetery stands as a powerful memorial to the 70,000 men who gave their lives. More than 6000 American soldiers were killed on the first day alone. Row after row of white crosses and Jewish stars, many unmarked, form a dizzying pattern across the land. The **Pointe du Hoc,** a sheer 100-ft. cliff just west of Colleville, concealed six 155mm German guns that covered both Utah and Omaha beaches. At 7:10am on June 6, 1944, 225 U.S. Rangers, led by Lt. Col. Rudder, stormed the point and within an hour destroyed the guns, thus neutralizing the threat to the Allies landing below. The rangers then held out under German counterattack for two days and nights before being relieved by a U.S. regiment. Underground German command tunnels pass between yawning craters.

Ten km north of Bayeux on D514 is Arromanches, a small town at the center of Gold Beach. Here the British built Port Winston in one day on June 6, 1944, using retired ships and mammoth blocks of concrete towed across the Channel at 1½ miles per hour and sunk in a wide semi-circle a mile out to sea. The enormous artificial harbor provided shelter while the Allies unloaded their supplies. The **Musée du Débarquement,** on the beach (tel. 31 22 34 31), houses fascinating relics and photographs of the British and Canadian landings. A film included in the price of admission is in French, but English films can be arranged for groups. (Open daily 9am-6:30pm, Sept.-June 9-11:30am and noon-5:30pm. Admission 15F, students 10F.)

Juno Beach, the landing site of the Canadian forces, lies east of Arromanches. The Canadian cemetery is located at **Bény-sur-Mer-Reviers,** near Courseulles, and there are commemorative monuments at Bernières, Courseulles, and St-Aubin. The second British beach, "Sword," continues east from Juno Beach. There are British cemeteries at **Hermanville-sur-Mer** and **Ranville.** Like their American counterparts, the British and Canadian paratroops spent the first hours of the June 6 invasion in confusion as they tried to organize at predetermined rallying points. War museums at **Benouville** and **Merville** recall the battles fought in the pre-dawn twilight.

The easiest way to see the D-Day beaches is through **Bus Fly,** 24, rue Montfiquet (tel. 31 22 00 08). The tour includes all of the beaches, the American cemetery, and the **Musée du Débarquement** entrance fee. The bus leaves from the Family Home at 9am and 2pm daily (100F).

Bus Verts serves **Port-en-Bessin** and other points west (bus #70; Mon.-Sat. 3 per day). Bus #74 serves **Arromanches** and other points east with three daily departures (12:18pm, 1:20pm, and 6:18pm). Alternately, rent a bike for the trip to Arromanches or Colleville from Bayeux (10km). All routes are relatively flat. Restaurants in this area tend to be both substandard and expensive; an exception is the country inn of **M. et Mme. Gerouard,** 14710 Trevieres, Asniers-en-Bessin, off N13 (tel. 31 22 44 14), which serves savory and ample *menus* from 65F (reservations appreciated).

There is a fairly large, municipal campground at Arromanches, av. de Verdun (tel. 33 22 36 78). Slightly better is **Camping Reine Mathilde** at Etreham, near Porten-Bessin, 2½km from the sea, 7km from Omaha Beach, and 9km from Bayeux (31 21 76 55). Both are fully equipped—and densely packed. (18F per person, 20F per tent. Open weekends in May, June to mid-Sept.)

Cotentin Peninsula

The road from Cherbourg to Avranches passes through the rugged, hilly Cotentin countryside and a handful of picturesque, historic towns. Transportation is no problem; most towns are connected by train, SNCF bus, or an STN bus based in Cherbourg. Hitchhiking is often unsuccessful as most major roads are used by heavily-packed cars arriving by ferry and hurrying south to their final destinations. Biking may well be preferable to waiting in stations; novices, however, may end up spending more time pushing than riding.

Cherbourg

At the northern tip of the peninsula, Cherbourg, nicknamed *"Port de la Libération"* during WW II, is now a major port with numerous ferry and train connec-

tions. The tides of ferry passengers that wash in and out have sparked the development of an active nightlife featuring discos, casinos, and fine restaurants.
Unfortunately, aside from its after-hours activity, Cherbourg has little appeal; there
is little reason to linger here between connections.

Irish Ferries, Gare Maritime Sud (tel. 33 44 28 96), runs ferries to Rosslare, Ireland (2-5 per week, 17 hr., 470-705F, students 430-670F; Oct.-May 355F, students
310F; also serves Le Havre. Information office open Mon. and Wed.-Fri. 9am-noon
and 2-6pm.) **P&O European Ferries** (tel. 33 44 20 13) serves Portsmouth, England.
(1 per day, 170-250F, students 145-175F. Also serves Le Havre.) **Brittany Ferries**
(tel. 33 43 43 68) sails to Poole, England six times per day, May through September
(140-220F). **Hoverspeed** (tel. 33 20 43 38) connects Cherbourg and Portsmouth,
England daily (280F).

The **train station** (tel. 33 57 50 50) is a 10-minute walk from the ferry terminal,
on the southern side of the Bassin du Commerce. Walk straight off the pier onto
quai de l'Ancien Arsenal, which turns into quai de l'Entrepôt, turn right onto av.
François Millet. The train station will be on your left. (Open Mon.-Fri. 6am-noon
and 2-6:30pm, Sat. 9am-noon and 2-6pm, Sun. 9am-noon and 2-5pm.) Trains run
to Paris (6 per day, 3¼ hr., 280F); Rouen (3 per day, 3 hr., 161F); Caen (6 per
day, 1¼ hr., 78F); Bayeux (9 per day, 1 hr., 63F); Avranches (3 per day, 3 hr.,
96F); Rennes (3 per day, change at Lison, 4 hr., 151F). An **SNCF** bus also runs
to Coutances (3 per day, 2 hr., 49F). There are luggage **lockers** (3F) at the station.
Across the street from the station is **Autocars STN** (tel. 33 44 32 22), which makes
infrequent runs to Auderville, Les-Pieux, Siouville, Carteret, Barfleur, St-Vaast, and
Carentan. (20-40F, open Mon.-Fri. 8am-noon and 2-6:30pm.)

The helpful Cherbourg **tourist office** (tel. 33 93 52 02), lies at the other end of
the Bassin du Commerce, has plenty of brochures on the Cotentin. (English spoken.
Open Mon.-Fri. 9am-noon and 1:30-6pm, Sat. 9am-noon at the main office; **annex**
at the Gare Maritime open June-Sept. daily 9am-noon and 1:30-6pm.) The **post office** is on rue de l'Ancien Quai, a 5-minute walk west of the Bassin du Commerce.
Major banks such as **Crédit Lyonnais** and **Banque Nationale de Paris** are located
on rue Gambetta, west of the Bassin du Commerce. You can also try the **Bureau
de Change** at the ferry terminal.

The **Auberge de Jeunesse,** 109, av. du Paris (tel. 33 44 26 31), about 300m east
of the train station, in the Centre Social et Culturel (36F per night, breakfast 14F,
sheets 12F) may be open in 1991. **Hôtel Divette,** 15, Rue Louis XVI (tel. 33 43
21 04), about a 5-minute walk north of the train station, has acceptable rooms with
sagging, canoe-like mattresses. (95F per person, 120F with shower. Breakfast 16F.)
Ask the tourist office for a free list of **bed and breakfast** accommodations. Most
offer singles beginning at 100-120F.

Along the canal and up many of the side streets are luxury hotels and seafood
restaurants, plus various casinos, cafés, and discos. The **Café du Théâtre,** pl. du Théâtre, recreates *fin-de-siècle* elegance with its glass exterior and plush decor. The
menu is expensive—stick to the delicious ice creams starting at 32F. (Open Tues.-
Sat. 8am-1am, Sun.-Mon. 8am-8pm). Across the street in the Place du Théâtre,
local vendors peddle fruit, cheese, and flowers in a huge **market** every Tuesday and
Thursday morning.

If you have time between connections, visit the **Musée de la Libération** (tel. 33
20 14 12), perched atop the Montagne du Roule in the old citadel, is about 1½ km
from the center of town and behind the youth hostel. If the large collection of German and American weaponry, photos, and documents doesn't thrill you, the panoramic view of Cherbourg and its surroundings may justify the strenuous hike.
(Open Wed.-Mon. 9am-noon and 2-6pm; Oct.-March Wed.-Mon. 9:30am-noon and
2-5:30pm. Admission 5F.) A somber incestuous love story marks the **Château de
Tourlaville,** a strikingly beautiful 16th-century structure in the Italian Renaissance
style, about 4km east of Cherbourg. Sixteenth-century siblings Julien and Marguerite de Ravalet lived here until Marguerite's vengeful husband exposed the liaison
and had the pair publicly executed in Paris. Only the surrounding park and gardens

are open to visitors, who may or may not be publicly executed in Paris. Take bus #1e (9F) and get off at Eglantines.

In **Lessay** stands a fine Romanesque abbey, which hosts the raucous Holy Cross Fair each September. Visit on any Sunday to hear the mass sung in Gregorian chant; call the town hall in Lessay (tel. 33 46 46 18) to check the mass time. Lessay lies midway between Cherbourg and Coutances and is accessible by STN buses. Otherwise, rent bikes at **LAMY**, 52, rue du Val de Saire (tel. 33 44 33 04) for 50F with a 100F deposit.

Coutances

Southeast of Lessay, Coutances is an attractive and peaceful religious center with three churches aligned on a hill. Its 13th-century **Cathédrale,** which Victor Hugo called the most beautiful cathedral since Chartres, survived the war unscathed (open daily 8am-7pm). Note the 12 small pointed towers tucked into the two main spires, a common feature of churches in the area.

On the opposite side of the town hall from the cathedral are the **Musée Quesnel Morinière** and the **Jardin des Plantes.** The museum houses a fairly interesting collection of 18th- and 19th-century paintings, as well as regional pottery and period costumes. (Open Wed.-Mon. 10am-noon and 2-6pm. Admission 12F.) Though the intricate formal garden may appear to be all that's worth seeing, check out the 18th-century 400-liter Norman cider press near the museum courtyard. (Open daily 9am-11:30pm, Oct.-March 9am-5pm, April-June 9am-8pm.) The 15th- and 16th-century **Eglise St-Pierre,** south of the cathedral, contains a unique baroque organ. (Same hours as the cathedral).

The **train station** (tel. 33 07 50 77) is a 15-minute walk downhill from the cathedral. (Open Mon.-Fri. 5am-8:30pm, Sat. 5:30am-8pm, Sun. 7:30am-10:45pm). Trains run to Rennes (2 per day, 1¼ hr., 81F); Caen (5 per day, 1½ hr., 104F); Granville (5 per day, 1 hr., 32F); Avranches (3 per day, 45 min., 34F). You can rent bikes for 40F per half-day or 50F per day, with a 500F deposit. **Buses** leaving from the train station connect Coutances with Cherbourg (2 hr., 56F); Granville (45 min., 65F); Mont St-Michel (1½ hr., 44F); St-Lô (1 hr., 75F). Call **STN** (tel. 33 05 65 25) in St-Lô for departure times. Coutances's ever-so-helpful, English-speaking **tourist office** is located at the public gardens (tel. 33 45 17 79). (Open Mon.-Fri. 9am-1pm and 2-7pm, May-Oct. 10am-12pm and 2-6pm). Nearby **Les Unelles** is an abbey newly restored as a cultural center. (Open Mon.-Fri. 9am-12pm and 2:30-6:30pm, Sat. 9am-12pm; Oct.-April Mon.-Fri. 9am-12pm.)

A 30-minute hike brings you to the **Foyer des Jeunes Travailleurs,** 20, rue Docteur Guillard (tel. 33 45 09 69), a dank lodging for rowdy and generally young male workers. From the train station, take the road directly in front of the entrance and turn right at the monument. Follow the serpentine route uphill past the old town. Take a right on the unmarked road by the large Codec supermarket, continue straight up the crest of the hill, bear right onto rue Docteur Guillard, and follow it as it curves right to the *foyer.* (Singles 100F with mandatory breakfast and one other meal. Kitchen. Open year-round.) The **Hôtel aux Trois Pilliers,** 11, rue des Halles (tel. 33 45 01 31), beside the cathedral, may actually be a better deal, considering its location. (Singles 80F. Doubles 100F. Showers 10F. Breakfast 15F.)

Fine *crêperies* line the cobbled streets of the *centre ville.* Health food fans may appreciate the fruit and regional cheeses at **GAM,** a well-stocked staples shop at 15, rue Geoffrey de Montbray. (Open Mon.-Sat. 7:30am-1pm and 2-7:30pm.) Coutances hosts a **Jazz Festival** each year in late May and sponsors concerts in the Jardin des Plantes and public squares around the the town.

Granville

Built on a rocky promontory, Granville (pop. 30,000) offers a little of everything: a bustling *ville basse* with narrow streets, an *haute ville* crowned by the massive 15th-century **Eglise de Notre-Dame,** and a limestone beach. The **Jardin Public**

Christian Dior, off av. de la Libération, a piece of oceanfront property donated by Dior a century ago, is the icing on the cake. (Open daily 9am-9pm. Free.) Granville welcomes its share of tourists in the summer, so don't expect solitude or even a surplus of hotel rooms, especially on weekends. Call ahead if you can. The crowds are especially thick during the weekly classical concerts in Eglise de Notre-Dame during July and August (40F).

Granville can be reached by car on D971; many hitchhikers find the going easy, as the roads leading into and out of the city are well traveled during the day. STN **buses** (tel. 33 50 77 89) connect Granville to Coutances (1 per day, 45 min., 27.80F); Avranches (3 per day, 1¼ hr., 26.80F); and Mont St-Michel (1 per day, 2 hr., 32F). The buses share the **train station** (tel. 33 57 50 50) with SNCF trains. To reach the station, walk 15 minutes from the center of town on rue Couraye, which becomes av. Maréchal Leclerc. Trains run to Paris (4 per day, 3½ hr., 172F); Cherbourg (3 per day, change at Folliniers and Lison, 3 hr., 96F); Avranches (3 per day, 1¼ hr., 29F). There are **lockers** in the station (3F, 3-day max.). (Open daily 9am-noon and 2-6pm.) From May through September boats leave daily for the Chausey Islands, an archipelago of anything from 52 to 365 islets, depending on the tide (1-3 per day, 50 min., round-trip 70F, children under 14 44F). Boats run less frequently October through April; for more information, contact **Vedette** at the Gare Maritime de Granville (tel. 33 50 31 81). **Emeraude Lines,** 1, rue Lecampion (tel. 33 50 16 36) also serves the Chausey islands (1-2 per day May-Sept., 70F, children under 14 43F) as well as Jersey and Guernsey (1 per day April-Sept., 95F-270F same day return). For more information, contact Granville's **tourist office,** 15, rue Georges Clemenceau (tel. 33 50 02 67), across from the casino. (Open Mon.-Sat. 9am-12:30pm and 2-7pm, Sun. 9am-7pm). The train station rents **bikes** (50F per day, open daily 8:30am-noon and 2-4:30pm); newer 3-speeds with panniers go for 50F per day at **Action,** 11, rue Clément-Desmaison (tel. 33 50 04 13).

There is no youth hostel here, but **Hôtel Michelet,** 5, rue Jules Michelet (tel. 33 50 06 55), has cheap rooms and a friendly reception. (Singles 70F. Doubles 80-95F, with shower 135F. Breakfast 20F.) Weary travelers arriving at the train station might opt for a spacious room at the **Hôtel Terminus,** pl. de la Gare (tel. 33 50 02 05). (Singles 90-120F. Doubles 120-165F. Showers in some rooms. Breakfast 18F.)

A few small coastal towns dot the pristine countryside and gorgeous beaches near Granville: **Hauteville-sur-Mer** and **Coutainville** are particularly worth a visit. These towns are served by STN buses, but the schedules are so inconvenient that you will do better renting a bike.

Avranches

The most delightful of the peninsula's larger towns, Avranches (pop. 9000) lies southwest of Granville on D973 and on the Caen-Rennes train line. Perched atop a butte in a northern corner of the bay of Mont St-Michel, this mountain town is an invigorating uphill hike from the station. (Take the pedestrian path to the right and in front of the station, not the weaving highway to the left.) Those unmoved by the manicured gardens of the **Jardin des Plantes** in the west end of the city may melt at the view of majestic Mont St-Michel. Every night from July to September, the Mont is lit up like a blazing, cognac-drenched armadillo. From June through August, the garden itself is lit each night at 10pm to classical music. The **Musée de l'Avranchin,** on pl. St-Avril (tel. 33 58 25 15), houses manuscripts and books saved from destruction when the Mont's abbey was sacked during the French Revolution. The museum also gives an interesting 30-minute slide show (in French) complete with period music and Gregorian chants. (Open Wed.-Mon. 9:30am-noon and 2-6pm. Admission 17F, children 8.50F.)

The central **tourist office** on rue Général de Gaulle (tel. 33 58 00 22) is next to the town hall. (Open daily 9am-noon and 2-7pm, Sept.-May Mon.-Fri. 9:30am-noon and 2-7pm.) A smaller branch presides over the entrance to the Jardin des Plantes (open May-Sept. Mon.-Sat. 10am-12:30pm and 2-7:30pm, Sun. 10am-12:30pm and

2-7pm). The main tourist office shares its building with the **STN bus station** (tel. 33 58 03 07), which sends one bus per day to Mont St-Michel and back (July-Aug. only; leaves Avranches at 10:25am, returns from Mont St-Michel at 4:10pm; 30 min.; 28F, round-trip 42F). Buses also leave for Granville (Mon.-Sat. 3 per day, 1¼ hr., 27F). (Open Mon.-Tues. and Thurs.-Fri. 10:30am-12:15pm and 3:30-6:30pm, Wed. 10am-noon and 3:30-6:30pm, Sat. 9:30am-noon.)

Avranches has a wonderful **Auberge de Jeunesse,** 15, rue de Jardin des Plantes (tel. 33 58 06 54), near the Jardin des Plantes. You may not find space during the off-season, when the hostel fills up with young workers. (Reception open Mon.-Fri. 5:30-9pm. Closed Sat. 2-6:30pm and after 8pm, closed Sun. 10am-6:30pm. Curfew 10pm, but you can get a key. 48F per person. Breakfast included. Superb kitchen facilities. Sheets 20F. Open year-round.) If the hostel is full, the **Hôtel la Renaissance,** rue des Fossés (tel. 33 58 03 71), behind the town hall, is not far. The young-at-heart, extremely friendly owners have sunny rooms, and the jovial bar downstairs is always filled with neighbors. (Singles and doubles 90-125F. No showers. Breakfast 20F.) **Hôtel le Select,** 11, rue de Mortain (tel. 33 58 10 62), features an equally friendly proprietor who loves *Let's Go* readers, as well as nicely furnished rooms. (Singles 85F. Doubles from 85F, with bath 128F. Showers 15F. Breakfast 15F.) **Les Mares Camping,** rue de Verdun (tel. 33 58 05 45), about a 15-min. walk south of the center, has a grocery store and pool. (Adults 15F, children 10F. Open April to mid-Sept.) Across the street from Hôtel Le Select at #6, **Le Valois,** an enticing gourmet shop and grocery store, sells take-out hot meals for 8-16F per portion. (Open Jan.-June 20 and July 15-Dec. Mon.-Sat. 8am-1pm and 3-5:30pm, Sun. 3-5:30pm.) There are lots of cheap *brasseries* and restaurants around the tourist office. **L'Express Bar,** rue des Fossés, has indoor and outdoor seating and plenty of appetizing *galettes* for 7-20F. (Open daily 9am-1am.)

Mont St-Michel

You will be awed by Mont St-Michel. Rising abruptly out of a huge expanse of land and sea, this dazzling structure is visible for kilometers in every direction. The stone buildings, built painstakingly over nine centuries on a tiny island, are a hodgepodge of major continental styles of architecture from 966, when the abbey was founded on the ruins of an 8th-century chapel, to the 19th century. Understandably, the Mont now attracts even more camera-wielding tourists than it did gift-bearing pilgrims in the Middle Ages. Try to get there in the morning; the crowds are as irritating as the Mont is unforgettable.

Orientation and Practical Information

Reaching Mont St-Michel is not a problem, but a little planning is necessary. **Trains** continue no farther than **Pontorson,** where STN buses (across from the *gare,* tel. 33 60 00 35) shuttle passengers the remaining 10km to the Mont (6 per day, round-trip 19F, railpasses not valid); the last STN bus from the Mont to Pontorson leaves at 5:50pm. If coming by train from Paris-Montparnasse, change at Dol for Pontorson (2 per day, 4¼ hr., 215F). The last train from Pontorson to Dol leaves at 9:12pm. You can also reach Pontorson from Paris by changing at Foligny (2 per day, 180F). **SNCF buses** (tel. 33 66 00 35) also connect Dol and the Mont but run on an inconvenient schedule. **Courriers Bretons et Normands** (tel. 33 60 11 43) offers regular service to Avranches, Granville, Villedieu, Caen, and St-Lô. For more information, stop in at the office by the train station in Pontorson. (Open Mon.-Fri. 8:30am-7pm.) Don't bother buying the museum tickets that the driver sells after the journey. The bus may be your best bet, though reliance on it precludes any evening view of the Mont. Hitchhiking is difficult. You can rent a **bike** at the Pontorson train station (tel. 33 66 00 35; open daily 8am-noon and 2-8pm) for a half-day (40F), a day (50F), or a week (285F), with a 500F deposit. The road is straight and covers mostly flat farmland.

A city in itself, the Mont centers on one central rampart, the Grand-Rue. Most hotels, restaurants, and sights are located along this thoroughfare.

Tourist Office: Boîte Postale 4, 50116 Le Mont St-Michel (tel. 33 60 14 30), behind the stone wall to your left after you pass through the Porte du Roi. Sells posters and books at lower prices than the stores. Ask about organized 2-hr. hiking expeditions over the sand to the **Ile de Tombelaine** (April-June and Aug.-Sept. at low tide). Avoid the **currency exchange** here and elsewhere on the Mont. Ask for the useful *Horaire des Marées,* a schedule of high and low tides. Open Mon.-Sat. 9am-6pm; in off-season Mon.-Sat. 9am-noon and 2-6pm.

Post Office: Grand-Rue, near the Porte du Roi. Open Mon.-Fri. 9am-noon and 2-7pm, Sat. 9am-noon. **Postal Code:** 50116.

Buses: All buses leave from the Porte du Roi. Tickets available on board. **STN buses** (tel. 33 60 00 35) connect the Mont to Pontorson and from there to other cities in the region, **SNCF buses** (tel. 33 66 00 35) run irregularly to Pontorson, and **Courriers Bretons et Normands** service Avranches, Granville, Villedieu, Caen, and St-Lô.

Luggage Storage: There are no lockers, but for 10F the bathroom attendant by the Porte Bavole will store your bags in a tiny cubicle behind the toilets.

Police: Emergency, tel. 17.

Accommodations, Camping, and Food

Spending the night in Mont St-Michel may prove expensive, so you should consider staying in St-Malo, Avranches, or Pontorson instead. Most of the listings below are in Pontorson (**postal code:** 50170), a small village reminiscent of old Normandy.

Centre Duguesclin (IYHF), rue Général Patton (tel. 33 60 18 65), a 10-min. walk through downtown Pontorson. Turn right on rue Général Patton. Opened in 1990, this hostel has a fully equipped kitchen, a terrace, and dormitory-style accommodations. Convenient location and newly renovated facilities make it quite popular. Registration open 8:30-10:30am and 5-10pm daily. Members 55F.

Pleine-Fougères (IYHF), rue de la Gare (tel. 33 48 75 69), about 5km from Pontorson. Count on walking both ways because buses to Pleine-Fougères run only in the morning and leave the town only in the afternoon. No curfew. Members 65F. Open July-Aug.

Hôtel de la Croix Blanche, rue Grande Pontorson (tel. 33 60 14 04), in Mont St-Michel. Located in the thick of the souvenir shops and seething throngs of visitors. Not unreasonable, considering its location. Some rooms with a view. Singles 105F. Doubles 180F. 53F *menu* in the restaurant downstairs. Reservations necessary at least 1 month in advance. Open March 15-Nov. 1 7am-2am.

Hôtel de l'Arrivée, pl. de la Gare (tel. 33 60 01 57), near the station in Pontorson. Friendly owners make this an excellent choice. Singles 57-87F. Doubles 57-120F. Breakfast 18F. Bar and restaurant downstairs.

Hôtel de France, 2, rue des Rennes (tel. 33 60 29 17), across from the train station in Pontorson. A decent establishment, but tiny rooms. Open 8am-11pm. Singles from 50F. Breakfast 18F. Showers 15F.

Camping: Camping Pont d'Orson, Cours de la Victoire (tel. 33 60 00 18), 10 min. from the station in Pontorson. Simple but adequate site by the river. 5F per person, 2F per tent. Hot showers included. Open April-Sept. **Camping du Mont St-Michel,** P.B. 8, 50116 Le Mont St-Michel (tel. 33 60 09 33). As close to the Mont as you will get (1.8km), at the junction of D275 and N776. Clean, pleasantly shaded sites. Next door is **Motel Vert** (doubles with shower 150F) and a supermarket. Best location for viewing the Mont at night, but fills fast. 12F per person, 10F per car or tent. Reserve in advance. Open April-Sept. **Camping St-Michel,** route du Mont St-Michel (tel. 33 70 96 90), by the bay. A bit far from the Mont (9km), but the Granville bus stops 200m from the entrance. Buses go to the Mont at 10:30am and 5pm; ask the helpful proprietor for the return schedules. The sites are quiet and equipped with a common room and telephone. Gates open 24 hs. 14F per person, 8F per tent. Open April-Sept.

Overpriced and lackluster snack bars infest the Mont; its specialties are instead roast lamb *pré-salé* (bred on the salt meadows surrounding the island) and *omelette poulard,* a fluffy soufflélike dish (about 30F). Ask for a recipe at the tourist office.

One of the more attractive places, **La Sirène,** on the Grand-Rue serves delicious *galettes* and omelettes (11-25F) in the middle of the action. Pack a picnic and eat in the abbey gardens near the top of the hill (a few flights below the entrance to the abbey), or on the beach at low tide. Provisions are available at the **Shopi** supermarket at 5, rue Couesnon, in Pontorson. (Open Mon.-Thurs. 9am-12:30pm, Fri.-Sat. 9am-12:30pm and 2:30-7:15pm.)

Several cheap eateries line rue Couesnon in Pontorson, but the best is **Le Grillon,** a snack bar at #37, with *crêpes* (5-20F), sandwiches, and a grill *menu.* **La Cave,** 37, rue de la Libération, is an overpriced hotel with a particularly varied and tasty 48F *menu.*

Sights

In 708, the archangel St-Michel appeared three times in the dreams of the Bishop of Avranches, instructing him to build a place of worship on a barren and rocky island north of Pontorson. Over the centuries, the modest original church expanded to its present size and has attracted millions of religious pilgrims and tourists. Only a few stones remain from the original oratory, and endless additions in various styles have buried them under tons of rock stacked up 156m above sea level. The additions began in 966, when a group of Benedictine monks made a pilgrimage to the Mont and were so inspired by its beauty and power that they began the construction of an even larger church on the original site. The monks lived without interruption on the Mont and received religious pilgrims until 1789, when the revolutionary government turned it into a state prison. Mont St-Michel remained under government control from then on, continuing to serve as a prison until Emperor Napoleon III recognized its historical value and began renovations in 1874.

Enter via the **Porte Bavole,** the only break in the outer walls, and then through the **Porte du Roi** onto Grand-Rue, a winding pedestrian street full of souvenir stands and restaurants. After climbing several flights of stairs, you will arrive at the **abbey** entrance, the departure point for all the obligatory one-hour tours. (Open daily 9:30am-6pm; Sept. 15-May 15 9-11:30am and 1:30-5pm. Tours in English daily at 10am, 11am, noon, 1:30pm, 2:30pm, 3:30pm, 4:30pm, and 5:30pm. Tours in French every 20 min. Admission 28F, ages 18-25 and over 60 16F, ages under 18 5F, Sun. ½-price.) For a special treat, take one of the more detailed *visites conférences.* These two-hour tours in French allow you to walk atop a flying buttress and creep inside the darkest crypts. (Daily at 10am, 11am, 2pm, 3pm, and 4:15pm. No reservations necessary. 39F.)

The church balances on the highest point of the island, directly above some frigid crypts and deliberately exposed to the skies for communion with the heavens. Passing through the refectory, you will descend into the dark and astonishingly chilly church foundations where the walls are 2m thick at some points. **La Merveille,** an intricate 13th-century cloister housing the monastery, encloses a seemingly endless web of passageways and rooms. If you're not impressed with its architectural complexities, the mechanical simplicity of the Mont's treadmill will surely catch your attention. Prisoners held in the Mont during the French Revolution would walk here for hours, their foot labor powering the elaborate pulley system that carried heavy stones up the side of the Mont.

Bertrand du Guesclin, the governor of Pontorson, built the **Logis Tiphaine** in 1365 to protect his young wife Tiphaine, an astrologer, from the English while he was fighting in Spain. (Open daily 9am-6pm. Admission 15F, students 10F, children under 12 5F.)

After the tour, escape down the ramparts and into the abbey garden, where you can reflect upon both the soaring stone buttresses that wrap around the entire island and the coasts of Normandy and Brittany. To avoid the asphyxiating crowds on the main street, descend to the Porte du Bavole via the ramparts.

Do not wander off too far on the sand at any time of day. The bay's tides are the highest in Europe, shifting every six hours or so. During high-tide days, or *mascaret,* the water recedes for 18km and rushes in at 2m per second, flooding the beaches along the causeway. While the tides were once said to rush in "faster than a horse at full gallop," the water now seldom moves faster than a brisk walking pace. To see this spectacle, you must be within the abbey fortifications two hours ahead of time.

When darkness falls, Mont St-Michel is lit up, its brilliance reflected in the surrounding water. As Milton might have said, the best view comes to those who wait, either at the entrance to the causeway or across the bay in Avranches. The Mont is illuminated during all church festivals and feasts, on high-tide nights, and nightly from July to September (dusk-11pm). Those who like *son* with their *lumière* should visit in July and August, when **Les Heures Musicales du Mont St-Michel,** takes place in the abbey. (Admission 70F per concert, students 35F.) Buy tickets at the door, or contact the tourist office in Avranches for more information. From mid-June through mid-September **Les Nocturnes** night program enlivens the Mont (50F, students 30F, Thurs., Fri., and Sat. 9-11pm) with a light show inside the abbey itself. On a more pre-industrial note, May flowers bring a spectacular folklore festival, **St-Michel de Printemps.**

Channel Islands (Iles Normandes)

US$1 = £0.61   £1 = US$1.64

Though King John lost the last of the Duchy of Normandy to the French in 1204, the Channel Islands remained under the protection of the crown of England and have remained so through several French attempts to reclaim them. When Hitler's troops invaded the islands, residents evacuated to England and returned after the war with English ideas and slang. In return for loyalty to the British, the islands enjoy favorable trade regulations and almost complete autonomy. Jersey has its own volunteer State Assembly, as does the Bailiwick of Guernsey, a federation of Guernsey and the smaller islands that surround it. As this home-rule suggests, the Channel Islands depend on neither of their powerful neighbors for government. In speech, manner, custom, and cuisine, however, the Channel Islands appear ever so British. English is spoken everywhere, although the islands lie closer to France and French is in fact the official language of Jersey.

Both Guernsey and Jersey issue their own currencies, of the same denominations and value as British sterling. French currency is accepted by some and British currency by everyone. To avoid any difficulties, exchange your francs upon arriving.

Most ferry companies offer modest round-trip fares to either Jersey or Guernsey, but one-way travel to and from either island can be expensive. When making travel plans, don't forget the time difference: the Channel Islands are one hour behind France.

Jersey

Jersey is famed for sweaters, stamps, and package-tour holidays; fortunately, the island continues to survive the swarms of tourists that descend on its lovely beaches and countless duty-free shops. Since Jersey does not impose a sales tax, luxury goods are less expensive than they are in either France or England. Avoid the built-up coast between St-Helier and Gorey. Instead, explore the cliff paths along Plemont and Bonley Bay, and relax on the *croissant*-shaped St-Oven's beach.

Reaching Jersey from either France or England is not difficult, but it can be expensive if you stay more than three days. In July and August be sure to book ferries at least a week in advance, as boats fill almost immediately. Most ferries from France leave the *gare maritime* in **St-Malo** and take roughly two hours to reach Jersey, with the exception of **Condor Hydrofoil**, Commodore Travel, 28 Conway St. and Albert Quay (tel. 721 63), in St-Helier, which makes the voyage in an unbeatable hour from St-Malo (5 each way per day 220F, same-day return 245F, 3-day return 380F, after 72 hr. 400F).

Emeraude Lines (tel. 99 40 48 40 in St-Malo; 744 58 in Jersey) runs three or four ferries per day (one way 220F, same-day return 245F, 72-hr. return 380F, after 72 hr. 400F). Emeraude Lines also connects Granville to the Channel Islands (1 per day, similar prices and times as those at St-Malo). In addition, **Condor** and various companies in Britain offer ferries from the Channel Islands to **Weymouth,** England (2 per day, 3½ hr., 350F, round-trip 625F). All ferries have reduced fares for children.

Cycling is the best way to see the natural beauty of Jersey, although the long hills of the coast will almost certainly challenge you. If you're renting a bike, you'll have to make do with a 3-speed, as 10-speed rentals are not available. In general, most rentals cost £3 per day and £15 per week, with a £5 deposit. If you're over 18 and have an international driver's license, you can rent a moped for £9 per day, £35 per week from **Kingslea's,** 77, Esplanade (tel. 247 77). Hitchhiking in Jersey is difficult since most drivers are tourists.

St-Helier

The capital and only real "city" of Jersey, St-Helier boasts a booming tourist trade and a surprisingly vibrant nightlife. Unfortunately, like the rest of the island, the city is geared toward the *New York Times* travel set. The tenacious bargain hunter, however, can unearth a number of reasonably priced bed and breakfasts and many cheap restaurants. To reach the tourist office, turn right at the end of Albert Pier; the office lies about 100m to your left. The pedestrian shopping district begins at the corner of Conway St. and King St., the main intersection of the city.

Orientation and Practical Information

Tourist Office: The Weighbridge Station (tel. 247 79, for accommodations 319 58), near the docks. Open Mon.-Sat. 8am-9:15pm, Sun. 8am-noon and 6-9pm; Nov.-April Mon.-Fri. 8:45am-12:30pm and 1:45-5pm, Sat. 9am-12:30pm.

Currency Exchange: The major banks, Lloyds and Barclays, give the best exchange rates and charge the lowest commisions (open Mon.-Fri. 9:30am-3:30pm). **Thomas Cook** is open Saturdays as well (9am-4pm). Avoid the exorbitant surcharges at independent "currency exchanges."

Post Office: Broad St. (tel. 262 62). You must use Jersey stamps on all mail. Currency exchange. General Delivery. Open Mon.-Fri. until 5:30pm, Sat. until 4:30pm. No postal code.

Telephone Code: 534.

Flights: Aurigny Air Services, Weighbridge Station (tel. 357 33) offers expensive but efficient service to Guernsey (19-21 flights per day, one way £15.40, round trip £30.80).

Buses: All buses leave from Weighbridge Station (tel. 212 01), across from the tourist office. Service is frequent and fast. To: Gorey Village (Mon.-Sat. every 30 min., Sun. every 90 min.; 20 min.; 70p); Rozel Bay (every hr., ½-hr., 858p); the Zoo via La Hougue Bie (every 1-2 hr., last bus at 6:15pm, ½-hr., 85p); the German Underground Hospital (every hr., 15 min., 70p); St-Brelade's Bay (every hr., 25 min., 85p); St-Ouen's Bay (every hr., 40 min., 90p). Explorers Tickets provide three consecutive days of unlimited travel around the island (£5.75).

Ferries: Condor Hydrofoil, Commodore Travel, 28 Conway St. and Albert Quay (tel. 712 63) runs five hydrofoils per day between Jersey and St.-Malo. **Emeraude Lines,** Albert Quay (tel. 744 58) also runs three to four ferries per day between Jersey and St.-Malo.

Bike Rental: Shops abound along the Esplanade. **Zebra,** 9 Esplanade (tel. 365 56), has a large selection at £3 per day, £15 per week with a £5 deposit. Open Mon.-Fri. 8am-6pm, Sat.-Sun. 8:30am-5pm.

Luggage Storage: Across from terminal 2 in the Condor Hydrofoil office. £1 per day. Open 7:45am-6:30pm.

Laundromat: Sunshine Launderette, 77 New St. Wash and dry £2.50. Open Mon.-Sat. 8am-8pm, Sun. 9am-7pm. **Launderette,** 51 David Place, across from Royal Lives Assurance Co. Wash and dry £2.50. Open daily 8am-8pm. Last wash 7:45pm. Bring plenty of 10p and 50p coins.

Beach Guards: St-Ouen's Bay, tel. 820 32. **Plemont Bay,** tel. 816 36.

Pharmacy: Charing Cross Pharmacy, 16 Charing Cross (tel. 322 42). Open Mon.-Fri. 8:30am-6pm, Sat. 9am-6pm, Sun 10am-2pm.

Hospital: General Hospital, Gloucester St. (tel. 590 00). Free clinic Mon.-Fri. 9am-noon, Sat. 10-11am; Oct.-April Mon., Wed., Fri. 9-11am. Prescription charge £1.

Emergency: Tel. 999 (no coins required).

Police: Rouge Bouillon, tel. 699 96.

Accommodations and Camping

Finding a room on your own in the summer is nearly impossible. Fortunately, the tourist office runs a free and fantastic accommodations service: when all the hotels and B&Bs are full, it makes public radio and TV appeals asking Jersey citizens to open up their homes to tourists. Many B&Bs will take only visitors who stay for a few days or even a week. If you arrive late in the day during July or August, be prepared to pay as much as £25. All of the following accept reservations by phone but may also require written confirmation and/or deposit. Make reservations up to a year in advance.

The Fairholme, Roseville St. (tel. 321 94). Friendly, family-run B&B about 100m from the beach and a 5-min. walk from the town center. £14.50 per person.

La Fontaine, 59 David Pl. (tel. 233 03). One of the cheaper B&Bs, but pleasant nonetheless. £13.50 per person. Doubles with shower £15 per person. Open March-Nov.

Bromley, 7 Winchester St. (tel. 239 48), near the city center off Val Plaisant. Pleasant dining room; even the garrets are spacious and comfortable. Speak French if you can; the proprietors do. £15 per person with breakfast.

Les Avenues, Les Platons (tel. 610 93), in Trinity. If driving, turn right onto the C97 from the B63. The house is on your right, marked by a tiny wooden sign—take the bumpy dirt road to the B&B at the back of the farm. Or take bus #4 to Les Platons, and ask the driver to let you off near the radio towers (last bus at 5:45pm, 70p). Peaceful, pastoral, and spacious. No singles. 3 doubles £12.

Les Ruettes, St-Lawrence (tel. 629 88), in the center of the island next to Carrefour Selons off the A10. Peaceful guest house surrounded by pastures. £11 per person. Open May 30-Sept. 30.

Camping: Camping outside official sites is illegal. Most of the island's campgrounds have facilities and services such as general stores with refrigerated goods, TV and game rooms, swimming pools, and hot showers. Reservations are necessary. **Beauvelande Camp Site,** in St-Martin (tel. 535 75), off route A6 from St-Helier. Take bus #3, disembark at St-Martin's school, continue in the same direction, take the second right, and follow the signs; it's a 30-minute walk (last bus at 11:20pm). Tends to attract families with extremely energetic children. Excellent **bikes** £3 per day, £11 per week. Adults £4, children £3. Open July-Aug. **Rozel Camping Park** (tel. 597 97) south of Rozel Bay. From St-Helier, follow the A6 to St-Martin's church and continue straight through the intersection along the B38—the campground is on the right. June-Sept. £4; April-May £3.50. Tent rental £2-4. Open April-Sept. 20. **St-Brelade's Camping Park** (tel. 413 98) off route A13, halfway between St-Aubin and St-Ouen's Bay. Quiet spot with inexpensive dinner and breakfast menus. Adults £5, children £3, £4 per tent, £1 per car. Open May-Sept.

Food

Jersey restaurants are adequate and often inexpensive. Some B&Bs serve dinner for about £5, but you can usually do better in a restaurant. Ask the tourist office for a list of winners in the Good Food Festival. A large open **market** is held Monday to Saturday (7am-5:30pm) at Halkett Pl. For a cheap meal, try one of the numerous pubs in the harbor area.

Albert J. Ramsbottom, 90/92 Halkett Pl. Noisy, popular seafood restaurant filled with locals and tourists. Chicken or fish special with fries and ice cream £2.95. Open daily 11:30am-2pm and 5-10pm.

Broadway Restaurant, 24 Esplanade. A few theatrical names for some excellent food. Minelli or Streisand burger £2.60-2.90. Try the deep-fried rings of fresh squid (£2.10). Open noon-2pm and 6-10pm.

The Waterfront, Chicago Pizza Restaurant, 10 Wharf St. Yes, MTV and pizza delivery have even reached Jersey. Rock music shakes this tavern-style place. Pizza £3-3.65. Apple pie £1.75. Open daily noon-11pm.

Juice Bar, 12 Beresford St. Cheap sandwiches and every kind of juice imaginable. Try the carrot parsley (£1.10). Open Mon.-Sat. 10am-7pm.

Graham's Restaurant, 37 David Pl. (tel. 705 97). Basic fish and chips in a basic diner. Hamburgers and chips £1.80, apple pie 80p. Open daily 7am-2pm and 5-8pm.

Sights and Entertainment

At low tide, you can walk from St-Helier's thin and grimy beach out to **Elizabeth Castle,** a Tudor fortress in the middle of the harbor. The castle is strong on anecdote but weak on visual impact. Helier himself, a pious, 6th-century hermit later decapitated by invading Vandals, brooded on **Hermitage Rock** at the castle's south side. (Open March-Oct. daily 9:30am-6pm. Admission £1.) A second castle, the Napoleonic **Fort Regent,** has been converted into a modern sports and entertainment complex that has almost destroyed the character of St-Helier's center. The heated pool is open Mon.-Fri. 9am-7:30pm, Sat.-Sun. 9am-5:30pm. The disco sponsors free vodka nights every night in March, 9:30pm-1am. You pay for only the mixers. (Entire complex open 9am-10pm; in off-season 10am-5:30pm. Admission £4, in off-season £3.)

Relics of old Jersey history slumber beneath the fort in the **Jersey Museum,** 9 Pier Rd. The somewhat dull **Barreau Art Gallery** on the second floor features a Gainsborough charcoal sketch (considered one of the earliest representations of a Jersey cow), watercolors by Blampied for the first edition of Barrie's *Peter Pan,* and local oils of Jersey dating from the German occupation. (Open Mon.-Sat. 10am-5pm. Admission £1.50, students £1.)

A series of flower shows throughout the summer leads up to the cataclysmic **Battle of Flowers** in early August. Some 30 floats covered with hundreds of thousands of blooms parade belligerently down the main thoroughfare. Festivities continue during the week with bands and entertainment. In days past, the procession of flower-decked floats culminated in an orgy of destruction as people pulled the entries apart and pelted one another with petals. In the interest of order, however, the tourist office has decreed that winning floats be preserved in the **Battle of the Flowers Museum** (in La Robelaine, Mont des Corvées St-Ouen), full of mummified blooms. (Open March-Dec. daily 10am-5pm. Admission £1.25.) You must get bleacher seats in advance for the Battle Parade (£5-6). For tickets, contact the Jersey Battle of Flowers Association, Burlington House, St-Savior's Rd., St-Helier (tel. 301 78).

Nightlife in St.-Helier is amazingly diverse for such a small city. **Thackery's** on the Esplanade specializes in trendy disco evenings that are popular with locals, as does **Lord's** on Beresford St. The **Red Lamp** on Peter St. caters to a college-age crowd, while **Friday's** on Halkett Pl. attracts a slightly older clientele. Buy the *Evening Post* for a listing of current movies (£3) or shows at the Opera House. Free weekly concerts with brass bands or jazz groups take place throughout the summer in **Howard Davies Park.**

Local restaurants compete in the four-day **Jersey Good Food Festival** in late May. While many gastronomic events cost upwards of £8-14 per person, there's plenty of free wine, *crêpes,* and seafood. In June, the **Festival France and Jersey** celebrates the close ties between Jersey and Normandy with folk dancing, jazz and classical concerts, art exhibitions, cabaret, and theater. During this festival, the entire French school system visits Jersey for a year-end spree. (For more information, call 267 88.)

Jersey Countryside

Although it consists of only three streets, **Gorey Village,** less than 10km from St-Helier, is Jersey's second largest town. The town's main attraction is **Mont Orgeuil Castle,** a massive and ruggedly beautiful 13th-century fort. Its key role in such major historical events as the English Civil War and World War II make it an excellent stop for history buffs. Local actors perform Shakespeare here on August evenings. (Open late March-Oct. daily 9:30am-5:30pm, last admission at 5pm. Admission £1.20, students 60p.) Restaurants, souvenir shops, and expensive hotels line the bay below the castle. To reach Gorey Village by bike, follow the A6 out of St-Helier and turn right onto the B28, which winds its way to the castle. Routes A3 and A4 to Gorey Village are shorter, but not nearly as beautiful. Buses to Gorey Village depart every 30 minutes Mon.-Sat., every 90 minutes Sun. (20 min., 70p).

On the way to Gorey Village along the B28 is **La Hougue Bie,** an intriguing religious complex. At the base of a large hill lies the entrance to a 50-meter-long dolmen. Outside, the tomb is covered by a 60-foot mound, capped by two medieval chapels. The tiny 12th-century **Notre Dame de la Clarté** has a simple eloquence and marvelous acoustics. Abutting this marvel is the dark and unexciting 15th-century **Jerusalem Chapel.** Nearby are the **Railway Museum, Agricultural Museum, Archaeological Museum, Geological Museum,** and **German Occupation Museum.** All except the Occupation Museum are terribly dull. (Open March-Nov. Tues.-Sun. 10am-5pm. Last ticket issued at 4:15pm. Admission £1.50, students £1.)

To the north of La Hougue Bie on the B46 is author Gerald Durrell's **Jersey Zoo,** in Les Augres Manor. Protected by the Jersey Wildlife Preservation Trust, the 20-acre zoo is home to a variety of endangered species. (Open daily 10am-6pm. Last ticket issued at 5pm. Closes at dusk in winter. Admission £3, children under 14 £1.50.) During the German Occupation, the Channel Islands became one of the most heavily fortified areas in Western Europe; bunkers and fortifications crop up frequently along the coastline. An exhibit in the **German Underground Hospital,** Meadowbank, St-Lawrence, details the 1940 bombing of a fleet of potato lorries, which a German squadron mistook for military vehicles. (Open March-Nov. daily 9:30am-5:30pm. Admission £2, children under 14 90p.) To reach the underground hospital from St-Helier, follow either the A1 or A2 out of town along St-Aubin's Bay, turn right onto the A11, and then continue straight onto the B99. Buses leave St-Helier for the hospital every hour (15 min., 70p).

The **Strawberry Farm** (tel. 836 24) lies in St-Peter's Valley, off the A11. Avoid the dull museum. You need not pay £1.25 for the ready-made desserts on the counter—just ask for a punnet of strawberries (50p); the cream and sugar are served free. (Farm open March-Oct. daily 10am-5:30pm.)

Three Jersey churches merit detours. In the **Fisherman's Chapel,** by the old parish church of St-Brelade, Norman murals still hang on the walls. From St. Helier, take the A1 west and turn right onto the B66. **St-Matthew's Church,** in Millbrook between St-Helier and Coronation Park on the A2, is known as the "Glass Church" for its Lalique. **St-Saviour's Church,** near St-Helier, was administered 150 years ago by Deacon Le Breton, Lillie Langtry's father, and the Jersey Lily herself is buried in the family plot in the graveyard.

Jersey has recently constructed several excellent cliff paths. All are satisfying day hikes, and some are illuminated at night. A vigorous mile separates Plemont point and romantic **Castle Grosnez** with its Cyrano de Bergerac-style promontory (open daily 9:30am-5:30pm; admission £1). Other hikes take you from St-Aubin's to Corbière, and between Crabbe, Sorel, and Devil's Hole. The tourist office has trail maps.

The shore on Jersey ranges from gently curving bays to harsh, rocky cliffs. Beautiful **St-Brelade's Bay** has the most popular beach, but the surf at **St-Ouen's Bay** is the roughest and most spectacular. You'll find the dudes with boards here. **Anne Port** and **St-Catherine** to the east are gentler, with small coves and rippling waves. All of the beaches suffer from a strong undertow and swiftly rising sea levels; the tourist board's list warns you about the danger spots.

Guernsey Channel Islands (Iles Normandes)

Despite their tiny size, Guernsey and neighboring islands Sark, Herm and Alderny form an independent country. The people of the Bailiwick take great pride in their autonomy—the quickest way to insult Guernseyans is to refer to them as "British." Having avoided tourism on the massive scale of nearby Jersey, Guernsey preserves precisely that sleepy way of life that most tourists seek.

From France, **Condor Hydrofoil,** North Pier Stops, St-Peter Port (tel. 261 21), skims the water from St-Malo to Guernsey (4-5 per day; 1 hr.; 220F, same-day return 245F, 3-day return 380F, after 72 hr. 400F). Condor also connects Guernsey to Jersey (3-4 per day; 1 hr.; 158F, 1-day return 189F). **Emeraude Lines,** New Jetty White Rock, St-Peter Port (tel. 71 14 14), connects St-Malo to Guernsey daily (255F, open return 480F). Between Jersey and Guernsey, **Aurigny Air Services,** South Esplanade, Guernsey (tel. 234 74), makes 15-minute flights almost every half-hour (£15.40, same-day return £30.80).

Guernsey comprises only about 24 square miles. *Perry's Guide* (£1.95), with detailed maps and suggested walking paths for all the islands in the Bailiwick, is useful if you're planning to explore on foot or by bike. Pick it up at the tourist office or at bookstores around the island. Hitchhiking is almost impossible in St-Peter Port but becomes somewhat more feasible away from the city. All buses leave from the terminal outside **The Picquet House** (tel. 72 46 77), which hoards maps and information on the extensive bus system. An islandwide **Rover bus ticket** will give you unlimited bus travel for a week (£11). Though Guernsey is hillier than Jersey, cycling is still possible.

St-Peter Port

Guernsey's capital, like its sister-city St-Helier, is a bustling and popular port city. Its smaller size and more provincial nature, however, make it more open and friendly to visitors. American-style restaurants and hotels crowd the Esplanade facing the harbor; walk beyond the church onto St-Peter Port's winding back roads for a more authentic perspective on the city.

Orientation and Practical Information

Tourist Office: Crown Pier (tel. 235 52, for accommodations 235 55), Victoria Pier. Free, efficient help with accommodations. Free map and tourist guide, *What's On in Guernsey.* Open Mon.-Sat. 9am-7pm, Sun. 10am-1:30pm and 5:30-7pm. Open July-Aug. nightly until 7:30pm.

Currency Exchange: Many banks in town, e.g., Lloyds, Barclays. Open Mon.-Fri. 9:30am-3:30pm, Sat. 8:30am-noon. **Thomas Cook,** Le Pollet St. Open Mon.-Fri. 9am-5:30pm, Sat. 9am-4pm. Most take a £3 commission. **Condor Ltd.,** North Pier Steps, in the only place to change on Sunday (open daily 9am-5pm).

Post Office: Smith St. (tel. 262 41). You must use Guernsey stamps on your cards and letters. You can have your letter postmarked with an ornate collectors' stamp. General Delivery. Open Mon.-Fri. 8:30am-5pm, Sat. 8:30am-noon. No postal code.

Telephone code: 481.

Flights: Aurigny Air Services, The Picquet House (tel. 246 77) runs about 20 flights per day to Jersey (£15.40 one-way, £30.80 round-trip).

Buses: The Picquet House (tel. 72 46 77). Extensive service around the island with special coastal excursions in summer. Most fares 75-85p.

Ferries: Condor Hydrofoil, North Pier Steps (tel. 261 21) operates 4-5 hydrofoils per day between Guernsey and St-Malo (245F). **Emeraude Lines,** New Jetty White Rock (tel. 71 14 14), also sails to St-Malo (255F). **British Ferries,** New Jetty White Rock (tel. 247 42) links Guernsey to Poole, England.

Taxis: Central Taxi, tel. 230 47 (open daily 6am-1am).

Bike Rental: Moullin's Cycle Shop, St-George's Esplanade (tel. 215 81). Decent 3-speeds and a few 5-speeds £3 per day; no deposit if you give them your vacation address. Open Mon.-Sat. 9:30am-12:30pm and 2-6pm. **Millard and Co.,** Victoria Rd. (tel. 207 77). 3-speeds £3 per day, £12 per week. Mopeds £7 per day, £25 per week. Motorcycles and scooters £9 per day, £35 per week. Open Mon.-Wed. and Fri.-Sat. 8:30am-12:45pm and 2-5:30pm, Thurs. 8:30am-12:30pm.

Sport Center: Beau Séjour Leisure Centre, tel. 285 55. Swimming, saunas, squash, and roller-skating. Tourist membership (£1.50) gets you swimming, badminton, and table tennis. Open 9am-11pm daily.

Laundromat: 59 Victoria Rd. Wash and dry about £2. Open daily 8am-7pm. Last wash 6pm. **Launderette,** Albert Pier, is conveniently located. Wash and dry about £2. Open daily 8am-10pm. Use 20p or 50p coins. **Pharmacy: Boots Chemists,** High St. (tel. 235 65). Open Mon.-Fri. 8:45am-5:15am, Sat. 8:45am-5pm.

Hospital: Princess Elizabeth, tel. 252 41.

Emergency: Tel. 999 (no coins required).

Police: Tel. 72 51 11.

Accommodations and Camping

Guernsey has manacled its tourist industry; all guesthouses are graded in the official accommodations list available at the tourist office. Rooms are nearly impossible to find in July and August. There are no youth hostels but plenty of campgrounds.

Friends Guest House, 20 Hauteville (tel. 211 46). Luxurious rooms in a house where Victor Hugo and his family lived from 1855-56. Friendly proprietors. Back porch has a great view of the port. £11.50 per person. Breakfast included. Open year round.

Les Granges Manor, Ivy Gates (tel. 209 39). A good example of early 17th-century architecture. Built in 1603 by Pierre de Beauvoir, this beautiful home is now filled with African and Oriental curios collected by its kind and elderly proprietor. A 15-min. hike from the harbor, but well worth it. £10 per person. Breakfast included.

Cordier Hill Bungalow, Cordier Hill (tel. 230 41). A 15-min. trek from St-Peter Port, but cheap. £10 per person.

Camping: Guernsey's 5 campgrounds are all accessible by bus from St-Peter Port, and most will rent equipment, especially if you book in advance. **Vaugrat Camp Site,** Les Hougues, route de Vaugrat (tel. 574 68) in St-Sampson (bus H1 or H2), is nearest. £2.75 per night. Rents bikes. Near St-Sampson, in Guernsey's northern interior, Vale (bus J1 or J2) has 2 sites: **L'Etoile Site,** Hougue Guilimine (tel. 443 25). £2.20 per night. Open June-Aug. **La Bailloterie,** (tel. 445 08). £1.90 per night. Open June-Sept. In adjacent Castel (bus D1 or D2): **Fauxquets Valley Farm** (tel. 554 60). £2.50 per night. Open mid-May to Sept. 14. Finally, in Torteval (bus C1 or C2): **Laleur,** (tel. 632 71). £2.50 per night. Open May-Sept.

Food

For dinner, try the streets near La Pollet or above Mill and Mansell St. For baked goods and four o'clock tea, try **Maison Carré,** at the Arcade between Market and High St.

The **Golden Lion** on Market St. is a small, comfortable pub with Guernsey's own potent Pony Ale on tap. The **White Hart** is the island's largest pub; beneath it lurks the **Golden Monkey** disco.

Whistler's, 1 Hauteville (tel. 258 09), near Pedvin St. One of the island's most famous restaurants—and one of its most expensive. Steak and mushroom pie £5, grills £5 and up. Try the "nearly mousse" (£2) for dessert. Make reservations. Open Mon.-Sat. 7-11pm.

Partner's, High St. Popular restaurant with burgers and vegetarian menu. Famous for its desserts. The geographically confused should try the Mississippi Mud Pie (£1.95). Open Mon.-Sat. noon-2pm and 6:30-10:30pm; Sun. 6:30-10pm.

Valentinos, on the Quay opposite the tourist office. Mexican menu with pizza too. Super nachos £2.95. Open Mon.-Tues. and Thurs.-Sat. noon-2pm and 7-11pm, Sun. 6-10pm.

Terminus Café, next to the bus terminal. Meager portions and dubious atmosphere, but the cheapest place for a meal. Sandwiches 75-85p, unappetizing pizza £1.50. Open Mon.-Sat. 8am-5pm, Sun. 9:30am-1:30pm.

Sights

Up the hill from the town church, the **market halls** display the abundant produce of Guernsey's soil and sea. The oldest part, now known as the **French Halles,** was built in 1780 and restricted to the produce of Brittany after the Victorian meat market was built. In the fish market, you may come across some ormer (from *oreille de mer,* "sea-ear") shells for sale, but they are now mysteriously rare. The animal itself is considered a delicacy, and the increasing shortage is something of a local sorrow. Along the Halles is a retail shop of the state dairy. You can sample the milk of the famous Guernsey bovine Bess; steer clear of the medicinal-tasting milkshakes.

The **Guernsey Traditional Market,** held most Thursday afternoons from May to September on Market St., sells local specialties. Contrary to Guernsey's usual policy, the market and the evening entertainment are crowded and enlivened for tourists. Continuing up Cornet St. to 38 Hauteville, you'll find Guernsey's most compelling attraction—the **Victor Hugo House** (now the property of the city of Paris). Here Hugo spent 15 years, and wrote his greatest works, including *Les Misérables.* Exiled from France between 1855 and 1870, Hugo designed and decorated the interior; the house is preserved as the author left it. The house can only be visited by guided tours, which last 15 to 30 minutes and are conducted in French and English. (Open Mon.-Sat. 10-11:30am and 2-4:30pm. Admission £1, students 50p, children and ages over 60 free.)

A statue of Hugo, cape and beard flowing, watches over the **Candie Gardens** on Candie St. Also in the gardens, the **Guernsey Museum and Art Gallery** has a fairly interesting permanent collection on witchcraft and local archaeology, and various temporary exhibitions. (Open daily 10:30am-5:30pm. Admission £1, students 40p, ages over 60 50p)

At 20 Smith St., near the post office, the **Channel Island Stamp Company** sells attractive local stamps. (Open Mon.-Sat. 9am-5pm.) The States of Guernsey, the governing body, meets at the **Royal Court,** at the top of Smith St., on the last Wednesday of every month except August. You can hear the formalities (in French) and the debate (in English) from the gallery. Proceedings begin at 10am; the opening ceremonies are particularly interesting, so arrive 10 to 15 minutes early. The queen sends a representative to the island parliament, but Guernsey sets its own laws and taxes. The island's only military obligation to England is to rescue the sovereign if he or she is captured and to help recover England if it is taken from the Crown.

Those of a military bent can wander off the quay to the **Castle Cornet,** a complex of fortresses occupied and attacked by everyone from King John to the Nazis. (Open daily 10:30am-5:30pm. Admission £1.50, ages under 14 50p, ages 60 and over 70p. Tours daily at 10:45am and 2:15pm.) More Nazi memorabilia awaits inside the **German Occupation Museum** in St-Andrew's. (Open daily May-Sept 10am-5pm; Nov.-April, Sun., Tues., and Thurs., 2-4:30pm. Admission £1.50.)

The closest beaches to town are to the south on **Havelet Bay** (take the coast road). Alternately, follow the cliff path up the stairs at the junction of Val des Terres. A five-minute walk puts you at **Soldier's Bay,** a surprisingly peaceful, pebbly beach that was once reserved for the troops of Fort George.

In summer, concerts of mostly classical music abound in St-Peter Port. The **Festival de Musique de Notre Dame** sponsors one concert per week in July and August.

Guernsey Countryside

Tiny bays ring the island of Guernsey, which has a different character on each side. The east coast, facing France, is fortified with cliffs to the south and castles to the north. While tiny, sandy bays form the south coast, bolder sweeps of sand and rocky headlands mark the west coast. The best way to explore the countryside is by bike, but be warned that the southeast corner of the island has steep hills. Bus service, though extensive, is not very frequent, and hitchhiking can be difficult and dangerous.

The archaic beauty of the island is most visible outside of St-Peter Port. The **cliff path** starting from Val des Terres south of St-Peter Port begins quite tamely, but steep inclines aren't far off. By the end, near Torteval, the cliffs are nearly deserted, and if you wander from the path, you'll be wading through shoulder-high ferns and brambles. Early birds get to see green **Fermain Bay** uncongested and explore the German fortifications in solitude. Near the beginning of the path, Guernsey's **Aquarium** is housed in a set of tunnels fortified by Soviet and Eastern European prisoner labor during the Occupation. Look for the defiant hammer and sickle chiseled into a wall of the second tunnel. (Open daily 10am-sunset. Admission £1.50)

An hour and a quarter by bike from St-Peter Port, you'll pass **Fermain Bay** and then reach **Telegraph Bay** and **St-Martin's Point.** If you're short on time, take the Jerbourg Road bus. One of the most beautiful spots on the island, St-Martin's Point's small grove of evergreens grows on land gently sloping down to the sea. Across Telegraph Bay, the peculiar rocks called "peastacks" protrude at the island's southern tip. Follow the path from here along the cliff to the **Doyle Monument,** from which you can see a splendid view of the nearby isle of Herm.

Continuing around Jerbourg Point, you next reach **Moulin Huet Bay;** take your pick of the beaches here. **Petit Port,** only accessible by a narrow flight of 250 steps, has perpendicular cliffs and white, crescent-shaped beaches. **Water Lane** at Moulin Huet, a lane with a stream in the middle, is typical of paths all over the southern bays.

As you continue around the bay to **Icart Point,** turn inland for cream tea at **Icart Tea Gardens,** one of the finest tea houses on the island. (Open daily 10am-5pm. Pot o' tea 35p, cream tea £1.) If you turn inland anywhere before Icart, you'll be near **St-Martin's,** the parish adjacent to St-Peter Port. *La Grande Mère du Climquière,* a stone figure dating from 700 BC, serenely guards the **St-Martin Parish Church Cemetery.**

Continuing inland toward the east, you'll soon come to the **German Underground Hospital** in St-Andrew's. It is preserved just as it was the day the Germans abandoned it: damp walls, rusted beds, and fetid atmosphere. (Open April-Oct. daily 10am-noon and 2-5pm. Admission £1.20, ages under 14 60p.) Also in St-Andrew's is the bizarre **Chapel of Les Vauxbelets,** which claims to be the smallest chapel in Europe. It's just large enough for a priest and two parishioners. The exterior is decorated with shells and bits of broken china—one monk dedicated his life to building the chapel out of broken dishes sent to him by the faithful. (Always open. Free.)

Rejoin the cliff path from the Occupation Museum (one mile south of the chapel) and follow it to the end. In lovely **Torteval,** a few minutes from St-Peter Port, the **Imperial Hotel** on Pleinmont St. serves excellent, cheap pub lunches (from £1.95) and good dinners. Along the eastern coast, the grand sprawling expanses of the flat bays—**Roquaine, Vazon, Grand Havre**—are best seen at high tide. Low tide in Guernsey drops as much as 40 feet, which means a lot of walking over slippery rocks to reach knee-deep water. At low tide, however, you can walk across to **Lihou Island,** between Roquaine and Perelle Bays, and see the ruins of the **Priory of St-Mary.**

Legend has it that Guernsey witches based themselves in Perelle Bay at **Le Catriorc,** one of the island's many ancient dolmens (underground graves). The best place to make your flesh crawl is the **Dehus Dolmen,** a prehistoric chambered tomb dating from 2000 BC, at the northern tip of the island, near the yacht marina in the Vale. Take the bus to Beaucette Marina from St-Peter Port. Though witchcraft has not made a popular resurgence in the island, as recently as 1914 one Mrs. Lake was accused of weaving a spell over one Mrs. Outin and her husband. The husband fell ill and died, as did all of Mrs. Outin's cattle.

The smaller islands around Guernsey are accesible by boat from St-Peter Port. **Sark,** which allows no cars on the island and is ruled by the Grand Duchess of Sark, is served by **Isle of Sark Shipping Company,** White Rock (tel. 240 59; 3-6 boats per day). **Alderny** (pop. 2000), the northernmost of the Channel Islands, is linked to Guernsey by Condor Hydrofoils, North Pier Steps (tel. 261 21).

Brittany (Bretagne)

As France's westernmost province, Brittany is geographically, politically, and culturally removed from the rest of France. Unlike most of their compatriots, the Bretons are a Celtic people whose ancestors crossed over from Britain to escape Anglo-Saxon invaders in the 5th and 6th centuries. They settled in the ancient Kingdom of Armor, converting its remaining inhabitants to Christianity and renaming it Little Britain, or Brittany. Although locals' frequent claim that they are Bretons first and French second may seem on the surface to have little meaning in the era of fax machines and acid-washed demin, distinctive customs endure in many villages. The traditional costume of Breton women, the black dress and lace *coiffe* (an elaborate headdress), can be seen in museums, at reenacted folk festivals, and even at some markets. While the lilting *Breizh* (Breton) is spoken most energetically at the pubs and the ports in the western part of the province, some children still learn the old Celtic tongue in school.

Bretons parade their cultural heritage in grand fashion during the village *pardons,* ancient church rites held on the Feast of the Assumption and on days honoring the most beloved of the region's several hundred local saints. Still considered days of repentance rather than displays for tourists, these festivals include a morning mass and an afternoon procession of costumed locals carrying banners, candles, and statues of the saints. The secular dances which follow tend to play modern music, but the lucky may hear ancient melodies played on traditional instruments. The *binou* descends from the Scottish warpipes and the Irish *uillean* pipes. The *vielle,* whose strings are sounded with a wooden disk attached to a crank, adds a scratchy, fiddlelike whine to the piper's jigs and reels. The best-known *pardons* take place at Tréguier in May, at Quimper's Festival de la Cornouaille between the third and fourth Sunday in July, at Ste-Anne-d'Auray in late July, at Perros-Guirec in mid-August, at Ste-Anne-La-Palud a week later, and at Josselin in early September. Also of note is Lorient's Festival Interceltique, held the first two weeks of August. For information, contact a tourist office in any large town.

Industrialization and modernization have come only in the post-war period to this relatively poor province, but in places they have come with a vengeance. Traditional vocations like farming and fishing have become increasingly difficult to pursue, and many younger people have emigrated to Paris and other cities throughout France. In the past, economic difficulties have fueled an active separatist movement. Recently, however, the French government has granted more autonomy to the local Breton leadership and has begun to support the preservation of Breton culture. In June 1979, under Giscard d'Estaing's administration, students were allowed to replace one language section of the *baccalauréat* exam with Breton. Mitterand made Brittany more easily accessible to the rest of France with his extensive road building project in the 1980s, thus diffusing the bottled-up energy of of the Breton movement. Discrimination against the Bretons, however, has not ended. One poster publicizing a recent Breton candidate for national office depicted a father telling his daughter that she can marry a man of any nationality, ethnic group, or race—just not a Breton.

However they may treat the Bretons, the rest of the French have great affection for the spectacular beaches and misted, almost apocalyptic headlands that ring this province. If you balk at crowds, beware visiting in July and August. June is a perfect month to see Brittany, as the weather is mild, the restaurants and hotels open, and the towns not yet swarmed. In the off-season, many of the coastal resorts such as St-Malo, Quiberon, and Concarneau essentially shut down, but the churches, cobblestones, beaches, and cliffs will be yours in eerie and romantic solitude. Whatever the season, try to spend some time on the crowded but pristine islands off the mainland—Batz, Ouessant, and Bréhat, in particular—and in the the smaller towns of the Argoat, where tourists are fewer and the Breton traditions less disturbed.

Both the Breton islands and the mainland lay claim to some inscrutable archaeo-logical treasures. Little is known of the neolithic people who settled here before the Gauls and erected the thousands of megalithic monuments visible today, sometimes in altered form. (The Romans, who conquered the area in 56 BC, decorated some of these monuments and incorporated them into their own rituals. Later, the Christian Bretons capped some standing stones with crosses or carved Christian symbols onto them.) Menhirs are large single stones weighing between 25 and 100 tons and pointing towards the heavens. Enormous menhirs usually stand alone, but some stand in circles to form cromlechs like the famous one at Er Lannic on a small island in the Gulf of Morbihan. Dolmens, smaller stones stacked to form roofed passages, may have been altars or tombs. The Merchant's Table in Locmariaquer, in the Gulf of Morbihan, is an impressive example.

The region's 1800-odd crêperies set their tables with more than just the famed regional specialty. *Galettes* of ground buckwheat flour (*sarassin*) wrapped around eggs, mushrooms, seafood, or ham, take their place alongside *crêpes* made of ground wheat flour (*froment*) and filled with chocolate, fruit, and jam. These are accompa-nied by *cidre brut* (the local cider) or by the sweeter *cidre doux,* while such delecta-ble seafood dishes as *coquilles St-Jacques* (scallops), *saumon fumé* (smoked salmon), and *moules-marinières* (steamed mussels in a white wine-based broth) are served with *Muscadet,* a dry white wine from the vineyards around Nantes. Brittany's con-tributions to French pastry windows include *kouign amann* (flaky layers dripping with butter and sugar) and the custard-like *far breton.*

Cycling is the best way to travel, especially since the most beautiful sights are also the least accessible by public transportation. The terrain is relatively flat, though it gets a bit hillier in the Argoat region. Hikers can choose from a number of routes, including the long-distance footpaths ("Grandes Randonnées") GR341, GR37, GR38, GR380, and the spectacular GR34 along the northern coast. ABRI offices in Rennes and Nantes, as well as the larger tourist offices, can help you coor-dinate your hiking or biking tour. Many people find hitchhiking easiest along the major roads such as D786 from Morlaix to St-Brieuc. The quickest hitching route to Paris is via Avranches in the north and Nantes, Angers, and Le Mans in the south, rather than the less-developed road through Rennes.Although trains and buses can be dependable and efficient, they are often infrequent in isolated areas and nearly nonexistent in the off-season.

Rennes

In 1720, a drunken carpenter knocked over his lamp and set most of Rennes ablaze. Despite this misbegotten bonfire, which consumed all but the heart of the half-timbered *vieille ville,* Rennes (pop. 250,000) survived to become the administra-tive center of Brittany, if not its tourist center. Unlike other towns in the region, Rennes is most active during the school year, when 36,000 students—apparently oblivious to the lesson of the 18th-century carpenter—return to the bars and cafés and rouse the city from its long summer nap. The charming but small old city war-rants an afternoon's wander in any season, but those looking for more than a glimpse of traditional Breton culture may find themselves itching to get out of town. When planning your excursions, consult the tourist office, the Association Bretonne des Relais et Itinéraires (ABRI), and the Centre d'Information Jeunesse Bretagne.

Orientation and Practical Information

Rennes is two hours from Paris (Gare Montparnasse) by TGV (3½ by regular train) and easily accessible from Normandy via Caen. The **Vilaine River** cuts the city in two, with the station to the south and most of the sights and shopping to the north. From the station, **av. Jean Janvier,** straight ahead, takes you to the river. To reach the tourist office, turn left along the river and walk five blocks to the Pont de Nemours. The *quais* which flank the Vilaine River are filled with shops and offices; art and antique shops crowd the narrow streets behind the Cathédrale St-Pierre and pl. St-Germain.

Tourist Office: Pont de Nemours (tel. 99 79 01 98). Lots of information and extremely friendly help. Ask for the free map of monuments in Rennes or for the guide with history, shopping, and cinemas (20F). Camping booklets, hotel listings, and other city maps also available. Open Mon.-Sat. 9am-7pm, Sun. 10am-1pm and 3-5pm; Sept. 16-June 17 Tues.-Sun. 10am-12:30pm and 2-6:30pm. **Association Bretonne des Relais et Itinéraires (ABRI):** 9, rue des Portes Mordelaises (tel. 99 31 59 44). Devoted to helping you discover Brittany on foot, on horseback, or by canoe. Free lists of travel shelters (*gîtes d'étape*). A 30% reduction on SNCF travel in Brittany available to groups of 10 or more. Open Tues.-Fri. 9:30am-12:30pm and 2-6:30pm; Sat. 10am-12:30pm and 2-6pm.

Post Office: pl. de la République (tel. 99 79 50 71). **Currency exchange** with respectable rates. Open Mon.-Fri. 8am-7pm, Sat. 8am-noon. **Postal Code:** 35000.

Trains: pl. de la Gare (tel. 99 65 50 50), at the end of av. Jean Janvier. To: St-Malo (11 per day, 1 hr., 55F); Paris (12 per day, 3½ hr., 195F); Caen (3 per day, 3 hr., 144F); Nantes (7 per day, 2 hr., 91F); Dinan (7 per day, 1½ hr., 57F). Information office open Mon.-Sat. 8am-7:30pm, Sun. 9am-7:30pm. Telephone information Mon.-Sat. 7:30am-10pm, Sun. 9am-9:30pm.

Buses: bd. Magenta (tel. 99 30 87 80), off pl. de la Gare. To: St-Malo (2 per day in summer, 6 per day in winter, 2 hr., 43.50F); Nantes (3 per day, 3 hr., 86F); Vannes (2 per day, Sun. 1 per day, 2¾ hr., 83F); Dinard (4 per day, 2 hr.; Sun. 2 per day, 1½ hr., 53F). Service to tiny local towns is more frequent on weekdays during the school year. *Courriers Bretons* makes direct trips to Mont St-Michel (1 per day, 50F, round-trip 95F). Information office open Mon.-Thurs. 8-11:30am and 1:30-5pm, Fri. 8-11:30am and 2:30-6pm, Sat. 8-11:30am. Ticket office open Mon. 6:15am-6:45pm; Tues.-Thurs. 8am-6:45pm; Fri. 8am-7pm; Sat. 9-11:45pm.

Taxis: At the train station (tel. 99 30 66 45), and the *mairie* (town hall) in pl. de la Mairie (tel. 99 79 59 69). 24 hrs., but harder to find at night.

Car Rental: Hertz, 10 av. de Mail, which runs westward from pl. Mal Foch at the town's western end (tel. 99 54 26 52, reservations 05 20 42 04). From 251F per day and 4F for each kilometer.

Bike Rental: The train station rents decent Peugeot 10-speeds locally and for one-way trips to Dinan, St-Malo, Dol, Combourg, and Messac. (30F per ½ day, 40F per day; for a more robust bike, 40F per ½ day, 50F per day. Deposit 500F or major credit card.)

Hitchhiking: Provoya, Maison du Champ de Mars, 6, cours des Alliés (tel. 99 30 98 87), on the 2nd floor. Next to CIJB. Arranges ride-sharing. Open Mon.-Fri. 2-6:30pm, Sat. 9am-noon.

Camping Store: Service Camping, 11bis, rue du Vieux Cours, off bd. de la Liberté. Sells equipment and repairs tents. Also rents tents and trailers. Open Mon. 2-7pm, Tues.-Sat. 9am-noon and 2-7pm.

Women's Center: 50, bd. Magenta (tel. 99 30 80 89). Free advice and information. Welcomes individuals and groups. Open Tues.-Wed. and Fri. 10am-5pm, Thurs. 1-5pm.

Youth Center: Centre d'Information Jeunesse Bretagne, Maison du Champ de Mars, 6, cours des Alliés (tel. 99 31 47 48), on the 2nd floor. Provides a comprehensive list of inexpensive hotels in Rennes as well as information on cycling, cultural events, work opportunities, and more for all of Brittany. Free babysitting service. Friendly staff. Open during school vacations and July-Aug. daily 10am-6pm, other times 2-6:30pm.

Pharmacy: Pharmacie de la Mairie, pl. de la Mairie (tel. 99 79 31 66). Conveniently located in the center of town. Every Rennes pharmacy stays open all night (sometimes you must ring a bell), except Sat. when they take turns; look for the name and address of the late-night pharmacy (*pharmacie de garde*) posted on any pharmacy door.

Hospital: Hôpital de Pontchaillon, rue Henri Le Guilaux (tel. 99 59 16 04).

Medical Emergency: SAMU, tel. 99 28 43 15. **Anti-Poison Center:** 24-hour hotline (tel. 99 28 42 22).

Police: rue d'Echange (tel. 99 65 00 22), off pl. St-Anne. **Emergency,** tel. 17.

Accommodations and Camping

Accommodations shouldn't be a problem in Rennes, except in early July during the Tombées de la Nuit festival. The spacious youth hostel is a 30-minute walk from the train station. There are also a number of small, moderately-priced hotels to the east of av. Janvier between quai Richemont and the train station.

Auberge de Jeunesse (IYHF), 10-12, Canal St-Martin (tel. 99 33 22 33). IYHF card required. From the train station, follow av. Jean Janvier straight to the canal. Take a left onto quai Chateaubriand, then a right onto rue d'Orléans. Go through the pl. de la Mairie and onto rue le Bastard. Rue Pont-aux-Foulons, curving on your left, leads to pl. St-Anne, and from there rue St-Malo leads north straight to the hostel. You can also take bus #20 or 22 (#2 on weekends) to Coëtlogon (every 20 min. until 7:30, 3F). From the bus stop, continue in the same direction to the intersection and then turn sharply right; look for signs. Newly renovated house in ideal location. Disabled access. Cafeteria and bar; 5 laundry machines (15F per token). Also 25% discount coupons for local cinemas (weekdays only). Ask for a free map of Rennes. 4 beds per room max., some single rooms. Excellent showers and fluorescent bed lamps in all rooms. Reception open Mon.-Fri. 7:45am-11pm, Sat.-Sun. 8-10am and 6-11pm. Midnight curfew. 64.50F in 1- to 2-bed rooms, 50F in 3- to 4-bed rooms. Rooms with TV available for 12F more and 50F deposit. Breakfast included. Sheets 13F.

Cité Universitaire: Every July and August, one or two university dorms open their doors to travelers for short stays (50F, 31F each additional night). Housing is comfortable, but try the hostel first. To check availability, call or visit **CROUS**, 7, pl. Hoche (tel. 99 36 46 11); open Mon.-Fri. 8.30-11.30am and 1-4pm.

Hôtel de Léon, 15, rue de Léon (tel. 99 30 55 28), near the Vilaine River off quai de Richemont. Large, comfortable rooms. Excellent location; friendly owners who love to talk about travel. Singles 110F. Doubles 120F. Breakfast 20F. Closed 2 weeks in Aug.

Hôtel le Magenta, 35, bd. Magenta (tel. 99 30 85 37). A 5-min. walk from pl. de la Gare. Bd. Magenta runs straight from the train station, a little to the left. Recently and tastefully remodeled. Reception at the bar open Mon.-Sat. 7am-9pm. Singles 85F. Doubles 100F. Showers 15F. Breakfast 20F.

Hôtel Riaval, 9, rue Riaval (tel. 99 50 65 58). Turn right as you leave the train station, and immediately turn right again onto the stairs just past the gas station. Follow the path over the railroad tracks to the end; when you emerge, peaceful rue Riaval will be in front of you, branching off slightly to the left (about 5 min.). The bridge over the tracks is perfectly safe during the day. Charming despite location away from the centre-ville. Singles and doubles from 78F. Breakfast 18F.

Hôtel le Saint-Malo, 8, rue Dupont des Loges (tel. 99 30 38 21). Take av. Janvier from the train station and make a right on rue Dupont des Loges. Clean and quiet rooms. Singles from 100F. Breakfast 20F.

Garden Hotel, 3, rue Duhamel (tel. 99 65 45 06), off av. Janvier just before the river and a block from the museum. Nice courtyard and small, quiet rooms. Wash cabinet and bedside telephone. Singles 105F. Doubles 140F. Breakfast in your room or downstairs 25F.

Camping: Municipal des Gayeulles, near Pare des Bois (tel. 99 36 91 22). Take bus #3 from rue de Paris, the southern border of the Jardin de Thabor, to parc Les Gayeulles. A grassy, scenic, 2-star site with beautiful flower beds. Isolated from the main road. Around 10F per person, 12F per site, 4F per car. Open Easter-early Oct.

Food

In Rennes, as in most of Brittany, crêperies are the cheapest places for a light meal; there are a number scattered about the old quarter and on rue St-Melaine near the university and gardens. You might also want to take fruit or some bread and cheese and sit on a bench at the beautiful Jardin du Thabor (remember that most merchants close for lunch around 1-3:30pm). A covered **market** is held Tuesday through Saturday from 7am to 6pm in a different place every day. Ask the tourist office or any local where it is. For a more interesting and extravagant meal, try one of Rennes's Afghan, Indian, Pakistani, Spanish, or Italian restaurants.

Restaurant des Carmes, 2, rue des Carmes (tel. 99 30 73 12), off bd. de la Liberté. Spare, elegant interior with lace curtains. Popular; wide selection of salads, pizzas, and meat dishes.

Four courses 40F, 5 courses 55F. Open Mon.-Fri. 11:45am-2pm and 7-10pm. Closed for a month in June-July at owner's discretion.

Le Boulingrain, 25, rue St-Melaine (tel. 99 38 75 11). Formerly a prison, now a small, friendly place with probably the best buy for *crêpes* in town. Try the scallops in cream sauce (29F). Three-*crêpe menu* 39F. Try the *boulingrain,* the restaurant's namesake: a *crêpe* stuffed with apples, caramel, and almonds (24.50F). Open Mon.-Sat. 11:30am-2pm and 6:30-11pm.

Au Jardin des Plantes, 32, rue St-Melaine (tel. 99 38 74 46). Good crowd and lovely half-timbered house. Four-course *menus* 43F and 60F. Open Mon.-Sat. noon-2pm and 7:15-10pm.

Le Moule et Co., 13, rue St.-Malo (tel. 96 63 70 71), on the way to the hostel. Delicious mollusks, shrimp and other seafood 30-40F. Catch of the day 32F. Open Tues.-Sun. noon-2pm and 7-11pm.

L'Escale, 178 rue St-Malo (tel. 99 59 19 55), near the youth hostel. Cross the bridge in front of the hostel and walk down rue St-Malo; the restaurant is on your right. Smoky and cozy with a local clientele. Cheap red wine and blatantly American music. *Galettes* 10-30F, *crêpes* 6-22F, entrees 20-50F. Open Sept.-July, Tues.-Sun. 7:30-11pm.

Crêperie des Portes-Mordelaises, Portes Mordelaises (tel. 99 30 57 40); near pl. des Lices at the foot of a 15th-century tower. In an old and rustic corner of town. Check out the nearby **Cathédrale St.-Pierre.** Try the *galette andouille* (about 17F). Open Tues.-Sat. 9am-2pm and 6:45-9:30pm, Sun. and Mon. 7:30-9:30pm.

Sights and Entertainment

Entertainment in Rennes ranges from visiting rock groups at the Maison de la Culture to marionette performances of *Peter and the Wolf* at the rue de la Paillette MJC. The pamphlet *Spectacles, informations* at the tourist office lists everything, even the blooming periods of Rennes's flowers, bushes, and trees. In early July, Rennes holds the festival **Les Tombées de la Nuit,** nine days of non-stop music, dance, theater, song, and mime by internatioanl performers who take over the streets from noon to midnight. For information, write to the Office de Tourisme, Festival de TN, 8 pl. du Maréchal Juin, 35000 Rennes. The annual **Festival International des Arts Electroniques,** brings candlelight to the canal and displays of electronic art and sculptures to the streets in June of every even year. Be sure to visit the startlingly green, well-kept **Jardin du Thabor** (open daily 7am-9:30pm) behind the Renaissance **Eglise Notre Dame** and the **Cloître Ste-Melanie.** To reach the gardens, follow the continuation of rue Jean Janvier across the river and turn right on rue Victor Hugo. The **Musée de Bretagne** (tel. 99 28 55 84) and the **Musée des Beaux Arts** (tel. 99 28 55 85) are housed in the same building at 20, quai Emile Zola, by the canal. The Musée de Bretagne provides an informative introduction to the region's history and traditions, with tools, costumes, and jewelry from the prehistoric to present times. The Musée des Beaux Arts displays local landscapes as well as an interesting (if obscure) collection of art from the 14th century to the present. Both museums emphasize the archaeology of the region. (Open Wed.-Mon. 10am-noon and 2-6pm. Admission to each 11F, families and students with ID 5.50F. Admission to both 17F, students with ID and families 8.50F.)

Those unimpressed by the large, bland, modern buildings that dominate the Rennes skyline, can stroll through the narrow streets between pl. du Palais and Palais St-Georges for a view of half-timbered medieval houses with overhanging upper stories designed to maximize space. If you long for Americana, go to pl. du Colombier, south of the old city and near the train station, right off bd. de la Liberté, for an afternoon of shopping at the new Rennes mall, complete with a McDonald's.

Summer visitors looking for truly raucous student nightlife may find themselves waiting around until September. If a café or drink is all you want, stay within the picturesque *vieille ville.* Extra energy (or *crêpes*) can be danced off at the popular **Le Pyms,** 27, pl. du Colombier (tel. 99 67 30 00). For 80F (Sun.-Thurs. 60F) the lucky will meet some fun Rennes people and probably not want to leave. It doesn't close until 5am. Pink-pillared **L'Espace,** 43, bd. de la Tour d'Auvergne (tel. 99 30 21 95), is also worth a try. (Sun.-Wed. 50F, Thurs. 60F, Fri. 70F, Sat. 80F; open daily 10:45pm-4:45am.) The older or more reserved may prefer **Charleston Café Dansant**, 2, av. du Mail (60F).

St-Malo

Geographically isolated yet economically prosperous, the original St-Malo was an island fortified with granite; it stood proud, aloof, and fierce in its fight for independence. Centuries spent capturing enemy vessels earned St-Malo the status of a free city in 1308, and for hundreds of years, it resisted French domination as strongly as it did Norman and English invaders. The Malouin people expressed their attitude in the city's motto: "Neither French, nor Breton, I am from St-Malo." Eighty percent of the town was destroyed in the effort to reclaim it from the Germans in 1944, but it has been scrupulously reconstructed.

Although St-Malo has surrendered to the mainland and built a connecting isthmus, this still former stronghold of shipbuilders, merchants, and privateers, still seems to belong to the sea. Standing on the ramparts, surrounded by the ocean on three sides, you might well imagine that the distant cod trawler is setting sail for the New World under the *fleur-de-lis* and command of *St-Malouin* Jacques Cartier, who discovered Canada in 1534. The celebrated poet, Chateaubriand, now buried off the St-Malo shore on the Ile de Grand Bé, spent his youth roaming the port. Today, the *corsaires* are gone and the vacationers crowding the sand show no sign of budging, but in St-Malo, the only Breton city to have preserved its cod fishing fleet, one can still sense the sailor spirit.

Orientation and Practical Information

St-Malo consists of the old walled city (called *intra muros*) and a complex of three former towns. The long beachfront promenades of **Paramé** and **Rothéneuf** lie to the southeast; **St-Servan**, to the southwest, dates from Gallo-Roman times. The *vieille ville* and the tourist office are a 10-minute walk from the station. Turn right, cross bd. de la République, and follow av. Louis-Martin. Various city buses make the trip to the walled city (the stop is porte St-Vincent), including the red #2 and 3 and the purple #4, which run every 20 minutes from bd. de la République (6.20F).

Tourist Office: esplanade St-Vincent (tel. 99 56 64 48), near the entrance to the old city. Busy staff speaks English. Request the city map that indexes street names. Also pick up a free list of local campsites. Open Mon.-Sat. 8:30am-8pm, Sun. 10am-6:30pm; Sept.-June Mon.-Sat. 9am-noon and 2-6:30pm.

Budget Travel: BCE Voyage (tel. 99 40 41 85), in the building facing the tourist office. Train, boat, and plane tickets. **Currency exchange** charges a grim 18F tariff per exchange. At least it's open Sun. Open April-Oct. daily 9:30am-7pm.

Post Office: 1, bd. de la Tour d'Auvergne (tel. 99 56 12 05), at the intersection with bd. de la Liberté. **Currency exchange** at this office only. Open Mon.-Fri. 8am-7pm, Sat. 8am-noon. **Branch office**, pl. des Frères Lamennais in the *vieille ville.* Open Mon.-Fri. 8:30am-6:30pm, Sat. 8:30am-12:30pm; Sept. 17-June Mon.-Fri. 8:30am-12:30pm and 1:30-5pm, Sat. 8:30am-12:30pm. To have mail held, address it: "Instance, Poste Restante"; "35401 St-Malo Principal" for the main office, or "35402 St-Malo *intra muros*" for the old-city branch. **Postal Code:** 35400.

Trains: pl. de l'Hermine (information in Rennes tel. 99 65 50 50; reservations in St-Malo 99 56 15 33). To: Paris-Montparnasse via Rennes (6 per day, 5 hr., 245F); Rennes (12 per day, 8 per day on weekends, 1 hr., 52F); Caen (10 per day, 118F); Rouen (10 per day, 187F); Brest (4 per day, 170F; 14F extra for high-speed TGV); Morlaix (4 per day, 148F). For Caen and Rouen change at Dol; for Brest and Morlaix change at Rennes. Open 5:30am-8pm.

Buses: Information offices for all buses in the pavilion opposite the tourist office, esplanade St-Vincent. (Information on the St-Malo city buses tel. 99 56 06 06.) **Tourisme Verney** (tel. 99 40 82 67). To: Rennes (Mon.-Sat. 3 per day, 2 hr., 43.50F); Dinan (3 per day, 1 hr., 28F); Dinard (12 per day, 5 on Sun.; 1 hr.; 16F); Cancale (1-2 per day Mon.-Sat., 50 min., 18.50F). Daytrips to the Côte d'Emeraude 105F (includes boat crossing of the Rance). Buses leave from the esplanade and stop briefly at the train station. Office open mid-June to mid-Oct.,

Mon.-Sat. 8:30am-noon and 2-6:30pm; mid-Oct. to mid-June Mon.-Fri. 8:30am-noon and 2-6:30pm, Sat. 8:30-noon. **Courriers Bretons** (tel. 99 56 79 09). To Pontorson (3 per day, 1 hr., 37F). Round-trip tickets from St-Malo to Mont St-Michel 80F. To Cancale (7 per day; Sun. 3 per day; ½-hr.; 16F, seniors 50% discount, ages 4-7 20% discount, under 4 free). Summer daytrips to other points along the Côte d'Emeraude and the Côte de Granite Rose. Office open Mon.-Fri. 8:30am-12:30pm and 1:30-6:45pm, Sat. 8:30am-12:30pm and 1:30-4:30pm; Sept.-June Mon.-Fri. 8:30am-12:15pm and 2-6:15pm, Sat. 8:30am-12:15pm.

Ferries: Voyages Pansart, esplanade St-Vincent (tel. 99 40 85 96), in pavilion with the bus offices. Information and booking for all ferries. Ask about their special autocar excursions to Mt. St. Michel, Quimper, Cap Frehel, Quiberon (80-140F). Open Mon.-Sat. 8am-12:30pm and 2-7pm, Sun. 8:30am-noon and 4:00-6:30pm; Sept.-May Mon.-Sat. 9am-noon and 2-6:30pm. **Brittany Ferries,** Gare Maritime du Naye. To Portsmouth (1-2 per day; 8½ hr.; 320F, round-trip 630F; Sept.-June 290F, round-trip 600F). **Emeraude Lines,** Gare Maritime de la Bourse (tel. 99 40 48 40). To: Jersey (1-2 per day, erratic departures Oct.-March; 2½ hr.; about 220F); Guernsey (May-late Sept. 1 per day, 4 hr., about 255F); Cap Fréhel (round-trip 105F); the St-Malo estuary (round-trip 55F, 110F if you stay more than 60hr.). One-way excursions to the Côte d'Emeraude (Dinard, 19F; Dinan, 75F; the Ile de Cézembre, 45F; the Iles Chausey, 53F). **Condor Hydrofoils,** Gare Maritime de la Bourse (tel. 99 56 42 29). To: Jersey (1-4 per day, 70 min., about 220F); Guernsey (May-Oct. 1-2 per day, 2½ hr., about 255F); Sark (4-6 per week, 2 hr., about 250F); Weymouth (late March-Oct. 1-2 per day, 4 hr., about 407F).

Car Rental: Thrifty Location, 46, bd. de la République (tel. 99 56 47 60). Opel Corsa 190F per day plus 1.20F per km, or 300F per day with unlimited mileage. Deposit 2000F per day or the estimated cost of the rental, to be adjusted upon return. Will meet you at the Gare Maritime free of charge. Open daily 8am-12:15pm and 1-8pm. **Avis,** Gare Maritime du Naye (tel. 99 81 73 24). **Europcar,** 16, bd. des Talards (tel. 99 56 75 17). **Hertz,** 48, bd. de la République (tel. 99 56 31 61) has cars starting from 350F with 250km included. Open Mon.-Fri. 8am-noon and 2-5pm, Sat. until 6pm, Sun. 9am-noon. Closed Sun. and Sept.-May.

Bike Rental: Diazo, 47, quai du Juaytrouin (tel. 99 40 31 63). Cheaper than at the station and only 300m away. The **train station** rents 10-speeds at 50F per day, deposit 500F. Longer rentals discounted.

Windsurfer Rental: Quai 34 Surf School, 7, rue Courtoisville (tel. 99 40 07 47). Walk along the Grande Plage until you see the signs. 70F per hour, 180F per ½ day. Deposit of passport or other identity card required. Open June-Aug. 9am-6:30pm, Sept.-May 9am-4pm.

Laundromat: 3, rue Ernest Renan, at bd. de la République, 2 blocks from the station. Washer 12F, dryer 2F per 7½ min., detergent 2F. Open daily 7am-10pm.

Pharmacy: Several St-Malo pharmacies, both inside and outside of the walled city, take turns staying open all night. Check posted list to see which one is open.

Hospital: Centre Hospitalier de St-Malo, 2, rue Laennec (tel. 99 81 60 40).

Ambulance: 16, av. Waldeck-Rousseau (tel. 99 40 02 02 or 99 56 30 64). 24 hrs.

Police: Place des Frères Lamennais (tel. 99 40 85 80). **Emergency,** tel. 17.

Accommodations and Camping

St-Malo is lovely, and unfortunately, everybody knows it. People with rooms in the hotels in July and August probably made reservations before you were born. To stay in the hostel, arrive early. Do not sleep on the beaches—even if the water is 350m away when you lie down, it will dash you against the wall within six hours.

Auberge de Jeunesse (LFAJ/IYHF), 37, av. du Père Umbricht (tel. 99 40 29 80). To avoid the 25-min. walk from the station, catch red bus #2 (3 per hr., 6F, last bus 7:30pm) on av. Jean Jaurès behind the station (3 right turns). Get off at Courtoisville. If the buses have stopped, continue down av. Jean Jaurès to bd. Gambetta. Take a left and follow this road until you reach av. du Père Umbricht. Turn right, pass the supermarket, and look for the hostel (and the flags) on your left. Pretty, ivy-covered building, fronted by tennis courts and beautiful pink flowers. The beach is just 3 blocks away. Reception open daily 9-10am, 5-6:45pm, and 7:30-8pm; lockout 10am-5pm, but you can still check in 10am-noon and 2-5pm. 55F, without a hostel card 59F (card required in July and August). Breakfast 13F. Lunch or dinner 32F (not served on weekends). Sheet sacks 13F. Tennis equipment available free. Next door, the **Foyer des Jeunes Travailleurs** has color TV, a pool table, and a higher ratio of French people. They might accept hostellers if there's no room at the hostel (36F per person).

Auberge de Jeunesse (IYHF), 13, rue des Ecoles (tel. 99 56 22 00), southeast of the center of town in Paramé. Dignified stone mansion with a greenhouse and friendly staff, but farther from town than the other hostels and often full. Take bus #2 from av. Jean Jaurès to Les Chênes (the last stop). Reception open Oct.-Feb. 9am-noon and 2-6pm., March-Aug. 8am-noon and 2-8pm. 37F per night in the house, 35F in fun bungalows with kitchens, 30F in the circus tents. Breakfast 12F. Call before coming; in summer, ask about the bungalows if they say there's no room.

Auberge Au Gai Bec (The Jolly Beak), 4, rue des Lauriers (tel. 99 40 82 16). This personable hostel offers very competitive prices, and the location inside the walls tips the scale in its favor. Small, clean rooms with big beds and multiple mirrors that reflect the hotel's past. Exceptionally friendly owners run a delicious restaurant downstairs. Singles (1-2 people) 95F. Doubles have 2 double beds, 1-2 people 135F, 3-4 people 190F. Shower free. Breakfast 20F. Reservations and credit cards accepted.

Hôtel le Neptune, 21, rue de l'Industrie (tel. 99 56 82 15). Close to the beach, with newly redecorated, impeccable rooms and a spacious bar downstairs. Singles 110F. Doubles 130F. Showers (free in some rooms) 15F. Breakfast 20F. Phone reservations accepted.

Hôtel Le Vauban, 7, bd. de la République (tel. 99 56 09 39). Clean, decent-sized rooms. Reception open daily; Oct.-April Mon.-Sat. Singles and doubles 100-120F. Showers 8F in summer, free otherwise. Breakfast 18F. 45-52F *menus*. Restaurant open noon-2pm and 7-10m. Telephone reservations accepted.

Information on all municipal campgrounds is available at the tourist office, or call 99 40 71 11. **Camping de la Cité d'Aleth**, near promenade de la Corniche in St-Servan (tel. 99 81 60 91), is the closest and most scenic campground, equipped with running water and hot shower. From July-Aug., you can take bus #1 to Aleth. (Adults 10.55F, children 5.27F, 5.49F per car, 6.97F per tent.)

Food

The outdoor **market** takes place from 8am to 12:30pm on Monday, Thursday, and Saturday, behind Eglise Notre-Dame-des-Grèves; on Tuesday and Friday, on pl. Bouvet in St-Servan and at the **Marché aux Légumes** *intra muros;* and on Wednesday and Saturday, on pl. du Prieuré, in Paramé. **Intermarché**, bd. Théodore Botrel, stocks bags of *craquelins de St-Malo,* crunchy flour biscuits that melt in your mouth. (Open Mon.-Fri. 9am-12:30pm and 3-7:15pm, Sat. 2:30-7:30pm.) *Craquelins* are also available inside the walls at the well-stocked **R. Cornu**, 4, pl. de Marché aux Légumes. During the off-season, the *vieille ville* has more seafood restaurants than you can shake a fishing net at.

Crêperie Chez Chantal, 2, pl. aux Herbes (tel. 99 40 93 97), near the *intra muros* post office. If by some bizarre mishap you haven't tried *crêpes* yet in Brittany, try them here. Great service, fun atmosphere, and the best prices inside the walls. Try the *galette aux fruits de mer* (seafood) for 32.50F. *Crêpes* 9-29F. Open daily noon-11pm.

Auberge Au Gai Bec, 4, rue des Lauriers (tel. 99 40 82 16). A seafood place to beat all others. Homelike atmosphere, good food, and a loveable owner. Tour France via their extensive wine list. *Menus* (79-148F) and entrees (30-50F) worth the money. Open Tues.-Sun. noon-2pm and 7-10pm. Closed for lunch Sat.

Restaurant L'Escale, 15, rue Jacques Cartier (tel. 99 40 94 13). Very filling four-course *menu* 66F. Try the grilled salmon (60F). Friendly and attentive service. Open Wed.-Mon. noon-2pm and 7-10pm.

La Corvette, 4, rue Jacques Cartier (tel. 99 40 15 04). Delectable seafood more than compensates for erratic service. 4-course *menu* 64F. Open Feb.-Nov., Tues. and Thurs.-Sun. noon-3pm and 6:30-11pm, Wed. 6:30-11pm.

Sights and Entertainment

The best way to see St-Malo is to explore the ramparts—you'll have the old town at your feet on one side and a long stretch of sea on the other. The scale of the tourist office map may deceive you, as the *vieille ville* is quite compact and manageable on foot. Begin at the staircase marked *Accès aux remparts* near porte St-Vincent, which opens onto lively pl. Chateaubriand. Not far from the entrance, porte St-Thomas looks out onto the **Fort National,** accessible only at low tide. Farther along, at the **Tour Bidouane,** climb down to the beach and continue along the stone walkway to **Le Grand Bé.** This small island holds the lonely grave of the Romantic poet Chateaubriand, who asked to be buried near the sound of the wind and the sea. The independent spirit of St-Malo and Brittany flares up three yards behind him. On the plaque engraved with the words "*Un grand écrivain français a voulu reposer ici*" (a great French writer wanted to rest here), someone has drawn a line through the word "français" and scrawled above it "Breton." Don't set out for the island if the sea is within 10m of the submersible walkway; you may be dangerously stranded in the wind and the wet for a good six hours until the tide recedes.

A casualty of 1944 bombings, the old town is largely a reconstruction, but some 17th-century houses and tiny streets with curious names remain: rue du Chat qui Danse (Street of the Dancing Cat) and rue de la Pie qui Boit (Street of the Drinking Magpie). Intricate leaded windows adorn one facade along rue Pelicot, and the last house before the anti-car barricade exemplifies fortified residential architecture. Farther down, you will see l'Escalier de la Grille (though the *grille* (gate) has been replaced with wooden doors), and to the right at 2, cour la Houssaye, lies the former residence of the Duchesse Anne de Bretagne, whose marriages to Louis XII and Charles VIII indirectly united Brittany with the rest of France. Gothic **Cathédrale St-Vincent** has also been extensively restored—the combination of a dark, 12th-century nave and fiery, modern stained-glass windows creates an eerie effect. (Open June-Aug. 8am-7pm and Sept-May 8am-noon and 2-7pm).

Built into the ramparts near porte St-Vincent, the excellent **Musée de la Ville** (tel. 99 40 71 11) makes its contribution to the continuing hullabaloo over Chateaubriand, St-Malo's very own Dead Poet. In addition, the winding staircase leads you through caches of maps, models, maritime documents and other pirate paraphernalia. It ends in the turret, the highest public vantage-point on this part of the Côte d'Emeraude, with a phenomenal view of St-Malo. (Open daily 9:30am-noon and 2-6:30pm; Oct.-May Wed.-Mon. 10am-noon and 2-6pm. Admission 12F, students with ID 5F.) At pl. Vauban, the **Aquarium** (tel. 99 40 91 86) and the **Exotarium** (tel. 99 40 86 21), house an eclectic array of both aquatic and land-lubbing reptiles. (Open daily 9am-11pm; mid-Sept. to July 9am-noon and 2-7pm. Admission 18F, students 13F. Admission to both buildings 31F, students 26F.) Over 300 dolls and furnished dollhouses are preserved in the **Musée de la Poupée,** 13, rue de Toulouse (tel. 99 40 15 51), inside the walled city. (Open July-Aug. daily 10am-noon and 2-7pm. Admission 15F, students 10F.) Those venturing outside the walls can visit the **Musée International du Long Cours Cap-Hornier** (tel. 99 81 66 09) at the Tour Solidor in St-Servan, which offers both nautical history and a present-day view of the Rance estuary. (Guided visits daily 10am-noon and 2-6pm; Sept.-June Wed.-Mon. 10am-noon and 2-6pm. Admission 10F, students 5F. Bus #2 to St-Servan every 20 min. from rue Jean Jaurès, behind the station, and from esplanade St-Vincent.)

When the sun goes down and you haven't quite had enough of endearing St-Malo, try the **Angelus Bis,** a popular and interesting bar, complete with circular red couches, Greek statues, and a large video screen. (Open 10pm-5am.) Currently fashionable **Le Pacha** holds court on the chaussée du Sillon, outside the walls (18 and over; no tennis shoes; drinks start at 50F, cover charge 60F.) The older, richer, or luckier might try the large **casino** on esplanade St-Vincent (both tel. 99 56 00 05), just outside the walled city. For a minimum bet of 5F, you can gamble at *la boule,* a roulette-like game (18 and over; cover charge 60F; Wed.-Sat. 9:30pm-4am, Sun. 9:30pm-12:30am.)

Near St-Malo

St-Malo is a crowded but convenient base from which to explore the Côte d'Emeraude. To the east lies **Cancale,** famous for its oysters (serviced by Tourisme

Verney and Courriers Breton buses), and scenic **Pointe de Grouin.** Thirty-six kilometers southeast of St-Malo lies Combourg, about which Chateaubriand once wrote, "It was in the woods of Combourg that I became what I am." If the prospect of becoming a cape-wearing Romantic poet doesn't scare you, visit the well-preserved **Château de Combourg** (tel. 99 73 22 95). The poet spent childhood nights in the *Tour du Chat* (Cat's Tower), which was supposedly haunted by a previous inhabitant's wooden leg and a black cat intent on using the terrified limb as a scratching post. (Open Wed.-Mon. Park 9am-noon and 2-5:30pm, Interior 2-5:30pm; Nov.-March Sun. 2-5pm.) Farther east is **Mont St-Michel,** a convenient daytrip from St-Malo (you probably can't afford to stay there). The cheapest and most convenient round-trip is an excursion run by Courriers Bretons (June 3 per week, July to mid-Sept. 3 per day; 80F). Buses leave from esplanade St-Vincent at 9:30am and return at 6:30pm. **Bateaux de la Baie du Mont St-Michel,** Gare Maritime Le Vivier-sur-Mer (tel. 99 48 82 30), tours the bay of Mont St-Michel in an amphibious boat (April-Oct. 4-5 per day, 78F). You may have trouble getting to Le Vivier-sur-Mer, 21km southeast of St-Malo. The most helpful staff at Voyages Pansart gives information on bus or boat tours of Vivier, Mont St-Michel and the Côte d'Emeraude. Emeraude Lines cruises out to the 70m cliffs of Cap Fréhel, 50km to the west (2½ hr., 105F).

Accessible by bus or a 15-minute boat ride, **Dinard** is the Breton haven for the Great Gatsby set, described by a fluttering *St-Malouine* as "oh la la, très chic" (Emeraude Lines runs 9:30am-6:15pm, from the Gare Maritime complex; 19F, round-trip 30F, bikes and mopeds 13F.) You can watch pedal boats, windsurfers, and sailboats from Dinard's excellent beach or swim in the Olympic-size swimming pool with heated sea water. The town itself supports some ugly high-rises and amusement park-type fast food stands, but it's worth a daytrip (Dinard has few affordable restaurants and hotels). Be sure to walk around both the **Pointe du Moulinet** and the **Pointe des Etetés,** where stone steps overgrown with rosebushes wind upward to mansions and viewpoints. Emeraude Lines also sails up the Rance to Dinan once a day with the tide (2 hr., 75F, round-trip 105F); boats stop in Dinard, but there's no time to get off. Several ferries operate between St-Malo and the **Channel Islands,** which claim unspoiled beaches and lower prices than the mainland.

Dinan

Dinan flaunts its status as the best-preserved medieval town in Brittany. Less crowded and commercial than Dinard and St-Malo, its northern neighbors at the mouth of the Rance Valley, Dinan and its 14,000 residents rest easy in their place out of the tourist spotlight. In the *vieille ville* 66m above the Rance, you can explore cobblestone streets lined by half-timbered houses dating from the 15th century. Challenging paths descend to the port, as well as a fascinating castle and museum.

Orientation and Practical Information

The tourist office in the *vieille ville* is a 10-minute walk from the station. Bear left across pl. du 11 Novembre 1918 onto rue Carnot, then right onto rue Thiers, which brings you to a large rotary intersection, pl. Duclos. Head up the hill to the left on rue du Marchix, which becomes rue Ferronnerie. Turn left at the sign for the tourist office, cross the square, take rue Ste-Claire, and turn left on rue de l'Horloge.

Tourist Office: 6, rue de l'Horloge (tel. 96 39 75 40). A granite-pillared 16th-century mansion next to a weeping willow. Helpful staff speaks some English. Walking tours of the town July-Aug. daily at 10am and 3pm (20F, children 5F). Map and excellent guide to the town's sights (in French, 6F). Free illuminated push-button map across the street. Open Mon.-Sat. 9am-7pm, Sun. 9am-12:30pm and 2-5pm; Oct.-April daily 9am-noon.

Post Office: pl. Duclos (tel. 96 39 25 07). **Currency exchange.** Open Mon.-Fri. 8:30am-7pm, Sat. 8:30am-noon. **Postal Code:** 22100.

Trains: pl. du 11 Novembre 1918 (tel. 96 39 22 39, information 96 94 50 50). To: Rennes via Dol (6 per day, 2 hr., 54F); St-Brieuc (Mon.-Sat. 3 per day, 1 hr., 42F); Paimpol (1 per day, change at St-Brieuc and Guingamp; 4 hr.; 74F); Morlaix (3 per day, Sun. 2 per day, change at St-Brieuc; 2 hr.; 87F); St-Malo (7 per day, change at Dol; 1¼ hr.; 37F). Lockers 3-5F. Ticket office open daily 5:30am-6:30pm. Information office open 8am-noon and 2-6:30pm; information tel. answered Mon.-Sat. 8:30am-noon and 2-6pm.

Buses: CAT/TV (tel. 96 39 21 05), at the train station on the other side of the *gare*'s baggage office. July-Sept. service to St-Malo only (3 per day, 27F, round-trip 40F). Excursions to points along the northern coast, Mont St-Michel, and the Gulf of Morbihan in July and Aug. only. Information office open Mon.-Fri. 8am-noon and 2-6pm, Sat. 8am-noon. TAE (tel. 99 50 64 17). Buses to Dinard and Rennes. Call for information.

Ferries: Emeraude Lines, quai de la Rance (tel. 96 39 18 04). May-Sept. 1 excursion per day downstream to St-Malo, return by bus (2½ hr. down by boat, ¾-hr. back by bus; 75F, round-trip 105F). Bikes 27F.

Taxis: pl. Duclos (tel. 96 39 06 00), outside the post office. 24 hrs., but scarce at night.

Bike Rental: M. Scardin, 30, rue Carnot (tel. 96 39 21 14). 40F per ½-day, 50F per day. Motorcycles for rent, too. Open Tues.-Sat. 8:45am-12:15pm and 2-4:20pm. The **youth hostel** charges 25F per day, deposit 200F.

Canoe/Kayak Rental: Port de Dinan (tel 96 39 85 01 or 96 85 33 85). Look for the yellow and black sign. Canoes/kayaks 40F/30F per hr., 60F/50F per 3 hr., 100F/80F per 7 hr. Open July-Aug. Mon.-Sat. 2-5pm.

Laundromat: 33, Grand' Rue, opposite the Eglise St-Malo. Wash 12F, dry 2F (1F and 2F coins). Open Mon.-Sat. 8:30am-8pm.

Hospital: rue Chateaubriand (tel. 96 39 27 60), at Léhon.

Police: pl. Duguesclin (tel. 96 39 03 02). **Emergency,** tel. 17.

Accommodations and Camping

Dinan has many campsites, a comfortable youth hostel, and a few cheap hotels that often have room in the summer, although calling ahead might be smart.

Auberge de Jeunesse (IYHF) (tel. 96 39 10 83), Moulin du Méen in Vallée de la Fontaine-des-Eaux. Unfortunately, there's no bus to this wooded hideaway. Fortunately, the walk is pleasant whichever route you take. From the train station, turn left from the main exit, turn left across the tracks, and follow the signs (a ½-hr. walk). If you're already in town, go down the very steep rue Petit Fort (not for those with weak knees or hearts), turn left on rue du Quai, and walk about 15 min. Follow the signs and look left. A wonderful, friendly place situated by a stream and weeping willows. Good facilities, including a kitchen, common room with fireplace, books on Breton culture, 2 guitars, Ravi's giant furry molar, and a small record collection. Dorms are usually mixed. Reception open daily 9am-noon and 5-11pm. Curfew 1am. Lockout 11am-5pm. 37F per person (IYHF card required). Breakfast 13F. Healthy lunch or dinner 38F. Beautiful, green, private **camping** nearby. Ask about the new 3½-hr. trail through the woods. Cots in huge tent 28F. Decent bikes 25F per day. Deposit 200F. Lockers 5F.

Hôtel du Théâtre, 2, rue Ste-Claire (tel. 96 39 06 91), around the corner from the tourist office in the *vieille ville*. Comfortable but poorly lit rooms, congenial owner, and great location. Singles and doubles 70-135F. Breakfast 18F. Phone reservations accepted.

Hôtel-Restaurant de l'Océan, pl. du 11 Novembre 1918 (tel. 96 39 21 51), across from the station. Friendly owner and clean rooms. Singles and doubles 90F, with shower 120F. Breakfast 20F.

Camping: The campground at the **youth hostel** is in a beautiful location (16F per night). The tourist office provides a list of other sites, the closest of which is **Camping Municipal,** 103, rue Chateaubriand (tel. 96 39 11 96). If you face the post office in pl. Duclos, rue Chateaubriand is to your right. Unspectacular site with decent facilities. 8.90F per person, 7.70F per site, 5.60F per car. Open May-Nov.

Food

Place du Champ and pl. Duguesclin in the *vieille ville* have been the site of the town's outdoor **market** for a millennium. (Thurs. 8am-noon). Take a picnic of fruit and "*crêpes* to carry" and dine *al fresco* in the beautiful Jardin Anglais behind the church.

Crêperie des Artisans, 6, rue du Petit Fort (tel. 96 39 44 10). Popular place featured in the *New York Times.* Feast on two *galettes* and 2 *crêpes* (38-52F) under the warm wooden rafters or on the terrace. . Open daily noon-10:30pm; April-June and Sept. Tues.-Sun. noon-10:30pm.

La Kabilie, 48, rue du Petit Fort (tel. 96 39 62 76). Tucked into the steepest hill in Dinan, this place serves excellent *couscous* with your choice of meat 48-74F. Terrific family owners. Open daily noon-2pm and 7-11pm; Sept.-May Wed.-Sun. noon-2pm and 7-11pm.

Le Connétable, 1, rue de l'Apport (tel. 96 39 06 74), in the *vieille ville.* Reputedly the oldest *crêperie* in Dinan. Wonderful *crêpes* in a 15th-century dark-timbered house. Pizza with ham, broccoli, and almonds 42F. Crepes flambées (with Grand Marnier, Kirsch, etc.) 20-22F. The best ice cream cones around (5-15F). Open daily 11:30am-9:30pm.

Le Papillon, 27, rue du Quai (tel. 96 39 93 76), at the port. Airy English salon by the sea brings relief from the *crêpe* onslaught. Generous omelettes and hamburgers. Apple pie 22F. Most entrees 35-45F. Open daily 9:30am-midnight; lunch and dinner only in winter.

Sights and Entertainment

The **Promenade des Petits-Fossés** begins near the post office and follows the looming ramparts to the 13th-century **Porte du Guichet,** the entrance to the intimidating **Château de la Duchesse Anne.** Before you ascend into the 14th-century *donjon,* pause to enjoy the antics of the **Jardin du Val Cocherel's** peacocks, roosters, and goats. (Open daily 8am-7:30pm. Free.) Inside the oval tower, the **Musée de Dinan** displays 18th-century polychromed statuettes and bas-reliefs and a selection of medieval and Roman weapons and artifacts. The nearby **Tour de Coëtquen** houses additional galleries with temporary exhibits, and a small but memorable collection of *gisants* (tomb sculptures). (Château and museums open daily 10am-noon and 2-6:30pm; Sept.-Oct. and March-May 10am-noon and 2-6pm; Nov.-Feb. Wed.-Mon. 1:30-5:30pm. Last ticket 4:50pm. Admission 13F.)

As you reenter the *vieille ville* through porte St-Louis, a right on rue Général de Gaulle will bring you to the **Promenade de la Duchesse Anne,** at the end of which stand the magnificently shaded **Jardin Anglais** and the **Basilique St-Sauveur.** The church blends a 12th-century facade, a lovely buttressed apse, and a curvilinear three-tiered steeple from the 17th century, its sleek tiles bearing a bizarre resemblance to an armadillo. The garden looks out over the Rance River, the viaduct, and the port below. At the far end, a path and a tiny staircase lead down to the river. Across the small Gothic bridge and under the viaduct, a winding path leads to the cloisters and ruined priory at **Léhon,** about 40 minutes away. (You can also reach Léhon by road (about 3km). Take rue Chateaubriand from the post office and turn left at the sign.)

From the port, reenter the walled city by **rue du Petit Fort,** which becomes **rue du Jerzval,** one of Dinan's prettiest (and steepest) roads. Interrupt your hike up or down this challenging path with visits to traditional artisans.

Back in the center of town, on Grand' Rue, **Eglise St-Malo** contains a remarkable polychrome organ, built by the Englishman Alfred Oldknow in 1889. (For a schedule of live organ concerts, contact the tourist office.) Flamboyant colors of 1920s stained-glass windows light the church's interior. The second window from the rear on the right side commemorates Dinan soldiers killed in WWI. Finally, on rue de l'Horloge, the 15th-century **tower** commands a *vachement chouette* view of Dinan's jumbled medieval streets and the surrounding countryside. (Open June-Aug. daily 10:45am-1pm and 3-6pm. Admission 9F. Call the tourist office if you wish to tour the tower during the off-season.)

The last weekend in September brings the annual **Fête des Remparts,** complete with 6,000 medieval costumes, chevalier combat, and the once-a-year chance to explore the inside of the town's otherwise forbidden ramparts. The modern-minded can quench their thirst year-round at **Le River's Club,** Le Vieux Port (tel. 96 39 31 64), a vivacious club open nightly, or **L'Hostellerie du Vieux St-Sauveur,** 19, pl. St-Sauveur (96 39 04 63), next to the church, a comfortable local bar with a pool table and board games.

Côtes d'Armor (Northern Coast)

The northern coast's three principal geographic regions—the Côte d'Emeraude, the Côte de Granite Rose, and the Ceinture Dorée—feature some of the most spectacular scenery in France. Conveniently located near the most worthwhile sites, youth hostels and *gîtes d'étape* range in quality from the rugged tent-camp near Cap Fréhel to the well-equipped hostel in Brest. (Motorists cannot stay in most *gîtes d'étape*.) The steadily increasing presence of tourists hasn't marred the appeal of this region. Although patience will prove essential in your journey, the wild beauty of France's northern coast will reward your efforts every time.

Transportation will be your biggest problem, but don't let it deter you. Unless you enjoy using your thumb, always check routes there and back. The Paris-Brest line brings frequent service to St-Brieuc, Guingamp, Plouaret, Morlaix, Landivisiau, and Landerneau, with the following connecting **trains** (or SNCF buses) running northward: from Guingamp to Paimpol (4 per day, 45 min., 31F); from Plouaret to Lannion (7-9 per day, fewer on Sun.; 15 min.; 14F); from Morlaix to St-Pol-de-Léon (3-4 buses or trains per day, ½-hr., 17F to St-Pol-de-Léon) and from Morlaix to Roscoff (3-4 per day, 45 min., 27F).

Private bus lines fill in only some of the gaps between train stations. Most train stations rent three- and 10-speed bikes (around 50F per day, deposit from 300F), and one-way rentals are not uncommon. Several hostels rent bikes to IYHF members (roughly 30F per day, deposits up to 300F). Tourist offices have information on local rentals, and many stock the *Guide Touristique Côtes-du-Nord* (5F), which lists all bike and car rental concessions in the region and provides a wealth of information on outdoor activities. Even the main roads, which pass through fields edged by Queen Anne's lace, are well-paved, scenic, and relatively flat. Many trains will carry your bike for free, and some bus companies charge only a small fee. Hikers can trace the northern coast on the GR34, which follows the sea from Cancale, east of St-Malo, to Morlaix. Hiking is easy in this area.

Tourisme Verney, located on esplanade St-Vincent in St-Malo (tel. 99 40 82 67), serves the Côte d'Emeraude in Dinard, St-Lunaire, St-Briac, Lancieux, Ploubalay, and St-Jacut. Eleven buses per day (9 on Sun.) run as far as St-Briac on weekdays. In July and August, two buses continue to St-Jacut (15F per bicycle).

Companie Armoricaine de Transports (CAT) has offices in St-Brieuc (tel. 96 33 36 60) and Lannion (tel. 96 37 02 40) and runs east to west from St-Brieuc to Le Val-André, Sables d'Or, Le Vieux-Bourg, and St-Cast. A second line links St-Brieuc and Paimpol (6 per day, 1½ hr., 37F) with connections to Pointe de l'Arcouest and Lézardrieux.

Côte d'Emeraude

Between Dinard and St-Brieuc, high cliffs and rocky points break up endless stretches of sand. As in most of Brittany, public transportation is scarce here, so you should coordinate train and bus schedules in advance.

On the Paris-Brest train line, industrial **St-Brieuc** is the best place to begin excursions on the Côte d'Emeraude, but it won't top any other lists. If you're stuck here between connections, visit the stoutly buttressed **Cathédrale St-Etienne,** built in the 13th and 14th centuries. To get to the cathedral from the train station, take rue de la Gare to rue du 71ème Régiment d'Infanterie and continue in the same direction on rue des Lycéens-Martyrs, bearing left at the fork. Bear right on rue de Rohan and take the next left. Before wheeling out of town in quest of more promising landscapes, ponder the fact that champion racer Bernard Hinault used to deliver mail here.

St-Brieuc's new youth hostel, **Manoir de la Ville Guyomard (IYHF)** (tel. 96 78 70 70) is a former farm vamped up with hot pink doors and black wood furniture. Singles and rooms with skylights and lofts are available, as are individual rooms for couples and disabled persons. Twenty dormitory beds, 20 cots in a big tent, and eight sites for campers are available. Bicycles are rented for 25F per day (deposit 200F), and kayaks are rented to groups only. Ask about the ceramic studio. (38F per person. Breakfast 13F. Sheets 13F.) From the train station, take bus #1 from pl. du Champ de Mars/pl. Duquesclin (last bus about 7pm), and follow the signs. The walk along the well-marked route takes about 30 min. The **tourist office,** 7, rue St-Gouéno (tel. 96 33 32 50) is in the center of town, a 10-minute walk from the train station. Follow the signs toward the *centre ville* and then toward the tourist office. **Trains** link St-Brieuc to: Dinan (2-3 per day, 44F); Morlaix (10 per day, 1 hr., 57F); Rennes (12 per day, 1 hr., 65F). There's an information office at the train station (tel. 96 94 50 50; open Mon.-Sat. 8am-noon and 1:30-7pm, Sun. 8am-12:25pm and 2-7pm).

Northeast of St-Brieuc, **Cap Fréhel** is a windswept cape with enormous red and gray cliffs covered by ferns and yellow flowers. It provides little solitude in summer, when cars and tour buses bring armies to admire the view, but it is awe-inspiring nonetheless. CAT in St-Brieuc (tel. 96 33 36 60) runs **buses** from St-Brieuc to Vieux-Bourg (2 per day, 35F). From there, you're on your own; the Cap is 5km northeast on the D34A. Don't take the bus to Fréhel—it's nowhere near the Cap. Emeraude Lines in St-Malo (tel. 99 56 63 21) runs a cruise that passes by but could not possibly dock at the 70m cliffs of the cape (16 departures in June, daily departures July-Aug. from St-Malo and Dinard; 2½ hr.; round-trip 90F). A pioneer spirit prevails at the **Auberge de Jeunesse Plévenon (IYHF)**, Kerivet, la Ville Hardrieux (tel. 96 61 91 87), a tent camp 4km from the Cap on the eastern coast of the peninsula (25F per person). Take the D16 out of Plévenon toward Cap Fréhel, and watch for signs.

Across the bay to the southeast lies **Pointe de St-Cast,** only 2km outside the town of the same name. Pointe de St-Cast juts far out into the sea and offers a truly spectacular view of St-Malo and the coastline. To get to St-Cast from St-Brieuc, take the SNCF train from St-Brieuc to Lamballe and then the SNCF or CAT bus from Lamballe to St-Cast (1¾ hr.). SNCF buses run from Lamballe to St-Cast in July and August only (2 per day, 1½ hr., 25F). **Camping Municipal la Mare,** just to the west of the promontory on Plage de la Mare and **Camping Municipal les Mielles** (tel. 96 41 87 60), 100m from the Grande Plage, are both inexpensive and within easy walking distance. (Both 7F per person, 4F per tent, 3.30F per car, 2F per bike.) About 4km from town on the east side of the *pointe* are the **Pen Guen** beach and uncrowded **Camping de la Ferme de Pen-Guen.** Mme. Grouazel, the director (tel. 96 41 92 18) can pick you up from the bus stop in St.-Cast for the cost of gas (around 8F; 6F per person, 3.50F per tent, 3.50F per car, bicycles free.) Ask for information on other campgrounds at the **tourist office** in St-Cast on pl. Charles de Gaulle (tel. 96 41 81 52). (Open Mon.-Sat. 9am-12:30pm and 2-7pm, Sun. 10am-noon and 3-5:30pm; Sept.-March Mon.-Sat. 9am-noon; April-June Mon.-Sat. 9am-noon and 2:30-5:30pm.)

There are several affordable hotels in St-Cast: **Hôtel du Commerce** in St-Cast Bourg (tel. 96 41 81 37) is pleasant for the price (singles and doubles 90-110F, breakfast 20F). The cheapest are **Hôtel de la Marine,** rue Frégate-Laplace (tel. 96 41 85 28), with doubles for 90-120F, breakfast 24F; and **Hôtel la Poste,** pl. de la Libération (tel. 96 41 84 92) with a view of the sea and doubles for 70-140F. Other possibilities include **Hôtel Angleterre et Panorama,** rue de la Fosserolle (tel. 96 41 84 92; open June 10-Sept. 4), with doubles for 90-110F, breakfast 21F; and **Hôtel de Paris,** bd. Duponchel (tel. 96 41 80 89; doubles 85-130F, breakfast 18F). **Le Bretan'or,** pl. A. Le Braz (96 41 92 45) has delicious *crêpes* (45-67F). Try their eponymous specialty (19F). The tourist office's handy guide to hotels, restaurants, and campgrounds indicates the locations of all these hotels, as well as the campgrounds. Ask about boat trips to Cap Fréhel and Fort la Latte.

East of St-Cast, the coast is dotted with small resorts. **Lancieux** and **St-Jacut** are particularly pleasant; both are accessible by Tourisme Verney buses from St-

Malo and Dinard. Buses run hourly to Lancieux (45 min. from St-Malo, 29F), continuing to St-Jacut in July and August only (2 per day, 37F from St-Malo).

Côte de Granite Rose

Pampiol and Ile de Bréhat

Transportation is difficult along this stretch of coast, where the rocks are rosy and, in high season, the water is warm. Although hardly Grand Central Station, Pampiol may be the best base for exploring Ile de Bréhat and the coastal towns to the west.

Paimpol (pop. 8000) anchors the eastern end of the Côte de Granite Rose. Historically a launching site for fishing expeditions to Newfoundland and Iceland, Paimpol retains the devil-may-care, swaggering air of a seafarer's town. Tourism is not yet the main industry, as both the giant fish market (Tues. mornings on rue de l'Oise/pl. Gambetta, alongside the vegetable market) and the Breton-speaking clientele of the port's numerous bars attest. Try **Le Pub** (tel. 96 20 91 74; open after 6pm), on rue des Islandais off quai Morand; **Le Cambridge,** 50, rue de l'Eglise (tel. 96 20 81 12; open until 2am); or **La Taverne,** rue des Islandais (open after 8:30pm), with a mixed gay and straight crowd. The first week of June, carnival rides, cotton candy, hot dogs, and blaring American megatunes take over the ancient port. The first week of August brings the *Fête du Chant de Marin* with over 500 musicians and 100 old ships.

Dol makes a superior starting point for exploring the coast, but is itself worth a visit if only for the exemplary **Auberge de Jeunesse/Gîte d'Etape (IYHF)** at Château de Keraoul (tel. 96 20 83 60), 25 minutes from the station. Turn left on av. Général-de-Gaulle, take a right at the first light and a left at the next light (even if the signs point straight), then follow the signs to "Keraoul." Take a left at the end of rue de Pen Ar Run. The hostel will be the second driveway on the right, just before the road bends sharply uphill to the right. The hostel, an old castle, sits in a large, peaceful park full of horses. The management's laissez-faire policies (no lockout, no curfew) make you feel at home. With a communal atmosphere all hostels should emulate, it's a great place to stay for a few days, make friends, and catch up on sleep (6 bunks per room. 37F per person. Breakfast 13F. Dinner 38F, including wine. Sheets 13F. IYHF card required.) Located across the hall from the hostel's dormitory, the *gîte d'étape* has kitchen facilities and showers. (37F per person. Dinner 38F.) Options in town include the **Hôtel Berthelot,** 1, rue du Port (tel. 96 20 88 66), with immaculate, airy rooms and a friendly proprietor. (Singles 95F. Showers 10F. Breakfast 20F.) From pl. de la République, walk down to the port; rue du Port is off quai Morand, which will be to your left. The area has numerous campgrounds. Sunny **Camping Municipal de Cruckin,** near the Plage de Cruckin (tel. 96 20 78 47), is closest. From the tourist office, take a left on rue de la Marne, another left onto av. du Général de Gaulle, then veer right and follow schizophrenic rue du Général Leclerc as it twists along four identity changes: Général Leclerc to Prof. Jean Renaud to Commandant Charcot to Commandant le Conniat. Rue de Cruckin branches off to your left from rue du Commandant le Conniat. (5.40F per person, 4.50F per site, 3.80F per car. Showers 5F. Open mid-June to mid-Sept. Tues.-Sat. 8-11am and 6-8pm, Mon. 8-9am and 5:30-7:30pm, Sun. 10-11am.) A block farther down rue Commandant le Conniat lies **Camping de Beauport.** (Tel. 96 22 09 87. 8F per person, 7.50F per site and per car. Showers 5F. Open April-Sept.) The Abbaye de Beauport is down the road to the left. **Rohou** (tel. 96 55 87 22) in Arcouest remains open year-round. You can also camp in the park in front of the youth hostel.

If Paimpol's bevy of cheap creperies and boulangeries seems uninspiring, treat yourself to the elaborate 68F seafood *menu* at the **Restaurant du Port,** quai Morand. The **post office** and **bank** are across the street from the train station. Paimpol can be reached by train via Guingamp (4 per day, ¾ hr., 28F), the next stop from St-Brieuc on the Paris-Brest line (8 per day, 20 min.). A ticket from St-Brieuc to Paimpol via Guingamp costs 46F. Taking your bike is no problem; the little Guingamp-Paimpol bus on rails and most of the St-Brieuc-Guingamp trains have a baggage car where you can stash it for free. Six CAT buses run daily direct from St-Brieuc to Paimpol (1½ hr., 37F).

Visit the friendly **tourist office,** rue Pierre Feutren (tel. 96 20 83 16), in the city hall near the church of Notre Dame, for information on the surrounding area. From the train station, turn left, then right at the light; near the top of the hill, look for the sign and turn right again. From anywhere in town, just walk toward the church. They are friendly and will help you in any way they can. (Open Mon.-Sat. 9am-noon and 2-7:30pm, Sun. 9am-noon; mid-Sept. to June Mon.-Sat. 9am-noon and 2-5pm.) You can rent brand-new 10-speed bikes at **Cycles du Vieux Clocher** (tel. 96 22 71 61), pl. de Verdun (80F per day, deposit 2000F). The rental fee and deposit are far lower 5km away in Plovézech at **Garage Ropert.**

In Paimpol the **plage de la Tossen,** a small sandy beach, provides the obligatory view of the bay. One kilometer south of town, a 10m menhir looms over the Field of Grief. According to local legend, the rock fell to earth and is slowly sinking, its complete disappearance timed to coincide with the end of the world. Just east of Paimpol along the D786 are the ivy-covered ruins of the **Abbaye de Beauport.** Well worth the time, the abbey dates from 1202, when monks of the order of Prémontré escaped to Brittany from Normandy. The tour guide re-creates the daily life of the monks, entirely without the aid of smoke, mirrors, or clap-activated electronic devices. (Open July and August daily 9am-noon and 2-7pm. To visit at other times, call M. Lecalvez at 96 20 81 59. Admission 15F, students 11F.) Walk down the pebbled, primrose-bordered lane to the rear of the abbey for a view of marsh and the Bay of Poulafret. The path winding along the coast is the European long-distance route GR 34, which can take you back to the Paimpol port.

If you're near Paimpol, jump on a boat to flower-laden **Ile de Bréhat.** Five hundred people call one half of this tiny, Oz-like island home. After oohing and aahing at the Munchkinesque cottages and gardens, escape to the uninhabited western and northern sides of the island, punctuated by imposing moss-covered rocks that rise out of the sea at low tide. **Vedettes de Bréhat** (tel. 96 55 86 99) runs boats from Arcouest to Ile de Bréhat every hour, every two hours from Sept. to May. (Last boat from Bréhat at 7pm, 10 min., round-trip 44F.) To reach Arcouest, catch a bus from the train station in Paimpol or go 6km north on the D789. Once there, you can also detour to **Pointe de l'Arcouest,** with its red and black cliffs and rocky shoreline. (10 buses per day from Paimpol, 15 min., 10F, round-trip 18F.) To the west, the D786 runs through artichoke fields to the enchanting town of **Lézardrieux** (5km). Guegan Voyages (tel. 96 22 37 05 or 96 20 59 50) runs two buses daily from the Paimpol train station (10 min., 7.90F).

Lézardrieux to Trégastel

The northernmost section of the Breton coast, from Lézardrieux to Perros-Guirec, is wild, sparsely inhabited, and low on public transportation. Breton farmers are known for letting people camp on their land in these parts, but campgrounds are also plentiful and two *gîtes d'étape* provide economical shelter near the coast. One is located at **Min ar Goas** (tel. 96 22 90 68), near the town of Lanmodez, about 7½ km north of Lézardrieux on the D20 (25F per person, meals 46F). Every May 19, the cathedral in **Tréguier** is the site of a popular *pardon* honoring St-Yves, one of Brittany's favorite saints, patron (incongruously) of both lawyers and the poor. A medieval song tells un that "Saint Yves was a Breton, a lawyer but not a thief, a thing which amazed the people." From Tréguier, the D8 continues 10km north to **Pointe du Château,** another of the coast's scenic promontories. On your way, stop at **Chapelle St-Gonéry** in Plougrescant (17km), and the chapel at **Port-Blanc,** also the site of a small, white-pebbled beach. Tréguier's **Hôtel de l'Estuaire** (tel. 96 92 30 25) has singles from 70F and doubles from 80F. The town is served by the Guegan Voyages bus via Lézardrieux (2 per day, 20 min., 12F).

Twenty-one km farther west is **Perros-Guirec,** a popular resort with a harbor and two gorgeous, well-protected, sandy beaches. Watch for the bilingual road signs along the D6 to Perros-Guirec/Peroz-Gireg. A spectacular walk awaits those who try the **Sentier des Douaniers,** a cliff path that threads its way along the sparkling seacoast from Perros-Guirec's main beach to Pors Rolland in **Ploumanach,** à picturesque fishing resort. In Ploumanach, you'll find the massive red granite quarries that give the Côte de Granite Rosé its name. The **tourist office** in Perros-Guirec, 21, pl. de l'Hôtel de Ville (tel. 96 23 21 15), has information on both Perros-Guirec and Ploumanach, as well as information on transportation and accommodations; ask for a list of *gîtes d'étape.* The office runs a **currency exchange** when the banks are closed on Monday. (Open daily 9am-8pm; Sept.-June 9am-noon and 2-7pm.) **Cycles Henry,** bd. Aristide Briand (tel. 96 91 03 33), rents bikes for 70F per day. Perros-Guirec has few cheap hotels, but many campgrounds. Try **West-Camping,** Carrefour de Ploumanach. (Tel. 96 91 09 19. 11F per site, 5F per car, 8F per tent. Hot showers included. Open June 15-Sept. 15.) **Camping la Claire Fontaine,** rue de Pont-Hélé (tel. 96 23 03 55), lets you pitch your tent at similar prices (open mid-June to mid-Sept.). There is also a *gîte d'étape* at **Villa Stella Maris** (tel. 96 23 15 62), in the nearby town of Louannec. From Perros-Guirec's *centre ville,* head south toward Lannion for roughly 2km, then turn left onto the D6 for 3km to reach Louannec. (Dorm beds 23F. Kitchen facilities but no meal service.)

Three km northwest of Perros-Guirec off the D788 stands the granite chapel (rose, of course) of **Notre Dame de la Clarté,** where a *pardon* takes place August 15. Farther north, don't miss the collection of rocks called the **Château du Diable,** where extreme weather has sculpted large stones into various shapes, some resembling animals. If you've always hoped to see a puffin, take a three-hour boat tour of the sea bird sanctuary on **Sept Iles,** a group of islands off the coast. There is a one-hour stop at the Ile aux Moines. (April-Sept. 2 per day from Trestraou; round-trip 80F, students 50F). For information and tickets contact Emeraude Lines, 1, rue Emile Bac (tel. 96 23 22 47).

The resort of **Trégastel** commands attention with the strange beauty of its rocks. Avenue de la Grève Blanche leads from the D788 to the white shore; a path follows the cliff to sandy **plage de Coz-Pors,** passing a series of rocks worn by wind and sea into fantastic shapes. Around to the right you'll find yet more rocks and a quiet, sandy cove. If you're continuing on to Trébeurden, take a few detours from the main road to see a more deserted and equally spectacular coastline. Local campgrounds include **Le Golven** (tel. 96 23 87 77; 12F per person, 6F per car, 12F per tent, hot showers included; open May to mid-Sept.) and **Tourony** (tel. 96 23 86 61; 11F per person, 6F per car, 10.50F per tent; open May-Aug.). Le Golven lies off the D788 between Trégastel and Trébeurden, and Tourony off the same route as it approaches Trégastel from Ploumanach. Tidy, green-shuttered **Hôtel de la Corniche,** 35, rue Charles le Goffic (tel. 96 23 88 15), has 70-90F rooms, breakfast (17F) and a 55F *menu* in the restaurant downstairs. (Open June-Sept. 15.) Rue Charles le Goffic becomes the D788 as it leaves town.

Ceinture Dorée

The coast of Brittany from Trébeurden to Brest well deserves the title of Ceinture Dorée, or "gilded belt". While the mild climate and fertile soil of the interior nourish impeccably aligned regiments of artichokes, potatoes and cauliflowers, rougher contours lure hikers and bikers to the coastline. Those just scurrying through to Brest for a ferry connection should not merely settle for seeing this area through a train window.

If approached with tenacity, the sometimes intimidating logistics of public transportation will fall into place. **Cars Verts,** 1, rue de Kergonan (tel. 96 23 50 32), in Trébeurden, sends five **buses** per day to Trébeurden from the rail station at Lannion. (Office open Mon.-Fri. 8:30am-noon and 2-6:30pm, Sat. 8:30am-noon.) You can rent **bikes** from the station in Lannion (50F per day, deposit 250F). The **Auberge de Jeunesse Trébeurden (IYHF),** 4km north of Trébeurden on the D788 (tel. 96 23 52 22), is pretty basic but on a better shorefront site than most hotels. In fact, it's right next to the Hôtel Toenot, whose big toe signs should help you find the hostel. (37F. Breakfast 13F. Sheets 13F. IYHF card required.)

Morlaix and St-Pol-de-Léon

Inland to the southwest, the attractive 18th- and 19th-century houses of **Morlaix** (pop. 17,000) sit at the base of steep green hills. Don't worry: the town's rather unwelcoming motto, "S'ils te mordent, mords les!" (If they bite you, bite them!), refers only to 16th-century British invaders. Morlaix makes a good daytrip from Brest, St-Brieuc, and coastal points north, or an easy (and often required) connection between the Côte de Granite Rose and the Finistère (land's end). It is also the best place to begin a trip to Brittany's wooded Argoat region or the western coast.

Morlaix is on the main Paris-Brest line; seven to nine daily **trains** run to St-Brieuc (1 hr., 60F) and other points east. The same number of trains connect Brest to Morlaix (¾-hr., 42F). Trains also travel to Quimper (80F) and Roscoff (24F). Call 98 80 50 50 or 98 88 55 00 for rail information daily 9am-noon and 2-6:30pm. A **CAT bus** (in Lannion tel. 96 37 02 40) runs to Morlaix from Lannion daily at 8:30am.

To enjoy Morlaix itself, pick up the self-guided walking tour (3F) at the **tourist office,** pl. des Otages (tel. 98 62 14 94). (Open July 14-Aug. Mon.-Sat. 9am-12:30pm and 1:30-7:30pm, Sun. 10am-12:30pm; Sept.-June Tues.-Sat. 9am-noon and 2-6:30pm.) Look for the unique 16th-century oak construction of **La Maison de la Reine Anne,** rue du Mur. The apparently collapsed staircase in the left-hand corner of the house was designed this way to connect the opposite walls by a narrow indoor bridge. (Open Mon.-Sat. 10:30am-noon and 2:30-6pm.) The office also leads trips to the parish closes of **St-Thégonnec** and **Guimiliau,** two masterpieces of Breton church architecture 10km to the west. You can rent **bicycles** at the station or at Cycles Henri le Gall, 1, rue de Callac (tel. 98 88 60 47), for 50F per day with the deposit of a passport or other ID. All-terrain bikes are 53F per half-day, 80F per day, and 130F per three days. Ask about one-way rentals to neighboring towns. (Open Mon. 2-6pm, Tues.-Sat. 8:30am-noon and 1:50-7pm.)

Cheap restaurants are not hard to find in Morlaix. As for cheap accommodations, you get what you pay for. When you've seen the hotels, you'll be happy to stay at the **Auberge de Jeunesse (IYHF),** 3, route de Paris (tel. 98 88 13 63), which just manages to peep its roof over the inclined roadway. Step over the threshold like Alice into the rabbit hole and find yourself in a rambling building whose bottom drops two stories from the front door to the street below. Though spartan, the hostel is a nice enough place with decent kitchen facilities. From the bottom of the train station steps, turn left and then right. Go down another set of endless steps, and turn left to pl. Emile Souvestre. Follow rue Carnot, take a right on rue d'Aiguillon, a left on rue de Paris, and then another left on route de Paris. The hostel is around the curve to the right, about a 20-minute walk from the station. (Reception open 8-11am and 6-9pm. Lockout 10am-6pm. Curfew 10pm. IYHF card required. 37F per person. Breakfast 13F. Sheets 13F.) There are two **gîtes d'étape** within 10-15km of Morlaix: in the town of **Garlan** (contact the mayor's office, tel. 98 88 19 04) and near the town of **Plougonven,** 12km along the D9 in Troyellou (contact Monsieur Kerharo, tel. 98 78 68 01). Campers should try **Camping Municipal Lannorgant** in Plouvorn (tel. 98 61 35 06), about 6km northwest of Morlaix (open June 15-September 15). For something a bit more luxurious, or at least indoors, **Hôtel Les Arcades,** 11, pl. Cornic (tel. 98 88 20 03), has friendly folks and comfortable singles for 80F and doubles up to 120F. (Open daily 8am-1am. Breakfast 20F.)

Northwest of Morlaix, the village **St-Pol-de-Léon,** local supplier of artichokes, potatoes, and onions, is a sweet town with little to see and only one hotel. The **Hôtel Cheval Blanc,** 6, rue au Lin (tel. 98 69 01 00), has pleasant, airy rooms and a friendly proprietor who speaks English. (Singles and doubles 90-130F. Showers 17F. Breakfast 21F.) To reach the **Ancienne Cathédral,** which enshrines St-Pol's bones, follow av. de la Gare from the train station to Pen-ar-Pont and turn right. Follow rue Cadiou and then rue Général Leclerc for 10 minutes to pl. de Guebriant, site of the cathedral. (Open daily 7-11:45am and 1-7:30pm.) St-Pol's pride is the magnificent belfry of its **Chapelle de Kreisker,** next to the train station on rue Cadiou. For 4F, you can crawl up 246 feet of tiny, circular stairs to see a magnificent view of the coast and surrounding towns. (Open 10-11:30am and 2-6pm; enter by the altar.)

The **tourist office** (tel. 98 69 05 69) lies beyond the cathedral. The **municipal campground,** Trologot (tel. 98 69 06 26), is open May 20 through September (5F per person, 3F per tent, 3F per car). There is a well-equipped private campground, **Ar Kleguer** (tel. 98 69 05 39), at Le Vrennit (10F per person, 11F per site, 4F per car. Hot showers included. Open April-Sept. daily 7:30-11am and 6-8pm.) The campgrounds are located 500m apart along the windy bay. To get to both camp-grounds from pl. de Guebriant, take a right onto rue du 4 Août 1944 and follow the signs. At rue Vezen Dan and rue des Minimes is the **Crêperie Ty Korn,** whose crisp 5-25F *crêpes* are local favorites. Hôtel Cheval Blanc also has a reasonably priced restaurant. **Briez Bar,** 16, pl. au Lin, is a favorite haunt of Breton locals. There is a **gîte d'étape** in the town of **Tréflaouénan,** roughly 11km southwest of St-Pol-de-Léon on the D788. (Contact the proprietor at Moulin de Kerguiduff, tel. 98 29 51 20.)

SNCF trains and buses run from Morlaix to St-Pol (4-6 per day, 25. min., 18F).

Roscoff and Ile de Batz

In the 17th century, **Roscoff** (pop. 3700), 8km northwest of Morlaix, marked the beginning of the feared Pagan Coast. Lawless brigands lit bonfires along the rocky shore from Roscoff to Brignogan, beguiling hapless seafarers and pillaging their wrecks. These days, you can bronze yourself safely on Roscoff's sands or depart unmolested from the harbor for stunning Ile de Batz, whose **Auberge de Jeunesse** will save you from hotel tariffs that verge on piracy. While in Roscoff, don't miss the striking **Eglise de Notre-Dame de Croas-Batz,** whose Renaissance belfry resem-bles an Antoni Gaudí building more than a church tower. Ask the **tourist office** at the port (tel. 98 69 70 70) about three new attractions in town, the **aquarium,** the **Jardin Exotique,** and, most importantly, the **Thalado** seaweed exhibition. (Of-fice open March-Nov. 10am-noon and 2-6pm.)

Roscoff does have some affordable hotels, like **Hôtel les Arcades,** 15, rue Amiral Réveillère (tel. 98 69 70 45), in whose chic bar and seaside restaurant you'll find every Roscoff inhabitant and tourist under 30. After you weary of the nightlife, re-tire to a clean, adequate room upstairs. (Singles 80F, with double bed 95F. Showers 20F. Breakfast 20F). If you're feeling rich, dine on the terrace or in the elegant res-taurant overlooking the bay toward Ile de Batz (65F *menu*). (Hotel and restaurant open April to mid-Oct.) Roscoff's elaborate **Hôtel des Bains** (tel. 98 61 20 65), on the water and right at pl. Lacaze Duthier, greets the over-30 crowd with reasonable prices. (Singles 120F. Doubles 130F. Family rooms with 2 double beds and 1 single bed 330F.) Campers can stake out a piece of Roscoff's **Perharidy** campground (tel. 98 69 70 86; 4.80F per person, 3F per tent, 2.60F per car; open Easter-Sept.) or the private campground at **Manoir de Kerestat** (tel. 98 69 71 92).

SNCF trains and buses run from Morlaix to Roscoff (4-6 per day, ½-hr., 24F). **Brittany Ferries** (tel. 98 29 28 28) sails to Plymouth, England from Roscoff (5-6 hr.; 322F, July-Sept. 332-348F). Round-trip discounts are available to students ages 18-26. Ferries leave at 8am, noon, 4:30pm, and 11:30pm, but call ahead. Ferries also leave for Cork, Ireland (15 hr.); ask the tourist office for more details.

To escape postcard stands and film vendors, head for unspoiled **Ile de Batz** (*Enez Vaz* in Breton). A 15-minute ferry ride from the Roscoff port, its charming old town of 750 inhabitants seems worlds apart, with few tourists and plenty of undiscovered beaches. Go, but keep it a secret (as we announce this to tens of thousands of read-ers). Protected by natural rock jetties, its rugged shoreline presides over an emerald seascape. As on the islands of Ouessant, Bréhat, and Groix, Breton farming and seafaring still coexist here despite modest tourist incursions. A *pardon* honoring Ste-Anne takes place the last Sunday in July, with an open-air mass and a *fête.*

Frequent **ferries** serve Ile de Batz from Roscoff (July-Sept. 13 per day in each direction, Oct.-Feb. 8 per day, March-June 9 per day. Round trip 25F. No bicycles.) For more information, check with the Roscoff **tourist office** at the port or **Vedettes Blanches** (tel. 98 61 77 75). Once on the island, you can rent purple or blue bicycles at the dock from Monsieur Le Saôut (tel. 98 61 77 65) for 40F per day, 30F per ½-day. The **tourist office** (tel. 98 61 79 90) is at the dock. (Open Mon.-Fri. 10am-noon and 2-5pm, Sat. 10am-noon.)

To reach the island's gem of an **auberge de jeunesse (IYHF)** (tel. 98 61 77 69), walk straight up the hill from the dock and follow the signs for AJ/Centre Nautique (less than 10 min.). Looking out on an expanse of water and rocks, this airy cabin in the pines has an upstairs loft lined with mattresses, bunks downstairs, and new kitchen facilities. The summer overflow crashes on cots in tents. The avuncular director serenades his guests vigorously but wants no business from those who do not respect the communal hostel atmosphere. (37F per person. Cots in tents 33F. Breakfast 13F. Dinner 38F. Reception open 8:30-9:30am and 6:30-7:30pm, but leave your bags anytime. No lockout. Canoeing, kayaking, and sailing lessons in July and August.)

You can buy food from the island's small grocery stores and *boulangeries.* In July and August, the **Crêperie Ty Yann** serves a 35F *menu* of three *crêpes,* cider, and coffee; it's just across from the hostel. (Open July-May 12:30-4:30pm and 7:15-10:30pm.)

Brest and Ile d'Ouessant

To the west, **Brest** is a large, modern port and military base with 220,000 inhabit-ants, ships galore, and a few museums. Before hopping a ferry from the Port de Commerce to Ile d'Ouessant or the Crozon Peninsula, check out the impressive new aquarium, **Oceanopolis Brest** (tel. 98 34 40 40), Port de Plaisance. From the stop across from and to the left of the train station parking lot, take bus #72 (every ½ hr. until 7:40, 5.50F) to Port de Plaisance. (Aquarium open June to mid-Sept. Sun.-Fri. 10am-7pm, Sat. 10am-10pm; mid-Sept to May Tues.-Fri. 10am-5pm, Sat. and Sun. 10am-7pm.) The **Auberge de Jeunesse (IYHF)** is located next to an artifi-cial beach at le Moulin Blanc, rue de Kerbriant (tel. 98 41 90 41), about 4km from the train station and right near Oceanopolis. From the Port de Plaisance bus stop, take the first left and turn left again at the first street. (Four bedrooms 37F per per-son. Breakfast 13F. Bikes 35F per day. Lockout 10am-6pm. Reception 8-9am and 6-7pm. Curfew 11pm. IYHF card required.) Alternately, try **Hôtel Le Ponant,** 20, rue de la Porte (tel. 98 45 09 32; singles from 60F, showers 10F, breakfast 17F). From the center of town, follow rue de Siam toward the water and cross the bridge to rue de la Porte. **Hôtel des Sports,** 4, rue du Vercors (tel. 98 02 01 65), just off rue Jean Jaurès, has singles from 65F. The **tourist office,** pl. de la Liberté (tel. 98 44 24 96), has a complete list of the hotels in the region. For a good, cheap meal, go where many *Brestois* go: the tidy **Crêperie des Fontaines,** 44, rue Jean Macé. From the *gare,* take a right on bd. Clemenceau, a left on rue du Château, and a right onto rue Jean Macé. (Three-*crêpe menu* 35F, substantial salads 22-32F. Open Mon.-Fri. 9am-9:30pm, Sat. 6-9:30pm.) The **post office** (tel. 98 44 02 11) is one block away at place Général Leclerc.

A pleasant 2½-hour boat ride away from Brest is windswept **Ile d'Ouessant** (Ush-ant in Breton), its green pastures dotted with gray sheep and white stone crosses. Fabled among sailors as the *Ile des Prêtresses* (Isle of Priestesses), this island's typi-cally Breton division of labor often leaves the farming to its indefatigable women while men voyage with the merchant marine or in lobster boats. Ushant tradition dictates that women propose marriage.

Boats dock at **Port du Stiff** on the northeastern shore, and the main town of **Lam-paul** is just a 45-minute southwestern stroll across the island. You can rent a **bike** at the dock (40F) or hop from the ferry into a **bus** (8F). In Lampaul, you'll find the **tourist office** (tel. 98 48 85 83) complete with maps. (Open daily 9:30am-12:30pm and 2:30-5:30pm; Sept. 7-July 7 daily 10:30am-12:30pm and 3:45-4:45pm.)

At the **Ecomusée du Niou-Huella,** about 1km northwest of Lampaul, you can take a look inside a traditional Ouessantine home. Take the D81 uphill out of town and watch for the turnoff sign. The guide will show you the beam where slaughtered pigs were hung and the porcelain racks still lined with *faïencerie* The stone house's ingeniously spare design includes a kitchen table that opens to reveal a *laverie* and well-positioned windows that keep the rooms bright from dawn to dusk. (Open Wed.-Mon. 2-6pm, tours (in French) 2:30-5:30pm every ½-hour.) If you continue away from town on the road outside the museum, you'll reach expanses of flowered heath.

Although exploring Ouessant on foot is enjoyable, cycling proves more efficient. Two shops in town rent **bicycles** to tourists: **Savina** (tel. 98 48 80 44) and **Malgorn,** (tel. 98 48 83 44), just outside the church. Both send vans loaded with bikes to meet the ferries. (40F per day. No deposit.) If you have your own bike, leave it in Brest since the round-trip ferry cost (46F) exceeds the rental fee. There are four hotels on Ile d'Ouessant; all are located in Lampaul and have comparable prices. **Le From-veur** (tel. 98 48 81 30) has rooms from 90-110F, **Duchesse Anne** (tel. 98 48 80 25) from 80-95F, **L'Océan** (tel. 98 48 80 03) from 80-125F, and **Roch ar Mor** (tel. 98 48 80 19) from 95-120F. You can **camp** at **Pen-ar-Bed** (tel. 98 48 84 65), 2km from the port (7.70F per person, 5.20F per tent).

From July to mid-September, **boats** leave Brest's Port de Commerce daily for Le Conquet (45-min.) and then continue to the island. From the end of March through the first week of July, service is suspended on Friday. The return trip leaves Ile d'Ouessant at 5pm. (2-3 hr. from Brest, 69F, round-trip 112F; 1¼ hr. from Le Conquet, 56F, round-trip 93F.) **Cars de St-Mathieu** (tel. 98 89 12 02) at Brest's *gare routière* information office (tel. 98 44 46 73) buses landlubbers west along the D789 from Brest to Le Conquet (daily at 7:30am from the Brest *gare routière,* 80 min., 25F). In winter, the passage from Brest can get rough. Tickets are sold at both ports, but it's best to make reservations a day or two in advance with the Service Maritime Départemental (tel. 98 80 24 68).

Argoat Interior

Although *Argoat* (roughly pronounced ARE-gwaht) still means "wooded country" to Breton ears, centuries of clearing have made the rocky Argoat Interior one of the least forested regions in France. The Parc Régional d'Armorique, the rolling hills of the Monts d'Arée, and the one-car/two-cow villages surrounded by pasture contain plenty of hydrangea bushes bursting with blue, pink, and purple, but precious few trees. The Argoat's relative baldness, however, scarcely diminishes its beauty. The one-hour bus ride along the D769 from Morlaix to Huelgoat provides a mere introduction to the area. Here in Brittany's interior, the people are friendlier, the prices lower, and the scenery no less remarkable than along the coastline.

The hilly terrain is better suited to walking than cycling. The **Fédération Française de la Randonnée Pédestre** has excellent topographical maps that include detailed hiking tours. The organization **ABRI** has designed routes that follow scrupulously marked trails from one *gîte d'étape* to the next (26F per night). These maps are available for 20-45F each at several tourist offices, including those at Morlaix and Huelgoat.

Huelgoat

A small town on a sparkling lake, Huelgoat (pop. 1745) sits among the curious grottoes and rocks of the **Parc Naturel Régional d'Armorique.** Megaliths, parish closes, and the Arée Mountains are only a bike ride away. Huelgoat is one of the Argoat's more accessible towns; an early morning and an afternoon SNCF bus connect it to Morlaix to the north (on the busy Paris-Brest line) and Carhaix to the south. Those hitching or cycling from Morlaix can take the D769 to Berrien and the D14 to Huelgoat (30km altogether). Unless you have a car or don't mind the bus rides, Huelgoat is not a one-day trip. Reasonable accommodations are available in town, and there is a comfortable *gîte d'étape* 6.5km south in Locmaria-Berrien, the next stop on the bus route from Morlaix.

Orientation and Practical Information

Huelgoat's center is on the eastern bank of the lake. All SNCF buses stop in pl. Aristide Briand, less than a minute's walk from both the lake and the tourist office.

Tourist Office: pl. Aristide Briand (tel. 98 99 72 32), behind the church. Regional guide and map of surrounding forest (5F), topographical maps (33F), and detailed book of hikes (75F). Open Mon.-Sat. 10am-noon and 2-4pm; Sept. 16-June 14 inquire at the mayor's office next door. Open Mon.-Fri. 8:30am-noon and 1:30-5:30pm, Sat. 8:30am-noon.

Currency Exchange: All banks closed Sun.-Mon. No exchange at post office. **Crédit Agricole,** 14-16, rue des Cendres, off the main *place,* in direction of tourist office. Open Tues.-Wed. and Fri. 8:30am-12:15pm and 1:30-5:30pm, Thurs. 9am-12:15pm, Sat. 8:30am-12:15pm and 1:30-4:30pm.

Post Office: 22, rue des Cieux. Open Mon.-Fri. 9am-noon and 1:30-5:30pm, Sat. 9am-noon. **Postal Code:** 29218.

Buses: Buses stop in front of the *boulangerie-pâtisserie* in pl. Aristide Briand, across from the church. Schedules posted in the window. Mon.-Fri. 2 per day, Sat. 3 per day, Sun. 2 per day. To: Morlaix (1 hr., 25F); Carhaix (16F); Locmaria-Berrien (7F). For information, call 98 80 50 50 or 98 90 50 50.

Ambulance: tel. 98 99 73 96 or 98 99 75 35.

Police: route des Carrières (tel. 98 99 71 45). **Emergency,** tel. 17.

Accommodations and Camping

You can usually find a room here in the summer, but call ahead to be safe. Cheap beds await those who make the 6km hike to the *gîte* in Locmaria-Berrien. (You can also take the bus, but try to look a little dusty when you arrive. *Gîtes* are intended for horseback riders, hikers, and bikers.)

Gîte d'Etape, l'Ancienne Ecole, Locmaria-Berrien. Obtain key at the *mairie* (tel. 98 99 73 09) Mon.-Fri. 8am-noon and 2-5pm. Mon.-Fri. after 5pm and Sat.-Sun. 9am-9pm, go to the green-shuttered house opposite the church and ask Mme. Morvan for the key. You can also inquire at the café across the street. If all else fails, try M. Blaize (tel. 98 99 95 08) or M. le Guern (tel. 98 99 70 75), or stop in the bar just beyond the café. If you can't get the key, at least you can have a drink. 2 buses per day from Morlaix (20F) via Huelgoat (7F); 1 extra bus goes early Sat. afternoon. From the bus stop, follow the signs 1.2km up the hill to the café and church. Turn right; the *gîte* and *mairie* are on your right. Well-equipped kitchen, new toilets and showers, and a pay phone nearby. Women might not want to go alone in June, as the *gîte* is likely to be empty and others have keys to the building. 26F per person, 20F per horse. Two-day max. stay. Absolutely no cars.

Hôtel de l'Armorique, 1, pl. Aristide Briand (tel. 98 99 71 24), across from the bus stop. Fairly large, simple rooms with comfortable mattresses. Pleasant owners speak English and Spanish. Local bar downstairs. Reception open daily 8am-1pm; in off-season Tues.-Sun. Singles and doubles 80-100F. Triples with 2 beds 160F. Quads 170F. Showers 15F. Breakfast 22F.

Hôtel du Lac, 12, rue Général de Gaulle (tel. 98 99 71 14), on the waterfront. Decent but small rooms with soft mattresses. Singles and doubles 95-110F, with shower 140-170F. Triples (2 beds) with shower 135F. Breakfast 23F. Nice restaurant serves seafood dishes (50-120F) and pizza (40-50F).

Camping: Camping Municipal du Lac, rue du Général de Gaulle, (tel. 98 99 78 80), 5 min. from bus stop. Sunny and well-tended lakeside location with hedges separating sites. Often crowded. Reception open June-Sept. 15 Mon.-Fri. 7:30-11:30am and 4-8pm, Sun. 8-11am and 4-7pm. 20F per person, 30F per 2 people, car and site included. **Camping de la Rivière d'Argent,** 3km from town on the way to Carhaix (tel. 98 99 72 50 or 98 99 70 56). Quiet, wooded spot on the river. 12F per person, 12F per site. Open June-Sept.

Food

Conveniently located for *gîte* dwellers, **Chez Anne,** at the Locmaria-Berrien bus stop (tel. 98 99 75 03), serves a filling 53F *menu* but no *à la carte* dishes. Breakfast is 15F. (Open daily 8:30-10am, noon-2pm, and 7-9pm.) Unfortunately, there is no grocery store near the *gîte.* Huelgoat's **market** takes place on the first and third Thursday of the month from 8:30am to 5pm in pl. Aristide Briand and along rue du Lac. Place Aristide Briand has a small supermarket (open Mon.-Sat. 8:30am-12:30pm and 2:30-7:30pm) as well as a few bakeries and *crêperies.*

La Chouette Bleue, 1, rue du Lac. A spacious place by the lake with an upbeat atmosphere. It's a bar, crêperie, snack bar, and full restaurant. Entrees 20-49F, *crêpes* 5-27F. Try a dozen escargots for 54F. Bar open 10pm-1am. *Crêperie* open daily noon-10:30pm. Full restaurant open noon-2:30pm and 7-10:30pm. In off-season open Fri.-Sun. only.

Crêperie des Myrtilles, 26, pl. Aristide Briand (tel. 98 93 62 66). *Crêpes* prepared while you watch (4.50-25F). 34F *menu* with 3 *crêpes,* including *crêpes myrtilles* for dessert. Open daily noon-9:30pm; April-June and Sept.-Oct. Tues., Wed., and Fri.-Sun. noon-9:30pm; Nov.-March Fri.-Sun. noon-9:30pm.

L'Oasis, 25, pl. Aristide Briand. Have mussels and "french fries" (30F) or an all-you-can-eat buffet (cold meats, salads, boiled eggs, etc.) on the grassy terrace overlooking the lake. Open July-Sept. 15 daily 11am-1am.

Sights

A terrible hurricane in October 1987 destroyed many of the trees in Huelgoat's state forest. The enormous uprooted oaks under living, vine-twined ones coerce the place into resembling the site of a troll fight.

The tourist office sells a map (5F) indicating Huelgoat's best-known geological oddities. One footpath begins at the end of rue du Lac, where the lake empties into the Argent river. Twisting through piles of enormous granite boulders, the path leads to the **Grotte du Diable.** Descend the iron staircase into the dark, clammy chasm formed by overlying boulders. The footpath threads its way onto the **Roche Tremblante,** Huelgoat's greatest claim to fame. If you can't budge the 137-metric ton boulder, watch with shame as any local 10-year-old (wearing a tourist office armband) pushes on the precise point where the rock moves without effort. Other sights in the immediate vicinity include the **Chaos de Moulin** and the **Ménage de la Vierge,** two thought-provoking piles of rock, the second of which is said to resemble the Virgin's house-cleaning equipment.

The path **Allée Violette** (½km) leads you to the road from Carhaix, just past the bridge over the Argent. You may either turn right and head back into town or turn left and look for signs to the **Promenade du Fer-à-Cheval,** a half-hour stroll through more unbeatable woods. As the paths end, you are once more on the main road to Carhaix. Turn left to head home, right to find the **Gouffre,** where the Argent River crashes into a deep cavity and disappears for some 150m. The **Allée du Clair Ruisseau** also starts on the D764 to Carhaix and leads to the **Mare aux Sangliers,** a pretty pond surrounded by, you guessed it, more rocks (about 600m from the road). A 6km jaunt brings you to **Locmaria-Berrien,** its sturdy 18th-century church surrounded by 17th-century oaks. Follow the directions to the *gîte.* Within 2km is the Obelix's **Menhir de Kérampeulven,** an impressive solitary structure. Take the D14 toward Morlaix and turn left after roughly 1.5km.

Near Huelgoat

Although traffic can get heavy on the the D764 toward Brest, this route offers head-turning scenery, especially near the enchanting little town of **La Feuillée,** 8km from Huelgoat. Back roads—especially the one from La Feuillée to Litiez—wind past isolated farmhouses and tiny villages, but you'll need a detailed map of the area and a very sturdy bike to tackle them. The roads become hillier and the landscape more desolate as you approach the Arrée Mountains. **Roc Trévezel** (365m) is one of the highest points, and may be reached from La Feuillée by taking either the tiny road through Litiez or the larger D764 and then turning left on the D785. The two routes are comparable in length; the Roc is about 14km from Huelgoat. Continue south on the D785 for roughly 8km, and turn right onto a steep little road for 1km to reach the **Montagne St-Michel,** no relation to the famous religious complex to the north. From the back of the chapel at the summit, you can see the **Yeun Ellez,** a huge peat bog. In winter, the fog becomes so thick and the atmosphere so sinister that Breton tradition calls its center the "*portes aux enfers*" (gates to

Hell). An artificial lake at the same spot once supplied a vehemently opposed (and no longer open) thermonuclear station at Brennilis.

Brasparts lies 6.5km farther down the D785. The small, typically Breton **parish close** includes the church, a fantastically detailed calvary carved in stone, and a charnel house. For 250F per day, **Les Cavaliers de Kerjean St-Michel** in Brasports will rent you a horse for riding in the Monts d' Avrée (call 98 81 40 08 during meal-times). Exit by the D21, then pick up the D14, which leads back to Huelgoat via the small parish closes of Lannedern and Loqueffret. The church in **St-Herbot** has a Flamboyant square tower with a cliché-ridden view of the countryside. Outside stands the *calvaire*, a characteristically Breton ornament in the form of a wayside, tridentlike cross dating from 1571. At this point you'll be only 6km from Huelgoat; the entire circuit is roughly 52km.

The town of **Pleyben**, 26km southwest of Huelgoat, is the site of **Eglise St-Germain l'Auxerrois.** With its domed Renaissance bell tower and the magnificently ornate *calvaire*, a sort of four-way *arc de triomphe* depicting the life of Jesus, this is one church in Brittany definitely worth seeing. On the first Sunday of August, a *pardon* takes place in the *calvaire.* To reach Pleyben, leave Huelgoat via the road to Quimper, which becomes the D14. After 20km, turn left on the D785.

To the south of Huelgoat, **Carhaix** is a small town worth skipping. Do not be lured here by false rumors of a 100m wooden statue of France's favorite American, Jerry Lewis. SNCF buses (tel. 98 93 00 01) from Carhaix run to: Morlaix and Brest (2 or 3 per day; to Morlaix 1½ hr., 36F; to Brest 2½ hr., 65F); Quimper (2 per day, 2 hr., 47F); Chateaulin for a connecting bus to Camaret (2 per day, 1¼ hr., 58F); Loudeac (3 or 4 per day, 1½ hr.); Guingamp (3 or 4 per day, 1 hr., 35F). Cheap beds, hot showers, ample kitchen facilities, and a friendly welcome await you at the **gîte d'étape** in **Port de Carhaix,** a 5km hike out of town along the D769. Call the *mairie* (tel. 98 93 00 13) or M. Kergona (tel. 98 99 54 42); pick up the key at the Café Priol, on the D769 across the road from the *gîte.* The bus to Quimper stops in Port de Carhaix, near the *gîte.*

Crozon Peninsula

This rugged, cruciform peninsula has some of Brittany's finest seacoast. You can brood over the ocean from the height of a towering cliff, or approach it more inti-mately from one of the fine, broad beaches. The peninsula's gentler inlets shelter small towns and modest resorts. From the Mènez-Hom peak (330m), you'll get a view of just about everything. Like much of Brittany, the area takes effort and perse-verance to enjoy. **SNCF buses** (tel. 98 90 50 50) run four times per day (twice Sun.) from Quimper to Crozon, Morgat, and Camaret (railpasses valid). **Autocars Douguet** (tel. 98 27 02 02) runs buses between Brest, Camaret, and Crozon. The bus ride from Brest to the peninsula takes a good two hours. The far more efficient Vedettes Armoricaines boat runs from Brest to Le Fret, with a connecting bus to Crozon, Morgat, and Camaret. This ferry helps cyclists avoid going all the way around on the coastal road, where the wind and the steep hills make progress diffi-cult. Tourist offices in Camaret, Crozon, and Morgat have a leaflet with all public transport timetables for the peninsula.

Camaret

Camaret (pop. 2980) has towering cliffs, wide stretches of white sand, rows of enigmatic menhirs, and a monstrous annual lobster crop. Although it does reel in its share of tourists, Camaret is hardly as overburdened as its coastal neighbors.

Orientation and Practical Information

Camaret lies at the end of both the SNCF bus line and the Autocars Douguet bus line from Brest. For a scenic approach from Brest, take the Vedettes Armori-caines (tel. 98 44 44 04 or 98 90 60 00) boat to Le Fret, where a connecting bus brings you to Camaret, Crozon, or Morgat. The boat from Brest leaves from the Port du Commerce, as do boats to Ile d'Ouessant. (3 boats and buses per day at 7:30am, 12:30pm, and 5:45pm April-Sept.; 45 min.; 44F, round-trip 80F. Bikes 20F each way. Students 38F from Oct.-June.)

In town, follow quai Toudouze and then take a right onto quai Styvel. The tourist office, hotels, and restaurants are on the adjacent main streets.

Tourist Office: quai Toudouze (tel. 98 27 93 60), behind you when you get off the bus. It's the boxy beige building with the brown trim. Ask for a list of *gîtes d'étape* in the area. Open Mon.-Sat. 9:30am-12:30pm and 2:30-7:30pm, Sun. 10am-noon; Oct.-June Tues.-Sat. 10am-noon and 2-5pm. If it's closed, call the mayor's office at 98 27 94 22.

Currency Exchange: Crédit Agricole (tel. 98 27 94 19), on pl. Charles de Gaulle across from the tourist office. Open Tues.-Fri. 9am-noon and 2-5pm, Sat. 9am-noon and 2-4pm.

Post Office: 2, rue de Verdun (tel. 98 27 92 51). From pl. St-Thomas, take rue de la Mairie, which becomes rue de Verdun. **Currency exchange.** Open Mon.-Fri. 9am-noon and 2-5pm, Sat. 9am-noon. **Postal Code:** 29129.

Buses: SNCF and Autocars Douguet buses stop outside **Café de la Paix,** 30, quai Toudouze (tel. 98 27 93 05). Buy tickets inside. **SNCF** buses to Quimper via Crozon-Morgat (3 per day, additional buses Mon. and Fri. during the school year; 42F to Quimper, 8.50F to Crozon-Morgat). **Autocars Douguet** (tel. 98 27 02 02) to Brest (Mon.-Fri. 2 per day, Sat. 1 per day; 42F). **Vedettes Armoricaines** buses stop in pl. Charles de Gaulle to pick up passengers for the boat trip to Brest. The bus stops at Crozon, Morgat, and Le Fret (3 per day; 44F boat ticket includes bus).

Bike Rental: Cycles Motobecane, 19, rue de Reims (tel. 98 27 80 57), parallel to quai Toudouze. Baggage bikes once again, but this time they're glow-in-the-dark green. 50F per day, 250F per week, deposit 150F. Open Tues.-Sat. 9am-noon and 2-7pm.

Laundromat: way down quai Toudouze. Wash 25F, dry 15F. Open daily 8am-6pm.

Police: Tel. 98 27 00 22. **Emergency,** tel. 17.

Accommodations, Camping and Food

The five hotels in Camaret couldn't possibly accommodate the crowd of summer visitors. Either call ahead or cross your fingers and be prepared to spend.

Auberge de Jeunesse de l'Iroise (IYHF) (tel. 98 27 98 24) route de Toulinguet. Walk down the quay (along the port), and turn left in front of Hôtel Styvel. Bear right and walk up the hill about 200m. The hostel is on the left. The reception office is the first building on your right, the hostel the second. If no one is at the office, go to the hostel anyway and pay the next day. Less than perfect bath and kitchen facilities and only 18 beds, but the view behind that hedge out the back window is worth it all. 37F per person. Meals for groups only. Open mid-June to Sept.

Hôtel Vauban, 4, quai Styvel (tel. 98 27 91 36). Spacious and sunny with a bar downstairs. Singles and doubles 115-175F. Showers 15F. Breakfast 22F. Open Feb.-Nov.

Hôtel du Styvel (tel. 98 27 92 74), on quai Styvel. Nicely decorated but not much better than the less expensive place next door. Singles and doubles from 160F, with shower 200F. Showers 25F. Breakfast 22F. Nice restaurant downstairs with 58F *menu.*

Camping: Camping Municipal de Lannic (tel. 98 27 91 31), off rue du Gronnach, fairly close to town center. Go to the end of quai Toudouze, take a left at quai Styvel, ascend the hill, and take a right at the sign. Scenic beach nearby. 6.40F per person, 4.90F per site, 3.70F per car. Showers 5.90F. Open June 15-Sept. 15. **Camping de Lambezen** (tel. 98 27 91 41 or 98 27 93 72), 5km away in Lambezen. Take a left off the road to Crozon just after you've ascended from Camaret. There's a sign at the turn-off, but it faces the other direction. From there on, follow the signs. 35F per 2 people, showers included. Open Easter-Sept. There are also 6 campgrounds in the Crozon-Morgat area; ask at the tourist office.

Camaret's top-notch seafood fetches high prices. For a special meal, **La Licorne,** 12, quai Toudouze, has a country-club atmosphere, professional service, and a good 60F *menu* with mussels or salad, fish or steak, and dessert. (Open daily for lunch and dinner; in off-season Tues.-Sun.) For those with smaller appetites and budgets, the town has several good *crêperies.* Try **Crêperie Rocamadour,** 11, pl. Charles de Gaulle, which serves plump dinner *crêpes* (12-20F), an excellent seafood *crêpe* (32f), and a 32F 3-*crêpe menu.* It's diagonally across from the tourist office. (Open Feb.-Nov. 15, Tues.-Sun. noon-11pm.)

Sights

The 17th-century Tour Vauban at the end of the pier houses Camaret's **Musée Naval,** a small collection of engravings, paintings, and model ships. (Open June-Sept. daily 10am-7pm. Last entry 15 min. before closing. Admission 11F.) Nearby **Chapelle de Notre-Dame-de-Rocamadour** continues the marine theme; model boats dangle from the ceiling, lifesavers hang from the walls, and the altar resembles a ship's stern. A *pardon* and a blessing of the sea are held here on the first Sunday in September.

The most spectacular sights lie outside town. Just beyond the edge of town on the D8 is a modest circle of stone menhirs. The **Pointe de Penhir,** just 3.5km away on the D8, is one of the finest capes in Brittany. A memorial to the Bretons of the Free French forces stands on the cliff; from there, it's a dizzying 76-meter drop to the deep blue sea. Climb out onto the rocks for a magnificent view of the isolated rock masses of the **Tas de Pois.** Vedettes Sirènes (tel. 98 27 29 90 or 98 27 22 50) runs birdwatching cruises to this area (1 per day, 1½ hr., 50F). Amazingly, a grassy plain on the leeward side of the point leads down to a sheltered beach. Farther north, the road passes another stone circle, the **Alignements de Lagatjar,** some 100 menhirs arranged in intersecting lines and ending in a Stonehenge-like circle. These prehistoric stones are believed to have been installed in 2500 BC for sun-worshipping rites. The D355 leads to the **Pointe des Espagnols,** another dramatic promontory with a view over Brest and the Plougastel Peninsula. South of Camaret is **Pointe de Dinan,** where you can cross a natural arch and survey the Atlantic.

Morgat and Crozon

The relationship between these two towns is easily expressed: Morgat is Crozon's beach (joint pop. 8000). Morgat provides sun and surf as inland Crozon feeds and houses you. Morgat is a bit more spruced up for the tourists than Camaret, but be prepared to pay for the pleasant surroundings. If you plan to spend the night, pleasant **Hôtel Julia** (tel. 98 27 05 89) is the cheapest roofed place, with singles and doubles from 120F. (Open Feb. 15-Oct.) Finish a day of sunshine and sand by eating at **A la Grange de Toul-Bass,** pl. d'Ys, a restaurant/antique shop with a farmyard outside. Enormous *crêpes* (8-25F) and seafood dishes (35-40F) are served next to the antique plow on the terrace (5F surcharge). (Open April-Sept. daily 10am-midnight.)

The Morgat **tourist office** (tel. 98 27 07 92) waylays visitors just before town on bd. de la France-Libre. (Open July-Aug. Mon.-Sat. 9:30am-7pm, Sun. 10am-1pm; June and Sept. Tues.-Sat. 9:30am-noon and 2-6pm.) Two companies offer tours of Morgat's magical, mystical **marine caverns.** Try to go at twilight. **Vedettes Sirènes** (tel. 98 27 29 90 or 98 27 22 50) departs every 25 minutes (May-Sept. 15, 45 min., about 40F). **Vedettes Rosmeur** (tel. 98 27 09 54 or 98 27 10 71) runs four daily tours (75 min., about 50F). Tickets are sold on quai Kader in Morgat. On Sundays in July and August, Vedettes Rosmeur makes the one-hour crossing to Douarnenez at 6:15pm (50F, round-trip 62F).

Three km north of Morgat, landlocked **Crozon** is smaller but no less congested. From 8am to noon daily, an open **seafood market** takes place in pl. de l'Eglise; go just to marvel at the colorful *fruits de la mer* dragged in from local shores. Should your stomach not howl for crab, try the pizzas (26-40F) at **Restaurant L'Océanic,** 24, rue du Camaret (tel. 98 27 02 70). (Open Sun.-Mon. and Wed.-Fri. 7pm-midnight, Sat. 7pm-dawn; in off-season Wed.-Mon. noon-2pm and 7pm-midnight.) A number of supermarkets in town and the **Intermarché** off route de Camaret will stock you for the road.

The well-equipped Crozon **tourist office** (tel. 98 26 17 18), on rue St-Yves next to the *gare routière,* distributes a helpful map of the Crozon-Morgat area and accommodations information. (Open Mon.-Sat. 9am-8pm; Sept.-June Tues.-Sun. 9am-

12:30pm and 2-6pm.) Crozon's **post office** is located on rue Alsace-Lorraine (open Mon.-Fri 8:30am-noon and 2-5pm, Sat. 8:30am-noon); the **postal code** is 29160. **Peugeot Station,** 34, rue de Poulpatre, off the marketplace in Crozon, rents mediocre bicycles. (Open Tues.-Sat. 8:30am-noon and 2-7pm; about 40F.) Carless travelers can head for two new Crozon **gîtes d'étape: de Larrial** at Crozon and **St-Hernot** at Cap de la Chèvre, south of Crozon and Morgat. (Both 26F. For de Larrial, call the Le Bretons at 98 27 62 30; for St-Hernot 98 27 15 00.) **Hôtel Moderne,** 61, rue Alsace-Lorraine (tel. 78 27 00 10), has clean, comfortable rooms from 104F; they don't come any cheaper in Crozon. (Showers 20F. Breakfast 23F.) If the Crozon *gîtes* are full, cyclists or ambitious walkers can head for the **gîte d'étape** (tel. 98 21 91 04) by the bay in Kerdilès, 4km outside of Landérennec. From Crozon, go east on the D887 for 5km, branch left onto the D791 for 7km, branch left again on the D60, and keep an eye out for signs after about 2km. The *gîte* has 26F beds and kitchen facilities; call in advance for a prepared meal. The *mairie* (tel. 98 81 90 44) in Le Faou has details about all *gîtes*. Inquire at the **ULAMIR** (Union Locale des Animations de Milien Rural), in the SIVOM building on route du Camaret (tel. 98 27 01 68), for a list of local *gîtes* and maps of hiking trails between them. If you have wheels, look into *chambres d'hôtes* (bed and breakfasts). Singles, including breakfast, range from 90-120F; doubles 100-190F.

Crozon has its share of campgrounds. **Les Pieds dans l'Eau** (tel. 98 27 62 43), 6km northwest of Crozon in St-Fiacre, lives up to its name with a magnificent view of the sea. (12F per person, 11F per site, 5.50F per car. Showers included. Fresh bread and croissants every morning. Office open June 15-Sept. 15 daily 9am-noon and 2-8pm.) **Pen-Ar-Ménez** (tel. 98 27 12 36) is close to the Crozon SNCF station on bd. de Pralognan (*direction* "Camaret"). (12F per person, 7F per tent, 17F per car. Open April-Sept.)

Getting to Crozon and Morgat is no problem. Vedettes Armoricaines **buses** from Brest or Camaret stop in Morgat, and Autocars Douguet (tel. 98 27 02 02) run two buses per day between Crozon and Morgat. Buses to Crozon proper include SNCF's connection with Camaret (3 per day, 10F) and Vedettes Armoricaines's Camaret-Crozon-Morgat-Brest line. Also, the three daily **boats** from Brest to Le Fret each connect with buses to Crozon and Morgat. Many people hitch with ease here.

Quimper

Historically the capital of La Cornouaille, the oldest region of Brittany, Quimper (KEM-pear; pop. 100,000) has managed to grow while retaining its delightful Breton flavor. This affordable touring center has something to please everyone: museums, theaters, shopwindows full of the famous local pottery, and—of course—scenery. On the fourth Sunday in July, Quimper holds the most important regional folk festival, the **Festival de Cornouaille.** The celebrations usually begin the preceding Tuesday and include concerts, films, parties, and plays in both Breton and French. While the city certainly caters to the tourist crowd, Quimper's year-round efforts to preserve its heritage are more than merely cosmetic. Some women wear traditional dress in church as well as in the marketplace, stores prominently display Celtic records and books, and one local high school conducts its classes in Breton.

Orientation and Practical Information

To get to the center of town from the train station, which lies to the east, turn right and follow av. de la Gare to the river. Cross the bridge, and turn left on bd. Amiral de Kerguélen. A right onto rue du Rois Gradlon leads to the cathedral and entrance to the old city. In the old city, Quartier St-Mathieu lies to your left; the Musée des Beaux Arts is behind the cathedral to your right.

Tourist Office: Should be in a brand-new building at pl. de la Résistance by Jan. 1991 (tel. 98 95 04 69). Follow av. de la Gare from the station. It becomes Boulevard Dupleix before ending at pl. de la Résistance. These people will do just about anything for you. Ask for the free booklet with public transportation schedules for Quimper and surrounding areas. 1½-hr. guided tours in French (July-Aug. Mon.-Sat., 2 per day, 25F). Also sells bus excursion tickets to such nearby wonders as Pointe du Raz. English spoken. Open Mon.-Sat. 8:30am-8pm, Sun. 9:30am-noon, longer during the festival; Sept. to mid-June Mon.-Sat. 9am-noon and 2-6pm.

Budget Travel: Nord-Sud Voyages, 5, bd. Amiral de Kerguélen (tel. 98 95 40 79). Eurotrain/BIJ. Open Mon. 2-6:30pm, Tues.-Fri. 9am-noon and 1:30-6:30pm, Sat. 9am-noon.

Currency Exchange: Banks in Quimper are open Tues.-Sat., except for **Crédit Agricole,** pl. St-Corentin (tel. 98 95 46 33), opposite the cathedral. Open Mon. and Sat. 8:30am-12:30pm and 2-4:40pm, Tues-Fri. 8:30am-12:30pm and 2-5:30pm. Good rates, but an 18F commission.

Post Office: (tel. 98 95 65 85), at bd. Amiral de Kerguélen and rue de Juniville. Open Mon.-Fri. 8am-7pm, Sat. 8am-noon. Branch office, rue du Calvaire, near the hostel. Both have **currency exchange.** Open Mon.-Fri. 8:30am-noon and 1:30-6pm, Sat. 8:30am-noon. **Postal Code:** 29000.

Flights: Brittany Air International (tel. 98 62 10 22 or 98 94 01 28). To London's Gatwick Airport via Brest daily. **Air Inter** (tel. 98 84 73 73) in Brest. 3-4 flights per day to Paris from Quimper's airport in Plugaffan (8km away, served only by taxi).

Trains: av. de la Libération (tel. 98 90 50 50, reservations 98 90 26 21). To: Paris (7-12 per day, 6½ hr., 274F); Rennes (6-10 per day, 3 hr., 133F); Nantes (5 per day, 3 hr., 138F); Brest (5 per day, 1½ hr., 62F). Information office open daily 8am-8pm; Sept.-June 9am-6:45pm. Inquire about one-way bike rentals. The station's *consigne* stores baggage for up to one full day (5-12F). Open 8am-8pm.

Buses: Many dependable private lines operate out of Quimper; ask at the tourist office or peruse the schedules posted around the parking lot next to the train station. **Cars de Cornouaille** (tel. 98 87 40 05). Service south to Pont l'Abbée, Loctudy, and Lesconil (4-5 per day, Sept.-June Mon.-Sat. 3 per day; 1 hr.; 8.20F to Pont l'Abbée, 7.70F to Loctudy, 21F to Lesconil). **Transports Départementaux du Finistère** (tel. 98 90 17 83). Information office in the small, squat building next to the train station. (Open Mon.-Fri. 9am-noon and 2:30-5:30pm). Service to Pont l'Abbée (17F), Guilvinec (24.50), Penmarch (27.50F), St-Guénolé (20F). Buses also stop alongside the Breton Museum near the cathedral. SNCF buses to Douarnenez (4 per day, 18F) and Camaret (4 per day, Sun. 2 per day; 42F). Railpasses valid. Buy tickets at train station. **CAT/TV** (tel. 98 95 02 36). Service to many spots. To: Plogoff (2 per day, 35.50F); Brest (6 per day, Sun. 2 per day; 59F); Morlaix (Mon.-Sat. 1 per day, 70F). All buses stop at (Sun. buses stop *only* at) 5, bd. Kerguélen, in front of the travel agency. **Cars Caoudal** (tel. 98 56 96 72) in La Forêt-Fouesnant. To: Concarneau (½-hr., 17.80F); Pont-Aven (1 hr., 26F); Quimperlé (1¾ hr., 33.50F). 4-6 daily buses leave from Café Nantais, av. de la Gare (tel. 98 90 07 84), right across from the train station. They also stop downtown near the tourist office in Nouvelles Halles. Also service to La Forêt-Fouesnant. Buy tickets at the café. No student discounts.

Public Transportation: Buses, pl. de la Résistance (tel. 98 90 72 40). Tickets 5.20F, good for 40 minutes. Schedules available in the office. Open Mon.-Sat. 10am-noon and 2-6pm.

Bike Rental: At the **train station** luggage department. 40F per ½-day, 50F per day, deposit 500F or credit card. The "½-day" is either 6:30am-1pm or 1-9:30pm. One-way rentals to Châteaulin, Douarnenez, Concarneau, and Rosporden. Office open daily 8am-8pm. If they're out, ask at the tourist office for private companies in town. If you're headed to the coast, try **Velodet,** 4bis, av. de la Mer (tel. 98 57 04 60), 16km from Quimper in Bénodet.

Laundromat: Au Raton Laverie, 4, rue Jacques Cartier, just west of the train station. Wash 20F, dry 15F. Open daily 7am-10pm. **Lav' Seul,** 9, rue de Locronan, right off pl. de Locronan. Wash 18F, dry 24F. Open daily 7am-10pm.

Pharmacy: Check the doors for the address of the late-night pharmacy on weekend nights.

Hospital: Centre Hospitalier Laennec, 14bis, av. Yves-Thépot, tel. 98 52 60 60.

Police: rue Théodore le Hars (tel. 98 90 15 41). **Emergency,** tel. 17.

Accommodations and Camping

Between July 15 and August 15, written reservations will make your life easier. If you don't have reservations, start looking early in the day. The tourist office can direct you to private homes that offer bed-and-breakfast (150F and up for 2 people).

For accommodations during festival week, make arrangements as early as you can—March, if possible.

Unfortunately, the youth hostel, formerly at 6, av. des Oiseaux (tel. 98 55 41 67), 25 minutes from the station in the Bois de l'Ancien Séminaire, had to close for the summer of 1990 because of conflicts with the city over funding. The verdict for 1991 is not yet out. Be sure to call or ask at the tourist office before heading out.

Hôtel de l'Ouest, 63, rue le Déan (tel. 98 90 28 35), near the train station. From the station, walk right on av. de la Gare and take a left on rue du Dr. Guillard, just before the fork. Rue du Dr. Guillard will lead you to rue le Déan (5 min.). Clean, spacious rooms and incredibly friendly owner. Singles and doubles 95-160F. Showers 12F. Breakfast 18F.

Hôtel le Terminus, 15, av. de la Gare (tel. 98 90 00 63). Directly across from the train station. Clean, attractive rooms, but street below can be noisy, especially on weekends. Singles 90F, with shower 140F. Doubles 140F, with shower 160F. Shower 15F. Breakfast 22F. Reception open daily until 9pm. Telephone reservations.

Hôtel Celtic, 13, rue de Douarnenez (tel. 98 55 59 35), on the edge of the old quarter, 1 block up from Eglise St-Mathieu. A little musty but nicely decorated; firm mattresses. Friendly management speaks English. Reception open noon-midnight. Singles and doubles 85F, with shower 110F. Showers 12F. Breakfast 20F. *Menus* from 55F in the restaurant below. Open June-Sept. 15 daily; Oct. 15-May. Mon.-Sat.

Hôtel de l'Odet, 83, rue de Douarnenez (tel. 98 55 56 75). Quite a hike from the station, but worth a try if other places are full. From the station, go right, follow the river, then turn right onto rue Amiral which becomes rue de Douarnenez. Adequate rooms. Singles 90F. Doubles 100F, with shower 125F. Breakfast 18.50F. 54F *menu* in restaurant below. Telephone reservations accepted. Open Jan.-Nov.

Camping: Camping Municipal, av. des Oiseaux in the Bois du Séminaire, next to the hostel. You can pitch your tent in the woods, well away from the campers below. Hot water and showers. Office open July-June 14. Call the mayor's office (tel. 98 98 89 89) for information. Mon.-Sat. 9-11am and 1-7pm. 4F per person, 2.50F per tent. Showers 3.70F.

Food

Quimper has the usual collection of *crêperies*. Try **Crêperie Victoria,** rue Ste-Catherine, or **Le Blé Noir,** across the street. A remarkable **covered market** in Les Halles in the old quarter along rue St-François gathers the area's freshest produce, seafood, bread, cheese, and pastries under one roof. (Open Mon.-Sat. 8am-1pm and 3-7pm, Sun. 9am-noon.) An **open market** takes place in the parking lot between the cathedral and the Musée des Beaux Arts. (Open Wed. and Sat. 9am-6pm; in off-season Wed. and Sat. 9am-2pm or later.)

CamyfloBar, 4, rue St-Catherine, next to the movie theater. Much more than a restaurant, it's a fun and popular bar, *saladerie, glacerie,* etc. Bright colors and delicious salads, quiches, and seafood dinners for less than 45F. Open daily 11am-1am.

Le Jardin d'Eté, 15, rue du Sallé. A charming place full of flowers. Outdoor *terrasse.* Miami Salad with asparagus, chicken, avocado, banana, and tomato (40F). Dozen *escargots* 42F. Open daily noon-2:30pm and 7-10:30pm.

Le Steinway, 20, rue des Gentilshommes. Elegant, intimate place knows how to *tuna* fish. Seafood *plat du jour* for lunch 40F, fish or meat dishes for lunch or dinner 45-70F. *Panaché de poissons* 42F. Open July-Aug. Mon.-Thurs. noon-2pm and 7:30-10pm, Fri.-Sat. noon-2pm and 7:30-10:30pm; open Sun. of the festival; Sept.-June Tues.-Sat. same hours.

Sights and Entertainment

At the entrance to the old quarter sits the majestic **Cathédrale St-Corentin,** dedicated to Quimper's patron saint, one of the many Breton saints unrecognized by Rome. The spiritual adviser of King Gradlon, this 6th-century bishop is said to have lived off a single fish. After eating his fill, Corentin would throw half the fish back in the river, only to have a regenerated version return obediently the next day. A statue of the king, added in 1856, stands between the cathedral's two distinctive spires.

From the small cathedral garden, climb to the old city ramparts for a good view of the cathedral and the Odet River as it flows from Quimper. (Open daily 8am-6pm.) Within the garden is the entrance to the **Musée Départemental Breton** (tel. 98 95 21 60), closed for remodeling until April 1991. Their fine local pottery collection is worth a look. (Open June-Sept. 10 daily 10am-7pm; Oct.-May 10am-noon and 2-5pm. Admission 10F, students and seniors 5F.)

The **Musée des Beaux Arts,** near the cathedral and the Hôtel de Ville, houses works by Rubens, Fragonard, Corot, Boudin, and Quimper's own Max Jacob. It also displays a wonderful collection of Flemish still-lifes and yet another collection inspired by the Breton landscape. (Open Wed.-Mon. 9:30am-noon and 2-6:30pm. Admission 20F, students and seniors 10F, Sun. in winter free.)

In the old quarter, shop windows along **rue Kéréon** and **rue du Salle** display handsome Breton furniture and pottery. Chic boutiques stock the latest clothing, jewelry, and shoes, but Quimper shops also provide a taste of contemporary Breton culture. The three record stores in the old quarter will play any selection of your choice—ask for the popular Breton group Tri Yann. Quimper's renowned pottery tradition celebrated its 300th birthday in 1990. Numerous shops sell the colorfully patterned pieces, each handmade, for roughly a fourth of what they fetch in North America. To see the artisans at work, visit one of the two **faïenceries** (porcelain studios) in town that are open to the public. Both sell factory seconds at a 20% discount. **Les Faïenceries de Quimper H. B. Henriot,** rue Haute (tel. 98 90 09 36), across from Notre-Dame de Locmaria, gives guided tours in French (and English if requested in advance). (Open Mon.-Thurs. 9:30-11:30am and 1:30-4:30pm, Fri. 9:30-11:30am and 1:30-3pm. Admission 12F, ages 8-14 6F.) One km out of town on route de Bénodet, the **Faïenceries Keraluc** (tel. 98 53 04 50) gives free tours. (Open Mon.-Fri. 9am-noon and 2-6pm.)

Those who miss the Festival de Cornouaille can still catch other celebrations of Breton culture. Every Thursday from late June to early September, festival week excluded, the cathedral gardens fill with traditional **Breton dancers** in costume, accompanied by lively *biniou* and *bombarde* players (9pm, 17F). The first three weeks in August, Quimper holds its **Semaines Musicales.** Some of Europe's finest orchestras, choirs, and soloists perform nightly in the Théâtre Municipal, the cathedral, and other churches. (Tickets 80F, students and children 50F, discounts for 3 or more concerts. Make reservations at the tourist office.)

For a night of live music, try **Chez Paul,** 52, av. de la Libération (tel. 98 90 04 31), a bistro-cabaret and hot spot for local singers and musicians. (Open Wed.-Sat. 6pm-1am, Tues. and Sun. 8pm-1am.) Torn from the bosom of their ancient culture, alienated Breton youth and other victims of modernity dance alone at **L'Arlequin,** 440, route de Bénodet (tel. 98 52 03 76) and **Le Sagittaire,** 2, rue Haute (tel. 98 90 18 78; cover charge 50F).

Near Quimper

Biking around here is arduous, but bus connections from Quimper to nearby sights are frequent and reliable. At least seven buses each day go from Quimper to the **Crozon Peninsula** (1-1½ hr., around 40F). **Vedettes de l'Odet** (tel. 98 57 00 58) will sell you down the Odet River and buy you back for 80F (July and Aug. only; tickets at the tourist office). The route down the east bank of the Odet River via the D34 leads to the tourist resort of **Bénodet,** 15km from Quimper. However, you're better off with the scenic D20 and D144, which snake through tiny villages along the west bank.

Halfway between Bénodet and Pont-l'Abbé on the D44 lies the **Jardin Botanique** (tel. 98 56 44 93), 8½ acres of camelias, azaleas, rare roses, and other exotic flora. (Open May-Sept. daily 10am-noon and 2-7pm. Oct.-April Sun. 2-7pm or by appointment. Admission 15F.) Farther along the D44 towards Bénodet is the **Musée de la Musique Mécanique** (tel. 98 56 36 03), a collection of organs, player pianos, and other mechanized musical instruments. (Open May-Sept. daily 2-6pm. Admission 20F, includes guided tour.) Buses in Quimper serve Bénodet, Pont-l'Abbé, and neighboring villages. Farther south and also accessible by bus, the tiny villages of the **Penmarch Peninsula** continue to practice the old Breton customs in spite of the crowds already jockeying for the best view of the 1992 Olympic sailboarding competition.

Flatter terrain makes for easier cycling north of Quimper. Twenty-two km north-west along the D765, lovely but smelly **Douarnenez** is an active fishing port and canning town. The fishing boats come in at 11pm; the mackarel, sardines, and shell-fish are auctioned off at 6am. The big market every Monday, Wednesday, and Friday is quite a sight. **La Cotriade**, 46, rue Anatole France, is one of the more remarkable restaurants in town. Douarnenez is well-connected to Quimper by bus (4 per day). In July and August, a ferry cruises from Douarnenez to Morgat on the Crozon Peninsula.

The **Pointe du Raz** is the westernmost point of all of France. Nearby lies the tiny village of **Plogoff**. During the late 70s, when a nuclear power plant was undergoing construction at Pointe du Raz, this community rejected all government support and declared "independence" for nearly three weeks. The people actually imprisoned the mayor and swore in their own leader. The plant is now dismantled; you *can* fight city hall. CAT buses serve the Pointe du Raz. Bikers should take the D765/D784 35km to **Audierne** and continue 15km to Pointe du Raz.

Concarneau

Those coming to Concarneau (pop. 19,000) expecting St-Malo's seaside elegance will be disappointed. Although Concarneau has all the trappings of a popular summer resort, it remains a working, seafaring town. For every souvenir-vendor trying to snag a tourist, there's a working person trying to net a tuna. Concarneau's identity as France's third-largest fishing port is well-disguised, but you'll scent it along quai Carnot, lined by warehouses packing the daily catch.

Orientation and Practical Information

Rail service to Concarneau is limited to freight (and bicycles) only. The tourist office adjoins the bus station, in the little building overlooking the port's parking lot. To get to the freight station (should you need to pick up your bicycle), take a right onto av. de la Gare and walk ½km. The *ville close* (walled city) lies beyond the tourist office in the other direction, accessible on the right by a small bridge.

Tourist Office: (tel. 98 97 01 44), on quai d'Aiguillon next to the bus station. Information on boat trips, bike rentals, and festivals. Good free maps and bus schedules. Ask about *gîtes d'étape* and *chambres d'hôte* in the area. Open daily 9am-8pm; Sept.-May Mon.-Sat. 9am-noon and 2-6pm; June Mon.-Sat. 9am-12:30pm and 2-7pm.

Budget Travel: Sterne Voyages, 8, av. de la Gare (tel. 98 97 50 55). Sells Transalpino/BIJ tickets, and does all a travel agent should. Open Mon.-Fri. 9am-noon and 2-6:30pm, Sat. 9am-noon and 2-4:30pm.

Currency Exchange: Crédit Mutuel de Bretagne, 1, rue des Ecoles. No commission. Open Mon.-Fri. 8:30am-noon and 1:30-5:30pm.**Crédit Agricole**, pl. du Général de Gaulle. Open Tues., Wed., and Fri. 8:15am-12:15pm and 1:45-5:15pm, Thurs. 8:45-12:15pm and 1:45-4:15pm, Sat. 8:15am-12:15pm and 1:45-5:15pm. Commission 18F. Also at the **post office**.

Post Office: 5, quai Carnot (tel. 98 97 04 00). **Currency exchange.** Open Mon.-Sat. 8am-7pm; Sept.-June Mon.-Fri. 8am-6pm, Sat. 8am-noon. **Postal Code:** 29900.

Trains: No service, but plenty of information at the **SNCF station,** av. de la Gare (tel. 98 97 00 66). Inquire about shipping your bike. The station will hold it for you. Open Mon.-Fri. 7am-6:30pm, Sat. 9am-1pm and 2-5:30pm.

Buses: av. Pierre Guéguin at quai Carnot, in the port's parking lot. To Rosporden (3-4 per day, 20 min., 13F) for rail connections on the main Paris-Quimper line. To Paris (3-4 per day, 6 hr.). All SNCF buses stop at the SNCF freight station, av. de la Gare, and at the port's parking lot near the tourist office. **Cars Caoudal** (tel. 98 97 35 31 or 98 56 96 72) information and ticket office, across the parking lot near quai Carnot. To Quimper (Mon.-Sat. 4-6 per day, ½-hr., 17.80F) and Quimperlé via Pont-Aven (4-6 per day; to Pont-Aven 20 min., 11.80F; to Quimperlé 1 hr.; 23F). Luggage 7F extra, even when bus is empty. Bikes 11F. Open Mon.-Fri. 8:45am-1:20pm and 2:45-6:45pm.

Bike Rental: At the **SNCF station.** 40F per ½-day, 50F per day, deposit 500F. Lower rates after 2nd and 10th days. Also at the **hostel.** 35F per day, deposit 200F, but even they recommend the better bikes at the station.

Laundromat: Lav'Seul, pl. Hôtel de Ville, near the hostel. Wash 20F. Dry 2F. 10F coins only. Open 7am-10pm daily.

Taxis: Tel. 98 97 24 18.

Youth Center: Permanence d'Accueil Jeunes (tel. 98 97 17 28), on pl. Jean Jaurès. Information on sports and cultural activities, student travel, women's issues. Advice for disabled people. Open Mon. 9am-noon and 1-4pm, Tues.-Fri. 9am-noon and 1-5pm.

Pharmacy: Check the doors to find which is open late. Poison hotline at tel. 99 59 22 22.

Hospital: rue du Trégunc, tel. 98 50 30 30.

Ambulance: 30, rue Dupetit Thouars (tel. 98 50 62 66).

Police: av. de la Gare (tel. 98 97 17 17). **Emergency,** tel. 17.

Accommodations and Camping

Finding a hotel room in summer is difficult but not impossible. Concarneau has numerous campgrounds and an excellent, large hostel which could easily be full in July or August. Word travels fast in the hostel circuit—Concarneau's is not one to miss. In July and August, it's best to make phone reservations at all places.

Auberge de Jeunesse (IYHF) (tel. 98 97 03 47), on quai de la Croix beside a little chapel. From the bus station follow the main street, av. Pierre Guéguin, which becomes quai Peneroff, toward the water. It becomes quai de la Croix (10 min.) around to the right. Superb location next to the beach and town. Through the bedroom and kitchen windows you get a salty wind and a view of the bay. Multilingual staff and easy-going atmosphere. Eek! co-ed bathrooms. Office open daily 8-10am and 6-8pm. Kitchen and bathroom areas stay open during the day, but bedrooms are locked. Midnight curfew. 37F per person. IYHF card required. Breakfast 13F. Filling 38F lunch or dinner *menu* may be available during the summer. Call ahead June-Aug.

Hôtel de la Crêpe d'Or, 3, rue du Lin (tel. 96 97 08 61), just off quai Carnot. From the bus stop at train station, take a right onto av. de la gare, a left onto quai Carnot, walk about ½ km and take a left onto rue du Lin. The hotel will be on your right. A clean, well-lighted place. Singles and doubles 100F, with shower 135F. Shower 12F. Breakfast 18F. Nice restaurant downstairs has 60F *menu* and 30-70F *à la carte.*

Hôtel des Voyageurs, 9, pl. Jean Jaurès (tel. 98 97 08 06). Great location diagonally across from the bus station. Spacious, comfortable rooms and bar downstairs. Singles and doubles from 110F, with shower 150F. Hall showers free. Breakfast 25F.

Hôtel Renaissance, 56, av. de la Gare (tel. 98 97 04 23). Take a right from the bus station and walk 5 min. Clean rooms on a noisy street near the station. Nothing fancy. Doubles from 95F, with shower 145F. Extra bed 40F. Breakfast 19F. Telephone reservations accepted. Closed 15 days in Oct.

Hôtel du Lin, 58, av. Alain Le Lay (tel. 98 97 09 92), close to the train station. Take a right onto av. de la Gare and a left onto av. Alain Le Lay. The street below gets noisy, but the owners and rooms are nice. Singles (1-2 people) 130F. Doubles with 2 beds (2-3 people) 150F. All rooms have showers. Breakfast 18F.

La Bonne Auberge (tel. 98 97 04 30), on plage du Cabellou. Far away, but worth it. Take bus #2 from the *gare routière* (4.40F, 18 per day; last bus at 6:40pm) and get out at Le Cabellou, the last stop. In a peaceful rural area overlooking a sandy beach, this place resembles a country home more than a hotel. Comfortable rooms. Doubles 120-200F, with shower 160F. Breakfast 19F. Open May to mid-Sept.

Camping: Camping du Dorlett (tel. 98 97 16 44), near plage des Sables Blancs. Take bus #1 from the bus station to Le Dorlett (4.40F, 13 per day, last bus at 6:20pm). 9F per person, 16.50F per site. Showers included. Open June to Sept. **Camping de Kersaux** (tel. 98 97 37

41), about 2km out of town next to plage du Cabellou. Take bus #2 from the bus station to Le Cabellou, and backtrack along the road. The campground will be on your right, shortly after the beach ends. 11.50F per person, 6.80F per site, 4F per car. Showers included. Open June 15-Sept. 10. **Camping Rural de Lochrist** (tel. 98 97 25 95), about 4km out of town. Take bus #1 from the bus station to La Maison Blanche and follow route de Quimper away from town. Also rents tents. 10F per person, 10F per site, 5F per car. Showers 4F. Ask the tourist office for a list of other campgrounds.

Food

Seafood *menus* start at 50F and sprint quickly up to 80-100F. As usual, you'll probably resort to *crêperies.* Some good ones show their faces near the youth hostel. Across the street and to the left, **Ti Clémentine** rolls the little buggers for 10-37F. (Open Thurs.-Tues. noon-3pm and 6:30pm-they decide to close, also open Wed. in the summer.)

Fish is sold Monday through Friday from 8am to noon near the port by the tourist office. There's a covered **market** daily from 9am to 1pm in pl. Jean Jaurès, as well as an open-air market outside on Monday and Friday mornings. Provisions are cheaper at **Rallye Supermarket,** quai Carnot. (Open Mon.-Fri. 9am-7:15pm, Sat. 9am-7pm.)

Taverne de la Ville-Close, 42, rue Vauban. Rustic yet elegant. 68F *menu* includes *moules marinières* or grilled steak. Hefty, healthy, hearty peasant salad 30F. Open June-Aug. daily noon-2pm and 7-10:30pm, Sept.-Nov. and April-May Thurs.-Tues. only.

L'Escale, 19, quai Carnot. Full dinner *menu* 38F. Music is loud and the look a bit weathered, but the food is fine. Open 10am-midnight.

Restaurant/Crêperie de la Porte au Vin, 9, pl. St-Guénolé. Less expensive than others in the *ville close,* and just as good. The 48F *menu* includes a full salad or marinated mussels, a *crêpe* with green eggs, ham, and cheese, and a *crêpe* or ice cream for dessert. Open March-Nov. 10am-midnight.

Sights

The usually deserted ramparts of the old town offer a fine view of the harbor, but you'll have to pay to reach the most extensive section. (Admission 3.60F, children 1.80F. Open April-June 15 10am-12:30pm and 2-7pm, June 16-Sept. 10am-7:30pm.) Although the rest of the old town is worth visiting, there is little to see but other tourists, souvenir shops, and a few mildly interesting art galleries. The **Musée de la Pêche,** rue Vauban, in the *ville close,* houses a large exhibit on the fishing industry, but only fishing fanatics would want to pay the admission. (Open daily 9:15am-8:30pm, Sept.-June 10am-12:30pm and 2:30-6pm. Admission 25F, ages 5-18 15F.) Between midnight and about 6am, the quays by the large warehouses on the port come alive as fishing boats unload their catch. At 7 and 10am, you can bid for the big ones yourself at the *criée* (auction).

Concarneau's beaches are fairly conventional despite the startlingly clear water and smooth sand; the extreme tides deposit heaps of seaweed and muck on the rocks. The **plage des Sables Blancs** is the best place to swin. Take bus #1 from av. Pierre Guéguin near the port to Sables Blancs or Cabellou, the resort on the other side of town (18 per day, last bus from beach leaves at 6:40pm).

During the last week in July, music, dance, and parades in ethnic costume round out Concarneau's annual **Festival International.** A more local folk festival, **Les Filets Bleus** (The Blue Nets), was first held in 1905 to aid Concarneau's sardine fishermen. The extravaganza now benefits the tourist industry more than the fishing trade. During the next to last week in August, the entire city turns into a giant playground, complete with four platforms of frenzied Terpsichoria, nocturnal Bacchanalia, and general pigging out. On the last day of the festival, the next to last Sunday in August, it costs 30F to enter the gates.

Quimperlé

Two rivers, L'Ellé and L'Isole, meet at Quimperlé (pop. 12,000) to form La Laïta, which winds south some 15km through the Forêt de Carnoët and then into the sea. This confluence of rivers gives the city its name—the Breton word "*kemper*" means "junction." The city's *basse ville* sits on the island created by the grand intersection. The jewel of the *basse ville* is the 11th-century Eglise Ste-Croix, which borrows the cloverleaf shape and all the grandeur of Jerusalem's Holy Sepulchre but none of the kitschy sectarian clutter. Flick the lightswitch over your head before descending into the 11th-century crypt under the altar. The 15th-century houses on rue Brémond d'Ars also warrant a look. Up the hill (and it's quite a hill), Quimperlé's *haute ville* is the site of the 14th- to 15th-century **Eglise Notre-Dame,** so tightly wedged into its surroundings that the steep streets pass under its arched buttresses.

Built between 1470 and 1500, the **Maison des Archers,** 7, rue Dom Morice, just off rue Brémond d'Ars in the *basse ville,* housed the town's crack commando squad of archers. Now a museum of local lore, it includes the room of Théodore Hersart de la Villemarqué, who wrote the famous *Barzaz Breiz,* the traditional Breton chorus. (Open July-Aug. 31 Tues.-Sun. 10am-noon and 2:30-7pm. Admission 12F.) The tourist office supplies a complete list of cloisters and abbeys found in and around the town. They can also direct Gauguin devotees to **Pont-Aven,** the artist's one-time stomping ground.

Orientation and Practical Information

If you arrive by bus from Quimper or Concarneau, stay on past the SNCF station to the stop by the rivers of the *basse ville.* The tourist office is on rue de Bourgneuf, on the east bank of the Laïta River, just across the Ellé from pl. Charles de Gaulle. Otherwise, the walk from the station to the *basse ville* takes about 15 minutes and serves as a good introduction to the town. From the station take a left on bd. de la Gare, then a right on rue de l'Hôpital Fremeur. Go up the hill, then cross pl. St-Michel diagonally to the right, pass the church on your left, and take rue Brouzic (which becomes rue Savary) to the jumble of cobblestones that passes for a staircase on rue Jacques Cartier. Cross the bridge to pl. Charles de Gaulle and turn right for the tourist office.

Tourist Office: (tel. 98 96 04 32), on rue du Bourgneuf in the *basse ville.* Helpful maps and a brochure describing architectural highlights. English spoken. Open Mon.-Sat. 9:15am-noon and 2:15-6:30pm.

Currency Exchange: Banks are as easy to find in Quimperlé as cobblestones. Most are open Mon.-Fri. 9am-noon and 1:30-5pm.

Post Office: pl. Charles de Gaulle, in the *basse ville.* Open Mon.-Fri. 8am-noon and 1:30-6:30pm, Sat. 8am-noon. **Postal Code:** 29300.

Trains: (tel. 98 39 24 24), on bd. de la Gare in the *haute ville.* On the main Paris-Quimper line. To: Paris (6 per day, 5½ hr., 256F); Lorient (8 per day, 15 min., 16F); Quimper (9 per day, 40 min., 34F). Information desk open daily 6am-noon and 1:30-6pm.

Buses: Two lines connect Quimperlé to nearby towns. **Cars Caoudal,** tel. 98 56 96 72. Information and tickets at Café de la Gare, across from the train station. Six buses per day (4 on Sun.) to: Pont Aven (¾-hr., 15.80F); Quimper (1¾ hr., 33.50F); Concarneau (1 hr., 23F). All buses stop outside the SNCF station next to the café Au Retour de Toulföeh in the *basse ville,* across the Isole River from the post office. Luggage 7F. **Ellé Laïta,** 19, rue Brémond d'Ars (tel. 98 96 13 77). To: Lorient (Mon.-Sat. 3 per day, ½-hr., 11.50F); Le Pouldu (Mon.-Sat. 3 per day, ½-hr., 16F); Le Faouët (Mon.-Sat. 2 per day, 45 min., 13.50F). Buses stop at the SNCF station only. Office open Mon.-Fri. 9am-noon and 2-6:30pm, Sat. 9am-noon.

Bike and Moped Rental: Cycles Peugeot, 5, rue de la Tour d'Auvergne (tel. 98 96 05 18), in the *basse ville.* Decent 5- and 10-speeds 40F per day, 180F per week, deposit 400F. Mopeds 51F per day, 279F per week, deposit 650F. Open July-Sept. 15 Tues.-Sat. 8:30am-noon and 2-6:30pm. **Cycles Guigoures,** rue Leuriou (tel. 98 96 08 98). 5- and 10-speeds 40F per day, 180F per week, deposit 400F. **Fontaine Sports,** 2, rue de Pont-Aven (tel. 98 96 05 30). Bikes 45F per day, 75F per 2-day period, 230F per week, deposit 1000F or ID.

Boat Rental: Take rue Audran to quai Surcouf on the banks of the Ellé River (open July-Aug. 1:20-6pm), or contact M. Meleard (tel. 98 96 05 94). Canoes 30F per hour, 70F per ½-day, 100F per day, deposit 2000F. Kayaks 30F per hour, 60F per ½-day, 90F per day, deposit 2000F.

Laundromat: (tel. 98 96 12 95), on bd. de la Gare just opposite the station. Wash 20F per 7kg, dry 2F. Open daily 8am-11pm, Sept.-May 8am-10pm.

Public Showers and Baths: 6, rue Mme Moreau. Showers 6F. Baths 9.70F. Open Fri. 3-8pm, Sat. 8am-noon and 3-8pm, Sun. 8am-noon. In July and Aug. also Wed. 5-8pm.

Hospital: Hôpital la Villeneuve (tel. 98 96 04 46).

Medical Assistance: Ambulance, 34, bd. de la Gare (tel. 98 39 12 75).

Police: Gendarmerie (tel. 98 96 00 58), on pl. Charles de Gaulle. **Emergency,** tel. 17.

Accommodations and Food

Hôtel-Restaurant Moderne, 22, pl. St-Michel (tel. 98 96 01 32), in the *haute ville*. One-star hotel in a good location. Clean and bright singles and doubles 75-90F, with shower 120F. Showers 10F. Breakfast 20F. Restaurant downstairs has 57F *menu*.

Hôtel-Restaurant de l'Europe, 32, bd. de la Gare (tel. 98 96 00 02). The huge, pale pink façade across from the train station hides red and green hallways; aesthetes beware. Dimly lit rooms 70F, with shower or bath 90F. Doubles 110F. Phone reservations accepted.

Hôtel les Tilleuls, 25, rue du Bourgneuf (tel. 98 96 07 97), near the tourist office in the *basse ville*. Decent rooms. Singles 65F. Doubles 100F. Triples 120F. Breakfast 20F. Workers' restaurant downstairs with a 42F *menu*.

Gîte d'Etape, 10km from Quimperlé in Locunolé. 26F beds. Call M. Primas at 98 71 35 52.

Camping: Camping Municipal de Quimperlé (tel. 98 39 31 30), just out of town on the N165. Two-star site with showers, swimming, and TV. 11F per person, 8.50F per site, 4.50F per car, 3.50F per bike. Electricity 7F. Open June-Sept.

Crêperies and pizzerias are everywhere. Halfway up the crumbling staircase of rue Jacques Cartier is **La Vache Enragée,** 5, rue Jacques Cartier, the ill-natured cousin of *La Vache qui rit* of cheese fame. Tasty 61F *menu*. Open Wed.-Mon. for lunch and dinner; Nov.-May Tues.-Sun. afternoon. **Crêperie Croqu' Odile,** 16, rue l'Hôpital Fremeur, continues the angry animal theme, serving *crêpes* (4-24F), salads (26-39F), omelettes (17-33F), and sandwiches (13-19F). More expensive and interesting is the **Bistro de la Tour,** 2, rue Dom Morice (tel. 98 39 29 58), in the *basse ville*. Don't mistake it for an antique shop. The pricier *à la carte* has more interesting options than the 54F *menu*. There are also two **markets:** one Monday through Saturday 8:30am to 1pm, with fresh fish stinking up the area opposite Eglise Ste-Croix; the other Friday 9am to 6pm and Sunday 9am to noon at pl. St-Michel in the *haute ville*. Grab your supermarket grub at the **Intermarché** on bd. de la Gare. (Open Mon.-Thurs. 9am-12:15pm and 2:15-7pm, Fri.-Sat. 9am-7pm.)

Near Quimperlé: Pont-Aven and Lorient

As you head west toward Quimper, the countryside becomes a colorful mass of yellow flowers. To see how such natural beauty has inspired human talent, visit **Pont-Aven,** Paul Gauguin's residence before he left France for Tahiti and now home to some of the finest art galleries in Brittany and the Trou Mad cookie factory. (Their decorative *galette* tins may be the closest you'll come to owning local art.) The **tourist office,** pl. de l'Hôtel de Ville (tel. 98 06 04 70), suggests mildly distracting walks along the river Aven through the **Bois d'Amour,** subject of many over-rated Impressionist canvases, and on to the 16th-century **Chapelle de Trémalo,** whose somewhat impressive crucifix provoked Gauguin's *Yellow Christ*. (Tourist office open Mon.-Sat. 9am-1pm and 2-7:30pm, Sun. 10:30am-12:30pm and 3-6:30pm; April-June and Sept. Mon.-Sat. 9am-12:30pm and 2-6:30pm, Sun. 10:30am-12:30pm and 3-6:30pm; Nov.-March Mon.-Sat. 9am-12:30pm and 2-6:30pm.) Each year the **Musée Municipal** in the Hôtel de Ville features the works of a contemporary Breton painter or a painter in Gauguin's Pont-Aven group. The museum's permanent collection includes Gauguin's drawings and letters as well as a number of Breton works dating from 1860 to 1940. (Open late March-Dec. 10am-12:30pm and 2-7pm. Admission 18F, 12F Sept.-May.) The town may disappoint those hoping to see an extensive exhibition of Gauguin's paintings: there are a few here, but the great ones are elsewhere. The calvary next to the 15th-century church at **Nizon,** about 1.5km northwest of Pont-Aven, inspired Gauguin's *Green Christ* (now at the Musées Royaux des Beaux Arts in Brussels). The tourist office suggests a scenic bicycle route to Nizon that returns along the rue des Grands Chênes. You can rent **bikes** at the BP service station on rue Emile Bernard (tel. 98 06 02 77). From the bus stop and tourist office, take a right onto rue Emile Bernard and follow it around the bend to the station. (40F per day, 160F per week, deposit 200F or passport. No one-way rentals.)

Despite the number of proverbially starving artists in town, hotel prices are geared to the wallets of the rich. You can easily make Pont-Aven a daytrip. The cheapest place in town, two-star **Ajoncs d'Or,** next to the tourist office at 1, pl. de l'Hôtel de Ville (tel. 98 06 02 06), is not cheap enough (singles and doubles 190F. Breakfast 24F. Open May-Sept). Better ideas include **Chez Pierre,** Ragvénés-Plage in Nevez (tel. 98 06 81 06), about 7km outside of Pont-Aven near the beach. (Singles and doubles from 115F. Breakfast 24F. Open April-Sept.) Ask the English-speaking tourist office about B&B in private homes. They'll let you look through a photo album of places in and around Pont-Aven and then call to see if the one you want is available. Prices run 120-225F. The campground closest to Pont-Aven is **Roz Pin** (tel. 98 06 03 13), a three-star spot five minutes from the beach. Take the rue des Abbés Tanguy to the intersection at Kergoz, take a left (*direction* "Nevez"), and follow the signs. (11F per adult, 5.50F per child, 19F per site, 5.50F per car. Electricity 7F. Open May-Sept.) There are seven other campgrounds in neighboring towns. Ask the tourist office for more information. Cyclists should pedal to the rustic *gîte d'étape* in Riec-sur-Belon (26F per night). Signs to the *gîte* appear on the D783 to Quimperlé. At least six buses run daily to Pont-Aven from the café across from the train station (45F, 15.80F).

Lorient (pop. 125,000), on the coast 40km south of Quimperlé, was founded in the 18th century as the main post of the powerful French East India Company. Named for "l'Orient," the area the company exploited until the British took over, Lorient remains a major fishing port. Although heavy bombing during WWII destroyed most of its historic buildings, the city hauls in 200,000 visitors to its annual **Festival Interceltique.** During the first two weeks in August dancing, music, and films on Celtic tradition from Ireland, Scotland, Wales, and the Isle of Man distracts the city from its preoccupation with the finny tribe. (Tickets 25-100F. Call the tourist office at 97 21 07 89 for information, or call a special information office at 97 21 24 29 or 97 21 20 51. A superb **Auberge de Jeunesse (IYHF)** sits by the ocean at 41, rue Schoelcher (tel. 97 37 11 65), about 3km from the train station. Built into the side of a hill overlooking a lake, this comfortable modern bunker has excellent kitchen facilities, hot showers, and clean rooms. Television, game rooms, a bar, and facilities for disabled travelers are available. The front doors lock at 10pm, but the kitchen door is always left open. (Reception open daily 8:30-10am and 5:30-7:30pm. IYHF card required. 37F per person. Camping 20F. Breakfast 13F. Dinner 38F. Sheets 13F. Closed mid-Dec. to Jan.) Take bus C from the train station (*direction* "Kerroman") every 15 minutes before 8pm (5.80F); get off at the stop marked *Auberge de Jeunesse,* and then follow the signs for 5-10 minutes. Efficient **trains** from Lorient travel to Quimper (20 per day, 45F), Auray (30F), Vannes (40F), and Paris (15 per day, 260F) via Nantes (120F) or Rennes (105F).

Lorient is also the departure point for ferries to **Ile de Groix,** a small, island less popular than Belle-Ile, its closest rival, but no less spectacular. (Four to eight ferries make the round-trip in summer (71F).) Most of the interesting sights can only be reached by foot—the well-marked paths along the coast are generally too narrow and rough for even a mountain bike. The eight km by four km island is small enough to explore in a day, but you'll probably end up wanting to stay longer. The **Ecomu-**

sée de l'Ile de Groix (tel. 97 05 84 60), 50m from the port where the ferry docks, merits a visit for its minutely detailed displays on island history and for its permanent geological, aquatic, and costume exhibits. Maps of 13-14km hikes are available here. (Open 9:30am-12:30pm and 3-7pm, Sept. 9-June 24 Tues.-Sun. 10am-12:30pm and 2-5pm.)

Two km from Port Tudy is an **Auberge de Jeunesse (IYHF)** (tel. 97 05 81 38), a one-time German gun emplacement that makes an excellent base for exploration and a *very* safe place to sleep. From the ferry dock, turn left, follow the signs up the hill, and turn left again. (Office open 8:30-11:30am and 6-11pm. 37F per person. Hot showers 6F. Open May 20-Sept. 20.) A little closer to the port is a less peaceful *gîte d'étape* (tel. 97 05 89 87). Walk left from the port for two minutes; you can't miss it. (26F per night, 6F extra to stay during the day. Showers and kitchen facilities included.) Campers should head for **Camping des Sables Rouge** (tel. 99 64 13 14), a three-star site at Port Coustic, near the Pointe des Chats on the southern tip of the island. (12.50F per person, 16.50F per site, 6F per car. Open April-Sept.) Bike rentals and food supplies are available in Port Tudy and Le Bourg, 1km south. Buy what you need here; civilization ends abruptly after these two towns.

Quiberon and Belle-Ile

Everyone comes to Quiberon (pop. 4860) in summer to find a quiet beach and escape the crowded cities—with the inevitable results. The crowded **Grande Plage** is smooth, sandy, and surprisingly clean, considering its location in the heart of town. To escape the congested port area, head for smaller, rockier **Plage du Goviro** near the campgrounds. From the port, follow bd. Chanard east along the water as it becomes bd. de la Mer and then bd. du Goviro. Back in town, the canneries on quai de l'Océan provide a glimpse of working life on Brittany's southern coast.

To appreciate the true beauty and character of the area, get out of town. Spectacular Belle-Ile is just a ferry ride away, and the craggy Côte Sauvage stretches a wild and windy 10km along the western edge of the Quiberon peninsula. Heed the signs marked "baignades interdites" (swimming forbidden): many have drowned in these tempting but treacherous waters. Cycling is a popular and convenient means of touring both the island and the coast.

Orientation and Practical Information

The Quiberon peninsula lies 140km southeast of Quimperlé and 50km southwest of Auray. The town itself occupies the southern tip of the peninsula. Train service to Quiberon operates only in July and August; the off-season buses, however, are frequent and dependable.

Tourist Office: 7, rue de Verdun (tel. 97 50 07 84). The enthusiastic staff will give you a giant tuna of a brochure with a detailed road map of the southern half of the peninsula. They also suggest cycling tours of the Côte Sauvage and book accommodations for the price of a phone call. English spoken. Open Mon.-Sat. 9am-8pm, Sun. 10am-noon and 5-8pm; Sept.-June Mon.-Sat. 9am-12:30pm and 2-6:30pm.

Currency Exchange: Crédit Mutuel, rue de la Gare, opposite the SNCF station. Open Tues.-Thurs. 8:45am-12:15pm and 1:30-6pm, Fri. 8:45am-12:15pm and 1:30-5pm, Sat. 8:45am-12:15pm and 1:30-4:30pm.

Post Office: pl. de la Duchesse Anne, near the church. **Currency exchange.** Open Mon.-Fri. 9am-7pm, Sat. 9am-noon; Sept.-June Mon.-Fri. 9am-noon and 2-5pm, Sat. 9am-noon. **Postal Code:** 56170.

Trains: (tel. 97 50 07 07), on rue de la Gare. Trains in July and Aug. only. Trains to Plouharnel (near Carnac) are most frequent (10 per day, ½-hr., local service 6F, "express" 11F). All other destinations require a transfer in Auray (6 per day, 40 min., 23F). To: Paris (4 per day, 6-7 hr., 246F); Vannes (4 per day, 1½ hr., 34F); Nantes (4 per day, 2¾ hr., 102F). Open year-round for bus information and **luggage storage** (12F per bag per day) 9am-noon and 2-5:30pm. Tickets sold daily 7am-8pm and 10-10:45pm. Information office open daily 9am-noon and 12:45-6:45pm.

Buses: All buses stop at the train station, Port Maria (the ferry dock), and pl. Hoche. **Transports le Bayon** (in Auray tel. 97 24 26 20). To: Plouharnel (7 per day, ½-hr., 11F); Carnac or Carnac *plage* (6-7 per day, ¾-1¼ hr., 16F); Auray (7 per day; 1½-2 hr.; 31F). To get from Auray to Locmariaquer, take the last bus to Auray (around 5pm) and a bus or taxi from there (1 per day, 1¾-2½ hr.). **TTO** to: Plouharnel (4 per day, ½-1 hr., 13.50F); Carnac or Carnac *plage* (4 per day, ¾-1¼ hr., 16F); Auray (4 per day, 1½-2 hr., 31F); Vannes (4 per day, 2-3 hr., 48F).

Ferries: Compagnie Morbihannaise, Port Maria (Quiberon tel. 97 50 06 90, Belle-Ile tel. 97 31 80 01). To Le Palais on Belle-Ile (July-Aug. 10-12 per day, Sept. 8-10 per day, Oct.-late March 4-6 per day, late March-June 6-10 per day; 45 min.; round-trip 71F; bikes 30F). Information and ticket office open 6am-9pm; Oct. to mid-March 7-11am and 1-8:30pm. The same company also runs the high-speed **Vedettes Gourinis** from Port Maria to Sauzon on Belle-Ile (May-Sept. 3 daily, 25 min., round-trip 82F).

Bike and Moped Rental: Cyclomar, 17, pl. Hoche (tel. 97 50 26 00). Three-speeds 38F per day, 160F per week, deposit 300F. Mopeds 110F per day, 500F per week, deposit 400F. Ten-speeds also available. Open daily July-Aug. 8am-midnight; March-June and Sept.-Dec. 8am-12:30pm and 2-7:30pm. **Cycles Loisirs,** 3, rue du Manémeur (tel. 97 50 10 69), behind the tourist office. Nicer bikes. 46F per day, 150F per week, deposit 400F. Mopeds 110F per day, 500F per week, deposit 500F. Open daily 9am-12:15pm and 2:30-7pm. **Cycles Lenoble,** 4, rue de la Poste (tel. 97 50 18 11). Open 9am-12:30pm and 2-6:30pm.

Medical Assistance: Auray-Hôpital Général le Pratel, 1, rue Docteur Laennec (tel. 97 24 15 51).

Ambulance: 10, rue de la Gare (tel. 97 50 10 52).

Police: av. Général de Gaulle (tel. 97 50 07 39). **Emergency,** tel. 17.

Accommodations, Food, and Entertainment

Quiberon's accommodations are scarce and expensive. Reserve several months in advance for July and August. Camping is a better option, but even the dozens of campgrounds fill up fast. Always call ahead for a bed at the hostel.

Auberge de Jeunesse (IYHF), 45, rue du Roch-Priol (tel. 97 50 15 54), a 15-min. walk from the station. Turn left and out of the station, bear right as the road curves around, then take a left on Rue de Puits. Turn right on bd. Anatole France and left onto rue du Roch-Priol. Small hostel with a raucous, communal atmosphere. Nice kitchen. Reception open 8:30-10am and 6-10pm. No lockout or curfew. IYHF card required. 37F per person, cots in open tent 30F. Camping 15F. Breakfast 13F.

Au Bon Accueil, 6, quai de l'Houat (tel. 97 50 07 92). Don't let the dingy hallways deceive you—the rooms are clean and comfortable. Pension required only for stays over 2 days. Singles and doubles from 95F, with shower 115F. Three beds 220F. Showers 15F. Breakfast 20.50F. Restaurant downstairs has a popular 61F seafood *menu.* Call ahead; almost always booked July-Aug. Open mid-March to mid-Nov.

Hôtel le Guerveur, rue de Pont-Maria (tel. 97 50 15 79). Decent singles and doubles 130-160F. Breakfast 20F.

Le Corsaire, 24, quai de Belle-Ile (tel. 97 50 15 05), at Port Maria. Good location and reasonable rooms. Dried-up pirates haunt the hallway wallpaper. Singles and doubles from 157F. Often full July-Aug. Restaurant below open late March-Oct.

Camping: Most of the campgrounds are located on the east side of the peninsula, where the beaches are broader and more spacious than in Quiberon proper. Most of the nine campgrounds fill in summer. Two-star **Camping du Goviro,** bd. du Goviro (tel. 97 50 13 54), is 50m from the beach. 8F per person, 4.20F per tent, 4F per car. Showers 5F. Right behind is the slightly more spacious **Camping Bois d'Amour** (tel. 97 50 13 52). Two stars, same prices. Open May-Oct.

Even the *crêperies* are overpriced here. Time for "Cooking in Quiberon." In the morning, fishing boats bring their catch to rue de Verdun and sell it right from the basket. Go to quai de l'Océan at any time of the day and see which of the canneries are open—many sell fish to people like you. The carnivalesque **market** in pl. du Varquez, right behind the tourist office, has loads of free samples (Sat. 8am-1pm). Buy groceries at **Super-Rallye supermarket** on rue du Port Haliguen, near the youth hostel; at **Stoc** on rue de Verdun (open Mon.-Sat. 8:45am-12:30pm and 3-7:15pm);

or at **Intermarché** on rue de Port de Pêche. A local specialty is *niniches*, tasty caramel-type candies; look for the signs on the Grande Plage. The **Restaurant La Goursen,** on the quai, usually offers a seafood *plat du jour* (47-62F), but their other dishes exceed the modest budget. Call 97 50 07 94 for reservations on summer weekends. **Le Retro,** on quai de Belle-Ile and the beach, is an upbeat pink place for *crêpes,* if you can still bear to look at them. The prices are a little higher than most *crêperies,* but what a view! (*Crêpes* 12-35F, 40F *menu,* service not included. Open in summer until 11:30pm.)

Even after a day of cycling, swimming, and sunning, Quiberon shows no sign of fatigue. If you still have the energy to stand and sway, check out chic **Excalibur,** 24, rue de Port-Maria (tel. 97 50 07 86). A large video screen playing California surf scenes is the backdrop to this cozy bar with good music, good wine, and good folk. (Open 8am-noon and 5pm-2am.) Afterward try **Le Suroit,** 29, rue de Port-Maria, a disco with a boat for a bar and a striking view. (Open 11pm-4am. Cover 50F, first drink 50F.)

Near Quiberon

The mysterious megalithic stone alignments northeast of the Quiberon peninsula and the ageless natural rock formations on the coast of Belle-Ile, Brittany's largest island, are each only 40 minutes away by boat, train, or bus. Although daytrips are possible, lower prices and greater tranquility recommend a night spent away from Quiberon.

Belle-Ile

At least ten boats depart daily from Quiberon's Port-Maria for **Belle-Ile,** an island off the coast that lives up to its name. The island's own magnificent coast merges high cliffs, small creeks, and crashing seas. Farther inland, thick patches of heather, gorse, and ferns color the fields. The crossing takes 25-45 minutes; you can take a bike with you.

The best way to see the island is by bicycle. Louis Banet (tel. 97 51 50 70) rents sturdy **bikes** for 40F per day, plus a 300F deposit. The garage is on quai Gambetta, just before the bridge to the citadel. (Open daily 9am-12:15pm and 2-7pm.) Three francs nets you a helpful map from the **tourist office** (tel. 97 31 81 93) near the gangplank. (Open Mon.-Sat. 9am-noon and 2:30-7:30pm, Sun. 9am-noon; Sept.-June Mon.-Sat. 9am-noon and 2-6pm, Sun. 9am-noon.) The terrain along the coast is flat enough for easy cycling, but formidable hills plague the inland routes. Watch for "*cyclistes ralentir danger*" (cyclists, slow down, danger) signs that indicate a steep descent. The well-marked trails are safe for prudent cyclists and hikers.

No matter what, get out of **Le Palais,** the island's largest town. Bike or walk 6km to **Sauzon,** a tiny fishing port with picture-book façades. You can even take a rapid **Vedettes Gourinis** boat directly from Quiberon to Sauzon and rent bikes at the port from the mysterious **Claude.** From Sauzon, sally forth another 4km to the **Pointe des Poulains,** at the northernmost tip of the island. This storm-battered spot, surrounded by water and rock, proves that the Apocalypse is at hand.

Four km southwest lies the impressive **Grotte de L'Apothicairerie** on the Côte Sauvage. The grotto took its name from the cormorant nests that once lined the rocks like the bottles in an apothecary's shop. Remember that you are not as invulnerable to these powerful waters as the rocks. Heed the signs warning of mortal danger, and do not follow other hapless, ignorant tourists who are climbing down toward the cave. People die in this grotto, and no apocalyptic apothecary can help them. Seriously.

On a more pleasant note, the nearby deserted fort was home for many years to actress Sarah Bernhardt. Although off-limits to visitors, it is worth a look. From the grotto, follow the D25 south to the rough **Aiguilles de Port-Coton,** which Claude Monet approximated in an 1886 painting, and the nearby **Plage de Port-Donnant,** where waves crash onto the sandy beach between high stone cliffs.

Inexpensive accommodations on the island include two campgrounds, three *gîtes d'étape,* and an **IYHF youth hostel.** The hostel (tel. 97 31 81 33) is located in Le Palais, a 20-minute hike from the port. Turn right from the port and follow the quai to the citadel; cross the bridge and walk up the hill. Here you'll pass popular **Camping Les Glacis** (5.80F per person, 4.50F per tent), which also has **public showers.** (Open Mon.-Sat. 9-11:30am and 5-7:30pm, Sun. 9-11:30am.) Continuing on to the hostel, turn left at the top through a residential area, then right at the *gendarmerie,* and look for signs. Despite its dubious past as military barracks and a juvenile prison, the hostel has comfortable two- and four-bed rooms, plus decent kitchen and bathroom facilities. You can also camp on the lawn. (IYHF card required. Office open 8:30-10am and 6-8pm. 37F per person. Camping 30F. Breakfast 13F. Sheets 13F.) The *gîte d'étape* in **Port Guen** (tel. 97 31 55 88), about 3km south of Le Palais, has 26F beds in a colorful barn and priceless fresh vegetables. The second *gîte* in **Locmaria** (tel. 97 31 70 92), 11km from Le Palais, is neither as pleasant nor as accessible. Heading south on the D25, continue past the sign indicating that you've entered Locmaria and take the first left. Stop at the pink house 1km down the road to pick up the key from the Carios. (Arrive after 6pm. 26F per person. Open March-Nov.) Campers can pitch their tents at the **Trion Guen** farm (tel. 97 31 85 76). A new *gîte* with 100F beds has just been built in Sauzon; call the *mairie* at 97 31 62 79 for more information. Sauzon also has the one-star, portside **Hôtel du Phare** with rooms from 150F. The tourist office in Le Palais has information on B&B in private homes.

La Chaloupe, 8, av. Carnot in Le Palais, has an enormous variety of reasonably priced *crêpes* and *galettes;* **Café de la Cale,** quai Guerveur in Sauzon, prepares delicious seafood and salads (30-50F). While in Sauzon, visit Jean-Marie at **Bleu Marine** on the quai. Tell him Christy says "salut."

Carnac and Auray

Majestic stretches of countryside with great pine forests and open heaths lie northeast of the Quiberon Peninsula. Mesolithic people roamed this area of Brittany as early as 10,000 years ago; their Neolithic heirs settled here between 4800-1700BC, leaving formidable menhirs and dolmens, once incorrectly thought to be the work of druidic wizardry, scattered throughout the area.

Just a few kilometers east of Plouharnel in **Carnac** stand the mysterious **Alignements du Ménec.** Here, more than 1000 menhirs, some over 3m tall, stretch in a line over 2km toward the horizon. The purpose of this 10,000-year-old megalithic arrangement remains an inscrutable mystery. Also in Carnac lies the **Tumulus de St-Michel,** an immense burial chamber within an earthen mound. Be prepared for long lines to get inside the passageways, stripped of most of their original decoration. (Open 10am-6pm. Tour 15 min., 3.75F, students 2F.) Introduce yourself to the history behind the tumulus and other dolmens by visiting the **Musée Miln le Rouzic,** which displays *moulages,* large stones incorporated into dolmen constructions. (Museum open daily 10am-noon and 2-6:30pm; Sept.-June Wed.-Mon. 10am-noon and 2-6:30pm. Admission 16F, students 8.50F.) Ask the **tourist office** in Carnac *ville,* pl. de l'Eglise (tel. 97 52 13 52) for more information on the various prehistoric sites. (Open July-Aug. Mon.-Sat. 9am-1pm and 2-7pm, Sun. 10am-12:30pm and 5-7pm; Sept. Mon.-Sat. 9am-noon and 2-7pm; Easter-June Tues.-Sat. 9am-1pm and 3:30-7pm), or the tourist office on the beach, 74, av. des Druides (same tel.; open Tues.-Sat. 9am-noon and 2-6pm).

To get to Carnac, take the **bus** from Quiberon (at least 7 daily, 16F) or from the Auray SNCF station (17F). You can also take the train to Plouharnel and catch a bus from there. The bus stop *Carnac-ville* puts you close to the museum, a five-minute walk up rue du Tumulus from the Tumulus de St-Michel. The Alignements du Ménec are 10-15 minutes from either the museum or the Tumulus. Go north on rue de Courdriec, rue de Poul Person, or rue des Korrigans until you see the menhirs on route des Alignements.

In Carnac, **Robert Lorcy,** 6, rue de Courdriec (tel. 97 52 09 73), rents **bicycles** for 30F per half-day, 40F per day, or 110F per week, with a 500F or passport deposit. (Open Mon.-Sat. 8:30am-12:30pm and 2-7pm, Sun. 8:30am-12:30pm; Sept.-June Tues.-Sat. and sometimes Sun. 8:30am-12:30pm and 2-7pm.) On the beach, **Agence ABC/Cyclo-Loisirs,** 62, av. des Druides (tel. 97 52 02 33), charges 19-27F per hour, 35-47F per half-day, 50-60F per day. **BMX,** 20, av. des Druides, has comparable prices. All of the above are often short of bikes in July and August.

If you're serious about prehistoric Brittany, you can stay in any one of a dozen campgrounds around Carnac, including three on the route des Alignements. The two-star **Alignements de Kermario** (tel. 97 52 16 57) is across the road from the megaliths. (8.70F per person, 13F per tent, 3.50F per car. Open June-Sept.) **Camping Kerabus** (tel. 97 52 17 89) is about three minutes away from the big old rocks on allée des Alouettes off route d'Auray. (7.50F per person, 5.50F per tent, 4F per car. Hot showers 4F. Open June-Sept. 15.) The tourist office has a complete list of campgrounds. **Hôtel D'Arvor,** 5, rue St-Cornély (tel. 97 52 96 90) has one dim star and singles from 95F, but it could easily be full. (Open March-Nov.) Most other hotels in Carnac are outrageously overpriced. Wander around town a little and look for **"chambres à louer"** (rooms for rent) signs on private houses. More can be found in the nearby village of **La-Trinité-sur-Mer,** which enjoys one of the largest pleasure ports in France and a phenomenal view across the Bay of Quiberon.

Another base for exploring the area's megaliths is **Auray,** a picturesque fishing village with a handful of affordable hotels. The Auray River meanders south from Auray through wooded terrain dotted by châteaux, passing several oyster-fishing villages before finally emptying into the Gulf of Morbihan. Six km north is the village of **Ste-Anne-d'Auray,** which holds one of the largest *pardons* in Brittany on July 26 and 27. (Hotels fill up at this time.) Smaller, less-touristed *pardons* take place beginning in March. **Transports le Bayon** (tel. 97 24 26 20) runs one bus every Monday to Ste-Anne-d'Auray from the Auray train station (15 min.). In Auray, **Hôtel le Moderne,** 20, pl. de la République (tel. 97 24 04 72), is a faded, cavernous place that can't live up to its name; it's agreeable nonetheless. (Singles and doubles for 90-120F. Showers 15F. Breakfast 19F. Open March-Nov. 15.) The **tourist office,** pl. de la République (tel. 97 24 09 75), will gladly help with accommodations. (Open July-Aug. Mon.-Sat. 8:45am-7pm, Sun. 9am-noon; Jan.-June and Sept. Mon.-Fri. 9am-12:30pm and 2-6:15pm, Sat. 9:30am-12:30pm.) The train station, about a 20-minute walk from town, rents **bikes** for 40F per ½-day or 50F per day, plus a 300F deposit. The Quiberon-Auray train runs only in July and August, but frequent buses run year-round. Auray lies on the main Brest-Bordeaux, Brest-Toulouse, and Paris-Quimper train lines.

Vannes

Moving north from Quiberon along the coast, the waters of the Gulf of Morbihan wash into the port of the city of Vannes (pop. 48,550). Most people use Vannes as a base to explore the islands of the Gulf, but the city also has some decent museums and a few interesting shops tucked away in the walled *vieille ville.*

Orientation and Practical Information

The train station lies north of the center of town. Turn right out of the station, follow the road to the bottom of the hill, and turn left on av. Victor Hugo. After several blocks, a right on rue J. le Brix and a left at the *mairie* on rue Thiers will bring you to the post office in pl. de la République (15 min.). From there, the *vieille ville* lies to your left, the tourist office 100m ahead on your right, and the port straight ahead. Alternately, take bus #3 or #7 from the train station to pl. de la République. Between the two you shouldn't have to wait more than 20 minutes (5F; no service Sun.).

Tourist Office: 1, rue Thiers (tel. 97 47 24 34), in a 17th-century house. From the train station, follow the signs to *centre ville* and then to the tourist office. Information on the Gulf of Morbihan, and a booklet with public transport timetables for the area. In July and Aug., 1½-hr.

guided tours of the city (in French) leave twice per day (20F, ages under 25 10F). Open Mon.-Fri. 9am-7pm, Sat. 9am-12:15pm and 2-6:15pm, Sun. 10am-noon; Sept.-June Mon.-Sat. 9am-noon and 2-6pm.

Budget Travel: Dubreuil Voyages, 18, rue Billault (tel. 97 47 41 76). BIJ/Eurotrain tickets. Open Mon.-Sat. 9am-noon and 1:30-6pm.

Currency Exchange: Crédit Agricole, 9, pl. Henri IV (tel. 97 63 35 44). Open Tues.-Fri. 8:30am-5pm, Sat. 8:30am-4pm. On Mon. try the branch at 11, bd. de la Paix. Open Mon.-Fri. 8:30am-12:15pm and 1:45-5:15pm. Commission 20F.

Post Office: pl. de la République, 100m to the right of the tourist office. Label Poste Restante mail "Recette Principale" to direct it here. American Express and Visa checks changed. Open Mon.-Fri. 8am-7pm, Sat. 8am-noon. **Postal Code:** 56000.

Trains: (tel. 97 42 50 50), on av. Favrel et Lincy, north off av. Victor Hugo. To: Paris (8-11 per day, 5 hr., 238F); Rennes (7 per day, 1¼ hr., 76F); Quimper (12 per day, 1¼ hr., 74F); Nantes (9 per day, 1½ hr., 82F). July-Aug. to Plouharnel (near Carnac) and Quiberon via Auray (6 per day; 1½ hr.; to Plouharnel 26F, to Quiberon 33F). Information office open daily 8am-7pm; Sept.-June 8am-noon and 2-6:30pm.

Buses: Transports et Tourisme de l'Ouest (TTO), rue du 116e R.I. (tel. 97 47 29 64). Line 20bis to Muzillac (Mon.-Sat. 2-4 per day, ½-hr., 23F) and Nantes (Mon.-Sat. 1-2 per day, 2¾ hr., 96F). Line 16 to Rennes and points between (Mon.-Fri. 2 per day, 3 hr., to Rennes 83F). Line 23 (4-5 per day) to Carnac (1 hr.; 34F to the *ville*, 36F to the *plage*) and Quiberon (2 hr., 48F). Office open Mon.-Fri. 8am-noon and 1-6:30pm, Sat. 8:30am-noon and 2-6:30pm. Buses stop in front of office; buy tickets on board. **Tourisme Verney/Compagnie des Transports Morbihan** (tel. 97 47 21 64), at pl. de la Gare opposite SNCF station. Line 3 to Pontivy and points between (Mon.-Sat. 2-3 per day, 1½ hr., 38.50F). Line 5 to Muzillac and points between (Mon.-Sat. 2 per day, 1 hr., 21F). Buses stop behind the office and at the *préfecture* in town. Numerous excursions throughout Brittany. Office open for tickets Mon. 8am-noon and 2-6pm, Tues.-Fri. 9am-noon and 2-6:30pm, Sat. 8am-noon. **Transports du Pays de Vannes (TPV)** (tel. 97 47 21 64) runs city buses. Information and schedules at the Tourisme Verney window. Connections to *centre ville,* train station, and nearby suburbs. Basic fare 5F. Central stop at pl. de la République in front of the post office.

Ferries: Take your pick. The most useful is **Vedettes du Golfe,** Gare Maritime (tel. 97 63 79 99), 1½km from town toward Conleau. To Belle-Ile (June-Aug. 1 per day, Sept. Wed. and Sun. 2 per day, Tues. and Sat. 1 per day; Mar. 25-April 16 Wed., Fri., and Sun. 2 per day; Tues., Thurs., and Sat. 1 per day; April 17-May Wed., Sun., and holidays 2 per day. All departures at 7:45, 8:30, or 10am. 140F). Tour of the Gulf of Morbihan, including stop on Ile-aux-Moines (June 15-Sept. 15 4 per day, Sept. 15-30 and late March-May 2 per day, June 1-15 3 per day; 4-9 hr.; 100F). Tour of Gulf and the River Auray, with up to 3 stops, at Ile aux Moines, Bono, and Locmariaquer (June-Sept. 15 4 per day, 6½-9 hr., 120F). Plenty of other services from neighboring ports. **Vedettes Blanches Armor** (tel. 97 57 15 27). From Larmor-Baden to Gavrinis (March-Sept. 25 9-11:30am and 1:30-5:30pm every ½-hr., 20 min., round-trip 20F). Tour of the Gulf of Morbihan including 1½ hr. stop on Ile-aux-Moines all year (at least one per day, 4 hr., 60F). Office open daily 8:30am-noon and 1:15-6pm. J. Pasco's **Vedettes l'Angelus** (tel. 97 57 30 29) leave from Locmariaquer's Port du Guilvin. Tour of Gulf (June-Aug. 4 per day, 40-85F), Belle-Ile (July-Sept. 21 Sun. 1 per day, 2 hr., round-trip 110F). Student discounts. All ferry services request reservations.

Car Rental: Avis, 4, rue Joseph Le Prix (tel. 97 47 54 54) or at **train station.** Opel Corsa 200F per day plus 3.20F per km.

Youth Information: (tel. 97 54 13 72), at the *mairie,* pl. Maurice Marchel. Information on jobs, schools, contraceptives, and vacation logistics; drug counseling. Open Tues. and Thurs.-Fri. 1:30-6pm, Wed. 10am-12:30pm and 1:30-6pm, Sat. 10am-noon.

Laundromat: 5, av. Victor Hugo, opposite the Foyer des Jeunes Travailleuses. Wash 20F, dry 2F per 7 min. 2F and 10F coins. Open daily 7am-9pm.

Pharmacy: Check on any pharmacy door to see which is open late that night.

Hospital: Centre Hospitalier Chubert (tel. 97 42 66 42), on pl. Docteur Grosse.

Police: 13, bd. de la Paix (tel. 97 47 19 20). **Emergency,** tel. 17.

Accommodations and Camping

Hotels in Vannes fill quickly, but student accommodations are never hard to find. The two *foyers* have clean, comfortable, and cheap rooms.

Foyer des Jeunes Travailleuses, 14, av. Victor Hugo (tel. 97 54 33 13). Clean and spacious singles for women, although the friendly staff usually accepts males, too. Register before 10pm. Curfew 1am, weekends 11pm. Keys available. 45F per night. Showers included. Breakfast 10F. Lunch and dinner (Mon.-Fri., Sat. lunch only) 28.50F. Sheets 20F.

Foyer du Jeune Travailleur, 2, rue Paul Signac (tel. 97 63 47 36), 20 min. from the station. Dormitory singles primarily for men, though women occasionally find rooms here. Office open Mon.-Fri. 8am-12:30pm and 2-8pm, Sat. 11am-12:30pm. 45F per person. Showers, breakfast, and sheets included. Dinner 33F.

Hôtel la Chaumière, 12, pl. de la Libération (tel. 97 63 28 51). From the train station, turn right off av. Victor Hugo onto bd. de la Paix and walk 3 blocks. Cheerful, clean rooms with outdoor bathrooms for 85F. The spoiled must shell out 120-130F for indoor bathrooms. Showers 15F. Breakfast 22.50F. Lively bar downstairs. Phone reservations accepted.

Hôtel au Relais Nantais, 38, rue Aristide Briand (tel. 97 47 15 85). From the station head onto rue Olivier de Clisson and turn left on av. St-Symphorien/bd. de la Paix to rue Aristide Briand. Uninspired decor and somber hallways, but centrally located. Clean doubles 105F, with shower 130-140F. Two beds 120-140F. Breakfast 22F. Busy bar downstairs with pool table. Phone reservations accepted.

The Gulf area is crawling with campgrounds, and in summer each and every one is crawling with campers. Nearest to town, **Camping Municipal de Conleau** (tel. 97 63 13 88) is a three-star wooded site near the beach. From the Hôtel de Ville, take blue bus #2 (*direction* "Conleau") and get off at the "Camping" stop. Those coming on foot from pl. Gambetta at the head of the port or rue Thiers should follow rue du Port along the harbor for 3km. (10F per person and per tent. Open March-Oct.) Ask the tourist office about other sites.

Food

Those who feel like doing a bad imitation of Julia Child can pick up supplies at the **Stoc** supermarket on 19, rue du Mené (open Mon.-Sat. 9am-12:30pm and 2:30-7:15pm) or the enormous **open market** that fills pl. Lucien Laroche, pl. du Poids Public, and pl. des Lices (Wed. and Sat. 8am-noon). *Crêperies* line practically every street in the old quarter, but this is one town where you might want to skip the little buggers for the following reasons:

La Paillote, 8, rue des Halles, in the *vieille ville.* A bustling local favorite. Salads 11-36F, Creole dishes 28-45F, big pizzas 26-45F. The 45F "Super Paillote" pizza groans under the weight of mussels, *coquilles St-Jacques,* and cognac. Open Mon.-Fri. noon-2pm and 7-10pm, Sat. 7-10pm.

Chez Carmen, 17, rue Émile Burgault, near the cathedral in the *vieille ville. Couscous* 45-70F; try the lamb varieties. Good *paella* 69F. Open Tues.-Sat. noon-2pm and 7-10pm.

Hôtel-Restaurant le Mirage, 19, rue de la Boucherie. A *restaurant ouvrier* (workers' restaurant), which means cheap, huge meals. 32F buys soup, appetizer, bread, pork and potatoes, noodles, cheese or fruit, and ice cream. 42F gets you a steak as well. Open noon-2pm and 7-8pm.

Cafeteria les Arcades, in the mall facing the *préfecture.* A comfortable and cavernous self-service place with *plats du jour* (20-42F), pizza (18F), steak (22.50F), and desserts (12F). Open Mon.-Fri. 11:30am-2pm and 6:30-10pm, Sat.-Sun. 11:30am-10pm.

Sights and Entertainment

In the center of the old district stands the half-Romanesque, half-Gothic **Cathédrale St-Pierre.** A pretty park next to this confused cathedral contains the remains of the cloister's **arcade.** On the other side, typical medieval Breton houses crowd **rue St-Guénahel,** their overhanging second stories braced by diagonal timbers that rest on sculpted heads (look for #17-19). At the bottom of this street, the heavily fortified and still intimidating 14th- and 15th-century **Porte Prison** gives access to the ramparts (open daily until 7pm), which are illuminated at night in July and August. **Rue St-Vincent** raises eyebrows a millimeter or two with the 18th- and 19th-century houses that accommodated the members of Parliament and their families after Louis XIV exiled the Parliament of Brittany from Rennes to Vannes in 1675. **Porte St-Vincent,** at the end of the street, replaced the fortified medieval gates at one end of the old city in 1704. Those overwhelmed by these obscurely historical structures will find relief in the pleasant, green void of the **Jardin de la Préfecture,** flanked by a river that murmurs in bad French as it rolls by.

The tiny **Musée de Préhistoire** (Museum of Prehistory), 2, rue Noé, has a clever display of artifacts from the megaliths at Carnac and other nearby sites. (Open Mon.-Sat. 9:30am-noon and 2-6pm. Admission 15F, students 10F.) **Musée de la Cohue,** containing both the new **Musée des Beaux Arts** and the **Musée de la Golfe,** is around the corner on rue des Halles, in a beautifully restored 16th-century house. The first has several works by Rodin, but its specialty is art inspired by the Breton landscape and inhabitants. The second has displays on the history of the Gulf of Morbihan. (Open Wed.-Sat. 10am-noon and 2-6pm; July-Aug. daily 10am-noon and 2-6pm; Sept.-May Tues.-Sat. 10am-noon and 2-6pm. Admission to both 12F, students 6F.) Unless you're bored while waiting for a ferry, avoid the overpriced (39F) and much-touted **Aquarium** (tel. 97 40 67 40); a few small tanks of tropical fish make it about as exciting as an elaborate pet shop.

At the end of July or the beginning of August, an annual four-day **Jazz Festival** swings in the Jardins de Limur. (Tickets 50-90F. Student discounts.) For more information, call the Palais des Arts at 97 47 47 30.

Near Vannes: Gulf of Morbihan

Warmed by the Gulf Stream, the waters of the Gulf of Morbihan (Breton for "little sea") nourish 50-odd islands, some no larger than a giant's little toe. **Vedettes du Golfe** (tel. 97 63 79 99) cruises around the gulf (100F) and up the River Auray (an extra 20F). Your ticket allows you to get off at any stop and pick up a later boat (get a timetable). Boats leave four times per day in late June, July, and August, less often in the off-season. The largest island in the gulf, **Ile-aux-Moines,** is a 6km sliver of soothing pine groves and pleasant beaches. Palm trees, mimosa, oranges, and lemons all thrive in this near-tropical microclimate. Anywhere on the island, you're never farther than 450m from the sea. Try to get to the other end of the island, where dolmens, vast heather moors, and deserted little roads compete for attention. Bike rentals on the quay are well worth the price (20F per ½-day); pick up a map at the tourist office (tel. 97 26 32 45). The fishing economy and the dearth of cars attest to the endurance of Breton ways here. The tiny town contains some very typical Morbihan thatched-roof cottages and the ever-present granite church.

Vedettes Vertes also passes, but doesn't stop at, the fascinating **Tumulus de Gavrinis,** an ancient burial mound 100m in circumference, made of stone and covered with earthworks. Archaeologists continue to explore the mound and its artifacts, estimated to be 7000 years old. To reach the tumulus, take a TTO bus from Vannes to Larmor-Baden (Wed. and Sat. 3 per day, ½-hr., 15.50F). From there, **Vedettes Blanches Armors** (tel. 97 57 05 31) runs boats (March-Sept. 25 every ½-hr. 9-11:30am and 1:30-5:30pm, 20 min., round-trip 20F). A stop at **Port Navalo** will put you on the less tourist-infested **Presqu'Ile de Rhuys,** which has a fine campground near the tip of the peninsula: **Camping Municipal de Port Navalo,** right up from the ferry stop.

Across from Port Navalo, **Locmariaquer** remains one of the prettiest villages in Brittany; white houses line the port, and a solitary church steeple breaks the skyline in the distance. Just beyond are the **Grand Menhir** and **Table du Négociant,** the broken remains of a 11,104,000-ounce menhir and a ritual tomb with remains of rare drawings. The Merchant's Table is composed of three huge "tables" suspended on points to form the galleries. The less massive **Dolmen des Pierres-Plats,** 1km out of town in the opposite direction, is not half as spectacular as the beach—on a good day you'll get a wide view of the coast toward Quiberon and Belle-Ile. Several campgrounds accommodate visitors to this mild and breezy land's end. **Vedettes l'Angelus** (tel. 97 57 30 29) sails from Locmariaquer's Port du Guilvin around the gulf (60F), around the gulf and up the River Auray (85F), and to Belle-Ile (round-trip 110F; you get 6½ hr. on the island). A whole fleet of ferries leaves from other ports near Vannes (see Practical Information).

The formation of the gulf makes for unpredictable tides and some of the strongest currents anywhere. If you're experienced and the tide is coming in toward the gulf, the waters of the eastern part may be navigable. Ask at the tourist office about sailing schools that can offer advice.

Nantes

In Nantes, as in so many of France's respectable *grandes villes,* the stately grey buildings have served as the backdrop for events both grisly and grand. Best known as the pulpit from which Henry IV proclaimed religious freedom for Protestants in the 1598 Edict of Nantes, the 15th-century château also imprisoned the infamous Maréchal de Retz, who was executed for sacrificing several hundred children in unspeakable rites and inspired the Bluebeard legends. During the Terror of 1793, Carrier's November *noyades* (drownings) sent hundreds of men and women, bound together in couples, plunging into the Loire. The elegant homes of 18th-century slave traders may smile placidly on the streets where Carrier rounded up these roy-alist rebels from the Vendée, but the somber African *mascarons* (huge stone heads designed to support window arches) recall the horrors that built these elaborate resi-dences.

Nantes is either at the southern tip of Brittany or on the western edge of the Val du Loire, depending on who you ask. (The *Nantais* generally claim the former.) Under the rule of the great Ducs de Montfort, François I and II, Nantes was firmly established as the administrative center of Brittany. But it was also in this city, in 1532, that Brittany was finally ceded to the French crown. Nantes bears much re-semblance to its adopted capital Paris, with wide boulevards marking the bounda-ries between administrative *arrondissements.* Like the capital, Nantes molts in sum-mer when the students leave and the tourists arrive. Stuffed to the gills with historic sights, diverse museums, and nightclubs, Nantes deserves more than a lazy after-noon of sightseeing.

Orientation and Practical Information

Nantes spreads for kilometers on both sides of the Loire with a 40-story sky-scraper, the Tour Bretagne, at its center. The city's major axes are **cours John Ken-nedy,** which becomes **cours Franklin Roosevelt,** running west from the train station, and **cours des 50 Otages,** which runs north to the tower. To get to the center of town and the tourist office, turn left out of the station onto bd. de Stalingrad, which becomes, interestingly enough, cours John Kennedy. Place du Commerce and the tourist office are 1km ahead. The hostel is a 10-minute walk from the station in the other direction.

Tourist Office: (tel. 40 47 04 51), on pl. du Commerce in the 19th-century commerce building, a stone's throw from McDonald's. If you ask nicely, the calm staff may give you a 200-page guide to the city and its architecture for free; otherwise, you get an adequate map/brochure. English spoken. Guided tours of Quartier Feydeau at 10am and Vignoble at 2pm June-Aug. Open Mon.-Fri. 9am-7pm, Sat. 10am-6pm.

Budget Travel: CROUS, 14, rue Santeuil (tel. 40 73 73 84). Information on student travel. BIJ tickets. Many other branches. Open Mon.-Fri. 10am-12:30pm and 1:30-5:30pm. **ABRI,** 7, rue de la Clavurie (tel. 40 20 20 62). Organizes cycling tours of Brittany. Good topographi-cal maps. Ask about the 120 *gîtes d'étape.* Open Tues.-Sat. 9am-12:30pm and 2:30-6pm. **Cen-tre Régional d'Information Jeunesse,** 28, rue du Calvaire (tel. 40 48 68 25). Youth travel information and a babysitting service to boot. Open Mon.-Fri. 10am-1pm and 2-7pm, Sat. 10am-12:30pm and 2-5pm.

Currency Exchange: Crédit Agricole, 2, pl. Ladmirault (tel. 40 73 06 64), and 6, rue de Gorges (tel. 40 89 46 03). Open Sat. until 4pm. Commission 20F. The post office also changes foreign currency for a 1% commission, but they are *slow*.

Post Office: pl. de Bretagne. **Currency exchange.** Open Mon.-Fri. 8am-7pm, Sat. 8am-noon. **Postal Code:** 44000.

Trains: Gare d'Orléans, 27, bd. Stalingrad (tel. 40 50 50 50). To: Paris-Montparnasse (11-14 per day, 3-4 hr., overnight trains 5 hr., 202F); Bordeaux (5-8 per day, 4 hr., 187F); Poitiers (5 per day, with change at Tours, 3-4 hr., 158F; via Cholet, longer trip, 106F); Quimper (7-10 per day, 3½ hr., 138F); Rennes (7 per day, 2 hr., 87F); Quiberon (July-Aug. 4 per day, with change at Auray and sometimes Redon, 2¾ hr., 102F); Angers (5 per day, 45 min., 58F). Also high-speed TGV to Paris (224F, plus 14F reservation). Information office open Mon.-Sat. 8:30am-7pm, Sun. 9:30am-12:45pm and 2:15-7pm.

Buses: TTO, tel. 40 89 27 11. Buses leave from the station on rue de Mayence near Champ de Mars. From the Duchesse-Anne tram stop near the château, take av. Carnot south, turn right on rue Jenmapes, and left onto rue de Mayence (5 min.). Or take city bus #26, 27, 28, or 29 to Champ de Mars. To: La Baule (2 per day, Sun. 1, 2¾ hr., 56F); Rennes (2-3 per day, 2½ hr., 86F); Vannes (Mon.-Sat. 1-2 per day, 2½ hr., 86F). Information office open Mon.-Sat. 8:15am-12:15pm and 3:30-6:30pm. Buy tickets on the bus when office is closed. Buses also stop opposite the branch office, 4, allée Duquesne (tel. 40 20 45 20), parallel to cours des 50 Otages. A host of smaller companies stop at the *gare routière* behind pl. Elisa Mercoeur, near allée Baco. Schedules posted at information office (tel. 40 47 62 70), near the *tabac.* **Cars Brisseau** (tel. 40 48 03 21). Two buses per day to Montaigu (25F) and Les Herbiers (39.50F). **Car Groussin** covers St-Philbert and points between (Mon.-Sat. 2-3 per day, 45 min., 21.50F). Service is more frequent during the school year. Central stop for **city buses** is pl. du Commerce. One ticket buys you unlimited travel on buses and trams for one hour (5.50F).

Taxis: tel. 40 69 22 22 or 40 63 66 66. 24 hrs.

Hitchhiking: Allostop-Provoya, 10, rue Lafayette (tel. 40 89 04 85) at the CRIJ. Give them 3-4 days notice and 60F, and they'll find you a driver entitled to charge you 0.16F per km for gas and tolls. Rides under 200km 20F; 6-month subscription 180F. Open Mon. 2-6pm, Tues.-Fri. 10am-1pm and 2-7pm, Sat. 10am-noon and 2-5pm.

Women's Center: Centre d'Information Féminin et Familial, for counseling, and **Délégation Régionale aux Droits des Femmes,** for crisis intervention. Both at 5, Maurice Duval (tel. 40 48 13 83). Open Mon. 2-5:30pm, Tues. 9:30am-noon and 2-5:30pm, Thurs. 9:30am-5:30pm, Fri. 9:30am-12:30pm and 2-5:30pm.

English Bookstore: Librairie Beaufretow, passage Pommeraye, near the tourist office. Respectable collection of classics and light reading (we sneer) from 49F. Open Tues.-Sun. 9:15am-12:30pm and 2-7pm.

Laundromat: 56, rue Maréchal Joffre, 5 min. from train station. Wash 15F, dry 2F, soap 4F. Open 7am-8pm.

Hospital: Centre Hospitalier Régional (tel. 40 48 33 33), on pl. Alexis Ricordeau.

Medical Assistance: SAMU, tel. 40 48 35 35.

Police: (tel. 40 37 21 21), on pl. Waldeck-Rousseau. **Emergency,** tel. 17.

Accommodations and Camping

Nantes has plenty of cheap hotels, and in summer lots of student dormitory space opens up. Although the hostel operates only in July and August, the *foyers* welcome travelers all year.

Auberge de Jeunesse (IYHF), 2, pl. de la Manufacture (tel. 40 20 57 25). From the station, turn right onto bd. de Stalingrad, left into the Manufacture complex opposite the tram stop, and right to the farthest corner of the complex (10 min.). Or take the tram from the train station to stop "Manufacture" (5.50F). Lots of space, a few 2-bed rooms, primary co′ kitchen, and TV. Warm, English-speaking staff. Office open 7-10am and 6-11pm. N staff if you wish to leave early or stay out late. 38F per person. Breakfast 12F. Sh(Open July-Aug.

Centre Jean Macé, 90, rue du Préfet Bonnefoy (tel. 40 74 55 74), a 15- to 20-min. wa the station. Turn left onto cours John Kennedy (also called bd. de Stalingrad), the at pl. de la Duchesse Anne onto rue Henri IV, which becomes rue Sully. The center is on rue Sully at rue du Préfet Bonnefoy. Alternately, take bus #12 from the SNCF station to pl. Maréchal Foch and continue up rue Sully. Clean if dimly lit rooms. Reception open 8am-8pm. 58F per person for a 2-bed room, 47F for a 3-bed room. Showers included. Breakfast 14F. Plain but filling meals 32F, Sunday meal 34F.

Foyer Nantais de la Jeune Fille, 1, rue du Gigant (tel. 40 73 41 46). From the train station, take the tram to pl. du Commerce, walk up cours des 50 Otages to either stop "St-Nicolas" or "Cathédrale." From there, catch bus #21, 22, or 23, and get off at stop "Edit de Nantes." The foyer is across the street. Both men and women welcome. Office open daily 9am-6pm. Private rooms with showers 52.50F. Lunch or dinner 31.50F.

Foyer des Jeunes Travailleurs, Beaulieu, 9, bd. Vincent Gâche (tel. 40 47 91 64). From the train station, take the tram to pl. du Commerce and, from there, take bus #24 (*direction* "Beaulieu") to Albert (5.50F). Coed bathrooms and 2-bed rooms. Office open 8am-10pm; doors never close (so why do they have locks?). 75.50F, with sleeping bag 70F. Breakfast included. Kitchen facilities and 35F meals. **Annex,** 1, rue Porte Neuve (tel. 40 20 00 80). From the train station, take the tram to pl. du Commerce and catch bus #40, 41, or 36 from across the street on cours des 50 Otages to "pl. Viarme" stop. Reception open 8am-8pm.

Hôtel Roosevelt, 28, rue des Petites Ecuries (tel. 40 47 17 00), 15 min. from the train station. Turn left on cours John Kennedy, right on cours Franklin Roosevelt, and right onto rue des Petites Ecuries. Rooms are small, but management obliging and mattresses firm. Amazing postcard store next door. Singles 75F. Rooms with 2 beds 95F. Showers 11F. Breakfast 15F.

Hôtel Calypso, 16, rue de Strasbourg (tel. 40 47 54 47), off cours John Kennedy. Clean, comfortable rooms with double bed 90F, with shower 105F. Rooms with 2 beds 120F and 155F. Extra bed 10F. Showers 12F. Breakfast 16F.

Hôtel d'Orléans, 12, rue du Marais (tel. 40 47 69 32), off cours des 50 Otages. One-star hotel with nice, spacious rooms. A few rooms 60F, most 85F, with shower 105F, with color TV 85F, with shower and color TV 125F. Showers 16F. Breakfast 16F. Open Aug.-July 23.

Camping: Camping du Val de Cens, 21, bd. du Petit Port (tel. 40 74 47 94), 3km from town. Take bus #42, 43, 54, or 55 from pl. du Commerce to Petit Port. A four-star site with hot water and showers. Wow. 7.80F per person, 12F per site. Open April to mid-Oct. No telephone reservations accepted, so arrive early in the morning in summer.

Food

You won't have trouble finding more than *crêpes* and seafood in Nantes. Lebanese, Italian, Indian, Chinese, and Vietnamese cuisines are there for the taking. Try the specialties of Nantes: its white wines *Muscadet* and *Gros Plant,* and its delicate and delicious white fish, prepared *au beurre blanc* (with butter sauce). **Markets** take place Tuesday through Sunday 9am to 1pm in pl. du Bouffay and at the **Marché de Talensac,** along rue de Bel Air near pl. St-Similien. A Decré **supermarket** is in the basement of Nouvelles Galeries, rue du Moulin, in the *centre ville.* (Open Mon.-Sat. 9am-7pm.)

Chez Rémy-La Brasserie des Sportifs, rue de la Bâclerie, off pl. du Bouffay, which is off cours J. Kennedy. Festive atmosphere, outdoor *terrasse.* Try the mountain of delicious *couscous* for 50-95F. Share a single serving with someone else; it has the same amount of everything but meat. *Paella* for two 160F. Open Tues.-Sat. noon-2pm and 7-11pm.

Crêperie Jaune, 1, rue des Echevins, off pl. du Bouffay. Students pack this casual place. Come early for a seat. The *plat du jour* costs only 38F, but everyone comes for the house specialty, an immense, meaty, double-decker *galette* called *pavé nantais* (37-45F, depending on ingredients). Vegetarian versions available. Open Mon.-Sat. noon-3pm and 7pm-2am.

Friterie de la Gare, 22, bd. Stalingrad, between train station and hostel. A *restaurant ouvrier* (workers' restaurant) in the "grease it, salt it, serve it" tradition. 40F and 45F *menus.* Open Mon.-Fri. noon-2pm and 7:30-10pm, Sat. noon-2pm.

La Mangeoire, 16, rue des Petite Ecuries. A quieter, more elegant place with a 45F *plat du jour.* A beautiful, if not too filling, 58F *menu* of salads, *escargots,* rabbit, chicken, fish, and spiffy desserts. Open Tues.-Sat. noon-2pm and 7-9pm.

Sights and Entertainment

Thanks to their lightweight Vendée stone, the Gothic vaults of **Cathédrale St-Pierre** soar some 37m above worshipers' heads, higher than the arches of Notre Dame in Paris. The original church took over four centuries to build (1434-1893), and its elaborate façade was finally crowned with plain towers in the 1930s. (Cathedral open daily 8:45am-noon and 2-7pm.) Behind the cathedral, on rue Malherbe (off rue Henri IV), **Chapelle de L'Immaculée** has an eerie aerial Virgin for a spire. To the right of the chapel, at 4, rue Malherbe, a smaller iron Virgin prays from a Flamboyant perch.

Built by François II, Nantes's heavily fortified 15th-century **château** (tel. 40 47 18 15) once held Gilles de Rais (Bluebeard), who was convicted of sorcery in 1440. Henri IV signed the Edict of Nantes here in 1598, granting religious freedom to Protestants and unleashing a capitalist frenzy. The best of three museums inside the château, the **Musée des Arts Populaires Régionaux,** gives a close look at traditional Breton costumes and furniture. The **Musée des Arts Décoratifs** sponsors temporary exhibits of the work of international contemporary artists. The **Musée des Salorges** presents Nantes's commercial history since the 18th century. (Château and museums (tel. 40 41 56 56) open Wed.-Mon. 10am-noon and 2-6pm. Entry to the courtyard and ramparts free. Admission to all 3 museums 15F, students 7F, Sun. free. Take Tramway or bus lines #24, 26, 28, or 29 to the "Duchesse Anne" stop.)

Two blocks from the cathedral, at 10, rue Georges Clemenceau, is Nantes's **Musée des Beaux Arts** (tel. 40 41 65 65), which once prompted Henry James to reflect on his peculiar fondness for provincial museums: "The pictures may be bad, but the place is often curious; and, indeed, from bad pictures, in certain moods of the mind, there is a degree of entertainment to be derived." James's assessment notwithstanding, the large collection includes fine canvases by Rubens, Courbet, de la Tour, and a gaggle of contemporary artists. (Open Wed.-Mon. 10am-noon and 1-5:45pm, Sun. 11am-5pm. Admission 5F, students 2.50F, Sun. free. Take bus #11, 12, 21, or 23 to stop "Trébuchet.") The **Musée Thomas Dobrée**, pl. Jean V (tel. 40 89 34 32), contains a library of rare books and manuscripts, including two rooms chronicling Nantes's rapport with China in the early 1800s. (Open Wed.-Mon. 10am-noon and 2-6pm. Admission 7F.) The **Musée Archéologique**, pl. Jean V (tel. 40 69 76 08), displays Neolithic and Merovingian artifacts as well as interesting temporary exhibits. (Open Wed.-Mon. 10am-noon and 2-6pm. Admission 7F. Bus #11; tram stop "Médiathèque.") The **Musée d'Histoire Naturelle**, 12, rue Voltaire (tel. 40 73 30 03), crawls with reptiles and insects from the region. (Open Tues.-Sat. 10am-noon and 2-6pm, Sun. 2-6pm. Admission 5F, students 2.50F. Bus #11, stop "Jean V.") Let your imagination run wild at the innovative **Musée Jules Verne**, 3, rue de l'Hermitage (tel. 40 69 72 52), near the river in pl. M. Schwob, which tries to re-create the world of Captain Nemo and other Verne characters through a collection of the author's novels, letters, and photographs. A *Nantais* born and bred, the 11-year-old Verne made an ill-fated attempt to stow away on a sailing ship before resigning himself to imaginary voyages. (Open Mon. and Wed.-Sat. 10am-noon and 2-5pm, Sun. 2-5pm. Sat.-Sun. free. Bus #21, stop "Garennes.") The nearby **planetarium** at 8, rue des Acadiens (tel. 40 73 99 23), off pl. Moysan, rounds out Nantes's impressive museum collection with galactic vistas. (Showings Tues.-Sat. at 10:30am, 2:15pm and 3:45pm; Sun. at 2:15pm and 3:45pm. Bus #21, stop "Garennes.")

West of the château are a gaggle of elegant buildings dating from the city's period of wealth and expansion in the 18th century. Prosperous sea merchants used the spoils of the slave trade to build lavish houses on **Ile Feydeau**, between allée Turenne and allée Tuouin. In 1938 the city filled in the water and built streets, but the *Nantais* say Feydeau is "toujours une île" (always an island). Walk down **rue Kervegan** for the best view. Even more stately 18th-century **place Royale** and **rue Crébillon** lead to **place Graslin**. Locals have so perfected the art of loafing, lounging, and lingering here that the verb "crébilloner" has entered their vocabulary. Off this street, poke around the **Passage Pommeraye**, a 19th-century gallery in iron and glass, executed with typical Victorian fussiness. The wealthy (or temporarily wealthy) can quench their thirst at **Cigale,** a belle-époque café that once hosted Sarah Bernhardt and other regulars from the nearby Théâtre Graslin.

Often overlooked, Le Corbusier's **Cité Radieuse** is a place of pilgrimage for architecture and Corbu buffs. Take bus #31 from the "Commerce" stop on cours Franklin Roosevelt.

The students at **Université de Nantes** do their share for the Breton regionalist movement, but they seem largely intent on continuing the city's strong cosmopolitan tradition. Fine bookstores cluster near pl. St-Pierre. Although university buildings are scattered through the city, the area north of rue Crébillon is most popular in the evening, and rue Scribe has an array of late-night bars and cafés. Every evening at 10, a live jazz ensemble tunes up at **The Tie Break Club,** 1, rue des Petites Ecuries. (Open Mon.-Sat. 10pm-3:30am.) Dance to the music of Africa and the Antilles at **Le Samba,** 8, rue Fouré (tel. 40 20 09 32), off the Champ de Mars. The tourist office has a long, complete list of Nantes's discos and piano bars.

During the first two weeks of July, Nantes hosts the annual **Les Fêtes de l'Eté,** a harmonic convergence of more than 1000 dance, music, and theater groups. (Tickets 30-120F, festival pass 240F.) For information and reservations, contact the Office du Tourisme de Nantes, pl. du Commerce, 44000 Nantes (tel. 40 47 04 51).

Near Nantes: La Baule and Pornic

La Baule ("La Belle") boasts that it has the most beautiful beach in Europe, and it may well be true. One smooth curve of sand stretches for kilometers along the coast, gently lapped by the warm Atlantic. Unsurprisingly, like Pornic to the south, La Baule is densely populated in summer and always expensive. **Trains** connect Nantes to La Baule (1 hr., 52F). Buses from Nantes (change at St-Nazaire) are half as fast and more expensive. There are two train stations: La Baule-les-Pins, east of the center in a quiet area close to camping, and La Baule-Escoublac, close to the busy center. From this station, take av. Serbie to av. Georges Clemenceau, and turn right to reach the **tourist office** (tel. 40 24 34 44; open daily 9am-7:30pm; Sept.-June Mon.-Sat. 9am-12:30pm and 2:15-6:30pm). From here, av. du Général de Gaulle runs to the beach.

La Baule has very few inexpensive hotels that don't require pension. Try to book in advance. The **Almanzor,** 17, av. des Pétrels (tel. 40 60 28 93), near pl. de la Victoire, is a small hotel with clean and attractive rooms. (Singles and doubles from 105F, with shower 130F. Extra bed 20F. No hall shower. Breakfast 18F. Open March-Nov.) The **Violetta,** 44, av. Georges Clemenceau (tel. 40 60 32 16), close to the station, is neither as clean nor as attractive. (Singles 75F. Doubles 120F, with wash basin 90-135F. Showers 20F. Breakfast 16F.) **Camping Municipal** (tel. 40 60 17 40 or 40 60 11 48) at av. P. Minot is a three-star site. (48.50F per 2 people and tent, 11F per additional person. Open March 25-Sept. 30.) Six km from St-Nazaire and approximately 12km from La Baule, a peaceful *gîte d'étape* occupies a dusty old stone farmhouse with two fireplaces and a complete kitchen. 26F includes hot showers. Call 40 22 56 76 or 40 66 05 66 for directions. A large and lively **market** fills av. Marché at av. des Pétrels in the afternoon. **La Bôle,** 36, av. de Gaulle, is a typical *crêperie* down the street from the tourist office with typical *crêpe* prices. Otherwise, count on spending a lot of money for food.

The **Côte de Jade,** a sunny crescent of rocky coast curving south from the mouth of the Loire through **Pornic,** boasts the breakers, the beaches, and even the menhirs you'd expect from the rest of Brittany, but all an easy one-hour train ride from Nantes. Trains run from Nantes to Pornic on their way to St-Gilles-Croix-de-Vie (4-6 per day, 45F). Make this a daytrip; after 24 hours the souvenir shops selling Donald Duck inner tubes provoke violent thoughts. Cycles Becquet at 24, rue de la Maine (tel. 40 82 26 80), rents **bikes** for 30F per day with a 250F deposit. (Open Mon.-Sat. 8:30am-12:30pm and 2:30-6:30pm.)

The **tourist office** in pl. de Môle (tel. 40 82 04 40) is a five-minute walk from the station in a pavilion on the harbor. From the station, go right, head across the canal, and turn left on quai Leray. The friendly staff will give you a streamer trunk full of pamphlets and suggest walks, but they aren't much help with accommodations. (Open Mon.-Sat. 9am-12:30pm and 2-6pm, Sun. 9:30am-12:30pm.) The few moderate hotels are packed for the season. **Relais St-Gilles,** 7, rue Fernand de Mun (tel. 40 82 02 25), has rooms with a double bed and wash cabinet for 111F. (Showers 14F. Breakfast 16F.) Ask at the tourist office about *chambres meublées,* boarding-house rooms for one or two people (70-100F). Food in Pornic is mostly *crêpes.* **La Sarrasine,** 28, rue des Sables, behind the casino, is better than most and also serves seafood. (Open Mon.-Sat. noon-2pm and 7-9pm.)

The quick and canny, jaded by the not-too-spectacular city of Pornic, will head in droves for one of the beaches west of town. As you follow them, notice the 9th-century château, restored in 1830. It's just a prop for the harbor—you can't go in. A promenade on the townward side of the new harbor, **Port de Plaisance,** was a favorite of Flaubert and Michelet. Rising on the high ground behind the castle, the megalithic stones, known as the **Mousseaux,** are a bit disappointing for Brittany but not bad for a stroll within city limits. More magnificent ocean views and less crowded beaches—**Grandes Vallées, Sablons, Porteau,** and **Gordière**—await along the coast toward Ste-Marie.

Loire Valley (Val du Loire)

Once a trade route but now unnavigable due to accumulated sand, the Loire shares its fertile valley, vineyards, history, and châteaux with less well-known rivers, including the Indre, the Cher, the Vienne, and the Maine. The fabled châteaux of the Loire Valley can be anything from grim medieval military ruins to elegant country mansions. Although most were built in the 16th and 17th centuries, when French monarchs forsook Paris and ruled from the countryside around Tours, some structures remain from the days before the region belonged to the French crown. Henry II and Richard Cœur de Lion mobilized two of the oldest communities, Chinon and Beaugency, to defend the region from the Capetian monarchs in the 11th century. The English and French squabbled over the Loire until Joan of Arc helped win it for the French during the Hundred Years' War. During the Renaissance, the French monarchy consolidated the region through both martial and marital activity. Under the Valois kings, a united France reveled in a period of unparalleled prosperity, and the nobility transformed functional fortresses into splendid country estates. Strongholds sprouted more decorative features and began to accumulate works of the Italian masters. Some of the finest châteaux, notably Blois and Chambord, were built in this era of court scandals and infamous mistresses. One such mistress, Diane de Poitiers, directed the construction of the magnificent Chenonceau.

The valley today mingles thriving vineyards, industrial complexes, sedate villages, and two nuclear power plants. In the last century, many renovated châteaux have opened their doors to the public. Chambord, Chaumont, and Cheverny are notable for their interiors; others, especially Azay-le-Rideau and Chenonceau, rest in sigh-inspiring settings. Only ruins of Chinon and Saumur remain, but their delightful towns recommend them. Standing firm at the western end of the valley, stout Angers guards many celebrated tapestries.

Although even the cuisine of royal chefs remained quite crude until the late 18th century, the rich regional specialties served by modern *cuisiniers Loirois* would have done justice to the châteaux's ornate dining rooms. Specialties include *rillettes* (a cold minced pork *pâté*), *fromage de chèvre* (goat cheese), and the creamy, sweet Port Salut cheese. After a long day of biking, sit down to veal *escalope, coq au vin, champignons* (mushrooms) marinated in wine, and *asperges* (asparagus) steeped in butter. The Loire is most famous for its light white wines, such as *muscadets,* Touraine, Montlouis, and Vouvray, and its fragrant reds Chinon, St-Nicolas-de-Bourgueil, and Saumur. Nearly every town has a local wine worth sampling. On rural roads, look for signs marked *cave/dégustation,* which indicate tours and free samples.

There are many ways *not* to explore this region. Blindly taking three-châteaux blitz bus tours from Tours or Orléans will make you yawn from boredom and exhaustion. The excellent hostels in Blois, Chinon, and Saumur are comfortable bases, but they pose daunting logistical challenges to those without their own wheels. Public transportation routes fan out of the larger cities, and infrequent service can leave you stranded. Trains don't reach many châteaux, and when they do, they are scheduled at inconvenient hours. The city of Tours (connected by rail to 12 châteaux) is best if you plan to travel only by train. Every train station distributes the useful booklets *Les Châteaux de la Loire en Train Eté '91,* and *Châteaux pour Train et Vélo* with train schedules, distances, and information on SNCF bike and car rental. Buses are not much better. Ussé, Villandry, and Chambord can be reached only by bicycle, car, tour bus, or bus circuits that require the purchase of half-day or all-day passes. At least five or six days should be set aside for a train tour of the major châteaux. Generally, a group of four renting a car can beat tour bus prices. Bikes, without doubt, are most suited to this flat, fertile region. Distances between châteaux and hostels tend to be short, and many small roads cut through fields of brilliant sunflowers. Rental bikes are available in almost any Loire town; if you rent from the Tours, Langeais, Amboise, Chinon, Loches, Onzain, Blois, or Vendôme train stations, you can return them to any other station on this list. Think about buying or renting *panniers* or *sacoches* (saddle bags) and leaving your backpack and other luggage in a locker. Those spending more than a day in the saddle should definitely pick up Michelin's road map of the region. Its meticulous detail will help you escape the truck-infested highways and steer you onto delightful meandering routes. Even hardcore Eurailpass users should consider biking to the least accessible châteaux. Hitchhikers find the less-traveled routes hard going; don't expect quick lifts since many of the cars traveling between châteaux are already overstuffed with families and luggage. Whatever the form of locomotion, take it slowly: one or two châteaux per day is a healthy dose.

In 1952 at Chambord, M.P. Robert-Houdin gave the first *son et lumière* show, a bombastic, melodramatic history lesson accompanied by darting floodlights. Although potentially a tiresome form of torture, *son et lumière* shows, including the original, often scintillate with wit, anecdotes, and impressive illumination. The best of the bunch takes place at Château Le Lude, which coordinates a water, fireworks, and costume spectacle worthy of Cecil B. DeMille. (Mid-June to Aug. Fri.-Sat. nights at 10 or 10:30pm. Admission 60-80F. English translation available. For more information call 43 94 62 20 or write Spectacle du Lude, B.P. 35, 72800 Le Lude.)

Orléans

In 1429 Joan of Arc went to battle to liberate Orléans, then the most important city in France after Paris. Mounted on a white steed, she rode into the besieged city, declaring herself its God-given savior. Inspired by this miracle, the Orléannais surged forward to dispel the disheartened English invaders. Whether Joan would do the same for the modern city is anybody's guess. Although the old city's Renaissance buildings survived devastating bombings in 1940 and the new city has maintained a clean, fresh façade despite the industrial onslaught, Orléans itself does not merit an extended visit. The many supermarkets, laundromats, and an American Express office make it an ideal place to stop en route to château country. Those exploring the upper part of the Loire countryside, the Loiret, may decide to base themselves in one of Orléans's many affordable hostels.

Orientation and Practical Information

The train station, the bus station, the tourist office, and most of the inexpensive hotels lie on the north side of the old city above the Loire. To reach the main square, **place du Martroi,** cross the large intersection at pl. Albert 1er and follow rue de la République for five minutes. To the south, the streets between pl. du Martroi and the Loire are lined with shops and cafés. One block south of the square, **rue Jeanne d'Arc** runs east-west between the cathedral and the museum. The restaurant-rich pedestrian area of **rue de Bourgogne** lies one block south of rue Jeanne d'Arc and one block north of the river. Across the Loire is the university and the Parc Floral, easily accessible by bus "S."

Tourist Office: (tel. 38 53 05 95), on pl. Albert 1er next to the new shopping center connected to the train station. Energetic staff will book hotel rooms (6F, outside of Orléans 22F, 50% deposit required for both) and load you with brochures. English spoken. A walking tour in French leaves from the office July-Aug. Wed. and Sat. at 2:30pm (32F, students 16F). Cassettes detailing a walking tour are available for rent in English (37F, deposit 250F). Open daily 9am-7pm; Sept.-June Mon.-Sat. 9am-7pm.

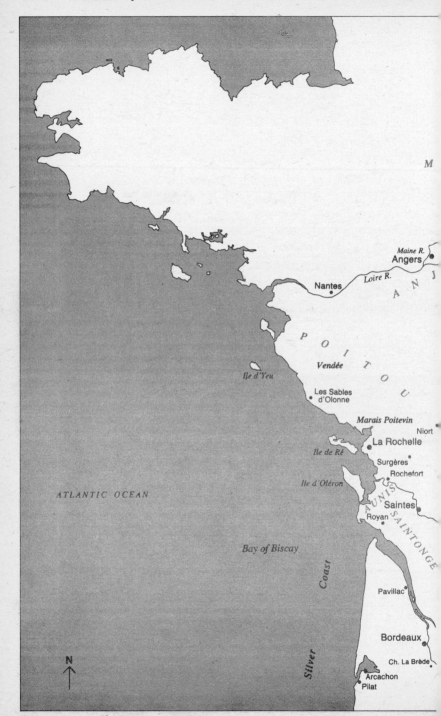

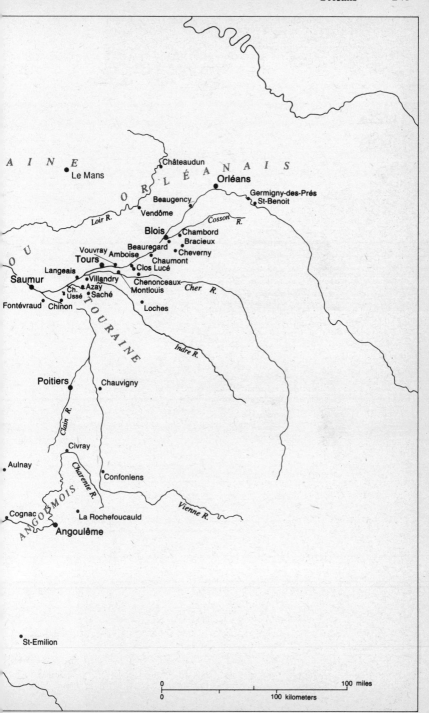

A I N E

Le Mans

Châteaudun

O R L É A N A I S

Orléans

Germigny-des-Prés
St-Benoit

Beaugency

Vendôme

Loir R.

Cosson R.

Blois

Chambord
Bracieux

Beauregard

Vouvray   Cheverny
Amboise
Tours   Chaumont
Clos Lucé

Langeais

Saumur   Villandry
Ch. Azay   Chenonceaux
Ussé Saché   Montlouis   *Cher R.*

Fontévraud   Chinon

Loches

O U

T O U R A I N E

Indre R.

Poitiers   Chauvigny

Clain R.

Civray

Aulnay

Charente R.   Confolens

A N G O U M O I S   *Vienne R.*

Cognac   La Rochefoucauld

Angoulême

St-Emilion

0   100 miles
0   100 kilometers

Budget Travel: Arlina Voyages, 116, rue Faubourg Bannier (tel. 38 62 13 49). BIJ tickets. Also flights to cities on 5 continents. Open Mon. 2-7pm, Tues.-Sat. 9am-noon and 2-7pm.

Currency Exchange: Crédit Lyonnais, 7, pl. du Martroi (tel. 38 75 63 33). Open Tues.-Fri. 8:25am-12:15pm, 1:25-5pm, Sat. until 4pm.All banks in Orléans close Mon., but you can change money at the main post office, its branch office, or American Express.

American Express: 12, pl. du Martroi (tel. 38 53 15 16), 5 min. from the train station along rue de la République. Changes most traveler's checks and Amex checks commission-free at an unexceptional rate. Open Mon.-Fri. 9am-12:30pm and 1:45-6pm.

Post Office: pl. du Général de Gaulle (tel. 38 41 35 14). Open Mon.-Fri. 8am-7pm, Sat.-Sun. 8am-noon. Branch office next to the train station with same hours. **Postal code:** 45000.

Trains: pl. Albert 1er (tel. 38 53 50 50). To: Paris-Austerlitz (25 per day, 1¼ hr., 75F); Tours (15 per day, 1¼ hr., 72F); Blois (10 per day, ½-hr., 41F); Amboise (5 per day, ¾-hr., 60F). Connections from Tours to Poitiers (121F) and Bordeaux (221F). Information office open Mon.-Fri. 8am-8pm, Sat. 8:30am-8pm, Sun. 9am-noon and 2-6:30pm. Ticket booths open 4am-1am.

Buses: Halte Routière, 300m behind the train station. The starting point for most local routes serviced by **SEMTAO.** For schedules and information try the booth here (open Mon.-Sat. 8:30am-12:30pm and 3-6:30pm) or on pl. du Martroi (open Mon.-Sat. 9am-12:30pm and 2:30-6pm). Operates every 15 min. 5:30am-9pm. The "S"-line, which goes from pl. Albert 1er to the university and beyond to Parc Floral and the Loire, operates until midnight. SEMTAO runs a 45-min. minitrain tour of Orléans in French or English June-Sept. 9 daily at 3, 4, and 5pm (25F, ages 14 and under 5F). Also night tours July-Aug. Tues., Fri., Sat. at 9pm. For information, visit or call the tourist office. Individual bus tickets 7F, *carnet* of 10 50F. Ticket is good for corresponding bus lines up to 1 hr. after initial use. **Les Rapides du Val de Loire,** av. du Münster (tel. 38 53 94 75), a block away from the train station. Follow the signs that read *gare routière.* To: Beaugency (11 per day, ½-1 hr., 25F); St-Benoit-sur-Loire (5 per day, 1 hr., 30F); Germigny-des-Prés (5 per day, 1 hr., 27F); Châteauneuf-sur-Loire (11 per day, ¾-hr., 25F); Blois via Beaugency (4 per day, 1½ hr., 40F); Chartres (4 per day, 1½ hr., 60F); Sully (5 per day, 1 hr., 36F). Information office open Mon.-Sat. 6:30am-12:20pm and 3:40-7:20pm.

Taxis: Taxi Radio Orléans (tel. 38 53 11 11), at pl. Albert 1er. 24 hrs.

Bike Rental: The best deal of all is at the **IYHF hostel,** which charges 37F per day (until 10pm) with a passport as deposit. **Societé Alexis,** 14, rue des Carmes (tel. 38 62 63 50). 50F per day, deposit 300F. Open Tues.-Sat. 8:30am-noon and 2-7pm. Also at the **train station.** 40F per ½-day, 50F per day, deposit 500F.

English Bookstore: La Foire Aux Images, 200, rue Bourgogne (tel. 38 62 26 40). A few shelves of cheap, used classics. Open Tues.-Sat. 10am-12:30pm and 2:30-7pm.

Laundromat: Lav Club, 113, rue Faubourg Bannier, around the corner from Hôtel Coligny and 15 min. from the station. Wash 17F per 6kg, dry 4F per 15 min. Open daily 7:30am-10pm.

Crisis Line: SOS Amitiés, tel. 38 62 22 22. A friendly voice.

Hospital: Centre Hospitalier Régional, 1, rue Porte Madeleine (tel. 38 51 44 44).

Medical Emergency: SAMU, tel. 38 63 33 33.

Police: 63, rue du Faubourg St-Jean (tel. 38 81 63 00; reception tel. 38 81 63 63). **Emergency,** tel. 17.

Accommodations and Camping

Several superb, inexpensive hotels cluster near rue Faubourg Bannier, north of pl. Gambetta. The comfortable youth hostel is not far from the center of town. Rooms fill by early evening, so schedule your arrival carefully or call ahead; three days notice is enough for most hotels. A deposit is unnecessary.

Auberge de Jeunesse (IYHF), 14, rue du Faubourg Madeleine (tel. 38 62 45 75), on the west side of town. Take bus B (*direction* "Paul-Bert") from in front of the train station (7F, until 8:20pm). If on foot, turn right outside the station onto pl. Gambetta. Follow bd. Rocheplate, which becomes bd. Jean Jaurès, and turn right onto rue du Faubourg Madeleine. The hostel will be on your right (15 min.). Surprisingly serene, given its proximity to the city. Two birds, a dog, excellent kitchen facilities and *sympa* native Orléannais managers with advice on everything from florists to bike routes. Office open daily 7-9:30am and 5:30-10pm; in winter Sun.-Fri. only. Lockout 9:30am-5:30pm. Curfew 10:30pm; keys available. 34F per person. IYHF card required. Sheets 11F. Bike rental 37F per day, deposit 300F or a vital document. Open Feb.-Nov.

CROUS, 17, av. Dauphine (tel. 38 63 68 57), in Les Hêtres. Take bus S from pl. du Martroi or from the front of the train station to La Source-Université (7F). Students 45F per person. Sheets 15F. Open late June-Sept.

Hôtel Coligny, 80, rue de la Gare (tel. 38 53 61 60), on the continuation of bd. Châteaudun north of the city center. From the station, take av. de Paris to rue de la Gare. A little dark but well-kept. Singles 85F, with shower 95F. Doubles 90-105F, with shower 120F. Showers 8F. Breakfast 15F.

Hôtel Touring, 142, bd. de Châteaudun (tel. 38 53 10 51), northwest of town. A little farther out than Coligny. Walk or take bus A (not the "Olivet" bus) to rue Trannier at rue Châteaudun. Clean and comfortable with welcoming owner. Singles 78F, with shower 99F. Doubles 95F, with shower 120F. Triples 115F, with shower 165F. Showers 18F. Breakfast 18F. Call 3-4 days in advance for a weeknight.

Hôtel de Paris, 29, rue Faubourg Bannier (tel. 38 53 39 58), a 3-min. walk across pl. Gambetta from the train station. Pretty pastel rooms. Proprietor likes to speak English. A good bet if you arrive in town exhausted. Singles 90F, with shower 105F. Doubles 105F, with shower 120F. Showers 10F. Breakfast 18F.

Camping: Camping Municipal Olivet (tel. 38 63 53 94), on rue du Pont-Bouchet. The closest. Take bus N, O, or S to Aumône. A 2-star site. Open June-Oct. 15. **St-Jean-de-la-Ruelle** (tel. 38 88 39 39 or 38 43 00 44), on rue de la Roche. A 2-star site. Take bus B from pl. Albert 1er to the Roche aux Fées stop. Open June-Nov. **La Chapelle-St-Mesmin** (tel. 38 43 60 46), on rue des Grèves. The municipal campsite of the châteaux. Take bus D and ask for the campground stop on the riverbank. Open June-Nov.

Food

Orléans's cheese is *frimault cendré,* a savory relative of *camembert.* Wash it down with the local *Gris Meunier* wine, available at any local shop, the Monoprix on rue Jeanne-d'Arc, or the one at 47, Faubourg Bannier (open Mon.-Sat. 8:30am-7pm). Inexpensive Chinese, Lebanese, Greek, Indian, Pakistani, and Moroccan restaurants jockey for customers on rue de Bourgogne. You'll also find most of Orléans's clubs and discos here. A permanent market thrives at **Les Halles Châtelet,** on the way to the river. (Open Tues.-Sat. 7:30am-7pm, Sun. 7:30am-12:30pm.) Another market changes location daily. Check at the tourist office.

Le Picotin, 1, rue Pothier, in the shadow of the cathedral. High-quality *crêperie* with reasonable prices. *Crêpes* from 16F, *galettes* from 22F, big mixed salad 26F. Open Mon. 7-10pm, Tues.-Sat. noon-2pm and 7-10pm.

Le Viking, 237, rue du Bourgogne, down the street from the above. Roister in the bowels of Leif Eriksson's ship. Delicious *gratin* dishes for 20-26F and a 39F *menu* (not available Sat. night) that includes *crudités,* dinner *crêpe,* drink, and dessert. Open Tues.-Sat. noon-2pm and 7-11pm, Sun. 7-11pm.

Le K. T. Self, 13, rue des Pastoureaux, right off rue Jeanne d'Arc before the cathedral. Cafeteria packed with locals at lunchtime. Charo ate here. Tasty, generous portions at unbeatable prices. Steak, sausage, or *plat du jour* 25-30F. Salad 13F. Desserts 10F. Open Mon.-Sat. 11:30am-1:15pm.

Fleurs d'Asie, 154, rue de Bourgogne. The most varied *menu* among those offered by a string of Vietnamese and Chinese restaurants. Excellent cuttlefish. Fish sautéed in coconut milk 30F. 42F *menu,* service and drink not included. No *menu* Sat. night. Open Wed.-Mon. noon-2pm and 7-10:30pm, Tues. 7-10:30pm.

Sights

The tourist office's fine walking tours include places you would not otherwise get to see, such as the 15th-century crypt of **Eglise St-Aignan.** (July-Aug. Wed. and Sat. 2:30pm, 32F, students 16F.) If you decide to explore on your own, stroll through the Renaissance back streets to see Orléans's contribution to France's unanimous tribute to Joan of Arc: **Cathédrale Ste-Croix,** which features a Joan of Arc chapel and a series of stained-glass windows depicting the life of this homegrown hero. Badly damaged by the Huguenots in 1568, the cavernous cathedral was rebuilt in Gothic style. (Open daily 9am-noon and 2-6pm.) The remains of the church's 4th-, 8th-, and 11th-century incarnations include fragments of a Carolingian floor mosaic (the only one in France) and a 4th-century Roman baptismal font (admission 8F.) The older man who guides visitors is a riot—but only if you understand French. English descriptions are available for the subterranean excavations.

The **Maison de Jeanne d'Arc,** 3, pl. de Gaulle, off pl. du Martroi, celebrates the shepherdess's contribution to Orléans and France. Joan of Arc stayed on the site in 1429, and the house was lovingly reconstructed after the 1940 bombing. The period costumes on display and the audio-visual re-creation (in English upon request) of the siege of Orléans are well worth the admission price. (Open Tues.-Sun. 10am-noon and 2-6pm; Nov.-April Tues.-Sun. 2-6pm. Admission 8F, students 4F, under 13 free.) The nearby **Centre Jeanne d'Arc,** upstairs at 24, rue Jeanne d'Arc (tel. 38 42 22 69), has mountains of documents on Orléans's savior. The accommodating staff shows movies about Joan for free, including the Ingrid Bergman version; Call ahead to arrange a screening time. (Open Mon.-Thurs. 9am-12pm and 2-5:30pm, Fri. 9am-12pm and 2-4:15pm.) On May 7 and 8, the town stages a tremendous festival honoring Joan of Arc, who delivered Orléans from the hands of the English on May 7, 1429. Street musicians, flower sellers, a big parade, fireworks, and more of those darn mimes all contribute to the revelry.

The 16th-century **Hôtel Groslot d'Orléans,** now the town hall, opens its sumptuously decorated rooms and delicate garden to the public as long as no one's getting married inside. (Open Sun.-Fri. 10am-noon and 2-5pm. Free.)

Next to the *cité universitaire* and the new high-rise city of Orléans-la-Source, the **Parc Floral** cultivates extensive fields of purple and white irises and a few tulip beds in the spring. The park surrounds one source of the Loire River, a branch of which flows past haughty pink flamingos to the village of Olivet, a few kilometers to the west. (Parc Floral open 9am-7pm, admission 16F, students 8F; Nov.-March 2-5pm, admission 8F.) Take bus S from pl. Albert 1*er* in Orléans (6.50F; last bus back to Orléans at 11:45pm).

Near Orléans

Beaugency, 30km southwest of Orléans, treats daytrippers to picturesque riverside scenery. The shades of 12th-century Beaugency, which was badly damaged during the Wars of Religion, are thickest around pl. Dunois. Although not very interesting in itself, **Château Dunois** houses an appealing jumble of local lacework, costumes, furniture, and children's games more formally known as the **Musée Régional de l'Orléannais.** (Open Wed.-Mon. 10am-noon and 2-4pm; June-Nov. until 6pm. Admission 15F, students 10F.) On pl. Dunois, 12th-century **Eglise Notre-Dame** is noteworthy for its gently sloping Romanesque architecture. You may need to wear earplugs while wandering; every street corner has a speaker that spews forth a bewildering range of American music on weekends.

The **tourist office,** 28, pl. du Martroi (tel. 38 44 54 42), distributes information on the surrounding region. (Open Mon.-Sat. 9am-12:30pm and 2-7pm, Sun. 9:30am-12:30pm.) The **IYHF hostel** 3km out of town on route de Châteaudun (tel. 38 44 61 31), draws crowds all summer; call ahead. (37F per night. IYHF card required. Breakfast 13F. Brunch and dinner 37F. Office open March-Dec. 8:15-9:30am and 5-9pm.) The cheapest hotel in town is the pleasant **Hôtel des Vieux Fossés,** 4, rue des Vieux Fossés (tel. 38 44 51 65). Campers can pitch their tents on the bank of the river April through November (tel. 38 44 50 39). The tiny, subterranean **Crêperie de la Tour,** 26, rue de la Cordonnerie (tel. 38 44 83 93), serves a 38F lunch *menu.* (Open Tues.-Sun. noon-2pm and 7pm-midnight.) Frequent trains connect Beaugency with Blois and Orléans; eleven daily buses make the trip to and from Orléans. Fares run 25-30F. Cyclists making the comfortable ride from Orléans must endure only a few short highway stretches. The train station rents **bikes** (50F per day, deposit 500F).

About 35km southeast of Orléans stands **St-Benoît-sur-Loire,** an ancient Benedictine monastery and basilica. The tranquility of this cloistered church may tempt you to join the order. Vespers are sung in Gregorian chant Monday to Friday at noon. One of the purest examples of Romanesque architecture in France, the open tower has columns decorated with scenes from the Book of Revelation. The nearby **Hôtel de la Madeleine** (tel. 38 35 71 15), 65, rue Orléannaise, has rooms from 75F. Le Port (tel. 38 35 70 92), the municipal **campground,** is close to town and open April through November.

The tiny Carolingian church of **Germigny-des-Prés,** founded in 806 by Théodulfe, Bishop of Orléans and friend of Charlemagne, awaits in the tiny town of the same name 3km from St-Benoît. The church's Byzantine mosaic, the only one in France, depicts the Ark of the Covenant with dazzling glass cubes transported from Italy by the Emperor himself. The curator will take you on a guided tour through this largely reconstructed church, believed to be the oldest in France. (Tours Mon.-Sat. at 11am and 3pm, Sun. 3:15pm and 4:30pm.) The modest 14th-century château of **Sully-sur-Loire** presides over cobblestone-street 8km farther downstream. (Château open daily May-Sept. 9-11:45am and 2-5:45pm; April and Oct. 10-11:45am and 2-5:45pm; March and Nov. 10-11:45am and 2-4:45pm. Admission 12F, students 6F.) Sully's **tourist office** (tel. 38 36 23 70) is at 3, pl. de Gaulle. (Open May-Sept. Mon.-Sat. 9:30am-12:30pm and 2:30-7pm, Sun. 10am-12:30pm.)

St-Benoît, Germigny, and Sully are all accessible by bus from the *halte routière* in Orléans (5 per day; 1 hr.; 27F to Germigny, 30F to St-Benoit, 36F to Sully). Biking is the ideal way to take in the countryside of the *Loiret;* the most distant town is Sully, an easy 8km ride from St-Benoît and a challenging 90km round-trip from Orléans. Start out early and take the tiny *Levée* route on the south bank of the Loire. After winding through tiny villages and sunflower fields, this delightful road to Sully will drop you off at St-Benoit if you cross the river. Be advised that the wind blows west to east.

South of Chartres en route to the Loire is **Châteaudun,** where fortress walls merge with sheer cliffs to form an imposing and impregnable front. (Open daily 9:30-11:45am and 2-6pm; Oct.-March 10-11:45am and 2-4pm. Admission 24F, students 12F.) The **tourist office,** 3, rue Toufaire (tel. 37 45 22 46), shares a building with a flock of stuffed birds, a few old rocks, and the other possessions of the **Musée Ornithologique.** A small, simple **IYHF hostel,** with kitchen facilites is on av. des Martineaux. (36F per person. Open mid-March to Sept.) The two-star municipal campground, **Moulin à Tan,** lies 2km from town on rue de Chollet (tel. 38 45 05 34; open mid-March to mid-Oct.). Orléans is 55km northwest on D955. Buses to Châteaudun leave from Chartres only.

Blois

Upon gliding into Blois by carriage in 1882, Henry James noted with disappointment that the château did not overhang the river, as he had romantically allowed himself to imagine, but instead preened on a hillside above the town. Nevertheless, this most stoic of travelers still found Blois "a sympathetic little town," one which "presents a bright, clean face to the sun, and has that aspect of cheerful leisure which belongs to all white towns that reflect themselves in shiny water." Visitors today are as likely to share James's opinion as his mode of transportation. Although the lovely château and *vieille ville* do their best to preserve the flavor of lost centuries, modern Blois responds with an explosion of commerce surprising for a town of only 50,000. The châteaux of Chambord, Cheverny, and Chaumont—three of the Loire Valley's finest—all repose in unadulterated settings nearby.

Orientation and Practical Information

On the north bank of the Loire, Blois is a major stop on the Orléans-Tours rail line. The station is north of the château and the center; take av. Jean Laigret five minutes south to the tourist office. Continue in the same direction past the château on your right and you will reach the *centre ville* almost immediately. Take the pedestrian street **rue du Commerce** or the store- and café-lined **rue Denis Papin** to the Loire and cross the bridge. On the other side, the more serene **avenue Wilson** contains a number of cheaper hotels and restaurants. On Monday all banks are closed, and most stores are open only in the afternoon.

Tourist Office: 3, av. Jean Laigret (tel. 54 74 06 49 or 54 78 23 21), in the lovely Renaissance pavillion of Anne de Bretagne. Books rooms for 5F plus a deposit of half the price of 1 night's stay. Changes bills under $100 and traveler's checks (commission 22F). Complete information on châteaux, including tickets for bus circuits and shows at the Blois château. English spoken. Open Mon.-Sat. 9am-7pm, Sun. 10am-1pm and 4-7pm; Oct.-March Mon.-Sat. 9am-noon and 2-6pm.

Currency Exchange: try **Crédit Lyonnais,** 41, rue Denis Papin. Good rates and 24F commission. Open Tues.-Fri. 8:30am-12:10pm and 1:35-5:15pm, Sat. until 4:15pm, or **Crédit Agricole,** 9, av. Wilson. 20F commission. Open Tues.-Fri. 8:45am-12:30pm and 1:30-5:30pm, Sat. until 4:30pm. The post office charges a 1% commission on traveler's checks.

Post Office: (tel. 54 78 08 01), on rue Gallois near pl. Victor Hugo, in front of the château. **Currency exchange** and **telephones. Branch office** on rue Ronceraie, across the river, the 3rd left after the bridge. Both open Mon.-Fri. 8am-7pm, Sat. 8am-noon. **Postal code:** 41000.

Trains: (tel. 54 78 50 50), on top of the hill on bd. Daniel Dupris, a 10-min. walk from the tourist office up av. Jean Laigret. To: Paris via Orléans (6 per day, 1 hr., 99F); Tours (10-12 per day, 1 hr., 41F); Amboise (8 per day, 20 min., 26F); Angers via Tours (10 per day, 3 hr., 92F); Chaumont's Onzain station (5 per day, 15 min., 15F). Information and reservations booth open Mon.-Sat. 8am-noon and 2-7pm, Sun. 9:30am-noon and 2-7pm.

Buses: Autocars STD, 2, pl. Victor Hugo (tel. 54 78 15 66), 2 min. from the tourist office. Conducts two bus circuits with the TLC line, allowing you to create your own itinerary of château visits. ½-day bus pass 60F, students 50F, ages 5-10 20F. One day bus pass 80F, students 70F, ages 5-10 30F. The passes give you reduced admission to the châteaux. Buy tickets at the bus station or tourist office, or on board. Buses leave from the train station. Regular service to: Vendôme (3 per day, 4 hr., 32F); Cheverny (get off at Scierie; 5 per day, Sun. 2; ½-hr.; 16F); Montlivault (2 per day, ¾-hr., 15F). For more schedule information, go to the tourist office or bus office. Open Mon. 8:30am-12:15pm and 1:30-6:30pm. Tues.-Fri. 8am-12:15pm and 1:30-6:30pm, Sat. 8:30am-12:15pm and 1:30-5pm.

Bike Rental: At the station (tel. 54 74 24 50). 50F per day, deposit 500F or major credit card. Call a week in advance mid-July to mid-Aug. Open daily 6am-9pm. **Atelier Cycles,** 44, levée des Tuileries (tel. 54 74 30 13), across the river from the campground. Decent 5- and 10-speeds 40-50F per day, deposit passport. Open daily 9am-10pm. **S.M.C. S.A.R.L. Sports Motos Cycles,** 6, rue Henri Drussy (tel. 54 78 02 64). 50F per day, deposit 300F. Open Tues.-Sat. 9am-7pm.

Youth Center: Bureau d'Information Jeunesse de Loir-et-Cher, 7, av. Wilson (tel. 54 78 54 87), across the river from the *centre ville.* Eager staff. Advice on personal problems. Information on travel throughout France and work (mostly babysitting) in the Blois area. Sightseeing concerns promptly punted to the tourist office. Open Mon. 2-7pm, Tues.-Sat. 10am-7pm.

Laundromat: 1, rue Jeanne d'Arc, near the river. A social center for poor backpackers who can't afford the bars around the corner on rue Foulerie. Wash 20F. Dryer demands many, many 2F pieces. Open Mon.-Sat. 7am-8:30pm, Sun. 9am-8:30pm.

Hospital: Centre Hospitalier de Blois, Mall Pierre Charlot (tel. 54 78 00 82).

Medical Assistance: SAMU, Tel. 54 78 78 78.

Police: 42, quai St-Jean (tel. 54 55 17 99). **Emergency,** tel. 17.

Accommodations

The summer throng of visitors can make finding a room in Blois an ordeal. In July and August, travelers stay usually only one or two nights, but their vacated rooms are taken in the afternoon by the next wave. Call a day in advance to reserve a place or you may wash up (illegally) on the granite banks of the Loire.

Auberge de Jeunesse (IYHF), 18, rue de l'Hôtel Pasquier (tel. 54 78 27 21), 4.5km outside of Blois in Les Grouets. Take bus #4 (*direction* "Les Grouets") and get off at Eglise des Grouets (last bus at 7:30pm). A secluded, rambling building with 2 single-sex dorm rooms. Excellent kitchen facilites, hot showers, and a relaxed evening atmosphere. Closed 10am-6pm. Curfew 10:30pm. 33F per person. Breakfast 13F. Sheets 13F. 48 beds often full in summer; call ahead. Open March-Nov. 15.

Hôtel de la Croix Blanche, 24, av. Wilson (tel. 54 78 25 32), a few blocks over the bridge. Comfortable rooms above a bar are kept spic-and-span by the young couple who run this pleasant hotel. Singles and doubles 95F, with shower 130F. Triples 140F, with shower 175F. Showers 20F. Breakfast 19F. You will pass 2 other hotels of similar quality before you get to this hotel. First, **Le Pavillon,** 2, av. Wilson (tel. 54 74 23 27), suffers from lots of street noise. Immaculate rooms with 1-3 beds 85-140F, with shower 160F. Showers 15F. Breakfast 22F. Bar downstairs. **La Sologne,** 20, av. Wilson (tel. 54 78 02 77), has warmly furnished singles and doubles for 80-120F, with shower 130-150F. Triples 150F, with shower 160F. Showers 10F. Breakfast 15F.

Saint-Jacques, 7, rue Ducoux (tel. 54 78 04 15). Orderly and professionally run, with spacious and bright rooms. Lounge with color TV. One 80F room, other singles and doubles 125F, with shower 160F, with shower and toilet 190F. Bath 15F. Delicious breakfast 21F.

Hôtel St-Nicolas, 2, rue de Sermon (tel. 54 78 05 85). Clean rooms 85F and 105F. Showers 10F. Breakfast 18F. Open Feb.-Dec. 15.

Etoile d'Or, 7-9, rue Bourg Neuf (tel. 54 78 46 93). Adequate rooms. Owner not keen on backpackers, but it's worth a try. Singles from 80F. Doubles 110F. Some rooms with boob tube. Showers 10F. Breakfast 20F.

Camping: La Boire (tel. 54 74 22 78), 2km out of town. 20F per person, 8F per tent. 30F with electricity. Showers included. Open March-Nov. A little farther out is **Lac de Loire,** tel. 54 78 82 05. A campground for the upwardly mobile, this facility offers 1-, 2- and 3-star sites. Open June-Oct. A shuttle bus runs July-Aug. from the train station to both campgrounds (frequent departures, about 5F).

Food and Entertainment

Restaurants in Blois charge high prices, but you may still want to luxuriate in the ambience of those near the château. Restaurants cluster around rue St-Lubin and along the Loire banks. Several *très chic* bars and yet more eateries line rue Foulérie. Rue Denis Papin bursts at its double reinforced seams with *boulangeries*, fruit stands, and supermarkets.

La Tosca, 36, rue Foulérie. Delicious fondues and the Swiss potato-and-cheese specialty *raclette* (as well as more familiar fare) served in a cozy atmosphere. *Menu* 68F. Cheese fondue 59F. Open daily noon-2pm and 7-11:30pm except Sunday lunch Oct.-April.

Packman, 25, rue Denis Papin (tel. 54 74 11 88), in the center of town. There are "three good reasons" to patronize this crass, loud cafeteria: it's cheap, it's clean, and every salad (16F and up) comes with a free roll. Open Sun.-Thurs. 6am-11pm, Fri.-Sat. 6am-1am.

Les Glycines, 54, rue Foulérie. Slick beach pastels and white decor. Slightly cheaper than similar places on the street. 65F *menu* is good but has only 3 courses. Pizza 30-44F. Salads from 26F. Open Mon.-Fri. noon-2pm and 7-11pm, Sat. 7-11pm.

La Manhattan, 39, av. Jean Laigret, a few blocks from the train station toward the *centre ville.* By far the best of the restaurants near the station. Treat yourself to a surprisingly tasty 65F *menu* or a 52F version (served only in the less posh section). The impecunious might try the *salade verte* (lettuce only), which comes with tons of bread (15F). Open Tues.-Sun. noon-2pm and 7-9pm.

Le Maidi, 42, rue St-Lubin. Eat in the shadow of the château in an old wooden house with exposed beams. Traditional 50F and 70F *menus,* plus couscous (38-55F) and appetizers (16-22F). Open Fri.-Wed. 11:30am-2:30pm and 7-10pm.

Sights

Home to French monarchs Louis XII and François I, whose court numbered 15,000, Blois was a Renaissance seat of power comparable to Versailles in subsequent ages. Most memorable of the château's attractions is the spiral staircase crawling with stone salamanders (François I's emblem and a symbol of immortality). Inside, the rooms reek of intrigue. Foot pedals open hidden panels, and tapestries conceal secret doors. Take the interesting guided tour (given frequently in English or French), or walk through on your own. Start with the Aile François I, fronted by a grand, ornamental staircase connecting several fine Renaissance rooms. In 1588 Protestant King Henri III hid in a small antechamber while his assassins fatally stabbed the Duke of Guise, a Catholic rival for the throne. Henri emerged from his hiding place, surveyed the perforated Duke, who measured almost seven feet tall, and said coolly, "He looks even bigger dead than alive." The next day Henri dispatched the Duke's brother, Cardinal de Guise, in a similar fashion, but his luck ran out when he himself was murdered eight months later. The basement of this wing houses the **Musée Archéologique,** full of funerary urns and other regional artifacts. Continue into the **Salle des Etats,** the only part of the château, along with one tower, surviving from the 13th century. The 15th-century Aile Louis XII next door contains the small **Musée des Beaux Arts** and the **Musée d'Art Religieux.** (Château and museums open daily 9am-6pm; Oct.-May 9:30am-noon and 2-5pm. Admission to both 24F, students 13F.) The château's *son et lumière,* unveiled every evening at 10:30pm in French and 11:15pm in English, is one of the less impressive but more affordable shows in the valley (22F, ages 5-12 and over 65 16F).

South of the château lies the impressive **Abbaye St-Lomer.** A lantern, a cupola ringed with stained glass, caps the broad ambulatory ringed with chapels in typical late Romanesque style; the Gothic nave was added more than a century later. A pleasant garden leads from the church to the river through the one-time cloister of a Benedictine abbey. Blois's **Cathédrale St-Louis** is a 17th-century reconstruction of a Gothic church destroyed in a 1678 hurricane and rebuilt at the urging of Colbert's wife, a native of Blois. The **Crypt St-Solenne** under the altar crackles with a funny, informative tape (in English) about the church's construction. The cathedral stands just north of the old quarter, a wonderful place for wandering among half-timbered houses and ancient archways. Also worth perusing is the **Eglise St-Vincent,** a faintly Italianate structure misplaced in pl. Victor Hugo, in the *centre ville.*

Châteaux Near Blois

Over the river and through the woods south of Blois are some of the most remarkable châteaux of the region. Unfortunately, all except Chaumont are inaccessible by train from Blois. Eurailpass holders should go to Tours, connected by rail to several châteaux. The cheapest bus trips, however, leave from Blois; STD in Blois sends buses on the TLC line to the châteaux all day. Their half- or full-day passes allow you to create your own itinerary and grant reduced admission to the castles, although the regular student price is often lower. Best of all, the châteaux are all within easy bicycling range of the town. Because Blois is smaller than Orléans to the east and Tours to the west, cycling in and out of town is a less stressful experience. Ambitious cyclers can pedal over the beautiful, largely flat trails to several châteaux in one day. Many people hitch. While you'll need an hour to get from Blois to Chambord, the trip from Blois to Cheverny, which lies just 2km off D956, is much quicker.

The largest and most extravagant of the Loire châteaux, **Chambord** is so enormous that not even summer's daily deluge of sightseers clutters its grand halls. Chambord's mix of dormers, turrets, and arcades seems a bit haphazard, but the château assumes a Renaissance harmony when viewed from afar. Risking accusations of bad taste, the ever-quotable Henry James opined that this behemoth had " . . . altogether a little of that quality of stupidity. . . .One feels to a certain extent the contrast between its pompous appearance and its specious but somewhat colourless annals." The colorful star of these colorless annals, François I, commanded this lavish production as the royal hunting retreat. Parts of the palace were inspired by the similarly enormous St. Peter's Cathedral in Rome. Although some claim Leonardo da Vinci played an important role in its construction, most credit the lesser-known Domenico de Cortona. Seven hundred of François I's trademark stone salamanders lurk on Chambord's walls and ceilings.

At the heart of the symmetrical château rises a spectacular double-helix staircase, constructed so that one person can ascend and another descend simultaneously without seeing one another. This design was initially intended to facilitate the rapid movement of large numbers of soldiers in fortresses. At the pleasure dome of Chambord, the intertwined spiral flights connect the downstairs ballroom with the apartments above, easing the amorous dalliances of the royal court. Equally remarkable is the rooftop terrace, where hundreds of turrets and spires combine to form a tiny village. The terrace commands a 360-degree view of Chambord's vast grounds, thus allowing the court ladies to follow the progress of the hunt. The château was a favorite address of Louis XIV, who sponsored the premieres of Molière's *Pourceagnac* and *Le Bourgeois Gentilhomme* here. To improve the setting, the Sun King diverted the river Cosson and planted the magnificent kilometer-long, treelined avenue approaching the château.

The cheapest way to see Chambord is by wandering around on your own. Rooms are adequately labeled in English, and the English pamphlet (3F) clarifies the castle's complex layout. Tourist traffic is efficiently and artfully routed on a path that circulates from airy balconies to splendidly furnished rooms. An excellent guided cassette tour is designed primarily for architecture and history buffs (22F, 32F per 2 listeners). Focusing on the château's creation, the lengthy, guided tour in French includes a few rooms not open to the unescorted public (38F, under 25 30F, under age 18 20F). Chambord's grounds, still a hunting reserve, are surrounded by a 32km wall, one of the longest in France. (Château open daily 9:30am-6:45pm; Sept.-June 9:30am-11:45am and 2-4:45pm. Admission 27F, students 15F, children 6F.)

Much of the château's appeal lies in its isolation; only one hotel (Hôtel St-Michel, doubles from 190F) and a few souvenir shops violate the verdure. Campers can play house at **Camping Huisseau-sur-Cosson,** 6, rue de Châtillon (tel. 54 20 35 26), about 5km southwest of Chambord on D33. (8.50F per person includes tent. Showers 5F. Open June-Nov.) The campground in **Bracieux,** on route de Chambord (tel. 54 46 41 84) has a swimming pool, tennis court, and free showers. (8.50F per person, 5F per tent. Gate open March 26-Oct. daily 7:30am-11pm.) Take D956 south for 2-3km and turn left onto D33 for 11km to get to Chambord from Blois.

Carefully manicured **Cheverny** preserves a rare dignity. Its stately Renaissance façade inspired Moulinsart, the mansion in the popular comic-book saga of Tintin. Owned by the same family for 700 years, Cheverny is the only château whose interior fulfills the luxurious promise of its façades. Among the treasures inside are antique furniture, Delft vases, an impressive array of arms and armor, and splendid tapestries, notably a Gobelin of *The Abduction of Helen.* The current count still inhabits the third and fourth floors, and jealous tourists crane their necks to see photos of his family. A compound on the grounds houses mixed English-Poitevan bloodhounds; you can see all 70 gulp down whole bins of ground meat in less than 60 seconds. (Mon.-Sat. at 5pm, Sept.-March Mon. and Wed.-Fri. at 3pm.) The park around the château has attractive formal gardens, but an electrified fence ensures that commoners see nothing without paying. (Open daily 9:15am-6:45pm; Sept. 16-May 9:30am-noon and 2:15-at least 5pm. Admission 23F, students 16F.) In town, the Cheverny **tourist office** (tel. 54 79 95 63) can guide you to the **Camping-Cour Cheverny du S.I.** (tel. 54 79 90 01; 8.50F per night, open June 2-Sept.). The tourist office is righ at the entrance to the château but moves in winter to av. de la République. (Open July-Aug. Mon.-Sat. 10am-noon and 3-7pm, Sun. 10am-noon; April-June and Sept. 3-6pm.)

Beauregard, a smaller, less crowded château, sits pretty 9km south of Blois. Beauregard is most notable for the upstairs portrait gallery, the largest in Europe, with over 350 portraits dating from 1328 to 1643. The tour guide gives an amusing run-down of European history in French, pointing out bloodlines between the royalty portrayed. (Open daily 9:30am-6:30pm; Sept. and June daily 9:30am-noon and 2:30-6:30pm; Oct.-May Thurs.-Tues. 9:30am-noon and 2-5pm. Admission 18F, students 13F. Tours given frequently.) Although difficult to reach by public transportation (the only bus runs infrequently and stops several km away), Beauregard makes an interesting and not too challenging daytrip by bike from Blois. The most direct route takes you along a busy four-lane highway; ask at a bike rental shop for touring routes. Hitchhikers head south on D956 to get rides.

Perhaps the most underrated of all the châteaux in the area, **Chaumont-sur-Loire** serves as a reminder that castles were first built to defend kingdoms, not to be filmed in *Brideshead Revisited*. With its towers, turrets, moat, and drawbridge, this com-pact feudal fortress dominates the river and valley below. Catherine de Medici lived here with her astrologer until the death of her husband, Henri II. She then forced Henri's mistress, Diane de Poitiers, to vacate the more desirable Chenonceau in ex-change for Chaumont. Obviously, Diane could have done worse. The château is best known for its luxurious *écuries* (stables), where the horses were fed from porce-lain troughs in richly upholstered stalls. Even before it was installed in the château, electricity lit the elegant lamps that hang just above the stalls as early as 1906. (Châ-teau open daily 9am-6pm; April-June and Sept. 9:15-11:35am and 1:45-5:35pm; Oct.-March 9:15-11:35am and 1:45-3:50pm. Admission 23F, students 12F.) A shel-tered **campground** is close by at Camping "Grosse Grève," just off the bridge on the southern bank of the Loire (tel. 54 20 93 95; 9F per night). Chaumont is accessi-ble by train from Blois (8 per day, 10 min., 15F) and Tours (8 per day, ½-hr., 32F). The **train station** (tel. 54 78 50 50) lies in Onzain, 2km north of Chaumont.

Honoré de Balzac spent some of his undistinguished scholastic career in **Ven-dôme**, a small Loiret city surrounded by gently rolling farmland. The abbey-church of **La Trinité,** with its impressive façade, was designed in the 16th century by Jean de Beauce, architect of the north tower of Chartres's cathedral. Inside, look for ma-jestic arches and the *Vitrail Notre Dame de Vendôme,* the oldest existing stained-glass image of Mary as the Virgin Mother. Try to come around 5pm, when you can climb the tower and watch the evening bells peal. Walk up the hill to the ruined **château,** dismantled by Henri IV in 1589. The fragments of the defending walls and the half-standing towers enclose a lovely garden and terrace with a view. (Open April-Oct. Tues.-Mon. 9am-noon and 2-6pm. Free.) The **tourist office,** pl. St-Martin (tel. 54 77 05 07), is at the riverside base of the ramp leading to the castle. On the banks of the Loire just outside town, three-star **Camping Municipal des Grands Prés,** rue Geoffrey Martell (tel. 54 77 00 27), has a swimming pool and lots of room (5F per person, 7F per tent). Buses to Vendôme leave daily from Blois but cost a steep 32F. Hitchhikers often take D957 32km northwest from Blois.

Amboise

Set on a steep hillside over the Loire, Château d'Amboise was home to Charles VIII, who ascended the throne and began expanding the royal residence at age 13. The château itself, partly destroyed after the Revolution, is neither as ornate as Chambord nor as graceful as Chenonceau, but its view of the Loire rivals any other. Although upstaged by the château, the small town below (pop. 12,000) makes the most of its status as Leonardo da Vinci's adopted hometown. Aside from the hostel and campground, there are few reasonable accommodations here. Amboise's loca-tion midway between Blois and Tours makes it a convenient daytrip.

Orientation and Practical Information

To reach either the château or the tourist office, walk straight from the station along rue Jules Ferry and cross the first bridge onto the tiny **Ile d'Or,** an island largely devoted to camping facilities. Continue straight and cross the next bridge into the *centre ville.* The château is on your left and the tourist office down the quay to your right.

Tourist Office: (tel. 47 57 09 28), quai Général de Gaulle. Bus schedules, advice on château visits, and a much-needed free accommodations service. English spoken. Open Mon.-Sat. 9am-12:30pm and 1:30-6:30pm, Sun. 10am-noon; March 19-June 17 and Oct. same hours except open Mon.-Sat. at 9:30am; Nov.-March 18 Mon.-Sat. 10am-12:30pm and 3-6pm.

Currency Exchange: All banks in Amboise charge a commission and are usually open Tues.-Sat. 8:30am-noon and 2-5pm.

Post Office: On quai Général de Gaulle, down the street from the tourist office. **Currency exchange** (with commission). Open Mon.-Fri. 8:30am-12:15pm and 1:30-6:15pm, Sat. 8:30-noon. **Postal code:** 37400.

Trains: (tel. 47 57 03 89), on bd. Gambetta, 15-min. from the center of town across the river. On the main Paris-Tours line. To: Tours (10-12 per day, ½-hr., 20F); Blois (8 per day, 10-15 min., 26F); Beaugency (6 per day, 20 min., 42F); Orléans (6 per day, 1 hr., 57F); Paris (6 per day, 2½ hr., 128F). Station open daily 6am-10pm.

Buses: Les Rapides de Touraine (in Tours 47 46 06 60) runs 3 buses daily from Amboise to Tours (20.60F) and 2 or 3 daily to Chenonceau (30F round-trip). Buses leave from the parking lot next to the tourist office. Don't be confused by the transports du Loir-et-Cher (TLC) schedules posted; these are only for people who have purchased special TLC day bus passes in Blois or, possibly, on board. Don't ask. We don't know either.

Bike Rental: at the train station. 50F per day, deposit 500F. Open daily 7am-9pm. **Cycles Richard,** 2, rue de Nazelles (tel. 47 57 01 79), near the station. 70F a day, deposit 500F.

Hospital: Centre Hospitalier Robert-Debré, rue des Ursulines (tel. 47 23 33 33).

Police: Gendarmerie Nationale, rue de Blois, right at the bridge across the river. **Emergency,** tel. 17.

Accommodations, Camping, and Food

Amboise's accommodations are expensive and generally rather ordinary. Beware hotels that require you to eat their overpriced meals. In summer it's a good idea to call at least a few days ahead. In July and August the youth hostel is usually booked by groups, but individuals should still give it a try.

Maison des Jeunes—Centre Charles Péguy/Auberge de Jeunesse, Ile d'Or (tel. 47 57 06 36), a 10-min. walk from the train station. Turn right after the first bridge. Nice location. If office is closed, go around to the back of the building, ring the bell, and ask for the warden. Reception open 3-10pm, Saturday until 8pm. No lockout or curfew. No kitchen. 2-6 bed rooms 42F. Sheets 25F. Breakfast 14F (groups only). Come early in summer. Closed Mon.; in off-season Sun.-Mon., but management may let you in if you call ahead.

Hôtel à la Tour, 32, rue Victor Hugo (tel. 47 57 25 04), across from the château. Six well-kept rooms with wood floors. Fall down the tiny spiral staircase into the bar. Singles 80F. Doubles 120F. Triples 180F. Breakfast 20F. Showers 10F. Often full in summer; call 2-3 weeks in advance. Open Dec.-Oct.

Hôtel le Chaptal, 13, rue Chaptal (tel. 47 57 14 46), on a quiet street off rue Nationale. Near the town center. Adequate rooms. Reception open in summer daily; in off-season Tues.-Sun. One 90F room, one 125F room, others 160-240F. Extra bed 30F. No hall shower. Breakfast 22.50F. Large family restaurant with 56 and 75F *menus.* In summer, call 2 weeks in advance.

Hôtel Les Platanes, bd. des Platanes (tel. 47 57 08 60), in a drab neighborhood behind the train station. Quiet and immaculate rooms. Singles 90F. Doubles 130F. Showers 15F. Breakfast 18F. 55F *menu* required of 1-night hotel guests.

Camping: The best place to stay in Amboise is at the fine campground on the Ile d'Or (tel. 47 57 23 37), across from the château. Showers and hot water. 10.80F per person, 13F per tent. In summer, crowded swimming pool 8F. There's usually a spot, but call ahead. Open April-Sept.

Amboise has an excess of overpriced street cafés but redeems itself with the exemplary **Chez Roger,** 7, rue du Général-Foy (tel. 47 57 61 53), not far from the château. Roger puts on lunch every weekday, and all the locals show up for the 43F lunch *menu* which includes four generous, tasty courses and all the bread and wine you want (coffee 2.50F). If Roger's mess-hall meat-and-potatoes style doesn't appeal to you (feel guilty, it should), you can dine in a comfortable 16th-century house at **L'Ecu,** 7, rue Corneille, off rue Nationale. (Dessert and cheese *crêpes* 12-20F. More substantial offerings 25-40F. Open Mon.-Sat. noon-3pm and 7pm-midnight, Sun. 7pm-midnight.) The **Restaurant de la Poste,** 5, rue d'Orange (tel. 47 57 01 88), near the postal museum, serves 45F and 64F traditional *menus.* (Open daily noon-2pm and 7-9:30pm; Nov.-Easter Tues.-Sun.)

Sights

After having spent three years beautifying the **Château d'Amboise,** his childhood home, Charles VIII died here in the 16th year of his reign when he struck his head on a doorway. Apparently, he was hurrying to watch a suspenseful game of cards being played in the moat. Undaunted, Louis XII and François I finished the castle in a luxurious, highly decorative style influenced by the Italian Renaissance and by Leonardo da Vinci, who came to help and never left. First buried in the church of St-Florentin, the remains of the original Renaissance Man were unearthed and scattered during the Wars of Religion. In the north transept of the château's Chapelle St-Hubert, a plaque makes the questionable claim that Leonardo's recovered bones lie below. The church and three-quarters of the original château fell prey to pillaging stone-bandits after the Revolution. Unfortunately, only one wall of the original rectangular set of fortifications remains. This portion, the **Logis du Roi,** is lavishly furnished in late Gothic style. In 1560, La Renaudie and other Protestants were condemned to death in the great hall, and 275 years later the great Algerian leader Abd el-Kader spent five years in exile here. Best of all is the **Tour des Minimes,** a giant, spiraling, five-story ramp for bringing horses and carriages into the château. Perched high above the Loire, the château's terraces present a striking view, which on a clear day extends to Blois and Tours. As you exit through the **Tour Heurtrault,** revel in the resounding chords and pornographic sculptures. (Château open daily July-Aug. 9am-6:30pm; April-June 9am-noon and 2-6:30pm, Jan.-March until 5 pm, Sept.-Dec. until 5:30pm. Admission 25F, students 15F. Obligatory tour in French, with printed English summary.)

Every evening from June through August, over 400 locals stage an extravagant Renaissance *A La Cour Roy François.* Lighting effects, period costumes, fireworks, and 16th-century music are thrown in for 60F per person. Information and reservations (5F) are available at the ticket booth on the ascending ramp (tel. 47 57 14 47).

From the château, walk along the cliffs on rue Victor Hugo among centuries-old *maisons troglodytiques,* hollowed out of the hill and still inhabited today. Just down the road is the **Clos Lucé,** the gracious manor where Leonardo da Vinci, under the patronage of François I, spent the last years of his life. The generally unsatisfying museum displays some fine furnishings and tapestries, but most highly touted are three rooms of models based on the master's drawings. Unfortunately, the models don't measure up to da Vinci's visionary plans, and the obligatory guided tour in French goes a bit too fast. (Tours July-Aug. only. Open daily June-Sept. 9am-7pm; Oct.-Dec. and Feb.-May 9am-12:30pm and 2-7pm. Admission 29F, students 20F, ages 7-15 15F.)

The unassuming **Musée de la Poste,** 6, rue Joyeuse (tel. 47 57 00 11), in the Hôtel de Joyeuse, presents the sinister history of mail delivery in France. The eclectic exhibit ranges from the uniforms worn by Napoleonic mail carriers to the first stamp printed in France to the Thurn and Taxis muted posthorns. (Open May-Sept. Tues.-Sun. 9:30am-noon and 2-6:30pm; Oct.-Dec. and Feb.-April Tues.-Sun. 10am-noon and 2-5pm. Admission 12F, students and ages under 10 6F.)

Near Amboise

Sheltered by an ancient forest, graceful **Chenonceau** cultivates an intimacy with its natural surroundings that resists even the most ferocious of crowds. Arching effortlessly over the Cher River, tons of white stone appear suspended in air, capped with slate-gray peaks. The gallery served as a military hospital during World War I. The privileged position of the château during World War II, half in the free zone south of the Cher and half in the occupied territory, allowed thousands of refugees to flee the Nazis. You need not take a guided tour; pick up a pamphlet in the language of your choice and just wander. Chenonceau's stunning exterior, viewed from the spacious garden or from a 10F rowboat, will touch even the most jaded castle-goer. (Open March 16-Sept. 15 daily 9am-7pm; Sept. 16-Sept. 30 9am-6:30pm; Oct. and March 1-15 9am-6pm; Nov. 1-15 9am-5pm; Nov. 16-Feb. 15 9am-4:30pm; Feb. 16-28 9am-5:30pm. Got it? Admission 30F, students and ages 7-15 20F.)

The **Musée de Cires,** a collection of wax figures in period costumes, illustrates the history of the château. (Museum open same hours as château, and only with admission to château, 8F.) The *son et lumière* presentation at Chenonceau is a nice diversion if you're staying nearby but not worth the elaborate transportation plans otherwise. Although not immune to hokey historical narration, it wisely concentrates on the beauty of the grounds. Bring insect repellent. (Shows July-Sept. daily at 10:15pm; May-June on selected evenings. Admission 30F. Call the château for information at 47 23 90 07.)

Three **trains** per day connect the village of Chenonceau to Tours (Sun. 1; ¾-hr., 28F). The station is 2km from the château. Follow the mob up the road from the station, left onto rue Bretonneau, and then left again onto rue du Château. **Les Rapides de Touraine** (tel. 47 46 06 60 in Tours) runs five buses per day from Tours to Chenonceau (Sun. 2; 1 hr., 36F) via Amboise (½-hr., 20.50F) and stops at the château gates.

Because the *son et lumière* ends at 11:30pm, you'll have to stay in or near Chenonceau to see it. The only reasonable prospect in town is the comfortable, two-star **Hostel du Roy,** 9, rue Docteur Bretonneau (tel. 47 23 90 17), minutes from the château. (Singles 100F. Doubles 135F. Showers included. Obligatory breakfast 25F. Dinner from 55F. Open Feb.-Nov.) Otherwise, try **La Taverne** (tel. 47 29 92 18), 2km away on the route to Tours, or **Chez Madeleine Badier** (tel. 47 29 92 48), a little farther on the route to Tours. Both hotels have rooms for 100-150F and inexpensive restaurants. In Chenonceau itself, **Le Gâteau Breton,** 16, rue Bretonneau, cooks both *à la carte* dishes and 52F *menus.* Chenonceau's tiny **campground** (tel. 47 23 90 13) is a few blocks left of the château entrance. (5.80F per person and per tent. Open April 15-Sept.) You can also camp in nearby **Civray** (tel. 47 23 92 13), about 1km away, or at a one-star site in **Chisseaux,** about 2km from the château (tel. 47 23 86 18; 8F per person, 10F per tent).

Tours

Tours, straddling both the Loire and the Cher, floats like an industrial island in the agricultural heartland of France. Employed mainly in electronics and metallurgy, the 250,000 *Tourangeaux* live and work within 60km of some of the loveliest châteaux and on the doorstep of Vouvray, Montlouis, and the other fine wine-growing towns of the Touraine. Bus and train connections to the châteaux are reasonably frequent, and the budget traveler will find a profusion of affordable accommodations. If you are looking for an urban base from which to explore the Loire Valley, search no further.

In addition to the usual glitzy pedestrian zone, august public buildings, and demure residential areas, Tours has an old quarter with buildings dating from the Renaissance. An educational center since the Middle Ages, the city is home to a large, cosmopolitan student population and a stodgy bourgeoisie, who claim to speak the purest French in the country.

Orientation and Practical Information

Tours lies only 2¼ hours from Paris-Austerlitz. The bus station is located in front of the train station; the tourist office is across the street from both stations and to the left. The city's focal point is **place Jean Jaurès,** a two-minute walk west from the tourist office along bd. Heurteloup. From here, numerous sidewalk cafés stretch southward along av. Grammont, and rue Nationale, Tours's answer to the Champs-Elysées, cuts a northward path to the Loire. The *vieille ville* lies to the left of rue Nationale along rue du Commerce and rue du Grand Marché; the cathedral and the Musée des Beaux Arts stand off rue Colbert about 1km to the right. Most of the inexpensive accommodations and many restaurants lie within a 10-minute walking radius of the station.

Tourist Office: (tel. 47 05 58 08), in pl. de la Gare across from the train station and to the left. Brochures galore. Some English spoken. Will book accommodations (6F plus 50-100F deposit) and arrange bus tours to the châteaux. A general bus tour including only the exteriors of sites (at 10am, 2½ hr., 49F) and a detailed historical tour on foot (at 3pm, 2½ hr., 25F) both depart daily from the office mid-June to early Oct. Another branch, at the Hôtel de Ville across the street (same tel.), handles reservations for tours. Disabled travelers should call 47 64 06 84 for a welcome and advice. Tours global museum ticket 50F. Open Mon.-Sat. 8:30am-8pm, Sun. 10am-noon and 3-6pm; Sept.-May Mon.-Sat. 9am-noon and 2-6pm. **Services for disabled people:** The tourist office provides guides for people in wheelchairs staying in Tours, *Tours en Fauteuil Roulant,* and in all France, *Touristes Quand Même.*

Budget Travel: Frantour, in the train station (tel. 47 05 68 45). BIJ and plane tickets with student and youth discounts. Open Mon.-Fri. 9am-noon and 2-6pm.

Currency Exchange: SOS Hôtels France, in the train station. Change all brands of traveler's checks for 10F. Best deal is at the **Crédit Agricole** booth, next to the tourist office, which gives an acceptable rate and charges no commission except Sun.-Mon. (20F), when most banks are closed. Open June 15-Sept. 15 Tues.-Sat. 8:30am-1:30pm and 5-9pm, Sun. 9:30am-2:30pm, Mon. 8:30am-9pm.

Post Office: 1, bd. Béranger (tel. 47 21 50 15). All services. This is the *recette principale.* Open Mon.-Fri. 8am-7pm, Sat. 8am-noon. **Postal Code:** 37000.

Trains: 3, rue Edouard Vaillant (24-hr. tel. 47 20 50 50). Many long-distance trains require you to change at St-Pierre-des-Corps, an industrial stop 5 min. outside Tours, so check schedule carefully. To: Chinon (3 per day, 1 hr., 29.50F); Angers (7 per day, 1½ hr., 67F); Poitiers (12 per day, 1½ hr., 67F); Bordeaux (12 per day, 2½ hr., 184F); Paris (1-2 per hr., 2 hr., 134F). Châteaux served by train include: Azay-le-Rideau (2-4 per day, ½-hr., 22F); Chenonceau (Mon.-Sat. 3 per day, Sun. 1; ¾-hr.; 28F); Loches (Mon.-Sat. 3 per day, Sun. 1; 1 hr.; 36F); Langeais (Mon.-Sat. 6 per day, Sun. 2; ½-hr.; 21F); Blois (10 per day, 35 min., 39F); Amboise (10 per day, ½-hr., 20F). Train information available at **Acceuil** desk by tracks (open 24 hrs).

Buses: (tel. 47 05 30 49), in pl. Maréchal Leclerc across from the train station. **Les Rapides de Touraine,** tel. 47 46 06 60. Around 4 buses per day (fewer Sun.) to Amboise (½-hr., 20.60F) and on to Chenonceau (1 hr., 35F). **Cars Coudert,** tel. 47 59 06 23 in Loches. Four buses per day to Loches (1 hr., 25F). **Eurolines,** tel. 47 66 45 56. Amazing deals on travel throughout Europe, North Africa, and the U.K. (Tours-London round-trip 760F, students 580F. Tours-Casablanca round-trip 1600F.) Most buses with bar and video. Information office open Mon.-Sat. 10-11:30am and 2-6:30pm.

Châteaux Bus Tours: The expensive but excellent option for English-speaking château-seekers is the small, personal **Touraine Evasion** service. *Sympa* drivers give minibus passengers colorful and intimate commentary. To: Blois, Chambord, and Cheverny (175F, entrance fees 70F); Chenonceau and Amboise (100F, entrance fees 55F). Groups of 5-7 can create their own itineraries. Call 47 66 52 32 Mon.-Fri. 9am-6:30pm and 47 66 63 81 Sat.-Sun. for information and reservations, or contact the tourist office at the Hôtel de Ville. Tours leave from there. **Service Touristique de la Touraine** (tel. 47 05 46 09). A large outfit run out of the train station. Half-day tours average 79F, entrance fees 45F (leave at 1:15pm from platform 20, return at 7pm). Summer *son et lumière* trips too; prices include admission. To Azay-le-Rideau (95F), Le Lude (125F), and Amboise (115F). There are 2-3 departures per week late March-early Oct. with French and English commentary from guide on bus. Office open Mon.-Sat. 8-11am and 3:30-7pm, Sun. 8-11am. Reserve here or at the tourist office (in the Hôtel de Ville) a day in advance.

Bike Rental: At the train station (tel. 47 44 38 01). 50F per day, deposit 500F. **Au Col de Cygne,** 46, rue du Docteur Fournier (tel. 47 46 00 37), 1.5km from the tourist office and train station. Ten-speeds 49F per day, 260F per week, deposit 300F. Mountain bikes 85F per day, 494F per week, deposit 600F. Bike bags 14F per day. Reservations wise in summer; must send a 30% deposit. Visa and Mastercard accepted. Open Tues.-Sat. 9am-noon and 2-7pm, Mon. 2-7pm. **Grammont Cycles,** 93, av. de Grammont (tel. 47 66 62 89). Mountain bikes 80F per day, deposit 400F. Open Tues.-Sat. 9am-noon and 2-7pm. **M. Barat,** 156, rue Giraudeau (tel. 47 38 63 75), has cheaper rates. **Montaubin,** 2, rue Nationale (tel. 47 05 62 27). Mountain bikes 70F per day, deposit 400F. It may be easier to rent bicycles in smaller towns such as Azay-le-Rideau if rentals in Tours are cleaned out. Phone reservations a week in advance will almost guarantee you a bike even in summer.

English Bookstores: La Boîte à Livres de l'Etranger, 2, rue du Commerce (47 05 67 29). Complete collection of Penguin classics. Visa, Mastercard, and Amex traveler's checks accepted. Open Tues.-Sun. 9:15am-noon and 2:15-7:30pm, Mon. 2:15-7pm. **Magic Livres,** 20, rue Marceau (tel. 47 05 81 47). Wide selection. Open Mon. 2-7pm, Tues.-Sat. 9:30am-7pm.

Laundromat: 20, rue Bernard Palissy, 5 min. from the station. Wash 8-25F, dryers 2F per 5 min. Detergent 3F. 1F, 2F, and 5F coins. Open daily 7am-9pm.

Crisis Line: SOS Amitié, tel. 47 54 54 54. For a friendly talk.

Medical Assistance: SAMU, tel. 47 28 15 15. **Hôpital Trousseau,** rue de Loches (tel. 47 47 47 47).

Police: 85, rue Roger Salengro (tel. 47 61 12 09). **Emergency,** tel. 17.

Accommodations and Camping

Cheap hotels abound near the train station. If you arrive before noon and it's not a holiday, reservations are never needed. The hostel and *foyer* both draw crowds in summer.

Auberge de Jeunesse (IYHF), av. d'Arsonval, Parc de Grandmont (tel. 47 25 14 45), 4km from the station in a park by the freeway. Buses #2 and 6 (bus #1 on Sundays) shuttle to the center every 12 min., but the last departure to the hostel is at 8:30pm (5.50F). Large rooms with 2-8 beds. Good kitchen facilities, TV, and phone. Reception open 5pm-midnight. Lockout 10:30am-5pm. Curfew 11pm. 37F per person includes breakfast of bread and coffee (8-9am). Sheets 14F. Small dinner 40F. Reservations recommended in summer. IYHF card preferred, but rooms usually go to the first arrivals.

Le Foyer, 16, rue Bernard Palissy (tel. 47 05 38 81), across bd. Heurteloup from the tourist office and down rue Bernard Palissy. Good location and big rooms. Accepts both sexes ages 16-25, but they rarely check for age. Office open Mon. afternoon-Sat. morning. Centrally located. Singles 65F. Doubles 60F per person. Good and cheap cafeteria. Breakfast 7F. Very crowded June-July, less so in Aug.

CROUS (tel. 47 05 17 55), Parc de Grandmont. Take bus #1 to Parc Sud (last bus 8:30pm). University rooms available July-Sept. You must appear in person at Bâtiment A (9am-1pm or 2:30pm). Call ahead. Considering the location and price (50F), you're better off in a hotel. Obtain tickets in advance to eat in the cafeteria (15F).

Hôtel Vendôme, 24, rue Roger Salengro (tel. 47 64 33 54), 1 block off av. Grammont. Four generations of family make this a homey place. Excellent rooms with telephones. Singles 75F. Doubles 90F, with shower 95-130F. Showers 15F. Breakfast 15-18F.

Mon Hôtel, 40, rue de la Préfecture (tel. 47 05 67 53). Friendly, quaint, and immaculate. Singles and doubles 80F, with bath 100-120F. Showers 12F. All-you-can-eat breakfast 18F.

Hôtel le Lys d'Or, 21-23 rue de la Vendée (tel. 47 05 33 45). Spotless rooms and gracious management. Accepts Amex traveler's checks. Singles and doubles 72-95F, with shower 110-125F. Showers and breakfast 18F.

Olympic Hôtel, 74, rue Bernard Palissy (tel. 47 05 10 17). Simple rooms are not the cleanest. Singles 85F. Doubles 100-120F, with shower 135F. Breakfast 20F. Shower 20F.

Hôtel Le Comté, 51, rue Auguste Comté (tel. 47 05 53 16), off rue Blaise Pascal. Haggard rooms are not exactly spotless, but *sympa* management and quiet location. Singles 61-73F. Doubles 76-95F. Showers 8F. Bath 17F. Breakfast 17F.

Hôtel Les Capucines, 6, rue Blaise Pascal (tel. 47 05 20 41). A tad musty, but the price is right. Come on down. Singles 85-95F, with shower 120-125F. Doubles 100-130F, with shower 150-160F. Breakfast 18F.

Camping: There are dozens of campgrounds within a 20-mile radius, most near châteaux and along the Loire. Pick up a list from the tourist office. **Camping Tours Edouard Peron** (tel. 47 54 11 11), on N152 is closest to the city. Take bus #6 ("Ste-Radégonde," 5.50F). For information, call 47 54 11 11 or the mayor's office at 47 66 29 94 (*poste* 46). Open May 21-Sept. 11.

Food

The Touraine region, the garden of France, is famous for food and wine, but not for bargains. Thanks to the large student population, Tours has scores of cheap (though not necessarily good) restaurants. You'll find restaurants serving *cuisine tourganelle* along rue Colbert and around pl. de la Lampraie in the old quarter. Try some of the local fish, especially salmon or trout, with one of the light white wines from Montlouis, Vouvray, or Touraine. There is a small produce market at pl. des Halles. (Open Sun.-Tues. and Thurs.-Fri. 8-9:30am.)

Le Foyer, 16, rue Bernard Palissy. Lively and local, frequented by young French workers. You *must* purchase a membership card at the foyer office (3F). Four-course menu 31F; meat and vegetables 23F. Open Mon.-Fri. 11am-1:30pm and 7-8pm, Sat.-Sun. 11:45am-1:30pm; Aug. Mon.-Fri. 11:45am-1:30pm and 7-8pm and Sat. 11:45am-1:30pm.

Le Point de Jour, 38bis, av. de Grammont. From the train station, follow rue Gilles and turn left on av. de Grammont. Cordial couple help you eat healthily and cheaply. Filling 3-course vegetarian *menus* at lunch (49F) and dinner (59F). With any student ID you can feast on an entree and salad for 30F. Vegetarian *pâté* in pastry (8.50F). Chemical-free fruit and wine. Store open daily 10am-11pm, meals daily 11:30am-2pm and 7-10pm.

Athènes, at the intersection of rue Nationale and rue Colbert. Authentic, tasty Greek cuisine. Entrees 40-70F. Salads 20-38F. Lunch *menu* 49F. Souvlaki-to-go 19F. Open Mon.-Sat. noon-2pm and 7-11pm.

Le Continental, 17, rue Blaise Pascal, near the train station. An unassuming place with particularly filling 44-62F *menus.* Chicken and shrimp *paella* 53F per person (2-person minimum). Diet/health platter of *crudités* and ham 38F. No alcohol. Open Mon.-Sat. noon-2pm and 7-9:30pm, Sun. noon-2pm.

Aux Trois Canards, 16, rue de la Rôtisserie, in the *vieille ville.* Elegant restaurant and bar on a quiet street. 44F and 65F *menus.* Open Mon.-Fri. noon-2pm and 7:30-10pm, Sat. 7:30-10pm.

Sights

Though the old quarter suffered serious damage during World War II, several buildings in the area around rue Briconnet and rue du Change survive. Renaissance houses, some open to the public, dot the quarter. The tourist office has a free annotated map and sells a 50F global pass to all of Tours's museums. Their theme visits focus on the cathedral, the city's Renaissance façades, *vieux* Tours, and the city's churches (daily at 3pm from the tourist office, 2½ hr., 25F).

At the **Hôtel Goüin,** 25, rue du Commerce (tel. 47 66 22 32), a fine Renaissance façade conceals a mildly interesting archaeological collection. (Open May-Sept. daily 10am-7pm; mid-March to April daily 10am-12:30pm and 2-6:30pm; Feb. to mid-March and Oct.-Nov. Sun.-Thurs. 10am-12:30pm and 2-5:30pm. Admission 15F, students 11F.) Flanking rue des Halles, the **Tour de l'Horloge** and the **Tour de Charlemagne** remain as fragments of the 11th-century Basilique St-Martin, a gargantuan Romanesque masterpiece that stood on the pilgrimage route to Spain. Enter at 3, rue Descartes. The **Nouvelle Basilique St-Martin,** a turn-of-the-century church of Byzantine inspiration, overlaps the foundation of the old structure, allowing St-Martin to slumber on undisturbed. (Open daily 7:30am-noon and 2-6pm.)

To the east is **Cathédrale St-Gatien,** probably Tours's most compelling sight. Walk around the church to appreciate the exterior details and the flying buttresses—one of which plants itself in the courtyard of a neighboring house, providing a setting for Balzac's novel *Le Curé de Tours*. With the attendant's permission, you can see the cloister adjoining the cathedral. (Open daily 8:30am-noon and 2-8pm; in off-season closes at 5pm.)

A short walk down rue Jules-Simon, the **Musée des Beaux Arts** occupies the former episcopal palace at 18, pl. François Sicard (tel. 47 05 68 73). The collection includes works from the Italian Renaissance, several paintings by Delacroix, and one Rembrandt. (Museum open Wed.-Mon. 9am-12:45pm and 2-6pm. Admission 20F, students 10F. Gardens open daily 7am-8:30pm, close 6pm in winter.)

Even more interesting is the unique **Musée de Compagnonnage,** 8, rue Nationale, Clôitre St-Julien (tel. 47 61 07 93), which commemorates the forerunner of the trade union and displays a bizarre array of pre-industrial artisan craftworks. (Open Wed.-Mon. 9am-noon and 2-7pm. and Oct.-March 9am-noon and 2-5pm. Admission 10F, students with ID 5F.) Downstairs, the **Musée des Vins de Touraine** (tel. 47 61 07 93) fills an ancient wine cellar. Unfortunately, this clever shrine to wine does not include free samples. (Same hours as the Compagnonnage. Admission 10F, students 5F.) Down the street at the intersection of rue Colbert and rue Lavoisier is the **Historial de Touraine,** a spiffy new museum where 165 wax characters, including Charlemagne, Rabelais, and da Vinci, bring Touraine history to life. (Open daily mid-June to mid-Sept. 9am-6:30pm, mid-Nov. to mid-March 2-5:30pm, mid-March to mid-June and mid-Sept. to mid-Nov. 9-11:30am and 2-6:30pm. Admission 28F, students 20F. Guide booklet in many languages 3F.)

A 15- to 20-minute bus ride from the *centre ville* (bus #7 from pl. Jean Jaurès, 5.50F) will bring you to **Plessis-Les-Tours** (tel. 47 37 22 80), Louis XI's favorite abode. The austere brick-and-stone manor does not soar, swoop, or otherwise inspire, but you can see the king's furnished bedroom and examine documents on the castle's history. (Open Feb.-Dec. Wed.-Mon. 10am-noon and 2-5pm.)

Châteaux Near Tours

In the 15th century young Prince Charles of France was sold out by his mother, who conceded the French throne to the English during the Hundred Years' War. The indignant Dauphin fled from Paris to Tours, one of his domains, to take his rightful place as king. Charles settled permanently in the Touraine, making the region a seat of power and prompting the construction of numerous châteaux. Thanks to this royal relocation, something interesting awaits you in every direction from the modern city. Before hitting the châteaux, make a pitstop at the many *caves* offering *dégustations*. There are five in **Vouvray**, 9km east of Tours on the N152 and accessible by bus #61 from pl. Jean Jaurès (Mon.-Sat. 5 per day, 20 min.) and several more in **Montlouis**, across the river to the south (11km) and accessible by bus from the Tours bus station (Mon.-Sat. 5 per day, 20 min.).

Loches (pop. 7000), 40km south of Tours, once struck fear into the hearts of the enemies of the French kings. Today it makes a nice daytrip for those tired of the tapestries-and-bedrooms châteaux tours. Here, the grim dungeon shares the hilltop with the delicate Renaissance *logis* (residence). After her June 1429 victory at Orléans, Joan of Arc came here to implore the Dauphin Charles to be crowned at Reims. Climb the four walls of the towering 11th-century **donjon** for views of the medieval town and an encounter with cawing, defecating birds. A 40-minute tour covers the sinister dungeons, where Ludovico Sforza, Duke of Milan, covered every inch of his cell with mystic messages and symbols. From June to September, you can visit the apartments and the *donjon* with or without a guide; at other times a tour is required. (Open daily 9am-6pm; March 15-June and Sept. 9am-noon and 2-6pm; Oct.-March 14 Thurs.-Tues. 9am-noon and 2-5pm. Admission to castle and dungeon 21F, students 14F.) The castle also stages a *son et lumière* show about Joan of Arc's adventures. (July-Aug. 2 or 3 shows weekly at 8:30 or 9pm. Tickets 50F. Call 47 59 01 32 or the Loches ticket office for information and reservations.)

Two daily buses travel from Tours to Loches (1 hr., 36F). The **tourist office** (tel. 47 59 07 98), in a pavilion near the station on pl. de la Marne, can help with accommodations. (Open July-Aug. daily 9:15am-8pm, Sept.-June Tues.-Sat. 9:15am-

12:30pm and 2-6:15pm.) In July and August they sponsor walking tours of the illu-minated medieval city (Mon.-Wed. at 9:30pm; 20F, students with ID 15F). Two-star **Tour St-Antoine,** 2, rue des Moulins (tel. 47 59 01 06), has a few rooms for 110-130F. (Breakfast 26F. Reserve early in summer.) **Hôtel Moderne,** 21, pl. des Verduns (tel. 47 59 05 06) has rooms for 100-150F. The beautiful **Camping Munici-pal,** rue Guintefol (tel 47 59 05 91), has an indoor swimming pool. Take N143 south, and follow route de Châteauroux to Stade Général Leclerc. (5.75F per person, 11F per site. Open April-Sept.) For lunch or dinner, visit **Le Charles VII,** 8, Grande-Rue, on the way to the château, where pizzas (22-34F), salads (7-25F), omelettes (16-24F), and desserts (24F) come in only one size—large. For something more lav-ish, try the refreshing and shaded terrace of **La Gerbe d'Or,** 22, rue Balzac (tel. 47 59 06 38), below the castle on the way into town (4-course *menu* 75F).

Lush **Villandry** maintains fantastic formal gardens with swan pools, vine-covered walkways, and three terraces of sculpted shrubs, flowers, and vegetable plants. Skip the château and invest your time and money outside. Most interesting is the inter-mediate terrace, where knee-high hedges are arranged in various patterns: a Maltese Cross, a Croix de Lorraine, and a charming reproduction of the **Carte du Tendre** with its four types of love (tender, courtly, passionate, and flighty). The uninterest-ing 40-minute tour is redeemed by the concluding 15-minute slide show, which in-cludes some spectacular seasonal shots of the château. (Gardens open daily 9am-7pm; castle open March 15-Nov. 15 daily 9am-6pm. Admission to gardens 20F, students 16F. Admission to the castle an additional 12F, students 10F.)

Cyclists should take heed of tiny D16, a narrow, paved marvel that winds along the bank of the Loire from Villandry to Ussé.

Ussé's pointed towers, white turrets, and chimneys inspired Charles Perrault's transcription of the *Sleeping Beauty* folktale. Surrounded by the thick woods of the Forêt de Chinon, the 15th-century château rises above terraced gardens and the Indre River. You don't have to take the tour to see models of the Sleeping Beauty story in 18th- and 19th-century French costume. If the admission seems steep, you could just picnic outside and revel in the view. (Château open April 15-Sept. daily 9am-noon abd 2-6pm; Oct. 10am-noon and 2-6pm. Admission 39F. For more infor-mation, call 47 95 54 05.)

Raised on one of a series of islands in the Indre River, **Azay-le-Rideau** rivals Che-nonceau in beauty. Built according to the whims of François I's corrupt financier (who was away embezzling in Italy), the château embodies the purity and vigor of the Renaissance. The interior is well-appointed, although many of the furnishings are either restorations or flat-out fakes. The only way to see the rooms is to take the obligatory tour in French. Go early, especially in high season, to catch the guides before they wilt from the crowds and heat. (Château open daily 9am-6:45pm; April-June and Sept. 9:30am-12:15pm and 2-5:45pm; Oct.-March 10am-12:15pm and 2-4:45pm. Admission 23F, students 12F.) The *son et lumière* performance allows for nocturnal wandering through gardens but is spruced up with costumed actors in boats. (Shows May-July at 10:30pm; Aug.-Sept. at 10pm. Admission 40F, children 30F. Information tel. 47 45 44 40.)

The château is a 2km walk from Azay-le-Rideau's train station. Turn right out-side the station and head left on D57. The **tourist office,** 26, rue Gambetta (tel. 47 45 44 40), will help with accommodations, few of which are cheap. Ask about buses to **Saché** (tel. 47 26 86 50) Balzac's home, located 7km east of Azay. (Open daily July-Aug. 10am-noon and 2-7pm; March 15-June and Sept. 9am-noon and 2-6pm; Oct.-Nov. and Feb.-March 14 Thurs.-Tues. 9am-noon and 2-5pm. Admission 18F, students 5F.) Two-star **Camping Parc du Sabot** (tel. 47 45 42 72), across from the château on the banks of the Indre, has canoe and kayak rentals and plenty of room. (8F per person, 5F per tent. Showers included. Open May-Nov.) Rent 10-speed bikes at the station or at **Le Provost,** 13, rue Carnot (tel. 47 45 40 94), which charges 25F per ½-day and 37F per day. (Open Tues.-Sat. 8am-noon and 2-7pm.)

Between Villandry and Ussé lies the forbiddingly feudal **Langeais,** one of the last medieval fortresses built for defense. Constructed from 1465 to 1469 for Louis XI, Langeais guarded the route from Brittany through the Loire Valley. Here in 1491, the marriage of Charles VIII of France and Anne de Bretagne consummated Brittany's union with the crown; one room of the castle contains wax figures of the bride and groom at their actual height, or lack thereof. (Recall that this 4' ruler died after somehow managing to hit his head on a doorframe.) The tour (in French) includes a walk along the upper fortifications, where stone slabs, when drawn back, reveal holes for hurling the proverbial boiling oil, pitch, and stones at attackers. The ruins of the original 11th-century fortress stand in the small château courtyard. (Château open daily 9am-6:30pm; Nov.-March 15 Tues.-Sun. 9am-noon and 2-5pm. Admission 23F, students 15F. Call 47 96 72 60 for more information.)

Several trains per day stop in Langeais on their way to Saumur or Tours. The **train station** (tel. 47 96 82 19) is a ¼km walk from the château; signs will point you in the right direction. The station rents **bikes** for 50F per day, with a 500F deposit or credit card. (Open daily 8am-8pm.) Hitchhikers find the 10km hitch north from Azay-le-Rideau on D57 to Langeais fairly easy; the 10km bike ride on D16 from Villandry or Ussé is delightful. The tourist office (tel. 47 96 58 22) is at pl. du 14 Juillet. (Open June-Sept. Tues.-Sat. 9am-noon and 2-6pm, Sun. 10am-noon.) The small town of 4000 has little in the way of indoor accommodations, but there is a **Camping Municipal** (tel. 47 96 85 80) on N152, 1km from the château. (5F per person, 5.50F per tent, 5F per site. Hot water included. Open June-Sept. 15). A new 40-bed *gîte d'étape* (tel. 47 96 67 29) awaits in La Rouchouze, 10km out of Langeais and within 20km of Langeais, Azay-le-Rideau, Ussé, and Villandry. (35F per night. Call the Langeais town hall at 47 96 71 62 for information and reservations.)

Chinon

Having ducked both heavy tourism and heavy industry, Chinon (pop. 9000) clings to a hillside capped by a ruined château. The restored *vieille ville*, birthplace of the great 16th-century comic writer François Rabelais (in whose *Gargantua* and *Pantagruel* Chinon's red wine is celebrated), presents a delightful maze of alleyways, chimneys, and medieval timber-frame houses, some with fine sculptural detail. A comfortable hostel and bucolic campground make Chinon an ideal spot to rest and plan your sallies to nearby Azay, Ussé, Villandry, and even Saumur—all accessible by train or bike.

Orientation and Practical Information

Chinon lies an hour southwest of Tours by train, and 30km southeast of Saumur, where the Vienne meets the Loire. To reach the town center, walk straight from the train station along rue du Docteur Labussière, bear left onto rue du 11 Novembre, continue straight along quai Jeanne d'Arc, and bear right before the bridge. Chinon's modest shopping square is pl. Général de Gaulle, which opens onto rue Voltaire and the unparalleled *vieille ville* on the left. The château perches atop the medieval rêverie of rue Haute St-Maurice, a continuation of rue Voltaire.

Tourist Office: 12, rue Voltaire (tel. 47 93 17 85), about 15 min. from the station. Wonderfully helpful staff arranges bus trips to nearby châteaux, suggests out-of-the-way destinations, books hotel rooms for the price of the call, and changes money when banks are closed. Rents a few bikes, too (35F per day, 100F deposit). English spoken. Open Mon.-Sat. 9am-7:30pm, Sun. 10am-12:30pm; Sept.-April Mon.-Sat. 9am-12:15pm and 2-6:30pm.

Currency Exchange: Crédit Lyonnais, quai Jeanne d'Arc (tel. 47 93 02 65), before the bridge. Open Tues.-Fri. 8:35am-12:25pm and 2-5:30pm, Sat. 8:35am-12:25pm and 2-4pm.

Post Office: 10, quai Jeanne-d'Arc (tel. 47 93 12 08). Open Mon.-Fri. 8am-noon and 1:30-5:45pm, Sat. 8am-noon. **Postal Code:** 37500.

Trains: (tel. 47 93 11 04), av. Gambetta at av. du Docteur Labussière. To Tours (2 per day, 1 hr., 35F). SNCF buses, not trains, connect Chinon to Thouars (2 per day, 1¼ hr., 35F); railpasses are valid. Open Mon.-Sat. 6am-7:30pm, Sun. 10:15-11:50am and 3:15-8:30pm.

Buses: stop at pl. Jeanne d'Arc. 5 daily buses to the Port-Boulet station. For information, call **Les Bus de Chinonais** at 47 93 08 30 or check at the train station. Also to Tours (Mon.-Sat. 2-3 per day, 1 hr., 35F).

Bike Rental: At tourist office: tired cycles for about 35F per day, deposit 100F. At station: 40F per ½-day, 50F per day, deposit 500F or credit card. You can return to Tours or Langeais. Free transport on many trains. Open daily 10am-7pm.

Medical Assistance: Clinique Jeanne d'Arc, rue des Quinquenays (tel. 47 93 17 78), off rue de Tours.

Police: 1, rue Voltaire (tel. 47 93 08 30, *poste* 320). **Emergency,** tel. 17.

Accommodations, Camping, and Food

Bargains are scarce so arrive early, call ahead, or plan on staying in the youth hostel. The hostel is uncrowded, relaxed, and worth a try even if you don't have an IYHF card.

Auberge de Jeunesse (IYHF) (tel. 47 93 10 48), on rue Descartes, about ½ km from the center of town and only a 5-min. walk from the train station. A combination youth hostel, *foyer*, and youth cultural center, this large, modern building has clean 4- to 6-bed rooms. Good kitchen facilities and mellow atmosphere. Reception open 6-10:30pm. Lockout 2-6pm. Curfew 10:30pm. 38F per person. Sheets 13F. Closed 15 days in late December.

Hôtel le Point du Jour, 102, quai Jeanne-d'Arc (tel. 47 93 07 20), 5 min. from the station. Popular, family-run place has one room without shower for 85F. Singles and doubles with shower 115-140F. Breakfast 18F. Reservations necessary (1 month in advance July-Aug.).

Le Jeanne-d'Arc, 11, rue Voltaire (tel. 47 93 02 85), above a café opposite the tourist office. Elegant, surprisingly quiet, and extremely clean. Singles and doubles 120F, with shower 140F. Triples and quads 210F. Showers 10F. 18F breakfast includes exceptionally buttery croissants. Call at least 2 days ahead in summer.

Camping: Camping Municipale de Chinon (tel. 47 93 08 35), across the river at Ile-Auger off RN749. Pleasant sites only 10-15 min. from the tourist office. 6.60F per person, 4.80F per tent. Shower 4F. Open April-Nov.

The old quarter has a real sense of style—and an eye on your wallet. Splendid French cuisine awaits at **Les Années 30,** 78, rue Voltaire (tel. 47 93 37 18), which has a tasteful indoor dining room and covered terrace. (Four-course *menus* 70 and 100F. Open Thurs.-Tues.) Not just another flash in the pan, **Du Grand Carroi,** 30, rue du Grand Carroi, off rue Voltaire, fries great *crêpes* for 20-30F. (Open Tues.-Sun. noon-2pm and 7:30-11pm.) Save room for the 11F dessert *crêpes* at **Rabelais,** 3, rue Voltaire.

Sights

Let your imagination recreate the crumbling **Château de Chinon** (tel. 47 93 13 45), now a clifftop ruin overlooking the river Vienne. This hulking rockpile was never destroyed but fell into decay through neglect under Cardinal Richelieu and, later, Napoleon. Originally built by Henry II of England to protect his holdings in France, it passed into French hands when King John lost it to King Philippe in 1205. This eminently defensible château consisted of three parts: the main **Château de Milieu, Château du Coudray** to the west, and **Fort St-Georges,** which once stood on the hill next to the present-day entrance. An optional guided tour (in French or English) leads through the **Logis Royaux,** partially reconstructed since 1970. The *logis* contain some medieval tapestry and sculpture, but the focus is on history. (There is a genealogical chart or official document on display in almost every room.) The ruined great hall contains a plaque marking the site where Joan of Arc prophetically recognized Charles VII, then the beleaguered Dauphin, in 1429.

After the tour, you are free to wander around the impressive fortifications, which contain the king's secret entrance, a narrow staircase leading into the *logis* from the ravine separating the châteaux. The only other entrance was through the 15th-century **Tour de l'Horloge,** which now houses an informative Musée Jeanne d'Arc, complete with multi-language audiotapes on each floor describing Joan's exploits (in a most opinionated fashion). (Open July-Aug. 9am-7pm; May-June daily 9am-6pm; Sept. 9am-6pm; Oct.-Nov. and Feb. to mid-March 9am-noon and 2-5pm; and mid-March-April 9am-noon and 2-6pm. Admission 20F, students 14F.)

Chapelle St-Radagonde, a 12th-century ruin, is about a 25-minute walk from the center. Follow rue Jean-Jacques Rousseau onto a mountain road lined with *maisons troglodytiques,* comfortable caves cut in the chalk where families live year-round. Behind is an elaborate complex of caves now containing regional art, tools, and utensils. The caretaker, who speaks inspired English, will spend 40 minutes guiding one visitor. The chapel is open only when the caretaker is there (usually throughout all school vacations—about July-Aug. 15), so check with the tourist office before making the trek. (Open daily 10am-7pm. Admission 10F.)

The **Musée du Vieux Chinon,** 44, rue Voltaire, has loads of local pottery, model boats, and lace bonnets. Don't say we didn't warn you. (Open 10am-12:30pm and 2:30-6:30pm. Admission 15F, students 10F.) For free, the **Cave Plouzeau,** 94, rue Voltaire (tel. 47 93 16 34), conducts tours and pours out some of their superb white and red Chinon wine. Be subtle as you nip from the 30 or so bottles; you can show your appreciation by taking a 25-30F bottle home. (Open Tues.-Sun. 10am-noon and 2-6pm.) You may also want to visit the kitschy but entertaining **Musée Animé de Vin,** 12, rue Voltaire (tel. 47 93 25 63), which illustrates the wine-making process with "automatons" who lace their speech with Rabelais quotations and end with the exhortation "drink always and never die." Shows are given in both English and French. (Open Fri.-Wed. 10am-noon and 2-6pm. Admission 16F, including a glass of Chinon wine.) Chinon also has its very own discotheque at **L'Acropole,** 13, rue Jean-Jacques Rousseau (tel. 47 93 03 30), where dancing automatons punctuate their smooth talk with more scatological quotations from the Bard of Chinon (cover 50F). There is a large, all-day **market** every Thursday in pl. Hôtel de Ville. On the first weekend of August, Chinon holds its popular **Marché Médiéval.** Medieval peddlers and artisans crowd the streets, bars serve food and drinks under the trees, and those in vaguely period costume may explore the château and town museums for free (anachronists must pay 35F).

Saumur

Immortalized in Balzac's novel *Eugénie Grandet,* Saumur bears few traces of the provincial idyll from which Eugénie watched life go by. The vines that made old Grandet rich still provide the town's main source of income, but the heavy traffic on the cobblestone streets adds a distinctly modern jangle to this city of 30,000. Saumur offers a variety of sights and museums, many of a horsey bent because of the resident *Cadre Noir* equestrian corps. This agreeable town merits a day's exploration. Plan ahead if you intend to stay overnight.

Orientation and Practical Information

Frequent trains running between Nantes and Tours serve Saumur; destinations farther away often require a change, usually at Tours. Most of the town is on the southern bank of the Loire, across from the train station. Take local bus A to the tourist office at pl. Bilange; otherwise, it's a 10-15 min. walk. Go right out of the train station, then turn right on the bridge. Cross Pont des Cadets, follow av. du Général de Gaulle across the island, and follow Pont Cessart to the tourist office.

Tourist Office: (tel. 41 51 03 06), in pl. Bilange. Helpful staff will book beds (5F), change money (commission 5%), and give information on tours of châteaux and vineyards. English spoken. Open Mon.-Sat. 9:15am-7pm, Sun. 10:30am-12:30pm and 3-6:30pm; Sept. 16-June 14 Mon.-Sat. 9:15am-12:30pm and 2-6pm.

Currency Exchange: Crédit Lyonnais (tel. 41 67 64 01), on rue de Gaulle. Accepts all travel-er's checks with the standard 24F commission. Open Mon.-Fri. 9:20am-12:30pm and 2:30-6:30pm.

Post Office: rue Volney (tel. 41 51 22 77). Have your Poste Restante mail addressed to "Sau-mur Volney," or it will be delivered to the main office on rue des Près (tel. 41 50 13 00), ½-hr. out of town. Open Mon.-Fri. 8am-6:30pm, Sat. 8am-noon. **Branch office** across from the station open the same hours. **Postal Code: 49400.**

Trains: (tel. 41 67 50 50), on av. David d'Angers. From pl. Bilange in *centre ville,* take bus A toward St-Lambert or Chernin Vert. Eleven per day to Tours (¾-hr., 42F) and Angers (20 min., 33F). You can get off at Port-Boulet (13F) and take a bus to Chinon (call **Les Bus du Chinonais** at 47 93 08 30 in Chinon for information). The station arranges connections to more distant destinations such as Sables d'Olonne (1 per day, 3-5 hr., 107F).

Buses: (tel. 41 51 27 29), on pl. St-Nicolas on the southern banks in front of a church. Go 2 blocks west of pont Cessart, then 1 block south. To: Doué-la-Fontaine (2-3 per day, ½-hr.); Angers (4 per day, 1½ hr.); Fontevraud (3 per day, 35 min.). Three or 4 buses per day to Angers and Tours. **Local buses** depart from pl. Roosevelt (tel. 41 51 11 87); tickets 9.20F, in *carnet* 4.50F.

Bike Rental: Brison, 49, rue Maréchal Leclerc (tel. 41 51 02 09). Best bikes and the best deal. 22.50F per ½-day, 34.50F per day, 140F per week, deposit 250F. Open Tues.-Sat. 8am-noon and 2-7pm. Also at the **train station.** 40F per ½-day, 50F per day, deposit 500F. **Cycles Carlos,** 57, quai Mayraud (tel. 41 67 69 32), 30F per ½-day, 55F per day, 275F per week, whopping 1200F deposit. **Cycles Briand,** 50, route de Rouen (tel. 41 67 63 50), 32F per day, 130F per week, 500F deposit.

Laundromat: 12, rue Maréchal Leclerc. Cheap, modern, and efficient. Wash 10F, dry 2F per 8 min. 2F and 10F coins. Open daily 7am-9:30pm.

Medical Assistance: Centre Hospitalier, rue Seigneur (tel. 41 53 25 00). **SAMU,** tel. 41 48 44 22. Ambulances.

Police: (tel. 41 51 04 32), on rue Montesquieu. **Emergency,** tel. 17.

Accommodations and Camping

Good values are painfully scarce; call ahead in summer.

Auberge de Jeunesse (IYHF)/Centre International de Séjour, rue de Verden (tel. 41 67 45 00), on Ile d'Offard between the station and the tourist office. Large and modern hostel next to a 3-star campsite on a delightful island. Good kitchen facilities and washing machine. Re-ception open 8-10am and 5-10pm. Lockout 10am-5pm. Curfew 10pm; ask for a key if you'll be out late. 39F per person. Sheets 17F. Breakfast 15F.

Hôtel Bretagne, 55, rue St-Nicholas (tel. 41 51 26 38). Noisy location but attractive rooms with wood floors and firm mattresses to sooth the bicycle back, an epidemic that strikes the region each tourist season. Rooms 130-150F, with shower 180F. Showers 15F. Breakfast 20F.

Hôtel de la Croix de Guerre, 9, rue de la Petite Bilange (tel. 41 51 05 88), off pl. Bilange. Spacious, comfortable rooms make the low-rent downstairs bar and rickety stairs bearable. Singles and doubles 95-115F, with shower 155F. Showers 15F. Breakfast 20F.

Camping: Camping Municipal de L'Ile d'Offard (tel. 41 67 45 00), at the end of rue Verden on Ile d'Offard, next to the hostel. A 3-star rapidly becoming a 4-star. 16F per person, 27F per site. ELectricity 14F. Open Mon.-Fri. 8am-noon and 2-10pm, Sat.-Sun. 8-10am and 5-10pm. Also **Camping Chantepie** (tel. 41 67 95 34), 6km out of Saumur in St-Hilaire-St-Florent. 17F per person, 20F per site. Electricity 15F.

Food

Saumur's name proudly graces a fine white, a subtle rosé, and an earthy red wine. The *caves* are outside town; ask the tourist office about tours and *dégustations.* Thinly sliced *champignons* (mushrooms) marinated in wine are a local specialty. Small fresh produce markets fill pl. de la République (Sat. morning) and av. de Gaulle (Thurs. morning). A modern, covered market, **Les Halles,** pl. St-Pierre, has all a picnicker desires. (Open Tues.-Fri. 8am-12:30pm and 3-7:30pm, Sat. 7am-1pm

and 3-7:30pm, Sun. 9am-12:30pm.) The streets around pl. St-Pierre shelter some
good restaurants.

La Pierre Chaude, 41, av. du Général de Gaulle, on the island. Catherine and Patrick welcome you with duck, whiskey flambée, and 58F and 95F *menus.* Open Mon.-Fri. noon-2pm
and 7:30-10pm, Sat.-Sun. 7:30-10pm.

Le Chianti, 65, rue St-Nicholas. *Magnifique* pizza (31-48F) and Italian fare. Open Sun.-Fri.
noon-2pm and 7pm-late, Sat. noon-2pm.

Le Quichenotte, 41, rue Haute St-Pierre, next to the church. Imaginative *crêpe* combinations
at low prices. Norwegian *crêpe* with spinach and salmon, 38F. Steak tartare 40F. Open
Thurs.-Tues. noon-2pm and 7-9:30pm.

Sights and Entertainment

The picture-book 14th-century **château** stands aloof above the city's otherwise
unassuming skyline. Designed for defense, it is better preserved but has fewer fine
touches than its Loire Valley counterparts. Duke René of Anjou tried to make it
more comfortable in the 15th century, and it proved useful to the Protestant governor of the town during the Wars of Religion and to the members of Saumur's cavalry school, who resisted the German army in 1940. Although the castle lacks grace,
the museums inside definitely compensate.

The **Musée des Arts Décoratifs** (tel. 41 51 30 46) has assembled a fascinating
collection of medieval painting and sculpture, 15th- and 16th-century tapestries,
and *faïence.* The **Musée du Cheval** upstairs, with its bridles, bits, horseshoes, and
horse skeletons, will interest true equestrians and those who, like Marcey Bailey,
haven't outgrown their horse phase. The guided tour, in French or English, blitzes
through both museums in an hour, locking doors behind it; ask the guide if you
want to see anything in more detail afterwards. If you don't mind shaky staircases,
climb the **Tour de Guët** for a great screw, er, *view* of the environs. (Château and
museums open daily 9am-6:30pm; July-Aug. also 8:30-10:30pm; Sept. 16-June 14
9am-11:30am and 2-5pm; Nov.-March 9am-11:30am and 2-5pm Wed.-Mon. Admission 22F, students 14F, 2F less Sept.-June.)

Saumur's tradition as an equestrian center goes back to its establishment in 1763
as the training ground for the royal cavalry. The French cavalry still trains here,
though in 1943 the school was enlarged to house "modern cavalry," or artillery.
About 10 minutes from the center of town stands the palatial **Ecole de Cavalerie,**
founded in 1814 and still home to the nation's elite equestrian order, the Cadre Noir.
Competitions and public presentations are held periodically throughout the summer. Contact the tourist office for dates. Nearby, the **Musée des Blindés** (tank museum) may amuse Saddam Hussein and other artillery buffs. (Open daily 9am-noon
and 2-6pm. Admission 15F, student 13F.) Real French soldiers drive real tanks
around the buildings near the museum like bumper cars.

Despite Saumur's status as Europe's leading producer of Carnival masks, local
celebrations are staid and orderly. In late July the cavalry school shows off in the
celebrated annual **Carrousel.** After the two hours of jumping, dressage, and stunts,
the spectacle degenerates into a three-hour motorcycle show and dusty tank parade.
(Admission 40-90F.) Every week in July and August various performances occur
at pl. de l'Hôtel de Ville.

Near Saumur

From its founding in the 11th century until the Revolution, **Abbaye de Fontevraud** enjoyed quiet fame as a monastic center for royalty and nobility. More than
half of the governing abbesses were of royal blood. The guided tour leads through
the cupola-capped abbey church past the remains of the tombs of the Plantagenets:
Henry II, Eleanor of Aquitaine, Richard Cœur de Lion, and Isabelle of Angoulême,
the wife of King John of England. The original tombs were destroyed during the
Revolution; afterward the British government repeatedly but unsuccessfully sought
the transfer of the royal remains to Westminster. The Plantagenets, the French gov-

ernment maintains, were Dukes of Anjou first and Kings of England second. As elaborate as the tombs and church is the enormous octagonal kitchen in the twenty-chimneyed **Tour Evraud.** In July, the abbey also hosts the **Centre Culturel de l'Ouest de la France,** an institute that brings art and architecture exhibits, concerts, and plays to this historic setting. Call 41 51 73 52 for reservations and tickets (40-120F). (Abbey open June-Sept. 15 Wed.-Mon. 9am-7pm; Sept. 16-Oct. Wed.-Mon. 9:30am-12:30pm and 2-6pm. Admission 22F, students 15F.) Three **buses** per day run from Saumur to Fontevraud (about 15km).

A daytrip to the countryside allows you to visit the local wine and mushroom *caves.* Most are 3km west of Saumur on D751 in St-Hilaire-St-Florent; pick up a list at the tourist office. (Generally open Mon.-Sat. 9-11:30am and 2-5:30pm.) A bit farther along D751, the **Musée du Champignon** organizes tours through some of the mushroom *caves.* Originally mined for stone to build the nearby châteaux, the *caves* now grow 70% of France's mushrooms in about 500km of underground tunnels. (Open mid-March to mid-Nov. daily 10am-12:30pm and 2-5:30pm. Admission and obligatory tour 18F, students 12F.) Take the local bus from pl. Roosevelt to St-Hilaire-St-Florent, and walk the 1km from the last stop.

Angers

Guarding the western gateway to the château region, the massive stone walls of Angers once daunted potential attackers of the Dukes of Anjou. Although Angers retains only its château and cathedral from its illustrious past as the Plantagenets' capital, the city unfairly condemned by a certain 19th-century novelist and travel writer as "stupidly and vulgarly modernized" still attracts visitors to its atmospheric, shop-lined streets. Home to the magnificent Tapisseries de l'Apocalypse, a 75-panel representation of the book of Revelation, this city of 200,000 raptured inhabitants makes a fitting End to a Jamesian tour of château country.

To get to the **château,** follow rue de la Gare to rue Talot onto bd. du Roi-René, and then continue left for a few blocks. A deep moat surrounding the thick gray walls has been converted into a colorful garden and deer park. Most of the buildings on the inside were constructed during the 15th-century reign of Anjou's last and greatest duke, René le Bon, who not only commanded an empire that included Sicily, Piedmont, and Lorraine, but also found the time to write several romances and volumes of poetry. The small Gothic chapel houses an exhibition of his work. After René, the château went downhill fast, eventually becoming a prison. It narrowly escaped destruction during the Wars of Religion, when Henry III ordered its demolition. (Fortunately, he died before his plans were carried out.) Walk around the ramparts for a view of the gardens, the city, and the Maine river.

Angers's richest attraction, the **Tapisseries de l'Apocalypse,** was woven of wool and gold thread from 1375 to 1380. Recognized as a masterpiece of European medieval art, the tapestry is noted for the consistency of its figures, the flamboyance of its multi-headed lions and serpents, and the graphic dialogue attributed to its characters. The childhood drawings of **Lucus,** in the kitchen downstairs, are worth a puzzled look. (Château open mid-March to June 9am-noon and 2-6:30pm; July-Sept. 9am-7pm; Oct. to mid-March 9:30am-noon and 2-5:30pm. Admission 23F, students 12F.) The tapestry was originally housed in the **Cathédrale St-Maurice,** on rue St-Maurice in the *vieille ville,* where several individual works remain. (Open daily 6:45am-7pm.)

Even in summer, unless you happen to arrive on a holiday, getting a place for the night is not a problem. The **Centre d'Accueil du Lac de Maine,** route de Pruviers (tel. 41 48 57 01), has singles for 53F and breakfast for 14.50F. Excellent accommodations and extensive sports facilities make the bus ride (#6 to Accueil Lac de Maine, 5F) worth it. Call ahead to see if there's space. (Open June 15-Sept. 15.) To reach the **Foyers des Jeunes Travailleurs** on rue Darwin (tel. 41 48 14 55), take bus #6 (*direction* "Val-de-Maine"). There are lower prices (36F per night) but not as many amenities. (Open July-Aug.) Family-run **Les Négociants,** 2, rue de la Roë (tel. 41 87 70 03), near the bus station, has clean singles and doubles for 118F, 148F with shower. Across the street from the train station, **La Coupe d'Or,** 5, rue de la Gare (tel. 41 88 45 02) has small but comfy rooms for 90-115F. If you must bathe, shell out 130-160F for room with a shower. There is no hall shower in the annex. (Breakfast 18F. Call ahead in summer.) There are two campgrounds close to Angers. **Camping du Lac de Maine** (tel. 41 73 05 03), next to the Centre d'Accueil, has a sandy lakeside beach. (27F per person and tent, hot water and shower included.) Almost as nice, **Camping du Parc de la Haye** (tel. 41 69 33 63), 4km out of Angers by bus #3 to Val d'Or, is near a pond and riding facilities. (Open June 15-Sept. 15.)

The pleasant pedestrian district around pl. Romain has many enticing sidewalk cafés, *pâtisseries,* and *charcuteries,* but Angers's most remarkable cheap fare awaits at Les Halles, a covered **market** at rue Plantagenet behind the cathedral. (Open Tues.-Sat. 8:30am-7:30pm, Sun. 8:30am-1pm.) **La Treille,** 12, rue Montault, serves an original 60F *menu* near the cathedral. (Open Mon.-Sat. noon-2pm and 7-9pm.) The best of the restaurants near the train station is **Le Signal,** rue de la Gare, which serves salads (25-35F) and a 55F *menu.* (Open daily noon-2pm and 7-9pm.) Noisy, fun **Chantegrille** at 25, bd. Foch, has a 55F all-you-can-eat buffet. (Open 11:45am-2:15pm and 7-11pm daily.) **Sur la Pouce,** on rue Bressigny, offers a 30F student *menu* of Greek and Turkish specialties.

The **train station,** rue de la Gare (tel. 41 88 50 50), is The Place to hop a train to Saumur (½-hr., 33F), Tours (1 hr., 64F), Orléans (2¼ hr., 123F), and Paris-Austerlitz (2¾ hr., 163F). The station rents **bikes** for 50F per day with a 500F deposit. (Open 8am-7:40pm daily.) From the bus station at pl. de la République (tel. 41 88 59 25; open daily 7am-8pm), buses leave about twice per day for Saumur (35.50F), Mont-Bellay (39.50F), Sable-Sarthe (40.50F), Châteaubriant (52F) and Rennes (81F). The **tourist office** (tel. 41 88 69 93) is across the street from the château at pl. Kennedy. The unruffled English-speaking staff organizes trips to châteaux and changes money when the banks are closed. (Open Mon.-Sat. 9am-7pm, Sun. 10:30am-6:30pm; Oct.-May Mon.-Sat. 9am-12:30pm and 2-6:30pm.) The **post office** is in the center of town at 1, rue Franklin-Roosevelt (tel. 41 88 45 47). Poste Restante mail should be addressed "Angers-Ralliement"; otherwise it will be shunted off to the rue Bamako office, a half-hour walk south of town. You can change money here, too. Angers's **postal code** is 49052. (Office open Mon.-Fri. 8am-7pm, Sat. 8am-noon.)

Poitou-Charentes

Granddaughter of the first troubadour and celebrated in song, mother of European royalty and shrewd politician, Eleanor of Aquitaine left her mark on the region that stretches from just south of Brittany to just north of Spain, much of which is now Poitou-Charentes. Eleanor married the French dauphin, Louis VII, was crowned queen of France, went on crusade, and then divorced Louis. By marrying Henry Plantagenet, who was to become king of England, Eleanor made English holdings in France nearly as great as those of the French monarchy.

It was around Eleanor's time that the pilgrimage route to St-Jacques de Compostelle, or Santiago de Compostela, brought thousands of people through this region every year. Saint Jacques was revered as the patron saint of the Franks in their wars against the Spanish Muslims, so it was fitting that many of the pilgrims pass by way of Poitiers, site of the battle at which Charles Martel turned back the Muslims in 732. Hostels, hospitals and Romanesque churches sprouted up along these routes to accommodate both the devout and the "false pilgrims" (such as the poet Villon) who robbed others along the way. An early travel guide for this pilgrimage route told pilgrims where to stay and included such cultural notes as "The Bordelais speak roughly, but their wine is excellent."

That excellent Bordeaux wine enchanted the English, who possessed the area during the Hundred Years' War and called the wine "claret." In the 17th century, the *Charentais* began distilling their wine to make cognac, which the English also adopted with usual zeal under the name "brandywine," after the Dutch words for "burned wine." *Pineau,* a more affordable mixture of cognac and grape or pear juice, is a local favorite.

The area again served as a battleground in the Wars of Religion, when the Protestant stronghold of La Rochelle fell to Cardinal Richelieu, and during the Revolution, when conservative peasants in the Vendée rebelled and were savagely repressed by the revolutionary government.

Now less tumultuous, Poitou-Charentes is blessed with a luminous climate, its beaches receiving more sun (and tourists) than any area of France except Provence. Its unifying characteristic is the constant proximity to the ocean. Fishing—for lobster, oysters, tuna, sardines, and other *fruits de la mer*— is still an important part of the economy. Other regional specialties include *farcis* (stuffed-meat dishes), *chabichou* (a rich goat cheese), and snails; desserts include *clafoutis* (a cherry tart) and chocolate candies called *marguerites* or *duchesses* after the famous Duchess Marguerite of Angoulême.

Trains in Poitou-Charentes run efficiently and frequently to all major towns. Bicycling is an enjoyable way of seeing the countryside, and many people hitch. For a vacation of a different sort, travel by boat down one of the region's main rivers, the Clain or the Charente.

Poitiers

A city on a hill above the rivers Clain and Boivre, Poitiers has attracted invaders, settlers, and visitors for centuries. From the ramparts of this balcony town, you can see much of the Poitou region, including modern Poitiers, home to 120,000. Although rather unremarkable at first glance, Poitiers hides a number of grand old buildings with interesting stories to tell. Recent archaeological excavations have unearthed a Bronze Age fortress, and remains of a Roman theater and kilns are still visible in Vieux Poitiers. From the 10th to the 15th century, the powerful Counts of Poitou and Dukes of Aquitaine ruled the expanding city. The impressive Palais de Justice and several remarkable churches remain from this period. In 1432, Charles VII established what was then one of France's most prestigious universities in Poitiers. The city suffered centuries of cultural stagnation after the Wars of Religion, but the arrival of a Michelin tire factory in 1972 and subsequent economic and cultural growth rejuvenated the capital of Poitou.

Orientation and Practical Information

Poitiers, 350km southwest of Paris, is neatly enclosed by train tracks to the west and a semi-circular stretch of the River Clain to the east. The city's street life centers on the stores and cafés near **place Maréchal Leclerc** and **place Charles de Gaulle,** three blocks north. Buses #1,2,3,7,8 and 16 run from the station to the Hôtel de Ville in the center of town; otherwise, it's a 15-minute hike.

Tourist Office: 8, rue des Grandes Ecoles (tel. 49 41 21 24). Good information on the Poitou-Charentes region. Plenty of free brochures, including a city map. Interesting guided tours change daily (10am and 3pm; 22F, under 25 12F). Will find you a room in town (10F) or in the region (20F). Free list of *hôtels pas chers,* (cheap hotels). Open Mon.-Sat. 9am-7pm, Sept.-June Mon.-Fri. 9am-noon and 1:30-6pm, Sat. 9am-noon and 2-6pm. **Regional,** 15, rue Carnot (tel. 49 41 58 22), near pl. Maréchal Leclerc. Start at the tourist office above, but this office also has excellent information. Open Mon.-Fri. 9am-noon and 2-5pm.

Budget Travel: Agence Touristique de l'Ouest, 2, rue Claveurier (tel. 49 01 84 84). Reduced rates on Air France travel. Open Mon.-Sat. 9am-noon and 2-6:30pm.

Currency Exchange: Crédit Agricole, 65, rue Gambetta (tel. 49 41 02 34). Competitive rates with 24F commission. Open Tues.-Fri. 9:15am-12:30pm and 2-6pm, Sat. 9:15am-12:30pm and 2-4pm.

Post Office: 16, rue Arthur Ranc (tel. 49 01 83 80). **Telephones, currency exchange,** and **Poste Restante.** Open Mon.-Fri. 8:30am-7pm, Sat. 8:30am-noon. **Postal Code:** 86000.

Trains: (tel. 49 58 50 50, reservations 49 55 81 64), on bd. du Grand Cerf. TGV service began Nov. 1990. To: Angoulême (12-16 per day, 1¼ hr., 67F); Saintes (4-8 per day, 1¾ hr., 110F); La Rochelle (7-9 per day, 1¾ hr., 84F); Les Sables d'Olonne (3-4 per day, at least 4 hr., 158F); Bordeaux (12-16 per day, 2 hr., 133F); Paris (10-14 per day, 3 hr., 173F). Information office open Mon.-Sat. 8:30am-7:10pm and Sun. 9:15am-noon and 2-7pm.

Buses: Rapides du Poitou, 20, rue de la Plaine (tel. 49 46 27 45). To Chauvigny (2-4 per day, 1 hr., 23F) and St-Savin-sur-Gartempe (2-3 per day, 1½ hr., 31F). Buses also run to Civray and most of the smaller towns nearby. All buses stop at the train station. **Local buses:** tel. 49 61 07 71. 6F buys an hour of bus transport.

Bike Rental: Cyclamen, 49, rue Arsène Orillard (tel. 49 88 13 25). Ten-speeds 39F per day, 144.50F per week. *Sacoches* (bike bags) 7.70F per day, 27.30F per week. Open Tues.-Sat. 9am-noon and 2-7pm.

Youth Information: Centre d'Information Jeunesse (CIJ), 64, rue Gambetta (tel. 49 88 64 37), near the Hôtel de Ville on a pedestrian street. A gold mine of clues on places to stay, cultural activities, sports, and employment, even a ride board. Free maps. *Carte Jeune* (70F) gives discounts on everything everywhere. Open Mon.-Fri. 10am-7pm, Sat. 10am-noon and 2-6pm.

English Bookstore: Maison de la Presse, 39, rue de la Gambetta. A few shelves of mind-occludingly light reading. Open Tues.-Sat. 9am-7pm, Mon. 9am-noon and 2-7pm.

Laundromat: rue de René Descartes Philosophe at pl. de la Liberté. Wash 15F, dry 2F per 5 min. Soap 2F. 10F, 2F and 1F coins. Open Mon.-Sat. 8am-6:30pm. Also at 2bis, rue de Carnot. Same prices, but 10F, 5F and 1F coins. Open daily 8am-8pm.

Hospital: 15, rue Hôtel Dieu (tel. 49 88 02 10).

Medical Assistance: Ambulance, tel. 49 88 33 34.

Police: 45, rue de la Marne (tel. 49 88 94 21). **Emergency,** tel. 17.

Accommodations and Camping

The hostel, university housing, and campgrounds are all far from the center of town. With or without the tourist office's list of cheap hotels, you should be able to find a reasonable place downtown. As always, it's best to call ahead in July and August.

Auberge de Jeunesse (IYHF), 17, rue de la Jeunesse (tel. 49 58 03 05), 2½km from the station. Take bus #3 from the station (Mon.-Sat. every ½-hr. until 7pm, 6F) or turn right at the station and walk along bd. du Pont Achard. Large building with municipal pool next door (5F a dip.) Clean 2- and 3-bed rooms. Reception open Mon.-Fri. 11am-1pm, 5-7pm, 8-10:30pm; Sat.-Sun. 7-10pm. Curfew 11pm. 52F per night. IYHF card required. Breakfast 13F. Incredible lunch or dinner 38F.

University Housing, 42, rue du Recteur Pineau (tel. 49 44 52 31), at the Résidence Descartes. Take bus #1 from the Hôtel de Ville. Clean dormitory singles with bed, sink, and desk. Call ahead if arriving late. 65F per person. Several nights 57F per person. Breakfast 7F at the university restaurant across the street.

Hôtel Jules Ferry, 27, rue Jules Ferry (tel. 49 37 80 14), near Eglise St-Hilaire on a pleasant street. Clean, renovated rooms with beds you'll get lost in. Heroic manager speaks English and Spanish. Singles and doubles from 100F, with shower 130F. Showers 15F. Breakfast 20F. Garage 15F.

Hôtel du Poitou, 79, bd. Grand Cerf (tel. 49 58 38 06), close to the station on the left. Not the cleanest or brightest rooms you've seen, but the best prices near the station and better than a late-night walk to the hostel. Singles and doubles from 80F, with shower 120F. Bath 16F. Breakfast 16F. Open Sept.-July daily. Call ahead; often full June-July. Restaurant downstairs serves a solid 55F *menu* (open Sun.-Fri.).

Hôtel le Carnot, 40, rue Carnot (tel. 49 41 23 69). If you don't care much for socializing with the managers or taking a shower, stay here in 1 of the 70F rooms. Extra bed 15F. Breakfast 16F. Popular local bar/restaurant downstairs serves a 5-course *menu* (45-55F, drink included). Meals served Mon.-Sat. noon-2:30pm and 7-10:30pm.

Camping: Le Porteau (tel. 49 41 44 88), on a hill 2km out of town. Take bus #7 and ask to be dropped off *"devant le terrain"* (in front of the field). Clean bathrooms, showers, and a patch of grass just waiting for a tent. 5F per person, 2F per site. Electricity 3.45F. Parking 2F. **Camping St-Benoît,** route de Passelourdin (tel. 49 88 48 55), 5km from Poitiers. Take bus #2 from the train station, transfer to bus #10, and get off at St-Benoît. Open April-Sept.

Food

Poitevin chefs cook an interesting mélange of northern and southern cuisine. Try the *fromage de chèvre,* the local *andouillette* (spicy sausage), and, if you're up to it, the *anguilles* (eels). Baked goods are also superb, from the *brioche* and *clafoutis* (a cherry tart) to the *tarteau au fromage* (sweet cheese sponge). Most hotel bars post five-course *menus* for around 55F. Avoid the overpriced cafés on pl. Maréchal Leclerc; you need only wander out a block or two to find better values. Few places open on Sunday. You'll find the usual histrionics at the **outdoor market** on pl. Charles de Gaulle (Tues., Thurs., and Sat. until noon). **Monoprix,** on rue des Cordeliers at rue du Marché Notre Dame, has anchovies, underwear, and other necessities. (Open Mon.-Sat. 9:15am-6:15pm.) **Santé et Vie,** 68, rue de la Cathédrale, sells life-prolonging legumes and other healthy staples. (Open Tues.-Sun. 9am-12:30pm and 2:30-7pm.)

Le Roy d'Ys, 51, rue de la Cathédrale. A plain but noble *crêperie* with great *galettes* (12-35F). If you like fungus, try *pavé nantais* (29F) or one of the other 15-odd mushroom selections. Killer peach melba 25F. Open Mon.-Sat. noon-2pm and 7pm-midnight.

Flunch, 2, rue de Petit Bonneveau at rue Carnot, 1 block south of the Hôtel de Ville. An upbeat cafeteria with boulder-sized portions at rock-bottom prices. Tasty fish or steak with serve-yourself vegetables 20-30F. Salads 6-15F. Open daily 11am-10pm. Only customers eating full meals allowed 11am-2:30pm and 8-10pm.

Le Poitevin, 76, rue Carnot. Regional cuisine worth busting your budget for. Finish the 75F *menu* and the muscular staff will roll you out the door. Open Mon.-Sat. noon-2pm and 7-10pm.

Casa Nostra, bd. du Grand Cerf, across from the train station. Colorful and noisy Italian resto. Pizza 38F. Salads 37F. 50F *menu.* Open daily 11:30am-2:30pm, 7-10pm.

Sights and Entertainment

The churches that pepper the old town are worth a long look. Follow rue Gambetta away from the jostling crowds of the *centre ville* and step into eccentric 12th-century **Notre-Dame-la-Grande.** Like an ancient mural gorgeously misplaced in a medieval church, the columns painted in warm earth tones depict the stories of the Annunciation, the Visitation, the Nativity, and Joseph's meditation. (Open daily 8am-7pm.)

Impressive Notre-Dame may seem to be "the Cathedral," but this appellation really belongs to the larger **Cathédrale St-Pierre,** a few blocks down rue de la Cathédrale. Constructed on the orders of Eleanor and Henry Plantagenet, this 12th-century cathedral imposes with its sheer size and surging horizontal lines. Above the central door, irreverent pigeons hop from heaven to hell and back during the Last Judgment. (Open daily 8am-7pm.)

West of the Cathédrale St-Pierre, the Mediterranean **Baptistère St-Jean** dates from the 6th century—the oldest existing Christian structure in France. The octagonal font built into the floor dates from the 4th century, and recent diggings have uncovered older aqueducts. The remarkably sturdy stone-and-brick structure houses carved sarcophagi and friezes from the Roman and early Christian eras. (Open daily 10:30am-12:30pm and 1-6pm; Oct.-March Wed.-Mon. 1-6pm. Admission 4F.)

Next to the baptistery, the wonderful **Musée Ste-Croix** contains innumerable relics from Poitiers's Bronze Age and Roman settlements, as well as a fine collection of Dutch and Flemish paintings. (Open Mon. and Wed.-Fri. 10am-noon and 1-6pm, Sat.-Sun. 10am-noon and 2-6pm. Free.) **Devenir,** just across the street, houses sophisticated exhibits on technology. (Open Tues.-Fri. 10am-7pm, Sat.-Sun. 2-7pm. Admission 20F, students 12F. Admission to TV room free with ID as deposit for TV headset.)

Heading east on rue Jean Jaurès from the *baptistère,* cross pont Neuf and turn left on bd. Coligny, which becomes bd. du Colonel Barthal. Follow the road as it curves near the golden statue of the Virgin. As you pause to take in the face-slapping view of Poitiers, try to count all the little orange roofs. Turn right at the sign for **Hypogée Martyrium** at the top of the hill, left at the *gendarmerie,* and right at the next sign (a 20-min. walk). The Hypogée, a 17th-century underground chapel, rests on a site where 72 Christian martyrs were buried by the Romans. (Open Wed.-Mon. 10am-noon and 2-6pm; Oct.-April 10am-noon and 2-4pm.) In the northern end of the city, **Eglise Montierneuf** has a plain Romanesque front, the towers that seem to be *de rigueur* in Poitiers, a simple barrel-vaulted interior, and a surprisingly elegant apse floating on the lightest of flying buttresses. (Open Mon.-Sat. 9am-7pm. Closed to visitors Sun. during services.) For a taste of more secular Romanesque architecture, check out the **Palais de Justice,** pl. A. Lepetit in the *centre ville,* the former palace of the Dukes of Aquitaine. You can wander freely through the vast 12th-century timber-roofed King's Hall that once echoed with the ballads of troubadours, plans of crusading knights, and the verse of Eleanor of Aquitaine's *Courts of Love.* (Open Mon.-Fri. 7am-6pm.)

During the first two weeks of May, Poitiers hosts **Le Printemps Musical de Poitiers** (tel. 49 41 58 94), a harmonic convergence of concerts, exhibits, and debates. (Tickets 30-60F.) The concert series **Rencontres Musicales de Poitiers** features mostly classical works in biweekly concerts from late October through late April. (Tickets 55F, ages under 26 38F; available at kiosk in pl. Maréchal Leclerc.) *L'Affiche Hebdo,* available at the tourist office, lists all local cultural events. Another list includes nightclubs and discotheques.

Near Poitiers

Only 10km north of Poitiers looms **Futuroscope,** a science-oriented amusement park with one foot well through the door of the 21st century. No playground for squealing kiddies, this high-tech Valhalla boasts "Kinemax" (the largest flat screen in Europe), the "Showscan" (which produces a staggeringly realistic image at 60 frames per second, compared to the normal 24), the Dynamic Simulator (with moving seats, synchronized with the action on the screen), and the 360-degree Global Image. There is also a park exclusively for the aforementioned kiddies, an animated show, and an amphitheater on the banks of an artificial lake. The Innobus rolls to Futuroscope from the Poitiers train station (9:30 and 10:50am) and back (6:10pm) for 15F round-trip. (Park open July-Aug. 9am-7:30pm; April-June 9:30am-7pm, Sept. Wed.-Sun. 9:30am-6:30pm. Admission to Futuroscope 95F, children 65F.)

About 20km east of Poitiers lies the typically Viennois town of **Chauvigny**, its medieval walls clenched around a spectacular hilltop site. Inside the town's defenses stands the Romanesque **Eglise St-Pierre**, notable for its intricate sculpture. **Abbaye St-Savin-sur-Gartempe**, 10km to the east, displays a remarkable collection of frescoes even finer than those of Notre-Dame-la-Grande in Poitiers. Guided tours are available in July and August; call the tourist office at 49 46 39 01 or the mayor's office at 49 46 30 21. Three to five daily buses run to Chauvigny and St-Savin (23-31F). Some people find the hitch along N151 fairly easy. In Chauvigny, the riverside **Hôtel du Chalet Fleuri** (tel. 49 46 31 12) rents singles from 70F, doubles 90-160F.

Halfway to Angoulême on D1, the town of **Civray** claims one of the finest Romanesque churches in France, **Eglise St-Nicholas.** The sculptural work on its classically ordered west façade is remarkable. After seeing the church, there's little to do but fish in the Charente river or camp at **Les Coteaux.** (Open May-Sept. Call 49 87 17 24 or the mayor's office at 49 87 00 49.) Buses run from Poitiers to Civray.

Les Sables d'Olonne

If you like education with your leisure, don't stop at Les Sables d'Olonne. An uninteresting pile of stones constitutes the town's church, there's not a château in sight, and the alleged local folk tradition survives only in postcards and a few farm houses. What Les Sables does have is sand, sweeping in magnificent arcs along the Vendée coast. Although the advancing phalanx of high rises and less orderly regiments of sunbathers have spoiled things a bit, the beach in town remains clean and pleasant. **Plage de Tanchet,** farther east near the lake campground, begins the sandy chain along the east road. To the northwest lies the **Forêt d'Olonne** reserve, where huge dunes tumble from dry woodlands to the sea.

If disaster strikes and it rains, spend the day with the 120-odd cars and motorcycles in the popular **automobile museum** (tel. 51 22 05 81), 8km from town on route de Talmont. (Open daily April-Sept. 9:30am-noon and 2-7pm. Admission 28F, children 14F.) The **Musée de l'Abbaye Saint Croix** (tel. 51 32 01 16) on rue de Verdun houses the town's prehistoric, traditional, and contemporary art in a fairly small building. (Open June 15-Sept. daily 10am-noon and 2:30-6:30pm; Nov. 2-June 14 Tues.-Sun. 2:30-5:30pm. Admission 4F, children 2F. Free Wed. and Sun.)

Orientation and Practical Information

The train station lies off av. de Gaulle, which leads north to pl. Liberté. From the fountain and trees of pl. Liberté, rue de l'Hôtel de Ville branches west toward the port and quai Dingler. Rue Travot plunges south to the crescent beach and to sweltering, crowded promenade Georges Clemenceau.

Tourist Office: (tel. 51 32 03 28), on rue Maréchal Leclerc. From the station take a right onto av. de Gaulle, which leads to pl. Liberté; head diagonally across the square onto rue Leclerc. Remarkably patient staff will outfit you with a map and list of hotels. Some English spoken. Open daily 9am-12:15pm and 2-6:30pm, Sat. 9:15am-12:15pm and 2-4:30pm, Sun. 10:15am-12:30pm and 2:15-5:15pm; Sept.-June Mon.-Fri. 9am-12:15pm and 2-6:30pm, Sat. 9am-noon and 2-5:30pm. The branch at pl. Navarin gives maps and some information. Open 8:30pm-10:30pm.

Budget Travel: Hervouet Agence de Voyages, 12, av. du Général de Gaulle (tel. 51 32 02 54), a stone's throw from the train station. BIJ/Eurotrain tickets. Helpful staff. Open Mon.-Fri. 9am-noon and 2-7pm, Sat. 9am-noon and 2-6pm.

Currency Exchange: Crédit Agricole, 33, av. de Gaulle (tel. 51 21 05 02). Good rates with 24F commission. Open Mon.-Thurs. 9am-12:30pm and 1:30-5:30pm, Fri. until 4:45pm. On Saturday, go to the av. d'Aquitaine branch. Open 8:45am-12:15pm.

Post Office: Rue Nicot, off av. du Général de Gaulle. **Telephones.** Photocopies 1F per page. Open Mon.-Fri. 8:30am-6pm, Sat. 8:30am-noon. **Postal Code:** 85100.

Trains: (tel. 51 32 00 20), on av. Général de Gaulle. More than 8 trains per day to La Rochelle (2 hr., 82F) via La Roche-sur-Yon (29F). Also to Nantes (1½ hr., 67F) and Paris (5 hr., 235F). All trains to Paris except one a day are TGV and require a 30F reservation. Open Mon.-Thurs. 5:45am-8pm, Sat. 5:45am-9pm, Sun. 6am-9:15pm. Information office open daily 9am-noon and 2-7pm.

Buses: To the left of the train station. **CFIT,** tel. 51 32 08 28. Line #8 provides early morning service to the ports in St-Gilles-Croix-de-Vie (22F), St-Jean-de-Monts, Fromentine (44F), Nourmourtiers, and other small towns. Office open Mon.-Fri. 8-11:30am and 3-6:30pm, Sat. 8-11:30am. **Sovetours,** tel. 51 95 18 71. To La Rochelle (68F) and La Roche-sur-Yon (23.40F). Office open daily 9:30am-noon and 2:30-6:30pm, Sat. 9:30am-noon.

Bike and Moped Rental: Le Cyclotron, 66, promenade Clemenceau (tel. 51 32 64 15). Bikes 33F per day, 150F per week, deposit 500F. 10-speeds 39F per day, 190F per week. Beat-up mopeds from 280F per day, deposit 5000F. Free helmet. You can also rent brightly-colored pedecabs that seat 2-8 people for 45-125F per hour. Deposit 50F. Open daily July-Aug. 9am-midnight (bikes due back at 7pm); April-June 10am-noon and 2-6:30pm. The **train station** has only 6 bikes. 40F per ½-day, 50F per day, deposit 500F.

Surfboard Rental: Pacific Surf Shop, 13, promenade Clemenceau (tel. 51 95 96 94). 100F per day. Open daily 10am-12:30pm and 2:30-7:30pm.

Windsurfer and Sailboat Rental: call 51 95 15 09, the port at 51 32 51 16, or the mayor's office at 51 21 16 50. At la Base des Dériveurs on the west end of the beach. Windsurfers 45F per weekend, 70F per week. Sailboats 150F per week. Open daily 9am-7pm.

Laundromat: 33, bd. Castelnau. Wash 20F, dry 2F per 5 min. Takes 10F and 2F coins. Open 7am-10pm.

Hospital: bd. Pasteur (tel. 51 21 86 33).

Medical Assistance: Ambulance, tel. 51 95 32 52 or 51 32 49 09.

Police: Rue de Verdun (tel. 51 21 14 43). **Emergency,** tel. 17.

Accommodations, Camping, and Food

Masses descend on Les Sables in July and August. By the beginning of June, most hotels are booked solid. The small hostel has no telephone; send one night's payment well in advance to reserve a space. Hotels may accept telephone reservations. Finding a room shouldn't be difficult October through May.

Auberge de Jeunesse (IYHF), rue du Sémaphore (no phone), in neighboring La Chaume. Don't attempt the dusty 50-min. walk from the station; take the bus from pl. Liberté (*direction* "Côte Sauvage," 1 per hr. until 6:30pm, 5F), get off at Armandeche, and walk up rue de Sémaphore. The hostel will be on the left. Small and sandy with cool outdoor showers and toilets (indoor showers for women), but a fantastic view of the rocky Côte Sauvage and a low-key atmosphere. Great kitchen facilities. They have big plans to remodel and expand over the next 2 years. No lockout or curfew. 37F per person. 25F in tent outside. Open July 10-Aug., longer after remodeling.

Hôtel le Merle Blanc, 59, av. Aristide Briand (tel. 51 32 00 35), close to the beach and supermarket. Clean as a whistle with paper-thin walls. Friendly folks. Singles 75F. Doubles 100-130F. All with bidet and sink. Breakfast 20F. Open March 15-Sept. Call ahead.

Hôtel les Olonnes, 25, rue de la Patrie (tel. 51 32 04 12), not far from the beach. Average doubles 110F-170F. Showers included. Breakfast 19F. Open mid-June to Sept.

Le Majestic Hôtel, 24, quai Guiné (tel. 51 32 09 71), near beaches and center of town. Small but comfortable rooms. Guests received until 11pm. Singles and doubles with shower 110F. Breakfast 20F. Four-course 64F *menu* in the restaurant downstairs.

Hôtel Beauséjour, 96, rue Léon David (tel. 51 32 05 88), a 15-min. walk from the center of town. Clean rooms and helpful management. Lilliputian bathrooms. Singles and doubles from 100F. Good 5-course 60F *menu* in restaurant below. Open April-Sept.

Le Relais des Voyageurs, 84, av. Alcide Gabaret (tel. 51 95 15 96). One-star hotel. Slightly cramped doubles from 180F. Showers 15F (large bathtub and great shower). Breakfast 20F. Restaurant downstairs Call in Jan. or Feb. for summer reservations.

Camping: There are dozens of sites in and around Les Sables—camp your heart out. The most convenient are always booked: **Le Lac** (tel. 51 95 13 35), on bd. Kennedy. Two-star. **Les Dunes** (tel. 51 32 31 21), L'Aubraie-La Chaume, on top of a dune. Four-star. Open June 15- Sept. 15. No reservations accepted. **Les Roses** (tel. 51 95 10 42), on rue des Roses. Four stars and a long waiting list. Open April-Oct. 15. The tourist office has a list of many more.

The promenades and quais of Les Sables have a netful of seafood restaurants, each as charming and expensive as the next. Journey one street inland to **Le Théâtre,** 20, bd. Roosevelt, where good 46-140F *menus* include the daily catch. (Open July-Aug. daily noon-2pm and 7-10pm, Feb. 15-June and Sept.-Oct. Same hours except Tues. night and Wed.) Follow Keith Sikes and his attendant paparazzi to flamboyant **La Salsa: Chez Carmine,** quai Guiné, where pizzas cost 49-59F, lasagne 59F, a seafood platter 85F, and *bouillabaisse* 150F. (Open daily for lunch and dinner.) If you're staying at the hostel, convenient and cheap **Restaurant Rosemonde,** 10, quai George V (tel. 51 95 25 81), in La Chaume, serves a filling 45F *menu* of Schwarzeneggerian mussels. **Arôm' Café,** 30, rue Hôtel de Ville, sells delicious homemade ice cream for 6.50F a scoop. (Open Mon.-Sat. 9am-12:30 and 2-7:30pm, Sun. 10am-12:30pm.) Fresh fish and produce are there for the buying at **Les Halles,** just south of the church. (Open Mon.-Sat. 8am-1pm. Big market days Wed. and Sat. 7am-1pm.) **Monoprix,** 15, rue Hôtel de Ville, will also fill your picnic basket. (Open Mon.-Sat. 9am-12:30pm and 2:15-7:30pm, Sun. 10am-12:30pm.)

The Islands

The islands scattered of the Poitevin coast from Les Sables d'Olonne to Royan make excellent daytrips from these and other towns on the mainland. Although all four islands endure their share of summer visitors, transportation difficulties and scarce accommodations ensure that fewer sunbathers clog their beaches than those near Les Sables or La Rochelle. Transportation to and among these islands is handled by innumerable ferry lines and three different bus line: Océcars, Citram, and Aunis et Saintonge (AS). They work well together (however intricately), their offices are usually close, and they will point you to the next office with a smile.

Ile d'Yeu

Reclusive monks christened this scrap of earth Ile Dieu (God's Island) in the 9th century. Although in recent years this seclusion has been marketed, the beauty that inspired the first monks remains. This tiny island of farms and hedges ringed by a splintered coast busies itself with fishing most of the year and endures tourists only in summer. The island even has a microclimate; one coast might be sunny when the opposite coast is soaked with rain, and palm trees thrive with no threat of frost.

The island stretches roughly northwest to southeast. **Vieux Château,** about 3.5km south of Port-Joinville, perches precariously on rocks in the port. Occupied in turn by Roman, English, and Spanish troops, the château was originally built in the 9th and 10th centuries by monks who now turn anxiously in their graves at the thought of the **nudist beach** nearby. Farther east on the island in **Port de La Meule,** climb up large rocks to see 16th-century **Notre Dame de Bonne Nouvelle,** whose simple white silhouette dignifies the gnarled shoreline. Moving east from Port de la Meule, you will find the soft sand beaches of **L'Anse des Vieilles,** a cove named not after old women but for a local species of fish called *"vieilles."* Northwest of Les Vieilles stands **St-Sauveur,** the island's oldest church.

Ile d'Yeu remains isolated: problematic public transport ensures that only the most determined travelers ever reach the island. Ferries to the island leave from Fromentine, St-Gilles-Croix-de-Vie, and Noirmoutier. **Fromentine** is accessible by bus from Nantes and Les Sables d'Olonne (4 per day, 44F). Three or four ferries per day make the trip to Ile d'Yeu. Make reservations and arrive at the port 30 minutes before departure time; call 51 68 52 32 for information. **St-Gilles** is accessible by train from Nantes (5 per day, 51F) or La Roche-Sur-Yon (2 per day, 35F) and by bus from Les Sables (ask the driver to drop you off at the *embarcadère*). From May through September, ferries from St-Gilles make three to six round-trip sailings per week to Ile d'Yeu (1½ hr., 35F round-trip). Call for reservations (tel. 51 54 15 15) or drop by the offices of **Navix-Vedettes**, 36, bd. de l'Egalité. St-Gilles's **tourist office,** bd. de l'Egalité (tel. 51 55 03 66), 500m east of the port, can help you with accommodations and the details of your trip. From Noirmoutier, accessible by bus from Les Sables, two to four daily ferries make the 45-minute trip between the port and Ile d'Yeu (round trip 160F). Call 51 39 00 00 for information and reservations.

Once on the island in Port-Joinville, you can rent **bikes** at Loca-Cycles (tel. 51 58 40 31), Vélo Plein 'Air (tel. 51 58 36 08), or Vélo-Prom'nade (tel. 51 58 43 22). The bike shops are all located at the port and are open daily 8:30am-7pm. The **tourist office** is on pl. du Marché (tel. 51 59 32 58; open Mon.-Sat. 10am-12:30pm and 4-6pm). The island makes room for a few expensive hotels and one **municipal campground** (tel. 51 58 34 20), located at Pointe de Gilberge, about 1km from the ferry landing and close to the beaches. If you don't stay overnight, you'll have only six or seven hours on the island. Food is deplorably expensive, so buy supplies on the mainland before departing. Port-Joinville has a **supermarket** on rue de Calypso, five minutes from the port. Take a left from the port and a right on rue de Calypso (the first stoplight). (Open Mon.-Sat. 8:45am-12:45pm and 3:30-7:30pm, Sun. 9:30am-12:15pm.)

Ile de Ré

Ile de Ré is linked to the town of La Pallice by a newly constructed 3km toll bridge (82F per car). Hike over the bridge or take one of the several daily buses from the bus station. **Citram** (tel. 46 99 01 36 in Rochefort, 46 41 04 57 in La Rochelle) sponsors a day-long excursion to the island. The bus leaves Rochefort at 9am from the bus station, 9:15am from Thermes (140F), stops in La Rochelle to pick up others at 10am (120F), and then takes you to the island's major cities, leaving enough free time for sunbathing and lunch. From La Rochelle, **Aunis et Saintonge** runs around five bus trips daily to Ile de Ré. (Return 62F. Call 46 93 21 41 in Saintes for information.) Also from La Rochelle, **Interîles** runs a bus and boat service to Sablanceaux on the island (2 per day, return 40F, children 30F). You can continue to Ile d'Aix for an additional 30F. Call 46 50 51 88 for more information.

The bridge leads to the town of **Rivedoux.** Go straight for about 10 minutes. On the left you will see the **tourist office,** pl. de la République (tel. 46 09 80 62), more shack than office, which has plenty of information on the island. (Open in summer 9am-noon and 5-7pm.) Locasport (tel. 46 09 65 27) rents **bicycles** for 68F per day with a 100F deposit or a passport. One hotel, **L'Hippocampe,** 16, rue Château des Mauléons (tel. 46 09 60 68), has singles for 70F and doubles for 110F. (Breakfast 16F.) The other hotels start around 150F and fill up quickly. Between the tourist office and the bridge is the huge **Camping Municipal** (tel. 46 09 84 10), which doesn't take reservations. (Office open Mon.-Sat. 9-11:30am and 2-9:30pm. 9.30F per person, 7.70F per site. Hot showers included. Open April-Sept.) For information on other campgrounds, call 46 09 80 04.

Beginning in July, French youth descend upon the island's 60km of beachs to surf, sunbathe, and party around the clock. Nightclubs are everywhere, but they charge at least 50F and are generally not worth it. Stick to such simple pleasures as a midnight swim or a clambake on the beach.

Ile d'Aix

South of Ile de Ré lies tiny, carless **Ile d'Aix**, barely 2km long but big enough to have sheltered Napoleon I's bruised ego during the emperor's last days on French soil in July 1815. Mediterranean-style cottages line dusty streets on this island, which only 200 permanent residents call home. During the summer, countless beach-fanatics occupy the tiny island. The **Musée Napoléon** houses a fairly substantial collection of Napoleon memorabilia, including some of His clothing. (Open Thurs.-Tues. 10am-noon and 2-6pm.)

Ramparts encircle the southern tip of the island; drawbridges provide the only entrances. **Fouras Aix Ferries** (tel. 46 84 60 50) runs from Pointe de la Fumée, 3km west of Fouras and 14km west of Rochefort. (Daily 8am-8pm, roughly every ½-hr., return 45F; Sept. 23-Dec. 22 and March 20-June 19 6-8 per day, return 30F; Dec. 23-March 19 4-6 per day, return 17F.) **Buses** leave Rochefort for La Fumée four to five times per day (½-hr., 13.50F). Two or three buses per day connect La Rochelle and Fouras (45 min., 22.40F). In summer round-trip cruises leave from La Rochelle almost every day. About seven hours on the island can be yours for 120F. Inquire at Océcar's main location, 14, cours des Dames (tel. 46 41 78 95; open Mon.-Fri. 8:30am-noon and 2-7pm, Sat. 9am-noon) or at pl. de Verdun.

The campground on the island, **Camping Municipal de Fort la Rade** (tel. 46 84 50 64), offers superb campsites on the ramparts from April to September. The island has but one (expensive) hotel.

Ile d'Oléron

The larger **Ile d'Oléron,** affectionately dubbed "luminous island" by its inhabitants, claims no fewer than 20 fine sand beaches along a 70km coastline, a thriving oyster industry, a château, and—of course—crowds. The citadel, in the town of **Le Château d'Oléron,** remains stalwart despite encroaching grass. The low ramparts and the slanted walls that deflect rather than absorb cannonball blows (don't try this at home) were innovations in fortress building. One of Europe's longest toll bridges (3km, toll 33F) connects the island with the mainland town of **Le Chapus.** Citram bus connections to Le Chapus from La Rochelle are lousy; Océcar's round-trip excursions by start at 90F, including a stop at Ile d'Aix. AS's better bus service runs from the towns of Rochefort (4-5 per day, 1½ hr., 37F) and Saintes (4-5 per day, 1¾ hr., 43F). Citram (tel. 46 99 01 36) does, however, have good connections from Rochefort's train and bus stations. (6 per day, 1½ hr., 32F.) Once you reach the island, bus service will easily take you anywhere (8F). Day-trippers should head for **St-Trojan** (sister city to Condom in Gascony) and the beautiful Gatseau beach.

Le Château d'Oléron is at the end of the toll bridge, 3km from the main road. Hotel accommodations start at 100F, so consider staying at the hostels in Saintes or Rochefort and making Oléron a daytrip. For **camping** in Le Château, try **Les Remparts,** bd. Philippe Daste (tel. 46 47 61 93; open April-Sept.) or **La Brande,** rue des Huitres (tel. 46 47 62 37; open March 15-Nov. 15.). Campsite fees range from 15-20F per person. The **tourist office** on pl. de la République (tel. 46 47 60 51), distributes free maps, brochures, lists of campgrounds and bike rental companies. (Open daily 9am-12:30pm and 3-7pm, Sun. 10am-noon; Sept.-June Tues.-Sat. 10am-noon and 2:30-6pm.) **Lacellerie Cycles,** 5, rue Maréchal Foch (tel. 46 47 69 30), rents bikes for 40F per day, deposit 600F. (Open daily 8:30am-12:30pm and 2-7:30pm.) Picnickers can give their money to **Supermarché Bravo** on rue des Antioches. (Open Mon.-Sat. 9am-12:30pm and 3-7:30pm.) The **tourist office** (tel. 46 47 11 39) is on pl. Gambetta in St-Pierre d'Oléron, the administrative center of the island. (Open Mon.-Sat. 9am-8pm; Sept.-June Mon.-Sat. 2:30-6pm.) Le Château d'Oléron's **postal code** is 17480.

La Rochelle

Named after the soft rock on which the earliest settlers built their homes in the 12th century, La Rochelle later became the coastal power of Aquitaine and profited from its position as a port city vital to both France and Britain. In the 17th century, the powerful and unscrupulous Richelieu saw this Protestant stronghold as an obstacle to uniting France and convinced Louis XIII to besiege the town. After a large portion of the population had starved to death, the city finally surrendered. The city Dumas immortalized in *The Three Musketeers* did not regain its former wealth until the 20th century, when vacationers rediscovered its white sand beaches and elegant old buildings.

Orientation and Practical Information

The main seaport of Charentes-Maritimes, La Rochelle lies about halfway between Nantes and Bordeaux on the main railway line. To get from the train station to the center of town, follow the directions given for the tourist office below, or take a short ride on bus #1 (6.50F).

The city stretches north from its old port, where **Tour de la Chaîne** and **Tour de la Lanterne** withstand frothing tides of backpackers. **Rue du Palais,** sewn in between arcades and shops, bisects the town longitudinally. **Place de Verdun** lies north of the old port and to the left of rue du Palais. The more colorful pedestrian district is just one block up from quai Duperré to the right of rue du Palais. Along the harbor, **Cour des Dames** is packed with cafés, ice cream vendors, and street performers.

Tourist Office: (tel. 46 41 14 68), on quai de Gabut. Follow av. du Général de Gaulle, from the train station to pl. de Motte Rouge. The office will be to your left; watch for signs. Good, free maps and brochures. Accommodations service 10F. English spoken. Open Mon.-Sat. 9am-8pm; June and Sept. Mon.-Sat. 9am-7pm; Oct.-May Mon.-Sat. 9am-12:30pm and 2:30-6pm.

Currency Exchange: Crédit Lyonnais, 19, rue du Palais. Open Mon.-Fri. 8:20am-12:10pm and 1:35-5pm. Also at the post office.

Student Travel: Centre Départemental d'Information Jeunesse (CDIJ), 14, rue des Gentilshommes (tel. 46 41 16 36 or 46 41 16 99), near Hotel Henri IV. BIJ/Wasteel tickets. *Carte Jeune* 70F. Bulletin boards listing apartments and jobs. Free ride/rider matching service and list of rides. Open Mon.-Fri. 10am-noon and 2-6pm, Sat. 10am-noon.

Post Office: pl. de l'Hôtel de Ville (tel. 46 41 92 88). **Currency exchange** and **telephones.** Open Mon.-Fri. 8:30am-6:30pm, Sat. 8:30am-noon. **Main office** on av. Mulhouse, by the train station. **Poste Restante.** Open Mon.-Fri. 8am-7pm, Sat. 8am-noon. **Postal Code:** 17000.

Trains: bd. Maréchal Joffre (tel. 46 41 50 50). To: Poitiers (*beaucoup*, 1½ hr., 84F); Bordeaux (4-5 per day, 2 hr., 110F); Paris-Austerlitz (7 per day, 5 hr., 222F); Nantes (4-5 per day, 2 hr., 102F); Rochefort (23F). About 3 per day to Lyon (303F) and Nice (446F). Office open Mon.-Sat. 8am-6:20pm, Sun. 9am-noon and 2-6:40pm.

Buses: Local buses (tel. 46 41 32 93) run to campgrounds, the *centre ville* (bus #1 from the train station), and La Pallice (also bus #1). Fare about 6.50F. To go anywhere else, it's best to start at the new bus station in pl. de Verdun. **Citram,** tel. 46 41 04 57. To Surgéres (50 min., 24.50F), Angoulême (84F), and other towns in the area. Office open Mon.-Fri. 9am-5:30pm. **Océcars,** tel. 46 41 20 40. To: Châtelaillon (6.50F), Fouras (22.40F), Rochefort (22.40F), Royan (54F), and points between. Office open Mon.-Sat. 8am-noon and 2-7pm. **Aunis et Saintonge (AS),** tel. 46 93 21 41. To Angoulême (3 hr., about 83.50F).

Ferry: Bus de Mer (tel. 46 41 32 93), near the youth hostel. Runs from the old port to port de Plaisance des Minimes, near the hostel (every ½-hr., 8F). Open Easter-Oct. daily 8am-8pm.

Bike Rental: Vélos Municipaux, quai Valin. With ID as deposit, will lend (for free) 1-speed bikes for 2 hr., 4F per hr. thereafter. Open daily 9am-12:30pm and 1:30-7pm. At **train station,** 40F per ½-day, 50F per day, deposit 500F. **Locasport,** plage de la Concurrence (tel. 46 41 66 33, Mme Benard). From the port, walk south past the Tour de la Chaîne and follow the shoreline to the beach. Bikes 45-56F per day, passport as deposit. Open daily 9:30am-noon and 1:30-6:30pm; in off-season shorter hours. At the **hostel,** first day 33F, additional days 25F, any ID as deposit.

Laundromats: 20, rue de la Pépinière (tel. 46 67 56 25), or rue St-Jean du Pérot, near the Tour de la Lanterne. Wash 28F, dry 9F per 15 min. Open daily 9:30am-7:30pm. Also at 8, rue des Dames. Wash 20F, dry 2F per 5 min., soap 2F. Open daily 7:30am-8pm. Also at the hostel. Wash 10F, dry 5F. Open daily 8-10am and 3-11pm.

Hospital: rue du Docteur Schweitzer (tel. 46 27 33 33).

Medical Assistance: SAMU, tel. 46 27 15 15.

Police: 2, pl. de Verdun (tel. 46 51 36 36). **Emergency,** tel. 17.

Accommodations and Camping

Hotel prices run high here. Cheaper places line the east side of the harbor, from the train station to just above pl. du Marché. Reservations are almost always required July through August; La Rochelle's few unreserved rooms usually fill by early afternoon.

Centre International de Séjour, Auberge de Jeunesse (IYHF), av. des Minimes (tel. 46 44 43 11), 2km south of the station. Take bus #10 from the station (every ½-hr. until 7:15pm, 6.50F). Otherwise, walk past the tourist office to av. Marillac, which becomes allée des Tamaris and then quai Marillac before intersecting with av. des Minimes (20-min. walk). An attractive, modern building with the look of a hospital but the mood of a party. Great facilities include snack machines, coffee machine, and laundry room. The 234 beds occasionally fill up in summer. Reception open daily 8-noon and 3-11pm. Lockout 10am-12:30pm. IYHF card required. 54F per person in 6-bed room. Breakfast included. Singles 84F. Camping 28F. Filling lunch or dinner 39F. Bike rental 33F per day. To reserve, call ahead or write with 1 night's payment.

Hôtel Printania, 9-11, rue du Brave Rondeau (tel. 46 41 22 86), off rue Thiers near pl. du Marché on rue du Brave Rondeau. Small living room for guests. Open all day. Fifteen decent singles and doubles 100F. Triples 150F, with shower 170F. Quints 220F. Breakfast 16F. Showers 6F. Call at least a month ahead for July-Aug.

Hôtel le Florence, 2, rue Marcel-Paul (tel. 46 41 17 24), 10 min. north of the *centre ville.* A bit of a hike, but decent prices for La Rochelle. Friendly owner serves cheap snacks and chats with locals in bar downstairs. Singles 105F. Doubles 125F. Breakfast 22F.

Hôtel Henri IV, on pl. de la Caille (tel. 46 41 25 79) at rue St-Saveur and rue du Temple. Great location but often full. Respectable doubles 130F, with shower 150F. 22F breakfast obligatory in summer. Open until 11:30pm. Call 2-3 months ahead for summer.

Hôtel le Bordeaux, 45, rue St-Nicolas (tel. 46 41 31 22), off quai Valin, about 5 min. from the station. Facing a pleasant pedestrian street. English-speaking management. Nine renovated doubles with phones 115F. Showers included. Breakfast 22F. Open Feb.-Nov. Call two months ahead for summer.

Camping: Camping Municipal, bd. A. Rondeau (tel. 46 43 81 20). Take bus #1 from pl. de Verdun to Port Neuf. Two-star site surrounded by factories. Elbow room for 500. 10.20F per person, 6.10F per tent, 4.10F per car. **Camping des Minimes** (tel. 46 44 42 53), on av. Marillac. Two-star site only 15 min. from the center of town; take bus #10 from pl. de Verdun. 10F per person, 4.70F per small tent, 5.20F per big tent, 4.20F per car. Open June-Sept. 15. The tourist office has a list of other sites—all more distant. Free-lance camping prohibited.

Food

The **market** in pl. du Marché sells fresh fish, fruit, and vegetables daily until 1pm (Fri. until 7pm). Outdoor stands near the harbor groan under the weight of mussels, oysters, and shrimp. Unsurprisingly, restaurants specializing in *les fruits de mer* (seafood) abound. The outdoor restaurants near pl. de la Chaîne will gladly relieve your wallet of at least 90F; better bargains exist on the other side of the harbor and near pl. du Marché. Expect to pay 20-30F more at any restaurant with a harbor view.

Le Pilote, 18, rue du Port, off quai Dupérré. A tiny seafood restaurant on a crowded street near the action. Friendly staff deposits a 3-course 58F *menu* and a more ambitious 95F *menu* on your table. Open daily noon-3pm and 7-10pm, Tues.-Sun. in winter.

Café de l'Arsenal, 12, rue Villeneuve. No view of the H2O, but this cafeteria may have the cheapest, most filling meals in La Rochelle. Finger-lickin' chicken or fish dishes 20-30F. Don't leave without some *mousse au chocolat* (7.50F) on your chin. Open daily 11:30am-2:30pm and 7-10pm. **Café Bravo,** 30, bd. Santel, has the same food and hours farther away.

Le Cordon Bleu, 20, rue du Cordouan, north of pl. du Marché. Casual place without the portside prices. Salads, steaks, sausages, oysters, and desserts. 40F and 45F *menus.* The 32F *plat du jour* comes with wine. Open Tues.-Sat. 11:45-2pm and 7-9:30pm.

Pizzeria-Grill Don Arturo, 46, rue St-Nicolas. Largely local clientele. 45F and 54F *menus.* Pizzas 31-39F. Open noon-2pm and 7:30-10pm.

Il Vesuvio, 24, cours des Dames. Crowded, outside seating by the port. Pizza (30-33F) and other Italian dishes. Seafood and squid erupt on the Pescatore Pizza (38F). 54F seafood *menu.* Open daily noon-11:30pm; Sept.-June noon-2pm and 7-11pm.

Sights

The famous 14th-century towers that guard La Rochelle's port allowed the city to thrive as a commercial center in the Renaissance. Originally, a chain passed between the forbidding **Tour St-Nicolas** and the **Tour de la Chaîne,** sealing off the harbor whenever enemies came to call. The chain now stretches between low stone pylons in pl. de la Chaîne. Tour de la Chaîne has a rather hokey *son et lumière* and a model of the town from Richelieu's day. (Tour de la Chaîne and its miniature village open April-June 15 Tues.-Wed., Sat.-Sun., and holidays 10am-noon and 2-7pm; June 16-Sept. daily 10am-noon and 2-7pm; Oct.-Nov. Sun. and holidays 10am-noon and 2-6pm. Admission 12F, students 8F.) A low rampart runs from Tour de la Chaîne to **Tour de la Lanterne,** also known as **Tour des Quatre Sergents.** In 1822, the Restoration Monarchy imprisoned four sergeants here for the heinous crime of crying "*Vive la République.*" Topped by a Flamboyant Gothic steeple, the 45m provides a view of the Ile de Ré on clear days. (Tour de la Lanterne and Tour St-Nicolas open daily June-Aug. 9:30am-7pm; Sept.-May shorter hours. Admission to either 16F, ages 18-25 and over 60 9F. Admission to both 25F.)

Beyond the whitewashed townhouses of the harbor stretch La Rochelle's elegant arcaded streets, built during the city's 18th-century heyday. Walk underneath the 14th-century **Grosse Horloge** (clock tower) and up rues du Palais and Chaudrier. At 10, rue du Palais, stands the renovated **Palais de Justice,** originally completed in 1789. Step into the *chambre correctionnelle* and watch the lawyers and judges go at it. Vicious rumors accuse the ornate Renaissance **Hôtel de Ville** of having more chandeliers per square meter than any building in Europe. (Open Mon.-Fri. 9:30-11am and 2:30-5pm, Sat.-Sun. 10am-12:30pm and 2-5:30pm; Oct.-March Mon.-Fri. 2:30-5pm.) France's largest **aquarium,** at port des Minimes (tel. 46 44 00 00), near the youth hostel, may also boast France's steepest admission prices. Join the Rockefellers on bus #10. (Open daily 9am-11pm; June 9am-7pm; Sept.-May 10am-noon and 2-7pm. Admission 37F, children 20F.) Sailing buffs will be blown away by **Musée de la Voile** (tel. 46 45 40 77), next to the aquarium. (Open daily 10am-noon and 2-7pm. Admission 27F, children 20F.) The **Musée des Automates** (tel. 46 41 68 08), on rue de la Désirée, houses 300 mechanical dolls. (Open 9:30am-6:30pm; Sept.-May 10am-noon and 2-6:30pm. Admission 30F, children 15F.)

For a quiet walk or picnic, take allée du Mail and choose a spot under the shady trees facing the beach or in the adjacent park and its well-kept gardens. The tourist office has a list of nightclubs and discos with at least a 70F cover; the portside bars and cafés are both livelier and cheaper. During the first two weeks of July, La Rochelle holds its **Franco Folies,** a six-day music festival with groups and audiences from all over Europe. To see the best groups will cost between 40F and 110F. Call 46 50 55 77 or the tourist office for more information.

Niort and the Marais Poitevin

Although Henry Plantagenet II and Eleanor of Aquitaine left a few noteworthy legacies here, Niort (pop. 70,000) is of interest to visitors only as a gateway to 100,000 hectares of marshland east of Niort. Unrippled by the vacationing mobs who frolic in the Atlantic surf, the slow-moving canals and waterways that criss-cross the marsh have earned this placid area the nickname "Green Venice." The grand canal outlines a triangle whose vertices are **Marans, Fontaines,** and **Coulon.** At the center of this triangle lies the county seat, **Maillezais.**

Orientation and Practical Information

Niort is accessible by train from La Rochelle, Poitiers, and Paris. The compact town center is near pl. de la Breche and the pedestrian zone, a 10-min. walk north-west from the train station. From the station, head up rue de la Gare; the tourist office will be on the right, hidden behind some trees.

Unfortunately, Maillezais and the other towns along the grand canal are not eas-ily accessible by public transportation. Furthermore, this traffic makes hitching dif-ficult. Your best bet is to rent a bike in Niort. To reach Maillezais by car or bike from La Rochelle, follow the N11 for 5km, turn left onto the D137 for 15km, and right onto the D938 for 14.5km. Turn right onto the smaller D25. In the small town of Maillé, turn left onto D15 and continue for 5km. From Niort, take rue du Ribray out of town, following the signs to Marais Poitevin. At Coulon, continue through the only intersection with a stoplight. After passing through the village of **Glands,** turn left at the first intersection. Go straight until **Le Mazeau,** and then follow the signs to Maillezais. It is extremely easy to lose your way on these back roads; don't hesitate to ask directions.

Tourist Office: Niort (tel. 49 24 18 79), on pl. de la Poste. Maps and plenty of advice on trips into the Marais Poitevin. They book hotel rooms in Niort (10F) and outside the Deux-Sèvres region (15F). Open July-Aug. Mon.-Sat. 9:30am-6:30pm, Sept.-June Mon.-Sat. 9:30am-noon and 1:30-6pm. **Coulon** (tel. 49 35 99 29), on pl. de L'Eglise. Open June 15-Sept. 15 daily 10am-6pm. **Maillezais** (tel. 51 87 23 01 or 51 00 75 18), inside the Camping Munici-pal. Open July-Aug. Mon.-Sat. 11am-noon and 3:30-6:30pm.

Currency Exchange: Crédit Agricole, 23, rue Brisson, across from Les Halles. Good rates and a 24F commission. Open Tues.-Fri. 9am-12:15pm and 1:30-6:15pm, Sat. 9am-12:30pm. Also try the post office.

Post Office: (tel. 49 24 84 03), on pl. de la Poste in Niort. **Currency Exchange.** Open Mon.-Fri. 8:30am-7pm, Sat. 8:30am-noon. **Postal Code: 79000.**

Trains: (tel. 49 24 50 50), rue de la Gare. To: La Rochelle (6-7 per day, ¾ hr., 45F); Poitiers (6-8 per day, 1 hr., 52F); Paris (8 per day, 4 hr., 201F). Two SNCF buses per day to Coulon (7F). Information office open daily 9:15am-6:30pm.

Bike Rental: The **train station** rents mediocre bikes for 40F per ½-day, 50F per day, deposit 500F. **J.F. Mainguenaud,** 105, av. des Limoges (tel. 49 28 20 38). Better bikes 100F per day, deposit 1000F. *Sacoches* (panniers) included. Open Tues.-Sat. 8:30am-noon and 2-7pm.

Medical Assistance: SAMU, tel. 15.

Hospital: 35, av. St-Jean-d'Angely (tel. 49 79 40 98).

Police: rue de la Préfecture (tel. 49 24 06 48). **Emergency:** tel. 17.

Accommodations, Camping, and Food

Niort has no youth hostel and few cheap accommodations. The **Foyer des Jeunes Travailleurs,** 8, rue St-André (tel. 49 24 50 68), in Niort, is usually full in July and August and is available only for stays of 2 weeks or more. If they have room, you'll pay 60F per night. If you have no luck here, try the branch at 147, rue du Clou Bouchet (tel. 49 79 17 44). **Hôtel St-Jean,** 21, av St-Jean d'Angély (tel. 49 79 20 76), has attractive 80F singles and 100F doubles. (Showers 15F. Breakfast 17F.)

Modern Hôtel, 113, rue de la Gare (tel. 49 28 13 34), next to the train station, has clean, simple rooms. (Singles 100F. Doubles 115F. Shower included. Breakfast 22F.) Also try cheery **Hôtel de la Paix** (tel. 49 24 17 90) next door. (Singles 80F. Doubles 110F. Breakfast 18F.) **Camping Municipal** on bd. S.-Allende (tel. 49 79 05 06), next door to the stadium in Niort, is open April to October. Take bus #6 from pl. de la Breche. (6F per person.) A covered **market** takes place at Les Halles Mon.-Fri. 9am-6pm, Sat. 9am-noon. The usual cheap provisions fill the shelves at **Prisunic,** 12-14 av. Victor Hugo. (Open Mon.-Sat. 9am-12:30pm, 2-7pm.)

In Coulon, **Camping Municipal** (tel. 49 35 90 26) is your best option. (Open mid-June to mid-Sept. In June or Sept., register at the tourist office.) In Maillezais, the **Hôtel des Etrangères** (tel. 51 00 70 15) has decent rooms for 80F and a restaurant with 40F and 50F *menus.* (Open daily noon-2pm and 8-9pm; in off-season Mon.-Sat. noon-2pm and 8-9pm). Campers can head for the **Camping Municipal de Maillezais** (tel. 51 00 70 79), also in town. (7F per person, 4.30F per tent. Open April-Sept.)

Sights and Entertainment

Niort's well-preserved **donjon** provides a remarkable view from atop its battlements. Destroyed during the Wars of Religion, Henry Plantagenet II's 700m ramparts once enclosed a small city within the borders of rues Brisson, Thiers, l'Abreuvoir, and the river Sèvre Niortaise. Today, the keep maintains a simple collection of local relics, tools, and costumes. (Open Wed.-Mon. 9am-noon and 2-5pm. Admission 13F, students free.)

In **Maillezais,** take the 45-minute boat tour past poplar-lined marsh banks and deceptively peaceful cows. The tiny plants on the water are so profuse that the canals appear to be paved with lime-green paint. The boat seats six and charges a flat 58F. (Tours Easter-Oct. daily 9:30am-12:15pm and 1:30-6:30pm. Tours are also available in Coulon (72F per boat) and Le Mazeau (58F per boat).

Before you step off Maillezais's firm ground, visit the ruins of **Abbaye St-Pierre** (tel. 51 00 70 11). Built on the site of a castle belonging to the Duke of Aquitaine, the abbey rose to prominence under the direction of the Benedictine Order. The abbey has a stormy history, having also been a bishopric under the charge of 22 abbots and then a Protestant stronghold complete with garrison. Confiscated by the revolutionary government in 1791 and demolished by mercenary deconstruction workers equipped with **jennies,** the abbey fell into the hands of a family hellbent on rebuilding it. One family began to preserve the remains in 1840. (Open daily 9am-8pm, Sept.-June 9am-noon and 2-6pm. Admission 13F, students 8F.)

Ruined Romanesque abbeys and churches litter the **Saintonge** region southeast of Niort. About 40km southeast of Niort lies the town of **Aulnay** (inaccessible by train or bus) with its dazzling **Eglise St-Pierre.** In town, **Hôtel-Restaurant Le Donjon,** rue Porte-Matha (tel. 46 33 17 31), has clean, attractive rooms. **Camping** is allowed on the grass next to the stadium, across the street from the church.

Rochefort

Rochefort (pop. 30,000) sits quietly inland, just far enough from the neighboring resorts to avoid the crowds but close enough to allow trips down the coast and excursions to Ile d'Aix and Ile d'Oléron. In the 17th century, Rochefort claimed the greatest naval arsenal in Europe and an intricate town planning scheme to boot. Aside from the outrageously decorated Maison de Pierre Loti, Rochefort's staid museums reflect its maritime heritage.

Orientation and Practical Information

The Charente River borders Rochefort to the south, east, and west. Place Colbert marks the center of town. To get to the tourist office from the train station, head down av. Wilson, turn right on av. Pelletan, left on rue Denfert Rochereau, and left again on av. Sadi Carnot.

Tourist Office: on av. Sadi Carnot (tel. 46 99 08 60). Good free maps. English spoken. Open daily 10am-7pm; Sept.-June Mon.-Sat. 9am-12:30pm and 2-6:30pm.

Post Office: (tel. 46 99 07 00), on rue du Docteur Peltier next to the tourist office. **Currency exchange** and **telephones.** Open Mon-Fri. 8am-7pm, Sat. 8am-noon. **Postal Code:** 17300.

Trains: bd. Aristide Briand (tel. 46 99 15 11). More than 6 trains per day to: La Rochelle (20 min., 24F); Saintes (½-hr., 35F); Royan (change at Saintes, 1 hr., 55F). **Lockers** 3F. Information office (tel. 46 41 50 50 in La Rochelle) open Mon.-Sat. 9am-noon and 1:30-6:50pm. Bike rental.

Buses: Océcars, on pl. de Verdun (tel. 46 99 23 65). To Royan (3 per day, 1½ hr., 36.50F) and La Rochelle (3 per day, 1¼ hr., 22.40F). Office open Mon.-Fri. 8:30am-noon and 2-7pm, Sat. 8:30am-noon. **Citram,** pl. de Verdun (tel. 46 99 01 36). To Ile d'Oléron (6 per day, 35-60F, Le Château d'Oléron, 25.50F) and Le Chapus (6 per day, 24F). Connecting buses from Le Château to other towns on Ile d'Oléron (8F). To La Fumée for connecting ferries to Ile d'Aix (4-5 per day, ¾-hr., 13.50F). Office open Mon.-Fri. 8am-12:15pm and 2-6:30pm, Sat. 8am-12:15pm.

Bike Rental: Barajas, 30, rue Gambetta (tel. 46 99 08 56). Only 5 bikes. 40F per day, deposit 800F. Open Tues.-Sat. 9am-noon and 2-7pm. Also at the **train station.** 40F per ½-day, 50F per day, deposit 500F.

Laundromat: pl. de la Gare, across from the train station. Wash 20F. Dry 7F per 10 min. Bring 10F, 5F, and 1F coins. Open daily 8am-7:30pm.

Hospital: rue de l'Hôpital, (tel. 46 87 10 33).

Medical Emergency: SAMU, tel. 46 27 15 15.

Police: 42, av. Jean Jaurès (tel. 46 87 26 12). **Emergency,** tel. 17.

Accommodations and Food

The surplus of vacationers from La Rochelle tends to fill Rochefort in July and August. Reserve a room in June or even earlier. Rochefort is quite tranquil in the off-season. The small **Auberge de Jeunesse (IYHF),** 20, rue de la République (tel. 46 99 74 62), has excellent kitchen facilities, immaculate 4-bed rooms, and no lockout or curfew. From the train station, follow av. Wilson to rue Begon; turn right on rue Pujos and then left on rue de la République. (IYHF card required. 37F per person. Camping 16F per person. Breakfast 13F. Sheets 13F. Bike rental 10F per day with 100F deposit. Call a week ahead in July-Aug. Send a 30% deposit if reserving more than a week in advance.) The **Hôtel Colbert,** 23, rue Audry de Puyravault (tel. 46 99 08 28), has clean doubles for 90-180F. (Call a month ahead in July-Aug.) The **Hôtel Roca Fortis,** 14, rue de la République (tel. 46 99 26 32), has one room for 120F, and others for 150-185F. (Breakfast 21F.) The unremarkable **Camping Municipal** (tel. 46 99 14 33), on av. de la Fosse aux Mats, requires a 15-minute walk from the center of town (6.10F per person, 4.10F per tent).

The local **market** convenes at the intersection of av. Charles de Gaulle and rue Jean Jaurès on Tuesday, Thursday, and Saturday morning; take your bread and cheese to the gardens near the *corderie.* **Chez Nous,** 72, rue Jean Jaurès, serves a filling 43F *menu* with a generous supply of bread and wine to eager *Rochefortais.* (Open Mon.-Fri. noon-1:30pm and 7-9pm, Sat. noon-1:30pm.) **Le Galion,** 38, rue Toufaire, a self-service cafeteria near the entrance to the naval museum, offers substantial meals for 30F. (Open Mon.-Sat. 11:45am-2pm and 6:45-9:30pm, Sun. 11:45am-2pm.)

Sights

Rochefort's most curious treasure is **La Maison de Pierre Loti,** 141, rue Pierre Loti (tel. 46 99 16 88), the former home of gadabout and writer Pierre Loti. This eclectic (to say the least) abode includes a mosque on the top floor, a Spanish banquet hall, and a Turkish smoking room (where Loti wrote and smoked hashish) somewhere in between. (Mandatory tours July-Sept. at 10am, 11am, 2pm, 3pm, 4pm, and 5pm (Wed. and Fri. also at 8:30pm); Jan. 20-June and Oct.-Dec. 20, Wed.-Mon. at 10am, 11am, 2pm, 3pm, and 4pm. Admission 25F, students 15F.) **La Corderie Royale** (the royal ropeworks) is, at 372m, the longest building in France. Built solely for the manufacture of rope, this now restored edifice went up in flames at the end of World War II. (Open daily July-Aug. 9am-8pm, spring and fall 9am-7pm, winter 9am-6pm. Guided tour at 3pm. Admission 20F, with tour 25F.) The **Musée de la Marine,** pl. de la Gallissonière, houses France's largest naval collection outside Paris, including an interesting set of vessel models built in the 17th century. (Open Nov. 15-Oct. 15 Wed.-Mon. 10am-noon and 2-6pm. Admission 18F, students 10F.) In July and August, the tourist office gives tours of Rochefort by van in French and English (25F, students 15F).

Saintes

Saintes (pop. 28,000) stretches peacefully along the banks of the green Charente River, amid flat expanses of fields that extend 30km to the sea in one direction and 25km to Cognac in the other. Originally the Roman capital of southwestern France, Saintes adopted Christianity in the 3rd century and spent much of its time thereafter fending off pyromaniacal invaders, who nonetheless wormed their way in and burnt the city to the ground several times. When things calmed down in the 11th century, the citizens of this provincial town breathed a sigh of relief and set about building churches. Today, the capital of Saintonge draws crowds to its music festivals in July and a sizeable number of stragglers the rest of the year.

Orientation and Practical Information

Saintes lies halfway along the main La Rochelle-Bordeaux railway line, about 20 minutes from the coast. Activity centers around the **Arc de Triomphe** and the **Pont Palissy.** The center of town is a simple 15-minute walk from the station. As you leave the train station, take a left, follow av. de la Marne two blocks south, turn right on av. Gambetta, and follow it to the river. You will see the arch on your left. Cross the bridge and continue straight for about five blocks. The tourist office will be on the right.

Tourist Office: 62, cours National (tel. 46 74 23 82). Helps with accommodations (fee 5F in town, 10F in region), gives tours of the city (Mon.-Sat. 10am and 3pm, 27F), and organizes cruises on the Charente (55F and up). Open Mon.-Sat. 9am-7pm, Sun. 10am-12:30pm and 3-6pm; Sept. 20-June 15 Mon.-Sat. 9am-noon and 2-6pm.

Currency Exchange: Crédit Agricole, 31, av. Gambetta. Average rates and 10F commission. Open Mon.-Fri. 9am-12:30pm and 1:45-5pm.

Post Office: 8, cours National (tel. 46 93 05 84), near the bridge. **Telephones.** Open Mon.-Fri. 8:30am-7pm, Sat. 8:30am-noon. **Postal Code:** 17100.

Trains: (tel. 46 92 50 50 or 46 92 04 19), on av. de la Marne. To: La Rochelle (6 per day, 1 hr., 45F); Bordeaux (7-8 per day, 1¼ hr., 72F); Cognac (6 per day, 20 min., 21F); Angoulême (6 per day, 1 hr., 49F). Baggage *consigne* open daily 8am-8pm, Sun. 9am-noon. Information office open daily 8:30am-noon and 2-6:30pm.

Buses: Autobus Aunis et Saintonge, 1, cours Reverseaux (tel. 46 93 21 41). To Cognac (3 per day, 1 hr., 24.50F) and Royan (3 per day, 1 hr., 26F). To points along Ile d'Oléron: Le Château (3 per day, 1½ hr., 44F); centre St-Pierre d'Oléron (3 per day, 2 hr., 49.50F); St-Denis (3 per day, 2¼ hr., 64F). Open Mon.-Fri. 8am-noon and 2:15-6:45pm. **Branch office** at rue Jean Moulin across from the train station. Open Mon.-Fri. 8am-noon and 2-6pm.

Bike Rental: Héline, 177, av. Gambetta (tel. 46 92 04 38). 33F per day, 110F per week, deposit 400F or passport. Open Tues.-Sat. 8:30am-12:30pm and 2-7:30pm. **Groleau Cycles,** 9, pl. Blair (tel. 46 74 19 03). 40F per day, 65F per 2 days. Open Tues.-Sat. 8:30am-12:15pm and 2-6:45pm.

Medical Assistance: Hospital, pl. du 11 Novembre, tel. 46 92 76 76. **Ambulance (SAMU),** tel. 46 27 15 15 or simply 15.

Police: rue du Bastion, tel. 46 93 52 53. **Emergency,** tel. 17.

Accommodations and Camping

Many hotels fill up during the mid-July festivals, but rooms are otherwise easy to find. The youth hostel usually has space.

Auberge de Jeunesse (IYHF), 6, rue du Pont Amilion (tel. 46 92 14 92), near the center of town next to the Abbaye-aux-Dames. From the train station, take av. de la Marne to rue Gambetta, turn left on rue du Pérat, right on rue St-Pallais, and left on rue Pont Emilion. Quiet, relaxed atmosphere. Two huge rooms full of bunkbeds for men and women. Great kitchen and bathrooms. No lockout. Office open 7am-noon and 6-11pm. Open mid-Jan. to mid-Dec. Doors close at 11pm, but the mellow management will give you a key. 38F per person. Camping 23F. IYHF card required. Sheets 15F.

Hôtel Parisien, 35, rue Frédéric-Mestreau (tel. 46 74 28 92), 1 minute west of the train station. Simple and clean. Singles 100F. Doubles 120F, with shower 140F. Breakfast 23F. Hall shower included. Reserve by phone a month in advance for July-Aug. and confirm by letter.

Hôtel St-Palais, 1, pl. St-Palais (tel. 46 92 51 03). Great location in the abbey's courtyard. Lively bar downstairs, clean rooms, and cheap to boot. Manager speaks English. Singles 85F. Doubles 100F. Hall shower included. Breakfast 20F. Call a month ahead for festival time, a week ahead during the rest of the summer.

Hôtel de la Gare, 46, rue Frédéric-Mestreau (tel. 46 93 06 12). Fairly large rooms, but a bit dingy. Singles 80F. Doubles 91F. Rooms with 2 big beds 120F. Showers 8F. Breakfast 15-20F. Restaurant downstairs has 45F *menu.* Open Oct.-Aug.

Le Gambetta, 72, av. Gambetta (tel. 46 93 02 85). Small, central, and cheap. Locals hang at the *brasserie* downstairs. Doubles 87-95F, some with showers. Rooms with 2 big beds 125F. Hall showers 15F. Breakfast 18.50F. Open Oct.-Aug. Tues.-Sun. until 1:30am.

Camping: Camping Municipal, 6, route de Courbiac (tel. 46 93 08 00). Two-star site spread over green fields along the banks of the Charente, next to the municipal swimming pool. A good ½-hr. walk from the train station, but only 900m from *centre ville.* Follow av. Gambetta across the river and turn right on quai de l'Yser. 6.80F per person, 4.80F per tent, 2.50F per car. Open May 15-Oct. 15 7am-10pm.

Food

Escargots cooked in garlic and parsley are the specialty here. A boisterous **market** takes place on cours Reverseaux Tuesday and Friday, at the base of Cathédrale St-Pierre Wednesday and Saturday, and at av. de la Marne and av. Gambetta near the station Thursday and Sunday (all open 8am-12:30pm). The **supermarket** E. Leclerc is located to the east of the hostel, 2 blocks up rue Pont St-Emilion. (Open Mon. 3-7:15pm, Tues.-Thurs. 9am-12:30pm and 3-7:15pm, Fri. 9am-8:15pm, Sat. 9am-7:15pm.) Take your goodies to the pleasant riverside **Jardin Public,** south of the tourist office.

Café Germanicus, 10, rue Arc de Triomphe. Self-serve cafeteria with friendly folks and a Roman air. Steak 28F, ham 24F, vegetables extra. Open Mon.-Sat. 11:30am-2pm and 7-10pm, Sun. 11:30am-2pm.

Crêperie Victor Hugo, 20, rue Victor Hugo. Rustic, friendly place in the *centre ville.* Galettes 11-43F, dessert *crêpes* 9-28F. Try the Franco-American "Gourmande," a hamburger *crêpe* (39F). 50F *menu* with a salad, a *crêpe,* and ice cream. Open Tues.-Sat. noon-2:30pm and 4:30-10pm.

Le St-Michel, 28, rue St-Michel. Where the market people eat after a morning's work. Well-prepared food and family-style service. 55F and 75F *menus.* Open daily noon-2pm and 7:30-9:30pm.

Pizza-Bojo, 17, rue de la Poste. Big, cheap pizzas 26-37F. Try the "Super Bojo," a mushroom, ham, egg, artichoke, cheese, anchovy pizza monstrosity (37F). 57F lunch *menu* includes salad, pizza, and *crêpes* or ice cream for dessert. Open Mon.-Fri. noon-2pm and 7pm-midnight, Sat. 7pm-midnight.

Sights and Entertainment

Rising unexpectedly between street and river in the *centre ville,* the first-century Roman **Arc de Triomphe** marks the spot where a bridge linked the two sides of town. An inscription still visible along the top dedicates it to Tiberius, Germanicus, and Drusus. From the arch, take rue Arc de Triomphe/rue St-Pallais to the **Abbaye-aux-Dames,** one of the most beautiful of the many Romanesque churches in the region. The interior was redone with Angevin vaulting in the 12th century. The west façade and the Poitou-style central tower are particularly fetching. The **Musée Archéologique,** on esplanade André Malraux next to the arch, is an intriguing forest of Roman columns, friezes, and cornices piled into two buildings and scattered across a small square. Most date from the demolition of the town's ramparts during the 3rd century. (Open Wed.-Mon. 10am-noon and 2-6pm; Oct.-May Mon. and Wed.-Sat. 2-5pm, Sun. 10am-noon and 2-6pm. Free.)

Across the river from the arch stands the 15th-century **Cathédrale St-Pierre,** its imposing, unfinished bell tower capped not by a spire but by a small dome. Inside, the massive 35-year-old organ will impress. From the cathedral, walk up rue des Jacobins, climb the stairs, and work your way up to cours Reverseaux. Take a left and then a right on rue St-Eutrope toward **Eglise St-Eutrope,** a split-level Gothic-Romanesque hybrid on the pilgrimage routes to St-Jacques de Compostelle in Spain. Descend into the gloomy crypt; illumination will set you back 2F, a small price to pay.

Away from St-Eutrope and the *centre ville,* signs mark the 15-minute walk to the **Arènes Gallo-Romaines,** a crumbling amphitheater overgrown with grass. Built in 40 AD, the tunnel entrance and several of the supporting arches still stand. At one time the structure could seat 20,000 people. (Open in summer 9am-8pm; in winter 9am-6pm. Free.)

Saintes's several summer festivals attract interesting characters and armies of Boy Scouts. The **Jeux Santons,** a weeklong celebration of folk music from around the world, takes place the second week in July. Some events are free; others cost 50-80F. (Call 46 74 47 50 for dates, or inquire at the tourist office.) The **Fête de Musique Ancienne** takes place the first two weeks of July (tickets 80F, students 60F). For information, call the Institut de Musique Ancienne de Saintes at 46 92 51 35 or stop by the tourist office. Tickets are usually available at the door.

Cognac

More than three centuries ago, the *vignerons* of Cognac discovered that, when distilled, their mediocre white wines became a rich *vin brulé* (burnt wine)—and one which avoided the heavy tax levied on regular wine exports to boot. Today Cognac (pop. 20,000) is not just the heart of cognac production in France; with its chalky soil and mild, sunny climate, the 150,000 surrounding acres are the only region in the world capable of producing the amber brandy called cognac. Within the confines of the city stand the distilleries of Hennessey, Martell, Rémy-Martin, and every other world-famous exporter of cognac.

The very air reeks of the stuff—but not the bars. Nearly all of the local specialty is exported, and the residents stick to less expensive wine or to *pineau,* an aperitif made of cognac and grape juice and aged at least three years. *Pineau* comes in white or rosé and costs at least 35F per bottle. Cognac comes only in amber, the color resulting not from the grape but from the tannins of the Limousin oak casks used for aging. Cognac is categorized by age: VS (very special) or VSOP (very superior old pale) cognac is at least five years old, while *Paradis* blends brandies between 50 and 180 years old. Remember: the stuff does not age in the bottle. A cognac made in 1865 and bottled in 1870 will always be five years old.

Orientation and Practical Information

Sitting pretty on the northern bank of the Charente, Cognac makes an easy daytrip from Angoulême, Saintes, and even La Rochelle if you plan ahead. Place François 1er, near shops, hotels, and the tourist office, is a 10-minute walk from the train station.

Tourist Office: 16, rue du 14 Juillet (tel. 45 82 10 71). Pleasant staff will find you a room for the price of a phone call. Currency exchanged when the banks are closed. Free maps with all the cognac houses clearly marked. English spoken. Open Mon.-Sat. 8:30am-7pm; Sept. 16-June 14 Mon.-Sat. 9am-12:30pm and 2-6:15pm.

Budget Travel: Transatco Agence de Voyages (tel. 45 82 28 27), on pl. Martell. BIJ/Eurotrain tickets. Open Mon.-Fri. 9am-noon and 1:30-6:30pm, Sat. 9am-noon.

Currency Exchange: Crédit Lyonnais, pl. François 1er. Open Tues.-Sat. 8:30-11:55am and 1:35-5:15pm.

Post Office: (tel. 45 82 08 99), on pl. Bayard at the other end of rue du 14 Juillet from pl. François 1er. **Currency exchange** and **telephones.** Open Mon.-Fri. 8:30am-7pm, Sat. 8:30am-noon. **Postal Code: 16100.**

Trains: (tel. 45 82 03 29 or tel. 45 38 50 50 in Angoulême), at pl. de la Gare off bd. de Paris. Limited service. To Angoulême (5 per day, 1 hr., 37F) and Saintes (6 per day, 20 min., 21F). Only four 3F lockers available. Station open Mon.-Sat. 6am-9pm, Sun. 8am-midnight.

Buses: Autobus Citram (tel. 45 82 01 99), at pl. Gambetta. To La Rochelle (1 per day, 3 hr., 57F) and Angoulême (6 per day, Sun. 2, 1 hr., 35F). Information office open Mon.-Fri. 7:45am-noon and 2-6:15pm, Sat. 9-11am.

Car Rental: Transatco (tel. 45 82 28 27), on pl. Martell. Friendly staff will contact any rental agency for you. Open Mon.-Fri. 9am-noon and 1:30-6:30, Sat. 9am-noon.

Bike Rental: J.F. Dupuy, 18, rue Elisée Mousnier (tel. 45 82 10 31). Good 10-speeds 50-60F per day, deposit 400F. Open Mon.-Fri. 8:30am-noon and 2-6:30pm, Sat. 9am-noon.

Youth Center: INFO 16, 53, rue d'Angoulême (tel. 45 82 62 00). Information on youth activities, including **Allostop** and nearby *foyers.* Smaller city maps free. There's also a ride board and baby-sitting services. Sells Eurotrain/Wasteel tickets and Carte Jeune (70F). Open Tues.-Fri. 10am-noon and 2-7pm, Sat. 10am-noon and 2-6pm.

Hospital: rue Montesquieu, (tel. 45 35 15 15).

Medical Assistance: Ambulance, tel. 45 32 19 30 or 45 35 35 00.

Police: 14, rue Richard (tel. 45 32 11 01). **Emergency,** tel. 17.

Accommodations and Camping

Foyer Ste-Elizabeth makes a delightful substitute for a hostel, if they have room. In July and August, call at least two weeks in advance for reservations, although there is usually room somewhere.

Foyer Ste-Elizabeth, 12, rue Saulnier (tel. 45 82 04 90), close to *centre ville* and the Hennessey plant. Newly refurbished building in a new location. Really for workers, but travelers accepted when there is room. Nice folks. No lockout or curfew. Your own clean single with desk and skylight 40F per night. Breakfast 7F. They hope to open a *gîte* next door in the spring of 1991 (30F per night).

Hôtel du Cheval Blanc, 6-8, pl. Bayard (tel. 45 82 09 55), across from the post office. Adequate, with good prices for a 1-star hotel. Reception open daily until 9:30pm but closes 3-6pm. Six singles 80F each. Four doubles 95F. Doubles with 2 beds 120F. Showers 10F. Breakfast 23F. Call ahead in summer. Closed around Christmas.

La Résidence, 25, av. Victor Hugo (tel. 45 32 16 09). Clean, airy 2-star hotel with nice English-speaking management and lots of room. Only one single 99F. Doubles 119F. Family room (2 big beds and shower) 190F. Showers 10F. Breakfast 24F. Telephone reservations advisable in summer.

Tourist Hotel, 166, av. Victor Hugo (tel. 45 32 09 61), 10 min. from the train station. Take bd. de Paris to the right. Decent rooms over an unappealing bar. Attractive courtyard in the back. Private parking. Doubles 85F. Rooms with 2 beds 130F. Showers included. Breakfast 18F. Closed Sun. and Aug. No telephone reservations.

Camping: Camping Municipal de Cognac, bd. de Chatenay (tel. 45 32 13 32), 15-min. walk from pl. François 1er. Follow rue Henri Fichon to the campground. 5F per person, 2.25F per tent, 2.30F per car. Electricity 4.50F. Open May 15-Oct. 15.

Food

Most of the cognac houses offer tours which conclude with a free dégustation or miniature bottle. The cheapest place to buy a bottle of cognac or *pineau* is probably **Prisunic,** pl. François 1er (cognac 90F and up, *pineau* 35-40F; open Mon.-Sat. 8:30am-7:15pm.)

An indoor **market** fills pl. d'Armes daily from 7am to 1pm.

Le Sens Unique, 20, rue du 14 Juillet. The locals' choice. Small and cozy, with a lot of decent food (including oysters). Three-course 49F *menu* and 4-course 60F *menu.* Open Mon.-Sat. noon-2pm and 7:30-10pm.

Duguesclin, just off pl. François 1er on rue du 14 juillet. A busy place with good service, good food, and lots of variety. Pasta dishes 31-40F, pizza 29-41F, *crêpes* 9-28F, and meat dishes 45-73F. Open Mon.-Sat. noon-1:45pm and 7-10pm.

Pizza Le Bojo, 42, rue Henri Fichon, also just off pl. François 1er. A cool, lively place with courteous service and water served in goblets. Endure Top 40 music. Pizzas or pasta 18-40F. Open Tues.-Sat. noon-2pm and 7-10pm, Mon. noon-2pm.

Le Chantilly, 146, av. Victor Hugo. A local spot with a simple restaurant-bar. Eat whatever the boss feels like serving: 47F or 60F includes *plat du jour,* coffee, and a bottle of wine. Lunch daily noon-2pm. Dinner Mon.-Fri. 7-9pm.

Sights

The joy of visiting Cognac lies in making your way from one brand name to the next, touring the warehouses, listening to the films about the history of each house, and collecting your nip bottles of golden brandy. All have frequent tours in English led by charming young guides. On rue de la Richonne, 5 min. from the *centre ville,* **Hennessy** offers an informative tour which includes a *short* boat ride across the narrow Charente. (Open Mon.-Fri. 9am-5:30pm; Sept. 16-June 14 Mon.-Fri. 9am-noon and 1:45-4:30pm. Last tour at 5pm in summer. Free.) **Martell's** fascinating tours include a peek at special storage rooms dubbed "Paradise" and "Purgatory" and a trip through the assembly-line bottling plant. They win extra points for offering both *dégustation* and free nip bottles. (Mon.-Sat. 8:30-11am and 1:30-5pm; June and Sept. Mon.-Fri. 8:30-11am and 2-5pm; Oct.-May 30 Mon.-Thurs. 8:30-11am and 2-5pm, Fri. 8:30-11am. Free.) **Otard,** bd. Denfert Rochereau (tel. 45 82 40 00), is the only major house open on Sunday; their tour is entertaining and more historically interesting than the others. The *dégustation* is free, but the nip bottles cost 15F. (Tours daily 9am-5:30pm; Oct.-March Mon.-Fri. 9-11am and 2-5pm. Free.) **Rémy-Martin** (5km) and **Polignac** (4km) and several other *chais* (distilleries and storehouses) are located outside of town. Get a complete list from the tourist office.

Cognac has few claims to fame besides drink. By the second half of the 14th century, the city was a bustling wine and salt port. In 1448, a certain Charles d'Angoulême brought his new wife, Louise de Savoie, to stay for a while. Their son François (who later became king of France) was born in the château here. His statue stands in the center of town, and the château in which he was born now serves as the *chais* of Baron Otard.

The **Musée du Cognac,** located in the Jardin Public, provides a relief from dank storehouses. Examine the collection of late 19th-century liquor bottles. Also on display is an gargantuan wooden boat discovered on the banks of the Charente in 1979; it dates back to 2590 BC. (Open Wed.-Mon. 10am-noon and 2-6pm; Oct.-May Wed.-Mon. 2-5:30pm. Admission 15F, students 10F.)

Eglise du Sacré Cœur, among the city's 15th-century half-timbered houses on rue de Bellefonds, stands out as Cognac's most impressive architectural work. Picnic among the swans in stunning **Jardin de l'Hôtel de Ville,** on bd. Denfert-Rochereau. (Open daily 7am-10pm; in winter 7am-8pm.)

When you tire of trudging through the warehouses, where 2,000,000 potential bottles of cognac evaporate through the pores of the barrels each year (the "angels' share"), venture out into the countryside where the actual distilling takes place. There are six *crus,* or regions, in which official cognac grapes grow. The *cru* closest to Cognac, Grande Champagne, is the most prestigious; the most distant bears the banal title Bois Ordinaire. Numerous small distilleries also operate in the region. Unfortunately the *chais* are spaced far enough apart (at least 6km) to make a walking tour difficult. If you are on wheels, head for rue Gande in the *vieille ville,* follow it downhill to porte St-Jacques, and turn right on quai Papin. Take the bridge across the Charente, and look to your right for the D731, in the direction of St-Jean-d'Angély. You will be in the region of vineyards known as the Borderies; several distilleries lie within 5km of Cognac. Unfortunately, none is accessible by bus. Thin traffic makes biking pleasant and hitchhiking difficult.

Angoulême

From its dignified perch above the Charente River, Vieil Angoulême surveys modern Angoulême (pop. 46,000) with the same suspicion and disdain Balzac observed when he came here to gather material for *Lost Illusions.* Once known for its paper mills, this pleasant if a bit ramshackle town deserves an afternoon's wander.

Orientation and Practical Information

Angoulême lies in the upper Charente Valley, about halfway between Bordeaux and Poitiers on the main rail line. Trains also run here from Saintes via Cognac. The old town, the most interesting part of Angoulême, sits high on a plateau just south of the Charente and southwest of the train station.

Tourist Office: 2, pl. St-Pierre (tel. 45 95 16 84). The best views in Angoulême right out its door. *Good* free maps, hotel lists, and self-guided walking tours. Guided tours by foot (1-1½ hr., 18F, children 10F); by bus (½-day, 55F, children 35F; whole day 90F, children 55F); by horse carriage (50F, children 35F). Tourist office open Mon.-Sat. 9am-7pm, Sun. 10:30am-12:30pm; Sept.-June Mon.-Fri. 9am-12:30pm and 1:30-6:30pm, Sat. 10am-noon and 2-4pm. **Information kiosk** (tel. 45 92 27 57), outside the train station, has maps. Open Mon.-Sat. 9am-noon and 2-6pm.

Currency Exchange: Crédit Lyonnais, av. du Général de Gaulle. Decent rates. Open Mon.-Fri. 8:05am-noon and 1:35-5pm.

Post Office: pl. du Champ de Mars, (tel. 45 95 23 11). **Currency Exchange** and **telephones.** Open Mon.-Fri. 8am-7pm, Sat. 8am-noon. **Branch office,** on pl. Francis Louvel. Open Mon.-Fri. 8am-6:45pm, Sat. 8am-noon. **Postal code:** 16000.

Trains: pl. de la Gare,(tel. 45 38 50 50). More than 6 trains per day to: Bordeaux (1½ hr., 83F); Poitiers (1 hr., 70F); Saintes via Cognac (1 hr., 51F); Royan (1½ hr., 70F); La Rochefoucauld (3 per day, 24F). Information office open Mon.-Fri. 9am-7pm, Sat. 9:30am-noon and 2-6pm.

Buses: Autobus Citram (tel. 45 95 95 99 or 45 95 56 40), at pl. du Champ de Mars. To: Confolens (1 per day, 2 hr., 40F); Niort (1 per day, 3 hr., 92.50F); Cognac (7 per day, 1 hr., 35F); Jarnac (7 per day, 45 min., 26.50F); La Rochelle (2 per day, 3½ hr., 83.50F). TGV requires 13F reservation. Office open Mon.-Fri. 8am-noon and 3-6pm. **STGA** (tel. 45 91 55 22), at pl. du Champs de Mars. Urban bus tickets cost 6F. Ask for schedule at the tourist office.

Bike Rental: Ets. Pelton, 5, rue des Arceaux (tel. 45 95 30 91). Mostly bike and motorcycle sales, but rents some decent bikes for about 34F per day. Mountain bikes for 70F per day, deposit 1500-3000F or credit card. Sat. afternoon-Tues. counts as 1 day. Open Tues.-Sat. 9:15am-noon and 2-7pm.

Youth Center: Centre d'Information Jeunesse, 6, pl. Bouillaud (tel. 45 92 86 73), next to the Hôtel de Ville. Information on just about everything. BIJ and bus tickets. Carte Jeune 70F. Open Mon.-Fri. 10am-12:30pm and 2-6pm, Sat. 2-6pm; Sept.-June Tues.-Sat. 10am-7pm.

Laundromat: 3, rue Ludovic Trarieux in Vieil Angoulême. Wash 15F, dry 2F per 6 min. Soap 5F. Open daily 7am-8pm. Also at 11, rue St-Roch. Wash 20F, dry 8F per 15 min. Open Mon.-Sat. 8am-7pm.

Hospital: Hôpital de Girac, rue de Bordeaux (tel. 45 24 40 40).

Ambulance: SAMU, tel. 45 92 92 92 or simply 15.

Police: pl. du Champs de Mars, (tel. 45 38 05 55). **Emergency,** tel. 17.

Accommodations and Camping

Finding cheap accommodations in Angoulême should never be a problem. Decent and affordable hotels cluster near the intersection of av. Gambetta and the pedestrian precinct, which leads downhill from the *vieille ville*.

Auberge de Jeunesse (IYHF), on Ile de Bourgines (tel. 45 92 45 80), almost 2km from the station next to the campground. Take bus #7 (every 15 min. until 9pm) from pl. du Champ de Mars and Cathédrale St-Pierre. 85 beds in a modern building on a small wooded island. Obliging management. Free passes to outdoor, Olympic-sized municipal swimming pool next door. Free use of canoes and kayaks on the Charente. TV and iron. No lockout. Curfew 11pm. 37F per person. IYHF card required. Breakfast 13F. Good meals 38F. Sheets 13F. Often booked by groups in summer.

Hôtel du Cheval de Bronze, 7, rue St-Roch (tel. 45 95 02 74), just off av. Gambetta. A somewhat noisy 1-star place. Clean, comfortable doubles 70F. Rooms with 2 beds 130F. Showers 10F. Breakfast 18F.

Hôtel de l'Eperon, 68, rue de la Corderie (tel. 45 95 20 41), off av. Gambetta. Not elaborate, but clean and pleasant rooms. Singles 80F. Doubles 90F. Triples 125F, with shower 130F. Showers 15F. Breakfast 16F. Open Jan.-Nov.

Hôtel Le Palma, 4, rampe d'Aguesseau (tel. 45 95 22 89). A handful of singles 80F. Doubles (1 or 2 beds) 100F. Hall showers included. Breakfast 20F. Good restaurant downstairs. On the tourist office's list, so usually full; call ahead. Open Mon.-Sat.

Hôtel les Messageries, pl. de la Gare (tel. 45 92 07 62), a few steps to the right of the train station. Kind manager treats you like family. Singles and doubles 90F. Rooms with 1 big and 1 small bed (2-3 people) 120F. Showers 15F. Breakfast with croissant 16F. Open Sept.-July Mon.-Fri. and Sat. morning. Receptionist may tell callers it's full; stop by to check.

Hôtel de Lille (tel. 45 95 03 01), on rue de Périgueux near Eglise St-Martial. Stay in this comfortable old hotel just to meet the charming character who runs it. Singles and doubles with shower 90-100F. Breakfast 20F.

Camping: Camping Municipal, on Ile de Bourgines (tel. 45 92 83 22), right next to the youth hostel. Great location. 20F per person. Showers included.

Food

Angoulême's specialty is *marguerite* chocolates, named for the sister of François 1er. Squeeze the cheapest, freshest produce in town at the **covered market** on pl. des Halles Centrales, two blocks down rue de Gaulle from the Hôtel de Ville. (Open Mon.-Sat. 7am-1pm.) You can do the same at the Prisunic **supermarket** on rampe d'Agesseau. (Open Mon.-Sat. 8:45am-12:45pm and 2:15-7pm.) Excellent but sometimes expensive restaurants crowd the winding streets of Vieil Angoulême west of the market. The finest picnic spots are on the ramparts by the streams of the **Jardin Vert** or behind the hostel by the small dam.

Le Chat Noir, on pl. des Halles. Go where the young go. Not a thrillingly diverse menu, but a fun place that's open when you're hungry. Sandwiches and big salads 25-32F. Open Mon.-Sat. 7am-1am.

Le Mektoub, 28, rùe des 3 Notre Dames, near Eglise St-André. An eclectic place with good service, phriendly pholk, and delicious Asian and Middle Eastern food. Meat entrees 40-50F. Open Mon.-Sat. noon-2pm and 7pm-midnight, Sun. 7pm-midnight.

Le Palma, 4, rampe d'Aguesseau. A pretty restaurant under a hotel. Good food at decent prices: 46F, 68F, and 110F *menus*. Open Mon.-Sat. 11:45am-2pm and 7:30-9:45pm; in off-season 11:45am-2pm and 6-9:15pm.

Marest, 26, rue de Périgueux, near Eglise St-Martial. Self-service cafeteria with abundant victuals food. Meat entrees 25-40F. Salads 6-10F. Open daily 11am-2:30pm and 6:30-9:30pm.

Sights and Entertainment

Rumor has it that on a clear day you can see Cognac from the ramparts. Follow the ramparts far enough and you'll reach the **Cathédrale St-Pierre.** Its dome and the square *campanile* may make you think you're in Italy, but the façade's distinctive towers and close-packed decoration is pure Aquitaine. (Open daily 9am-7pm.)

Behind Cathédrale St-Pierre, the **Musée des Beaux Arts** (or **Musée Municipal**) (tel. 45 95 07 69) in the restored bishop's palace, displays medieval art, 16th- and 19th-century paintings, ceramics, African art and pottery, and Oceanic art. Check out the bizarrely lit comic strip displays and temporary exhibits from Angoulême's art school students. (Open Wed.-Mon. 10am-noon and 2-6pm. Admission 15F, students 5F, under 18 free.) The **Musée Archéologique,** 44, rue Montmoreau (tel. 45 38 45 17), displays regional treasures from the Gallo-Roman era to recent centuries. (Open Wed.-Mon. 10am-noon and 2-5pm. Free.)

The center of Vieil Angoulême is **Eglise St-André,** redone in a Gothic style but retaining the original Romanesque tower and entrance. Gothic **Eglise St-Martial** rises in the center of town near the pedestrian zone. The extraordinary **Maison St-Simon,** 15, rue de la Cloche Verte (tel. 45 92 34 10), a 16th-century building with walls nearly a meter thick, houses avant-garde art expositions. (Open Wed. 2-6pm, Thurs.-Fri. 9am-noon and 2-6pm, Sat. 2-7pm. Free.)

If you're in Angoulême in January, join the other 200,000 visitors at the world-famous **Salon International de la Bande-Dessinée,** three days of brilliant, free comic strip exhibits. Call 45 95 87 20 for more information. In May, groups from France, South Africa, Jamaica, Nigeria, Italy, Great Britain, and the United States converge at Angoulême's **Festival International de Jazz et Musiques Métisses.** Call 45 95 43 42 for information.

La Rochefoucauld

A half-hour train ride from Angoulême *(direction* "Limoges," 24F) lies La Rochefoucauld (pop. 30,400), the site of a splendid 16th-century château complete with dungeon, chapel, and galleries. (Open late June-early Sept. Admission 20F, tel. 45 63 54 94.) The town's simple but handsome **Cathédrale Notre-Dame-de-l'Assomption** was built in the 13th century, attacked three times by Huguenots, and repeatedly reconstructed in one style or another. The tranquil cloisters of the **Couvent des Carmes** have left many a harried travel writer speechless.

In summer, the tourist office in Angoulême showers tourists with ads for La Rochefoucauld's *son et lumière* stampede of 500 costumed locals and plenty of horses. The historical hoopla is presented at least a dozen times from the end of June through the end of July; it begins in the château's courtyard at 10:30pm. (Tickets 60F, children 25F. Call 45 63 02 33 or the La Rocehfoucauld tourist office for more information.)

If you're staying the night, consider tidy and tasteful **Hôtel de France,** 13, Grande Rue (tel. 45 63 02 29). Doubles run 85-110F. (Breakfast 17F. Open March-Jan. Sun.-Thurs. until 10pm.) Clean, two-star **camping** awaits just around the corner from the château, next to the municipal pool. (5F per person, 3F per tent, 3F per car. Showers 3.50F. Open May-Sept.)

The town's attractions are a short walk from the train station. Look to your right for av. de la Gare, and take a left on rue Porte Marillac, which becomes rue des Halles. (If driving or biking from Angoulême, turn left on rue des Halles at the signs for the château.) From rue des Halles, turn left at the ivy-covered wall for the cathedral or right at the two large stone flower boxes for the cloisters; for the château and the serene waters of **La Tardoire**, continue straight. The **tourist office,** rue des Halles (tel. 45 63 07 45), is next to the cloisters. (Open late June to mid-Sept. Tues.-Sat. 9am-noon and 3-6pm, Mon. 2-6pm.) A cheery fruit and vegetable **market** occupies 18, rue des Halles. (Open Mon.-Sat. 8am-12:30pm and 2:30-7:30pm, Sun. 8am-12:30pm.) The **postal code** is 16110.

North of La Rochefoucauld is **Confolens,** a well-preserved medieval town with the usual half-timbered houses, Gothic bridge, and 12th-century church. Confolens hosts a well-known **International Folklore Festival** around the second week of August. Fifteen countries send dance groups in picturesque garb. For information, contact the Confolens **tourist office,** pl. des Marronniers (tel. 45 84 00 77; open Mon.-Sat. 9am-noon and 2-4pm). The **Hôtel de Vienne,** 4, rue de la Ferrandie (tel. 45 84 09 24), has fine singles and doubles from 80F. (Showers 14F. Breakfast 15F. Open until 10pm.) There's also a two-star municipal **campground** on route de St-Germain. (4.70F per person, 3.60F per tent, 2.30F per car. Open April-Oct.) Confolens is accessible only by bus.

Bordeaux

When Eleanor of Aquitaine married Henry Plantagenet in the 12th century, her sizable dowry included the port city of Bordeaux (pop. 700,000). The marriage soured Anglo-French relations for three centuries but sweetened the pot of *Bordelais* merchants, whose crates of red wines found rabid customers in the English. France's premier industrial port, modern Bordeaux is far from idyllic. A thin layer of grime covers the acclaimed High Gothic churches, grandiose remnants of its prosperous mercantile past, and the Garonne River flows a delicate shade of brown. Beyond the showy boutiques, you will find a city at once magnificent and polluted, crowded and diverse, and never boring. The inexpensive city is a good stopover as well as a springboard to the awe-inspiring Dune du Pilat at Pyla-sur-Mer.

Orientation and Practical Information

Bordeaux's train station is a healthy half-hour walk from the center of town. Bus #7 or 8 makes the trip to pl. Gambetta every 10 minutes (7F). Be sure to pick up a decent map at the information booth in the station or a better map from the information panel with rotating advertisements (2F). The neighborhoods around the hostel and the train station are depressed but not dangerous during the day. Many a *Bordelais,* however, will warn you to watch your valuables, as theft is rampant.

Tourist Office: 12, cours du 30 Juillet (tel. 56 44 28 41). Take bus #7 or 8 from the train station. Large office, usually crowded, orchestrated by expert English-speaking help. Good map, lists of hotels, camping information hotline (July-Aug.), and more. Carte Jeune 70F. Good bus tour of nearby wineries and advice on private companies' tours. Ask about the Carte Bordeaux Découverte, the cheap all-day bus ticket (17F). Open Mon.-Sat. 9am-7pm, Sun. and holidays 9am-3pm; Oct.-May Mon.-Sat. 9am-6:30pm. Also at the **airport.** Mon.-Sat. 8am-6:30pm, Sun. noon-6pm. **Information booth** at train station. Open Mon.-Sat. 9am-12:30pm and 1:30-6pm; Sun. 9am-3pm; Oct.-May Mon.-Sat. 9am-12:30pm and 1:30-6pm, Sun. 9:30am-12:30pm.

Budget Travel: Havas Voyages, 54, cours du Châpeau Rouge (tel. 56 90 93 00), near the Grand Théâtre. Any tickets you want, including BIJ, Air France, and SNCF. Open Mon.-Fri. 9am-6pm, Sat. 9am-noon.

Consulates: U.S., 22, cours Maréchal Foch (tel. 56 52 65 95). Open Mon.-Fri. 9am-noon and 2-5pm. Visa section open Mon.-Fri. 9am-12:45pm. Visa processing takes 2 days. **U.K.,** 15, cours de Verdun (tel. 56 52 28 35). Open Mon.-Fri. 9am-noon and 2:30-5pm.

Currency Exchange: Banc Pinto Sotto Mayor, 18, cours du Chapeau Rouge (tel. 56 48 03 31), close to the tourist office. Open Tues.-Fri. 9am-12:30pm and 2-6pm, Sat. 9am-12:45pm and 2-4:30pm. On Sat. also try the **post office** or the **Banque Franco-Portugaise,** 10, rue Claude Bonnier (tel. 56 98 73 93). Open Tues.-Sat. 9am-12:30pm and 2-6pm. **Thomas Cook** (tel. 56 91 58 80) at the train station. Not the greatest rates, but open on Sunday. Open daily 8am-8pm.

American Express: 14, cours de l'Intendance (tel. 56 81 70 02). Both a travel agency and a currency exchange. Good rates and 10F commission. Open Mon.-Fri. 8:45am-noon and 1:30-6pm.

Post Office: 52, rue Georges Bonnac (tel. 56 48 87 48). Mark Poste Restante letter "Recette Principale" for this office. Branch office on cours de la Marne, 5 blocks from the train station. Open Mon.-Fri. 8am-7pm, Sat. 8am-noon. **Postal Code:** 33000.

Trains: Gare St-Jean (tel. 56 92 50 50), on rue Charles Domercq. Information upstairs and ticket sales downstairs. City maps available at the information desk. **Lockers** 12F, 20F, or 25F. Open 5am-11pm. **Showers** 15F, open until 10:30pm. To: Paris (10-14 per day; 4½-5½ hr. by day, up to 8 hr. by night; 260F); Angoulême (8-12 per day, 1 hr., 79F); Poitiers (10-14 per day, 2½ hr., 133F); Saintes (5-8 per day, 1-1½ hr., 72F); Nantes (5-8 per day, 4 hr., 187F); Toulouse (9-11 per day, 2½ hr., 138F); Nice (4-5 per day, 9-10 hr., 375F); Arcachon with bus connections to the Dune du Pilat (12-16 per day, 45 min., 39F); St-Emilion (2 per day, 45 min., 34F). Helpful information office open daily 8am-8pm; be sure to pick up a number before lining up at the windows.

Buses: Citram, 14, rue Fondaudege (tel. 56 81 18 18). To: Pauillac (1 hr., 37.50F); St-Emilion (5-7 per day, 1¼ hr., 32F). Information booth open Mon.-Sat. 9am-noon and 2-6:15pm. Buy tickets on board. Many smaller lines serve Bordeaux; inquire at the tourist office for schedules. Carte Bordeaux Découverte, available at the tourist office or train station, provides unlimited travel for one (17F) or three (38F) days.

Bike Rental: The **train station** rents mediocre bikes for 50F per day with 500F deposit. Inquire at the baggage desk. Open 24 hrs. The only other bike rental is in the suburb of Mérignac (accessible by bus or on foot): **Ecocycle,** 47, av. Aristide Briand (tel. 56 96 07 50).

Hitchhiking: Allostop, 49, cours de l'Argonne (tel. 56 91 06 79), right off pl. de la Victoire. Give them 3-4 days' notice and a 40F subscription fee, and they'll find you a ride for 0.16F per km. 30F subscription for journeys under 300km. Open Mon.-Fri. 9am-1pm and 2-6pm, in winter also Sat. 10am-noon.

English Bookstore: Mollat, 83-91, rue Porte Dijeaux. Big, expensive selection. Open Mon. 2-6:45pm, Tues.-Sat. 9am-6:45pm.

Womens Center: Centre d'Information sur les Droits des Femmes, 5, rue Jean-Jacques Rousseau (tel. 56 44 30 30). Information and counseling. Open Mon. 10am-4pm, Tues. 2-7pm, Thurs. 10am-4pm.

Youth Centers: Centre d'Information Jeunesse d'Aquitaine, 5, rue Duffour Dubergier (tel. 56 48 55 50). Information about activities, jobs, etc. BIJ and train tickets. Carte Jeune 70F. Open Mon.-Fri. 9am-6pm. **CROUS:** 18, cours du Hammel (tel. 56 91 98 80). They can tell you which university restaurants are open but can't sell you tickets. Open Mon.-Fri. 9am-12:30pm and 1:30-4pm.

Laundromat: Take your pick. The most convenient is on cours de Marne, 5 min. from the station and hostel. Wash 12F, dry 2F per 5 min. Open daily 7am-10pm. Also at 27, rue de la Boëtie. Wash 15F, dry 2F per 5 min. No 1F coins at either location. Open daily 7am-9pm.

Medical Assistance: SAMU, tel. 56 96 70 70. Ambulance service. **Hôpital St-André,** 1, rue Jean Burguet (tel. 56 79 56 79). 24-hr. emergency room. Free VD treatment Mon.- Tues. and Thurs.- Fri. 5-6pm.

Police: 87, rue Abbé de l'Epée (tel. 56 90 92 75). **Emergency,** tel. 17.

Accommodations and Camping

Bordeaux is a popular place to spend several days as well as a convenient stop on the way to or from Spain. In July and August, it's advisable but not imperative to call ahead. The hostel is an adequate and convenient place to sleep, but the strict lockout and curfew might limit your carousing. Plenty of cheap hotels and an elegant student *maison* round out the abundant affordable lodgings in this city. Hotels

Photograph by Christine Michelini, mother, Salem, Massachusetts.

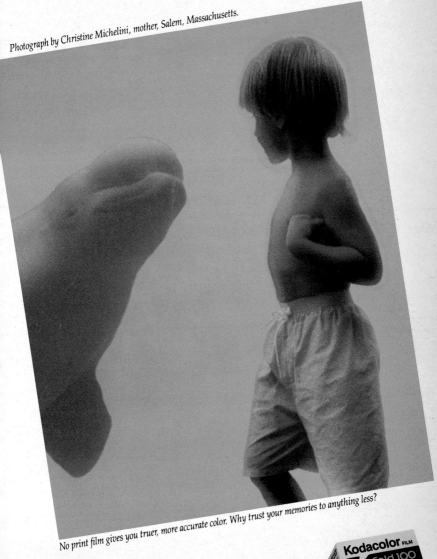

No print film gives you truer, more accurate color. Why trust your memories to anything less?

Show Your True Colors.™

CARRY-ON RELIEF.

When you're traveling abroad, it's nice to hear a familiar voice.

Bobbi Coney
AT&T Operator
Pittsburgh, PA

The language may be difficult.
The food may be different.
The customs may be unfamiliar.
But making a phone call back to the States can be easy.

Just dial the special *AT&T* **USADirect**® access number for the country you're in.

Within seconds, you're in touch with an *AT&T Operator* in the U.S. who can help you complete your call.

Use your *AT&T Calling Card* or call collect. And not only can you minimize hotel surcharges but you can also save with our international rates.

Only *AT&T* **USADirect** *Service* puts you in easy reach of an *AT&T Operator* from over 75 countries around the world.

And it's just another way that AT&T is there to help you from practically anywhere in the world.

So call **1 800 874-4000 Ext. 415** for a free information card listing *AT&T* **USADirect** access numbers.

And see how making a phone call from distant lands can become familiar territory.

AT&T **USADirect**®*Service.*
Your express connection to AT&T service.

AT&T
The right choice.

farther from the station are cleaner and less crowded, but you'll be surprised what you can find close to the station at good prices. Some university dorms open their doors July through mid-September at village #5 on the university campus in Talence (tel. 56 80 74 34). Take bus F (7F) from pl. de la Victoire.

Auberge de Jeunesse (IYHF), 22, cours Barbey (tel. 56 91 59 51), 10 min. from the station and 20 min. from the *centre ville*. Bear right out of the station, left onto cours de la Marne, then left again onto cours Barbey. The 250 beds often fill in summer. Businesslike management, good kitchen and bathrooms, and spacious 8-bed rooms. Office open 7-9:30am and 6-11pm. Strict lockout 9:30am-6pm and curfew 11pm. 37F with an IYHF card, 42F with a passport. Breakfast 16F. Sheets 16F. No telephone reservations. Arrive early in July and August.

Maison des Etudiantes, 50, rue Ligier (tel. 56 96 48 30). Take bus #7 or 8 from the station to Bourse du Travail, and continue in the same direction on cours de la Libération to rue Ligier. If walking from the station, follow cours de la Marne though pl. de la Victoire to cours Aristide Briand. Turn right on rue Ligier (30 min.). The Maison is on the righthand corner. Single rooms. Quiet, clean, and closer to the center of town than the hostel. Ping-pong and TV downstairs. Kitchen lacks pots, pans, and silverware, but you might be able to borrow some. A few beds only for women Oct.-June. Coed July-Aug. Plenty of beds during summer. No lockout or curfew. 55F, 45 with ISIC. Showers and sheets included. Telephone reservations accepted.

Hôtel la Boétie, 4, rue de la Boëtie (tel. 56 81 76 68, fax 56 81 24 72), a quiet street between pl. Gambetta and the Musée des Beaux Arts. Comfortable, spacious rooms and friendly management. Reception open 8am-11pm. Singles 95-110F. Doubles 110-125F. Triples 150F. All rooms with shower and TV. Breakfast 16F. The same family also runs two other *centre ville* hotels of similar quality and with the same prices: **Studio Hôtel,** 26, rue Huguerie (tel. 56 48 00 14), and **Hôtel Lafaurie,** 35, rue Lafaurie-de-Monbadon (tel. 56 48 16 33).

Hôtel d'Amboise, 22, rue de la Vieille Tour (tel. 56 81 62 67), in the *centre ville*. Attractive rooms overlooking pedestrian streets. English-speaking management. Open 7am-9:30pm. A few singles 70F. Doubles 80F, with shower 105F. Showers 8F. Breakfast 16F. Telephone reservations accepted.

Hôtel Huguerie, 67, rue Huguerie (tel. 56 81 23 69), in the *centre ville*. Tidy, tasteful singles and doubles 70-85F, with shower 110F. Showers 8F. Extra bed 20F. Breakfast in bed 15F.

Hôtel-Bar-Club Les 2 Mondes, 10, rue St-Vincent-de-Paul (tel. 56 91 63 09). Turn right from the station and left onto rue St-Vincent de Paul (3 min. on foot). One star. Spacious, clean rooms. Singles 80F. with shower 90F. Doubles 95F, with shower 95-115F. Triples 165F. No hall showers. Breakfast 17F. Reservations only held until 6pm.

Camping: There are no campgrounds in the city itself, but one lies in the immediate vicinity. **Camping les Gravières,** Pont-de-la-Maye in Villenauve d'Ornon (tel. 56 87 00 36). A 3-star campground in a forest by the river. 200 sites. Reception open 8am-11pm. 15.10F per person, 13F per tent, 21F per tent and car. **Camping Beausoleil** (tel. 56 98 17 66) is a 3-star site 10km out of town in Gradignan. Take bus G from pl. de la Victoire. Both sites open all year.

Food

Known in France as *la région de bien boire et de bien manger* (the region of fine drinking and dining), Bordeaux offers a variety of specialty restaurants. Along with the celebrated wine, you'll find plump oysters, tender *confits* of duck and goose (a delicacy of meat preserved in its own fat, and often fried with potatoes), and *champignons* (mushrooms) as light as truffles. Bordeaux has restaurants in all price ranges, including some of the cheapest in France. These cluster around pleasant **place St-Michel,** a multi-ethnic neighborhood located at a safe distance (but a short walk) from downtown madness. The restaurants near the **Grosse Cloche** in rue St-James post slightly more expensive *menus*. The area around pl. Général Sarrail, especially along rue des Augustins, also has some moderately priced establishments. For a look at more costly *menus*, walk along **rue des Faussets,** off pl. St-Pierre. This ancient, newly renovated pedestrian street is lined with restaurants, each more atmospheric and elegant than its neighbor; most offer main dishes and *menus* for under 65F.

There is a cheap Auchan **supermarket** near the Maison des Etudiantes at the huge Centre Meriadeck on rue Claude Bonnier. (Open Mon.-Sat. 8:30am-10pm.) **Mar-**

kets are scattered all over town. The market on allées de Tourny (moving to pl. des Grands Hommes in 1991) is upscale and expensive; the marché des Capucins, off cours de la Marne at the end of rue Clare, is a madhouse and much more fun (open Mon.-Sat. 6am-1pm). Look for more stalls near Eglise St-Louis, on rue Notre-Dame, at the foot of rue Montesquieu (open Mon.-Sat. 6am-1pm), and on cours Victor Hugo at pl. de la Ferme de Richemont. On Sunday, settle for the grocery stores along cours Victor Hugo. **Flunch,** a self-service cafeteria on cours de l'Intendance, has 30-40F meals. (Open daily 11am-10pm.)

> **University Restaurant:** If you figure out which branch is open, you can eat a decent 25F all-you-can-eat meal. Better yet, buy a ticket with your ISIC card or your Carte Jeune and eat for 12F. Tickets are easily bought from students at the door and officially obtained at the restaurant. CROUS (tel. 56 91 98 80) can tell you where to go. Otherwise, stop by any location and look for posted schedules. Tickets sold Mon., Wed., and Fri. 11:30am-1pm at the restaurants. **Lebec,** rue de Cursol (tel. 56 91 79 96), is usually open July-Aug. and Oct.-May. Sun.-Fri. 11:45am-1:30pm and 6:45-8:10pm.

> **Restaurant Kim-Long,** 187, cours de la Marne, a 2-min. walk from the station. The 3-course 39F Vietnamese dinner is fresh and filling. First breadless meal you'll have in France and still feel full. Main dish (chicken, pork, or beef) with rice and interesting desserts. 39F *menu* not available weekends. *A la carte* dishes from 30F. Open Mon.-Sat. noon-1:30pm and 7-10:30pm, Sun. 7-10:30pm.

> **La Perla,** 3, rue Gaspard Philippe. Abundant if unspectacular food. The place is not extremely clean, but it has its own charm. 38F buys soup, hors d'oeuvres, vegetable, meat, dessert, and wine. Spanish specialties. Open Mon.-Sat. 10:30am-1:45pm and 6:30-8:45pm.

> **L'Athenée,** 44, rue des Trois Conils, 1 block east of the cathedral. A cozy place with appetizing 40F, 63F, and 72F *menus.* Delicious desserts 8-20F. Open Mon.-Fri. noon-2pm and 8-10:30pm, Sat. noon-2pm.

> **La Flambée,** 26, rue du Mirail. A memorable 80F or 120F feast includes a plate of *fruits de mer gratinés* (seafood with melted cheese) and Burgundy fondue. You won't be disappointed. Open Mon.-Sat. noon-2pm and 7:30-10pm.

Sights and Entertainment

Bordeaux's prosperous past is unambiguously indicated by two full-scale High Gothic masterpieces, **Cathédrale St-André** and **Eglise St-Michel.** The cathedral, built between the 11th and 16th centuries, is remarkable for its extravagant façade, numerous and well-preserved grimacing gargoyles, and a strange assortment of flying buttresses. Just to the right of the main portico sits a 16th-century buttress composed of a string of slender columns; the one next to it resembles a ribbon of flames. Eleanor of Aquitaine first dabbled in matrimony here with Louis IX. (Cathedral open to the public 8am-noon and 2-5:30pm. Free organ recital every other Tues. evening mid-June to mid-Sept. Call 56 81 78 79 or 56 52 68 10 for information.) Across town, Eglise St-Michel is accompanied by an immense, free-standing 15th-century bell tower. Even if such architectural overstatements leave you cold, investigate the old St-Michel neighborhood. Nearby **Eglise Ste-Croix,** a 12th- and 13th-century Benedictine abbey, has a façade with Romanesque arches and statuettes. One of Bordeaux's showpieces, its **Grand Théâtre,** will be closed in 1991-92 for long-needed renovations. Vandalized during the Revolution and subsequently used as a target range by the army, the **Jardin Public** has been gradually renovated and redesigned in the English style since 1856. Today these 25 green acres in the center of Bordeaux contain the botanical gardens. (Open daily 7am-9pm, in winter 7am-6pm.) The **Musée des Beaux Arts** (tel. 56 90 91 60, ext. 1380), on cours d'Albret near the cathedral, houses a fine collection of canvases by Titian, Giordano, de Cortone, Rubens, Délacroix, Corot, Renoir, Matisse, and other European painters. (Open Wed.-Mon. 10am-noon and 2-6pm. Admission 13F, students 6F, Wed. free.) The **Musée d'Art Contemporain,** rue Foy (tel. 56 44 16 35), has temporary shows of contemporary art. (Open Tues.-Sun. 11am-7pm, Wed. until 10pm. Admission 20F, students 15F, noon-2pm free.) **Musée d'Aquitaine,** cours Pasteur (tel. 56 90 91 60) houses treasures from Bordeaux's agricultural, maritime, and commercial endeavours over the centuries, as well as good information on the Aquitaine region and its history. Of note is the 2000-year-old *Vénus à la Corne.* (Open Wed.-Mon. 10am-6pm. Admission 13F, students 6F. Free Wed.) The museum also oversees archaeological sites throughout the city. Bordeaux's great efforts to restore the 16th- and 17th-century houses around pl. du Parlement have created a nice walking circuit.

During the school year, nightlife centers on the students cafés around pl. de la Victoire. The **Alligator,** pl. Général Sarrail (tel. 56 92 78 47), is a popular jazz club with no cover. Drinks, however, will take a 40-60F bite out of your wallet. **Le Pacha,** route Arcachon Pessac (tel. 56 36 66 30) and **Le Twenty,** quai Brazza (tel. 56 40 36 49) are two trendy discos.

Wine and Wineries

There are three main families of red Bordeaux wine: Medocs and Graves; St-Emilion, Pomerol, and Fronsac; and Bordeaux and Côtes de Bordeaux. All except Graves, which takes its name from the small pebbles in the soil, are named after the region from which they come. The whites—both dry (sold in a green bottle) and sweet *liquoreux* (in a clear one)—are made by different processes. The dry grapes are harvested and fermented like most wines, but grapes (such as the Sauternes) for the *liquoreux* gain their aroma from the "noble rot," a microscopic fungus that attacks the over-ripe grape.

Just opposite the tourist office, the **Maison du Vin/CIVB,** 1, cours du 30 Juillet (tel. 56 00 22 66), is the place to ask all your oenological questions. The only house within Bordeaux to offer free tastings, they can give you a list of small wine châteaux in the area. (Open Mon.-Fri. 8:30am-6pm, Sat. 9am-12:30pm and 1:30-5pm, Sun. 9:30am-12:30pm and 1:30-4pm.) The **Vinothèque,** 8, cours du 30 Juillet (tel. 56 52 32 05; open Mon.-Sat. 9am-7:30pm), the **L'Intendant,** 2, allées de Tourny (tel. 56 48 01 29; open daily 10am-7:30pm) (both within 50m of the tourist office), and **Magnum,** 3, rue Gobineau (tel. 56 48 00 06; open Mon.-Sat. 9am-7:30pm), have knowledgeable salespeople who will answer your questions and sell you a bottle of Bordeaux red in the 10-10,000F range. In general, wine in the city of Bordeaux is no cheaper than anywhere else in France; however, wine bought at the châteaux usually costs 10-20F less.

A visit to the major wine-producing châteaux requires, at the very least, a preliminary phone call. Remember to be bold; you don't get anything without asking. Many huge houses, such as **Château Haut-Briond** (tel. 56 98 33 73), manage to sell their wines without the help of backpack-laden small fry. Ask them how they may be reached by bus and they are likely to suggest you take a cab; hesitate, and it's all over. Enlist the support of the tourist office to help you make reservations. The Maison du Vin has a list of smaller houses that accept walk-in visitors. Get a list from the Maison du Vin. The tourist office's **bus tours** are a good way to see many wine châteaux quickly. (Open mid-May to mid-Oct. Admission 100F, students 85F. Reserve in the morning for the 1:45pm tours.)

Near Bordeaux

About 38km east of Bordeaux, the medieval market town of **St-Emilion** boasts beautiful cloisters and a splendid hillside view of more than 1000 wineries and billions of grapes. More than 29 wine-producing châteaux in St-Emilion bear the mark of highest distinction—*Grand Crus.* The view from atop the **donjon** may slap even the jaded across the face. (Admission 3F. Open daily 9am-12:30pm and 2:30-6:45pm.) St-Emilion's intriguing **Eglise Monolithe** was painstakingly carved from a single, massive piece of rock. The guided tour passes through the ancient catacombs adorned with open sarcophagi and an occasional bone or two. Tours leave daily from the tourist office about every 45 minutes beginning at 10am (45 min., last tour at 5:45pm, 25F). Trains run to St-Emilion twice per day (¾-hr., 34F). Take a right on the main road from the station and walk the 2km to St-Emilion.

The **tourist office,** pl. des Créneaux (tel. 57 24 72 03), sits at the foot of the church tower. (Open daily 9:30am-12:30pm and 1:45-6pm.) The tourist office organizes tours (some in English) of the different châteaux (July-Sept. 15 Mon.-Sat., 2½ hr., 50F). These include a round-trip bus ride to the winery, a guided tour of the château, and a free *dégustation.* If you feel like striking out on your own, ask the tourist office for a list of châteaux that offer tours in English.

Southeast of Bordeaux, toward Leognan, lies the beautiful 13th-century **Château de la Brede** (tel. 56 20 20 49), former home of the 18th-century *philosophe* Montesquieu. (Open, in theory, July-Aug. Wed.-Mon. 2:30-5:30pm.)

Trains leave Bordeaux about every hour for **Arcachon** (50 min., 39F). *Get on one of these trains.* Arcachon, a popular seaside resort with a beautiful sandy beach, is not the main attraction. The real reason to visit, the sublime **Dune du Pilat** at **Pyla-sur-Mer,** lies 10km south of town. At 117m above sea level, the spectacular dune is the largest in Europe, massive enough to absorb the summertime throngs effortlessly. In the late afternoon especially, you'll have plenty of room to ski or roll or jog down this golden Alp's forgiving but steeply-raked slopes—and to slog painfully back up. Buses leave for Pyla (a short walk from the Dune) from the Arcachon station (about 20 per day, last return at about 7:45pm, 40 min., 7.50F). Those who hitch get there in half the time. Take food and water with you. There are average-priced restaurants behind the dune (meaning you have to climb back over after lunch) and a snack bar on the beach whose steep prices rival the dune. The snack bar has no running water and charges 10F for half a liter of Vittel.

Arcachon's **tourist office** on pl. Roosevelt (tel. 56 83 01 69) is a stone's throw left of the station. (Open daily 9am-7:30pm; Sept.-June Mon.-Fri. 9am-noon and 2-7pm, Sat. 9am-noon and 2-6pm.) Pyla's tourist office, rond-point du Figuier (tel. 56 54 02 22), provides lists of hotels. You almost certainly won't be able (or willing) to pay for a single one, especially in July and August when prices are inflated 50-80% and the cheapest rooms top the 100F mark. (Open 10am-1pm and 3-7pm; Sept.-June 9am-5pm.) Instead, try the three-star **Camping les Abatilles** (tel. 56 83 24 15), on allée de la Galaxie in Arcachon (open April to mid-Oct.), or choose from four campgrounds in Pyla, including a three-star spot on the Dune, **Camping de la Dune** (tel. 56 22 72 17; open May-Sept.). Freelance camping is prohibited in the area. Across the bay from Arcachon in **Cap-Ferret** is an **Auberge de Jeunesse,** 87, av. de Bordeaux (tel. 56 60 64 62; open July-Aug.). Cap-Ferret is accessible by ferry from Arcachon's **Jetée Thiers** (every ½-hr., 9am-noon and 2-7pm; 27F, return 35F; tel. 56 54 83 09). Arcachon oysters are delightful when washed down with a bottle of Graves—but most of the restaurants here are as expensive as the hotels. Across from Arcachon's station, the **Coquille,** 63, bd. du Général Leclerc, includes oysters and mussels in its five-course 75F *menu.*

Périgord-Quercy

For roughly 30,000 years the winding grottoes of Périgord and Quercy have sheltered graceful maroon etchings of stampeding bison, frolicking wild horses, and panicked reindeer fleeing a hunter's arrows. While such prehistoric beasts still loom large in the imaginations of locals and tourists alike, the millennia since Cro-Magnon artists first turned to the walls of Lascaux and other caves have brough smaller, less threatening fauna into the *périgordin* diet. Local farms are the temporary safe haven for plump geese innocently pecking at their feed, oblivious to the market value of the *foie gras* made from their enlarged livers. Hungry pigs hunt the large Boletus mushrooms know as *cêpes* as well as the black truffles found at the root of oak trees from November to March. Local goats make their contribution to regional feasts in the form of *cabécon,* a tart cheese that complements the smoother taste of *foie gras.* You'll find all these specialities along with the odd Cro-Magnon statuette at the local markets. Eschew the canned stuff for the fresh produce available at Bergerac and Périgueux (Wednesday and Saturday) and at Brive, Cahors, and Sarlat (Saturday morning).

In addition to an incomparable collection of prehistoric art *in situ* and some of the most seductive gourmet tables in France, Périgord-Quercy offers some fine and relatively uncrowded scenery. The Dordogne river passes dozens of châteaux and feudal *bastides* as it makes its wild and woolly way westward from the Massif Central to the Gironde, a finger of the Atlantic poking inward toward Bordeaux. Although Hautfort and a few other châteaux recall an era of elegant leisure, most were defensive strongholds built during the Hundred Years' War. Domme, Beynac, and La Roque-Gageac (all near Sarlat) are among the most stunning hilltowns in France. Rocamadour, the most impressive of them all, draws both tourists and religious pilgrims to the clifftop site where the pious hermit St-Amadour lived.

Bus and train connections in the region are neither frequent nor convenient. Many *sentiers de grandes randonnées,* clearly marked long-distance footpaths, pass through remote areas and connect such cities as Limoges, Les Eyzies, Sarlat, Souillac, and Cahors. Inquire at Dordogne's **Comité Départemental de Tourisme,** 16, rue Wilson (tel. 53 53 44 35) in Périgeux for maps and information on canoeing or kayaking along the Lot, Dordogne, Isle, or Vézère rivers. Although hitching long distances can be very difficult on the small, curving roads, many people make smaller hops to the tourist towns quite easily.

Périgueux

In Périgueux, the Isle River winds past Roman ruins, a Byzantine-Romanesque cathedral topped with an outrageous number of domes, and the properly tangled streets of the *vieille ville.* As the capital of Périgord-Quercy, the city has enough supermarkets and moderately priced accommodations to recommend it as a touring base. A short walk from the *centre ville* leads to attractive wooded countryside, but don't neglect longer daytrips to the cave paintings of Les Eyzies and the fortified *bastides.*

Orientation and Practical Information

Located at the center of the triangle formed by Bordeaux, Limoges, and Brive, Périgueux is a one- to two-hour train ride from any of these cities. The *vieille ville* and tourist office are a 10- to 15-minute walk from the train station. Turn right on rue Denis Papin and left on rue des Mobile-de-Coulmiers, which becomes rue du Président Wilson. On your right, you'll pass rue Lafayette, which leads to the Roman ruins clustered around the train tracks. Continue straight on rue du Président Wilson; the tourist office will be on the left up av. d'Aquitaine. The *vieille ville* will be directly ahead, perched on the western banks of the Isle River and enclosed by cours de Tourny, bd. de M. Montaigne, and rue Taillefer.

Tourist Office: 1, av. d'Aquitaine (tel. 53 53 10 63). English-speaking staff has bus schedules, topographical maps and hiking guides, and lists of alternative accommodations (farms and campsites). Grab the invaluable free brochure *La Fête en Périgord.* Guided tours of town, sometimes in English, July-Aug. (15F, students 10F). Ask about organized bus tours of surrounding towns in summer (150-200F). Open Mon.-Fri. 8:30am-noon and 1-7pm, Sat. 9am-noon and 2-5pm. **Regional Tourist Office:** 16, rue du Président Wilson (tel. 53 53 44 35). Even better information on the Dordogne region. Brochures on camping, festivals, and shows in the city. Busy staff—be persistent. User-friendly computer outside puts loads of info at your fingertips (in French). Open Mon.-Fri. 9am-noon and 2-6pm; Oct.-May Mon.-Fri. 9:30am-noon and 2-4:30pm.

Budget Travel: HAVAS **Agence de Voyages,** av. d'Aquitaine (tel. 53 08 12 62), across from the post office. BIJ/Eurotrain tickets. Student discount airfare tickets. Open Mon.-Fri. 8:30am-noon and 1:30-6pm.

Post Office: rue du 4 Septembre, near the tourist office. **Telephones** and **currency exchange.** Open Mon.-Fri. 8am-7pm, Sat. 8am-noon. **Postal Code:** 24000.

Trains: rue Denis Papin (tel. 53 09 50 50 daily 4am-midnight; reservations 53 03 23 00). To: Paris (6-7 per day, 5-6 hr., 235F); Lyon (4 direct per day, 7-8 hr., 230F); Toulouse (6-8 per day; 4 hr.; 144F via Brive, 140F via Agen); Limoges (10-13 direct per day, 1¾ hr., 63F); Bordeaux (11-13 direct per day, 2 hr., 77F); Sarlat (3-4 per day, 1½ hr., 61F); Les Eyzies (4 per day, ¾ hr., 30F; take the 7:15am train to see the cave paintings); Brive-la-Gaillarde (6 per day, 1-1½ hr., 51F). Information office open Mon.-Thurs. 8:30am-7:45pm, Fri. 9am-7:40pm, Sat. 9am-noon and 2-7:45pm, Sun. 10am-noon and 2-7:45pm.

Buses: pl. Francheville (tel. 53 08 76 00). Regional bus information upstairs; city bus information downstairs . Schedules are confusing and fluctuate often. **Gonthier Nouhaud** (green and white buses) goes to Mussidan and Hautefort. Other lines to Riberac, Verteillac, Payzac, Limoges, Excideuil, Sarlat via Montignac, Brantôme, and Bergerac. Check at the tourist office or station for schedules. Most lines also stop at the SNCF station.

Car Rental: Europcar, 14, rue Denis Papin (tel. 53 08 15 72), across from the train station. The most reasonable rates in town and still expensive. Ask about weekend specials. From 295F per day.

Bike Rental: Au Tour de France, 96, av. du Maréchal Juin (tel. 53 53 41 91). Mountain bikes, mopeds, panniers. Open Mon.-Sat. 8:30am-12:30pm and 2-7:30pm. **Huot Sports,** 41bis, cours St-Georges (tel. 53 53 31 56).

Youth Center: Centre d'Information Jeunesse (CIJ), 1, av. d'Aquitaine (tel. 53 53 52 81), next to the tourist office. Tons of information on concerts, excursions, and other youth activities. Helps find student lodging (free). Open Mon.-Fri. 9am-noon and 2:30-6:30pm, Sat. 9am-noon and 2:30-5:30pm.

Hospital: Centre Hospitalier, 80, av. Georges Pompidou (tel. 53 07 70 00).

Medical Assistance: SAMU, tel. 53 08 81 11.

Police: Commissariat, rue du 4 Septembre (tel. 53 08 17 67). **Emergency,** tel. 17.

Accommodations and Camping

Several inexpensive hotels cluster around the train station. A few more are scattered on the way into the *vieille ville* and in the pedestrian area. The hostel is not marked at all and can be difficult to find. Use the map outside the station for orientation before making the trip. **Farms** in the region sometimes let rooms or camping space. The tourist office and the computer outside on rue Wilson have a list. Whether you plan to sleep indoors or out, in the city or on a farm, reserve a few days in advance in summer.

Foyer des Jeunes Travailleurs Résidence Lakanal, off bd. Lakanal (tel. 53 53 52 05). From the tourist office (see directions above), go back down av. Aquitaine, cross rue Wilson onto rue Ernest Guillier which becomes rue E. Lafont after the church. At Rond-Point Durant, bear to the left onto bd. Bertrand de Born and then turn right onto rue des Thermes, which curves parallel to the track. The *foyer* is at the end of the street, to the left, facing away from you as you enter the parking lot (10 min.). Reception open Mon.-Fri. 5-7pm, Sat.-Sun. after

8pm. Cramped dorm rooms with bunk beds. 55F per person. Sheets, showers, and breakfast included. Cafeteria lunch 30-35F. Dinner 35F.

Hôtel du Midi et du Terminus, 18-20, rue Denis Papin (tel. 53 53 41 06), opposite the train station. Run by a kindly manager and his family. Comfortable, attractive rooms (some small) on a noisy street. TV lounge. Reception closed Sun. 2-6:30pm. Singles with a small skylight in the turret 80F. Doubles 90F, with shower 110F. Two big, comfortable beds 125F. Hall showers included. *Croissant* breakfast 19F. Excellent *menus* from 57F served daily noon-2pm and 7:30-9:30pm. Call a day ahead. Open Oct. 7-Sept. 25.

Hôtel des Voyageurs, 22, rue Denis Papin (tel. 53 53 17 44), across from the station. No-frills accommodations; definitely cheap. The *voyageurs* whose voices you hear are actually inside the trains. Reception open Mon.-Sat. Doubles 80F. Two beds 83F, with shower 90F. Showers 8F. Breakfast 17F. Call a day in advance. Closed 3 weeks in summer, usually in Aug.

Hôtel des Arènes, 21, rue du Gymnase (tel. 53 53 49 85), between Eglise St-Etienne-de-la-Cité and Tour de Vésone. Convenient, comfortable, and quiet. Reception closed after 11pm and Sat.-Sun. noon-6pm. Airy doubles with telephone 90-110F, with shower 125F. Extra bed 45F. Showers 22F. Breakfast 18F, 22F, and 30F.

Camping: Barnabé-Plage, 80, rue des Bains (tel. 53 53 41 45), 1½km from Périgueux in Boulazac. Take the city bus (*direction* "Cité Belaire") from cours Montaigne or the SNCF station. A riverside site packed in July and Aug. Canoe rentals. 9.80F per person, 9.30F per tent, 6.40F per car. Open daily 8:30am-midnight. **Camping de l'Ile,** route de Brive (tel. 53 53 57 75), 3km from town in Boulazac. 14F per person, 10F per tent, 10F per car. Open April-Sept. daily until 11pm.

Food

The most notable of *périgourdin* specialties are truffles and *pâtés*. *Charcuteries* along rue Limogeanne are palaces of *pâté de foie gras* and other delicacies. Budgetarians (and vegetarians) may have to settle for the fresh produce at the daily morning **market** in pl. du Coderc; meat steams in the adjacent covered **Halles**. There is also a larger market near the cathedral on Saturdays. **Monoprix,** on pl. de la République in *centre ville,* has a mediocre supermarket upstairs. (Open Mon.-Tues. and Thurs. 9am-12:30pm and 2:15-7pm, Wed. and Sat. 9am-1pm and 2-7pm.) The garden bordering the ruins of the Arènes Romaines, or the more central pl. St-Louis, are pleasant places to spread your picnic blanket. Most hotels serve 50-60F *menus;* the Hôtel du Midi's is particularly delicious.

If you hanker for Asian food, try the excellent delicatessen and take-out store, **Tan Phat,** 42, rue Limogeanne. On pl. St-Louis, the chic cafés **Le Benson** and **Le St-Louis** combine atmosphere, elegance, jazz, and overpriced coffee.

Café-Bar Le Gambetta, 18bis, rue Gambetta. Interesting salads (33-45F) and light meals. *Plat du jour* 39F. Open Mon.-Fri. 11am-5pm.

Le Canard Laqué, 2, rue Lammary, off pl. St-Louis. The namesake dish combines duck, pork, chicken, and seafood in a delicious stew (55F). Thai specialties, such as *canard Chiangmai* (duck with eggplant and curry), an amazing 40F. Large portions of everything. Open Tues.-Sun. noon-2:30pm and 7-10:30pm.

La Grignotière, 6, rue du Ruy Limogeanne, in a quiet courtyard off pl. St-Louis. Great for hearty salads, Try the *Salade du Périgorde,* packed with nuts, duck, *foie gras,* and everything else you've seen at the market (40F). Gawk at the *jeunes cadres* (yuppies).

Restaurant Le Charbol, 22, rue Eguillerie, just off pl. St-Louis. Expensive, but the 58F lunch *menu* served on the terrace will make you feel like a likely candidate for *foie gras.*

Febus, 11, rue Notre-Dame. Umbrageous but casual bar-restaurant with young, regular crowd. Mexican cuisine. Light but savory 45F *menu,* good salads 20-30F, chili and *plats du jour* 25F. Umbrella-topped cocktails and beers. Open for meals daily noon-midnight; open for drinks until 2am.

Pizzeria Les Coupoles, 7, rue de la Clarté, near Cathédrale St-Front. Good-sized pizzas 30-55F. Open Tues.-Sat.

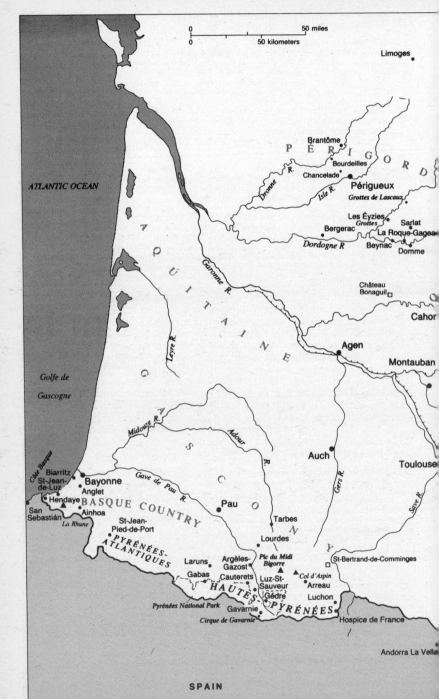

0 ___ 50 miles
0 ___ 50 kilometers

ATLANTIC OCEAN

Limoges

PÉRIGORD

Brantôme
Bourdeilles
Chancelade
Dronne R.
Isle R.
Périgueux
Grottes de Lascaux
Les Éyzies
Grottes
Sarlat
Bergerac
La Roque-Gagea
Dordogne R
Beynac
Domme

A Q U I T A I N E

Garonne R.

Leyre R.

Château
Bonaguil
Cahor
Q

Golfe de

Gascogne

Agen

Montauban

Midouze R.

G

A

S

Adour R.

Auch

Toulouse

Gers R.

Côte Basque
Biarritz
St-Jean-
de-Luz
Anglet
Hendaye
San
Sebastián
La Rhune
Ainhoa
Bayonne
Gave de Pau R.
BASQUE COUNTRY
Pau
C
O
Save R.

St-Jean-
Pied-de-Port
PYRÉNÉES-
ATLANTIQUES
Laruns
Gabas
Argèles-
Gazost
Cauterets
Luz-St-
Sauveur
HAUTES-
Pyrénées National Park
Gavarnie
Cirque de Gavarnie
Tarbes
Lourdes
Pic du Midi
Bigorre
Gédre
PYRÉNÉES
Col d'Aspin
Arreau
Luchon
N
Y
St-Bertrand-de-Comminges
Hospice de France

Andorra La Vella

SPAIN

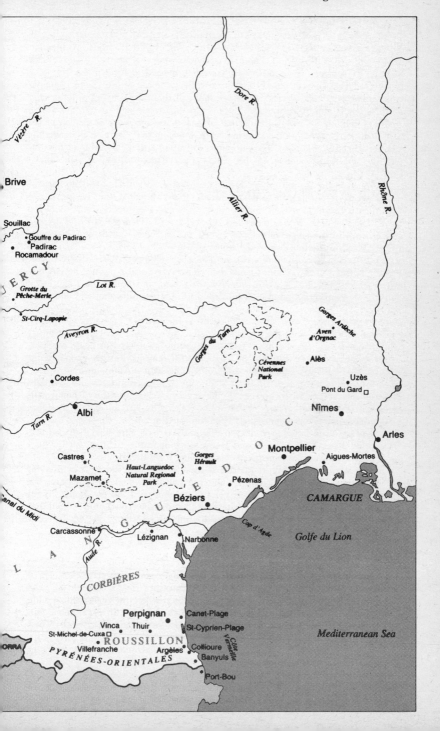

Sights and Entertainment

As *vieille villes* go, Périgueux's is exceptional. Expensive *charcuteries* border crowded *salons de thé* and eclectic shops which sell everything from Cro-Magnon man sculptures (authentic, of course) to regional costumes to mineral jewelry. Place St-Louis is perfect for people-watching, rue Limogeanne for window-shopping (which often degenerates into blatant drooling). While rue de la Miséricorde hides Renaissance *hôtels* and obscure stairways, sunny pl. du Coderc bustles with the daily market. Hours slip by easily here.

Along allée de Tourny, Neanderthal Man and his ancestors await you at the **Musée du Périgord.** Note the amusing death notice on the glass case enclosing the Chancelade Man's remains. The museum's collection also includes Stone Age implements and Roman artifacts. (Open Thurs.-Tues. 10am-noon and 2-5pm. Admission 5F.)

As you face the station on rue Denis Papin, look to your left for the narrow, camel-backed footbridge across the train tracks to av. Maréchal Juin. Turn left, then take rue du Président Wilson for the *vieille ville* and the tree-lined waters of the river **l'Isle,** the great white domes and 70m belfry of **Cathédrale St-Front** floating above. Built in the shape of a Greek cross, the cathedral successfully combines Sacré-Coeur's Byzantine domes, the Abbey of Cluny's Romanesque arches, and the stylish turrets of a reformed fortress. In 1852, the architect of Paris's Sacré Coeur, Abadie, added more Byzantine turrets than conservative critics deemed decent, creating a most bodacious house of worship. (Free tours in summer daily 8am-noon and 2:30-7:30pm, upon request. Admission to the 9th-century cloisters and crypt 10F.)

One km southwest, just across the tracks, is the massive, cut-away cylinder of the **Tour de Vésone,** once the marble-encased temple of an important first-century Gallo-Roman city. Legend has it that the break in the tower was made when St-Front shooed away the last demons worshipped by pagans. Farther on stands the Romanesque **Eglise St-Etienne-de-la-Cité,** its unmistakable Aquitaine dome resembling a hovering armadillo. Up from St-Etienne are the palm trees and fountains of **Jardin des Arènes,** where you can see the remains of the 1st-century Roman stairwells and the ancient arena's vomitorium. Relax, it's just an exit area. (Open 7:30am-9pm; Sept.-April 8am-6pm.) From the garden, take av. du 50*ème* R.I. and turn right onto rue Turenne to modest **Château Barrière,** a fortified medieval residence with Roman foundations and Renaissance apertures. Unfortunately, some local yokels seem to have mistaken this building for a dump.

On summer evenings, join the flower of local youth in the sidewalk cafés along bd. Montaigne. The **Café St-Louis,** 26bis rue Eguillerie, sometimes features live jazz. (Open Mon.-Sat. 8pm-2am.) If you crave disco, try **L'An des Roys,** 51, rue Aubarede (tel. 53 53 01 58), a favorite with the younger crowd. (Open Wed.-Sat. from 10:30pm, Sun. from 2:30pm.) Under-40s might try **L'Ubu,** 3, rue des Jacobins, a *club privé* that might not let you in. (Ppen Tues.-Sun.)

Near Périgueux

Twenty-five km north of Périgueux lies **Brantôme,** a bucolic village encircled by the Dronne River. Charlemagne founded the **abbaye** in 769 AD. Take the fascinating tour of the monastic buildings and the grottoes, where the earliest inhabitants carved out a chapel and a mill. (Daily tours in French only 10-11am and 2-5pm on the hour, 11F.) The monks took refuge in the **Grotte du Jugement Dernier** whenever the abbey was attacked; the eerie apocalyptic reliefs are extraordinarily striking. The rest of the abbey buildings are now the town hall and the **Musée Fernand-Desmoulin,** which exhibits paintings by its obscure namesake and a collection of local prehistoric artifacts. (Open daily 10am-noon and 2-7pm; Sept. 16-June 15 Wed.-Mon. 10am-noon and 2-5pm. 11th-century bell tower tours July-Aug. 10-11am and 2-7pm on the hour. Admission a steep 10F.)

Brantôme's **tourist office** (tel. 53 05 80 52), on av. de Pierre de Bourdeille near the abbey, sells maps with walking circuits of Brantôme and its environs (2F). (Open daily 10am-noon and 3-5pm.) The **Hôtel de la Posté**, rue Gambetta, posts a four-course *menu* with wine for 60F. Rooms upstairs range from 70-110F. (Reception open Mon.-Sat.)

Getting to Brantôme is not so pleasant: only one bus per day runs on Friday and Saturday during the school year (45 min., 22.20F). In July and August, the tourist office organizes bus tours of the Dronne Valley (including Bourdeilles and Brantôme) that depart Wednesday at 8am and return at 6pm. Check with the tourist office or call the station (tel. 53 08 43 13) for details. As the bus tour costs 140F (student discount 10%), biking is the way to go. Though there are sometimes too many cars for comfort, the route passes through peaceful countryside and gets hilly only toward the end. Hitching is impossible.

The châteaux of Périgord are best reached by car, as the biking can be hilly. Although "bargain" rentals start at a ridiculous 270F, Europcar in Périgueux has a better weekend rate. Seven km southwest of Brantôme on the Dronne lies **Bourdeilles,** site of a medieval castle, bridge, and town. In July and August, daily canoe and kayak rentals at Porte des Réformés, Brantôme (tel. 53 05 80 46) enable you to paddle your way to Bourdeilles. (80F includes the return to Brantôme by van.) You can also walk from Brantôme or board an erratic CFD bus from Périgueux. On the same line as Brantôme lie **Chancelade,** a once great but now crumbling abbey with a museum of its own 10th- to 12th-century art, and **Villars,** where there are several cave paintings. Ruins of a 12th-century castle abide in **Excideuil,** a one-hour bus ride from Périgueux (1 or 2 per day). The château at **Hautefort,** its medieval towers and Renaissance façades wholly intact, is more impressive but just as difficult to reach by bus.

South of Périgueux between Bergerac and Agen are the feudal **bastides,** small fortress-towns built by the English and French when both countries claimed sovereignty over the area during the Hundred Years' War. The *bastides* share a common design: rows of rectangular blocks, cut at right angles by narrow streets and surrounded by square ramparts. The English fortress of **Monpazier,** the best preserved, retains its church, arcaded town square, and fortifications. It is also quite close to the intimidating medieval castle of **Biron.** Other *bastides,* including **Lalinde, Villeneuve, Villeréal,** and **Puylaroque,** can be covered in a day by bike or car. The scenery is so stunning it is almost exhausting, making a trip here worth any effort and expense.

In addition to the excursion to Brantôme and the Dronne Valley, Périgueux's tourist office arranges **bus tours** from mid-June to mid-September to Sarlat, Domme, La Roque-Gageac, and Beynac (Tues. at 9am, return 6:50pm, 150F), as well as the *bastides* and the château in Biron (Thurs. at 7:50am, return 7:20pm; 165F). Another excursion includes the Thot museum, the re-created Lascaux II caves, and the museum (but not the caves and paintings) in Les Eyzies (Fri. at 7:50am, return 7pm, 175F). Call a day ahead to confirm departures. In July and August make it a few days, as departures may fluctuate to meet demand. Buses leave from outside the tourist office and 5-10 minutes later from the *gare.* Students get a 10% discount.

Brive

Since 1347 this city has proudly borne the name Brive-la-Gaillarde (Brive the Jolly or, more appropriately, Brive-the-We-Thumb-Our-Collective-Nose-at-You). During the Hundred Years' War, the city's thick walls and courageous residents managed to repel the English forces. Continuing this tradition of strength and pride, Brive became the first town in France to liberate itself from the German Occupation in 1944. These days of peril have passed, however, and modern Brive, surrounded by the countryside of Périgord and Quercy, has embraced its humbler role as regional center and touring base.

The center of Brive is dominated by the 12th-century **Collégiale St-Martin,** named after the Spaniard who happened to introduce Christianity to Brive in the early 5th century. Martin interrupted the feast of Saturnus, loudly proclaiming his faith and smashing idols; the shocked worshippers chopped off his head, unknowingly making a martyr of him. In 1986, excavations at St-Martin's Press uncovered ancient walls and a bell foundry. (Tours July-Aug. Sun. at 4pm; or call 55 24 10 82 one day in advance to request a tour.) **Musée Edmond-Michelet,** 4, rue Champanatier (tel. 55 74 06 08), close to pl. de la Liberté, is a 5-minute walk northwest from the train station. The building was the home of a local leader in the Resistance and now commemorates the fight against the Nazis. (Open Mon.-Sat. 10am-noon and 2-6pm. Free.) An excellent collection of archaeological finds from southern France, formerly housed in the **Musée Ernst-Rupin,** rue Massenal (tel. 55 74 90 15), has been transferred to **Hôtel de la Benche** (tel. 55 24 19 05), 2 blocks away on rue Blaise Raynal. The archaeological archives, however, remain on display at the Ernst-Rupin. (Open Wed. 3-6pm, Sat. 4-6pm.)

One of the biggest in the area, Brive's **market** occupies a huge chunk of pl. du 14 Juillet. Everything from cheap clothes to **gerbils** to stereo equipment can be unearthed in the stalls. The prices at the food market are dirt cheap and the shopping is serious—no catering to tourists here. Hold on tight to your purse or wallet. (Open Tues., Thurs., and Sat. (the big day) 8am-noon.)

The **Auberge de Jeunesse,** 56, av. du Maréchal Bugeaud (tel. 55 24 34 00), is one of the photogenic places featured in the IYHF catalogue. The renovated building has a kitchen, TV room, and smallish, single-sex dorms. From the station (25 min.), follow av. Jean Jaurès (*ignore* the sign to turn right on bd. Clémenceau—it's longer). Cross bd. Ed. Lachaud at the bottom of the hill, turn onto rue de l'Hôtel de Ville, and head for the church in the center of town. At the church, turn to the right, keeping the church to your left, and take rue Dr. Massenat to the main intersection with bd. Jules Ferry. Turn left and proceed one block to the sign at av. Maréchal Bugeaud; turn right and follow to the end. The hostel is on the right. (Lockout 11am-6pm. Strict 11pm curfew. 50F per person. 8am breakfast included.) The cheapest hotels line av. Jean Jaurès, which starts at the train station. **Hôtel de l'Avenir,** 39, av. Jean Jaurès, provides good-sized singles for 70F, doubles 90F, and quads 120F. (Currency exchange. Reception open Mon.-Sat. 7am-11pm. Showers 10F. Breakfast 18F.) **Hôtel de la Gare** (tel. 55 74 14 49) has equally good rooms a bit closer to the station. (Singles 60-70F. Doubles 80F. Quads with 2 big, saggy beds 115F, with shower 135F. Breakfast 18F.) **Camping Municipal des Iles,** bd. Michelet (tel. 55 24 34 74), charges 9F per person and 6F per tent. (Showers included. Open daily 7am-10pm.)

Le Quercy, 3, pl. du 14 Juillet serves generic but tasty 35-60F entrees and 55-75F *menus.* (Open Tues.-Sun.) **Brasserie Le Molière** at pl. Molière, behind the tourist office, fries large, filling omelettes for 22-50F. (Open Mon.-Thurs. 11am-2pm and 7-8:30pm, Fri.-Sat. open later.) The **Monoprix** supermarket, 10, rue de l'Hôtel de Ville, right near the church in the center of town, stocks cheap supplies upstairs. (Open Mon.-Sat. 8:45am-noon and 2-7pm.) Buy produce here only if the market (see above) is closed or picked over.

The **tourist office** is in Immeuble Château d'Eau, pl. du 14 Juillet (tel. 55 24 08 80). From the train station, follow av. Jean Jaurès to St-Martin and continue on av. de Paris which runs slightly to the right. The tourist office towers on the right. (English spoken. Open Mon.-Sat. 9am-12:30pm and 2:30-7pm, Sun. 10am-1pm; Sept.-June Mon.-Sat. 10am-noon and 2:30-6pm.) The **Gare Routière,** recently relocated to av. Léo Lagrange, opposite the municipal sports complex, is a 20-minute walk from the youth hostel. Avenue Léo Legrange branches eastward off bd. Voltaire, away from the town center. Buses shuttle from the *gare routière* (often making stops at the SNCF *gare* and other points in Brive) to such nearby towns as Tulle (5 per day, 1 hr., 59F); St-Privat (2 per day, 2 hr., 107F); and, during the school year, Perpezac-le-Noir (Mon.-Sat. 3 per day, 1½ hr., 91F). One bus per day runs from the train station to Montignac (Mon.-Sat. at 6pm, 1 hr., 21F). The only return bus leaves the Montignac depot at 6:45am. To see Lascaux II, you'll have to spend two nights and a full day in Montignac or, if your brave, try your luck hitchhiking; there is no train connection within 10km of the town. From the **train station** (tel. 55 23 50 50), you can get to major cities and many towns in Périgord-Quercy. Trains go to: Rocamadour (4 per day, 45 min., 33F); Souillac with 4-5 connecting buses to Sarlat (4 per day, ½-hr., 29F); Cahors (9 per day, 1½ hr., 64F); Paris (18 per day, 4 hr., 227F); Toulouse (10 per day, 2½ hr., 117F); Aurillac (6 per day, 1 hr., 64F); Montauban (9 per day, 5 hr., 92F); and Bordeaux (6 per day, 3 hr., 114F).

Les Eyzies

Some of the world's best-preserved prehistoric cave paintings hide in the limestone cliffs above Les Eyzies-de-Tayac. The town itself can get unpleasant when too many tourists assemble, but the carefully monitored solitude of the caves is not to be missed. A visit requires starting early (ideally from Périgueux) and killing a few hours between buying your ticket and starting your tour. A good place to rest is on the banks of the rivers Vézère and Dordogne, which quietly join forces about 1½km southwest of the caves. Try to visit at the end of the week. All the caves and museums at Les Eyzies are closed on Tuesday, except Combarelles, which shuts its gates on Wednesday, and the Musée l'Abri Pataud, which closes on Monday.

Orientation and Practical Information

Les Eyzies is linked by train to Agen, Périgueux, Le Buisson, and Sarlat. There are also weekly tourist buses from Sarlat and Souillac. To get to the center of town from the train station, turn right and walk 1km down the village's only street. The Grotte de Font-de-Gaume lies 2km down D47.

Tourist Office: pl. de la Mairie (tel. 53 06 97 05), 5 min. from the train station. Excellent list of nearby caves, advice on getting scarce tickets, **currency exchange** (traveler's check fee 5.48F), and, in summer, tours of the museum and outlying area. Tours to Beynac, Les Milandes, Castelnaud, La Rogue Gageac, Montfort, Carsac, and Domme (Fri. at 9am, 155F) as well as Lascaux II, Le Thot, and St. Amand de Coly (Sun. at 9am, 115F). Call a day or two ahead in summer to book tours and check the schedule; the tour days often change during the year. Also rents bikes (see below). Information on car and canoe rentals, horse trails, and camping. Sells cycling and hiking guides. Open July-Aug. Mon.-Sat. 9am-7pm, Sun. 10am-noon and 2-6pm; March-June and Sept.-Nov. Mon.-Sat. 9am-noon and 2-6pm; Jan.-Feb. Tues. and Thurs. 9am-noon and 2-6pm.

Currency Exchange: Crédit Agricole, beyond the post office. Open Tues.-Fri. 9am-12:30pm and 1:30-5pm, Sat. 9am-noon. Also at the post office and the tourist office.

Post Office: Down the street from the tourist office. **Currency exchange.** Open Mon.-Fri. 9am-noon and 2-5pm, Sat. 9am-noon. Postal Code: 24620.

Trains: Tel. 53 06 97 22. To Périgueux (6-7 per day, 30-45 min., 31F) and Sarlat (2-3 per day, change at Le Buisson, 1 hr., 35F). Information office open in summer daily 6am-1pm, 2-5:30pm, and 7-11pm.

Bike Rental: At the train station 50F per day, deposit 500F. At the tourist office 25F per ½-day, 37F per day, 180F per week, deposit 50F plus ID.

Hospital: (tel. 53 59 00 72), in Sarlat.

Police: Tel. 53 29 20 17. **Emergency,** tel. 17.

Accommodations, Camping, and Food

Les Eyzies would be a pleasant place to stay if rooms weren't so expensive and hard to find. Reserve months in advance, or add years to your life by stepping 3km out of town to the idyllic *gîte d'étape*. Another option is a bed in a private house in town (120-150F), fine if two people share a room. The tourist office has a list of these B&Bs, which often put up signs announcing *chambres*.

Gîte d'Etape: **Ferme des Eymaries,** route de St-Cirq (tel. 53 06 94 73). From the tourist office in Les Eyzies head out of town on route de Périgueux, and cross the train tracks and the river Vézère. Look for the route de St-Cirq immediately on your left, take this for 1½km, turn right just before more train tracks, and follow the signs for 1km (25 min.). Cozy buildings at the base of cliffs with a superb view of farmland and more cliffs. Usually has space, but reservations are required. Kitchen facilities. 32F per person. Breakfast 14F. Dinner 45F with advance notice (Mon.-Fri. only). Open April-Oct. daily 6am-10pm. Call for reservations July-Aug.

Hôtel du Périgord, on D47 near the Grotte de Font-de-Gaume (tel. 53 06 97 26). Singles and doubles 100-175F. Breakfast 20F. Reservations necessary. Open March 20-Oct. 14 daily 10am-9pm.

Hôtel de France (tel. 53 06 97 23), on rue du Musée. Spacious, airy rooms 100-140F, with shower 140-200F. Breakfast 25F. Open mid-March to mid-Nov. 7:15am-midnight. Reservations necessary June-Aug.

Camping: Usually plenty of room. **La Rivière** (tel. 53 06 97 14), just out of town on route de Périgueux. Take a left out of the train station and continue just past the river. Reasonable snack bar and restaurant, pool, washing machines, and canoe rental. 16F per person, 15F per tent or car. Electricity 12F. Also has 8 doubles with shower (150F). Breakfast 18F. Open March 15-Oct. 15 daily 8am-9pm. **Camping Le Pech** (tel. 53 06 95 84), 3km from the train station, mostly uphill. Walk to the end of the main street and follow the signs. Call ahead and the kind managers will come and pick you up. 8.50F per person, 8F per tent and car. Electricity 8F. Hot showers 2F. Open daily 8:30am-midnight; in off-season 8:30am-10pm.

Restaurants here serve very expensive, well-prepared meals. Try to bring a picnic from Périgueux, as even the town's one *épicerie* is suspiciously overpriced. For those who can't bear doling out 25F for another skinny *croque-monsieur,* the **Halle Paysanne des Eyzies,** on route de Sarlat brings relief in the form of local produce and tins of *foie gras.* They have occasional free tastings of the expensive stuff. (Open June-Sept. 15 daily 9am-1:30pm and 2:30-7pm.) A small **market** is held in town Monday morning; the fourth Monday of the month brings a larger market. **Resto Mentalo,** just past the Halle Paysanne, serves pizzas at outdoor tables (26-35F). **Restaurant de Laugerie-Basse,** near the caves and away from Périgueux on D47, posts 45F, 47.50F, 55F, and 87F *menus.*

Sights

By far the most important sight is the **Grotte de Font-de-Gaume** (tel. 53 06 97 48), 2km down D47. Inside the cave are 20,000-year-old drawings of horses, deer, and bison—faint, but still amazing. During peak season, 20 people are admitted at half-hour intervals in closely monitored groups. Because of these restrictions, and because many of the tickets are bought in advance by tour groups, the road to the famous cave is paved with hard-luck stories. In summer, come as early in the day as possible; the 7:14am train from Périgueux arrives at 7:50am. If you arrive by 8am, you'll probably get a late-morning or afternoon ticket—at the very least, you'll have a few hours to wait. You should return at least 15 minutes before your 45-minute tour begins. (Be aware that it takes 15 min. to climb to the mouth of the cave.) Although the tours are in French, the adept guides armed with flashlights get the message across. Several people in the group will usually translate in hushed tones. (Open Wed.-Mon. 9-11:15am and 2-5:15pm; Oct.-March Wed.-Mon. 10-11:15am and 2-4:15pm. Admission 23F, ages 18-25 and over 60 12F, ages 7-18 5F, ages under 7 and artists or art students free.)

The **Grotte des Combarelles,** 2km farther down the road (tel. 53 06 97 72), contains dazzling prehistoric carvings in a more intimate atmosphere thatn Grotte Font-de Gaumes. Visitors are admitted in groups of six for the slightly rambling one-hour tour. Tickets are available at 9am for morning tours and 2pm for afternoon tours. Yes, they go quickly. (Same hours and prices as the Grotte de Font-de-Gaume, but closed Wed. instead of Tues.)

In the town of Les Eyzies, the **Musée National de Préhistoire** (tel. 53 06 97 03) exhibits a vast collection of weapons, tools, bones, cave drawings, and carvings. (Open Wed.-Mon. 9:30am-noon and 2-6pm; Dec.-March Wed.-Mon. 9:30am-noon and 2-5pm. Admission 10F, ages 18-25 and over 60 and Sun. 5F, ages under 18 free.) A two-minute saunter from the train station, fortified **Eglise de Tayac** impresses with its slate-roofed bell towers and narrow fortress windows. Unfortunately, it is only open at the discretion of the local priest.

Opened on April 1, 1990, the **Musée L'Abri Pataud** already outshines the older national museum next door. The site of the museum and adjacent archaeological display is on the former property of a local farmer, M. Pataud. As the story goes, practically every time Monsieur Pataud pulled up a tree or attempted to plant a small crop, he unearthed bones or stone tools. No wonder—his farm was built on one of the most archaeologically rich sites in Europe: the shelter (*abri*) for several groups of reindeer hunters over a span of 20,000 years. It was not until Harvard professor Hallum L. Movius spent 12 years (1953-64) digging here that the extent of the find was realized. Guests are supplied with headsets which pick up recordings (in French) corresponding to 16 windows. Simple English and German translations are available, and as 1992 approaches, the museum will cater more to English- and German-speaking tourists. The sculpture on the ceiling of the museum, visible in a mirror, was found accidentally: when technicians were scaling the cliff to decide where to put electrical lines, one worker's flashlight illuminated it. (Open July-Aug. Tues.-Sun. 9:30am-7:30pm; Sept.-Dec. and Feb.-June 10am-noon and 2-5:30pm. Last entry 45 min. before closing. Admission 20F.)

Near Les Eyzies

The hills around Les Eyzies are pock-marked with caves and rock formations. You'll run across a series of roadside attractions northwest of the village along D47. The tourist office runs weekly tours to those beyond walking distance (see above). Call ahead to reserve and verify the day of the tour. Most interesting is the **Grotte du Grand Roc** (tel. 53 06 96 76), 1½ km from town, which lies halfway up the chalk cliffs and commands a blistering view of the Vézère Valley from its mouth. It has no cave paintings, just impressive stalactites and stalagmites. (Open daily July 1-Sept. 15 9am-6:30pm; March 12-July 1 and Sept. 16-Nov. 11 daily 9am-noon and 2-6pm. Admission 25F, ages 6-12 12F. 25-minute tour.) Next to the Grand Roc, the **Laugerie-Basse** (tel. 53 06 97 12) and the **Laugerie-Haute** (tel. 53 06 92 90) display cross-sections of geological strata containing human remains and bison droppings. (Laugerie-Basse open June 1-Sept. 30 daily 9:30am-6pm. Admission 18F, ages 6-12 12F. 35-min. tour. Laugerie-Haute open March 1-Sept. 30 daily 9am-noon and 2-6pm; Nov. 2-Feb. 28 Wed.-Mon. 10am-noon and 2-5:15pm; Oct. and March Wed.-Mon. 10am-noon and 2-4:30pm. Admission 15F, ages 18-25 and over 60 9F, 7-18 5F. 45-min. tour.) Carved bison and groups of horses cavort on the stone walls of the **Abri du Cap-Blanc** (tel. 53 59 21 74 or 53 29 66 63) in Marquay, 6km from Les Eyzies. (Open daily July-Aug. 9:30am-7pm; late March-June and Sept.-early Nov. 10am-noon and 2-5pm. Admission 17F, ages under 12 9F.)

The town of **Montignac**, 20km northeast of Les Eyzies on N704 (*direction* "Brive"), preserves the 20th century's most elaborate salute to the artistic cave-dwellers: a complete re-creation of the caves of **Lascaux**, pithily dubbed **Lascaux II** (tel. 53 53 44 35). The exhibit, inaugurated in 1983 (20 years after the caves were closed to prevent the deterioration of their paintings by breathing tourists), is the work of painter Monique Peytral and a team of a dozen sculptors. Peytral's art is interesting in its own right and is shown occasionally in the area. (Open July-Aug. daily 9:30am-7pm; Feb.-June and Sept.-Dec. Tues.-Sun. 10am-noon and 2-5:30pm. Tickets sold at pl. Tourny in Montignac starting at 9am. Admission 40F, ages under 12 18F. 40-min. guided tour.) Trains run from Brive to Montignac (Mon.-Sat. 1 per day, 1¼ hr.).

Sarlat

Despite the tourist-besieged main street lined with vendors of *foie gras,* t-shirts, and cheap jewelry, Sarlat remains a town with an uncommon medieval atmosphere. Thanks to the 1965 renovations, most of the old quarter looks as if it were carved from a single block of golden sandstone. Such movie-set perfection attracts the gaze of more than a few cameras, but the crowds aren't a good enough reason to skip the narrow streets, hidden corners, and unique doorways of Sarlat's *vieille ville.*

Orientation and Practical Information

Popularity has made train service to Sarlat simple and efficient. Both Brive and Périgueux are less than 2 hours away. Sarlat's *vieille ville* is neatly bisected by the modern commercial thoroughfare, **rue de la République,** known locally as la Traverse. To the east lie most of the sights and all the tourists. The west side tells a quieter story, and some of the picturesque, flower-potted streets might even qualify as deserted.

Tourist Office: pl. de la Liberté (tel. 53 59 27 67). A busy but helpful office housed in the 16th-century Hôtel de Maleville. Free maps of the *vieille ville.* Information on excursions, camping, and bike tours. Accommodations service (5F plus 100F deposit). Currency exchange on days when the banks are closed. The accommodations service is not oriented toward budget travelers. Their free booklet, *Informations Générales,* includes transport schedules and excursions. Guided tours of the town (in French and English) July-Aug. Mon.-Fri. 4 per day, Sat. and Sun. 2; June and Sept. Mon.-Sat. 2 per day, Sun. 1. Tours 17F, students 10F. Open Mon.-Sat. 9am-7pm, Sun. 10am-noon and 4-6pm; Sept. 16-June 14 Mon.-Sat. 9am-noon and 2-6pm.

Currency Exchange: Banks open Tues.-Sat. On Mon. go to the post office. To change American Express checks or any checks in British pounds, go to **Crédit Agricole,** rue des Consuls. Open June 15-Sept. 15 Mon.-Sat. 9am-1pm and 2-7pm.

Post Office: pl. du 14 Juillet (tel. 53 59 12 81). **Telephones** and **currency exchange.** Open Mon.-Fri. 8am-noon and 1:30-6:30pm, Sat. 8am-noon. **Postal Code:** 24200.

Trains: route de Souillac (tel. 53 59 00 21). Ticket booths open daily 5:45am-9pm. To: Bordeaux (3-4 per day, 2½ hr., 93F); Brive (4 per day, 1 hr., 42F); Périgueux (3 per day, 1½ hr., 61F), via Les Eyzies (3 per day, 1 hr., 36F); Le Buisson (4 per day, 1½ hr., 24F). The Les Eyzies and Le Buisson connections to Paris are ill-timed and indirect. The route via Souillac, served by SNCF bus, is better. The same buses to Souillac connect with trains to Toulouse (4 per day, 3 hr., 110F). The ride from the station to *centre ville* is free.

Buses: SNCF buses and **Trans-Périgord** buses stop at the train station and in pl. Pasteur. Trans-Périgord to Souillac (4-5 per day, 45 min.). SNCF to Le Buisson (2-3 per day, 1 hr., 23.70F). **Cars Pezin,** in a funeral parlor in pl. Pasteur (tel. 53 59 21 25), runs to Domme (Sat. 2, ½-hr.). **Cars Correspondances** (tel. 55 24 29 93) to Brive from pl. Pasteur (Mon.-Sat. 1 per day, ½-hr.). Complete schedules printed in *Informations Générales,* free at the tourist office.

Bike Rental: At the train station. 40F per ½-day, 50F per day, 290F per week, deposit 500F. **Garage Matigot,** 52, av. Gambetta (tel. 53 59 03 60). Three- and 10-speeds 30F per day, 180F per week, deposit 100F. Mopeds 75F per day, 350F per week, deposit 200F. Open Mon.-Sat. 8:30am-noon and 2-7pm; Oct.-June Tues.-Sat. 8:30am-noon and 2-7pm.

Laundromat: 24, av. de Selves. Down the street from the hostel. Wash 25F per 7kg, dry 2F per 10 min. Open daily 6am-10pm.

Hospital: Centre Hospitalier, Jean Le Claire (tel. 53 59 00 72).

Police: Commissariat, pl. Grande Rigandie (tel. 53 59 05 17). **Emergency,** tel. 17.

Accommodations and Camping

Sarlat's youth hostel operates only July 1 through October 15. Hotels tend to be expensive and crowded; reserve up to a week in advance for summer and weekend visits. The tourist office keeps track of vacant hotel rooms and can also find you a room in a local home (5F charge if they make the reservation). Before July 1 it may be more affordable to base yourself in Brive's hostel, an easy one hour trip by train.

Auberge de Jeunesse (IYHF), 15bis, av. de Selves, route de Périgueux (tel. 53 59 47 59), 30 min. from the station but only 5-10 min. from the *vieille ville*. From the station, follow av. de la Gare and signs to *centre ville*. Take rue de la République (which becomes av. Gambetta) through the town center and bear left onto av. de Selves at the fork. The hostel is on the right, just before the supermarket. Easy-going atmosphere. Somewhat cramped dorm space, clean exterior toilets and showers, well-equipped kitchen. Office open 9am-1pm and 6pm-midnight. Lockout 11am-6pm, but someone might be there in the afternoon. No lockout when it rains. No curfew. 32F per person. Camping site 16F. Sheets 12F. Occasionally chock-full of large groups of campers; call one day in advance. Open July 1-Oct. 15.

Hôtel Marcel, 8, av. de Selves (tel. 53 59 21 98), opposite the youth hostel on a noisy street. The cheapest rooms in town, but clean and comfortable, if you can get them. Reception open until 10pm. A few singles and doubles 90F, with shower 100F. Most rooms 130-160F. Breakfast 25F. Respectable restaurant downstairs serves a 5-course 61F *menu*. Call at least one week ahead to get cheap rooms.

Hôtel des Récollets, 4, rue Jean Jacques Rousseau (tel. 53 59 00 49), up the little ramp after rue Papucie. Great location in the quiet half of the *vieille ville*. Clean rooms. Doubles 110F, with shower 117F. Breakfast 25F. Call a week ahead in July-Aug.

Camping: Expect crowds everywhere. **Les Perières,** ¾km out on D47 (tel. 53 59 05 84), is the closest to town. Swimming pool, tennis courts, game room, library, and bar. Usually full July-Aug. Minimum price 110F per 3 persons, including tent and electricity. Open Easter-Sept. 30 9am-noon and 2-7pm. **Les Acacias** (tel. 53 59 29 30; for information 53 59 15 56), at La Canéda. Slightly farther away (2½km) and slightly cheaper. Pool, bar, restaurant, and hot water. 16F per person, 15F per tent. Electricity 15F. Open Easter-Sept. 30.

Food

Pick up groceries at the enormous **Intermarché** supermarket, just across from the youth hostel. (Open Mon.-Fri. 9am-12:30pm and 3-7:15pm, Sat. 9am-7:15pm.) *Boulangeries* and *charcuteries* line rue de la République. The celebrated Saturday **market** has bargains on truffles and *foie gras* all day; a smaller market takes place Wednesday mornings. Both are trumped up a bit for tourists in summer.

Restaurant du Commerce, 4, rue Albéric Cahuet. Outdoor seating and satisfied customers. 43F *menu* includes delicious soup, meat and potatoes, salad, and dessert (such as *crème caramel* or chocolate mousse). 55F entitles you to tender *confit de canard* (duck in aspic); 75F, a truffle salad. Open April-Nov. daily 8am-5pm and 7-11pm; Jan.-March Tues.-Sun. 8am-5pm and 7-11pm.

Hostellerie Marcel, 8, av. de Selves, opposite the hostel. Well-known and well-liked. Five-course 55-75F *menu* includes *poulet basquaise*. Open daily; mid-Nov. to Jan. Tues.-Sun.

Pizzeria Napoli, rue La Calprenede, off av. Gambetta. Sit on the patio and enjoy some greasy French-style Italian cuisine. Pizzas 30-45F. Open daily noon-2:30pm and 7pm-midnight.

Auberge du Bon Chabrol, 2, rue des Armes, off rue de la République. Périgordin cuisine served either inside or outside an old *hôtel particulier*. 50F lunch *menu* Mon.-Fri.; 4-course 72F dinner *menu* (service 10%). Open daily noon-2pm and 7-9pm; Oct.-May Thurs.-Tues. noon-2pm and 7-8:30pm.

Sights and Entertainment

The tourist office's free walking map points out places that otherwise might evade even the most rabid observers of architectural trivia. Keep your eyes on doors throughout the *vieille ville*. The buildings have no shortage of bizarre orifices, a few of which may lure you in. While the interior of the **Cathédrale St-Sacerdos** stands out for its windows and Atlurian grand organ, a walk behind the cathedral reveals some of the structural sleight-of-hand for which Sarlat is famous. The small arches in the wall surrounding the nave are supposed to have been tombs. Who knows how they fit bodies in there . . . Music lovely enough to raise the dead often fills the cathedral in July and August (tickets 30-80F). **La Lanterne des Morts,** a 12th-century beehive of a monument, baffles even the experts. No one can understand why the architects left no access to the second-story chamber in the conical part of the structure.

Next to the cathedral are the **Palais Episcopal** and the **Maison de la Boétie.** Built in the 16th century, the Maison's pointed gable and highly decorated windows exemplify Italian Renaissance style. It now serves as the Chambre de Commerce et d'Industrie, and its lower common room frequently houses small exhibitions.

On the other side of the main thoroughfare, the **Musée de la Chapelle des Pénitents Blancs,** on rue de la Charité at rue Jean-Jacques Rousseau, maintains a small but impressive collection of polychrome statuettes and ecclesiastical garments. Of note are the 17th-century statue of the Virgin gingerly holding a leper's skull and the mannequin clothed in a penitent's white robes and pointy hat. If you ask, the friendly caretaker will explain the historical connections between the Crusades, the plague, the penitents, the Spanish explorers of the New World, the white costumes (similar to those of the Ku Klux Klan), and the Bavarian Illuminati. (Museum open Easter to mid-Oct. daily 10am-noon and 3-6pm. Admission 10F, students 5F.) For a change of scenery try the **Musée Aquarium** on rue du Commandant Maratuel. (Open daily 10am-7pm; Sept. 16-June 14 daily 10am-noon and 2-6pm. Admission 19F, students 16F, ages 2-16 12F.)

For two weeks in late July and early August, Sarlat hosts the **Festival des Jeux du Théâtre,** a series of plays in the open-air theater in pl. de la Liberté. (Tickets 80-150F. 10% discount with Carte Jeune.) For reservations, write Festival des Jeux du Théâtre de Sarlat, B.P. 53, 24200 Sarlat. For information, call Hôtel Plamon (tel. 53 31 10 83).

Near Sarlat

Sarlat makes an ideal base for touring the area's ineffably spectacular attractions. If ever there were a moment to utter the words "Let's Go," this is it. Some 14km from Sarlat, the fortified village of **Domme** perches high on a cliff overlooking the Dordogne Valley. From the **Belvédère de la Barre,** you can see the plain and its poplar-lined river, the villages of Beynac and La Roque-Gageac, the châteaux of Montfort and Giverzac, and wee cows the size of ladybugs. The caves where Domme's inhabitants took refuge during the Hundred Years' War and the Wars of Religion contain a few odd bones of Ice Age bison and rhinoceri. **Cars Pezin,** pl. Pasteur (tel. 53 59 21 25), in Sarlat, runs Saturday buses to and from Domme. The tourist office in Souillac also sponsors tours (see below).

SNCF buses to Le Buisson (Mon.-Sat. 2-3 per day) stop at the village **Beynac,** whose golden castle and cliff survey the castles of Marqueyssac, Castelnaud, and Fayrac, all set in a magnificent pastel countryside. Stop in **La Roque-Gageac,** a lovely village between the Dordogne and a high cliff. Trans-Périgord buses bound for Souillac also stop at **Carsac,** whose 11th-century Romanesque church merits a brief visit. More convenient than SNCF or Trans-Périgord buses, the SNCF excursion bus stops at Carsac, Domme, and La Roque-Gageac. (From Sarlat June 13-Sept. 12 on Tues., same-day return. Tickets 120F, students 110F. Reserve at the tourist office.) To swim in the Dordogne, head for **Vitrac Port,** 7km from Sarlat on the D46 towards Bergerac. The open-sided barge "Les Norbert," modelled after the *gabarres* which once carried merchants and travelers down the Dordogne, leaves from La Roque-Gageac on its 12.5km cruise past La Malartine, Le Lacoste, Castlenand, Marqueyssac, and Beynac. (Open Easter-Sept. Every 15 min., 1¼ hr. Adults 40F, children 20F. English-speaking guide. For information, call 53 29 40 44; for reservations call 53 59 47 48.) Beg, borrow, or steal transport to this area of the Dordogne Valley—all of it is truly spectacular.

Souillac

Souillac is like a hole in a doughnut: though there's nothing much in the town itself, the castles, caves, hills, and valleys of the surrounding countryside are Dordogne at its finest. Unfortunately, hotels are booked solid in summer and cheaper accommodations are nonexistent. Souillac in season (last week in June to the end of August) is for cycling campers only. The challenging, rollercoaster bike ride between Souillac and Rocamadour passes through 20km of vistas which mere adjectives cannot quite describe.

Orientation and Practical Information

Souillac squats on the Paris-Toulouse line, only 45 min. from Brive. Bus and train departures in all directions are frequent and generally convenient. To reach the *centre ville* go straight from the station exit, left onto av. Jean Jaurès, and right onto av. du Général de Gaulle. The tourist office and *vieille ville* are on the right (20 min.). To reach the Dordogne, go 1½km farther along av. de Toulouse.

Tourist Office: bd. Louis-Jean Malvy (tel. 65 37 81 56). Information on summer SNCF excursions to Les Eyzies (120F); Rocamadour and the Gouffre de Padirac (120F); Domme, La Roque Gageac, Beynac, and Sarlat (100F). Decent maps. Inquire about *gîtes d'étape* in the *département* of Lot, *chambres d'hôte,* and hiking tours. Open Mon.-Sat. 9am-1pm and 2-7pm, Sun. 9am-12:30pm and 4-7pm; Oct.-May Mon.-Sat. 9am-noon and 2-6pm.

Currency Exchange: Banque Populaire, 31, av. Gambetta. Open Mon.-Fri. 8am-noon and 1:30-5pm. Currency exchange until 4pm only. On Sat., try the **post office.**

Post Office: 11, bd. Louis-Jean Malvy. Open Mon.-Fri. 8am-12:30pm and 2-5:30pm, Sat. 8am-noon. **Postal Code:** 46200.

Trains: tel. 65 32 78 21. To: Toulouse (6-8 per day, 2 hr., 95F), via Gourdon (15 min., 18F); Cahors (7 per day, 1 hr., 40F); Paris (4-6 per day, 5-6 hr., 241F) via Brive-la-Gaillarde (15-30 min., 27F); Limoges (5 per day, 1½ hr., 77F).

Buses: Information at the train station. **Trans-Périgord** buses to Sarlat (Mon.-Sat.) stop at the train station and 4 min. later on av. de Sarlat (Mon.-Thurs. 4 per day, Fri.-Sat. 5 per day, Sun. 3; ¾-hr.). SNCF buses to St-Denis-Près-Martel stop at the station and 2 min. later at Hôtel Renaissance (Mon.-Sat. 3 per day, Sun. 1; ¾-hr.; 15.50F).

Bike Rental: SNCF station. 40F per ½-day, 50F per day, 285F per week, deposit 500F or ID. **Bi-Causse,** pl. de la Halle (tel. 65 37 03 64). Mountain bikes 40F per ½-day, 60F per day, 150F deposit. Open daily 9am-noon and 2-7pm; Sept.-June Tues.-Sun. 9am-noon and 2-7pm.

Police: Gendarmerie, route de Sarlat (tel. 65 32 78 17). **Emergency,** tel. 17.

Accommodations, Camping, and Food

The only way to find a hotel here in July or August is to start early, cross your fingers, and go down the list provided by the tourist office. The attractive **Auberge du Puits,** pl. du Puits (tel. 65 37 80 32), provides comfortable doubles from 110F, with shower 120F. (Reception open 7:30am-10:30pm. Hall showers 12F. Breakfast 22F. Restaurant *menus* from 50F.) In a noisy area, the less stunning **Nouvel Hôtel,** 21, av. du Général de Gaulle (tel. 65 32 79 58), lets simple doubles from 80F, with shower 100F. (Breakfast 22F. *Menus* from 50F.) Quieter, smaller, and cheaper is the **Hôtel Beffroi,** pl. St-Martin (tel. 65 37 80 33). (Singles and doubles 85-130F. Breakfast 15F.) Another option is **Hôtel L'Escale,** 36, av. Louis-Jean Malvy, in the center of town. (Singles 75F. Doubles 100F. Showers included.) The bar downstairs is a lively hang-out.

Scenic, well-equipped camping sites crop up in this area as often as cliff-hanging châteaux. All are crowded in July and August. Nearby **Camping Municipal Les Ondines,** av. de Sarlat (tel. 65 37 86 44), on the banks of the Dordogne, makes a good first choice. (9F per person, 5.50F per tent. Electricity 4.50F. Open July-Sept. 7am-8pm.) Quieter **Camping de Lanzac** (tel. 65 37 02 58) is a 20-minute walk farther on the other side of the river, next to pont de Lanzac (9F per person, 6F per tent). Another chic possibility is 4-star **Camping La Paille Basse,** route de Borrèze (tel. 65 37 85 48 or 65 32 73 51; 23F per person, 38.50F per tent; open July-Aug. 8:30am-

12:30pm and 1:30-9pm, May 15-June and Sept. 1-15 shorter hours). Ask at the tourist office about other sites.

Most of Souillac's hotels offer reasonably filling 50-60F *menus*. You'll get the best deal at the **Hôtel Beffroi,** known to loyal locals as "Chez Jeanette." The informal, unhurried service delivers delicious meaty *menus* for 50F, 70F, and 90F. (Open Sun.-Fri. noon-2:30pm and 7-9:30pm, Sat. noon-2:30pm; in winter open Mon.-Sat. same hours.) **La Crêperie,** 33, rue de la Halle, serves *crêpes, galettes* and occasionally *paella* in a quiet atmosphere (9-38F). Decent salads fetch 18-24F. (Open Mon.-Sat. noon-midnight.) The **farmer's fair** comes to pl. de la Halle the first and third Friday of the month (9am-4:30pm). A smaller **market** is held here each Monday and Wednesday morning from about 8am to 12:30pm. The fresh produce puts supermarket veggies to shame.

Sights

The town itself has only a few intriguing features. The recently opened **Musée de l'Automate** (tel. 65 37 07 07), pl. de l'Abbaye, is a celebration of mechanical toys, from the very first 19th-century models to the modern robot. Bring the tykes. (Open daily 10am-1pm and 3-7pm; April-June and Sept.-Oct. Tues.-Sun. 10am-noon and 3-6pm; Nov.-March Wed.-Sun. 2-5pm. Admission 25F, students 20F, ages 5-12 15F.) The **Eglise Abbatiale,** an extravaganza of domes and octagonal chapels, claims three cupolas similar to those of the Byzantine-Romanesque cathedrals of Périgueux and Cahors. Devils and fantastic monsters preen with resignation on the portal columns. They, like the New Kids, know they are being exploited. Near the cathedral in pl. St-Martin stands the partially demolished **beffroi,** a 12th-century bell tower now reduced to a shadow of its former self.

Souillac's annual **jazz festival,** held the third week of July, is one of the better Quercy festivals. Although the general hoopla in the streets is free, tickets for the nightly concerts run 80-120F, or 220F for three nights. Get yours at the tourist office or, after July 1, from the people at Festival de Jazz, B.P. 99, 46200 Souillac.

Rocamadour

The precarious location and full-circle views of Rocamadour have earned this tiny hamlet the title of *"deuxième site de France"*—second most visited site in France. Rocamadour's harsh beauty exceeds the reputation which draws 1,500,000 pilgrims and tourist annually. In the 12th century a perfectly preserved body—supposedly that of a hermit who lived out his life on the cliff—was unearthed near the small chapel of Notre-Dame-de-Rocamadour. This discovery of the *roc amator* (lover of the rock) gave the cliff town its name.

Orientation and Practical Information

Getting here is painful by bicycle and difficult by public transport. The 45 min., 5km walk from the Rocamadour-Padirac SNCF station is pleasant; getting a lift from the chefs picking up supplies is usually a snap. Sarlat, Souillac, and Brive's tourist offices run tour buses in the summer only, generally for a steep 90-100F. Don't let any of this nonsense deter you; minor hassles are diminished by the major reward.

The only thing harder than getting to Rocamadour is getting lost once you're there—the town has only one curling, crowded street that runs parallel to the cliff and is bookended by two 13th-century fortified gates.

Tourist Office: Hôtel de Ville (tel. 65 33 62 59). **Currency exchange** Thurs.-Tues.; there's no bank. Office open daily July-Aug. 10am-noon and 3-8pm; April-June and Sept. 10am-noon and 3-7pm. Another tourist office at **L'Hospitalet** (tel. 65 33 62 80), on the road to town from the train station. Though their sign says they only handle hotel reservations, they may be just as helpful as the main office. Open July-Aug. 9am-noon and 3-8pm.

Post Office: rue Roland le Preux. Open Mon.-Fri. 9am-noon and 2-5pm, Sat. 9am-noon. **Postal Code:** 46500.

Trains: tel. 65 33 63 05. A brisk 45-min. walk (5km) from town. Rocamadour is most easily reached via Brive (5 per day, 45 min., 33F). From the south, catch a bus at Sarlat or Souillac for St-Denis-Près-Martel (Mon.-Sat. 3 per day, 45 min. from Souillac, 16F). Trains from St-Denis (3-4 per day, 15 min., 14F). Bike rental 30F per ½-day, 40F per day, deposit 500F. Open Mon.-Fri. 8:30am-10:30pm and Sat.-Sun. 10am-noon and 1:30-7:30pm.

Taxis: For a steep 30F each way, a briskly efficient woman (tel. 65 33 62 12) will run you to and from the train station. If there's a group of 8 or more people—which is rare—she'll take you in her van (9F each way). Many hitchhikers find passage from the station shockingly easy.

Police: Commissariat, tel. 65 33 60 17. **Emergency,** tel. 17.

Accommodations, Camping, and Food

Congested Rocamadour is better suited to daytrips (preferably on the 8am train from Brive) than overnight stays. Hotels are not cheap and are booked solid in summer. Make phone reservations one month in advance for July and August. **Hôtel du Lion d'Or,** Porte Figuier (tel. 65 33 62 04), has doubles for 80F (1 bed) and 90F (2 beds). If you snag one of these, feel lucky because their other rooms go for 100-200F. (No hall shower. Breakfast 22F. Open April-Oct.) **Hôtel Terminus,** pl. de la Carretta (tel. 65 33 62 14), lets two rooms at 80F (90F for 2 people) and three more rooms at 110F. (Showers 10F. Breakfast 24F. *Menus* from 48F. Open April-Oct.) Campers pitch their tents in campgrounds and in nearby fields. **Relais du Campeur,** above Rocamadour at L'Hospitalet (tel. 65 33 63 28), has hot showers, a grocery store, and a free pool. Check in at the *épicerie* next to the campground. (15F per person, 14F per site. Electricity 8F. Hot showers included. Open April-Sept.) Camp closer to the train station at **Camping Les Tilleuls.** Turn left from the station, cross the tracks, and take a right on the main road (10 min.). (13F per person, 13F per tent. Electricity 8F. Pool free. Open daily 7am-noon and 7:30-11pm.)

Several restaurants serve 45-60F *menus.* Good hotel food awaits at the **Lion d'Or,** which serves a 60F *menu.* The quick service at **Le Bellevue** at L'Hospitalet, delivers a 55F four-course *menu* and a 70F gourmet *menu* to a flower-lined terrace overlooking the Alzou Canyon. On Rocamadour's main street by the tourist office **Chez Anne Marie** beams with a pleasant ambience and a 54F *menu.* Just outside the train station **Restaurant des Voyageurs** serves a 45F *menu,* including *plat du jour, crudités,* and ice cream. *Crêpes,* pizzas, and sandwiches are sold all along the street in Rocamadour, and there is one overpriced, under-stocked *épicerie.* Daytrippers should bring a picnic and eat at the small park on the cliff road between l'Hospitalet and the château.

Sights

Ascending steeply beside the town's main street is the **Escalier des Pèlerins;** even today some pilgrims still kneel in prayer at each of its 216 steps. It's worth making the uphill journey to see the sacred **Cité Religieuse,** also accessible by elevator (7F, round-trip 9.70F; 7:45am-10pm every 3 min.). The Cité encompasses the impressively fortified **Evêché,** once the palace of the bishops of Tulle, and the 11th-century **Basilique St-Saveur,** home to an evocative 16th-century sculpture of Christ. Most notable among the Cité's several small chapels is the **Chapelle Notre-Dame,** to which generations of pilgrims have come. The ancient sword thrust into a rock above the door is reputedly the sword of Roland. Legend says that an unwed woman who touches the sword, which Roland tossed to Rocamadour before he died, will be married within a year. Don't touch it! **Chapelle St-Michel** opens only for the free guided visits that start at the basilica in summer. If the Cité is not crowded, the guide may also give you a free guided tour of the entire area. Around and in between the chapels are free exhibitions, crypts (open only to guided tours), and the **Trésors Musée,** which houses items related to the sanctuaries. (Museum open

July-Aug. 9am-6pm; April-June and Sept.-Oct. 9am-noon and 2-6pm. Admission 10F, children 6F. Tours of the crypts in French only daily 9am-noon and 2-6pm.)

Still higher up—accessible by the zigzagging **Chemin de Croix Blanche** and soon by elevator as well—stands the **château,** built in the 14th century to protect the pilgrims below and now inhabited by the chaplains of Rocamadour. All the public may see is the view from the **ramparts.** (Open July-Aug. 9am-7pm; April-June and Sept.-Oct. 9am-noon and 1:30-8pm. Admission 6F, under 18 4F.)

The annual *pèlerinage* to Rocamadour takes place during the week of September 8. Pilgrims began gathering here for shelter in the early Middle Ages, and from 1170 on, both kings and popes came to Rocamadour to worship. The site's renown increased with the spread of a rumor that St-Amadour, the hermit who lived in the cliffs, was in fact the Zacchaeus of the gospel. In the later Middle Ages, Rocamadour and its oratory became associated with the grandiose Benedectine order, and the little church of Notre-Dame became increasingly popular as a center for organized pilgrimages. The Wars of Religion stunted Rocamadour's growth, but in 1853, local clergy rekindled the pilgrimage that today draws thousands on their way to Lourdes.

For a less orthodox diversion, visit the 150 friendly monkeys who inhabit the **Forêt des Singes** (tel. 65 33 62 72) 1.5km outside Hospitalet. The monkeys, some of them belonging to rare species, roam freely. (Park open June 16-Aug. daily 9am-7pm; April 1-June 15 and Sept. 1-Oct. 15 10am-noon and 2-6pm.) Next door, flora and fauna rock on at the **Jardin des Papillons,** which has two greenhouses full of live butterflies from Asia, Africa, America, Australia, and—gasp!—Europe. (Open daily July-Aug. 9am-6:30pm; April-Oct. 10am-noon, 2-5:30pm. Admission 22F.)

Twenty km from Rocamadour, 15km from the train station, and 100m underground is the astounding **Gouffre de Padirac,** more intriguing than any subterranean realm imagined by Jules Verne. At the end of the 19th century, a speleologist explored Padirac's enormous sinkhole or *gouffre*—held by local superstition to be the site of a bout between St-Martin and Satan—only to discover these enormous underground caverns. A 1½-hour tour descends to the bottom of the *gouffre* and below it, to the underground river that carved the dank passageway. Bring a raincoat, as it rains incessantly in one of the vaults. (Open July daily 8:30am-noon and 2-6:30pm; Aug. 8am-7pm; April-June and Sept.-Oct. 9am-noon and 2-6pm. Admission 28F.) From July 7 through September 1, Arcoutel et Cie (tel. 65 33 62 12) runs excursions to the *gouffre* from Rocamadour's train station every Wednesday and Friday at 8:45am (3hr., 50F). The same company sends buses once a week from Rocamadour to Sarlat, Souillac, Beynac, La Roque Gageac, Domme, Montfort, and Carsac (110F, reserve a few days in advance). Daytrippers should take the early train to Rocamadour from Brive, which arrives at about 8:45am; then take the excursion, explore the town, and take the train back to Brive at 7:02pm (no evening train on Sat.). An excursion bus also leaves Brive's bus station in pl. du 14 Juillet at 1:30pm (July-Aug. daily) and covers Martel, the *gouffre,* Rocamadour, and Souillac, before returning to Brive at 7pm (100F). Contact the Brive tourist office (tel. 55 24 08 80) for reservations. Group excursions to the *gouffre* leave from Souillac once per week from June 22 to September 7 (120F); contact the Souillac tourist office (tel. 65 37 81 56). Cyclists may consider heading for the **Auberge de Jeunesse (IYHF),** pl. du Monturu (tel. 55 91 13 82), 30km northeast of Padirac in Beaulieu-sur-Dordogne. (Open Easter-Sept.)

Cahors

Spanish flavor spices up life in Cahors, the only town in Quercy where *foie gras* makes room for *paella* and Byzantine domes melt into red-tiled roofs. A tight loop in the murky Lot river and high cliffs on the opposite banks have protected Cahors through centuries of war and Spanish invasion. 19th-century activist Léon-Michel Gambetta of street, square, and avenue fame, was born in this sun-baked town in 1838.

Orientation and Practical Information

Situated on the main Paris-Toulouse line, Cahors lies just over one hour from Brive to the north and Toulouse to the south. Clermont-Ferrand sits, lies, squats, and stands two hours to the east.

A 15-minute walk from the train station brings you to the center of town. Turn right onto av. Jean Jaurès and take the third left onto rue Wilson. (A right would take you away from the center and to the Luciferian medieval bridge.) Continuing straight on rue Wilson toward *centre ville,* you arrive at **boulevard Gambetta,** Cahors's liveliest thoroughfare, which runs north-south. The *vieille ville* spreads in front of you between the Lot and bd. Gambetta. The tourist office is one block south, on the right.

Tourist Office: pl. Aristide Briand (tel. 65 35 09 56), near rue Wilson at bd. Gambetta. Free map, information on camping and canoeing, a book of suggested routes for hiking and bicycling, and a guide to regional wines. Daily tours of the *vieille ville* in summer (15F, at 10am and 3pm). Minibus tours offered at these times (from 70F) often end with a wine-tasting session at the *caves.* Open Mon.-Sat. 9am-12:30pm and 1:30-6:30pm; Sept.-June Mon.-Sat. 9am-noon and 2-6pm.

Budget Travel: Voyages Belmon, 2, bd. Gambetta (tel. 65 35 59 30). Excursions to Rocamadour, the Gouffre de Padirac, Sarlat, La Roque Gageac, Domme, Gourdon, Château de Bonaguil, and the Lot Valley. Reserve a few days in advance at their office, the train station, or the tourist office. Open Mon.-Fri. 9am-noon and 2-7pm, Sat. 9am-noon.

Currency Exchange: The only exchange offices open on Mon. are the post office and **Crédit Agricole,** 22, bd. Gambetta (tel. 65 30 10 35). Open Mon.-Fri. 8:30am-noon and 1:30-5:30pm; exchange 8:30-11:30am and 1:30-4:30pm.

Post Office: rue Wilson, between pont Valentré and the tourist office. **Telephones** and **currency exchange.** Open Mon.-Fri. 8am-7pm, Sat. 8am-noon. **Postal Code: 46000.**

Trains: av. Jean Jaurès (tel. 65 22 50 50). To: Paris (7 per day, 5-6 hr., 275F); Brive (8 per day, 1¾ hr., 64F); Souillac (6 per day, 1 hr., 44F); Montauban (11 per day, ½-hr., 43F); Toulouse (12 per day, 1¼ hr., 70F). Information booth open 5:30am-12:30am.

Buses: SNCF buses in front of the train station. To Capdenac (3-4 per day, 2 hr., 78F) via St-Cirq-Lapopie and the Figeac *gare.* To Monsempron-Libos (4-6 per day, 1¼ hr.) via Puy L'Eveque and Fumel (near the Château de Bonaguil).

Bike Rental: Combes, 117, bd. Gambetta (tel. 65 35 06 73). 35F per day, 175F per week, deposit 220F plus ID. Open Tues.-Sat. 8:30am-noon and 2-7pm. Also at the **train station.** 40F per ½-day, 50F per day, deposit 300F.

Women's Center: Centre d'Information sur les Droits des Femmes, 50, rue St-Urcisse (tel. 65 30 07 34), off rue Clemenceau. Open Mon.-Fri. 9am-noon and 2-5pm.

Youth Center: Maison de Jeunes et de la Culture (MJC), 42, impasse de la Charité (tel. 65 35 06 43), behind and to the right of the cathedral. Canoe trips, occasional concerts and films, arts and crafts. A friendly hang-out for ping-pong and cards. Open Tues.-Thurs. and Sun. 2-7pm, Mon. and Fri. 2-7pm and 8:30-11:30pm. Bar open 10am-7pm and during *soirées.*

Laundromat: Laverie Laveco, on rue de la Prèfecture at rue Cathala, which becomes rue Coture. Wash 20F, dry 1F per 3 min. Soap free. Open daily 8am-8pm.

Hospital: Centre Hospitalier, rue Wilson (tel. 65 35 47 97).

Police: rue St-Gery (tel. 65 35 27 00). **Emergency,** tel. 17.

Accommodations and Camping

Finding a room shouldn't be a problem if you start looking early in the day.

Foyer des Jeunes Travailleurs Frédéric Suisse, 20, rue Frédéric Suisse (tel. 65 35 64 71). From the train station bear right onto rue Anatole France and take the 2nd left onto rue F. Suisse. The *foyer* is at the end on the left (10 min.). Loads of character: wooden floors, iron balustrades, and mosquitoes big enough to carry your pack away. TV and ping-pong.Reception open Mon.-Fri. 9-11:30am and 2-7pm, Sat. 10-11:30am. No lockout or curfew. Singles and doubles 40F, showers included. Breakfast 8.50F. Lunch (noon-1pm) or dinner (7:15pm) 36F; order in advance. Sheets 11F.

Foyer de Jeunes en Quercy, 129, rue Fondue Haute (tel. 65 35 29 32), off bd. Gambetta. Both sexes and all religions welcome. Kind sisters, good meals, respectable rooms. Reception open daily 8am-10pm. Singles 47F, shower included. Breakfast 10F, lunch 30F, dinner 27F.

Hôtel l'Escargot, 5, bd. Gambetta (tel. 65 35 07 66), up the hill. Cheerful owners and reasonable rooms. Reception open mornings Tues.-Sun. Rooms 75-120F. Breakfast 17F. Pleasant local restaurant downstairs with a 50F *menu*.

Hôtel de la Paix, pl. St-Maurice (tel. 65 35 03 40), overlooking the covered market. Adequate, clean rooms. Reception open Mon.-Sat. 7am-9pm. Singles and doubles 90-95F, with shower 105F. Showers 10F. Breakfast 20F.

Camping: Camping Municipal St-Georges (tel. 65 35 04 64), on the river bank 5 min. from the tourist office. Follow bd. Gambetta across pont Louis Philippe. Behind the campground, an alley leads to a path up Mont St-Cyr. 16F per person, 16F per tent. Electricity 10F.

Food

Although the big **markets** take place Wednesday and Saturday until 12:30pm in front of the cathedral, produce stands often pop up other days of the week. Check out the covered market nearby. (Open Tues.-Sat. 7:30am-12:30pm and 3-6pm, Sun. 9am-noon.) Stroll behind the tourist office to reach the **Prisunic** supermarket. (Open Tues.-Fri. 9:15am-12:15pm and 3-7pm, Mon. and Sat. 9:15am-12:15pm and 2:30-7pm.) Be sure to sample the town's full-bodied red wine, advertised as "the wine of kings and of the Russian Orthodox Church" but known simply as "vin de Cahors."

L'Orangerie, rue St-James, off pl. St-Maurice. Surprise—a vegetarian restaurant in provincial France. Good combination of veggies and regional specialties. Tremendous rice, veggie, tofu, tomato platter (36F). Open Tues.-Sun. 11:45-2:30pm and 7-10pm.

Pizzeria La Pescara, 163, quai Champollion. Huge pizzas and delicious salads with tomato-ricotta dressing. Three dining rooms and a vine-entwined terrace. Pizza 20-40F, salads 15-37F, pasta 26-31F, lasagne 34F. Open Tues.-Sat. noon-1:45pm and 7:30-11:30pm, Sun. 7:30-11:30pm.

Le Champ de Mars "Chez Piche," 17, bd. Gambetta (tel. 65 35 04 80). Standard *brasserie* with a filling 44F *menu*. Open Mon.-Fri. 9:30am-9:30pm, Sat. 10am-4pm.

Le Melchior Bar-Restaurant, pl. de la Gare, across from the train station. Satisfying *plats du jour,* such as jitterbugging chitterlings, beef bourguignon, and vegetable tart (37F). Unspectacular 58F *menu*. Open daily 12:15-1:45pm and 7:15-9:30pm.

Marie Colline, 173, rue Clemenceau. Shock. Two vegetarian restaurants in one town, although this no-frills place just barely qualifies as a restaurant. Tasty victuals, low prices, small portions. Eggplant parmesan 30F. Steamy soups and crunchy salads 17F. Desserts 15F. Open Tues.-Sat. 11:45am-2:30pm.

Sights

Though the 14th-century **Pont Valentré's** three towering turrets seem fantastic and impractical (except, perhaps, for picnics), they helped repel invaders during the Hundred Years' War and the Siege of Cahors in 1580. Legend has it that the architect bargained with the devil to hurry the bridge's construction. He tricked Beelzebub of his due, however, and in revenge, the fiend repeatedly toppled the central tower. When a 19th-century architect replaced the tower, he added a small carving of the devil struggling to pull it down, visible from the middle of the bridge.

Like the church at Souillac, **Cathédrale St-Etienne** is topped by three domed cupolas of Byzantine inspiration. The northern Romanesque portal, formerly the front entrance on the west side, was moved in the 14th century to allow the construction of the fortresslike façade, appropriate to the church's function as a refuge for monks during the religious wars. The northern wall's beautifully sculpted tympanum, dating from 1135, depicts Christ's Ascension. To the right of the choir, a door leads to the **cloître,** built around 1500. The cloister overlooks the cathedral domes and is next to the **chapelle musée,** which contains a remarkable fresco of the Last Judgment. (Cathedral open daily 8:30am-6pm. Museum open 10am-7pm; Sept. 15-June go next door to l'Agence des Bâtiments de France and ask for the key to the museum.)

For three or four days around July 14, Cahors's **Festival de Blues** convenes prominent blues artists such as Magic Slim and B.B. King. Tickets cost 60-100F at the tourist office.

Near Cahors

There is far more to see outside Cahors than within. **Safaraid** (tel. 65 36 23 54) at Bouziès, where the river Célé joins the Lot, arranges somewhat expensive river trips lasting up to two weeks (mid-May to mid-Sept. only). Trips include gentle white-water rafting, canoe parties, or lazy *bateau mouche* crawls—prices vary considerably. The tourist office provides more information on canoe routes and rentals.

Thirty-six km from Cahors, the exquisite medieval houses of **St-Cirq-Lapopie** peruse the river from atop a cliff. The view from the ruins of **Château Lapopie** sweeps over the village, river, cliffs, and broad plains below. Buses run from Cahors's *gare routière* to a point at the base of the hill, 2km from the castle (3-4 per day, 35 min., 22.50F). Ask the driver to let you off at the stop marked "Tour de France, Gare SNCF."

Several km north of St-Cirq-Lapopie and inaccessible by public transport is the **Grotte du Pech-Merle** (tel. 65 31 23 33). Discovered in 1922, this one-mile natural art gallery is an incredible Stendhalian display of art from the Paleolithic era. Between June and August, tickets sell *fast*. (Open Easter-Sept. daily 9:30am-noon and 2-6pm; in off-season call 65 31 27 05.) Ask the Cahors tourist office about Monday excursions to Pech-Merle and St-Cirq-Lapopie (6 hr., 130F.)

Farther from Cahors in the western corner of the Lot Valley, 16th-century **Château de Bonaguil** remains as an immense and commanding fortress despite vandalism suffered during the Revolution. (Open March-Sept. 10am-noon and 2:30-6pm.) Reserve tickets for the castle's concerts and stage productions (July-Aug. 60-90F) at the Fumel tourist office (tel. 53 71 13 70). To get to Bonaguil from Cahors, take the SNCF bus to Fumel (4-6 per day, 1 hr., 37F) and follow D673 for 4½km and D158 for 3½km. Inquire at Cahors's tourist office for bus schedules.

Basque Country (Pays Basque)

An afternoon *pelote* match, a cross shaped like four spiraling teardrops, and the ubiquitous rope-soled espadrilles all at first seem surface tokens of someone else's culture, carried over from the past to stock the shelves of souvenir shops. But the Basque culture is very real, and its survival is extremely important to the Basque people. The Basques hold that Euzkadi (the Basque Country) is one nation, now unjustly divided between France and Spain. While Spain's four Basque provinces are highly industrialized, the three in France live mostly on agriculture and tourism. Since the death of the unsympathetic Franco in the late 70s, the Spanish Basques have seen a strong revival in their language and customs. More insouciant than their Spanish counterparts, the French Basques have watched their language disappear and have begun more and more to identify with France rather than with the Euzkadi state. The Basque beach towns, lapped by some of the world's best surfing waters, attract more bronzed, neon-shorted youths than attention from the French government. In addition, the mountain enclaves of Euzkadi have steadily lost younger Basques to the big cities and are beginning to lose ground in the wool market. The nationalist movement, supported by several political parties in the 1960s, has also lost much popular support because of alleged connections with the ETA (the militarist Spanish Basque liberation front Euzkadi Eta Askatasum, meaning "Euzkadi and Freedom"). Despite their more subdued attitude, the French Basques still shelter their Spanish cousins from French police investigations and threats of Spanish extradition. In past years, arrests and acts of violence have scared visitors away; now, the most you have to fear is a sunburn.

Although most of the region is poorly served by rail, Bayonne and Biarritz are fairly easy to reach and St-Jean-Pied-de-Port is an easy and beautiful hour's ride through the mountains from Bayonne. Trains run from Bordeaux in the north and Pau in the east. Along the coast from Biarritz to Hendaye, inexpensive buses make up for the scanty rail service. Excursion buses travel to a few towns in the interior, but many people find hitchhiking and cycling the best ways to penetrate the hills.

The typical *neo-Basque* architecture of the region, characterized by white walls and visible timbers painted in bright colors, imitates old Basque farmhouses where the animals lived on the ground floor. Another architectural peculiarity of the Basque country is found in the churches, notably the one in St.-Jean-de-Luz. Wooden galleries, often exquisitely carved and usually somewhat frightening to sit in, hang above the nave. Constructed in the 16th century to support the burgeoning population of newly-Catholocized Basques, the balconies were occupied by the men, whose voices still blend in the many hymns so popular in the region.

The regional sport *pelote*, known as jai alai in the U.S., is the fastest game played with a ball. Burly players hurl a hard ball at speeds up to 200kmph at a wall by means of a *chistera* (basket appendage) laced to the wrist. Try to get to a *fronton* (outdoor arena) or a *trinquet* (indoor arena) to appreciate the speed and skill of the local players. Tickets to the world cup matches in St-Jean-de-Luz, which are played all summer, start at 30F.

In general, Basque *fêtes* involve several days of drinking, dancing the fandango, playing the *ttun ttun* and *txistu,* and, in most traditional villages, whitewashing all the farmhouses. The most famous, the *fête de Bayonne,* occurs in the first week of August. For a complete list of festivals and events, pick up the free guide, *Fêtes en Pays Basque,* at a tourist office. The popularity of these festivals makes accommodations extremely difficult to find in August, but reservations are possible as late as July. The months from November to March will find the coast almost deserted.

Basque cuisine is distinctive and inexpensive. Although the renowned Bayonne ham, densely pressed and cured, may not be delectable to those averse to almost-raw meat, Basque fish stew rivals the frothiest *bouillabaise*. *Pipérade* is an omelette made with tomatoes, green peppers, and ham. Don't let the modest appearance of the *gâteau basque* (Basque cake) fool you. The light pastry filled with cream or jelly outdoes fancier *chantilly*-capped concoctions. The **Pâtisserie Etchebaster** in Bayonne and St-Jean-de-Luz offers the most acclaimed version of this *gâteau*. The tangy Ardigazna cheese made from sheep milk is best when a bit dry. Once a major wine-producing region, the Pays Basque is making a comeback with some vigorous reds, notably *vin d'Irouleguy*. The local herbal liqueur Izarra, distilled in Bayonne, is a sweeter cousin of chartreuse.

The French Basque country is a land of hot sun and bold colors, blue skies and beautiful beaches, but it is more than another tourist resort. It's a culture to respect, a place to ask questions and get involved. To a lot of people there's something very important going on. You can bet the tourist office didn't spraypaint the word "Euzkadi" at the bus stop.

Bayonne

Capital of the Pays Basque, Bayonne (pop. 43,000) lies just kilometers away from surf beaches, the Pyrenees, tiny Basque villages, and the Spanish border. While enjoying cosmopolitan accoutrements, Bayonne retains its small-town charm. Lively markets crowd narrow streets, and rivers lead to two wonderful museums, a citadel, and a Gothic cathedral. After the first Tuesday in August, Bayonne drops its façade of cool charm for the festival—five days of concerts, fandangos, bullfights, fireworks, and a chaotic race between junk heaps masquerading as boats. Crisscrossed by the Adour and Nive Rivers, Bayonne has served as a major port, military base, and industrial center since the 12th century. Chocolate first came to France through its port, and the martinets of this city invented the bayonet.

Orientation and Practical Information

Six hours from Paris by train, Bayonne is linked by bus to the nearby towns of Anglet and Biarritz, both directly west. The merging rivers split Bayonne into three main areas. **St-Esprit,** on the northern side of the Adour, contains the train station and pl. de la République. Pont St-Esprit arches across the Adour to **Petit-Bayonne,** home of Bayonne's two museums, several inexpensive hotels, and some lively bars. Five small bridges cross the Nive River and connect Petit-Bayonne to **Grand-Bayonne,** on the west bank of the Nive. The oldest part of town, Grand-Bayonne has a pedestrian zone lined by alluring shops and *pâtisseries*. The center of town is easily manageable on foot and an excellent bus system covers the outskirts and beaches.

Tourist Office: (tel. 59 59 31 31), in Hôtel de Ville, pl. de la Liberté, in Grand-Bayonne under the arcade on the side facing the river. Excellent maps of Anglet and Bayonne, but the staff can't find you a room. Pick up the *Programme des Fêtes en Pays Basque.* Guided tours of the city July-Aug. Mon., Wed., Fri. at 10am and Tues., Thurs., Sat. at 3pm (25F). Tues. and Fri. in English. Open Mon.-Sat. 9am-noon and 2-7pm; Oct.-May Mon.-Fri. 9am-noon and 2-6:30pm, Sat. 9am-noon.

Budget Travel: Pascal Voyages, 8, allée Boufflers (tel. 59 25 48 48), in Petit-Bayonne. BIJ/Eurotrain tickets. Airline student discount tickets. No credit cards or checks accepted. Open Sept.-July Mon.-Fri. 8:30am-noon and 2-6:30pm, Sat. 9am-noon; Aug. Mon.-Fri. 8:30am-noon and 2-6:30pm.

Currency Exchange: 17, rue Thiers (tel. 59 59 70 70), 50m from the tourist office. Good rates. Open Mon.-Sat. 9am-6:30pm. Also at **post office.**

Post Office: rue Jules Labat, in Grand-Bayonne. **Telephones** and **currency exchange.** Open Mon.-Fri. 8am-6:30pm, Sat. 8am-noon. **Branch office,** on bd. Alsace-Lorraine, closer to the train station. **Telephones.** Open same hours. **Postal Code;** 64100.

Trains: (tel. 59 55 50 50), off pl. de la République. To: Paris (7 per day, 5½-6½ hr., 331F); St-Jean-Pied-de-Port (6 per day, 1¼ hr., 37F); Hendaye (11 per day, 45 min., 29F); St-Jean-de-Luz (11 per day, ½-hr., 18F); Bordeaux (6 per day, 2 hr., 110F). Information office open 7am-11pm. Baggage check open 6am-midnight.

Buses: STAB (tel. 59 59 04 61), on pl. du Réduit on the riverside. Pick up bus map here or at the tourist office. Also outside the Hôtel de Ville in Grand-Bayonne (tel. 59 63 20 89). Lines #1 and 2 go to Biarritz. Line #2 also goes to the hostel in Anglet (25 min.), and Biarritz's Gare la Négresse (45 min., 6.50F). Hostelers can also take line #4 to La Barre and switch to #6 (direction Arcadie), to be dropped off in front of the hostel. Buses leave every 30-40 min. Tickets 6.50F, *carnet* of 10 50F, carnet of 5 25F.

Taxis: at the train station (tel. 59 55 13 15). Call 59 63 17 17 for 24-hr. service.

Bike Rental: Location Vélos, at the train station (tel. 59 55 05 88, ask for *service des bagages*). 40F per day, discounts after 3 days for salamanders. 210F per week. Deposit 500F plus ID. Call in advance to reserve. Open daily 7am-1:15pm and 1:25-8pm.

Hiking Guide: M. Pierrick d'Aleman, 50, quai des Corsaires (tel. 59 59 12 10). Organizes 4- to 5-hr. hikes in July and Aug. (150F per person). Call for reservations.

Laundromat: 16, rue Pointrique, in Petit-Bayonne. Wash 12F, dry 2F per 8 min. 10F and 2F coins. Open daily 7:30am-9:30pm.

Hospital: rue Jacques Loeb, St-Léon (tel. 59 63 50 50). Take bus #3.

Medical Emergency: SAMU, tel. 59 63 33 33.

Police: (tel. 59 25 77 00), on rue Jacques Laffitte in Petit-Bayonne opposite the Musée Bonnat. **Emergency,** tel. 17.

Accommodations and Camping

Cheap hotels abound in Bayonne. The commute to and from the beach will often cost less than a hotel in Biarritz or St-Jean-de-Luz. In St-Esprit, start looking around the train station. The hotels in Grand-Bayonne are generally more expensive; in Petit-Bayonne look around **rue Pannecau** and **place Paul Bert.** Although always advisable, reservations are only imperative in August during the festival. The closest hostel is in Anglet. Take bus #2 (stop "pl. Leclerc") or #6 (stop "Auberge de Jeunesse").

Hôtel Paris-Madrid, pl. de la Gare (tel. 59 55 13 98). A large, newly renovated establishment right next to the train station. English-speaking reception open 24 hrs. Singles 70F, with shower 110F. Doubles 100F, with shower 110F. Triples with shower 170F. Quads with shower 200F. Extra bed 20F. Breakfast 18F.

Hôtel du Moulin, 12, rue Ste-Catherine (tel. 59 55 13 29), 2 blocks from the station. A small hotel in a quiet location with a bar downstairs. Simple rooms with gorgeous old furniture. Singles 60-70F. Doubles 70-85F. Showers 7F. Breakfast 18F.

Hôtel des Arceaux, 26, rue Pont Neuf (tel. 59 59 15 53), 15 min. from the station in Grand-Bayonne's charming pedestrian district. Clean and pleasant rooms. Singles and doubles 90-110F. Quads 240F. Extra bed 35F. Breakfast 20F. Showers included. Call ahead.

Hôtel des Basques, 4, rue des Lisses (tel. 59 59 08 02), in Petit-Bayonne off pl. Paul Bert, facing Caserne au Château-Neuf. Noisy during the festival; ask for a quieter room that does not overlook the square. Singles and doubles 68-108F, with shower 85-148F. Breakfast 18F.

Camping: Barre de l'Adour, 130, av. de l'Adour (tel. 59 63 16 16). Two-star site in an unpleasantly industrial setting at the mouth of the river in Anglet. Take the bus (*ligne verte*) from Bayonne's Hôtel de Ville. Reception open 8am-9pm. 9.50F per person, 12.40F per tent, 4.10F per car. Open June-late Sept. **Camping de la Chêneraie** (tel. 59 55 01 31), on RN117 north of town behind St-Esprit. A 4-star facility with everything. 15F per person, 25F per tent or car. Open June-Sept. 15 7am-11pm, but reservations not taken until noon.

Food

Food in Bayonne is varied and affordable. The streets of Petit-Bayonne have a number of small restaurants and cafés, most of them with 50-60F *menus.* There are also some good, cheap restaurants on the side streets of St-Esprit. Sardines and anchovies are always fresh and unlike anything you've ever had from a can. Basque fish stew is a spicy treat, but be warned that anything can go in your soup—seashells and bones included. The *charcuteries* and *traiteurs* display plump vegetables *farci* (stuffed with meat) and salads, all perfect for a picnic on the *quais*. Bayonne is known for its hams, chocolate, and its local liqueur Izarra, three things which rarely occur in the same dish. All this and more awaits at the **marché municipal,** on the quai Roquebert by the Pannecau bridge, under the parking area. (Open daily 5am-1pm and 3-7pm, Mon. 5am-noon.) **Prisunic,** to the right of the Pannecau bridge, offers standard grocery store fare. (Open Mon.-Fri. 8:30am-7pm and Sat. 8am-7pm.

Restaurant Irintzina, 9, rue Marengo, in Petit-Bayonne. Down-home food in attractive white-washed interior. The 48F *menu* leaves you stuffed to the gills with an omelette, meat, vegetable, bread, and dessert. Open Mon.-Sat. noon-2pm and 7-9:30pm.

Restaurant Dacquois, 48, rue d'Espagne, in Grand-Bayonne. Regional specialties, local clientele, and a filling 49F *menu.* Open Mon.-Sat. noon-2pm and 7:30-10pm.

El Mosquito, on rue des Augustines, in Petit-Bayonne. Eat mounds of chili (39F) in a cozy den decorated with Persian rugs. Pancho plays South American music Fri. and Sat. night (cover 10F). 70F *menu* includes 3 courses, wine, and coffee (served 7:15-8:30pm). Drinks 20-30F. Open daily 7:15pm-3am.

Bar des Amis, 13, rue des Cordeliers, in Petit-Bayonne on a street parallel to rue Pannecau. The food is good and plentiful (4-course, 40F *menu*), but don't go for the decor or atmosphere. *Menu* served daily noon-2pm and 8-9:30pm.

A la Femme Sans Tête, 18, quai Chaho, on the Nive. Don't let the name scare you away from the delicious Vietnamese specialties. Slightly expensive, but a welcome break from *poulet basquaise.* Main courses from 50F. Open daily noon-1:30pm and 7-10pm.

Chex Catal', 14, bd. Alsace-Lorraine. Enormous pizzas served with a smile. Pizzas run 30-40F, pasta 25-35F, and desserts 10-15F. Open daily 11:30am-10pm.

Chocolat Cazenave, 19, arceaux Pont-Neuf. Taste the chocolate Bayonne introduced to France. Not to be missed. Open daily 11am-6pm.

Sights and Entertainment

Cathédrale Notre-Dame was built 700 years ago in the purest Gothic style, with graceful lines, golden stone, and twin peaks. The sacristy contains a few paintings and carved stone portals but is usually closed. Stone *Bayonnais* bishops line up nearby. (Cathedral open Mon.-Sat. 7am-12:30pm and 2:30-7:30pm, Sun. 8am-12:30pm and 3:30-7:30pm.)

The **Musée Basque** (tel. 59 59 08 98), at quai des Corsaires and rue Marengo in Petit Bayonne, is one of the finest folklore museums in France. Among the extensive displays are rounded Basque tombstones shaped like giant keyholes, a motif which reappears in Basque decorative arts and on the front wall of *pelote* arenas. The museum doors should reopen in 1991 after extensive repairs. A library in the same building as the Basque museum houses over 10,000 volumes, including most everything published concerning the Basques. (Open to scholars Mon.-Fri. 10am-noon and 2-5pm.)

Bayonne's recently renovated museum of fine arts, the **Musée Bonnat,** 5, rue Jacques Lafitte (tel. 59 59 08 52) in Petit-Bayonne, bears the name of a celebrated 19th-century *Bayonnais* painter who bequeathed his extensive collection to the city and then directed the construction of the museum. Rich in English, Italian, French, and Spanish paintings from the 13th through 19th centuries, this small museum includes an impressive colleciton of Rubens and a few works by Delacroix, Degasm and Antoine Bayre. Bonnat's own grandiose, classical works fill several rooms. (Open Wed.-Mon. 10am-noon and 3-7pm; in off-season Mon. and Wed.-Thurs. 1-7pm, Fri. 3-9pm, Sat. 10am-noon and 3-6pm, Sun. 10am-noon and 3-7pm. Admission 15F, students 5F, seniors free.)

Free tours and tastings of Izarra, the heavy Basque liqueur, are given at **Izarra Distillery,** 9, quai Bergeret (tel. 59 55 09 45), in St-Esprit off pl. de la République (entrance on rue de Belfort). Izarra is sold cheaply here; the sweet *framboise* (raspberry) liqueur goes for 75F per 70cl bottle, while the yellow (32 herbs used) and green (48-herb) liqueurs cost 75F and 95F, respectively. Only three people in the entire distillery possess the secret herbal recipe for Izarra. (Could one of them be the Colonel?) English tours are available. (Open July-Aug. daily 8:30am-7pm; Sept.-June Mon.-Fri. 9-11:30am and 2-4:30pm.)

Throughout the year, fast and furious *pelote* matches can be seen Thursday at 4pm in the Trinquet St-André. The orchestra Harmonie Bayonnaise puts on a less harrowing, free show in the pl. de Gaulle gazebo Thursday at 8:30pm in July and August. In August and early September, Bayonne holds four **corridas** (bullfights) in the large Plaza de Toros. As a Spanish-style nod to the Basques' French citizenship, a bullfight is also held on Bastille Day. Tickets run 50-300F and sell out fast. For ticket information, write or call Bureau des Arènes Municipales, 5, rue du 49ème, Bayonne (tel. 59 59 25 98). Tickets also go on sale at the Bureau du Théâtre (tel. 59 59 07 27), next to the tourist office. (Open Mon.-Sat. 10am-12:30pm and 3-7pm.) The **Jazz aux Remparts** festival lures Count Basie and his ilk in mid-July. Tickets are available at the tourist office (120F).

Anglet

Wedged between Bayonne and Biarritz, Anglet (hard T) is a bland suburb redeemed by fine beaches, the only hostel within 50-odd miles, and a 370-acre pine forest with coastal hiking paths. Efficient buses run to Bayonne and Biarritz every half-hour from 7am to 8pm (6.50F).

Although there are a number of reasonable hotels in Anglet (singles 50-90F), avoid staying anywhere but the the well-equipped **Auberge de Jeunesse (IYHF)**, 19, rue de Vignes (tel. 59 63 86 49). Bus #6 (*direction* "La Barre") runs there about every 40 minutes from the Biarritz Hôtel de Ville. (Service Mon.-Sat. 7:23am-7:52pm, Sun. 9am-7:35pm; 6.50F.) From Bayonne, take bus #4 (6:45am-8:20pm every 20 min.; 6.50F) from the *gare* SNCF to La Barre, and switch to bus #6 (*direction* "Arcadie"). Located amid suburban split-levels, this 95-bed hub of the southwestern France surfing subculture packs in beautiful, tanned wave-worshipers who have come to teach surf, learn surf, and do surf. (No lockout. Open 8:30-10am and 6-10pm. 54F per person. Camping 33F. Cot in one of five circus-style tents 50F. Breakfast included.) Lunch and dinner are served in the summer but you must purchase tickets before 10am (40F). Day-long rentals of surfboards (60F), boogie boards (50F), or wetsuits (30F) may be arranged at the reception 9-9:30am and 6-6:30pm. The hostel is usually packed—make reservations a month beforehand or arrive at least an hour before opening. There are no kitchen facilities in summer, but the basement *brasserie* serves generous portions of spaghetti *à la bolognaise* (30F), *poulet basquaise* (30F), and *steak-frites* (28F). (Open for brunch 9:30-11:30am and from 6:30pm to around midnight). The hostel organizes camps for surfing, sailing, golf, and other sports. Prices for activities, meals, and lodging start at 1800F. Write to the hostel in April for information.

Three of Anglet's campgrounds have two stars. All are well-situated and fully equipped. **Chambre d'Amour,** route de Bouney (tel. 59 03 71 66), offers 265 sites May through September. Follow the signs down rue Chambre d'Amour, a five-minute walk from Cinq Cantons. (Reception open 9am-noon and 2-7pm. 14F per person, 14F per tent, 6F per car. Showers included.) **Barre de l'Adour,** 130, av. de l'Adour, opens its 200 sites from June through mid-September. Take the green bus from Bayonne or the "Navette des Plages" shuttle bus (#4) to the northern end of the line. (Reception open 8am-10pm. 10.50F per person, 12.40F per tent, 4.10F per car. Showers included. Reservations accepted.) **Fontaine Laborde,** av. de Fontaine Laborde (tel. 59 03 89 67), has 100 sites. From the hostel, go down the hill toward the beach. (11F per person, 11F per site, 5F per car. No caravans. Open June-Sept.)

The main **tourist office** on pl. du Général Leclerc (tel. 59 03 77 01) has information on accommodations. (Open Mon.-Sat. 9am-12:30pm and 1-7pm, Sun. 10am-noon; Sept.-June Mon.-Fri. 9am-noon and 1-6:30pm, Sat. 9am-noon.) The **post office** is next door; Anglet's **postal code** is 64600.

Even if you don't intend to tame the waves, Anglet's beaches deserve the trip. Although the 4km of fine sandy stretches are reputedly patrolled by the highest concentration of lifeguards anywhere on the coast, swimmers should be careful of the strong cross-current pull. Beneath the lighthouse, **Chambre d'Amour** beach faces a bay surrounded by large cliffs. Larger waves and more beachfront shops attract the surfing elite to adjacent **Sables d'Or** beach. Here, the **Waïmea Surf Shop** (tel. 59 03 81 18) rents mountain bikes (100F per day), wetsuits (50F per day), and surfboards (30F per hr., 70F per 4 hr., 100F per 8 hr., 360F per week, deposit 500F). (Open daily 9:30am-noon and 2-7:30pm.) Farther north lie the beaches of **Les Corsaires** and **Les Cavaliers.**

All the beaches are within walking distance of the hostel and Cinq Cantons and are accessible by the blue **Navettes des Plages** shuttles with surf scenes on the side, which run between Biarritz and La Barre. Part of the STAB system, the *navettes* depart 12 times per day (July-Aug. Mon.-Fri. 7:23am-7:52pm, Sun. 9am-7:35pm; 6.50F).

Biarritz

Strolling in Biarritz in the late evening, as Jaguars and Mercedes prowl narrow streets and the sounds of crashing waves compete with the echolalia of music, laughter, and clinking silverware, makes you feel you've just walked into the pages of *The Great Gatsby.* You have. Off-season, however, the town is a mere shadow of its summer self. With only one open casino, a chilly Atlantic surf, and far fewer fireworks and festivals, Biarritz sinks into hibernation. With the first blossoms of blue and pink hortensia, however, the garden boulevards and promenades regain their postcard splendor. The warm waves buttering a yellow *croissant* of soft, sandy beach make up for a winter of misplaced suns and a millenium of awful puns. You will probably want to stay for a while, as Biarritz (pop. 25,000), ritzy resort ambiance aside, *is* accessible to budget travelers. The town where Napoleon III, Bismarck, and Queen Victoria summered has now acquired cheap snack bars, reasonable hotels, and even California-style surf shops.

Orientation and Practical Information

Getting to Biarritz is not as easy as it was in the grand old days when luxury trains ended their journeys in the now-deserted station. Today, trains run through **Biarritz-la-Négresse,** 3km out of town. To get to the center, take blue bus #2, which travels to Bayonne via Biarritz and Anglet (6:30am-8pm every 20-40 min.). As many Paris-Hendaye trains don't stop in Biarritz, get off in Bayonne and take a bus to downtown Biarritz. Red bus #1 runs regularly from Bayonne to the Biarritz Hôtel de Ville (daily 6:35am-11:20pm; in off-season Mon.-Sat. 6:35am-8:45pm). Bus #2 leaves from the Bayonne train station (Mon.-Sat. 6:25am-8:10pm). All buses cost 6.50F.

Tourist Office: Javalquinto, pl. d'Ixelles (tel. 59 24 20 24), off av. Edouard VII. The extraordinarily gregarious staff dispenses free map and loads of brochures. Be sure to get *Biarritz Service.* They'll track down a room or a campsite for you, but there's no guarantee you can afford it. Cheap ones go fast. Open Mon.-Sat. 9am-7:30pm, Sun. 10am-12:30pm; Sept. 16-June 14 Mon.-Fri. 9am-12:30pm and 2:15-6:15pm, Sat. 10am-12:30pm and 3-6pm.

Currency Exchange: The post office and most banks are open Mon.-Sat. **Change Plus,** rue Mazagran, in the heart of town. No commission, but rates probably lower. Do some checking. Open daily 10am-8pm. **Comptoir Bayonnais d'Or et de Change,** 3, av. Edouard VII. A class operation with good rates. Open daily 9am-8pm.

Post Office: (tel. 59 24 23 71), on rue de la Poste. **Poste Restante.** Open Mon.-Fri. 8:30am-7pm, Sat. 8:30am-noon. **Postal Code:** 64200.

Trains: Biarritz-la-Négresse station is 3km out of town (tel. 59 23 15 69), but you can ask all of your questions at the office at 13, av. Foch (tel. 59 24 00 94; open Mon.-Sat. 9am-noon and 2-6pm). Frequent 6.50F buses run to the station (take #2). To: Bayonne (11 per day, 10 min., 10F); Hendaye (11 per day, ½-hr., 22F); St-Jean-de-Luz (11 per day, ¼-hr., 11F); Bidart (7 per day, 5 min., 7F). Station office open 5:45am-midnight.

Buses: ATCRB (tel. 59 24 36 72), on rue Joseph Petit, in the same building as the tourist office. To St-Jean-de-Luz (7 per day, ½-hr., 12.60F), with ill-timed connections to Hendaye (45-60 min. wait, 23F). In July and August, half-day excursions to La Rhune (80F), St-Jean-Pied-de-Port (90F), and other regions in southeast France. Full-day excursions to the Iraty Forest and the Kakvetta Gorge (135F), Gavarnie (140F), and St-Sebastian (110F).

Car Rental: At the train station (tel. 59 23 58 97). Open 6am-11pm. **Avis,** 25, av. Edouard VII (tel. 59 24 33 44). Opel Corsa 260F per day plus 2.78F per km and gas (ouch!). Open Mon.-Sat. 8am-noon and 2-7pm.

Bike Rental: SOBILO, 24, rue Peyroloubilh (tel. 59 23 39 52). Bikes 35F per day, mountain bikes 45F per day, mopeds 80F per day, deposit 1000F plus ID. English spoken. Reservations accepted. Open daily 9am-7pm; Oct.-May Mon.-Sat. 9am-7pm.

Surfboard Rental: Plums, 5, pl. Clemenceau (tel. 59 24 08 24). 50F per ½-day, 90F per day. Wetsuit 40F per ½-day, 60F per day. Open daily 9:30am-1pm and 3-8pm.

English Bookstore: Bookstore, on rue Gardère at av. Edouard VII. An elegant shop with a small selection of English books. Open Mon.-Sat. 9:15am-12:45pm and 3-7:30pm. Also try the rack of cheesy airport novels at **Maison de la Presse,** av. Edouard VII, across from the Hôtel de Ville. Open Mon.-Sat. 8am-12:45pm and 2-7:30pm, Sun. 9:30am-12:30pm.

Student Information Center: Hôtel de Ville, av. Edouard VII (tel. 59 24 52 50). About as helpful as OCS, but give them a try for job placement or information for women and families. Look on the board on the right as you enter. Open Mon.-Thurs. 8:30am-12:30pm and 2-6pm, Fri. 8:30am-12:30pm and 2-5pm.

Laundromat: 5, rue du Port-Vieux, toward the beach. Wash, dry, and soap 34F. Open 9am-10pm. Another at 4, av. Jaulerry, across from the post office. Wash 24F, dry 2F. 2F and 10F coins. Open daily 7am-10pm.

Public Showers: rue d'Alsace. 10F. Open Wed.-Thurs. 3:30-7pm, Sat. 8:30am-12:30pm and 3:30-7pm, Sun. 8:30am-12:30pm.

Hospital: av. Jacques Loëb (tel. 59 63 50 50).

Medical Emergency: SAMU, tel. 59 63 33 33.

Police: rue Louis-Barthou (tel. 59 24 68 24), opposite the tourist office. **Emergency,** tel. 17.

Accommodations and Camping

Hotels in Biarritz have enough stars to start a small galaxy; bargains, however, do exist. They're spread all over town, some even in excellent locations. Write a month or two ahead for a space in July or August. Otherwise, arrive early and enlist the help of the tourist office to find a room and find some others to split the cost. You might try commuting from Anglet's hostel or Bayonne.

Hôtel Barnetche, 5bis, rue Floquet (tel. 59 24 22 25). Take rue du Helder from pl. Clemenceau. Helpful management. Rooms from 140F. Obligatory breakfast 24F. In summer 12-bed dorms 65F per person, breakfast and shower included. *Demi-pension,* which includes breakfast and one other meal, preferred in the summer (160F). Telephone reservations not held after 2pm. Open May-Oct. Restaurant has an excellent 22F *menu.* (Open daily noon-2pm and 7:30-10pm.)

Hôtel Berhouet, 29, rue Gambetta (tel. 59 24 63 56). A little bit run-down, but clean and pleasant enough and in a good location. Often full. Singles and doubles from 90F, with shower from 130F. Hall shower included. Breakfast 18.50F. Expensive restaurant downstairs.

Hôtel le Dahu, 6, rue Jean Bart (tel. 59 24 36 38). Only seven rooms, but they're delightful and equipped with telephones and showers. Superman agement and excellent restaurant (see below). Singles and doubles 140-160F. Quads 230F. Breakfast 20F. *Demi-pension* deal worthwhile for 1 person (180F) or a pair (340F).

Hôtel Arokenia, 15, rue Gardague (tel. 59 24 23 44). Not the cleanest place, but a healthy *laissez-faire* attitude prevails. Girl-and-grandmother team will keep you charmed. Superb location near the beaches. Singles and doubles from 120F (number of people negotiable). Showers 10F. Breakfast 20F. Prices may rise after renovations.

Hôtel Atlantic, 10, rue du Port-Vieux (tel. 59 24 34 08). Clean rooms and phriendly pholks, but often full. Singles and doubles 140F. Triples and quads with shower and bathroom 220F. Showers 15F. Breakfast 20F. *Demi-pension* 335-430F per 2 people.

Camping: The coast crawls with 'em. **Municipal** (tel. 59 24 52 50), on av. Kennedy, quartier de la Négresse. Nearest the station and least expensive. 9.80F per person, 11.70F per tent, 4.70F per car. Open June-Sept. **Splendid** (tel. 59 23 01 29), on rue d'Harcet. 12F per person, 15F per tent, 4.50F per car. Tax 1F. Hot shower included. Open April-Sept. 9am-10pm. **Biarritz,** 28, rue d'Harcet (tel. 59 23 00 12). Cleverly named. 17F per person, 15F per tent, 5F per car. Shower included. Open April 29-Sept. 24 hrs. Try to arrive early in the morning. Splendid and Biarritz are closer to the beach and about 2km from the station. To get to all 3 campgrounds, take av. Kennedy from the station and follow the signs.

Food

Even places that look cheap probably aren't. The unwealthy and wise should check out the **marché municipal** on rue des Halles (open daily 7am-1pm). An evening picnic on the beach, with some cold *poulet basquais,* good Bordeaux red wine, bread slathered with *fromage de brebis,* and *gâteau Basque,* may be the best idea.

Le Dahu, 6, rue Jean Bart. Take av. Foch from pl. Clemenceau and veer left. Come here even if you're not staying at the hotel above. Nice atmosphere for the prices. 65F *menu* will buy soup or salad, meat or fish, and dessert or cheese. The 35F *plat du jour,* meat or fish with vegetable, is available Mon.-Fri. Open daily 12:30-2pm and 7:30-10pm.

Le Gascogne, 11, av. du Maréchal Foch. Pleasant indoor-outdoor atmosphere not far from the beach. 82F *menu* includes mussels or fruit, spaghetti, fish, and dessert. 55F express *menu* includes *plat du jour,* coffee, and dessert. Snacks include 28-35F salads, french fries, hamburgers, squid kebabs, and such. Open noon-2pm and 7-10pm for meals, all day for snacks.

Le Zoulou, 6, rue du Port-Vieux. Bright colors and lively atmosphere make the 65F *menu* taste even better. Seafood dishes 35-50F. A great place to hang out in the evening.

La Goulue, 3, rue Port-Vieux. Although this place won't win any ambiance awards, it's clean, cheerful, and one of the cheapest places around. Perfect for lunch or snacks. No *menu,* but good *à la carte* dishes (omelettes, cheeseburgers) around 30F. Wide choice of salads 20-35F. *Plats garnis* 38F. Drinks 10-26F. Freshly squeezed fruit juices 20F. Open 10am-midnight.

L'Amphore, 12, rue du Centre. Fantastic Greek specialties. Moussaka 45F. Open daily 7:30-10pm.

Hôtel-Restaurant Atlantic, 10, rue du Port-Vieux. An unexciting atmosphere, but great food in a good location. Mussels 35F. *Poulet basquais* 42F. Open May-Sept. daily noon-1:30pm and 7-9pm.

Epicerie Fauchon, 41bis, rue Mazagran. Part of the Paris-based chain. Not a restaurant, but a great place to pick up some delicious, homemade picnic food. Try the quiche (9F) and the peppery squares of Spanish potato omelette (10F). Obligatory cherry- or cream-filled *gâteau basque* (9.50F per slice). Open Mon.-Sat. 7am-8:30pm.

Sights and Entertainment

Dominated by two casinos, **Grande Plage** teems with bathers and surfers. Just north are **plage Miramar,** nestled against the base of the cliffs, and **Pointe St-Martin,** where bathers escape the crowds and peacefully repose *au naturel* (butt nekkid). Protected from the violent surf by jagged rock formations, the old **Port des Pêcheurs** harbors colorful small craft. The scuba diving school near the steps to the Plateau de l'Atalaye hosts scuba initiation excursions for 70F in July and August.

Jutting out into the sea from the **Plateau de l'Atalaye,** the **Rocher de la Vierge** provides spectacular views of the coastline stretching north to the lighthouse and southward along the **Plage des Basques,** located at the foot of still more thrilling cliffs. Check the tide schedule before venturing onto the rocks. At low tide, this beach boasts the cleanest water and the most open sand in Biarritz. Directly below, iron crosses embedded in the half-sunken rocks commemorate sailors lost at sea. Inland from the crags, the **Musée de la Mer** offers a simple display of North Atlantic marine life and fishing lore. The seals are fed at 10:30am and 5pm. (Open July-Aug. daily 9am-7pm; June 15-July 1 and Sept. 1-14 9am-noon and 2-7pm; Sept. 15-June 15 9am-noon and 2-6pm. Admission 22F, under 16 12F.) East of the Musée, the small **plage du Vieux Port** wedges between its cliff walls a calm bit of Atlantic quite a few families undaunted by the filthy water.

The *Programme des Fêtes,* published by the tourism and festival committee in Biarritz, lists the flurry of daily activities from July through October. Events range from firework displays, triathalons, and acrobatic water-skiing to conventional cocktail soirées and dancing. A series of frisbee, beach bum, and beach volleyball tournaments justify Biarritz's currently-touted and rather embarrassing nickname: "Californie de l'Europe." Look for the free art exhibits at the Hôtel du Palais.

Basque culture isn't totally absent from Biarritz, at least not when there are tourists to entertain. In July and August, *pelote* and folklore exhibitions take place in Parc Mazon Mondays at 9pm, matches of *cestapunta* (a complicated traditional game) at the jai alai arena Wednesday and Saturday at 9:30pm, and bullfight-parodying *courses de vaches* (cow races) in Parc Mazon Thursday at 9:15pm. Tickets start at 30F. Nights in July and August burble with the sounds of jet-setters and surf-demigods. Hang out at **Le Port des Pêcheurs** until midnight, when the *boîtes de nuit* start to burble. The **Brasilia Copacabana,** 24, av. Edouard VII (tel. 59 24 65 39), plays good music and doesn't admit burblers in beach wear. (Cover 30F.) Across the street, the **Blue Note** tunes up a bit later with live jazz. (Cover 60F.)

Near Biarritz: Côte Basque

Some of the most spectacular sand and scenery lie south of Biarritz along the Côte Basque. The frequent trains running to the Spanish border occasionally stop at the smaller towns on the way, as do ATCRB buses (about 10 per day to Hendaye, near the border; Mon.-Sat. 4 per day to San Sebastian, fewer Sun.) All leave from pl. d'Ixelles in Biarritz, outside the ATCRB office. Ask the train conductor to make an *arrêt facultatif* at Bidart or Guéthary. Otherwise the train may not stop.

Superb beaches await at **Bidart** ("crossroads" in Basque), a picturesque pipsqueak of a town perched atop a cliff. The hard sand promontory commands one of the highest vantage points on the Côte Basque. To the south, less rocky and more crowded beaches are graced with fine sand, fine waves, and fine bronzed youths clasping fine surfboards. Rue de la Grande Plage runs down the steep cliffs to the popular **Plage du Centre.** The **tourist office,** rue de la Grande Plage (tel. 59 54 93 85), will try to help you find a room in July and August, when most of the hotels are booked solid. Make reservations in April. (Open Mon.-Sat. 9am-7pm, Sat. 9am-noon and 2-7pm, Sun. 9am-noon; in off-season Mon.-Sat. 9am-noon.) The **post office** is nearby on pl. Sauveur Atchoarena (open Mon.-Fri. 9am-noon and 2-5pm, Sat. 9am-noon); the **postal code** is 64210.

There are 10 one-star hotels in Bidart; beware those with two-star prices. **Hôtel Itsas-Mendia,** rue de la Grande Plage (tel. 59 54 90 23), offers the best rooms. (Singles and doubles from 135F, showers included). The restaurant downstairs serves a 70F *menu.* In the center of town, **Hôtel Fronton** (tel. 59 54 90 63) has pleasant rooms barraged by bopping-ball sounds from the *pelote* court next door and non-stop radio music from the town hall loudspeakers. (Rooms 90-135F. Shower included. Breakfast 20F. No phone reservations.) Campsites are plentiful, but make reservations. Try the two-star **La Plage** (tel. 59 54 92 69; open June 20-Sept.), off N10 (called rue de la Gare) near plage de l'Uhabia, or the nearby two-star **Le Parc** on rue Maurice-Pierre (tel. 59 26 54 71; 10.70F per person, 9.70F per tent, 5.45F per car; electricity 9F; open June-Sept. 7:30am-10pm).

Bidart lies on the Bayonne-Hendaye rail line with more than 10 trains per day to Biarritz and Bayonne in the north and 10 trains to St-Jean-de-Luz and Hendaye in the south. **ATCRB** buses from Biarritz also stop in Bidart on their way to St-

Jean-de-Luz (about 10 per day). For the center of town, get off at the stop marked *église.* The **train station,** on the other hand (open May-Sept. 6am-9:45pm) is a 15-minute walk to town. Take the small tree-shaded path to your right, cross a wooden bridge, and walk through the cornfield. Make a quick left on the main road, then a right on the street by Camping Ur-Onea. Make a right at the top of the hill, then a left on rue des Ecoles. Cross rue Nationale, then take rue de l'Eglise (by the church) up the hill to the central square.

St-Jean-de-Luz

Home to whalers from the 10th to the 16th century, St-Jean-de-Luz ("Donibane Lohitzun" in Basque) today contents itself with being the tuna capital of France and the touristic second city of the Pays Basque. No ugly stepsister to glitzier Biarritz, *néo-Basque* St-Jean has a pedestrian zone and port full of lovely whitewashed buildings with the traditional colored shutters and wooden beams.

Orientation and Practical Information

At the mouth of the Nivelle river, St-Jean-de-Luz lies a half-hour from Bayonne by train, 20km south of Biarritz, and only 8km from the Spanish border. **Place Louis XIV,** next to the port, is the center of town and the beginning of **rue Gambetta,** the crowded pedestrian artery. To get here from the train station, go up av. de Verdun and continue straight for three minutes until you see the tourist office, bus station, and *centre ville.*

Tourist Office: (tel. 59 26 03 16), on pl. Foch. Maps and information on events and excursions. Accommodations booking service. Open Mon.-Sat. 9am-12:30pm and 2-7:30pm, Sun. 10am-noon; Oct.-May Mon.-Sat. 9am-12:30pm and 2:30-6:30pm.

Currency Exchange: Change Plus, 32, rue Gambetta (tel. 59 51 03 43). As always, read the fine print. Open daily 9:30am-8pm. Banks are open Tues.-Sat.

Post Office: (tel. 59 26 01 95), on bd. Victor Hugo. **Telephones** and **currency exchange.** Open Mon.-Fri. 9am-6pm, Sat. 9am-noon. **Postal Code:** 64500.

Trains: (tel. 59 26 02 08), on av. de Verdun. To: Biarritz (11 per day, 11F); Bayonne (11 per day, 18F); Bidart (8 per day, 8F); Paris (5 per day, 350F); Guéthary (4 per day, 5F). Office open 5:40am-7:25am and 8:35-11:15pm.

Buses: pl. Foch, by the tourist office. **ATCRB** sends 12 buses per day to Biarritz (12.60F) and Bidart (9F). Also to: Bayonne (16.20F); Guéthary (5.40F); Hendaye (12.60F); St-Sebastian, Spain (19F). Excursion trips to St-Jean-Pied-de-Port, La Rhune, Lourdes, and Gavarnie (70-100F). Call 59 26 06 99 for reservations. Office open Mon.-Sat. 8am-noon and 1:30-6:30pm. Another private line, **Basque Bondissant,** 100, rue Gambetta (tel. 59 26 25 87 or 59 26 23 87), runs 4 buses per day to Ascain, Col de St-Ignace, and Sare. (Mon.-Sat., 30 min., 10F). Buses leave from opposite the Hôtel du Commerce by the train station. **Pullman Basque,** 33, rue Gambetta (tel. 59 26 03 37), also runs excursions into the interior (70-125F).

Bike and Moped Rental: Peugeot, 5-7, av. Labrouche (tel. 59 26 14 95), 1 block from the station. Bikes 43F per day, 235F per week, deposit 500F. Mopeds 80F per day, 370F per week, deposit 600F. Open Mon.-Sat. 9am-noon and 2-7pm.

Boat Excursions: Le Tourisme Basque, 100, rue Gambetta (tel. 59 26 25 87) or at the port in front of the Hôtel de Ville. Four-hr. fishing excursion, including equipment (100F). Two-hr. cruises along the Spanish coast (55F). Open July-Aug. daily 9am-6pm.

Hospital: route de Bayonne (tel. 59 51 45 45). **Polyclinique,** rue Biscarbidéa (tel. 59 26 21 41). 24-hr. emergency service.

Police: route de Bayonne (tel. 59 26 08 47). **Emergency,** tel. 17.

Accommodations, Camping, and Food

Hotels fill up rapidly in summer, and reservations might be hard to make. Most budget places save their rooms for regular, long-term guests. Arrive early, especially in August. You may have better luck commuting from Bayonne or Biarritz.

Hôtel Toki-Ona, 10, rue Marion Garat (tel. 59 26 11 54), 1 block from the station. Formal, immaculate, and usually full—but a good deal. Singles and doubles 110F. Triples 140F. Showers 10F. Breakfast 20F. Telephone reservations accepted. Open Easter-Sept.

Hôtel Bolivar, 18, rue Sopite (tel. 59 26 02 00), off bd. Thiers. Pretty rooms in the center of town. Doubles 120-240F. Breakfast 20F. Open June-Sept. Telephone reservations accepted.

Hôtel Kapa-Gorry, 9, rue Paul Gélos (tel. 59 26 04 93), a short walk out of town along the beach. Worth the effort, and might have room when the others are full. Doubles 150F. Large triples 200F. Showers 10F. Breakfast 20F. The name means "red hat" in Basque. Holden Caulfield did not stay here.

Hôtel de Verdun, 13, av. de Verdun (tel. 59 26 02 55), across from the station. Clean, simple rooms with agreeable management. Singles (1-2 people) 150-165F. Showers 10F. Breakfast 20F. Restaurant next door serves a 3-course 52F *menu.*

Camping: There are 14 sites in St-Jean-de-Luz proper and 13 more within 13km, most of them 3-star. Incredibly, most fill up; the tourist offices in Biarritz and St-Jean-de-Luz will try to find you a spot. **Camping Chibaou Berria,** chemin de Chibaou (tel. 59 26 11 94 or 59 26 21 90; 13 per person, 19F per tent and car; electricity 8.50F; open 8am-9pm), and **Camping de la Ferme** (tel. 59 26 34 26; 12F per person, 18F per tent and car, tax 1F) are all in Quartier Erromardie north of downtown. Take the ATCRB bus from pl. Maréchal Foch (*direction* "Biarritz", 7am-noon and 2-8pm every hr., 6.50F).

The Basque and Spanish specialties in St-Jean-de-Luz are the best north of the border, but cheap meals are harder than usual to find. **Crustacés Sardines Grillés,** at the corner of the covered market's *poissonerie* on bd. Victor Hugo, is a lively, laid-back place popular with everyone but the crustaceans. Eat tuna *pipérade* (43F) or *moules marinières* (25F) at the outdoor tables engulfed in a fish smell. (Open daily 11am-11pm.) **Restaurant Ramuntcho,** 24, rue Garat (tel. 59 26 03 89), serves a 68F *menu* with two plentiful entrees and dessert. Wash down a steaming heap of mussels with Corbières, the unusual red wine (16F per ½-bottle). (Open noon-2pm and 7-9:30pm.) Bustling **La Vieille Auberge,** 22, rue Tourasse, serves a popular 70F *menu* that also features dessert and two dishes. Choose from *moules marinières, soupe de poisson,* or *salade Luzienne* for the first course; Basque specialties such as *poulet basquais* with rice for the second. (Open May-Oct. daily noon-2pm and 7-11pm.) The **Pavillon de Jade,** av. de Verdun, across from the station, serves a 55F lunch *menu* and a 70F dinner *menu* of Vietnamese dishes. (Open daily noon-1:30pm and 7-9pm.) Plenty of food shops front bd. Victor Hugo and rue Gambetta; some are even open mid-day. The **market** on pl. des Halles is the place to shop (open daily 7am-1pm) before picnicking on one of the town's many small squares. **Chez Dodin,** av. Gambetta, scoops the best local ice cream in its 1960s style *salon de thé.* The purported champion in the *gâteaux basques* bakeoff is **Chez Etchebaster,** also on rue Gambetta (open Tues.-Sun.).

Sights and Entertainment

The museum in the **Maison Louis XIV** has been redone in an interesting 17th-century style, but the 25-minute guided tour is not worth the price. (Open June 8-Sept. 15 Mon.-Sat. 10:30am-noon and 3-6:30pm, Sun. 3-6:30pm. Admission 15F, students 12F.) Louis XIV stayed at this house, owned by the Lohobiague family, for 40 days in 1660, when the 22-year-old monarch came to St-Jean-de-Luz to sign the Treaty of the Pyrenees. The king stayed here again when he returned to marry Maria Teresa of Spain. In the nearby **Eglise Ste-Jean Baptiste,** a portal was ceremoniously sealed forever after the newlyweds exited the church—look to the right of the main entry. Check out the bilingual prayer books in French and Basque and notice the unusual wooden galleries, where men traditionally sat. (The women had the more comfortable seats in the nave.)

Blighted by an ugly concrete pavilion packed with snack bars and souvenir shops, the stretch of sand along **promenade Jacques Thibaud** remains festive until about midnight. Watch a volleyball match or rent a James Bondesque catamaran pedal-boat. (25F per ½-hr., 35F per hr.) Protected by dikes, St-Jean-de-Luz's beach and harbor form the best windsurfing area on the coast. Rent a board on the beach for 65F per hour (July-Aug.). The swimming here can be unpleasant as the Nive river dumps debris into the harbor, but it's far safer than along the rest of the coast. The summer season abounds with Basque festivals, bullfights, concerts, and the world cup of *cestapunta*. Ask the tourist office for the free guide, *St-Jean-de-Luz en Fêtes*. Tickets to *pelote* matches cost 30F and up. Matches are played Monday, Thursday, and Saturday evenings (at 5:30pm, 7:30pm, and 9:30pm) throughout the summer and well into September. Bullfight parodies involving clowning matadors, cows, and a swimming pool occur Wednesday at 9:30pm in the Erromardie Arena. The **Toro del Fuego,** complete with fireworks and manic dancing, ignites at about 10:30pm on Tuesdays and Sundays. The biggest annual festival is the **Fêtes de St-Jean,** which lasts for three days beginning on the weekend closest to St-Jean's Day (June 21). At the **Fêtes du Thon** (the Saturday closest to July 7), the whole town gathers around the harbor to eat tuna, toss confetti, and dance under fireworks. The **Nuit de la Sardine** is not a horror movie but an evening in mid-July at the Campos-Beri jai alai stadium that features up to 2000 participants, one orchestra, lots of fireworks and Basque singers, and one giant sardine (20F).

Near St-Jean-de-Luz

Ten km southeast of St-Jean-de-Luz lies miniscule **Col de St-Ignace,** which isn't a town so much as a welcoming center for **La Rhune,** the most spectacular viewpoint in the Basque Country. Stop in Col de St-Ignace only to board the wooden, two-car cog-train that crawls laboriously up the mountainside to La Rhune. At each turn you will be confronted with dazzling views of plunging forests and the quilted farmland below. The lucky might see herds of wild Basque ponies ("pottok" horses) and a daring mountain biker (El Becca) navigating the rocks. At La Rhune, 900m above sea-level (it can be chilly, even in July), a fabulous panorama of the ocean, the Forêt des Landes, and the Basque Pyrenees greets those who checked the weather forecast. You will see nothing on a misty day.

La Rhune lies on the Spanish side of the French-Spanish border, and shop-owners and workers converse in both French and Spanish. Because of its duty-free status, the shops here overflow with liquor bottles at reduced prices. It's best not to indulge if you're planning to descend the mountain by foot. The only way to return directly to Col de St-Ignace is to follow the train tracks—not too dangerous, as the train rumbles along not much faster than you will. Alternatively, take the well-marked path to the left of the tracks down to Ascain, and walk the tortuous 3km on D4 back to Col de St-Ignace (1-1½ hr.). You might be able to get a ride from hikers returning to their cars at the foot of the path. From July through September, the two trains ascend and descend daily every half-hour 9am to noon and 1:30 to 5:30pm. From May through June and October through November 15, trains depart on Sunday only at 10am and 3pm. Purchase tickets from the **VFDM** office (tel. 59 54 20 26) at the end of the tracks in Col de St-Ignace (22F, round-trip 40F). In summer, expect an hour-long wait. **Le Basque Bondissant** (tel. 59 26 25 87 or 59 26 23 87) runs four buses from St-Jean-de-Luz to the departure point, one of which is too late in the evening to ascend to La Rhune (one way 10F).

Buses stopping in Col de St-Ignace from St-Jean-de-Luz continue 3km farther down D4 to the tiny village of **Sare** (10 min., 3F). The **tourist office** in the *mairie* in pl. de Sare (tel. 59 54 20 14) will help you find a room, a difficult task in August. (Open Mon.-Fri. 9:30am-12:30pm and 2:30-6:30pm.) Try **Hôtel de la Poste,** pl. de Sare (tel. 59 54 20 06). Nice rooms with firm mattresses go for 120F, with shower 150F. (Showers 12F. Breakfast 18F.) Although reservations are recommended in August, one of Sare's three campgrounds usually has a spot. **Camping de la Petite Rhune,** 2km from town (tel. 59 54 23 97), has three stars, a tennis court, and 100 spaces. (9F per person, 11F per site, 4.50F per car. Hot showers included. Open June-Sept. 8am-10pm.) **Camping Goyenetche,** on D306, route des Grottes (tel. 59 54 21 71), is open April to September and has cheaper rates (32F per 2 people).

The terrace of **Restaurant Mendi-Bichta** overlooks rolling Basque countryside. The 55F *menu,* which includes *pipérade* and *gâteau basque,* is as symphonic as the view. **Hôtel-Restaurant Lastiry,** next to Hôtel de la Poste in pl. de Sare (tel. 59 54 20 07), has a cozy, oak-beamed dining room and a three-course 55F *menu.* (Open daily noon-2pm and 7-8:30pm.) The **Hôtel de la Poste** also whips up a 48F *menu* and 35F omelettes. (Open May-Nov. daily noon-2pm and 7-10pm. The *gâteaux basques* sold in the square are as mouthwatering as they are cheap (10F). While you're waiting for the bus to St-Jean-de-Luz, visit the traditional cemetery in the church by the tourist office. On September 13, Sare paints itself red for a 24-hour *fête* featuring musicians and merrymaking in the streets, food and drink, and a large ball named Hank. Should you be in Sare in October, ask the tourist office about opportunities to watch a *chasse à la palombe,* a traditional ring-dove hunt. The fascinating **Fête de la Palombe,** held on a Sunday in mid-October, is still dedicated to solemn ritual rather than antics for tourists. It begins in the morning, with a mass in the church and a parade of ring-dove hunters in full regalia.

St-Jean-Pied-de-Port

Nestled in the Pyrenees along the trout-filled Nive, St-Jean-Pied-de-Port marks one of the few passages through the Pyrenees, at the *col de Roncevaux* of *Song of Roland* fame. Narrow, cobblestone **rue de la Citadelle** climbs up through the *haute ville* to the old fortress, while **rue d'Espagne** spans the calm Nive and stretches lazily toward Spain, only 5 miles away. Rounded by centuries of the pilgrims' footsteps on their way to Santiago de Compostela (St-Jacques de Compostelle), these cobblestones are still trodden by modern pilgrims, recognizable by the *coquille St-Jacques* (scallop shell) on their clothing. Although St-Jean-Pied-de-Port seems to have become everyone's favorite daytrip, this ancient capital of the inland Pays Basque, a pleasure in itself, also gives access to some less-trodden territory.

Orientation and Practical Information

St-Jean-Pied-de-Port is 8km from the Spanish border, 55m from Bayonne, and 76km from the Navarese capital and iced-chocolate haven Pamplona. The only rail access to St-Jean-Pied-de-Port is a wonderful one-hour train ride through the mountains from Bayonne (6 per day, 38F). The picturesque *haute ville* spreads behind the ramparts below the *citadelle.* The modern *basse ville,* of no particular interest unless you want to take a dip in the municipal swimming pool on rue de Ste-Eulalie (10F), lies even farther down.

Tourist Office: 14, pl. Charles de Gaulle (tel. 59 37 03 57), in the center outside the old city walls. Free maps. Good walking and hiking itineraries (15F). Ask for hiking information on the nearby Forêt d'Iraty. Pick up a free copy of *Programme des Festivités.* They won't book you a room but know which hotels have vacancies. Open July-Aug. daily 9am-12:30pm and 2-7pm; in off-season Mon.-Fri. 9am-noon and 2-5:30pm, Sat. 10am-noon.

Currency Exchange: Crédit Agricole, rue de la Poste. Commission 20F. Open Mon.-Fri. 9am-12:15pm and 1:45-5pm. On Sat. try **La Caisse d'Epargne,** route d'Uhart.

Post Office: rue de la Poste. **Telephones.** Open Mon.-Fri. 9am-noon and 2-5pm, Sat. 9am-noon. **Postal Code:** 64220.

Trains: av. Renaud (tel. 59 37 02 00). To Bayonne (4-6 per day, 1¼ hr., 38F). The friendly station master may let you leave your pack here free of charge. Station open 5:30am-10pm.

Bike Rental: Chez Steunou (tel. 59 37 25 45), in pl. du Marché in the center near the tourist office. 40F per day, deposit 500F and ID. Open daily 8am-7:30pm. **Garazi Cycles** (tel. 59 37 21 79), in pl. St-Laurent. Good mountain bikes 80F per day, deposit 500F.

Hospital: Fondation Luro, Ispoure (tel. 59 37 00 55). For taxi-ambulance, call 59 37 05 70 or 59 37 05 00.

Police: (tel. 59 37 00 36), on rue d'Ugagne. **Emergency,** tel. 17.

Accommodations and Food

Hotels are few and prices high. **Hôtel Ramuntcho,** above the old city walls and porte de France (tel. 59 37 03 91), has rooms with pleasant views and a terrace to stretch out on. (Singles and doubles 125-165F. Showers included. Breakfast 22F.) The owner runs an excellent restaurant with a 65F *menu.* (Room, breakfast, and a meal 175F.) Recently remodeled **Hôtel Itzalpea,** pl. du Trinquet (tel. 59 37 03 66), outside and just opposite the old walls, has clean and cheerful rooms. Tell the proprietors if you plan to leave early in the morning so they can chain Ozzie, the prowling watchdog. (Singles and doubles with telephone 100F, with shower 120F. Triples and quads with shower 200F.) **Hôtel des Remparts** (tel. 59 37 13 79), has rooms from 145F. Breakfast costs 19F. (Open April-Oct. daily, Nov.-Mar. Mon.-Fri.) Ask at the tourist office for a list of *chambres d'hôte,* rooms in private homes (80-90F). St-Jean-Pied-de-Port has a nice two-star **Camping Municipal** (tel. 59 37 00 92), on the Nive riverbank, a *pelote*'s throw from the municipal *fronton;* cross the bridge from the tourist office and continue straight. (9F per person, 5F per tent.) **Camping Bidegainia** (tel. 59 37 03 75 or 59 37 09 09) 1km away from St-Jean-Pied-de-Port, is a popular two-star site with trout-fishing. (5F per person, 6F per tent. Showers 3F. Open April-Aug. daily 7am-11pm.) Four-star **Europ' Camping** (tel. 59 37 12 78), 1.5km from St-Jean on D918 to Bayonne, has a restaurant, free pool, and sauna. (22F per person, 30F per tent and car. Electricity 12F. Showers included. Open Easter-Oct. 8am-10pm.) All campgrounds are usually full from July 15 to August 15. Make reservations.

Fresh rainbow trout—often sreved with head, eyes, and tail—star in the superb collection of Basque specialties prepared in St-Jean. **La Vieille Auberge** (also known as **"Chez Dédé"**), outside the city walls on rue de France, serves a delicious four-course 55F *menu estival* (summer menu) including *truite meuniére* and *poulet basquais,* wine, coffee, and service. (Pizzas 35F. *Plat du jour* 35F. Open daily 9am-2am.)**Hôtel Itzalpea's** restaurant assembles a generous 58F *menu* with soup, trout, a choice of meats, and dessert. (Open daily noon-2pm and 7-9pm.) The **Restaurant Hillion,** on pl. du Trinquet as you enter the *haute ville* from the train station, cooks a 40F *menu* that includes *crudités* and *gâteau basque,* with *truite de pays, poulet basquais,* or *pipérade* (an omelette with tomatoes and ham) as the main course. It also serves bigger 60F and 75F *menus.* (Open daily noon-2:30pm and 7:30-10pm.) Soft ice cream fans should not miss the *glace maison* at the **Pâtisserie Barbier Millox,** 17, rue d'Espagne (generous single cone 6F, double cone 11F) Farmers bring their Ardigazna (tangy, dry cheese made from sheep's milk) and other products to the Monday **market.**

Sights and Entertainment

St-Jean's streets and picture-book location are thc main attractions. The ancient *haute ville,* bounded by **Porte d'Espagne** and **Porte St-Jacques,** consists of one narrow street, rue de la Citadelle, bordered by houses made from the dark red stone of the region. Along the Nive, at the bottom of rue de la Citadelle, stands **Eglise Notre-Dame-du-Bout-du-Pont,** a church that once doubled as a fortress (open daily 7am-9pm). Vauban fortified the city in 1685, and rue de la Citadelle serves as a ramp up to his fortress. The public can no longer go inside the steep walls. From the top of the arch, to the left as you face the valley, a postern staircase of 269 steps descends to the Porte de l'Echangette behind the church near the Nive. Farther down rue de la Citadelle at #41, the 13th-century **Prison des Evêques** opens its vaulted underground cell to gawkers. (Open 10am-12:30pm and 2-7pm. Admission 5F.) A pleasant and wooded walk leads from the church along the Nive to the **Pont Romain** (about 2km). The area around the Roman bridge on allées d'Eyheraberry is ideal for picnics. If you wish to venture farther than the Pont Romain, call the **Foyer Rural Haïzoblian**, rue Ste-Eulalie (tel. 59 37 22 27). The guides will help you plan an itinerary or take you on their organized hike. The foyer also rents horses and bikes. (Telephone before 8am or after 8pm.)

In the summer, a different activity enlivens St-Jean every night. *Bals* (street dances) and concerts frequently offer free entertainment, and *cours de vaches* (mock bullfights), Basque choirs, and daily *pelote* matches add local color. Admission to the *fronton* is 30F, but you can easily watch a match from the fence. For schedule information, check at the tourist office or listen to the loudspeakers. Each weekend one of the region's villages holds a festival that includes public dancing until 3am on Saturday and Sunday. Around August 15, St-Jean-Pied-de-Port celebrates its patron, St-John the Baptist, with fireworks, late-night revelry, and local edibles.

Near St-Jean-Pied-de-Port

Sturdy pilgrims still trek up into the mountains along the trail of Santiago de Compostela (St-Jacques de Compostelle) which stretches from Paris to the Atlantic coast of Spain. Hitchhiking is difficult and dangerous on the narrow, winding roads. Hiking and biking require calves the size of Warren Beatty's ego. Pick up the *Ensemble de Circuits de Randonnées dans et autour de St-Jean-Pied-de-Port* from the St-Jean tourist office (15F). This excellent publication indicates five marked trails which leave from the office and take one to five and a half hours. Superb yet easy hiking awaits in the **Forêt d'Iraty**, 28km southeast of St-Jean-Pied-de-Port along D18. Unfortunately, no public transportation runs to this forested valley near the Spanish border. The tourist office in St-Jean has pamphlets and guides that map out 5 to 28km excursions in the surrounding mountains and villages, including one path leading to the Forêt d'Iraty. These excursions may be more realistic alternatives for those without wheels since they begin in St-Jean-Pied-de-Port.

Serious hikers should buy a *Carte de Randonnées, 1/50,000 Pays Basque Est* (47F), the most complete and detailed hiking map for the Basque Pyrenees. Travel shelters are indicated on the GR10 and GR65, longer paths fanning out of St-Jean-Pied-de-Port. Once in the **Pointe d'Iraty**, consider taking the 9km **Larreluche** trail, which ascends a breathtaking slope of green mountains sometimes topped by *blondes d'Aquitaine* (cows) or pottok horses (Basque ponies) let loose for the summer. Located at the end of most of the trails, **Chalet Pedro** and its 90F *menu* will remind you always to bring a picnic. If you don't have your own provisions, try their polychrome trout (30F) from the stream behind the restaurant. The *Randonnées Pyrénées* guide, free at tourist offices, lists the *gîtes d'étape* indicated on the *Carte Randonnée*. If you prefer to see the Pyrenees on four legs, reserve a day ahead for a guided trail ride (60F per hour) organized by the **Centre Equestre** (tel. 59 28 51 29) in July and August. In winter, the trails in the Forêt d'Iraty are frequented by cross-country skiers. Red signs posted on trees are for skiers only; ignore the warning *access interdit* if you are there in summer.

Gascony (Gascogne)

Though Gascony contains the most visited city in France, Lourdes, the essence of the region lies in its densely misted mountains, which climax in the **Pique du Vignemale** (3298m). In 1967, the French government voted to protect the habitat of the renowned *isards* (mountain antelopes) by designating a strip of the Pyrenees south of Pau as the **Parc National des Pyrenees.** One of only five national parks, the antelope reserve also shelters eagles, vultures, and the few remaining *ours des Pyrénées* (a small brown bear).

Trains from Toulouse in the west and Bordeaux in the east serve the larger cities, and an excellent bus system covers the mountainous backcountry where the best hiking bases are found. Many of the buses are run by the SNCF, and accept Eurail and other passes. Be sure to coordinate the train and bus schedules beforehand; connections can be made only infrequently.

Mountain accommodations are inexpensive. The **Club Alpin Français (CAF),** the **Comité des Sentiers de Grande Randonnée,** and the **Parc National** all maintain simple *gîtes* along major trails, and shepherds' cabins are available in summer along wilder routes. Reservations are usually not necessary, but you may want to write to the Parc National offices in Cauterets or Gavarnie. The **Grande Randonnée** No. 10 (GR10) connects the Atlantic to the Mediterranean, winding through some of the chain's most splendid scenery. If you plan to follow any part of this, pick up the guide *GR10* (51F) in a bookstore. It provides good trail directions and up-to-date listings of refuges along the route. Also essential is at least one of the four detailed purple 1:25,000 maps of the Parc National (47F), also available in bookstores.

To most, Gascony also means excellent eating. Henri IV, the *bon roi* who glorified good eating and temporarily calmed the religious wars with the Edict of Nantes, was born in Pau. Gascony still produces the best *foie gras* and goose and duck *pâtés* in the south. Abundant fresh fish and superb rosé wines, the *vins de Béarn,* complete regional feasts. Local farmers use cow and sheep milk to make various *fromages des Pyrénées,* which range in flavor from mild to sadistically strong.

Hiking

Exercise caution. Trails may be well traveled, but you'll still be hours away from emergency services in town. Watch out for sliding rocks. Avoid wearing sneakers on the often-slippery trails, and carry only the bare essentials—map, compass, army knife, trail food, sweater, matches, first-aid kit—in your pack. Bring a container filled with water, as many sources in the hills contain *giardia,* a serious parasitic disease transmitted by sheep. **Never** drink the mountain water from its source. Camping is allowed only when you are more than an hour from a refuge and/or a road. Travel with somebody, leave a copy of your itinerary with the local CAF or police station, and check the local weather report before you leave. Storms often rush through the valleys with alarming swiftness. Once on a trail, stick to it. On a first trip, join a guided hike. Contact the Club Alpin Français office in Pau for details, or a Parc National office in St-Lary, Luz St-Sauveur, Gavarnie, Cauterets, Anens-Marsous, Gabas, or Bedous. Mountain boots, ice picks, and clamps can be rented in Pau or in Cauterets and Gavarnie, both more convenient bases.

Pau

A graceful city of gardens set against the Pyrenees, Pau (pop. 85,000) prides itself on having produced two kings. Henry IV was born in the château here and, during his reign as King of France, kept Béarn an independent country and Pau its capital. Under Henry's son Louis XIII, however, Béarn was annexed to the kingdom of France and reduced to the provincial status. Another *Palois*, J.B. Bernadotte, took off from bourgeois origins to become King of Sweden in the early 19th century. Simultaneously, Pau's decline was reversed, and the city became a popular winter gathering place for the English well-to-do. When Queen Victoria took her 1889 winter holiday in Biarritz instead, Pau once again slipped out of the international limelight. Vestiges of the town's old glory remain: the château, the boulevards, and the extensive resort facilities created for the English colony. Never lacking in concerts and cultural events, Pau makes a good place to relax, socialize, and stock up on necessities before trekking into the lonely mountain heights.

Orientation and Practical Information

Pau lies 195km and 2½ hours by train west of Toulouse. A steep uphill walk separates the train station from the center, but you and your bicycle can take the free funicular across the street, which climbs to bd. des Pyrénées every five minutes. Even if it looks closed, it's probably open. Wait a few minutes until someone comes; get on if the gate is open. (Runs Mon.-Sat. 7am-9:40pm, Sun. 1:30-9pm.)

Tourist Office: (tel. 59 27 27 08), next to the Hôtel de Ville in pl. Royale. Well-equipped office distributes cool 3-D maps. Guided tours of the city Tues., Thurs., and Sat. (1½ hr., 25F, under 18 15F). Free accommodations service. Pick up a free copy of *Les Fêtes du Béarn*, a calendar of the region's summer activities. Open daily 9am-6:30pm; Sept.-June Mon.-Sat. 9am-noon and 2-6pm, Sun. 10am-1pm and 2-5pm. **Service des Gîtes Ruraux**, 124, bd. Tourasse (tel. 59 80 19 13), in the Cité Administrative, gives advice on trails and mountain lodgings. English spoken. Open Mon.-Fri. 9am-12:30pm and 2-5pm.

Budget Travel: Aquitaine Tourisme, 84, rue Emile Guichenné (tel. 59 27 88 82). BIJ/Eurotrain tickets. Open Mon.-Fri. 9am-7pm, Sat. 9am-noon.

Post Office: (tel. 59 27 76 89), on cours Bosquet at rue Gambetta. **Currency exchange** and **telephones.** Open Mon.-Fri. 8am-6:30pm, Sat. 8am-noon. **Postal Code: 64000.**

Currency Exchange: Crédit Agricole, 2, bd. Alsace-Lorrain, at the intersection with av. Edouard VII. Open Mon.-Fri. 9am-4:30pm, Sat. 9am-4pm. Be careful: no Sun. exchange in town.

Trains: (tel. 59 30 50 50), on av. Gaston Lacoste at the base of the hill dominated by the château. To: Bayonne (6 per day, 1¼ hr., 64F); Biarritz (6 per day, 1½ hr., 69F); Bordeaux (6 per day, 128F); Lourdes (14 per day, ½-hr., 30F); Nice (3 per day, 360F); Paris (4 per day, 342F); Toulouse (7 per day, 118F). Open daily 5am-11pm. Information desk open in summer Mon.-Sat. 9am-6:25pm. Luggage storage open 8am-8pm.

Buses: CITRAM—Courriers des Basses Pyrénées, 30, Palais des Pyrénées, rue Gachet (tel. 59 27 22 22). To: Oloron-Ste-Marie. (2 per day) and Aubisque via Laruns (4 per day, 34F). Excursions to Gavarnie and Spain. Open June-Sept. Mon.-Fri. 8:30am-12:15pm and 2-6:15pm, Sat. 8:30am-12:15pm; Oct.-May Mon.-Fri. 8:30am-12:15pm and 2-6:15pm. Buses leave from pl. Clemenceau and the base of the funicular. **Société TPR**, 2, pl. Clemenceau (tel. 59 27 45 98). Regularly to Lourdes and Biarritz. Expensive excursions (95-130F). **STAP** (tel. 59 27 69 78), on rue Gachet. Information on city buses. Tickets 5F, *carnet* of 10 24F. Open Mon.-Fri. 8:50am-noon and 2-5:30pm; Sept.-June Mon.-Fri. 8:50am-noon and 2-5:30pm, Sat. 8:50am-noon.

Taxis: pl. Clemenceau (tel. 59 02 22 22).

Bike and Hiking Equipment Rental: Romano Sport, 41, av. Général de Gaulle (tel. 59 80 21 31). They've got it all, from boots to clamps. Bikes 50F per ½-day, 100F per day. Hiking boots 22-27F per day. Open Mon.-Sat. 9am-noon and 2-7pm.

Hiking Information: Club Alpin Français (CAF), 5, rue René Fournet (tel. 59 27 71 81). Open Mon.-Wed. and Fri. 5-7pm, Thurs. 5-8pm.

Womens Center: Maison des Femmes, 12, rue René Fournet (tel. 59 82 82 54). Open Sun.-Tues. and Thurs.-Fri. 2-5pm.

Laundromat: Lavo Self, 11, rue Castetnau (tel. 59 83 77 85). For 28F, they'll do it. Open Mon.-Fri. 8:30am-noon and 2-7pm; Sept.-June Mon.-Fri. 8:30am-noon and 2-7pm, Sat. 8:30am-noon and 2-5pm. **Lavomatique Foirail,** 3, rue de Bordeu. Wash 12F, dry 5F. No 1F coins. Open daily 7am-10pm.

Medical Assistance: Hospital, 145, av. de Buros (tel. 59 02 82 70). **SAMU,** tel. 59 27 15 15.

Police: (tel. 59 27 94 06), on rue O'quin. **Emergency,** tel. 17.

Accommodations and Camping

A number of inexpensive hotels dot the busy downtown area. A good 20-minute walk from the station (no buses), the hostel is by far the best deal.

Auberge de Jeunesse/Foyer des Jeunes Travailleurs (IYHF), 30, rue Michel Hounau (tel. 59 30 45 77). From the station, take the *funiculaire* and cross pl. Royale to rue St-Louis. Follow rue St-Louis to rue Maréchal Joffre and turn right. Walk about 10 min. along this main drag, which becomes rue Maréchal Foch and then cours Bosquet. Turn left onto rue E. Garet, and continue to the rue Michel Hounau, again on the left. A friendly place with a bit of luxury at low prices. Single rooms, hot showers in every 2nd-floor room, laundromat, kitchens, a lively bar and self-service cafeteria, and a game room. Singles for those with a hostel card and/or under 25, 50F; otherwise 69F. Breakfast included. Good 4-course meals served Mon.-Fri. 11:45am-1:15pm and 7-8:15pm, Sat. 11:45am-1:15pm (34F). Rooms almost always available June-Sept. Call ahead Oct.-June.

University Housing: CROUS, (tel. 59 02 88 46, reservations 59 02 73 35), on av. Poplanski at the Cité Universitaire Gaston Phébus. Take bus #4 from *centre ville.* Open 9am-11:30am and 2-6:30pm. Rooms around 30F with student ID. Available July-Sept. only.

Hôtel de la Pomme d'Or, 11, rue Maréchal Foch (tel. 59 27 78 48), on the main boulevard off pl. Clemenceau. Friendly owners and a homey atmosphere. One single on the street 60F. Other singles 75F, with shower 90F. Doubles 85F, with shower 110F. Quads 130F, with shower 170F. Breakfast 18F.

Hôtel Le Béarn, 5, rue Maréchal Joffre (tel. 59 27 52 50), on the side street opposite Cinéma Béarn. Wonderful rooms, a well-kept dining room, and an elevator. Singles and doubles 75F, with shower 110-120F. Breakfast 15F. Shower 10F.

Hôtel Ossau, 3, rue Alfred de Lassence (tel. 59 27 07 88), off rue Louis Barthou. Smiling management and a view of the mountains. Singles 85-95F. Doubles 90-105F. Breakfast 18F.

Camping: Camping Municipal de la Plaine des Sports et des Loisirs (tel. 59 02 30 49), a 6km trek from the station. Take bus #A4. Three stars. 43F per 2 people. Open April-Nov. **Camping du Coy** (tel. 59 27 23 11) in Bizanos, a 10-min. walk east of the train station. Two stars. Open daily 8am-10pm.

Food

Rue Léon Daran and other streets leading to the university have plenty of inexpensive restaurants, but in Pau a little extravagance may be justified. The region that brought you Béarnaise sauce has many other specialties: salmon, pike, *oie* (goose), *canard* (duck), and the *assiette béarnaise,* a platter which usually includes gizzards, duck hearts, and baby asparagus. Elegant little restaurants serving regional dishes fill the side streets around the château. **Epicerie de Nuit,** 21, rue Montpensier, will satisfy late-night grocery cravings. (Open Sun.-Wed. 10pm-3am; Thurs.-Sat. 10pm-4am.)

Le Panache, 8, rue Adoue, next to St-Martin. A feast worthy of Henry IV with appropriate decor. 69F *menu.* Try the *aiguillettes de canard.* Open daily noon-2pm and 7-11pm.

Pappadum, 9, imp. Honset, off rue Henri IV. An Indian place. Try the scrumptious *beignets de légumes* (28F) or the curries (40-50F). Open daily noon-1:30pm and 7-10pm.

Chez Maman, 6, rue du Château. A cute, lively place with good *crêpes* (10-42F). Filling 45F *menu.* Salads 20-49F. Open daily noon-2pm and 7-10:30pm.

Chez Olive, 9, rue du Château. Friendly and unpretentious serving simple but well prepared food. Tasty 85F *menu;* an even better 120F one. Try the *bouchées aux fruits de mer* (seafood in a puff pastry) and *truite pochée au beurre blanc* (poached trout). Open Mon. 7-10pm, Tues.-Sat. noon-1:30pm and 7-10pm.

El Mesón, 40, rue Maréchal Joffre. Spicy *bar à tapas* (10-28F) which makes a good meal. Also a lively night spot. Not much English or French spoken. Open daily 10:30am-3am.

Sights and Entertainment

On a clear day the view from bd. des Pyrénées stretches some 50km over the vineyards and hills to the distant, jagged heights. An exceptionally beautiful French garden blooms below the walkway; adjoining the boulevard is Parc Beaumont, filled with bright flowers, a lake, and a small waterfall.

A rambling structure with six square towers, the château overlooks the river from the highest point in Pau. Built by the Viscounts of Béarn in the 12th century, the castle later housed the Kings of Navarre. Fifty glorious Gobelin tapestries, well-preserved royal chambers, elaborately decorated ceilings, and several ornate chandeliers (some weighing over 300kg) grace the castle. In Henry IV's bedroom, the guide will show you the tortoise shell that served the royal infant as a cradle. It was believed that the tortoise would bestow its fabled longevity on the toddling *dauphin.* (Open daily 9:30-11:45am and 2-5:45pm; in off-season 9:30-11:45am and 2-4:45pm. Last guided tours ½-hr. before closing. Admission 22F, students 12F, ages under 18 free.) The Musée Béarnais on the third floor has an exhibition of local traditions and crafts, as well as displays of preserved butterflies, birds, and bears. (Open daily 9:30am-12:30pm and 2:30-6:25pm; in off-season 9:30am-12:25pm and 2:30-5:30pm. Admission 6F.)

The Musée des Beaux-Arts, rue Mathieu Lalanne, possesses a small but engaging collection of paintings, including notable works by El Greco, Ribera, Zurbarán, Miranda, Rubens, and Degas, as well as an impressive collection of contemporary art. (Open Wed.-Mon. 10am-noon and 2-6pm. Free.) For those interested in Scandinavia and in the anomalies of history, the Musée Bernadotte, 8, rue Tran, is a fascinating place to spend an afternoon. Well-informed, English-speaking guides lead guests through the birthplace of J.B. Bernadotte, whose brilliant military career catapulted him to the Swedish throne in 1818. (Open Tues.-Sun. 10am-noon and 2-6pm. Free.)

Held from the last week of June to the first week of July, the annual Festival de Pau brings classical plays, concerts, recitals, and ballet performances to the château courtyard and other venues. (Admission 90-130F per event.) As soon as the festival ends, the festival committee sponsors a free program of firework displays, *pelote* tournaments, poetry readings (worthy of Rimbaud's later days and Jenny's pet tuna), a leg of the Tour de France, and jazz, rock, ballet, and reggae performances. Pick up a schedule at the tourist office.

Although the Pyrenees are easily reached from Pau, the city is too far from the trails to make a good hiking base. The Librairie des Pyrénées, rue St-Louis (tel. 59 27 33 19), offers excellent maps and itinerary advice. (Open Mon.-Sat. 9am-noon and 2:30-7pm.) SNCF and private buses link the town to Laruns, north of the Parc National (4 per day, 1 hr.). From here, catch a local bus or hike to Gabas, a good base with camping and a CAF refuge. Other accessible sights—some of the finest in the Pyrenees—include the Col d'Aubisque mountain pass, the Pic du Midi d'Ossau (2884m), and the Lac d'Artouste, all with CAF mountain refuges nearby. Many people find Laruns to be a good departure point for hitchhiking and biking. Take advantage of local transportation and make side trips to mountain villages such as Cauterets and Gavarnie. During the last two weeks of July, Etoile Bus (tel. 59 02 45 45) sends a fleet from pl. de Verdun at 5:30pm for the Festival des Pyrénées at Gavarnie. (See Cauterets and Near Cauterets.)

Lourdes

A town of 18,000 inhabitants, Lourdes is overrun each year by 5,000,000 pilgrims. Since the 1858 apparitions of the Virgin to 14-year-old Bernadette Soubirous, who was canonized by Pope Pius XI in 1933, the miracle of Lourdes has blossomed into a pre-packaged tourist industry. Special trains, buses, and charter flights from all over the world bring entire parishes to the sacred site, and the streets are jammed with souvenir stands selling empty Virgin-shaped water bottles, plastic rosary beads, and more statuettes than Europe produced during the entire Renaissance. Perhaps the **Caverne des Apparitions,** where Bernadette had the visions that transformed the town, is still conducive to spiritual feelings, but probably less so than a cool green trail through the mountains. Be prepared for long lines and many ill people. The concrete echo chamber known as **Basilique Pius X** won an international architecture prize in 1958 despite its looking like a cross between Madison Square Garden and a parking garage. Fortunately, most of this behemoth slumbers underground. Designed for use as an atomic bomb shelter, the basilica accommodates up to 20,000 people. On Easter weekend, the Festival International de Musique Sacrée fills the local holy buildings with Bach and Mozart. Tickets are available through the tourist office (80-150F).

Orientation and Practical Information

Lourdes is a major train stop. The train station is located on the northern edge of town; the *centre ville* is 10 minutes away. The grotto, basilica, and souvenir shops all cluster in the northeastern section of town, 15 minutes from the tourist office.

Tourist Office: pl. Champ Commun (tel. 62 94 15 64). Turn right from the train station, then turn left at the Chaussée Maransin and walk for about 10 min. Good maps, free brochure, and a list of Lourdes's 380 hotels. Staff handles their Herculean task with cheer. Posts a board of available rooms outside but won't find you one. Open Mon.-Sat. 9am-noon and 2-7pm, Sun. 10am-noon; Oct. 16-Easter Mon.-Sat. 9am-noon and 2-6pm. Information booth **Touristes et Pélerins Isolés,** in the arcades to the right of the basilica. Has the scoop for a pilgrimage visit.Open 7am-noon and 2-6pm.

Currency Exchange: Société Lourdaise de Change, 38, rue de la Grotte (tel. 64 42 07 11). Open daily 9am-noon and 2-7pm.

Post Office: At rue de Langelle and chaussée Maransin. **Telephones** and **currency exchange.** Open Mon.-Fri. 8am-7pm, Sat. 8am-noon. **Postal Code: 65100.**

Trains: on av. de la Gare (tel. 65 94 10 47). The terminus of one of the Pyrenees lines. To: Pau (7 per day, ½-hr., 30F); Paris (5 per day, 7-9 hr., 357F); Toulouse (9 per day, 2½ hr., 99F); Irun (5 per day, 4-5 hr., 107F); Cauterets (change at Pierrefitte, 3-4 per day, 1 hr., 30F). SNCF buses to Cauterets accept Eurail passes. Many other excursion companies post schedules in front of the station. Luggage storage 12F. (Open 7:40am-7pm.) Information office open 8:30am-noon and 2-6pm.

Buses: (tel. 62 94 31 15), in pl. Capdevielle below the tourist office. To Argelès and Pierrefitte (9-10 per day; 11-15F). Open Mon.-Fri. 8am-noon and 2-6:45pm, Sat. 8am-noon. Local buses run from the station to the cave every ¼-hr. (Easter-Oct., 6F.)

Bike Rental: (tel. 62 94 28 25) at the train station. Ask at the baggage claim. 30F per ½-day, 40F per day. Deposit 500F. Open daily 7:40am-7pm.

Taxis: Tel. 62 94 31 30. Timed for train arrivals. Open 6am-11pm.

Hospital: 2, av. Alexandre Marqui (tel. 62 94 78 78).

Police: 7, rue Baron Duprat (tel. 62 94 02 08). **Emergency,** tel. 17.

Accommodations and Camping

Lourdes is best visited as a daytrip, if at all. More hotels than in any French city but Paris accommodate those who must linger here. The best place to look is around **rue Basse** in the center of town (from the train station turn right after you've crossed the bridge). Also try the **route de Pau.** Two lower-priced alternatives, both Christian organizations, have the pilgrim rather than the tourist in mind. The hostel-like **Centre des Rencontres "Pax Christi,"** 4, rue de la Forêt (tel. 62 94 00 66), is a 10-minute walk up the road behind the basilica. Dinner, bed, and breakfast cost 74F. Although there is usually space, you can reserve through **Les Amis de Pax Christi,** 18, rue Cousté, B.P. 133, 94234 Cachan (tel. 46 63 10 30). If you're under 25, stay at **Camp des Jeunes, Ferme Milhas,** rue Mgr-Rodhain (tel. 62 94 03 95), a 10-minute uphill walk out of town. Dorm accommodations cost 22F per person; camping in your own tent is 15F. You'll need a sleeping bag, but showers are included. You are strongly encouraged to participate in evening services and community activities. Ask for directions and reserve a place at the Service Jeunes booth in the big plaza by the sanctuaries. (Open April-Sept.)

Cauterets

Set 1000m up in a breathtaking valley on the edge of the **Parc National des Pyrénées Occidentales,** Cauterets makes the best base for exploring nearby towns and mountains. In winter, some of the best skiing in the region is a gondola, chairlift, or T-bar ride away. Long, white runs drop hundreds of meters down the slopes, while cross-country ski trails delve into the heart of the national park. In summer, green pastures and an extensive network of hiking paths lure an international crowd of hikers.

There isn't much to see in Cauterets itself other than a covey of well-heeled visitors soaking in the *thermes.* Thought since Roman times to treat sterility, these sulfuric hot springs inspired the Romantic dalliances of Victor Hugo, George Sand, and Chateaubriand. At the **Palais des Attractions** on esplanade des Oeufs, you'll find lots of youths, loud music, a game room, exhibits, a swimming pool, a library, and a club that you can enter for free after 10:30pm. The Place de la Mairie remains lively until about 10pm.

Orientation and Practical Information

About 12km from the Spanish border, Cauterets is most accessible by SNCF bus from Lourdes (1 hr., 30F). From the station, turn right and walk up av. Général Leclerc to the tourist office, which is on the right. The city climbs a hillside along the river Gave.

Tourist Office: (tel. 62 92 50 27), in pl. de la Mairie. List of hotels (with prices) available. **Currency exchange** July-Aug. Sat.-Sun. Information center open July-Aug., Christmas, and French winter holidays Mon.-Sat. 9am-7pm, Sun. 9am-noon and 4-7pm; in off-season Mon.-Sat. 9am-12:30pm and 2-6pm, Sun. 9am-noon. **Maison de la Montagne** (tel. 62 92 58 16), next door, arranges 6- to 7-hr. guided hikes. (200-220F per person.) Check the board in front for departure times (usually before 8am). Office open daily 10am-12:30pm and 4-7:30pm.

Post Office: on rue de Belfort (tel. 62 92 54 00). **Telephones** and a good **currency exchange.** Open Mon.-Fri. 9am-noon and 2-6pm, Sat. 8am-noon. **Postal Code:** 65110.

Buses: (tel. 62 92 53 70), in a chalet in pl. de la Gare. Cauterets is served by Lourdes Les Pyrénées buses (tel. 62 94 22 90), which also run to Gèdre and Gavarnie. To Gavarnie via Pierrefitte (2 per day, 36F) and Lourdes (6 per day, 30F). From Lourdes, change buses at Pierrefitte to Gèdre, Gavarnie, and Luz-St-Sauveur. Buses also stop in Luz-St-Sauveur twice a day (30F). Pick up the complete schedule in any regional tourist office or train station. Open Mon.-Fri. 9am-noon and 3-6:30pm and Sat. 9am-noon.

Bike and Mountain Equipment Rental: Skilys, route de Pierrefitte at av. de la Gare. Ten-speeds 35F per day. Mountain bikes plus guided tour (3 hr.-1 day) 73-200F. Tours run May-Oct. Mountain boots 20-30F per day. Downhill skis 42-112F per day. Ski boots 26-80F. Cross-country skis and boots 45F per day. Passport required for deposit. Open daily 9am-12:30pm and 2-7pm.

Hiking Information: Parc National des Pyrénées, Maison du Parc (tel. 62 92 52 56), in pl. de la Gare. Hiking trips, nature films, a Pyrenean flora and fauna exhibit, and information on the park and its trails. Open April-Sept., Dec., and Feb. daily 9:30am-noon and 3:30-7:30pm.

Ski Information: Régie Municipale des Sports de Montagne (tel. 62 92 58 10), on av. Docteur Domer.

Weather Update: Tel. 62 32 97 77 for High Pyrenees. 24-hr. recording. For a forecast for the mountains around Cauterets, call **Météo-Montagne** (tel. 62 32 90 01).

Mountain Rescue Service: Tel. 62 92 54 69.

Police: Emergency, tel. 17.

Accommodations and Food

Make reservations in summer and avoid the hotels that require *pension*. The **Center UCJG "Cluquet,"** av. Docteur Domer (tel. 62 92 52 95), is a friendly and affordable place with free sheets, showers, and excellent kitchen facilities. Pitch your own tent for 15F, sleep in a 14-bed tent for 28F, or take a bed in a cabin for 38F. (Open June 15-Sept. 13.) In town, the *gîte d'étape* **Le Pas de l'Ours,** 21, rue de la Raillère (tel. 62 92 58 07), warmly receives hikers, climbers, and skiers. Continue past the tourist office and up the hill. Co-ed accommodations in big, communal rooms with bunkbeds are 45F (showers included). Good cooking facilities for your food and yourself (sauna 45F, 70F per 2 people). Breakfast costs 23F. **Hôtel du Béarn,** 4, bd. Général Leclerc (tel. 62 92 53 54), lets go of large, clean rooms with immense windows. (Singles and doubles 62-105F. Triples 135F. Breakfast 17F. Open Dec.-Sept.) **Hôtel-Restaurant Christian,** 10, rue Richelieu (tel. 62 92 50 04), has friendly management and immaculate rooms. (Singles and doubles 100-120F, with shower 120-160F. Open April-Sept.)

Pick up your gorp at the covered **market** in the center of town. (Open daily 8:30am-12:30pm and 2:30-7:30pm.) On Friday in July and August, check out the open air **market** held all day in front of the cable car station on pl. de la Gare. The supermarket **Codec,** on av. Général Leclerc, has groceries galore but is not nearly as much fun. (Open daily 8:30am-12:30pm and 4-7:30pm.) Jovial M. Lafon, at 3, rue de la Raillière, engineers succulent *sacristains* (a light, twisted pastry) and the best *chocolatines* around. Appropriately named **La Flore,** 11, rue Richelieu concocts a delicious 60F *menu* featuring *escalope à la crème* (veal in cream sauce). The owners raise dwarf bunnies; ask to meat one. (Open daily noon-3pm and 7pm-2am.) At #10, **Restaurant Christian** serves a good 65F *menu*. (Open April-Oct. daily noon-2pm and 7-9pm.) After a long day of hiking, treat yourself to a four-course, family-style meal at **Hôtel Dulau,** 7, rue du Raillère. (Open Mon.-Sat. 12:15-2pm and 7:25-10pm.) Across the street at #8, **Le Silver Tree** serves whole roast ring-doves big enough for two (140F). **Royalty Crêpes,** esplanade des Oeufs, makes good, phenomenally cheap *crêpes* in a festive atmosphere. Four of the little buggers will only set you back 15-20F. (Open Mon.-Sat. noon-2pm and 6-9:30pm.)

Near Cauterets

Before taking off for the mountains, read the general advice in the Gascony introduction. Pick up one of the purple 1:25,000 maps of the Parc National des Pyrénées (55F); for the Cauterets region use *Balaïtous*. The invaluable *Promenades en Montagne* series on the Vallée des Cauterets (available at the tourist office and the Parc National for 31F) details numerous itineraries and lists area refuges. **La Civette,** a bookstore opposite the tourist office in Cauterets, sells a complete selection of maps. (Open daily 9am-noon and 3-7pm.) Understand that a "refuge" usually means a roof with or without any amenities beneath it. The comparatively luxurious *gîtes d'étape* normally have beds, kitchen facilities (or a restaurant), and a resident caretaker.

The **GR10** passes through Cauterets and continues to Luz-St-Sauveur by two different paths. The easier one crosses the plateau of Lisey, while the other leads past **Lac de Gaube,** glaciated fields of the Vignemale 3200m up, Gavarnie, and the village of Gèdre. Start your mountain ramblings with the easy two-hour hike to **Col d'Ilhéou** (1198m). Refuel at the **Refuge d'Ilhéou** (tel. 62 92 82 38) and continue along the path to **Col de la Haugade** (2311m), another (and a more difficult) one and a half hours away. From there descend to **Plant du Cayan** (1625m), a plateau with plenty of wildlife and good camping. The route leading southwest from here to **Refuge Wallon** (tel. 59 33 90 47) is well-known; seek your solitude elsewhere.

Another good base for trips to the mountains is the **Fruitière** (1371m), a 10-minute drive or a one-hour walk from Cauterets. Hike one and a half hours to **Lac d'Estom** (1804m), and then continue along the more difficult route to **Lac de Labas** (2281m). Go farther only if you are a serious hiker. Past Lac Glacé is **Col Gentianes** (2729m), from where you descend—and pay close attention while you do it—to **Refuge Baysellance** at 2651m. (60F per night. Open July-Sept.) This area is close to the **Pique du Vignemale,** the highest mountain in the French Pyrenees (3298m). The hike down to Cauterets from here is difficult. Stay overnight in one of the refuges unless you are in very good shape. Snow on the steep slopes can make this path treacherous all year. Proper equipment, including an ice pick, and a thorough knowledge of hiking are crucial.

Luz St-Sauveur, in the Vallée du Toy, is another excellent launching pad into the Pyrenees. The **Maison du Parc National et de la Vallée** (tel. 62 92 87 05), off the pl. St-Clément, disgorges valuable, precise information for anyone interested. (Open Mon.-Fri. 10am-noon and 2-7pm, Sat.-Sun. 2-7pm.) If you plan to stay in the area, ask the tourist office at pl. du 8 Mai (tel. 62 92 81 60) about the **Ticket Toy,** which provides discounts on many activities in this animated valley. **Camping les Cascades** (tel. 62 92 82 15), near the church in the *vieille ville,* has free laundry service, a small grocery store, kitchen facilities, hot showers, a small mountain of puppies, and a great view. (10F per person, 11.50F per tent.) An Americanophile brother/sister team runs both the campground and the **auberge de jeunesse/gîte d'étape** next door (41F per night). The campground restaurant offers breakfast (15F) and a hearty regional *menu* for 50F. Luz-St-Sauveur can be easily reached by the SNCF Lourdes-Les Pyrénées **buses** (tel. 62 94 22 90) from Cauterets (3 per day, 26F).

The bus also connects Luz-St-Sauveur with the postcard-perfect **Gavarnie** on the Massif du Marboré (15F). Hikers can take the GR10 between the two towns. Many people find hitching to be a breeze; follow the av. de la Poste down past the swimming pool. In winter Gavarnie's ski slopes are less packed than those of nearby resorts. During the rest of the year, its spectacular scenery draws adventurers from all over France. From **Col de Boucharou** in Gavarnie, hike the 11km to the **Brèche de Roland,** one of the many places where Charlemagne's nephew is said to have struck the ground with his sword. Less traveled than the rest of the area's paths, this half-day's route should be tackled only by experienced hikers. The **Refuge de la Brèche** (or des Sarrodets) (tel. 62 92 48 24) awaits in the forest of the Brèche de Roland. The grandiose, snow-covered **Cirque de Gavarnie** and its mist-wreathed waterfall are also nearby. Hordes of tourists heave themselves onto horses for the trip to the Cirque (round-trip from the village about 70F, 2-3 hr.). To avoid being trampled, take the path marked *rive droite.*

During the last two weeks of July, the **Festival des Pyrénées** occurs at the foot of the Cirque de Gavarnie. The nightly performance begins as the sun sets over the mountains; afterwards, torches are distributed to light the way back to the village. Past festivals have featured Shakespeare's *Macbeth* and *A Midsummer's Night Dream;* the latter, complete with pyrotechnics and galloping horses, brought its mobile audience to three different settings. Tickets cost 90F (70F for students) at tourist offices, bookstores, banks, and hotels throughout the region.

Some 8km from Gavarnie is the cute town of **Gèdre,** also within walking distance of (ta-dah!) spectacular scenery. The **tourist office** here (tel. 62 92 48 26) will gleefully help you plan your itinerary. The buses from Cauterets stop here after Gavarnie.

Auch

A graceful, pleasant town with curious streets, a golden cathedral, a crumbling tower, and a somewhat charming dullness, Auch makes a relaxing daytrip from Toulouse. Rental bikes are hard to find, but try to do some pedaling along the tree-lined roads in the surrounding area. Mean hills will test your mettle, but you'll pass sunflower and rose fields, vineyards, windmills, châteaux, and pigeon houses. You can see all this equally well on foot; the hiking paths GR 65, 652, and 653 pass through here.

Orientation and Practical Information

One and a half hours from Toulouse by train, Auch is divided into the *basse* and *haute villes* by the Gers river. A bus leaves from the train station for the *mairie* every half-hour from 7am-7pm (4F). The uphill walk takes about 15 minutes.

Tourist Office: 1, rue Dessoles (tel. 62 05 22 89), on pl. de la République in front of the cathedral. Free tours of the museum and cathedral. English spoken. Open Tues.-Sat. 9am-noon and 2-6:30pm, Sun.-Mon. 2-6:30pm; Sept.-June Tues.-Sat. only.

Currency Exchange: On Sun. and Mon., when the banks are closed, change currency in the Hôtel de France, pl. de la Libération. **Banque Nationale Populaire,** pl. de la Libération, is one of the few places that changes traveler's checks. Open Tues.-Fri. 8:15-11:45am and 1:15-5:15pm, Sat. 8:15-11:45am and 1:15-4:30pm.

Post Office: rue (what else?) Gambetta. **Telephones.** Open Mon.-Fri. 8am-7pm, Sat. 8am-noon. **Postal Code:** 32000.

Trains: (tel. 62 05 00 46), on av. de la Gare in the *ville basse.* To: Toulouse (6 per day, 1½ hr., 56F); Montauban (1 SNCF bus per day, 1½ hr., 56F); Agen (7-8 SNCF buses per day, 49F). Information, reservations, and ticket service open Mon.-Sat. 5:15am-9:45pm; Sun. 6:30am-12:30pm, 1:15-7pm, and 8-9:45pm.

Buses: allées Baylac, pl. du Forail (tel. 62 05 76 37). To: Condom (2-3 per day, 1 hr., 25F); Bordeaux (1 per day, 4 hr., 90F); Toulouse (2 per day, 1¼ hr., 44F). Open daily 7:30am-noon and 2-6:30pm.

Bike Rental: In July and Aug. from the Maison de Gascogne. 30F per day, 150F per week, deposit 300F.

Taxis: Tel. 62 05 00 48, 62 05 66 25, or 62 05 27 40.

Youth Information: AJIR, 9, rue Espagne (tel. 62 05 07 63). Well-organized and enthusiastic. Information on sight-seeing, transportation, sports, and cultural activities. Open Mon.-Fri. 1-6pm.

Medical Assistance: (tel. 62 05 11 10), on av. des Pyrénées.

Police: Tel. 62 05 24 01. **Emergency,** tel. 17.

Accommodations and Camping

Unless you want to lug your pack uphill, try to find a hotel in the *ville basse.* The youth hostel usually has plenty of space. A *gîte d'étape* 4km from town sits in the shadow of a château.

Auberge de Jeunesse, Foyer des Jeunes Travailleurs, in the building complex Cité Grand Garros (tel. 62 05 34 80). Catch bus #2 from the station and get out at Grand Garros (last bus 7pm). Luxurious for a youth hostel. No kitchen facilities, lockout, or curfew. First night 48F per person, each additional night 36F. Breakfast 9.80F (served 7-7:45am). Lunch or dinner 35.20F. Almost always has space, but call before making the trek.

Gîte d'Etape, Château St-Cricq, on the route de Toulouse (tel. 62 63 10 17), 4km from Auch. Sleep in the castle annex. Twenty beds available to hikers, horseback riders, and cyclists. 30F per person. Call before 5pm.

Hôtel de Paris, 38, av. de Marne (tel. 62 63 26 22). Carved wood furniture and quiet halls. Singles from 110F, with showers 140F. Doubles from 130F, with shower 170F. Breakfast

20F. Shower 15F. Extra bed 10F. The excellent restaurant on the ground floor offers a 60F *menu* complete with *pâtisserie* concocted by the owners' son. Restaurant open Mon.-Sat. noon-2pm and 7:30-9:30pm. Hotel open Dec.-Oct.

Hôtel-Restaurant Modern, 10bis, av. Pierre-Mendés-France (tel. 62 05 03 47). Clean rooms with high ceilings and low prices. Singles 110F. Doubles 140F. Triples 170F. Breakfast 18F, shower 8F.

Camping: Camping Municipal (tel. 62 05 00 22), 1-2km from the train station on av. des Pyrénées. 10.50F per person, 6.50F per tent. You can also pitch your tent at a local farm and help with the chores for about 15F per night or 75F per week.

Food

Resign yourself to paying a little more than usual and eating heartily. Look for the regional specialties: *tourins à l'ail* or *à l'oignon* (garlic or onion soup), *palombes* (ring-doves), *maigrets* (lean duck), and *pastis gascon* (layered apple or plum cake). The *basse ville* holds an **open market** on av. Hoche every Thursday until 1pm; the *haute ville* holds another near pl. de la Libération in front of the cathedral each Saturday until 6pm. A **Codec** supermarket on rue Bourget in Grand Garros is convenient for hostel dwellers. (Open Mon.-Sat. 8:30am-7pm.)

La Crêpe, on pl. Porte Trompette next to Nouvelles Galeries in the *basse ville*. A lively new place with good prices and good food. 39F *menu* includes salad, *crêpe*, dessert, and a ¼-bottle of wine. Meat dishes also available. Open Mon.-Sat. noon-11pm, Sun. 2-11pm.

Les Trois Mousquetaires, 5, rue Espagne, off pl. de la République. Excellent service makes the 55F *menu* even better. Soup, appetizer, meat, and dessert included. Open daily noon-2pm and 7:30-10pm.

Les Grenadines, 165, rue Victor Hugo. The 20-min. walk ascends to a view of the surrounding hills. Fish specialties and a 49F lunch *menu* featuring grilled beef and *salade humeur du chef* (whim of the chef salad). Young crowd. Open Tues.-Sat. noon-2pm and 6-11pm.

Resto Quick Seguin, 6, rue Dessoules, across from the tourist office. Wood-beamed *salon de thé* that doubles as a cafeteria. Small pizzas 8F. Hamburgers 10F and 16F. Chicken or steak with salad and french fries 30F. Open Tues.-Sat. 9am-7:30pm.

Sights and Entertainment

Try to catch the classical west façade of otherwise Gothic **Cathédrale Ste-Marie** at dawn or sunset, when the cathedral shimmers like a golden armadillo. The masterworks of this 15th- and early 16th-century beauty are the ornately carved choir stalls. (Choir open daily 8:30am-noon and 2-6pm. Admission 5F.) The 16th-century Gascon painter Arnaut de Moles created the 14 stained-glass windows in the apsidal chapels. If you're taking one of the three free daily tours, try to convince your guide to take you into the treasury and up the winding stairs. While you're at it, request a walk on the roof. (Cathedral open daily 7:30am-noon and 2-8pm; in off-season 8am-noon and 2-6pm.)

A weathered monolith near the cathedral, the **Tour d'Armagnac** once served as a prison. Leading down to the river from the tower is the **escalier monumental,** a formidable staircase offering expansive views of the *basse ville* and the countryside. In the middle stands a statue of the most famous of Louis XIV's musketeers, d'Artagnan, who was born near Auch in 1615 and later immortalized by Alexandre Dumas and Hollywood. The road from pl. Salinis leads under medieval **Porte d'Arton** to the steep and narrow *pousterles* (stairways).

The **Maison de Gascogne,** rue Gambetta, is a mall where regional crafts and specialties (largely culinary and alcoholic) are showcased and sold in July and August. (Open Sat.-Thurs. 10am-12:30pm and 2:30-7:15pm, Fri. 10am-12:30pm and 2:30-10:30pm.) You can sample (mostly free) baked goods such as the flaky *croustade* (3F), practically dripping with sugar, and the fiery *armagnac,* Gascony's sweeter and somewhat more herbal answer to cognac. Set in a former convent, the **Musée des Jacobins,** pl. Louis Blanc, has temporary exhibits of contemporary art, a collection of regional arts and crafts, and a selection of rare furniture from Auch. (Open

Tues.-Sun. 10am-noon and 2-6pm; Oct.-June Tues.-Sat. 10am-noon and 2-4pm. Admission 5F, students 2.50F.)

At the end of September, Auch holds the well-known and well-attended **Festival de Musique et Danse Contemporain** at the Maison de Gascogne which brings in excellent new music and dance groups from all over France. Even better known is the **jazz festival,** one of the biggest in France, held 25km from Auch in **Marciac.** The Auch tourist office has tickets (106-206F).

If you're tempted to visit wine cellars, ask the tourist office for a list of local *caves.* You can engage in safe sightseeing in **Condom,** a small town to the north with seven churches and the **Musée de l'Armagnac,** which demonstrates in detail the production of Armagnac, the regional liqueur. Erected in the 13th century, the **Château de Cassaigne** (tel. 62 28 04 02) once housed the Bishops of Condom. (Open daily 9am-noon and 2-7pm.) In late October a large antique show takes over the **Halle des Expositions** next to the municipal campground (admission 15F). The first week in June brings a group of international musicians to the **Festival de Musique.** (Admission 45-100F, students 20% off.)

Languedoc-Roussillon

A hinge between France and Spain, Languedoc-Roussillon still bears the marks of the ethnically diverse peoples drawn by its strategic importance. The impressive Roman aqueducts and arenas in and around Nîmes, the Moorish *palais des rois de Majorques* in Perpignan, the crumbling *châteaux Cathars* (the last digs of a heretical sect near Carcassonne), and the Jacobins (the tremendous Catholic Church in Toulouse) all bear testimony to the populations whose conflicts and passages have shaped this region of southern France. Modern political divisions cut the region into the **Midi-Pyrénées,** which spreads south of Toulouse to the Pyrénées, and the official **Languedoc-Roussillon,** which begins on the coast and continues inland to Carcassonne.

The name Languedoc-Roussillon indicates the two cultures which have maintained the strongest influence in the area. Languedoc refers to the culture which dominated most of southern France from the 9th to the 13th centuries. The people spoke the *langue d'oc* (named for its word for "yes," "oc," as opposed to the northern *langue d'oïl*); their courts enjoyed a literary blossoming with tales of adventure and courtly love recounted by the wandering troubadours. Heretical sects seemed to sprout more easily here than in other regions of France, and they, along with the erotic aesthetics of the troubadours, drew the attention of a Catholic Church at the height of its power. Accustomed to war and frustrated by unsuccessful crusades, the northern French nobility needed little prodding to seize upon its neighbor as a land ripe for conquest. King Philippe August allowed Pope Innocent III to preach a crusade against the area's Cathar or Albigensian heretics, and dispatched Simon de Montfort, an opportunistic baron from the Ile-de-France, on the Albigensian crusade, a campaign of conquest against all of Languedoc. After his armies crushed the province in 1213, the *langue d'oc* faded, and in 1539 the Edict of Villiers-Cotterets imposed the northern *langue d'oil.*

In the following centuries, Parisian politics often disrupted local traditions, leading to poverty, resistance, and homegrown leftist ideology. Languedoc has proudly maintained its socialist tradition, despite recent tendencies to the right. The newspapers on the stands today, such as *L'Humanité* and *La Dépêche du Midi,* are direct descendants of the 19th-century journals founded by Jean Jaurès and other leftist politicians. The *langue d'oc,* now more commonly known as *occitan,* hasn't completely disappeared. Students can learn the language at school and count it as a foreign language on the *bac,* the national university qualifying exam. The *occitan* banner, yellow and red vertical stripes with a black cross, flies throughout the region.

"Roussillon" refers to the Catalan region around Perpignan. Another medieval power, Catalonia extends into Spain, with Barcelona as its capital. *Catalan* is also offered as a subject in school and a large literary center thrives in Perpignan.

This complex cultural heritage makes peregrinations through Languedoc-Roussillon both fascinating and confusing. Ask tourist offices for itineraries which lead you *sur les traces des Cathares* (on the tracks of the Cathars) or along the old Roman roads. Try to get to know some of the exceedingly generous people. Enjoy the clean, sprawling beaches, but don't miss the mountains. In addition to an intricate web of hiking trails, the Pyrenees attract skiers to excellent resorts such as Bonascre (near Ax-les-Thermes) and Font Romeu (near Perpignan). Frequent trains to both the mountains and the Mediterranean run from the hubs of Toulouse and Narbonne. Its locks visible in the centers of Toulouse and Perpignan, the Canal du Midi also links some towns in the region. The hilly countryside makes cycling a bit difficult, and the sparse traffic reduces hitching possibilities. Unfortunately, drought has greatly reduced the canal's navigability.

One of the most popular dishes of the hearty southwestern cuisine is *cassoulet,* a stew of white beans, sausage, pork, mutton, and goose. Along the coast, chefs often toss octopus into the pot. South of Nîmes in the Camargue, try the tender bull meat. In Roussillon, choosy eaters prefer *cargolade* (snails stuffed with bacon) to the many other seafood offerings. The tangy fermented Roquefort and St-Nectaire cheeses complement the panoply of luscious fruits grown in the Garonne Valley. Wash your meals down with a glass of one of the region's full-bodied red wines such as Minervois or Corbières. For dessert or as an aperitif, sip the sweet white wines of Lunel, Mireval, and St-Jean-de-Minervois.

Toulouse

One of the fastest growing cities in France, Toulouse (pop. 370,000) has spent much of this century fashioning itself as the technopolis of the future. During World War I, the French Air Force chose this city far from the raging front as its construction center. In the 1920s, Antoine de St-Exupéry (known to most students as the author of *The Little Prince*) and other pilots launched mail service from Toulouse to Africa and South America. In recent decades, these adventurers have ceded their places to the researchers at the Aérospatiale, the European aeronautic research center where the Ariane rockets (which launch most of the world's satellites) and the Airbuses (the most technologically advanced jumbo jet) are made.

Unlike many high-tech centers, Toulouse is a city with a grand past to match its present. The Occitan flag, sporting a cross on a red and yellow background, still flies throughout this cultural and political capital. Home to the oldest literary society in France, the 14th-century Académie de Jeux Floraux, Toulouse continues to support both Occitan and mainstream arts and to renovate its impressive collection of Renaissance *hôtels particuliers.* Although oddly unimpressed by *la ville rose,* whose history he found "detestable, saturated with blood and perfidy," novelist Henry James did find ample cause for admiration in Toulouse's splendid churches, especially St-Sernin. Indeed, those who come here simply to change trains are missing some of the most distinctive architecture in France.

Orientation and Practical Information

Toulouse sprawls on both sides of the Garonne Valley, but the museums, interesting churches, and sights are located within a compact section east of the river, bounded by the rue de Metz in the south and the boulevards Strasbourg and Carnot to the west and north. To get to the tourist office, turn left from the station and then right on the broad allées Jean Jaurès. When you reach pl. Wilson bear right, and then take a right onto rue Lafayette. The tourist office is in a small park on the left of the intersection with rue d'Alsace-Lorraine. The tourist office map verges on useless. Try to get the one published by *Galeries Lafayette,* available in many hotels and at the store.

Tourist Office: Donjon du Capitôle, rue Lafayette (tel. 61 23 32 00), in the little park behind the Capitôle. Don't expect lavish attention. Efficient staff makes accommodations reservations in other cities, including Aix, Paris, and Marseille (May-Sept., free). Walking tours of the old city (30-45F) and bus excursions to nearby sights (120F). Most tours leave daily from July 1 through September 30. Ask for brochure. Sells train tickets. **Currency exchange** May-Sept. Sat.-Sun. and holidays 11am-1pm and 2-4:30pm. Open daily 9am-7pm; Oct.-April Mon.-Sat. 9am-6pm. English spoken. Also an **information service** at the station (tel. 61 63 11 88). Open July-Sept. Mon.-Fri. 9am-noon and 2-6pm.

Budget Travel: Wasteels, 1, bd. Bonrepos (tel. 61 62 67 14), across the canal and to the left from the train station. BIJ tickets and Cartes Jeunes. Open Mon.-Sat. 9am-noon and 2-7pm.

Currency Exchange: Banque Populaire, at the station. Open Tues.-Sat. 6-9am, noon-2:15pm, and 7-8pm, Sun.-Mon. 6am-8pm. Also at the tourist office, the post office, several banks

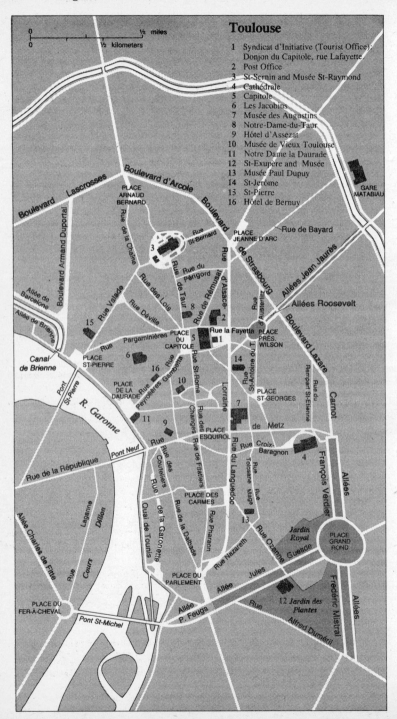

Toulouse

1 Syndicat d'Initiative (Tourist Office);
  Donjon du Capitole, rue Lafayette.
2 Post Office
3 St-Sernin and Musée St-Raymond
4 Cathédrale
5 Capitole
6 Les Jacobins
7 Musée des Augustins
8 Notre-Dame-du-Taur
9 Hôtel d'Assezat
10 Musée de Vieux Toulouse
11 Notre Dame la Daurade
12 St-Exupère and Musée
13 Musée Paul Dupuy
14 St-Jérôme
15 St-Pierre
16 Hôtel de Bernuy

around pl. du Capitôle, and the airport Toulouse-Blagnac. The post office often has the best rates (and long lines).

Post Office: 9, rue Lafayette (tel. 61 22 33 11), opposite the tourist office. **Poste Restante, currency exchange,** and **telephones.** Open Mon.-Fri. 8am-7pm, Sat. 8am-noon. **Postal Code:** 31000.

Trains: (tel. 61 62 50 50; reservations 61 62 85 44), on bd. Pierre Sémard. To: Paris (9 per day, 8 hr., 306F); Bordeaux (10 per day, 2¾ hr., 138F); Lyon (6 per day, 6 hr., 256F); Marseille (11 per day, 4½ hr., 204F); Albi (14 per day, 1 hr., 49F); Castres (8 per day, 1½ hr., 54F); Montauban (every hr., ½ hr., 37F). Station open 24 hrs.

Buses: 68, bd. Pierre Sémard (tel. 61 48 71 84), next to the train station. Frequent connections to Albi (10 per day, 1½ hr., 49F) and Castres (8 per day, 1½ hr., 54F). Less frequent to Carcassonne (2 per day, 2½ hr., 56F), Moissac (3 per day, 35F), and Foix (30F). SNCF buses accept Eurail passes. Buy tickets in train staion.

Public Transportation: Buses (tel. 61 41 70 70), on pl. du Capitôle. Tickets 5.50F (1 zone), 7.80F (2 zones); *carnet* of 10 40F (1 zone), 59F (2 zones). Route maps are available at the bus station's ticket booths and the tourist office.

Taxis: Tel. 61 80 36 36 (24 hr. service) or 61 62 37 34.

Hitchhiking: If you chose to hitch, take bus #2 to RN113 for Carcassonne. For Paris, take bus #10 to start. For Auch and Bayonne, take bus #64 to RN124. For Albi, take bus #16 or 19.

English Bookstore: The Bookshop, 17, rue Lakanal (tel. 61 22 99 92), down from Les Jacobins. *Let's Go* prominently displayed. Impressive selection of novels, non-fiction, comic books, and dictionaries. Trade in your used paperbacks. Open Tues.-Sat. 10am-noon and 2:30-7pm; Sept.-June Mon.-Sat. 9:30am-1pm and 2-7pm.

Youth Center: Centre d'Information Jeunesse, 17, rue de Metz (tel. 61 21 20 20). Information on sports, leisure, travel, and education. Foreigners welcome. Open Mon.-Fri. 10am-noon and 2-6pm, Sept.-June also Sat. 10am-noon.

Laundromat: Laverie Self-Service, 20, rue Cujas. Wash 12F, dry 2F per 7 min. Open daily 7am-9pm. Same prices at 14, rue Emile Cartailhac, near St-Sernin. Open 6am-10pm. Bring 10F and 2F coins to both.

Public Showers: At the train station. Showers 11F. Bath 16F. Open 5am-9pm.

Hospital: C.H.R. de Rangueil, chemin de Vallon (tel. 61 53 11 33). **Medical Emergency,** tel. 61 49 33 33.

Night Pharmacy: 17, rue Rémusat (tel. 61 21 81 20).

Police: (tel. 61 29 70 00), on Rempart St-Etienne. **Emergency,** tel. 17.

Accommodations and Camping

There are plenty of inexpensive hotels near the train station, especially on rue Caffarelli, off allées Jean Jaurès. However, the hotels in this unpleasant and unsafe neighborhood are no cheaper than budget hotels scattered beyond pl. Wilson in the *centre ville*. If you must stay near the station, know that the *concierges* tend to be suspicious and inhospitable; ask about curfews.

Auberge de Jeunesse (IYHF), Villa des Rosiers, 125, rue Jean Rieux (tel. 61 80 49 93). Call ahead before making the ½-hr. walk. Take bus #14 (*direction* "Purpan") to pl. du Puy and change to bus #22 (*direction* "Gonin-La Terrasse"). Ask the driver for the stop closest to the hostel. Small, somewhat run-down, and remote—but very friendly. Office open 8-10am and 4:30-11pm. Card required. 42F per person. Breakfast 12F. Sheets 12F. Kitchen available. Open Feb.-Dec.

Hôtel des Arts, 1bis, rue Cantegril (tel. 61 23 36 21), at rue des Arts off pl. St-Georges. Run by a delightful English-speaking young couple. Lively, central neighborhood. Singles 75-95F, with shower 115F. Doubles 110-120F, with shower 135F. Quads with shower 200F. Large breakfast 22F. Showers 15F per room. Luggage storage. Take bus #14 from the station; get off at Musée des Augustins.

Hôtel du Grand Balcon, 8, rue Romiguières (tel. 61 21 48 08) at a corner of the pl. du Capitole. An incredible deal. Saint-Exupéry and his cronies stayed here. Ask to see his room; the charming *concierge* will explain the history. Doubles 105-115F, with shower 165F. Quads with shower 180F. Breakfast 20F. Open Sept.-July.

Hôtel de l'Université, 26, rue Emile Cartailhac (tel. 61 21 35 69), near pl. St-Sernin. Attractive, newly-renovated rooms in a quiet neighborhood. Attentive owner. Doubles 80-90F, with shower 110-130F. Breakfast 18F.

Hôtel du Pays d'Oc, 53, rue Riquet (tel. 61 62 33 76) to the left off allées Jean Jaurès, 10 min. from the station. Tidy and cheap rooms, but the neighborhood ain't the greatest. Singles 55-85F. Doubles 100F, with shower 120F. Showers 5F. Breakfast 12F.

Nouvel Hôtel, 13, rue du Taur (tel. 61 21 13 93), off pl. du Capitôle. Ideal location and newly redecorated rooms. Doubles 125F, with shower 145F. Triples with shower 170F. Breakfast 20F.

Hôtel St-Antoine, 21, rue St-Antoine (tel. 61 21 40 66), off pl. Wilson. Sumptuous pastel rooms in an excellent neighborhood. Doubles 105F, with shower 165-180F. Breakfast 20F.

Camping: There are excellent campgrounds outside the city. You need a car or a lot of energy to get to the last three. **Pont de Rupé** (tel. 61 70 07 35) on av. des Etats-Unis (RN20 north), chemin du Pont de Rupé. Take bus P from the staion. Swimming pool. 26.25F for two people. **Camping Municipal du Ramier,** Roques-sur-Garonne (tel. 61 72 56 07). 14F per person, 6.50F per site. Open May-Oct. **La Bouriette,** 201, chemin de Tournefeuille (tel. 61 49 64 46), at St-Martin-du-Touch along RN124. Hot shower available. 13F per person or site. **Les Violettes** (tel. 61 81 72 07), on RN113 after Castanet. Showers included. 13.25F per person or site.

Food

Inexpensive restaurants crowd the city. Markets occur Tuesday through Sunday mornings at pl. des Carmes and on bd. Victor Hugo; gobble down your purchases in the Jardin Royal or the Jardin des Plantes. On Wednesday the pl. du Capitôle becomes an outdoor department store. Restaurants abound on the tiny streets on either side of rue St-Rome, but the most economical eateries lie along the rue du Taur on the way to the university. **Les Halles,** on the ground floor of the Parking Victor Hugo, has a truly frightening number of food stands, all open daily. A grocery store slumbers in the basement of the **Nouvelles Galeries,** 6, rue Lapeyrouse. (Open Mon.-Sat. 8:30am-7pm.) **Le Moulin,** 40, rue Peyrolières, has fava bean toothpaste, goat's milk coffee creamer, and other life-prolonging products. (Open Mon. 4-7:30pm, Tues.-Fri. 9:30am-12:30pm and 3-7:30pm, Sat. 9:30am-12:30pm and 4-7:30pm.)

Auberge Louis XIII, 1bis, rue Tripière. Tucked away in a quiet street off rue St-Rome. Enter through Sleeping Beauty's tangled garden. Interesting student crowd. 40F and 55F *menus*. Open Sept.-July Mon.-Fri. noon-2pm and 7-9:45pm.

Place du May, 4, rue du May, off rue St-Rome next to the Auberge Louis XIII. A stylish terrace with mercifully soft background music and a creative 49F lunch *menu* (without dessert or appetizer 39F). 79F dinner *menu*. Open Mon.-Sat. noon-2pm and 8-11pm, Sun. 8-11pm.

Salade Gasconne, 75, rue du Taur. Excellent regional specialties served *wiki wiki*. Popular with students. Eat your *brochettes du cœur* (heart shish kebabs) out. 49F *menu*. *Plat du jour* 39F. Open Mon.-Sat. noon-2pm and 7:30-10pm.

Au Coq Hardi, 6, rue Jules-Chalande, off rue St-Rome. Popular with students. Traditional family-style meals. 3-course, 51F lunch *menu*. 69F dinner *menu*. Open Mon.-Fri. noon-2pm and 7-10pm, Sat. noon-2pm.

Les Caves de la Maréchale, 3, rue Jules-Chalande, off rue St-Rome on a narrow pedestrian street. Sophisticated restaurant in an old wine cellar. Pamper yourself with some of Toulouse's most refined food. The 65F lunch *menu,* which resembles their dinner menu at nearly half the price, includes hors-d'oeuvre buffet, *plat du jour,* dessert, wine, and coffee. Open Tues.-Sat. noon-2pm and 8-11pm, Mon. 8-11pm.

Le Chat Dingue, 40bis, rue Peyrolières. A tiny restaurant with a big . . . painting? Excellent 55F lunch *menu.* Open Mon.-Sat. noon-2pm and 8-11pm.

Le Pavillon d'Argent, 42, rue du Taur. Fantastic Vietnamese specialties served with *nouvelle cuisine* flair. 59F lunch *menu.* Open Mon.-Sat. noon-2pm and 7:30-10pm.

Le Ciel de Toulouse, Nouvelles Galeries, 6, rue Lapeyrouse (tel. 61 23 11 52). Not typically French, but fun. On the 6th floor of a department store, this place serves hundreds of people in five bar-like units. Pizza 15F, big *plats du jour* 24-40F. Open Mon.-Sat. 11:30am-3pm; serves as a *salon de thé* 3-6pm.

Cafétéria Casino, on pl. Wilson. Looks like the other expensive cafés on the *place,* but the prices here are some of the lowest in town. Entrees 26-45F. Rib steak with fries 43.80F. It's a *salon de thé* in the afternoon. Open Mon.-Sat. 11am-11pm, Sun. 11am-10pm.

Sights

An unwavering Catholic stronghold in a region torn by wars of religion, Toulouse possesses several of France's most architecturally distinctive and historically important religious monuments. Start your ecclesiastical tour by heading up rue du Taur from pl. du Capitôle. You will reach the **Basilique St-Sernin,** the largest Romanesque structure in the world and one of the most magnificent. The oldest part of the church, the brick west façade, is a modest, even dull prelude to the grandeur that lurks inside. Crossed by a transept nearly 70m wide, the 100m nave boasts more reliefs, statues, paintings, altars, chapels, crypts, and reliquaries than an army of Siamese twin centipedes can count on their fingers and toes. St-Dominique, most vigilant of Cathar-hunters, preached his inquisition from this church. (Open Mon.-Sat. 8-11:45am and 2-5:45pm, Sun. 2-5:45pm. Crypt open 10-11:30am and 2:30-5pm. Admission 8F.)

Down rue du Taur is **Eglise Notre-Dame-du-Taur,** originally known as St-Sernin-du-Taur after Saturninus, the first Toulousain priest, who was martyred in 250 AD. Legend has it that he was tied to the tail of a wild bull that dragged him to his death; the building marks the alleged spot where his corpse finally rested. His name was corrupted over the years to St-Sernin, and his remains were long ago moved to the crypt of the cathedral.

While Basilique St-Sernin is one of the finest southern Romanesque churches, **Les Jacobins,** rue Lakanal, holds the honor for southern Gothic, or *gothique du Midi.* (The name of the church derives from a monastic order founded some eight centuries earlier, whence came the designation for the radical French revolutionaries, who first met in a Jacobin monastery.) The extraordinary stained-glass and the calm cloister, site of weekly summer piano concerts, complement the elegant proportions of the church. A modest crypt inside contains the ashes of the philosopher, Saint Thomas Aquinas. (Church open Mon.-Sat. 10am-noon and 2-6pm, Sun. 2:30-6pm. Admission to the cloister 6.50F. Concert tickets from 60F available at the tourist office.)

Four different attempts to transform a simple 11th-century Romanesque church into a grand cathedral based on northern models resulted in **Cathédrale St-Etienne.** In the 13th century, the rose window (copied from Notre-Dame in Paris) was added. Later additions include a Flamboyant Gothic choir. Ask the tourist office about occasional concerts on the 17th-century. (Open 7:30am-7:30pm; Oct.-May 2-7pm.)

Although Toulouse's museums tend to be a bit dull, a few deserve a visit. The **Musée des Augustins** (tel. 61 22 21 82; entry on 21, rue de Metz, off rue Alsace-Lorraine) houses not only an unsurpassed deposit of Romanesque and Gothic sculpture, but also an excellent collection of Romanesque capitals. Especially noteworthy are the 15 sniggering gargoyles from Les Cordeliers, an abbey that was pillaged mercilessly after burning to the ground in the 19th century. (Museum open Thurs.-Mon. 10am-6pm and Tues.-Wed. 10am-10pm; Oct.-June Wed. 10am-noon and 2-10pm, Thurs.-Mon. 10am-noon and 2-5pm. Admission 6.50F, free Sun. Free guided tours July-Aug. Ask for a brochure at the museum.) Cozy **Musée de Vieux Toulouse,** rue de May, contains haphazard exhibits on Toulouse's history and popular culture. (Open June-Sept. Mon.-Sat. 3-6pm; May and Oct. Thurs. 2:30-5:30pm. Admission 6.50F.) Slicker and better organized, the small **Musée Paul Dupuy,** 13, rue de la Pleau (tel. 61 22 21 83), shows an extensive collection of popular arts, including *faïences,* arms, instruments, and costumes. (Open Wed.-Mon. 10am-noon and 2-6pm, Sun. 2-6pm. Admission 6.50F, Wed. students free.) Next to St-Sernin, the **Musée St-Raymond** (tel. 61 22 21 85) displays the town's archaeological finds and interesting temporary exhibits. (Open Wed.-Mon. 10am-noon and 2-6pm, Tues. 2-6pm. Admission 6.50F.)

Toulouse's secular architecture is worth a look. During the Cathar revolt, the life of the Church's ban on interest led to an explosion of economic activity by the *Capitouls* (named for the post-Carolingian consuls who ruled the city) which did not abate even after the Church regained control. Though the greatest souvenir of the Capitouls is the Place du Capitôle, a few towers which survived the revolution poke up above the rooftops on rue St-Rome. Profits from the pastel-blue dye produced here until indigo shipped from India took over the market built splendid *hôtels particuliers,* over 50 of which remain. Many date from before the 17th century; some are restored and still inhabited. Perhaps the finest is the **Hôtel d'Assezat,** pl. d'Assezat, on rue de Metz. Constructed to resemble the Louvre, the *hôtel* now houses the ancient literary society, *l'Académie des Jeux Floraux.* Entrance to the lovely **Hôtel Bernuy** on rue Gambetta, now a high school, should be no problem for anyone who looks vaguely like a student. Ask the tourist office for a list of other *hôtels particuliers* tucked away in *vieux Toulouse.*

The **Jardin des Plantes** and the more formal **Jardin Royal** across the street offer shade with plenty of benches and a few drinking fountains. For bicyclists seeking a bit of greenery, the **Grand Rond** unfurls into allée Paul Sabatier, which just keeps rolling to the Canal du Midi. On Sunday mornings, a rather impious *marché aux puces* (flea market) surrounds the Basilique St-Sernin.

Entertainment

Whatever your feet's beat, Toulouse's late-night *caves* and bars can match it. The least expensive and most off-the-wall places lie along rue des Blanchers. Place St-Georges is the center of student life. Gay bars are concentrated on rue de Colombette. The weekly journal of entertainment, *Flash,* gives complete club listings (5F at newsstands).

> **Le Broadway,** 11, rue des Puits-Clos (tel. 61 21 10 11). Popular with both gay and straight people. Regarded as the city's leading nightclub by *les branchés* (the hip). Open daily 11pm-6 or 7am. Cover charge 40F.

> **Le Chapo,** 6, rue St-Rome (tel. 61 21 73 27). An attractive interior packed with a slightly younger crowd than the Broadway's. Open Tues.-Sat. 11pm-6am. Cover charge 50F.

> **L'Ubu,** 16, rue St-Rome (tel. 61 23 26 75). The jet-set landing pad for over 20 years. The doorman will let you in if you have *le look.* Plan on coming late, then arrive even later. With 70F drinks and the inevitable stuffiness, it might not even be worth it.

> **Le Florida,** 12, pl. du Capitôle (tel. 61 21 87 59). A great place for before and after the *boîte de nuit* (nightclub). The best-looking café on the square. Open daily 7am-2am.

> **Le Van Gogh,** 21, pl. St-Georges (tel. 61 21 03 15), on the ever-lively pl. St-Georges. Lend them your ear. A café with live piano music on weekends. Open daily 7am-2am.

The free *Regard* magazine, available in newsstands and *tabacs,* lists concerts and theater events in the area. Pick up a copy of *50 festivals de musique en Midi-Pyrénées* from the tourist office. From July to September, the **Musique d'été** brings classical concerts, jazz, and ballet in a variety of outdoor settings, concert halls, and churches. (Tickets 40-60F sold at the tourist office and on location before the performance.) The **Fête de la Musique,** nationally celebrated on June 21, is especially festive and free-form in Toulouse. Last year, one chorus of 20 people dressed as trash cans sang their ecological plea through a filter of rotting garbage. The pl. Wilson is filled with movie theaters which often show American films in English. Look for "V.O" (*version originale*).

Near Toulouse: Pays de Foix and Ax-les-Thermes

Nestled in the eastern Pyrenees 85km south of Toulouse, the tiny town of Foix (pop. 10,000) was home to Gaston III, the great 14th-century warrior who gave Foix its motto—*Toco y se gausos* (Don't you dare meddle). On first view of the imposing château (tel. 61 65 56 05), it's not hard to imagine the dejection of Simon de Montfort, the powerful count of Toulouse who never mustered the force to conquer Foix. Inside this extraordinarily well-preserved medieval fort is the **Musée d'Ariège**, which displays archaeological findings dating from Roman and medieval times. (Château and museum open daily May-Sept. 9am-noon and 2-6:30pm; Oct.-April 10am-noon and 2:30-6:30pm. Admission 10F.) Don't you dare fail to appreciate the charm of the top-heavy medieval houses on place Parmentier, the fowl of a fountain on pl. de l'Oie, and the other surprises tucked away in the tiny streets.

In July and August, Foix relives its medieval glory with the **Médiévales Gaston-Phébus.** Parades, mounted jousts, medieval concerts and feasts, and a fantastic *son et lumière* (75-85F) animate the city for two weeks The **tourist office** on av. Gabriel Fauré (tel. 61 65 12 12) has full information on the festival and sends English-speaking guides to the château. (Open July-Aug. daily 9:30am-noon and 2:30-6:30pm; Sept.-June Mon.-Fri. only.) To reach the office, turn right out of the train station and then right onto the main road RN20. Follow the highway to the bridge, cross it, and follow av. Gabriel Fauré to the tourist office.

To take in the prehistoric caves and almost immodest beauty of the surrounding countryside, you'll have to stay overnight. A modern hostel, the **Foyer Leo Lagrange**, 16, rue Peyrevidal (tel. 61 65 09 04) provides clean attractive rooms and plenty of vacation ideas. *Demi-pension*, which includes breakfast, one meal, and a bed, costs 130F. Full pension, which includes all meals, costs 160F. Weeklong stays, which include daytrips in the region and full pension, start at 1050F. (Open July and Aug. 24 hrs.; Sept.-June 7am-9pm. Call ahead to reserve.) The friendly **Hôtel Eychenne**, 11, rue Peyrevidal (tel. 61 65 00 04), with its elegant wooden interior and firm beds, may be a better deal for those who would rather eat in the excellent local restaurants. (Doubles 80-130F, with shower 120-150F. Quads with shower 200F. Showers 15F. Breakfast 18F.) **Hôtel Echauguette**, rue Paul Laffont (tel. 61 65 02 31), has quiet rooms in a pleasant but less central location. (Singles 120F, doubles with shower 180F.) **Camping La Barre** (tel. 61 65 11 58), 3km on foot up RN20 toward Toulouse, is a large riverside site. (7.50F per person, 6.40F per tent.)

The capital of the *département* of Ariège, Foix is an excellent place to try out some *ariègeois* specialties. The *truite à l'ariègeoise* (trout) and the *écrevisses,* crayfish which make fantastic (if messy) finger food, are highlights of the hearty cuisine. Try Gaston Phébus's drink, the stiff, herbal *Hypocras.* Make sure it's served cold.

A jolly prize-winning pastry chef runs attractive **Le Médiéval**, 42, rue des Chapeliers (tel. 61 02 81 50). Despite his affection for chantilly, the 65F *menu* includes a few low-calorie options; the 90F *menu* includes rich *ariègeois* specialties. (Open Mon.-Tues. and Thurs.-Fri. noon-2pm and 7:30-10pm, Sat. 7:30-10pm and Sun. noon-2pm.) At the **Crêperie des 4 Saisons,** 11, rue La Faurie, friendly English-speaking owners post a 38F *menu* which includes a meat *crêpe,* a salad, a dessert *crêpe,* and wine. (Open Mon.-Fri. noon-2pm and 7-9pm, Sun. 7-9pm.) The **Auberge Miranda,** 36, rue Labistour fixes a copious 45F *menu* of Spanish specialties, *vin compris.* (Open Dec.-July 10 Mon.-Sat. for lunch and dinner, July 10-Sept. 15 Mon.-Sat. for lunch only, Sept. 16-Oct. 15 daily for lunch and dinner, and Oct. 16-Nov. Mon.-Sat.) An **open-air market** fills pl. St-Volusien on Friday mornings.

The Ariège boasts some of the most spectacular caves in France. To best explore them, rent a mountain bike from **Itineraire VTT,** 8, allées de Villote (tel. 64 02 66 44). The rental fee includes accessories, help with itineraries, and transport into the mountains. (70F per ½-day, 110F per day, 85F per day after 4 days. Guided tours 130F. Open daily 8:30-9:30am and 6-7pm.) An hour-long boat ride takes visitors through the cavern at **Labouiche** (tel. 61 65 04 11), 6km from Foix. (Open Palm Sunday to early June Mon.-Sat. 2-6pm, Sun. 10am-noon and 2-6pm; mid-June to Sept. 3 daily 9am-noon and 2-6pm. The **Grotte de Niaux,** 16km south of Foix, contains herds of leaping bison, deer, and horses. Don't panic; these 20,000-year-old beasts are only pictures. Ask the Foix tourist office about entry into this and other prehistoric caves. Rising high above the plain 35km southeast of Foix along the D9, the **Château de Montségur** served as the funeral pyre for Cathar *parfaits* (or "perfect ones") who chose death by fire over allegiance to the pope in 1244. A ticket to the château includes entrance to the museum in the village below, which displays artifacts found in the castle. (Open daily March-Sept. 10am-7pm; Oct.-Feb. Sat.-Sun. 10am-1pm and 2-7pm.)

Trains connect Foix with Toulouse (6 per day, 1 hr.), La Tour de Carol (5 per day, 1½ hr.), and Ax-les-Thermes (45 min.). The **train station** (tel. 61 65 27 00) is north of town off RN20. The **post office** is on av. Gabriel Fauré; Foix's postal code is 09000. The **hospital** (tel. 61 05 40 40) is also on av. Gabriel Fauré. Contact the **police** at tel. 61 65 52 55. In an emergency, call 61 65 00 17.

St-Louis sent his soldiers suffering from leprosy to bathe their feet in the *Bassin des Ledres* in **Ax-les-Thermes,** a small resort town 50km southeast of Foix and 130km south of Toulouse. Though most visitors are sedentary types who come to Ax seeking cures in the sulfuric thermal baths, the city also makes an excellent base to explorations of the *Pyrénées Ariégeois.* The **tourist office** (tel. 61 64 20 64) on pl. du Breilh has information on local spas and nearby ski areas. (Open Mon.-Sat. 10am-noon and 2-7pm and Sun. 9am-noon and 2-6pm.) To reach the office, turn left out of the train station and follow RN 20 to the pl. du Breilh. The **Office du Tourisme de la Vallée d'Ax** (tel. 61 64 60 60) in Perlos et Castelet, 3km from Ax on the road to Toulouse, has excellent information on hiking trips and cave visits.

Several paths passing near Ax offer both easy, year-round rambles and hikes that lead to snow even in July. The *grandes randonnées* 10 and 7 are rather difficult. The easier *sentier Cathar* and the *Tour des Vallées d'Ax* accommodate year-round hikers of all levels. The **Office de la Montagne de la Haute Vallée de l'Ariège** (tel. 61 64 05 61 or 61 64 28 34), next to the tourist office, offers guided tours. (Open daily July-Sept. 5:30-7pm.) Otherwise, the *Topoguide d'un Village à l'Autre* or *100 Randonnées en Ariège,* published by Editions Randonnées Pyrénéennes will help you go it alone. Call 61 66 40 10 or write to **CIMES Pyrénées,** BP 88, 09200 St-Girons; ask for information on the Ariège.

Oxygène, av. du Docteur Gomma (tel. 61 69 21 09), rents mountain bikes for 60F per half day, 90F per day, and 150F per week. One and a half hours on foot from Ax in the *Réserve d'Orlu,* M. Huez (tel. 61 64 44 72) rents donkeys for 160F per day.

Eight km above Ax, **Bonascre** (tel. 61 64 21 81) offers excellent, challenging, and relatively warm skiing with great moguls. (Lift pass 63F per ½-day, 86F per day. Rent skis and boots in front of the lifts for 56F per day. Agence Ferrer (tel. 61 64 20 53) runs four shuttles per day between Ax and Bonascre from December through April when there is snow. (July-Aug. 3 per day, 24F roundtrip.)

Ax has a number of comfortable places to rest after a day of soaking, skiing, or bushwhacking. Kind Spanish owners keep the **Hôtel la Terrasse,** 7, rue Marcaillou (tel. 61 64 20 33), a clean place with a river view. Large rooms make up for a somber entrance filled with scary hunting trophies. (Singles with shower 110F. Doubles with shower 190F. Triples with shower 250F. Quads with bunks and showers 310F. The **Hôtel le Breilh,** pl. du Breilh (tel. 61 64 24 29) offers simple, pretty rooms with balconies. (Doubles 190F. Triples with shower 260F. Breakfast 25F.) The snack bar on the ground floor serves cheap pizzas (12F) from 8am-10pm. (Open Dec.-Oct.) The less welcoming Hôtel de la Paix, pl. Breilh (tel. 61 64 22 61) has rooms from 85F. (Open Feb.-Nov. 15.) The rapid service restaurant posts filling 55F and 85F *menus.* (Open Thurs.-Tues. noon-2pm and 7-10pm.) Excellent pizzas are cooked while you wait on the pl. Roussel (25-35F). For excellent food and a piping hot welcome, walk up route d'Espagne for 10 minutes to **L'Orry Le Saquet** (tel. 61 64 31 30). The 85F *menu* includes such *ariégeois* exotica as duck, crayfish, and kiwi tarts. The entire menu is translated into English, and a charming English-speaking hostess will explain the preparation to you.

Trains connect Ax with Toulouse (72F), Pamiers (15F), La Tour de Carol (36F), and Foix. You can check your packs and skis at the station between 5am and 8:30pm. Agence Ferrer, pl. du Breilh (tel. 61 64 20 53) runs daily afternoon buses to Pas de la Case in Andorra (28F). From June to October, they run somewhat expensive excursions to Lourdes, Perpignan, Collioure, and Carcassonne. Reserve a day ahead. Exchange currency at the **post office** on pl. Roussel (tel. 61 69 22 71); the **postal code** is 09110. The St-Louis **hospital** (tel. 61 64 20 35) is on pl. du Breilh. Call the police at 61 64 20 17.

Montauban

The town of Montauban (pop. 55,000) was born out of the townspeople's 12th-century struggle against the oppressive abbey at Montauriol ("golden mountain"). In 1144 Alphonse Jourdain, Count of Toulouse, helped the enraged population sack the abbey and use its bricks to build Montauban (originally Montalban, "white mountain"). Lacking a true *vieille ville*, the town sprang up after urban planning made right angles common. Although working to restore old *quartiers* and revive the economy, Montauban itself has little to please visitors aside from an Ingres museum. Either make the town a daytrip from Toulouse(50km to the south), or spend your time in the lovely towns nearby.

The centerpiece of town, **Place Nationale** was once officially called pl. Commune, then pl. Royale under Louis XIV, and pl. Impériale under Napoleon. But it's always been *les couverts* to the townspeople, mindful more of the triple row of covered arches than shifting political winds. From the train station, walk down av. Mayenne and across pont Vieux; continue on côte de Bonnetiers and turn right on rue Princesse. To reach the **tourist office,** hop across pl. Nationale diagonally to rue Fraîche, which becomes rue Bessières. Bus #3, timed for train arrivals, saves you the 15-minute walk; get off at bd. Midi-Pyrénées (4F). The tourist office at 2, rue du Collège (tel. 63 63 60 60) organizes detailed walking tours in French. (July-Aug. Mon.-Sat. at 10am, 1½ hr., 12F. Open Mon.-Sat. 9am-noon and 2-7pm, Sun. 10am-noon and 3-6pm; Sept.-June Mon.-Sat. only.)

The belfry of **Eglise St-Jacques** shows holes gouged by Louis XIII's cannon shots during an unsuccessful siege of this Protestant stronghold in 1621. When neighboring towns surrendered to royal forces, Montauban was at last conquered; in 1629 Catholicism was reimposed. After the revocation of the Edict of Nantes (which had guaranteed religious freedom) in 1685, Louis XIV ordered the construction of the **cathédrale.** To the left of pont Vieux stand the monasteries where women who refused to convert were imprisoned until they agreed to marry Catholic men.

To the right of the bridge as you face town, the Palais Episcopal is now the **Musée Ingres.** The *Montalbanais's* corpus is remarkable not only for the exotic luster of canvases such as *Jesus et les Médecins, La Rêve d'Ossian,* and the *Portrait de Madame Gonse,* but also for the drawings and preparatory studies on rotating display, which reveal a great deal about Ingres's technique. Many works of the well-known native sculptor, Bourdelle, hang on the ground floor. A visit to the museum also includes the **Palais des Evêques** (bishop's palace), with partially furnished rooms, painted walls, and a dank basement glinting with torture instruments. (Open daily 9:30am-noon and 1:30-6pm; Sept.-June Tues.-Sun. 10am-noon and 2-6pm. In winter closed Sun. afternoon. Admission 12F, students 8F. Free Wed. Sept.-June if no temporary exhibit.)

Some hotels languish in the dingy area near the train station. Look for rooms closer to pl. Nationale. **Hôtel du Commerce,** 9, pl. Roosevelt (tel. 63 66 31 32), has small but attractive rooms near the cathedral. (Singles 70-75F. Doubles 90-120F. Showers 10F. Breakfast 15F.) **Le Bristol,** 12, allée Mortarieu (tel. 63 63 06 89), an extension of bd. Midi-Pyrénées, has unspectacular rooms above a bar. (Doubles 70F, with shower 110F. Triples with shower 110F. Breakfast 20F.) **Hôtel de la Poste,** 17, rue Michelet (tel. 63 63 05 95), off pl. Nationale, has adequate rooms. (Singles 80F. Doubles 85F. Triples and quads 150F. Showers 10F.) The closest

campground (tel. 63 31 00 44) is a three-star site 8km north in Albias. Take the Caussade bus from pl. Lalique. Another three-star site (tel. 63 30 52 73), 10km south in Montbartier, stays open June 15-September 15. Take the Toulouse bus. For both, you must ask the driver to stop at the *camping.* The tourist office lists other sites accessible by car.

A **market** fills pl. Nationale Tuesday through Saturday until 12:30pm. Many inexpensive restaurants line rue d'Elie and rue d'Auriol, off pl. Nationale. Friendly locals enjoy the robust 50F *menu* and *cassoulet* (24F) at **Restaurant Toulousain,** 2, rue Gillaque. (Open Sept.-July Mon.-Sat. noon-1:30pm, until 10pm as a café.) You'll find pressed wildflowers on the wall and fresh vegetarian *plats* (35F) and salads (15F) on the table at **La Clef des Champs,** 3, rue Armand. (Open Tues.-Sat. 11:45am-2pm.) **Don Quichotte,** 8, pl. de Franklin Roosevelt, opens at 10am and is still tilting at windmills at 2am. Beware—the cost of *tapas* adds up quickly. (Squid 20F, tortillas 16-20F, salads 20F.)

Trains roll from the station on rue Salengro (tel. 63 63 50 50) to Paris (9 per day, 5½ hr., 291F), and Toulouse (every hr., 1½hr., 39F), Bordeaux (9 per day, 2 hr., 116F), and Moissac (6 per day, ½hr., 24F). (Information office open 6am-midnight.) Down av. Mayenne in pl. Lalique, the **bus station** (tel. 63 63 88 88) sends buses to Albi (1 per day, 3 hr.), Moissac (2 per day, 1 hr.), Toulouse (5 per day, 1 hr.), Bruniquel (1 per day, 45 min.), and Penne (1 per day). (Information office open daily 7am-12:30pm and 2:30-6:30pm.) Also in pl. Lalique, **Harle** (tel. 63 63 15 80) rents cars for 219F per day plus 1.62F per km or 2368F per week with unlimited mileage. (Open Mon.-Sat. 8am-noon and 2-6pm.) Rent **bikes** (40F per day) and mountain bikes (70F per day) from **Gury,** 26, av. Gambetta (tel. 63 63 19 10). Open Tues.-Sat. 8am-noon and 2-7pm.) THe **hospital** is at 14, rue du Docteur Alibert (tel. 63 03 91 19); the **police station** is at 30, bd. Alsace-Lorraine (tel. 17).

Near Montauban

A strong contender for the title of world's most beautiful cloister lies a bus or train ride away at the 6th-century **Abbaye de Moissac.** Though anti-clerical revolutionaries hacked off most of their carved faces, the cloister's 76 columns still manage to convey stories from the Old Testament and the lives of the saints. The brightly painted interior of the church is best appreciated from atop the cloister staircase. (Cloister open July-Aug. daily 9am-7pm; Sept.-Oct. and April-May 9am-noon and 2-6pm; Nov.-March 9am-noon and 2-5pm. Admission 18F, students 9F.) Your ticket also admits you to the **Musée Moissagais,** a former nunnery now full of treasures from the cathedral and 19th-century memorabilia. (Open July-Aug. daily 9am-noon and 2-7pm; Sept.-June same hours as cloister.) From June to August, **Moissac** (pop. 12,000) holds a series of classical concerts in the church and cloister. (Admission 80F, students 60F. After June 15, call 63 04 06 81 for more information. Otherwise, contact the tourist office.) The **tourist office** is next to the cloister (tel. 63 04 01 85; open Mon.-Sat. 10am-noon and 2-6pm; Nov.-Feb. Mon.-Sat. 2-5pm). In town, **Le Relais Auvergnat,** 31, bd. Camille Pelthil (tel. 63 04 02 58), has respectable doubles for 80-100F and triples for 120-140F; the restaurant downstairs posts a 50F *menu* and serves 20F breakfasts. **Camping Beauséjour,** 53, av. Jean Jaurès (tel. 63 04 01 28), is a small three-star site with a supermarket, 15 minutes from the center and 1km from the train station in the direction of Montauban. (6.50F per person, 6F per tent. Showers 4F. Office open 8am-7:30pm. Open March-Dec.)

Montauban's tourist office distributes a map of the *circuit des bastides,* a route through Bruniquel, Penne, and the other fortified towns in the Tarn region. The tiny hill village of **Bruniquel,** east of Montauban and accessible by bus, has attracted troubadours and 19th-century literati of Romantic persuasion, including poet Charles Nodier. Its 13th-century **château** overlooks the confluence of the Aveyron and Vere Rivers. (Open July-Aug. daily 10:30am-12:30pm and 2-7pm; June and Sept. Mon.-Fri. 2-6pm and Sun. 10:30-12:30pm and 2-6pm; May and Oct. Sun. only. Admission 6F, with guided tour 12F.) The local chronicler Pierre Malrien, who has written three books on the village and its neighbor, Penne, always likes to meet visitors interested in learning more about Bruniquel (tel. 63 67 25 18). Although tourists storm the castle daily, the village itself is not crowded. The discreet hotel **Etape du Château** (tel. 63 67 25 00) has basic doubles with shower for 120-140F. **Le Payssel** (tel. 63 67 25 95), a campground less than 1km outside of the village, has swimming facilities. (11.50F per person, 15F per site.) The mayor's office handles inquiries from Tuesday to Friday (9am-noon and 2-7pm) and on Saturday (9am-noon).

The imposing ruins of the château in **Penne** also lie on the *circuit des bastides.* The tiny **tourist office** (tel. 63 56 36 68), has information on canoeing and kayaking daytrips in July and August (60F per person, 100F for 2). The **Camping à la Ferme Auri Feuilles** (tel. 63 93 05 17) lies in the direction of Vaours (19F per night, 120F per week). Buses leave Montauban twice per day for Bruniquel and once per day for Penne but don't return until the following morning. Call the bus station in Montauban (tel. 63 63 88 88).

Agen is a busy industrial town along the Garonne River, between Montauban and Bordeaux. Although known for its plums and champion rugby team, it warrants a visit only for its museum, which is housed in four 16th- and 17th-century *hôtels.* Among its Gallo-Roman antiquities is a marble *Vénus* found in the Mas d'Agenais. Five works by Goya, including a self-portrait, anchor a strong collection of paintings. (Open Wed.-Mon. 10am-noon and 2-6pm. Admission 6-10F.) **Cathédrale de St-Caprais,** its Romanesque capitals depicting the life of the structure's namesake, may also be worth a look.

The **tourist office** (tel. 53 47 36 09), down bd. Carnot from the train station, dispenses a city guide and gives free tours of the *vieille ville* in summer Monday at 10am and Thursday at 9pm. (Open Mon.-Sat. 9am-noon and 2-7pm; Oct.-March Mon.-Fri. 9am-noon and 2-6pm, Sat. 9am-noon.) The comfortable **Auberge de Jeunesse (IYHF)**, 17, rue Lagrange (tel. 53 66 18 98), 1½km outside of town, has kitchen facilities. Walk or take the bus from the station *(direction* "Lalande") to Léon Blum. Turn left on bd. Dumon, left again on av. Barbusse, cross over a bridge, and turn right on bd. du Docteur Messines. (IYHF card required. Curfew 10pm. 34F per person. Open June-Aug. all day; Sept.-May 6pm-10am.) The **Camping Municipal** (tel. 53 68 27 18) has access to hostel facilities all year (3.50F per person, 7.70F per tent). Down bd. Carnot from the train station, **Hôtel Coq d'Or,** at #96 (tel. 53 66 05 33), offers modest singles and doubles (80-90F). A covered market is held every morning at **Les Halles** on pl. des Laitiers. Each weekend a farmers' market fills pl. du Pin.

Albi

Albi unhappily gave its name to the Albigensian Crusade, a campaign orchestrated by Pope Innocent III against the heretical Cathars (or *Albigeois)* spread throughout Languedoc-Roussillon. These heretics, particularly concentrated in Albi, regarded all material things, including those used in Catholic sacraments, as evil. In stark opposition was the soul, which could expect repeated reincarnations until attaining "perfection" and joining God in the predetermined mass victory of good over evil. This unorthodox doctrine made the Church fume at the thought of lost souls and lost mass attendees. After a prolonged and bloody crusade, the heresy was squelched for good in 1302 by Bishop Bernard de Castanet.

An energetic city of 90,000, Albi now attracts many fans of the works of native son Henri de Toulouse-Lautrec. An extraordinary assemblage of his art graces the local museum, and the magnificent cathedral stands right next door.

Orientation and Practical Information

The capital of the *département du Tarn,* Albi makes an easy daytrip from Toulouse (76km southwest). To reach the tourist office and the center of town, turn left in front of the station onto av. Maréchal Joffre. Make another left on av. Général de Gaulle, and then bear left over pl. Laperouse to the cobbled pedestrian streets of the *vieille ville,* where signs will direct you to the tourist office.

Tourist Office: pl. Ste-Cécile (tel. 63 54 22 30). **Currency exchange** (commission 25F) Sun.-Mon., when banks are closed. Accommodations service 10F. Detailed map of the city 14F. English spoken. Open Mon.-Sat. 9am-7pm, Sun. 10:30am-12:30pm and 4:30-6:30pm; Sept.-June Mon.-Sat. 9am-noon and 2-6pm.

Post Office: on pl. du Vigan (tel. 63 45 76 02). **Telephones** and **currency exchange.** Open Mon.-Fri. 8am-7pm, Sat. 8am-noon. **Postal Code:** 81000.

Trains: (tel. 63 54 50 50), at the end of av. Maréchal Joffre. To: Toulouse (14 per day, 1 hr., 49F); Rodez (5 per day, 1½ hr., 52F); Brive (6 per day, 4 hr., 173F). Open 5:30am-9:30pm.

Buses: Gare Routière Halte des Autobus (tel. 63 54 58 61), on pl. Jean Jaurès. To Toulouse (7 per day), Rodez (2 per day), and Castres (4 per day). Open Tues.-Fri. 8am-noon and 2-6:15pm, Sat. 9am-noon. **Cars Bécardit** (tel. 63 54 03 79), on rond-point du Lude. Excursion to nearby Castres and Cordes once per day in July and Aug.

Taxis: Albi Taxi Radio, tel. 63 47 62 84 or 63 47 51 11. 24 hrs.

Bike Rental: At the train station. 30F per ½-day, 40F per day, deposit 500F. Open 6am-9pm.

Laundromat: 8, rue Emile Grand. Wash 12F, dry 2F. Bring 10F and 2F coins. Open daily 7am-9:30pm.

Medical Assistance: Centre Hospitalier, rue de la Berchere (tel. 63 47 47 47).

Police: 23, rue Pompidou (tel. 63 54 12 95). **Emergency,** tel. 17.

Accommodations and Camping

Tourists pour into Albi's few hotels. Reserve in May for July and August, and call a couple of days ahead during the rest of the year.

Maison des Jeunes et de la Culture, 13, rue de la République (tel. 63 54 53 65). Clean, hostel-like lodging open to all at rock-bottom prices. Overflows with activities and bulletin boards. Coed bathrooms and a largely male clientele. No kitchen. Check in 6-7pm. No lockout or curfew. Dorm bunks 22F. Breakfast 12F. Filling homecooked meals 37F. You can leave your backpack until 4:30pm. Closed 4:30-6pm and weekends Sept.-June.

Hôtel Regence, 27, av. Maréchal Joffre (tel. 63 54 01 42). From the train station, turn left and walk one block. The closest you'll come to sleeping in a Laura Ashley shop. Swoon on the sun porch. Singles 85F. Doubles 120F, with shower and TV 145F. Extra bed 40F. Showers 10F. Large breakfast 22F.

Hôtel Le Vieil Alby, 25, rue Toulouse-Lautrec (tel. 63 54 14 69), in the *vieille ville.* Very proper rooms. Owner is friendly, but picky about upkeep of rooms (no food). He requires that you eat in his excellent restaurant in summer (69F *menu,* wine included). Singles 105F. Doubles 110-120F, with shower 140F. Triples with shower 200F. Breakfast 23F. Hotel and restaurant open Tues.-Sun. afternoon.

Hôtel du Parc, 3, av. du Parc (tel. 63 54 12 80). From the train station follow av. Maréchal Joffre which becomes bd. Carnot. On the left across from a park. Exceptionally clean, quiet rooms. Doubles 120F, with shower 155-170F. Breakfast 22F.

Camping: Parc de Caussels (tel. 63 60 37 06), 2km east of Albi on D99 (route de Millau). Take bus #5 from pl. Jean Jaurès (every ½-hr. until 7pm). Ask the driver for the stop near the campground, next to the **L'Univers** store. Swimming pool nearby. Hot showers included. 37F per 2 people.

Food

Treat yourself to *cassoulet* and *tripes,* some of the typically hearty dishes of this region. Albigensian stew should be washed down with the local reds, Guillac or Cunac. You'll find good deals at the large indoor **market** on pl. du Marché (Tues.-Sun. until noon) or at the supermarket/cafeteria **Casino,** 39, rue Lices Georges Pompidou. (Store open Mon.-Sat. 8:30am-8pm. Cafeteria open daily 11am-10pm.) A large, open-air market fills pl. Ste-Cécile on Saturday morning. Somewhat expensive health food awaits at **La Vie Claire,** 23, rue Séré-de-Rivières (open Tues.-Sun.

9am-12:30pm and 2:30-7pm), and **Les Aliments Naturels,** 1, rue Puech Bérenguier, in the *vieille ville* (open Tues.-Sat. 9am-noon and 2:30-7pm; Mon. 2:30-5pm).

Auberge St-Loup, 26, rue de Castelviel, behind the cathedral. Local specialties served in a intimate medieval inn. Real men and women eat the *gras double* (made with sheep tripe). 60 and 70F *menus*. Open Tues.-Sun. noon-2:30pm and 7-10pm.

La Pastaciutta, 11bis, rue de la Piale (tel. 63 54 40 30), across from the cathedral in a sunken old street. Good homemade pasta with subtle sauces (30-35F). Attentive staff and owner. Weekday lunch *menu* 55F, wine and service included. Open Mon.-Sat. noon-2pm and 7pm-1am. Reservations needed Sat. night.

Le Saint-Salvy, 27, pl. Saint-Salvy, behind the church. Salads (32-39F), *crêpes* (34-42F), and a 70F *menu*. Try the Salade St-Jacques, made with scallops. Open daily noon-2pm and 7:30-11pm.

Le Bateau Ivre, 17, rue d'Engueysse, down the hill past the tourist office. *Nouvelle cuisine* served with flair in an attractive brick interior. Immense salads 60-90F. Succulent *menu* 80F. Adolescent poets welcome.

Sights and Entertainment

Born to an aristocratic family, Henri de Toulouse-Lautrec turned posters into an art form and created storms of controversy with his unique interpretation of form and color and his candid view of French society. Until his death in 1901 at the age of 37, he kept his distance from the Impressionist circle and academic taste—for this reason, the collection of works gathered by the artist's assiduous mother and ferreted away in the **Musée Toulouse-Lautrec** is the best anywhere. Located in the Palais de la Berbie, the museum contains not only all 31 of the famous posters of Montmartre nightclubs, but also dozens of oils and pastels and rooms full of the master draftsman's sketches and drawings. Upstairs is a fine collection of contemporary art, including sculpture and paintings by Degas, Dufy, Matisse, and Rodin. The museum also contains a chapel and a few archaeological exhibits. (Open daily 9am-noon and 2-6pm; Oct. 2-Easter Wed.-Mon. 10am-noon and 2-5pm. Admission 18F, students 9F. Guided tours in several languages 10F.) The artist's birthplace in Vieil Albi, the **Maison Natale de Toulouse-Lautrec** is still owned by the family and normally opens its doors daily from July to mid-September (9:30am-1pm and 2:30-7pm).

The **Basilique Ste-Cécile,** built in 1282 after the papal crusaders quashed Albi's heretics, was designed to serve as a fortress as well as a church. Bright 16th-century frescoes cover the interior. Carved entirely out of soft stone, the choir depicts 30 Old Testament figures in astounding detail. (Open daily 8:30-11:45am and 2:30-5:45pm. Admission 2F.) The basilica is lit inside and out nightly from June 15 to September. Guided tours leave between 8:45am and 10:30pm (15F, students 8F). On Wednesday afternoons in July and August, the organ at the back of the church (the largest in France) bursts into song.

In intimate **Eglise St-Salvy,** the radiant violet light of the stained-glass windows fills the humble pews. While the fragrant garden of the cloister is usually accessible, the church opens only from 8:30am to 12:15pm and from 2:30 to 5:45pm. A pathway next to the entrance to the cathedral leads to the narrow pedestrian streets of Vieil Albi, where artisans make and sell wares in a somewhat artificial atmosphere.

Albi entertains visitors with a number of summertime festivals and celebrations. The **Feu de la St-Jean** on a Saturday night around June 24 kicks off the season with nimble Jacques jumping over a giant log fire. The **Festival du Théâtre** takes place during the last week of June and the first week of July. The six-day **Festival International du Film 9.5mm** features a busy agenda of screenings and banquets during the first week of August (tickets free at the tourist office; another festival in October runs short films. The **Festival de Musique,** a fine series of concerts, opera, ballet, and flamenco guitar recitals, resounds from July 25 through the first week in August. The **Bureau de Festival** (tel. 63 54 26 64), opposite the tourist office, sells tickets (80-140F); buy them in advance. The **Centre Culturel de l'Albigeois,** pl. Edmond Canet (tel. 63 54 27 17), shows foreign films in their original languages all year long. Pick up a schedule at the Centre. (35F, students and ages over 60 18F).

Near Albi

Albi perches on the western tip of the Tarn Valley, an expansive stretch of cliffs, forests, and quiet towns. **Château du Bosc** (tel. 65 69 20 83), where Toulouse-Lautrec spent a happy childhood, hides in a forest 45km from Albi. (Open Easter-Dec. 9am-noon and 2-7pm. In off-season call for reservations.) The **Gorges du Tarn,** a region with high limestone cliffs, grottoes, and caves, await nearby. The **tourist office,** av. Alfred Merle (tel. 65 60 02 42), in **Millau,** has extensive information on the region and will direct you to **Le Rozier,** the best place to begin your descent. Pick up *Le Guide Millau-Grands Causses Rocquefort-Gorges du Tarn-Lézevou* (25F) at any tourist office in Tarn. Irregular buses leave Albi for both Millau and **Le Rozier;** ask at pl. Jean Jaurès. Contact the **Centre Equestre Albigeois** (tel. 65 54 46 91) about horse rentals.

Twenty-four km from Albi, the small 13th-century city of **Cordes** served as sentinel on the frontier of the Cathar territories during the 13th-century Albigensian Crusade. Jutting out high above the fertile valley of the Cerou River, the walled city has been extensively renovated, largely thanks to artist Yves Brayer, who arrived in 1940. **Eglise St-Michel** rests at the summit. Albert Camus (not Isaac Newton) came to Cordes-sur-Ciel (Cordes in the sky) to roll a boulder up the hill and watch it roll down again. The tourist office (tel. 63 56 00 52) is on pl. de Halle. (Open daily 10am-12:30pm and 2:30-6pm; Nov.-Easter Sat.-Sun. 10am-12:30pm and 2:30-6pm). The **Musée Yves Brayer** is worth visiting only for its colorful and fanciful renditions of the town (admission 5F). The **Musée Charles Portal** has interesting exhibits on local customs and a reconstructed farmhouse interior. (Open July-Aug. Mon.-Sat. 1-6pm; Sept. and June Sun. and holidays 2-5pm. Admission 10F.) If you're in the region on Bastille Day, don't miss the **Fête du Grand Fauconnier,** which sends Cordes back 500 years. Townspeople wrap their homes in garlands and medieval bunting and cavort as queens, princes, knights, and fair damsels, celebrating with a banquet and a torchlit procession in a festival unrelated to the French national holiday. (Entrance is 40F, unless you're in costume.) The church and pl. des Halles reverberate with classical music performed by international groups during a music festival in July and August. (Tickets 50F, with discounts for students; available at the tourist office.)

Cordes is prohibitively expensive. The **Auberge de la Bride** (tel. 63 56 04 02) on pl. des Halles has clean, airy singles and doubles with showers for an exorbitant 175-210F. Breakfast is 28F. For slightly less expensive rooms, try the handful of hotels in the lower town. Three-star **Camping le Moulin de Julien** (tel. 63 56 01 42), 1km out of town, has a swimming pool, lake, and mini golf. (50F per 2 people. Open Easter-Sept.) For information on *chambres d'hôte* ask at the tourist office or write to ATTER, Maison des Agriculteurs, BP 89, 81003 Albi CEDEX (tel. 63 54 39 81). With doubles from 105-165F, these bed-and-breakfast farmhouses make seeing the countryside a breeze. Avoid the overpriced restaurants near the Halle and in the rest of the old city. Bring a picnic or treat yourself to a "chaudwich," in the tropically decorated **Cordes Raid,** Grande Rue. The English-speaking owner serves 44F, 54F, and 69F *menus* as well as delicious 'wiches from 18F.

Getting to Cordes can be a logistical nightmare. Buses leave pl. Jean Jaurès in Albi early in the morning on Mondays and Wednesdays through Fridays. On Thursdays and Saturdays, one departs in the late morning. Normally, a bus returns each day in the afternoon. An easier route involves two trains and a taxi or a bike. Take the train from Albi to Gaillac and change there for Vindrac-Cordes. Once at the station rent a bike (30F per ½-day, 40F per day) and ride 5km uphill to Cordes. **Minicar** (tel. 63 56 14 80) will pick up the linguine-legged at the station for 18F. The station (open 5:30am-10:30pm) runs six daily trains to Toulouse (49F). Most find hitching possible only in July and August. From Vindrac, go to the junction of bd. de Strasbourg, av. Deusbourg, and rue Albert Thomas.

Castres

Celebrated journalist and politician Jean Jaurès put his hometown on the map. Jaurès leapt into prominence as leader of the striking glass-workers of Carmaux in 1896 and later joined other socialists, notably Emile Zola, in vociferous defense of Captain Richard Dreyfus, the Jewish officer framed as a traitor by French generals. After the turn of the century, Jaurès fought a losing battle against rising militarism and sought in vain to avert war by forging an agreement between the French and German working classes. In 1914, his fate as a martyr was sealed when he was assassinated in a Parisian café. Perhaps more out of lack of imagination than true respect, his name is given to a prominent street in every city in France.

Built on both sides of the Agoût river, Castres (pop. 48,000) now emphasizes the arts over politics. The Musée Goya maintains the largest collection of Spanish art in France. Magnificently pruned gardens adorn this somewhat narcoleptic city.

Orientation and Practical Information

Castres lies 72km from Toulouse and 65km north of Carcassonne. Eight direct trains from Toulouse *(direction" Mazamet")* roll in daily. To reach the center of the town from the station, turn left onto av. Albert 1er and then bear right onto bd. Henri Sizaire. At pl. Alsace-Lorraine, turn left onto the rue de l'Evêché. The tourist office is in the Théâtre Municipal. Along with the tourist office and the Hôtel de Ville, museums, shops, and banks cluster on the west side of the river, connected by the pedestrian streets of the old city. Rue Alquier Bouffard and its continuation, rue Villegoudou, cross the pont Neuf and lead to **place Soult,** café central.

Tourist Office: (tel. 63 59 92 44), on pl. de la République in the Théâtre Municipal. Information on the national park nearby. English-speaking staff suggests walks and car excursions in the Tarn region. Open Mon.-Sat. 9:15am-12:30pm and 2-7pm, Sun. 10:30am-12:30pm; Sept.-June Mon.-Sat. 9:15am-12:30pm and 2-6:30pm.

Post Office: (tel. 63 59 28 54), on bd. Alphonse Juin near the tourist office. **Telephones** and **currency exchange.** Open Mon.-Fri. 8am-7pm, Sat. 8am-noon. **Postal Code:** 81100.

Trains: av. Albert 1er (tel. 63 59 22 00). To: Toulouse (8 per day, 1 hr., 57F); Carcassonne via Toulouse (8 per day, 2½ hr., 103F); Albi via St-Sulpice (7 per day, 2 hr., 62F). Information office open daily 5:20am-9:30pm.

Buses: pl. Soult (tel. 63 35 37 31). To: Carcassonne (Mon.-Tues. and Thurs.-Sat. 1 per day, 1 hr., 65F); Toulouse (Mon.-Sat. 4 per day, Sun. 2, 41.50F); Albi (Mon.-Sat. 4 per day, 22F).

Taxis: tel. 63 59 99 25, 24 hrs.

Bike Rental: At the train station (tel. 63 59 22 00). The 10 bikes are often rented (40F per ½-day, 50F per day, 500F deposit. Office open 8am-8pm.

Hospital: 20, bd. Maréchal Foch (tel. 63 71 63 71).

Police: tel. 63 35 40 10. **Emergency,** tel. 17.

Accommodations and Camping

The lonely neighborhood near the train station offers nothing of interest. Try to make the 15-minute hike to the center of town. There is no youth hostel, but the tourist office can direct you to some *gîtes d'étape.*

Hôtel du Perigord, 22, rue Emile Zola (tel. 63 59 04 74), in *centre ville.* Large rooms with high ceilings and good furniture. Singles and doubles with shower 75-85F. Breakfast 15F. Restaurant downstairs posts a 53F *menu,* wine included. Open Sept.-July Sun.-Fri. morning.

Splendid Hôtel, 17, rue Victor Hugo (tel. 63 59 30 42) off pl. Jean Jaurès. Spacious, clean doubles 80F, with shower 100F, with 2 beds 136F. Breakfast 18F.

Hôtel Carcassés, 3, rue d'Augue (tel. 63 35 37 72), off pl. Soult. Family establishment has gigantic rooms with sloping floorboards. Room prices based on the number of double beds (65F each). Showers included. Breakfast 17F.

Camping: Camping Municipal (tel. 63 59 56 49), on av. de Roquecourbe near *centre ville.* Cross the canal and turn left on av. Luicien-Coudert. On the riverbank. 20F perr 2 people.

Food

A large **market** convenes on pl. Jean Jaurès (Tues. and Thurs.-Sat. mornings). Bring a *baguette* and the local *roquefort* and *bleu* cheeses to the shady Jardin de l'Evêché, beside the Hôtel de Ville. Restaurants cluster off pl. Jean Jaurès and near rue Villegoudou.

Les Sarrasines, 34, rue Villegoudou. Lavender and lace decor, and art exhibitions on the wall. *Crêpes* 11-32F, salads 11-29F. 35F *menu.* Open Tues.-Sat. noon-5pm and 7pm-midnight.

L'Eau à la Bouche, 6, rue Malpas. Turn left at pl. Jean Jaurès before the Banque Nationale Populaire. White wicker furniture and lots of baby blue. Refined 65F *menu,* wine included. Open Tues.-Sat. noon-2pm and 7-10pm, Sun. noon-2pm.

Restaurant Carcassés, 3, rue d'Augue, off pl. Soult. Workers' restaurant with filling but no frills 50F *menu, vin compris.* Open noon-2pm and 7-10pm.

Sights and Entertainment

Next to the sculpted shrubbery of the **Jardin de l'Evêché** in the Hôtel de Ville stands the **Musée Goya** (tel. 63 59 62 63, ext. 1512). Strengthened by the canvases of early Catalonian and Aragonese masters, the museum's Goya collection spans a period of over 50 years. (Open July-Aug. open daily 9am-noon and 2-6pm; April-June and Sept. Tues.-Sun. 9am-noon and 2-6pm, Sun. 10am-noon and 2-6pm; Oct.-March open Mon.-Sat. 9am-noon and 2-5pm. Admission 10F, students 5F, under 14 free. Free Nov.-March Wed. and Sun.) Castres's other great museum, the **Musée Jaurès,** pl. Pélisson (tel. 63 72 01 01), is packed with pamphlets, trenchant political cartoons, old photographs, and faded newspaper articles that catch the flavor of Jean Jaurès's spirited, often bitter rhetoric. (Open daily 9am-noon and 2-6pm; April-June and Sept. 1-22 Tues.-Sat. 9am-noon and 2-6pm; Sept. 23-March Tues.-Sat. 9am-noon and 2-5pm. Admission 10F, students under 26 5F, under 14 free.) The **Centre d'Art Contemporain,** marooned in a lovely 18th-century *hôtel particulier,* features exhibits often hung by the artists themselves. (Open Mon.-Sat. 9am-noon and 2-6pm; Sun. 10am-noon and 2-6pm. Admission 5F, students free.) The **quai des Jacobines** presents a fine view of the medieval textile merchants' houses across the Agout River. The wooden galleries were used for drying, while the arched entryways opening onto the river facilitated shipment. Today little of the industry remains; the dilapidated houses have been renovated by the government to provide rent-controlled housing.

From June through August, the **Festival Goya** celebrates Spanish music, dance, art, and theater; tickets (60-120F) are available at the Théâtre Municipal (tel. 63 72 11 73). On the first weekend in July, the **Festival Occitan** reenacts "the tragedy of Occitanie" from Simon de Montfort to the 19th century. Fireworks provide comic relief. The tourist office has tickets (80F).

Accessible by train from Castres (6 per day, 16F), **Mazamet** makes an excellent base for the **Montagnes Noires** in the Parc Natural Régional du Haut Languedoc. For information on hiking routes and *gîtes,* write to the Parc Naturel Régional du Haut Languedoc, 13, rue du Cloître, 34220 Saint-Pons (tel. 67 97 02 10), or buy the brochure *Sidobre, Monts de Lacaune, Montagne Noire* at the Mazamet tourist office (tel. 63 61 27 07). The area of the **Sidobre,** 28km from Castres in the northwest corner of the park (tourist office tel. 63 50 64 25), has provided southern France with grantie since the 11th century. Explore the area on bike or with the Castre-based **Tourisme Vert** (tel. 63 35 54 67). Call three days ahead to book tours.

Carcassonne

According to medieval legend, the name "Carcassonne" dates from the 8th-century occupation of the city by the Saracens. Charlemagne supposedly laid siege to the city for five years, annihilating the defending army. The wife of the Moorish king, however, valiantly continued to defend the city alone. Dame Carcas rushed around the ramparts moving dummies to make the enemy believe that soldiers still protected the city. To complete the illusion of continuing prosperity, she forced the last pig to eat the last bag of wheat and then tossed the unfortunate porker over the outer wall. When Charlemagne saw the exploded pig, he called off the attack. If after five years the besieged population still had enough food to feed their pigs, he thought, his army had clearly failed. But in medieval folklore Charlemagne can't lose; the story goes on. Dame Carcas rang the bell to signal to the retreating King that she wanted to draw up a treaty. The King's men called to him, "Carcas sonne!" (Carcas rings).

Carcassonne's double-walled fortress with turrets and towers (known as "la Cité") seems to encourage such fanciful tales. An agglomeration of fortifications from Gallo-Roman times to the 13th century, the Cité fell into disrepair after the Wars of Religion. So rapaciously did villagers pillage the walled town in search of building materials that for centuries little more than a few crumbling walls remained. In 1844, Viollet-le-Duc, famous architect and chief of the newly created government department of historic monuments, decided to grimthorpe the ancient fortress. Although Viollet's grandiose visions were not matched by his attention to historical detail, he created a living museum of medieval urbanism.

Orientation and Practical Information

The Cité, nicknamed *La Pucelle du Languedoc* (The Maiden of Languedoc), perches imperiously above its ugly stepsister, the modern *ville basse* (pop. 45,000). Most shops, offices, and hotels—as well as the train station—are down below. To reach the Cité, catch the black #4 bus from the train station (every ½-hr. until 6:53pm, 4.50F) or from pl. Gambetta (every ½-hr. until 7:02pm, 5 min.). Otherwise, it's a 30-minute hike.

Tourist Office: 15, bd. Camille Pelletan, pl. Gambetta (tel. 68 25 07 04). Turn left from the train station, and then turn right on bd. Jean Jaurès. **Currency exchange** on weekends when the banks are closed (10F commission). Open Mon.-Sat. 9am-7pm, Sun. 10am-noon; Sept. and April-June Mon.-Sat. 9am-noon and 2-7pm; Oct.-March Mon.-Sat. 9am-noon and 2-6:30pm. **Annex** in the porte Narbonnaise (tel. 68 25 68 81), to your right as you enter the Cité. Open July-Aug. 9am-7pm; April-June and Sept.-Oct. 9am-12:30pm.

Post Office: rue Jean Bringer. **Currency exchange, telephones** and Poste Restante. Open Mon.-Fri. 8am-7pm, Sat. 8am-noon. Branch office, rue Vicomte Trencavel, in the Cité. Open Mon.-Fri. 9am-noon and 2-5pm, Sat. 8:45-11:45am. **Postal Code:** 11000.

Trains: (tel. 68 47 50 50), behind Jardin St-Chenier. Carcassonne is a major stop between Toulouse (11 per day, 50 min., 60F) and points north and east, such as Montpellier (10 per day, 2 hr., 93F), Nîmes (7 per day, 2½ hr., 115F), Lyon (3 direct per day, 5½ hr., 232F), Marseille (every 2 hr., 3 hr., 180F), Toulon (5 per day, 4 hr., 204F), Nice (5 per day, 6 hr., 256F), and Narbonne (10 per day, 1 hr., 55F). Information office open daily 8am-noon and 2-6:30pm. Baggage storage open 5am-2:45am.

Buses: (tel. 68 25 12 74), on bd. de Varsovie. Check complete schedule posted at the station or ask the tourist office. To: Lezignan (5 per day, in winter 2, 50 min., 23F); Toulouse (3 per day, 2½ hr., 51F); Narbonne (2 per day, 1 hr., 31F); Foix (1 per day, 3 hr., 43.50F). Information office open Mon.-Fri. 8am-noon and 2-6pm. **Cars Teissier** (tel. 68 25 85 45), across from the Café Bristol in front of the station. Service offered to Lastours and other nearby towns. Office open Mon.-Sat. 8am-noon and 2-6pm.

Taxis: tel. 68 71 50 50.

Bike Rental: At the train station (tel. 68 71 79 63). 40F per ½-day, 50F per day, 285F per week, 500F deposit. Open 9:30am-8pm.

Laundromat: LAV2000, 68, rue Jean Bringer. A soap odyssey. Wash 20F, dryer 2F per 8 min. No 5F coins. Open 7am-9pm.

Medical Assistance: SAMU, tel. 15; **Centre Hospitalier,** route de St-Hilaire D342 (tel. 68 25 60 30).

Police: 40, bd. Barbès (tel. 68 77 49 00). **Emergency,** tel. 17.

Accommodations and Camping

The large, comfortable youth hostel will put you smack in the middle of the Cité. When the hostel is full, find a hotel in the *ville basse*—those in the Cité are ferociously expensive. The **M.J.C. Centre Internationale de Séjour,** 91, rue Aimé Ramon (tel. 68 25 86 68), is for groups, but may accept desperate individuals.

Auberge de Jeunesse (IYHF) (tel. 68 25 23 16), on rue de Vicomte Trencavel. Friendly and immaculate dorm accommodations. Bed and breakfast 52F. 12F surcharge without hostel card and sheet sleeping sack. Showers included. Open July-Aug. daily 8-11am and 6-midnight; June and Sept. until 11pm; April until 10:30pm; Feb., March, and Nov. until 10pm. Call a few days in advance, especially in June.

Hôtel de l'Octroi, 106, av. Général Leclerc (tel. 68 25 29 08), at the foot of the Cité. Take bus #4 every ½-hr. to the "Leclerc" stop. Appealing singles and doubles 78-100F, with shower and toilet 150F. Triples 115F. Showers 12F. Breakfast 18F. Arrive promply if you make a reservation.

Le Cathare, 53, rue Jean Bringer (tel. 68 25 65 92), near the post office. Cozy rooms. Singles 85F. Doubles 100F, with shower 132F. Showers included. Breakfast 21F. Downstairs restaurant has a 55F *menu*.

Hôtel St-Joseph, 81, rue de la Liberté (tel. 68 25 10 94), 5 min. from the station. Large frilly rooms. Singles 65F. Doubles 68-80F, with shower 125F. Triples 136F. Quads 145F, with shower 165F. Showers 10F. Breakfast 18F.

Hôtel de la Poste, 21, rue de Verdun (tel. 68 25 12 18), also near the post office. Worn rooms above a bar. Singles and doubles 95F, with shower 125F. Quads 150F, with shower 190F. Showers included. Breakfast 18F.

Hôtel Bonnafoux, 40, rue de la Liberté (tel. 68 25 01 45). From the station, follow rue G. Clemenceau and turn at the second right, rue de la Liberté. Simple rooms with a friendly owner. Doubles 68-80F, with shower 113F. Triples 113F, with shower 150F. Quads 130F, with shower 165F. Showers 10F. Breakfast 18F. Open Feb.-Nov.

Camping: Camping de la Cité (tel. 68 25 11 77), across the l'Aude from the modern town. A 3-star site with exchange office, swimming pool, and access to the *Cité*. July-Aug. 58F per 2 people; Easter-June and Sept.-Oct. 40F per 2 people.

Food

Most of the surprisingly inexpensive restaurants in the Cité serve the regional specialty *cassoulet,* a stew of white beans, herbs, and some form of meat (usually lamb or pork). For provisions, visit the **market** in pl. Carnot (also known as pl. aux Herbes; open Tues., Thurs., and Sat. until 1pm), or the **covered market** at pl. d'Eggenfelden, off rue Aimé Ramon. In the *ville basse,* simple but affordable restaurants line bd. Omer Sarraut. Restaurants in the Cité tend to shut down in winter.

Au Bon Pasteur, 29, rue Armagnac, in the *ville basse* near Eglise St-Vincent. A friendly, English-speaking owner and a 60F *menu, vin compris.* Excellent *cassoulet* and *confit de canard* (preserved duck). Open Feb.-Dec. 23, Tues.-Sat. noon-2pm and 7-9pm.

L'Ostal des Troubadours, 5, rue Viollet-le-Duc, in a 15th-century building. A fun place for coffee or drinks. Musicians play Provençal songs, Irish ballads, blues, rock. The restaurant serves some of the cheapest *menus* around (39F and 59F, service not included). Drinks 10-15F. Open noon to midnight. *Menus* served noon-2pm and 6-10pm. Open noon-2pm and 6-10pm.

La Taverne Médiévale, 4-7, rue Cros Mayrevieille, on the Cité's main thoroughfare. A cafeteria serving decent food. Pleasant, wood-beamed room. Meat with choice of vegetable 30F, *cassoulet* 50F. Open Fri.-Wed. 11:30am-3pm and 6:30-10pm.

La Rotonde, 13, bd. Omer Sarraut, in the *ville basse* across from the train station. A late-night *brasserie* and café, with a quick 48F *menu* of veal and pork dishes. Also an unlimited hors-d'oeuvre bar with lots of vegetables and pâté, and a limited dessert bar. Open daily 6:30am-2am.

Le Sénéchal, 6, rue Viollet-le-Duc. Somewhat expensive dinner *menu,* but it's a small price to pay for excellent food and a beautiful courtyard setting. 62F *menu.* Open daily noon-1:45pm and 7-9:45pm; Oct.-June Tues.-Sat. noon-1:45pm and 7-9:45pm, Sun. noon-1:45pm.

Sights and Entertainment

Occupying a strategic position on the road between Toulouse and the Mediterranean, the original fortifications at Carcassonne date back to the Roman Empire in the first century and the Visigoths in the 5th century. An early fortress here withstood Clovis, King of the Franks, in 506 AD, and subsequent invaders, but Carcassonne fell with Languedoc during the Albigensian Crusade in 1209. When the Cité passed to the control of the French King Louis IX (St-Louis), the monarch ordered the construction of the second outer wall, copying the double-walled fortress design French crusaders had seen in Palestine. The city lapsed into neglect until Viollet-le-Duc reimagined it, rather controversially, in 1844. The blue slate roofs used for the towers of the inner ring of fortresses are so out of place among the red-tiled roofs of the Midi that local authorities here recently embarked on a scheme to reroof them using local materials.

The coolest place in the *Cité* on a scorching summer day, the **Basilique St-Nazaire** stuns visitors with some of the loveliest rose windows in southern France. (Open daily 9am-noon and 2-6pm.) Entrance to the grounds and outer walls is free, but entrance to **Château Comtal** and the inner towers requires a guided tour. Tours in French run continuously; two or three English tours run daily in July and August. All start inside the château's gates. (Open July-Aug. 9:30am-12:30pm and 2-7:30pm; May-June and Sept. 1-15 9:30am-12:30pm and 2-6:30pm; Sept. 16-April 9:30am-12:30pm and 2-5pm. Admission 23F, ages 18-25 and over 60 12F, under 18 8F.) Those not qualifying for a reduction can pick up the three-monument pass for the Château, the Fort de Salses, and the Remparts d'Aigues-Mortes at any of the three sights.

Though a bit unsightly by day, the *ville basse* is livelier than the Cité at night, especially from September to June. The streets, which meet at prosaic right angles, hold their share of churches. With its round steeple and rose windows, the **Cathédrale St-Michel** exemplifies 14th- and 15th-century *gothique languedocien.* **Eglise St-Vincent** features only one lonely nave and a 54m tower. Pilgrims flocked to **Notre-Dame de Santé,** a tiny 16th-century chapel to the right of pont Vieux, on the way to the Cité.

Last year the opera *Carmen* and Ray Charles animated the eclectic **festival,** which returns each July to the restored theater of the Château Comtal (admission 80-260F). For information, contact Festival de la Cité, Théâtre Municipal, 11005 Carcassonne (tel. 68 71 30 30). In August, the entire Cité returns to the Middle Ages for the **Médiévales.** People dressed as medieval folk talk to visitors, display their crafts, and pretend nothing has changed in 800 years. In addition, jousts clang daily at 6pm; contact the tourist office for ticket information (30F). On summer nights, the Cité stages an elaborate sound and light show. (Admission 80F; call the tourist office for reservations.)

Perpignan

Perpignan's strategic location between the Mediterranean and the Pyrenees was used to military advantage between 1276 and 1344, when the kings of Majorca established their royal residence here. A part of France only since 1659, Perpignan (pop. 113,000) reigns as the northern capital of the **Catalogne-Française** (French Catalan), with Barcelona as its southern counterpart. Friendlier and less pretentious than vacation destinations on the Côte d'Azur, Perpignan remains a quiet and dull spot despite a summer deluge of backpackers. Once called the "center of the world" by the rather decentered Salvador Dali, Perpignan's train station (yes, the *train station*) provides connections to the surrounding Catalan region, Spain 50km south, white sand beaches 13km east, picturesque fishing villages 25km south, and the Pyrenees, whose foothills begin rolling 30km west.

With its immense arcaded courtyard and two curiously superimposed chapels, the restored **Palais des Rois de Majorque** is still the city's most impressive sight. The **citadelle,** whose forbidding walls still surround the palace, was used as an arsenal in the last century, and is just now being restored. (Gates open Wed.-Mon. 9:30am-noon and 2:30-6pm. Admission 10F, students 5F, ages under 10 free.) Guided tours in French leave from the entrance of the palace at 10am, 11am, 3pm, 4pm, and 5pm. Ask the tourist office for a list of summer concerts held in the gardens.

Housed in the enchanting brick **Castillet** (castle), **La Casa Païral,** pl. de Verdun (tel. 68 66 30 66), displays exhibits of Catalan culture and folklore. (Open Wed.-Mon. 9:30-11:30am and 2:30-6:30pm; Sept. 16-May Wed.-Mon. 9am-noon and 2-6pm. Free.) For more information on Catalonian traditions, contact the **Musée Puig,** 42, av. de la Grande Bretagne (tel. 68 35 66 30).

The **Fête de la St-Jean** occurs every June 23, when the sacred fire is brought from the **Canigou,** a nearby mountain. According to popular legend, jumping over a bonfire lit by the *feu de St-Jean* cleanses the spirit. Along with the rest of the *Pyrénées-Orientales,* Perpignan explodes into spectacular firework displays.

Orientation and Practical Information

From the train station, walk up av. Général de Gaulle and turn right before the large *place* onto cours Lazare Escarguel, which crosses the canal. Turn left immediately after crossing the bridge; the regional tourist office is on your right on quai de Lattre de Tassigny (15 min.). Place Arago and pl. de la Victoire lie farther along the canal from the regional tourist office.

Tourist Office: in the Palais des Congrès, pl. Armand Lanoux (tel. 68 34 13 13 or 68 66 30 00). Unhelpful, crowded, and on the other side of the planet (a solid ½-hr. walk from the train station). Follow the canal to bd. Wilson, and walk along the Promenade des Platanes to the Palais des Congrès. Walking tours leave daily at 3:30pm (20F, under 12 10F). Office open June-Sept. 9am-8pm, Oct.-May Mon.-Sat. 8:30am-noon and 2-6:30pm. **Regional Tourist Office,** quai de Lattre de Tassigny (tel. 68 34 29 94). The English-speaking staff is better prepared to distribute information on the city and the Roussillon region. Information on hotels, camping, *gîtes d'étape,* restaurants, walks, train and bus schedules, and festivals. City maps. Open daily 9am-8pm; Sept. 16-June 14 9am-noon and 2-7pm.

Currency Exchange: Eurochange, 35m av. du Général de Gaulle (tel. 68 34 44 34). Excellent rates and no commission. (Open Mon.-Sat. 9am-noon and 2-7pm; Sun. 9am-noon). Rates at the train station are a pisser. (Open daily 8-11am and 5-7pm.)

Post Office: quai de Barcelone. **Exchange** with good rates. **Telephones.** Open Mon.-Fri. 8am-7pm, Sat. 8am-noon. **Postal Code:** 66020.

Trains: (tel. 68 35 73 11), on rue Courteline. To: Narbonne (30 per day, ½-hr., 42F); Paris (6 per day, 10 hr., 382F); Villefranche (7 per day, 50 min., 34F); Prades (7 per day, 40 min., 31F); Collioure (12 per day, ½-hr., 21F); Salses (5 per day, 15 min., 13F). Office open Mon.-Sat. 4am-7:30pm and Sun. 8am-noon and 2-6pm.

Buses: 17, av. Général Leclerc (tel. 68 35 29 02), near pl. de la Résistance. To: Narbonne (Mon.-Sat. 2 per day, 1½ hr.); Béziers (Mon.-Sat. 1 per day, 21/3 hr.); the airport (Mon.-Sat. 3 per day, 15 min.). **Car Inter 66,** 17, av. Général Leclerc (tel. 68 35 29 02). 4 buses per day to all the beaches from le Barcarès to Cerbère. 10 buses connect individual beaches. Schedules available at both tourist offices. Car Inter 66 offers a **tourist pass** good for one week within the *département* (110F). Office open Mon.-Thurs. 8am-noon and 2-6pm; Fri. 8am-noon and 2-5pm; Sat.-Sun. 8am-noon and 2-6pm.

Public Transportation: Buses, tel. 68 61 01 13. City bus #1 goes to Canet-Plage June-Aug. Mon.-Sat. 22 times per day (last bus at 7:30pm, last return from Canet-Plage at 8pm, 25 min.). Buses leave from pl. des Platanes (10F, day pass 30F). Intra-city bus tickets 5F.

Taxis: tel. 68 34 59 49 or 68 51 11 84. 24 hrs.

Laundromat: Lavomatique, 5, pl. Jean Payra (tel. 68 34 15 89). Gregarious English-speaking woman in charge will watch your stuff. Wash 20F. Dry 2F. Soap 4F. Open daily 9am-7pm.

Hospital: av. du Maréchal Joffre (tel. 68 61 66 30).

Police: Emergency, tel. 17.

Accommodations, Camping, and Food

Auberge de Jeunesse (IYHF), La Pépinière (tel. 68 34 63 32), off av. de la Grande Bretagne behind the Hôtel de Police and the Parc de la Pépinière. Kind and understanding management make up for somewhat archaic facilities (Turkish toilets). Bunk beds and a small kitchen which is open all day. Keys available for entrance after the 11pm curfew. Lockout 10am-6pm. 52F per person. Sheets 13F. Brekafast included (served 7:30-8:30am). Call ahead in July and Aug.

Hôtel le Bristol, 5, rue Grande des Fabriques (tel. 68 34 32 68), off pl. de Verdun. Spacious, quiet rooms in an excellent location. Singles 70-80F, with shower 110F. Double 90F, with shower 110F. Triple with shower 140F. Free hall shower. Breakfast 22F. Reserve for July and Aug.

Hôtel de la Poste, 8, rue Fabrique Nabot (tel. 68 34 42 53), near pl. de Verdun. Friendly management and spacious rooms. Singles 100F, with shower 165F. Doubles 120F, with shower 180F. Showers 10F. Breakfast 20F. Open Feb. 16-Jan. 14.

Hôtel le Berry, 6, av. de la Gare (tel. 68 34 59 02), in front of the train station. Large doubles 80F, with shower 100F. Triples with shower 130F. Extra bed 30F. Showers 15F. Breakfast 15-17F.

Hôtel de la Gare, 19, av. de Gaulle (tel. 68 34 56 16). The cheapest within reasonable geographic proximity to Dali's *centre du monde.* Doubles 80F, with shower 100F. Triples and quads 150F. Breakfast 20F.

Camping: La Garrigole, rue Maurice Levy (tel. 68 54 66 10). Take bus #2 from the station (5F). Shaded site with a pool. July-Aug. 59F per 2 people; Sept.-Nov. and Jan.-June 55F per 2 people. Open Jan.-Nov. **Camping Le Catalan,** route de Bompas (tel. 68 63 16 92). Take the "Bompas" bus from the station. Free pool and showers. July-Aug. 58F per 2 people; Sept.-June 42F per 2 people.

Place de la Loge and pl. de Verdun in the *vieille ville* are filled with restaurants and cafés that stay lively at night. More expensive restaurants line quai Vauban along the canal. An **open-air market** fills pl. de la République daily from 5am to 6pm. The grocery store in the basement of the **Nouvelles Galeries,** pl. de la Résistance, provides all the fixings for a beach picnic. (Open Mon.-Sat. 9am-7pm).

Le Perroquet, 1, av. Général de Gaulle, a stone's throw from the train station, offers surprisingly cheap, excellent food. Their 50F *menu* features a wide range of choices, such as *escargots* and *lapin* (bunny), both prepared with a Catalan twist. (Open Sat.-Wed. noon-1:45pm and 7-9m, Thurs. for lunch only.) The self-service cafeteria, **Le Palmarium,** pl. Argo, entices diners to its outdoor terrace overlooking the canal. *Plats du jour* run 25-35F. (Open daily 11:30am-2:30pm and 7-9:30pm.) **Le Canneton,** 12, rue Victor Hugo, serves a bland 30F *menu,* wine included. (Open Mon.-Sat. noon-2pm and 7-9pm.) Hard-to-find **La Mesa,** 3, rue de la Petite Monnaie (tel. 68 35 03 85), near the Palais des Rois de Majorques, offers excellent fish dishes and a 50F *menu* of Spanish specialties. (Open Mon. and Wed.-Sat. noon-1:30pm and 7:30-9:30pm; Tues. noon-1:30pm.)

Near Perpignan: Beaches, Prades, and Villefranche

The **Côte Vermeille,** extending from Perpignan into Spain, hosts more French tourists than any other region except the Côte d'Azur. Families spend a week or two of their vacations splayed on the wide beaches or in the clean waters bordering Roussillon. In July and August, beaches are crowded but not unbearable. Since hotels and campgrounds usually fill up during peak tanning months, you'll probably end up commuting from Perpignan.

Shuttles run to **Canet-Plage** from the promenade des Platanes in Perpignan (2 or 3 per hr., 25 min, 10F). The **tourist office,** pl. de la Méditerranée (tel. 68 73 25 20), will direct you to a campground.

Cars Inter 66, 17, av. Général Leclerc (tel. 68 35 29 02), connects Perpignan to the resorts of **St-Cyprien-Plage** (tourist office tel. 68 21 01 33; Mon.-Sat. 5 per day, Sun. 3, ½-hr., 18F); **Argèles-sur-Mer** (tourist office, pl. des Arènes (tel. 68 81 15 85); Mon.-Sat. 8 per day, Sun. 4, ½-hr., 22F), and **Banyuls-sur-Mer** (tourist office, 38, av. de la République (tel. 68 88 31 58); 4 per day, 70 min., 30F). These buses depart from the *gare routière* on av. Général Leclerc. Another bus links all of the coastal resorts from **Bacarés** to **Cerbère.** Pick up schedules in the Perpignan tourist offices or at the Car Inter 66 office at the bus station.

The 15th-century **Fort de Sales** looms 16km north of Perpignan. Built by King Ferdinand of Aragon in 1497, the fort housed 1500 soldiers charged with protecting the territory recently acquired by the Spanish sovereign. (Open Wed.-Mon. 9am-noon and 2-7pm; Oct.-April. 9am-noon and 2-5 pm; 23F, students 12F.) Visit the **tourist office,** 13, rue Gaston-Clos (tel. 68 38 66 13), for maps indicating châteaux in the area.

West of Perpignan, the train begins its ascent into the Pyrênées. **Prades** (pop. 6000) presides over the agricultural area called the **Conflent.** The 1000-year-old **Abbaye de St-Michel de Cura** lies 3km from the center of town. (Open daily 9:30am-noon and 2:30-6pm.) Get a map and directions from the friendly English-speaking staff of the **tourist office,** 4, rue Victor Hugo (tel. 68 96 27 58). From July 25-August 13, the *abbaye* hosts the **Festival Pablo Casals,** three weeks of classical music honoring the Catalonian cellist and exile from Franco's Spain who spent 23 years in Prades. Tickets (100-140F) are available from the festival office, **Académie,** rue Victor Hugo (tel. 68 96 33 07). Every Tuesday the flourishing **open-air market** draws the population out of the mountains (8am-1pm). Left-over hippies sell fascinating sculptures carved from woodlike mushrooms. Prades is also home to a number of European converts to Islam. Seven daily trains head for Prades from Perpignan (40 min, 36F). If you decide to stay in the city, call the *abbaye* (tel. 68 96 02 40) and ask the monks if there is any room at the inn. The **postal code** for Prades is 66500.

Originally the capital of the Conflent and known for its fine pink marble, **Villefranche-le-Conflent** occupies a prized location at the confluence of the Cady and Têt rivers and at the base of three mountains. The town's military ramparts are as well-preserved as the twenty-two 13th- and 14th-century façades registered as historical monuments. Built into the mountainside high above the town, 17th-century **Fort Liberia** was designed by chief French military architect Vauban to protect Villefranche after the 1659 Treaty of the Pyrenees established the nearby Franco-Spanish border. Although never attacked, the three levels of fortification formed an elaborate defense system that guarded Villefranche from every possible angle. (Open 9am-8pm. Admission 25F, children 10F.) On June 23, the Catalonian **Fête des Feux de la St-Jean** burns brightly in Villefranche. As in Perpignan, torches lit on nearby Canigou mountain bring the sacred fire back to the village, where locals dance the traditional *sardane,* drink wine, and jump over bonfires.

Guided visits of Villefranche and its *remparts* leave from pl. de l'Eglise at 3pm. (Mon., Wed.-Thurs., and Sat., 20F). The **tourist office,** also on pl. de l'Eglise (tel. 68 96 22 96), can help with lodging. The **Association Culturelle,** 38, rue St-Jean (tel. 68 96 25 64), has a remarkably dedicated staff who will give you information on historical hiking tours of the area. (Open Mon.-Fri. 9am-noon and 2-7pm). For exhaustive maps and information about hiking locally and throughout the Pyrenees, write to **Editions et Diffusions Randonnées Pyrénéennes,** BP 88, 09200 St-Girons (tel. 61 66 71 87). Hotels in Villefranche fill quickly in summer. **Hôtel Le Terminus,** outside the village next to the train station (tel. 68 05 20 24), lets attractive rooms for 80F. (Doubles with shower 120F. Breakfast 20F.) The town hall (tel. 68 96 10 78) on pl. de l'Eglise operates *gîtes communaux* where you can stay one or two nights if you have a sleeping bag. (Town hall open Mon.-Fri. 9am-noon.)

The same train which stops in Prades continues to Villefranche (7 per day, 45 min., 37F). Buses also run the same route from Perpignan. Schedules are available at the **Car Inter 66** office, 17, av. Général Leclerc (tel. 68 35 29 02) in Perpignan.

From Villefranche, catch the charming, open-air *petit train jaune* through the Pyrenees to **La Tour-de-Carol** (2½ hr., 73F), where trains connect to Toulouse and Barcelona. Six trains daily make the climb through the mountains, stopping at small villages along the way. The 63km stretch of track once transported iron and marble produced in the area. The Association Culturelle in Villefranche sells a guide, *Promenades et randonnées à partir de train jaune* (60F). The staff will show you the *boucles* (hikes) which can be made from each village where the train stops. These paths are well-marked and dotted with *gîtes* which facilitate longer stays in these spectacular Mediterranean mountains.

If visiting the area in winter, the fashionable ski area at **Font Romeu,** accessible by the *petit train jaune,* is fully equipped with snow machines and ski lifts. Day lift tickets cost 90F. Contact the **tourist office,** av. E. Brousse (tel. 68 30 02 74), for information on equipment rental.

Collioure

The uncanny, brightly-colored beauty of Collioure called to the unknown Matisse in 1905. Dérain, Gris, Dufy, Dali, and Picasso soon followed. In summer, painters still line the *quais* with their easels, trying to capture the decorated *barques* beached on the **plage Boramar.** For the price of a drink (try the local Banyuls, a sweet *apéritif*), you can marvel at the canvases covering every inch of wall space in the **Hôtel des Templiers,** quai de l'Amirauté (tel. 68 82 05 58). Matisse, Picasso, Dali and hosts of lesser artists donated their work in exchange for meals and unlimited lodging privileges. Caring more for local tradition than for profit, the proprietors have held on to these works in the face of an increasingly bullish art market.

With Perpignan only 27km north and Spain 20km south, Collioure inspired military artists as well, beginning with the Greeks in the 6th century BC. Louis XIV's strategist Vauban fortified the 13th-century **Château Royal** (tel. 68 82 06 43) in 1679. The palace now houses a hodge-podge of regional history and modern art exhibits. (Open June 20-Sept. Wed.-Mon. 10am-7pm, Oct.-Nov. and March-June 19 Wed.-Mon. 2:30-7:30pm, admission 16F.) The village's new **Musée de Collioure,** on the road to Port-Vendres, displays the work of artists who painted here. (Open July-Aug. Wed.-Mon. 2-7pm; May-June and Sept. Wed.-Mon. 2-7pm. Admission 12F, students 8F.) The 17th-century **Notre Dame des Anges** rises at the end of the crescent-shaped village. A gilded altar crafted by Catalonian sculptor Joseph Sunyer in 1698 brightens the dark interior. (Open 8am-noon and 2-5:30pm.)

Rocky beaches border the interior of the village. If you're thinking about beach bumming, take the Car Inter 66 **bus** which leaves from pl. Général Leclerc and from av. Général de Gaulle up or down the coast (4 per day to Argèles-sur-Mer-plage, 5 per day to Banyuls). The Centre International de Plongé, 2, rue de Puits-St-Dominique, in the *basse ville* (tel. 68 82 07 16), rents **windsurfers** (70F per hr., 290F per 5 hr., 500F per 10 hr.) and **canoes** (40F per hr., 100F per ½-day, 200F per day). The CIP offers training in scuba-diving and windsurfing from May through early November. The one-week courses include room and board at the center's clubhouse (950-1300F). Write ahead to: CIP Collioure, BP 38, 66190 Collioure.

The **féria de Collioure** takes place each August 14-18. Humane Portuguese-style bullfights (the bull isn't killed) and fireworks make braving the crowds worthwhile. During July and August, you can join into the *sardanes,* traditional Catalonian dances which occur rather spontaneously in village squares. It's a good idea to make hotel reservations for these months as early as February.

Hotels here are expensive. The **Hôtel des Templiers** (tel. 68 82 05 58) might have room in their annex (doubles 150F). **Hôtel Le Majorque,** 16, av. Général de Gaulle (tel. 68 82 29 22), provides simple, clean rooms. (Doubles 150F, with shower 190F. Quads 190F. Open March-Nov.) **Hôtel Triton,** 1, rue Jean Bart (tel. 68 82 06 52), in the *basse ville,* offers rooms overlooking the port d'Avall all year. (Singles 148F. Doubles with shower 198F. Breakfast included.) **Camping Les Amandiers** (tel. 68 81 14 69), 150m from the beach, has free hot showers. (17F per person, 14F per tent. Open April-Sept.) For directions, go to **Hôtel La Frégate,** av. Camille Pelletan (tel. 68 82 05 58).

A fantastic **market** on the pl. du 8 Mai 1945, offers inexpensive, locally grown fruit and artisanal *charcuterie.* Somewhat less expensive than the hotels, Collioure's restaurants serve the renowned *sardines a la braise* as well as other locally caught fish. **L'Albatros,** 48, rue de la Démocratie, in the *basse ville* facing the port, has a small, bright interior decorated like a Matisse paper collage. Eat it or wear it. (Mussels 30-38F, pizza 30-40F. Open Thurs.-Tues. noon-3pm and 7pm-midnight, Wed. 7pm-midnight.) **Le Chiberta,** 18, av. du Général de Gaulle, also in the *basse ville,* offers a 62F *menu*of Catalonian specialties cooked by the owner. (Open daily noon-2pm and 7-10pm, Oct.-June 19, Fri.-Wed. same hours.) Off av. Général de Gaulle, **Le Welsh,** 5, rue Edgar Quinet, drowns *lapins* (bunnies) in the local Banyuls wine for the sake of their 56F *menu.*

The **train station** (tel. 68 92 05 89), at the end of av. Aristide Maillol, sends trains north to Perpignan and Narbonne (8 per day, 21F) and south to Port Bou (6 per day, 13F) and Barcelona (5 per day, 56F). **Luggage storage** costs 12F per day. (Station open daily 5:30am-11:30pm.) For **bus** schedules and prices, call Car Inter 66 (tel. 68 82 15 47) or inquire at the **tourist office,** pl. de la Mairie (tel. 68 82 15 47). The tourist office's brochure, **Collioure, Joyau de la Côte Vermeille,** is helpful when planning short hikes from the village. (Open June-Sept. Mon.-Sat. 9:30am-noon and 3:30-7pm, Sun. 10am-noon; Oct.-May Mon-Tues. and Thurs.-Sat. 9:30am-noon and 2-5pm.) The **post office,** rue de la République, has telephones. (Open Mon.-Fri. 9am-noon and 2-5 pm, Sat. 8:30-11:30am). The **postal code** for Collioure is 66190.

Montpellier

In his *Mémoires d'un Touriste,* Stendhal called Montpellier "la seule ville française de l'intérieur qui n'a pas l'air stupide" (the only French city of the interior that doesn't look stupid). Claiming to admire Stendhal's memoir despite his "often singularly false" taste and "perversely colourless" style, rival 19th-century literary traveler Henry James called Montpellier "one of those places that please, without your being able to say wherefore." Despite the city's history of damningly faint praise, the charm and vitality of Montpellier (pop. 250,000) is infectious. Springing up in the 10th century at the crossroads of the salt trade route and the pilgrimage route to St-Jacques-de-Compostelle, relatively young Montpellier remains an important economic center. IBM and other high-tech industries have set up factories in this *technopôle.* Close enough to the beach to torture its students through spring exams, the university in Montpellier has schools of medicine and law renowned since the 12th century. The 40,000 students erupt into jubilant activity after dark. During the day, narrow and surprisingly quiet streets entice visitors into the *vieille ville,* which hides many 17th- and 18th-century *hôtels particuliers.* Cafés on pl. de la Comédie, fondly known to *Montpellierains* as *l'Oeuf* (the egg), offer expensive coffee and hours of four-star people-watching. An international modern dance festival and numerous theatrical productions enliven the city yet more during the summer.

Orientation and Practical Information

Trains run directly to Paris, Avignon, Nîmes, Marseille, Nice, and Perpignan. The modern town center is the Place de la Comédie, a combination of slick office buildings, 19th-century hotels, and a large open space that springs to life at night with street musicians, dancers, and the occasional roving trouvère. The *place* lies on the southwestern corner of the *vieille ville.* Known as the *écusson* (coat of arms), the old city can be confusing without a map. Get one at the tourist office in the train station. To get to the main tourist office from the train station, walk up rue Maguelone and turn right onto the pl. de la Comédie. Go across the *place* and turn right onto the allée Jean-Milhau. **Le Triangle,** the building on your left, houses the tourist office.

Tourist Office: allée du Tourisme (tel. 67 79 15 15), le Triangle. Excellent maps as well as information on Montpellier and Languedoc-Roussillon. Hotel reservation service and currency exchange. English-speaking staff. Guided tours of the city in French (1-2 per day 34F, student 21F) and English (Mon. 41F, students 27F). Open July-Aug. 9am-8pm; Sept.-June 9am-6pm.**Budget Travel: Atoll Voyages,** 1, rue de l'Université (tel. 67 66 03 65). **BIJ/Eurotrain** tickets. Good information on charter flights. Open 9:30am-12:30pm and 3:30-6:30pm Mon.-Fri. **Post Office:** pl. Rondelet (tel. 67 92 48 00). **Currency exchange** and **telephones.** Open Mon.-Fri. 8am-7pm, Sat. 8am-noon. **Branch office** at pl. des Martyrs de la Résistance. **Postal Code:** 34000.

Trains: pl. Auguste Gilbert (tel. 67 58 50 50). A small **tourist office** (open Mon.-Fri. 9am-noon and 2-6pm) and an **exchange** desk with excellent rates (open daily 8am-9pm). To: Avignon (16 per day, 1 hr., 62F); Carcassonne (16 per day, 2 hr., 92F); Marseille (8 per day, 2 hr. 10 min., 102F); Béziers (½ hr., 30F); Narbonne (every hr., 50 min., 62F); Nîmes (almost every hr., ½-hr., 40F); Nice (8 per day, 4½ hr., 200F); Toulouse (every hr., 3¼ hr., 136F); Perpignan (10 per day, 1 hr. 50 min., 95F); Paris (9 per day, with change in Lyon, 5 hr., 356F plus 14F TGV reservation).Information office open Mon.-Sat. 8am-7pm, Sun. 8:15am-noon and 2-5:15 pm.

Buses: (tel. 67 92 01 43), on rue Jules Ferry, next to the train station. Line #17 to: Palavas (2-3 per hr., 8F); Aigues-Mortes (1½ hr., 29.10F); Béziers (every hr., 1½ hr., 43.60F); Carnon (2 per hr. 20 min., 15.10F); Nîmes (every hr., 1¾ hr., 39.30F); Alès (4 per day, 1¾ hr., 58.10); La Grande Motte (2 per hr., 45 min., 19.10F). Information office open daily 9am-noon and 2-7pm.

Taxis: tel. 67 41 37 87 or 67 92 04 55. 24 hrs.

Bike Rental: At the train station near the baggage storage. 50F per day, 40F per ½-day, 500F deposit. Open daily 8am-8pm.

English Bookstore: Bookshop, 4, rue de l'Université (tel. 67 66 09 08). Large selection includes *Let's Go France* and *Let's Go Europe,* newspapers, periodicals, and video rental. Extremely helpful staff glad to give advice on restaurants, accommodations, and the like. **American Library:** 11, rue St-Louis (tel. 67 58 13 44). Huge collection of current periodicals and large selection of books. Membership (150F per year, students 100F per year) required to check out materials. (Open Mon. 2-6:30pm, Tues. 10am-6:30pm, Sat. 10am-noon.) **French-American Center:** 4, rue St-Louis (tel. 67 92 30 66). Has a bookstore (tel. 67 58 13 44). All anglophones welcome. Open Mon.-Fri. 9am-noon and 2-6:30pm.

Laundromat: Le Lavoir, 30, rue de Candolle. Lively, cozy café-laundromat with bright decorations and comic strips on the walls. Wash 16F, dry 2F per 5 min. Soap 2F. They'll do it for 42F. Open daily 7:30am-10pm.

Crisis Lines: SOS Amitié, tel. 67 63 00 63. 24-hr. crisis line. **SOS Femmes,** tel. 67 75 61 63. Helps women in need. 24 hrs.

Hospital: St-Eloi, 2, av. Bertin Sans (tel. 67 33 90 50).

Medical Assistance: SAMU, tel. 67 63 00 00.

Police: 22, av. Georges Clemenceau (tel. 67 22 78 22). **Emergency,** tel. 17.

Accommodations and Camping

In addition to the youth hostel and *foyer,* Montpellier has many one-star and no-star hotels. During the summer, find a hotel room in the morning; they may all be full by afternoon.

Auberge de Jeunesse (IYHF), 2, impasse de la Petite Corraterie (tel. 67 79 61 66). Take bus #5 from the train station and get off at bd. Louis-Blanc. Otherwise, ask directions to rue de Ecoles-Laïques. The hostel is off this street. Plain dormitory accommodations. (Open 8-10am and 6pm-1am). IYHF card required (on sale for 96F). 51F per person. Sheets 12F. Breakfast included.

Foyer des Jeunes Travailleurs, 3, rue de la Vieille (tel. 67 52 83 11), past pl. de la Comédie and left off rue de la Loge. In a renovated 14th-century mansion 10 min. from the train station. Clean, modern facilities include a washing machine and Kurtzbergian TV room. But is the wallpaper flowery? Friendly management. 3-day min. stay. Reception open daily until 10pm. Singles 65F. Doubles 55F per person. Sleeping bag required. Breakfast included. Lunch and dinner 36F. Terrace dining above the street always available. Call ahead. Rooms, and then only a handful, available June 15-Sept. 15.

Hôtel Plantade, 10, rue Plantade (tel. 67 92 61 45). From the train station, bear left on av. de la République, which becomes bd. du Jeu de Paume. Turn left on rue du Faubourg du Courreau; it's the first right. Friendly, English-speaking proprietor. Interesting decor. Singles 73F, with shower 95F. Doubles 85F, with shower 115F. Showers 6F. Breakfast 15F. Usually full in June and September.

Hôtel Majestic, 4, rue du Cheval Blanc (tel. 67 66 26 85), 3 blocks down rue des Etuves from pl. de la Comédie. Good location. Not majestic, but cheap. Singles 70F. Doubles 90F, with shower 100-130F. Triples with shower 160-200F. Showers 20F. Breakfast 15F. Reserve by mail.

Nova Hôtel, 8, rue Richelieu (tel. 67 60 79 85), down the street from the Majestic. Rather stuffy and faded rooms. Doubles 100-120F, with shower and toilet 158F. Triples and quads 180-229F. Showers 16F. Breakfast 20F.

Hôtel Fauvettes, 8, rue Bonnard (tel. 67 63 17 60). The street runs by the Jardin des Plantes, and the hotel has its own garden. Basic singles 70F. Doubles 85F. Triples and quads 150F. Showers 10F. Breakfast 14F.

Hotel France, 3/4, rue de la République (tel. 67 92 68 14). Down the street from the station. Huge hotel with spacious rooms. Doubles 110-140F, with shower 165F.

Food

Rue des Ecoles Laïques in the old city offers interesting ethnic choices. The **university restaurants** are **Arceaux,** rue Gustave; **Boutonnet,** rue Emile Duployé; **Triolet,** rue Prof. Joseph Anglada; and **Vert-Bois,** 209, rue de la Chênaie. Check at **CROUS,** 2, rue Monteil, to see which are open in summer. You must show an ISIC card to buy a meal ticket. Morning **markets** are held daily around the *préfecture,* pl. Cabane, and pl. Jean Jaurès. Inexpensive groceries leap off the shelves of **Monoprix,** pl. de la Comédie. (Open Mon.-Sat. 9am-7pm.)

Les Lutins, 5, rue de la Petite Loge. An Aveburyesque place tucked away in a corner. Excellent *tartes salées* (savory tarts) 45F, 55F and 68F. Open daily noon-2pm and 7:30-11pm.

Yakanooga, 10, rue du College Duvergner, on pl. de la Chapelle Neuve. Beautiful flowered balcony terrace in summer; inside seating is light and pleasant. Fish specialities. Seafood salads 28-35F. 49F lunch *menu.* Open Tues.-Fri. noon-2pm and 7-10pm, Mon. and Sat. 7-10pm.

Ramses, 26, rue des Ecoles Laïques. Exquisitely presented and delicious Egyptian specialities. Vegetarian plate 38F. 68F *menu.* Try the mint tea after dinner. Open daily 7-11pm.

Le St-Côme, 7, pl. St-Côme. Terrace seating. Try the *boeuf camarguaise.* Copious 49F *menu.* Open May-Sept. 8pm-midnight.

Le Viel Ecu, 1, rue des Ecoles Laïques, on pl. de la Chapelle Neuve. Good food served in a 16th-century chapel or on the popular terrace. *Terrine de saumon aux legumes* 32F. 85F *menu.* Open Tues.-Sat. noon-2:30pm and 7-11:30pm, Sun.-Mon. 7-11:30pm.

Le Feu Follet, 10, rue du Petit St-Jean. White stone walls and wooden beams. Large selection of salads (18-42F). Somewhat dull 42F *menu* includes salad, pizza, and dessert. 59F *menu,* too.

Sights and Entertainment

The *écusson* (Montpellier's *vieille ville*) is bounded by bd. Pasteur and bd. Louis Blanc to the north, the Esplanade Charles de Gaulle and the bd. Victor Hugo to the east, and bd. Jeu de Paume to the west. The old city's pedestrian streets, bookstores, and the sprawling pl. de la Comédie offer some of the best entertainment in Montpellier, all of it free. The tourist office offers a walking guide and will indicate which of the 100-odd *hôtels particuliers,* built in the 17th and 18th centuries by the emerging bourgeoisie, open their doors to the public.

In the northwestern corner of the "coat of arms," the **promenade du Peyrou** links a large **Arc de Triomphe,** erected in 1691 to honor Louis XIV, to the **Château d'Eau,** the arched terminus of a beautifully preserved aqueduct. The arch and pool are illuminated in the evenings. Midway along the promenade stands the impressive equestrian statue of Louis XIV, which was resurrected in 1839 after being destroyed during the Revolution and has survived all subsequent turmoil. Follow bd. Henri IV to the **Jardin des Plantes,** France's first botanical garden. Designed in 1593 to allow the botany school to study medicinal herbs, the garden is now an historical monument. (Open April-Nov. 15 9am-noon and 2-6pm, Nov.16-March 8:30am-noon and 2-5pm. Free.) The lower side of pl. la Comédie leads to the most recent architectural additions to the city. **Antigone** is an exceptional neoclassical housing complex designed by Catalonian architect Ricard Boffil. The pride of Montpellier, these buildings were designed as shops, offices, and low-cost housing for people of all income groups. In addition, Montpellier plans to construct **Port Marianne,** a project to regain access to the sea. (The port had filled up with sand by the end of the Middle Ages.)

The **Musée Fabre,** 13, rue Montpelliéret, near the tree-lined esplanade, presents an important collection of works by Courbet, Gericault, and 17th-century Dutch and Flemish painters. The top floor exhibits contemporary and local art. (Open Tues.-Fri. 9:30am-noon and 2-5:30pm, Sat.-Sun. 9:30am-noon and 2-5pm. Admission 15F, Wed. free.) The **Collection Xavier-Atger** (tel. 67 66 27 77), next to the cathedral at the Faculté de Médecine, rue de l'Ecole-de-Médecine, contains drawings and preliminary sketches by Fragonard, Watteau, Caravaggio, and others. (Open Oct.-May Mon.-Fri. 1:30-4:30pm. Free.)

From late June through early July, the **Festival International Montpellier Danse** brings international performances, workshops, and films to local stages and screens (admission 50-150F). Call 67 61 11 20 for information and 67 60 41 10 for reservations. The festival office at 7, bd. Henri IV, is open Friday from 9am-2pm and 3-7pm. The **Festival de Radio France et de Montpellier** sponsors performances of opera, jazz, and classical music during the final weeks of July (admission 50-150F). Call 67 52 07 07 for information, 67 52 83 83 for tickets. Early June witnesses an array of theatrical presentations; contact the **Printemps des Comédiens,** av. des Moulins. (tel. 67 61 06 30). For year-round information on plays and concerts, contact the **Théâtre Municipal,** pl. de la Comédie (tel. 67 66 31 11). The **Centre Culturel Irlandais,** 10, rue du Berger (tel. 67 66 22 66), off rue des Ecoles Laïques, sponsors classical guitar concerts and Irish singing.

Although some clubs slow down during the summer, **Rockstore,** on rue Verdun (tel. 67 88 70 10) off pl. de la Comédie, keeps hoppin' all year with a mostly tourist crowd doing the Zorach. Live bands perform occasionally. The 50F cover charge includes the first drink. If you arrive before 11pm when there is no band, the cover may be waived. The **Sax'aphone,** 24, rue Ernest Michel (tel. 67 58 80 90), one km south of the train station, plays Caribbean music 11pm to 3am. The **Rimmel,** also off the pl. de la Comédie, rue de Clos René, packs a **branché** crowd into a shockingly white interior. Don't even *think* about arriving before 1am. (Cover 70F.)

Near Montpellier

West of Montpellier lie the condominia, pine groves, and long beaches of **Cap d'Agde.** Take one of the frequent trains to the town of Agde (½-hr., 37F), then catch the hourly shuttle bus to Cap d'Agde, 7km away (10F). At the last stop is a nudist beach (*plage naturiste*), visible from the crenellated roof of the cathedral in Agde with powerful binoculars.

Northwest of Montpellier, the spectacular **Gorges de l'Herault** stretch for 50km along the Herault River, which runs parallel to the D4. Nearby **St-Guilhem-le-Desert** has interesting ruins of castles, fortifications, and an abbey. The abbey cloisters now reside in the Cloisters Museum in New York City. To reach the Gorges, take a bus from Montpellier to Gignac or Ganges. To reach New York, take a plane from Toulouse. The **tourist office** in Gignac, pl. Général-Claparède (tel. 65 57 58 83 or 67 57 50 02) can help map out hiking tours.

Narbonne

While Narbonne (pop. 45,000) contains Roman and religious monuments, most of the town's summer visitors are would-be sunbathers, responding to the bewitching siren song of the nearby beach developments at **Narbonne-Plage** and **Gruisson-Plage.** Before heeding the call, pay your respects to the city's main attractions, clustered together in the *vieille ville.* The **Cathédrale St-Just et St-Pasteur,** an imposing Gothic structure, is only half as large as its architects intended it to be. Construction began in 1272 but stopped in 1340 during a long, bitter zoning dispute between the archbishops and city hall. Fortunately, the church lost. Further construction would have given Narbonne France's largest cathedral but would have damaged the existing fortified walls, which saved the city when the English Black Prince attacked in 1355. Pay the extra francs to climb up to the second level under the spidery buttresses.

All museums sell a 10F global ticket, good for two days. The opulent **Palais des Archevêques,** next to the cathedral, testifies to the wealth and power of the former archbishops of Narbonne. Inside, the **Musée Archéologique** displays prehistoric and Gallo-Roman artifacts. Across the courtyard at the **Musée d'Art et d'Histoire,** 17th-century paintings from the French and Flemish schools fill the old apartments of the archbishops. **L'Horreum,** an uncovered Roman grain warehouse, is Narbonne's only remaining ancient monument and is not yet completely excavated. The **Maison Vigneronne** is a restored 17th-century powderhouse containing displays of maps, photographs, and traditional tools related to winemaking. The church of **Notre-Dame de LaMourguier** has a lapidary museum with Roman stones, inscriptions, sculptures, and sarcophagi found in the area. (All museums open July-Sept. 15 daily 10-11:50am and 2-6pm; Sept. 16-May Mon.-Sat. 10-11:50am and 2-5:15pm.)

The large and clean **Foyer des Jeunes Travailleurs "Le Capitole,"** 45, av. de Provence (tel. 68 32 07 15), has luxurious singles with private bathrooms for 75F, breakfast included. (Meals 33.50F, served Mon.-Fri. noon-1pm and 7:15-7:45pm. Kitchen facilities available. Key deposit 50F or ID.) **Hôtel le Novelty,** 33, av. des Pyrénées (tel. 68 42 24 28), has immense rooms. (Singles 70F, with shower 80F. Doubles with shower 90-100F. Triples 110F. Quads 150F, with shower 170F. Breakfast 18F.) **Chez Feliz,** 20, bd. Général de Gaulle (tel. 68 32 10 67), has simple cabin-like rooms which up to three people can share for 80F. The restaurant below serves a 39.50F *menu* with wine. (Open daily noon-2pm and 7:30-9pm, Sept.-June Mon.-Sat. noon-2pm and 7:30-9pm.) There are also several campgrounds in the Narbonne area. Those on the coast are usually full and always crowded. **Camping le Languedoc** (tel. 68 65 24 65), 1km southeast, has washing machines and a currency exchange.

L'Escargot, 9, rue Corneille, on a small street off rue de l'Ancien Courrier near Monoprix, serves trout (30F), chicken (31F), and salads (10-25F). (Open daily Oct.-Aug. noon-2pm and 7:30-10pm.) **La Paillote,** passage de l'Ancien Courrier, has a pleasant outdoor terrace for afternoon snacks or a more extravagant meal, *vin compris.* Try the excellent *escargots* (27F). (Open daily noon-2:30pm and 7-10pm.)

Narbonne's **tourist office,** pl. Salengro (tel. 68 65 17 52), is a 10-minute walk from the train station. Turn right onto bd. Frédéric Mistral. After 5-10 min., turn left onto rue Chennebier, which leads into pl. Salengro; the tourist office will be on your left. The staff exchanges currency and offers the usual information. (Open daily 8am-7pm; Sept. 15-June 15 Mon.-Sat. 8:30am-noon and 2-6pm; Sun. 9:30am-12:30pm.) Ask about the guided walking tours of the city (July-Sept. 15 Mon.-Sat. at 10am and 4pm, Sun. 10am; 1½ hrs.; 15F). The **post office,** 25, bd. Gambetta, has **telephones** and a **currency exchange.** (Open Mon.-Fri. 8am-7pm, Sat. 8am-noon.) In the summer, **Sail Toute La Presse,** 15bis, bd. Gambetta (tel. 68 65 31 56), has a small shelf of English books to stick in your beach bag. The **train station** (tel. 69 32 16 38) lies close to the main sights and the downtown area. (Open Mon.-Fri. 7:30am-12:30pm and 2-7:30pm, Sat. 3-7:30pm.) Trains go to Perpignan (14 per day, ¾ hr., 42F), Toulouse (13 per day, 1½ hr., 87F), Béziers (12 per day, 15 min., 21F), Nîmes (12 per day, 1 hr. 20 min., 84F), and Montpellier (12 per day, 55 min., 59F). The **gare routière** (tel. 68 32 16 38) at the end of quai Victor Hugo sends buses to Port la Nouvelle, Perpignan, and Carcassonne. (Open Sun.-Thurs. 8am-noon and 2-7pm.)

Beaches near Narbonne

Jean-Jacques Beneix's steamy *37°2 le matin (Betty Blue)* was filmed in **Gruisson,** an old fishing village 15km from Narbonne. Although you must bring your own loony lover, you may be able to rent a windsurfer on the beach. (If you rent one in town, you'll have to lug it all the way to the water yourself.) An information office (tel. 68 49 09 00) in the new port on bd. Pech Maynard has information on watersports (sometimes safe) and other *passe-temps.* (Open daily 9am-noon and 2-6pm.) Hotels in Gruisson are expensive; the cheapest, Hôtel de la Plage (tel. 68 49 00 75), has 200F doubles, breakfast included. You may want to commute from Narbonne. The **Camping Municipal** (tel. 68 49 07 22) puts you right by the beach. (8F per person, 12F per tent. Open June-Sept.)

Five km from Narbonne, **Narbonne Plage's** huge beach attracts families all summer long. Three good campgrounds obviate the commute from Narbonne. **Camping des Côtes des Roses** (tel. 68 49 83 65) has a Gothic mini-golf and a foodstore (48F per 2 people. Open Easter-Oct.). **Camping Soleil d'Oc** (tel. 68 49 86 21) rents tents (50-60F per 2 people; open Easter-Nov. 15). **Camping la Falaise** (tel. 68 49 80 77) has washing machines (52F per 2 people; open April to early Oct.). Six daily buses leave for both resorts from Narbonne's quai Victor Hugo and train station (20 min., 30F).

Béziers

For 2000 years Phoenicians, Greeks, Romans, Arabs, and other conquering tribes have plagued the *Bitterois.* Once a liberal religious center, Béziers refused to cooperate when Pope Innocent III tried to purge it of heretics in 1209. Everyone was slaughtered, and the buildings went up in smoke. Not until wine production revitalized the local economy did the town begin to rebuild itself. In 1907, a disease which attacks grapevines, the *phylloxéra,* laid waste to the economy. Recently, this ill-fated city of 90,000 began to revive itself through tourism, and once again, wine. Though Béziers has traditionally been known for its simple table wine, the few remaining vineyards pride themselves on quality. For a taste of the new prosperity, try the Minervois or Fitou labels.

Any of the nearby private vineyards or *caves cooperatives,* central outlets for local wines, give tours ending with samples of the St-Chignon, Bourlou, and St-Saturnin wines. The **tourist office,** 27, rue du 4 Septembre (tel. 67 49 24 19), directs you to the local producers as well as the nearby beaches. (Open Mon.-Sat. 9am-7pm, Sun. 10am-noon; Sept.-June Mon.-Fri. 9am-noon and 2-6:30pm, Sat. 9am-noon and 3-6pm.) In 1681, native son Paul Riquet planned and built the **Canal du Midi,** which connects the Atlantic to the Mediterranean. Full-day cruises pass through the masterful system of nine locks in Béziers and on to local vineyards and a fish farm. For information, call 67 37 13 96 from 8am to 8pm or visit the offices on the quai du Neuf Port or at the top of the locks (open 5-8pm). Cruises leave at 9am and return about 5pm (210F, lunch included). The **Cathédrale St-Nazaire,** a Roman church built on the ruins of a pagan temple, was destroyed with the rest of the city in 1209 but rebuilt and enlarged by the 14th century. The functional fortified towers at the top of the cathedral are characteristic architectural features of the region.

Climb to the top for a, shall we say, *view* of the surrounding mountains and sea. The **Fabrégat des Beaux Arts**, pl. de la Révolution, and its annex, **Hôtel Fayet,** 9, rue des Capuces, house a medium-sized collection of 19th- and 20th-century paintings, including works by Dufy, Soutine, Delacroix, and Corot. (Open Tues.-Sat. 9am-noon and 2-6pm, Sat.-Sun. 2-6pm. Free.) Béziers's public garden, the **Plateau des Poètes,** in front of the train station, is a pleasant spot for picnicking or hiding from the sweltering sun (open 7am-10pm).

Several festivals animate Béziers in July and August. At the end of August, a **féria,** which earned Béziers the nickname the "French Seville," fills the evenings with *corridas* and traditional dancing. Tickets are available at the *Arènes,* av. Emile Claparède (tel. 67 76 13 45). A less frenetic festival at the end of July features classical music in local churches as well as the likes of Dizzy Gillespie. Buy tickets at the tourist office, the *Eglise St-Aphrodise,* or the cathedral (60F, ages under 18 or over 60, 30F). The third Sunday in October brings the **Fête du vin nouveau.**

Béziers has no youth hostel, but there are a handful of simple, inexpensive hotels. **Hôtel Angleterre,** 22, pl. Jean Jaurès (tel. 67 28 48 42), has quiet, clean rooms in the city center. (Singles 75F. Doubles 90F, with shower 140F. Quads with shower 230F. Breakfast 20F.) Up the street from the train station, the **Hôtel de Paris,** 70, av. Gambetta (tel. 67 28 43 80), has crisp, clean rooms, some of them cozy attic chambers with eaves. (Doubles 80-105F, with shower and toilet 150F. Quads 140F, with shower 155F. Extra bed 25F. Showers 15F. Breakfast 20F. Garage 30F.) **La Dorade,** 10, rue André Nougaret (tel. 67 28 83 11), off pl. du Général de Gaulle, is run by a kind Spanish mother-daughter team. Their affordable rooms fill up fast in summer. (Doubles 70F, with shower 80F. Quads with shower 104F. Breakfast 18F.) The restaurant downstairs serves a 45F *menu.* If price is everything, try **Hôtel Métropole,** 16, rue des Balances (tel. 67 28 45 50), in the center of the *vieille ville.* From allées Paul Riquet, take rue 4 Septembre—the hotel is on the second small street on your left. Call ahead; many of their incredibly cheap rooms are rented by the month. (Doubles 60F. Quads 90-120F. Communal shower 10F.)

Mykonos, 5, rue Bagatelle, near the top of Plateau des Poètes, serves economical house samplers (55-65F). Moussaka is 40F *à la carte,* baklava 22F. (Open Tues.-Sun. 7:30pm-midnight.) Down from the cathedral on rue Viennet, **Le Thé Retrouvé** serves salads (30-35F), quiche (25F), pastries (15F), and a light 45F *menu.* (Open Tues.-Sat. 2-11pm.) **L'Hacienda,** 14bis rue des Balances, posts a traditional 57F *menu.* (Open daily 2pm-midnight). The **market** on **place 14 juillet,** open all day Tuesday, has plenty of squeezable produce.

The bus station, pl. Jean Jaurès (tel. 67 28 23 85), sends four-wheeled behemoths to local beaches. Buses do run to Narbonne (5 per day, last bus 7:05pm; 40 min.; 23.20F), Pezenas (10 per day, last bus 6:50pm; 40 min.; 19.80F), and Montpellier (15 per day, 1 hr. 35 min., 43.60F). Frequent **trains** connect Béziers to Narbonne (20 per day, 20 min., 22F) and Montpellier (28 per day, 40 min., 49F). The station (tel. 67 28 53 44) is open from 6am to midnight.

Beaches near Béziers

City buses (tel. 67 76 90 10) leave pl. du Général de Gaulle for **Valras** beach (11 per day, last return 8pm, round-trip 22F). Fifteen km from Béziers, this onetime fishing village has developed into an all-purpose family entertainment beach resort complete with waterslide and ferris wheel. In the evening, join a game of *boules* or chow seafood caught by the returning fishing boats. On the same bus route, 5km from Béziers, **Serignan** has a wide, clean beach (11 per day; last return 8:05pm; 9.30F one way).

Provence: Rhône Valley

Although contemporary geographers define Provence as the region stretching from the east bank of the Rhône to the Alps and including the Côte d'Azur, the 19th- and 20th-century regionalist writers who put the region on the modern cultural map have defined Provence both more and less expansively. Frédéric Mistral, whose fellow Félibres sought to revive the ancient Provençal tongue and the spirit of the medieval troubadours, considered himself the spokesman for any patch of land buffetted by the fabled *mistral* wind and nurtured (or ravaged) by the mighty Rhône. Jean Giono, whose novels of the 1920s and 30s reveals a far less idealized vision of Provençal life, limited his imagination to the somewhat bleak area north of the Durance and Verdon rivers. In any case, mapless visitors may safely suspect they are in the region the Romans named Provincia (literally, "the province") when carpets of olive groves and vineyards begin to unroll between hills dusted with lavender and mimosa and a fierce wind carries the scent of sage, rosemary, and thyme, the musical *herbes de Provence*.

This enormously varied landscape includes undulating mountains to the east, haunting rock formations in the Delta, the flat marshland of the Camargue, and the rocky cliffs of the Vaucluse. Provence's high point is the white limestone peak of Mont Ventoux, which looms about 30km east of Orange. Soon after Petrarch recorded his climb to the summit in 1327, a small chapel at the top began to lure intrepid pilgrims. Petrarch also haunts the region's low point, the Fontaine de Vaucluse, a natural spring that gurgles about 25km east of Avignon. The poet wrote many of his sonnets to Laura next to the seemingly bottomless pool that, six centuries later, nearly swallowed Jacques Cousteau up for good. At all altitudes in between are the area's celebrated Roman monuments, the most impressive of which include the arenas at Nîmes and Arles, the Pont du Gard, and the extensive ruins at Glanum.

Provence is famous throughout France for its festivals; in the summer, even the smallest hamlets come alive with music, dance, theater, and outdoor antique markets. In Avignon you'll find theater and music (July to mid-Aug.); in Arles, photography (July); in Aix, music (mid-July to Aug.); in Orange, opera (mid-July to early Aug.); and in Vaison-la-Romaine, ballet and classical music (July-early Aug.). For a fairly complete listing of the summer's events, ask for *Provence, terre des festivals '91,* a thick booklet available at most tourist offices.

Ever since Julius Caesar exalted the Provençal wines in his *Commentaires,* the region has been exporting its sun-soaked nectar. Vintage wines include Châteauneuf-du-Pape, Gigondas, and Côtes du Rhône. In certain regions of Provence you can follow the *route de vin* and stop in at the local *caves* for tastings. The area's temperate climate yields a cornucopia of fruits and vegetables—dozens of types of olives, cherries, sweet figs, asparagus, herbs, and—of course—garlic. Eat the Cavaillon melons fresh before they grace the *haute* tables of Paris. Local cuisine includes *ratatouille* (a rich blend of eggplant, zucchini, and tomatoes); *bouillabaisse* (an often expensive fish soup), served with toasted bread and *rouille* (a saffron-flavored mayonnaise); and *soupe au pistou* (soup made with *pistou,* a fragrant basil-garlic sauce). *Aïoli,* a mayonnaisesque sauce made from olive oil and garlic, goes with hors d'oeuvres, vegetables, and fish soup. Honey here is made from lavender and other flowers.

Provence is also a major transport center, with quick connections to Languedoc and the Côte d'Azur. Within Provence, rail and bus service to cities and most towns is excellent. Many people hitch along the country roads but report long waits for rides out of cities like Aix and Avignon. To see the region properly, rent a car and take only the smallest roads or, even better, bike along them. Bicycle rentals are available at most train stations, as well as in many shops. Only a few kilometers from cities, even at the height of the season, you can be alone with Van Gogh's sunflowers and the scent of lavender. During festivals, make hotel reservations or arrive early in the day. Be prepared for higher food prices, as restaurants often serve only one *menu* (or none at all) during dinner hours.

Vaison-la-Romaine

Tucked away on the remote western edge of the French Alps, Vaison-la-Romaine (pop. 5800) presides over a varied landscape dusted with grapevines and lavender. Extensive ruins of the prosperous Roman city of Vasio, which reached its peak in 40 AD, have been excavated in the lower town. A 12th-century castle, once belonging to the Counts of Toulouse, watches over the medieval quarter below and provides a breathtaking view of the herbs and sunflower fields which carpet the upper Rhône Valley.

Orientation and Practical Information

The bus stops in pl. de Montfort, a knot of cafés and late-night *brasseries.* To get to the tourist office and the Roman ruins, take Grand'Rue for 2 blocks, through pl. de la Poste. To reach the *haute ville,* take Grand'Rue in the other direction, across the l'Ouvèze River.

Tourist Office: pl. du Chanoine Santel (tel. 90 36 02 11). Free wine tasting. Maps and historical information on the town. Guided tours of the Puymin area in French and English (July 10-Sept. 9 Wed. 10am, Sat. 11am), the *haute ville* (Wed., Fri. and Sun. 2pm), and the Cloître Cathedral (Mon., Thurs., Sat. 2pm). Tours cost 26F, students 15F, ages under 19 10F. Open daily 9am-7pm, Sept.-June daily 9am-6pm.

Currency Exchange: Banks open Mon.-Fri. 8am-noon and 2-5pm. **Tourist office** will also change money, but at a bad rate. Open daily 9am-7pm; Sept.-June 9am-6pm. Also at the post office. Open Mon.-Fri. 9am-noon.

Post Office: pl. du Chanoine Santel (tel. 90 36 06 40). **Currency exchange, telephones,** and **Poste Restante.** Open Mon.-Fri. 8:30am-noon and 2-5pm, Sat. 8:30am-noon. **Postal Code:** 84110.

Buses: Cars Lieutand (tel. 90 36 05 22; in Avignon tel. 90 86 36 75). To Avignon (Mon.-Sat. 5 per day, Sun. 2 per day; 1 hr. 20 min.; 30F), Orange (2-3 per day; ¾ hr.; 21.50F), and Séguret (Mon.-Sat. 5 per day, Sun. 2 per day; 15 min.; 11.50F).

Taxis: Clérand (tel. 90 36 00 04) or Berger (tel. 90 36 00 94).

Bike Rental: Borel, cours Taulignan (tel. 90 36 06 77). 35F per day. **Ditroit,** rue Bussaven (tel. 90 36 03 57). Mountain bikes 50F per ½-day, 90F per day. Open Mon.-Sat. 9am-noon and 2:30-7:15pm.

English Bookstore: Le Bouquiniste, 57, rue Trogue Pompée (tel. 90 36 14 38), next to the post office. Excellent selection of used books at a phenomenal 12-36F. Will buy books back at half-price.

Laundromat: La Lavandière, cours Taulignan. Wash and dry 24.50F per 5kg. Soap 5.50F. Open Mon.-Sat. 9am-noon and 3-7pm. **Pharmacy:** av Victor Hugo (tel. 90 36 14 06). Open Tues.-Sat. 9am-12:30pm and 2-7pm.

Medical Assistance: Centre Hospitalier de Vaison-la-Romaine, Grand'Rue, tel. 90 36 04 58. **Ambulance (Fire Department),** tel. 90 36 26 10 or 90 36 00 04. **Emergency,** tel. 18.

Police: (tel. 90 36 04 17), quai de Verdun and rue Gevandau. **Emergency,** tel. 17.

Accommodations and Camping

The few hotels in Vaison tend to be expensive and full during the summer. Fortunately, there will probably be room at the cultural center 1km outside town or at the youth hostel in Séguret, 8km away on the bus line.

Auberge de Jeunesse (IYHF) (tel. 90 46 93 31), 8km away in Séguret, on route de Sablet toward Orange. Tell the bus driver to drop you off. The last bus from Vaison leaves at 5:35pm, but some people try to hitch the short distance. An excellent hostel with a brand new swimming pool. Henri, the super-friendly manager, is a great chef. Dinner with wine 55F. Bed and breakfast 55F per person. Doubles 116F, with shower and toilet 130F (breakfast not included). Open May-Sept. Reservations accepted in winter.

Centre Culturel à Cœur Joie (tel. 90 36 00 78), on av. César Geoffroy, next to the campgrounds. A huge center with all kinds of sports and cultural facilities. Bare but spotless singles 90F, with shower 110F. Doubles 145F, with shower 153F. Breakfast included. Dinner 59F. No lockout or curfew. Office open daily 8am-9pm.

Hôtel du Théâtre Romain (tel. 90 36 05 87), on pl. de l'Abbé-Jautel near the tourist office. Large, comfortable, clean rooms. Friendly owners. A few small doubles 110F, with shower 175F, and toilet 190F. 5-person room with shower and private toilet 315F. Hall showers included. Breakfast 23F.

Les Voconces (tel. 90 36 00 94), on pl. de Montfort across from the bus stop. Small hotel. Large, clean, spartan rooms. Doubles 110F, with shower 150F. Triples and quads with shower 200F. Breakfast 20F.

Camping: Le Moulin de César (tel. 90 36 06 91), next to the Centre Culturel. A 3-star site that holds 260 people. Hot showers, laundromat, grocery store, volleyball courts, and bike rentals. 17.50F per adult, 7.80F per child under 11. 11-13F per tent. Open March 18-Oct.

Food

In 1483, Pope Sixtus II gave Vaison the right to hold a weekly **market,** a right which Vaison still exercises every Tuesday morning. This lively assemblage of sweet-smelling herbs, inexpensive fruits, vegetables, clothes, and pottery fills the town center from 8am to 1pm. **Supermarché Lion,** av. Victor Hugo (tel. 90 36 19 31), next to the *gare routière,* is an inferior indoor version. (Open Mon.-Fri. 8:45am-12:30pm and 2:30-7:30pm, Sat. 8:30am-7:30pm.)

Many of the *caves* in town offer *dégustations* of the local wines. You can taste the Ventoux rosés and the strong reds of Gigondas free if you show an interest in buying. Regional specialties include *tapenade* (an olive paste) and honey from Ventoux.

Auberge des Platanes, 12, pl. Sus Auze, off pl. Montfort. 45F *menu* includes various *hors d'œuvres,* roast beef or chicken, and dessert. Five-course *menus* 57-80F. Open daily noon-1:30pm and 7:30-8:45pm, Jan.-March Mon.-Sat. noon-1:30pm and 7:30-8:30pm.

La Grasihado, pl. du Chanoine Santel, next to the post office. Pleasant terrace. *Menus* at 59F (3-course) and 79F (4-course). Filling salads 15-38F. Omelettes 26-28F. Pizza 33-49F. Open daily noon-2:15pm and 7:15-11pm; Sept.-June Wed.-Sun. only.

Le Bacchus, 9, cours Taulignan, between the Puymin ruins and pl. Montfort. A top-notch restaurant serving French classics. Cheese plate 30F. *Escargots de Ventoux* (42F for 12). 3-course *menu* 69F. Open daily noon-2:30pm and 7-11:30pm;

Sights and Entertainment

In **Quartier de Puymin** and **Quartier de la Villasse,** the foundations and columns of Roman houses alternate with elaborate baths and remarkable mosaics. The ruins stretch over hills carpeted with roses, pine trees, and cypresses. The Puymin excavations reveal the ruins of a **théâtre.** Such faint details as pits for stage machinery and curtain holes evoke former grandeur. Tours of the ruins and the adjoining museum leave from the tourist office. (Ruins open July-Aug. daily 9am-7pm; Sept.-Oct. and May-June 9am-6pm; Nov.-April 9am-5pm. Admission to all monuments 26F, students 15F, ages 12-18 10F.)

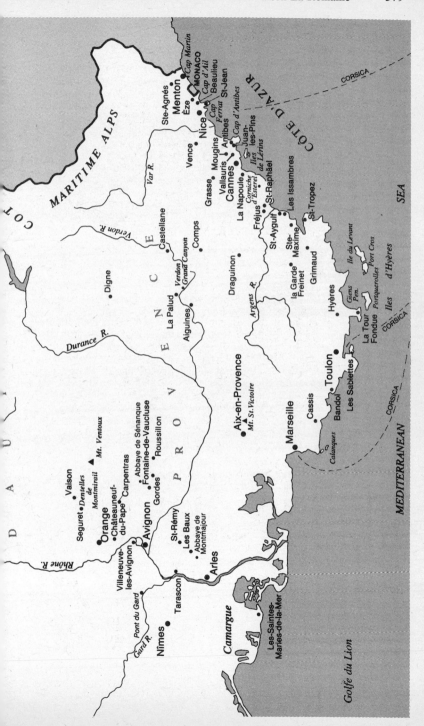

Near Quartier Villasse, **Cathédrale de Notre Dame** mixes styles and eras. The adjoining 11th-century **cloître** displays a unique double-faced Gothic cross. (Open same hours as ruins but closed noon-2pm daily.) Across the small Roman bridge spanning the l'Ouvèze and up the hill, narrow streets wind through the gardens of the medieval town. The tower of the 12th-century **fortress,** built under Count Raymond VI of Toulouse, offers a panorama of the new town, the vine-covered Ouvèze Valley, and fabled **Mont Ventoux** (1912m), looming 15km from Vaison. In the evenings, Vaison residents head for **Discothèque Eclipse** on route de Villedieu, where women enter free all summer. (Cover 70F. Open Wed.-Sun. 11pm-late.)

Just east of Vaison stretches a line of conical mountains, the **Dentelles de Montmirail,** which constitute the diminished western border of the Alps. Wrapped around one of them, 8km from Vaison, the picturesque 15th-century village of **Séguret** is renowned for its youth hostel, vineyards, lavender, and little else.

From early July to early August, Vaison's impressive **summer festival** brings ballet, opera, drama, and classical music to the Roman theater almost nightly. (Admission 100-200F.) Contact the Bureau du Festival, 84110 Vaison-la-Romaine (tel. 90 28 82 12; after April 1, 90 36 02 11). Every three years Vaison also holds its **Choralies,** a harmonic convergence of choral groups from around the world. The next is scheduled for early August 1992.

Orange

In 46 BC, Julius Caesar presented his triumphant seventh legion with Aurision, a new town built over the remains of a Celtic market. The Roman homes, arena, baths, and city walls have disappeared, but the ancient theater and the triumphal arch endure among the 12th-century houses that dot modern Orange (pop. 29,000). The Choregies, a prestigious opera and choral festival, revitalizes the theater each July. From the top of the St-Eutrope hill you can see over the city's appropriately orange rooftops to the acres of vineyards and sunflowers carpeting the neighboring valley of the Vaucluse. in this beautiful area between the Rhône and Durance Rivers, small villages sit perched among the rocky hills, awash in fragrant fields of lavender and spices. *Caves* scattered throughout the region produce red and rosé Côtes du Rhône wines.

Orientation and Practical Information

Avenue Frédéric Mistral, in front of the station, becomes rue de la République, which feeds into rue St-Martin after pl. de la République. Rue St-Martin goes straight to the tourist office. The Roman theater lies to the left of this street.

Tourist Office: cours Aristide Briand (tel. 90 34 70 88). English spoken. Maps and a booklet listing hotels and restaurants. Open Mon.-Sat. 9am-7pm, Sun. 10am-6pm; Oct.-March Mon.-Sat. 9am-5pm. **Annex,** pl. de Frère Mounets, across from the Roman theater. Maps and loads of information on the surrounding region. Open Aug. daily 10am-6pm.

Currency Exchange: Crédit Agricole, cours Aristide Briand (tel. 90 34 32 32), across from the tourist office. Open Mon.-Fri. 8:15am-5:45pm. The **tourist office** changes money on days when the banks are closed, including weekends.

Post Office: bd. E. Daladier on cours Portoulles (tel. 90 34 08 70). Open Mon.-Fri. 8am-7pm, Sat. 8am-noon. **Postal Code:** 84100.

Trains: (tel. 90 82 50 50), on av. Frédéric Mistral. Direct to: Avignon (20 per day, 17 min., 23F); Arles (9 per day, 40 min., 42F); Marseille (14 per day, 1½ hr., 84F); Cannes (11 per day, 3¾ hr., 176F); Lyon (16 per day, 2 hr. 10 min., 113F); Paris (14 per day, 4½ hr., 306F plus 14F TGV reservation). Information desk open daily 9am-noon, 2-5pm, and 5:30-6:45pm.

Buses: (tel. 90 34 15 59), on cours Portoulles in front of the post office. Schedule posted outside above the entrance door. To: Avignon (Mon.-Sat. 5:50am-6:45pm about every hr., Sun. 5; ¾-hr.; 21F); Vaison-la-Romaine (2-3 per day, 70 min., 21.50F); Séguret (2 per day, 65 min., 17F); Carpentras (5 per day, 50 min., 18.50F). Office open Mon.-Fri. 8am-noon and 2-6pm, Sat. 8am-noon.

Taxis: pl. de la République (tel. 90 34 15 55) or pl. de la Gare (tel. 90 34 57 42).

Bike Rental: Cycles Lurion, 48, cours Aristide Briand (tel. 90 34 08 77), across from the tourist office. 45F per day, deposit 500F. Credit cards accepted. Open Tues.-Sat. 8am-noon and 2:30-7:30pm.

English Bookstore: Librairie Victor Hugo, 39, av. Victor Hugo (tel. 90 34 02 45), off rue de la République. A small selection of new Penguin books (12-67F). Open Tues.-Sat. 9am-12:15pm and 2:30-7:30pm.

Laundromat: Laverie Libre Service, 5, rue St-Florent (tel. 90 34 74 04), off bd. Edouard Daladier. Wash 15F per 5kg, dry 2F per 7 min. Soap 4F. Open daily 7am-9pm.

Pharmacy: Pharmacy Pfister, 38, rue de la République (tel. 90 34 00 80). Open Tues.-Sat. 9am-12:30pm and 2-8pm, Mon. 2-8pm.

Hospital: Hôpital Maternité, cours Pourtoules (tel. 90 34 46 33). **Clinique Mistral,** 75, av. Frédéric Mistral (tel. 90 51 60 20). **Medical Emergency: SOS Médecin** (tel. 90 51 89 89). Doctors make house calls. Open 8am-8pm.

Police: Parc de la Brunette (tel. 90 51 71 04), next to the entrance to the *autoroute.* **Emergency,** tel. 17.

Accommodations and Camping

Hotels are booked well in advance for festival weekends in July and August. During the week, however, you should be able to find inexpensive lodging. The region's **youth hostel** (tel. 90 46 93 31), 20km away in Séguret, has a swimming pool and is accessible by bus from Orange (1pm and 6pm daily, 65 min., 21.50F). Bed and breakfast costs 55F per person (doubles 116F, with shower 130F).

Hôtel Freau, 3, rue Ancien-College (tel. 90 34 06 26), off pl. aux Herbes. In an old converted house. Kindly management, spacious rooms, and comfortable old furniture. Likely to have rooms during the week. Doubles 90F, with shower 110F. Triple 140F. No hall shower. Breakfast 18F. Open Sept.-July.

Arcotel, 8, pl. aux Herbes (tel. 90 34 09 23). Central location and spacious rooms with carpeting. Singles 80F, with shower 130F, and toilet 160F. Doubles 130F, with shower 180F, and toilet 200F. Breakfast 20F.

Hôtel le Français, 21, av. Frédéric Mistral (tel. 90 34 67 65), next to the train station. A 2-star hotel. All rooms have carpeting, direct telephones, and lots o' space. Doubles 100F, with shower 130F. Rooms with 2 beds 60F extra. Breakfast 20F.

Hôtel St-Florent, 4, rue du Mazeau (tel. 90 34 18 53), near pl. aux Herbes. Cramped, but clean and nicely furnished. TV room. Singles 100F, with shower 120F, and toilet 160F. Doubles 120F, with shower 150-180F, and toilet 180-250F. Hall showers 10F. Breakfast 20F.

Camping: Le Jonquier (tel. 90 34 19 83), off RN7 to Lyon. A luxury 3-star site with a restaurant, bar, hot showers, pool, mini golf, and tennis courts (55F per hour)—but no TV room. 22F per person, 21F per tent. Open May-Sept.

Food

The cafés in pl. aux Herbes and pl. de la République serve *pain bagna,* the traditional salad-filled sandwich of the Midi. Gather your supplies at the open **market** throughout the *centre ville* every Thurs. 7am-noon or at **Codec Supermarché,** pl. de la Mairie, off pl. de la République. (Open Mon.-Sat. 8:30am-7:15pm.)

La Roselière, 4, rue du Renoyer, off pl. Clemenceau. Great French food served indoors or out. 60F lunch *menu* on weekdays features *l'idée du jour* (the idea of the day). Expensive dinner *menus.* Open daily noon-2pm and 7-11pm.

Le Viet Nam, 51, av. de l'Arc de Triomphe, near the end of av. Victor Hugo. Decent Vietnamese food you can afford. Try the duck with mushrooms (38F) or the chicken with almonds (35F). 3-course 50F *menu.* Open Wed.-Mon. noon-2pm and 7-11pm.

Le Bosphore, 53, av. Charles de Gaulle, just past the tourist office on the left hand side. What it lacks in atmosphere it makes up for in the size of the portions. 45F *menu en semaine* of filling French specialties. Open daily 5:30am-10:30pm.

Restaurant Le Gaulois, 3-5, pl. Sylvain (tel. 90 34 32 51), next to the theater. 69F 4-course *menu* includes *truite* (trout), steak grilled with herbs of Provence, or *côte de veau à la crème* (veal with cream sauce). Open Mon.-Sat. noon-3pm and 7-11pm.

La Fringale, 10, rue de Tourre (tel. 90 34 62 78). Make a left off rue St-Martin onto Cours A. Briand and follow it to the end. Fast food (steak and fries 23F, sandwiches 10-13F) or slow food (*plat du jour* 35F, lasagne 40F, 45F and 65F *menus*). Either way it's cheap food. Open Mon.-Tues. and Thurs.-Sat. 11:30am-2:30pm and 6-11pm, Wed. and Sun. 6-11pm.

Sights and Entertainment

Orange's **Théâtre Antique** (tel. 90 51 80 06, *poste* 304), the best-preserved in France, boasts the only intact stage wall in Europe. A few majestic columns and friezes hint at the façade's former splendor. A statue of the Emperor Augustus, discovered and reconstructed in 1931, presides over the scene from above the central royal doorway. (Open daily 9am-6:30pm; Oct.-March daily 9am-noon and 1:30-5pm. Admission 22F, students 17F.) The ticket to the theater also admits you to the **Musée Lapidaire** (tel. 90 51 80 06, *poste* 319) across the street, which houses an interesting collection of stonework unearthed from the theater site as well as 17th- and 18th-century artwork from the region. (Open Mon.-Sat. 9am-6:30pm, Sun. 9am-noon and 2-6:30pm; Oct.-March daily 9am-noon and 2-5pm.)

Orange's other Roman monument, the **Arc de Triomphe,** stands on the ancient via Agrippa, which once connected Arles to Lyon. Take rue Victor Hugo to av. de l'Arc de Triomphe. This monument to Roman vanity and power, its northern façade depicting Caesar's gory victory over the Gauls, was the model for Napoleon's monument to his own vanity and power, the Arc de Triomphe in Paris.

From July 26 to August 6, 1991, the theater resumes its original function when the **Choregies,** a series of celebrated opera and choral productions, come to town. The 1991 program will feature *Electra* (July 20) and *Aïda* (Aug. 3 and 6). Information is available from the Maison des Choregies, pl. Sylvain, 84100 Orange (tel. 90 34 15 52 or 90 34 24 24), next to the theater. (Open Mon.-Fri. 9am-noon and 1-6pm; after June 10 Mon.-Sat. 9am-noon and 1-6pm.) Tickets cost 130F, 270F, 485F, or 650F, depending upon the performance. You can often buy a discounted ticket at the door.

Avignon

> *Avignon! Its shabby lights and sneaking cats were the same as ever; over-turned dustbins, the glitter of fish scales, olive oil, broken glass, a dead scorpion . . . It had always waited for us, floating among its tenebrous monuments, the corpulence of its ragged bells, the putrescence of its squares . . . Here it lay summer after summer, baking away in the sun, until its closely knitted roofs of weathered tile gave it the appearance of a piecrust fresh from the oven. It haunted one although it was rotten, fly-blown with expired dignities, almost deliquescent among its autumn river damps. There was not a corner of it that we did not love.*
> —Lawrence Durrell, Monsieur

Avignon (pop. 92,000) has had a reputation for melancholy squalor at least since the 14th century, when Petrarch denounced his adopted hometown as "the unholy Babylon, the hell of the living . . . , the sewers of the earth. . . . How shameful to see it suddenly become the capital of the world." Avignon became this figurative capital in 1309, when Pope Clement V moved the papacy to his native France partly to escape the regional warfare and corruption of feudal Italy, partly to oblige the more powerful French king Philippe le Bel, who had ruthlessly thwarted the

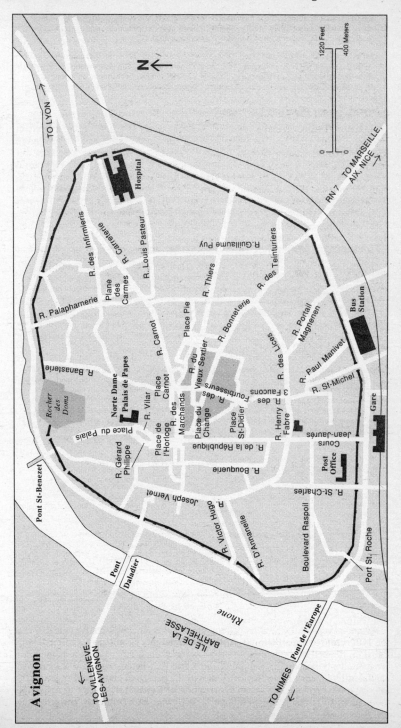

Avignon

N

TO LYON

TO MARSEILLE.
AIX. NICE

RN 7

1220 Feet
400 Meters

Hospital

R. des Infirmieris

R. Carreterie

R. Louis Pasteur

R. Palapharnerie

R.Guillaume Puy

R. des Teinturiers

Plane
des
Carmes

R. Thiers

R. Banasterie

Place Pie

R. Carnot

R. Bonneterie

R. Portail
Magnenen

Bus
Station

Rocher
des
Doms

Norte Dame
Palais de Papes

Place
Carnot

R. du
Vieux Sextier

R. des
Lices

R. Paul Manivet

R. St-Michel

Place du
Palais

R. Vilar

R. des
Marchands

R. des
Fourbisseurs

R. des
Faucons

R. Henry
Fabre

Gare

R. Gérard
Philippe

Place de
l'Horloge

Place du
Change

Place
St-Didier

Cours
Jean-Jaurès

R. de la République

R. Bouquerie

Post
Office

Joseph Vernet

R. St-Charles

R. Victor Hugo

R. D'Annanelle

Boulevard Raspoil

Port St. Roche

Pont St-Benezet

Pont.
Daladier

Rhone

ILE DE LA
BARTHELASSE

Pont de l'Europe

TO NIMES

TO VILLENEVE-
LES-AVIGNON

Church's political ambitions. The papal seat remained in Avignon for almost three quarters of a century, during which seven popes constructed and added to the Palais des Papes, a sprawling Gothic fortress of white stone. Innocent VI strove to protect the town's population by erecting the ramparts which endure today. In 1378 with the death of Gregory XI, the papacy turned to Rome, leaving behind only two ill-fated "anti-popes" and a number of highly trained artists.

Avignon remained an artistic and literary center even after 1790, when the French government took possession of the city, dispersed its large Jewish community, expelled all the religious orders, and shackled its thriving publishing houses with strict censorship laws. In 1854, Avignon became the center of the Félibrige, Frédéric Mistral's Provençal nationalist literary group. A century later the city became the site of Europe's most important theater festival and a riotous set of fringe events. From early July to early August, people from all over Europe descend on Avignon to enjoy both the official performances and the general Bacchinalia in the streets. Hotel prices and restaurant prices skyrocket, accommodations become scarce, and authorities crack down on visitors sleeping in the streets. A cultural hotspot even in the off-season, Avignon makes an excellent base for exploring the Rhône Valley.

Orientation and Practical Information

Situated on a bend in the Rhône River, Avignon lies on the TGV line between Paris (4 hr.) and Marseille (1 hr.). Inside its 14th-century ramparts the city itself is a maze of endless alleyways, small streets, and public squares. To reach the tourist office from the train station, walk straight ahead through porte de la République on cours Jean Jaurès, which becomes rue de la République, the main thoroughfare. The tourist office is on your right (5 min.). At night, lone travelers should avoid the area around rue Thiers and rue Philonarde, and travelers everywhere should be forewarned of Avignon's many car thieves and pickpockets.

Tourist Office: 41, cours Jean Jaurès (tel. 90 82 65 11), 3 blocks from the station. Their free brochure *A comme Avignon* lists hotels, restaurants, museums, and other useful addresses. Guided tours of town June-Sept. Mon.-Sat. (25-40F, students 20-30F). Office open Mon.-Sat. 9am-8pm, Sun. 9am-1pm and 2-6pm; Aug. 16-June Mon.-Fri. 9am-6pm; Sat. 9am-noon and 2-6pm. The **branch office** in the train station (tel. 90 82 65 11, for reservations, or 90 82 05 81) will book you a hotel room the same day (10-15F). Open daily 9am-8pm; Aug. 16-June Mon.-Fri. 9am-6pm, Sat. 10am-6pm. **Festival Information,** Bureau du Festival, BP 92 (tel. 90 82 67 43, for reservations 90 86 24 43).

Budget Travel: Frantour Travel (tel. 90 86 52 73), next to the train station. BIJ/Eurotrain tickets and student discounts. Open Mon.-Fri. 8:30am-noon and 3-6:15pm.

Currency Exchange: Banks along rue de la République. Open Mon.-Fri. 8:30am-noon and 1:30-4pm. Tourist office often changes money on days when banks are closed. No commission. Open 9-11:45am and 2-6:50pm. Exchange at the **post office** open Mon.-Fri. 8am-6pm, Sat, 8-11am.

Post Office: av. du Président Kennedy (tel. 90 86 78 00), inside the walls across from the train station. **Currency exchange, Poste Restante** and **telephones.** Open Mon.-Fri. 8am-7pm, Sat. 8am-noon. **Branch office,** pl. Pie. (tel. 90 86 40 30). **Poste Restante** (specify which branch on letters) and **telephones** upstairs. Open Mon.-Fri. 8am-6:30pm, Sat. 8am-noon. **Postal code:** 84000.

Trains: porte de la République (tel. 90 82 50 50). TGV to Paris (11 per day, 4 hr., 330F plus obligatory 14F reservation). To: Arles (12 per day, 25 min., 29F); Marseille (17 per day, 1¼ hr., 75F); Toulon (12 per day, 2 hr., 110F); Nice (9 per day, 4 hr., 184F); Nîmes (24 per day, ½-hr., 37F); Montpellier (24 per day, 1 hr., 62F); Orange (13 per day, 15 min., 24F); Dijon (11 per day, 4¼ hr., 213F); Carcassonne (7-8 per day, 3 hr., 144F); Toulouse (7-8 per day, 4 hr., 184F). Information desk open daily 9am-6:30pm.

Buses: bd. St-Roch, east of the train station. Doggone efficient. Departure times for buses are synchronized with train arrivals, especially the TGV. Information desk open Mon.-Fri. 8am-noon and 2-6pm. **Cars Lieutaud** (tel. 90 86 36 75). To Vaison-la-Romaine (2-3 per day, 1 ¼ hr., 30F) and Orange (3 per day, 40 min., 21F). **Rapides Sud-Est** (tel. 90 82 48 50). To Châteauneuf-du-Pape (5 per day, ½-hr., 14F). Indirectly to Orange (5 per day, 21F). **Cars**

Arnaud (tel. 90 38 15 58). To Fontaine-de-Vaucluse (7 per day, 55 min., 15F). **Cap Phocéen** (tel. 90 82 07 35). To Nice (at 7:30am, 5 hr. 20 min.) Within the city **TCRA** city buses, Touvelle de la République (tel. 90 82 68 19) across the street from the train station, runs line #10 (every 40 min., 5-10 min., 5.50F) to Villeneuve-les-Avignon. Information desk open Mon.-Fri. 8:15am-noon and 1:45-6:30pm, Sat. 8:15am-noon and 1:45-5pm.

Radio Taxi, pl. Pie (tel. 90 82 20 20). 24 hrs.

Bike Rental: Cycles Peugeot, pl. Pie (tel. 90 82 32 19). 40F per day, 219F per week. **Dopieralski,** 84, rue Guillaume Puy (tel. 90 86 32 49), corner of rue Ninon Vallin. 40F per day, 220F per week, 1200F deposit plus passport or credit card. Open Tues.-Sat. 8:30am-noon and 2-7pm, Sun. 8:30am-noon. **Transport Routier,** 11, av. Monclar (tel. 90 85 56 63), between the train station and the bus station. 30F per ½-day, 50F per day, 300F per week, 900F deposit or credit card. Open Mon.-Sat. 9am-noon and 2-7:15pm; Sept.-June Mon.-Fri. only.

Lost and Found: Police Municipale, Halte Routière (tel. 90 82 20 20).

French-American Center: Centre Franco Américain de Provence, 23, rue de la République (tel. 90 85 50 98). Organizes various cultural exchanges, *au pair* stays, language courses, and the well-publicized French-American Film Workshop. Tea party every Wed. 3-6pm. Open to all nationalities. **The English Bookstore** (tel. 90 85 50 98), at the same address, has an excellent collection of books. Open Mon.-Sat. 9:30am-noon and 2-7pm.

Womens Center: Vaucluse Information Femmes, 9, rue Carnot (tel. 90 86 41 00 or 90 82 76 56). Information on professional, social, legal, and familial rights. Open Mon.-Wed. 9am-noon and 2-6pm, Thurs. 9am-6pm.

Laundromat: Laverie, 19, bd. des Lices. Wash 12F per 5kg, dry 2F per 7 min. Dryers require 2F coins. Open daily 7am-9pm. **Lavomatique,** 9, rue du Chapeau Rouge, off pl. Pie. Wash 16F per 5kg, dry 2F per 5 min. Open daily 7am-8:30pm.

Pharmacy, 7, rue de la République (tel. 90 82 54 70). Open Mon.-Sat. 8:30am-7:30pm.

Disabled Services: La Commission Départementale des Handicapés, 70, rue Montfavet. A center for disabled people.

Hospital: Ste-Marthe Hôpital (tel. 90 82 99 28), bd. Limbert. **Hôpital de la Durance,** 305, rue Raoul Follereau (tel. 90 89 91 31).

Medical Emergency: SOS Médecins, tel. 90 82 65 00.

Police: Tel. 90 85 17 17. **Emergency,** tel. 17.

Accommodations

There are no "official" youth hostels; Avignon's four excellent *foyers* usually have room, but things get tight during the festival. The handful of reasonable ones are reserved long in advance; expect to pay at least 90F for a single. The tourist office has a list of organizations that set up inexpensive dormitory accommodations during the festival. If you are sleeping outside, buy some insect repellent and use it generously; the Rhône breeds bloodthirsty bugs. Consider staying in Nîmes, Orange, or Arles and commuting by the frequent, speedy trains.

Foyers: Foyer Bagatelle, Ile de la Barthelasse (tel. 90 86 30 39), across the river, just over Pont Daladier. 250-bed *foyer* in the middle of a campground. All the essentials—hot showers, clean bathrooms, spacious dorm rooms (6 beds per room), snack bar, cafeteria, and mini-market—and the cheapest prices in town. No curfew or lockout. 41F per person. Sheets 13F. *Demi-pension* 103.10F. Often full of large groups; call ahead.

The Squash Club, 32, bd. Limbert (tel. 90 85 27 78). Walk 30 min. along the walls from the train station or take bus #2 from the station. Chummy management may give you a discount if you can beat them at squash. Bring your own racquet, and don't count on it. Spacious 16-bed rooms 44F per person. Breakfast on the squash courts (mandatory in summer) 14F. Sheets 14F. Lockout 11am-5pm. Curfew 11pm. Office open 8-11am and 5-11pm.

Foyer YMCA, 7bis, bd. de la Justice (tel. 90 25 46 20), in Villeneuve, across Pont Daladier, the first left after the train bridge. A ½-hr. walk, or take bus #10 (5.50F) from the post office across from the train station. Curfew midnight. Opens at 5pm daily. 45F per person. Breakfast 15F. *Demi-pension* 92F. Open April-Sept.

Centre Pierre Louis Loisil (tel. 90 25 07 92), on av. Pierre Sémard in Villeneuve *centre ville*. Take bus #10 from the post office across from the train station. No curfew. Dormitory-style quarters with 3-4 beds per room. 50F per person. Breakfast 12F. *Demi-pension* 92F. Sheets 19F.

Hôtel Saint-Roch, 9, rue Paul-Mérindol (tel. 90 82 18 63), outside porte St-Roche. A 10-min. walk left of the train station. Turn left at the highly noticeable Hôtel Arcade. Charming management, spotless rooms, beautiful garden. Singles with shower 95F. Doubles with shower and toilet 140F. Triple with bath, toilet, and TV 220F. Quad with shower, toilet, and TV 300F. Breakfast 23F.

Hôtel Central, 31, rue de la République (tel. 90 86 07 81). Right in the middle of it all. A small terrace shielded from the central street. Sweet rooms each with carpeting, desk, dresser, and telephone. TV room. Singles 94-118F, with shower 145F, with shower and toilet 183-219F. Doubles 118-155F, with shower 145-176F, with shower and toilet 183-268F. Breakfast 22F.

Hôtel le Parc, 18, rue Perdiguier (tel. 90 82 71 55), off cours Jean-Jaurès near the tourist office. Clean, pleasant, and highly recommended. Singles 90F. Doubles 100F, with shower 130F. Triple with shower 160F. Quads available. Breakfast 15F. Tax 2F per person per day.

Pacific-Hôtel, 7, rue Perdiguier (tel. 90 82 43 36) off cours Jean-Jaurès near the tourist office. Large, airy rooms and friendly management. Singles 90-110F, with shower 125F. Doubles with shower 150F. Triples and quads with shower 200F. Breakfast 15F.

Hôtel Mignon, 12, rue Joseph Vernet (tel. 90 82 17 30). Lemon-fresh rooms with telephone, TV, and carpeting. Doubles 115F, with shower 160F, and toilet 175F. Doubles with 2 beds 210-290F. Breakfast 17.80F.

Hôtel Splendid, 17, rue Perdiguier (tel. 90 86 14 46), off cours Jean-Jaurès near the tourist office. Spotless and spacious rooms, all with shower, carpeting, and a garden view. TV room. Singles with shower 140F, and private bathroom 180F. Triples with shower 150F, and private bathroom 210F. Quads with shower 220-230F. Breakfast 18F.

Hôtel Innova, 100, rue Joseph Vernet (tel. 90 82 54 10), near corner of rue de la République. Worn, bungalow-like rooms. Singles and doubles 100F, with shower 140F. Triples 170F. Quads 210F. Breakfast 18F.

Camping

Bagatelle (tel. 90 86 30 39), across the river on Ile de la Barthelasse. Take bus #10 (5.50F) or walk (30 min.) over Pont Daladier. The closest to town. An immense campground made in the shade. A 3-star site with over 1200 places. Hot showers, cafeteria, laundromat, and supermarket. 13F per person, 5.25F per tent.

Camping Municipal St-Bénezet (tel. 90 82 63 50), Ile de la Barthelasse, 5 min. past Camping Bagatelle. Take Bus #10 (5.50F). A 4-star site with tennis and volleyball courts, washing machines, supermarket, restaurant, and hot showers. 14.10F per person, 8.10F children. 11F per tent. 16F per caravan. Electricity 12F. Open March-Sept. 8:15am-9:45pm.

Les Deux Rhône, chemin de Bellegarde (tel. 90 85 49 70), La Barthelasse. A 15-20 min. walk from Camping St-Benezet. Take Bus #10 (5.50F). 100 places. A 2-star site with a bar, restaurant, hot showers, a pool, and tennis courts (40F per hour). 12.10F per person, 6.10F per child under 7. 5F per tent. Electricity 9.50F. Open June 1-Sept.

Camping du Parc des Libertés (tel. 90 85 17 73), Ile de la Barthelasse. Really difficult to reach and far away from town, but quiet, cheap, and in a beautiful lakeside location. Take bus #10 (5.50F) to Camping les Deux Rhônes and then walk the 2km. 13.10F per adult, 7.600F per child. 9F per tent.

Food

The cafés filling pl. de l'Horloge are better suited for coffee after dinner, when the clowns, musicians, and mimes have appeared on the streets. **Parc de Rocher des Doms,** overlooking the Rhône, offers many scenic spots for a picnic and has an outdoor café near the pond. Buy provisions in Les Halles, the large indoor **market** in pl. Pie (open Tues.-Sun. 7am-1pm), at the less expensive open-air **market** outside the city walls near porte St-Michel (Sat.-Sun. 7am-10pm), or at **Shopi Supermarché,** 23, rue de la République (open Mon.-Sat. 8:30am-7:15pm). The tourist office lists restaurants with meals for 80F or less. The shaded old **rue des Teinturiers** has small, interesting cafés and restaurants that are popular meeting places during the festival.

Arrête des Salades, 4, rue Pavot, in a narrow alley off rue des 3 Faucons midway between pl. des Corps Saints and pl. St-Didier. Cheap and delicious food. Huge 30F salads. Try the 35F "*formule rapide*": salad, *tarte du jour,* and wine. 59F *menu* with homemade *plats du jour.* Run by a friendly French-American couple who are genuinely interested in your dining pleasure. Open daily in summer noon-3pm and 6:30-10pm.

Restaurant Danh, 31bis, rue Bonneterie, corner of rue Bernheim-Lyon. Small, family-run Vietnamese restaurant with great food and even greater prices. Curry chicken 27F. Beef dishes 27-34F. Open daily 11am to 2 or 3pm and 6-11pm.

Cafeteria Flunch, 11, bd. Raspail, off rue de la République. A full meal costs next to nothing. Roast chicken with two vegetables 14.90F. Open daily 11am-10pm.

Tapas, 10, rue Figuière, off pl. St-Didier. Tasty small dishes are best for a light lunch or snack. Wide variety of hot and cold foods and salads, including fried mushrooms, fried squid, pork, gazpacho, and other Spanish dishes served amidst matadorian decor. 10F per serving. Open Mon.-Sat. noon-1:30pm, Sun. 6:45pm-1:30am.

Le Pain Bis, 6, rue Armand-de-Pontmartin. A small place with some outdoor seating, pastel colors, and contemporary art. All the ingredients are *biologique* (organic), and most dishes are vegetarian. Sandwiches and cold plates for lunch, and 54F (lunch only) and 67F *menus.* Open daily noon-2:30pm and 7pm-midnight, Sept.-June Mon.-Sat. noon-2:30pm and 7:30-11pm.

Tache d'Encre, 22, rue des Teinturiers. A pleasant *café-théâtre* with live music on most weeknights and excellent French cuisine. 47F (3-course, lunch only), 62F, and 89F *menus* featuring pork or chicken or veal in mushroom sauce, vegetables, and dessert. *Plat du jour* 35F. Open daily noon-3am.

Le Magnanen, 19, rue St-Michel, off pl. des Corps Saints. Not far from the station and near porte Magnanen. Tiny and popular with locals. *Plat du jour* 37F. Three-course 52F *menu.* Open Mon.-Fri. 11:45am-2pm and 6:45-8:30pm, Sat. 11:45am-2pm.

Sights

Smooth granite unifies the towers and battlements of the **Palais des Papes** (tel. 90 86 03 32), one of the finest examples of French Gothic military architecture. Benoît XII, the third of the *Avignonnais* popes, began the construction of the building in the 14th century. Aggrandized by Clement VI and other popes, the palace became a residence for papal legates and vice-legates during the 17th and 18th centuries and was converted to military barracks in 1906. Warmly colored frescoes grace the interior of **Chapelle St-Martial.** (Open July-Sept. daily 9am-7pm; April-June and Oct. 9am-12:15am and 2-6pm; Dec.-March 9-11:15am and 2-4:15pm. Admission 22F, students and ages over 65 15F. English guided tours daily 10am and 3pm. 29F, students 20F.)

Adjacent to the Palais sits 12th-century **Cathédrale Notre-Dame-des-Doms,** a rather heavy Romanesque church with a richly decorated interior. Popes Benoît XII and Jean XXII lie ornately entombed within. Traces of a Simone Martini fresco, *The Virgin Surrounded by Angels,* can be seen above the porch. (Open daily 11am-6pm. Free.) At the far end of pl. du Palais is the austere **Petit Palais** (tel. 90 86 44 58) once home to cardinals and now to fine Italian primitive, Gothic, and Renaissance paintings and sculpture. (Open Wed.-Mon. 9:30-11:50am and 2-6pm. Admission 16F, students 8F; Oct.-March Sun. free.)

The **Musée Calvet,** 65, rue Joseph Vernet (tel. 90 86 33 84), houses a collection of 13th- to 15th-century Italian paintings, and 12th- to 15th-century *Avignonnais* paintings and sculptures. It is closed for repairs and is not scheduled to re-open until 1992.

Le Rocher des Doms (open daily 7:30am-9pm), a lovely park with a pond full of ducks and fish, has sightlines to Mont Ventoux, the fortifications of Villeneuve-les-Avignon, and 12th-century **Pont St-Bénezet.** The "Pont d'Avignon" of nursery-rhyme fame, rue Ferruce (tel. 90 85 60 18) ends abruptly halfway across the Rhône, only four of its original 22 arches intact. Avignon legend tells that in 1177 a shepherd boy, St-Bénézet, was instructed by angels to begin the 11-year task of erecting the bridge. To dance where *"on y danse, on y danse,"* those over 12 will have to pay 3-5F. (Open daily 9am-6:30pm; Oct.-March 9am-5pm.) Newer **Pont Daladier,** which makes it all the way across the river to the campgrounds, is a good vantage point from which to see both the broken bridge and the towering Palais des Papes—and it doesn't cost a red centime.

Across the river rises **Villeneuve-les-Avignon,** guarded by the the **Tour de Philippe le Bel,** a 14th-century fortification standing where pont St-Bénézet used to end. (Open Wed.-Mon. 10am-12:30pm and 3-7:30pm; Oct.-March Wed.-Mon. 10am-noon and 2-5pm. Admission 6.30F, students 4F.) Villeneuve was France's southeastern outpost until 1790, when this papal possession was ceded to the new French Republic. **Fort St-André** (tel. 90 25 45 35) is celebrated for its magnificent sunset view of Avignon. (Open daily 9am-noon and 2-6:30pm. Admission 16F, ages 18-25 and over 60 9F.) You'll have to pay an extra 7F to enter the attractive terraced gardens graced with wildly twisting olive trees like carded wool. **Chartreuse du Val de Bénédiction** (tel. 90 25 05 46), a monastery founded in 1352 under Pope Innocent VI and now being restored, gathers various artists-in-residence. (Open July daily 9am-6:30pm; April-June and Aug.-Sept. 9am-noon and 2-6:30pm; Oct.-March 10am-noon and 2-5pm. Admission 23F, ages 19-25 and over 60 12F, ages 7-18 5F.) Bus #10 runs between Avignon and Villeneuve about every half-hour in summer (5.50F), but it follows two routes. Ask if the bus goes to Villeneuve first.

Entertainment

From early July through early August, the riotous **Festival d'Avignon** brings small explosions of plays, dance, mime, and everything else from Gregorian chants to an all-night reading of the *Odyssey.* (Admission varies with event.) Hardly a cloister, church, or basement stands without a play in its innards, or an archway without a sitarist or puppeteer. The official festival, the most prestigious theatrical gathering in Europe, has at least 12 different venues, the courtyard of the Palais des Papes and the municipal theater being the most impressive. (Events start 9:30-11pm.) The fringe festival has at least 65 different locations, and an even fringier free-for all takes over the streets. The movie houses in town show an average of five different movies each day; afternoon and midnight showings are usually cheaper. During and after the festival, there is plenty of good jazz around pl. Grillon and theater near pl. de l'Horloge. On Bastille Day, Avignon ignites an impressive fireworks display. For information contact the Bureau de Festival, B.P. 92 (tel. 90 82 67 08, for reservations 90 86 24 43).

Although it calms down the rest of the year, Avignon hardly goes into hibernation. The **Théâtre du Balcon,** 38, rue Guillaume Puy (tel. 90 85 00 80) stages dramatic performances almost every weekend. (Tickets 30-70F.) Regular performances of opera, drama, and classical music are held in the **Opéra d'Avignon,** pl. de l'Horloge (tel. 90 82 23 44). The **Centre d'Action Culturelle,** 8bis, rue de Mons (tel. 90 82 67 08), provides information on jazz clubs and theater groups. Rue des Teinturiers is lined with theaters, including the **Théâtre du Chien qui Fume** at #75 (tel. 90 85 25 87) and **La Tache d'Encre** at #22 (tel. 90 85 46 03). The **Utopia Cinema,** 15, rue Galante (tel. 90 82 65 36), off rue de la République, is an avant-garde movie theater that screens a wide variety of flicks throughout the year (27F, card for 10 showings 220F). The **Maison Jean Vilar,** 8, rue de Mons (tel. 90 85 59 64), shows free videos, but the schedule varies and it may be necessary to make a reservation. The **Palace Cinema,** 38, cours Jean Jaurès (tel. 90 86 13 94), shows five movies per day in French only. (Admission 38F; students, under 18 or over 65 28F.)

For more improvised nightlife, join the raucous French and American student crowd at **Pub Z,** pl. Pie. Place des Corps Saints (Holy Bodies) is the unfortunately named working turf of Avignon's prostitutes and the unlikely location of three lively bars. The popular **Grand Siècle** (tel. 90 85 13 08) has outside seating and a huge video screen inside. (Open Mon.-Sat. 7am-3am, Sun. 6am-3am. Beers 8F.) **Célestins** (tel. 90 82 02 42) plays loud rock 'n' roll all day and all of the night to a predominantly French crowd. (Open daily 7am-3am. Beer 9F.) **4 Coins** is a small local bar with a video screen and few tourists. (Open daily 8am-1:30am. Beer 8.50F.) Avignon has only three nightclubs: the **Ambassy Club,** 27, rue Bancasse (tel. 90 86 31 55), off rue de la République (open Aug.-June Mon.-Sat. 10:30pm-late); **Club 5.5,** porte St-Roch (tel. 90 85 46 76, open Wed.-Mon. nightly 10:30pm-late); and **Le Sholmès,** Rochefort du Gard (tel. 90 31 73 43, open nightly 10:30pm-late).

Near Avignon: The Vaucluse

Buses link Avignon to several attractive towns, but service can be erratic. **Carpentras** (pop. 26,000), where Petrarch spent his childhood, is graced with a small triumphal arch, a magnificently decorated **synagogue** built in 1367 (the oldest in France and the second oldest in all of Europe; open Mon.-Fri. 10am-noon and 3-5pm; free), and **Cathédrale St-Siffrein,** Flamboyant and Gothic hybrid. From mid-July to mid-August, the lighthearted **Festival Passion,** brings 19th-century operettas, ballet, drama, and classical music to the open-air theater. (Admission 80-300F, students from 30F.) For information contact Festival, B.P. 113, 84200 Carpentras (tel. 90 63 46.35). After July 1, the festival office is at pl. d'Inguimbert (tel. 90 63 05 72). If you plan to spend the night, the Carpentras **tourist office,** 170, av. Jean Jaurès (tel. 90 63 00 78 or 90 63 57 88), has a list of hotels but won't make reservations. (Open Mon.-Sat. 9am-7pm, Sun. 9:30am-12:30pm; Sept-June Mon.-Sat. 9am-12:30pm and 2-6:30pm.) Try **Hôtel La Lavande** on bd. Alfred Roger (tel. 90 63 13 49). Doubles are 100F, none have showers, and there are only eight of them. Hourly buses run from Avignon to Carpentras (6:50am-9pm, last return 7:15pm, 45 min. 15.50F). For more information call **Cars Contadins,** 38, av. Wilson (tel. 90 67 20 25).

The tiny village of **Fontaine-de-Vaucluse** hides the largest natural spring in Europe. Even Jacques Cousteau has yet to explore the 400m-deep pool at the source of the spring just below the cliffs. Above water, the site which lured 14th-century Italian poet Petrarch is overcrowded, overpriced, and quite dull. You may, however, end up agreeing with Henry James who concluded that "Vaucluse is indeed cockneyfied, but . . . I should have been a fool, all the same, not to come." **Camping Municipal Les Prés** (tel. 90 20 32 38), a two-star site with hot showers and a restaurant, is only ½km out of town on the right. (9.70F per person, 8.60F per tent.) A relaxed **Auberge de Jeunesse(IYHF),** chemin de la Vignasse (tel. 90 20 31 65), occupies an emerald setting 1km out of town. Cross the bridge and follow the yellow brick road; you'll see signs at the town limit. (Lockout 10am-5:30pm. 11:30pm curfew. 37F per person or tin man in dorm rooms (7-8 beds per room). Breakfast 13F. Kitchen facilities. Open Feb.-Nov. daily.) Fontaine-de-Vaucluse's **wizard office** is on pl. de l'Eglise (tel. 90 20 32 22; open Easter-Oct. Mon.-Sat. 9am-noon and 2-6:30pm).

The village of **Châteauneuf-du-Pape** (pop. 2070) was named after the castle built for Pope John XXII from 1316 to 1333 and destroyed by four escaping German soldiers in August, 1944. One wall remains visible on the outskirts of town. To understand what drew the popes here, visit the **Musée des Vieux Outils de Vignerons,** av. Bx Pierre de Luxembourg (tel. 90 83 70 07), a small museum of winemaking in the Père Anselme *cave,* down the hill from the center of town. You might even get lessons on proper wine-tasting techniques. (Open daily 8am-noon and 2-6pm. Free.) The **tourist office,** pl. du Portail (tel. 90 83 71 08), in the center of town, provides a long list of *caves* accepting visitors. (Open July-Aug. Tues.-Sat. 9am-12:30pm and 3:30-8pm; Sept.-Oct. and Dec.-June Tues.-Sat. 9am-12:30pm and 2-6pm.) Tasting the famous grape is free at all of these (as long as you look like a serious buyer), but small *caves* will give you more personal attention. One such place is **Domaine Perges,** 8, av. St-Joseph (tel. 90 83 71 34), which sells both white and red wines at 35-45F a bottle. (Open July-Aug. Mon.-Sat. 11am-6pm; April-June Sat.-Sun. 2-6pm.) For more information on area *caves,* contact the Fédération des syndicats de Producteurs de Châteauneuf-du-Pape, route d'Avignon (tel. 90 83 72 21). Four buses per day leave Avignon for Châteauneuf-du-Pape (17F).

You can sleep at **La Mère Germaine,** pl. de la Fontaine (tel. 90 83 70 72), next to the tourist office. (Doubles 150F, with shower 160F.) Two km away by foot lies the two-star campground **Islon St-Luc** (tel. 90 83 76 77; 13F per person, 10F per site; open April-Sept.). All of Châteauneuf's restaurants consider their cuisine *haute* and charge accordingly. You'll find less expensive but good regional cooking at **La Mule du Pape,** pl. de la Fontaine, next to the tourist office. (Sandwiches 13-18F; 4-course *menu* 55F. Open daily noon-5pm and 7pm-midnight.) Buses leave from Avignon to Châteauneuf-du-Pape (30 min., 14.50F) 5 times per day during the week and once on Saturday afternoon. Contact **Les Rapides du Sud-Est** (tel. 90 82 51 75) for more information.

Isolated on a hill, the stone village of **Gordes** (pop. 2000) was left in ruins when the Germans, angered by the Maquis's assassination of a German soldier, set fire to the city, blew up a number of houses, and executed 13 people before a monk from the abbey at Sénaque stopped them. Since 1944, the combined efforts of the permanent population and summertime vacationers have transformed Gordes into an attractive town with shaded outdoor cafés, restored buildings, and high-quality galleries. A fashionable retreat for Avignon festival directors and actors, the village puts on its own music and theater **festival** the first week of August (tel. 90 72 08 14; admission 120F). Free fringe shows by international performers occupy the squares. An exhibit of Vasarely's vibrant geometric paintings fills the **Château de Gordes** (tel. 90 72 02 89), a medieval castle restored during the Renaissance. (Open July-Aug. daily 10am-noon and 2-6pm; Sept.-June Wed.-Mon. 10am-noon and 2-6pm. Admission 15F, students 10F.) Two km south of Gordes is the odd little **Village des Bories,** a cluster of dome-shaped stone huts built in the 17th-century, possibly to quarantine victims of the Marseille plague of 1720. Occupied until the 19th-century, they now house a good museum of rural life. (tel. 90 72 03 48; open daily 9am-sunset). South of Gordes on the Beaumettes road, stained-glass artist Frédéric Durand and his wife maintain the **Moulin des Bouillons.** The house contains a wonderful old olive press and exhibits on olive growing since Greek times, as well as samples of Durand's own work. Enclosed in its own peaceful valley only 3km north of Gordes, the 12th-century **Abbaye de Sénanque** (tel. 90 72 02 05) has exhibits on Saharan nomads as well as the abbey's own history. A group of Cistercian monks still lives here. (Open Mon.-Sat. 10am-noon and 2-6pm, Sun. 2-6pm. Admission 14F, students 10F.) The **Chemin des Bilais,** a 4km footpath to the abbey, begins just outside the town center after the Hôtel du Domaine de l'Enclos on route de Sénanque.

The Gordes **tourist office,** pl. du Château (tel. 90 72 02 75), has information on Gordes, the Village des Bories, the Moulin de Bouillons, and the Abbaye de Sénanque, as well as camping and lodging in the Vaucluse region. It does not change money, however, and there are no banks in Gordes. (Open daily 9:30am-12:30pm and 3-7pm; Sept.-April Mon.-Sat. only.) The only semi-affordable hotel is luxurious **Le Provençal,** pl. du Château (tel. 90 72 01 07), where doubles with bath go for 185F, triples for 240F. The closest campground, the no-frills **Camping Municipal des Chalottes** (tel. 90 72 05 38), is 9km away in Murs. (Hot showers. Open Jan.-April and June 16-Sept. 15.) Unfortunately, Gordes is difficult to reach by public transportation. To get there from Avignon, you must first go to Cavaillon (5-10 per day, 35-40 min.) and then catch one of the infrequent, inconveniently timed buses to Gordes. (Mon.-Sat. 3 per day. Last bus from Cavaillon to Avignon at 5:45pm.)

Aix-en-Provence

In Aix, when a blind man thinks it's raining, if he
could see without his stick, he would behold a thou-

sand blue fountains sing praise of Cézanne.
—*J. Cocteau*

Aix (pronounced EX), where Paul Cézanne was born and carried out most of his work, radiates *joie de vivre* and gentle grace. While it may take pride in its pedigree as the oldest Roman settlement in Gaul, this somewhat snobbish university city retains no monuments from that era. Rather, the rows of sand-colored townhouses with iron grillwork housed wealthy magistrates from the Parlement, the supreme court of justice which operated in Aix between 1487 and the Revolution. The carved dolphins and cherubs that spray water in seemingly every square are one happy legacy of the Plague of 1721, which made it necessary for the city to renew its water supply. The morning flower market in the pl. Hôtel de Ville infuses the *vieille ville* with radiant color.

Every summer in June and early August, Aix hosts characteristically elegant music festival complete with ushers in tuxedos. Less formal, more exuberant performances take place in the streets, particularly in and around cours Mirabeau.

Orientation and Practical Information

The main axis of Aix is **cours Mirabeau,** a wide promenade that sweeps through the center of town, linking the tourist office at the west end with the churches and the Catholic college at the east. **La Rotonde,** at the west end of cours Mirabeau and just north of the train station, is the central terminus for city buses. To get here from the train station, go straight out on av. Victor Hugo and bear left at the fork, staying on av. Victor Hugo (5 min.) until it feeds into La Rotonde.

Tourist Office: 2, pl. du Général de Gaulle (tel. 42 26 02 93). A busy office with the usual services: hotel reservations, **currency exchange** (open May-Sept. daily Mon.-Sat. 9am-noon and 2-6pm), and guided tours of the city (daily at 10am, 3:30pm, and 9pm; tours in English Wed. at 10am; 40F, students 20F). Pick up a plan of Aix with suggested walking tours. The monthly guide to events in Aix, *Le Mois à Aix* (free), is useful during the festival. Open daily 9am-10pm; Nov.-Feb. daily 9am-8pm. **Festival Information:** For the music festival only, go to the Palais de l'Ancien Archevêché (tel. 42 23 11 20 or 42 23 37 81). Reserve tickets by mail or phone before July 1. Open Feb.-June 9am-noon and 2-6pm; July-Jan. 10am-1pm and 3-7pm. The green booth in the courtyard outside sells tickets during the festival Mon.-Sat. 9am-1pm and 3-7pm, Sun. 10am-noon. The kiosk outside the tourist office distributes information on the dance festival only.

Budget Travel: Council Travel, 12, rue Victor Leydet (tel. 42 38 58 82), off pl. des Augustins. Books international and domestic flights at reduced student prices. Check Air Inter prices for domestic flights, as some are as cheap (if not cheaper) than 2nd-class train tickets. Special prices on flights within Europe for Americans and Canadians under 25. Open Sun.-Fri. 10am-1pm and 2-6pm.

Currency Exchange: L'Agence Voyages-Change, 15, cours Mirabeau. No commission, good rates, and open on weekends. Open summer Mon.-Sat. 9am-9pm, Sun. 10am-1pm and 4-7pm; winter Mon.-Fri. 9am-7pm, Sat. 9:30am-5:30pm. Another **bureau de change** at the post office, 2, rue Lapierre. Commission 1%. Open Mon.-Fri. 8am-7pm, Sat. 8am-noon. The large banks on cours Mirabeau keep ridiculously short hours and slap on a steep commission.

Post Office: 2, rue Lapierre (tel. 42 27 62 45), across La Rotonde from the tourist office. **Poste Restante** and **telephones.** Open Mon.-Fri. 8am-7pm, Sat. 8am-noon. The less crowded **Postal annex** (tel. 42 23 44 17), 1, pl. de l'Hôtel de Ville, provides the same services until 6:30pm daily in Aug. **Postal Code:** 13100.

Trains: (tel. 91 08 50 50 in Marseille) at the end of av. Victor Hugo, off rue Gustavo Desplace. To get just about anywhere from Aix, you have to go to Marseille via the hourly trains (40 min., 31F, last train 9:40pm). To Nice (3 hr., 143F) and Cannes (2½ hr., 128F). Station open daily 6am-10pm.

Buses: rue Lapierre (tel. 42 26 01 50), behind the post office. A very confusing place. About 10 different companies run independently. **SATAP** (tel. 42 26 23 78) goes to Avignon (6 per day; 1½ hr.; 58F, with Carte Jeune 40F). **SCAL** (tel. 42 26 29 13) travels to Nice (3 per day; 2¼ hr.; 108F, with Carte Jeune 75F) and Cannes (3 per day; 1¾ hr.; 100F). Other companies go to Arles (5 per day; 1½ hr.; 55F) and Marseille (every 15 min.; 45 min.; 10.50F, students 20.50F return. Buses within the city 5.60F, 10 tickets 32F. Information office open Mon.-Sat. 8am-noon and 2:30-6pm.

Taxis: Tel. 42 27 71 11 6am-9pm, tel. 42 26 29 30 9pm-6am.

Hitchhiking: If you chose to hitch, be aware that although the autoroute A8 swings right through Aix, hitching can be tricky. You're better off waiting for the long haul rather than taking a short ride and being dropped off on the highway. For Avignon, follow bd. de la République until it becomes A8. For Nice, follow cours Gambetta.

English Bookstore: Paradox, 2, rue Reine-Jeanne (tel. 42 26 47 99), behind the Roi René Hôtel on bd. du Roi René. Excellent selection of new books. Open Tues.-Sun. 9:30am-noon and 3-7pm. **The Bookshop of Aix-en-Provence,** at French-American Center of Provence (see directly below). Fair selection of new and used classics and bestsellers from 20F. Open daily 9am-noon and 2-7pm.

French-American Center: Centre Franco-Américain de Provence, 24, pl. des Martyrs de la Résistance (tel. 42 23 23 36), ancienne pl. de l'Archevêché. Organizes exchanges, *au pair* stays, and 3- to 4-week crash language courses. Unofficial flat-finding service for members only. Membership (150F) and services open to all nationalities. Open daily 9am-noon and 2-7pm.

Women's Center: Information Femmes—C.I.D.F., 24, rue Mignet (tel. 42 20 69 82), in the *sous-préfecture.* Not a lot of English spoken but loads of information. Open Mon.-Tues. and Thurs.-Fri. 9am-noon and 2-4pm and by appointment noon-2pm.

Laundromat: Off La Rotonde on the corner of rue Bernadines and rue de la Fontaine. Wash 15F per 4.5kg, dry 2F per 7½ min. Open daily 7am-8pm. **Inter-Laverie,** bd. Carnot, opposite the Ecole d'Arts et Métiers. Wash 14F for 5kg, dry 2F for 6 min. Open daily 7am-8pm. The hostel has its own laundry facilities (soap, wash, and dry 20F).

Pharmacy, 3, cours Mirabeau (tel. 42 26 12 15). English spoken. Open summer daily 9am-12:30pm and 2:30-7:30pm; winter daily 9am-12:30pm.

Medical Emergency: Centre Hospitalier Général, av. Tamaris (tel. 42 33 50 00). **SOS Médecins:** tel. 42 26 24 00. Available 24 hrs. **SOS Amitié,** tel. 91 76 10 10. 24 hr. crisis hotline.

Police: 8, pl. Jeanne d'Arc (tel. 42 26 04 81). **Emergency,** tel. 17.

Accommodations and Camping

There are few inexpensive hotels near the center, and during the festival they are all booked in advance. Do likewise, or arrive early and hope for cancellations. The crowded youth hostel is a 25-minute hike outside of town, but buses run until 8pm. Be sure to call before setting out.

Auberge de Jeunesse (IYHF), 3, av. Marcel Pagnol (tel. 42 20 15 99), quartier du Jas de Bouffan, next to the Fondation Vasarely. A 25-min. walk from the center of town. Bus #12 makes the trip from La Rotonde (every ½-hr. until 8pm, 5.60F). A modern hostel in a newly-developed neighborhood. Strict proprietor. Laundry facilities (20F wash and dry). No kitchen facilities. Lockout 9am-5:30pm. Curfew 11pm. Bed (9 beds per room) and obligatory breakfast 62F first night, each additional night 51F. Meals 38F. Sheets 10F, no sleeping bags. TV room, bar, tennis courts, and volleyball net. Call ahead to make sure there's room or make a reservation (5F deposit required). Office open 7:30-10am and 5:30-10pm.

CROUS: Cité des Gazelles, 38, av. Jules Ferry (tel. 42 26 33 75), outside the center. The university occasionally offers 55F singles with a 2-day min. stay in July-Aug.

Foyer des Abeilles, av. de Maréchal Leclerc (tel. 42 59 25 75), a 10-min. walk from the hostel towards town. Ask for Mike. Doubles 70F per person. Quads 50F per person. Hall showers included. Dinner 44F. Breakfast 16F. Often filled with large groups. No reservations from individuals accepted.

Hôtel Vigoureux, 27, rue Cardinale (tel. 42 38 26 42), between pl. des Dauphins and the Musée Granet. A boarding house for university students in winter. Clean and spacious rooms are simple but elegant. Singles 100F. Doubles 200F, with shower and toilet 230-250F. Breakfast 25F.

Hôtel Vendome, 10, cours des Minimes (tel. 42 64 45 01), from La Rotonde walk up bd. de la République; cours des Minimes meets République at a rotary on the left hand side (5 min.) Hot rooms with Bibles; pray for air conditioning. Cheapest hotel in town. Adequate but not great. Singles and doubles 100F, with showers 150F. Breakfast 20F.

Hôtel du Casino, 38, rue Victor Leydet (tel. 42 26 06 88). off cours Mirabeau. Excellent location. Adequate rooms. Singles 110-130F, with shower 150F. Doubles 165-175F, with shower 175F, and toilet and TV 260F. TV room. Breakfast 25F.

Camping: All campgrounds lie outside of town. THe 3-star sites relatively close by all cost around 34F per person and tent. The last one is likely to have room even in summer. **Arc-en-Ciel** (tel. 42 26 14 28), Pont des Trois Sautets, route de Nice, 3km from the center of town (bus #3). A 4-star site with a pool and hot showers. **Chantecler** (tel. 42 26 12 98), val St-André, by route de Nice, 3km from the center (bus #3). Swimming pool and hot showers. 1 person with tent 43.70F, 2 people 62.80F. **Le Felibrige** (tel. 42 92 12 11), in Puyricard, off the RN7 or the RN de Manosque, also 3km from Aix. Take the bus to Puyricard from cours Sextius (Mon.-Sat. every ½-hr.). A pleasant campground conveniently located next to a pool. 1-3 persons with tent 80F; 9F each additional person.

Food

Although the restaurants in Aix serve delicious regional specialties often seasoned with the garlic *aïoli* sauce, the city's culinary reputation comes from its *confiseries* (confections). In France, most prepared almonds used in cakes and cookies originate in Aix; its most famous confection is the *calisson d'Aix* (a small iced almond cookie). Other regional specialties include the soft nougat and the hard praline candy. Check out the *pâtisseries* on rue d'Italie or rue Espariat.

The cafés on cours Mirabeau often serve bland and overpriced meals and are better suited for after-dinner drinks and people-watching. Affordable restaurants with terrace seating cluster in the area around pl. des Cardeurs. Several inexpensive, interesting places can also be found in the rue Van-Loo area off cours Sextus. There is a **Supermarket Casino** at 1, av. de Lattre de Tassigny, off bd. de la République (open Mon.-Sat. 8:30am-8:30pm) and a **Monoprix Supermarket** on cours Mirabeau (open Mon.-Thurs. and Sat. 8:45am-7:15pm, Fri. 8:45am-8pm). Better yet, head for the **market**, held on Tuesdays, Thursdays, and Saturdays at pl. de Verdun in front of the Palais de Justice (7am-1pm).

Hacienda, 7, rue Mérindol, west of pl. des Cardeurs. Outdoor seating, quick service, and an excellent value. The 53F *menu* includes veal, steak or fish, fries or vegetables, dessert, and wine. Great salads 28-38F. Open Sept. 4-Aug. 5 Mon.-Sat. noon-2pm and 7-10:30pm.

Djerba, 8bis rue Rifle-Rafle, a tiny street off pl. des Pêcheurs. Busy outdoor restaurant with Tunisian specialties. 66F lunch *menu* (Mon.-Fri. only) features pork or steak. 105F dinner *menu. Plat du jour* 35F. *Couscous* 46-70F. Open daily noon-3pm and 7pm-midnight.

Chez Lorraine, 18, rue Portalis, off bd. Carnot. Small and cozy restaurant serving Lorraine specialties. *Plat du jour* 39F. *Quiche lorraine* 36F. Lorraine omelettes 25F. Open Tues.-Sat. 10:30am-2:30pm and 7-11pm, Sun.-Mon. 10:30am-2:30pm.

Restaurant Chahé, 6, rue de la Paix, off rue Van-Loo. Greek, Lebanese and Armenian dishes at a price you can afford. *Tabouleh* (25F), hummus (25F), *mousaka* (50F) and kebab (55F). Open daily noon-2pm and 7-10:30pm.

Alimentation Nguyên-Thành, 16, rue Gaston de Saporta, not far from the Hôtel de Ville. A take-out with appetizing East Asian specialties. Makes a wonderful picnic. Chicken curry 15F. Cantonese rice 8.70F. Open Tues.-Sat. 10am-1:30pm and 4-8pm.

La Cigale, 48, rue Espariat, off pl. des Augustines and not far from cours Mirabeau. 51F (3-course) and 65F (4-course) *menus* with French and Italian specialties. Lasagne and ravioli both 42F. Super salads 28-30F. Open Thurs.-Tues. noon-2pm and 7-11pm.

Cafeteria Flunch, 2, av. des Belges, next to the tourist office. Super cheap and filling fare. Roast chicken with 2 vegetables 14.90F. Open daily 11am-10pm.

Sights

Cultured Aix supports several museums of note. A fine collection of Beauvais tapestries from the 17th and 18th centuries hangs in the **Musée des Tapisseries**, pl. des Martyrs de la Résistance (tel. 42 21 05 78), at ancienne pl. de l'Archevêché.

A handout in English is available at the door. (Open Wed.-Mon. 9:30am-noon and 2-5:45pm. Admission 20F, students 10F.) The **Musée Granet,** pl. St-Jean-de-Malte (tel. 42 38 14 70), displays a collection of Roman sculptures and Egyptian mummies, a large number of Dutch and classical paintings, and exhibitions of contemporary art. The current pride and joy of the museum is the recent acquisition of eight small paintings by Cézanne. (Open daily 10am-noon and 2-6pm, Sept.-May Wed.-Mon. same hours. Admission 12F, students 7F, under 12 free.) The **Musée du Vieil Aix,** 17, rue Gaston de Saporta (tel. 42 21 43 55), not far from pl. des Martyrs de la Résistance, contains an eccentric collection of exhibits on local history and popular customs. A display of marionettes explains the *jeux de Fête-Dieu,* a local pageant-puppet show, allegedly started by Good King René. Supposedly symbolic of Christian triumph over heathens, the religious procession is joined by secular games and a fair on the cours Sextus. (Open April 16-Oct. 1 Tues.-Sun. 10am-noon and 2:30-6pm; Nov. 1-April 15 Tues.-Sun. 10am-noon and 2:30-5pm. Admission 10F, children 5-14 free. English guidebooks 5F.)

The stunning and defiant **Fondation Vasarely,** 1, av. Marcel Pagnol (tel. 42 20 01 09), Jas de Bouffan, can be found outside town near the youth hostel. Take bus #12 (5.60F) from La Rotonde to Vasarely. The black and white pattern of the building makes an apt backdrop for Victor Vasarely's enormous, vibrant experiments with color. The museum houses 42 of Vasarely's monumental works, known as "mural integrations," which fool the careless viewer into thinking that they are 3-dimensional. All the rooms are hexagonal—a patriotic gesture to six-sided France. (Open Wed.-Sun. 9:30am-12:30pm and 2-5:30pm. Admission 25F, ages 7-18 10F.) After this visual stimulation, you can relax in the park outside, one of the quietest spots in Aix.

The ardent Cézanne devotee may want to visit the **Musée d'atelier Paul Cézanne,** 9, av. Paul Cézanne (tel. 42 21 06 53), five minutes out of town. His studio remains much as he left it in 1906, with his easel, a smock, and an unfinished canvas. Some of his paintings, as well as a few etchings and drawings, abide here. (Open Wed.-Mon. 10am-noon and 2:30-6pm; in winter Wed.-Mon. 10am-noon and 2-5pm. Admission 10F; students, children, and seniors 5F.)

Cathédrale St-Sauveur is an architectural melange of additions and carvings from 11th-century Romanesque to late Flamboyant Gothic. The main attractions, beautiful 16th-century carved panels of the main portal, remain in perfect condition, thanks to their protective wooden shutters. The interior's claim to fame, the *Triptych du Buisson Ardent,* depicts King René and his queen in odd juxtaposition with the Virgin and Child and the burning bush of Moses. This work is usually closed away, but for a small tip, the parlous guard may show it and the front panels to you. Adjoining the church, the delicate 13th-century **Cloître St-Sauveur** has a wooden roof over the galleries instead of the usual heavy arches. During the festival, mass is held Sunday at 10:30am. (Church open Wed.-Mon. 8am-noon and 2-6pm. Free.) **Bibliothèque Méjanes,** 8-10, rue des Allumettes (tel. 42 25 95 95), just next to the *gare routière,* displays an impressive collection of illuminated manuscripts and, often, works of contemporary artists. (Open Tues.-Wed. and Fri. noon-6pm, Sat. 10am-6pm. Free.) The **Fondation St-John Perse,** in the same building (tel. 42 25 98 85) stores materials and manuscripts related to the 1960 Nobel prize-winning poet, St-John Perse (open Tues.-Wed. and Fri. noon-6pm. Free.)

Entertainment

Aix is famous for its **International Music Festival,** held from mid-July to early August, which attracts first-rate musicians and renowned orchestras from around the world. Tickets are expensive, seats scarce, and student discounts rare. The program features opera in the **Théâtre de l'Archevêché** (admission 240-680F); concerts in **Cathédrale** and **Cloître St-Louis,** 60, bd. Carnot (admission 120-380F); and recitals by advanced music students at **Cloître St-Sauveur** (admission 75F). Beginning the second week of June, all of Aix takes the opportunity to celebrate with a less formal, but no less interesting, two-week jamboree of big-band jazz, classical quartets, and wind ensembles. Most concerts are free, and each evening the streets of the *vieille ville* fill with conservatory students playing everything from rock to classical music. The tourist office's program *Aix en Musique* lists concerts and locations; call 42 63 06 75 for more information. For the first two weeks of July, Aix holds its international **Dance Festival,** with performances ranging from classical ballet to modern and jazz. (Tickets 70-150F, students 50-120F.) Contact the Comité Officiel des Fêtes on cours Gambetta (tel. 42 63 06 75), at the corner of bd. du Roi René, for information on the Music and Dance Festivals.

Although Aix's primary source of entertainment is the never-ending parade on cours Mirabeau, excellent jazz shows, frequented by a lively, appreciative crowd, often go bop in the night. The **Marathon Théâtre,** 23, bd. de la République (tel. 42 26 36 50), an avant-garde/radical theater, usually lists the time and place of each jazz show and also puts on excellent shows of its own most weekends (tickets 65F). The **Théâtre de Verdure,** parc Paysage du Jas de Bouffan (tel. 42 59 38 30), runs an inexpensive outdoor theater that goes into high gear during the music festival.

One of Aix's better nightclubs is **La Palette Club 60,** 21, rue Lisse des Cordeliers (tel. 42 26 44 05), on a small street just before the intersection of rue Cordeliers and cours Sextius. Here you can rock around the clock to 50s and 60s music. (Open Wed., Fri. and Sat. 10:30pm until late.) **Le Mistral,** 3, rue Frédéric Mistral (tel. 42 38 16 49), next to the restaurant Gu et Fils, attracts a mature student crowd. (Open nightly 11pm until sunrise. Admission 80F.) **Le Scat,** 11, rue Verrerie (tel. 42 23 00 23), is an excellent club with live jazz and blues every night at 10:30pm. (Open Mon.-Sat. 10pm until sunrise). **La Chimère,** montée d'Avignon (tel. 42 23 36 28), quartier des Plâtrières, outside the town, attracts a sizable gay crowd to its bar and disco. (Open Tues.-Sun. 10pm-6am.) Another Aix hotspot is **Hot Brass,** chemin Départ (tel. 42 21 05 57).

The Forum des Cardeurs, behind the Hôtel de Ville, is lined with chic cafés and bars, some lit up by candlelight after dark. Try the **Croquet Bar** or the **Royal Bar,** both open daily from 7:30pm until everyone's gone.

The **Cézanne** cinema, 21, rue Gayraud (tel. 42 26 04 06) plays 10 movies every night, some in their original language (32F). **Le Mazarin,** 6, rue Laroque (tel. 42 26 99 85), also shows good *version originale* films. (6 per night, 32F, children under 13 22F.)

Near Aix

As you walk toward the Montagne de Ste-Victoire, you can retrace Cézanne's easel stops along the D17, now called **route de Cézanne.** The road winds its way to the hamlet of **Le Tholonet,** 5km from Aix. French and English minibus tours leave Thursday from the tourist office (April-Sept., at 1:45pm, 130F); call the tourist office or Cie Autocars de Provence (tel. 42 23 14 26) for information. (Tours in French and English).

Picasso devotees can seek out the master's grave in **Vauvenargues,** 16km east of Aix. Three or four buses per day run from Aix. For more info call **RDT 13,** 42 26 01 50. Although visitors are not allowed entrance to the 19th-century château where Picasso lived, some of the artist's sculptures are on display in the park.

Nîmes

Nîmes (pop. 140,000), like Rome, was built with Roman labor on seven hills; 2000 years later it still competes with Arles for the title *la Rome française*. Visible throughout the city, an enchained crocodile commemorates Emperor Augustus's victory over Anthony and Cleopatra in Egypt. Arriving in France, Augustus made the pathetic figure a symbol of Egypt's demise and gave Nîmes to his troops as a Rome away from Rome. In addition to the well-preserved *arènes* (Roman arena), where summer bullfights and concerts take place, Nîmes also possesses an elegantly articulated Roman temple and the Maison Carrée.

In 1860, an Austrian named Levi-Strauss began exporting a heavy cloth from Nîmes to California to serve as tent cloth for gold diggers. Produced here since the 17th century, this fabric *de Nîmes* still indicates its origins in its name, denim.

In 1985 the city declared its older, historical section a conservation zone and began renovating the area. In addition, Nîmes has planned a new center of contemporary art and media, the **Mediathèque,** which will be similar in function to Paris's active Georges Pompidou Center.

Orientation and Practical Information

The arena marks the center of the city. Most of the interesting sights lie within the area bordered by bd. Victor Hugo, bd. de la Libération, and bd. Admiral Courbet. The first two fan out from the arena. To get to the tourist office from the train station, go up av. Feuchères, veer left around the small park, and go around the arena; then continue straight on bd. Victor Hugo for five blocks. Just after the Maison Carrée, signs direct you to the tourist office.

Tourist Office: 6, rue Auguste (tel. 66 67 29 11, recorded announcement in French 66 67 86 86). Free accommodations service. Information on bus and train excursions to pont du Gard, the Camargue, and nearby towns. Guided tours of the city July-Aug. daily at 10am (30F). Exhaustive festival information. **Currency exchange** available during office hours (1% commission). Open Easter-Sept. Mon.-Fri. 8am-7pm, Sat. 9am-5pm, Sun. 10am-3pm; Oct.-Easter Mon.-Fri. 8am-7pm, Sat. 9am-noon and 2-5pm, Sun. 10am-noon. **Branch office** in the train station distributes a map with important telephone numbers. Open Mon.-Sat. 9:30am-12:30pm and 1:30-5:30pm, Sun. 9:30am-12:30pm and 2-6:30pm. **Regional Tourist Office,** 3, pl. des Arènes (tel. 66 21 02 51). Yet more information on Nîmes and the surrounding area. Open Mon.-Sat. 8:45am-7:30pm, Sun. 9am-noon. All 3 offices staffed with English speakers.

Post Office: bd. de Bruxelles (tel. 66 76 67 06), near pl. de la Libération at the end of av. Feuchères. **Telephones** and **currency exchange.** Branch office on bd. Gambetta. Open Mon.-Fri. 8am-7pm, Sat. 8am-noon. **Postal code:** 30000.

Trains: av. Feuchères (tel. 66 23 50 50). Nîmes is on the major line between Bordeaux and Marseille. Direct to: Toulouse (16 per day, 3 hr., 160F); Arles (33F); Montpellier (1 or 2 per hr., ½-hr., 38F); Paris (6 per day, 4½ hr., 337F plus obligatory 14F TGV reservation); Orange (6 per day, 1¾ hr., 50F); Marseille (77F). **Information office** open Mon.-Fri. 8am-6pm, Sat. 9am-12:15pm and 2-6:15pm. **Lockers** 20F per 72 hrs.

Buses: (tel. 66 29 52 00) on Rue Ste-Félicité, behind the train station. Complete, up-to-date timetable posted in the station. Friendly, professional staff. Open Mon.-Fri. 8:30am-noon and 2-6:30pm. **Société des Transports Départementaux du Gard (STDG),** tel. 66 29 27 29. To: Vers (3 per day, 50 min., 24F); Uzès (Mon.-Sat. 8 per day, Sun. 2 per day, 50 min., 24F); Pont St-Esprit (4 per day, 1¼ hr., 53.50F); Pont-du-Gard (8 per day, ½-hr., 24F); Avignon (7 per day, 1¼ hr., 31.50F). **Cevennes Cars,** tel. 66 29 11 11. To: Aigues-Mortes (6 per day, 55 min., 28F); Le Grau du Roi (6 per day, 1 hr., 31F); La Grande Motte (5 per day, 1¼ hr., 36.50F); Alès (5 per day, 1½ hr., 40F). **Les Rapides de Camargue,** tel. 66 85 30 28. To St-Gilles (4 per day, 35 min., 20F). **Les Courriers du Midi,** tel. 66 92 05 00. To Montpellier (every hr., 1½ hr., 39.50F).

Public Transportation: Buses, tel. 66 38 15 40. Tickets 5F, *carnet* of 5 19F.

Bike Rental: At the train station (tel. 66 29 72 41). 10 bikes, often all rented. 50F per day, 285F per week. Deposit 500F. Office open daily 8am-8pm.

English Bookstore: Librairie Anglaise, 8, rue Dorée (tel. 66 21 17 04). Limited collection of Jane Austen bodice-rippers. Behind the Hôtel de Ville. Open Mon.-Fri. 9am-noon and 2-6pm.

Womens Center: Droits de la Femme, 1, rue Raymond Marc (tel. 66 67 70 21, ext. (*poste*) 1746 and 1743), on the fourth floor of the *préfecture.* Open Mon.-St. 8:30am-12:30pm and 1:30-5:30pm.

Laundromat: 26, rue Porte de France. 14F wash, 2F per 8-min. dry. Open 7am-8:30pm. Also at 47, rue de la République.

24-Hour Doctor and Pharmacy: The commissariat on av. Feuchères (tel. 66 67 96 91) has a list.

Hospital: Gaston Doumergue, 5, rue Hoche (tel. 66 27 41 11).

Medical Emergency: Tel. 66 21 60 01. **SAMU,** tel. 15.

Police: 16, av. Feuchères (tel. 66 67 96 91). **Emergency,** tel. 17.

Accommodations and Camping

Hotels cluster around the arena and off bd. Admiral Courbet. Fairly inexpensive rooms are easy to find except during the week-long *férias* in February, June, and September. During these festivals, reservations are essential.

Auberge de Jeunesse (IYHF) (tel. 66 23 25 04), chemin de l'Auberge de Jeunesse, a continuation of chemin de la Cigale 3½km from the station. Take bus #20 (Mon.-Sat. every hr., 6am-8pm) from the train station to the Cigale stop, then walk 500m uphill. To walk, go past the *jardin,* take route d'Alès, and follow the signs. Friendly, informal hostel in a peacful setting. 78 beds and camping space available. Snack bar and well-equipped kitchen. Open 7-10am and 6pm-midnight. 50F per person. Breakfast included. Sheets 12F. Often full from March 15-June 30, so call ahead and arrive by 5:30pm during these months.

Hôtel de France, 4, bd. des Arènes (tel. 66 67 47 72), in front of the arena. Excellent location. Oddly shaped singles with shower 80F. More conventional doubles with private toilet 120F. Triples and quads with shower 140-180F. Breakfast 15F.

Nouvel Hôtel, 6, bd. Amiral Courbet (tel. 66 67 62 48). Warm owners in an attractive building. Some rooms have separate breakfast nooks. All rooms have showers. Singles 115F. Doubles 150-180F. Triples and quads 220F. Breakfast 22F.

Hôtel Majestic, 10, rue Pradier (tel. 66 29 24 14), off av. Feuchères near the train station. Two-star hotel with big, simple rooms and bathrooms that swivel back into the wall when not in use. All rooms have a shower and toilet. Singles 150-170F. Doubles 170-190F.

Le Lisita, 2, bd. des Arènes (tel. 66 67 62 48). Two-star hotel. Well-furnished rooms. Alphonse, the mockingbird, greets you sarcastically. Singles 85-100F. Doubles with shower and private toilet 180F. Breakfast 20F.

La Couronne, 4, pl. de la Couronne (tel. 66 67 51 73). Grim but cheapish. Rooms 110-120F, with shower 140-190F. Breakfast 17F.

Camping: Domaine de La Bastide (tel. 66 38 09 21), on route de Générac about 4½km from the train station. Until 8pm, take bus #4 from bd. Gambetta or av. Feuchères, near the train station (5F). A 3-star site. 26F per person including tent. 46F for 2 people.

Food

Specialties include *brandade de morue* (a puree of codfish with olive oil and spices) and *herbes de Provence* (a mixture of herbs and olive oil used on *canapés* as hors d'oeuvres). For dessert, try a *croquant villaret* (a crispy almond cookie) or a *caladon* (a cookie with almonds and honey). In summer the gardens are the perfect place for a picnic. Buy your fruits and vegetables in the **market** in the Halles, rue Général Perrier, near the Maison Carrée (Wed. 8am-1pm), in the **Prisunic** off bd. de la Libération (Open Mon.-Sat. 9am-7pm), or in the **open-air market** (Mon. 8am-1pm).

Les Persiennes, 5, pl. de l'Oratoire. Refined atmosphere, a 53F unlimited hors d'oeuvre bar, and a 68F *menu.* Try the curried chicken kebab or any of the fish *pâtés.* Open Sept.-July Tues.-Sat. noon-2pm and 8-10pm.

La Baie d'Halong 5, bd. Victor Hugo. Vietnamese specialties served next to a goldfish pond. 40F lunch *menu* includes *nems* (spring rolls) and *porc laquée.* Open daily noon-2pm and 7:30-11pm.

L'Oeuf à la Côte, 29, rue de la Madeleine, in the *vieille ville.* High ceilings and stone walls like eggshells. Terrace seating available. Menu features eggs and poultry. 46F *plat du jour* with appetizer. A *salon de thé* between meals. Open daily noon-midnight.

Les Hirondelles, 13, rue Bigot, at rue Porte de France. A lunchtime restaurant with a local crowd. 45F traditional *menu* includes wine and changes daily. Open Sun.-Fri. noon-2pm and 7-10pm.

Pizzeria Cerutti, 25, rue de l'Horloge, behind the Maison Carrée. Pizza and pasta 40F. For night owls. In summer try the sangria. Open daily noon-2pm and 7pm-1am.

Sights

Most of the Roman monuments in Nîmes are concentrated in two areas—near the *arènes* and near the *jardins*—which are within easy walking distance of each other. Admission to all the monuments and museums (except the Arena and free sights) is 12F.

Smaller than the one in Arles, Nîmes's **Amphithéâtre Romain** is preserved in frayed but magnificent entirety. In summer, bullfights and concerts draw crowds who either shout for blood or hold up cigarette lighters, depending on the occasion. (Open 8am-8pm. Admission 17F.) Nîmes's **Maison Carrée** (Square House) is actually rectangular, its length (26.5m) being almost exactly twice its width (13.5m). Built in the 1st century BC and dedicated to the grandsons of the Emperor Augustus, this Roman temple is accented by fluted Corinthian columns and exquisite decorations, still visible through 2000 years of **grime**. The newly restored **Musée Archéologique,** 13, bd. Amiral Courbet, contains statues, mosaics, and other antiquities. Attached to the Musée Archéologique, the **Musée d'Histoire Naturelle** crawls with incredible two-headed monstres and more conventional critters which will make taxidermists beam and everyone else feel sick. (Open Mon.-Sat. 9am-7pm, Sun. 1:30-7pm; Oct.-May Mon.-Sat. 9am-noon and 1:30-6pm, Sun. 1:30-6pm. Free.) Also recently renovated, the **Museé des Beaux Arts** exhibits temporary art shows and permanent collections of modern sculpture and painting. (Open daily 9am-7pm; Sept. 16-June 14 daily 9am-noon and 1:30-6pm.) The **Musée du Vieux Nîmes,** Palais de l'Ancien Evêché, pl. aux Herbes, displays regional popular arts including 17th- and 18th-century furniture, textiles, and ceramics. (Open daily 10am-6pm. Free.)

While away the afternoon in the **Jardins de la Fontaine,** left along the canals from the Maison Carrée. The spring which feeds the fountain and the canal originally enticed the Romans to settle in Nîmes. From the top of the **Tour Magne,** one of the towers on the Roman city walls built by Augustus in 15 BC, From the top, you can see at least five churches in different parts of the city. Of these, we deem the most interesting to be **Cathédrale St-Castor,** with a spacious if short Romanesque nave and an sculpted façade depicting scenes from the Old Testament. We could be wrong. On your way down the hill, inspect the ruins of the Roman **Temple of Diana,** uncovered during the construction of the garden in 1745. The tourist office keeps a list of plays to be performed here in the summer months. Maréschal, a military engineer who designed the gardens, was criticized by contemporaries who thought his masterpiece looked more like a soldiers' parade ground than an ornament for the city. In any case, the park makes a quiet retreat from the town, especially on summer evenings when the ponds are illuminated. (Park, temple, and tower open June 16-Sept. 15 9am-7pm; Sept. 16-Oct. and March-June 15 9am-noon and 2-6pm; Nov.-Feb. 9am-noon and 2-5pm.)

Ancient history buffs may want to head northeast of the garden to the **Castellum,** off bd. Gambetta, the scant and unremarkable remains of the Roman plumbing system which was linked to the **Pont du Gard** and distributed water from the Eure to different parts of the city. The only relic of this kind in the world, the basin has 10 small holes that once diverted water into five different canals leading to each village quarter.

Entertainment

From June to September, the nightlife in Nîmes centers around the arènes. A big-name rock concert (150F) as well as an opera (tickets from 80F) are produced each year. In the first half of July, various concerts fill the city, including some at the Temple of Diana (admission from 50F, tickets at door). The tourist office has a calendar.

The home of France's major school of **bullfighting**, l'Ecole Française de Tauromachie, Nîmes sponsors three important *corridas*. In February, June, and September, the streets resound with the clattering hooves as the bulls are herded to their deaths. Tickets (from 90F) may be purchased two weeks before the bullfight from the **Bureau de Location des Arènes,** rue Alexandre Ducros (tel. 66 67 28 02). "Courses Camarguaises" offer more humane entertainment; the aim of the fighters is to strip the bull of the decoration on his horns and forehead, rather than to kill him.

Café-Théâtre le Titoit de Titus, 6, rue Titus (tel. 66 67 64 73), off the canal, sponsors innovative drama, comedy, and concerts throughout the year. Pick up a current calendar at the theater; shows usually take place on weekend nights (60F, students 50F). **Musique en stock,** 28, rue Jean Reboul (tel. 66 21 73 73), offers junkyard décor and live bands on Friday and Saturday nights. The excellent cinema **Le Sémaphore,** 25a, rue Porte de France (tel. 66 67 88 04), one block over from bd. Victor Hugo, mounts a great summer film festival during July and August. Foreign films play in their original language year-round; the theater also hosts occasional concerts and lectures by filmmakers. Pick up a schedule in front of the box office.

Near Nîmes

Pont du Gard and Uzès

A legend recorded by Frédéric Mistral recounts that the devil built the **Pont du Gard** in return for the soul of the first creature to cross the bridge. A hare was first to make the trip and the devil, infuriated by his poor catch, flung himself into the river. Twenty km from Nîmes toward Avignon, this mortarless Roman aqueduct was built 2000 years ago to bring water from the Eure into the Nîmes Castellum. Three levels of graceful arches support the water canal, enclosed except for periodic breaks that allow for ventilation and maintenance. You can walk across the narrow top of the aqueduct—an exhilarating experience since no guardrails separate you from the rock-filled river 50m below. Sometimes people jump into the river from the center of the bottom level. Perform this imitation of the devil's stunt at your own risk.

The *région Pont du Gard* which includes Nîmes, Avignon, the Pont du Gard, and Uzès, can only be reached by bus. From Nîmes buses go to Uzès (6 per day, 24F) and to the Pont du Gard (8 per day, Sun. 4; 40 min.; 24F). Check schedules posted at the *gare routière* in Nîmes (behind the train station). Buses also leave for the Pont du Gard (6 per day, ½-hr.; 24F) from Avignon. During July and August, a 55F ticket allows you one full day of unlimited travel between Pont du Gard, Nîmes, Uzès, and Avignon; buy it before boarding the bus. The ticket is a good investment for those stopping at the Pont or in Uzès on their way between Avignon and Nîmes.

At the Pont du Gard, visit the **tourist office** (tel. 66 37 00 02) across the bridge from the Hôtel de Vieux Moulin and on the left. They have information on campgrounds, boar rental, and hiking as well as a currency exchange. (Open daily June-Aug. 9am-6pm, Sept.-May 10am-5pm.) The English-speaking staff will also direct you to **Collias,** 4km away toward Uzès, where **Kayak Vert** (tel. 66 22 84 83) rents canoes for two people (50F per hr., 140F per day). For 150F, you can paddle downstream from Collias to the Pont du Gard and then shuttle back to Collias. In Collias, **Camping le Barralet,** rue des Aires (tel. 66 22 84 52), offers a pool in addition to river bathing. (27F per person, open Easter-Sept.)

Thirty-five km from Nîmes is the small city of **Uzès,** the childhood home which André Gide recalled in his poems. Standing formidably in the center of the *vieille ville,* the **Duché d'Uzès** has been inhabited for 1000 years by the noble family of the Crussol d'Uzès. The family is at home when the flag flies from the castle tower. Inside the *duché* are paintings, tapestries, Louis XIII and Louis XIV furniture, and a 15th-century Gothic chapel. (Open June-Aug. daily 9:30am-noon and 2:30-6pm; Sept.-May 9am-noon and 2:30-5:30pm. Admission 30F.)

The six-story, cylindrical **Tour Fenestrelle** has a (non-leaning) Tower of Pisa-style bell tower uncommon in France. **Place aux Herbes,** next to the castle, is the site of a lively **market** on Saturday. If you can come for the summer **féria,** or **fête votive** (patron saint's day), usually at the beginning of August, you will be greeted by bulls stampeding through the streets and raging torrents of *pastis,* Uzès's alcoholic drink of choice. An international music festival, the **Nuits Musicales d'Uzès,** takes place the second half of July. Tickets (from 40F-140F) are available from the **tourist office,** av. de la Libération (tel. 66 22 68 88). The friendly office distributes transportation information, changes money, and can help with lodging. It also has a list of nearby farms which accept campers. (Open Mon.-Fri. 9am-6pm, Sat. 10am-noon and 3-5pm; Sept.-June Mon.-Fri. 9am-noon and 3-5pm, Sat. 10am-noon.) **La Taverne,** 4, rue Sigalon (tel. 66 22 13 10), has doubles for 130F, 200F with shower; breakfast is 25F. The hotel's restaurant, down the street toward the cinema, posts a 60F *menu.* **Camping Municipal Vallée de l'Eure** (tel. 66 22 11 79) has sites not far from Uzès. (10F per person, 4F per tent. Open June 15-Sept. 15.)

Uzès is easily reached by **bus** from Nîmes (7 per day, Sun. 4; 55 min.; 24.50F) or from Avignon (3 per day, 1 hr., 34.50F).

Alès and the Gorge de l'Ardèche

Alès lies 44km northeast of Nîmes at the heart of the **Cévennes** region. The unique **mining museum,** chemin de la Cité Ste-Marie (tel. 66 30 45 15), takes visitors back to Zola's *Germinal.* Don a hard hat before descending 650m into the human mole-hole. A one-hour guided tour and a 20 minute video complete the visit. (Open July-Aug. daily 10am-12:30pm and 3-7:30pm, Sept.-Nov. 11 and April-June 9am-12:30pm and 2-5:30pm. Admission 29F, under 12 13F.) In contrast, the **Musée Bibliothèque Pierre André Benoît,** montée des Lauriers (tel. 66 86 98 69) presents an impressive collection of modern art, including works of Picasso, Picabia, Braque, and Viera de Silva. (Open daily 11am-7pm, Sept. 16-June 14 Wed.-Sun. 11am-7pm. Admission 15F, students 7.50F, under 14 free.) Situated immediately west of the **Parc National des Cévennes,** Alès also makes a good base for forays into this region of closely packed mountains. *Sentiers de grandes randonnées* (hiking trails) lace the park. The **tourist office,** Alès's Chambre de Commerce, rue Michelieu (tel. 66 78 49 10), has information on the town and park. (Open Mon.-Fri. 8am-noon and 1:30-5:30pm.) From April through September an **annex** operates in the pavilion, pl. Gabriel Péri (tel. 66 52 32 15), in the center of town. (Open Mon.-Sat. 9am-noon and 1:15-7pm, Sun. 10am-noon and 1-4pm.) **Hôtel de Flore,** 23, bd. Victor Hugo (tel. 66 30 09 84), has doubles for 80F (with shower 120F) 30m from the station. **Camping Les Châtaigniers,** chemin des Sports (tel. 66 52 53 57), maintains a pool and organizes horseback excursions. (10.50F per person, 6.50 per tent. Open June-Sept.) Seven trains and three buses leave Nîmes daily for Alès. Two daily buses connect Alès and Uzès.

North of Nîmes in the **Gorges de l'Ardèche,** between Vallon Pont d'Arc and Pont-St-Esprit, the sparkling Ardèche River winds between precipitous white cliffs and buttes. The spectacular, rugged canyon is sparsely forested with scrub pine. For challenging driving, follow the twisting *route touristique* (D290) above the cliffs along the northern bank. You'll find views (and space to park) at every turn.

The place to start any tour of the Gorges de l'Ardèche is **Vallon Pont d'Arc,** itself an ugly tourist trap. Accessible by bus from Alès, the town lies a few kilometers from the natural bridge that spans the gorge. The **tourist office** (tel. 75 88 04 01; open Mon.-Sat. 9am-6pm) provides useful trail maps and lists of boat rental agencies. Standardized prices on two-person canoes (260F per day) include the descent from Vallon to Sauze and the taxi service back. Try **Ardèche Bateaux,** Camping la Rouvière, on the river at Vallon Pont d'Arc (tel. 75 30 10 07). For a one-day descent into the gorge, you must leave before 9am. You can also do a mini-descent of 6km. All boat trips start from the riverhead at Vallon Pont d'Arc. June is the best month for more experienced paddlers.

There are plenty of places to pitch your tent near Vallon; ask the tourist office for a complete list. Two municipal sites on the river at **Gaud** and **Gournier** have no amenities (5F per night). **Mondial Camping,** route touristique (tel. 75 88 00 48), has a store and a tennis court. (60F per two people.) **Ardèche Bateaux,** also on the route touristique (tel. 75 37 10 07), runs a site and rents boats (42F per 2 people).

While in the Ardèche Valley, visit the immense caverns of the **Aven d'Orgnac** (tel. 75 38 62 51). The yawning vault known as Grand Chaos reaches 50m. (Open daily March-Nov. 9am-noon and 2-6pm. Admission 30F, students 25F, ages 6-14 17F.) Neither trains nor buses stop nearby, but the 17km hitch from Vallon Pont d'Arc is relatively easy. Also near Vallon, **Ma Magnagerie,** route de Ruomes (tel 75 88 01 27), demonstrates the entire life cycle of the silkworm, once the source of an important local industry. (Open June-Aug. Mon.-Sat. 9am-noon and 2-6pm, May-Sept. Mon.-Sat. 10am-noon and 2-5pm.)

Aigues-Mortes

South of Nîmes in the wild swamps of the Camargue, the 13th-century ramparts of **Aigues-Mortes,** city of the "dead waters," mark the beginning of French dominance in the region. In 1229, the count of Toulouse sacrificed the Camargue to Louis IX (St-Louis). Himself involved in a 20-year crusade against the *Albigeois,* the Count cut his losses and gave the French new access to the Mediterranean. St-Louis launched both of his crusades from Aigues-Mortes. On August 25-26, the **Fête de la St-Louis** commemorates the king with historical reenactments, jousting, and a medieval market. Although never attacked, the remarkable fortress **Tour de Constance** remains equipped with the latest in medieval strategic defense initiative. Its 6m-thick walls also prevented dozens of Huguenots from escaping in the 17th and 18th centuries. One woman languished in the 10m diameter tower for 35 years. (Open June daily 9am-6pm, July-Sept. 15 9am-7pm, Sept. 15-30 8am-noon and 2-5:30pm, Oct.-March 9:30am-noon and 2-4:30pm, April-May 9am-noon and 2-5:30pm. Admission 22F, students and over 60 12F, ages 7-17 5F.) The **tourist office,** Cloître des Capucins, pl. St-Louis (tel. 66 53 73 00), has information on walking, cycling, and horseback-riding (60F per hr.) in the Camargue region. (Open daily 9am-8pm; Oct.-June 19 9am-noon and 2-6pm.) They also organize tours of the nearby salt beds and refinery; the **Companie des Salins du Midi** produces 400,000 tons of salt per year—more than enough for all of France. (July-Aug. Mon. and Wed. 1:30pm; 3½ hr.; 40F, children 20F.)

The city sponsors a festival of new and classical French theater and dance during the last week of July and the first week of August. (Tickets 70F and 88F, available at the tourist office.) For information call 66 53 91 96 or 66 53 76 95. Held during the first two weeks of October, the **Fête Votive** involves "harmless" bullfighting games that only citizens of the most civilized nation on earth could imagine. One of these elegantly named games, the **Toro Piscine,** requires that participants entice or coerce a bull to jump into a small swimming pool at the center of the stadium.

Hôtel l'Escale, av. Tour de Constance (tel. 66 53 71 14), just outside the town walls, provides spacious and relatively inexpensive rooms. (July-Aug. doubles with shower 223F. Sept.-June doubles 110-150F. Breakfast included.) **La Petite Camargue,** Quartier le Môle (tel. 66 53 84 77), has camping in a luxurious four-star setting. (100F per 2 people. Open April-Sept.) A **market** is held along the outer walls on Wednesday and Sunday morning. The **Place St-Louis** has many restaurants with terraces, but you'll find affordable places elsewhere. Try the regional specialties presented by the English-speaking staff at **La Dudende,** 16, rue Amiral Courbet. The **cave cooperative "Les Remparts"** has free *dégustations* of the *vin de sable,* an extremely sweet wine made from grapes planted in sandy soil. (Open June-Aug. 8am-8pm, Sun. 8am-12:30pm, Sept.-May Mon.-Sat. 8am-noon and 2-6pm.)

Buses for Aigues-Mortes leave from Nîmes (7 per day, 55 min., 28F) and Montpellier (2 per day). Five daily trains also connect Aigues-Mortes and Nîmes.

Arles

Arles (pop. 50,000) has a little of everything for which Provence is famous. The sturdy arches of its *Arènes Romaines* have survived the centuries beautifully and now watch over summer bullfights, just as the Roman *Théâtre Antique* approximates its original function as an elegant stage for concerts and dance performances. The lighting and landscape of Arles drew the likes of Van Gogh, who spent several years (and lost one ear) here, and Picasso, who loved Arles so much he donated the collection of drawings now on display. The museums, monuments, and ancient walls and aqueducts silently preserve much of the history of the town, and evenings here can be just as quiet. The intriguing marshland of the Camargue and the beaches at Les Saintes-Maries-de-la-Mer and Piemanson lie less than an hour away by bus.

Orientation and Practical Information

Arles is a 20-minute train ride from both Nîmes and Avignon; lower prices make it a superior base for exploration. The interesting section of town lies between the Rhône and bd. des Lices. To get from the station to bd. des Lices and the tourist office, veer left through pl. Lamartine (the first square after the station), follow bd. Emile Combes for 1km as it bends between high walls and railroad tracks, and then turn right onto bd. des Lices at the end of the ancient city wall on your right.

Tourist Office: (tel. 90 96 29 35), in esplanade Charles de Gaulle off bd. des Lices and across from the Jardin d'Eté. Follow the signs from the station to the *centre ville*. Guided tours of the city, including a Van Gogh tour. (Every Tues. and Fri. at 5pm; 2 hr.; 20F, students 10F.) English spoken. Accommodations service 4F. Open Mon.-Sat. 9am-8pm, Sun. 9am-1pm; Oct.-March Mon.-Sat. 9am-6pm. **Currency exchange** with evil rates open same hours. **Branch office** in the train station (tel. 90 49 36 90) has an equally helpful English-speaking staff. Open Mon.-Sat. 9am-8pm, Sun. 9am-2pm; Sept. 16-June 14 Mon.-Sat. 9am-1pm and 2-6pm.

Post Office: 5, bd. des Lices (tel. 90 96 07 80). **Currency exchange, telephones,** and **Poste Restante.** Open Mon.-Fri. 8:30am-7pm, Sat. 8:30am-noon. **Postal Code:** 13200.

Trains: av. Tallabot (tel. 90 82 50 50 in Avignon). Arles is on the Paris-Marseille and Bordeaux-St-Raphaël lines, with frequent service to Avignon (about every hr., 20 min., 28F); Nîmes (15 per day, 25 min., 34F); Orange (8 per day, 35 min., 44F); Montpellier (15 per day, 70 min., 59F); Toulouse (9 per day, 3½ hr., 180F); Marseille (16 per day, 1 hr., 57F); Aix-en-Provence (10 per day, 1¾ hr., 75F). **Luggage lockers** 5F per day. Tourist information booth open Mon.-Sat. 9am-noon and 2-6pm.

Buses: Modern and efficient terminal across from the train station (tel. 90 49 38 01). All schedules posted outside. **Les Carts Verts de Provence,** 5, chemin de Brissy (tel. 90 93 74 90 or 90 93 76 75). To: Orlay Airport (12 per day 7am-9:25pm, 70 min., 30F); Aix-en-Provence (5 per day, weekends 2 per day; 1 hr. 50 min., 55F); Marseille (5 per day, Sat.-Sun. 2 per day; 2 hr., 25 min.; 70F); Les Baux (4 per day, ½-hr., 23F); Piemanson Plage (May-Sept. 3-5 per day, 70 min., 40F). **Les Cars de Camargue,** 4, rue Jean-Mathieu (tel. 90 96 36 25). To: Stes-Maries-de-la-Mer (8 per day, 1 hr., 29.50F); Nîmes (6 per day, 20 min., 27F). **Cars Ceyte et Fils,** 5, chemin de Brissy (tel. 90 93 74 90). To Avignon (5 per day, 45 min., 30F).

Taxis: Radio Arlésiens (tel. 90 96 90 03). 24 hrs.

Bike Rental: Dall' Oppio, 10, rue Portaguel (tel. 90 96 46 83). 50F per day, 500F deposit. Mountain bikes 100F per day, 1000F deposit. Open Tues.-Sat. 8am-noon and 2-7pm.

Hitchhiking: To hitch north to Les Baux, follow av. Lamartine 2km out toward Avignon to the D17. For the Camargue, cross the Rhône and take av. de la Camargue. For Nîmes, follow the N113.

English Bookstore: Librairie Méjan, quai Marx Dormoy (tel. 90 93 37 28) in the Restaurant Méjan. A few new books at reasonable prices. Open Mon.-Sat. 9am-9pm.

Laundromat: Washmatic, 16, av. de Stalingrad (tel. 90 96 26 37), just after Monoprix. Wash 12F per 5kg. Dry 1F per 7 min. Soap 4F (8 ½F pieces needed). Open Mon.-Sat. 8:30am-12:15pm and 2:30-7pm.

Pharmacy, 31, rue de l'Hôtel de Ville (tel. 90 96 01 46). Open Mon.-Sat. 8:30am-7:30pm.

Medical Assistance: Centre Hospitalier J. Imbert, Quartier Fourchon (tel. 90 49 29 29).

Police: bd. des Lices (tel. 90 96 02 04). **Emergency,** tel. 17.

Accommodations and Camping

Inexpensive hotels are numerous and densely packed around pl. du Forum and pl. Voltaire. During the first two weeks of July, when the photography festival is in full swing, it is absolutely necessary to call ahead.

Auberge de Jeunesse (IYHF) (tel. 90 96 18 25), on av. Maréchal Foch, 5 min. from the center and 20 min. from the station. Take bus #4 from the station (4F) and transfer to bus #3 at bd. des Lices. Get off at "Fournier" stop. Last bus at 7pm. To walk, take bd. Emile Combes to pl. de la Croisière, and follow the signs. Near the municipal swimming pool. Clean, modern, and friendly. Everyone gets a personal locker. Bar open until 2am. Dorms with 8 beds. No sleeping bags allowed. Office open 7-10am and 5pm-midnight. Curfew 2am. 63F for first night, 50F thereafter. Shower and breakfast included. Supper 40F. Sheets 13F. No kitchen facilities. Often lots of groups, so call ahead.

Terminus Van Gogh 5, pl. Lamartine (tel. 90 96 12 32), 1 block from the train station. Charming M. and Mme Garrigues offer small but well-decorated rooms. Doubles 80-110F, with shower 120-140F, and toilet 160-170F. Showers 20F. Breakfast 22F.

La Gallia Hôtel, 22, rue de l'Hôtel de Ville (tel. 90 96 00 63). A real gem. Spacious, spotless rooms in an excellent location. Super-friendly managers. Singles or doubles with shower 80-90F. Doubles with shower and toilet 100-110F. Breakfast 23F.

Hôtel de Provence, 12, rue Chiavary (tel. 90 96 03 29), off rue du 4 Septembre, on a straight line into town from the train station. Fine place, kind proprietor. Rooms with a view of the arena. Small but clean singles 90F, with shower 130F, and toilet 150F. Doubles 100F, with shower and toilet 160F. Showers 15F. Breakfast 18F.

Hôtel Camarguais, 44, rue Amédée-Pichot (tel. 90 96 91 23), off rue du 4 Septembre. Gracious owner. Small rooms are clean and pleasant. Above a neighborhood bar. Doubles 100F, with shower 130F. Extra bed 40F. Showers 15F. Breakfast 17F.

Hôtel Rhodania, 1, rue du Pont (tel. 90 96 08 14), just off quai Marx Dormoy. Clean and comfortable rooms with a view of the Petit Rhône. Single or double 100F, with shower 150F. Triple 140F, with shower 190F. Quad 180F. Showers 15F. Breakfast 20F.

Hôtel Voltaire (tel. 90 96 13 58), on pl. Voltaire. Some spacious bathrooms and restaurant below; owner doesn't want food in the rooms. Singles or doubles 110F, with shower 130F. Hall shower included. Breakfast 18F.

Hôtel de France, 3, pl. Lamartine (tel. 90 96 01 24), just left of the train station. Often filled by afternoon with train travelers. Singles 80-108F, with shower 135F. Doubles 88-108F, with shower 141F. Triple or quad 150-184F. Showers 20F. Breakfast 15F.

Hôtel-Pizzeria de Studio, 6, rue Réattu (tel. 90 96 33 25), by the Musée Réattu. Clean, fairly spacious, and dirt cheap. Some mildly questionable clientele. Singles 60F. Doubles 90F, with shower 120F. Triple with shower 120F. Breakfast 20F.

Camping: There are several sites in the area, but none within walking distance. The closest is **Camping-City,** 67, route de Crau (tel. 90 93 08 86), a 2-star with a pool, snack bar, washing machine, hot showers, and room for 150. Take the "Pont de Croix" bus and get off at the "Greauxeaux" stop. 12.30F per person. 11.50F per tent. Open March-Oct. Two other 2-star sites in nearby Raphèle on RN453: **Du Gardian** (tel. 90 98 46 51), with hot showers, a pool, snack bar, and washing machine (14F per person, 13F per tent) and **La Bienheureuse** (tel. 90 98 35 64), with everything Du Gardian has plus bike rentals. (13F per person, 13F per tent.) To get to the last two take the bus from Arles to Marseille and ask the driver to let you off at the campgrounds.

Food

Many of Arles's small restaurants serve fish, rabbit, and veal *à la provençale.* Local *Arlésien* specialties include *fougasse,* a pretzel-shaped bread often containing bits of ham, and a *saucisson* made out of donkey. Compared to those in most other cities in Provence, the restaurants in Arles are high in quality and low in price. Three-course meals with wine average 50F. Wednesday morning, a colorful **market** lines bd. Emile Combes (7am-12:30pm). On Saturday morning, an all-purpose market takes over bd. des Lices, in front of the tourist office (7am-12:30pm).

The best cafés for watching and sipping are on **place du Forum,** where everyone comes for breakfast armed with croissants from nearby *boulangeries,* and where, come nightfall, everyone knows everyone else. You'll also enjoy the cafés on **place Voltaire** by the arena, strung merrily with colored lights and barraged with rock or jazz music on Wednesday nights in summer. As a rule, cafés on bd. des Lices are noisy, crowded, and overpriced.

> **Lou Gardian,** 70, rue du 4 Septembre (tel. 90 96 76 15), at the end of rue de l'Hôtel de Ville. Family-run place serving Provençal specialties. Attracts more hungry tourists than locals but the food is great and the portions large. 50F (4-course), 65F (5-course), and 85F (6-course) *menus* include service. Crowds pour in as soon as the doors open, so make reservations or come late. Open Mon.-Sat. 11:45am-2pm and 6:45-9:30pm.

> **Le Criquet,** 21, rue Porte-de-Lauve, on the hill behind the Jardin d' Eté. Four-course 55F *menu* includes wine and the *specialité de la maison,* veal in white wine sauce with herbs *provençales.* Seats only 23, so you get lots of personal attention. Open Sat.-Thurs. noon-2pm and 7:15-9:45pm.

> **Le Restaurant du Méjan,** quai Marx Dormoy. Appetizer: leafing through books. Main course: local specialties. Dessert: watching a movie (30F). Nightcap: looking at photography. You can spend an entire evening at this movie theater-bookstore-gallery-restaurant. Films in original language. Try the *formule rapide:* salad, dessert, wine, and coffee 55F. Entrees 30-35F, *plat du jour* 50F, omelettes 27-35F. Open daily noon-2pm and 7-11pm.

> **Magali** 12, rue Chiavary, just off rue du 4 Septembre. Run by same management as Hôtel de Provence. 55F *menu* includes *salade niçoise* or *pâtés,* choice of steak, pork, or chicken, and dessert. Outdoor seating, but candlelit dining indoors. Open daily noon-2pm and 7-11pm.

> **La Gueule du Loup,** 39, rue Arènes. Run by a gregarious Australian woman and her French husband who is the chef. Try the delicious *magret de canard* (breast of duck) and warm *chèvre.* 82F and 120F *menus. A la carte* available. Open daily 6-10pm.

Sights and Entertainment

If you plan to visit all the monuments and museums in town, buy the economical *"Forfait 3"* global ticket sold at most of the attractions (40F, students 28F). Other global tickets include the major monuments (26F, students 18F) and the museums and cloister (23F, students 17F).

The elliptical **Arènes** (tel. 90 96 03 70), measuring 136m by 107m and one of the largest remaining amphitheaters in France (seating approximately 12,000 people), dates from the first century AD. In the 8th century it was converted into a fortified stronghold; three of the four original towers still stand. The bullfights that take place here sporadically from Easter through September (tickets 60-190F, children 30F) are as cruel and bloody as anything the Romans staged. The top of the structure commands a fine view of the Rhône, the Camargue, and surrounding plains. (Open June-Sept. daily 8:30am-7pm; Oct. and March 9am-12:30pm and 2-6pm; Nov.-Feb. 9am-noon and 2-4:30pm; April 9am-12:30pm and 2-6:30pm; May 9am-12:30pm and 2-7pm. Admission 15F, students 7.50F.)

The **Musée Réattu,** rue du Grand Prieuré (tel. 90 49 37 58), houses a collection of contemporary art, as well as watercolors and oils of the Camargue by Henri Rousseau and two rooms of canvases by the neoclassical painter Réattu. The museum takes most pride, however, in the 57 drawings that Picasso donated to this town in 1971, not long before his death. Upstairs are temporary exhibits by noted modern European photographers and artists. (Open June-Sept. daily 9:30am-7pm; Oct.-March 10am-12:30pm and 2-5:45pm; April-May 9:30am-12:30pm and 2-7pm. Admission 15F, students 7.50F.) The **Musée Arlaten,** rue de la République (tel. 90 96 08 23) is the extraordinary folk museum founded in 1896 by Frédéric Mistral, who used the money he received from his Nobel Prize in literature to buy the 16th-century townhouse it occupies. The attendants wear regional dress, and the signs are in the local dialect. (Open daily 9am-noon and 2-7pm; winter Tues.-Sun. 9am-noon and 2-5pm. Admission 10F, students 7F.)

The nearby **Théâtre Antique** (tel. 90 96 93 30) retains the plan, if little of the elevation, of the original Augustan construction. Of the original stage wall, only two admirable marble columns remain to lend an eerie effect to summertime drama and dance spectacles. (Hours and admission same as the arena.) The **Jardin d'Eté**, behind the theater on bd. des Lices, is a pleasant picnic spot, but don't even consider sitting on the manicured lawns. The beautiful capitals of 12th- to 14th-century **Cloître St-Trophime** (tel. 90 49 36 36) merit a visit. (Admission 15F, students 10F.) The **Thermes Constantin,** now in ruins, once served as public baths for the Romans. (Hours same as the arena. Admission 11F, students 5.50F.) The **Musée d'Art Chrétien** (tel. 90 49 36 36) possesses one of the world's richest collections of early Christian sarcophagi, second only to that of the Vatican Museum. Many of the more interesting ones come from the Alyscamps, an ancient Roman burial ground later consecrated for Christian use by St-Trophime. In the Middle Ages, this cemetery, referred to by Dante in his *Inferno,* enjoyed such fame that bodies flocked to it from great distances. Beneath the museum lie the **crypto-portiques,** four extensive, forbidding galleries dating from the Roman era. (Museum open daily 8:30am-7pm; Oct.-April daily 9am-noon and 2-5pm. Admission 11F, students 5.50F.)

The tourist office organizes guided tours of specific monuments such as the cloister (Mon.-Sat. at 10:30am, 1½ hr.), and the Alyscamps (Mon.-Sat. 4:30pm, 1½ hr.). (Each tour 18F, students 12F, with global ticket 12F, students with global ticket 6F.) **Le Petit Train d'Arles** leaves from the tourist office on Wednesday and Saturday at 9pm and offers a one-hour tour (in French) of the old city (25F).

The **Rencontres Internationales de la Photographie** in July is a slick and exciting festival that is not to be missed. During the first two frenetic weeks, undiscovered photographers roam around town with their portfolios under their arms, trying to attract agents. More established photographers give shows in some 15 sites (including parked train cars and a salt warehouse), conduct nightly slide shows (50F each, 200F for all 6) and debates, and offer workshops. When the festival crowd departs, you can still see the remarkable exhibits they leave behind (10-20F per exhibit; global ticket 120F, students 100F). For more information, visit the tourist office or contact "Rencontres," 10, Rond-Point des Arènes (tel. 90 96 76 06).

After the photography festival ends, the **dance and music festival** moves into the Théâtre Antique and other sites. In 1990 the August music festival featured Spanish Baroque guitar, classical Arab music, and music from Elizabethan England. (Tickets 100-120F, students with ID 70-84F.) Contact the Festival d'Arles, 28, rue de l'Hôtel de Ville (tel. 90 93 91 11), for more information.

On May 1, the ancient *Confrérie des Gardians* (the people who herd the Camargue's wild horses) parade through town and then gather in the arena for the **Fête des Gardians,** a traditional but tame version of a rodeo. On the last weekend in June and the first in July (June 28-30 and July 1 in 1991), bonfires blaze in the streets and locals wear traditional Provençal costume to the beautiful **Fête de la Tradition.** The *Reine d'Arles,* a young woman chosen to represent the region's language, customs, and history, is crowned at the end of the festival.

Near Arles

"There is nothing terrible and savage belonging to feudal history of which an example may not be found in the annals of Les Baux," wrote the 19th-century historian John Addington Symonds. Eighteen km from Arles, **Les Baux de Provence** (pop. 484; 5,000 with tourists) is a magnificent site of ancient pottery, feudal ruins, a demolished castle, and gracefully restored Renaissance homes. The **Cité Morte,** the crumbled remains of the lords of Baux's 13th- and 14th-century citadel, commands an exquisite view of the **Val d'Enfer** (the Valley of Hell) and of patchworked vineyards and olive fields. (Open June-Aug. daily 8:30am-7pm; Sept.-May daily 9am-6pm.) Once the site of a regional court frequented by the finest troubadours, the *centre ville* has been taken over by souvenir shops, expensive ice cream stands, overpriced cafés, and more than enough tourists to support them. A few legitimately starving artists have galleries scattered throughout the town. To avoid the clutter and crowds, walk through **Porte Eyguières** ("water door" in Provençal), once the town's only entrance, to the Cité Morte above.

The **tourist office** in the Hôtel de Ville (tel. 90 97 34 39 or 90 54 34 39), about halfway up the hill between the parking lot and the Cité Morte, has maps, information on the surrounding region, and operates a **currency exchange** without commission. (Open April-Nov. 10 daily 9:30am-12:30pm and 2:30-6:30pm.) Don't make plans to stay here, however. The hotels, with a single exception, are all beyond the budget range. **Le Mas de la Fontaine,** at the foot of the village (tel. 90 54 34 13), has old furniture, a garden, and a pool. (Doubles from 165-230F.) Most backpackers bring picnics to eat in the Cité Morte; you can buy supplies at the small *épicerie* in the parking lot. (Open daily 7am-7pm.) Better yet, stop at the Monoprix in Arles before you leave.

To reach Les Baux, take the bus from bd. Clemenceau in Arles, outside the Cars Verts de Provence office (tel. 90 93 74 90), or from the bus station (Mon.-Sat. 4 per day, ½-hr., 35F round-trip). Buses also travel from Avignon (July-Aug. 2 per day, 55 min., 34F) and from St-Rémy (2 per day, 15 min., 12F).

The Popes of Avignon summered at the **Abbaye de Montmajour** (tel. 90 54 64 17), 2km from Arles toward Les Baux. The rectangular 12th-century towers, Romanesque church, cloisters, and nearby **Chappelle Ste-Croix** perch serenely above the surrounding fields of sunflowers. (Open Wed.-Mon. 9:30am-7pm; in off-season Wed.-Sun. 9am-noon and 2-5pm. Admission 16F.)

St-Rémy (pop. 9400), 21km from Arles, and the birthplace of Nostradamus, has two predictably well-preserved Roman monuments. One km south of town on av. Pasteur, the **Mausolée,** virtually intact and decorated with bas-reliefs of battles, contains statues of Caius and Lucius Caesar, grandsons of the emperor Augustus. The **Arc de Triomphe,** ornamented with fine sculpture, is the oldest in the region. **Don't** miss the **Ruines de Glanum** (tel. 90 92 23 72) across the road. Founded in the 6th century BC by Phocaean traders from Asia Minor, the city was destroyed in the 2nd century BC, restored by the Romans around the turn of the century, and sacked once and for all in the 3rd century. Only fascinating ruins of old houses, temples, and baths remain. (Open daily 9am-noon and 2-6pm; Oct.-March daily 9am-noon and 2-5pm. Admission 23F, ages 18-24 and over 60 12F.) Van Gogh devotees can make the pilgrimage to the **Monastère de St-Paul-de-Mausole,** the tranquil 12th-century monastery where mad Vincent was treated from May 1889 to May 1890. (Open daily 9am-noon and 2-6pm.)

The **Grand Hôtel de Provence,** 36, bd. Victor Hugo (tel. 90 92 06 27), is an old hotel with small rooms overlooking a garden. (Doubles with showers 130F. Triples with showers 170F.) **Camping Monplaisir** (tel. 90 92 22 70) squats just outside of town on chemin de Monplaisir. (10F per person, 13.50F per tent. Open March-Oct.) The **tourist office** (tel. 90 92 05 22), on pl. Jean Jaurès, provides a free guide to bicycle tours of the region, including a three-hour trek to Les Baux. (Open Mon.-Sat. 9am-noon and 2-7pm, Sun. 9am-noon.) To get to St-Rémy, take the bus from Les Baux (2 per day, 6F), Avignon (9 per day, 40 min., 23.50F), or Tarascon (3 per day, ½-hr.).

Midway between Arles and Avignon, the remarkable, sprawling castle of **Tarascon** dominates the banks of the Rhône. In town, the relaxed and friendly **Auberge de Jeunesse (IYHF),** at 31, bd. Gambetta (tel. 90 91 04 08) has kitchen facilities and bike rentals. (Bed 37F, 53F without IYHF card. 8 beds per room. Curfew 11pm. Open March-Dec. 7-10am and 5:30-11pm.) On the last Sunday in June, Tarascon holds a traditional Provençal parade with regional costumes, dancing, and music; the mythical green dragon *Tarasque,* symbol of Tarascon, is wheeled rapidly through the streets. To reach Tarascon, take the bus from St-Rémy (3 per day) or Avignon (3 per day); or take the train from Arles (10 per day, 20 min., 13F) or Avignon (20 per day, 10 min., 16F).

The Camargue

Between Arles and the Mediterranean coast stretches a wedge-shaped region, bounded by the Grand-Rhône and Petit-Rhône rivers, known as the Camargue. Pink flamingos, black bulls, and the famous white horses roam freely across the vast expanse of wild, flat marshland, carefully protected by the officials of the natural park. The area's inhabitants include *gardians,* rugged herdsmen with wide-brimmed hats, and large numbers of gypsies who pass through intermittently. The rice fields in the northern sections of the marshland supply the tables of Provence with *riz de Camargue.* A small zone is accessible to tourists without a permit, but entry into the **Réserve Naturelle Zoologique et Botanique de la Camargue,** one of Europe's most celebrated natural sanctuaries, is limited to keepers, scientists, and researchers. Fortunately, you'll glimpse some wildlife outside the preserve, whose borders are marked by biking and hiking paths.

The best way to see the Camargue is on horseback. Geared mostly to beginners, organized rides follow fairly limited routes. However, advanced riders can have more freedom. The tourist office in Les Stes-Maries-de-la-Mer has a list of all the horse rentals in the area (65F per hr., 170F per ½-day (3 hrs.), 300F per day, meal included). Rates do not vary from one establishment to another. Although most of the trails are open only to horseback riders, touring by bicycle is another way to see much of the area. Keep in mind, however, that the bike trails are sandy and sometimes become impossible to ride on. If you insist on bicycling, get a trail map from the tourist office at Stes-Maries-de-la-Mer and be sure to bring an ample supply of fresh water—it gets hotter than Hades and there *aren't* any Coke machines. A two-hour ride will reveal some of the area, but you'll need a whole day if you plan to stop on the miles of wide, deserted white-sand beaches near the bike trail. **Camargue Safaris** (tel. 90 97 86 93) offers jeep tours of the Camargue—or at least the limited portion accessible to cars (55F per hour, ½-day 200F, full day 320F, meal included). One-hour cruises ply the interior waters of the Camargue (1¼ hr., 50F, under 7 25F). Schedules vary throughout the year; call Le Tiki III (tel. 90 97 81 68 or 90 97 81 22) for more information. Although they have no official address, frequent signs direct you to their office west of Stes-Maries-de-la-Mer, near the camping area.

Les Stes-Maries-de-la-Mer

The unofficial capital of the Camargue, Les Stes-Maries (pop. 2200) boasts some 40km of beach leading straight into the natural reserve as well as a medieval quarter swamped by white cottages and tourist stores. According to legend, the town was founded by Mary Jacobé and Mary Salomé, two refugees from Palestine who landed here with the risen Lazarus and their Egyptian servant Sarah, patron saint of the gypsies. In the 19th century, gypsies began attending the annual **Pèlerinage des Gitans,** held on May 24 and 25. On these days and during a smaller version in mid-October, nomadic people assemble from all over Europe and, amid flowers and fanfare, carry Sarah's statue from the crypt of the fortified church down to the sea. The church tower has a magnificent view of town, sea, and Camargue. (Open daily 10am-12:30pm and 2:30-7pm. Admission 10F.)

Whatever its saintly origin, the town today plays host to myriad sun-worshippers and would-be windsurfers. Stes-Maries comes alive in the summer, when its beaches are packed and there are nightly "Camargue-style bullfights" (the bull is not killed) at the modern arena, **Les Arènes** (tickets 70-230F; tel. 90 97 85 86). If you continue past the camping area east of town, you'll have 25km of beach and dunes to explore. A 15-minute bicycle ride along the coastal trail will take you to fine white sand where you won't see another soul. Six km out of town you can bask in the nude in the twilight *zone naturiste.*

Those interested in the area's flora and fauna should stop in at the **Centre d'Information de Ginès** (tel. 90 97 86 32) along the D570. (Open daily 9am-noon and 2-6pm, Oct.-March Sat.-Thurs.) Next door, the **Pont de Gau** bird park (tel. 90 97 82 62) houses several rare local species in its aviaries and marks out ornithological trails in the marsh near by. (Open Feb.-Nov. 9am-sunset.)

Orientation and Practical Information

Tourist Office: 5, av. van Gogh (tel. 90 97 82 55), next to the arena. English spoken. Information on horseback riding and camping. Maps for walking tours. **Currency exchange** Oct.-May. Open daily 9am-1pm and 3-7pm; Oct.-May daily 9:30am-noon and 2:30-6pm.

Currency Exchange: No great deals anywhere. **Bureau de Change,** 3, av. Van Gogh, next to the tourist office. 10F min. commission or 1% or total transaction. Open June-Sept. daily 9am-1pm and 3-6pm. Also at the **tourist office** Oct.-May daily 9:30am-noon and 2:30-6pm.

Post Office: av. Gambetta. **Poste Restante** and **telephones.** Open Mon.-Fri. 9am-noon and 2-5pm, Sat. 8:30-11:30am. **Postal Code:** 13460.

Buses: Regularly from Arles (8 per day, 3 on weekends, 55 min., 29.50F). Buses leave from the area opposite the Station Bar on bd. des Lices in Arles and from the *gare routière*. In Les Stes-Maries the buses stop just north of pl. Mireille. To Arles (3-5 per day, 55 min., 32F). Call **Les Cars de Camargue,** 4, rue Artaud (tel. 90 96 36 25) in Arles for more information. Several companies in Arles conduct excursions through the Camargue.

Bike Rental: Le Vélociste (tel. 90 97 83 26 or 90 97 86 44), next to the church on pl. des Remparts. The friendly folks here rent the best bikes and will point you in the right direction. 20F per hr., 42F per 4 hr., 70F per 10 hr., 90F per 24 hrs. Open daily 9am-midnight; Sept.-June daily 9am-7pm. Passport required as a deposit. **Camargue Vélo,** 27, rue Frédéric Mistral (tel. 90 97 94 55 or 90 47 94 55). 60F per day. Deposit passport and 200F. Open Feb.-Nov. daily 8:30am-8:30pm. **Delta Vélos,** rue Paul Peyron (tel. 90 97 84 99), directly across from the tourist office. 20F per hr., 40F per 4 hr., 60F per day. Open daily 9am until 7 or 8pm.

Taxi: Tel. 90 97 82 09 or 90 97 80 74. Open 6am until 8 or 9pm.

Pharmacy: rue Victor Hugo (tel. 90 97 83 02). Open Mon.-Sat. 9am-12:30pm and 3-7:30pm, Sun. 10am-noon.

Police: (tel. 90 97 89 50), on route d'Arles 570. **Emergency,** tel. 17.

Accommodations and Food

The best and almost the only way to spend the night here is to camp. Sleeping on the beaches is illegal, but rows of sleeping bags decorate the sand at night. Hotels fill up quickly in summer; you'll be hard pressed to find any with rooms for under 100F. You can always base yourself in Arles and make the town a daytrip.

Auberge de Jeunesse (IYHF), Hameau de Pioch Badet (tel. 90 97 91 72), a regular bus stop between Les Stes-Maries and Arles (6 per day from Ste-Maries, 15 min., 18F; from Arles 40 min., 23F). Get off at "Pioch Badet" stop. In summer fills up early in the day. Take the 8am bus from Arles or arrive earlier. Open daily 7:30-11am and 5pm-midnight; Oct.-June daily 7:30-11am and 5-11pm. Bed 34F, under 15 26F. IYHF card required. Sheets 13F. Breakfast 13F. Dinner 38F. Bike rental 35F per ½-day, 60F per full day.

Hôtel Méditerranée, 4, bd. Frédéric Mistral (tel. 90 97 82 09), off rue Victor Hugo. Plush, spotless, comfortable rooms. Singles 130F, with shower 160F, with shower and toilet 220F. Breakfast 20F. Tax 5F per person per day.

Hôtel de la Plage, av. de la République (tel. 90 97 84 77), in the center of town, around the corner from the tourist office. Dimly lit and bare, but definitely clean. Single with shower 90F, with bath 130-180F. Double with shower 100F, with shower and 2 beds 150F, with bath 200F. Tax 4F per person per day.

Hôtel Le Delta, pl. Mireille (tel. 90 97 81 12), around the corner from Hôtel de la Plage. Very clean rooms with *loud* flowery wallpaper. Doubles with shower and toilet 200F. Triples with shower and toilet 360F. Quads 380F. Breakfast 22F.

Camping: La Brise (tel. 90 47 84 67), an oceanside site 5 min. from the center of town. 20.60F per person, ages 5-12 9.30F, 18.20F per tent. **Le Clos du Rhône** (tel. 90 97 85 99), 2km on the other side of town on the banks of the Petit Rhône. Quieter 4-star site with pool and open-air theater. 26.10F per person, 14.05F ages 5-12, 23.80F per tent or caravan. Open April 15-Sept. Reservations accepted.

One of the Camargue's main crops is rice, and you will find it in gelatinous cakes sold at *pâtisseries*. Local supermarkets include **Casino** on av. Victor Hugo (open daily 7:30am-8pm; Aug. 16-July 14 7:30am-12:30pm and 4-7:30pm) and **Co-op supermarket,** 12, route de Cacharel (open Mon.-Sat. 8:30am-12:30pm and 3:30-7:30pm, Sun. 8:30am-12:30pm). A **market** fills pl. des Gitanes Monday and Wednesday (7am-2:30pm). A burger, fries, and drink come to 27F at the **Snack Restaurant,** 4, rue du Capitaine Fouque. Their 56F *menu* features French classics. (Open daily 11am-midnight.) **Les Montilles** 11, rue du Capitaine Fouque, serves superb lasagne, ravioli (30F) and pizza (28-30F). (Open daily 7pm-midnight.) The self-service cafeteria **Les Amphores,** 2, av. van Gogh, across from the tourist office, on the second floor, serves relatively inexpensive pizza, spaghetti (25F), omelettes (18F) near the beach. (Open daily noon-3pm and 7-10pm.) **Les Flamants Roses,** 49, av. F. Mistral, has an eccentric bright pink interior and terrace. Local specialties such as *soupe de poisson, moules marinières,* and melon grace its 4-course 68F *menu*. The *spécialité de la maison* is a creamy *bouillabaisse* (210F for 2 people).

Provence: Côte d'Azur

> *You desire to know the state of the arts and sciences at Nice; which, indeed, is almost a total blank. I know not what men of talent this place may have formerly produced; but at present, it seems to be consecrated to the reign of dullness and superstition. It is very surprising to see a people established between two enlightened nations, so devoid of taste and literature.*
> —Tobias Smollett, *Travels Through France and Italy*

> *Why cross the sea to Algiers, why go to semi-barbarous Spain, when we have but to come to the South of France to change dark November into smiling June?*
> —Lord Brogham

Ever since 18th- and 19th-century travelers like Smollett and Lord Brogham advertised the vices and virtues of Nice and Cannes, respectively, countless French and foreign visitors have made the trip to the uncommonly beautiful coast between Marseille and the Italian border. Transportation was more difficult, to say the least, in the days when the English and Russian aristocracy came to the unspoiled fishing villages to cure ailments from consumption to hangnails and to ride along the newly built promenades in hopes of seeing Queen Victoria or the ill-fated Tsarevitch Nicholas. Historically a winter resort, the Côte became a favorite destination of French sunseekers only after World War II, when a government-mandated increase in vacation time and new highways and railroads made the area accessible to millions of average working people with a few weeks on their hands. However unsightly visitors may find the condo complexes, postcard shops, and encampments of backpackers in any train station or on any beach that will tolerate them, the Côte remains a stunning tableau of pastel Belle Epoque villas, remarkably blue waters, and natural gardens of olive trees, roses, and mimosa. Inland, a diminishing population of farmers make their living by growing grapes, oranges, and olives, as well as by cultivating silk.

While the Côte of today may seem more likely to provoke a sociological treatise on the dangers of mass tourism, remember that this is the landscape that inspired many of the 20th century's greatest artists. Were he to visit the area today, the curmudgeon Smollett would surely retract his statement that "Here are no tolerable pictures, busts, statues, nor edifices." Nearly every town along the eastern stretch of the Côte lays claim to a chapel, room, or wall decorated by Matisse or Chagall, and there are good museums everywhere. Look for the Fauves at St-Tropez's Musée de l'Annonciade, the excellent temporary exhibits at the Maeght Foundation in Vence, the Matisse and Chagall museums in Cimiez (near Nice), the Picasso cache in Antibes, the Cocteau stash in Menton, and the dozens of other collections scattered serendipitously throughout the region. Jass festivals go on throughout the summer; the Cannes Film Festival is held in May, Nice's *Carnaval* in February, the Monte Carlo Rally in January, the Grand Prix in May, and Monaco's Fireworks Festival in August. If you feel like celebrating your own occassion, order a steaming cauldron of *bouillabaisse* (a hearty fish soup), *soupe au pistou* (a brew of pine nuts, fresh basil, and the ubiquitous garlic), or some fresh seafood laced with the malodorous herb. Whatever your feast, wash it down with the flavorful whites or reds of

Cassis (no relation to the blackcurrant liqueur produced in Dijon), the fruity rosés of Côte de Provence, or one of the region's other respectable vintages.

The coast from Marseille to Italy is well served by frequent, inexpensive trains and buses. Most of the famous attractions lie along the coastal rail line from St-Raphaël to Menton, a two-hour stretch served by frequent trains. Trains for the Côte leave Paris's Gare de Lyon every hour in summer, and the trip takes seven to eight hours on the TGV to Marseille. You might want to base yourself in one of the larger cities (Nice, for example) and make daytrips to quieter beaches and smaller coastal locales. If city convenience sours to urban blues, retreat to the many campgrounds scattered across the region or to small-town hostels at Menton, Antibes, and Cap d'Ail. Groups should consider renting a car to explore the spectacular coast—firms will often waive the 500F deposit if you have a credit card. Mopeds rent for about 70-90F per day (plus a 1000F deposit); larger firms have better machines. Some people hitchhike between smaller towns but report fairly bleak prospects along the main *autoroute*.

Beaches

Familiarize yourself with the Côte before you lie down and bake. In general, the largest towns have the worst beaches. Marseille has an artificial beach, and the Nice beaches are rocky. At Cannes, they are private, and at Monte Carlo, remote. Seek out the quieter beaches between towns: Cap Martin (between Monaco and Menton) and Cap d'Ail (between Monaco and Nice) are both lovely. West of Nice, Antibes and Juan-les-Pins both have long, white-sanded *plages* with clear water and fine swimming; the privacy of the beaches around the *calanques* (mini-fjords), accessible only by moped, is rarely enforced. St-Raphaël has smooth, public, and fairly crowded stretches of sand right off the train line and equally fine but less peopled beaches nearby. Some of the finest sandy expanses stretch *between* St-Raphaël and St-Tropez. Since almost all of the towns on the Côte lie along one local rail line, it's worthwhile to hop off and on at small stations to see what you can find. Do not neglect the less-frequented coastal islands. The Porquerolles and Ile du Levant off Toulon and the Iles de Lerins off Cannes all have fine rock ledges and secluded coves.

If you've come just for the sun, try to arrive in early June or in September, when the air and water are warm but the beaches aren't obscured by droves of fashionable beached lemmings. In summer, optimal swimming tends to be during the two-hour period before the 9pm sunset. Bring a towel and a woven reed mat (10F at the supermarkets in Nice and Cannes); even the sand beaches are a bit rocky. Many bathers of both genders bare breasts and, in the *zones naturistes*, even more.

Accommodations are extremely tight in high season; youth hostels and hotels are often booked months in advance. Although it is illegal, many travelers end up sleeping where they lay their towels during the day. A number of beaches provide showers, toilets, and even towels for a small fee (10-15F). Those who spend the night on the beaches at Nice, Cannes, and Juan-les-Pins may run afoul of more than the law. You may find yourself bedding down next to groups of often "respectable"looking youths whose summer job consists of unburdening tourists of their mopeds, jewelry, and walkmans. Daytrippers can make use of the lockers (15F-20F) available at most train stations—always hide the key. Even in stations where lockers have been closed because of vandalism, you can always check your luggage for 12F.

Marseille

A fine town, Marseille. This human ant-heap, this
smutty vulgarity, this squalor. They don't kill each
other as much as they say in the alleys of the Vieux

Port—but it's a fine town all the same.
                              —Jean Anouilh, Eurydice

Although Nice may actually harbor more of the French mafia these days, it is grimy Marseille (pop. 1.1 million) that enjoys a universal reputation for roguishness and danger. Ever since Hellenic civilization entered Gaul here in 600 BC, the city that Dumas called "the meeting place of the entire world" has seen black, white, and brown, rich and poor live side by side, if not always amicably. Recently, resentment of the large immigrant population has fueled a surge of support for the ultra-rightist national politician Jean-Marie Le Pen. But don't let the bad press scare you away from France's swaggering second city, which counts an active nightlife, gorgeous nearby beaches, and steaming pots of *bouillabaisse* among its virtues.

Orientation and Practical Information

The heart of Marseille is the humming **Vieux Port** (Old Port) and the adjacent streets of the **vieille ville.** At night, these areas can be dangerous for lone travelers of either sex but groups are usually safe. Shooting straight out of the port is Marseille's main artery, **La Canebière,** affectionately known to English sailors as "Can o' beer." Jammed in the day but empty after 10pm, La Canebière can also be dangerous. Avoid the streets adjoining La Canebière (especially cours Belsunce and bd. d'Athènes) for the same reasons. Between the train station and La Canebière twist the narrow, dusty streets of the **North African quarter,** roughly bounded by bd. Nedelec, bd. d'Athens, rue d'Aix and La Canebière. In the day, the stores and restaurants are intriguing and inexpensive, but at night the streets' beggars are replaced by muggers. Finally, the area in front of the opera (near the port) is often the meeting ground for prostitutes and their customers. Exercise caution in this corner of Marseille after dark. When in doubt, stay in a group or call a cab; they operate 24 hours. It is virtually impossible to make a phone call without a phone card in Marseille except in the train station and at the post office.

Finally, directions. As you leave the train station, turn left and descend the majestic steps. Continue straight down bd. d'Athènes until you arrive at McDonald's and La Canebière; the tourist office and port are on your right.

Tourist Office: 4, La Canebière (tel. 91 54 91 11), near the Vieux Port. Well-staffed, English-speaking office with information on boats, festivals, and youth activities. Free accommodations service. SNCF information and reservations. Bus tours in English leave mid-June to mid-Sept. Mon.-Sat. at 10am (90F). Pick up a copy of *Marseille Poche,* which lists the activities for the week. Open daily 8am-8pm; Sept.-May Mon.-Sat. 9am-7:30pm, Sun. 10am-5pm. **Annex,** at the train station (tel. 91 50 59 18) performs the same services. English spoken. Open Mon.-Sat. 8am-8pm; Sept.-June Mon.-Fri. 9am-12:30pm and 2-6:30pm.

Budget Travel: Voyages Wasteels, 87, La Canebière (tel. 91 50 89 12), sells BIJ/Eurotrain tickets. Open Mon.-Fri. 9am-12:15pm and 2-6:30pm, Sat. 9am-12:15pm.

Youth Information: Centre d'Information Jeunesse: 4, rue de la Visitation (tel. 91 49 91 55), off bd. Françoise Duparc, just north of the Palais Longchamp. Information on sports and activities, including climbing excursions to the *calanques.* They also have a *Guide des Loisirs* for disabled people (10F). Open Mon. 1-7pm, Tues.-Fri. 9am-7pm. **CROUS,** 38, rue du 141e R.I.A. (tel. 91 95 90 06) has information on housing, work, and travel for students.

Consulates: U.S., 12, bd. Paul Peytral (tel. 91 54 92 00), off rue Paradis and near pl. de la Préfecture. Open Mon.-Fri. 8:30am-noon and 1-5:30pm. **Canada and U.K.,** 24, av. du Prado (tel. 91 77 54 01), a 15-20 min. walk northeast of the port. Open Mon.-Fri. 9am-noon and 2-5pm. All other consulates reached through the **Secretariat du Corps Consulaire,** 56, La Canebière (tel. 91 54 24 34), at the Senegal Consulate. Ask for M. Valéry. Open Mon.-Fri. 2-3pm only.

Currency Exchange: Almost every place charges commission and has relatively poor rates. **Change de la Bourse,** 72, La Canebière (tel. 91 56 15 78) has competitive rates and no commission. Open daily 8:30am-noon and 2-6pm. Open Mon.-Fri. 8:30am-8pm, Sat. 9am-7pm; Sept.-May Mon.-Sat. 9am-7pm. **Comptoir de Change Méditerranéen** (tel. 91 84 68 89), at the train station, charges a 10F minimum commission (1% if over 100F). Open daily 6am-9pm; Oct.-June 8am-6pm. **American Express,** 39, La Canebière (tel. 91 90 18 33). Buys and sells travelers checks and exchanges money only. Open Mon.-Fri. 8:30am-6pm, Sat. 8:30am-noon and 2-5pm.

Post Office: 1, pl. Hôtel des Postes (tel. 91 90 31 33), at the intersection of rue Colbert and rue Barbusse. **Poste Restante** in same building, around the corner at 8, rue du Colonel J.B. Pétré. **Currency exchange** at this branch only. Open Mon.-Fri. 8am-7pm, Sat. 8am-noon. **Branch offices,** 11, rue Honnorat (tel. 91 50 89 25), near the train station (open Mon.-Fri. 8:30am-6:30pm, Sat. 8:30am-noon); and pl. de Stalingrad, at the end of La Canebière (open Mon.-Fri. 8am-6:30pm, Sat. 8am-noon). **Postal Code:** 13001.

Flights: Aéroport Marseille-Provence (tel. 42 78 21 00; info tel. 91 50 59 34). Flights to Corsica, Paris, and Lyon. Buses connect the airport with Gare St-Charles (5:30am-9:50pm every 20 min., 25 min., 35F). **Air France,** 1, pl. de Gaulle (tel. 91 54 92 92), off La Canebière. Open Mon.-Fri. 9am-7pm.

Trains: Gare St-Charles (tel. 91 08 50 50). Nearby *bureau d'accueil* (reception desk) open daily 4am-1am. Information and reservation desk open Mon.-Sat. 8am-8pm. Marseille is a major rail center with connections to nearly all major towns in the south. Also to: Cassis (every ½-hr., 30 min., 22F); Paris (4 TGV per day, 4¾ hr., 374F plus 14F required reservation); Lyon (about every 2 hr., 3½ hr., 178F); and Toulon (every 20 min., 1 hr., 46F). **SOS Voyageurs** (tel. 91 64 71 00), in the train station. Cheery senior citizens will help orient you and find lodgings. Open Mon.-Sat. 8am-8pm.

Buses: (tel. 91 08 16 40), on pl. Victor Hugo behind the train station. Open Mon.-Sat. 8am-6:30pm. **Cars Phocéens** (tel. 91 50 57 68). To: Cannes (3 per day by *autoroute,* 1¾ hr., 103F, students 75F; 1 by the *nationale,* 3 hr., 72F) and Nice (3 per day by *autoroute,* 2¾ hr., 114F; 1 by the *nationale,* 4 hr., 74F). The **Société Cars et Autobus de Cassis** (tel. 42 73 18 00). To Cassis (17 per day, 50 min., 18F). **Autocars SATAP** (tel. 91 62 32 98). To Avignon (4 per day, 2 hr., 73F). **Société des Transports Régionaux** (tel. 42 23 14 26). To Aix-en-Provence (6 per day, 45 min., 18F). **Les Cars Verts de Provence** (tel. 90 93 74 90). To Arles (Mon.-Fri. 4 per day, 2 hr., 62F; Sat. and Sun. 2 per day). **Société Varoise de Transport (SVT)** (tel. 42 70 28 00). To Toulon (Mon.-Fri. 2 per day, 1¾ hr., 40F).

Municipal Transportation: A practical network of buses and metros run by **RTM,** 6, rue des Fabres (tel. 91 91 92 10). Exact change or tickets (7F; 30F for 6; sold at metro and bus stops). The ticket is good on bus or metro for 70 min. after first use. Metro lines #1 and 2 both have stops at the train station. The former ("M2") will take you to the Vieux Port (*direction* "Castellane"). The tourist office has a free *RTM Plan-Guide du Réseau.*

Ferries: ENTMW, 61, bd. des Dames (tel. 91 56 32 00), off rue de la République. Information and tickets for boats to Corsica, Sardinia, and North Africa. Cheaper and less frequent Oct.-April. Open Mon.-Fri. 8am-5:45pm, Sat. 8-11:45am. **Sealink Ferries** (tel. 47 42 86 87) connect Marseille with England and Ireland (1-2 per day). Ask for information at the train station information desk. Tickets sold at windows 15 and 17.

Taxis: Available 24 hrs. Phone requests taken. Prices are based on zone and time of day, and drivers have been known to overcharge. **Maison du Taxi** (tel. 91 95 92 50). **Marseille Taxi** (tel. 91 49 91 00). Call the mayor's office in case of complaints (tel. 91 77 16 00).

English Bookstore: Librairie Fuerï Lamy, 21, rue Paradis (tel. 91 33 57 91), off La Canebière. Small selection of new books (40F and up). Open Tues.-Sat. 9am-12:30pm and 2-7pm, Mon. 2-7pm.

Laundromat: Laverie Libre Service, corner of rue Iosard and rue Consulat, just off of bd. Longchamps, not far from the palace. Wash 15F per 5kg, dry 5F per 10 min. Open daily 7am-9:30pm. 2nd location at 27, bd. National, off of cours Belsance and rue d'Aix. Wash 15F per 5kg, dry 2F per 6 min.

Special Services: SOS Amitié (tel. 91 76 10 10). 24-hr. crisis line. **CORPS** 48, rue de Bruys (tel. 91 94 19 91). A gay center. Open in summer around 8pm. **CODIF,** 81, rue Sénac (tel. 91 47 17 05). Information for women. **Office Municipal pour Handicapés et Inadaptés,** 128, av. du Prado (tel. 91 81 58 80). An excellent center for disabled people. Open Mon.-Fri. 9am-noon and 2:30-6pm. For transportation service, call 91 78 21 67 (8am-noon and 1-6pm) a day ahead. Service operates daily 6am-midnight. **Association d'Aide aux Victimes de la Deliquence (AVAD),** 56, rue Montgrand (tel. 91 54 81 00). Will aid victims of crime. The sympathetic staff will even replace stolen train tickets and provide emergency accommodations. Open Mon.-Fri. 8:30am-noon and 1:30-5pm.

Pharmacy: 166, La Canebière (tel. 91 48 20 66). Open Tues.-Sat. 8am-9pm, Mon. 2-9pm.

Hospital: Hôpital Timone, bd. Jean Moulin (tel. 91 92 12 12). Take bus #6 to pl. Brossolette.

Medical Emergency: For a home visit call 91 52 84 85. **SAMU ambulances,** tel. 91 49 91 91.

Police: 2, rue Antoinne Becker (tel. 91 91 90 50). Also in the train station on Esplanade St-Charles (same tel., ask for *poste* 4017). **Emergency,** tel. 17.

Accommodations and Camping

Inexpensive hotels abound in Marseille, especially on rue Breteuil and rue Aubagne. Resist the temptation of cheap accommodations in the North African quarter; the area is dangerous after dark and some of the hotels front prostitution. Unfortunately, both hostels are far from the center of town.

Auberge de Jeunesse de Bois-Luzy (IYHF), 76, av. de Bois-Luzy (tel. 91 49 06 18). Take bus #6 from pl. de la Libération or #8 from La Canebière by day or bus K after 8:20pm from La Canebière (7F). This former château overlooking the city and the sea has clean, well-kept rooms, kitchen facilities, and hot showers, but also many noisy school groups and an 11pm curfew. Office open 7:30-10am and 5-10:30pm. 37F per night, 53F without IYHF card. Cooking and camping facilities 29F per night, but you must buy breakfast (13F).

Auberge de Jeunesse Bonneveine (IYHF), 47, av. J. Vidal (tel. 91 73 21 81). From the station, take the metro to pl. Castellane (6.50F), then bus #19 to Les Gatons Plage or bus #44 to pl. Bonnefon (same ticket). Very large, but often filled. Probably not worth the extra dough. Office open 7-10am and 5-11pm. No curfew. 68F per night. Breakfast included. Other meals 38F. Cooking facilities.

Hôtel Moderne, 11, bd. de la Libération (tel. 91 62 28 66). Follow La Canebière to rue du Montsabert, which becomes bd. de la Libération. A great bargain. M. Reynaud keeps very clean rooms and has been known to give discounts to tapdancers. Singles 60F, with shower and TV 120F. Doubles 110F, with shower 140-150F. Triple with shower 170F. Shower 15F. Breakfast 18F. Fills early.

Hôtel Moderne, 30, rue Breteuil (tel. 91 53 29 93). From the train or bus station, take bd. d'Athènes (which becomes bd. Dugommier), turn right on La Canebière to the Vieux Port, and look for rue Breteuil. The second most "moderne" hotel in these listings. Immaculate rooms, winding staircases, and funky murals. A real gem. Singles 85F, with showers 100F. Doubles (most with shower, toilet, TV, and radio) 175-200F. Breakfast 20F.

Hôtel Gambetta, 49, allées Léon Gambetta (tel. 91 62 07 88). Centrally located and near the train station. Spacious, spotless modern rooms. Singles 82F, with shower 102F. Doubles with shower 134-164F, and toilet 180F. Showers 15F. TV in room and breakfast each 20F.

Hôtel Trianon, 12, rue de la Grande Armée (tel. 91 50 73 10), near pl. Stalingrad. From bd. Athènes (which becomes bd. Dugommier) make a left on bd. de la Libération and another left onto rue de la Grande Armée at the branch post office. Clean rooms and some of the lowest prices in town. Management is eager to please. 11pm curfew. Singles 46-56F. Doubles 66-81F, with shower 105F. Shower 15F. Breakfast 13F.

Hôtel Montegrand, 50, rue Montegrand (tel. 91 33 33 81), off rue Paradis. Charming owner keeps the place squeaky clean. Singles 100-110F, with shower 120-140F, and toilet 150F. Doubles with bath and toilet 160-180F. Triples with bath and WC 160-220F. Breakfast 18F, in room 20F.

Hôtel Azur, 24, cours Franklin Roosevelt (tel. 91 42 74 38), about 15 min. from the train station. Take allée Gambetta from bd. d'Athènes. Costs a bit more, but you get what you pay for. Immaculate, spacious rooms overlooking a small garden, many with color TV, telephone, and carpeting. Singles 122-144F, with shower and TV 140F. Doubles 140F, with shower 160-180F, with shower and toilet 180-200F. Showers 15F. Breakfast 22F.

Hôtel Le Provençal, 32, rue Paradis (tel. 91 33 11 15), near rue Montegrand. Pink rooms with telephones. Plain, but the cute kids put the Brady bunch to shame. TV room. Singles 92F. Doubles with shower 124F. Triple with shower 176F. Breakfast 21F.

Hôtel Edmond Rostand, 31, rue Dragon (tel. 91 37 74 95), corner of rue Edmond Rostand in the center of town off rue Paradis. A charming, intimate hotel run by 2 real gentlemen. Rooms a bit worn, but clean and well-kept. Singles with shower 103F. Doubles 72F, with shower 99-120F. Triples 120F. Showers 15F. Breakfast 18F or 22F. Reservations advisable in summer.

Hôtel Beaulieu Glaris, 1, pl. des Marseillaises (tel. 91 90 70 59), to the right after you descend the stairs from the train station. Small, clean rooms, some very noisy. Singles 100F, with shower 140F, and toilet 170F. Doubles 120F, with shower 150F, with shower and toilet 180F. Triples with shower 200F. Breakfast 20F. In summer, preference is often given to those who pay for *demi-pension* (breakfast and another meal).

Capucines Hôtel, 25, allées Gambetta (tel. 91 62 17 99), near the train station. Excellent location and excellent prices. The rooms, however, are not excellent. Singles 50-60F. Doubles 85F, with shower 120-130F. Triple 120F. Quad 150F. Showers 14F. Closes at 2am.

Hôtel Beauséjour, 13, rue Saint-Saëns (tel. 91 33 80 59), by the Vieux Port. Slightly grim but cheap. Singles 68-76F. Doubles 78-106F, with shower 140F. Shower 15F. Breakfast 25F.

Camping: The **Auberge de Jeunesse de Bois-Luzy** (tel, 91 49 06 18) is cheapest and closest to town. (29F per person, compulsory breakfast 13F). All other campgrounds are south of the central city near the Parc Borely, a large, densely-wooded park with an English garden. Take bus #44 from the Castellane metro stop (7F). **Les Vagues**, 52, av. de Bonneveine (tel. 91 73 76 30), is not far from the sea. (54F per 2 people and tent, 72F per 3 people and tent. Open July-Aug.) Take bus #44 and get off at the "Bonneveine" stop.

Food

Marseille is the home of *bouillabaisse,* a fish stew cooked with saffron. Mussels, eel, lobster, and anything else that swims may be thrown into this local specialty. Expect to pay 70-170F, depending on the quality. The slightly more expensive restaurants on quai du Port serve better *bouillabaisse* and include a view of Notre Dame de la Garde. Freshly caught ingredients are available on quai des Belges at the base of La Canebière; come early for the best quality and the most colorful scene. Bargain *couscous* restaurants abound near **rue Longue des Capucins,** but the neighborhood is dangerous at night. Meat and produce stands roost near the junction of rue Vacom and rue Aubagne. A **Monoprix** supermarket does the same at 59, La Canebière. (Open Mon.-Sat. 9am-7pm.)

Le Vaccares, 64, rue de La République (tel. 91 56 16 76), west of quai des Belges. Amiable staff and ample portions. Delicious *escargots de Bourgogne* 35F. Pizza 20-30F. 48F *menu* with tasty lamb or pizza, fries, and wine. Open Mon.-Sat. noon-2:30pm and 7:15-11pm.

Le Jardin d'à Côté, 65, cours Julien (tel. 91 94 15 51). A chic café. Large outdoor parasols and appetizing salads. The blue and white interior is pleasant when the wind picks up. *Plat du jour* with wine 40F. Large salads 45F. Open daily noon-2:30pm and 8pm-1am.

La Dent Creuse, 14, rue Sénac (tel. 91 42 05 67), off La Canebière. Spirited staff cook up a storm, and *fast* in this popular, rustic restaurant. 55F lunch *rapide menu* includes all-you-can-eat salad bar. Open Tues.-Fri. and Sun. noon-2pm and 7pm-midnight, Sat. 7pm-midnight.

Le Mondial, 68, rue Tilsit, off rue de Lodi near cours Julien. Cheap hole in the wall locals love to crawl into. 4-course 34F *menu* includes French classics. Open Sept.-July Mon.-Fri. noon-2:30pm and 7-10pm.

Chez Soi, 5, rue Papère (tel. 91 54 25 41), off La Canebière. Quality Provençal specialties. 60F *menu* with steak, omelette, or ham. Delicious omelettes 17F. Grilled steak 32F. Pork and fries 26F. Other entrées 26-52F. Open mid-Aug. to mid-July Tues.-Sun. 11:30am-2pm and 6:30-11pm.

Country Life, 14, rue Venture (tel. 91 54 16 44), off rue Paradis. Vegetarian *menu* 48F. Scrumptious "light" (ha) pastries 7-15F. Open Mon.-Fri. 11:30am-2:30pm.

Sights

The 19th-century **Basilique de Notre Dame de la Garde,** originally a chapel and a fort, keeps watch over Marseille. This Second Empire Basilica is crowned with a gilded virgin and lined with multicolored marble, but you will probably only have eyes for the view of the harbor islands, the Château d'If, and the surrounding mountains. Take bus #60—or follow rue Breteuil, turn right on bd. Vauban, and then turn onto rue Fort du Sanctuaire. (Free. No shorts.) The **Jardin du Pharo,** at the mouth of the Vieux Port, contains a castle Napoleon III built for Empress Eugénie.

North of the port, off av. Robert Schumann on pl. de la Major, stands the **Ancienne Cathédrale de la Major,** which has a Romanesque altar reliquary from 1122

AD, a delicate ceramic relief by Luca Della Robbia, and a 15th-century altar dedicated to Lazarus. (Open Wed.-Mon. 9am-noon and 2-6:30pm. Free.) The **Abbaye St-Victor** (tel. 91 33 25 86), perched atop the end of quai de Rive Neuve, evokes the ascetic beginnings of Christianity. The 5th-century catacombs and basilica contain an extensive array of both pagan and Christian relics, including the 3rd-century remains of two martyrs.

The gaudy 19th-century **Palais Longchamp** at the eastern end of bd. Longchamp, contains the eclectic **Musée des Beaux-Arts** (tel. 91 62 21 17). Particularly strong in Provençal painting, the museum also exhibits paintings of Marseille's early history and devotes one room to Honoré Daumier (1808-1879), the satirical caricaturist from Marseille. Works by Ingres, David, and Rubens, and some early Dufy landscapes round out the display. (Open Mon.-Fri. 10am-5pm, Sat.-Sun. noon-7pm. Admission 10F, students 5F, over 65 free.) The palace also houses the little-known **Musée d'Histoire Naturelle** (tel. 91 62 30 70) with a new aquarium (scheduled to open in 1991) and rotating exhibits on wildlife. (Open Sun.-Mon. and Thurs.-Sat. 10am-noon and 2-7pm, Wed. 2-7pm. Admission 10F, students 5F, over 65 free.) The new fish palace will have a hard time surpassing the **Aquarium del Prado,** pl. Amiral Muselier (tel. 91 71 00 46), at Promenade de la Plage by the Plage du Prado. Over 8000 exotic fish of 350 different species swim in 400 tons of water—now *that's* what we call *bouillabaisse.* Take Bus #19, 83, or 72 (7F). (Open Sun.-Thurs. 10am-7pm, Fri.-Sat. 10am-midnight. Admission 35F; students, seniors, and children 25F.)

Marseille has more than its share of small museums. **Musée Cantini,** 19, rue Grignan (tel. 91 54 77 75) features modern art from Fauvism to the present in constantly changing exhibitions. The house alone, a 17th-century mansion with an elegant courtyard, merits a visit. (Admission 15F, students 7.50F, over 65 or under 10 free.) **Musée Grobet-Labadié,** 140, bd. Longchamp (tel. 91 62 21 82), is also in a mansion and displays musical instruments, some medieval sculptures, Middle Eastern tapestries, Flemish paintings, and a few Corot landscapes. (Admission 10F, students 5F, over 65 or under 10 free.) **Musée du Vieux Marseille,** Maison Diamantée, 2, rue de la Prison, traces the port city's story through *santons* (tiny clay figures), displays of maritime history, and maps. (Admission 10F, students 5F, over 65 or under 10 free.) The three above museums are all open Monday through Friday 10am-5pm, Saturday and Sunday noon-7pm. The **Musée d'Histoire de Marseille,** Centre Bourse (tel. 91 90 42 22), at the Jardin des Vestiges, contains the remains of an ancient Roman ship discovered underground in the middle of the city in 1974. (Open Mon.-Sat. noon-7pm. Admission 10F, students 5F, over 65 or under 10 free.)

GACM (tel. 91 55 50 09) runs motorboats from the Gare Maritime on quai des Belges to **Château d'If** which Alexandre Dumas immortalized in *The Count of Monte Cristo.* (20 min., round-trip 35F. Office open daily 7am-7pm.) Originally designed to defend Marseille, the fortress later imprisoned Mirabeau and a number of Huguenots. Foreign ships have never threatened Marseille; the cannons inside the chateau's three stark turrets have only been fired in salute. Boats will also take you to **Ile de Frioul** (25 min., round-trip 35F). Round-trip tickets for both islands cost only 55F. In summer, boats can take you around the *calanques* (90F). All boats run more or less every hour from 6:45am to 7pm.

Along bd. Michelet (en route to the *calanques*), Le Corbusier's 1950s **Cité Radieuse** is a vast concrete box standing on many short, curved legs.

Entertainment

France's oldest city is far from tired. Don't let Marseille's reputation send you to bed early; do take some basic precautions.If you're careful, you can enjoy the nightlife too. Neither men nor women should cruise the streets of Marseille alone after dark. Even groups should be careful, especially around the Vieux Port. Avoid the North African quarter, cours Belsunce, and bd. d'Athènes altogether after 10pm.

The best of the many nightclubs on pl. Thiers is **Ascenseur.** Slip into this *boîte* to hear late-night jazz and Brazilian music. (No cover. Open nightly 11pm until late.) **Le Couvent,** 13, rue J.-F. Leca (tel. 91 90 39 41 or 91 56 66 78), brings jazz to a 17th-century convent. If you have your own instrument (and a lot of nerve), center stage will be yours. (Open Wed.-Sat. 10:30pm until late.) The **London Club,** 73,1 corniche John Kennedy (tel. 91 52 64 64) plays rock, disco, and new wave all night long. (Cover and first drink 80F. Open nightly 11pm until late.)

Cours Julien and the adjacent rue Vian are well suited to evening promenades and people-watching. The popular **Il Caffe,** 63, cours Julien (tel. 91 42 02 19), is an ideal spot for coffee or fresh juice (13F). (Open Mon.-Sat. 9am-9:30pm.) **L'Avant Scène,** 59, cours Julien (tel. 91 42 19 29), is a modish *café-théâtre* with a gallery, newsstand, and restaurant. (Open Tues.-Sat. No theater in Aug.) Everyone from Sid Vicious to Bob Marley haunts the **Maison Hantée,** a concert-café at 10, rue Vian (tel. 91 92 09 40) is a concert-café offering everything from punk to reggae. (Open nightly 7pm-late. Concert starts at 10pm.) An intriguing mix gathers down the street at **Les Thés Tard,** 2, rue Vian (tel. 91 42 29 74; open daily noon-2pm and 7pm-2am).

In December, Marseille hosts its annual international **Festival de Musique** at l'Abbaie de Saint-Victoire; call the tourist office for ticket information. Theater buffs can check the offerings at the **Théâtre National de Marseille,** quai de Rive Neuve (tel. 91 54 70 54). (Tickets 75-120F. Box office open Tues.-Sat. 11am-7pm.) For complete nightlife information, pick up *Marseille Poche* (free) at the Tourist Office, la FNAC at centre Bourse by the Vieux Port or at most cinemas.

Near Marseille

Between Marseille and Toulon zigzag the **calanques,** inlets of clear blue water surrounded by walls of jagged rock. The most impressive are at **En Vau.** At **Port Miou,** the craggy rocks have a five o'clock shadow of blooming heather. You'll find a small, tree-studded beach lies between the angular walls of **Port Pin.** During July and August, the **Société des Excursionnistes Marseillais,** 16, rue de la Rotonde (tel. 91 84 75 52), conducts free walking trips of the *calanques* once or twice per week. Their boat trips leave from quai des Belges daily in summer (round-trip 90F). You can also take bus #21 (*direction* "Luming," 7F) to the end of the line—near *calanques* Morgiou and Sormiou.

Twenty-three km (and as many minutes by train) from Marseille is **Cassis,** an idle, rich, and carless resort town. Immaculate white villas are clumped around the hills above Cassis, while the town itself—a network of winding staircases, slender alleyways, and gardens thick with flowers—rests beside a devillishly bright port and the deep blue sea. Swimmers should follow the signs to the Calanque de Port-Pin, about twenty minutes east of town along a footpath. From there, it's another half-hour of difficulty walking to En Vau.

Getting there can be a bit tricky, as the train leaves you 3km out of town. Several **buses** run from Marseille to Cassis (17 per day, 50 min., 18F); call Société Cars Autobus de Cassis (tel. 42 73 18 00) for exact schedule information. The bus drops you at the **tourist office,** pl. Baragnon (tel. 42 01 71 17), right in the middle of town. (Open July-Sept. Mon.-Sat. 9am-7:30pm, Sun. 9am-12:30pm; Oct.-June Mon.-Sat. 9am-noon and 1-6pm, Sun. 9am-12:30pm.) The only affordable lodging is the **Auberge de Jeunesse La Fontasse (IYHF)** (tel. 42 01 02 72), 10km away from Marseille on the B559. The hostel is open year-round (37F per night, 53F without IYHF card) but has no hot water, and even the nearest bus leaves you 4km away (*direction* "Les Calanques"). You might prefer the **Camping Les Cigales** (tel. 42 01 07 34), 10 minutes away on av. de la Marne. (1 person with tent 40F, 20F for each additional person or tent.)

Toulon

Although more modest in size than Marseille, the salty, sassy city of Toulon (pop. 185,000) is hardly tame. In this, France's leading naval base and second largest port, uniformed sailors wander the streets like children on a school outing. Because Toulon is small, a good neighborhood rapidly blends into an unsafe one; solo travelers should exercise care after 7pm on the streets between rue Jean Jaurès and the port.

Orientation and Practical Information

Toulon is connected by frequent trains to Marseille, St-Raphaël, and St-Tropez. The center of the city lies between the train station and the shore. Between bd. Strasbourg and rue Jean Jaurès around pl. Victor Hugo and pl. Dauphius there is a pleasant pedestrian zone of shops and cafés. The North African quarter, with its narrow streets and colorful shops, spreads from rue Jean Jaurès south to the port. Although dangerous at night, this area provides some of the best daytime strolling in Toulon. To get to the tourist office and the center of town, walk left out of the train station for three blocks and turn right on av. Colbert.

Tourist Office: 8, av. Colbert (tel. 94 22 08 22), at rue Victor Clapier. Makes free reservations for hotels in the city and knows which campsites have space—a valuable service in July and Aug. English spoken. Open Mon.-Sat. 8am-7pm; Sept.-June Mon.-Sat. 8:30am-6:30pm. **Annex** in the train station (tel. 94 62 73 87). Same services as above. English spoken. Open daily 7:30am-8pm; Sept.-June Mon.-Sat. 7:30am-noon and 2-8pm, Sun. 8:30am-noon and 2-6:30pm.

Currency Exchange: Best rates at **Comptoir de Change,** av. Jean Moulin, at corner of bd. Leclerc. Open Mon.-Sat. 9am-noon and 2-7pm. **Bureau de Change,** 15, quai Stalingrad, at the port, charges 10F commission for exchanges less than 500F and 20F for those from 500-1000F. Open daily 9am-7pm. Also in the **train station.** Open daily 9am-noon and 2-6pm.

Post Office: rue Jean Jaurès at rue Guiol (tel. 94 92 36 04), at the western end of the pedestrian zone. **Poste Restante** and **telephones.** Open Mon.-Tues. and Thurs.-Fri. 8am-7pm, Wed. 8am-6pm, Sat. 8am-noon. The *recette principale* is at the post office on rue Raymond Poincaré, about 15 min. east from the center of town. Open Mon.-Fri. 8am-6:30pm, Sat. 8am-noon. **Postal Code:** 83000.

Trains: on bd. Toesca, (tel. 94 91 50 50). Information office open Mon.-Sat. 8am-7pm. Tickets sold daily 5am-midnight. About every ½-hr. to: Marseille (55 min., 46F); St-Raphaël (55 min., 60F); Nice (2 hr., 93F); Cannes (80 min., 77F). Buses and ferries leave for St-Tropez from St-Raphaël. Also to: Bandol (every ½-hr., 15 min., 14F); and Hyères (3 per day, 5 min., 17F). Baggage storage open daily 7:30am-8:30pm. Lockers (20-25F) open 6am-10pm.

Buses: (tel. 94 93 11 39), across from the train station. Open daily 8:30am-7pm. Buses depart from the front of the train station, except for the green **S.A.R.C.V.** bus (tel. 94 74 01 35) to Bandol (every ½-hr., 45 min., 14F), which leaves from the corner of av. du Maréchal Leclerc and av. Vauban. **Autocars Raynaud** (tel. 94 93 07 45). To: La Brusc (4 per day, 40 min., 11.50). **Francelignes** (tel. 91 98 32 05). To: Aix-en-Provence (2 per day, 75 min., 68F, students 34F). **Sodetrav** (tel. 94 92 26 41). To: St-Tropez (7 per day, 2½ hr., 76F) with many stops such as Hyères (1 per hr. 6:30am-9:25pm, 35 min., 30F); Le Lavandou (1 per hr. 6:30am-9:25pm, 50 min., 48F); Cavalaire (7 per day, 80 min., 65F); La Foux (7 per day, 2 hr., 73F).

Ferries: SNCM, 21 and 49, av. de l'Infanterie-de-Marine (tel. 94 41 25 76 or 94 41 01 76) at the far end of the port. To Corsica (2 per day; 10 hr.; 2nd-class round-trip 530F, ages 4-12 290F). In the "blue" period (Oct.-April), reductions for married couples on cabin tickets; 12-25 30% off; over 60 50%. **Transmed 2000,** quai Stalingrad (tel. 94 92 96 82), at the port, sends 4 ships a day July 14-Sept. 2 to Porquerolles (40F, round-trip 70F), Port Cros (70F, round-trip 120F), and Ile du Levant (80F, round-trip 140F). From Sept. 3 to July 13, 1 boat per day (9:30am) leaves for Porquerolles.

Taxis: near the train station (tel. 94 93 51 51 or 94 93 51 84). 24 hrs.

English Bookstores: Les Kiosques, rue Paul Ferrero (tel. 94 92 29 88), next to the rue Jean Jaurès post office. Look for the mannequins on the roof. Small selection of sleazy beach reading. Will buy books, tapes, and records. Open Mon.-Sat. 8am-8pm. **Le Bouquiniste,** rue Paul Ferrero (tel. 94 91 31 30), across the streets from Les Kiosques. Small selection of used books.

Laundromat: Laverie, 25, rue Baudin. Cheerful murals and best prices. Picasso came here to find inspiration. Wash 10F per 7kg, dry 2F per 5 min. Open daily 7am-9pm.

Pharmacy: 9, av. Vauban (tel. 94 92 37 42), directly south of the train station. Posts location of late night pharmacy each day. Open Tues.-Sat. 8:30am-noon and 2:30-7pm, Mon. 2:30-7pm.

Medical Emergency: SAMU, tel. 94 27 07 07. **SOS Medecins,** tel. 94 62 50 50.

Hospital: Ste-Anne (tel. 94 09 90 00), bd. Ste-Anne off av. Victoire de 8 Mai 1945, just behind the train station.

Police: rue Xavier Savelli (tel. 94 09 80 00). **Emergency,** tel. 17.

Accommodations and Camping

Toulon has an excellent youth hostel and over twenty one-star hotels. Even in July and August, inexpensive lodging should be easy to find. Head for the areas of the upper *vieille ville*, safer than the questionable neighborhoods near the port. A number of cheap hotels cluster on and off rue Jean Jaurès in the middle of the pedestrian zone.

Auberge de Jeunesse, 21, bd. Louis Picon (tel. 94 24 34 96 July-Aug.; in winter for reservations 94 91 87 17), a 15-min. walk from the station. Exit and after 4 blocks make a right onto av. du Maréchal Leclerc, which soon changes into av. Maréchal Foch. Make a right on pl. Bidouré, which will become bd. Picon. The hostel is on the left. Bus #3 makes the trip. Spotless modern rooms, lots o' space, and a *super sympa* atmosphere. No curfew or lockout. Dorm bed (12 beds per room) and breakfast 42F. No card needed. Open 24 hrs. June 30-Aug. 31 only.

Hôtel Molière, 12, rue Molière (tel. 94 92 78 35), on pl. Victor Hugo. An ideally situated gem with management as bright and cheerful as the fresh flowers. TV room. Telephones in all rooms. Singles 70-75F, with shower 100F. Doubles 85F, with shower 115F or (155F with 2 beds). Triples with shower 170F. Breakfast 20F.

Hôtel Lutetia, rue Jean Jaurès (tel. 94 93 07 75), in the middle of the pedestrian zone near the theater. Not exactly luxury, but cheaper than all the others and nicer than most. Singles 50F. Doubles 68F (1 bed), 75F (2 beds), with shower 115F. Triple 85F, with bath 155F. Quad 95F. Breakfast 18F.

Hôtel Little Palace, 6-8 rue Berthelot (tel. 94 92 26 62), just off pl. Puget in the middle of the pedestrian zone. The German manager, M. Schmidt, keeps the small, dimly-lit rooms immaculate. Singles 70-75F.

Hôtel de Provence, 53, rue Jean Jaurès (tel. 94 93 19 00), in the middle of the pedestrian zone and across from the post office. Plainer than a 747, but cheap and centrally located. Friendly managers. Singles 60-80F, with shower 110F. Doubles 85-90F, with shower 120-140F. Triple with shower 150F. Quad with shower 160F. Breakfast 18F.

Hôtel des Trois Dauphins, 9, pl. des Trois Dauphins (tel. 94 92 65 79). across from Hôtel Little Palace, near pl. Puget. Spacious rooms, each with carpet, desk, and dresser. Joel Kurtzberg memorial TV room. Singles 70-90F, with shower in hall 85-95F, with shower 110F. Quad 160F. Breakfast 17-20F.

Hôtel de Strasbourg, 10, rue Leblond St-Hilaire (tel. 94 92 84 78), near the end of rue Jean Jaurès, a 10-min. walk from the station. Large, comfortable rooms with a gentle family in charge. Bring your own air freshener. Several singles 70F, with shower 120F. Doubles 130F, with shower 160F. Triples with shower 200F. Showers 15F. Breakfast 18F.

Hôtel Lux, 52, rue Jean Jaurès (tel. 94 92 97 46), in the pedestrian zone. Personable managers but dingy quarters. Singles 80-90F, with shower 120F. Doubles 130F, with shower 160F. Triples 160F, with shower 200F. Showers 15F. Breakfast 20F, 24F in room.

Camping: Camping Beauregard (tel. 94 20 56 35), in La Garde, quartier Ste-Marguerite, 6km from Toulon and 400m from the sea. Bus #7 or 23 to the Promised Land ("La Terre Promise" stop). 11.50F per person, 10.30 per tent.

Food

You will find plenty of restaurants in and around the pedestrian zone. For seafood, look around the Vieux Port, but remember that the places on the waterfront charge for the view. Try rue du Pomet and rue Poncy near the opera, but be careful at night, when sailors and prostitutes take control of the streets nearby. A fruit and vegetable **market** takes place on cours Lafayette every morning from 6am to noon. **Prisunic Supermarket,** 42, bd. Strasbourg (tel. 94 22 03 23) is open Mon.-Sat. 8:30am-7:30pm.

Piano Crêperie, 45, rue Victor Clappier, near the tourist office. Over 50 *crêpes* (31-66F) and as much variety in the jazz played. Huge video screen to boot. Better than *Cats*. Open Tues.-Sun. 7pm-1am. Nightly concert 9pm-midnight.

Le Murat, 52, rue Jean Jaurès. You're invited to see chef Bernard do his thing in the kitchen, and that don't mean pizza. Great French classics on a 75F *menu*. *Plat du jour* 45F, *pêche du jour* 50F, and "suggestions of the day" 40-50F. Open Fri.-Sat. and Mon.-Wed. noon-1:30pm and 7-10:30pm, Sun. noon-1:30pm.

Al Dente, 30, rue Gimeli, a few blocks from the tourist office at rue Dumont d'Urville. Eight varieties of fresh homemade pasta in an incongruously slick environment. Ravioli Roman-style (heavy on the cheese and herbs) 38F. *Spaghetti au pistou* 32F. On weekdays lunch *menu* 46F. Open daily noon-2pm and 7:15-11pm; Sept.-June Mon.-Sat. noon-2pm and 7:15-11pm, Sun. 7:15-11pm.

Trois Bonheurs, 5, rue Notre-Dame, off rue Jean Jaurès. Vietnamese delicacies served with speed. Sauteed duck with black mushrooms 42F. Pork, chicken, and beef dishes 30-40F. Open Thurs.-Tues. noon-2pm and 7-10:30pm.

Le Jardin des Delices, 2, rue Ferdinand Pelloutier, in the middle of the pedestrian zone on pl. Puget. Pleasant both inside and out. Eating on the terrace costs 10% more. Appetizing veal 43F. *Plat du jour* 44F. Filling salads 18-33F. Steak tartare (50F). Open Mon.-Sat. 7am-8pm, full meals served noon-3pm only.

Cafeteria du Centre, rue Chavannes at corner of rue Gimelli. Huge portions at low prices. Roast chicken and vegetables 19.50F. Open daily 7am-1am.

Sights and Entertainment

Bus #3 runs to the small, uncrowded, and relatively isolated beaches at **Mouril-lon** from in front of the train station and Galeries Lafayette on bd. Leclerc (8F). Be sure to amble through the North African quarter (before dark), where everything from army surplus gear to Persian rugs languishes in the windows and stalls. **Musée Naval,** pl. Ingénieur Général Monsenergue (tel. 94 02 02 01), has the collection of models and replicas of old ships. (Open July-Aug. daily 10am-noon and 1:30-6pm; Sept.-June Wed.-Mon. 10am-noon and 1:30-6pm. Admission 20F, students 10F.) Next door at Point de la Mître Le Mourillon, the 16th-century **Tour Royale** (tel. 94 02 17 99) provides a good view of the coast. (Open June-Sept. 15 Tues.-Sun. 2-6pm; Sept. 16-May Tues.-Sun. 3-6pm. Closed Nov.-Dec. 22 and Jan. 4-March 1. Admission 10F, children 5F.) For an even better view, take the *téléphérique* (tel. 94 92 68 25) to the top of Mont Faron from bd. Perrichi, several blocks behind the station. (Open Tues.-Sun. 9:15am-noon and 2:15-6:45pm. One way 19F, return 28F, students and children 19F return.) At the top, the **Musée du Débarquement** (tel. 94 88 08 09), has exhibits on the 1944 Allied landing. (Open July-Aug. Tues.-Sun. 9:30-11:30am and 2-5:30pm. Admission 18F, under 13 8F.) Also at the top is an excellent **zoo** (tel. 94 88 07 89). (Open June-Sept. daily 10am-noon and 2-6:30pm; Sept.-May daily 2pm until sundown. Admission 30F, children 4-10 20F.) Two free museums, the historical **Musée Toulon** (tel. 94 93 15 54; open daily 1-7pm) and the **Musée d'Histoire Naturelle** (open daily 10am-noon and 2-6pm) share a building at 113, bd. Maréchal Leclerc.

Boat tours of the port leave from quai Stalingrad (tel. 94 91 50 50), as do one-hour boat trips to the isthmus of **St-Mandrier** and the ancient fort on the isthmus of **Tamaris.** (Ferry to either 9F; admission to fort about 20F.) **Le Petit Train** (tel. 94 92 78 64) offers a 50 min. tour of the city leaving on the half-hour from 2:30 to 5:30pm from quai Stalingrad. (July-March daily; April-June Tues.-Sun.) From late May to mid-July, Toulon hosts an **international music festival** that attracts re-nowned groups from as far away as Moscow and a wide range of non-classical performers. Tickets to the first few shows in May are free. After that tickets cost 50-180F and are sold at the tourist office (tel. 94 93 52 84). The Centre Culturel Châteauvallon, 5km from Toulon, hosts the **Festival de la Danse et de l'Image** throughout July. (Festival tickets 80-160F.) Call 94 24 11 76 for information.

The **Piano Crêperie,** 45, rue Victor Clappier (tel. 94 91 93 04) has live jazz music every night. (Open Tues.-Sun. 7pm-1am. Concerts begin at 9pm and end at mid-

LET'S GO Travel
1991 CATALOGUE

LET'S PACK IT UP

Let's Go Pack/Suitcase:
Lightweight and versatile. Carry-on size
(24" x 14" x 10"). Hideaway suspension (internal
frame). Waterproof Cordura nylon. Lifetime
guarantee. Detachable day-pack.
Navy blue or grey.

10014 Suitcase   **$144.95**
Free shoulder strap and
Let's Go travel diary.

Passport/Money Case:
Zippered pouch of waterproof nylon.
71/2" x 41/2". Navy or grey.
10011 Passport Case   **$6.50**

Undercover Neck Pouch:
Ripstop nylon and soft Cambrelle. 61/2" x 5".
Two separate pockets. Black or tan.
10012 Neck Pouch   **$6.95**

Fanny Pack:
Pack cloth nylon. Three compartments.
Charcoal or Marine Blue.
10013 Fanny Pack   **$13.95**

Let's Go Travel Books:
Europe; USA; Britain/Ireland;
France; Italy; Spain/Portugal/Morocco; Greece;
Israel/Egypt; Mexico; California/Hawaii; Pacific
Northwest; London; New York City.
1016 Specify USA; Europe   **$13.9**
1017 Specify Country   **$12.9**
1018 Specify New York or London   **$9.9**
This is $1.00 off the cover price!

International Youth Hostel Guide for
Europe and the Mediterranean:
Lists over 3,000 hostels. A must.
10015 IYHG   **$10.9**
FREE map of hostels worldwide.

Sleepsack: (Required at all hostels)
78" x 30" with 18" pillow pocket. Durable
poly/cotton, folds to pouch size. Washable.
Doubles as a sleeping bag liner.
10010 Sleepsack   **$13.9**

LET'S G[O] Travel

We w— to the book on budget travel

1991-1992 American Youth Hostel Card

(AYH): Recommended for every hosteler, this
card is required by many hostels and brings
discounts at others. Applicants must be US
residents. Valid internationally.

10022	**Adult AYH (ages 18-55)**	**$25.00**
10035	**Youth AYH (under age 18)**	**$10.00**
10023	**Plastic Case**	**$0.75**

FREE directory of hostels in the USA.

ET'S SEE SOME I.D.

91 International Student
entification Card (ISIC): Provides
scounts on accommodations, cultural events,
fares and, this year, increased accident/
edical insurance. Valid from 9/1/90–12/31/91.

020 ISIC **$14.00**
*REE "International Student Travel Guide"
d insurance information.*

91 International Teacher Identification
ard (ITIC): Similar benefits to the ISIC.
024 ITIC **$15.00**
*REE "International Student Travel Guide" and
surance information.*

91 Youth International Education
change Card (YIEE): Similar benefits
the ISIC. Available for non-students under
e age of 26. Valid by calendar year.
021 YIEE **$14.00**
REE "Discounts for Youth Travel."

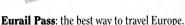

Eurail Pass: the best way to travel Europe.

First Class

10025	15 Day	**$390.**
10026	21 Day	**$498.**
10027	1 Month	**$616.**
10028	2 Months	**$840.**
10029	3 Months	**$1042.**

Flexipass

10030	5 Days within 15	**$230.**
10031	9 Days within 21	**$398.**
10032	14 Days in 1 month	**$498.**

Eurail Youth Pass (Under 26)

10033	1 Month	**$425.**
10034	2 Months	**$560.**
10036	15 days in 3 months	**$340.**
10037	30 days in 3 months	**$540.**

Child Passes (age 4-12) also available.

*All Eurail Pass orders include FREE: Eurail Map,
Pocket Timetable and Traveler's Guide.*

LET'S G⊕® Travel

One source for all your travel needs.

LET'S GET STARTED

PLEASE PRINT OR TYPE. Incomplete applications will be returned.

International Student/Teacher Identity Card (ISIC / ITIC) application enclose:
- ❶ Dated proof of current FULL-TIME status: letter from registrar or administration or copy of transcript or proof of payment.
- ❷ One picture (1 1/2" x 2") signed on the reverse side. Applicants must be at least 12 years old.

Youth International Exchange Card (YIEE) application enclose:
- ❶ Proof of birthdate (copy of passport or birth certificate). Applicants must be age 12 – 25.
- ❷ One picture (1 1/2" x 2") signed on the reverse side.
- ❸ Passport number _____ ❹ Sex: M   F

Last Name_____First Name_____

Street_____

Continental U.S. Addresses only. We do not ship to P.O. Boxes

City_____State_____Zip Code_____

Phone ( )_____—_____Citizenship_____

School/College_____Date Trip Begins_____/_____/_____

ITEM NUMBER	DESCRIPTION	QUAN-TITY	UNIT OR SET PRICE	TOTAL PRICE
		Total Price		
		Total Shipping and Handling		
		Optional Rush Handling (add $9.95)		
		Mass. Residents (5% sales tax on Gear, Books & Maps)		
			TOTAL:	

Shipping and Handling
If your order totals: Add
Up to 30.00 $2.00
30.01 to 100.00 $3.25
Over 100.00 $5.25

Please allow 2-3 weeks for delivery.
RUSH ORDERS DELIVERED WITHIN
ONE WEEK OF OUR RECEIPT.
Enclose check or money order payable to
Harvard Student Agencies, Inc.

LET'S GO® Travel

Harvard Student Agencies, Inc.   Thayer Hall–B   Cambridge, MA   02138
(617) 495-9649   1-800 5LETSCO

night.) Bars galore, both gay and straight, line the streets around **rue Pierre Semard** and **rue des Riaux,** but the area is unsafe. Although the police patrol these streets, lone visitors will feel uneasy as early as 7pm. A disco in a safer neighborhood is **Le Hi-fi Club,** 44, bd. de Strasbourg (tel. 94 92 31 14), near the tourist office. (Cover and first drink 70F, 2nd drink 40F.) There's also a selective *club privé,* **Les Clefs d'Or,** 2, rue Corneille (tel. 94 92 34 33), off of rue Jean Jaurès, near the theater; steer clear of the 600F bottles of champagne. (Open nightly 10pm-sunrise. 80F cover. Dress appropriately.) The **Femina Cinéma,** 20, rue Victor Clappier (tel. 94 92 39 31), near the tourist office, plays 10 films (original version with French subtitles) per night. (Admission 37F, Mon. 27F.)

Near Toulon

The islands off the coast of Toulon are known as the **Iles d'Hyères,** or the Golden Isles, a reference to the color of the sun's reflection off the mica rock. Reaching these treasured isles can be expensive, but few regret the trip. **Porquerolles** (pop. 350), the largest island, was home to a religious order until François I declared it an asylum for criminals who agreed to defend the mainland against pirates. The convicts, however, soon transformed the island into a base for their own pirate forays. Louis XIV finally ended their raiding decades later.

Some of the best unspoiled Côte d'Azur awaits you at the **Calanque de l'Oustaou de Dieu,** across the island from the village. Perched on the island's south side, a giant nite-lite of a lighthouse looks out over rocky cliffs plunging into blue waves. You can get there by walking straight through town from the port and continuing through the island's dry but pleasant interior. Both the *calanques* and the lighthouse are easily accessible by bicycle or foot. To reach the yacht-filled cove at **Plage d'Argent,** turn right just outside the port (look for signs). The beaches are thinner on the other side of the village, but so are the crowds. A shop 100m left of the port rents bikes for 40-55F per day with a 500F deposit. Try to get a sturdier mountain bike. The English-speaking **tourist office** (tel. 94 58 33 76) at the port has a list of accommodations on yachts (100-300F per night). For info on yacht accommodations, call 94 58 34 15.

The neighboring **Ile du Levant,** originally settled by monks, now harbors one of Europe's most famous nudist colonies, **Héliopolis.** Except for the western tip where ferries land, the entire island goes *au naturel.* Visitors are welcome—if they're willing to bare it all. The two one-star hotels, **H. Gaëtan** (tel. 94 05 91 78) and **La Brise Marine** (tel. 94 05 91 15) are booked well in advance throughout the summer. Rough it in the buff at the island's three campgrounds: **Le Colombéro** (tel. 94 05 90 29; open Easter-Oct.), **Les Eucalyptes** (tel. 94 05 91 32), or **La Pinède** (tel. 94 05 90 47; open April-Oct.).

You're more likely to run across Adam and Eve clad in modest fig leaves on hilly **Port-Cros,** the least corrupted of the islands. This colorful wildlife preserve is privately owned and camping is prohibited. The tranquil "Valley of Solitude" walk lives up to its name, unless you come on a weekend in high season. Fewer attempt the longer hike to **Port-Man.** Fine beaches and well-equipped **campgrounds** grace **La Capte** on the **Glens Peninsula.**

Boats for the islands (tel. 94 92 96 82) depart from quai Stalingrad in Toulon. Boats go to Porquerolles (40F, round-trip 70F), Port Cros (70F, round-trip 120F) and Ile du Levant (80F, round-trip 140F) four times per day, once in off-season. The trips last between one and a half and two hours. Boats also depart for the islands from Port d'Hyères, accessible from Toulon by train. (3 per day, 5 min., 17F) and bus (every hr., 35 min., 30F).

If you find yourself back on the mainland in **Hyères** (pop. 50,000) savor the carefully maintained elegance of this oldest of Riviera resorts. The **tourist office** in Hyères at Roton de Jean Salusse, av. de Belgique (tel. 94 65 18 55), has lists of campgrounds and hotels. (English spoken. Open daily 8:30am-8pm; Sept. 16-June 14 Mon.-Sat. 9am-noon and 2-6pm.) International talents crowd the town in mid-July for the weeklong **Jazz Festival.** Tickets (95F) are available at the Théâtre Denis, cours Strasbourg (tel. 94 65 22 72) or in Toulon at the Phonothèque, pl. de la Liberté (tel. 94 32 27 30).

Inland, two excellent wine-growing regions, small Bandol and Côtes de Provence, lie west and east of Toulon, respectively. They produce mostly rosé, but also some white and red wines. Once a refuge for Bertholt Brecht and Thomas Mann, **Bandol** (pop. 6714) is now popular with less luminous Germans, and even more so with the French. Its white, twisting streets surround a delightful town square, which doubles as marketplace and nighttime dance floor. Bandol's **tourist office** (tel. 94 29 41 35), on allées Vivien near the bus station, changes money in summer. (Open Mon.-Fri. 9am-12:30pm and 2:30-9pm, Sat.-Sun. 9am-12:30pm; Sept.-June Mon.-Fri. 9am-noon and 2-6pm, Sat.-Sun. 9am-noon.) Regional sailing regattas are visible from the port in May and June. Rent a windsurfer at Hookipa Beach (tel. 94 29 53 15) for 60F per hour (discounts for longer rentals). You may have to cut between private condominiums to get to the perfect public beaches west of town, but this is common practice. Buses to Bandol leave the Toulon train station twice every hour from July to September. Call **S.A.R.C.V. Littoral Cars** at 94 74 01 35 for a schedule. Ten daily trains stop in Bandol on the way to Marseille in summer (25 min., 15.50F).

About 10km north of Bandol lies the quaint if overcrowded village of **Le Castellet.** On your way there, don't forget to sample the local wines in the many vineyards. Public transportation cannot take you directly to Le Castellet. Your best bet in to the bus trom Toulon to Marseille (7 per day) and get off at the "Le Beausset" stop, 5.6km from Le Castellet. Many people hitch. In Bandol, **Kit-Provence,** 118, av. du 11 Novembre (tel. 94 29 60 40), rents bikes for 40F per day, deposit 500F. (Open Mon.-Sat. 8am-noon and 2-5pm.) Small roads from Le Castellet lead to **La Cadière-d'Azur,** a Lilliput of a village with three chapels and a view of the Provençal valley.

St-Tropez

St-Tropez has played host to crazed bands of star watchers and paparazzi since just after World War I, when novelist Colette and Edward VIII, the soon-to-be Mr. Wallis Simpson, bought villas in this tiny port village. Yet it took an actress named Brigitte Bardot, who frolicked nude on St-Tropez's beach in *And God Created Woman* and began to play house here for real in 1958, to make this resort the overdeveloped, spoiled paradise for overgrown, spoiled children that it is. In 1961, the ever-apocalyptic *Paris-Match* prophesied that "Phoney St-Tropez will die of asphyxiation under the assault of the bogus, the bluff, and the counterfeit." The fiery holocaust that ripped through the Riviera's desiccated forests during the summer of 1990 spared this fair spot, but next time St-Tropez may not find such grace. Repent, and wear Saint-Laurent!

St-Tropez is best visited as a daytrip, but be aware that there's no place to store luggage. The famous beaches are all 3-8km from the center of town. **Plage de Pampelonne** (6km away) has the most sand, **Plage de Tahiti** (4km) the most wealth, and **Plage des Salins** (4km) the most public space. Sodetrav buses (tel. 94 65 21 00) run to Pampelonne (15 min., 7F) and Tahiti (10 min., 5F). Hitchhikers, despicable creatures by St-Tropez's standards, will find stiff competition for rides. You're better off renting two wheels from **Louis Mas,** 5, rue Quaranta (tel. 94 97 00 60), where bicycles go for about 40F per day (deposit 500F), mountain bikes for 68F per day (deposit 2000F), and mopeds from 73F per day (deposit 2000F, gas 25F). (Helmets 4F. Open April-Oct. 15 Mon.-Sat. 9am-7:30pm, Sun. 9am-12:30pm.) Great swimming and good climbing rocks await at **Plage de l'Escalet,** 15km away; the Sodetrav beach bus from St-Tropez stops at the village of l'Escalet twice per day (5F). Otherwise, you can walk to **Les Canoubières,** a smaller, quieter beach 10 minutes out of town on chemin des Graniers, or the small **Plage des Graniers,** just east of town past the marine cemetery on route des Salins. Don't worry about being underdressed at any of these beaches, which range from merely topless to completely nude, but be prepared to have your body critically assessed by all.

The **tourist office,** quai Jean Jaurès (tel. 94 97 41 21), has information on sports and may be able to find you a room. (Open Mon.-Sat. 9am-7:30pm, Sun. 10am-1pm and 2:30-7pm; April-May Mon.-Sat. 9am-7pm, Sun. 10am-1pm and 2:30-7pm; Oct.-March Mon.-Sat. 9am-6:30pm, Sun. 10am-1pm and 2:30-7pm.) The **branch office** at the *gare routière* (tel. 94 97 20 66) performs the same services during the same hours. Pick up the small fortune needed to pay for your room at the **American Express** office (tel. 94 97 20 66), 23, av. du Général Leclerc. (Open May-Sept. 9am-8pm daily; Oct.-April Mon.-Fri. 9am-12:15pm and 2-5:30pm. 10F exchange fee on notes.) Even by mid-June, the few affordable hotels are booked nearly solid. Call ahead or hope for the best at **Hôtel le Mediterranée,** bd. Louis Blanc (tel. 94 97 00 44), across from the Hôtel de Paris. (Singles and doubles 120F, with shower 240F, with toilet 350F. Breakfast 25F.) **Lou Cagnard,** 18, av. Paul Roussel (tel. 94 97 04 24 or 94 97 09 44), has spacious rooms with carpeting and telephones. (Doubles 190F, with shower and toilet from 220F. Obligatory breakfast 27F.) Camping is by far the cheapest option, but again, make reservations. The tourist office will tell you which sites have space, but few will in July and August. Try four-star **La Croix du Sud** (tel. 94 79 80 84), route de Pampelonne (20F per person, 30F per tent. Open Easter-Sept.), or **Kon Tiki** (tel. 94 79 80 17; 60F per tent). Both lie just behind the Pampelonne beach. Toward l'Escalet is **Les Tournels,** route du Phare de Camarat (tel. 94 79 81 38; 35F per person, including tent). Camping on the beach is illegal and this law is enforced. There are no youth hostels nearby.

Find a less expensive restaurant for dinner, but don't skip the ritual coffee (12F) at the portside **Café Senequier,** quai Jean Jaurès, next to the tourist office. (Open daily 8am-3am.) **Café des Arts** on pl. des Lices fills with St-Tropez's bohemian stragglers. (Open daily 8am-3am. Coffee 7.80F.) **Pasta** (36-47F) and pizza (36-42F) wait to be devoured at the **Trattoria di Roma,** av. du Général Leclerc, near the bus station. (Open May-Aug. daily noon-2:30pm and 7-10:30pm.) **Mario,** 9, rue Aire du Chemin and rue de la Miséricorde, off rue Gambetta, offers a 65F French and Italian *menu* on a lavendar leather terrace. (Open daily noon-7pm.) You'll probably end up heading for **Prisunic** supermarket, 7, av. du Général Leclerc (open Mon.-Sat. 8am-8pm, Sun. 8am-1pm) or the outdoor *grand marché* in pl. des Lices (open Tues. and Sat. 6:30am-1pm).

Climb up the **citadelle** (tel. 94 97 59 43) for a panoramic view of the entire gulf. The dungeon of this 16th-century fortress houses a naval museum. (Open June 15-Sept. 15 Wed.-Mon. 10am-6pm; Sept. 15-Oct. and Dec.-June 14 Wed.-Mon. 10am-4:30pm. Admission 17F, students 8F.) In the serene confines of an ancient chapel, the **Musée de l'Annonciade,** rue de la Nouvelle Poste, exhibits a wild collection of Fauvist and neo-Impressionist paintings. (Open June-Sept. Wed.-Mon. 10am-noon and 3-7pm; Oct. and Dec.-May 10am-noon and 2-6pm. Admission 20F, students 8F, under 12 free.)

Each year from May 16 to 18, St-Tropez goes all out for its defiant *bravade* in honor of its patron saint, who was beheaded by Nero and then set adrift with a cock and a dog aboard, only to arrive intact in this town. To commemorate the event, locals (who would seem to have more in common with Nero) don religious costumes and race through the streets firing guns for two days.

The town lies well off the rail line but can be reached by **bus** from St-Raphaël (8 per day, 1½-3 hr., 39F), Toulon (8 per day, 2½-4 hr., 76.60F), or Hyères (6 per day, 2-3 hr., 60F). Call **Sodetrav buses** (tel. 94 97 62 77), or ask the tourist office for more information. A more enjoyable alternative is the boat from the port in St-Raphaël (mid-June to mid-Sept. 3-4 per day, April-June and Sept.-Oct. 1-2 per day; 50 min.; one way 40F, round-trip 80F). Boats also leave from Ste-Maxime and Port-Grimaud July to the beginning of September (about every ½-hr., 20 min., one way 16.50F, round-trip 32F). Contact **Gare Maritime de St-Raphaël** (tel. 94 95 17 46) for more information. (Open daily 9am-noon and 2-6pm.) St-Tropez's **postal code** is 83990.

St-Tropez to Cannes: The Var

Known to the French as the "land of blue, green and gold," the wonderfully varied coast and hinterland between St-Tropez and Cannes provides minimal relief to tourist-weary tourists. Although you probably cannot afford most of the Riviera's restaurants, this relatively uncrowded countryside is at least a sumptuous feast for the eyes.

The nearby hill town of **Grimaud** beguiles with shady lotus trees, an old fortress, and an 11th-century barrel-vaulted church. It is on the St-Raphaël-Toulon bus line, with a connection at La Foux (from St-Raphaël 8 per day 6:30am-8pm, 50 min.-3 hr. (in summer traffic), 39F; from Toulon one direct, several indirect lines per day; 2½-4 hr.; 78F). The bus from Toulon goes on to the less frequented, more picturesque village of **La Garde-Freinet**, 15 minutes from Grimaud. The three-star **Camping Municipal St-Eloi** (tel. 94 43 62 40), has free hot showers, a swimming pool, and a snack bar. (8.50F per person, 10F per tent. Open June 15 to Sept. 15.) The friendly **tourist office** (tel. 94 43 67 41; open Wed.-Mon. 9:30am-12:30pm and 5:30-7:30pm) flanks the youth hostel in **Chapelle St-Eloi.** The *Guide des Campings Var* lists campsites in the region.

In the early 1960s, hoping to recreate a typical Mediterranean fishing village, the people of **Port Grimaud** let the sea flow into canals dug throughout town, creating avenues of water. Boats have indeed replaced cars, which must be left outside the town limits, but Port Grimaud's wealth can't help but clash with its humble ideal. In any case, the artificial beaches are clean and uncrowded. There are large campgrounds just outside town, including the tremendous 1400-spot **Les Prairies de la Mer** (tel. 94 56 25 29) at Saint-Pons les Mûres, equipped with a minimarket, restaurant, bar, tennis courts, hot showers, and (of course) a TV room. (50F per 1-2 people in a tent. Open April-Oct.) Port Grimaud is accessible from St-Tropez by ferry (tel. 94 96 51 00; 24F, 45F round trip) and by a bus which stops at nearby St-Pons (7.50F). Another ferry (tel. 94 95 17 46) runs from St. Raphael Monday and Saturday at 2:30pm (80 min., round trip 90F). Most hitchhikers who wend their way back to St-Tropez from Port Grimaud find the best prospects from the parking lot at the town exit.

Nearby **Ste-Maxime** has a sandy, crowded beach. Fifteen daily buses (two in winter) roll into town. The **tourist office,** av. Général de Gaulle (tel. 94 96 19 24), has a helpful English-speaking staff. (Open daily 9am-7pm; Oct.-June Mon.-Sat. 9am-noon and 1:30-6pm, Sun. 10am-noon and 3-5pm.) On the same bus line, **Les Issambres** (½-1 hr., 16.50F from St-Raphaël) and **St-Aygulf** (20 min., 6F) have slightly more appealing beaches. Grimaud, Port Grimaud, and La Garde Freinet cluster relatively close to St-Tropez in the west.

St-Raphaël (pop. 27,000) lies midway between Cannes and St-Tropez, and, although frowned upon by snobs to the east and west, makes a good base for exploring the Var. The train line from Cannes ends here (28F; 25 min., 5:43am-11:30pm). A fleet of buses make the trip from St-Tropez (11/3-2hr. in summer traffic, 39F); a ferry leaves from St-Tropez's Gare Maritime (50 min., 40F). Call 94 95 17 46 in summer to make reservations. A prominent resort even in Roman times, St-Raphaël had its two days in the sun when Napoleon landed here on his return from Egypt in 1799 and set sail for the exile of Elba from here in 1814. Although the town still attracts the affluent, expanses of public beaches, a bevy of cheap hotels, and refreshingly unassuming locals await those on the other end of the financial spectrum. The **Comité Départemental de Tourisme,** (tel. 94 40 49 90) located in the train station above the tracks, can tell you everything you ever wanted to know about the Var and suggests car and bike routes. Unfortunately, this wonderful office run by equally wonderful Collette Allongue may close permanently in 1991. (Open Tues.-Wed. 8:15am-noon and 1:45-6pm, Fri. 8:15am-noon and 1:45-5pm.) The somewhat less knowledgeable English-speaking **tourist office**, pl. de la Gare (tel. 94 95 16 87 or 94 95 19 70) can tell you about hotel room availability, a significant problem in July and August. They do not, however, make reservations. (Open May-

Sept. Mon.-Sat. 8:15am-12:30pm and 1:30-7pm; Oct.-April Mon.-Sat. 8:15am-noon and 1:30-6pm.)

Hôtel des Pyramides, 77, av. Paul Doumer (tel. 94 95 05 95), has clean, comfortable rooms just off the beach but near train tracks that become active shortly after 6am. How to get to the beach should be obvious. (Singles 75F. Doubles 120F, with showers 150-190F. Breakfast 22F.) **Les Templiers,** rue de la République (tel. 94 95 38 93), behind the train station, is a jolly hotel which correctly claims to be "not luxurious but very clean." (Singles 90F. Doubles 120F. Free hall shower. Breakfast 25F.) The plush oceanside **Centre International du Manoir** (tel. 94 95 20 58), in Boulouris, has dormitory rooms in the annex, a bar, and a disco. (Lockout 4-5pm. 90F per person. Rooms with 1-6 beds 133F per person. Breakfast included. Meals 47F.) A bus makes the 5km trip to the hostel from St-Raphaël approximately every half-hour until 6:30pm (5F).

The bar at Les Templiers hotel, patronized by crusty old-timers and local youth, is not literally a riot, but worth a visit nonetheless. The 45F, 55F, and 65F *menus* are deliciously French. (*Plat du jour* 35F. Open daily noon-1:30pm and 7-11:30pm.) Most other restaurants in St-Raphaël are more expensive; buy your own fixings at **Monoprix,** bd. de Félix Martin, off av. Alphonse Karr near the train station (open Mon.-Sat. 8:30am-12:30pm and 2:30-7pm) or at the daily morning **market** on pl. de la République, just behind the train station (8:30am-12:30pm). If you make a right out of the train station and continue all the way down, you will soon enter the city of Fréjus (pop. 42,418) where you will find a few cheap waterfront **pizzerias** (36-45F per pizza) in a sea of expensive restaurants. You'll also find most of St. Raphaël's nightlife across the border in Fréjus. Popular **L'Odyssée Disco,** bd. de la Libération rocks all night long. Take a right from the St-Raphaël train station and follow the road for about 5 minutes. (Open nightly from 11pm until the wee hours. Cover and first drink 80F.)

While the city of **Fréjus,** founded by Julius Caesar in 49 BC, lies only a few minutes away by foot from the St-Raphaël train station, the *centre ville* is a good 5km bus ride (every ½-hr., 10 min., 5F). This small and sedate town can either be very relaxing or quite dull. The partially reconstructed Roman **amphitheater** (*Les Arènes*) is unremarkable until the bullfights begin on July 17 and Aug. 15. (Open April-Sept. Tues.-Sun. 9:30-11:45am and 2-6:15pm; Oct.-March Tues.-Sun. 9-11:45am and 2-4:15pm; admission 6F, free for children under 7; tel. 94 51 34 31.) Fréjus's **cathedral,** at pl. J.-C. Formige (tel. 94 51 26 30), off rue Bretagna in the northwest corner of *centre ville,* has a 4th-century baptistry that makes it one of the oldest buildings in France; the original mosaics merit a visit. (Open April-Sept. daily 9am-7pm; Oct.-March daily 9am-noon and 2-7pm. Admission 16F, students or senior 9F, children (7-17 years) 5F.) **Le Petit Train du Far West** (tel. 94 83 77 36) offers a tour of the city's Roman ruins (in French) and leaves from *Les Arènes* every day at 3:30, 4:30, and 5:30pm. (Admission 25F, 3-10 years 12F.)

The staff at the **tourist office** on 325, rue Jean Jaurès (tel. 94 51 54 14) speaks good English and is slightly more in the know than the one on pl. Calvani (tel. 94 51 53 87). (Jean Jaurès office open July-Aug. Mon.-Sat. 9am-7pm; Sept.-June Mon.-Sat. 9am-noon and 2:30-7pm. Calvani office open Mon.-Fri. 9am-noon and 3-6pm, Sat. 9am-noon.) The **Auberge de Jeunesse Fréjus (IYHF),** perched atop Chemin de Counillier, has military-style single-sex bunkers with six beds (50F, 66F without card) and camping (21F per person). (Office open 8-10am and 6-8pm. Lockout 10am-6pm. Curfew 11pm. Dinner 38F.) Buses leave from St-Raphaël's *gare routière* every 30 min. until 6pm (5F). However, the only return bus runs at 9:25am; unless you want to make the 5km hike back to St-Raphaël, plan to stay in Fréjus. At the hostel bus stop is a well-stocked **Intermarché supermarket.** (Open Mon.-Thurs. 8:30am-12:30pm and 2:30-7:30pm, Fri.-Sat. 8:30am-7:30pm.)

Outside of the *centre ville,* but still in Fréjus, is the **Parc Zoologique Safari de Fréjus le Capitou** (tel. 94 40 70 65), a huge animal safari park that you can visit by car or—if you're brave—by foot. Take the "Fayence-St-Raphaël" bus line from St-Raphaël to the "Le Camps le Coq" stop. Go right at the fort and continue for about 10 minutes. (Open daily 10am-5:30pm. Admission 48F, ages 3-10 26F.) Also outside the *centre ville,* but in the other direction, is Fréjus's **Aquatica,** rue Capitaine Blazy (tel. 94 52 01 01), a huge water fun fest with slides, scooters, and the biggest wave pool in all of Europe. Take the bus from St-Raphaël to Fréjus and get off at the "Géant Casino" stop. (Open June-Sept. daily 10am-8pm; May-June, Sat. and Sun. 10am-6pm. Admission 78F, children under 12 58F.)

A bit further east of Fréjus, along **Corniche de l'Estérel** in Villa Solange flourishes the cheap but usually full **Auberge de Jeunesse Le Trayas/Théoule-sur-Mer (IYHF),** 9, av. de la Veronese (tel. 93 75 40 23). (Bed and breakfast 51F, 67F without card. Dinner 38F. Lockout 10am-5pm. No curfew.) To reach the hostel, take one of eight daily trains to Le Travas from St-Raphaël (16F, until 5:30pm) and Cannes (12F, until 5:30pm), or one of the eight daily buses from either city (½-hr., 10-12F). A bus makes the 2km uphill trip to the hostel.

The *massif* (rock mass) between St-Raphaël and La Napoule overlooks the *calanques* (coves)—the most spectacular scenery on the Côte. Blood-red rocks flecked with the rich green of olive trees and the brilliant yellow of mimosa plunge abruptly into the glowing blue of the Mediterranean. Local trains and buses spend most of their time underground; the best way to see the stunning cliffs is by minibike rented in St-Raphaël. Try **Dewil Cycles,** av. Victor Hugo (tel. 94 51 03 66), off rue Mermoz, just right of the train station. (Bikes 20-70F per day, deposit 600-1200F. Mopeds 70-120F per day, deposit 2000-3000F.)

In the village of **La Napoule** a medieval château (tel. 93 49 95 05) prevents the bizarre works of American sculptor Henry Clews from seeing the light of day. You'll have to enter the dark castle to see the grotesque menagerie of scorpions, lizards, and gnomes. (Open Wed.-Sun. 2-4pm only. Admission 25F, students and seniors 20F.) Not the place for a long visit, this traffic-ridden city lies on the train and bus lines between St-Raphaël and Cannes. (8 trains and buses per day from St-Raphaël, 50 min., 18-21F. Buses from Cannes 8F.)

About 80km northwest of Cannes the **Grand Canyon de Verdon,** 630m deep and 20km long, reigns as the deepest canyon in Europe. Here, massive cliffs streaked with yellow and pink plunge to swift rivers and forested valleys. Seek out the vertiginous views at Point Sublimes and at the Balcons de la Mescla. The tourist offices in St-Raphaël have hiking maps and information on the canyon. The cheapest and easiest way to see the canyon is by bus tour. **Havas Voyage,** av. Karr (tel. 94 95 33 43), to the right of the train station, by the port in St-Raphaël, runs tours every Thursday from the St-Raphaël bus station (June-Sept., departure 8am, return around 7pm, 80F.) Reservations are advised. (Office open Mon. 9:30am-noon and 2:30-6:15pm, Tues.-Fri. 9am-noon and 2:30-6:15pm, Sat. 9:30am-noon.) Similar tours leave twice per week (April-Sept.) from Antibes and Cannes (both 107F), and weekly from Nice (150F). You'll have more fun in a car. **Europcar,** pl. de la Gare (tel. 94 95 56 87), across from the St-Raphaël train station, will rent to anyone over 21 with a license and a credit card. (400F per day. Open Mon.-Sat. 7am-8pm, Sun. 7am-noon and 6-8pm.) **Avis,** next door to Europcar (tel. 94 95 60 42 or 94 95 61 24) has the same requirements and charges 326.25F per day plus 4F per km. (Open Mon.-Sat. 6:45am-12:30pm and 2-7:30pm, Sun. 7-10:30am and 6-7:30pm.)

Once there, you can also get hiking maps and information on shelters and camping in the canyon from the **tourist office** (tel. 94 70 21 84), in the mairie in **Les Salles-sur-Verdon.** Les Salles sits just outside Aiguines, which is connected daily by bus with **Draguignan;** infrequent buses from Cannes and almost hourly buses from St-Raphaël (65 min., 22F) run to Draguignan. Draguignan's **tourist office,** av. Georges Clemenceau (tel. 94 68 63 30), also has information on the Verdon Canyon. Buses run once per day from Draguignan to Comps and Castellane at the eastern end of the canyon. Midway between Aiguines and Castellane, the **Auberge de Jeunesse (IYHF)** at La-Palud-sur-Verdon (tel. 92 74 68 72), is accessible by bus from Castellane. (35F per person. Camping 20F. Open March-Nov.) Pleasant lodging is also available at the **Auberge du Point Sublime,** 17km from Castellane (tel. 92 83 60 35). Call before hitching or taking a taxi. (Doubles with shower 100F. Breakfast 20F.)

Cannes

All preconceived notions of the French Riviera materialize in Cannes (pop. 69,000). Its surrounding hillsides encrusted with opulent villas, this renowned city smugly flaunts its pricey cafés, plush hotels, purse-pulverizing boutiques, and palm-lined boardwalk. Cannes has changed almost beyond recognition since Lord Brogham established the tiny fishing village as a fashionable resort among English aristocrats. The medieval citadel in Le Suquet still cuts a fine figure at the east end of town, but an unsightly festival and conference center has replaced the grand old Cercle Nautique, site of Queen Victoria's consumptive son's fatal encounter with slick marble and a number of happier aristocratic rendezvous.

Aside from windowshopping and sunbathing, visitors will find little to do but attend one of Cannes's many obscure festivals, such as the recent Advertising Festival or the regular Clairvoyancy and Hairdressing Festivals. April showers bring May's much ballyhooed **Festival International du Film** and its three-ring circus of directors, actors, producers, and paparazzi, but few of the 350 screenings are open to the public. Tickets for the 1991 festival (May 8-21) go on sale a week in advance at the *billetterie* of the Palais des Festivals. Cannes, the appropriate sister city of Beverly Hills, also holds a **Festival Américain**. The gala begins on July 4 and ends on July 14, Bastille Day, thus celebrating revolutions on both sides of the Atlantic. Tickets for the football game and the jazz and country music concerts are available at the ticket office.

Orientation and Practical Information

Most points of interest lie between the **train station, le Suquet** (take lovely, carless rue Meynardier up the hill), and **boulevard de la Croisette,** a long and lavish promenade that runs beside the sea. On one side of the road stand palatial luxury hotels; facing them are their parasol-studded private beaches. Don't despair: if you walk far enough westward down la Croisette, a small block of public beach appears. Other sandy public beaches lie beyond Port Canto and Palm Beach (on pl. Franklin Roosevelt). Windsurfing lessons are offered at the one near Palm Beach. As an alternative to the sea and sand, explore the tiny streets and tile-roofed shops between rue Marechal Joffre and le Suquet.

Tourist Office, 1, bd. de la Croisette (tel. 93 39 01 01 or 93 39 24 53), in the Palais des Festivals next to the *vieux port.* Expert staff speaks excellent English. Loads of information on Cannes and the surrounding area. Free accommodations service and bike and car rental suggestions. Open daily 9am-7:30pm; Sept.-June Mon.-Sat. 9am-6:30pm. Extended hours during festivals. **Branch office,** 1, rue Jean-Jaurès (tel. 93 99 19 77), upstairs in the train station. Another helpful office with accommodations service. English spoken. Open daily 9am-7:30pm; Sept.-June Mon.-Sat. 9am-12:30pm and 2-6:30pm.

Budget Travel: Frantour Tourisme, just outside the train station (tel. 93 39 20 20). BIJ/Transalpino tickets. Open Mon.-Fri. 9am-noon and 2-6pm, Sat. 9am-noon. **C.I.T.,** 9, bd. de la Croisette (tel. 93 39 47 82). Handles student travel and offers cheap fares.

Currency Exchange: Office Provençal, 17, rue Maréchal-Foch (tel. 93 39 34 37), across from the main train station. No commission and a good location, but so-so rates. Open daily 8am-8pm. **Bank of Credit and Commerce International,** 6, rue des Serbes (tel. 93 38 23 43), off bd. de la Croisette. Good rates and no commission. Open Mon.-Fri. 9am-1pm and 2-4pm.

American Express: 8, rue des Belges (tel. 93 38 15 87), on the corner of rue Notre Dame and not far from rue Bivouac Napoléon. Full range of services. 10F commission on currency transactions. Open Mon.-Sat. 9am-8pm. **AmEx Bank,** 3, bd. de la Croisette (tel. 93 39 84 67). Also sells traveler's checks and exchanges money. Open Mon.-Fri. 9am-noon and 2-5pm.

Post Office: 22, rue Bivouac Napoléon (tel. 93 39 14 11), off of rue Jean de Riouffe. Open Mon.-Fri. 8am-7pm, Sat. 8am-noon. **Branch office,** at 37, rue Mimont (tel. 93 39 33 15), behind the train station. Open Mon.-Fri. 8am-6:30pm, Sat. 8am-noon. Both branches have **telephones** and **Poste Restante. Postal Code:** 06400. In July and Aug. there is a mobile **telephone office** on quai St-Pierre. Open daily 9am-10pm.

Trains: 1, rue Jean-Jaurès (tel. 93 99 50 50). Cannes lies on the major coastal line, with connections approximately every ½-hr. (6:11am-11:59pm). To: St-Raphaël (25 min., 26F); Juan-les-Pins (10 min., 7F); Antibes (15 min., 9F); Nice (35 min., 24F); Monaco (50 min., 34F); Menton (1 hr., 37F). Also hourly (6:30am-11:05pm) to many towns including Toulon (1¼ hr., 74F) and Marseille (2 hr., 107F). Station open 6am-midnight. Information desk open 8:30-11:50am and 2-6pm. Ticket sales 5:45am-11pm. Baggage service open daily 6am-1:40pm and 2-9:40pm.

Buses: Gare Routière (tel. 93 39 31 37), next to the train station. Information office open Mon.-Tues. and Thurs.-Sat. 9am-noon and 2-6:30pm. To: Grasse (every ½-hr., 50 min., 16F); Mougins via Grasse (1¼ hr., 23.50F); Golfe-Juan (every 40 min., 15 min., 10.10F); Vallauris (every hr., 40 min., 9F); Nice Airport (every 40 min. 6am-7:40pm, 60F (45 min.) or 40.50F (1½ hr.)). Most buses leave from **Gare des Antibes,** pl. de l'Hôtel de Ville (tel. 93 64 50 17). Every 20 min. to Juan-les-Pins (15 min., 9.50F), Antibes (30 min., 10.50F), Nice (1½ hr., 25.50F). Also to St-Raphaël (8 per day, 70 min., 22F), stopping along the way at La Napoule (10 min., 7F), Le Trayas (30 min., 10F), and Grasse (16F). **Local buses** 5.90F, *carnet* of 6 19.80F or 25.90F.

Taxis: tel. 93 38 30 79, in front of the train station.

Bike Rental: 2 Roues, 5, rue Allieis (tel. 93 39 46 15 or 93 99 21 41), off pl. Gambetta in front of the train station. Bicycles 38F per day, deposit 1000F, mopeds 173F per day, deposit 4000-5000F. Gas included. Helmet 3.60F. Discounts for longer rental. Credit cards accepted. **SNCF Train Vélo** (tel. 93 90 33 50), in train station. Bicycles 50F per day, deposit 500F. Open daily 6am-1:40pm and 2-9:40pm.

English Bookstore: The English Bookshop, 11, rue Bivouac Napoléon (tel. 93 65 41 78), off rue Jean de Riouffe. Good selection of new books. Paperbacks 48F and up. *Let's Go: France* a measly 180F. Open July-Aug. Mon.-Sat. 9:15am-7:30pm; Sept.-June. Mon.-Sat. 9:15am-1pm and 2-7pm.

Youth Center: Cannes Information Jeunesse, 5, quai St. Pierre (tel. 93 68 50 50), facing the port. General information for the jejune. Open Mon.-Fri. 9am-12:30pm and 2-6pm. **Cannes Jeunesse,** 2, quai St-Pierre (tel. 93 38 21 16) has information on water sports and activities. Open Mon.-Wed. 9-11am and 2-4:30pm.

Showers: (tel. 93 68 52 13), on rue Jean Hibert in the *vieille ville.* Open mid-Sept. to mid-Aug. Wed.-Fri. 3-6pm, Sat. 8-11am and 3-6pm, Sun. 8-11:30am.

Pharmacy: pl. Gambetta (tel. 93 39 11 37). Picasso came here to find inspiration. Open Tues.-Sat. 8:30am-12:30pm and 2:30-7pm, Mon. 2:30-7pm.

Hospital: Pierre Nouveau, 13, av. des Broussailles (tel. 93 69 91 33). From train station take a left and eventually a right on av. de Grasse. Bear right at the fork on av. Broussailles.

Medical Emergency, tel. 93 38 39 38 or 93 99 12 12. English sometimes spoken.

Police: 15, av. de Grasse (tel. 93 39 10 78), 10 min. west of the train station. **Emergency,** tel. 17.

Accommodations and Camping

Although most of Cannes's hotels have more stars than you can afford, there are a few bargains to be found just off rue d'Antibes and close to the beach. Single prices may melt the lenses in your sunglasses. Double and triple prices are less apocalyptic. Try to book ahead—an absolute must in July and August. If you arrive early in the day, the tourist office can usually find you a room.

Hôtel National, 8, rue Maréchal-Joffre (tel. 93 39 91 92), a few blocks to the right of the station. English manager keeps bare rooms squeaky clean. Singles 100-120F. Doubles 150-170F, with showers 250-300F. Showers 15F. Breakfast 20F.

Hôtel Cybelle, 14, rue du 24-Août (tel. 93 38 31 33), a small street one block to the right from rue des Serbes as you leave the station. The price is right. TV room. Single 100F, with shower 120F. Doubles 120F, with shower 150F.

Hôtel Chanteclair, 12, rue Forville (tel. 93 39 68 88), a few streets from the western end of rue Félix-Faure. Follow the signs to the sheltered courtyard. Jean-Claude Hautcœur keeps clean, comfortable rooms with bright flowery wallpaper (and no roosters). Singles 120-160F. Doubles with shower 140-200F, and private toilet 250F. Triple with shower 213F. Shower 10F (usually automatically added). Breakfast 17F.

Le Florian Hôtel, 8, rue du Commandant André (tel. 93 39 24 82), off rue d'Antibes. Friendly Italian manager, Giordano, keeps clean rooms, all with showers and telephones. TV room. Singles 130-150F. Doubles 150-170F. Breakfast 18F.

Hôtel Albert Ier, 68, av. de Grasse (tel. 93 39 24 04), off pl. de la Gare. Take a right out of the station, then a right uphill on av. de Grasse. A charming place with a beautiful garden in a quiet neighborhood. Single or double 140F, with shower 170F, with private toilet 230F. Breakfast 22F. Tax 2F per person per day.

Hôtel de Bourgogne, 13, rue du 24-Août (tel. 93 38 36 73), a small street one block to the right from rue des Serbes as you leave the station. Central location. Spotless rooms with carpeting and telephones, some with TVs. Kitchen available. TV room, amazingly enough. Singles 150-180F. Doubles 170-220F, with shower 180-250F. Triple with shower 270F. Breakfast 20F. Tax 2F per person per day. Open Jan.-Nov.

Hôtel du Nord, 6, rue Jean-Jaurès (tel. 93 38 48 79), across from the train station. Outgoing owner loves the USA. Eat breakfast among pictures of the Grand Canyon. Spotless—but not soundproof—rooms. Singles and doubles 140-180F, with showers 200-220F. Triples with showers and private toilet 240-400F. Hall showers included. Breakfast 20F. Open Dec. 16-Nov. 14.

Robert's Hôtel, 16, rue Jean Jaurès (tel. 93 38 66 92), in front of the train station. Clean but a bit cramped. Singles 145F. Doubles 145-190F, with shower 190-240F. Breakfast 20F. Open March-Dec.

Camping: Le Grand Saule, 24-26, bd. de la Frayere (tel. 93 47 07 50), in nearby Ranguin. Take the bus from pl. de l'Hôtel de Ville towards Grasse or the local train (every hr., 12 min.). Three-star site with pool and hot showers. Sometimes crowded. 99F per 2 people, tent included. Open Easter-Oct. **Caravaning Bellevue,** 67, av. M. Chevalier (tel. 93 47 28 97), in Cannes-La Bocca. 211 spaces. 64F per person, tent included. Open Jan.-Oct. **Le Ranch Camping,** chemin St. Joseph (tel. 93 46 00 11), in Rochville, 2km from town. Take bus #10 from the station. 1-2 persons 50F on foot (you bring the tent), 66F with car/caravan. On Sat. 1-2 persons 60F on foot, 72F with car/caravan.

Food

The elegant sidewalk cafés on bd. de la Croisette, Cannes's center of conspicuous consumption, attract violinists and accordion players but cost an arm and a leg. Keep your legs and walk to **Monoprix Supermarket,** 9, rue Maréchal Foch, across from the train station. (Open daily 8:45am-7:30pm.) The **Casino Supermarket,** 55, bd. d'Alsace, has a better selection but higher prices. The upstairs cafeteria is good for a quick bite. (Entrees 14.80-46.50F; open daily 11am-10pm.) Better yet, try the **outdoor markets** in pl. Gambetta and rue Forville (Tues.-Sun. 7am-1pm).

Chez Mamichette, 1, rue St-Antoine, off the western end of rue Félix Faure. A tiny, delightful Savoyard restaurant on a hill near the Vieux Port. Reasonable prices in a ritzy area. Try the *fondue savoyarde* (50F), the 65F *menu*, the *plat du jour* (40F), or if you're really hungry, the ribsticking *raclette* (85F). Open Mon.-Sat. noon-3pm and 7-11pm.

Restaurant le Pacific, 14, rue Venizélos, across from the train station on the right. Excellent pizzas (32-50F), a 4-course 52F *menu,* and *steak-frites* (33F). Open Sun.-Thurs. 11:30am-2:30pm and 6:30-9:30pm, Fri. 11:30am-2:30pm.

Au P'tit Creux, 82, rue Meynadier, at the corner of rue Docteur Gazagnaire. Four hearty varieties of Tunisian *couscous* (from 52F) and a 59F *menu* with French classics. Outdoor seating. Open Tues.-Sat. noon-2:30pm and 7-10pm, Sun. noon-2:30pm.

Le Bouchon, 10, bd. de Constantine, off rue d'Antibes. A 10-min. walk left of the train station. Dine among seagulls. Varied 68F and 95F *menus* feature *canard à l'orange* (duck with orange sauce) and *aïoli* (Provençal garlic mayonnaise dip with raw vegetables). Open Jan.-Nov. Tues.-Sun. noon-2pm and 7-10pm.

Le Santorin, 5, pl. de la Gare, across from the train station. Tasty pizzas (28-35F) served in a hall of painted mirrors. 50F and 80F *menus. Plat du jour* 40F. Dine indoors or out. Open Mon.-Sat. noon-2pm and 7-10pm.

Sights and Entertainment

Cannes's **Le Casino Croisette,** 1, get. Albert Edoef (tel. 93 38 12 11), near the main tourist office has slots as well as blackjack, roulette, and French roulette. (Gambling daily 5pm-4am, open for slots at 11am. No shorts. Must be 18. Free.) The **Nautilus** (tel. 93 99 62 01), a glass-bottomed seafaring aquarium, leaves every hour from the Gare Maritime next to the main tourist office. (Runs daily 10:30am-2:30pm. Admission 60F, over 60 50F, under 22 40F, under 10 30F.)

Cannes certainly knows how to entertain its guests at night. **Le Blitz,** 22, rue Massé (tel. 93 39 31 31), off bd. de la Croisette, with both disco and video bar, is the most popular nightclub. You must be 18 to enter, but the crowd usually isn't much older. (Open nightly 11pm-7am. Cover 60F.) **Club du 10,** 10, rue Teisseire (tel. 93 39 24 67), at the corner of pl. Gambetta, is a new-wave nightclub that rocks during the day. (Open Wed.-Mon. 3-7pm. Cover 30F. Drinks 30F.) **Les 3 Cloches** (tel. 93 68 32 92), is another local favorite.

International types favor the video jukebox at **Bar du Port,** 2, rue de la Rampe (tel. 93 39 78 98), right off quai St-Pierre. (Open daily 7:30am-2:30am. Beer 8-22F. Mixed drinks 25-40F.) Fooze while you booze at **La Boum,** rue Fery (tel. 93 39 91 82), off rue Félix Faure, near the port. (Open Tues.-Sun. 11am-2:30am. Beers 10F.)

Cannes has about as many gay nightspots as straight ones. **Le Bar Basque,** 14, rue Macé (tel. 93 39 35 61), off bd. de la Croisette, has been a favorite gay bar for 50 years. (Open daily 7pm-7am. Beers 15F.) The **Club 7 Disco,** 7, rue Rouguière, near the port, is newer but no less popular. (Open nightly 11pm until morning. Cover 90F. Drinks 25-35F.) **Zanzi-Bar,** 85, rue Félix Faure (tel. 93 39 30 75), attracts a mixed crowd. Everyone shrieks cacophonously at the top of their lungs. (Open daily 2pm-4am. Beer 16F.)

Cannes to Nice

If you are based in Cannes or Nice, many a daytrip by rail or by boat awaits you. Both the **Iles de Lérins** provide a welcome respite from fast-paced Cannes. The smaller island, **St-Honorat** harbors pine forests and an active monastery, the **Abbaye de Lerins,** where Cistercian monks live in silence, obedience, and chastity. (Open daily 10am-2:30pm. Free.) Nicer and more densely forested, **Ile Ste-Marguerite,** is famous for the fort Cardinal Richelieu built in 1712. Both islands, but particularly St-Marguerite, offer terrific tanning spots, far less wind, and far fewer people than the mainland beaches. Twelve boats per day leave between 7:30am and 4pm from the Gare Maritime des Iles (tel. 93 39 11 82), across from the Cannes tourist office on bd. de la Croisette. (Round-trip Cannes to St-Honorat ½-hr., 35F; Cannes to Ste-Marguerite 15 min., 30F. Both islands round-trip 40F. Ages 4-10 ½-price.) Boats to both islands also leave from Golfe-Juan and Juan-les-Pins. (Round-trip to both islands 55F, ages 4-10 28F.)

Grasse, in the hills outside Cannes, was known for its leather until a 16th-century passion for leather gloves made it the perfume capital of the world, a position it maintains today. The *parfumiers* lead free tours around their factories and offer their products at wholesale prices; the **Fragonard Parfumerie,** 20, bd. Fragonard (tel. 93 36 44 65) is the largest (open daily 8:30am-6:30pm). Aside from the little bottles, there's little to see here. Even the local hero, Rococo painter Fragonard, got bored and fled for Paris. The **Villa-Musée Fragonard,** 23, bd. Fragonard, exhibits some of his and his family's work. (Open Mon.-Fri. and the 1st and last Sun. of each month 10am-noon and 2-6pm; Oct.-June Mon.-Fri. 2-5pm. Admission 8F, children free.) Buses leave from both bus stations in Cannes, near the train station and at pl. de l'Hôtel de Ville (every 30 min., 50 min., 16F).

Set on a hill 8km from Cannes, **Mougins** hides peaceful streets behind its old fortified walls. Picasso came here in 1924 to find inspiration. Walk through the streets of this old fortified town, and climb to the top of the monastery tower for an unrivaled view of the coast and a glimpse of the snowy Alps to the northeast. The Cannes-Grasse bus stops at Val du Mougins (every 30 min., 20 min., 7.50F); from there it's a pleasant one-hour climb past gracious villas to the old town.

Most towns on the Riviera stay up late, but no place burns the midnight oil like **Juan-les-Pins.** Boutiques remain open until midnight, cafés until 2am, and nightclubs until 4 or 5am. Most clubs charge a cover of 60-100F. If you have any money left after clubbing, you may want to gamble the rest of the night away at the **Eden Beach Casino.** (Open nightly 8pm-4am. Minimum age 21. No shorts or sneakers. Free.) Famous for its age-old pine trees, the *Pinède* of Juan-les-Pins is the site of the **Festival International de Jazz (Jazz à Juan),** an outstanding annual musical program which runs the second week in July. (Tickets 145-250F, available at Juan-les-Pins and Antibes tourist offices.)

Juan-les-Pins is accessible by train from Nice (27 min., 20F) and Cannes (12 min., 8F). The English-speaking staff at the **tourist office,** 51, bd. Guillaumont (tel. 93 61 04 98), distribute maps and make hotel reservations. To reach the tourist office from the station, turn right and go to the end of the street by the beach; take a left on Guillaumont and then look to your left. (Open July-Aug. Mon.-Sat. 9am-8pm, Sun. 9am-1pm; Sept.-June Mon.-Fri. 9am-noon and 2-6:30pm, Sat. 9am-noon.) A good room is nearly impossible to find in July or August. Spotless **Hôtel Eden,** 16, av. Louis Gallet (tel. 93 61 05 20), around the corner from the tourist office, is the nicest of the budget hotels. All rooms have telephones and beautiful views of the ocean. (Singles 170F, doubles 180-200F, with shower 200-260F, with shower and toilet 300F. Extra bed 70F. Breakfast 20F.) **Hôtel Trianon,** 14, av. de l'Estérel (tel. 93 61 18 11), one block farther away from the beach than av. Louis Gallet, has clean but bare rooms. (Singles 140F, with shower 160F. Doubles 160F, with shower 200F. Triples 200F. Shower 15F. Breakfast 25F. Open Dec.-Oct. 15.) **Hôtel Parisiana,** 16, av. de l'Estérel (tel. 93 61 27 03), next door to Trianon, has clean, cramped rooms. (Singles 130-160F. Doubles with shower 160-210F. Breakfast 25F.) **Hôtel de la Gare,** 6, rue du Printemps (tel. 93 61 29 96), at the end of av. de l'Estérel, is a homey establishment with clean, airy rooms. (Single or double 160F. Triple 270F. 5-person suite 450F. Hall shower included.) Restaurants in Juan-les-Pins are generally expensive; deign to stock up on essentials at **Supermarché Robert,** 22, av. Amiral-Courbet. (Open Mon.-Sat. 8:30am-12:30pm and 4-7:15pm.)

An agreeable walk or a five-minute bus ride south will take you to the **Cap d'Antibes,** a small, sunny peninsula with gorgeous pine forests. Walk along the seaside on bd. Guillaumont, past the Juan-les-Pins tourist office. Take a right on av. Edouard Baudoiun, which eventually becomes av. Maréchal Juin and leads into the heart of Cap d'Antibes. At the end of av. Maréchal Juin also lies the **Musée Naval et Napoléon,** av. Kennedy (tel. 93 61 45 32), which combines naval history with Napoleonics. The museum's Sella tower overlooks the remains of an old military battery. (Open Wed.-Mon. 9-11:45am and 2-6:45pm; winter Sun.-Mon. and Wed.-Sat. 9-11:45am and 2-5:45pm.)

If you go back up the other side of the peninsula, you will soon hit **Antibes,** a glamorous sea-side resort that is a bit less hectic than some of its neighbors. Antibes is accessible by train from Nice (25 min., 18F) Cannes (14 min., 12F) and Juan-les-Pins (2 min., 4F). *Vieil Antibes* and Juan-les-Pins are linked by **Le Petit Train** (tel. 93 65 08 41), a trolley which shuttles back and forth hourly. Catch it on the half-hour at the Juan-les-Pins Promenade du Soleil on bd. Baudoin, and on the Antibes pl. de la Poste, on rue Piétonne. (10am-11pm; 40 min.; 25F, under 10 15F.)

Home to celebrated English writer Graham Greene and a gaggle of other artists, Antibes takes great pride in the **Musée Grimaldi-Picasso** (tel. 93 34 91 91) in the Château Grimaldi on pl. Mariejol. Hanging onto a seaside cliff for dear life, this château housed Picasso for a productive six months in 1946. Several small rooms display drawings, ceramics, and a sampling of the paintings Picasso executed here. The top floor features his *atelier* (studio) and paintings by young contemporaries, such as de Staël, Hartung, and Mathieu. (Open June 15-Aug. Wed.-Mon. 10am-noon and 3-7pm; Sept.-Oct. and Dec.-June 14 Wed.-Mon. 10am-noon and 2-6pm.

Admission 20F, students 10F, children under 10 free. Free Dec.-May Wed.) The **Musée Archéologique** (tel. 93 34 48 01), along the waterfront in the Bastion St-Andrée sur les Remparts, illuminates archaeological digs of the area and the history of Antipolis (the ancient Greek city on the site). Temporarily closed in 1990, this museum will probably reopen in January 1991. (Open 9am-noon and 2-7pm; Sept.-Oct. and Dec.-June Wed.-Mon. 9am-noon and 2-6pm. Admission 6F, students 3F.) The **Musée Peynet**, pl. Nationale (tel. 93 34 36 64), presents over 200 creative masterpieces by local artist Raymond Peynet. (Open July-Sept. Wed.-Mon. 10am-noon and 3-7pm; Oct. and Dec.-June Wed.-Mon. 10am-noon and 2-6pm. Closed Nov. Admission 20F, students and ages 12-18 10F, under 12 free.)

The English-speaking **tourist office**, 11, pl. de Gaulle (tel. 93 33 95 64), off bd. Albert 1*er*, helps with accommodations and has a list of the 11 campgrounds in the area. (Open daily 9am-8pm; Sept.-June Mon.-Sat. 9am-12:30pm and 2-7pm.) Most of them are in nearby Biot (see below). If you insist on staying in *vieil Antibes*, check out the cozy rooms and 1930s tiled staircase at the **Modern Hôtel**, 1, rue Fourmillière (tel. 93 34 03 05). (Singles 140F. Doubles 172-182F, with shower and toilet 240F. Showers 15F. Breakfast 25F.) Better than any hotel is the Antibes **Relais International de la Jeunesse,** bd. de la Garoupe (tel. 93 61 34 40). Lean and cheap, this hostel by the sea consistently attracts a fun bunch of backpackers. Bottles of wine are sometimes available for 8F; the lighthouse above the hostel is an inspiring place to drain them. No individual reservations are accepted; call ahead to make sure a group has not booked it full. Take the *Garoupe* bus from the Antibes bus station (10 min., 4F) and ask the driver to stop at the hostel. (Lockout 9:30am-5pm. No curfew. 50F, breakfast (at 8am sharp) included. Meals 46F. Sheets 10F. Open June-Sept.)

In Antibes, most restaurants will devour your budget. At **Au Fruits de Mer Snack Bar,** galerie du Port at rue Fontvielle, off rue Lacan, enjoy delicious *crêpes* (10-35F), the *plat du jour* (35F), or a (50F) 3-course *menu* indoors or out. (Open daily 9am-10pm.) **La Palmeraie**, 6, rue Rostan (tel. 93 34 39 90), off rue de la République and near pl. Nationale, serves regional and North African dishes; five types of *couscous,* including vegetarian, run 60F and up. (Open daily noon-2pm and 7pm-midnight.) For some real Tex-Mex food, head for **Taco's Grille,** 41, rue James Close, right off pl. Nationale. (Tacos 30-38F. Chili *con carne* 70F. Open daily noon-2pm and 7-11pm.) If the restaurants are out of range, resign yourself to the **Codec-Top** supermarket on 8, av. Niqué, near pl. de Gaulle (open Mon.-Sat. 8:30am-7pm), or the morning **open market** at cours Masséna, near the Picasso Museum and the beach. (Open daily 6am-2pm.)

At the end of July or beginning of August, Antibes holds its annual **Eté Musicale** in front of the château. Tickets (100-220F) are available at the tourist offices in Antibes and Juan-les Pins. Also at the end of July or beginning of August is Antibes's **Festival de Théâtre;** pick up tickets at the tourist office (75F, students 60F).

Biot, one railway station east of Antibes, has gathered painter Fernand Léger's colorful, geometric depictions of mechanized modern life in the **Musée National Fernand Léger,** chemin du val de Pome (tel. 93 65 63 49 or 93 65 63 61). (Open Wed.-Sun. 10am-noon and 2-6pm; Oct.-March 10am-noon and 2-5pm. Admission 15F, students 8F.) A bus runs to the museum from the Antibes bus station, between the tourist office and the pl. de la Poste (every 2 hr., 20 min.). From the Biot train station, it's a pleasant, signposted hike along route de Biot (2km). Along route de Biot you'll also find a waterpark with gargantuan waterslides, a petting zoo with hamsters the size of woolly mammoths, and **Marineland** (tel. 93 33 49 49), a giant aquarium with one of the best watershows in Europe but, *hélas,* no rodents. (Open daily at 11am. Shows at 2:30, 4:30, and 6pm. Admission 78F.) The ancient walled town itself is known for its fine glassware; many glass-blowing shops are open to the public. Peek into **La Verrerie de Val de Pome** (tel. 93 65 03 78) on the way to the museum. (Open Mon.-Sat. 10am-12:30pm and 2-7pm, Sun. 2-7pm. Free.)

Biot has a handful of campgrounds, none of which rent tents. The best bargain is the monstrous 3-star **Le Logis des la Brague** (tel. 93 33 54 72), right across from the train stop. You'll find hot showers, washing machines, a supermarket, and a snack bar here. (1-2 people on foot 38F; 1-2 people in car or caravan 65-80F. Each additional person 16F. Electricity 12F. Open May-Sept. 8am-noon and 2-8pm.) **Idéal Camping,** pont de la Brague (tel. 93 74 27 07), right next door, is a smaller site with less to offer and inexplicably higher prices. (Tent 46-87F. Caravan 38-66.50F. Adults 17F, children under 7 10F. Electricity 12F. Open March 15-Oct. 10.) Wallow in luxury at four-star **Les Embruns,** 7, route de Biot (tel. 93 33 33 35), which has hot showers, washing machines, snack bar, minimarket, tennis courts, and that all-important TV room. (2-3 persons on foot 50F. 2 persons in a caravan 70F each. Additional person 20F, under 5 10F. Electricity 10F. Reception open May-Sept. daily 9am-12:30pm and 2:30-8pm.)

Vallauris, a few kilometers inland and east of Cannes, has long been known as the pottery capital of France. Picasso was fascinated by the town's ceramics and came here to work shortly after World War II. Most of the stores sell mass-produced, low-quality ware. The **Galerie Madoura** stocks high-quality reproductions, but at 1500F a plate, you might opt just to look. (Open Mon.-Fri. 9:30am-12:30pm and 2:30-6pm.) Vallauris hosts a bi-annual exhibition of ceramics and modern art from over 30 countries. To get to pottery land, take a bus (from near the train station or from pl. de l'Hôtel de Ville) from Cannes (every hr. 8am-7:30pm, 40 min., 9F), from Antibes (5 per day), or from Golfe-Juan (6:35am-8:15pm every ½-hr., 15 min., 5.50F). The **tourist office** is on 84, av. de la Liberté (tel. 93 63 73 12).

Nice

Nice (pop. 400,000) welcomes its influx of tourists each summer with all the usual accoutrements of a Riviera town—casual affluence, an ample beach, topnotch museums, flowery avenues—but without the affected aloofness of its neighbors. Furthermore, Nice is blessed with reasonably priced hotels, good local and regional transport, a population accustomed to visitors, and all the other conveniences of an authentic metropolis. Carry as little cash as possible here, as Nice's big-city appeal is coupled increasingly with big-city crime; lone women in particular may be targets. Be careful at night near the train station and in Vieux Nice. Tucked untidily into the southeastern pocket of the city and limited to pedestrians, Vieux Nice is anything but an outdoor museum. The labyrinth of tiny streets hides the boisterous bars, clubs, and restaurants which more poised Riviera towns lack. Colorful flower, fish, and vegetable markets fill cours Saleya Tuesday through Sunday from dawn until noon. Dotted with cafés, boutiques, and overpriced restaurants, the pedestrian zone west of pl. Masséna is an ideal place to plant yourself and watch the world go by. Port Lympia, a warren of alleyways, boulevards, *brasseries,* and *tabacs,* lies on the opposite side of the château and below Vieux Nice.

Arrive in Nice early in the day in the summer, or you'll almost certainly be forced to join the legion of visitors who camp outside the train station. Because of its convenient location, Nice endures an annual student invasion; the station moonlights as one of the largest and least safe bedrooms in France. Although police do sporadically enforce a law that prohibits sleeping on the beach, groups of young people often check their baggage at the concierge and head for the rocky waterfront.

Orientation and Practical Information

The SNCF train station (gare Nice-Ville) is in the center of town, next to the tourist office on **avenue Thiers.** The area around the station is fairly seedy and packed with cheap restaurants and hotels. To the left, **avenue Jean-Médecin** runs toward the water to **place Masséna.** Vieux Nice lies just south of pl. Masséna. Heading right from the train station, you'll run into **boulevard Gambetta,** the other main street running directly to the water. Sweeping along the coast, the majestic and festive **promenade des Anglais** is crowded, noisy, and rock-covered.

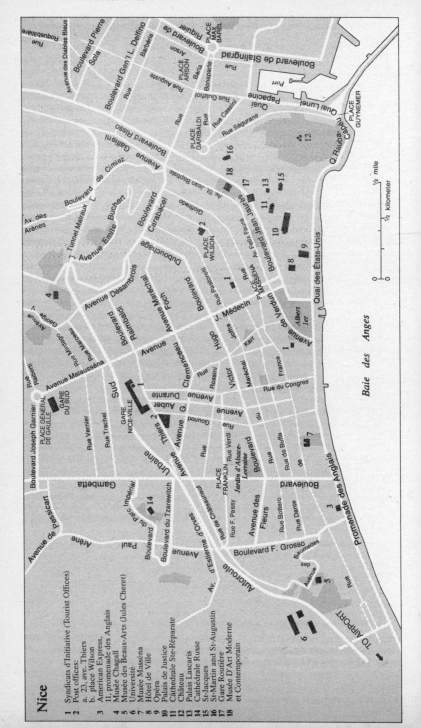

Nice

1 Syndicats d'Initiative (Tourist Offices)
2 Post offices:
    a. 23, ave. Thiers
    b. place Wilson
3 American Express,
    11, promenade des Anglais
4 Musée Chagall
5 Musée des Beaux-Arts (Jules Cheret)
6 Université
7 Musée Masséna
8 Hôtel de Ville
9 Opéra
10 Palais de Justice
11 Cathédrale Ste-Réparate
12 Château
13 Palais Lascaris
14 Cathédrale Russe
15 St-Jacques
16 St-Martin and St-Augustin
17 Gare Routière
18 Musée D'Art Moderne
    et Contemporain

Baie des Anges

Tourist office: av. Thiers (tel. 93 87 07 07), beside the train station. English spoken. Books a limited number of rooms after 10am. Stake out a place in line early. 10F for a reservation in a 1-star hotel and 20F for 2-star hotels, of which 10F will be deducted from your hotel bill. Crowded and a bit impersonal, but information on absolutely everything. Ask for their detailed map (5F), extremely helpful in Vieux Nice. Open daily July-Aug. 8:45am-7pm; Sept.-June Mon.-Sat. 8:45am-12:15pm and 2-5:45pm. Another office at 5, av. Gustave V (tel. 93 87 60 60), near pl. Masséna. Less English spoken, but much less crowded. Open June-Aug. Mon.-Sat. 9:30am-noon and 2-6pm; Sept.-May Mon.-Fri. 8:45am-noon and 2-6pm. A 3rd office at the airport (tel. 93 83 32 64), near the Ferber parking area. Not much English spoken. Free hotel reservations available on Signotel boards at the information desk. Open Mon.-Sat. 7:30am-6pm.

Currency Exchange: Cambio, 17, av. Thiers (tel. 93 88 56 80), across from the train station. No commission; good rates. Open daily 7am-midnight. Avoid Thomas Cook at the station. If you have American Express traveler's checks, the best deal is at the American Express office. **BEMO:** 7, av. Gustave V (te. 93 82 11 40), next to the downtown tourist office. No commission and less crowded than American Express. No Eurocheques accepted. Open Mon.-Sat. 9am-5pm.

American Express: 11, promenade des Anglais (tel. 93 87 29 82), at the corner of rue du Congrès. Expect long lines in the summer. Holds mail and cashes American Express traveler's checks at the best rate in the city. Open Mon.-Fri. 9am-6pm, Sat. 9am-noon; Oct.-April Mon.-Fri. 9am-noon and 2-6pm.

Post Office: 23, av. Thiers (tel. 93 88 52 52), near the train station. Open Mon.-Fri. 8am-7pm, Sat. 8am-noon. **Branch offices** at 18, rue Hôtel des Postes (tel. 93 85 98 63) at pl. Wilson (open Mon.-Fri. 8am-7pm, Sat. 8am-noon) and at 2, rue Clemenceau (tel. 93 88 72 88), off bd. Jean Médecin (open Sun.-Wed. and Fri. 8am-6:30pm, Thurs. 8:30am-6:30pm, and Sat. 8am-noon). Another office at the airport (open Mon.-Fri. 9am-5pm, Sat. 9am-noon). All offices have **Poste Restante** and **telephones.** Postal code: 06000.

Flights: Aéroport Nice-Côte d'Azur (tel. 93 21 30 30). Take the airport bus (every 20 min., 8F) from the *gare routière* by pl. Leclerc, or slower #9 from pl. Masséna or the port. An SNCF minibus runs between the train station and the airport 7:30am-7:15pm (14 per day, 15 min., 22F). **Air France,** 10, av. Félix-Faure (tel. 93 83 91 00), near pl. Masséna. One-way flights to Paris (571F, students 376-476F), New York (5630F), and Istanbul (3760F, students 1235F). Open Mon.-Sat. 9am-6pm. **Air Inter,** 4, av. de Suède (tel. 93 31 55 55), at the corner of av. de Verdun, the continuation of av. Félix Faure after pl. Masséna. Domestic flights only. Open Mon.-Sat. 9am-6pm.

Trains: Gare SNCF, av. Thiers (tel. 93 87 50 50). Information office open Mon.-Sat. 8am-7pm, Sun. 8am-noon and 2-6pm. Trains about every 20 min. (5:40am-midnight) to Cannes (40 min., 24F) and Antibes (25 min., 16F); about every 15 min. (6:05am-11:10pm) to Monaco (25 min., 13F) and Menton (35 min., 18F). Also to other coastal towns, northern France, Italy, and Spain. In summer, about 11 per day connect with the TGV express from Marseille to Paris (7½ hr.; 355F plus 15F required reservation). Showers at the station 12F, towels 3F, soap 1F. Toilets 1.50F. Open daily 7am-7pm. Next door at the **Cafétéria Flunch** (open daily 11am-10pm), the bathrooms are uncrowded and clean. **Lockers** 12F for 72 hr. Luggage stored for 12F per day per piece (open daily 5:30pm-midnight). **Gare de Sud,** 33, av. Malausséna (tel. 93 84 89 71 or 93 88 28 56), on the upper continuation of av. Jean-Médecin. Special trains, the *chemins de fer de la Provence,* leave for Digne through the southern Alps (5 per day: 3¼ hrs., 91F). Information booth, tel. 93 88 89 13. Open Mon.-Fri. 8am-12:30pm and 2-6pm, Sat. 8am-12:30pm.

Buses: Gare Routière, promenade du Paillon (tel. 93 85 61 81), off av. Jean Jaurès across from Vieux Nice. Open Mon.-Sat. 8am-6:30pm. Buses every 20 min. (6:30am-7:30pm) to: Villefranche (7.50F); St-Jean (10F); Eze (11.50F); Cap d'Ail (14.50F); Monaco (16.60F); Monte-Carlo (18F); Menton (45 min., 25F); last return bus leaves Menton at 8pm and Monte-Carlo at 8:30pm. Every 15 min. (6:15am-7:30pm) to: Antibes (20F); Juan-les-Pins (22F); Cannes (1½ hr., 25F). One per hr. to St-Paul (45 min., 16F) and Vence (55 min., 17.50F). Also to La Turbie (4 per day, 16.50F).

Public Transportation: Station Centrale, the TN (Transports Urbains de Nice) bus system at 10, av. Félix Faure (tel. 93 62 08 08), near pl. Général Leclerc and pl. Masséna. Information on city buses. Bus #12 from the train station goes to pl. Masséna and the beach (Mon.-Sat. 6am-1:30am, Sun. 7:45am-1:30am). All buses 8F per person. Buy *carnets* of 5 (25.80F) at av. Thiers tourist office, or at kiosks and *tabacs.* Buy 19F day passes on board.

Ferries: SNCM, quai du Commerce (tel. 93 13 66 66), at the port from which the boats sail. Take bus #1 or #2 from pl. Masséna. Passage to and from Corsican cities: Bastia, Caloi, Ile Rousse, Propriano, and Ajaccio (6-7 hr., one-way 230F, ages 4-12 130F). The cheapest and shortest route to Corsica from any French port, but not always convenient. Each Corsican city served only 1-2 times per week. Open Mon.-Fri. 8am-noon and 1:30-6pm, Sat. 8am-noon.

Taxis: (tel. 93 80 70 70). Avoid using taxis at all costs. Very expensive (about 30F to go around the block, even more if you don't speak French).

Bike and Moped Rental: Nicea Location Rent, 9, av. Thiers (tel. 93 82 42 71), near the train station. Friendly owners will help you with directions. Bikes 100F per day, deposit 2000F (accepts credit cards). Mopeds 150-180F per day plus 35F for gas, 3000-4000F deposit. Motor scooters 285-325F per day, deposit 6500F or 10,000F. Motorcycles 385F per day, deposit 10,000F. Helmet 15F. Open daily 9am-6:30pm Reduced rates on 3-day and weekly rentals. **Cycles Arnaud,** 4, pl. Grimaldi (tel. 93 87 88 55), near the pedestrian zone and beach. Tips on tours for hard-core cyclists. Bikes 70F, deposit credit card only. Mopeds 110F, including enough gas for a round-trip to Monaco, deposit credit card only. Motor scooter 160F, gas for moped and motor scooter 30F. Reductions for longer periods. Open Mon.-Fri. 8:30am-noon and 2-7pm.

English Bookstores: Riviera Bookshop, 10, rue Chauvain (tel. 93 85 84 61), off rue Gioffredo. Extremely friendly and well-stocked. New and second-hand books at 6F and up. Open Mon.-Sat. 9:30am-12:30pm and 2-6:30pm. **The Cat's Whiskers,** 21, rue Lamartine (tel. 93 80 02 66), behind Nice Etoile off bd. Jan Médecin. Better selection of new and used books than Riviera Bookshop, but a bit more expensive. Will buy books back at half price when you're done. *Let's Go: Europe* 190F. Open Mon.-Sat. 9:30am-12:30pm and 2:30-7:30pm.

Womens Center: Centre d'Information Droits des Femmes, rue de Grenoble (tel. 93 72 22 84), across from the Nice-Matin building. Take bus #9 or #10 from the central bus station. English sometimes spoken. For legal issues, walk-in service Mon.-Fri. 9am-3:30pm.

Youth Center: Centre d'Information Jeunesse, 19, rue Gioffredo (tel. 93 80 93 93), not far from the outermost edge of promenade du Paillton. Posts a bulletin board (in French) with summer jobs for students of any nationality. Jobs are tough to find (about 1-2 weeks); priority to citizens of the EEC. Jobs include baby-sitting and bartending. Open Mon.-Fri. 8:45am-6:45pm.

Laundromats: Taxi Lav, rue Pertinax, and **Point Laverie,** bd. Raimbaldi, both near the Let's Go Meublés hostel. Wash 14F for 6kg. Dry 2F per 7 min. Both open Mon.-Sat. 7am-8pm and Sun. 7am-1pm. **Laverie Self-Service,** 8, rue de Belgique, near the train station. Cross the street and make a left on the street that goes downhill. Wash, dry, and soap 28F per 5kg. Winsome manager will do it for you in 90 min. for an extra 10F. Open daily 7am-11pm.

Crisis Lines: SOS Amitié (tel. 93 26 26 26). 24-hour friendly ear. English spoken. **SOS Femmes en Battu:** Tel. 93 52 17 81. 24-hr. line for victims of sexual assault. English spoken.

Late-Night Pharmacy: Pharmacie, 7, rue Masséna (tel. 93 87 14 29), on the pedestrian walkway, where rue Masséna becomes rue de France. Open daily 9am-12:30pm and 2-6:30pm.

Hospital: St-Roch, 5, rue Pierre Devoluy (tel. 93 13 33 00). From av. Jean Médecin, turn left on rue Pastorelli, which turns into rue P. Devoluy.

Medical Services: SOS Medical Service (tel. 93 53 03 03). Available 24 hrs. No English spoken.

Police: Tel. 93 53 53 53, at the opposite end of bd. Maréchal Foch from bd. Jean Médecin and scattered throughout the city. **Emergency,** tel. 17.

Accommodations

Rooms in summer are like cigarettes in the Soviet Union: gone as soon as they're on sale. Arrive at the av. Thiers tourist office early for help in finding a room, or call individual hotels in advance. Managers are usually reluctant to accept phone reservations without a deposit through the mail. The greatest concentration of hotels is just outside the train station on the west side of av. Jean-Médecin. Most are pleasant, fairly inexpensive, and accustomed to English-speaking guests. If the ones listed are full, try either the area around rue d'Angleterre and rue d'Alsace-Lorraine or the area north of the train station between bd. Gambetta and av. Malausséna. There are also several hotels, some more expensive, on the other, more desolate side of av. Jean-Médecin away from the station. Nice's IYHF youth hostels are a distant and unattractive 8F bus ride away. University dorms are sometimes vacant in the summer (70F per day). Call **CROUS**, 18, av. des Fleurs (tel. 93 96 73 73) for reservations (Open daily 8:45am-12:15pm and 1:30-5:15pm).

Meublé Abadie, 22 rue Pertinax (tel. 93 85 81 21), 2nd floor. The strict but friendly manager, M. Abadie, says he's looking for "nice, smiling, clean people"—and he means it. The place itself is nice and clean, if a bit bare. All rooms with sink and bidet. Lockout 12:30-6pm. Midnight curfew. Dorm-style rooms 50F. Singles 70F. Doubles 110F. Triples 150F. Showers 15F. No reservations.

Hôtel Belle Meunière, 21, av. Durante (tel. 93 88 66 15), near the station. This quasi-villa with a large garden was a gift from one of Napoleon's generals to his mistress. The friendly, and "accommodating" family, the Marsels, keep the place immaculate. In summer, expect the atmosphere of a school dorm. 70F per person in 3-5 bed rooms. Singles 80F. Doubles 165F, with shower 230F. Triples 210F, with shower 290F. Showers 10F. Breakfast included. Parking 20F. Baggage room 5F. Open Feb.-Nov.

Hôtel Novelty, 26, rue d'Angleterre (tel. 93 87 51 73), near the train station. Clean rooms, but a bit cramped and frayed. There's a safe for valuables. Dorm rooms 60F. Singles 90-110F, with shower 120-150F, with toilet 190F. Doubles 150F, with shower 180F, with toilet 260F. Triples 220F, with shower 260F. Breakfast 20F. Two-day min. stay in summer.

Hôtel St-François, 3, rue St-François (tel. 93 85 88 69 or 93 13 40 18), in Vieux Nice near the morning fish market and across from the *gare routière.* Clean, quiet, and tiny rooms with sink and bidet on a tinier street. Lively Corsican manager speaks English. Singles 65-75F. Doubles 135F. Triples 175-190F. Showers 15F. Breakfast 13F.

Hôtel Mono, 47 av. Thiers (tel. 93 88 75 84), a few blocks west of train station along the same road. Removed from the hotel area south of the station, in an even dingier neighborhood. Clean and nicely furnished rooms with carpeting, telephones, sinks, and bidets. Street noise might get annoying. May have room when others are booked. Doors close at midnight. Singles 75-100F. Doubles 120F, with showers 145F. Triples 140F, with showers 180F. Shower 8F. Breakfast 15F.

Hôtel Idéal Bristol, 22, rue Paganini (tel 93 88 60 72), off of rue Alsace-Lorraine. M. and Mme Saelen keep spacious and spotless rooms, with sinks and bidets. Beautiful TV room. Dorm style rooms (3-4 in room) with kitchenette and refrigerator 70F. Single 100F. Double 115F, with shower 125-150F. Triple 165F, with shower 210F.

Hôtel les Orangers, 10bis, av. Durante (tel. 93 87 51 41), a 3-min. walk straight across from the station. Clean, quiet, and cramped rooms, some with kitchenettes and refrigerators. Two-night min. stay in summer. Discounts for longer stays. Six-bed dorms 70-80F. Doubles 170F. Triples with shower 250F. Breakfast 13F. Come early; no reservations. Open Dec.-Oct.

Hôtel Regency, 2, rue St-Siagre (tel. 93 62 17 44), off rue Pertinax near the train station. Take elevator to 2nd floor. Newly renovated, spacious duplexes with kitchenettes, refrigerators, and private bathrooms. The helpful manager, Paul, speaks English. Some 90F singles (shower 10F). Duplex doubles 150F, triples 240F, and quads 300F. Discounts for longer stays.

Hôtel de France, 24, bd. Raimbaldi (tel. 93 85 18 04 or 93 62 11 44), off of av. Jean Médecin. Plain, small rooms in a good location. Inquire after M. Boisgirard if you arrive in the afternoon. Singles 60-70F, with shower 90F. Doubles 120F, with shower 150F. Triples 180F, with shower 220F. Showers 15F.

Hôtel Lyonnais, 20, rue de Russie (tel. 93 88 70 74), near rue d'Italie. Fairly spacious and clean rooms with telephones. Singles 90-115F, with showers 155-175F. Breakfast included.

Hôtel Notre Dame, 22, rue de Russie (tel. 93 88 70 44), at the corner of rue d'Italie. Rooms are a bit small, but clean, quiet, and carpeted. Friendly management speaks well English. Single 90F, with private bathroom 130F. Double with shower 160F. Breakfast 15F. Shower 10F.

Hôtel Central, 10, rue de Suisse (tel. 93 88 85 08), off rue d'Angleterre. Small, clean, and airy rooms with modern bathrooms and telephones. Owners with miles o' smiles. Ask for Annette. Singles 110-160F, with shower 180F, with toilet 200F. Doubles 130-180F, with shower and balcony 200F. Triples with shower 240F. Showers 15F. Breakfast 17F. **Hôtel Select Serraire,** (tel. 93 88 18 45), in the same building. A bit cheaper, but not as good as Central. Singles and doubles 113-135F, with shower and kitchen 150F. Showers 15F. Breakfast 16F.

Hôtel Montreuil, 18bis, rue Biscirra (tel. 93 85 65 90), off av. Jean Médecin. Friendly manager. Slightly grim but clean. All rooms with TV. Singles 100F. Doubles 180F, with shower 200F. Hall showers included. Breakfast 15F. Discounts for longer stays.

Drouot Hôtel, 24, rue d'Angleterre (tel. 93 88 02 03 or 93 81 10 39), off of av. Jean Médecin. Newly renovated, immaculate rooms. The helpful managers, Ariel and Didier, speak English. Beautiful color TV room. Some rooms have kitchenettes. Singles (with hall showers) 110F. Doubles 160F, with shower 180F. Triple with shower 240F. Quad with shower 280F.

Hôtel St. Jacques, 27, rue d'Angleterre (tel. 93 88 80 96), right off of rue d'Alsace Lorraine. Smallish rooms are spotless, quiet, and cozy. Singles 100-120F. Doubles 145F, with kitchenette and TV 150-185F. TV 10F, color 20F.

Hôtel Darcy (tel. 93 88 67 06), across from Hôtel St. Jacques. Otherwise known as "the Tromanhause." Cramped but clean rooms. Singles 100-115F, with shower and toilet 170F. Doubles 120-150F, with shower and toilet 220F. Triples 180-225F. Breakfast 15F.

Auberge de Jeunesse (IYHF), route Forestière du Mont-Alban (tel. 93 89 23 64), 4km away from it all. Take bus #5 from the train station or walk to pl. Masséna, then take #14 from bd. Jean-Jaurès (every 25-40 min. until 7:30pm). Otherwise, a 45-min. walk. 62 beds. Opens 5pm. Lockout 10am-5pm. Curfew midnight. Bed, breakfast, and shower 50F. Required sheet rental 13F. Kitchen and fridge available. Laundry service 30F. IYHF card not needed.

Relais International de la Jeunesse "Clairvallon," 26, av. Scudérei (tel. 93 81 27 63), in Cimiez 10km out of town. Take bus #15 from pl. Masséna (every 10 min., 20 min.). A large, unofficial hostel in an old villa with a free swimming pool. Run by students. Luggage must be kept in a common storage room. 6 bunks per room. Check-in 6pm. Curfew 11:30pm. Bed and breakfast 50F.

Food

In general, restaurants in Nice are not budget traveler friendly. The area around the train station specializes in fairly inexpensive but mediocre fare. Seafood restaurants in Nice are expensive but worth it. Boulevard Jean Jaurès, opposite the fountain, or cours Saleya in Vieux Nice, are wellsprings of savory *bouillabaisse*. Just across the Mediterranean from North Africa, Nice offers delectable *couscous* and lamb and rice feasts. Quality Asian food can also be found here. *Pissaladière,* an onion, olive, and anchovy pizza, is a Niçois specialty. Avoid eating a meal at the overpriced tourist haunts on rue Masséna; they are more appropriate for people-watching, which can be enjoyed for the price of a drink or dessert. Few restaurants open before 7pm, and most stay open late. The **fruit market** east of pl. Masséna bustles each morning, as does the **fish market** in pl. St-François. You'll find everything else at **Prisunic,** 42, av. Jean Médecin (open Mon-Thurs. and Sat. 8:30am-7:15pm, Fri. 8:30am-8pm) or **Supermarché Casino** on rue Deudor, behind the Nice Etoile on av. Jean Médecin and off of rue Biscarra (open Mon-Thurs. and Sat. 8:30am-8pm, Fri. 8:30am-9pm). At both places, mineral water costs one-fourth of what street vendors charge. **CROUS,** 18, av. des Fleurs (tel. 93 96 73 73), lists the addresses of the many inexpensive student cafeterias liberally sprinkled throughout Nice (meals 9.60F). If you're not a French student, meals cost 32F. The convenient **Restaurant Université,** 3 av. Robert Schumann (tel. 93 97 10 20) is open from Sept-June. The cafeteria at **Montebello,** 96, av. Valrose (tel. 93 52 56 59), near the Musée Matisse, is usually open until mid-August. All student cafeterias open daily 11:30am-1:30pm and 6:30-8pm.

Cafeteria Flunch, av. Thiers, next door to the train station. A budget traveler's best friend. Good food, large portions, and the cheapest prices in town. ½ roast chicken or sausages with 2 vegetables 14.90F. Open daily 11am-10pm.

Le Pacific Pizzeria, 18, rue Miron, 5 min. from the station or the Chagall Museum. Savor the largest 35-45F pizzas in Nice amidst 50s and 60s American decor. *Plat du jour* 35F. Casual, tolerant management is a welcome change. Open daily noon-2pm and 7-11pm.

Le Panda, 26, rue Buffa, near rue Meyerbeer. Small and cozy restaurant/grill has 4-course 65F and 5-course 85F *menus.* Salads 25-40F. *Plat du jour* (usually chicken, fries, salad) 36F. Open daily noon-3pm and 7pm-midnight.

Palais de Chinois, 41, rue d'Angleterre, near the train station. Chinese and Thai food at reasonable prices. Beef, duck, pork, or chicken dishes 30-48F. 52F, 65F, and 88F *menus*. Open Sun-Wed. and Fri-Sat. 11:45am-2:30pm and 6:30-11pm, Thurs. 6:30-11pm.

Restaurant de Paris, 28, rue d'Angleterre, near the train station. Recommended by locals. Offers a variety of specialties at affordable prices, including beef fondue (with fries or salad 45F). Sometimes a special 25F *menu*. 32F, 38F, 49F *menus*. Open Dec.-Oct. daily 11:45am-2:30pm and 7:40pm-midnight.

Le Säetone, 8, rue d'Alsace Lorraine, off rue d'Angleterre near the train station. A comfortable restaurant serving regional dishes. Fills up quickly. Try the *soupe au pistou* and their special dessert, *mousse au café*. 43F, 50F, and 67F *menus*. *Plat du jour* 35F. Open Tues.-Sat. 11:30am-2pm and 6-9:30pm. **La Petite Biche**, across the street at 9, rue d'Alsace-Lorraine, is not as distinctive, but offers varied 50F and 70F *menus*. *Plat du jour* 37F. Open daily 11:45am-2pm and 6:45pm-10pm.

Le Faubourg Montmartre, 32, rue Pertinax, off av. Jean Médecin. Fantastic *couscous* 65F. Excellent bouillabaise 110F for two. 65F *menu*. The proprietor loves students. Open daily 1-3pm and 5pm-midnight.

Restaurant au Soleil, 7 bis, rue d'Italie, corner of rue de Russie. Filling French fare at reasonable prices. Fish soup, ½ roast chicken, french fries, and dessert 47F. 47F and 56F *menus*. *Plat du jour* 35F. Open daily 8:30am-1pm and 5-11pm.

Chez Davia, 11bis, rue Grimaldi, a short walk from pl. Masséna off bd. Victor Hugo. Excellent French and Italian food at great prices. Run by a charming Italian woman whose family has owned the establishment for 30 years. Wide selection. Four-course 50F *menu* and 5-course 70F *menu*. Try the *coq au vin* (36F). Sunday specialty is duck or rabbit. *Plat du jour* with dessert 36-38F. Lasagne or ravioli 30F. Open Thurs.-Tues. noon-2:30pm and 7-10:30pm.

Le Dalpozzo, 33, rue de la Buffa, 2 blocks from promenade des Anglais. a white-tablecloth-and-marble affair *sans* pretension. Dinner *menu* includes duck and wine (80F). Pizza 35-45F, pasta 44-55F. Open Sun.-Fri. noon-2:30pm and 9-11pm, Sat. 9-11pm.

La Gitane, pl. Rosseti in the center of Vieux Nice next to a beautiful fountain. Ample, family-style dishes. *Menu* 59F. *Plat du jour* 38F. Open daily noon-2pm and 6-11pm.

Sights

The most confirmed museum-hater will have a hard time resisting Nice's varied collections. Since most of the city's museums are hidden among attractive houses in quiet suburbs, visiting them gives you a respite from the beach and pl. Masséna as well as a glimpse of the luxurious residential areas. Furthermore, virtually all the museums are free. The tourist office's leaflet *Museums of Nice* provides more detailed information. Unfortunately, the pride of Nice's museum collection, the **Musée Matisse**, 164, av. des Arènes de Cimiez (tel. 93 81 75 75 or 91 53 17 70), is closed for renovations until March 1992.

The elegant **Musée National Marc Chagall**, av. du Docteur Ménard (tel. 93 81 75 75), is a 15-min. walk north of the station. Alternately, take bus #15 (every 20 min., 8F) to stop "Docteur Moriez." Like many museums on the Côte, this building makes radiant use of glass, space, and light. The 17 oil paintings devoted to Old Testament themes, including the vivid *Song of Songs,* exemplify Chagall's colorful inventiveness. The biblically-inspired collection contains mosaics, sculptures, tapestries, lithographs, and engravings—works into which Chagall said he could put all his sadness and happiness. (Open July-Sept. Wed.-Mon. 10am-7pm; Oct.-June. Wed.-Mon. 10am-12:30pm and 2-5:30pm. Admission 16F; students, seniors, and Sun. 8F. Library on history of art and religion open Tues.-Thurs. 10am-12:30pm.)

The **Musée des Beaux-Arts Jules Chéret**, 33, av. Baumettes (tel. 93 44 50 72), is a must for fans of the surreal. Take bus #38 or 40 from the Station Centrale to Chéret (8F). Among the artists whose works are displayed here is Gustave Albert Mossa (1883-1971), an undeservedly unknown Niçois painter, whose surrealist works are steeped in those crazy existential themes of love, sex, and death. The collection also includes works by Dégas, Monet, Sisley, Renoir, Bonnard, and Dufy. The sculpture garden blooms with the work of Rodin and Carpeaux. (Open May-

Sept. Tues.-Sun. 10am-noon and 3-6pm; Oct.-April Tues.-Sun. 10am-noon and 2-5pm. Closed 2 weeks in Nov. Free. Guided tour every Wed. at 5pm. 20F.)

The spanking new **Musée d'Art Moderne et d'Art Contemporain,** Promenade des Arts (tel. 93 62 61 62), at the intersection of av. St. Jean Baptiste and Traverse Garibaldi, contains over 400 French and American avant-garde pieces from 1960 to the present, including works by Roy Lichtenstein, Andy Warhol, Kenneth Noland, and Yves Klein. (Open Sat.-Mon. and Wed.-Thurs. 11am-6pm, Fri. 11am-10pm. Free.)

In town, visit the **Musée Masséna** (tel. 93 88 11 34 or 93 88 06 22), housed in an elegant villa at 65, rue de France, at the corner of promenade des Anglais. Take bus #12 from the train station to Meyerbeer (8F). It is furnished and decorated in First Empire style, and canvases by Renoir, Dufy, and Sisley adorn the upstairs walls. The third floor houses religious art and a small collection of 15th- to 18th-century armor. (Open Tues.-Sun. 10am-noon and 3-6pm; Oct.-April 10am-noon and 2-5pm. Free.) The **Musée International de Malacologie**, 3, cours Saleya (tel. 93 85 18 44), in Vieux Nice, will primarily interest young children and Jacques Cousteau groupies. The musueum has two aquariums and a collection of over 15,000 shells. (Open May-Sept. Tues.-Sat. 10:30am-1pm and 2-6pm; Free.) Other museums include a **Musée Archéologique,** 160, av. des Arènes de Cimiez (tel. 93 81 59 57). Take bus #15, 17, 20, or 22 to Arènes (8F) and visit the Gallo-Roman baths for 5F, 2.50 for students and seniors. (Guided visits every Sat. and Sun. at 3pm for 20F, students 10F.) (Open May-Sept. Tues.-Sat. 10am-noon and 2-6pm, Sun. 2-6pm; Oct. and Dec.-April Tues.-Sat. 10am-noon and 2-5pm, Sun. 2-5pm.) On the other end of the spectrum, the **Musée Alexis et Gustav-Adolf Mossa** 59, quai des Etats-Unis (tel. 93 62 37 11), exhibits works from the 1960s to the present and always has room for new talent. (Open Tues.-Sat. 10:30am-noon and 2-6pm, Sun. 2-6pm. Free.)

If you've had your fill of Gothic and Romanesque churches, take a look at the **Cathédrale Orthodoxe Russe St-Nicolas**, 17, bd. du Tsarévitch, off bd. Gambetta, a 5-minute walk from the train station. Before the Revolution, Nice was a favorite resort for wealthy Russians. Built between 1903 and 1912 in the style of the Iaroslav church in Moscow, this intimate church is topped by six onion domes roofed with typical Niçois tiles. Visitors wearing shorts or sleeveless shirts will not be allowed inside. (Open Mon.-Sat. 9am-noon and 2:30-6pm; in off-season 9:30am-noon and 2:30-5:30pm. Admission 10F.)

Nice maintains many parks and public gardens, the most central of which is the **Jardin Albert 1er.** Located at promenade des Anglais and quai des Etats-Unis, this quiet refuge has benches, fountains, and plenty of shade. Be sure to look at the ornate 18th-century Triton fountain. Jardin Albert 1er also contains the **Théâtre de Verdure** (tel. 93 82 38 68), a small amphitheater that hosts a variety of summer events. (Box office open daily 10:30am-noon and 3:30-6:30pm). In the public gardens around the Musée Matisse, old meets new head on as students from the nearby university sporting the latest in casual *chic* relax amidst the collection of Roman ruins from 200 BC.

Like many centers on the Côte, Nice has a colorful, convoluted old section known to residents as Vieux Nice. Sprawling out southeast from bd. Jean Jaurès, this *quartier* is a perilous mix of tourist trap cafés and shops and homes of the *vrai Niçois* ("real" *Niçois*). To experience the authentic old city, stick to the tiniest of the already tiny streets. Avoid the Galeries des Ponchettes and the area around the Cathédral Ste-Réparate where most establishments display American Express decals in the windows. The ruins of a **château** rest on the hills above Vieux Nice. Climb the stairs as medieval pilgrims did, or take the elevator. Between the exotic pines and unusual cacti, you'll catch a glimpse of the port and the Baie des Anges (Bay of Angels).

Entertainment

Capital of the hedonistic Riviera, Nice *gets down* all summer long. Most of the action is along rue Masséna, which is jammed with Anglophone tourists, and the less safe area around the edges of Vieux Nice. Connecting these two centers is rue François de Paule, an artery which clubgoers cruise until the early morning. The expensive bars along the waterfront cater to the piano-bar set. Bars around pl. Masséna attract the jukebox crowd. There are several smoky *bars américains* (bars that open late and close early the next morning) around Pier Lympia, but most are unmarked and hard to find. Most late-night clubs cost at least 50F to get in and about the same for each drink. Due to strict liquor license laws, most places without a cover charge can't stay open past 12:30am.

Chez Wayne, 15, rue de la Préfecture (tel. 93 13 46 99), in Vieux Nice near the Palais Justice (no sign, look for the imitation telephone booth outside), is the closest thing you'll find to a British pub on the Riviera. There's live music every night (usually classic rock but sometimes reggae, blues, or jazz) and British beer (can 15F, bottle 20F). (Open daily 10am-midnight.) **The Hole in the Wall,** 3, rue de l'Abbaye (tel. 93 80 40 16), about a block from rue de la Préfecture in Vieux Nice, also has a lively pub atmosphere with live pop and rock nightly at 9pm. Beer costs 18-28F a bottle, and the hamburger platters (45F with chips and salad) are popular with the Anglophone crowd. (Open Tues.-Sun. 8pm-midnight). **Jonathan's,** 1, rue de la Loge (tel. 93 62 57 62), in Vieux Nice off rue Centrale not far from the bus stop at av. Jean Jaurès, attracts a slightly older (21-27) and less touristy crowd with live folk music and soft rock every evening in a candlelit cellar. A bottle of beer costs 20F and a pitcher for 4 runs 60F. (Open nightly 8:30pm-12:30am) **Scarlet O'Hara's,** 22, rue Droite (tel. 93 80 43 22), off rue Rossetti in Vieux Nice, is a pub which attracts a predominantly French-speaking crowd. Beers run 20-23F. (Open Mon.-Sat. 7pm-12:30am.)

Nice's nightclubs are unrelentingly expensive. **Ruby's,** 8, descente Croh (tel. 93 62 59 60), along bd. Jean Jaurès opposite the Promenade de Paillon, plays reggae, ska, and calypso music to a multiracial crowd. (Cover 50F, 70F on Sat. Drinks 50F. Open nightly 11:30pm-6am). At **Le Centre Ville Discothèque,** 1, pl. Masséna (tel. 93 88 88 47), a young crowd (ages 17-25) moves to pop, funk, rap, and new wave. Women dance for free on Wednesday, Thursday, and Sunday. (Cover and first drink 70F, Sat. 90F. Open Wed.-Sun. 11pm-6am. Open nightly in July.) **Dan's Club,** 11, rue Alexandre Mari (tel. 93 62 61 96), right between pl. Masséna and pl. du Palais in Vieux Nice, rocks all night long and is a bit of a meat market. Those who don't enjoy being *boeuf Bourgignon* should skip the Wednesday night amateur strip tease. (Cover 50F, 60F on weekends. Women free until midnight. Open every night 5pm-6am.) **The Quartz Discothèque,** 18, rue Congrès (tel. 93 88 88 87), attracts a mixed gay and straight crowd to its long bar, comfy chairs, and a small dance floor; the doors open at 11pm.

The **Théâtre du Cours,** 2, rue Poissonerie in Vieux Nice, offers traditional dramatic performances Thursday through Saturday at 9pm and Sunday at 7pm (65F).The new **Central Dramatique National,** Promenade des Arts (tel. 93 80 52 60 or 93 13 90 90), at the corner of av. St. Jean Baptiste and Traverse Garibaldi, has a show almost every weekend (50-140F).

Nice's **Parade du Jazz** in mid-July at the Parc et Arènes de Cimiez (tel. 93 21 22 01), near Musée Matisse, attracts some of the most commercially successful European and American jazz musicians to its three stages. Tickets are available at the door or at the FNAC in Nice Etoile shopping center on av. Jean-Médecin (110F). The **Festival de Folklore International** and **Batailles des Fleurs,** pageants of music and flowers along promenade des Anglais, bloom in the heat from July 21 to August. (Reserved seats in the stands 60F.) From February 11 to March 3, fireworks fan across the city's skies as parades roll through the crowds celebrating Nice's **Carnaval.** *Semaine des Spectacles,* published every Wednesday, carries entertainment listings for the entire Côte and is available at newsstands (6F). The **Comité des Fêtes,** 5, Promenade des Anglais (tel. 93 87 16 28) has information about all the above events (open Mon.-Fri.).

Nice to Monaco

Nice is ideally suited for daytrips. You can leap on and off the train to Monaco, visiting the small towns en route. Buses circumscribe the towns of St-Paul-de-Vence, Vence, and Cagnes, three communities whose inland beauty brings relief from the surfocentric coastal towns. **Buses** leave Nice's *gare routière* about every ½-hour (6:15am-7:30pm) for St-Paul-de-Vence (50 min., 16F) and Vence (55 min., 17.50F). The same bus also stops at the train station at Cagnes (every ½-hr. 6:40am-7:55pm; 20 min. to St-Paul, ½-hr. to Vence). The last bus generally returns from Vence at 6:30pm, but prices and times change frequently. Special loop tickets (*billets circulaires*) available in Nice (35F) allow you to get on and off the buses all day.

The pride of carless **St-Paul-de-Vence** is the **Fondation Maeght** (tel. 93 32 81 63), a one km walk from the center of town. Get off at the second St-Paul bus stop, just outside the center of town on the way to Vence, and follow the signs up a steep, winding hill, Chemin des Gardettes. If you can go to only one museum in the whole Riviera, make it this one. The museum, designed by Josep Louis Sert, is actually part park, with fountains, wading pools, and split-level terraces. Works by Miró, Calder, Arp, and Zadkine are arranged with such care that, despite their innate abstractness, they seem natural in their garden setting. Stained-glass windows by Braque and Ubac are set in the garden chapel. Inside is an excellent permanent collection, as well as rotating exhibits usually devoted to a single artist. (Open daily July-Sept. 10am-7pm; Oct.-June 10am-12:30pm and 2:30-6pm. Admission 40F, students 25F, but worth every centime.) The **Musée d'Histoire Locale**, pl. de la Castre (tel. 93 32 53 09), next to the church, recounts the history of St-Paul from 1224 to 1875. From the bus stop, walk downhill and follow the signs into St-Paul Village. (Open April-May Thurs.-Tues. 10am-7pm, June-Oct. 10am-noon and 2-6pm. Admission 20F, children 14 and under 12F.)

St-Paul itself is among the best-preserved hill towns in France. For a panoramic view of the hills and valleys of the Alpes-Maritimes, walk along the ramparts, virtually unchanged since the 16th century. Studios, galleries, and expensive boutiques fill the lower floors of the houses in this artists' colony. The St-Paul **tourist office** is near the entrance of St. Paul Village, (tel. 93 32 86 95) at the beginning of rue Grande. (Open July-Sept. Mon.-Tues. and Thurs.-Sat. 10am-6pm, Sun. 2-6pm; Oct.-June Mon.-Tues. and Thurs.-Sat. 10am-noon and 2-6pm, Sun. 2-6pm.) If you need a place to stay, try clean and spacious **Les Remparts**, 72, rue Grande (tel. 93 32 80 64), a bit farther down the street from the tourist office. (Doubles 105F, with shower 180F, with private toilet 220F. 5F tax per person per day.) Restaurants are overpriced, so go on to Vence, where food is cheaper.

The most notable building in **Vence** is **Chapelle du Rosaire**, 1.5km from the last bus stop on av. Henri Matisse. The chapel's tiny interior was designed by Matisse, who considered the green, yellow, and blue stained glass his masterpiece. (Open Dec. 15-Oct. Wed., Fri., and Sat. 10-11:30am and 2:30-5:30pm, also by appointment if you call two days ahead. Free. Photographs forbidden). Vence's well-stocked **tourist office** (tel. 93 58 06 38) is in a booth in pl. du Grand Jardin beside the bus stop. (Open July-Aug. Mon.-Sat. 9am-12:30pm and 2-7pm; Sept.-June Mon.-Sat. 9am-noon and 2-6:30pm). This former Roman market town is known for its elegantly crafted pottery.

On your way back to Nice, try to stop at quaint **Cagnes-sur-Mer.** Get off the bus at the "Eglise" station, near the **tourist office** at 6, bd. Maréchal Juin (tel. 93 73 66 66 or 93 20 61 64). (Open Mon.-Sat. 8:45am-12:30pm and 1-7pm; in winter and spring 8:45-noon and 2:30-6:30pm.) Filling nine rooms of the house Renoir lived in from 1908-1919, the **Musée Renoir**, av. des Collettes (tel. 93 20 61 07), off av. des Tuilières contains works from the artist's "Cagnes period." (Open June-Oct. 15 Wed.-Mon. 10am-noon and 2-6pm; Nov.16-May Wed.-Mon. 2-5pm. Admission 20F, children 10F.) Cagnes's other attraction is the **Chateau-Musée des Cagnes,** Montée de la Bourgade (tel. 93 20 85 57), a 14th-century stronghold built after the Crusades to keep watch over both the sea and its own prisoners. At the top of the tower, 110m above sea level, there is a beautiful view of both the Alps and the coast from Cap d'Antibes to Cap Ferrat. (Open Wed.-Mon. Admission 5F, children 3F).

Another full and varied daytrip from Nice includes Villefranche-sur-Mer, St-Jean-Cap-Ferrat, and Beaulieu-sur-Mer. Villefranche and Beaulieu are on the rail line between Nice and Monaco (about every ½-hr., 10 min., 6F), and buses connect both of them to Cap-Ferrat. If you get off the train at Beaulieu, you can also make the 2km seaside walk to the Cap. St-Jean and Cap-Ferrat can also be reached by bus from Nice. (2 per hr. 8am-7:10pm, Sun. 11:30am and 7:15pm only; to St-Jean ½-hr., 10F; to Cap-Ferrat 11F.) On the way to St-Jean-Cap-Ferrat stands the **Fondation Ephrussi de Rothschild** (tel. 93 01 33 09), a pink Italianate villa built at the turn of the century to house the superb furniture and art collection of the Baroness de Rothschild. Works by Monet and Fragonard, Chinese vases, and Beauvais tapestries are complemented by spectacular gardens surrounding the villa. In 1991, additional 18th-century works will be added in rooms that have never been open to the public before. (Open July-Aug. Tues.-Sat. 10am-noon and 3-7pm, Sun. 3-7pm; Sept.-Oct. and Dec.-June Tues.-Sat. 10am-noon and 2-6pm, Sun. 2-6pm. Admission to museum and garden 25F, students 17F, garden only 10F. Admission for new rooms (*visite confidentiale*) an additional 15F, students 10F.) Also on the way to Cap-Ferrat, a little further than the museum, is St. Jean's **tourist office**, 59, av. Denis Séméria (tel. 93 76 08 90). Make a left at the museum; the office is about 300m up on the right. (Open Mon.-Fri. 9am-noon and 2-5:30pm). The **Zoo du Cap Ferrat** (tel. 93 76 04 98) is on bd. Général de Gaulle. (Open daily 9:30am-7pm, in winter and spring daily 9:30am-5:30pm. Admission 38F, children under 11 28F.) If you want to stay in Cap-Ferrat, try **Hôtel Bastide**, 3, rue Albert 1er (tel. 93 76 06 78), not far from the tourist office. (Doubles 180F, with shower and private toilet 230F)

The narrow streets and pastel houses of **Villefranche-sur-Mer** have attracted many writers, including Aldous Huxley and Katherine Mansfield. Trains run from Nice every ½-hour (6F). **Rue Obscure,** the oldest street in Villefranche and one of the most peculiar in France, was built in the 13th century. Its small, cramped houses huddle with their backs to the crescent-shaped bay full of sailboats. Jean Cocteau decorated the 14th-century **Chapelle St-Pierre,** quai Courbet, with boldly executed scenes from the life of St. Peter and the Camargue gypsies of Stes-Maries-de-la-Mer. (Open July-Sept. Sat.-Thurs. 9:30am-noon and 2:30-7pm; Oct.-Nov. 15 Sat.-Thurs. 9:30am-noon and 2-4:30pm; Dec. 15-March Sat.-Thurs. 9:30am-noon and 2:30-6pm; April-June Sat.-Thurs. 9:30am-noon and 2-6pm. Admission 10F.) The tourist office on Jardin François Binon (tel. 93 01 73 68) suggests excursions by foot, bus, or train to the small villages of the region. They do not make hotel reservations but will direct you to hotels or, for stays over a week, apartments. (Open June 15-Sept.15 9am-7pm daily; Sept. 16-June 14 Mon.-Sat. 9am-noon and 2-6pm.) There are two museums worth seeing, both located in the 16th-century **Citadelle.** The **Musée Volti** (tel. 93 76 61 00) displays the comtemporary art and sculpture of Villefranche resident Antoniucci Volti. The **Musée Goetz-Boumeester** (tel. 93 76 61 00) traces the works of Villefranche painter and sometime Surrealist Henri Goetz and his wife, Christine Boumeester. (Both open daily 10am-7pm; Oct.-June 10am-noon and 2-5pm. Free.)

Peaceful **Beaulieu**, also on the Nice-Monaco train line (every ½-hr., 6F) has relatively uncrowded gravel beaches and a relatively unpretentious casino (which may reopen in 1991). **Kérylos**, a seaside Greek villa, has been reconstructed with ivory-and-marble mosaics and frescoes. (Open July-Aug. Tues.-Sun. 2:30-6:30pm; Sept.-Oct. and Dec.-June Tues.-Sun. 2-6pm. Admission 18F, 10F students and children.) The **tourist office** on pl. de la Gare (tel. 93 01 02 21) makes hotel reservations for free. (Open Mon.-Fri. 9am-noon and 2:30-6pm, Sat.-Sun. 9am-noon.) The **Gare du Petit Train** (tel. 93 29 40 23), across from the *marché*, has a miniature "train" which goes from Beaulieu to St-Jean Cap-Ferrat every hour from 10am-6pm (in summer also from 9-11pm), with touristy historical info in French (15F one way, 25F round trip).

Next to Beaulieu on the train line, **Eze** is a run-of-the-mill seaside town in the shadow of an ancient château and fortified village. From the station you'll have a

45-minute climb up Chemin Friedrich Nietzsche, a foot path that is generally good for walking, but, in places, beyond evil. It was here that Zarathustra spake to the vacationing philosopher. The finest beach east of Antibes is unquestionably at **Cap d'Ail,** 20 minutes by train from Nice (every ½-hr., 10F). From the station walk down the stairs, under the tracks, and turn right. You'll find small, rocky coves to the east that are perfect for sunning or fishing but dangerous for swimming. A ½km walk west leads to pebbly *Plage de la Mala,* sheltered by cliffs; swimming is safe here. On the way to the beach, the **Relais International de la Jeunesse** on bd. de la Mer (tel. 93 78 18 58) is a glorious seaside youth hostel in an old villa. Men and women are housed in separate villas (60F), but but can stay together if they sleep in the 12-person tents with electric lights (50F). Breakfast is always included. As there's a midnight curfew (Fri.-Sat. 1am), don't stay here if you plan to gamble the night away at Monaco's casino. (Lockout 10am-5pm. Snack bar. Dinner 45F. Beer 6F, wine 10F.)

Monaco/Monte-Carlo

> *Shake off the shackles of this tyrant vice;*
> *Hear other calls than those of cards and dice;*
> *Be learn'd in nobler arts than cards of play;*
> *And other debts than those of honour pay.*
> *—David Garrick, The Gamester: Prologue*

The Monaco of legend glitters with majestic wealth and jet-set glamour. The Monaco of reality is clogged with unsightly high-rises and gaudy new hotels. Nevertheless, the sun, excitement, and liberating, self-indulgent atmosphere may eventually win over even the most reluctant visitors and moralistic critics. A tax-free haven for tennis players, Monaco proudly remains one of the last bastions of truly hideous conspicuous consumption.

Monaco is ruled by a hereditary Prince (now Rainier III, whose late wife American actress Grace Kelly is buried in the Monaco Cathedral), but there is not much to reign over. The *Monégasques* number only 5000, and their territory occupies less than 2 square km. The currency, electricity, and tap water are all French. In fact, stamps and tobacco are about all that this nominally independent principality does not sponge off France. This freeloading does not mean that state functions are not performed with comic self-importance. Whether through the zeal of its street cleaners or the pomp of the changing of its palace guard, Monaco is eager to prove and practice its statedom.

Orientation and Practical Information

Travelers should picture Monaco as a U-shape opening to the sea with the train station at the curved end. When you exit the station, go right on av. Prince Pierre for two blocks, left on av. du Port, and then left on quai Albert overlooking the harbor. Above you on the right sits the *quartier* of Monaco-Ville with its *vieille ville* and the Prince's palace. To the left of the port rises the fabled *quartier* of Monte-Carlo and its grand casino.

Tourist Office: 2a, bd. des Moulins (tel. 93 50 60 88), near the casino. Very helpful staff speaks English and makes reservations. An avalanche of maps and information. You can also call hotels from a special phone at the train station. Open Mon.-Sat. 9am-7pm, Sun. 10am-noon.

Budget Travel: Monaco Centre de la Jeunesse, 19, bd. Princesse Charlotte (tel. 93 15 29 29), at the corner of av. St. Michel. Actually a center for local students, but the English-speaking staff gladly helps foreigners. Information on camping, transportation, and odd jobs for those who lost it all at the casino. Open Jan.-July and Sept.-Dec. Mon.-Fri. 3-7pm.

Currency Exchange: Compagnie Monégasque de Change, parking des Pêcheurs (tel. 93 25 02 50), in the parking complex connected to the Musée de l'Océanographie. Commission only on French traveler's checks. Open daily 9am-7pm. Closed in Aug. and Dec. Another currency exchange inside the **train station.** Open daily 8:30am-noon and 2-4:30pm.

American Express: 35, bd. Princesse Charlotte (tel. 93 25 74 45). Mail and financial services. Open Mon.-Sat. 9am-6pm

Post Office: pl. Beaumarchais, Monte-Carlo. Monaco issues its own stamps, but unless you mail your postcards here, you'll have to start a stamp collection. **Telephones.** For **Poste Restante** specify Palais de la Scala, Monte-Carlo. **Branch office** across from the train station (tel. 93 30 10 14), with **telephones.** Both offices open Mon.-Fri., 8am-7pm, Sat. 8am-noon. **Postal Code:** MC 98000 Monaco.

Trains: av. Prince Pierre (tel. 93 87 50 50). Monaco lies on the St-Raphaël-Ventimiglia line with direct connections to: Nice (every ½-hr. 5:30am-11:07, 25 min., 14F); Antibes (every ½-hr. 5:30am-11:21pm, 45 min., 30F); Cannes (every ½-hr. 5:30am-11:21pm, 70 min., 35F). Less frequent service to other towns along the coast. To Menton (every ½-hr., 10 min., 6F). To and from Annot, Digne, and Lyon (4 per day, 26F). Information desk (English spoken) open daily 9am-6:45pm. Lockers 20F for 72 hr.

Buses: Buses to other cities leave from many locations. Buses to Nice, with stops at Cap d'Ail, Eze-sur-Mer, Beaulieu-sur-Mer, and Villefranche-sur-Mer (every hour Mon.-Sat. 6:30am-8:30pm, Sun 7:30am-8:30pm) leave from av. de la Costa, near bd. des Moulins and the tourist office. Buses to Menton (7:15am-8:15pm) leave from pl. des Moulins. For information on above buses call 93 85 61 81 or ask the tourist office. Buses to La Turbie and Italy leave from bd. des Moulins in front of the tourist office.

Public Transportation: tel. 93 50 62 41. Five routes link the entire hilly town every 10 min 7am-9pm. Bus #4 connects the train station to the Casino in Monte-Carlo. Tickets 6.50F.

Taxis: av. Prince Pierre (tel. 93 50 92 27) and 1 av. Henri Dunart (tel. 93 50 56 28). As usual, *very* expensive.

Bike and Moped Rental: Auto-Moto Garage, 7, rue de la Colle (tel. 93 30 24 61), near the station. Five-speed bikes 58F, mountain bikes 68F, deposit 1500F; mopeds 95F per day, deposit 1500F. Open Mon.-Fri. 8am-12:30pm and 2-7pm, Sat. 8am-noon.

English Bookstore: Scruples, 9, rue Princesse Caroline (tel. 93 50 43 52), near the train station. Fairly good selection of new books. Paperbacks 80F and up. *Let's Go: France* 241F. Open Mon.-Sat. 9:30am-noon and 1-7pm; Sept.-June 9:30am-noon and 2:30-7pm.

Hospital: Centre Hospitalier Princesse Grace, av. Pasteur (tel. 93 25 99 00).

Police: Tel. 93 30 42 46. Officers maintain a conspicuous presence around the casino. **Emergency,** tel. 17. **Lost and Found** at 3, rue Louis Notari (tel. 93 15 30 15).

Accommodations, Camping, and Food

Monaco is a nice place to visit, but you probably do not want (and can't afford) to sleep here. Most of the principality's lavish appeal can be soaked up in a day. Near the station, especially on rue de la Turbie, relative values can be unearthed. You might choose to exile yourself and go to **Beausoleil** (officially outside the borders of Monaco), a five-minute walk from Monte-Carlo, where hotels are slightly less expensive, especially along bd. du Général Leclerc. Wherever you go, reservations are essential from mid-June to August.

Centre de Jeunesse Princesse Stéphanie, 24 av. Prince Pierre (tel. 93 50 75 05), 100m up the hill from the train station. Built to accommodate the festival swarms of bedless youth, this otherwise excellent facility fails because it is only open as a hostel July 1-Oct. 1; the 40 beds are lotteried off at 2pm to the crowds who begin gathering at 10am. Only foreign students ages 16-26 (ID required) will be allowed to stay here. One-day max. stay. Open 7-10am and 2pm-12:30am. 45F per night. Breakfast included. Sheets 5-10F. No reservations.

Hôtel Cosmopolite, 4, rue de la Turbie (tel. 93 30 16 95), very near the train station. Homey and clean. Singles 120F, with shower 190F. Doubles 125-177F. Triples 200-320F. Showers 15F. Breakfast 26F.

Hôtel de France, 6, rue de la Turbie (tel. 93 30 24 64), near the train station. Small but elegant rooms. Kitchen and TV room. Ask for M. Dileau. Single 140F, with shower 220F. Double 190F, with shower 270F. Shower 15F. Breakfast 28F.

Hôtel Cosmopolite, 19 bd. du Général Leclerc (tel. 93 78 36 00), in Beausoleil. Airy, nicely decorated rooms. Singles with shower and TV 130F, with private toilet 165F. Doubles with private bathroom and TV 165-200F. Triples 280-300F. Breakfast 22F.

Hôtel Villa Boeri, 29, bd. du Général Leclerc (tel. 93 78 38 10), in Beausoleil. Owner, unlike *Let's Go* researchers, loves TVs: regular and cable in rooms and in the lobby, which is also inexplicably cluttered with pink parasols. Some rooms have balconies overlooking the sea; all are spotless. Doubles 200-290F. Triples 470F. Showers and breakfast included.

Hôtel Helvetia, 1bis, rue Grimaldi (tel. 93 30 21 71), on the way to Monte Carlo from the station. Costs a bit more, but worth it. Singles 192F, with shower 272F. Doubles 264F, with shower 384F. Triple with shower 491F. Breakfast included.

There are no campgrounds in Monaco, but there are spots between Roquebrune and Cap Martin, on the N7 toward Italy. **Point Accueil Jeunes de Beausoleil,** Quartier Fondivine (tel. 93 78 60 74), by rue Moyenne Corniche is open from June 15-Sept.30 and has only 20 spots. You *must* call in advance for reservations. (10F per night, 5 night maximum.) You can also camp in Menton (see Menton section) at **Municipal du Plateau St.-Michel** (tel. 93 35 81 23), or ask the tourist office about nearby sites.

Undistinguished but inexpensive sustenance lurks among trellises of plastic flowers near the station at **Le Biarritz,** 3, rue de la Turbie; the 35F, 55F and 75F *menus* reflect Italian influence. (Open daily noon-3pm and 6:30-10:30pm.) The **Pizza Grille** next door sells large pizzas for 35-50F and sandwiches for 13.50-20F. (Open daily 7:30am-11pm. Hours sometimes vary.) Also near the station, **Le Périgordin,** 4, rue de la Turbie (tel. 93 30 06 02), serves a 55F *menu* (lunch only, 72F for dinner) and French duck specialties in a refined atmosphere. The manager, Gérard Baigne, force-feeds ducks for three weeks in order to get a liver large enough for his special *pâté.* (Open Mon.-Sat. noon-2pm and 7:30-10:30pm.) **Garden Burger,** 22, rue Grimaldi, on the way to Monte-Carlo from the station offers "a good hamburger at a good price" (16F) and a wide variety of fast-food specialties. (Open Mon.-Sat. 10am-10pm.) For a late night snack, try the **Tip Top Snack Bar,** 11 av. des Spélugues, near the casino. (Sandwiches 23-32F, salads 24-60F, spaghetti 40F. Open nightly 8pm-6am.) Simple but elegant **L'Aurore,** 6 and 8, rue Princesse Marie de Lorraine, has Italian and *Monégasque menus* for 69F, 75F, and 103F. (Open daily 8am-5pm.) Picnickers should stop at the fruit and flower **market** at pl. d'Armes (open daily 6am-1pm), at the end of av. Prince Pierre or the supermarket, **Codectop,** 30, bd. Princesse Charlotte, near the corner of bd. des Moulins by the tourist office. (Open Mon.-Fri. 8:30am-12:15pm and 3-7:15pm, Sat. 8:30am-7:15pm.)

Sights and Entertainment

The resort which novelist Katherine Mansfield called "Real Hell, the cleanest, most polished place I've ever seen," is epitomized in its folly of a **Casino.** Surrounded by gardens overlooking the coast, the old casino building was designed by Charles Garnier and resembles his Paris Opera House. The interior, a shining paragon of 19th-century extravagance with red velvet curtains, gold and crystal chandeliers, and gilded ceilings, is worth visiting, even if you're not a gambler. Here Mata Hari once shot a Russian spy; here in 1891 the Englishman Charles Deville Wells broke the bank repeatedly and turned 10,000 gold francs into a million; and here Richard regaled Liz with the huge and rather vulgar diamond. Today, the rooms teem with backpackers and tourists. The slot machines open at noon, and the *salle américaine* (where blackjack, craps, and roulette require a 25F minimum bet) at 4pm; hardcore veterans don't arrive until after 10pm. Admission to the main room—or "kitchen"—is free (you must be over 21 and cannot wear shorts), but it costs 50F to enter the *salons privés,* where French games such as *chemin de fer* and *trente et quarante* begin daily at 3pm.

The casino also houses the sumptuous **Théâtre** (tel. 93 50 76 54), occasional stage to Sarah Bernhardt's smash-hit one-woman show and long-time venue of Diaghilev's Ballets-Russes. You can visit only by attending a ballet or opera performance; tickets cost 130-140F (students 70F), but here at least you are guaranteed a return for your money. Outside the theater, across the main lobby from the casino rooms, is an extensive display of costumes from the theater's opera productions.

For a taste of Monaco's new, democratic vulgarity, visit the **Loews American-style Casino,** a Vegas-style palace on av. Spelugues. As garish and brash as the older casino is elegant, the place has large Tarot-like cards on the walls and other random mythical decor. The tables open daily at 5pm (Free. Minimum age 21.)

Monaco-Ville is full of stately "sights." At 11:55am each day, you can see the changing of the guard outside the **Palais Princier,** a ritual which, given the size of the principality, resembles a Marx Brothers' routine. In their lily-white uniforms, the soldiers look about as functional as the palace cannons, strategically positioned to bombard the shopping district. Skip the uninteresting state apartments and the **Musée du Palais.** (Open daily 9:30am-6:20pm. Admission 25F.) You can have a much better time at the excellent **Musée de l'Océanographie,** av. St-Martin (tel. 93 15 36 00), directed by Jacques Cousteau (admission 45F, students with ID 23F). Only in Monaco could the first large room be devoted to pearl cultivation. (Open daily 9am-9pm; June and Sept. 9am-7pm; Oct.-May 9:30am-7pm.) Connected to this museum in parking des Pêcheurs is the new **Monte Carlo Story,** a creative, colorful 35 min. English film on Monaco's exotic history. (Mon.-Sat. every hour 10:30am-5:30pm. Admission 30F, students and ages over 65 18F, ages 6-14 14F.) The **Jardin Exotique** (tel. 93 30 33 65 or 66), with its devastating cactus collection, is privy to coastal views, as well as grottoes with stalagmites and stalactites. (Open June-Sept. 9am-7pm; Oct.-April 9am-noon and 2-6pm. Admission 29F, students 19F.)

The **Open Air Cinema,** on av. Princesse Grace (tel. 93 25 86 80) plays a different film (in English with French subtitles) each night at 9:30pm. Admission 30F. If you have to ask how much Monaco's indoor nighlife costs, you probably can't afford it.

Monaco hosts trapeze artists of the inward eye in May when the Grand Prix automobile race roars to a finish through its winding streets. The drama and excitement lie as much in the dynamics of the crowd as the race itself. The **Orchestre Philharmonique de Monte-Carlo** performs evening concerts in July and August at the Cours d'Honneur of the Palais Princier. (Admission 70-260F. Tickets available at the Atrium of the Casino de Monte-Carlo.) The royal family usually attends these concerts (program information available at the tourist office). One of the highlights of the summer season is the **Fireworks Festival,** an explosive international competition that lights up the sky in late July and early August. If for some reason you're in the area in winter, go to a night of **Festival International du Cirque,** which features the world's best circuses. A gala performance on the last night features the best acts from all the circuses (Jan. 31-Feb.4 1991). On February 30 of each leap year, the **Fête Lisa Monaco** honors the American Communist Party fundraiser whose career was destroyed by allegations of blood relationship to Prince Rainier and longtime ownership of an Hermès Grace Kelly bag. The dulcet strains of postfeminist pop fill the streets, where iced coffee and abstract nouns flow freely. For information on all annual events, call the **Comité des Fêtes** (tel. 93 30 80 04).

Menton

Bought by France in the 19th century, Menton (pop. 30,000) has done quite well for itself in the shadow of its neighbor and former owner Monaco. It is in this town, known for its tart lemons and Belle Epoque gentility, that those proverbial old gamblers who never die just fall asleep in sherbet-colored deck chairs. The snug embrace of green mountains and the intense heat (which residents claim is the most unrelenting in France) seems to have lulled this community of affluent retirees and their coiffed poodles into a permanent afternoon nap that not even summer clouds can interrupt. Follow rue de la Gare from the train station, turn right on av. Boyer until you reach the grandiose Palais d'Europe. Inside is the **tourist office**, 8, av. Boyer (tel. 93 57 57 00), with a refreshingly irreverent staff who will make reservations or direct you to available rooms. (Open June 15-Aug. 8am-8pm; Sept.-June 14 8:30am-noon and 2-6:30pm. English spoken).

Accommodations, Camping, and Food

Auberge de Jeunesse, (IYHF) plateau St-Michel (tel. 93 35 93 14). Follow rue de la Gare and cross under the train tracks at the bridge. Take the immediate first right up the hill, the second left onto rue des Terres Chaudes, and go up the 305 steps. Alternately, take the SNCF minibus that departs from the train station (7am-noon and 2-8pm, 20F for 1-2 people, each thereafter 8F.) A shipshape modern hostel. Spacious lounging area and soul-stirring view of Menton's bay more than make up for the elevator music. Be sure to call ahead; the place is often filled by groups. Open 5-11pm. Lockout 9:30am-5pm. Curfew 11pm. 51F per person (67F without an IYHF card); 47F in 8-person tents with pillows, beds, and electric lights. Breakfast included, dinner 38F. Wash and dry 35F. Required sleeping sheet 12F. No reservations. Open Jan. 16-Dec. 14.

Hôtel Mondial, 12, rue Partouneaux (tel. 93 35 74 18), around the corner from the tourist office. Clean rooms but a bit worn. Café downstairs. Fills up fast. Singles 110F. Doubles 130-203F. 1.50F tax per person per day. Breakfast 17F. Open Dec.-Oct. Office closed 1-5pm.

Hôtel Belgique, 1, av. de la Gare (tel. 93 35 72 66), near the train station. Small but clean rooms. Café downstairs. Singles 110F (small bed), 160F (big bed). Doubles 160-207F, with shower and private toilet 225F. Extra bed 60F. Breakfast 22F.

Le Terminus, pl. de la Gare (tel. 93 35 77 00), opposite the train station. Genial, English-speaking family welcomes you into their slightly frayed but satisfactory hotel. Singles and doubles 115F, with shower 175F. Extra beds 40F. Breakfast 22F. Showers included.

Hôtel Beauregard, 10, rue Albert 1er (tel. 93 35 74 08), behind and below the train station. A peach-painted wonder with a pretty garden in front. Cool, unpretentious Mme Erdmann keeps squeaky-clean rooms. Comfortable TV room. Singles and doubles 160F, with shower 210F. Triples with shower 300F. Breakfast 17F.

Hôtel Grimaldi, 7 bis, rue Partouneaux (tel. 93 28 30 30), around the corner from the tourist office. One of the best places in town. M. Palmar's rooms cost a bit more but are still a bargain. All have showers, color TV, carpeting, and a telephone. Singles 180F, with private toilet 200F. Doubles 225F, with private toilet 265F. Triple with private toilet 335F. 1.50 tax per person per day. Breakfast included.

Campground Municipal du Plateau St-Michel, by the hostel on route des Ciappes de Castellar (tel. 93 35 81 23), has Turkish toilets, hot water (except in July), a snack bar, and space for 516 campers. You need your own tent. (11F per person, 6F for children under 6 and dogs, 10F per tent. Cars 10F. Refrigerators 10F. Laundry service 30F. Open Mon.-Fri. 8am-noon and 3-8pm, Sat.-Sun. 8am-noon and 5-8pm.) **Fleur de Mai,** 67, route de Gorbio (tel. 93 57 22 36; 200 sites) provides tents for 200 campers. The site lies only 1.5km from a pool and tennis court. (1 or 2 campers and tent 52-73F, with car 63-83F. Hot showers 5.50F. Electricity 13F. Open April 1-Oct. 11 daily 8am-noon and 2-9pm).

Restaurant de la Poste, 1, impasse Bellecour, off rue Partouneaux offers a 4-course 55F *menu.* (Open Tues.-Sun. noon-2pm and sometimes 7-8:30pm.) **La Regence Cafeteria,** 23, rue Partouneaux, lacks atmosphere but offers large grilled steaks (35F), hot dogs (16F) and sandwiches (20F). (Open Mon.-Sat. 6:30am-9pm.) **Le Pub Snack Bar,** 10, rue Piéta, off of rue St. Michel, serves a mean lasagne (32F) in a room plastered with World Cup soccer pictures. (Open daily 7am-midnight.) Orphaned groceries languish on the shelves of the **Petit Marché Mentonnais,** 11, rue Partouneaux. (Open daily 8am-1pm and 3:30pm-8pm.)

Menton's modest **Casino du Soleil** at the end of av. Boyer, closed for the past two summers because of accounting irregularities, may reopen in 1991. Menton's prized possession is the **Musée Jean Cocteau,** quai Napoléon III (tel. 93 57 72 30), next to Vieux Port 18 and the *vieille ville* on promenade du Soleil. Best-known for his brilliant work in film and drama, Cocteau was also skilled in all the visual arts. Menton's 17th-century stronghold houses a representative collection of his work, which is rarely displayed elsewhere. (Open June 15-Sept.15 Wed.-Sun. 10am-noon and 3-6pm; Sept. 16-June 14 Wed.-Sun. 10am-noon and 2-6pm. Free.) Devoted Cocteau fans should also visit **La Salle des Mariages** in the Hôtel de Ville (tel. 93 57 87 87), a room the artist decorated like a Greek temple. (Open Mon.-Fri. 8:30am-12:30pm and 1:30-5pm. Admission 5F.) Across the street in the *vieille ville,* the **municipal market** displays quail, rabbit, goat, horse, cheese, fruits, and *pâtés.* (Open Tues.-Sun. 5am-1pm.) Rising above the *marché* is the bell tower of **Eglise St-Michel** (tel. 93 35 73 73), a fine 17th-century Baroque church with side chapels decorated by local artists. (Open Sun.-Fri. 10am-noon and 3-6pm, Sat. 3-6pm.)

In August, the **Festival de Musique** takes over the square in front of the church. September brings **piano recitals** to the **Théâtre du Palais de l'Europe.** (Tickets 30-220F for both events, available at the Palais de l'Europe, av. Boyer, tel. 93 35 82 22, or at the tourist office.) Every July, there is chorus music at the Théâtre du Palais (tickets 70-150F). To usher in the Mardi Gras, Menton devotes Sundays in early February to the **Fête Internationale du Citron.** (Feb. 16-March 3, 1991) This exaltation of the lemon includes a *Corso des Fruits d'Or* in which floats in various shapes and forms made of lemons are paraded through town. Considerably less inspiring is the town's pebbly, unremarkable, and lemon-free beach. You will find superior swimming and sunning along the rail line to the west. Near the Italian border, on av. St. Jacques Garavan, lies the **Jardin Botanique Exotique Menton** (tel. 93 35 86 72) and the **Musée National d'Histoire Naturelle.** (Both open May-Sept. Tues.-Sun. 10am-noon and 3-6pm; Feb.-April Tues.-Sun. 10am-noon and 2-5pm. Admission to both 10F.)

Corsica (Corse)

Known for centuries as the "Isle of Beauty," Corsica continues to live up to—and exceed—its reputation. Vineyards, twisting creeks, and *maquis* (scrub) cover the steep, craggy mountains of the interior, and along the jagged coastline white beaches line a placid, turquoise sea. Although industry and agribusiness have come to this most isolated of French *départements,* the air remains astonishingly clear and is bathed almost year-round by brilliant (and often scorching) sunshine. Travel here is an adventure unrivaled by sallies to other parts of France. Bus and train service along torturous mountain routes may be infrequent and inexpensive, but a relatively unspoiled paradise waits at the end of the line. Especially in the villages of the heartland, life is as robust and unadorned as the land itself. Although many Corsicans have emigrated since the first great wave in 1850, most of those who remain continue to live in the homes of their ancestors or uphold the tradition of returning to the small villages of their families on weekends. The island's contribution to the international vocabulary, *vendetta,* refers to the bloody family feuds that attempted to compensate for the Genoan occupiers' insufficient justice system.

Although a fierce streak of nationalism pervades the island, Corsica only knew independence for a brief 14 years. Attractive to would-be conquerors throughout the ages, the island has witnessed Greek, Roman, Pisan, Genoese, Saracen, and French invasions. Even today strategic 16th-century Genoese towers and *citadelles* dominate the hilly landscape, seeming to survey the Mediterranean for signs of attack. Genoa gained control of the island in 1347, when internal clan rivalry hobbled Corsican unification efforts. Despite internal unrest and external hostility, Genoa controlled the island for nearly four centuries. A series of uprisings in 1729 initiated the the Corsican War of Independence, otherwise known as the Forty Years' War. In 1755, the revered Pascal Paoli proclaimed the island an autonomous republic, created a university, and drafted a new constitution. The retreating Genoans ceded its protectorate to the French, who humiliated Paoli's army at Ponte Nuovo on May 8, 1969. Among the Corsican officers who quickly swore their allegiance to France was a certain Charles Bonaparte. On August 15, 1769, his second son, Napoleon, was born in Ajaccio.

However important they are economically, La Corse shrugs off its connections to the mainland. While most Corsicans speak French, they much prefer their own language, an unwritten Romance dialect related to Italian. Corsican was recently reinstituted in the public school system, a sign that the island, along with other French provinces, is gaining greater cultural autonomy. Referring to themselves proudly as Corsicans, some groups, notably the outlawed Front Libéral National Corse (whose initials adorn every graffiti-marked surface), continue to try to bomb their way to independence. Visitors are not in any real danger, as the bombs are carefully targeted at French officials.

It is best to visit Corsica in the off-season. Between June 14 and September, services are more widely available but prices soar. August 15, the nationally celebrated **Fête de l'Assomption** takes on special significance because it is also Napoleon's birthday. Every town on the island erupts with fireworks in favor of their ill-fated local hero. After most of the tourists leave in September, the weather is at its best and the Mediterranean waters their warmest.

Transportation

Air France and **Air Inter** fly to Bastia, Ajaccio, and Calvi from Paris (991F, with discount 541F), Nice (340F, with discount 238F), and Marseille (376F, with discount 276F). Discounts apply to people under 25 (students under 27) and senior citizens on several "blue flights" each week. Air France maintains offices at 3, bd. du Roi-Jérome, Ajaccio (tel. 95 21 00 61) and at 6, av. Emile Sari, Bastia (tel. 95

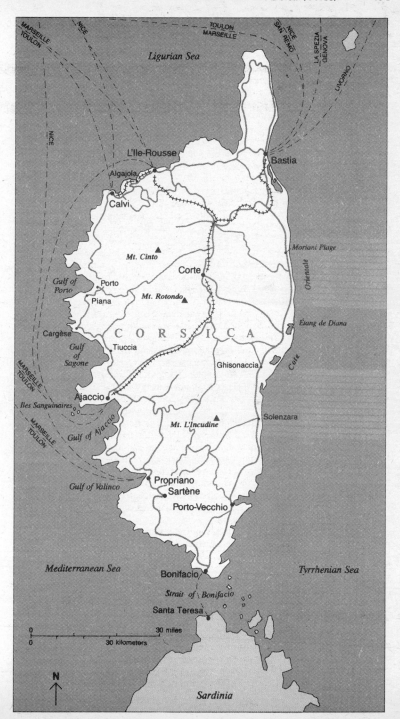

Ligurian Sea

MARSEILLE
TOULON

NICE

TOULON
MARSEILLE

SAN REMO

NICE

LA SPEZIA
GENOVA

LIVORNO

NICE

L'Ile-Rousse

Algajola

Bastia

Calvi

Mt. Cinto

Moriani Plage

Corte

Gulf of
Porto

Porto

Orientale

Piana

Mt. Rotondo

C O R S I C A

Étang de Diana

Cargèse

Gulf of
Sagone

Tiuccia

Ghisonaccia

Tavignano

Ajaccio

Iles Sanguinaires

Mt. L'Incudine

Solenzara

MARSEILLE
TOULON

Gulf of Ajaccio

MARSEILLE
TOULON

Gulf of Valinco

Propriano

Sartène

Porto-Vecchio

Mediterranean Sea

Tyrrhenian Sea

Bonifacio

Strait of Bonifacio

Santa Teresa

0   30 miles
0   30 kilometers

N

Sardinia

31 99 31). Air Inter's offices are at the airports in Ajaccio (tel. 95 21 63 06), Bastia (tel. 95 36 02 95), and Calvi (tel. 95 65 20 09). Telephone reservations are advisable and can be made at these numbers from 8am to 6pm daily.

The **Société National Maritime Corse Mediterranée (SNCM)** operates car ferries from Marseille, Toulon, and Nice on the continent to Bastia, Calvi, Ile Rousse, Ajaccio, and Propriano. Trips, many overnight, take six to 12 hours. About two boats per day travel to and from Corsica in off-season, and a few more cross the Mediterranean in summer each day. Don't depend on a boat connecting a given mainland city with a given Corsican city on the day that you want to leave. Call ahead to find out schedules, and always arrive at least ½-hr. before the departure. Tickets to the island from Marseille and Toulon cost 225F, from Nice 200F. People under 25 are eligible for a 30% reduction on journeys to Nice. During the "blue period" (about Sept. 15-June 15), people under 25 receive a 30% discount and those over 60 a 50% reduction. SNCM has offices in Ajaccio (quai l'Herminier, tel. 95 21 90 70), Bastia (Nouveau Port, tel. 95 31 36 63), Calvi (quai Landry, tel. 95 65 01 38), and Ile Rousse (av. J-Calizi, tel. 95 60 09 56). On the mainland, SNCM offices are located in Nice (quai du Commerce, tel. 93 13 66 66), Marseille (61, bd. des Dames, tel. 91 56 80 20), and Toulon (21, av. de l'Infanterie de Marine, tel. 94 41 25 76). **Corsica Ferries** provides crossings between the Italian ports of Livorno, Genova, and La Spezia (160-180F) and Bastia. From mid-May to mid-September, ferries run from Genova to Ajaccio and Calvi (180F). Corsica Ferries has offices in Bastia (5bis, rue Chanoine Leschi, tel. 95 31 18 09), Calvi (Port de Commerce, tel. 95 65 10 84) and Ajaccio (Port de Commerce, tel. 95 51 06 39). The central reservation center is in the Bastia office. In addition, **NAV.AR.MA. Lines** run to Bastia from La Spezia, Livorno, Piombino, and Porto San Stefano on the Italian mainland (140F); they also connect Bonifacio to Sardinia (60F). Call the office in Bonifacio (port de Bonifacio, tel. 95 73 00 29) for reservations to Sardinia.

Train service in Corsica is slow and limited. Four trains per day travel each way between Bastia and Ajaccio (4 hr., 97F) via Corte and Ponte Leccia; two per day run between Bastia and Calvi (3½ hr., 74F) via Ponte Leccia; and two per day connect Ajaccio and Calvi (5 hr., 113F) via Corte and Ponte Leccia. A special service connects Calvi and Ile Rousse (May to mid-Sept. 10 per day, 50 min., 21F). The Corsican rail system accepts no passes except InterRail (50% off) and does not connect with Bonifacio or Porto-Vecchio. **Buses** connect the island's major towns but are neither cheaper nor more frequent than trains. The rough route from Bastia to Ajaccio, for example, is served only twice per day in summer (3½ hr., 90F). Some exceptionally patient people have hitched short rides. Those who write "Je vous offre l'essence" (I will pay for gas) on a sign have better luck. Ten liters (about 55F) usually covers 100km on flat roads.

Renting a car is convenient but costs 120-250F per day for the least expensive models, plus 1.37-3.30F per km. Weekly rentals (from 1700F) usually include unlimited free milage. Bicycle rentals are rare and relatively expensive (about 70-100F per day with 1500F deposit). Mopeds (*mobylettes*) run about 150F per day (with 2500F deposit). Note that narrow, curving mountain roads make biking difficult and dangerous. Get a Michelin map which marks the roads less traveled. Even drivers should be careful; remember to honk before turning on the mountain roads. Summer crowds can make driving painfully slow. (The bus from Ajaccio to Bonifacio, for example, takes 4 hr. to cover 145km.) Gas is cheaper here than on the mainland and in Italy, but gas stations are few and far between. If you do run out of gas, call the local **Brigade de Gendarmerie.**

The **Grande Randonnée-20,** a superb 15- to 21-day trail, takes hikers high into the mountainous interior. About 10,000 people each year follow the trail from one end of the island to the other, and many hike shorter segments. Do not tackle this trail alone, and be prepared for cold, snowy weather, even in early summer. For further information, contact the **Comité National des Sentiers de Grande Randonée,** 8, av. Marceau, 75008 Paris (tel. 16 1 47 23 62 32), or **Parc Naturel Régional de la Corse,** BP 417, 20184 Ajaccio Cédex (tel. 95 21 56 54).

One tip for finding addresses: since the numbering and nomenclature in Corsica can be vague, you're better off asking for directions than relying on a map.

Accommodations, Camping, and Food

Food and hotel prices in Corsica are about 30% higher than on the mainland. Few inexpensive hotels exist, and all accommodations fill up early in the morning in July and August. However, reservations for July and August can be made as late as June. Campgrounds lie close to most major cities, and many rent tents. The government ban on unofficial camping is strictly enforced in most areas. Be aware of the frequent, spontaneous brushfires before bedding down in the *maquis*, even legally. Before tackling the Grande Randonnée-20, get a list of *gîtes d'étape* (about 40F per night) at any park office, or write to the Parc Naturel Régional de la Corse (see above). The beds at the *gîtes* fill on a first-come, first-served basis, but latecomers can usually pitch a tent unofficially. Ask for a list of *auberges de jeunesse* at any tourist office or hostel. There are about 30 hostels on Corsica, but most are inland and far from the major towns. You rarely, if ever, need a hostel card to stay at one, and most hostels have no age restrictions. Although reservations are often not accepted, it's a good idea to call ahead in July and August.

Corsican cuisine is hearty, fresh, fatty, and pungent. Seafood is excellent but expensive along the coast; try *calamar* (squid), *langouste* (lobster), *gambas* (prawns), or *moules* (mussels). In fall and winter you can order *nacres* (pink-shelled mollusks) and *oursins* (sea urchins). Other delicacies include *pâté de merle* (blackbird *pâté*), *saucisson* (pork sausages), *truite* (river trout), and *sanglier* (wild boar). Excellent cheeses include *brucciu* and *chèvre*, both white cheeses made from goat's milk which keep without refrigeration. Corsican *menus* are usually expensive (90-100F); grocery stores provide a more affordable taste of Corsica.

Fortunately, the heady, flavorful Corsican wines are as inexpensive as their cousins on the mainland (10-15F per bottle in a market). Tourist offices usually have leaflets on local vineyards open to visitors. The sweet *Muscat* and almost any label from *Sartène*, as well as several potent *eaux de vie* flavored with Corsican berries are particularly interesting. The unofficial official drink here, as in Provence, is *pastis*, a wickedly strong brew flavored with anise and imbibed at all hours.

Ajaccio

Despite its growing congestion and size, Ajaccio (pronounced ah-JACKS-ee-oh; pop. 60,000) still has the air of a small provincial town where old people pass the time in quiet cafés or play *boules* in the dusty squares. Although half the streets bear the Bonaparte name and souvenir shacks peddle dishtowels emblazoned with Napoleon's face, most locals seem uninterested in the legacy of "the little corporal." Instead, the younger inhabitants focus on attracting the industries, particularly aeronautics, which diversify their tourist-dependant economy.

Orientation and Practical Information

Ten hours by boat from the mainland, Ajaccio lies on the western coast, about 80km north of Bonifacio. Relatively frequent bus and train connections make this centrally located city an ideal place to begin your exploration of the island.

Cours Napoléon, which runs from pl. de Gaulle (formerly pl. du Diamant) to the train station, contains most of the city's services. The pedestrian **rue Fesch** starts at pl. Maréchal Foch (formerly pl. des Palmiers) and runs parallel to cours Napoléon. It is a livelier street, with smaller, more interesting stores and some restaurants. The *vieille ville* is bound by pl. Foch, pl. de Gaulle, and the Citadelle.

From the ferry dock on quai l'Herminier, bear left and walk toward the *citadelle* to pl. Foch and the tourist office. To reach cours Napoléon, walk through the *place* and up av. du 1er Consul. Avoid visiting Ajaccio on a Sunday, when everything is closed.

Tourist Office: (tel. 95 21 40 87), Hôtel de Ville, pl. Maréchal Foch. Does not make hotel reservations, but will tell you where there's room. Well-stocked with pamphlets listing all of the island's hostels, campsites, and hotels, as well as bus and boat excursion schedules. Pick up their excellent map and *Corsica . . . The Holiday Island!* a good brochure with practical information. English spoken. Open daily June 15-Sept. 15. 8:30am-10pm; Sept. 16-June 14 Mon.-Sat. 8:30am-6pm.

Currency Exchange: Decent rates offered at the **bus station** (tel. 95 51 23 43) and the **airport** (tel. 95 20 13 48). Open daily July-Aug. 7am-8pm; Sept.-June 9am-noon and 3-5pm.

Post Office: (tel. 95 21 41 78), on cours Napoléon at rue Ottavy. **Telephones** downstairs. Open Mon.-Fri. 8am-6:30pm, Sat. 8am-noon. **Postal Code:** 20000.

Flights: Campo dell'Oro (tel. 95 21 03 64), 7km away. Take bus #1 ("Ricanto") from cours Napoléon (every hour 7am-7pm; 13F). To: Nice (2-3 per day, 336F, 232F with discount); Marseille (2-3 per day, 376F, 266F with discount); Paris (5-6 per day, 991F, 541F with discount). Discounts apply during "blue" periods for students under 27, families, and people 60 and over. For information, call **Air France,** 3, bd. du Roi-Jérôme (tel. 95 21 00 61) or **Air Inter** (tel. 95 25 63 06), at the airport. Additional flights to London, Lisbon, Geneva, Brussels, and Amsterdam.

Trains: rue Jean-Jérôme Levie (tel. 95 23 11 03), between cours Napoléon and bd. Sampiero. To: Corte (4 per day, 2½ hr., 52F); Calvi (2 per day, 5 hr., change in Ponte Leccia, 113F); Ile Rousse (2 per day, 4½ hr., 100F); Bastia (4 per day, 4 hr., 97F). Open daily 6am-8pm.

Buses: (tel. 95 21 28 01), on quai l'Herminier, part of the Gare Maritime. **Ollandini** (tel. 95 21 06 30) offers regular bus service. Open Mon.-Sat. 7-8:30am and 2-6:30pm; July-Aug. 7am-6:30pm. To: Bonifacio (Mon.-Sat. 2 per day, 4 hr., 98F); Calvi (July 1-Sept. 15 2 per day, 10 hr. with a 3½-hr. stopover in Porto; Sept. 16-June 30 1 per day, 10 hr. with a stopover in Ponte-Leccia, 100F); Propriano (Mon.-Sat. 2 per day, 2 hr., 46F); Sartène (Mon.-Sat. 2 per day, 2 hr., 54F); Porto-Vecchio (Mon.-Sat. 2 per day, 4 hr., 98F); Corte (2 per day, 2 hr., 49F); Bastia via Corte (Mon.-Sat. 2 per day, 3½ hr., 90F). 30% discount to students and people over 60. 5F luggage charge. The only other regular service is offered by **Autocars S.A.I.B.,** 6, pl. de Gaulle (tel. 95 22 41 99). To: Porto (Mon.-Sat. 2 per day, 3hr., 55F).

Several firms organize excursions from July 15 to Sept. 15. Ollandini is the agent for SNCF tours, 16, pl. Maréchal Foch (tel. 95 21 14 08). To: Bonifacio (130F); Calvi (150F); Filitosa (a prehistoric site; 100F); and other sites. **Autocars Roger Ceccaldi** (tel. 95 22 50 34) runs to the Calanche de Piana on Tues. (120F). **Autocars Arrighi** (tel. 95 22 50 34) makes similar trips as well as going to Soccia via Tiuccia, Sagone end Vico.

Public Transportation: TCA buses (tel. 95 50 04 30), run daily on the hour from 7am-7pm. Take bus #1 from pl. de Gaulle to the train station and airport (13F) or down the cours Napoléon (6.50F). #5 from av. Dr. Ramaroni stops at Marinella and the beaches on the way to the Iles Sanguinaires (9.50F).

Ferries: (SNCM), quai l'Herminier (tel. 95 21 90 70), across from the bus station. Toulon and Marseille 220F, Nice 200F. During the "blue period," for those under 25 30% reduction, over 60 60% reduction. Two boats usually leave each day for one of several mainland cities. Check the schedules carefully or you may be stranded. Open Mon.-Sat. 8am-noon and 2-6pm.

Taxis: pl. de Gaulle (tel. 95 21 00 87). 24 hrs.

Car Rental: Locafab, at the airport (tel. 95 22 76 11). 122F per day plus 1.37F per km. Weekly rentals with unlimited mileage 1685F. Deposit 1500-2000F. Driver must be 23. **Balesi,** 5, rue Stéphanopoli (tel. 95 21 08 11). From 230F per day plus 3.33F per km. Drivers must be 21.

Bike Rental: Corsica Loisirs, 3, montée St. Jean (tel. 95 20 22 42), about 6 blocks past the train station and left off the cours Napoléon. In July and August, a second location on the quai de la Citadelle (tel. 95 21 49 84). Mountain bikes 100F per day with 1500F deposit. Mopeds 150F per day with 2500F deposit.

Hiking Information: Parc Naturel Régional, rue Général Fiorella (tel. 95 21 56 54). Maps for the Grande Randonnée-20 and other mountain trails, as well as information on shelters and trail conditions. Open Mon.-Fri. 8:30am-noon and 2-6:30pm.

Laundromat: rue Maréchal Ornano. Wash 34F; dry 50F. All coins except centimes and new, debased, 10F pieces. Open daily 7am-9pm.

Hospital: av. Napoléon III (tel. 95 21 90 90).

Medical Emergency: Tel. 95 21 50 50.

Police: Tel. 95 23 20 36. **Emergency,** tel. 17.

Accommodations and Camping

Hotels in Ajaccio are more numerous and pleasant than in most Corsican towns, but you can still expect to pay as much for mediocre lodgings here as you would for a plush den on the mainland. Call ahead to make reservations for July and August.

Hôtel du Palais, 5, av. Beverini (tel. 95 23 36 42), off cours Napoléon and 5 min. from the station. Courteous owner keeps a tidy 11-room hotel. Singles with shower 140F. Doubles with large bed and shower 150F; with twin beds 160F.

Hôtel Colomba, 8, av. de Paris (tel. 95 21 12 66). A small hotel in the center of town, near pl. de Gaulle. Three flights up, but pleasant rooms. Some rooms have a view of the gulf. Singles with shower 130F. Doubles and triples with shower 160F.

Hôtel Bonaparte, 1-2, rue Etienne-Conti (tel. 95 21 44 19). Neat, small rooms with a view of the port. June-Sept. singles with shower 194F, doubles with shower 248F. March-May and Oct. to mid-Nov. singles with shower 172F, doubles with shower 204F. Breakfast included.

Camping: Barbicaja (tel. 95 52 01 17), 3km away. The closest to town. Take bus #5 from av. Docteur Ramaroni just past pl. de Gaulle (last bus at 7pm). 26F per person, 10F per tent. Open all year. **U Prunelli,** tel. 95 25 19 23. Near the bridge of Pisciatello, next to Porticcio, which is accessible by ferries from Ajaccio (every ½-hr., round-trip 40F) and by bus (tel. 95 25 40 37). Friendly and cheerful. 19.50F per person, 7F per tent. Other campgrounds are more than 10km away. Ask the tourist office for a list.

Food

The morning **market** on bd. Roi Jérôme and in pl. César Campinchi behind the tourist office will fill your picnic basket (8am-noon). Pizzerias congregate in the *rues piétonnes* off pl. Foch towards the *Citadelle* (35-50F). At **L'Escale,** on the pl. Foch, the apéritif is free.

Le Petit Vatel, rue des Halles, near the Hôtel Bonaparte. Enjoy a 4-course meal (58F) outside under the canopy. Try the *brochette*. Open daily noon-2pm and 7-10:30pm.

Les Liserons, 50, cours Napoléon. The best deal in Ajaccio is hidden on the third floor. Simple 35F *menu* includes wine. Friendly owners like young people. Open daily noon-2pm and 7-10:30pm.

L'Artisanat, rue de la Porte, in a cobbled alley off pl. Foch towards the cours Napoléon. Spanish owner offers Corsican fish specialties from 65F. Eat in the garden. Open noon-2pm and 7-11pm.

La Serre, 91, cours Napoléon, past the train station. Cheery, stylish cafeteria. Hot entrees from 35F. Salads 20F. Complete the meal with chocolate mousse (13F). Open 11:30am-2:30pm and 7-11pm.

Chez Paulo, 7, rue Roi-de-Rome. For wealthy night owls. Munch on Corsican specialties (90F) and wait for sunrise. Open 7:30pm-dawn.

Sights and Entertainment

Modestly tucked away in the *vieille ville,* between rue Bonaparte and rue Roi-de-Rome, the birthplace and childhood home of Napoléon, the **Musée National de la Maison Bonaparte,** is well worth a visit. Ironically, this 18th-century house briefly sheltered Hudson Lowe, Napoléon's jailer on St. Helena. (Open June-Sept. Mon. 2-6pm, Tues.-Fri. 9am-noon and 2-6pm, Sat. 9am-noon; Oct.-May Mon. 2-5pm, Tues.-Fri. 10am-noon and 2-5pm, Sat. 10am-noon. Admission 16F, under 26 and over 60 8F.) On the second floor of the *hôtel de ville,* next to the tourist office, the **Salon Napoléonien** (tel. 95 21 90 15) offers a quick summary of Napoléon's accomplishments through a collection of commemorative coins. (Open Sept.-May,

Mon.-Sat. 9am-noon and 2-5pm, June-Aug. 9am-noon and 2:30-5:30pm. Admission 2F.) The recently renovated **Chapelle Impériale,** rue Fesch, is the final resting place of most of the Bonaparte family. (Open April-Sept. daily 8:30am-noon and 2-6:30pm. Free.)

Next to the Chapelle stands the **Palais Fesch,** which houses works by 15th- and 16th-century Italian masters; check for hours at the tourist office. The newest addition to Ajaccio's collection of museums is the **Musée à Bandera,** 1, av. Général Levie (tel. 95 51 07 34). Friendly guides will show you through five rooms of mostly military memorabilia tracing Corsican history from 6000 BC. (Open June-Aug. Mon.-Sat. 10am-noon and 3-7pm; Sept.-May. Wed.-Fri. 10am-noon and 2-6pm. Admission 15F, students 5F.) The **Musée du Capitellu,** opposite the *citadelle* at 18, bd. Danielle Casanova (tel. 95 21 50 57), maroons the work of contemporary artists among paintings and relics of important families. (Open Mon.-Sat. 10am-noon and 3-7pm. Admission 20F.)

Southwest of Ajaccio at the mouth of the gulf, the **Iles Sanguinaires** (the Bloody Islands) bathe in a scarlet glow at sunset. **Bateau des Iles** (tel. 95 23 22 16) and **La Silène** (tel. 95 51 05 56) run daily excursions from quai de la Citadelle (late May to mid-Sept., 75F). Call for reservations. La Silène also runs excursions to Porto and Girolato (290F) and Bonifacio (260F).

Visible from the excursion boats, the Genoese **Tour de la Parata** can also be reached by the hourly bus #5 from av. Dr. Ramaroni (7am-7pm; 9.50F). This bus also stops at numerous beaches along the way. On the other side of the bay, the sandy beaches in **Porticcio** are wide but crowded. Shuttle boats leave for this resort from the quai de la Citadelle every half-hour until 7pm (40F). In front of the airport, **Tahiti-plage** is long, relatively empty, and easily accessible via bus #1, which runs on the hour from pl. Charles de Gaulle (7am-7pm, 13F).

Most of Ajaccio's clubs and discos are on the route des Sanguinaires. Unfortunately, there is no public transportation after 7pm. If you do go, remember that most of these clubs open only on weekend nights and are usually full of lonely men nursing their martinis. Lively late-night cafés along the quai de la Citadelle provide a more comfortable option, especially for single women. High stakes, elegance, and glamour are absent at Ajaccio's **Casino,** bd. Lantivy (tel. 95 21 41 14; open until 5am).

Ajaccio to Calvi

Don't count on the bus ride north from Ajaccio to Calvi as a time to catch up on sleep. Both the spectacular scenery and the treacherous road will keep you awake. About 25km from Ajaccio lies the Golfe de Sagone. To enjoy some of Corsica's finest beaches, ask the bus driver to let you out 3km before **Tiuccia,** at the **Camping Le Calcatoggia** (tel. 95 52 28 31), a shady site open from May to August. (17F per person, 16F per tent.) **Cargèse,** at the end of the Golfe de Sagone, is a small Greek Orthodox community built into the cliffs. The **tourist office** (tel. 95 26 41 31; open Mon.-Sat. 8:30am-noon and 5-7pm) can provide a list of hotels. You can spend the night at the **Hôtel de France** (tel. 95 26 41 07; doubles 120F, triples 135F, showers included; open May-Oct.). Plage de Pero and its Genoese tower lie 1km north of the village.

Seventy km north of Ajaccio, **Piana's** quiet streets and gardens rest atop granite cliffs. This tiny town has no tourist office; ask anyone for directions to the **Hotel Mare e Monti** (tel. 95 27 82 14) where doubles run 180F (190F with a view). Be sure to make reservations in July and August. (Open April-Nov.) The **Calanches de Piana** lie one km along the road to Porto. Well-marked paths cross this park where natural forces have carved forms, like a dog's head, out of the stone. Early morning visitors may catch a glimpse of the rare African fish-eagle; this area is its only known European habitat.

The summer Ollandini bus between Calvi and Ajaccio usually stops in **Porto** (pop. 150) for about 3½ hours—just long enough for the driver to steady his nerves and for riders to rest on the beach beneath the red cliffs. The Porto **tourist office,** up the main road leaving the port (tel. 95 26 10 55), can help with camping and transportation and provide a list of *gîtes d'étape* (about 40F per night) in the area. Before mid-July, hotels are reasonable and easy to come by. The first two hotels down from the bus stop—the **Hôtel Bon Accueil** (tel. 95 26 12 10) and the **Hôtel Beau Séjour** (tel. 95 26 12 11)—are the most affordable. (Singles 100-150F. Doubles 130-200F.) In addition, a 26-bed **hostel** remains open all year in **Ota,** 3km from Porto (45F). **Autocars S.A.I.B.** runs two buses each day from Porto. Many hitch-hikers find the journey along this short stretch relatively easy. **Camping Les Oliviers** (tel. 95 26 14 49) is a two-minute walk outside of town in the direction of Ajaccio. (23F per person, 8.50F per tent. Open Easter-Oct. 31.) Make reservations if you plan to arrive at the end of July or August. The camp office rents bikes (60F per day) and mountain bikes (70F per day). At the top of the hill, **Le Pub** serves pizzas (35-40F) and salads (20-30F) from noon to midnight. (Open May-Oct.) **Le Belve-dere** offers great *crêpes* (35-50F) on a terrace overlooking the beach. (Open April-Oct. noon-2:30pm and 7-11:30pm.)

The Hôtel Monte Russo sells tickets for **Alpana Revellata** excursions to Girolata (tel. 95 26 17 10; May-Sept. 2 per day, 5 hr., 120F). Accessible only by boat or on foot, this sheltered part of the bay enjoys a ban on hunting, fishing, and building. The mountainous countryside is an osprey sanctuary. Alpana Revellata also runs cruises past the Calanche de Piana (2 hr., 80F).

Hitchhiking along the coastal route can be as slow and uncertain as waiting for a decent Queen album. It's probably best to make it a two-day trip. Slow buses leave Ajaccio for Calvi and return daily, but you won't have time to stop at the attractive beaches and small villages along the way if you plan on getting to Calvi the same day. **Cars Ollandini** (tel. 95 21 06 30) leaves Ajaccio and Calvi at 8am and arrives at 6pm (97F). **S.A.I.B.** (tel. 95 22 41 99) runs buses as far as Porto (May 15-Oct. 15 at 7:20am and 3:30pm, 55F). **Autocars Arrighi** (tel. 95 22 50 34) runs inland to the village of **Vico** (Mon.-Sat., 1 hr., 30F); there's a year-round **youth hostel** (tel. 95 26 60 55; 27F per person) in the Couvent St-François. Ask for Frère Martin. The bus continues to Soccia, a 1½-hour walk from the Lac de Creno. (Mon.-Sat. 1 afternoon bus to Tiuccia, Sagone, Vico, and Soccio. Returns the following morning.)

Calvi

Frequented by many French *vedettes* (stars) and hordes of others, Calvi is one resort which knows how to exploit its beauty without spoiling it. The population balloons from 3500 to 60,000 in July and August, as tourists arrive to roam the white beaches and peer into the well-preserved Genoan *citadelle*. People still living within this fortification cling to the dubious belief that Christopher Columbus was born here in 1451. Take refuge from the sun and the crowds in the **Oratoire Ste-Antoine,** a 15th-century building that is now a museum of ancient and medieval religious art.

Orientation and Practical Information

Calvi lies on the northwest corner of the island, about 200km from Ajaccio. **Avenue de la République** runs parallel to the port and leads from the train station to the tourist office next door, and then on to the citadel.

Tourist Office: on pl. de la Gare (tel. 95 65 16 67), immediately to the right as you leave the train station. Maps, hotel lists, and information on trains and excursions. Will not make hotel reservations, but will tell you where there's room. Has a list of rooms in private homes. English spoken. Open Mon.-Sat. 9:30am-noon and 3-6:30pm; Oct.-May Mon.-Fri. 9am-noon. For information, write to **Office Municipal du Tourisme de la Ville de Calvi,** Port de Plaisance, 20260 Calvi.

Currency Exchange: Accommodations and restaurants in Calvi will lighten your wallet considerably, but you can lose your money just as easily by exchanging it at banks. **Credit Agricole** on bd. Wilson charges a 20F fee. A change booth on pl. Porteuse d'Eau (turn right when leaving the station) is open daily 8:30am-8pm but has miserable rates.

Post Office: bd. Wilson (open Mon.-Fri. 8am-noon and 2-6pm.; Sat. 8am-noon). **Currency exchange** here. **Postal Code:** 20260.

Trains: pl. de la Gare (tel. 95 65 00 61). To: Bastia (2 per day, 3 hr., 74F); Corte (2 per day, 3 hr., change at Ponte-Leccia, 62F); Ajaccio (2 per day, 5 hr., 113F). Special trains to Ile Rousse run every hour May 12-Sept. 10 (50 min., 50F). Open 6am-8pm.

Buses: Ollandini, 6, av. de la République (tel. 95 65 06 74), near the youth hostel. To: Bastia (June-Aug. 2 per day, 2½ hr., Sept.-May 1 per day); Ajaccio (2 per day, change in Ponte-Leccia, 90F); Ile Rousse (2 per day, ½ hr.). Buses run daily, Sept. 15-June only Mon.-Sat. **Autocars-S.A.I.B.** (tel. 95 21 53 74) also runs buses to Porto (1 per day, 2½ hr., 55F) and Ajaccio (10 hr., 110F).

Ferries: Agence Tramar, quai Adolphe Landry (tel. 95 65 01 38). Handles SNCM boat trips to mainland France. Call for details. Open Mon.-Fri. 9-11:30am and 2-5:30pm, Sat. 9-11:30am. **Corsica Ferries** (tel. 95 65 10 84), next to the SNCM booth on quai de Commerce. Sails for Savona in northern Italy (early June to mid-Sept. approximately 3 per week, 5½ hr.). Open Mon.-Fri. 9am-noon and 2-6pm.

Taxi: (tel. 95 65 03 10), next to the train station on av. de la République. 24 hrs., but rates go up after 8pm.

Bike and Moped Rental: Garage Ambrosini, 4, Villas St. Antoine (tel. 95 65 02 13) near the pl. Bel Ombra. Bikes 40F per ½-day, 65F per day, deposit 1500F; mopeds 100F per ½-day, 150F per day, deposit 2000F. Ages 18 and over only.

Police: Emergency, tel. 17.

Accommodations, Camping, and Food

The prices in Calvi rise between June 1 and September 30. Often full of families, the hostel and the campgrounds are the only real options for budget travelers.

BVJ Corsotel, av. de la République (tel. 95 65 14 15). Enthusiastic owners turn this 120-bed hostel into a bustling "youth center." Rooms for 2-8 people. No curfew or lockout. Reception open late May-Sept. 6am-1pm and 5-10pm, March-May and Oct. 7am-1pm and 5-10pm. 85F. Huge breakfast included. Open late March to Oct. 31. Reservations are only accepted for week-long stays in July and August. Arrive early during the season.

Hôtel Laeticia, 5, rue Joffre (tel. 95 65 05 55). Seven clean, small rooms. Doubles with shower 175F. Open June 1-Sept. 30. Make reservations.

Hôtel du Centre, 14, rue d'Alsace (tel. 95 65 02 01). Pleasant rooms. Doubles with shower July 220F, June and Sept. 200F, August 240F.

Meublé de la Mer, 18, rue Clémenceau (tel. 95 65 18 70). On the third floor overlooking the port. Doubles with a view 240F July-Aug., 180F in June and Sept.

Camping: La Clé des Champs, tel. 95 65 00 86. Follow the road from the train station to Ile Rousse and watch for the sign on your right (15-min. walk). Or get off the train at the last stop before Calvi and cross the road to Ile Rousse (5 min.). Clean with lots of shade. 17F per person (July-Aug. 16F per person), 7F per tent. Tent rental 20F. Many other campgrounds at the entrance to the town and along the coast. Take the train to Ile Rousse or follow the road to find them. Open May-Oct.

Pick up supplies at the **market** near the church (Tues.-Sat. 8am-noon). While the restaurants along the port are expensive, the old pedestrian streets above the port are filled with moderately priced restaurants with outdoor seating. **Le Marly,** near the hostel on the av. de la République, offers Corsican entrées and 4-course *menus* (60-70F) all year. On the impasse bd. Wilson, **U Fournu** serves moderately priced fish dishes (65-70F) on a pleasant terrace. The least expensive restaurant on the quai Landry is **Cappucino.** Watch the boats while munching on pizza (35-50F). Most of Calvi's **clubs** are prohibitively expensive, so spend the evening on the lively waterfront. Cafés and bars stay open into the wee hours, and, like the restaurants, change ownership and close down frequently. You can try **La Camargue** (tel. 95

65 08 70), which runs a free shuttle service after 8pm. (Just call them.) Ask about the reputations of other clubs before you go; some are notorious hang-outs for off-duty Legionnaires.

Near Calvi

In 1758, Pasquale Paoli built **Ile Rousse** to compete with Calvi, which the agitator for an independent Corsica wanted to punish for its allegiance to Genoa. The stretch of coastline between the two famous rivals is among the most heavily touristed on the island, luring mostly middle-aged crowds with its powdery white sand and calm, shallow water. Shop for picnic supplies at the morning market off pl. Paoli from 8am-noon. **La Cave** is the least expensive restaurant on pl. Paoli, serving a traditional French *menu* (65F) and wine. A train covers the coast between Calvi and Ile Rousse (June to mid-Sept. 10 per day, May and mid-Sept. to Oct. 5 per day, Nov.-April 2 per day; 50 min.) The line is divided into three sections, at 7F per section; you can save money by purchasing a *carnet* of six tickets for 32F. Look for the trains marked **Tramways de la Balagne.** Several beaches and campgrounds lie along the route—just hop off the train when you see one you like. Ile Rousse's **tourist office** at the foot of pl. Paoli (tel. 95 60 04 35) can brief you on local camping. (Open Mon.-Fri. 10am-noon and 3-6pm.)If you're miraculously unimpressed by Ile Rousse's beaches, hop one of the SNCM boats to Nice (200F), Marseille (225F), or Toulon (225F). There are three or four departures per week. Agence Tramar, av. Joseph Calizi (tel. 95 60 09 56), sells tickets (open Mon.-Fri. 8:30am-noon and 2-5:30pm, Sat. 8:30am-noon).

Two stops and 14F from Calvi, **Algajola** is a village that has grown up inside and around the walls of a ruined fortress. Algajola has no tourist office. **Hôtel l'Esquinade** (tel. 95 60 70 19) faces the beach at the edge of the village. (Singles 124F. Doubles 194F. Triples 226F. Quads 276F. Showers included. Breakfast 15F.)

Five km from Ile Rousse on the D151, the hillside village of **Pigna** is home to CORSICADA, an eclectic group of shepherds, organ and lute makers, potters, and engravers who came to the ancient city in 1964 to found an artists' commune. To reach Pigna, take the train to Cantaretti and then follow the trail (20-30 min.). Every July 13 brings the **Paese in Festa,** a day of improvisational music and theater.

The **vineyards** surrounding Calvi often give tours of their *caves*. Many are within a few kilometers, and all are listed in the tourist office's brochure on Corsican wines. Visiting hours lengthen in September, when much of the wine is made.

Côte Orientale

The island's only relatively flat road stretches from Bastia to Porto-Vecchio, closely following the Côte Orientale. Mobbed by families who clutter the unattractive, granular beaches, the Corsica's eastern coast extends like one long suburb of Bastia. Inland, the **Plaine Orientale** includes orderly vineyards, clementine orange groves, and even kiwi farms, as well as the coarse *maquis* whose blooms are used to make an unusual tasting honey. **Castagniccia,** a low, hilly region filled with chestnut trees, lies east of Corte. Order a *tarte aux châtaignes* in a restaurant to taste the chestnut flour which was once a staple of the Corsican diet. **Kallistours** makes an excursion to Castagniccia from Bastia on Thursday afternoons in July and August. (80F). Make reservations at the Bastia agency (tel. 95 31 71 49). You'll need a car to explore the virtually untouched back roads of this area. The road southeast from Corte (N200) leads to the **Etang de Diana,** where the water is calm and abnormally salty.

On an inlet of the Tyrrhenian sea, **Porto-Vecchio** sits tight in its 16th-century Genoese walls. The **tourist office**, pl. de l'Hôtel de Ville (tel. 95 70 09 58), will help you find a hotel or campground. The English-speaking staff also provides information on transportation and hiking. (Open Mon.-Sat. 9am-noon and 4-7pm, Sun. 10am-noon and 5-7pm.)

A view of the **Plage de Palombaggia,** 7km south of Porto-Vecchio, adorns many of the island's brochures. **Trinitours** (tel. 95 70 13 83) runs shuttles to the beach in July and August. (Mon.-Sat. 10am, return from the beach 6pm. 30F.) **Rapides Bleus,** 7, rue Jean Jaurès (tel. 95 70 10 36), runs two buses per day (1 Sun.) between Bastia and Porto-Vecchio (3 hr., 90F). **Autocars Balesi** (tel. 95 70 14 50, in Ajaccio 95 21 28 01) sends a bus to Ajaccio at 6am. (July-Aug. Mon.-Sat., Sept.-June Mon., Wed. and Fri.; 3hr.; 80F.) **Ollandini** (tel. 95 70 13 83) sends buses to Bonifacio (2 per day, 30 min.), as does Trinitours (1 per day at noon, 46F).

Le Moderne, 10, cours Napoléon (tel. 95 70 06 36) offers attractive doubles (170F). In a less desirable location, the **Hôtel Panorama,** 12, rue Jean-Nicoli (tel. 95 70 07 96) has doubles with showers for 190F (Nov.-June 160F). If you plan to stay in a hotel, be sure to get off the bus in the city, not at the port. Near the port, **La Matonara** (tel. 95 70 35 05) is the least expensive campground. (6.90F per person, 8.50F per tent.) Get your picnic supplies at **Codec,** across from the post office on Av. Général Leclerc. (Open Mon.-Sat. 9am-12:15pm and 3:30-7:30pm.) If you find this place lacking in drama, check out the fish market near the Hôtel de Ville, where freshly caught octupi and blowfish peer up at shoppers with accusing eyes (Mon.-Sat. 7am-noon). Most restaurants group between rue Borgo and the Cours Napoléon. **A Stadda,** on rue Commandant l'Herminier, serves an 80F *menu* and an excellent *salade au chèvre chaud* (salad with warm goat cheese), 35F in a rustic interior.

Bonifacio

On the southernmost tip of Corsica, the fortified city of Bonifacio commands a majestic view of Sardinia, 13km away, and of the emerald straits between. Here the steep cliffs are chalky and white, unlike the dusty rose rocks of much of the rest of the island. Heavy stone walls, complete with drawbridges, encircle the original city, which was founded as a fortress. The French Foreign Legion still sets up camp here among the shops selling coral jewelry and beach gear. From June 15 to September 15, you can visit the **Steps of Aragon.** The invading soldiers of 15th-century King Alphonse d'Aragon supposedly carved the 149-step staircase out of the cliff in only one night.

From the **Port de Plaisance,** small craft leave several times an hour from April to October to explore the grottoes and impressive natural rock formations near Bonifacio (50 min., 50F). Excursions to the national park of the **Iles de Lavezzi** are also available (1½ hr., 100F). For more information, contact **La Méditerranée** (tel. 95 73 07 71) or **Thalassa** (tel. 95 73 05 43 or 95 73 01 17). To discover the countryside and the luxurious beaches nearby, rent a moped from **Corse Moto Services,** quai du Nord (tel. 95 73 15 16). (160F per day, 850F per week; 2000F deposit. Unlimited mileage.) Follow route du Phare, which runs west out of town to **Piantarella,** or take D58 to **Gurgazo** (6km). Both beaches offer friendlier waters than the treacherous **plage Sutta-Rocca,** which can be reached by descending the stairway next to **Chapelle St-Roch.** The **Aquarium de Bonifacio** displays a collection of fish and crustaceans caught by local fishermen. This is the place to check out dogfish eggs. (Open 10am-7pm, 20F.)

Practical Information

Although the city does not lie on a railroad, year-round **buses** make transportation relatively simple. Buses run between Bonifacio and Porto-Vecchio twice per day, with a connection to Bastia in the morning only (to Porto-Vecchio 46F, to Bastia 135F). Two buses per day connect Bonifacio to Ajaccio (98F). Contact the **Ollandini** office, 26, quai Comparetti (tel. 95 73 01 28), on the port. (Open Mon.-Fri. 9am-noon and 2-6pm, Sat. 9am-noon.)

You can also leave town by sea—on a ferry to Sardinia. **Saremar** (tel. 95 73 00 96) sails for **Santa Teresa** 3 times daily. (50 min., 47F, last boat 7:30pm. Office open daily 9:45-10:15am, 11:45am-2:35pm and 4-6pm.) **NAV.AR.MA. Lines** (tel. 95 73 00 29) also goes to Santa Teresa. (July-Sept. 7 per day, Oct.-June 4 per day; 60F. Office open daily 9am-7:30pm.) All boats leave from the **Gare Maritime** at the end of quai Comparetti, beneath the walls of the upper city. Buy tickets shortly before departure time. If you plan to bring a car, reservations are essential in July and August.

The **tourist office,** rue des Deux Moulins (tel. 95 73 15 16), in the *haute ville* (high town), will help you find a room. (English spoken. Open July-Aug. 9am-8pm, Sept.-June 9am-noon and 2-6pm.) The **post office** on nearby pl. Carrega (tel 95 73 00 15) **exchanges currency** at good rates and has **telephones.** (Open Mon.-Fri. 9am-noon and 2-5pm; Sat. 9am-noon.) The **postal code** for Bonifacio is 20169.

Accommodations and Camping

Bonifacio's inhabitants squeeze a year's living from the six-month season from April to October. Hotels are scarce and expensive, clustered with most of the restaurants along the port below the city. The tourist office has a list of hotels and campgrounds and information on rooms in private homes.

Hôtel les Voyageurs (tel. 95 73 00 46), quai Camparetti. Straightforward doubles 120F, with shower 180F. Triples 260F. Creative restaurant with wild tropical decor and stenciled green walls. *Menus* from 65F. Hotel and restaurant open from March to October.

Hôtel des Etrangers (tel. 95 73 01 09), on av. Sylvère Bohn at the entrance to the lower town, 300m from the port. Perfectly adequate doubles 160F. Open March-Oct.

Hôtel la Pergola, 13, quai Comparetti (tel. 95 73 13 56, in winter 95 73 06 16). Dark and expensive; try here when all else fails. Doubles with shower 180F.

Camping: There are several campgrounds in the area. Relais de a'Araguina, at the entrance to the city, is the closest, the most expensive, and the dustiest. July-Aug. 1-2 people 50F; Sept.-June 46F. Cavallo Monto (tel. 95 73 04 66), on route de Porto-Vecchio, 2km away. 20F per person, 8F per tent. Open April 15-Oct. 15. In the direction of the Phare de Pertusato (5km) is 4-star Camping des Iles. 17F per person, 9F per tent. Open Easter-Oct. 31.

Food

Every *boulangerie* in Bonifacio sells its own version of *pain des morts* ("bread of the dead"—a non-lethal raisin-and-walnut concoction), the town's self-declared contribution to Corsican cuisine. Restaurants line the port from April to October; the cheapest cluster at the end farthest from the *haute ville*.

Pub Royal, rue Fred-Scamaroni. Spacious dining room open all year. Pizzas 32-55F. 55F amd 65F *menus* include pasta and fish. *Moules farcies* (stuffed mussels) 40F. Open daily noon-10pm.

La Main à la Pâte, 8, rue Fred Scamaroni. Homemade pasta in a variety of sauces from 50F. Try the ravioli stuffed with *brocciu* (goat cheese). Open daily 9am-3pm and 5-7pm. In the summer, second location at 1, montée Rastello. Open daily May-Oct. 11am-2pm and 7-11pm.

La Grignotlère, 2, rue de la Loggia. Inexpensive *creêpes* and sandwiches (15-25F). Attractive modern decor in the heart of the *haute ville.* Open July-Aug. 9am-2am.

L'Agora, av. Carotolla, in the *citadelle*. A sophisticated terrace above the port with bar, restaurant, and an expensive disco downstairs. Dinner runs about 60F. Open 8pm-midnight. Disco open until 5am. (Cover 100F.)

l'Ancura, quai Camparetti (tel. 95 73 00 27). Great view of the marina. Select your own fish from the impressive showcase displaying the catch of the day. 65F *menu*. Don't miss the *soupe du poisson* (fish soup). Open June-Oct. noon-2pm and 7:30-11pm.

Near Bonifacio

The road from Bonifacio northwest to Ajaccio crawls through mountains and offers intermittent glimpses of the sea in the distance. Try to leave the main route and explore some of the isolated coastal villages. A stunning example of the unusual rock formations whipped out of the cliffs along the entire western coast, the **Rocher du Lion** crouches 55km from Bonifacio at **Roccapina**, adding his protection to that of the Genoese tower beside him.

Megalithic stones and fantastically shaped rock faces surround the town of **Sartène**, built on granite. Sartène sponsors **La Catenacciu**, a Good Friday procession imported from Seville, Spain. A red-hooded Christ bearing a wooden cross and dragging a long chain walks through the candlelit streets of the old town in a re-enactment of the Calvary drama. Traditionally a prisoner from a local jail, the actor always remains unknown. Although most of the local vineyards are now only terraces on the mountainsides, **La Cave Sartenèse** in pl. Porta (tel. 95 77 12 28) continues to pour the potent *vin Sartène* (3.50F per glass, bottles from 14F). The local specialties include peach and orange wines in a muscat base. **Camping Olva** (tel. 95 77 11 58), 5km from Sartène on the mountain road D69 has its own pool. (21F per tent, 8.50F per person. Open April-Sept.) The **tourist office** (tel. 95 77 15 40) is on rue Borgo. (Open Mon.-Fri. 9am-noon.) Sartène is a stop on the Ajaccio-Bonifacio bus line (2 per day, 2 hr. 36F).

To understand the popularity of **Propriano,** follow the beach path which extends for several kilometers south of this fishing village turned resort, or simply plop down on the sand right in town. The **tourist office,** 17, rue Général de Gaulle (tel. 95 76 01 49), stores baggage for 3F per day and exchanges currency. Although they do not make reservations, they can help with hotels and transportation. (Open Mon.-Sat. 9am-noon and 3-7pm.) Buses to Ajaccio leave twice per day (2 hr., 46F). Buses also run twice per day to Bonifacio (2 hr., 46F), Sartène (½-hr., 13F), and Porto-Vecchio (2 hr. 20 min., 54F). Buy tickets at the **Ollandini** agency at 22, rue Général de Gaulle (tel. 95 76 00 76). **Hôtel Le Bellevue**, 9, av. Napoléon (tel. 95 76 01 86), on the port, has big, clean rooms with an ocean view. (Doubles 150F, with shower 200F. Open April-Sept. Make reservations for July and Aug.) Two km from Propriano at the **Centre Equestre de Barachi,** an **auberge de jeunesse** (tel. 95 76 19 48) has slightly cramped co-ed dorm rooms, kitchen facilities, a restaurant, and a washing machine (50F per person).**Camping Colomba** (tel. 95 76 06 42), next to the youth hostel, also has a restaurant. (20F per person, 9F per tent. Open Easter to September.) There are other camping facilities nearby. **Restaurant Mal Assis** (tel. 95 76 01 49), on rue Général de Gaulle, joins other restaurants along the street in offering the venerable *steak-frites* with an hors-d'oeuvre and dessert for 45F. Other inexpensive restaurants cluster near the **Gare Maritime.** The **Sole e Mare,** 23, av. Napoléon, serves finger-licking *crêpes* (20-35F).

From June to September, a second **Ollandini** agency, 2, rue Général de Gaulle (tel. 95 76 05 36), makes excursions to **Filitosa,** where recently uncovered faces carved into stone monoliths watch the tides ebb and flow. (40F; office open Mon.-Sat. 8am-noon and 3-7pm, Sun. 8am-noon and 6-8pm.) **Valinco Accessoires** (tel. 95 76 11 84) rents bikes for 70F per day with an 800F deposit and mopeds for 150F per day with a 2500F deposit. (Open June-Oct., Mon.-Sat. 9am-noon and 3-7:30pm). From May through September, the good ship **Valinco** runs four tours per day to the **Golfe du Valinco.** Bring you suit; the boat stops for snorkeling. (100F, children 70F. Mask and snorkel included.)

Corte

Pascal Paoli, the "enlightened despot" who led Corsica to its short-lived independence (1758-1769), ran the island from Corte, a city nestled in the mountains halfway between Ajaccio and Bastia. Still known as the *capitale sentimentale de l'Ile,* Corte remains the most Corsican of the island's cities. The regional tongue is a required class at the university, which Paoli, a friend of Jean-Jacques Rousseau, founded in 1764 only to see it close after 16 years. In 1980, a new university opened, drawing 2500 students to this small town.

Easy to reach by bus or train, Corte's lovely setting and proximity to outstanding hiking trails make it an ideal stop when crossing the island or exploring the interior.

Trains which stop often for goats run from Bastia (4 per day, 2 hr., 46F), Ajaccio (4 per day, 2½ hr., 52F), and Calvi (2 per day, 3½ hr., change at Ponte-Leccia, 62F). The **train station** (tel. 95 00 80 17) is 1km out of town; to get to the center, turn right, cross the bridge, and climb up av. Jean Nicoli past the university. An old man at the station **hunts boar. Ollandini** buses (tel. 95 46 25 54) run to Bastia (Mon.-Sat. 2 per day, 1½ hr., 42F) and Ajaccio (2 per day, 2 hr., 49F). Buses depart from in front of the agency on pl. Xavier Luciani.

For **tourist information** (tel. 95 46 24 20), follow the signs to the entrance of the *citadelle*. Good, tours of the 15th-century *citadelle* (admission 5F, groups 3F per person) leave hourly from 9am to 8pm in July and August. In May, June and September, the tours leave from 9 to 11am and 2 to 7pm on the hour. A recorded explanation is available in English near the entrance for 2F. (Office open only in summer June-Sept. 9am-8pm; May and Oct. 9am-noon and 2-7pm.)

From July through September, students with ID can stay in university dorms for 53F. Contact the **CROUS** office at the university, av. Jean Nicoli, 20250 Corte (tel. 95 46 02 61; open Mon.-Fri. 9am-6pm). From May to October, **Hôtel de la Poste,** 2, pl. du Duc du Padoue (tel. 95 46 01 37), offers singles with showers for 110F, doubles with showers for 140-170F. (Open May-Oct.) From June to October, the **Hôtel du Nord,** 22, cours Paoli (tel. 95 46 00 68), has renovated doubles for 150-190F; avoid rooms overlooking noisy cours Paoli. Four **campgrounds** lie in the Restonic Valley, slightly southwest of the city. From the train station, turn left and then take the first right, which is an offshoot of N193. Walk for about 10 minutes to **Restonica** (tel. 95 46 11 59) and **Alivetu,** which face each other. (Both 16F per person, 9F per tent. Open late April to Oct.) **U Sognu** (tel. 95 46 09 07) is closest to the center of Corte. From pl. Paoli, go down av. Xavier Luciani and then turn right onto av. du Président Perucci. A five minute walk down hill will bring you to the campground and its clean, pleasant facilities. (18F per person, 11F per tent. Open March-Oct.) Continuing past U Sognu, turn left on chemin de Baliri. Ten minutes down the path, **U Tavignanu** (tel. 95 46 16 85), the only campground open all year, offers horseback riding. (13F per person, 8F per tent. Call for reservations.)

If a true Corsican meal has eluded you in the coastal cities, try the 74F *menu* at **A Piazzetta,** near pl. Gaffory on pl. de l'Eglise. *Crêpes,* salads, omelettes, and even a 49F *menu* are available here from May to early October. (Open daily noon-2pm and 7-10pm.) **Restaurant le Bip's,** 14, cours Paoli, is a relaxed place, with a traditional 60F *menu.* The entrance is off the parking lot. **U Spanu,** av. Xavier Lucciani (tel. 95 46 07 85), just off pl. Paoli, offers a 69F *menu* and a 90F *menu Corse.* Dine with the student crowd at **U San Sampiero** on av. Pierucci, across from the *lycée.*

Near Corte

Southwest of Corte, a tiny road stretches 15km through the **Gorges de la Restonica,** one of the island's loveliest and least populated areas. A crystal-clear, trout-filled stream slides through the fig, poplar, and chesnut trees covering the mountainside. Gnarled pines crowd the road as it climbs above 1600m, and you can see snowy peaks as late as June. Lakes offer chilly (18°) swimming in the summer. Follow the road in the direction of the river to the **Lac de Melo** (1-hr. hike), a snow-fed beauty at almost 2000m, surrounded by peaks that culminate with Mt. Cinto (2700m). You can continue to the **Lac de Creno** and join the **Grande Randonnée-20,** the challenging trail that winds its way across the entire breadth of Corsica. Be prepared for cold, even snowy weather as late as June. For more information, contact the **Parc Naturel Régional** in Ajaccio (tel. 95 21 56 54). The guides at the *citadelle* in Corte can help you map out trails (tel. 95 46 27 44; open June-Oct.). Write to Parc Naturel Régional de Corse, Citadelle de Corte, 20150 Corte, for trail maps and general information year-round.

Bastia

Its name derived from the word *bastiglia* (dungeon), Bastia gets a bum rap from Corsicans who consider it the most aptly titled city on the island. Maybe their antipathy stems from the city's historical position as a Genoese stronghold, or perhaps Corsicans simply prefer the extraordinary countryside covering the rest of the island. While Bastia shares Ajaccio's industrial character and traffic, its greater verve will be obvious to anyone who ventures more than 200m from the train station. After walking through the **place St-Nicolas**, a bustling 300m esplanade on the waterfront, and then climbing up the rue Napoléon into the *vieille ville,* you'll discover narrow streets and stone staircases meandering up to the Genoese *citadelle.* The buildings all seem to lean toward the charming *vieux ort,* where a traditional fish net repair shop still exists. Located in the 15th-century **Palais des Gouverneurs Génois** overlooking the port, the **Musée d'Ethnographie** offers a depiction of traditional Corsican life in different regions. (Open daily 9am-noon and 3-6pm.) For the best view of the *citadelle* and the port, walk to the end of the Jetée du Dragon.

Orientation and Practical Information

Corsica's economic center, Bastia is at the southwest corner of the Cap Corse. The new port and the train station are connected by **avenue Maréchal Sebastiani,** where you'll find the tourist office kiosk and the post office. The commercial bd. Charles de Gaulle, bd. Paoli, and rue César Campinchi run parallel to pl. St-Nicolas and lead to the old port and old town.

Tourist Office: 35, bd. Paoli (tel. 95 31 02 44). Information on the entire island. Some English spoken. Open Mon.-Fri. 8am-noon and 2-6pm, Sat. 8am-noon; Sept.-May Mon.-Fri. 9am-noon and 3-6pm. Another office at pl. St-Nicolas (tel. 95 31 00 89). Information and guided tours. Open daily June-Sept. 8am-7pm; in Oct.-May until 6pm.

Currency Exchange: The **post office** has the best rates (1% commission). Outside of post office hours, an exchange with rotten rates and sharp teeth lurks on the corner of av. Maréchal Sebastiani and bd. Paoli. Open daily 9am-noon and 2-9pm. Also try the Gare Maritime.

Post Office: av. Maréchal-Sebastiani. **Telephones** and **currency exchange** here. Open Mon.-Fri. 8am-7pm, Sat. 8am-noon. **Postal Code:** 20200.

Flights: Bastia-Poretta (tel. 95 36 02 03), 23km away. A bus timed for airplane departures leaves from pl. de la Gare, in front of the Préfecture (½-hr., 35F). To: Marseille (3 per day, 50 min., 376F); Nice (2-3 per day, 40 min., 334F); Paris (5-6 per day, 1½ hr., 991F). In the "blue" period, ages 25 and under, families, and seniors are eligible for discounts: to Marseille 266F, to Nice 232F, to Paris 541F. Daily flights to London via Paris, Geneva via Nice, and Amsterdam via Nice. **Air France,** 6, av. Emile-Sari (tel. 95 31 99 31). **Air Inter** at the airport (tel. 95 36 02 95). Air France and Air Inter also have booths in the SNCM office off pl. St-Nicolas. Open Mon.-Fri. 8-11:30am and 2-5:30pm.

Trains: pl. de la Gare (tel. 95 32 60 06), just off av. Maréchal Sebastiani. Corsica's most modern station. To: Calvi (2 per day, 3½ hr., 74F); Corte (4 per day, 2 hr., 46F); Ajaccio (4 per day, 4 hr., 117F). You can leave your luggage at the *consigne* for 13F per day, but remember that the station is only open Mon.-Sat. 6am-8pm and Sun. 8am-12:15pm and 1:15-6:45pm.

Buses: Rapides Bleus, 1, av. Maréchal Sebastiani (tel. 95 31 03 79). To Porto-Vecchio along the Côte Orientale (8:30am and 4pm, Sun. 8:30am; 3 hr., 90F). **Ollandini,** 9, av. Maréchal Sebastiani (tel. 95 31 44 04). To Corte (Mon.-Sat. 8:15am and 3pm, 1½ hr., 42F) and Ajaccio (3½ hr., 90F). For excursions around Cap Corse, inquire at the bus stop on rue du Nouveau Port (service runs July-Aug. only). **Kallistours,** 6, av. Mal Sebastiani (tel. 95 31 71 49), runs excursions around the Cap every monday afternoon in July and August (90F). Call for reservations. Trips to Porto (130F), Calvi (180F), and Bonifacio (130F). Open Mon.-Fri. 8am-noon and 2-6pm, Sat. 8am-noon.

Ferries: SNCM, Hôtel de la Chambre de Commerce (tel. 95 31 36 63). Open Mon.-Fri. 8-11:30am and 2-5:30pm. Generally 1-2 ferries to the mainland per day. Many overnight trips. Marseille and Toulon (225F), Nice (200F). During the "blue" period ages over 60 get a 50% reduction, under 25 receive a 30% reduction. **Corsica Ferries,** 5bis, rue Chanoine Leschi (tel. 95 31 18 09). To Italy: Livorno and La Spezia (4-5 hr., 150F) and Genova (8 hr., 180F).

NAV.AR.MA., 4, rue Commandant Luce (tel. 95 31 46 29). To Italy: Livorno (4 hr.) and Piombino (3 hr.). One way to both ports 140F.

Car Rental: Ginanni, 35, rue César Campinchi (tel. 95 31 09 02). 500F per day; unlimited mileage. **Mattei,** 7, rue Chanoine-Leschi (tel. 95 31 57 23). Citroën AX, Panda TO, Zorach Chouette, or Super5 for 2034.01F per week with unlimited mileage. Additional days 170.61F. Open 8am-noon and 2-6pm Mon.-Fri.; Sat. 8am-noon. Both agencies require the driver to be over 21 and to have had a license for 2 years.

Bike and Moped Rental: Locacycles, 40, rue César Campinchi (tel. 95 31 02 43). 10-speeds 84F per day, 504F per week, deposit 1000F. Mopeds 132F per day, 840F per week, deposit 2000F. Prices may be higher in Aug. Open Mon.-Fri. 8am-noon and 2-6pm; Sat. 8am-noon.

Taxis: tel. 95 34 07 00.

Hospital: Falconaja, route Impériale (tel. 95 30 30 30). Lots of Snoopy bandaids.

Police: (tel. 95 33 51 69), on rue Commandant Luce de Casabianca. **Emergency,** tel. 17. **Gendarmerie,** tel. 95 33 52 06.

Accommodations and Camping

Depressing hotels huddle near the train station and port. Venture up bd. Paoli into the old city to find more interesting and inexpensive digs. Although the tourist office does not reserve hotels, they have a complete list.

Riviera-Hôtel, 1bis, rue du Nouveau Port (tel. 95 31 61 04). A sleep factory near the port. Doubles 140F, with shower 180F. Extra bed 40F. Breakfast 18F. Make reservations for August.

Hôtel de l'Univers, 3, av. Maréchal Sebastiani (tel. 95 31 03 38), down the street from the train station. Cheerful rooms and management. Singles 100F. Doubles 130F, with shower 150F. Triples 150F, with shower 200F. Higher prices from July to Oct.

Hôtel San Carlu, 10, bd. Auguste Gaudin (tel. 95 31 70 65). Rooms with balconies overlooking the old city are worth the hike. Run by a friendly family. All rooms have showers. SIngles 120F. Doubles 160F.

Central Hôtel, 3, rue Miot (tel. 95 31 71 12). Excellent location between bd. Paoli and rue Campinchi. Double with shower 150F. Prices rise from July to October but go down the longer you stay.

Camping: Les Sables Rouges (tel. 95 33 36 08), closest to town. From the train station, take the small train which follows the coast (every ½-hr., 7F, last train 8pm). 8F per person, 10F per tent. Open June-early Oct. **Camping Casanova,** route du Tennis (tel. 95 33 91 42). Clean, pleasant location 5km north of Bastia. Take the bus marked **Erblanca** across from the tourist office kiosk (every ½-hr., 7:30am-7pm, 8F). 19F per person, 7F per tent. **Camping San Damiano** (tel. 95 33 68 02), on route de la Lagune de Pinette, 15km south of Bastia. Closer to the airport. 18F per person, 10F per tent. Open June-Oct.

Food

Restaurants ring the *vieux port,* many with terraces and fantastic views. At lunch or dinner, you can hear Corsican music at **U Cantarettu,** on the old port. (Open Wed.-Mon.) You won't find much near the train station except for sandwich stands.

Le Dépot, 22, rue César Campinchi. A cozy, intimate place with a winding wooden staircase and brick walls. Fire-cooked pizza 24-45F, *plats du jour* 50-70F. Open daily noon-3pm and 7-11pm.

Nanny, 28, rue César Campinchi. A chic café; excellent for lunch. *Crêpes* and *tartes salées* (savory tarts) as well as sandwiches (28-40F). Open daily 7am-8pm.

Le Pied Marin, Vieux Port. Excellent location. Try the *beignets de brocciu* (fried goat cheese) and the veal in Corsican sauce. 75F *menu.* A real splu#@*&%!.

Chez Gino, 11, av. Emile Sari (tel. 95 31 41 43), 5 min. from the ferry terminal. A lively neighborhood eatery, ideal for a pre- or post-ferry snack. Pizzas 18-48F. Open Tues.-Sun.

Near Bastia: Cap Corse

North of Bastia, a string of fishing villages and quiet inlets rim Cap Corse, a 48km peninsula which points toward France. The 113km road around the Cap passes sheltered coves and forest-covered mountains. Sprinkled amidst these hills of chestnut and lime trees and olive groves are fortified Genoese towns such as **Cagnano,** 5½km inland from the port of **Porticciolo.** On the coast you can see several Genoese towers, including the restored **Tour de Losse,** part of the elaborate system that once could warn every Corsican within two hours of an impending attack by barbarians or pirates.

Macinaggio, 40km from Bastia, is one of the few port towns where you can find services and supplies (including gas and a large supermarket). The **tourist office** (tel. 95 35 40 40) is open daily 9am-noon and 3-7pm. The **post office** has a **currency exchange.** (Open Mon.-Fri. 9am-noon and 2-4:30pm, Sat. 9-11:30am.) **Hôtel des Iles** (tel. 95 35 43 02) has clean rooms with a view of the port. (Doubles 220F, with shower 240F.) From July to September 15, **Camping de la Plage** (tel. 95 35 43 76 or 95 35 40 49) offers (surprise!) beach-side camping. Guided horseback tours leave from the campground. Call Jean Albertini at 95 35 43 76 for information.

Domaine de Gioielle (tel. 95 35 42 05 or 95 32 12 60) opens its *caves* to the public. Especially interesting in September, the vineyard is on the left, ½km toward Rogliano from Macinaggio. For a closer view of the islands of Elba, Monte Cristo, and Capri, rent a boat from **Nocéan Charter** (tel. 95 35 41 47). (July-Aug. 500F per day, Sept. 400F per day, Oct.-May 300F per day, June 400F per day. Deposit 2000F.)

Rogliano, Macinaggio's sister village 2½km inland, is solemn and undisturbed. Shaped like an amphitheater, it contains the ruins of a Genoan castle, **Château de San Colombano,** and a large 16th-century church, **San' Agnello.** Walk from Macinaggio to Rogliano, or take the free shuttle bus run by the **Restaurant u Sant Agnellu** (tel. 95 35 40 59), which has a 80F *menu* and spacious doubles with shower for 200F. The shuttle runs from April to October (7-8:30pm).

In the port of **Centuri,** on the other side of the peninsula, 57km from Bastia, boats bring in the daily catch of *langoustes, moules,* and fish. Sublimely picturesque, Centuri is often photographed as a pure example of an authentic fishing village. **Camping l'Isoluttu** (tel. 95 35 62 81) is near the beach. (Open April-Oct. 15F per person, 12F per tent, 8F per car.) In town, three one-star hotels all have high prices. **Le Centuri** (tel. 95 35 61 70) is a modern hotel with large rooms, all equipped with shower and private bath or toilet. (Open April-Oct. Doubles 250F.) Centuri's handful of restaurants all offer approximately the same mid- to high-priced meals. **U Fossu** serves the least expensive *menu* at around 58F. House wines tend to be top-notch. Look for *rapo,* a wonderful but seldom produced dessert wine.

Mirroring Bastia on the other side of the Cap (20km from Bastia on the inland road), **St-Florent** is a modern beach resort built around an old port. There's nothing to see here, and you won't even be able to find a *crêpe* at a decent price. Stop at **Patrimonio,** a tiny village 5km from St-Florent, for local wine at very good prices (5F per liter in your own bottle or sack, 10-15F per bottle). **Clos Marfisi** (tel. 95 37 01 16) and **Orenga** (tel. 95 30 11 38) provide *dégustations* right in Patrimonio.

Traveling along the *corniche* around the Cap is not particularly easy. Check with the tourist office in Bastia for excursions and up-to-date bus information. **Kallistours** (tel. 95 31 71 49) organizes afternoon circuits which include wine-tasting in Patrimonio. (Monday afternoons July-August, 90F.) Call the office for reservations. (Open Mon.-Fri. 9am-noon and 2-6pm, Sat. 9am-noon.) **Ollandini** (tel. 95 32 22 05) provides similar services in July and August. Ask at the bus stop on rue du Nouveau Port or contact their office. (Open Mon.-Fri. 7:30-9:3-am and 2-6:30pm, Sat. 7:30am-noon.) Hitchhiking is next to impossible here since the drivers are mostly tourists, and there are relatively few of them at that.

Alps (Savoie-Dauphiné)

After museum corridors and enervating urban centers, the majestic Alps and the glassy rivers that carved their valleys turn Paris smog into a distant memory. Commercialized resort and the occasional undisturbed hamlet may entertain or enchant visitors, but the natural architecture is the real attraction here. The curves of the Chartreuse Valley grow to rugged crags in the Vercors range, all climaxing in Europe's highest peak, Mont Blanc. Magnificent but hardly unspoiled, the region will host the 1992 Winter Olympics. Construction has already begun in towns around Albertville (the base city for the games) such as Les Saisies, Tignes, Val d'Isère, and even along the roads to Chambéry and Annecy. The new construction, however unattractive now, shouldn't destroy the area's charm. Decades of ongoing development have alerted the government to the need to protect the natural beauty that has earned the French Alps their popularity.

The Alps are shared by two regions, Savoie and Dauphiné. Dauphiné, the lower region, comprises the Chartreuse Valley and the Vercors Mountains, the sporting and university center of Grenoble, and magnificent, unspoiled mountain ranges. Grenoble has been the capital of the region since the 14th century, when Louis XI designated the town the permanent parliamentary seat. Numerous late medieval châteaux are scattered to the northeast of La Tour du Pin. Savoie bears the name of the oldest royal house in Europe. After 1000 BC this region of the Alps became the possession of Humbert aux Blanches Mains, founder of the House of Savoie and a vassal of the German emperor. Humbert established his capital at Chambéry and began extracting exorbitant tolls from neighboring kings who wanted to march unimpeded through the mountain passes. By the 14th century this powerful kingdom included Nice, the Jura, Piemonte, and Geneva, a choice expanse of territory that attracted the military attention of generations of French monarchs. In 1860, weary of centuries of invasion, a plebescite showed an overwhelming number of *Savoyards* in favor of becoming French.

The futuristic city of Grenoble is an ideal center for travel to Olympic events. Though smaller and less cosmopolitan, Chambéry is even closer to Albertville. Efficient train lines link the Alps's main cities to those in France, Italy, and Switzerland, while a thorough bus system serves the higher altitudes and more remote villages. Hitchhikers often find themselves stranded along the curving main roads; once in Albertville, many people find the short hops to the smaller resorts much easier.

After the cramped comforts of a TGV, bus, or car, the best way to stretch out is by heading in the most logical direction—up. After the spring thaw, flowery meadows, icy mountain lakes, and postcard-perfect views await experienced and amateur hikers alike. Most towns have sports shops that rent appropriate footwear for about 40F per day, even on Sunday; local tourist offices will often provide free trail guides. Trails are clearly marked, but serious climbers should invest in a *Topo-Guide* (hiking map). Talk to the experts at the **Club Alpin Français** or the **Compagnie des Guides** in Grenoble or Chamonix for updated information on trail and weather conditions, and suggested hikes. Skiing in the Alps has always been somewhat expensive, and the pre-Olympics hype has sent prices even higher. Begin making arrangements six to eight weeks in advance or, better yet, in September. The least crowded and cheapest months to go are January, March, and April. Most resorts close in October and November.

Perhaps the only thing richer than the average skier in Val d'Isère is the alcohol-heavy, Swiss-influenced *savoyard* cuisine. The first few bites make all diners ecstatic, but those who clean their plate will crawl away with light heads and leaden stomachs. The most deadly and delicious regional specialty is *fondue savoyarde,* a blend of 3 Alpine cheeses made with white wine and kirsch. Other cheesy dishes include *raclette* (scrapings from a strong Swiss cheese melted and served with boiled potatoes, pickled onions, and gherkins) and *gratin dauphinois* (a delicious concoction of potatoes baked in a cream and cheese sauce). The *Savoyards* and *Dauphinois* also cure excellent ham and catch superb trout from the cold mountain streams. The renowned *montagne* cheeses are mild and creamy: try Tomme de Savoie, St-Marcellin (half goat's milk), and Reblochon. Excellent regional wines include the whites of Apremont, Ayse, and Chignin and the rich reds produced in Montmélian and St-Jean-de-la-Porte. If you have any room for dessert, try the *roseaux d'Annecy* (liqueur-filled chocolates), *St-Genux* (a *brioche* topped with pink praline), or the *gâteau de Savoie* (a light sponge cake). *Eaux de vie,* strong liqueurs distilled from fruits, are popular here, especially when made from local *framboises* (raspberries).

Grenoble

Built on the site of a 4th-century Roman city, Grenoble relishes its role as the industrial, academic, and sporting capital of the Alps. Although the clean lines of a contemporary city hide most of historic Grenoble, the right bank of the Isère is packed with 18th-century Italian buildings, which now house mainly the city's busy (if not necessarily studious) student population. Founded in 1339 by Humbert II, Grenoble's science-oriented university is one of the largest in France. Its size accounts for the city's numerous cafés, shaggy radicals, dusty bookshops, and serious politics. Although a mountain view greets them at the end of each boulevard, the 392,000 *Grenoblois* endure their share of pickpockets, smokestacks, sky-blocking highrises, and other urban nuisances.

The city is well-situated for trips into the surrounding mountains. The imminent arrival of the 1992 Winter Olympics has improved transportation to the Chartreuse, Vercors, and Oisans ranges, but runaway development has made some areas less suitable for a true rural retreat. The main Olympic city, Albertville, is only 86km north of Grenoble.

Orientation and Practical Information

Both the downtown and the *vieille ville* of Grenoble are easily accessible on foot, and the train station is 10 minutes from the center. Nevertheless, public transportation in Grenoble is extremely efficient. The tramway and bus system (TAG) costs 6F a ride, 42F for a book of 10 tickets. The tramway runs about every 10 minutes from 5am-10pm, the buses from 6am-9pm. The central city is conveniently dotted with "you-are-here" maps, and each TAG stop has its own transit map.

You may want to invest 10F in the **Guide DAHU,** a guide to restaurants and nightlife written by Grenoble students with razor-sharp wits (available in English at the tourist office and some *tabacs*).

Tourist Office: 14, rue de la République (tel. 76 54 34 36), in the center of town. From the station, take the tramway (*direction* "Grand Place") to the Maison du Tourisme stop, take your first left and then your first right. Ample information on public transportation, trains, mountain excursions, and guided tours. Free map with an incomplete street index. For a steep 25F you can buy a better map at most *tabacs* and stationary stores. Will reserve hotel rooms in Grenoble (free) or anywhere in France (25F). Open Mon.-Fri. 9am-6:30pm, Sat. 9am-12:30pm and 1:30-6:30pm; in off-season Mon.-Sat. 9am-6pm. SNCF and TAG (local public transportation) offices on the premises. Open Mon.-Fri. 9am-6pm. Also, **Grenoble Spectacles,** a cultural center. Open Tues.-Sat. 10:30am-12:30pm, 1:30-6pm. **Annex** at train station (tel. 76 56 90 94). Maps and a fair supply of information. Open Mon.-Sat. 9am-noon and 1-6pm.

Hiking Information: Club Alpin Français, 32, av. Félix Viallet (tel. 76 87 03 73). Advice on all mountain activities. Organizes group hiking, mountaineering, ice-climbing, and parachuting trips. Map library. Supervises mountain refuges (54F per night, club members 27F). Club membership (mainly an insurance policy) 270F, ages 18-25 170F. Open Tues.-Wed. 3-7pm, Thur.-Fri. 3-8pm, Sat. 9am-noon. **CIMES (Centre Informations Montagnes et Sentiers),** Maison de la Randonnée, 7, rue Voltaire (tel. 76 54 76 00). Organizes hiking trips. Detailed guides of hiking, mountaineering and cross-country skiing routes for alpine areas (59F). Topo-Guides (55F). Open Mon.-Fri. 9am-6pm, Sat. 10am-noon and 2-6pm year-round.

Budget Travel: Jeunes sans Frontière-Wasteels, 50, av. Alsace-Lorraine (tel. 76 47 34 54), near the train station, and 20, av. Félix-Viallet (tel. 76 46 36 39). BIJ tickets and cheap excursion packages to Ajaccio (920F, roundtrip); flights to Biarritz (1250F, roundtrip) and Lisbon (1610F, roundtrip). Both offices open Mon.-Fri. 9am-noon and 2-7pm, Sat. 9am-noon and 2-6pm.

Currency Exchange: Banque Nationale de Paris, rue de la République, across from the tourist office. Open Tues.-Fri. 8:05-11:55am and 1:15-5:05pm, Sat. 8:05-11:55am and 1:10-4pm. No currency exchange after 4pm. **Barclays Bank,** av. Alsace-Lorraine, on the way from the train station. Open Mon.-Fri. 8:45am-12:10pm, 1:35-5pm.

Post Office: bd. Maréchal-Lyautey (tel. 76 76 14 14). **Currency exchange** and **telephones.** Open Mon.-Fri. 8am-6:45pm, Sat. 8am-noon. Branch office attached to the tourist office. Open Mon.-Fri. 8am-6:30pm, Sat 8am-noon. **Postal Code:** 38000.

Flights: Aéroport de Grenoble St-Geoirs, St-Etienne de St-Geoirs (tel. 76 65 48 48). Eight buses per day leave from the *gare routière* (15F).

Trains: pl. de la Gare (tel. 76 47 50 50; for reservations 76 47 54 27). Trains almost every hr. to: Valence (80 min., 59F); Chambéry (1 hr., 42F); Annecy (2 hr., 68F); Chamonix (5½ hr., 132F); Voiron (20 min., 19F); Avignon (3 hr., 122F); Lyon (2 hr., 74F). To Strasbourg (5-7 per day, 9 hr., 265F) and Paris (5-7 per day, 5-8 hr., 282F) via Lyon. Information office open Mon.-Fri. 8:30am-7:30pm, Sat. 9am-6pm.

Buses: Gare Routière, to the left of the train station. Four companies offer summer excursions plus service to ski resorts and surrounding towns. **VFD** (tel. 76 47 77 77) is the biggest. Office open daily 7:40-11:30am and 2:30-6pm. For other companies, call 76 87 90 31. To: Chambery (10 per day, 1 hr., 37F); Voiron (2 per day, 3 hr., 17.50F); Les Deux Alpes (2 per day, 1 hr., 72F); Alpe d'Huez (2 per day, 45 min., 59.50F); Chamrousse (2 per day, 1½ hr., 47F); Briançon (7 per day, 1 hr., 112F).

Taxis: Tel. 76 54 42 54. 24 hrs.

Bike Rental and Climbing Equipment: Borel Sport, 42, rue Alsace-Lorraine (tel. 76 46 47 46). Bicycles 60F per day, deposit 1000F. Rents mountain climbing equipment. Shoes 20-35F per day. Open Tues.-Sat. 9am-noon and 2:30-7pm. **Objectif Montagne,** 18, rue Marceau Leyssieux (tel. 76 51 58 76), way out in St-Martin d'Heres. Take bus #23 and get off at Cité Labeye. Specializes in renting mountaineering equipment. Shoes 35F per day. Open daily 9am-7pm.

Shoe Repair: Cordonnier, 78 quai Perrière, on the right bank of the Isère. Specializes in hiking boot repairs.

Hitchhiking: Alpestop, at the Centre Régional Jeunesse. Less than 300km 30F, more than 300km 60F, plus gas and road fee 0.18F per km. Open Mon.-Fri. 1-6pm. The area is well served by freeways, so the smaller roads see almost no through traffic, and hitching can be difficult. If you chose to hitchhike long-distances, you'll be best off taking a bus to Valence, where you'll have access to the major highways.

English Bookstore: Just Books, 1, rue de la Paix (tel. 76 44 78 81). Sizable, entirely English collection of paperbacks, including the full line of *everybody's* favorite budget travel guide. Open Tues.-Sat. 10am-noon and 2-7pm.

Womens Center: Centre d'Information Féminin, 9, rue Raoul Blanchard (tel. 76 54 08 19). Free advice and pamphlets. Open Mon.-Wed. and Fri. 1-6pm.

Youth Center: Centre Régional d'Information Jeunesse, 8, rue Voltaire (tel. 76 54 70 38), near the tourist office across from CIMES. Free ride board service. Information on housing, sports, and cultural events. Carte Jeune 60F. Open Mon.-Fri. 1-6pm.

Laundromat: 65, pl. St-Bruno (tel. 76 96 28 03). 12F per load. Open daily 7am-7pm. 4, rue Bayard. Wash 13F, dry 4F, soap 2F. Open daily 7am-9pm. 18, rue Chenoise. Wash 13F, dry 2F, soap 2F. Open daily 7am-9pm. 90, cours Berriat. Wash 12F, dry 3F. Open daily 7am-9pm. Rue Alphand, behind the tourist office. Wash 15F, dry 4F. Open daily 7am-10pm.

Snowfall Information Service, tel. 76 54 30 80.

Sports Office: Office Municipal des Sports, 3, Passage du Palais de Justice (tel. 76 44 75 61).

Mountain Rescue: Secours en Montagne, tel. 76 21 44 44.

Hospital: Centre Hospitalier Régional de Grenoble, La Tronche (tel. 76 42 81 21).

Medical Emergency: SAMU, tel. 76 42 42 42.

Police: bd. Marèchal Leclerc (tel. 76 60 40 40). **Emergency,** tel. 17.

Accommodations and Camping

A small but sufficient number of budget hotels cluster in the pedestrian zone. Grenoble's many *foyers* are especially suitable for longer stays. For rentals, see the tourist office board marked *Locations Meubles.*

Auberge de Jeunesse (IYHF), 18, av. du Grésivaudan, Echirolles (tel. 76 09 33 52), about 4km out of town. Take bus #8 from cours Jean Jaurès (1 block straight ahead from the train station) or from the tourist office to La Quinzaine. It's on the right a block behind the Casino market. If walking, follow cours Jean Jaurès and turn right just before the Casino market. A modern building with a garden, bar, game room, cooking facilities, and TV. As always, watch your valuables. Open daily 6am-11pm. Rooms with 4-6 people 60F. Doubles 65F per person. Breakfast included. Ask for the door combination if out late. Reservations accepted.

Le Foyer de L'Etudiante, 4, rue Ste-Ursule (tel. 76 42 00 84), near pl. Notre Dame. From the tourist office, follow pl. Ste-Claire to pl. Notre Dame and take rue du Vieux Temple. On a quiet street close to the center. Ordinary rooms in a friendly atmosphere. Kitchen facilities, TV, and a piano. Open daily 9am-noon and 2-5pm. Singles 60F. Doubles with 2 beds 40F. Sheets included. Make reservations a week in advance. Accepts men and women travelers mid-June to mid-Sept.

Foyer les Ecrins, 36, rue Christophe-Turc (tel. 76 09 40 74). Take bus #13 from pl. Victor Hugo. Looks like a run-down college dorm from the outside, but rooms are pleasant enough. Restaurant, TV rooms, and cafeteria. 3-day min. stay. Kitchenettes on each hall. Office open 4-6:30pm. Three nights 240F, 4 nights 300F, 5 nights 350F.

Hôtel de la Poste, 25, rue de la Poste (tel. 76 46 67 25), in the center of the pedestrian zone. Don't be put off by the dark entrance hall. Large, beautiful rooms in an old building. Singles 100F. Doubles 120F. Triples 150F. Showers included. Singles have beds for three. Breakfast 25F.

Hôtel Colbert, 1, rue Colbert (tel. 76 46 46 65), a 5-min. walk from the train station. Go right through pl. de la Gare, rue 4 Septembre, and onto rue Joseph Rey, hugging the tracks all the way. After about 200m, turn left onto rue Colbert. Spacious, sunny, and clean rooms with brass beds. Singles 95F. Doubles with 1 bed 110F. Doubles with 2 beds and triples 135F. Showers 15F. Breakfast 20F.

Camping: Camping Municipal, 15, av. Beaumarchais (tel. 76 96 19 87), on the way to the hostel. Take bus #8 towards the hostel (or walk along cours Jean Jaurès), and get off at Albert Reynier. Not particularly pleasant but passable. No reservations or long stays. Not ideal during winter months. 5F per person, 4F per student, 3F per site.

Food

Refugees from the fondue scene should head for the cheap North African restaurants on **rue Chenoise,** and **rue St-Laurent** on the right bank of the river (*menus* 45F). Pizza lovers can find good-sized pies (28-45F) on quai Perrière, on the right bank of Isère. **Prisunic,** across from the tourist office (open Mon.-Sat. 8:30am-7pm) or **Supermarket Casino,** at the youth hostel (open Mon.-Sat. 8:30am-9pm) will supply your *al fresco* feasts. Alternately, try the big **markets** at pl. St-Bruno, near the station on the other side of the tracks, and rue Joseph Rey, where cours Jean Jaurès meets the railroad tracks. (Both open Mon.-Sat. 8am-1pm.) The covered market in pl. Ste-Claire, near the tourist office, features fruit, meats, and regional cheeses every morning.

Le Cantilène, 11, rue Beyle-Stendhal, near the post office. Small and boisterous. 45F *menu.* Evening specials such as *moules-frites* (mussels with fries) 40F. Open Mon.-Thurs. 11:30am-2pm and 7-10pm, Fri.-Sat. 11:30am-2pm and 7-10:30pm.

La Panse, 2, rue de la Paix (tel. 76 54 09 54). Always crowded with loyal locals. Ambrosial French cuisine at reasonable prices. Simple 75F *menu,* and a gourmet 150F *menu,* including duck salad and *pâté de hareng aux whiskey et truffes* (herring *pâté* with whiskey and truffles). Open Mon.-Fri. 8am-2pm and 5-10:30pm.

Restaurant Indochinois, 13, rue Raoul Blanchard, behind the tourist office. Good, filling Vietnamese cuisine. Full meal (in and out in ½-hr.) 40F. Egg rolls at the counter 5F each. Open Mon.-Sat. 10:30am-10:30pm.

Le Tunis (tel. 76 42 47 13), rue Chenoise. Small restaurant, simple *menu.* If you're coo coo for *couscous,* this is the place for you. Lamb *couscous* 35F, chicken *couscous* 36F, *couscous royal* 65F. Open daily noon-2pm and 6-10pm.

Restaurant de la Plage, 2, rue St-Hughes, just off pl. Notre Dame. Follow pl. Ste-Claire from the tourist office. A beach, in the Alps? The restaurant that dares to be laid-back. *Plat du jour* 38F, *menu* 50F. Open Mon.-Fri. noon-2pm and 7:30-11pm.

Le Palais Slave, 20, rue Chenoise. Delectable Russian cuisine in an intimate setting. Be prepared to spend a palatial 100-150F. Liver strogonoff 45F, goulash 48F, and a superb 85F *menu* including zucchini caviar and *blînis* (Russian crepes). Open Mon.-Sat. 7:30-11:30pm.

University Restaurants: Scattered around town. One at 5, rue Arsonval. Call **CROUS** at 76 87 07 62 to find out what's open. Buy a ticket from a student waiting in line (10F). Open Sept.-May.

Sights and Entertainment

A futuristic bubble of a cablecar (the *téléphérique de la Bastille*) pops out of the city every three minutes from quai Stéphane-Jay (Gould?) and whisks visitors up to the imposing **Bastille,** with its truly spectacular view of Grenoble, and, on a clear day, Mt. Blanc. (Téléphérique open Mon. 11am-7:30pm, Tues.-Sat. 9am-midnight, Sun. 9am-7:30pm; Nov.-March daily 10am-6pm; April-June 15 and Sept. 16-Oct. Sun 9am-7:30pm, Mon. 10am-7:30pm, Tues.-Sat. 9am-midnight. 17F, round-trip 27F; students 9F, round-trip 14F. (Disabled access.) From the top, the ambitious can follow well-marked trails of varying difficulty. Walk—don't ride—down through the **Jardin des Dauphins** and **Parc Guy Pape.** (Open, weather permitting, daily 9am-7:30pm; April-May and Sept.-Oct. 9am-7pm; Nov.-Feb. 9am-4pm; March 9am-5:30pm. For general information on the *téléphérique,* call 76 44 33 65 or 76 51 00 00.)

Halfway down the hill from the Bastille, the **Musée Dauphinois,** 30, rue Maurice-Gignoux (tel. 76 87 66 77), is a noteworthy example of France's many (too many?) regional museums. Formerly the convent of Sainte-Marie-d'en-Haut, the 17th-century building has a fine collection of *dauphinois* folk art. (Open Wed.-Mon. 9am-noon and 2-6pm. Admission 9F, students and seniors 5F, Wed. free.)

Students and recent immigrants now occupy most of the 18th-century houses on the riverbank, Grenoble's most attractive neighborhood. Victorian **Pont St-Laurent,** an early suspension bridge, occupies the former site of a Gallo-Roman bridge. Overlooking the manicured **Jardin de Ville,** the elaborate Renaissance **Palais de Justice** has a set of intricately carved ceilings. The only organized visits depart from pl. St-André at 10am on the first Saturday of each month (8F, students 4F), but you can usually sneak a look.

Information-age street signs seem to point to an endless number of museums or houses, but only three are truly extraordinary. The **Musée de Peinture et de Sculpture,** pl. Verdun (tel. 76 54 09 82), has a well-organized collection of Egyptian art, Renaissance and Baroque paintings (including a few beautiful Tintorettos) and a notable modern collection (Chagall, Picasso, Matisse). A flashy room with geometric designs and works by Calder exits to the street through a tunnel. (Open Wed.-Mon. 10am-noon and 2-6pm. Admission 9F, students 5F, Wed. free. Tours on request.) The Alps were a stronghold of the Resistance; history buffs should make a point of visiting the **Musée de la Résistance,** 14, rue J.J. Rousseau (tel. 76 44 51 81; open Wed.-Sat. 3-6pm; free). A renovated warehouse at 155, cours Berriat (take tramway A to Berriat), houses **MAGASIN** (Center National d'Art Contemporain), an exhibition area for temporary displays of modern art (tel. 76 21 95 84; open Tues.-Sun. 12:30-7pm; admission 9F, ages under 25 5F). Guided tours of the *vieille*

ville leave from the tourist office at 4pm Monday through Saturday from July 1
to Sept. 30. (½-hr., 10F, students 5F.)

Heed the *Guide DAHU's* advice on Grenoble's hot nightspots with a young clientele. Bars and sidewalk cafés serve a wider age group, and are just as active as their
youthful competition. **King Charly Pub,** 2, rue de Sault (tel. 76 47 29 72), attracts
an international student crowd. (Open Mon.-Sat. 11:30am-1am.) **L'Entrepot,** rue
Auguste Gerin (tel. 76 48 21 48), spotlights local jazz and rock. (Cover 40F. Open
Mon.-Sat. from 8pm.)The upscale **Palazzo,** 7, av. de Vizille (tel. 76 96 07 97), is
packed six nights a week. (Cover 80F, cocktails around 60F. Open Mon.-Sat. 9pm-
1am) **Le Club des Etudiants,** 50-52, rue St-Laurent (tel. 76 42 00 68), is a favorite
student disco, but you might not feel comfortable alone. You must show student
ID to get in. (Cover about 35F. Open Thurs.-Sat. 10pm-3am. Often closed in summer.) **Le Crocodile,** 1, Grande Rue (tel. 76 42 74 45), is a chic café with live bands.
(Free. Open daily 2pm-1am.) **Le George V,** 124, cours Berriat (tel. 76 73 64 47),
is a popular gay disco. (Cover 60F. Open Wed.-Sun. 11pm-3am.) **L'Etalon,** 1, rue
Alphonse-Terray (tel. 76 49 20 95), has a reputation for being a meat market. (Cover
60F. Open Mon.-Sat. 3pm-1am.)

Grenoble suffers a shortage neither of the banal nor the bizarre. Annual offerings
including February ice car racing, an August 15 outdoor Summer Feast, and the
spectacular Bastille Day (July 14) fireworks at the Bastille, which includes high
school students dancing on the sides of buildings. The **Festival du Court Métrage**
(short films) takes place July 5-9. Contact the Cinémathèque Française, 21, rue
Génissieu (tel. 76 24 13 83), for details. The renowned **Festival International du
Roman et du Film Noir** occurs during the second week of October. Over 100 authors
from around the world come to Grenoble to sign, display, and sell their books. For
more information, contact Association Grenoble-Polar, 21, rue Génissieu (tel. 76
24 13 83) or **Le Cargo,** Maison de la Culture de Grenoble, at the tourist office. (Open
Mon.-Fri. 1-5:45pm, Sat. 10am-7pm (tel. 76 54 34 36).)

Near Grenoble

In 1605 the monks of the **Monastère de la Grande Chartreuse** tried to produce
the elixir of long life; they came up with the celebrated Chartreuse liqueur. The
all-natural recipe of 130 ingredients is now known only by three monks. Of course,
this does not stop local stores from selling "the real thing" in plastic bottles for
around 70F. The design of the actual monastery is the prototype for the "charterhouse style" that has influenced communal institutions and hermitages around the
world. You cannot visit the monastery (the monks still live there in silence and seclusion), but there is an excellent view of it from **Correrie,** about 1km from the main
road. The **museum** in Correrie (tel. 76 88 60 45) faithfully depicts the monks' daily
routine. (Open April-Sept. Mon.-Sat. 9am-noon and 2-6:30pm. Admission 12F.)
You can reach Correrie by taking a bus to nearby **Voiron** from Grenoble's *gare routière* (5 per day, 45 min., 18F). While in Voiron, take a free tour of the **Caves de
la Grande Chartreuse,** 10, bd. Edgar Kofler (tel. 76 05 81 77). It ends with a free
tasting of the colorful spirits. (Open July-Aug. daily 8am-6:30pm; Easter-June and
Oct. 1-8 8-11:30am and 2-6:30pm; Oct. 9-Easter Mon.-Fri. 8-11:30am and 2-
5:30pm.)

Swimming, sailing and camping await ten km north of Voiron at **Lac de Paladru,**
the largest in Dauphiné. Four buses per day run to the lake from Voiron (45 min.,
30F). Free beaches and more camping await at Charavines, Paladru, Bilieu, Le Pin,
and Montferrat. The local tourist office is in Charavines-Paladru (tel. 76 06 60 31).

Directly north of Grenoble, in the Chartreuse Valley, the scenic resort town of
St-Pierre de Chartreuse offers swimming, tennis, golf, and hiking during the summer. The 15km route near **St-Laurent du Pont** passes through some of the most
picturesque countryside in the Alps; locals consider this road a national monument.
The tourist office is located in St-Laurent du Pont (tel. 76 88 62 08; **postal code:**
38380). **Camping La Martinière** (tel. 76 88 60 36) is in nearby **Martinière** (40F per

2 people). The smaller and cheaper **Camping Charmant Som** (tel. 76 88 62 39) is in St-Hughes (13F per 2 people).

Site of the 1968 Winter Olympics, in which native son Jean-Claude Killy won all three downhill events, Grenoble is the gateway to some of the Alps' most renowned ski resorts. In general, enjoying the white stuff does not come cheap. Weekly passes run 500-800F; weekend passes average 90-150F. Ski equipment in most areas rents for 100-160F per day. In summer, weekly passes (120F-150F) provide access to pools, tennis courts, golf courses, and other facilities.

Alpe d'Huez lies at the heart of the Oisans, only 63km from Grenoble (tourist office tel. 76 80 35 41; **postal code:** 38750). The **Auberge de Jeunesse** is on Chemin de la Goutte (tel. 76 80 37 37). For snow conditions call 76 80 34 32; for general information, call 78 58 33 33. Buses run to Alpe d'Huez from Grenoble (4 per day, 2hr., 62F). Named for the union of two villages on Mont de Lans and Venosc, **Les Deux Alpes** (75km from Grenoble) is also served by bus from Grenoble (3 per day, 2½hr., 72F). Call the tourist office (tel. 76 79 22 00) for more information; the **postal code** is 38860). Closer to Grenoble (30km), **Chamrousse** (tourist office tel. 76 89 92 65; **postal code:** 38410) is also a major resort. The two **Auberges de Jeunesse (IYHF)** (tel. 76 89 91 14 and 76 89 91 31) are both 1½km away in St-Martin d'Uriage (both open June 15-Aug. 15 and Oct. 14-March 5).

Less glittery but somewhat more affordable resorts include **Villard-de-Lans** (tourist office tel. 76 95 70 38; open Dec.), **St-Nigier** (tourist office tel. 76 53 40 60), **Lans-en-Vencours** (tourist office tel. 76 95 42 62; open mid-Dec. to April), and **St-Pierre** (tourist office tel. 76 88 62 08; open mid-Dec. to April). All four areas are in the Vercors mountains, to the west of Grenoble.

To the east lie the Hautes-Alpes, with **Briançon** at their center. You can reach them through Val d'Isère, over the *Iseran* pass from the north, or by the scenic **route des Grandes Alpes.** Buses from Grenoble's *gare routière* make the trip twice a day (3 hr., 110F). In July, the renowned **Tour de France** bicycle race passes through on nearby N6, a steep and spectacular road.

Chambéry

Sitting at the foot of the Chartreuse and Bauges Mountains, in a valley bordered by Lac du Bourget and Val d'Isère, Chambéry (pop. 60,000) was the capital of Savoie for centuries. Before the Savoie region became a department of France in 1860, Chambéry's loyalties were split between France and Italy; the Dukes of Savoie had an affinity for Italy, but the citizens considered themselves French. The different buildings and styles of Chambéry's castle attest to the frequent French and Italian invasions of the 16th and 17th centuries. Happily, no tourist invasion has yet hit the lovingly preserved *vieille ville.*

Orientation and Practical Information

Chambéry lies on the Lyon-Chamonix line, about one hour from Grenoble and Annecy, three to four hours from Chamonix, 1½ hours from Lyon and Geneva, and five to six hours from Paris. It is also a convenient 50km from Albertville, the main site of the 1992 Winter Olympic Games. To reach the tourist office from the station, walk left for one long block, then cross pl. du Centenaire to bd. de la Colonne.

Tourist Office: 24, bd. de la Colonne (tel. 79 33 42 47). Disabled access from the other side at 19, av. des Ducs de Savoie. English-speaking staff has loads of pamphlets on the city and region. Bimonthly *15 jours à Chambéry* (free) lists activities. In summer, the office sponsors a nightly tour of the old quarter and 2 daily tours of the château (15F, students 10F). Accommodations information. Open Mon.-Sat. 9am-noon and 2-6pm. **Regional Tourist Office,** 24, bd. de la Colonne (tel. 79 85 12 45), in the same building. Information on the surrounding area and ski resorts. Open Mon.-Sat. 9am-noon and 2-6pm.

Post Office: (tel. 79 69 10 69), on pl. Paul Vidal. **Telephones** and **currency exchange.** Open Mon.-Fri. 8am-7pm, Sat. 8am-noon. **Postal Code:** 73000.

Trains: (tel. 79 85 50 50; reservations 79 62 35 26), on pl. de la R. Sommeiller. Trains at least every hour to: Lyon (1½-2 hr., 65F); Grenoble (1-2 hr., 43F); Aix-les-Bains (12 per day, 10 min., 12F); Annecy (12 per day, 45 min., 38F); Geneva (8 per day, 1½ hr., 70F); Paris via Lyon (many, 5½ hr., 240F). Information office open Mon.-Fri. 8am-12:20pm and 1:30-6:50pm, Sat. 8am-12:20pm and 1:30-5:50pm.

Buses: pl. de la R. Sommeiller, across from the train station. Many companies share this central depot. Try **VFD** first (tel. 79 68 28 78). For all other companies, call 79 69 11 88. To Le Chateland (3 per day, 1½ hr., 40F); Annecy (8 per day, 1 hr., 31F); Aix-les-Bains (8 per day, 20 min., 12F); Grenoble (6 per day, 1 hr., 38.50F). Excursions to: the Grande Chartreuse (105F); Chamonix (130F); Venice (420F); Geneva and Yvoire (131F); Turin (140F); Zermatt (195F); Strasbourg (230F). Call VFD for information on other trips. **STAC,** 18, av. des Chevaliers Tireurs (tel. 79 69 61 12). Local buses run every 10-15 min. Mon.-Fri. 1-4F.

Taxi: Tel. 79 33 39 14. 24 hrs.

Bike Rental: D. Brouard, 28, av. de Turin (tel. 79 70 13 54). In the Motobecane store on the way out of town, next to the fire station. Mountain bikes 50F per day plus deposit.

Hiking Information: Club Alpin Français, 70, rue Croix d'Or (tel. 79 33 05 52). Advice on hiking and mountaineering in the area. Open Tues.-Fri. 5:30-7:30pm, Sat. 10am-noon.

Car Rental: Car Go! 1, quai de Verdun (tel. 79 96 34 84). Despite the fantastic (and blatantly imitative) name, the average rental is only 96F per day.

Womens Center: Centre d'Information sur les Droits des Femmes, 22, rue Jawerie (tel. 79 85 49 13). General advice and pamphlets in French. Open on a walk-in basis Mon.-Fri. 2-5pm.

Youth Information Center: Centre d'Information et de Documentation Jeunesse (CIDJ), 4, pl. de la Gare (tel. 79 62 66 87), across from the train station. Information on sports, hostels, and *foyers.* Bulletin board posts rides, jobs, baby-sitting, and housing information. BIJ/Transalpino tickets. Open Mon.-Fri. 9am-noon and 2-6pm.

Laundromat: 37, pl. Monge. Wash 12F, dry 1F per 5 min., soap 4F. Open daily 7am-10pm.

Hospital: Centre Hospitalier (tel. 79 62 93 70), on pl. François-Chion.

Medical Emergency: SAMU, tel. 79 69 25 25.

Police: 585, av. de la Boisse (tel. 79 96 17 17). **Emergency,** tel. 17.

Accommodations and Camping

Chambéry's few budget hotels are pleasant and rarely full. The *foyer* is nicer than most hotels. All cluster in or near the pedestrian zone.

Maison des Jeunes et de la Culture (MJC), 311, Faubourg-Montmélian (tel. 79 75 13 23). From the train station, take bus B or E (5F) to stop "MJC." Otherwise an easy 10 min. walk from Tourist Office (turn right on Blvd. de la Colonne and head straight along the river). Friendly staff. No lockout. No guests after 9:30pm. Comfortable dorm singles 52F. Doubles 84F. Sheets 22F. Office open Tues.-Fri. 1-9pm, Sat.-Mon. 8am-8pm; Sept.-June daily 8am-8pm. Reservations recommended.

Hôtel le Maurennais, 2, rue Ste-Barbe (tel. 79 69 42 78), in the shadow of the château. The cheapest hotel in town. Singles 53F. Doubles 75F.

Hôtel du Château, 37, rue Jean-Pierre-Vaugrat (tel. 79 69 48 78). Also in the shadow, but sunny rooms. Singles 65F. Doubles 130F.

Hôtel de la Banche, 10, pl. de l'Hôtel de Ville (tel. 79 33 15 62). Small, half-timbered house in an excellent location. Bar downstairs. Singles 100F. Doubles 160F. Triples 180F. Breakfast 20F. Often booked; reservations accepted.

Hôtel Savoyard, 35, pl. Monge (tel. 79 35 36 55), not far from the center of town. A small, cozy hotel attached to a good restaurant. Singles and doubles 90F, with shower 135F. You must eat 1 meal per day, besides breakfast. Breakfast 20F. Restaurant serves 51-89F *menus,* as well as fondue and *raclette* (52-62F per person, 2 person minimum). Call ahead; sometimes randomly closed.

Camping: The nearest is **Camping le Nivolet** (tel. 79 33 19 48), north of town in Bessens. 8F per person, 8F per tent, 5F per car. Electricity 8F. Open May-Sept.

Food

Cheap pizzerias, *crêperies,* and a few regional restaurants beckon from the pedestrian zone in the center of town, especially on rue du Croix d'Or. *Charcuteries* and *épiceries* on pl. de Genève and at the foot of pl. St-Léger make gourmet meals cheap and easy. Les Halles on pl. de Genève house a covered **market** on Tuesday, Thursday, and Saturday (6am-noon).

Cafétéria Olympie, 2, av. de Bassens, in the same building as the Maison des Jeunes. Best quantity-to-price ratio. Full meals 30F. Open Mon.-Fri. 11:30am-3pm and 6:30-9pm, Sat. 11:30am-3pm.

Le Clap, 4, rue Ste-Barbe, next to Hôtel le Maurennais. No, you won't get it here. Sumptuous mussels, rice and salad combo (45F) served under the watchful gaze of Hollywood greats. Russian specialties include creamy *blinis* caviar (40F). Open Tues.-Sat. noon-2pm and 7-10pm, Mon. 7-10pm.

La Belle Vie, 40, rue d'Italie. Small servings of vegetables and health food (no red meat) served in a simple green setting. Salads 15-30F. Pike pâté 29F. Carrot and nut tart 28F. *Plat du jour* 38F. Vitamins, seaweed, and mudpacks also served. Open Tues.-Sun. 11:45am-9pm.

La Frite Dorée, 13, pl. Monge, near Hôtel Savoyard. Simple 40F *menu.* Hearty, garlic-laden portions of regional *charcuterie* 12F. No *frites . . .* Open Tues. noon-5pm, Thurs.-Sun. noon-9pm.

La Ha Tien, 26, rue de la Banque. A quiet restaurant with Vietnamese, Chinese, and Cambodian food. Curried pork 35F. Beef plates 30-35F. Open Tues.-Sun. noon-1:30pm and 7-10:30pm, Mon. 7-10:30pm.

Sights and Entertainment

For six centuries, independent Savoie's power emanated from the imposing **Château des Ducs de Savoie.** The château's last prominent master was King Vittorio Emmanuel, who presided over Italy's unification. Repainted in *trompe-l'œil* in the 19th century, **Ste-Chapelle** was the 16th-century home of Jesus' burial cloth. The frequent invasions by French kings eventually persuaded the Duke of Savoie to transfer the capital, and the Holy Shroud, to Turin, Italy, where it remains today. (Obligatory, energetic 1hr. tours July-Aug. 5 per day; June and Sept. 2 per day; March-May and Oct.-Nov. Sat. at 2:15pm, Sun. at 3:30pm. Admission 15F, students 10F.) From July 7 to September 8 the Château presents a short play, *Confessions d'un Chamberien,* complete with authentic 18th-century costumes and dialogue from Rousseau's *Confessions.* (Sat. at 9pm, 35F; reservations at Tourist Office.)

Take time to stroll through Vieux Chambéry and admire the Italian-style *hôtels particuliers* on rue Croix-d'Or and the pl. St-Léger. The tourist office has a list of the city's most interesting mansions. (Tours of the old city leave from pl. Château June-Sept. daily at 4pm; March-May and Oct.-Nov. Sat. at 4pm. Admission 15F, students 10F.) In July and August, a pleasant tour includes a free tasting of the wines of Savoie. (Daily at 9pm. Admission 18F.) For those with weary feet, the Little Train leaves from the pl. St-Léger daily (every hr. 10am-noon and 2-7pm; admission 22F). The **Fontaine des Eléphants**— the most photographed monument in Chambéry—serves as a good compass for discovering the city's other sites. Erected in 1838 to honor Count "Bubba" de Boigne, who made it big in India, the elephants' trunks still spout occasional showers. North of this aquatic stampede in place du Palais de Justice is the **Musée des Beaux Arts** (tel. 79 33 44 48), home of the second largest collection of Italian paintings in France (after the Louvre). (Open Wed.-Mon. 10am-noon and 2-6pm. Free.) The uncrowded **Musée Savoisien** (tel. 79 33 44 48), south of the elephants on bd. du Théâtre in an old Franciscan convent, displays some delightful primitives from Savoie in one of the cloister galleries. (Open Wed.-Mon. 10am-noon and 2-6pm. Free.)

Two km out of town on the uphill chemin des Charmettes stands the **Musée des Charmettes** (tel. 79 33 39 44), the house where Jean-Jacques Rousseau lived in vice and debauchery with Mme. de Warrens. The interior has been reconstructed and now displays Rousseau memorabilia; the garden has yet another **spectacular view.** From pl. Monge, take av. de la République to chemin des Charmettes; follow the mountain stream (uphill of course) until you run out of breath. (Open Wed.-Mon. 10am-noon and 2-6pm; Oct.-March Wed.-Mon. 10am-noon and 2-4:30pm. Admission 5F.)

Garden spots in the center of town include the **Jardins du Verney;** the **Clos Savoiroux,** with its statue of Rousseau; and the **Parc des Loisirs de Buisson Rond,** with its fine rose garden. On June 21, Chambéry hosts the outdoor **Fête de la Musique.** For 10 days in September, the **Foire de Savoie** raises local spirits, and in early October, a series of small festivals enlivens the town.

Aix-les-Bains

The small town of Aix-les-Bains lies scattered about translucent **Lac du Bourget,** France's largest natural lake. Renowned for its thermal baths, Aix has become an elegant *ville d'eau* (water town), attracting primarily an older, well-off crowd who come to cure their ailments—from rheumatism to *ennui*. Endless games of *boules,* manicured parks, and elegant 19th-century *hôtels* set the tone for this fountain of faded youth. Things pick up a little (but only a little) on the busy lakeside, where a more dynamic crowd mills about the restaurants, campsites, and beaches.

Orientation and Practical Information

Aix-les-Bains lies 10 minutes north of Chambéry on the main train line. The center of town is up the hill from the train station; the **lake** and **beach** are a 20-minute walk in the opposite direction. From the station, take bus #2 to the beach (every 10-15 min., 6.50F). To reach the tourist office and the center of town, follow av. Général de Gaulle (directly in front of the train station) and turn left before the Thermes Nationaux. The **tourist office,** pl. Maurice Mollard (tel. 79 35 05 92), distributes decent free maps (a more complete map costs 12F) and a glossy tourist guide. They also give free tours of the town Tuesday and Thursday mid-June to mid-September at 2:30pm. (Open Mon.-Sat. 9am-noon and 2-7pm, Sun. 10am-noon and 4:30-6:30pm; Oct.-March Mon.-Fri. 9am-noon and 2-6pm, Sat. 9am-noon.) The **post office** is on av. Victoria at av. Maris de Solms (tel. 79 33 15 15); the **postal code** is 73100. (Open Mon.-Fri. 8am-7pm, Sat. 8am-noon.) **Banque Populaire,** rue de Genève, exchanges currency. (Open Mon.-Thurs. 8:15am-12:15pm and 1:30-5:10pm, Fri. 8:15am-12:15pm and 1:30-4:10pm.) **Trains** leave almost hourly for Chambéry (10 min., 13.50F), Annecy (45 min., 33F), and Grenoble (1¼ hr., 52F). You can **rent bikes** at the baggage desk here (40F per ½-day, 60F per day, deposit 500F). For **taxis** call 79 35 08 05. The **hospital** is on bd. Pierpont-Morgan (tel. 79 35 71 28); the **police** can be reached at 79 35 61 98.

Accommodations, Camping, and Food

Like most thermal spas, Aix-les-Bains is loaded with hotels, many of which are reasonably priced. A few require reservations in summer. One-star hotels may attach a 1.50F nightly tax to your bill. Most hotels cluster between the rue de Genève and the beginning of ave. du Grand Port.

Auberge de Jeunesse (tel. 79 88 32 88), on promenade de Sierroz. Take bus #2 to the left of the station and get off at the Camping stop. The 30-min. walk from the *centre ville* can be enjoyable if you take a short-cut along the stream (*le Sierroz*). A beautiful, modern hostel with a cornfield out back and spacious dorm accommodations. Four min. from the lake. ISIC card required. Open 7-10am, 6-10pm. If out after 10pm, ask for key. 38.10F per person. Breakfast 16F, meals 38F. Sheets 12F. Open Dec. 15-Oct.

Hôtel Le Sporting, 58, rue de Genève (tel. 79 35 28 91). Excellent location. Clean rooms have enough room for vigorous bedtime calisthenics. The restaurant will flatten your wallet. Singles 70F. Doubles 110F. Shower 12F.

Avenue Hôtel, 16, av. du Grand Port (tel. 79 35 24 63). A little fancier than its neighbor. Singles 84F, with shower 90F. Doubles 75-90F. Shower on the floor below. Breakfast 19F.

Hôtel les Deux Savoies, 12, av. du Grand Port (tel. 79 35 14 86). Decent rooms with hardwood floors not too far from *centre ville.* Singles 70F. Doubles 100F. Breakfast 20F.

Hôtel-Brasserie de Savoie, 43, bd. Wilson (tel. 79 35 20 69), 1 block to the right of the train station. You'll be counting trains to get to sleep. Small, plain singles and doubles 85F, with shower 100F. Showers 13F. Breakfast 20F.

Camping: Camping Municipal Sierroz (tel. 79 61 21 43), conveniently located across from the lake about 2km from the station just down the street from the youth hostel. Large. Showers, grocery store, and volleyball. 12.50F per person, 23F per tent; 48F for 4 or more people. Electricity 12F. Reservations required 1 month in advance July-Aug. 3F discount Oct.-Nov. 15 and Feb. 15-May. Office open Feb. 15-Nov. 15 daily 8am-noon and 3-7pm.

Cheap, lively restaurants are rare. Look on rue de Genève and rue Albert 1er, behind the tourist office. For the more economically minded, a large **market** fills pl. Clemenceau on Wednesday and Saturday. There is also a **Prisunic** supermarket at 15, rue de Genève, and **La Provence,** Sq. Alfred Boucher, rue de Genève. **La Quimperoise,** 4, rue Albert 1er, serves excellent *crêpes* for 9-40F and a *crêpe* meal with green salad for 40F. (Open Tues.-Sat. noon-11pm, Sun. 7-11pm.) **Cafétéria Casino,** 8, rue du Casino, seems like it just rolled off the Indiana toll road. (Delicious fruit melba 14F. Steak and chips 34.50F. Open daily 11am-10pm.) **La Petite Auberge,** 76, rue de Genève, serves a 55F fondue and a 40F *menu.* Near the tourist office, **Campanus,** pl. du Revard, a lively café with outdoor seating, serves *crêpes* for 18-22F and omelettes for 22-25F. (Open Thurs.-Tues.)

Sights and Entertainment

The **Thermes Nationaux,** Aix-les-Bains's *raison d'être,* give tours of the new baths followed by a descent underground to view the remains of the ancient Roman ones. Outside, visit the grottoes and the sinus-clearing sulphur springs. Tours leave from opposite the tourist office on pl. Maurice-Mollard. (Mon.-Sat. at 3pm; Oct.-April Wed. and Sat. at 3pm, or call 79 35 38 50 for an appointment. Admission 5F.) Treatments in the baths involve mud, mineral water, massage, and money. An underwater massage runs 60-100F. (Reservations recommended July-Aug.) The **Musée du Docteur Fauré,** bd. des Côtes (tel. 76 61 06 57), diverts spirits sodden by bath water with works by Sisley, Pissarro, Renoir, Cézanne, and Rodin. (Open April 15-Oct. 15 Wed.-Mon. 10am-noon and 2-6pm; Oct. 16-March 30 Wed.-Sun. 10am-noon and 2-6pm. Admission 15F.)

The best reason to stay overnight in Aix-les-Bains is the morning excursion to the **Abbaye d'Hautecombe.** Gregorian chants emanate from this Benedictine abbey, which was completely restored in the 19th century and now houses the tombs of the princes of Savoie. (Free. Donations appreciated.) The only means of transportation is a boat that departs from Aix's Grand Port (July-Aug. Mon.-Sat. at 6 per day; June and Sept. Mon.-Sat. 3 per day; May and Oct. Mon.-Sat. 1 per day; 3¼ hr., 35F). A special Sunday trip to attend the mass at the abbey leaves at 8:30am. Call 79 35 05 19 or 79 61 45 75 for more information. Other water excursions include a two-hour trip to the southern end of the lake (July-Aug., 35F) and to **Canal de Savière,** at the northern tip (leaves at 2:15pm, 4 hrs., 75F).

The little town of **Le Revard,** a 20-minute bus ride from Aix, is surrounded by an extensive network of trails for cross-country skiing (Dec. 15-April 15) flanked by Lac du Bourget on one side and Mont Blanc on the other. Buses leave from the kiosk in the Parc de Verdure (Sept.-June daily at 10:50am and 1:15pm, 7F). For information call **Gonnet Excursions** (tel. 79 61 01 78). You can also take a two-hour hike up to Le Revard. The well-marked trail starts at the base of the Les Mentens *téléphérique* in **Mouxy,** 4km east of Aix-les-Bains. The bus excursions that leave from Chambéry all stop at Aix-les-Bains. (Call Frossard Excursions at 79 35 09 33 for more information.)

Aix hosts a variety of concerts (mostly free) in the **Théâtre de Verdure** in late July. Larger concerts take place at the Palais du Congress. For two or three days in the last week of August, Aix puts on a lakeside **Fête des Fleurs** (Flower Festival), with fireworks, singing, and the usual good clean fun. Check the blue kiosks around town for monthly information. Nightly entertainment in Aix-les-Bains is limited to a merry-go-round that whirls the young-at-heart around the pl. Carnot. (10F, 40F for 6 rides, 60F for 10 rides. Let's go!)

Annecy

With its winding cobblestone streets, overstuffed flowerboxes, turreted castle, and clear mountain lake, relentlessly photogenic Annecy is reminiscent of those high school homecoming queens that everyone resented for their perfection but fell in love with anyway. Despite the efforts of envious rivals, Annecy always comes in first. This capital of the Haute Savoie won the 1989 prize for the cleanest city in France, consistently cleaned up in the National Flower City contest (it is now out of competition), and carefully guards its reputation of having the purest lake in France. (It did, however, fail to merit a mention in the 1990 "Tattooed France" Competition.) This beauty even had a sitting with Cézanne, whose *Le Lac d'Annecy* may provide admirers with their only daytime glimpse of the lake free of the dense flotilla of sailboats and windsurfers that now skim its crystalline waters.

Orientation and Practical Information

Annecy is easily reached by rail from Chambéry, Lyon, Grenoble, and Paris. Most activity centers on the lake, southeast of the train station. The canal runs east to west through the old town, leaving the château elevated on one side and the main shopping area on the other, closer to the *centre ville*. It's hard to miss the modern tourist office: follow the rue Sommeiller from the station for one block, turn right and the left onto rue Vaugelas, and then go straight. The tourist office will be on your left, inside the greenhouse-style *bonlieu* (shopping mall).

Tourist Office: 1, rue Jean Jaurès (tel. 50 45 00 33), at pl. de la Libération on the ground floor of the *bonlieu*. Free, detailed maps. Information on hiking, hotels, campgrounds, rural lodgings, excursions to nearby towns, and mountain climbing. Guided tours (27F) daily at 10am and 3pm in summer (in English on Wed. at 3pm). Ask for the helpful booklet *Le Mois à Annecy*. **Currency exchange** open July-Aug. daily 5-6:30pm, June and Sept. Sat.-Sun. 9am-noon and 2-6:30pm. Office open daily 9am-6:30pm; Oct.-May 9am-noon and 1:45-6:30pm.

Currency Exchange: Bureau de Change, 2, Côté St-Maurice (tel. 50 45 59 97), in the *vieille ville*. No commission, good rates. Open daily 10am-noon and 2-7pm.

Post Office: 4, rue des Glières (tel. 50 45 10 19), around the corner from rue de la Poste, down the street from the train station. **Currency exchange** on the ground floor and **telephones** in the basement. Open Mon.-Fri. 8am-7pm, Sat. 8am-noon. **Postal Code:** 74000.

Trains: (tel. 50 66 50 50), on pl. de la Gare. To: Grenoble (9 per day, 2 hr., 72F); Aix-les-Bains (1 per hr., 15 min., 35F); Chambéry (10 per day, 45 min., 42F); Chamonix (8 per day, 2-2½ hr., 73F); Lyon (8 per day, 2 hr., 103F); Paris (by TGV 8 per day, 4½ hr., 281F with required 13-45F reservation; 1 night train per day, 6-8 hr.); Nice (4 per day, 6 hr., 296F). Information office open Mon.-Sat. 8am-7:15pm, Sun. 9am-7:15pm. Station open daily 5am-11:30pm.

Buses: Adjacent to the train station. Some English spoken at the information desk. **Voyages Crolard,** tel. 50 45 08 12. To: Talloires (9 per day, 1 Sun.; 25 min.; 10F); La Clusaz (4-7 per day, 1¼ hr., 31F); Chamonix (1 per day, none Sun.; 2½ hr.; 66F). Also 1-day excursions to: Geneva (July-Aug. daily, 79F); Turin (Sat., 130F); l'Abbaye d'Hautecombe (Wed., 70F). **Frossard,** tel. 50 45 73 90. Slightly cheaper day and ½-day trips in summer to: La Grande Chartreuse (Wed., 105F); Interlaken (Tues., 170F); l'Abbaye d'Hautecombe (Fri., 63F); Zermatt (Sat., 195F); Turin (Sat., 140F). Regular service to: Geneva (Mon.-Sat. 6 per day, 1¼ hr., 38.50F); Grenoble (4 per day, 2 hr., 50F); Lyon (2 per day, 4 hr., 77F). **Francony,** tel.

50 45 02 43. To: Chamonix (1 per day, 3 hr., 58F). Call **SAT** (tel. 50 37 22 13) for schedules and rates to Morzine and Avoriaz.

Public Transportation: SIBRA, tel. 50 51 70 33. Tickets 5.30F, *carnet* of 8 28F. Get a bus map and schedule from the tourist office or the kiosk on rue de la Préfecture (open Mon.-Sat. 8:30am-7pm).**Car rental: Car Go!** 29, av. de la Plaine (tel. 50 66 00 77). Around 96F per day.

Bike Rental: Loca Sports, 37, av. de Loverchy (tel. 50 45 44 33), 10 min. from the *centre ville.* 55F per day; lower rates for longer rentals. Also at the **train station.** 42F per ½-day, 50F per day, deposit 500F.

Hiking Information: Club Alpin Français, 38, av. du Parmelan (tel. 50 45 52 76), at rue de Mortillet. Information on mountain activities and organized group trips. Open Wed. 3-7pm, Fri. 5:30-7pm, Sat. 10am-noon.

Women's Center: Centre d'Information Féminin, 4, passage de la Cathédrale (tel. 50 45 61 25). Advice and pamphlets. Open Mon. and Thurs. 9am-noon and 2-5pm, Tues.-Wed. and Fri. 9am-noon.

Seniors Information: Information de Personnes Agées, 26, rue Sommeiller (tel. 50 51 40 76), leaving the tourist office, 1 block to the right off rue Prés. Fauré. Open Tues. and Thurs.-Fri. 9am-noon and 1:30-5:30pm.

English Bookstore: Persan Bleu, 9bis, rue Prés. Fauré. A small selection.

Laundromat: Pressing, in the Nouvelles Galeries complex on bd. du Lycée. Wash 14F, dry 5.50F per 15 min. Soap 3F. **Les Lavandières,** rue de Chausseurs. **Self-Laverie,** 9, rue Louis-Armand. Bring 1F, 2F, and 5F coins.

Public Showers: on quai des Clarisses (tel. 50 45 71 96). Not exactly sparkling. Showers 7F. Baths 11F. Soap, towel, and shampoo 6F. Open Wed. 5:45-7:15pm, Sat. 8:45-11:45am and 1:15-5:15pm.

Hospital: (tel. 50 88 33 33), av. des Trésums.

Medical Assistance: SAMU, tel. 50 51 21 21.

Police: 15, rue des Marquisats (tel. 50 45 21 61). **Emergency,** tel. 17.

Accommodations and Camping

Annecy has prices high enough to match its altitude. Try the Maison des Jeunes, the hostel, or one of the many small campgrounds. Reservations are indispensable; call at least two months in advance for high season and festival weekends.

Maison des Jeunes et de la Culture (MJC), 52, rue des Marquisats (tel. 50 45 08 80), on the lake, a 10-min. walk from *centre ville.* A modern building among the pines. Gorgeous view. Comfortable rooms. TV and recreation areas. Office open 24 hours. No curfew. Six-bed dorm-style rooms 45F per person. Doubles 65F per person. A strong shower, good breakfast with fruit, and sheets included. Cafeteria meals 34F. Call Mon.-Fri. 9am-3pm for reservations as far in advance as possible.

Auberge de Jeunesse "La Grande Jeanne" (IYHF), 16, route de Semnoz (tel. 50 45 33 19). Take the bus marked "Semnoz" across the street from the Hôtel de Ville (5.50F). A quiet chalet in the woods with basic dorm accommodations (4-6 per room). As always, watch your valuables. IYHF card required. Office open 5-10pm. No curfew. 50F per person, breakfast included. In off-season: 22F per person, breakfast 20F. Meals 36F.

Maison de la Jeune Fille, 1, av. du Rhône (tel. 50 45 34 81), at av. d'Aléry. Accepts men and women July-Aug.; women only Sept.-June. One-week min. stay. Office open Mon.-Fri. 8-11am and 5:45-7:30pm. No curfew. Clean, ordinary singles 85F. Obligatory breakfast and 1 meal included. 3 meals 106F. Separate cafeteria meals 30F.

Hôtel Savoyard, 41, av. de Cran (tel. 50 57 08 08), in a residential area behind the train station. The managers define hospitality (but in French). Clean, comfortable rooms. Good-sized singles or doubles 85F, with luxurious bathroom 160-190F. Triples 130F. Showers 10F. Home-cooked breakfast 15F. Open Feb.-Oct.

Hôtel des Alpes, 12, rue de la Poste (tel. 50 45 04 56). Centrally located near the post office and train station. Small and comfortable, though some rooms are noisy. Singles 80-115F. Doubles from 110F, with shower 148F. Extra bed 40F. Showers 15F. Breakfast 20F.

Rive du Lac, 6, rue des Marquisats (tel. 50 51 32 85). A fine location near the lake and *centre ville.* Large, sunny singles and doubles 95F. Doubles and triples from 112F, some with great French windows and small balconies. Showers 15F. Breakfast 20F. You can never reserve too early.

Hôtel du Château, 16, rampe du Château (tel. 50 45 27 66), up a winding ramp, near the castle in a secluded part of the old town. Grand old walls and climbing flowers. Singles and doubles with shower 130F. Two beds 140F. Triples 230F. Showers 10F. Breakfast 20F. Book early. Closed Oct. 16-Dec. 14.

Dozens of small **campgrounds** border the lake in the town of **Albigny,** which can be reached by Voyages Crolard buses or by following av. d'Albigny from the tourist office. The larger **Belvedere,** route de Semnoz (tel. 50 45 48 30), on the same road as the hostel, is closer and usually packed. The food store sells staples at reasonable prices. (Closed Oct. 16-Dec. 14.)

Food

Annecy has few affordable restaurants; lakeside picnics are probably your best bet. Pick up your fixings at the **markets** on Tuesday, Friday, and Sunday morning around pl. Ste-Claire, and Saturday morning on bd. Taine. The cafeterias at the MJC and the Maison de la Jeune Fille serve heaps of food to anyone who will pay 35F. The town has lots of small **Casino** supermarkets, and a **Prisunic** occupies the better part of the pl. de Notre Dame.

Chez Petros, 15, faubourg Ste-Claire, near the end of rue Ste-Claire. The only Greek restaurant, brags the owner/manager/cook, in the Haute-Savoie. Try the *guiros* (34F), with the *feuilles de vignes* (stuffed grape leaves) as an appetizer. Scrumptious baklava 16F. Open daily 11am-3pm and 6:30pm-1am; Sept.-April Mon.-Sat. only.

Taverne du Freti, 12, rue Ste-Claire. A find for those fond of fondue. *Fondue savoyarde* and many other varieties 45-60F. *Tarte paysanne* 30F. Open Tues.-Sun. 7-11:30pm.

Au Bord du Thiou, 4, pl. St-François-de-Sales. Scenic location on the canal near the Palais de l'Ile. Good for salads (10-30F), crepes (from 17F), and ice cream. The *"crêpe* Rock" includes Roquefort cheese, nuts, raisins, and cognac (26F). Open daily noon-2pm and 5pm-midnight; in off-season 5pm-midnight.

Le Cellier, 7, rue Perrière, in the heart of the old town. Less pretentious than its neighbors. Pizza 35-52F. *Plat du jour* 40F. Trout with almonds 50F. Open daily noon-2pm and 6:30-11pm.

Au Lilas Rose, passage de l'Evéché. Prize location in *vieille ville.* Everything from *fondue savoyarde* (55F per person) to trout (53F) to lamb cutlets with fries (59F) to pizza (30F). A unique "do-it-yourself" meat dish which you cook on hot stones and eat with vegetables and lettuce (89F, serves 2-3 people). Open daily 11:45am-2:30pm and 6:45-11pm.

Cafétéria Le Petit Pierre, 8, rue de l'Annexion. Plastic surroundings, but the best quantity-to-price ratio in town. Main dishes 20-34F. Open daily 11am-2:30pm and 6:30-11pm.

Sights and Entertainment

In the *vieille ville,* follow the swans along the canal du Thiou and past the baroque locks, to the formidable **Palais de L'Ile,** a 12th-century prison jutting out from a tiny island. For a view of the old town's aquatic labyrinth, climb up to the **Château d'Annecy** (tel. 50 45 29 66). In addition to the obligatory folklore collection, the château houses an ongoing series of expositions focusing on various periods and media. (Open July-Aug. daily 10am-noon and 2-6pm; June and Sept. Wed.-Mon. 10am-noon and 2-6pm. Admission 10F, students 5F. Free on Wed. Sept.-May.)

The justly famous scenery of the Lac d'Annecy is best appreciated by pedaled, motorized, or chauffered boat. **La Compagnie des Bateaux,** 6, pl. aux Bois (tel. 50 51 08 40), and at the quai Napoléon III, conducts various cruises which all dock frequently for photo breaks (5-6 per day; 1 hr., 45F, ages 5-14 35F; 1½ hr. 55F, ages 5-14 45F; mealtime cruises 58 and 148F). The main beach charges 13F (ages under 18 9F), but you can easily find free places to swim all along the shore. The **plage de Sevrier,** a few kilometers past the MJC on rue des Marquisats, allows some breathing space. The **Champs de Mars** is a premier sunning and Frisbee site. Around the Jardin Public you can rent windsurfers (70F per hr.), canoes and kayaks (50F for 2 hr.), sailboats, pedal boats, motor-launches, and small outboard boats (28-44F per hour).

The lakeside towns of **St-Jorioz, Doussard, Menthon-St-Bernard** (birthplace of St-Bernard, founder of the famed Hospices), **Duingt** (beloved of Cézanne), and **Talloires** are all within 20km of Annecy and accessible by bus. (Check with **Voyages Crolard** excursions; 2-3 per day in high season, 45-70F). The tourist office in Annecy has a brochure describing their main attractions. All offer a smorgasbord of swimming, boating, hiking, tennis, and evening entertainment. The **Fête du Lac** enlivens the first Saturday in August with fireworks and water shows (admission 45-190F). Each year the floats on the lake take on different themes; "Monsters and Legends," "Adventures in the Far West," and "Beyond the Planet Earth" have been themes in the past. The **Festival de la Vieille Ville** (1st 2 weeks in July) features free concerts, performances in the streets and churches, and a few big-time musical events.

Near Annecy

Ten km from Annecy, waterfalls roar over the scarred cliffs of the **Gorges du Fier,** a canyon carved by prehistoric glaciers. (Open March 15-Oct. 15 daily 9am-6pm. Admission a steep 20F for the 40-min. walk. Call 50 46 23 07 for more information.) The medieval **Château de Montrottier** (tel. 50 46 23 02) lies five minutes up the hill from the entrance to the gorges. The castle contains centuries-old East Asian costumes, armor, and pottery. (Open June-Sept. 15 daily 9-11:30am and 2-5:30pm; Easter-May and Sept. 16-Oct. 15 Wed.-Mon. 9-11:30am and 2-5:30pm. Obligatory, informative tour 20F; students 15F.) To get to the gorges and the château, take the Voyages Crolard (tel. 50 45 09 12) excursion bus (2-3 per week, 2:45pm, 75F). Alternately, take the train to **Lovagny** and then walk the 800m to the gorges (3 per day stop at Lovagny at odd hours, 10 min., 10F); or take bus A to the end of the line at Poisy and walk the 4km to Lovagny and the château.

Ask at the Annecy tourist office for a guide on hikes around the lake. **La Forêt du Cret du Maure,** next to the Parc Regional du Semnoz (near the youth hostel), is peaceful, flowery, and fragrant (tourist office guidebook 8F). **Talloires,** 13km from Annecy, makes a good starting point for hikes to **La Cascade d'Angon** (1 hr.) and the beautiful gardens of the **Ermitage de St-Germain** (45 min.).

In winter, hotel prices drop and the skiers pour in. The nearest ski resort is **La Clusaz** (accessible by bus). Contact the **tourist office** in La Clusaz (tel. 50 02 60 92; **postal code** 74220) for information. The **Auberge de Jeunesse Chalet "Marco-ret" (IYHF)** has dorm rooms for 55F. (Open 7-10am, 6-10pm. No curfew. Ask for key after 10pm.)

In the Facigny area north of Annecy, **Samoëns** boasts **Jardin Alpin,** eight acres of waterfalls, small ponds, and terraces. (Open daily 8am-noon and 1:30-7pm; in off-season 8am-noon and 1:30-5pm.) The **Auberge de Jeunesse "Beau Site" (IYHF),** in La Coutettaz (tel. 50 79 14 86), is one km outside the town of **Morzine.** A tough mountain leg of the Tour de France finishes there in the middle of July. **Lac de Montriond,** a sparkling mountain lake at an altitude of 1164m, splashes against the banks of **Avoriaz,** a chic resort without automobiles and accessible only by cable car. **Flaine,** dubbed the "intellectual's ski resort," is a relatively new establishment with avant-garde films, galleries, and remarkably good skiing in winter. For more information, contact the tourist office in Morzine (tel. 50 79 03 45; **postal code** 74110). The nearest train station is in Les Cluses, 30km away. Call **SAT** (tel. 50 37 22 13) for bus schedules.

Chamonix

Chamonix is literally the pinnacle of both cool Alpine beauty and sweaty Alpine athleticism. Snowcapped Mont Blanc (Europe's highest peak at 4807m) and its lesser cousins draw thousands of hikers, bikers, skiers, delta-planers, and parachutists to this city-in-the-clouds in summer and winter. Despite a slight parochial streak (only recently did the prestigious mountain guide school admit people not born in Chamonix), the city welcomes an international crowd whose multilingual snorts and grunts, followed by the inevitable oohs and ahhs, resound throughout the valley.

Directions and locations are often expressed in altitude—Chamonix is at 1035m and everything else is up. Chamonix comprises both the central town and the complex of nearby villages, scattered between forests and mountains. Les Bossons, Les Pèlerins, Les Praz, Les Bois, Les Tines, Lavancher, Les Chosalets, Argentière, Montroc, and Le Tour all spread along the narrow valley, bounded by the Mont Blanc range and the Aiguilles Rouges chain. Buses and trains serve the valley well, and a number of mechanical conveniences will carry you up the slopes.

Orientation and Practical Information

The center of town is at the intersection of the three main commercial streets: av. Michel Croz, rue du Docteur Paccard, and rue Joseph Vallot, each named for a past conqueror of Mont Blanc's summit. North of the river *Arve* is *Le Brávent*, and to the south, the entire Mont Blanc *massif.* From the train station, follow av. Michel Croz straight through town, take a left onto rue du Dr. Paccard, and then follow your first right to the pl. de l'Eglise and the tourist office. The detailed map in front of the train station will set you straight.

Tourist Office: (tel. 50 53 00 24), on pl. du Triangle. Efficient, modern center with a list of hotels and dormitories and a helpful map of campgrounds. Everything in English. Free hotel-finding service. Hotel reservations (tel. 50 53 23 33) require a 30% deposit. Sells the *Carte des Sentiers d'Eté* (hiking map, 20F) and *Chamonix Magazine,* a useful biweekly bulletin (3F, in winter free). Handy list of the area's *téléphériques* has hours, telephone numbers, and prices. A user-friendly computer system (in French and English) provides telephone numbers and weather conditions on a colorful screen. Open daily 8:30am-7:30pm; Sept.-June 8:30am-12:30pm and 2-7pm.

Currency Exchange: Société Générale, 205, av. Michèle Croz. No charge. Open Mon.-Fri. 8:30-11:45am and 1:45-5:45pm.

Post Office: (tel. 50 53 15 90), on pl. Jacques-Balmat. Disabled access. **Telephones,** telex, and Poste Restante. Open Mon.-Fri. 8am-7pm, Sat. 8am-noon; Sept.-June Mon.-Fri. 8am-noon and 2-6pm, Sat. 8am-noon. **Postal Code: 74400.**

Trains: (tel. 50 53 00 44), on av. de la Gare. To: St.-Gervais (35 min., 21F), change for banal but well-mannered Annecy (5 per day, 2 hr., 70F); Aix-les-Bains (6 per day, 2½ hr., 92F); Chambéry (6 per day, 3 hr., 95F); Lyon (6 per day, 4-5 hr., 147F); Martigny, Switzerland (6 per day, 1½ hr., 67F) with transfers to Montreux. Information office open daily 8am-noon and 2-6:30pm.

Buses: Chamonix Bus (tel. 50 53 05 55), on pl. de l'Eglise. Every ½-hr. in summer, every 15 min. in winter, and every hr. in off-season, buses go up and down the entire valley to Les Pèlerins, Les Praz, Les Houches, Argentière. Tickets 5.50-22F. *Carnet* of 6 tickets 30F, of 10 45F. Summer excursions to: Interlaken and Grindelwald (Tues., 190F); Venice (Fri., 360F); Zermatt (Sat., 190F); Turin (Sat., 180F). Tour of Lac Leman (Thurs., 155F) and Mont Blanc (Tues., 155F). **Société Alpes Transports,** at the train station (tel. 50 53 01 15). To: Annecy (2 per day, 2¾ hr., 70F); Grenoble (1 per day, 3½ hr., 132F); Geneva (1 per day, 2 hr., 135F); Courmayeur, Italy (6 per day, 40 min., 45F).

Taxis: Tel. 50 53 13 94. 24 hrs.

Car Rental: Budget, rue du Bouchet, pl. du Mont Blanc (tel. 50 55 86 66).

Bike Rental: Le Grand Bi, 240, av. du Bois du Bouchet (tel. 50 53 14 16). Three-speeds 35F per ½-day, 45F per day. Ten-speeds 40F per ½-day, 65F per day, 300F per week. Mountain bikes 65F per ½-day, 100F per day, 650F per week. Open Mon.-Sat. 9am-noon and 2-7pm. **Mountain Bike,** 138, rue des Moulins (tel. 50 53 54 76). High quality mountain bikes 70F per ½-day, 110F per day, 620F per week. Open May-Nov. 9am-7pm.

Hiking Equipment and Ski Rental: Sanglard Sports, 31, rue Michel Croz (tel. 50 53 24 70), smack in the center of town. Staff speaks English. Hiking boots 30F per day, mountain climbing boots 40F per day. Average pair of skis and boots 80F per day. Open daily 9am-12:15pm and 2:30-7:15pm. One of almost 20 choices.

Hiking Information: Maison de la Montagne, pl. de l'Eglise next to the church. The **Office de Haute Montagne,** tel. 50 53 22 08, stocks detailed maps (40F), a weather monitor, and a library of hiking and mountaineering guides. Open June 13-Sept. daily 8:30am-noon and 2:30-6:30pm; June 1-12 and Oct. daily 8:30am-noon; Nov.-May Mon.-Tues. and Thurs. 8:30am-noon. **Compagnie des Guides,** tel. 50 53 00 88. Organizes skiing and climbing lessons and leads guided hikes in summer, guided ski trips in winter. Open daily 8:30am-noon and 2-7:30pm. **Meteorological station,** tel. 50 53 03 40. Open daily 9-11am and 4:30-6pm. **Club Alpin Français:** 136, av. Michel-Croz (tel. 50 53 16 03). Information on mountain refuges and road conditions. Their bulletin board matches drivers, riders, and hiking partners. If you're considering a long stay, a 1-year membership gets you 50% off all Alpine refuges, insurance, and participation in their semi-professional skiing and hiking expeditions. Open Mon.-Sat. 9am-noon and 3:30-7:30pm; Sept.-June Mon.-Tues. and Thurs.-Fri. 3:30-7pm, Sat. 9am-noon.

Laundromat: Lav'matic, 40, impasse Primevère, to the left of rue Vallot a few blocks up from the supermarket. Wash 22F, dry 10F per 20 min. Soap 2F. 5F, 2F, and 1F coins. Open daily 8am-8:30pm.

Weather Conditions: Issued 3 times per day by the meteorological office in the Maison de la Montagne. Bulletins in the window of the Pharmacie Mont Blanc and the Club Alpin Français. Call 50 53 20 00 for a recording (in French) on the weather and road conditions. Also check tourist office computer.

Pharmacy: 3, rue Vallot (tel. 50 53 12 61), across from the tourist office. Open daily 9am-12:30pm and 2:30-7:30pm; in off-season 9:15am-12:15pm and 2:30-7:15pm.

Mountain Rescue: PGHM Secours en Montagne, 69, route de la Mollard (tel. 50 53 16 89). Accident victims or "their heirs" are responsible for all expenses. Cheap accident insurance available here, at the Club Alpin Français and at the Office de Haute Montagne. Register any serious hiking itinerary here. Open 24 hrs.

Medical Assistance: Hôpital de Chamonix (tel. 50 53 04 74), on rue Vallot. **Emergency,** tel. 50 53 02 10. **Ambulance,** tel. 50 54 40 36.

Police: 109, route de la Mollard (tel. 50 53 10 97). **Emergency,** tel. 17.

Accommodations and Camping

Mountain chalets with dormitory accommodations (5-6 beds per room, bare mattresses, hall showers) combine affordability with splendid settings: 35-40F per night buys you a bed far from our age of Docksiders and paperbacks. Many places close in the off-season (Oct.-Nov. and May). All hotels and many dormitories require reservations (preferably 6 weeks in advance) for the hectic school vacations (Dec. and Feb.) but usually have some space January, March, and April. The crowds start coming again in July and early August. If you camp, be prepared for chilly nights.

Auberge de Jeunesse (IYHF), 103, montée Jacques Balmat (tel. 50 53 14 52), in Les Pèlerins. Take the bus from pl. de l'Eglise toward Les Houches, get off at Pèlerins Ecole, and follow the signs uphill to the hostel. Simple and clean. 25% discount on all *téléphériques.* Kitchen facilities available. Office open Dec.-Sept. daily 8-10am and 5-10pm, but you can drop your bags off anytime. No curfew. 51F. Some doubles 61F per person. Nonmembers 15F more per night (up to 6 nights). Breakfast included. Meals 35F. Sheets 15F. Often full in winter; reservations accepted.

Gîtes d'Etape: Chalet Ski Station, 6, route des Moussoux (tel. 50 53 20 25). Friendly atmosphere. No kitchen but a space for cooking if you have a camp stove. Many long-term residents during ski season. Reception open 8am-11pm. No curfew. 40F per person. Shower 5F per 5 min. Sheets 10F. Open June 21-Sept. 19 and Dec. 21-May 14.

Chamoniard Volant (Chalet le Chamoniard), 45, route de la Frasse (tel. 50 53 14 09), 15 min. from the town center; follow av. du Bouchet east to La Frasse. Run by a young English-speaking French couple. Clientele a veritable global salad bowl. Kitchen facilities. Office open daily 10am-10pm. No curfew. Chummy co-ed dorms (4-6 per room) 40F per person. Continental breakfast 20F. Open year round.

Les Grands Charmoz, 468, chemin de Cristalliers (tel. 50 53 45 57). Run by a hospitable American couple. Phone ahead to reserve their comfortable rooms. Beautiful kitchen and occasional garden barbecue. Dorm accommodations 51F per person. Doubles 142F. Triples 185F. Showers and sheets included.

La Montagne, 789, promenade des Crêmeries (tel. 50 53 11 60). Want to get way from it all? This homey place lies a full ½-hour from town, deep in the Bois du Bouchet. Extensive logging, however, minimizes any sylvan feeling. Office open daily 5-10pm. Lights out 10:30pm, curfew 11pm. Bunk beds in a cramped dormitory 33F per person. Tepid showers included.

Le Corzolet, 186, av. du Bouchet, 10 min. from the station. Under construction in 1990. May open in 1991. Check at the tourist office.

Many people pitch tents in the Bois du Bouchet, but the police are cracking down on this illegal practice during peak winter and summer seasons. The tourist office dispenses a map and description of the 20 campgrounds in the area. Most have good views, hot showers, and refreshingly few trailers. Several campgrounds lie near the foot of the Aiguille du Midi *téléphérique*. **L'Ile des Barrats,** route des Pèlerins (tel. 50 53 11 75), is one of the nicest. From the *téléphérique,* turn left and look to your right (20F per person, 16F per tent; office open June 15-Sept. 15 8am-9pm). **Les Rosières,** 121, clos des Rosières (tel. 50 53 10 42), off route de Praz, the closest on the other side of Chamonix, is open all year and often has space. Follow rue Vallot for 1-2km or take a bus to Les Nants (15F per person, 8F per tent; office open 8am-9pm).

Smaller, neighboring villages maintain more secluded chalets away from the crowds. The tourist office has a list. **La Boerne,** in Tré-le-Champ (tel. 50 54 05 14), is outside Montroc and accessible by bus from Chamonix. Thirty-two francs buys you a bed in their cleverly renovated barn.

Food

Don't stray from the basics in Chamonix. Anything but fondue will probably break the bank. Luckily, most chalets have kitchens to relieve the restaurant-weary. The well-stocked **Supermarché Payot Pertin,** 117, rue Joseph Vallot, is by far the cheapest place to buy groceries (open Mon.-Fri. 8:15am-12:30pm, 2:30-6:30pm). **Markets** take place Saturday morning at pl. du Mont Blanc and Tuesday morning in Chamonix Sud, near the foot of the Aiguille du Midi *téléphérique.*

Le Fer à Cheval, 118, rue Whymper (tel. 50 53 13 22), at pl. du Mont Blanc. Follow your nose to this cozy roadside spot, but not without making reservations. *Fondue savoyarde* 40F, *fondue bourguinonne* 62F. Crepes 10-25F. Open daily noon-10:30pm.

Brasserie des Sports, rue Joseph Vallot. Simple food at affordable prices. *Fondue savoyarde* 42F; *menus* 55F and 72F. Open Wed.-Mon. noon-2pm and 6:30-9pm; in off-season Mon. and Wed.-Sat. noon-2pm and 6:30-9pm.

La Boule de Neige, 362, rue Joseph Vallot. A skier's restaurant run by a boisterous family. Steak and fries 34F. *Fondue savoyarde* 35F. 36F, 49F, and 60F *menus.* Open daily noon-2:15pm and 7-9pm.

Le Ski Rock, 30, rue Joseph Vallot (tel. 50 53 01 76). Casual *après-ski* hangout for weary jocks. 42F *menu.* Close-to-the-Italian-border lasagne 34F. Open daily noon-2:30pm, 6-9pm.

Le Ferme de la Côte, 250, route Henriette d'Angeville (tel. 50 53 13 24). Charming ambience, glorious view, and delicious food. *Raclette* 67F, *fondue savoyarde* 48F. Open daily noon-2pm and 7-10pm.

Le Fond des Gires, 350, rue du Bouchet. Big servings in a loud, cafeteria atmosphere. *Plat du jour* with roast chicken, roast beef, or fish 28-35F. Open Feb.-Dec. daily 11:45am-2pm and 7-9pm. In winter Mon.-Sat. 11:45am-2pm and 7-9pm.

Restaurant Robinson, 307, chemin des Crêmeries (tel. 50 53 45 87), in the Bois du Bouchet 20 min. from center. A beautiful wooded setting. Cupcakes in the pantry. Outdoor seating available. *Raclette* 65F. Omelettes from 18F. 72F *menu* includes veal. Open June-Sept. daily noon-2pm and 7-9pm.

Sights and Entertainment

The best place to go is up. An intricate web of trails covers the valley, each clearly marked by lines painted on trees indicating degree of difficulty. The 20F hiking map of the area available at the tourist office color-codes all the trails according to difficulty and is well worth the investment. Serious climbers should buy the IGN topographic map (40F), available at the Office de Haute Montagne and at local bookstores. The best trail guide is the pricy *Guide Vallot* (55F) available at the **Presse du Mont Blanc**, 96, rue de Docteur Paccard.

Whatever your skill, a few precautions are in order: bring layers of warm, waterproof clothing and wear sturdy shoes, preferably hiking boots. Be aware that the weather changes rapidly. Do not underestimate the length of your hike. The tourist office hiking map gives an accurate estimate of hiking times for most trails. Discuss any serious plans with the Office de Haute Montagne. *Téléphériques* give you access to the higher, more aesthetically rewarding trails quickly but can wreak havoc on your budget. A large board in the pl. de l'Eglise reports daily on which *téléphériques* and lifts are open.

One of the more spectacular trails leads up to **Lac Blanc**, a small, turquoise mountain lake dominated by snow-covered peaks. Take a bus (6F) or walk (25 min.) along rue Vallot/route de Praz to the town of Les Praz and the La Flegère *téléphérique* (26F, round-trip 42F; last descent 5:20pm). From the top of the *téléphérique*, turn right and climb the strenuous, well-marked trail for about 90 minutes. The more energetic can take the *téléphérique* of Le Brévent (tel. 50 53 13 18) up the hill from the tourist office (35F, round-trip 42F), follow the **Grand Balcon Sud** trail for two hours to the La Flegère *téléphérique* (tel. 50 53 18 58; 28F, round-trip 40F; open in summer 8am-5:30pm, last ascent 5pm) and continue up from there. The **Petit Balcon Nord** or the berry-lined **Petit Balcon Sud** are less demanding but worthwhile.

For a longer excursion, try the celebrated **Tour du Mont Blanc,** a six-day trail that passes through France, Italy, and Switzerland. Refuges are conveniently located about six hours apart. Available for anything from the shortest hike to the most difficult climb, guides are advisable for all but the most expert climbers. The Maison de la Montagne, Compagnie des Guides, and Club Alpin Français (see above) all have information. Many of their guides speak English.

The prices of the **Aiguille du Midi** *téléphérique,* the highest (3842m) and most spectacular in the world, are as steep as the trajectory but it's worth it. No one who survives the often suffocating crowds and interminable wait is disappointed. Cars leave regularly from the station in South Chamonix; go early, as crowds and clouds usually gather by mid-morning. The simplest trip takes you to Plan de l'Aiguille (40F, round-trip 50F), but most people continue through the clouds to the next *étape,* the Aiguille du Midi (92F, round-trip 120F from Chamonix; elevator to the summit for a slightly better view 10F). The round-trip to the summit takes at least one and a half hours. From the Midi, you can continue to a third stage, Gare Helbrouner in Italy (135F, round-trip 184F from Chamonix; take your passport), and if you've got money to burn, you can continue on to the Italian town of Courmayeur. No matter how far up the mountain you go, take warm clothes and expect a wait for the car back down. The Helbrouner station is also an approach to rather limited summer skiing. Inquire at the tourist office before you go; most sports stores in Chamonix rent skis. (*Téléphérique* open July-Aug. 6am-5pm, May-June and Sept. 8am-4:45pm, Oct.-Apr. 8am-3:45pm.)

A cheaper but less dazzling alternative is the two-part *téléphérique* Brévent at the north end of town, near La Mollard. The *télécabine* to Planpraz is 40F, round-trip 50F, and the *téléphérique* to Brévent is 43F, round-trip 64F. The walk down from Planpraz is not too strenuous.

One of the more arresting attractions in Chamonix is the **Mer de Glace,** a glacier that moves 30m each year. Special trains run from a small station next to the main train station (May-Sept. 8am-6pm; 30F, round-trip 47F), but you might prefer the one-hour hike. Accessible via *téléphérique* (10F) or a short hike, nearby tourist-laden **La Grotte de Glace** is a kitschy cave in which the ice has been carved a grand piano, a sofa set, and other imaginative shapes. (Admission 9F.)

Summertime Chamonix may seem to be a hiker's domain, but the resort has extensive facilities and opportunities for many other activities. In just one week's time, for a mere 2350F, you can learn to parachute from the highest peaks of the *massif.* For information, contact **Ecole Professionelle,** 278, rue Paccard (tel. 50 55 98 50), one of three schools in town (English spoken). Biking in the relatively flat Chamonix valley is a pleasant way to get around on the ground, and there is also an Olympic indoor ice-skating rink. (Open Thurs.-Tues. 3-6pm, Wed. 3-6pm and 9-11pm. Admission 18F. Skate rental 14F.) Chamonix has its own 18-hole golf course, tennis club, and *hydroglisse* school for shooting down the Avre on canoe or raft. (Rentals at **Centre Sportif,** promenade du Fori, tel. 50 53 55 70; open May 15-Oct. 15.) Fulfill your Olympic fantasies on **La Luge d'Eté,** which sends flattened human cannonballs down two concrete *pistes* behind the gare du Montenoers. (Tel. 50 53 08 97; open June-Sept. daily 10am-noon, 1:30-6pm; July-Aug. 10am-7:30pm; May, Oct., Nov. Sat.-Sun. 1:30-6pm.)

The **Musée Alpin,** off av. Michel Croz (tel. 50 53 25 93), is more interesting than most folklore museums and displays paintings and photographs of Mont Blanc from every conceivable angle. (Open daily June-Sept. 2-7pm; Christmas-Easter 3-7pm. Admission 10F.)

Skiing in Chamonix challenges even the best skiers, but there is plenty of mountain here for everybody. You can buy a day pass on one *téléphérique* (in La Flegère 95F per day) or a skipass, which allows you access to *téléphériques* up and down the valley (2-day skipass 300F, 3-day 450F, 1-week 850F). Unfortunately, you often have to take the shuttle bus from one *téléphérique* to another. Over 20 stores in Chamonix rent skis.

After a day in the mountains, kick back at **La Choucas,** 206, rue Docteur Paccard (tel. 50 53 03 23), a popular place with a bistro-café club atmosphere and a large video screen usually showing mountaineering and ski movies. (No cover. Open daily 9pm-1am.)

Val d'Isère

Val d'Isère will never be the same again—not since it was chosen as the site of the Men's Alpine Skiing events in the 1992 Winter Olympics. Its ideal location in a deep, green valley between snow-covered peaks a few miles from the Italian border, far enough from civilization to qualify as "the boondocks," is both its gift and its curse. This town, which has always struggled against the commercialization of the cherished valley, has become a concrete and metal construction site. Wildflowers still pave the banks of the Isère river, but new hotels, restaurants and ski-shops are popping up like weeds just about everywhere else.

There is a good reason why the town was chosen to host one of the most prestigious Olympic events; it makes no secret of its superb winter skiing conditions and better-than-average summer conditions. Mountaineers flock to this little town all year, and in the winter, its "white gold" attracts the jet-set. Luckily, the *formidable* skiing mitigates Val d'Isère's high prices and lofty pretensions.

Orientation and Practical Information

Val d'Isère lies tucked away in the Isère river valley, due east of Chambéry and a few kilometers from the Italian border. No trains run to Val d'Isère. The nearest train station is in **Bourg St-Maurice,** 30km north. Two to five trains per day arrive in Bourg St-Maurice and one train a night from Paris (9 hr.) and the others from Chambéry (2 hr., 72F). Nearly every 15 min., a bus leaves for Val d'Isère (45F). Take the bus to **Les Boisses** (39F) if you are going to the hostel.

There are no street names in Val d'Isère; fortunately there is only one main street. From the bus stop, walk up for about 100m and the tourist office will be on your left.

Tourist Office: (tel. 79 06 10 83 or 79 06 06 60), Boîte Postale 28. Free maps and glossy brochures, many in English. **Val Hôtel** (tel. 79 06 18 90), for hotel reservations, is upstairs. Open Dec.-March and June 25-Aug. 30 daily 8:30am-7:30pm; Sept.-Nov. and May-June 24 9am-noon and 2:30-7pm.

Currency Exchange: Banque Populaire (tel. 79 06 05 57), 75m down from the tourist office. Open Mon.-Thurs. 9am-noon and 2-5:30pm, Fri. 9am-noon and 2:30-4:30pm. No commission. On Sun., go to the **Galerie du Solaise**, 50m down and to the left of the tourist office. Open Dec.-April daily 9am-12:30pm and 3-8pm; July-Aug. 9:30am-12:30pm and 3:30-7:30pm.

Post Office: (tel. 79 06 06 99), across from the tourist office. Open Mon.-Fri. 9am-noon and 2-7pm, Sat. 9am-noon; in winter Mon.-Fri. 8:30am-noon and 2:30-7pm, Sat. 8:30am-noon. **Postal Code:** 73150.

Buses: Autocars Martin (tel. 79 06 00 42), 100m down the main street from the tourist office. Main office at pl. de la Gare (tel. 79 07 04 49), in Bourg St-Maurice. Open Wed.-Mon. 9:30am-noon and 2:30-7pm.Buses coordinated with trains. In winter, buses to Geneva airport (3 per day, Sat.-Sun. 5 per day; 4 hr.; 240F). Buses to and from Les Boisses and the youth hostel (5 per day, in summer 2-3 per day; 10 min.; 14F). Daily excursions to nearby ski resorts (57-165F) usually leave around 10:45am.

Bike Rental: Jean Sports (tel. 79 06 04 44), 100m up from tourist office. Ten-speeds 30F per ½-day, 50F per day. Mountain bikes 50F per ½-day, 80F per day. 500F per week. Open daily 8am-noon and 2:30-7pm.

Ski Conditions: Call tourist office at 79 06 06 60, or listen to 96.10 on the radio for ski, lift, road, and weather conditions. **Ski lifts,** tel. 79 06 00 35. **Ski Patrol,** tel. 79 06 02 10.

Police: (tel. 79 06 10 96), kittycorner from tourist office. **Emergency,** tel. 17.

Accommodations, Camping, and Food

Hotel rooms in Val d'Isère cost a bundle—reserve early at the hostel or the refuge. To rent an apartment for a week or more, contact the tourist office or **Val d'Isère Agence** (tel. 79 06 15 22) for a list of those available. Many of the cheaper places are already booked for Sept. 1991-April 1992; try either haggling viciously or crowding into an apartment or chalet. Prices may soar even higher by the time the Big Thaing arrives.

Auberge de Jeunesse "Les Clarines" (IYHF) (tel. 79 07 10 61), 10km out of town in Tignes. Take the bus marked "Tignes/Val Claret" from Bourg St-Maurice or Val d'Isère and get off at Les Boisses. Spotless rooms and a friendly atmosphere. Reserve in Sept. for Dec. and Feb.; 6 weeks ahead for Jan., March, and April. Booked Sept. 1991-April, 1992. Office open 5-10pm but you can drop off bags all day (the bus from Bourg St-Maurice gives you about 10 min. before heading to Val d'Isère). Ask for a key or code if out past 10pm. Quads with showers 45F. Nonmembers 15F more per night up to 6 nights. Good breakfast with cornflakes and yogurt 19F. Hearty meals 40F. Often requires a 92F ½-pension which includes dinner, room, and breakfast. Sheets 12F. Open mid-Nov. to mid-May and mid-June to mid-Sept., depending on ski season dates.

Gîte d'Etape: Refuge le Prarion (tel. 79 06 06 02). Head up from town for about 1 hr. to the National Park parking lot. (The shuttle to Le Fornet takes you about halfway.) From there it's an exhilarating (exhausting?), well-marked hike up to a mountain valley (45 min.). Cozy. Ski to and from ski lifts in spring. Popular base for cross-country skiing. 55F per person. Meals 50F. Breakfast 27F. Kitchen facilities available. Call ahead to reserve. Open March 15-May 20 and June 15-Sept. 15, depending on snow levels.

Hôtel le Floçon (tel. 79 06 04 19), 200m up from the tourist office off the main street. Best hotel deal in Val d'Isère but not cheap. All rooms with private bathroom. Breakfast included. Singles 118F, doubles 193F, triples 265F. In winter: singles 140F, doubles 230F, triples 310F. Quads available. Reserve early. Open Dec.-April and July-Aug., depending on snow levels.

Camping: Camping les Richardes (tel. 79 06 00 60), 500m up from tourist office. Plain campground in a beautiful setting with few trailers. 6.50F per person, 4.50F per tent, 3.50 per car. 5-min. shower 5F. Crowded in Aug. Office open June 15-Sept. 15 daily 7:50am-12:50pm and

2-8pm. Although free-lance camping is officially illegal, many travelers pitch a tent off the road above the campground. Camping in the National Park fetches a 450F fine.

Affordable restaurants are few and far between in Val d'Isère. The well-stocked supermarkets, **Supermarché Banco** and **Supermarché Unico,** are your only hope. The town's most popular pizzeria, **La Perdrix Blanche,** serves a 57F *plat du jour* and pizza from 35F. The **Bar/Restaurant L'Olympique,** 200m up and across the street from the tourist office, has a hearty 75F *menu* in a relaxing ambience. It also has a pricy *fondue savoyarde* with green salad (78F).

Sights and Entertainment

There's not much to see in Val d'Isère itself, but the slopes—some of the world's best—offer plenty to do. Over 100 lifts and *téléphériques* give access to 400km of trails. The trails may not be the trickiest in the Alps, but no skier will ever be bored. Lift tickets cost 115F per ½-day, 160F per day, and get progressively cheaper per day over longer periods. A new *téléphérique* and seven ski lifts serve a few mediocre ski runs on the **Glacier Pissaillas** in July and August. A summer ski lift ticket (good 7:30am-1pm) costs 110F.

Hikers should procure the profusely detailed *Guide des Promenades de Val d'Isère* (11F) and a hiking map (20F) from the tourist office. The 40 routes described include hikes to **Rocher de Bellevarde** and **Tête du Solaise,** the most popular hikes from Val d'Isère. A *téléphérique* can whisk you part way to Rocher or to the **Tête;** unrelentingly spectacular mountain vistas reward the next hour or so of legwork. The hike alongside a steep gorge up to the refuge raises spirits as well.

Val d'Isère is the town closest to the main Olympic sites—Albertville, Les Saisies, Tignes, Les Arcs, Les Menuires, Moribel, Courcheval, and La Plagne. All are easily accessible by frequent bus and TGV service.

Massif Central

The rugged Massif Central is often called the heart of France, and its history reveals a long tradition of symbolic association with French patriotism. *Auvergnats* remember with pride Vercingetorix, the Gaulish chief who defeated Caesar at the battle of Gergovia near Clermont-Ferrand. In the Middle Ages, pilgrims traveled through on their way to Spain, and popes, troubadours, and kings (the Bourbons) sprang from the Massif. During the Hundred Years War, this region was held first by the Duke of Berry and later by the dauphin Charles VII, whose capital at the time was Bourges and to whom the region served as a jumping-off point for the reconquest of northern France from the English.

Despite this tradition, the identity of the Massif Central as a region has long been in question. Invented in the 19th century, the term refers to the mountainous region that covers 15% of the country's surface area. Encompassing the regions of Auvergne, Limousin and Berry, it is a region of contrasts, with river valleys, forests, and ancient volcanic mountains, modern industrial cities and declining agricultural hamlets. Never sure whether they were speaking *langue d'oc* or *langue d'oïl*, the inhabitants of this region developed their own dialects, incomprehensible to foreigners and often to their neighbors. The town of Vichy, originally known for its pure, naturally carbonated water, became infamous as the seat of the decidedly impure Vichy government, which collaborated with the Nazis during World War II; yet at the same time, the surrounding region was a hotbed of both active and passive resistance, with Lyon as the capital of the Résistance. Perhaps the decisive characteristic of this area is that it has received little attention from the French and tourists alike. Lately, the region's potential for tourism has begun to be exploited. Skiing in winter, swimming and canoeing in summmer, and hiking and horseback riding year-round are among the outdoorsy delights of the Massif.

Folk traditions remain strong here. In late summer in Auvergne, villages hold traditional *fêtes patronales,* which culminate in the exuberant *bourrée,* a dance to the strains of the *cabrette* (a type of bagpipe). *Limougeauds* celebrate their patron saints with periodical *ostensions,* processions and displays of the authentic holy relics. Small châteaux and churches (often graced by black statues of the Virgin) dot the countryside. Bounding the Massif in the east and north, Lyon and Bourges are early commercial centers grown into energetic modern cities.

Railroads, including the TGV, run to the major cities and also make many small villages accessible, but more remote areas are served only by private bus companies with limited schedules timed for workers and local students rather than tourists. The steep, winding roads of much of the countryside make biking difficult but not impossible. Some people hitch successfully along the *routes nationales* and other main roads.

Lyon

Situated at the confluence of the Rhone and Saône rivers, midway between Paris and Provence, Lyon has been a transportation and economic hub for thousands of years. Bronze Age trade passed through the Rhone Valley, and the Gauls who settled here made Lugdunum (named for the god Lug) their religious capital. Paradoxically, this was one of the first places in Gaul to be converted to Christianity; in another twist of fate, Lyon also harbored the Waldensian heresy, one of the prominent renegade sects of the Middle Ages. The legacy of medieval fairs, the silk trade, banking (two major banks still bear Lyon's name), and printing made Lyon one of the most important commercial centers of Europe in the Renaissance. Many of Rabelais's works were first published here, and the city's own school of Petrarchan poets included Louise Labé and Pierre Ronsard.

Lyon's history has its dark clouds—prosperity won at the expense of the *canuts* (silk workers), enslaved to the terrible Jacquart loom—and its silver lining, as the capital of French Resistance during World War II. Today, Lyon (pop. 1.5 million) is known for three things: wealth, food, and a resolute *froideur* (coldness) toward outsiders. Old *lyonnais* wisdom has it that prosperous Lyon was plagued throughout the Middle Ages by pillagers. As a result, Lyon's citizens became suspicious of innocent interlopers and learned to hide their prosperity by eschewing extravagant dress and building a city with an austere façade. Epitomizing this distrustful attitude, the city's mascot—the opinionated marionette Guignol—has parodied government figures since 1808. Despite its attitude and status as an industrial center, this attractive, cultured city is a good place to visit.

Orientation and Practical Information

The Saône and the Rhône cleave Lyon into three parts. Vieux Lyon (the old city) unfolds on the west bank of the Saône. East of the Rhône is an area long considered uninspiring and colorless. Finished in 1975, the mammoth Part-Dieu commercial center, train station and alarmingly modern shopping mall, hasn't added much of a sparkle to this sprawling expanse of warehouses, private homes, and university buildings. Between the Saône and the Rhône, the pedestrian zone runs from the Perrache train station in the south to pl. Carnot, up rue Victor Hugo to pl. Bellecour, and along rue de la République to pl. des Terreaux. There is a tourist office in the Perrache train station. Like Paris, Lyon is divided into *arrondissements,* but there is no easy way to decipher this system.

To get to the main tourist office from Perrache, walk straight out onto rue Victor Hugo and follow it all the way down to pl. Bellecour. The tourist office is on the right. From the Part-Dieu station, go left out of the station and turn right onto av. Félix Faure. Follow this down and turn right on cours Gambetta. Continue over the bridge (Pont de la Guillotière) until you hit pl. Bellecour (a 30-min. walk). The tourist office is on your left.

Lyon is a reasonably safe city. Solitary travelers can walk at any hour in the area between the Perrache train station and pl. des Terreaux without taking more than the usual precautions.

Tourist Office: pl. Bellecour (tel. 78 42 25 75), 10-min. walk along rue Victor Hugo or 2 metro stops from the Perrache station. An incredibly efficient office with tons of information. Excellent introduction to Lyon *Lyon Vous Aimerez . . .* (free). Ask also for *Lyon Spectacles Evènements,* a comprehensive list of the year's shows and events, and *Lyon Nocturne,* a list of the ongoing nightlife (both free). Accommodation service 5F (1-star), 10F (2-star), 30F (outside Lyon). Open Mon.-Fri. 9am-7pm, Sat. 9am-6pm, Sun. 10am-6pm; Sept. 16-June 14 Mon.-Fri. 9am-7pm, Sat. 9am-5pm, Sun. 10am-5pm. **Annex** in the Centre d'Echange (tel. 78 42 22 07), attached to the **Perrache** train station. Same services as the Bellecour office, but not quite as efficient. Open Mon.-Sat. 9am-12:30pm and 2-6pm; Sept. 16-June 14 Mon.-Sat. 9am-12:30pm and 2-4pm. Another annex in **Villeurbanne,** 3, rue Aristide Briand (tel. 78 68 13 20), east of the Rhône. Open Mon.-Fri. 9am-6pm, Sat. 9am-5pm.

Budget Travel: Wasteels (tel. 78 37 80 17), at the Centre d'Echange. BIJ tickets and student discounts on flights. Open Mon.-Fri. 9am-6:30pm, Sat. 9am-5:30pm. Another office at 5, pl. Ampère (tel. 78 42 65 37), off rue Victor Hugo. Open Mon.-Fri. 9:30am-noon and 2-7pm, Sat. 9:30am-noon and 2-6pm. **Transalpino Travel,** 32, rue Sala (tel. 78 42 65 37), off rue Victor Hugo. BIJ/Eurotrain tickets. 25% student discount on everything. Open Mon.-Fri. 9:30am-12:15pm and 2-6:30pm, Sat. 9:30am-12:15pm.

Consulates: U.S., 7, quai Général Sarrail, 6ème (tel. 78 24 68 49), near Pont Morand. Open Mon.-Fri. 9am-12:30pm and 1:30-5pm. In a real emergency, however, there is *always* someone available (call). **U.K.,** 24, rue Childebert, 2ème (tel. 78 37 59 67), off rue de la République. Open Mon.-Fri. 10am-12:30pm and 2:30-5pm.

Currency Exchange: AOC, rue du Griffon (tel. 78 27 35 45), on pl. de l'Opéra, behind the Hôtel de Ville. No commission. Open Mon.-Sat. 9am-noon and 1:30-6pm. **Thomas Cook** (tel. 78 33 48 55), Part-Dieu train station. Poor rates and a 1% commission (min. 12F) but convenient location. Open daily 9:30-7:30pm.

American Express: 6, rue Childebert (tel. 78 37 40 69), up rue de la République from pl. Bellecour. Buys and sells traveler's checks. Money wired. 10F commission on exchange of bank notes. Open for exchange Mon.-Fri. 9am-noon and 2-5:30pm, Sat. 9am-noon; Sept.-April Mon.-Fri. 9am-noon and 2-5:30pm.

Post Office: pl. Antonin Poncet (tel. 78 42 60 50), next to pl. Bellecour. Regular service and **Poste Restante** open Mon.-Fri. 8am-7pm, Sat. 8am-noon. **Telephone** and telegraph services open Mon.-Sat. 8am-midnight, Sun. 8am-2pm. **Branch office,** rue Henri IV, near Perrache train station. **Postal Codes:** 69000-69009. (Main post office and *centre ville* is 69002.)

Flights: Aéroport Lyon-Satolas (tel. 72 22 72 21), 30km east of Lyon. Direct flights to Paris, London, Berlin, Casablanca. **Satobuses** leave from Perrache via Part-Dieu (Mon.-Fri. every 20 min. 5am-9pm, Sat. every 20 min. 5am-1pm and every 30 min. 1-9pm; Sun. every 30 min. 5am-9pm, 45 min., 37F). **Air France,** 69, rue de la République, 2*ème* (tel. 78 42 79 00). **Air Inter,** 100, rue Garibaldi, 6*ème* (tel. 78 52 84 30). Both open Mon.-Fri. 8:30am-12:30pm and 1:30-6pm, Sat. 8:30am-12:30pm.

Trains: Perrache (tel. 78 92 50 50), on the southern part of the land between the Saône and Rhône rivers. More central of the 2 stations. Sprawling mall with shops, bars, and **currency exchange** (open daily 5:15am-12:30pm and 1:15-8:30pm). SOS Voyageurs here provides wheelchairs, baby-changing facilities, and sick beds. *Le Mail* offers similar services as well as hot drinks, language translation, and a place to leave bags. SNCF information and reservation desk open Mon.-Sat. 8am-7:30pm, Sun. 9am-noon and 2-6:30pm. **Part-Dieu** (tel. 78 92 50 50), in the middle of the business district of the same name, southeast of Perrache. **Thomas Cook** Exchange office open daily 9:30am-7:30pm. Blissfully understanding SOS Voyageurs staff. SNCF information desk open Mon.-Sat. 8am-7:30pm, Sun. 9am-noon and 2-6:30pm. TGV trains to Paris (every hour 6am-9pm; 2 hr., 245F plus 14F mandatory reservation). Trains to: Dijon (8 per day, 2½ hr., 115F); Grenoble (24 per day, 2 hr., 77F); Strasbourg (6 per day, 5-7 hr., 231F); Geneva (11 per day, 2 hr., 98F); Marseille (13 per day, 3-4 hr., 188F); Nice (14 per day, 7 hr., 267F); Avignon (14 per day, 21/3 hr., 134F).

Buses: (tel. 78 71 70 00), on the bottom floor of the Perrache train station. Open Mon.-Sat. 7:30am-6:30pm; Sept.-June Mon.-Sat. 6:30am-5pm. **Philibert** (tel. 78 23 10 56). To: Annecy (2 per day, 4 hr., 62F). **CDL** (tel. 78 70 21 01). To: Vienne (23 per day, 35 min., 33F); Annonay (8 per day, 2 hr., 62F). **Cars Grery** (tel. 78 96 11 44). To: Grenoble (2 per day, 70F).

Public Transportation: TCL (tel. 78 71 80 80), outside the Part-Dieu train station. Open Mon.-Sat. 9am-6:30pm. **Subway** operates 5am-midnight. Tickets good for 1 hr. in 1 direction; bus and trolley connections included. 6.50F, 34.50F for a *carnet* of 6, 105F for 20. **Trolleys (funiculaires)** operate until 8pm and go from pl. St-Jean to the Théâtre Romain and the Musée Gallo-Romain. **TCL** network's Samedi Bleu tickets available on board the buses grant unlimited travel on Saturday. **Plan Guide Blay** (35F) gives the complete low-down on the public transport system (available at any *tabac*).

Taxis: Allô Taxi, tel. 78 28 25 23). **Taxi Radio de Lyon** (tel. 78 30 86 86). 24 hrs. Fares start at 9F (14F if you called for one) and go up 2.73F per km (7am-8pm) or 4.76F per km (8pm-7am).

Hitchhiking: If you choose to hitchhike, be aware that for Paris, the *autoroute* approaches are difficult to hitch on; taking bus #2, 5, 19, 21, 22, or 31, and standing past pont Monton at the intersection with the N6 less difficult. For Grenoble, take bus #39 as far as the rotary at bd. Pinel. Believe the tales of 3-day waits.

English Bookstore: Eton, 1, rue du Plat (tel. 78 92 92 36), one street west of pl. Bellecour toward the Saône. The only English bookshop in Lyon. Open Mon.-Fri. 9am-noon and 2-6pm.

Assistance for Disabled People: L'Association des Paralysés de France, 23, rue Sala (tel. 78 38 01 18), off av. Victor Hugo. Publishes an excellent guide, *Faire Face,* with loads of pertinent information and a guide listing disabled access for all of Lyon, *Guide d'Accessibilité pour Personnes Handicapées.* Both available at the pl. Bellecour tourist office. Open Mon.-Fri. 8:30am-5pm.

Youth Center: CROUS, 59, rue de la Madeleine (tel. 78 72 55 47). Information on university housing and cafeterias. Open Mon.-Fri. 1:30-4:30pm; Sept.-July 14 Mon.-Fri. 8:30am-12:15pm and 1:30-4:30pm. **IYHF,** 5, pl. Bellecour (tel. 78 42 21 88). Sells membership cards to those who can prove French residence (70F, over 26 80F) and student ID cards (45F). Information on all France's hostels and IYHF-sponsored summer trips. A week of horseback riding, meals included, 1600-2400F. Open Mon.-Fri. 2-6pm. **Centre Régional d'Information pour Jeunes,** 9, quai des Célestins (tel. 78 37 15 28). Lists of jobs, *au pair* opportunities, and sports. Open Mon. noon-7pm, Tues.-Fri. 10am-7pm.

Colmar

Mulhouse

Ronchamp
Belfort

Aube R.

Seine R.

Fontenay

Vesoul

Semur-en-Auxois

CÔTE
D'OR
Dijon

Doubs R.

Besançon

Biel

Nuits-
St-Georges

Ch. du Clos
Vougeot

Dole

Ornans

COMTÉ

L. Neuchâtel

de
ully

Ch. de
Rochepot

Beaune

Ch. du Meursault

Arbois

Pontarlier

SWITZERLAND

Autun

Chalon-sur-Saône

Ch. de
Couches

Grottes de
Baume-les-Messieurs

FRANCHE

JURA

Lons-le-Saunier

Ch. du Gevrey-
Cormatin

Tournus

Clairvaux
les
Rousses

Lausanne

Montreux

Berzé-le-
Châtel

Cluny

Berzé-la-Ville

L. Geneva

Ain R.

Lamartine

Bourg-
en-Bresse

Brou

Geneva

Saône R.

AIS

Lyon

Grenoble

Rhône R.

Isère R.

ITALY

MOUNTAINS

N

100 miles

100 kilometers

Laundromat: 10, rue Mourget. Take pont Bonaparte across the Saône to the old city, and follow the street. Bear left; the laundromat is on your left. Wash 15F per 7kg, dry 2F per 10 min. Open daily 7am-9pm. **Salon Lavoir GTI**, 38, rue Jean Jaurès. Wash 13F per 5kg, dry 2F per 7 min. Open daily 7am-9pm. **Laverie Eco**, rue Cuvier, near the corner of rue Garibaldi. Wash 13F per 5kg, dry 2F (2F pieces only). Open daily 7am-8:30pm.

Public Toilets: pl. des Terreaux (opposite the St-Pierre museum); pl. des Cordeliers (beside the Stock Exchange on the northern side); pl. des Jacobins (in the middle of the square). All cost 1F.

Special Services: CISL (tel. 78 76 14 22), an international center for visitors to Lyon. **SOS Friendship** (tel. 78 29 88 88). For the lonely traveler. **SOS Depression** (tel. 78 65 98 92). For when you're feeling blue. **SOS Racism** (tel. 78 30 04 44). **Rhône Accueil** (tel. 78 42 50 03). Regional service for women unfamiliar with Lyon. **Lost and Found** (tel. 78 42 43 82).

All-Night Pharmacy: Pharmacie Blanchet, 5, pl. des Cordeliers (tel. 78 42 12 42), in the *centre ville* between pont Lafayette and rue de la République. **Pharmacie Perret**, 30, rue Duquesne (tel. 78 93 70 96), just over Pont de Lattre de Tassigny.

Medical Emergency: Hôpital Edouard Herriot, 5, pl. Arsonval (tel. 78 53 81 11). Best-equipped to handle serious emergencies, but far from center of town. For little boo-boos, go to **Hôpital Hôtel-Dieu**, 1, pl. de l'Hôpital (tel. 78 42 70 80), near quai du Rhône. **SOS Médecin** (tel. 78 83 51 51). For home visits. **SAMU** (tel. 15 or 78 33 15 15) is on the scene in 10 min. by ambulance or helicopter. **Dental Emergency** (tel. 78 80 86 58). 24-hr. service. **Combat Against AIDS Association** (tel. 78 27 80 80).

Police: pl. Antonin Poncet (tel. 78 28 92 93), next to pl. Bellecour and the post office. **Emergency**, tel. 17.

Accommodations and Camping

A business and finance center, Lyon fills with suited people during the week. The centrally located hotels are often packed Monday to Thursday nights and then empty over the weekend. However, even if the hotels near Perrache are full, cheap accommodations abound in *centre ville*. Also try the hotels near pl. des Terreaux, which are less popular with business travelers.

Auberge de Jeunesse (IYHF), 51, rue Roger Salengro, Vénissieux (tel. 78 76 39 23, before 5pm 78 01 04 35), in a suburb of Lyon. Take the metro to Bellecour and bus #35 to George Lévy (30 min.); after 9pm, take bus #53 from Perrache to Etats-Unis-Viviani and walk ½km along the train tracks. From Part-Dieu, take bus #36 to Vivani Joliot-Curie (last bus at 11:15pm, but call ahead if you'll be late). Friendly cinderblock hostel with 130 beds, excellent kitchen facilities, a TV room, and a bar (food and drinks 10-20F until 10pm). Almost always room, but check in early in summer. Grape-picking jobs listed at the hostel, especially in Sept. Office and bedrooms closed 11:30am-5pm. Curfew 11:30pm. Dorm beds (6 per room) 37F per person. Breakfast 13F. Sheets 13F. 53F without hostel card, but 2nd and 3rd night at regular price.

Residence Benjamin Delessert, 145, av. Jean Jaurès (tel. 78 61 41 41). From Perrache, take any bus that goes to J. Macé, walk under the train tracks 5-10 min., and look to your left. From Part-Dieu, take the subway to Macé. Large, plain dorm rooms, all with telephones and comfortable beds. TV room. Singles 60F. Doubles 50F per person. Hall shower and sheets included. Breakfast 7.50F. Open July-Aug.

Hôtel Croix-Pâquet, 11, pl. Croix-Pâquet (tel. 78 28 51 49), in Terreaux. From either station take the subway to the Croix-Pâquet stop, or walk up rue Romarin from pl. des Terreaux to pl. Croix-Pâquet. Enter from the 4th floor off the courtyard. The LeClercqs keep these spacious rooms absolutely spotless. Singles 80-90F. Doubles 90-100F, with shower 120-130F. Showers 15F. Breakfast 15F.

Centre International de Séjour, 46, rue du Commandant Pegoud (tel. 78 01 23 45), far from the center of town. From Perrache, take bus #53 to Etats-Unis-Beauvisage (15 min., last bus at 11:30pm, 6.50F). From Part-Dieu, take bus #36 (every 20 min., last bus 11:15pm, 6.50F). A hopping polyglot place with 24-hr. check-in. Modern but crowded rooms as expensive as a hotel room in town. Singles 100F. Doubles 154F. Triples 198F. Quads 248F. Showers and breakfast included. Self-service meals from 30F.

Hôtel Vaubecour, 28, rue Vaubecour (tel. 78 37 44 91), about halfway between Perrache and Bellecour. Some of the cheapest and nicest rooms in town. Cozy but not cramped. Singles

73-82F, with shower 134F. Doubles 93-150F, with shower 145-191F. Breakfast 16F. No hall showers.

Hôtel Alexandra, 49, rue Victor Hugo, 2*ème* (tel. 78 37 75 79). A large, old hotel in an ideal location. Enormous rooms. No hall showers. Often close-to-full during the week. Singles 86-105F, with shower 166F, and toilet 181F. Doubles 110F, with shower 183F, and toilet 198F. Breakfast 19F.

Hôtel Le Terme, 7, rue Ste-Catherine (tel. 78 28 30 45), in Terreaux. Fairly small and unexciting rooms (all with TV and telephone) in an otherwise expensive area. Singles 90F. Doubles 138-145F, with shower 158-165F. Hall shower included. Breakfast 20F.

Hôtel de la Loire, 19, cours de Verdun (tel. 78 37 44 29), off pl. Carnot. Small, pleasant rooms with carpeting, desks, and telephones. Singles 97-115F, with shower 152F, and toilet 187F. Doubles 119-140F, with shower 177F, and toilet 219F. TV 20F. Breakfast 21F.

Hôtel de Vichy, 60bis, rue de la Charité (tel. 78 37 42 58), near pl. Bellecour. Sixteen adequate rooms. Single or double 77F, with shower 135F.

Camping: Dardilly, tel. 78 35 64 55. An easy bus ride from Lyon. From the Hôtel de Ville take bus #19 (*direction* "Ecully-Dardilly") to the Parc d'Affaires stop. One of the most beautiful campgrounds in the Rhône Valley. Hot showers, swimming pool, grocery store, bar, and restaurant. 42F per tent and car, 15F per extra person. Electricity 10F. Open March-Oct.

Food

Some of the best chefs in the world—Paul Bocuse, Georges Blanc, Jean-Paul Lacombe—have made Lyon famous for its *haute cuisine*. For authentic Lyon cooking you can afford, head for one of the city's *bouchons,* the descendants of inns where travelers would stop to dine and to have their tired horses *bouchoné* (rubbed down) with straw. Today, the 20 or so remaining *bouchons* serve *cochonailles* (hot pork dishes), *tripes à la lyonnaise* (heavy on the onions and vinegar), and *andouillette* (sausage made of chitterlings). The original *bouchons* can be found in Terreaux (the oldest is *Le Soleil,* 2, rue St-Georges). The most pleasant (and tourist-ridden) in Vieux Lyon will seat you outdoors on narrow, cobblestoned streets.

Rue Mercière, near pl. Bellecour, is not nearly so scenic, but has many restaurants with 50F *menus*.

The **university restaurants** in Villeurbanne serve cheap but unappetizing food. Ask at the tourist office for names and locations. Three large open **markets** are held at quai St-Antoine (Tues.-Sun. 7:30am-12:30pm), on bd. de la Croix Rousse (on the Rhône, Mon. 8am-12:30pm), and on quai Victor Augagneur (Tues.-Sun. 7:30am-12:30pm). The **Carrefour Supermarché**, one of the largest in France, looms across the highway from the hostel. (Open Mon.-Fri. 8:45am-10pm, Sat. 8:45am-8pm.)

Paul Bocuse, 50, quai de la Plage (tel. 78 22 01 40) in Collonges-au-Mont-d'Or, 9km north along the D433. Possibly the greatest of French chefs. Dinner will set you back 560F, 620F, or 660F—yes, those are zeros—but you get what you pay for. Dress appropriately. Open daily noon-2pm and 7-10pm. All credit cards accepted. Do it.

Elie et Henry, 21, rue Jean Larrivée (tel. 78 60 57 32), off rue Chapponée. Cross pont de la Guillotière to the east bank of the Rhône and continue straight; rue Jean Larrivée is on the left. Elegant atmosphere and good prices for seafood and traditional fare. 46F (lunch only) and 64F *menus* include salad, choice of steak or duck, and dessert. Open Mon.-Fri. noon-2pm and 7:30-10:30pm, Sept.-June Mon.-Sat. noon-2pm and 7:30-10:30pm.

L'Eau Vive, 65, rue Victor Hugo (tel. 78 42 32 92). Vegetarian cafeteria serving everything from watermelon juice (10F) to seaweed meals (24-30F). *Plat du jour* 24-30F. Open Mon.-Sat. 11:30am-2:30pm.

Café de Jura, 25, rue Tupin (tel. 78 42 20 57), the 6th block north on your left from Hôtel-Dieu. A true *bouchon* run by Henri, a charmer with a handle-bar mustache. New selection of entrees daily (34-70F). Open Mon.-Fri. at 7:30am; lunch noon-2pm, dinner 7:30-10:30pm.

Le Confort Impérial, 10, rue Confort (tel. 78 42 41 88), off rue de la République. 41.50F 3-course lunch *menu* and 62F dinner *menu*. Winner of the "Golden Chopsticks Award" for gourmet Chinese cookery. Open Mon.-Sat. noon-11pm.

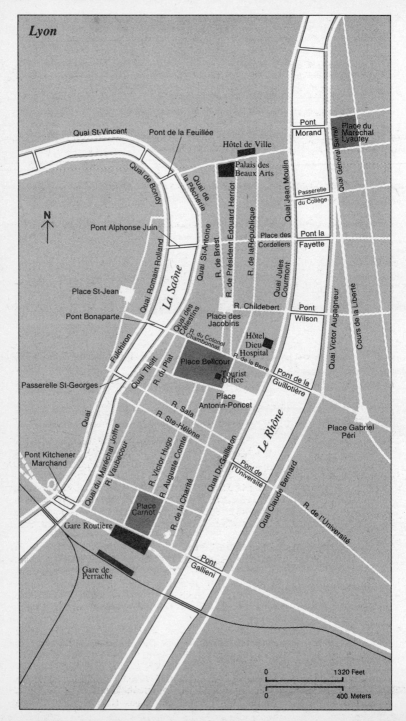

Lyon

Quai St-Vincent

Pont de la Feuillée

Hôtel de Ville

Palais des Beaux Arts

Quai de Bondy

Quai de la Pêcherie

Quai St-Antoine

R. de Brest

R. de Président Edouard Herriot

R. de la République

Quai Jean Moulin

Pont Morand

Place du Maréchal Lyautey

Quai Général Sarrail

Passerelle du Collège

N

Pont Alphonse Juin

Place des Cordeliers

Pont la Fayette

Quai Romain Rolland

Pont Bonaparte

Place St-Jean

La Saône

Quai des Célestins

R. Childebert

Place des Jacobins

Quai Jules Courmont

Pont Wilson

Quai Victor Augagneur

Cours de la Liberté

Fulchiron

Quai Tilsitt

R. du Piat

R. du Colonel Chambonnet

Place Bellcour

Hôtel Dieu Hospital

R. de la Barre

Tourist Office

Pont de la Guillotière

Passerelle St-Georges

Place Antonin-Poncet

R. Sala

Le Rhône

Place Gabriel Péri

Quai

Quai du Maréchal Joffre

R. Vaubecour

R. Victor Hugo

R. Auguste Comte

R. Ste-Hélène

Quai Dr-Gailleton

Pont de l'Université

Quai Claude Bernard

R. de l'Université

Pont Kitchener Marchand

Place Carnot

R. de la Charité

Gare Routière

Gare de Perrache

Pont Gallieni

0   1320 Feet

0   400 Meters

Titi Lyonnais, 2, rue Chaponnay 3ème (tel. 78 60 83 02), off cours de la Liberté on the east bank of the Rhône by pont Wilson. Popular with locals. 57F "quick" *menu* includes *entrée*, dessert, and coffee. *Cuisine lyonnaise* 65F *menu* with melon or salad; veal, beef, or fish of the day; dessert; and wine. Open Tues.-Sat. noon-2pm and 7:30-10:30pm, Sun. noon-2pm.

Chez Mounier, 3, rue des Marroniers (tel. 78 37 79 26), just north of pl. Antonin Poncet and the post office. Another authentic *bouchon,* whose *Gnafron* (sausage in fresh cream sauce) alone makes it worth a visit. 53F, 75F, and 88F *menus* change daily. Open Tues. and Thurs.-Sun. noon-2pm and 7-10pm, Mon. and Wed. noon-2pm.

Garioud, 14, rue du Palais-Grillet (tel. 78 37 04 71). From rue de la République, take a left onto rue Ferrandère; rue du Palais-Grillet is the first street on the right. Great *cuisine lyonnaise* by Paul Griard, a Bocuse acolyte. 72F, 116F, 146F, 162F, and 242F *menus.* Dress appropriately (no shorts). Open Mon.-Fri. noon-2pm and 7:30-10pm, Sat. 7:30-10pm.

Chez Carlo, 22, rue du Palais Grillet (tel. 78 42 05 70), near Restaurant Garioud. Great pasta and pizza (38-50F) in Lyon. Very popular with locals. Open Tues.-Sat. noon-1:30pm and 7-11pm, Sun. noon-1:30pm.

Sights

Whoever thinks there is nothing to do in Lyon has not yet cultivated a taste for *la flânerie* (strolling). Start at **place Bellecour,** fringed by shops and flower stalls and dominated by an equestrian statue of Louis XIV in the center. If you've been traveling through small towns in Burgundy and desire a big-city atmosphere, head out of the square along rue de la République (or its parallel, rue du Président Edouard Herriot) to **Terreaux,** a pleasant *quartier.* At pl. des Terreaux, the ornate Renaissance **Hôtel de Ville** stands guard opposite the **Musée des Beaux Arts.** Farther north around rue des Capucins and pl. Croix-Pâquet is a vibrant if somewhat dilapidated warehouse district next to a small park.

Those overwhelmed by the city might take one of the tourist office's theme tours. In the language of your choice, a guide will show you old Lyon, the *traboules,* or Bellecour. (July-Sept. 2 at 2:30pm, 40F, ages 8-18 20F. For info call 78 42 25 75.)

A brief walk across the Saône leads to the most intriguing part of town, **Vieux Lyon.** These renovated Renaissance buildings in the St-Paul, St-Georges, and St-Jean quarters are the most costly residences in Lyon. The intriguing *traboules* (from the Latin *trans ambulare,* to walk across) were built under and around the buildings to compensate for the lack of crosswalks. Connecting the neighborhood widthwise, these passages helped protect silk as it was transported through the city in stormy weather. The passages were also used by the Resistance (of which Lyon was the center) to thwart the Nazis, who couldn't find the entrances to the *traboules.* You will have equal trouble visiting the passages unless you have the *Liste des Traboules* from the tourist office. They are closed after dark, which is the best time to see the ancient buildings in Vieux Lyon highlighted by spotlights. A particularly interesting church in the St-Jean quarter is *bourguignon* style **Cathédrale St-Jean.** Its northern transept has an astronomical clock that shows the feast days from 600 years ago all the way to the year 2000. (Open Mon.-Fri. 7:30am-noon and 2-7:30pm, Sat.-Sun. 2-5pm. Free.)

Documents and photos of the Lyon Resistance are displayed in the **Musée de la Résistance,** 5, rue Boileau, on the east bank of the Rhône. (Open Wed.-Sun. 10:30am-noon and 1-6pm. Free.) The **Musée Africain,** 150, cours Gambetta, is dedicated to the culture of West Africa, an integral part of France's colonial history and current economy. Cross pont de la Guillotière to the east bank of the Rhône and continue a few blocks straight along cours Gambetta. (Open Wed.-Sun. 2-6pm. Admission 10F, students 5F.)

The **Fourvière Esplanade,** above Vieux Lyon, provides aesthetic high ground from which to peer down at Lyon's urban sprawl. On the summit of the hill rises the extravagant 19th-century **Basilique de Fourvière.** (Open daily 8am-noon and 2-6pm. Free.) On the descent, you will pass the **Théâtre Romain,** still used for everything from opera to rock. (Open daily 9am-nightfall. Free.) This hillside marks the site where Lugdunum, Julius Caesar's commercial and military center of Gaul, was founded in 43 BC. Also on the Fourvière hill, the **Musée Gallo-Romain,** 17, rue

Cléberg, displays a collection of mosaics, swords, rings, statues, and money from Lyon's Roman past. (Open Wed.-Sun. 9:30am-noon and 2-6pm. Admission 20F, students 15F, under 18 free.)

In disturbing contrast to Vieux Lyon, modern Lyon is made up of sleek buildings and space-age conveniences. The **District Part-Dieu** is worth a visit just to see its direly modern train station. The **Tour Crédit Lyonnais**, on the other side of the mall, symbolizes commercial Lyon. Next to it, the **Auditorium Maurice Ravel** proves that the functional can be beautiful.

There are 26 museums in Lyon—pick up a list at the tourist office. Starting in 1991, a 30F one-day ticket will cover all the museums. The **Musée des Beaux Arts** in the Palais St-Pierre at pl. des Terreaux, houses a large and rather exciting collection of paintings and sculpture that includes works by Spanish and Dutch masters, two rooms of Impressionism, and several rooms of excellent early 20th-century canvases. (Open Wed.-Sun. 10:30am-6pm. Admission 20F, students 15F, under 18 free.) Take a breather in the beautiful sculpture garden in the museum's courtyard. The *Musée d'Art Contemporain,* located in the same building but with an entrance at 16, rue Edouard-Herriot, houses some excellent temporary exhibitions of works from the last three decades. (Open Wed.-Mon. noon-6pm. Admission 20F, students 15F, under 18 free.)

Lyon seems to revel in its former position as center of the European silk industry. At the turn of the 18th century, 28,000 looms operated in Lyon. The *canuts* silk workers, who toiled in basement sweatshops, were driven to riot against the profiteers (St-Martins) who controlled the business. Although silk manufacturing is based elsewhere today, an extraordinary collection of silk and embroidery ranging from the Coptic to the Oriental remains at the **Musée Historique des Tissues,** 34, rue de la Charité. (Open Tues.-Sun. 10am-5:30pm. Admission 13F, students 7F.) The **Musée Lyonnais des Arts Decoratifs,** down the street at #30, displays porcelain, silver, and tapestry from various periods. (Open Tues.-Sun. 10am-noon and 2-5:30pm. Free with ticket from Musée des Tissues.) **La Maison des Canuts,** 10-12, rue d'Ivry (tel. 78 28 62 04), demonstrates the actual weaving techniques of the *canuts lyonnais.* (Open Mon.-Sat. 8:30am-noon and 2-6:30pm. Free. Guided tour in French 6F, students 5F.) The **Musée de la Marionette** at pl. du Petit Collège in Hôtel Gadagne exhibits the famous *lyonnais* puppets, including Guignol, as well as international specimens. (Open Wed.-Mon. 10:45am-6pm. Free.)

When urban fatigue sets in, leave the city noise behind for the roses of the **Parc de la Tête d'Or,** Lyon's botanical garden. Here you can bounce about on a pony or in a go-cart and tour the park in a minitrain. (Open daily 6am-10pm; in off-season 8am-8pm.) For something completely different, take a boat trip along the Saône and Rhône. Boats leave from quai des Célestins (April-Nov. daily 2, 3, 5, and 6pm for a 60-90 min. trip; 38F, ages under 10 27F). The boats also make a long, leisurely trip to Vienne. (July-Oct. Mon. and Wed.-Sun. at 9:30am; April 15-June Mon. and Thurs.-Fri. 8:15am and 2pm. 70F, under 10 45F. Reservations mandatory.) For more information, contact **Navig'Inter,** 13bis, quai Rambaud (tel. 78 42 96 81) or **Hermes,** quai Claude Bernard (tel. 72 73 23 60) at Pont de l'Université.

Entertainment

To find out what is going on in Lyon every week, pick up a copy of the *Lyon Poche,* available at newsstands for 8F. Lyon supports a variety of resident theaters as well as an opera company, but the highlight of its cultural activities comes in June with one of two annually alternating music and dance festivals. (Schedules available from the tourist office.) In May, Lyon draws musicians from all over Europe to its **Festival des Musiques Européennes.** (Contact the Centre Charlie Chaplin-Vaulx-en-Velin tel. 72 04 37 03) and its **Festival de Théâtre Amateur,** which gives aspiring thespians a chance to show their stuff. (Call 78 25 00 58 for information.)

The **Festival Hector Berlioz** is just that—a week of his music, performed and discussed. The festival takes place during the third week of September in odd-numbered years (Sept. 19-30, 1991) in La Côte St-André, not far from Lyon. For more information call 78 60 85 40 or write to Festival Berlioz, 127, rue Servient, 69431. On each December 8 since 1852, candles have lit the city's windows and streets have filled with parades for the **Fête de la Vierge,** honoring the Virgin Mary for having protected Lyon from the plague.

Starting on July 1, a host of international jazz celebrities come to **Vienne,** a town just outside Lyon and accessible by bus or train. The **Festival du Jazz à Vienne** lasts almost two weeks and features many free outdoor concerts by jazz stars of every style. (Tickets 120F, students 115F.) For information, call 74 85 00 05 or the Vienne tourist office (tel. 74 85 12 62) on 11, quai Reonded. There is a youth hostel in Vienne (tel. 74 53 21 97; 37F per night. Breakfast 15F. Sheets 15.50F. Lockout noon-6pm. Curfew 10pm.)

Lyon is a great place to see silver screen classics. **Cinema Opera,** 6, rue J. Serlin (tel. 78 28 80 08) and **Le Cinema,** 18 impasse St-Polycarpe (tel. 78 39 09 72) specialize in old black-and-white classics, all in *version originale* (28-34F). You'll find avant-garde flicks and oldies at the **CNP Terreaux Cinema,** 40, rue Président Edouard Herriot (32F).

Lyon may well have more pubs per capita than any other French city. **Eddie and Domino,** quai de Docteur Gailleton (tel. 78 37 20 29), off Pont de l'Université, is a British pub with a huge selection of whiskeys and a bartender who allows you to create your own cocktails. (Open Mon.-Sat. 6pm until dawn.) **Le Pub,** rue de la Baleine (tel. 78 42 47 44), near pont Alphonse Juin in the west, is another British pub with a young crowd slouching in red velvet chairs. (Open daily 6:30pm-3am.) For incredible nightly jazz, head for riverside **Le Bec de Jazz,** 9, quai de Bondy (tel. 78 28 79 48), across Pont de la Feuillée. **Place Mobile,** 2, rue René Leynaud (tel. 78 27 88 80), near pl. Croix Paquet, has concerts every weekend and plays reggae, jazz, blues, and rock during the week. Popular gay bars include the **Pirate's Bar,** 13-15, rue Therme (tel. 78 27 25 11) and **Naverie Night,** 3, rue Therme (tel. 78 30 02 01), both off rue d'Algérie, which is right off pl. des Terreaux. (Open nightly 6pm-late.)

There are nightclubs galore on rue Therme, off rue d'Algérie and near pl. des Terreaux. **Club Navire, Le Madras Discothèque,** and **Club Mona Lisa** are all open Thursday to Saturday. (10pm-sunrise, Sun. 3-8pm. No jeans. Cover 50-70F.) The **Africana Club,** 36, rue du Bœuf (tel. 78 37 39 37), near the Palais de Justice, plays reggae and alternative music to a good mix of locals and tourists. (Open Tues.-Sat. 10:30pm-dawn. Cover 70F.) **Le Club des Iles,** 1, grande rue des Feuillants (tel. 78 39 16 35), off petite rue des Feuillants by quai A. Lassagne, plays a big West Indian beat in a pseudo-island setting. (Open Fri.-Sun. 10pm-5am.) **Le Mylord,** 112, quai Pierre Scize (tel. 78 28 96 69), by Pont de la Feuillée on the Sâone, and **La Petite Taverne,** 12, rue René Leynaud (tel. 78 28 24 28) are exclusively for gay men.

Near Lyon: Bourg-en-Bresse

Once the center of a druidic cult, Bourg-en-Bresse, 60km northeast of Lyon, now puts everything into its poultry industry and large **animal fairs,** held on the first and third Wednesday of each month. Animal husbandry aside, you would do well to focus your attention on marvelous **Eglise de Brou,** a Flamboyant Gothic church constructed between 1505 and 1536 as a tomb for Margaret of Austria's husband. The tomb of Philibert le Beau lies in the middle of the building, flanked by the tombs of his wife and his mother. (Open daily June-Sept. 8:30am-1pm and 2-6:30pm; Oct.-March 10am-noon and 2-4:30pm.) Take bus #2 from the train station to the center of Bourg-en-Bresse (pl. Carriat), and change to #1 to Brou. Also worth a visit are the 16th-century Gothic **Eglise Notre-Dame** and **rue Bourgmayer,** where most of the remaining old houses of the city stand. The town puts on a *son et lumière* every Thursday, Saturday, and Sunday at 9:30pm June through September.

The **tourist office,** 6, av. Alsace-Lorraine (tel. 48 24 75 33), makes free room reservations and distributes a walking tour pamphlet. (Open Mon.-Fri. 8:30am-7pm, Sat. 8:30am-noon and 2-6pm; Sept. 16-June 14 Mon.-Sat. 8:30am-noon and 2-6:30pm.)

The **train station,** av. P. Sémard, has departures to Lyon every hour and frequent service to Dijon and Mâcon. Bourg is also a TGV stop on the Paris-Geneva line. You'll easily find accommodations on av. A. Baudin, opposite the station. Try **La Genève** at #24 (tel. 74 21 02 59), where singles go for 85F, with bath 135F. (Doubles 100F, with bath 140F. Breakfast 15F.) The **campground** (tel. 74 22 27 79) has hot showers, a restaurant, and a grocery store. (14F per tent, 9F per person; open March-Oct.) **Chez Mémé,** 24, bd. de Brou, serves good *menus* from 45F. (Open Tues.-Sat. noon-2pm and 7-9pm, Mon. noon-2pm.)

Moulins

Moulins came into being in the 10th century when Archambault, a member of the future royal family, had a château built on the river Allier for his mistress. While Archambault's humble gift, the **Château des Ducs,** may have fallen into ruin, Moulins itself seems to have discovered the fountain of youth. The courtyards and half-timbered houses of Moulins' *vieille ville,* as well as the entire pedestrian zone, are wired for sound. All summer from noon to sunset, citizens and tourists alike step to the beat of rock music blaring from inconspicuous speakers.

To be a French town is to have a 16th-century Jacquemart clock tower. The former capital of the Bourbonnais erected its specimen on pl. de l'Hôtel de Ville in the center of town. The mechanical couple Jacques and Jacquette, along with children Jacquelin and Jacqueline, make a noisy appearance every 15 minutes.

The tourist office's self-guided walking tour of the town provides a good introduction to Moulins' confusing *vieille ville.* While in quest of pious victory, Joan of Arc stayed in the elegantly perched **Château d'Anne de Beaujeu,** a highlight of the walk. Just across from Joan's house, the **Cathédrale Notre Dame** hides sundry treasures within its grey walls. Stained-glass windows of Anne de Beaujeu and Pierre II de Bourbon in prayer, a Flamboyant Gothic choir and ambulatory, and the famous **Triptyque du Maître de Moulins** all recommend this unusual cathedral. (Cathedral open daily 9am-noon and 2-6pm. Admission to *Triptyque* 9F, students 5F.) Two museums with rather unimpressive collections but housed in glorious buildings conclude the official walking tour. Egyptian and 19th-century artifacts shine in the otherwise dull collection of the **Musée d'Art et d'Archéologie,** pl. du Colonel Laussedat. (Tel. 70 20 48 47; open Wed.-Mon. 10am-noon and 2-6pm. Admission 10F, students 5F, under 18 free.) The endless exhibits at the **Musée de Folklore et des Moulins,** 6, pl. de l'Ancien Palais (tel. 70 44 39 03) contain farm tools, household irons, hats, dolls, and dusty religious statues. (Open Fri.-Wed. 10am-noon and 3-6:30pm. Admission 10F.)

The **tourist office,** pl. de l'Hôtel de Ville (tel. 70 44 14 14), across from the Jacquemart, offers free maps and a hotel and restaurant list. For 15F you can take a guided tour of the *vieille ville.* (Open Mon.-Sat. 9am-noon and 2-7pm, Sun. 9am-noon; Sept. 15-June 15 Tues.-Sat. 9am-noon and 2-6:30pm.) The **post office,** pl. Jean Moulin (tel. 70 20 13 86), has a **currency exchange** (open Mon.-Fri. 8am-7pm, Sat. 8am-noon); Moulins' **postal code** is 03000. About six trains per day run to Lyon (2¼ hr., 111F), Bourges (1 hr., 64F), and Nevers (40 min., 44F). More than 10 per day run to Clermont-Ferrand (1½ hr., 65F). (Information office open Mon.-Sat. 9am-6pm, Sun. 9am-noon and 2-6:45pm. Call 70 46 50 50.)

Hostel-living at its finest awaits young travelers at the **Foyer des Jeunes Travailleurs,** 60, rue de Bourgogne. There is almost always space in this old converted townhouse with a garden, TV room, ping-pong table, volleyball court, and several washing machines (8F). (Reception open Mon.-Fri. 6:30am midnight, Sat. 7am-midnight, Sun. 9am-midnight. Singles and doubles 40F, without hostel card 50F. Breakfast 12F. Lunch or dinner Mon.-Fri. 30F. Sheets 30F.) The **Hôtel de l'Agriculture,** 15, cours Vincent d'Indy (tel. 70 44 08 58), has an old-fashioned porch entrance and a jungle of a bar, complete with tall green plants, bird cages, and lots of chirping. (Singles 75F. Doubles 85F, with shower 130F. Breakfast 20F.) Closer to the center of town, **La Taverne de France,** 8, rue des Bouchers (tel. 70 44 04

82), offers doubles with stained carpets for 75F and a jolly bunch of locals in the bar downstairs. The **Camping Municipal** (tel. 70 44 19 29) is on the river, about 2km from the station and just south of Moulins's one-car bridge. (5F per person, 3F per site, 3F per car. Electricity 7F. Open June 1-Sept. 30.) A good alternative to the town's decent but touristy *brasseries,* **Pizzeria Le Gondole,** 5, rue de Bourgogne, serves salads (16-32F) and pizza (22-38F) Wednesday through Monday.

Nevers

Beautiful surrounding landscape and the cradle of the Loire and Nièvre rivers protect the small, unaffected city of Nevers. Rivers, canals, forests, and fields all converge on Nevers, which had its only brush with fame in Marguerite Duras's novel and screenplay, *Hiroshima, mon amour.* The city itself discreetly conceals carefully tended parks, modest squares, and a long tradition of excruciatingly detailed ceramics. If at first you aren't impressed by this reticent city, remember (and then forget) Duras's words, "To speak badly of Nevers would be an error of both the spirit and the heart."

The **Cathédrale St-Cyr et Ste-Juliette** was rebuilt five times between 502 and 1945. A gentle clash between Romanesque and Gothic styles, the cathedral is further confused by several modern stained-glass windows added after a 1944 bombing. The sundial currently being mapped out on a section of the stone floor will tell the date, time of day to the second, and Earth's position in the zodiac at any given moment. Opposite the cathedral, the Renaissance **Palais Ducal** sits under fairytale turrets with a view of the Loire. On pl. Charte, to the east of the cathedral and beyond the major pedestrian streets, the 11th-century **Eglise St-Etienne** consists of a series of circular chapels radiating from one circular nave. From a hovering zeppelin the church would look like a rose window or, more accurately, an upside-down *brioche.* The remains of Nevers's fortifications along the av. Général de Gaulle are rather minimal. One exception is the **Porte du Croux,** a strong tower which now harbors a dull Romanesque sculpture museum in the former guards' rooms. (Open Wed. and Sat. 2-4pm.) The old ramparts leading from Porte du Croux down to the river hide a few stretches of quiet, manicured gardens. A little more lively and much larger, the **Parc Municipal,** off pl. Carnot, usually hosts concerts during the summer and a few odd traveling carnivals. Nevers is also known for its fine ceramics, some of which languish in the **Musée de Faïences,** rue St-Genest. (Open Wed.-Mon. 10am-12:30pm and 2-6:30pm. Free.)

Life and traffic revolve around the pl. Carnot. From the train station, head straight on av. Général de Gaulle for four blocks. The **tourist office,** 31, rue du Rempart (tel. 86 54 07 03), is on the right, across the square. Ask for the brochure *Bienvenue à Nevers,* which describes architectural landmarks in the area, and for information on local châteaux accessible by car. (Open Mon.-Sat. 9am-12:30pm and 2-6:30pm.) The **post office,** pl. J.B. Thevenard, has a **currency exchange.** (Open Mon.-Fri. 8am-6:30pm, Sat. 8am-noon, and holidays that fall on Mon. or Sat. 8am-noon.) Nevers's **postal code** is 58000. The **Centre d'Accueil Universitaire,** 57, Faubourg du Grand Mouësse (tel. 86 30 00 02), helps travelers find cheap housing. **Trains** from the Loire Valley and the Massif Central pass through Nevers to Dijon (4-5 per day, 3 hr., 119F); Lyon (6 per day, 3 hr., 143F); Paris (8 per day, 2½ hr., 138F); and Bourges (5 per day, 1 hr., 43F). **Bike rental** is available at the station (40F per ½-day, 50F per day, deposit 300F).

The **Hôtel de la Paix,** 50, av. Général de Gaulle (tel. 86 57 30 13), would almost be elegant if it weren't for the peeling paint and the worn rugs. (Singles and doubles 80F, with shower 120F. Breakfast 17F. Lunch and dinner *menus* 55F.) The **Hôtel Villa du Parc,** 16-18, rue de Lourdes (tel. 86 61 09 48), across from the park, has bright, flowery rooms and a luxurious TV lounge. (Singles and doubles 85-95F, with bathroom 140F. Extra bed 37F. Breakfast 20F.) The **Hôtel de l'Avenue,** 38, av. Colbert (tel. 86 01 01 97), is a bit distant but a good bargain. (Singles 70F. Doubles 85F. Breakfast 17F. Ask for a key if out past 11pm.) The **Camping Municipal** (tel.

86 37 56 52), across the river, is near a swimming pool. From the cathedral, follow rue de la Cathédrale to the river, cross the bridge, and turn left. (5.10F per person, 2.20F per tent. Open March-Oct.)

Nevers's *vieille ville* is studded with rather expensive *brasseries*. Seek out the inexpensive, atmospheric places scattered in all directions from pl. Carnot. **La Scala,** 23, rue des Récollets, just off pl. de l'Hôtel de Ville, serves excellent pizzas (from 37F) and a 50F *paella menu* to a rowdy local crowd. (Open Tues.-Sun. 11:45am-1:30pm and 6:30-10pm. Around the corner at **L'Alhambra,** rue du 14 Juillet, Spanish chef Miguel puts Pillsbury Bake-Off champs to shame with his casserole of fish, prunes, and almonds (70F). His selection of tamer *couscous* starts at 60F. (Open Tues.-Sat. 6-10pm.) The **Cafétéria de Paris,** 7, pl. Guy Coquille, stresses quantity over quality. (*Menu* 37F. Entrees 8-25F. Open Mon.-Sat. 11am-2:30pm and 6-9:30pm.) The local **Supermarché Major** is a world unto itself. (Open Mon.-Sat. 9am-7:30pm.)

Near Nevers: La Charité-sur-Loire

Twenty-three km north of Nevers (25-min. train ride), the red roofs, church spire, and ramparts of La Charité-sur-Loire emerge from the greenery on the banks of the Loire. Founded in the 11th century by Cluniac monks, La Charité grew in power and wealth until it was known as "the older sister" of Cluny, with 400 dependent monasteries throughout Europe. Pilgrims often stopped here on the way to St-Jacques de Compostelle. Virtually annihilated by a 1559 fire and the Wars of Religion, La Charité continued to decline under subsequent Protestant control. Only 12 monks remained by the time of the Revolution, and the monastery has not quite recovered from a three-day fire in the 19th century that destroyed most of the buildings. A Romanesque monastery and fine stained-glass windows recommend the 12th-century **Eglise Notre-Dame.**

Tiny La Charité makes a pleasant day trip. Those wishing to spend the night can try the **Hôtel La Terminus,** 23, av. Gambetta (tel. 86 70 90 61). (Open Tues.-Sat. Singles 90F. Breakfast 17F.) Across the bridge, **Camping de la Saulaie** (tel. 86 70 00 83) is near a swimming pool, the Loire, and a beach. (Open June 15-Sept. 15.) The **Bar de la Plage,** across the river, to the right at the end of the bridge, gives its diners a view of the Loire and the city. The view comes cheaper if you picnic on the ramparts. The **tourist office,** 49, Grande-Rue (tel. 86 70 16 12), opposite the Hôtel de Ville, has information on the monastery and La Charité's other sights. (Open Mon.-Sat. 10:30am-noon and 3-6:30pm.) The **train station** (tel. 86 70 03 02) is on top of the hill to the east of town. Four trains per day run from Nevers (27F), fewer on Sunday and Monday. The station also rents **bicycles.**

Bourges

Bourges lies at the *coeur* (heart) of France. Its people like to think that it is *the* heart and lifeblood of France, and the city is appropriately decorated. Most of this warm, Valentine's-Day-overstock sentiment is due to Jacques Coeur, the surreptitious finance minister of Charles VII and one of the greatest merchants of the Middle Ages. In 1433 Monsieur Coeur decided to make his home where the heart is choosing Bourges as the site of his magnificent (heart-festooned) residence. Since then, this self-proclaimed intellectual and cultural stronghold, charming despite its civic decor, has not stopped beating with vigorous pride over its much-envied status as the capital of Berry.

Orientation and Practical Information

221km from Paris, Bourges sits on the major train route between Orléans (105km) and the Loire Valley to the north, and Montluçon (93km) and the Massif Central to the south. The medium-sized city is a maze of small streets within a roughly pentagonal traffic ring, the only thing the citizens haven't been able to make heart-shaped. Avenue H. Laudrier and its continuation, av. Jean Jaurès, lead directly south from the train station to this ring, in which rue Moyenne is the principal north-south artery.

Tourist Office: 21, rue Victor Hugo (tel. 48 24 75 33), by the cathedral. 15 min. from the train station. Head straight from the station on av. H. Laudier, which becomes av. Jean Jaurès. Bear left onto rue du Commerce, which becomes rue Moyenne and leads to the office. Efficient, English-speaking staff. Request the larger, more detailed map. Free accommodations service. Two-hr. walking tours (French only) leave July-Sept. daily (19F, students 13F); night tours July-Sept. Fri.-Sat. at 8:15pm (20F, students 16F). Open Mon.-Sat. 9am-7pm, Sun. 9am-1pm and 2:30-7pm; Sept. 16-June Mon.-Sat. 9am-noon and 2-6pm.

Currency Exchange: Banks closed Mon. except **Crédit Agricole,** 69, rue d'Auron. Open Mon.-Fri. 8:30am-noon and 1:45-5pm. More convenient to the center is **Banque Nationale de Paris,** 37, rue Moyenne. Open Tues.-Sat. 8:30am-noon and 1:40-5:15pm.

Post Office: 29, rue Moyenne (tel. 48 24 21 01). **Currency exchange** and **telephones.** The exterior architecture is a sight. Open Mon.-Fri. 8am-7pm, Sat. 8am-noon. **Postal Code:** 18000.

Trains: pl. Général Leclerc (tel. 48 65 50 50). Bourges is just off the main north-south train line. Many destinations require a transfer at nearby Vierzon. About 6 trains per day to: Paris (2½ hr., 130F); Orléans (1¼ hr., 67F); Tours (1½ hr., 87F); Lyon (3¼ hr., 166F). Ten per day to Clermont-Ferrand (2½ hr., 119F). Information office open daily 9am-7pm.

Buses: Gare Routière, rue du Champs de Foire (tel. 48 24 36 42). Easy connections to La Charité (11/3hr., 71F), Jussy-Champagne, and Châteauneuf (40 min. each, 41F). Unfortunately, buses leaving for the châteaux along route Jacques-Coeur depart in the evening and return the following morning. Reduced service during school vacations.

Car Rental: Locomat, 29, av. Jean Jaurès (tel. 48 24 02 94). 270F per day includes unlimited mileage and all taxes. Discounts on longer rentals. Deposit 2000F. Minimum age 23. No one-way rental.

Bike Rental: At the **youth hostel** (see below). Members only: 15F per ½-day, 30F per day, 150F per week, deposit 250F. Also at the **train station** (tel. 48 24 58 09). 40F per ½-day, 50F per day, deposit 500F.

Hitchhiking: If you chose to hitch to Lyon, the Alps, and the Midi, take rue Jean Baffier (bus #3 for N153). For Tours and Orléans, av. d'Orléans at av. des Près de Roi (N76). For Paris, av. de Général de Gaulle (N140).

Laundromat: 117, rue Edouard Valliant. Wash 20F, dry 5F per 12 min. Open daily 7am-8pm. Also at 79, av. Marcel Haegelan. Open daily 7am-8pm.

Public Showers: Centre Nautique Municipal de Bourges, 11, av. du 11 Novembre (tel. 48 24 42 90). Showers 7F, bath 8.50F. Open Thurs.-Sat. 9:30am-12:30pm and 1:30-7pm, Fri. 9am-12:30pm and 1:30-7:30pm, Sun. 8am-12:30pm.

Women's Center: Hotline for battered women, tel. 48 24 87 65.

Hospital: Centre Hospitalier, 34, rue Gambon (tel. 48 68 40 00).

Medical Emergency: SAMU Ambulance, tel. 48 65 15 15.

Police: 6, av. d'Orléans (tel. 48 24 42 46). **Emergency,** tel. 17.

Accommodations and Camping

Hotels in Bourges are scattered, rather expensive, and often closed in August. Calling a day or two in advance can smooth the ruffled feathers of many managers during July and August. The hostel is downright idyllic.

Auberge de Jeunesse (IYHF), 22, rue Henri Sellier (tel. 48 24 58 09), in a wooded site overlooking a stream. A 10-min. walk from the center of town and an easy 25 min. from the train station. Take av. H. Laudier onto av. Jean Jaurès at pl. Planchat. Follow rue des Arènes, which becomes rue Fernault Jacques and makes a sharp curve onto rue Henri Sellier. The hostel is set back slightly from the street. If your bags are getting you down, take bus #1 from the station. Get off at Château-d'Eau, turn right onto rue Château d'Eau, then right onto rue Charles Cochet, and right again onto rue Henri Sellier. Fine hostel run by a fantastic young family with green thumbs. Well-equipped kitchen, TV room, washing machines, and strong showers. Although popular with school groups, there is almost always space during the summer. Must have proper ID. Office open 6-10pm, but you can always leave bags in back. Ask for key if out past 11pm. 48F per person. Breakfast 12F. Dinner 36F. Sheets 12F.

Hôtel L'Etape, 4, rue Raphael Cassanova (tel. 48 70 59 47), just off rue Juranville. Tucked into a quiet street close to downtown. Kind managers. Clean singles and doubles 95F. Breakfast 17F.

Au Rendez-vous des Amis, 6, av. Marc Dormoy (tel. 48 70 81 80). A hike from the center, but a 5-min. walk from the train station. Turn left onto av. Pierre Semard from the station and then right after the overpass. The cheapest place in town. Singles from 80F. Doubles 95F. Breakfast 17F. Closed Dec. 25-Jan. 1.

Hôtel de la Nation, 24, pl. de la Nation (tel. 48 24 11 96). Slightly cramped but in a good location. Singles 85F. Doubles 95F. Showers 15F. Breakfast 20F. Open Mon.-Sat., closed last 2-3 weeks in Aug. and at the end of the year.

Camping: Camping Municipal, 26, bd. de l'Industrie (tel. 48 20 16 85). Follow directions to the hostel, but continue on rue Henri Sellier away from the *centre ville,* and turn right on bd. de l'Industrie. 10F per person, 12F per tent and car. Open March 15-Nov. 15.

Food

The side streets off pl. Gordaine in the *vieille ville* proudly display many slightly expensive, elegant restaurants. Tucked behind these establishments are a few local places without the red velvet and high prices. *Poulet en barbouille,* a winter specialty fortunately served year-round, is chicken roasted in a local aromatic red wine. Bourges has a number of produce **markets,** the largest of which fills pl. de la Nation on Saturday mornings. The other big market takes place on Thursday until 1pm at pl. des Marronniers. Smaller markets occur Wednesday at la Chancellerie, Friday at pl. Gordaine, and Sunday at pl. St-Bonnet.

Chez Charles, 19, rue des Ecoles (tel. 24 80 18 02), off rue Juranville. Small place, big meal. The 37F *menu* is satisfying; the Brobdingnagian 55F *menu* includes omelette, pizza, choice of meat, vegetable, cheese, and dessert. Open when it wants to be.

Au Rendez-vous des Amis, 6, av. Marx Dornoy (tel. 48 70 81 80), beneath the hotel of the same name. Friendly, family-style restaurant. Basic 5-course *menus* 40F and 45F. Open daily.

La Main à la Pat, 108, rue Bourbonnoux, behind the cathedral. Loud chattering and a wood fire for pizzas (28F and up). *Main à la Pat* salad with chicken and eggs 32F. Take-out available. Open Tues.-Sun. noon-2pm and 7pm-midnight.

D'Antan Sancerois, 50, rue Bourbonnoux (tel. 48 65 96 26). Popular with Bourgeois who linger over filling lunches of Berry specialties. *Poulet en barbouille* 46F. Succulent duck *à l'orange* 30F. Open Wed.-Sun. for lunch.

Sights and Entertainment

Undoubtedly one of the most magnificent cathedrals in France, Bourges' famous **Cathédrale St-Etienne** merits a long look. Five elaborately sculpted portals embellish the 13th-century façade. Only after the central portal representation of the Last Judgment was finished here did this particular theme become standard in most Gothic cathedral tympanums. By far the most awesome work is the set of stained-glass windows. The ten main windows (conveniently located near eye level) have recently undergone a massive restoration project, leaving them brilliantly clean. Throughout the summer, prominent international organists play on the cathedral's tremendous *grande orgue.* The schedule of free concerts is posted below the organ. (Open daily 7am-noon and 2-6pm.)

The Eglise Souterraine, or Underground Church, contains little more than a white marble figure of the Duke of Berry. Twelve large windows grace this crypt, so you won't be left completely in the dark. The times of the obligatory half-hour tour are posted next to the north entrance. (Open Mon.-Sat. 9-11:30am and 2-5:30pm, Sun. 2-5:30pm. Admission 16F, ages 18-24 and over 60 9F, ages 7-17 5F.) A half-hour audio-visual presentation with period music traces the artistic heritage of Bourges and Berry. (Tues.-Sat. at 10:30am, 2:30pm, 3:30pm, and 4:30pm, Sun. no morning shows; July-Aug. additional shows at 10am and 11am. Free.)

The intricate late medieval architecture of the **Palais Jacques-Coeur** is a testimony to the Man's own motto: "A vaillant Coeur, riens impossible" ("To the bold Heart, nothing is impossible"). The obligatory 45-minute tour winds past storerooms, reception halls, and bedrooms, none of which are alike. The tours are in French, but a printed English translation is available from the front desk. (Tours at 10:15am, 11:10am, 2:15pm, 3:15pm, and 4:10pm. Admission 16F, ages 18-24 and over 60 9F.)

For 26F (students 13F), you can buy a ticket to Bourges's three museums. **Musée du Berry** includes a collection of prehistoric and Gallo-Roman remains in an elegant 16th-century *hôtel* on rue des Arènes. (Open Wed.-Sat. and Mon. 10am-noon and 2-6pm, Sun. 2-6pm. Admission 10F, students 5F.) Built by a rich 15th-century merchant, the luxurious **Hôtel Lallemant,** rue Bourbonnoux, is furnished with pieces from different periods. (Open 10am-noon and 2-6pm; Oct. 16-March 31 Tues.-Sat. 10am-noon and 2-5pm, Sun. 2-5pm. Admission 11F, students 6F.) The **Musée Estève** 13, rue Edouard-Branly, houses the work of *Berrichon* artist Maurice Estève. (Open Wed.-Sat. 10am-noon and 2-6pm, Sun. 2-6pm, Mon. 10am-noon and 2-6pm. Admission 12F, students 6F.)

Well over 100,000 sets of ears crowd Bourges to enjoy the **Festival Printemps de Bourges.** Although most tickets cost 35-40F, some of the informal folk, jazz, and rock concerts are free. For information contact l'Association Printemps de Bourges, 5, rue Sampson (tel. 48 24 30 50). If all the hearts have gotten to your heart then stay in Bourges to celebrate the **Fête de Jacques-Coeur,** a marathon of general musical and cultural management from the last two weeks in June to Bastille Day. From mid-July through August the tourist office sponsors (heartfelt) **Ballades à Bourges,** yet another conflagration of classical concerts, rock, theater, and folk-dancing. Tickets go on sale one hour before showtime at the concert spot (often a church or park) or one week in advance at the tourist office. Most cost 35-70F.

Near Bourges: Châteaux on Route Jacques-Coeur

Stendhal once said that Bourges was "surrounded by plains of bitter ugliness." As usual, this cape-wearing charlatan of a novelist was wrong. Although less attractive than the Loire valley to the north, this stretch of château country has a certain charm. Bourges's tourist office provides helpful pamphlets with explicit maps, explicit photographs, and English descriptions of each château. Although none lie more than 90km from Bourges, daytrips are possible only by car or bike. Buses run only once per day to the châteaux and return the following morning. For more information on travel connections and occasional bus excursions, contact the Bourges tourist office.

Sixty-nine km south of Bourges on the Châteauroux-Montluçon train line, **Culan** (tel. 48 56 64 18) perches gracefully atop a steep crag. Joan of Arc was once a houseguest in this 11th-century château, now lavishly furnished with 15th- and 16th-century pieces. (Open daily 9:30am-6:30pm; Sept. 11-Nov. 30 and Feb. 1-May 14 9:30am-noon and 2-6:30pm. Admission 15F, students 9F.) A few miles north of Culan is the Italianate **Ainay-le-Vieil** (tel. 48 63 50 67), its octagonal Romanesque towers prompting the nickname "Little Carcassonne." (Open June-Oct. daily 10am-noon and 2-7pm; Feb. 3-March and Nov. Wed.-Mon. 10am-noon and 2-5pm. Admission 15F, students 9F.) Ainay is a stop on the train line between Bourges and Montluçon.

Set in a lovely park with a pond 35km south of Bourges, **Château Meillant** (tel. 48 63 30 58) incorporates elements of both medieval and Flamboyant Gothic style. (Open Feb.-Nov. daily 9-11:45am and 2-6:45pm. Admission 15F, students 9F.) Not far from Meillant, the 12th-century Cistercian abbey of **Noirlac** (tel. 48 96 23 64), shares its lovely symmetry with the surrounding gardens. (Open daily 10am-noon and 2-6pm; Oct.-March Wed.-Mon. 10am-noon and 2-5pm. Admission 12F, students 6F.) Other interesting châteaux in the area include **Menetou-Salon** (tel. 48

64 80 54), an unnecessarily ornate mansion from the end of the Renaissance (open March 26-Nov. 1 Wed.-Mon. 10-11:45am and 2-6pm), and **Jussy-Champagne** (tel. 48 25 00 61), a small 17th-century brick and stone château with a large garden (open March 25-Nov. 15 daily 9-11:45am and 2-6:30pm; admission 15F, students 8F). Forty km north of Bourges stands **La Verrerie,** a 15th-century Renaissance château by a small lake in the middle of a forest. (Open 10am-noon and 2-7pm).

Limoges

Celebrated for its fine porcelain, Limoges is an ordinary French university city and industrial center with little of interest to tourists. The old quarter and porcelain museums merit a day's visit at most. For a comparative study of the local product and its foreign competition, check out the **Musée National Adrien-Dubouché,** av. St-Surin, which houses the largest porcelain collection in Europe. (Open Wed.-Mon. 10am-noon and 1:30-5pm. Admission 15F, ages 18-25 and over 60 8F.) From July through September a free exhibit of porcelain and enamel is held at the Pavillon du Verdurier. (Open daily 9am-12:30pm and 2-6:30pm.) In the **Pavillon de la Porcelaine** (tel. 55 30 21 86), nonstop video and live demonstrations show the crowd how the stuff is made. (Open daily 8:30am-7pm.) The factory is in an industrial zone on av. John Kennedy; take bus #15 from the pl. de Jacobins near the Hôtel de Ville (*direction* "Magré"). The **Musée Municipal de Limoges,** next to the cathedral, displays an excellent exhibit of the town's enamel products, some dating from the 12th century. (Open daily 10-11:45am and 2-6pm; Oct.-June Wed.-Mon. 10-11:45am and 2-6pm. Free.)

You'll enjoy a good view of **Cathédrale St-Etienne** and its bell tower from the elegant and well-kept **Jardin de l'Evêché.** Of particular note is the façade of the north end of the transept, characteristic of the Flamboyant style. A district of narrow streets and medieval houses, **La Boucherie** has been home to the town's butchers since the 10th century. Vegetarians might want to skip Limoges in mid-October, when La Boucherie returns to the 13th century for its lively Feast of the Butchers' Brotherhood.

Limoges lies about four hours south of Paris-Austerlitz (10-12 trains per day, 180F). Other connections include Brive (10 per day, 1-1½ hr., 63F); Aurillac (6 per day, 3 hr., 110F); Lyon (4 per day, 6 hr., 200F); and Bordeaux (4 per day, 2 hr., 121F).

The city stretches roughly northwest from the Vienne river. The old city, called *La Boucherie,* lies southwest of the tourist office. From the train station, go left onto av. du Général de Gaulle and head across pl. Jourdan for the **tourist office,** bd. des Fleurus (tel. 55 34 46 87), which gives out good free maps and endless brochures. (English spoken. Open Mon.-Sat. 9am-noon and 2-6:30pm.) Their two-hour guided tours of the city run every Monday (4pm) and Thursday (10am) in July and August. (16F). The **Tourist Office Haut-Vienne,** 4, pl. Denis Dussoubs (tel. 55 79 04 04), has maps and information on the entire region. Their pamphlets describe several short walking tours. (Open Mon.-Fri. 9am-noon and 1:30-5:30pm, Sat. 10am-12:30pm and 1:30-5pm; Sept. 16-June 14 Mon.-Fri. 9am-noon and 1:30-5:30pm.) The **Centre d'Information Jeunesse,** 23, bd. Carnot (tel. 55 32 72 72), has the lowdown on student and cultural activities. (Open Mon.-Fri. 9am-6:30pm, Sat. 9am-noon and 2-5:30pm.) **CROUS,** rue Alexis-Carrel (tel. 55 01 46 12), has information for students on housing and university restaurants. **Urban buses** cost 5F per ride; ask at the tourist office for a bus map. Find truth in lint-covered underwear at the **laundromat** at 28, rue Delescluzes. (Open daily 7am-9pm. Wash 10F, dry 2F per 5 min.)

You will have no trouble finding a room in Limoges. The **Foyer des Jeunes Travailleuses/Auberge de Jeunesse,** 20, rue Encombe Vineuse (tel. 55 77 63 97), 15 minutes from the station, has sparkling clean singles for 52F (nonmembers 55F); take rue Théodore Bac to pl. Carnot, turn left onto av. Adrien Tarrade, and take the first left to the hostel. The *foyer* becomes a youth hostel only from June to August, but during the rest of the year they accept travelers for 55F per night if there is space, which there generally is. (Open 7am-2am. Breakfast 12F. Sheets 12F.) The **Hôtel de France,** 23, cours Bugeaud (tel. 55 77 78 92), two minutes from the station (follow the left side of the park) offers large, clean singles and doubles for 75-100F; the manager speaks English. The closest **campground** is Camping de la Vallée de l'Aurence (tel. 55 38 49 43), 5km east of Limoges.

The best restaurants cluster near **place des Bancs.** An indoor **market** occurs at pl. de la Motte every morning and a larger market Saturday mornings at pl. Carnot. **Café Leopold,** in old Limoges, 27, rue Haute-Vienne, offers a *plat du jour* plus three vegetables for 47F. (Open Mon. for lunch, Tues.-Sat. for lunch and dinner.) **Le Paris,** 7, pl. Denis Dussoubs, caters to a raucous student crowd. Their "menu of the moment" (about 43F) may include *moules gambrinues* (mussels with onions and brown beer) and a selection from their list of 51 beers, some of which are brewed on the premises. (Open Tues.-Sun. 11:45am-2pm and 7-10pm.) Several **university restaurants** also dot Limoges. Call **CROUS** (tel. 55 01 46 12) for information.

Near Limoges

The entire region around Limoges is littered with châteaux, inaccessible by public transport. **Coussac-Bonneval, Montbrun,** and **Brie** are just three of the feudal castles in the beautiful countryside.

On June 10, 1944, Nazi S.S. troops massacred all 642 inhabitants of **Oradour-sur-Glane.** Since that day, this martyred village has been left untouched. Obsolete electrical wires dangle from slanting poles and 1944 automobiles rust on the road. The women and children were slaughtered in the town church; fingernail imprints can still be detected on the walls. One of France's most vivid testimonies to the devastation of World War II, this town is not a place to take children. Two to three buses a day run from the bus station (tel. 55 77 39 04) on pl. des Charentes in Limoges (40 min., about 15F). Follow N141 to D9 (about 25km) if you chose to hitch.

The village of **Solignac,** 13km south of Limoges on D704, is dignified by the huge dome of a 12th-century church in the Périgordan style. Inside the choir, bas-reliefs decorate the curiously carved portal and the wooden misericords. A half-hour climb brings you to the ruins of the **Château de Chalusset,** an excellent example of medieval military architecture. Two to three trains per day run from Limoges, to Solignac (10 min., 10F).

Thirty km east of Limoges lies **St-Léonard de Noblet,** an ancient town that looks out over the Vienne river. The town's 12th-century Romanesque church is an amalgam of styles and techniques. Trains make the trip from Limoges about three times per day (25 min., 9F). In **Aubusson,** 50km east of Limoges, tapestry-weaving has been an art there since the 8th century. The town is full of private galleries displaying local handiwork. Get more information from the tourist **office** on rue Vielle (tel. 55 66 32 12) in the pedestrian zone. (Open Mon.-Fri. 9am-noon and 2-6:30pm.) Hiking trails skirt the cliffs surrounding the town; it's a 20km trek south to **Lac de Vassivière,** where dozens of campgrounds accommodate swimmers, canoers, sailors, and windsurfers. In the summer, free shuttle buses circle the lake and transport passengers 10km to the nearest train station in Eymontier. **Camping Château-court** (tel. 55 69 22 40) is in nearby Beaumont-du-Lac.

Le Puy

Le Puy (pop. 46,000) occupies one of the most extraordinary sites in France. At the conflux of the Borne and Loire rivers, its location in a fertile bowl of gentle mountains gives it a mild, almost meridional climate. But it is the rugged geography—the stark contrast between rolling green hills and cones of dark volcanic rock—that render Le Puy and its environs so beautiful. Three jutting needles of volcanic rock (giant versions of those used for making Le Puy's special lace) tower over the red-tile roofs of the city. The narrow cobblestoned streets trimmed with reddish volcanic stone ascend steeply to the magnificent Romanesque Cathédrale Notre-Dame, still an important pilgrimage site. A few days here are a good antidote to fast-paced, tourist-infested cities.

Orientation and Practical Information

Direct trains run regularly to Le Puy from St-Etienne (Châteaucreux) and Lyon, but if you're heading south from Clermont-Ferrand or north from Nîmes, you'll have to change at tiny St-Georges d'Aurac. From the train station, walk left along av. Charles Dupuy and turn left onto bd. Maréchal Fayolle. After five minutes you will reach two adjacent squares, pl. Michelet and pl. de Breuil. The tourist office and most of the hotels are here and on adjacent bd. St-Louis; the cathedral and *vieille ville* are just to the north up the hill.

Tourist Office: pl. du Breuil (tel. 71 09 38 41). Basic English spoken. Free hotel reservations. Hiking suggestions, a shower of brochures, tirades on lace making, and guided tours of the city in French (July daily 3pm, Aug. daily 9am and 3pm; 2 hr.; 25F). *Petit train touristique* gives 45-min. rides through the city (every hr. 9am-noon and 2-7pm, 25F, under 12 15F; July-Aug. also 9-10pm, 28F, under 12 22F). Summer excursions to Chaise-Dieu, St-Flour, Lac Bouchet, and nearby châteaux (1-2 per week, 50-350F). Open daily 8am-6:30pm; Sept.-June Mon.-Sat. 8am-noon and 2-6:30pm.

Post Office: 8, av. de la Dentelle (tel. 71 07 02 00), corner of av. Charles Dupuy, a 5-min. walk east of the tourist office. **Poste Restante** and **telephones. Currency exchange** has excellent rates and no commission, but no lace either. Open Mon.-Fri. 8am-7pm, Sat. 8am-noon. **Branch office,** 49, bd. St-Louis. Open Mon.-Fri. 9am-noon and 2:30-5:30pm, Sat. 9am-noon. **Postal Code:** 43000.

Trains: pl. Maréchal-Leclerc (tel. 71 02 50 50). To Lyon (11 per day, 2½ hr., 88F). To St-Etienne (Châteaucreux), where you can take a train to Lyon (8 per day, 11/3 hr., 57F). To Clermont-Ferrand via St-Georges d'Aurac (4 per day, 2-3 hr., 88F). Lockers 5F and 10F. Information office open Mon.-Sat. 9am-noon and 2-7pm.

Buses: (tel. 71 09 25 60), next to the train station. Useful free *Horaire Rail-Air-Route en Haute-Loire* has times for all transportation around the area. To: St-Etienne (2-3 per day, 2½ hr., 30F); Yssingeaux (2-3 per day, 45 min., 15F); La Chaise-Dieu (1 per day, 1 hr. 10 min., 27F). To Lyon via St-Etienne (4 per day, 4 hr., 67F). Open July-Aug. Mon.-Fri. 8:30am-12:30pm and 2:30-7pm, Sat. 8:30am-12:30pm and 2:30-6pm; Sept.-June Mon. 7:30am-noon and 2:30-7pm, Tues.-Fri. 8:30am-12:30pm and 2:30-7pm, Sat. 8am-12:30pm and 2:30-7pm.

Taxis: Radio Le Puy, pl. du Breuil (tel. 71 05 42 43). 24 hrs.

Laundromat: 12, rue Chèvrerie, at rue Boucherie Basse, off pl. Michelet. The place to take your lace. Wash 14F per 5kg, dry 8F per 20 min. Dry cleaning 44F. Open Mon.-Sat. 7:30am-8pm.

Public Showers: av. de la Cathédrale. Open Fri.-Sat. 8am-noon and 1:30-7pm, Sun. 8-11:30am. Free.

Pharmacy: Grande Pharmacie, 2, bd. Maréchal Maréchal Fayolle. Open Tues.-Sat. 9am-noon and 2-7pm, Sun.-Mon. variable hours. In emergency, dial 15 24 hrs. for the address and phone number of the late night pharmacy.

Medical Emergency: Centre Hospitalier Emile Roux, bd. Dr. Chantemesse (tel. 71 05 66 77), 10 min. from the center of town. If you injure yourself while making lace. Follow bd. St-Louis towards the highway to Clermont-Ferrand. **Clinique Bon Secours,** av. Maréchal Foch (tel. 71 09 05 84). **SAMU** ambulances, tel. 71 02 02 02.

Police: rue de la Passerelle (tel. 71 02 34 55). **Emergency,** tel. 17.

Accommodations and Camping

Numerous cheap hotels cluster around pl. du Breuil, especially on busy bd. Maréchal Fayolle. Phone reservations will usually be enough here. Even in July and August, rooms are usually available in the morning. The tourist office has lists of *foyers,* most of which are for women.

Centre Pierre Cardinal (IYHF), Jules Vallés (tel. 71 05 52 40). From pl. Michelet, take rue Porteil d'Avignon north to the dead end, and turn right on rue Général Lafayette. The hostel is up the hill to the left, in a beautiful building overlooking Le Puy (a 10-min. walk). Excellent hostel with a strict proprietor, friendly atmosphere, and great kitchen facilities. Usually open 7am-11pm; if closed during the day, check after 8pm. Curfew 11pm. 31F per night (4 beds per room). Breakfast 7.50F. Lunch and dinner (served if there are enough people) 28F; order a day in advance. Sheets 15.50F.

Hôtel des Cordeliers, 17, rue des Cordelières (tel. 71 09 01 12), off rue Crozatier, which is off bd. Maréchal Fayolle. The nicest budget hotel in Le Puy. Big rooms cleverly decorated by the somewhat wacky owner. Singles 90F. Doubles 135F, with bath, TV, and toilet 145F. Triple with shower and toilet 195F. Huge hall showers and baths included. Breakfast 18F. Restaurant downstairs.

Hôtel le Régional, 36, bd. Maréchal Fayolle (tel. 71 09 37 74), a short walk from pl. Michelet, on the noisy corner of av. Dupuy. Slightly small but clean rooms over a lively bar. Singles 70F, with shower 115F. Doubles 80F, with shower 115, and toilet 130F. Triples 190F, with shower 200F. Hall showers included. Breakfast 20F.

Hôtel de la Gare, 5, av. Charles Dupuy (tel. 71 02 29 20), across from the train station. Clean but not very clean, small but not very small. Singles 85F, with shower 120F. Double with shower 120F. No hall shower. Breakfast 18F.

Hôtel Les Voyageurs, 37, bd. Maréchal Fayolle (tel. 71 09 05 30). Kinder, gentler proprietors keep clean and comfortable rooms, all with carpeting and telephones. Not much nicer than other places, however, and it costs a bit more. Single or double 100F, with shower 150F. Hall shower 15F. Breakfast 19F.

Grand Hôtel Lafayette, 17, bd. St-Louis (tel. 71 09 32 85), in a quiet courtyard. Intriguing remains of a once-grand hotel. Cavernous halls, worn rooms filled with antiquated furniture, a now-defunct iron-grill elevator, and dusty silk flowers in the lobby. Less than grand service to boot. Singles 75-85F, with shower 120F. Doubles 85F, with shower 120F, and toilet 150F. Feeble hall showers 10F. Mandatory breakfast 18F. Open Jan. 1-Dec. 22.

Camping: Camping Municipal Bouthezard, chemin Rodéric (tel. 71 09 55 09), in the north-west corner of town. Walk up bd. St-Louis, continue on bd. Carnot, turn right at the dead end on av. d'Aiguille, and look on your left. Bus #7 makes the 2km trip (7 per day, 10 min., 5F). A 3-star site with hot showers and a restaurant. 17F per person with tent. 7F per additional person.

Food

A **farmer's market** fills pl. du Plot on Saturday (6am-12:30pm). Every bar and many stores (which often give free samples) serve the algae-hued after-dinner liqueur *verveine*, made from a collection of indigenous herbs (55-70F a bottle). **Supermarket Casino**, av. de la Dentelle, is open Mon.-Sat. 8:30am-8pm.

Restaurant des Cordeliers, 17, rue des Cordeliers, at the end of a small alley. Chummy neighborhood joint with a variety of tasty victuals. 29F lunch *menu* with roast chicken and potatoes. 47F *menu* with tomato and onion salad, choice of pork or chicken, lentils, and the *dessert du jour*. 5-course 69F *menu* has lots of choices. Open Mon.-Sat. noon-2pm and 7:30-9pm, Sun. noon-2pm.

Le Regina, 34, bd. Maréchal Fayolle. Appetizing pizza (32-45F) and such in elegant pink booths. Great *pâtés* (30-38F) and huge salads (22-39F). 40F *menu* includes appetizer, pizza or spaghetti, and dessert. Take-out available. Open daily noon-2:30pm and 7pm-midnight.

Café Le Palais, 27, pl du Breuil. Stylish café with 30F *plats du jour* and 32-43F *menus*. Open daily noon-2pm and 7-10pm.

Cafétéria Casino, av. de la Dentelle, a 2-min. walk southeast from pl. Michelet. On the 2nd floor of the supermarket of the same name. Surprisingly good cafeteria food for 24-47F. Wine 6F per 1/3-carafe. Open daily 11am-10pm.

Sights

A long procession of streets and steps climbs dramatically to the façade of **Cathé-drale Notre-Dame** (tel. 71 05 44 93), one of the most striking and unusual Romanesque churches in Auvergne. The Virgin Mary's black-skinned likeness, draped in lace, graces the main altar. These black Virgins are common throughout central France. Some dismiss the phenomenon as discoloration by the incense of countless church masses. More reasonable souls claim that its original creator (possibly St-Luke) modeled his statue after Judean women or that it was later painted that way to acknowledge the victims of the black plague. It is most likely, however, that crusaders brought the statue home from the Middle East, where artists endowed Mary with the tawny complexion she almost certainly had. The original Black Virgin went up in the French Revolution's flames, but its replacement is still paraded reverently through the streets on August 15 (Assumption Day). (Cathedral open daily 8:30am-7pm; Sept.-June 8:30am-noon and 2-6:30pm. Admission 16F, students and seniors over 60 9F, under 18 5F. Free tours leave from the nave July-Sept. at 3:30pm.)

A 26F global ticket entitles you to see the Cathédrale, Cloître, Chappelle St-Michel, and the Musée Crozatier (see below). The curiously appealing **cloître** next door displays a 13th-century fresco of the Crucifixion amid alternating bright red tiles and black volcanic rock on Byzantine arches. The intricate frieze of grinning faces and mythical beasts is barely visible under the edge of the roof. The 16F admission (students 9F, under 17 5F) includes entry to the **Trésor d'Art Religieux** and the **Chapelle des Reliques**. Tucked in the Trésor are walnut statues, jewelled capes, and paintings. The celebrated Renaissance mural *Les Arts Libéraux* hangs in the Chapelle des Reliques. Thought to be unfinished, the painting represents only four of the seven liberal arts: Grammar, Logic, Rhetoric, and Music. (Open July-Sept. 15 daily 9:30am-7:30pm; Sept. 16-30 and April-June 9:30am-12:30pm and 2-6pm; Oct.-March 9:30am-noon and 2-4:30pm.)

From the sacred city, you can climb up the **Rocher Corneille** for a tomato of a view. If high isn't high enough, a staircase takes you up the cramped statue of the Virgin and Child for a view from Mary's halo. (Open May-Sept. daily 9am-7pm; Oct.-March 15 10am-5pm; March 16-April 9am-6pm. Admission 8F.) On the edge of town, 10th-century **Chapelle St-Michel d'Aiguilhe** crowns a narrow, 80m spike of volcanic rock. The view from the top verges on the apocalyptic. (Open June 15-Sept. 15 daily 9am-7pm; Sept. 16-Nov. 12 daily 9:30am-noon and 2-5:30pm; Nov. 13-March 14 daily 2-4pm; March 15-31 daily 10am-noon and 2-6pm. Admission 7F, under 14 4F.) The **Musée Crozatier**, in the Jardin Henri Vinay, houses a small collection of archaeological items and artwork, including a display of Le Puy's needlework lace from the 16th to 20th century. (Open Wed.-Mon. 10am-noon and 2-6pm; Oct.-April Wed.-Sat. and Mon. 10am-noon and 2-6pm; Sun. 2-6pm. Admission 10F, students 5F.)

Saturday is market day in Le Puy, and practically every square in town puts on its own show. From 6am to 12:30pm, farmers bring what they've grown (fruits, vegetables) and made (cheeses, breads, jams, honey). Those in **place du Plot** throw in a few live chickens, rabbits, and puppies. The adjacent pl. du Clauzel hosts an all-day **antique market.** Bargaining for the items on sale, which include World War II medals, pipe paraphernalia, and old silverware, is *de rigueur* (Sat. until 6pm). In **Place du Breuil,** the biggest spread of them all includes new and used clothing, hardware, toiletries, and footwear galore (Sat. until 6pm). In the second week of September every year, all Le Puy goes Renaissance for the week-long **Fête Roi de l'Oiseau.** Locals dress in period costume, jugglers and minstrels wander the streets, food and drink in the *vieille ville* can be purchased only with the currency minted for the festival, and a different theatrical presentation takes the stage each day. The celebration culminates with the crowning of the town's best archer. (Admission to nightly shows at 9pm 50F, but you'll be expected to be in costume.) In the second week of July, Le Puy hosts its **Festival International de Folklore.** More than 15 countries send musicians and dancers in traditional garb to wander the streets and show their stuff. (For more information, call 71 09 13 91.)

A 5km walk from Le Puy (or a short bus ride from the *gare routière*), the **Forteresse de Polignac** once housed the most powerful family in the area. To reach the ruins, follow bd. St-Louis past the bridge to the N102. (Open May-Sept. daily 9:30am-noon and 2:30-7pm; in off-season call 71 05 70 74.) Fifty km north is the ancient mountain town of **La Chaise-Dieu,** best known for its Gothic Abbaye St-

Robert, which houses a chilling *danse macabre* fresco. (Open daily 9am-noon and 2-7pm; Sept.-June Wed.-Mon. 10am-noon and 2-5pm. Admission 11F.) In late August and early September, the abbey holds a festival of French and classical music. (Admission 50-390F.) La Chaise-Dieu's **tourist office** (tel. 71 00 01 16) is in pl. de la Mairie. (Open in summer Tues.-Sun. 10:30am-noon and 2-6pm; winter Tues.-Sat. same hours.)

Clermont-Ferrand

Home of the Michelin tire empire, Clermont-Ferrand (pop. 155,000) testifies to the recent industrialization of central France. The city hardly resembles the healthy, green Auvergne you know and love: factory chimneys spit out smoke onto a city which climbs the surrounding mountainsides. The main reason most travelers come here is to hop a bus or train to the extinct volcanoes and reassuring greenery nearby.

Some believe that the city occupies the site of ancient Gergovia, where Vercingetorix defeated Julius Caesar. If you, like Caesar, are stuck in Clermont-Ferrand, take bus #2 or #4 from the station (6F) to lively **place de Jaude.** If you'd rather make the 20-minute walk, go left from the station on av. de l'Union Soviétique and then right on av. Carnot; follow av. Carnot and av. Joffre west and down the hill to pl. de Jaude. To continue to the **tourist office,** on 69, bd. Gergovie (tel. 73 93 30 20), take rue Gonod, which becomes bd. Charles de Gaulle, and then turn left on bd. Gergovie. Bus #2 also goes to the tourist office. (Open Mon.-Sat. 8:30am-7pm, Sun. 9am-noon and 2-6pm; Oct.-May Mon.-Fri. 9am-6:30pm, Sat. 9am-noon and 2-6pm.) There is a **branch office** in the train station.

Once in the *ville noire* (built of black volcanic stone), follow rue de Port to the Basilique de **Notre-Dame-du-Port,** a heavy 12th-century church built in pure *auvergnat* Romanesque style. (Open daily 9am-noon and 2-6pm.) Built only a quarter of a century later than the basilica, Gothic **Cathédrale Notre-Dame** sends slender spires (constructed of volcanic stone brought from nearby Volvic) shooting gracefully upwards. Climb the steep, winding steps of the tower over the northern transept (3F) for a crimson view of the city and the Puy de Dôme to the west. (Open Mon.-Sat. 9:30am-noon and 2-5pm. Free. Guided tours in French Wed. and Sat. 3pm.)

Clermont-Ferrand was once two distinct cities: the episcopal city of Clermont and the 12th-century Montferrand, built by the dukes of Auvergne to rival their neighbor's power. The two merged in the 18th century. **Vieux Montferrand** is quiet and sparsely populated compared to its industrial neighbor. Buses #1 (every 15 min., 6F), 9, 10, and 16 (every 15 min., 6F) take you from the northeast corner of pl. de Jaude to pl. de la Fontaine, at the foot of picturesque **rue Guesde.** Continue up the hill to the 13th-century **Notre Dame-de-Prosperité.** Built out of volcanic stone, it stands on the site of the long-demolished château of the *auvergnat* dukes.

Clermont-Ferrand has more than its share of hostel-like lodgings. The **Centre d'Information Jeunesse Auvergne,** 8, pl. de Regensburg (tel. 73 35 10 10), behind the Home-Dôme *foyer,* can help you find a bed. The **Auberge de Jeunesse (IYHF),** 55, av. de l'Union Soviétique (tel. 73 92 26 39), near the station, has basic dorm accommodations with no hot water. (Open Dec.-Oct. 7-9:30am and 5-11pm. Curfew 11pm. 37F per person. Card required.) **Foyer St-Jean/Auberge de Jeunesse,** 17, rue Gaultier de Béauzat (tel. 73 92 49 70), is a nicer than usual place 10 minutes north of pl. de Jaude. (11pm curfew. Singles 60F, nonmembers 80F. Call ahead.) **Foyer International de Jeunes "Home-Dôme,"** 12, pl. de Regensburg (tel. 73 93 07 82), has plain dorm singles for 66F per person. Take bus #18 from pl. de Jaude (every ½-hr. until 8:30pm) or walk southwest on av. Julien, turn left on rue Bonnard, then right on bd. Pasteur, and then follow rue du 8 mai 1945. (10 min. from *centre ville,* 30 min. from station. Lockout noon-5:30pm. Curfew 11:30pm. No reservations, but call ahead.) Near the train station, **Hôtel d'Aigueperse,** 4, rue Aigueperse (tel. 73 91 30 62), has spacious, flowery rooms. (Singles and doubles 69-79F, with shower 103.50F. Double with 2 beds 158F. Shower 20F. Breakfast

16F.) Two blocks from pl. de Jaude, **Hôtel Foch,** 22, rue Maréchal Foch (tel. 73 93 48 40) pulsates with live and recorded bird chirping. (Singles and doubles 90F, with shower 115-120F. Doubles with 2 beds 180F. Triple 190F. Quad 200F. Showers 15F. Breakfast with homemade jam 18F.)

The two *foyers* listed above heap good, inexpensive cafeteria food on non-guests as well as guests (meals around 35F). Inexpensive ethnic restaurants and student hangouts cluster on rue St-Dominique, behind the cathedral. **Cafétéria Flunch,** 8, av. des Etats-Unis, north of pl. de Jaude, serves roast chicken or sausages with two fresh vegetables for a mere 15F. Whoever started this chain of cafeterias deserves the slavering affection of impoverished backpackers. (Open daily 11am-10pm.) **Restaurant La Tonkinoise,** 23-25, rue des Chausstiers, serves incredible Vietnamese grub. Try the Le My Sao, vegetables stir-fried with crab (37F), beef (35F), or chicken (33F). (3-course 48F lunch *menu* and 62F dinner *menu*. Open daily noon-2pm and 7-11pm.) Popular **Le Stramboli,** 18, rue du Cheval Blanc, serves good pasta (22-38F), pizza (28-45F), and a filling salad with hearts of palm and other exotica (28F). (Open Mon. 7-11:30pm, Tues.-Sat. noon-2:30pm and 7-11:30pm.) For affordable regional cuisine, try **Auberge Auvergnate,** 37, rue des Vieillards. Specialties of the house include *potée auvergnate* and *tripes.* The 3-course 60F and 4-course 80F *menus* change daily. (Open Mon.-Sat. 8am-1am.)

A large student population animates Clermont throughout the year. **Thoren's,** 16, pl. de Jaude (tel. 73 93 32 55), is a plush bar with a powerful sound system. (Open daily 10am-1am. Beer 13F.) Fooze while you booze at **Le Clown,** 65bis, rue Anatole France (tel. 73 92 17 75), a small bar behind the train station that sometimes attracts local musicians. (Open Mon.-Thurs. 4am-1am, Fri.-Sun. 4am-2am. Beer 8-14F.) The **Horn Pub,** 31, rue Anatole France, behind the train station, is a lively British pub that lures students with live music almost every weekend. (Open July-Aug. Tues.-Sun. 7:30pm-late; Sept.-June Tues.-Sun. 6pm-late. Admission to better shows 35F.) One of the better—and most exclusive—nightclubs is **Club L'Arlequin,** 2, rue d'Etoile (tel. 73 37 33 88), off av. des Etats-Unis. (Open Tues.-Sun. 11:30pm-late. Cover 60F. No jeans.)

Every year in late January and/or early February, filmmakers from all over Europe flock to Clermont-Ferrand's **Festival International du Court Métrage** (International Festival of Short Films). With up to 75 films in competition, the festival is an effort to publicize and reward the underappreciated short film industry. Ticket prices start at 40F. For information, contact Sauve Qui Peut le Court Métrage, 26, rue des Jacobins (tel. 73 91 65 73).

Clermont-Ferrand lies midway between Paris and Marseille. Direct trains connect the city with Mont Dore (49F); Riom (11 per day, 12 min., 12F); Vichy (11 per day, 37 min., 39F); Lyon (6 per day, 3 hr., 123F); Toulouse (4 per day, 7 hr., 194 or 201F); Marseille (7-8 per day, 6 hr., 208 or 260F); Paris (11 per day, 4½-5½ hr., 204F). Indirect trains run to Le Puy (5 per day, 21/3 hr., 84F) and Aurillac (5 per day, 3 hr., 94F). The station (tel. 73 92 50 50) is on av. de l'Union Soviétique. (Information desk open Mon.-Sat. 8am-7:30pm, Sun. 9:30am-noon and 2-7:15pm.) **Buses** run from the station (tel. 73 93 13 61; open Mon.-Sat. 8:30am-6:30pm) next to the tourist office to Riom (1 per day at 4pm, 1 hr. 45 min.); Moulins (2 per day 8am and 3:30pm, 1½ hr., 64F); Le Puy (1 per day, 3½ hr.); Vichy (2 per day, 8am and 5:45pm, 1½ hr.); and Riom (2 per day, ½-hr., 14-16F). The **Centre Communal d'Action Social,** 1, rue St-Vincent (tel. 73 92 80 80), has information for disabled travelers. **Pharmacie Ducher,** 1, pl. Delille (tel. 73 91 31 77) is open 24 hrs. The **Hôpital St-Jacques** is at 30, pl. Henri-Dunant (tel. 73 62 57 00). The **police station** (tel. 73 92 36 20) is in the Palais de Justice on pl. Philippe Marcombes. In an emergency, dial 17.

Near Clermont-Ferrand

If—nay, *when*—Clermont-Ferrand begins to seem dull, sooty, or worse, light out for the extinct volcanoes and fading historic towns in the surrounding area. Rather difficult to reach, the Auvergne Natural Volcano Park welcomes hikers, climbers, and binocularists. The historic, if somewhat dull, towns of Riom and Vichy at least have cleaner air and greener environs than Clermont-Ferrand. Both can easily be seen in a day.

Parc Naturel des Volcans d'Auvergne

The **Parc Naturel Régional des Volcans d'Auvergne** (tel. 73 65 67 19) was founded in 1967 to save the local scenery from industrial development and to preserve cottage industry and agriculture. Historical monuments in the park, including medieval castles built from volcanic stone and churches in the local Romanesque style, have been restored. Hiking paths through the most picturesque parts of the region are marked and are catalogued in a booklet available at the Clermont-Ferrand tourist office. The protected area includes three main sections—the **Monts Dore,** the **Monts du Cantal,** and the **Monts Dômes**—the last of which is the best place to examine extinct volcanoes and swim in one of the many lakes that fill their craters.

For a great view, head on up to **Puy de Dôme** (1465m), a massive flat-topped peak accessible by toll road and tour buses that leave Monday mornings in summer from the train station and pl. de Jaude. If you're up for a long walk, take city bus #14A from Clermont to Royat (every 20-30 min., 6F) and follow the Col de Ceyssat for about 6km to the *sentier de muletiers,* a Roman footpath which will lead you to the top in about an hour. The magnificent view from this summit extends over an eighth of France and approximately 6000 *boulangeries* when the weather is clear. Two small towns set among the most beautiful of the Monts Dore are **Orcival** and **St-Nectaire,** both with interesting Romanesque churches. Each is served by occasional buses from Clermont and excursion buses from nearby Mont Dore.

The **Comité Départemental de Tourisme du Puy du Dôme,** 26, rue St-Esprit (tel. 73 42 21 21) in Clermont-Ferrand, has loads of information on this area. (Open Mon.-Thurs. 8:30am-12:15pm and 1:45-5:30pm, Fri. 8:30am-12:15pm and 1:45-5pm). **Charmina,** 5, rue Pierre-le-Vénérable (tel. 73 90 94 82), also in Clermont, distributes maps and plans hiking and climbing trips in the Massif. (Open Mon.-Fri. 9am-6pm.)

Riom

In the 17th century, Riom and Clermont were great commercial and cultural rivals. Riom (pop. 20,000) lost its status as a powerful metropolis long ago, but not its sophisticated tastes. Although a wide circular boulevard has replaced the old city ramparts, many ornate *hôtels particuliers* (bourgeois mansions) and half-timbered houses remain from its days of glory only to house doctors' and lawyers' offices, plus the odd *masseur.* It should take no more than two to four hours to see the old town, the only thing in Riom worth a visit.

To get to the old town from the station, head straight on rue Jeanne d'Arc and turn right on rue du Commerce. The **tourist office,** 16, rue du Commerce (tel. 73 38 59 45), distributes an annotated walking tour of Riom's 16th-century *hôtels particuliers* and a good free map. (Open Mon.-Sat. 9am-12:30pm and 2-6:30pm; Oct.-April 9am-noon and 2-6pm.)

The most impressive *hôtels particuliers,* the **Maison des Consuls,** rue de l'Hôtel de Ville, and the **Hôtel Guimoneau,** 12, rue de l'Horloge, are no longer very impressive. The latter has a beautiful courtyard and sculptured stairway. More moving still is the celebrated 14th-century statue of the Madonna and Child, called the *Vierge à l'Oiseau,* sequestered in the relatively simple **Eglise Notre-Dame-du-Marthuret,** 44, rue du Commerce. The **Ste-Chapelle,** the only remaining vestige of the **Palais de Justice,** built in the 14th century by Jean de Berry, has exquisite stained-glass windows. (Obligatory tour given July-Aug. Mon.-Fri. 3-5:30pm; Sept. Wed. and Fri.; May-June Wed.. All year by appointment. Admission 12F.) To experience the Auvergne of old, visit the **Musée Régionale Folklorique d'Auvergne,** 10bis, rue Delille (tel. 73 38 17 31), near the Palais de Justice. Dedicated to the "strong and noble artisans and farmers of Auvergne," the museum shelters a fascinating collection of local arts and crafts, costumes and musical instruments peculiar to Auvergne. (Open Wed.-Mon. 10am-noon and 2:30-6pm. Admission 12F, students with ID 6F, Wed. free.) The beautifully renovated **Musée de Mandet**, 4, rue de l'Hôtel de Ville (tel. 73 38 18 53), in a 17th-century *hôtel particulier,* preserves a delightful collection of Gallo-Roman bronzes and pottery, early French and Flemish paintings and sculpture, and an extensive if unexciting collection of paintings from the 17th to the 19th centuries. More intriguing are the portrait gallery on the second floor and the excellent exhibits it sometimes houses (Miró in 1990). (Same hours and admission as the Musée Régional. Admission to both museums 16F.) Every year in June, Riom hosts the week-long **Piano à Riom,** an international piano festival. (Admission 40-100F per concert, ages under 25 35-50% reduction. For information call 73 63 54 60.)

Buses run between Riom and Vichy (12 per day, 25 min., 31F) and Clermont-Ferrand (8am and 5:45pm daily, ½-hr., 6F). The **post office** is at 25, rue Croseur, but the entrance is on rue du Commerce (open Mon.-Fri. 8am-7pm, Sat. 8am-noon.) In a **medical emergency,** call 73 27 33 33 for an ambulance. The hospital, **Hôpital Guy Thomas,** is on 1, bd. Clémentel (tel. 73 38 08 01).

Vichy

> So I took the waters this morning, my very dear one.
> Oh, how awful they are! . . . One drinks, and one
> makes a terrible grimace . . .
>
> —Madame de Sévigné

Perhaps best-known as the seat of Maréchal Pétain's collaborationist government during WW II, Vichy (pop. 30,000) today is chiefly preoccupied with restoring the health—especially the wine-sodden livers—of the silver-haired from *le tout Paris* (i.e. wealthy Parisians) who descend on the town in great numbers every summer to "take the water" and stroll around parks and gardens. Everyone seems to come to Vichy to go on a health kick—sports facilities cover almost as many acres as the entire *centre ville.* There is no denying that Vichy's lush parks are beautiful, or that the atmosphere becomes a bit festive during summer, but the town still lacks vigor.

Vichy occupies a bend in the Allier river, about 100km northeast of Clermont-Ferrand. The river borders the *centre ville* to the south and west (regardless of how it may appear on the tourist office map). The center of activity is the **Parc des Sources** across from the tourist office. From the station, walk straight on rue de Paris; at the fork, take a left on rue Georges Clemenceau and then a quick right on rue Sornin. The **tourist office,** 19, rue du Parc (tel. 70 98 71 94), is straight ahead across the park. The office has terrible free maps and a good 4F one. They help find rooms for free and operate a **currency exchange** on weekends and holidays for a 20F commission. They also provide a comprehensive booklet of suggested walking and car tours in Vichy and the region. (Open July-Aug. Mon.-Sat. 9am-7:30pm; Sun. 9:30am-12:30pm and 3-7pm; May-June and Sept. Mon.-Sat. 9am-7pm, Sun. 9:30am-12:30pm and 3-7pm; Oct.-April Mon.-Fri. 9am-noon and 2-6:15pm, Sat. 9am-noon.)

In the glass and white cast-iron **Halle des Sources** (tel. 70 98 95 37) at the edge of the Parc des Sources, you can sit among the palm trees and watch the *curistes* file into the surrounding establishments every morning to get their daily dose of the lukewarm carbonate-laden water. (Admission 8F, 1F per glass. Open Feb.-Dec. Mon.-Sat. 6:15am-8:30pm, Sun. 7:45am-8:30pm.) This stuff is horrid, but if you drink what they give you, you can refill your bottle with a weaker version from the **Source des Célestins** on bd. Kennedy (free). At 18, av. Thermale is the **Maison du Missionaire** (tel. 70 98 34 29), where religious orders stay while taking the cure. It houses a strangely uninteresting collection of mementoes from missions in former French colonies. (Open daily 4-6pm. Free.)

Across the river the **Maison des Jeunes,** *rive gauche* (tel. 70 32 04 68; open Wed.-Sat. 9am-11pm, Sun. 9am-10pm) shows films and sponsors activities throughout the year. The nearby **Centre Omnisport** (tel. 70 32 04 68) coordinates tennis courts, gymnasia, and kayaking on the river. You can rent windsurfers along the river. The seven-day *passeport sportif,* available at the Maison des Jeunes (400F), allows one week's use of the city's windsurfing equipment, sailboats, tennis courts, swimming pools, canoes, and kayaks. An outdoor **swimming pool** (tel. 70 32 27 20) and a sun-bathing beach (no swimming allowed) lie across the river by the campground and youth hostel. (Open Mon., Wed., and Fri.-Sat. 10am-7:30pm, Tues. and Thurs. 10am-9:30pm, Sun. 10am-7pm. Admission 10F, under 18 5F.)

The **Auberge de Jeunesse (IYHF),** 19, rue du Stade, Bellerive (tel. 70 32 25 14), across the river on the left after crossing pont de Bellerive, scrapes the bottom of the hostel barrel. Each room has 10 beds, and the pit toilets are in a shack outside. However, the rooms are clean, kitchen facilities are available 24 hrs., and the place is rarely full. For the hostel or for any of the campgrounds (see below), take bus #4 from the train station (2 per hour 6:13am-7:45pm, 5F) and get out after the bridge; cross the street and head straight toward the Le Bellerive sign atop the high-rise hotel. Follow the lamp-lined pavement onto rue du Stade and the hostel. (34F per person. No curfew or lockout. Open April-Oct. daily 8am-10pm.) The **Hôtel Antilles,** 16, rue Desbrest (tel. 70 98 42 86 or 70 98 27 01), close to the center, has pleasant singles and doubles off a courtyard for 70-90F, with shower 125-130F. (Breakfast 19F. Prices negotiable.) **Les Acacias,** rue Cl.-Décloître, by the river at Bellerive (tel. 70 32 36 22), is the nearest of several campgrounds along the river bank. (21F per person, 15F per tent. Electricity 11F. Sept.-June 15F per person, 10F per tent. Swimming pool and showers included. Open March 25-Oct. 25 8:30am-10pm.) Take bus #4 from the station (2 per hour, 5F) to the hostel. From the hostel, head down rue de la Grange to the river.

Restaurants abound in Vichy. Quality restaurants do not. **Le Fochotel,** 7, rue Foch, a popular self- or waiter-service spot, has salads (19-28F), pizzas (21-41F) and omelettes (17-21F) in an elegant setting. In the sit-down section there are 29-34.50F *plats du jour* and a 3-course 52F *menu.* (Open daily 11:15am-2:15pm and 6:45-10:30pm.) **L'Oasis Restaurant,** 15, rue Portugal, off rue de Paris, lacks atmosphere but serves fabulous Tunisian fare, including *couscous* (38-60F) and fish soup (16F). For dessert try some of their fresh pastries (5F). (Open Tues.-Sun. 9:30am-11pm.) **Restaurant de la Nièvre,** 17-19, av. de Gramont (tel. 70 31 82 77), just right of the train station, posts a 50F *menu* with a choice of salad, sausage, or *pâté de campagne* (pork *pâté*); chicken *cordon bleu* or *steak garni,* and dessert. (Open daily noon-2pm and 7-10pm.). The large covered **market** does its thing in pl. du Grand Marché (Tues.-Sun. until 12:30pm).

The **post office,** pl. Charles de Gaulle (tel. 70 59 90 90), has a **currency exchange** with competitive rates but a 1% commission. (Open Mon.-Fri. 8am-7pm, Sat. 8am-noon.) Vichy's **postal code** is 03200. The **train station,** pl. de la Gare (tel. 70 46 50 50), rents **bikes** at the baggage desk (40F per ½-day, 50F per day, deposit 500F). Trains run to Clermont-Ferrand (12 per day, 36 min., 39F), to Riom (12 per day, 25 min., 31F) and to Paris (6 per day, 3½ hr., 183F). (Information office open Mon.-Sat. 9am-6:30pm, Sun. noon-2pm.) **Urban buses** (tel. 70 97 75 75 or 70 98 77 04) cost 5F each way. Buses for the surrounding region and Montluçon (3-5 per day, 3 hr., 72F) leave from **gare routière,** pl. Charles de Gaulle (tel. 70 98 41 33). (Office open Mon.-Fri. 8am-noon and 2-6pm.) In a **medical emergency,** dial 15 for an ambulance. The **Centre Hospitalier** (tel. 70 97 33 33) is on bd. Denière. The **police** are on 35, av. Victoria (tel. 70 98 60 03).

Three km east of Vichy, the town of **Cusset** has gathered a grand collection of 15th- and 16th-century houses on rue St-Arloing. The tourist office in either Vichy or Cusset (2, rue St-Arloing; tel. 70 31 39 41) has a clear, well-annotated map of this area. To get to Cusset take bus #4 from Vichy's station to the end of the line (2 per hour, 40 min., 5F).

The area around Vichy has many remarkable Romanesque churches. To the north are **Bessay-sur-Allier** and **Toulon-sur-Allier.** To the south, the church at **En-**

nezat has a pure *auvergnat* Romanesque nave and a Gothic choir. All these towns make an easy daytrip from Vichy on the **CFIT** bus line, which departs from the *gare routière,* pl. Charles de Gaulle, in Vichy. All except Ennezat are also on train lines. **SNCF excursions** leave for various natural and architectural sights in the area (about 50F). **Châtel-Montagne** and **Château Lopalisse** are both about 25km from town, but inaccessible by public transportation.

Montluçon

A wall around Montluçon's medieval *cité* has kept it pristine, but a new tire industry and France's central Dunlop factory have commercialized the surrounding town. Although Montluçon has plenty of small-town charm, *hélas,* there just isn't that much to see. A daytrip from Clermont-Ferrand, Vichy, Limoges, or Bourges should more than cover it. At the core of the *cité* stands the imposing **Château des Ducs de Bourbon.** Constructed during the Hundred Years' War to defend the town against the English, it is the only remaining château of the Bourbon dukes. Inside, the **Musée du Château des Ducs de Bourbon** exhibits regional archaeological finds and rusting farm implements. An interesting collection devoted entirely to the traditional stringed instrument of Auvergnat folk music, *la vielle,* awaits at the top of the winding castle steps. (Open Wed.-Mon. 10am-noon and 2-6pm; Oct. 15-March 15 Wed.-Mon. 2-6pm. Admission 6F, students 4F. Oct.-June free on Wed.) **Eglise Notre-Dame** was begun in the 12th century as a Romanesque church. The choir, in Flamboyant Gothic, was not finished until the 15th century. To reach the château from the train station, follow av. Marx Dormoy from the train station past the tourist office and the post office. Boulevard de Courtais, the main commercial street, circles the walled city.

The exemplary **Auberge de Jeunesse Montluçon (IYHF),** 34, rue Notre-Dame (tel. 70 05 20 84), surrounds a garden courtyard in the old city. From the station, take av. Marx Dormoy to bd. Courtais, turn right and follow bd. Courtais to the Hôtel de Ville. Then turn left, climb up to rue Notre Dame, and turn right; the entrance is around the corner. During the year, the hostel functions as a **Foyer des Jeunes Travailleurs** and accepts travelers only if there is space (there usually is). Officially a hostel from June 15 through September 15, it provides spotless facilities, including a library, TV lounge, ping-pong table, and washing machines. (Singles 60F. Breakfast, sheets, and private shower included. Tasty meals 27F. Ask for a key if out past 11pm.) The **Hôtel le Celtic,** 5, rue Barathon (tel. 70 05 28 79), 1 block south of bd. Courtais (entrance at 1, rue Corneille), has cozy rooms with decent country furnishings and a friendly, English-speaking manager. (Singles and doubles 75-80F, with shower 100F. Breakfast 20F.) The **Hôtel des Deux Gares,** 7, rue de Bruxelles (tel. 70 05 06 58), two minutes to the right of the station, has spacious singles and doubles for 90F and a restaurant downstairs that posts a satisfying 50F *menu.* The **Camping Municipal,** route de Néris-Clermont (tel. 70 05 39 53), is a two-star site 5km out of town on RN144. Take bus #1 from rue des Forges and bd. de Courtais.

Monluçon's culinary specialty is *pâté de pommes de terre,* a pastry filled with a mixture of mashed potatoes and cream, eaten hot or cold. On Saturdays until 2:30pm, vegetable stalls take over the streets of the *vieille ville.* A less elaborate market also takes place Wednesday and Sunday mornings at Ville Gozet, across the river from *centre ville.* Of course, there's always **Monoprix,** at rue Marx Dormoy and bd. de Courtais. (Open Mon.-Thurs. 8:45am-12:15pm and 2-7:15pm, Fri. 8:45am-12:15pm and 2-8pm.) The **Jardin Publique Wilson,** off bd. Carnot, is a pleasant place to stage your own *déjeuner sur l'herbe.* **Chez Renée,** 33, rue des Forges, two blocks from bd. de Courtais, offers a substantial five-course *menu* for 42F. **La Vie en Rose,** 7, rue de la Fontaine, in the heart of old Montluçon, serves traditional specialties to a youthful crowd in a pink, fern-filled bar setting (*plat du jour* 32F).

Amateur musicians play just about every night at the friendly co-op bar **Le Guin-gois,** 8, rue de la Réunion (tel. 70 05 88 18; access to bar 15F, shows 25-70F). For the first half of July, the old city comes alive for **Montluçon en Fête.** The **Festival de l'Instrument de Musique** brings concerts, many of them free, during the third week in May.

Regular **trains** roll from the station (tel. 70 05 50 50) on rue de Bruxelles to Clermont-Ferrand (6 per day, 1 hr., 67F); Bourges (4 per day, 2 hr., 66F), Paris (4 per day, 3¾ hr., 180F); Tours (6 per day, 3 hr., 132F); and Limoges (5 per day, 2 hr., 93F). (Information office open Mon.-Sat. 9am-noon and 2-7pm, Sun. 9:15am-noon and 2:15-6:45pm. Station open daily 5:10am-8:50pm.) Four daily **buses** leave from the station (tel. 70 05 39 97) on quai Rouget de l'Isle, near the river Cher, for Culan (40F) and Moulins (70F). (Office open Mon. 10:45am-noon and 2-6pm, Tues.-Fri. 8:15am-noon and 2-6pm, Sat. 8:45am-noon.) The **tourist office,** 1ter, av. Marx Dormoy (tel. 70 05 05 92), at the foot of the castle, does little but distribute free maps and a meager booklet describing walking tours. (Open Mon. 10am-noon and 3-6:30pm, Tues.-Sat. 9:30am-noon and 3-6:30pm.) The **post office** is nearby on pl. Piquard; Montluçon's **postal code** is 03100. The **police station** (tel. 70 05 15 40) is at 1, rue Joseph Chantemille. The **Centre Hospitalier** (tel. 70 05 77 77) is at 18, av. du 8 Mai. In an emergency, jsut dial 17.

Le Mont Dore

Located in the heart of the Massif Central and in the middle of Auvergne's 1000 volcanoes, Le Mont Dore (pop. 2394) suffers from a split personality. In summer, thousands of *curistes* file into the Etablissement Thermale to inhale the carbonated gas that supposedly heals their rheumatism and respiratory ailments. In winter, ski-ers take over the resort town, taking advantage of the numerous jagged volcanic peaks, including the highest peak in the Massif Central. The spring thaw reveals emerald green slopes sliced by splendid hiking trails. Unfortunately, if you don't hike, ski, or ache, this town has little allure beyond its fine scenery. You might be amused by the tour offered by the **Etablissement Thermal** on pl. du Pantheon (tel. 73 65 05 10). (Tours given May-Sept Mon.-Sat. 11:15am, 11:30am, 3pm, 3:30pm, 4pm, and 4:30pm. 5F.) Five of the springs used today were first channeled by the Romans; and the center, built between 1817 and 1823, has grand arcades and granite Roman-style columns.

Although it is crowded during the winter and summer seasons, you can usually find a room in one of the 43 one-star hotels. The **Auberge de Jeunesse (IYHF),** route du Sancy (tel. 73 65 03 53), 5km uphill from the station, is a fantastic hostel with 8 beds per room, a mini-tennis court, mini-golf course, mini-TV bar, and mini-game room. Buses leave from across from the train station (1 per hour 9am-6pm, summer 2-6pm; 8.50F, 12.80F round-trip). Ask to be dropped off at the *auberge de jeunesse,* which is a chalet on a ski slope. If all else fails, call a taxi (tel. 73 65 09 32 or 73 65 01 05). Filled with families during the winter (reserve 2 weeks ahead), the hostel usually has space during the summer, but *always* call before you arrive. (37F per night. Breakfast 13F. Meals 38F. Sheets 12F. No lockout or curfew.) The **Hôtel du Centre,** 8, rue Jean Moulin (tel. 73 65 01 77) has respectable rooms over-looking the center of town. (Singles and doubles 65-70F. Triples 85F. Hall shower included. Breakfast 18F. Open Dec. 15-Nov. 15. daily.) **Hôtel Helvetia,** 5, rue de la Saigne (tel. 73 65 01 67), is cozy and clean with a good restaurant downstairs. (Singles and doubles 80-85F. Breakfast 18F. Hall shower included.) There are four **campgrounds** in and around Le Mont Dore. The most convenient by far is **Les Crou-zets,** av. des Crouzets (tel. 73 65 21 60), a 2-star site across from the train station. (10.20F per person, 5.10F per site, 3.60F per car; open Nov.-Sept. Mon.-Sat. 9am-noon and 2-6pm, Sun. 9-11:30am.) **La Plage Verte,** route de la Tour d'Auvergne (tel. 73 65 09 85) is a 2.5km walk from the station. (10.50F per person, 5.80F per tent. Open May 15-Sept. 25.) **Domaine de la Grande Cascade,** route de Besse (tel. 73 65 06 23), is another 2-star site 3km away from the station. (35F per 2 people with tent. 11F each additional person. Open June-Sept.) **L'Esquiladou,** route des Cascades (tel. 73 65 23 74), is a 3-star site 1km behind the train station (11.30F per person, 5.10F per tent. Open May 15-Sept. 30.)

Just about every restaurant in Le Mont Dore posts a 50-55F dinner *menu*. At **A Tout Va Bien,** rue Marie Thérèse (tel. 73 65 05 14), on the corner of av. Général Leclerc, you can grill your own meat without oil or grease in their *pierre chaude* (open daily noon-2pm and 7-10pm). A covered **market** occurs every day in pl. de la République (open 8am-6pm); an open-air market takes over on Friday (until 4pm). Before you hit the trail, stock up on groceries at the **Supermarché Suma,** av. de la Bourboule, directly behind the train station. (Open Mon. 9am-1pm and 2:30-7:30pm, Tues.-Fri. 9am-12:30pm and 2:30-7:30pm, Sat. 9am-1pm and 2:30-7:30pm, Sun. 9am-noon.)

From the train station, ascend av. Michel Bertrand and follow the signs to the **tourist office,** av. de la Libération (tel. 73 65 20 21), which distributes free maps and organizes hikes. Unfortunately, their free hotel reservation service (tel. 73 65 09 00) requires reservations 10 days in advance. They **exchange currency** without commission on Saturday and Sunday when banks are closed. (Open Mon.-Sat. 9am-12:30pm and 2-6:30pm, Sun. and holidays 10am-noon and 4-6:30pm; Oct.-Nov. Mon.-Sat. 9am-12:30pm and 2-6:30pm.) The **post office,** pl. Charles de Gaulle (tel. 73 65 09 86), has **telephones** and **Poste Restante.** (Open Mon.-Fri. 8am-7pm, Sat. 8am-noon.) Le Mont Dore's **postal code** is 63240. The **train station** is at pl. de la Gare (tel. 73 92 50 50). Twenty trains per day run to Laqueille (18 min., 12F) with changes to Clermont-Ferrand (1½ hr., 49F). Five trains per day run to Paris (1 direct at 11am, 8 hrs., 228F). (Information desk open daily 9:30am-12:30pm and 2-6pm.) In a medical emergency call **Centre Médico Thermal,** 2, rue du Cap-Chazotte (tel. 73 65 22 22). The **police station** (tel. 73 65 01 70) is on av. Michel Bertrand.

Near Le Mont Dore

Le Mont Dore is a medium-sized ski area; most hot-dog skiers go elsewhere. The base of the slopes is at **Le Sancy,** 5km out of town on route de Sancy and right next to the hostel. Buses leave on the hour from the train station and in front of the tourist office. (9am-6pm in winter, 2-6pm in summer, 8.50F, 12.80F round-trip.) Le Mont Dore and the surrounding area have recently been connected to the Super Besse area. You can buy lift tickets for just Le Mont Dore (65F per ½-day, 85F per day, 150F per 2 days) or for both powdery masses (90F per day, 210F per 3 days, 420F per 7 days). A 50% reduction goes into effect between January 5 and February 1 and between February 27 and March 4. In addition, 400km of cross-country trails run circles around Mont Dore.

During summer, don't miss the opportunity to get to the mountains via the Grande Randonnée and other rewarding trails. If you left your hiking gear at home, one of Le Mont Dore's eight sporting goods stores will happily outfit you. Try **Jacky Sports,** pl. Charles de Gaulle (tel. 73 65 06 79; open daily 9am-12:30pm and 2-7pm). The tourist office can recommend a route suited to your endurance. Before you set off on a serious hike (4 hr. or more), pick up their detailed map (40-60F). Contact the *gendarmerie* at the base of Puy de Sancy (tel. 73 65 05 03) and have them approve your route. **Vallée de Sancy** will give you an overview of the region. Start at the **Salon de Capucin** (1249m), which you can reach by foot or by a funicular (one way 8F). From there you can continue through the **Puy de Ciergue** (1691m) to the **Puy du Sancy** (1886m), the highest peak in Central France. The two-hour hike will take you along the *chemin de crètes* with all its old volcanoes and past the source of the Dordogne.

Less brave souls can also reach Puy de Sancy by *téléphérique* (every 15-20 min. 9am-noon and 1:30-5:30pm, 20F, return 26F); the summit is only a 20-minute climb away. Wildflowers carpet the protected **Vallée de Chaude-four,** east of Puy de Sancy. You'll see many endangered species of flora here. Volcanic lakes along the trail, including **Lac Serviéré** (20km northeast of Le Mont Dore), and **Lac de Guery**

(7km north), are suitable for windsurfing, sailing, and fishing, and (when warm enough) swimming. An alternate 25-minute walk on the route to Besse leads to the **Grande Cascade,** where you can stand under the projecting rocks behind falling water. If you'd rather not roam around on your own, **Tourisme Verney** (tel. 73 37 31 06) organizes reasonably-priced tours of the region's lakes, volcanoes, châteaux, cheese and honey factories, and more. (45-90F.) Reserve through the Mont Dore Tourist Office (tel. 73 65 29 21).

Five km away lies the mountain resort of **La Bourboule,** another *station thermale* and cross-country ski center. The town's natural setting rivals that of Le Mont Dore. The **swimming pool** (tel. 73 81 03 02) across from the bus station, open every afternoon, refreshes returning hikers. The **tourist office,** av. Agis Ledru (tel. 73 81 07 99), can help you organize your stay. For accommodations, try **Hôtel les Thermes,** bd. Georges Clemenceau (tel. 73 81 09 24), or **Hôtel Banne d'Ordanche,** av. Général Leclerc (tel. 73 81 09 57), above the train station. There is a **camping municipal** on av. de Lattre de Tassigny (tel. 73 81 10 20).

Aurillac

Aurillac (pop. 33,197), 110km southeast of Clermont-Ferrand, lies among steep green hills in a basin encircled by high volcanic ranges. In centuries past, isolated Aurillac managed to maintain faint ties with Languedoc and Aquitaine. The town's abbey produced the first French Pope, Sylvester II, in the 10th century. Unfortunately, the abbey, along with most of the town, was razed by Protestants in 1552 during the Wars of Religion. Today, a well-preserved *vieille ville,* a series of avant-garde festivals, and convenient bus service make Aurillac an attractive base for excursions into southwestern Auvergne.

Be aware that something strange happens between Clermont-Ferrand and Aurillac—phonemes shift. The *Cantaliens* tack on a nasal twang to words ending in "n," which end up rhyming with *meringue* (as in pie).

All that remains of the original 13th-century **Château St-Etienne** is a dingy tower overlooking the city. In the renovated château next door, the **Maison des Volcans** houses an extensive exhibit on the volcanoes and the geology of Auvergne. (Open July-Aug. Tues.-Sat. 10am-6:30pm; Sept.-June Tues.-Fri. 8:30am-noon and 2-5:30pm, Sat. 8:30am-noon. Admission 10F, students 5F.) The **Musée d'Art et d'Archéologie,** 8, pl. de la Paix, displays an interesting collection of rocks, minerals, regional flora and fauna, and archaeological finds. The **Musée de Parieu des Beaux-Arts** next door resigns itself to paintings from the 17th through 20th centuries and a collection of contemporary color photographs. (Both museums open Tues.-Sat. 10am-noon and 2-6pm, Sun. 2-6pm. Free.) The **Maison Consulaire,** also known as the **Musée du Vieil Aurillac,** 2, rue de la Coste traces the development of Aurillac's religious art and customs. (Open April-Sept. Wed.-Sat. 2-6pm. Free.) The **Musée de Cire,** pl. Gilbert, off cours Monthyon, displays wax figures of Charlemagne, Mitterand, and various luminaries that came between them. (Open June-Sept. Mon.-Sat. 10am-noon and 2-6:30pm, Sun. 2-6:30pm. Admission 12F, students 7F.) **La Sellerie,** next to pl. de la Paix in the Jardin des Carmes, is a recently converted stable devoted to contemporary photography. (Open June-Sept. Mon.-Sat 1-7pm. Free.)

In recent years the town has developed a surprising reputation as a center for avant-garde visual and performing arts. Last year's **Eclat d'Aurillac,** an international street-theater festival in the last week of August included plays in outdoor tents, store windows, and moving trains (most shows free, some 60F). The **Festival de Création Choréographique d'Aurillac** brings the work of post-modern Terpsichores to town for three days in mid-July. Aurillac's huge international film festival, held in late October, allows only films depicting rural life to compete. (Tickets 20F.) Throughout the summer, **Café Musique** brings jazz, funk, rock, blues, and reggae bands to the streets. For more information on all festivals, contact the Office Culturel d'Animations et Fêtes, 37, rue du 139*ème* Régiment d'Infanterie (tel. 71 48 86

00). (Open Mon.-Fri. 9am-noon and 2-7pm. In morning use side entrance and ring the bell. In the afternoon, use main entrance.)

From the station turn right, bear left onto rue de la Gare, and continue straight to pl. du Square, the center of town and location of the **tourist office** (tel. 71 48 08 56). The harried but pleasant staff will give you a good free map and information on the area, and can help you find a room. They also organize bus excursions (90-140F), hand out annotated walking tours, and operate a **currency exchange** in July and August when the banks are closed. (Open Mon.-Sat. 9am-12:30pm and 2-7:30pm, Sun. 10am-noon and 2-7pm; Sept.-June Mon.-Sat. 9am-noon and 2-6:30pm.) The **Comité Départemental du Tourisme,** av. Gambetta (tel. 71 46 22 00) in the Hôtel du Département building, first floor, distributes information on cheap lodging, camping, hiking, and food for the entire Cantal region. (Open Mon.-Thurs. 8:30am-noon and 1:30-5:30pm, Fri. 8:30am-noon and 1:30-5pm.).

Accommodations in Aurillac hotels seldom fill. The **Château St-Etienne** (tel. 71 48 49 09) offers simple rooms at extraordinarily low prices. Always make a reservations 3-4 weeks in advance, as it is almost always filled by groups. (Singles 52F. Doubles 104F. Special group price (5 or more) 32F per person. Kitchen facilities.) From pl. du Square, head up rue Delzons, bear right onto bd. d'Auriques, and take your first left onto rue du Château St-Etienne. The château is at the top of the hill. The **Foyer des Jeunes Travailleurs,** 25, av. de Tivoli (tel. 71 63 56 94), offers ordinary singles for 55F or studios for 80F. (Showers included. Breakfast 13F. Office open daily 8:30am-9pm.) Take bus #1 from the station or pl. du Square (*direction:* "Arpajon") and ask to be dropped off at the *foyer* (2 per hour, last bus 7:39pm, 5.50F). Otherwise, make the 25-minute walk. From the station, take a right on av. Milhaud and another right at the end on av. des Pupilles de la Nation. Bear right at the fork on av. des Prades and make a third left on av. de Tivoli. The **Hôtel Bosc-Lapier,** 19, av. du 4 Septembre (tel. 71 48 26 85), five minutes from the station, has nicely furnished rooms with hardwood floors. (Singles and doubles 70F, with shower 100F. Shower 8F. Breakfast 15F. 45F *menu* in restaurant.) More central is the **Hôtel Le Pont Rouge,** 1, bd. du Pont-Rouge (tel. 71 48 05 33). (Singles or doubles 80F, with shower 100F. 2 beds with shower 145F. Showers 10F. Breakfast 16F.)

By far the best meal bargain in Aurillac is the cafeteria at the *foyer* (guests welcome). A mere 37F buys you a surprisingly good, appallingly large five-course meal. (Open Mon.-Fri. noon-1pm and 7-8pm, Sat. noon-1pm. Call the *foyer* to confirm the hours.) Entertaining **Le Bistro,** 18, av. Gambetta serves economical *plats du jour* (32F), *steak-frites* (32F), and salads (12-40F). (Open daily noon-3pm and 7-11:30pm.) A covered **market** holds forth at pl. de l'Hôtel de Ville on Wednesday and Saturday morning. A **Supermarket Topco** looms across the street from the *foyer.* (Open Mon.-Fri. 8:30am-12:30pm and 3-7:30pm, Sat. 8:30am-12:30pm and 2:30-7:15pm.) Don't leave Aurillac without sampling the town's three different varieties of cheese: St-Nectaire, a soft, delicate hazelnut cheese; the potent Bleu d'Auvergne; and the hard Cantal cheese. You can tast them all for free at **Dégustation des Fromages d'Auvergne** (tel. 71 47 52 16), next to the Château de St-Etienne. (Open Tues.-Sat. 10am-1pm and 3-7pm.)

The **train station** (tel. 71 48 50 50) is on pl. Pierre Semard (information office open daily 7:30am-8pm). **Trains** run to Toulouse (5 per day, 3½ hr., 123F); Brive (5 per day, 1 hr. ¾-hr., 62F); Clermont-Ferrand (5-6 per day, 3 hr., 94F); and Paris (via Brive; 4 per day, 61/3 hr., 267F). You can rent a **bicycle** at the station (tel. 71 48 08 56) for 40F per ½-day or 50F per day plus a 500F deposit. (Open daily 7am-9pm). **Urban buses,** 8, rue Denis Papin (tel. 71 64 54 55), cost 5.50F a ride, 32F for a 10-ticket *carnet.* **Regional buses** to the surrounding Cantal region (Super Lioran, Ussel, St-Flour, Vic-sur-Cère) all stop at the *gare routière* in the parking lot to the left of the station. A schedule is posted in the train station. The main **post office** on rue Salvador Allende (tel. 71 45 62 00) has a currency exchange and telephones. (Open Mon.-Fri. 8am-7pm, Sat. 8am-noon.) The more convenient **branch office** (tel. 71 48 14 04) is at 3, rue Rieu. (Open Mon.-Fri. 8:30am-noon and 1:15-5pm, Sat. 8:30am-noon.) The **postal code** is 15000. Poste Restante letters must be marked "Préfecture" to arrive at the branch office. The only bank open on Mondays is **Crédit Agricole**, rue S. Allende. (Open Mon.-Fri. 8:30-noon and 1:30-5pm.) In a **medical emergency** call **Centre Hospitalier**, 83, av. Charles de Gaulle (tel. 71 63 62 44).

Cantal Countryside

Older and greener than the Monts Dôme to the northeast, the volcanic mountains of the Cantal are dotted with feudal *châteaux,* ancient *burons* (farmhouses), and bell-bearing bovines genuinely surprised to see people trotting down the country roads. Don't count on getting anywhere in the Cantal fast, unless you've got your own wheels or wings. Even then, the hilly terrain that challenges Tour de France veterans can torture the amateur cyclist. Masochists unfazed by steep hills can rent bikes at the Aurillac train station (tel. 71 48 08 50) for 50F per day plus a 500F deposit. (Open daily 7am-9pm.) Nonmasochists are better off basing themselves in Aurillac and traveling by train or bus.

Before you wander too far out into the countryside, pick up maps, guides, and accommodations listings at the Comité Départemental du Tourisme, av. Gambetta (tel. 71 46 22 00) in Aurillac. Although generally less comprehensive, the Aurillac tourist office has printed descriptions of towns, lists of campgrounds and hotels, and a free regional accommodations service. *La Montagne,* a local newspaper, usually lists events and festivals in the region (4F).

The region is not well served by **trains.** There are three main lines: Clermont-Ferrand to Aurillac to Toulouse (6 per day, 120F); Aurillac to Bort-les-Orgues (3 per day, 62F); Bort-les-Orgues to Neussargues (2-4 per day, 47F). SNCF's Service Voyageurs (tel. 71 48 89 46) organizes marathon train tours of the region (11 hr., 175F). Three daily SNCF buses run like heck from Bort-les-Orgues to Ussel. If you plan your trains ahead, you can see a good section of the countryside without too many delays.

In addition, sixteen private **bus** companies serve the region. Unfortunately, no office organizes them all. Check the schedules posted at the train station, or ask for a schedule at the tourist office. **STTAC**, 9, pl. du Square (tel. 71 48 48 33) covers Le Lioran (3 per day, 1 hr. 10 min.), St-Flour (3 per day, 2 hr.), and Vic-sur-Cère (1-2 per day, ½-hr.). Most buses leave from the *gare routière,* to the left of the Aurillac train station.

By sticking to the train line between Aurillac and Neussargues (on the way to Clermont-Ferrand), you can cover a lovely stretch of countryside. The first stop on the line is the tiny village of **Polminhac,** which cowers in the shadows of the **Château de Pesteils.** From 13th-century towers to the imposing dungeon, the fortress exudes the strength that rebuffed several invasions. Inside the tower are some beautiful 14th-century frescoes. The 17th-century wing contains finely-painted ceilings and furniture and Aubusson tapestries. (Open May-June and Sept. 2:30-5:30pm; July-Aug. 10am-noon and 2:30-6pm. Admission 17F, children under 10 8.50F.) If you insist on spending the night, the **tourist office** (tel. 71 47 40 07) will help you find a place. Nearby **Camping Val de Cère** is open June 15 to September 15. Prepare for chilly evenings.

The next train stop on the Aurillac-Neussargues line is **Vic-sur-Cère** (16F from Aurillac, pop. 2048), a popular summer resort in a beautiful valley by the Cère River. Once you've seen the handsome Romanesque church and old city, several walking paths will funnel you into the surrounding mountains. Walk toward Thiézac to the **Pas de Cère, Rocher de Muret,** or the **Grotte des Huguenots,** where the Huguenots held cabals during the Wars of Religion. The **tourist office,** Pavillion du Parc (tel. 71 47 50 68), recommends walking, cycling, and hiking routes. (Open June daily 9:30am-noon and 2:30-6:30pm; July-Aug. daily 9:30am-noon and 2:30-7pm; Sept.-May daily 9:30am-noon and 2:30-6pm.) **La Terrasse Hôtel,** av. du Docteur Jean Lambert (tel. 71 47 50 24), has clean and comfortable doubles for 88F (with shower 145F). If it's full, even the tentless will have to head for the **Camping**

Municipal, av. des Tilleuls (tel. 71 47 51 04), a three-star site with hot showers. (10F per person, 3.80F per tent. Open April-Sept.)

Also on the Aurillac-Neussargues line, **Le Lioran** (29F from Aurillac) is the Cantal's major ski resort. In summer its ski runs become hiking trails. A *téléphérique* whisks you to a short distance from the **Plomb du Cantal** (1855m). Turn left from the train station, take the first right, and climb the 1km up to the ski area and hiking trails. The **tourist office** (tel. 71 49 50 08) at the foot of the *téléphérique* distributes information on skiing, hiking, and the lambada. (Open Dec.-Sept. daily 9am-noon and 1-6pm; Oct.-Nov. Mon.-Fri. only.) There are no cheap hotels in Le Lioran. **Vallagnot Camping** (tel. 71 20 11 34) lies 5km outside town. (8F per person, 4.50F per tent. Open June-Sept.)

The old village of **Murat** (pop. 2813) is the last town of interest on the Aurillac-Neussargues train line. The **tourist office** on pl. de la Mairie (tel. 71 20 09 47 or 71 20 03 80), founded by 4th-century Episcopalians and other nonexistent groups, is not a tourist office. (Mon.-Sat. 9:30am-noon and 2-6pm and Sun. 10am-noon.) The main (and only) thing to see here is the **Maison de la Faune,** pl. Batat (tel. 71 20 00 52) a natural history museum with over 600 birds, 6000 insects, and other *auvergnat* fauna. (Open July-Aug. daily noon-2pm and 4-6pm. Sept.-June by appointment.)

To the east of the Aurillac-Neussargues train line, **St-Flour** sits pretty on a high plateau. To get to the *centre ville* from the station, turn right on av. de la République and make a left on rue du Pont Vieux when you hit pl. de la Liberté. Take a right on chemin des Chèvres and then start climbing like a mountain goat. When you reach the top you'll stumble upon the severe Gothic **Cathédrale St-Pierre,** the graceful interior of which shelters a beautiful 15th-century wooden crucifix called *le Bon Dieu Noir.* (Open daily 9am-6pm. Guided tours in English daily 9am-noon and 2-6pm.) The **Musée de la Haute Auvergne** next to the Cathedral in the Hôtel de Ville, contains several displays of *auvergnat* folklore and a few rooms devoted entirely to the traditional *auvergnat* instrument, the *cabrette* (similar to a bagpipe). (Open daily 10am-noon and 2-7pm. Admission 17F, students 8.50F.) The **Musée Douet,** in the **Ancienne Maison Consulaire** on pl. d'Armes contains several richly furnished rooms, ancient arms, and various paintings and sculptures. (Open daily 9am-noon and 2-7pm; Sept.-June Tues.-Sat. 8am-noon and 2-6pm. Admission 17F, students 8.50F.) **Musée de la Poste,** pl. des Jacobins, with its well endowed postcard and stamp collection, refused to give Joel Kurtzberg its telephone number. (Open daily 10am-12:30pm and 2-7pm. Admission 10F.) The **tourist office,** 2, pl. des Armes (tel. 71 60 22 50), next to the cathedral, often runs English tours of the city (15F). (Open daily 9am-noon and 2-7:30pm; Sept.-June closed Sun.) In July and August, the **annex** down below at pl. de la Liberté (tel. 71 60 26 29) distributes free maps. (Open July-Aug. Mon.-Sat. 9:30am-noon and 2:30-7pm.) The cheapest hotel is **Les Orgues,** av. des Orgues (tel. 71 60 06 41), where adequate singles and doubles cost 70F, 150F with shower. (Breakfast 16F.) **Camping de l'Ander,** rue de Massales (tel. 71 60 29 27) is a two-star site next to the covered market (6.15F per person, 5.30F per tent, 4.25 per shower.) **Camping les Orgues,** off av. du Dr. Mallet (tel. 71 60 44 01), has a restaurant, grocery store, and three stars. (8.45F per person, 5.40F per tent. Showers included. Open April-Oct.)

Ten km southeast of St-Flour reclines the **Viaduc de Garabit,** a huge (564m) metallic bridge designed by none other than Gustave Eiffel. There is no public transportation. So there. Hitchhikers find the best place to wait is along the N9. Thirty km south of St-Flour by bus (3 per day Mon.-Sat., 35 min., for information call 71 23 56 44) lies **Chaudes-Aigues** (pronounced showed-ZEG), an open-air spa which immerses the variously afflicted in Europe's hottest spa water (82°C from the Par Spring). The **tourist office,** 1, av. Georges Pompidou (tel. 71 23 52 75) has showers of information on the water's alleged powers. (Open Mon.-Sat. 10:30am-noon and 3-6pm.)

Two hours north by train from Aurillac is **Bort-les-Orgues** (pop. 4500) (3 trains per day, 62F). Itself unattractive, the town is a good place to start hikes in the beautiful valley of the Dordogne River and the nearby **Lac du Barrage de Bort.** Bort-les-Orgues is actually closer to Le Mont Dore (40km south on N89) than Aurillac but there is no train line from Bort to Le Mont Dore. **SNCF buses** connect Bort-les-Orgues to Neussargues (47F) and also run between Bort-les-Orgues and Ussel (36F). The **Hôtel du Barrage,** 851, av. de la Gare (tel. 55 96 73 22), barrages clean, ordinary travelers with clean, ordinary singles and doubles for 85F (breakfast 12F). Get a list of the many campgrounds in the area from the **tourist office,** pl. Marmontel (tel. 55 96 02 49; open daily 9am-noon and 2-7pm).

The 15th-century **Château du Val** (tel. 71 40 30 20) lies 6km from Bort in the tiny village of Lanobre. The six fortified round towers with pepper-pot roofs and a Gothic chapel once overlooked the sleepy Dordogne until the construction of the dam at Bort surrounded the castle with a lake. Although the castle tends to look more impressive on postcards, the rustic interior makes an interesting visit. (Open June 15-Sept. 15 daily 9am-noon and 2-6pm; Sept.-Oct. and Dec. 16-June 15 Wed.-Mon. same hours. Courtyard 3F. Castle with obligatory tour 14F.) To get there, follow N122 north for 5km out of Bort, and turn left on the well-marked road to the lake (2km). The busy roads are unpleasant to walk along.

About midway between Bort and Aurillac, **Salers** (pop. 450) is a beautiful if tourist-thronged old town set on a plateau overlooking the Maronne Valley. The somber **Eglise St-Mathieu** contains renowned *mise au tombeau* (entombment) sculpture and five Aubusson tapestries. The elegantly simple **Chapelle Notre-Dame de Lorette** (2 min. out of town off D680) shelters souls and an occasional chirping sparrow. The **esplanade de Barouze** provides picnickers with an appetizing view of the peaceful valley. Salers is inaccessible by public transportation; hitching a ride from Mauriac (on the Bort-Aurillac train line) is one (unattractive) possibility. More locals travel on the road from Salers to Mauriac (D22), so even if you're coming from or going to Aurillac, you should probably take this road. The **tourist office,** pl. Tissandier d'Escous (tel. 71 40 70 68 or 71 40 72 33) will direct you to hotels and campgrounds. (Open daily 10am-12:30pm and 2-7pm.)

The villages along the main road from Mauriac to Aurillac (D922) offer plenty of rustic charm, and, well, rustic charm. **St-Martin Valmeroux, St-Chamant,** and **St-Cernin** also contain enchanting 15th- and 16th-century churches. The majestic **Château d'Anjony** (tel. 71 47 61 67) languishes 5km off D922 in the village of Tournemire. (Open Easter-Oct. 2-6:30pm).

Burgundy (Bourgogne)

Encompassing the upper valley of the Saône and its surrounding hills—the Côte d'Or, the Plateau de Langres, and the wild, forested Morvan—Burgundy is best known for its Romanesque architecture and the 40 million bottles of wine it produces each year. Today, the hills that gave feudal lords control over important passes leading toward Paris and the northern provinces are covered with small vineyards that produce great wine. Beaujolais comes from the area south of Mâcon, fine white wines—notably the dry Pouilly-Fuissé—from the Mâconnais, white Chablis from Auxerre, and full-bodied reds—Vougeot, Chambertin, Nuits—from the Côte d'Or, which stretches from Santenay north to Dijon. Roads throughout the wine-producing areas are dotted with signs advertising *dégustations* (free tastings) at local *caves*).

While the wine certainly is, as the saying goes, Burgundy's best ambassador, the locals and their beautiful surroundings make Burgundy an ideal travel area. The Roman conquest of Gaul began in the area around Autun, and the impressive Gallo-Roman ruins of that city, combined with the thousands of Roman objects displayed in regional museums, constitute a fascinating historical legacy. The pamphlet *Bourgogne Archéologique,* free at most tourist offices, lists excavation sites and noteworthy museums throughout the region. Romanesque and Gothic architecture flourished in Burgundy, and each village church claims that its tympanum or altar *retable* is the most original in the province. Later, an 11th- and 12th-century building craze produced churches and abbeys decorated with an inexplicable and bewitching mix of biblical and fantastic, perhaps Celtic, stone carvings.

Making the most of its wine-based sauces, Burgundy's renowned cuisine includes such specialties as *boeuf bourguignon, coq au vin,* Dijon *moutardes* (mustard made with white wine instead of vinegar), and *kir* (a beverage concocted with white wine and blackcurrant liqueur). Other culinary delights include *gougère* (a soft bread made with *pâte à choux* and cheese), *escargots,* and *quenelles* (little dumplings). Luckily, these gastronomic masterpieces are (outside of Dijon) affordable works of art: *bourguignon* restaurants keep both customers and wallets fat and happy.

Hotels are relatively expensive, but hostels and *foyers* are common in the region. For a list of campgrounds, ask at the tourist office for *Camping en Bourgogne, 1990.* Burgundy is fairly well served by trains, and daily or twice-daily buses sometimes fill in the gaps. The famous wine routes and many of the most idyllic villages are most easily reached (or, in some cases, can only be reached) by car or bike; cheap rentals are easily found. Keep in mind that banking days vary from town to town; some are open Monday to Friday, others Tuesday to Saturday.

Summer brings a flurry of cultural festivals. From mid-July to mid-August, under the auspices of **Musique en Bourgogne,** classical and early music fills the cathedrals and churches of Sens, Beaune, Vézelay, Tournus, and other towns. Many of these events, and particularly those in Dijon, attract prestigious international groups. Ask any tourist office for the *Petit guide des manifestations musicales en Bourgogne.*

Opportunities to help in the annual grape *vendange* (harvest) are plentiful during September and October; be aware that the work is physically taxing. For information, contact the Centre Régional de Jeunes Agriculteurs, 41, rue de Mulhouse, Dijon (tel. 80 30 84 96); or the Agence Nationale pour les Emplois, 6, bd. St-Jacques, Beaune (tel. 80 22 16 72). You can also go directly to the local vineyards, where they are less picky about foreigners having a work permit. Youth centers also have information on grape and cherry harvest jobs; if your French is shaky, the staff might be persuaded to call around for you.

Those more interested in harvesting old rocks might volunteer on archaeological digs throughout the region. Contact Direction des Antiquités de Bourgogne, 39, rue Vannerie, 21000 Dijon (tel. 80 67 17 67).

Dijon

Dijon's prospects looked bleak in 1513 when 30,000 Swiss held the city in a vise-like siege. Negotiations faltered until, in a stroke of Burgundian brilliance, the *Dijonnais* sent a multitude of wine casks across enemy lines. The Swiss, with the generosity of utter inebriation, acquiesced and retreated, saving Dijon.

An important industrial center and home to a respected univesity, Burgundy's animated capital stands at the crossroads of two of the world's finest wine producing regions: the Côte de Nuits and the Côte de Beaune. Multiple turrets are stacked above the carefully restored *vieille ville* like so many salt cellars, peppermills, and—of course—mustard jars.

Orientation and Practical Information

Conveniently linked by train to most of France, Dijon is two and a half hours south of Paris, one and a half hours north of Lyon, and eight hours north of the Côte d'Azur. The city is relatively small and compact. The main east-west axis, the pedestrian zone of **rue de la Liberté**, runs roughly from **place Darcy**, where the tourist office and the Tromanhause are located, to **place St-Michel.** From the train station, follow av. Maréchal Foch straight to pl. Darcy, a few minutes away. The *vieille ville* and most of Dijon's other attractions are on the small streets radiating from rue de la Liberté to the north and south. The **place de la République**, northeast of pl. Darcy, is the central roundabout for roads leading out of the city.

Tourist Office: pl. Darcy (tel. 80 43 42 12). Accommodations service 6F plus 1.50F per star. **Currency exchange** without commission. English-speaking staff unleashes torrents of information, much of it in English. The pamphlet, *Circuits en Côte d'Or*, lists things to see and do in the region. Ask for the extremely useful guide *Divio 1990*. It's free; if they won't give you a copy, explain that you're staying in town a long time. Open Mon.-Sat. 9am-noon and 2-8:30pm, Sun. 10am-noon and 2-7:30pm; Aug. Mon.-Sat. 9am-8:30pm, Sun 10am-7:30pm. July-Sept. guided walking tours leave daily at 3pm and 4:30pm (1½ hr.; 20F, students 10F).

Budget Travel: Wasteels, 16, av. Maréchal Foch (tel. 80 43 65 34). BIJ tickets. Open Mon.-Sat. 9am-7pm. If you're under 26, you can get BIJ tickets for 25% less at **Autostop Bourgogne** (see Hitchhiking).

Post Office: (tel. 80 43 81 00), on pl. Grangier close to pl. Darcy. Open Mon.-Fri. 8am-7pm, Sat. 8am-noon. **Poste Restante, telephones,** and stamps available only until 11am on Sat. **Postal code:** 21000.

Trains: SNCF (tel. 80 41 50 50; reservations 80 43 52 56), at the end of av. Maréchal Foch. Station and ticket booth open 24 hrs. Some English spoken. Long wait. Reservation and information desk open Mon.-Sat. 8:30am-7pm, Sun. 9am-noon and 2-7pm. **SOS Voyageurs** (tel. 80 43 16 34) is open Mon.-Fri. 8am-7pm, Sat. 8am-6pm. To Paris by TGV (5 per day, 1½ hr., 168F plus 13F reservation). To: Lyon (every hr., 2 hr., 107F); Beaune (3 per day, ½-hr., 30F); Les Laumes (3 per day, 30 min., 25F); Besançon (10 per day, 1 hr., 60F); Gevrey-Chambertin (6 per day, 10 min., 13F); Strasbourg (1 per day, 4 hr., 174F); Nice (6 per day, 7½ hr., 340F).

Buses: (tel. 80 43 58 97), on av. Maréchal Foch, connected to the train station. Information and ticket booth open Mon.-Fri. 8:30am-12:30pm and 2:30-6:30pm, Sat. 8:30am-12:30pm, Sun. (in a small booth outside) 11am-12:30pm and 5-7:45pm. You can also by tickets aboard. To Avallon (2 per day, 2½-3 hr., 70F) via Semur-en-Auxois (1½ hr., 42F) and Gevrey-Chambertin (5 per day, Sun. 3; ½-hr.,; 11F). The most convenient and scenic way to travel the *route de vin* is on the 8 daily buses to Beaune (1 hr., 30F), Nuits St-George (40 min., 19F), and other towns. The 12:15pm continues all the way to Autun (2½ hr., 60F).

Public Transportation: Buses (STRD), (tel. 80 30 60 90), booth in pl. Grangier. Covers greater Dijon Mon.-Sat. 6am-8:30pm, Sun. 1-8:30pm. Tickets 5F, 12-trip pass 36F. Map available from tourist office.

Car Rental: Avis, 5, av. Maréchal Foch (tel. 80 43 60 76). Compacts from 167F per day plus 2.34F per km. Must be over 20. Open Mon.-Sat. 8am-noon and 2-7pm.

Bike Rental: Cycles Pouilly, 3, rue de Tivoli (tel. 80 66 61 75). 25F per ½-day, 40F per day, 200F per week. Deposit 500F.

Hitchhiking: If you chose to hitchhike to Paris via Sens, take av. Albert 1er. For the south, take av. Jean Jaurès (N74 for Chalon). **Autostop Bourgogne,** 14, rue Audra (tel. 80 30 71 55), in the same office as the youth center CIJB. They'll do their best to match you with a driver. 30F per voyage or 80F per year. Pay the driver 0.16F per km. Open Mon. noon-6pm, Tues.-Fri. 10am-6pm, Sat. 9am-noon; July-Aug. Mon.-Fri. only.

English Bookstore: Librairie Université, 10, rue de la Liberté. Has an English section. **Librairie Voyageur** across the street sells the *vachement chouette Let's Go: Europe* and *Let's Go: France* (each 163F).

Youth Information: Centre d'Information Jeunesse de Bourgogne (CIJB), 22, rue Audra (tel. 80 30 35 56). Friendly. Information on accommodations, French classes for foreigners, festivals, cheap restaurants, wine harvesting, sports, and travel throughout France. Willing to call around for work if you can't speak French. Open Mon. noon-6pm, Tues.-Fri. 10am-6pm, Sat. 9am-noon; July-Aug. Mon.-Fri. only. **CROUS,** 3, rue du Docteur Maret (tel. 80 30 76 33). Information on plentiful university housing and cafeterias. Open Mon.-Fri. 9-11:30am and 2-4:30pm.

Women's Centers: SOS Amitié, tel. 80 67 15 15. Friendly ear 24 hrs. Boîte Postal 354. **SOS Femmes Battues,** tel. 80 46 21 66. For women in need. **Solidarité Femmes,** 4, rue Choncelier de l'Hôpital (tel. 80 67 17 89).

Markets: Halle Centrale: Follow rue François Rude from rue de la Liberté. Everything under the sun; prices reasonable but not remarkable. Open Tues. and Fri. until 1pm, Sat. all day.

Taxis: Taxi Radio Dijon cour Gare, tel. 80 41 41 12.

Airport: Aéroport Dijon-Bourgogne (tel. 80 67 67 67), 6km from center in Longvic.

Laundromats: 36, rue Guillaume Tell, above the train station. Wash 22F, dry 2F per 6 min. Open daily 7am-9pm. Also rue J. J. Rousseau at rue d'Assas, pl. de la République. Wash 20F, dry 2F per 5 min. Open daily 6am-8:30pm. Also at 4, bd. des Martyrs-de-la-Résistance and 28, rue Berbisey.

Medical Assistance: Hôpital Général, 3, rue Faubourg Raines (tel. 80 41 81 41). **SAMU,** tel. 80 41 12 12.

Police: 2, pl. Suquet (tel. 80 41 81 05). **Emergency,** tel. 17.

Accommodations and Camping

From mid-June to mid-August and during the first week of September, the profusion of reasonably priced hotels fill quickly. Reserve a place early or use the accommodations service at the tourist office.

Auberge de Jeunesse (IYHF), Centre de Rencontres Internationales, 1, bd. Champollion (tel. 80 71 32 12), a 4km ride from the station. Take bus #5 from the "Bar Bleu" in pl. Grangier toward Epirey at the end of the line, or bus #6 from pl. Darcy. A classic concrete "megahostel," complete with electronic surveillance, a bar, disco, and shrieking school groups. Hosts language programs in summer for foreigners. Singles 80F. Doubles 70F per person. Dorms with 5-8 beds 50F per person. Breakfast included. Self-service dinner 36F. Fills quickly July-Aug., so call ahead and pick up keys early in the day.

Foyer International d'Etudiants (tel. 80 71 51 01), on av. Maréchal Leclerc. Take bus #4 (*direction* "St. Apollinaire"), and get off at Vélodrome; from av. Paul Doumer, turn right on rue du Stade, then first left for the *foyer*. A sleek, noisy place with 300 beds. One of the best deals in town. Rooms 49F. Breakfast 9F. Cafeteria lunch 20F. Normally long-term residents, but travelers admitted year-round if there's room.

University Dorm Rooms: Residence Universitaire (R.U.) Mansart (tel. 80 66 18 22), on bd. Mansart, and **Residence Universitaire Montmuzard** (tel. 80 39 68 01), on bd. Gabriel. Two stops away from each other on bus #9. Take the bus from the train station or pl. Darcy to Mansart (for R.U. Mansart) or to Faculté des Sciences (for R.U. Montmuzard). Clean, comfortable singles available July-Sept. Students 45F, others 65F. Often full in Aug., so call ahead. Cafeterias at Mansart (tel. 80 66 18 22) open in Aug. only, at Montmuzard (tel. 80

39 69 50) in July only. Breakfast 8F. Lunch or dinner 25F, with a student card (sometimes *any* student card) 10F.

Hôtel de la Gare, 16, rue Mariotte (tel. 80 30 46 61). From the train or bus station, go down rue A. Remy; rue Mariotte is on your left. Cramped and dilapidated, but clean and convenient. Usually has space before 7pm. Pleasant management and amusing door keys fashioned from tennis balls. Reception closes at 8pm. Singles 70-100F, with shower 120F. Doubles 120F, with shower 155F. Triples 150F, with shower 185F. Breakfast 20F.

Hôtel du Miroir, 7, rue Bossuet (tel. 80 30 54 81), off rue de la Liberté. Central but quiet, located down an alley and upstairs. Spacious, clean rooms and friendly management. Singles 70-80F, with shower 100F. Doubles 80-100F, with shower 130F. Triples 110-130F, with shower 150F. Quint 220F. Showers 18F. Breakfast in café below about 20F.

Hôtel du Sauvage, 64, rue Monge (tel. 80 41 31 21), near Eglise St-Jean and not far from pl. Darcy. The closest modern travelers can get to Asterix's Gaul. Rugged, wood-beamed building overlooks a quiet, vine-covered courtyard. Singles and doubles 100F, with shower 140F. Triples and quads with shower 220F. Shower 15F. Breakfast 20F. Open Jan.-Dec. 24.

Hôtel Confort, 12, rue Jules Mercier (tel. 80 30 37 47), on an alley off rue de la Liberté. Delightful rooms and a breakfast room mural that'll make you feel like royalty. Neat singles and doubles 95-110F, with shower 130F, and TV 160F. Triples with shower 170F. Baths 20F. Breakfast 22F.

Hôtel du Théâtre, 3, rue des Bons Enfants (tel. 80 67 15 41), on a quiet side street off pl. de la Libération. Average rooms, no hall showers. Especially full weeknights. Singles and doubles 80F, with shower 130F. Breakfast 20F.

Hôtel Monge, 20, rue Monge (tel. 80 30 55 41), up the street from Hôtel du Sauvage. Set away from the street over a courtyard. Clean and cozy rooms with flamboyant mattresses. Singles 103F, with shower 130F. Doubles 109F, with shower 135F. Triples and quads about 150F. Showers 15F. Breakfast 20F.

Camping: Camping Municipal du Lac (tel. 80 43 54 72), at bd. Kir and av. Albert 1er. On a beautiful lake about 1km behind the train station; follow the signs for Paris. Bus #18, direction Plombières, stop "Pont des Chartreux." Spacious, with good facilities. 9F per night. Open April-Nov. 15. **Camping l'Orée du Bois,** (tel. 80 35 60 22) on route d'Etaules, 9km out of town in Darois. A 2-star campground with a pool near by. 9F per night. Open May-Sept.

Food

Sadly, Dijon's reputation for good food (dating from Gallo-Roman times) has inflated restaurant prices. *Charcuteries* are a particularly good place to try different *dijonnais* specialties. Bring 100g of *jambon persillé* (a ham *pâté* with parsley), *tarte bourguignon* (a pie with meat and mushrooms in a creamy sauce), or *quiche aux champignons* (mushroom quiche) to the **Jardin de l'Arquebuse** behind the train station. *Dijonnais* chefs take every possible opportunity to garnish their delicacies with heavy portions of their vinegars, wines, and mayonnaise. University cafeterias stay open all summer; R.U. Maret, 3, rue Docteur-Maret (tel. 80 39 67 83), has an all-you-can-eat dinner for only 9.90F. (Open 11:45am-1:15pm, 6:40-7:45pm.) There is a large **supermarket** in the basement of the Nouvelles Galleries on rue de la Liberté, and a superb *Géant Casino* on bd. Clemenceau, in the direction of the *foyers* (open Mon.-Sat. 8:30am-9pm).

Au Bec Fin, 47, rue Jeannin. Rue Jeannin starts behind Notre Dame, about 1 block north of rue de la Liberté. 66F (noon only), 66F, and 85F *menus*. 60F buys 4 courses; try the *galantine de volaille* followed by a spicy *colombo de porc,* a choice of regional cheeses, and a delicious lemon mousse in raspberry sauce. Truly outstanding. Open Mon.-Fri. noon-1:30pm and 7:30-10:30pm, Sat. 7:30-10:30pm.

Le Grilladou, 29, rue J.J. Rousseau, off pl. de la République. Cooking like yesteryear: over a wood fire smack in the middle of the dining room. 45F lunch *menu* . Assorted *brochettes* 30F. 47F *menu* rotates daily. Smoked salmon salad 32F. Generous lunch/dinner *menu* 60F. Open Mon.-Sat. noon-2pm and 7pm-10:30pm, Sun. 7pm-10:30pm.

Au Moulin à Vent, 8, pl. Françoise Rudé, near the ducal palace and open market. Rustic carnivorous dining in a half-timbered house. White wrought-iron tables and chairs outside.

Generous 65F and 85F *menus.* Excellent *boeuf bourguignon.* Open Tues.-Sat. noon-2pm and 7-9:30pm.

Mélodine, 6, av. Maréchal Foch, straight down from the train station. Locals pack this pleasant self-service restaurant. Huge selection of salads, hot meals, cheese, and desserts. See how much chocolate mousse you can fit in an 8F bowl. Full meals 30-45F. If it's your birthday, they'll give you a surprise. (Don't lie.) Open daily 11am-11pm. 10% student discount 11am-noon and 1:30-11pm.

Restaurant La Soupière, 15-17, av. Maréchal Foch, in the Hôtel Climat de France, across from station. This large buffet with an orgasmic array of desserts floors *Dijonnais* students. *Menus* from 76F. Open daily 11:45-9:45pm.

La Vie Saine, 27-29, rue Musette, off pl. Grangier. A vegetarian outpost in *boeuf* country. Attached to a health-food store. Adequate leafy *menus* from 55F. Open Mon.-Sat. noon-2pm; Thur.-Sat. also 7-9:30pm.

Le Vinarium, 23, pl. Bossuet, by Eglise St-Jean in a 13th-century crypt. Four 115-160F *menus* from different parts of Burgundy. *Boeuf bourguignon, jambon persillé,* and *charlotte* (a cake made with ladyfingers). Expensive, but generally worth the investment. A tad touristy. Open Mon. 7:30pm-late, Tues.-Sat. noon-2pm and 7:30-10pm.

Sights

In their hundred-year heyday (1364-1477), the Dukes of Burgundy were fearless (Jean sans Peur), heroic (Philippe le Bon), and bold (Philippe le Hardi). Wielding power as great as the French kings', these leaders built the **Palais des Ducs de Bourgogne** on the pl. de la Libération at the center of the *vieille ville.* Most of the buildings currently house administrative offices. A climb up the 289 steps of the **Tour Philippe le Bon** ends with a spectacular view of all of Dijon and more importantly, a glimpse of the enormous palace kitchen below. (Open Easter-Nov. 1 Wed.-Mon. 9:30-11:30am and 2:30-5:30pm; Nov. 1-Easter Sun. 9:30-11:30am and 2:30-5:30pm, Wed. 2:30-5:30pm. Admission 5F, students free.)

Second only to the Louvre among French musea, the **Musée des Beaux Arts,** pl. de la Sainte Chapelle (tel. 80 30 31 11) fills the palace's attractive east wing with works by Caracci, Veronese, Titian, French canvases from Mignard to Manet, Flemish primitives, and medieval works. The attic houses an amusing, if not particularly extensive, selection of 20th-century sculptures, oils, and lithographs. The most famous gallery in the museum is the **Salle des Gardes,** dominated by the huge mausoleums of Philippe le Hardi and Jean sans Peur. Note the 41-statuette funeral procession at the base of Philippe's tomb, sculpted by the 14th-century master Claus Sluter. (Open Mon. and Wed.-Sat. 10am-6pm, Sun. 10am-12:30pm and 2-6pm. Admission 9F, students free.)

From the palace, any number of streets lead to 300 year old *hôtel* façades and hidden courtyards. The demure exterior of the **Hôtel Chambellan,** at #34, rue des Forges, gives no indication of the extravagant Gothic courtyard within. The owl is the beloved bird of Dijon, and **rue de la Chouette** (of the owl) boasts several noble residences. Gawk at the sumptuous renaissance portico of 17th-century **Hôtel de Voguë,** at #8. The grooved center of the pavement on **rue Verrerie** was the sewage conduit in the 17th century.

Its façade a morass of gargoyles, 17th-century **Eglise de Notre Dame** exemplifies the Burgundian Gothic style. A surprisingly haggard Mary, the church's dedicatee, rests to the right of the main altar. The **Horloge à Jacquemart,** which Philippe le Hardi commissioned in 1382 after his victory over the Flemish, ticks above the right tower. In 1610, the lonely male statue who sounded the hour was given a spouse, then a son to strike the half hour, and finally, in 1881, a daughter to announce the quarter hour. Man, these people are *loud.*

At the end of rue de la Liberté, the **Eglise Saint-Michel** is a Gothic and Renaissance hodge-podge. In a fit of fancy, one stoneworker mixed mythological and biblical themes together—behold the result over the central portal. In the last century, the church focused its devotion on a modern day saint, Elisabeth-de-la-Trinité. Communed at St.-Michel and enrolled into the Carmelite monasteries at an early age, Elisabeth died of a mysterious disease at 26 and has since been revered as an example of sacrificial devotion. The elegant 93 meters of apse and spire in the **Cathédrale St-Bénigne,** 4, rue Docteur Maret, memorialize a second-century missionary priest whose martyred remains were unearthed near Dijon in the sixth century. Rebuilt four times since the sixth century, the abbey houses a unique circular crypt dating from 1007. Across from the Cathédrale St- Bénigne, the **Musée Archéologique,** 5, rue Docteur Maret (tel. 80 30 88 54), depicts the mysterious past of the Côte d'Or. (Open June-Sept. Wed.-Sun.'9:30am-6pm; Oct.-May Wed.-Sun. 9am-noon and 2-6pm. Admission 9F, students free.) Across from the pl. de la Libération, the recently renovated **Musée Magnin,** 4, rue des Bons Enfants (tel. 90 62 11 10), houses a decadent display of 17th-century living, loving, and gorging. Though paintings by Poussin, David, and many others hang on the walls, the museum is most interesting for the elegance of its period furnishings. Look for the wood-paneled passageway on the second floor. (Open Wed.-Mon. 9am-noon and 2-6pm. Admission 12F.)

The tombs of Philippe le Hardi and kin, now in the Musée des Beaux Arts, once stood in Claus Sluter's **Chartreuse de Champmol** on the western edge of town. Partially destroyed in 1793, the sculpture group includes the **Puits de Moïse** (Well of Moses) and three portals depicting the prophets. To reach the Chartreuse (now on the grounds of a psychiatric hospital) from pl. Darcy, follow bd. de Sevigne, go under the train overpass, and continue on av. Albert 1er. The entrance is on bd. Chanoine Kir. (Open to the public 9am-6pm.)

The refreshingly non-Gothic and un-Romanesque **Galerie 6,** 6, rue Auguste-Comte (tel. 80 71 68 46), displays an interesting, varied collection of pieces from the 17th century through the 1930s. (Open Tues.-Sat. 9:30am-noon, 2:30-7pm.) No culinary pilgrimage is complete without a stop at the **Grey Poupon** store, 32, rue de la Liberté. This establishment has been making *moutarde au vin* since 1777 and displays an exhibit of exciting antique jars. Buy your decorated mustard pots here, not from those pandering in whispers down the road.

Entertainment

Throughout June, Dijon's **Eté Musical** lures many of the world's best symphony orchestras and chamber groups. From mid-June to mid-August, **Estivade** brings dance, music, and theater to the streets. Dijon devotes a week in the first half of September to the **Fête de la Vigne,** a now-famous celebration of the grape that first took place in 1946, just after the devastation of WWII. Call the tourist office ahead for tickets—they go fast.

The best source (besides *Divio 90*) of information on films, festivals, and Dijon's numerous amateur and professional theater productions is *Dijon Nuit et Jour,* available free from the tourist office and et *tabacs.* Opera, classical music concerts, and operettas are performed in season (mid-Oct. to late April) at the **Théâtre de Dijon,** pl. du Théâtre (tel. 80 32 78 00), a beautiful 18th-century opera house. (Tickets 150F, students 75F.) Investigate the shows at **Nouveau Théâtre de Bourgogne,** located at Théâtre du Parvis St-Jean, pl. Bossuet. The box office of this church-turned-theater opens at 5pm. Since 1989, a comedy group from Aix-en-Provence has entertained young and old *dijonais* at **Le Bistrot de la Scène,** 203, rue d'Anxonne (tel. 80 67 87 39). Meals, drinking, and lighthearted *bavardage* with the actors is included with each hysterical performance. (Thurs., Fri., and Sat. at 8pm.)

Le Carillon, 2, rue Musette (tel. 80 30 63 71), and **La Cathédrale,** 4, pl. St-Bénigne (tel. 80 30 42 10), are two popular student bars. **Le Messire Bar,** 3, rue Jules Mercier (tel. 80 30 16 40), in a dark nightclub with flashing lights and a chatty clientele. (Cover 30F. Open until 2am.) On the quieter side, **Le Bistrot** rue d'Ahuy, serves a wide selection of beers until 2am. Warm up with the friendly clientele and hostess Barbara at **L'Iceberg,** 47, rue De Vosges (tel. 80 72 41 41). Cocktails cost 30-60F. (Open Mon.-Sat. 4pm-2am; hot drinks only until 8:30pm.) For a complete list of bars, nightclubs, and restaurants, as well as shops and services of interest to young people, get a free copy of *Divio '90* from the tourist office.

Cluny

The **Abbaye** at Cluny was founded in 910 as part of an effort to purify monasticism. To halt creeping secularization, the Cluniacs demanded that the abbot have supreme control over the abbey and be responsible only to the Pope. For hundreds of years afterward, Cluny was the pillar of Christian power and the center of a vast ecclesiastical empire that reached from Poland to Portugal. Until the construction of St. Peter's in Rome, the abbey's church was the largest in all of Christendom. With power and opulence, however, came a relaxation of discipline. When the abbey fell under control of the French state, and one of the heirs to the Bourbon throne had a special chimney added to the church so that he wouldn't be chilly at mass, it was clear that Cluny's influence had waned. The anti-clerical fervor of the French Revolution touched off 25 years of uninterrupted destruction of the abbey. The French government continued to sanction the pillage of Cluny and eventually sold it to enterprising masons who dismembered the buildings and sold the stones. Although only a few structures remain, this deservedly popular town makes an easy daytrip from Mâcon or Chalon-sur-Saône or a longer daytrip from Lyon.

Orientation and Practical Information

Cluny sits in the Grosne River valley, about 20km west of the main Dijon-Lyon train line. From Chalon-sur-Saône or Mâcon, a SNCF bus (free with railpass) meanders through the beautiful farms and forests of the Beaujolais countryside. The bus stops at rue Porte de Paris. From there, turn left onto rue Filaterie, which becomes rue Lamartine then rue Mercière; this main road leads to the tourist office.

Tourist Office: 6, rue Mercière (tel. 85 59 05 34). Helpful staff in a well-stocked office. Free maps. Some English spoken. **Currency exchange** when banks are closed. Will call hotels or map out bicycle trips and other excursions. Walking tours of the town (July to mid-Sept. daily or depending on demand at 3:30pm, 11F). Open daily 9:30am-6:15pm; March-June 15 and Sept. 15-Oct. Mon.-Sat. 9:30am-12:15pm and 2:15-6:15pm; Nov.-Feb. Tues.-Sat. 2:30-5:30pm.

Post Office: On route D-980, adjacent to the Cluny Séjour and bus stop. Open Mon.-Fri. 8am-noon and 2-7pm, Sat. 8am-noon. **Postal Code:** 71250.

Buses: Information is available in Cluny at the station (tel. 85 59 07 72) on route 980, at the end of rue de la Digue and across the river. Also at **SNCF**, tel. 85 38 50 50 in Mâcon, 85 93 50 50 in Chalon-sur-Saône. All schedules are posted at the tourist office or at the more central stop outside Cluny Séjour, on rue Porte de Paris. To: Taizé (8 per day, 10 min., 10F); Cormatin (6 per day, 20 min., 15F); Mâcon (8 per day, ½-hr., 20F); Chalon-sur-Saône (6 per day, 1½ hr., 37F).

Bike Rental: Hôtel Moderne, Pont de l'Etang (tel. 85 59 05 65). 10F per hr., 30F per ½-day, 50F per day. Picnic basket 60F. Open 24 hrs. Also at the Cluny **bus station.** 50F per day, 30F per half-day.

Medical Emergency: SMUR, tel. 85 34 33 00.

Police: route de Mâcon (tel. 85 59 06 32). **Emergency,** tel. 17.

Accommodations and Camping

Cluny has few hotels and even fewer budget hotels. Reservations several days in advance are absolutely necessary in summer, particularly on weekends. The large hostel-like installation is better than most hostels but also requires reservations.

Cluny Séjour (tel. 85 59 08 83), on rue Porte de Paris behind the bus stop, a 3-min. walk from the abbey. Sparkling clean modern hostel in a renovated 18th-century building. Reception open 7-11am and 5:30-10pm. Strict curfew 10pm in the dorm; no curfew in individual rooms. Beautiful wooden bunkbeds in co-ed dorm 41F (sleeping bag or sheet sack required). Singles 100F. Doubles 120F. Triples 150F. Breakfast, hot showers, and bantering included.

Hôtel du Commerce, 8, pl. du Commerce (tel. 85 59 03 09). Comfortable place in the center of town. The largest, cleanest singles and doubles you'll find for 100-145F, with shower 135F. Hall showers 15F. Breakfast 22-25F. Make reservations. Closed Sun. Nov.-April.

Hôtel de l'Abbaye (tel. 85 59 11 14), on av. de la Gare, 5 min. from the center of town. Follow rue Lamartine/rue Filaterie down to pl. du Commerce, and bear right onto av. de la Gare. Elegant and popular. Singles and doubles 90-115F, with shower 145F. The restaurant downstairs has 70F and 95F *menus.* Be sure to reserve. Open March-Nov. Closed Sun. evenings March-May and Sept.-Nov.

Camping: Camping Municipal St-Vital (tel. 85 59 08 34), rue des Griottins. Follow rue Filaterie to rue de la Levée across the river, and turn right. 3-star site next to a swimming pool. Often full July-Aug.; usually space if you arrive in early afternoon. Office sells ice cream. Adults 8F, children 4F. 5F per tent or car. Office open June-Sept. 8am-10pm.

Food

Cafés and *salons de thé* outnumber restaurants in Cluny, which may be just as well for budget eaters. **Maximarché** is a large supermarket on av. de la Gare, past the Auberge du Cheval Blanc. (Open Tues.-Sat. 8:45am-12:15pm and 2:30-7:15pm, Sun. 9am-noon.) You can't miss the small **Casino** at 29, rue Lamartine in the center of town. (Open Mon.-Sat. 7am-noon and 3-7pm, Sun. 8-11am.) For coffee and dessert, try either of the two *salons de thé* on rue Lamartine, **Pâtisserie au Succès** and **Le Péché Mignon,** or the **Café de la Nation,** just off rue Lamartine.

Restaurant de la Renaissance, 47, rue Mercière, on the continuation of rue Lamartine. Serves large portions of regional fare to hungry working people. The back room is elegant but a bit stuffy. *Plats du jour* from 35F. 50F *menu.* Open Oct.-Aug. daily 7:30am-8:30pm.

Les Marronniers, 20, av. de la Gare. A casual bar and restaurant on the edge of the *centre ville.* Popular with locals. Tiny, shaded outdoor terrace perfect for devouring the 10-20F desserts. Large 57F *menu.* Open Tues.-Sat. noon-2pm and 7-8:30pm, Sun. noon-2pm.

La Petite Auberge, 18, pl. du Commerce. Salads 10-19F, good pizza 26-35F. *Côte de veau grillé* 43F. The staff hustles around to jazz tapes. Open Thurs.-Tues. noon-1:15pm and 7:15-9:30pm.

Auberge du Cheval Blanc, 1, rue Porte de Mâcon. A cozy, white stone building just outside the *centre ville.* Expensive but sumptuous 70F and 100F *menus* include Bourguignon specialties. Open Sun.-Fri. noon-1:30pm and 6-9pm.

Sights

The only remains of the once-proud abbey are the south transept of the church, a handful of storage buildings, and a collection of finely-carved capitals. A truly stellar explanation (in French) is given by Georges Levy, abbey connoisseur and one of the finest tour guides in France. Georges usually leads the first group of the afternoon at 2:15pm. (Tours 23F, ages 18-24 12F, children 5F. Open daily 9am-6pm, tours every ½-hr.; April-June and Oct. 9:30am-noon and 2-6pm, tours every ½-hr.; Nov.-March 10am-noon and 2-4pm, tours every hr.)

To grasp the extent of the abbey's former grandeur and influence, go to the 15th-century Palais Jean de Bourbon and peruse the well-documented artifacts at the **Musée Ochier.** (Open daily June 15-Sept. 15 9:30am-noon and 2-6:30pm; Jan. 15-June 15 and Sept. 15-Dec. 20 10am-noon and 2-6pm. Admission 5F.) You can get a magnificent overview of the abbey and the valley by climbing the **Tour des Fromages;** enter through the tourist office. (Same hours as tourist office. Admission 5F, students 3F.) The humble 12th-century **Eglise St-Marcel,** topped by a 16th-century steeple houses a mildly distracting, free exhibit on the not-so-free life of a Benedictine monk.

Don't leave Cluny without pausing to ponder the mystery of **Le Cellier de l'Abbaye** on rue Lamartine, which now houses a wine shop. The top floor dates from the 12th century, the middle from the 14th, and the bottom from the 16th. Even our good friend Georges doesn't know how the Cluniacs pulled that off.

Near Cluny

South of Cluny, the magnificently situated castle **Berzé-le-Châtel** overlooks the abrupt slopes and crags of the Bois Clair Pass. (Terrace open April-Oct. daily 9am-noon and 2-6pm. Free.) A few kilometers down N79 is **Berzé-le-Ville** (tel. 85 36 66 52) with its **Chapelle Monacale** and notable 12th-century frescoes. (Open Easter-Nov. Mon. and Wed.-Sat. 9:30am-noon and 2-6pm, Sun. 2-6pm. Admission 10F, students 5F.) Twelve km south of Cluny on D22, the **Château St-Point,** former home of the poet Lamartine, contains a small museum. Nearby **Lac St-Point-Lamartine** has sailboat rentals and camping. There is no public transport to any of the above, so you'll have to improvise.

Four buses per day make the one-and-a-half-hour trip to **Basilique de Paray-le-Monial,** a well-proportioned if smaller replica of the abbey at Cluny. St-Margaret Mary Alacoque, then a humble nun, had her vision of the Sacred Heart of Jesus here in the 19th century. Today the site draws pilgrims from all over the world. (Open May-Sept. 9am-noon and 1-7pm; April and Oct. 1-7pm. Free.) The **Musée d'Art Sacré du Hiéron** (tel. 85 88 85 80) is devoted to religious sculpture and paintings; the tympanum which decorated the arch above the door at Anzy-le-Duc is considered a masterpiece of Burgundian Romanesque sculpture. (Open May-Sept. daily 9am-noon and 1:30-6:30pm. Admission 10F.)

The road between Cluny and Tournus passes village after enchanted village, each with its own beautiful Romanesque church. The Chalon-Mâcon bus route stops at the religious community of Taizé, 10 minutes from Cluny. Brother Roger, its founder, settled here in the 1940s and sheltered political refugees in his home. Today, this small village with its modest 12th-century church has become a properly bustling religious center. Every summer several thousand young Christians congregate here for singing, serious religious discussion, and good clean fun. Phone ahead (tel. 85 50 14 14) if you intend to stay. Bring a sleeping bag for the tents or bunks; they charge about 25F or whatever you can pay. For more information write Taizé Communauté, 71250 Cluny.

Tournus

Situated midway between Chalon-sur-Saône and Mâcon on the Saône River, Tournus bridges the border of two distinct Burgundian regions. To the east lie the flat plains of Bresse, sliced by undulating rivers. To the west rise the hills of the *Maconnais* region, covered with vineyards and Romanesque churches. The central district of modern Tournus (pop. 7000) is itself a jumbled mélange. Friendly local bars and cafés filled with Tournus' farmers and metalworkers coexist with multiple souvenir shops on the main road—all in the solemn presence of the city's venerable religious buildings.

Orientation and Practical Information

This long and narrow town runs along the west bank of the Saône. The main drag, rue Docteur Privey (which becomes rue de la République, then rue Desiré Mathivet) saunters through pl. Lacretelle, pl. Carnot, and pl. de l'Hôtel de Ville, where the action, such as it is, can be found.

Tourist Office: (tel. 85 51 13 10), on pl. Carnot. From the station, walk right on av. Gambetta then left on rue Docteur Privey. Knowledgeable staff in a half-timbered building. Some English spoken. Excellent free city maps. Accommodations service. Brochures on châteaux and Romanesque churches (in English). Map of the small roads connecting the above (1F) especially useful for biking or hitching. **Currency exchange** Mon. in July-Aug. Open daily 9am-noon and 3-7pm; March-June and Sept.-Oct. daily 9am-noon and 2-6pm; Nov.-Feb. Tues.-Thurs. and Sat. 9am-noon.

Post Office: (tel. 85 51 15 16), rue du Puits des Sept Fontaines. Take the bridge under the train tracks at pl. de l'Arc and bear right, following the PTT signs. Open Mon.-Fri. 8am-noon and 2-6pm, Sat. 8am-noon. **Postal Code:** 71700.

Trains: (tel. 85 51 07 30), on av. Gambetta. Tournus is on the Paris-Lyon route. To: Paris (5 per day, 3½ hr.); Dijon (6 per day, 1½ hr., 61F); Chalon-sur-Saône (4 per day, 15 min., 20F); Mâcon (3 per day, 25 min., 27F); Lyon (6 per day, 1½ hr., 65F). Eight per day to Beaune (1 hr.), some requiring a transfer at Dijon.

Buses: Call the *gare routière* in Chalon-sur-Saône (tel. 85 48 79 04) or Mâcon (tel. 85 38 13 85) for information. Schedules posted at Café du Centre, 6, quai de Verdun (tel. 85 51 01 69). To: Chalon-sur-Saône (6 per day, 40 min., 20F); Mâcon (3 per day, 1½ hr., 24F); Lyon (1 per day, 3 hr.). Buses leave from quai de Verdun and from the train station.

Hitchhiking: If you chose to hitch north or south, take the RN6, which plows right through Tournus. Avoid lightly traveled D56 toward Cluny. It's easier to get rides for short distances.

Hospital: Hôpital de Belnay, route de St-Gengoux (tel. 85 51 02 22).

Ambulance: SARL, 5, av. du Clos Mouron (tel. 85 32 50 50).

Police: Gendarmerie, 9, av. de la Résistance (tel. 85 51 12 34). **Emergency,** tel. 17.

Accommodations, Camping, and Food

One reason to make Tournus a day trip from Chalon, Mâcon, or Dijon (20-40 min.) is the noticeable lack of cheap, comfortable hotels.

Hôtel-Gras: 2, rue Fénélon (tel. 85 51 07 25) to the right of the abbey. Simple rooms. Strong hall showers. Singles 85F. Doubles 110-180F. Triples 205F. Reception open Mon.-Sat. 7am-10pm.

Hôtel de la Madeleine, 15, rue Désiré-Mathivet (tel. 85 51 05 83). The bartender-manager maintains 4 neat rooms with a narrow passageway view onto the Saône. Singles and doubles 80F, with 2 beds 120F. No showers. Breakfast 17F.

Hôtel de l'Hôtel de Ville (tel. 85 51 07 33), on pl. de l'Hôtel de Ville. Family-run establishment with cozy rooms. Locals unwind in the bar downstairs. Singles and doubles 100-140F, with bath 160F. Extra bed 40F. Breakfast 22F.

Hôtel Aux Terrasses, 18, av. du 23 Janvier (tel. 85 51 01 74), on the continuation of the main street. Classy 2-star establishment. Singles 108F. Doubles 125F, with shower 135F. Triples and quads 175F, with shower 200F. Breakfast 24F. Often booked; call ahead if you plan to arrive on Sun.

Camping: Le Pas Fleury, tel. 85 51 16 58. Follow av. Général-Leclerc or av. du 23 Janvier out of town to N6 (*direction* "Lyon"), and turn left. One-star site at the river's edge, beyond Dennis Hopper and behind the track field. Pool and tennis courts nearby. English spoken. 5F per person, 4F per tent, 3F per car. Hot showers 4F. Open April-Sept. Crowded July-Aug. but usually has room for a tent. No reservations.

Tournus is probably the best place to try *quenelles au brochet,* dumplings made with *pâte à choux* and fish and drenched in a creamy sauce. Most hotel restaurants serve meals for about 60F. The outdoor **market** (Sat. mornings on rue de la République) stretches from one end of town to the other and sells just about everything. **Confiserie Fagot,** 42, rue de la République, confects *pain d'épices,* a dry, spicy cake common in the region. (Open Tues.-Sat. 9am-noon and 2:15-7pm.) Staples crouch, ready to spring into your arms from the shelves of **Supermarché Champion,** av. de la Resistance, off av. Gambetta. (Open Mon.-Thurs. 8:30am-12:30pm and 2:30-7pm, Fri. 8:30am-12:30pm and 2:30-7:30pm, Sat. 8:30am-7pm, Sun. 8:30am-noon.) **Au Bon Accueil,** 31, rue Chanay, a local favorite, cooks excellent *menus* from 57F. To get there, walk under the tracks on the continuation of rue Dorey. (Open Sun.-Fri. noon-2pm and 7-9pm.) **Le Voleur de Temps,** 32, rue Docteur Privey (tel. 85 40 71 93), features an uncontrived country atmosphere and an ambitious young chef. (Vegetarian *menu* 50F, flesh eaters' *menu* 61F. Open Thurs.-Mon.) Get your *quenelles au brochet* in the 70F *menu* at the elegant but touristy **Restaurant l'Abbaye,** 12, rue Lion-Godin. (Open daily noon-2pm and 7-10pm.)

Sights

Exposed red brick and unadorned columns lend **Abbatiale St-Philibert** a powerful simplicity. The gloomy **Chapelle Supérieure St-Michel,** above the narthex, accommodated both prisoners and pilgrims between the 10th and 17th centuries. The unique ribbing of the nave's barrel vaults embellishes the otherwise unremarkable interior of the abbey. The graceful cloisters and a series of small exhibits of the abbey's façade outside the church are, however, worth an extended visit. On the other side of the cloister, behind the abbey on rue A. Thibaudet, is the excellent **Musée Bourguignon,** rue Perrin de Puycousin. The somewhat dilapidated exterior conceals 18th-century Burgundian rooms filled with period costumes, utensils, textiles, and ironwork. (Open April-Oct. Wed.-Mon. 9am-noon and 2-6pm. Admission 6F, students 4F.) **Musée Greuze,** rue de Collège by pl. de Lacretelle, maintains a large collection of works by Greuze, a popular, sentimental 18th-century artist born in Tournus. (Open April-Nov. Tues.-Sat. 9:30am-noon and 2-6:30pm, Sun. 2-6:30pm. Admission 6F, students 4F.) In the old town, somber façades give way to ornate Renaissance courtyards, the most interesting of which are at #13, 21 and 63, rue de la République.

Charlieu

In the 9th century, Benedictine monks fleeing invading Normans established a new monastery at Charlieu. They called their settlement *carus locus* in Latin, *cher lieu* (dear place) in French. Over the next 200 years, Charlieu grew into an important commercial and military hub under the sway of nearby Cluny. In the 13th century, Charlieu was a teeming city of 5000 outnumbered only by Lyon. Charlieu fell into decline after the 15th century, when major byways were re-routed through Beaune, but was revived somewhat when Lyon's silk industry spread here at the beginning of the 19th century.

Orientation and Practical Information

Charlieu is located about 70km west of Vichy and about 90km northwest of Lyon. Getting there will make your day—your *whole* day. The nearest train station is in Roanne, 20km south of Charlieu, on the main rail line west of Lyon. Trains run every hour to Lyon (1¼ hr., 60F) and St-Germain-de-Fossé (40 min., 45F) with transfers to all points west. (Call 77 37 50 50 for SNCF information.) **Cars Michel** runs buses from Roanne to Charlieu. One bus leaves around 9am, another about 5pm (40 min., 12.80F). The bus station has a list of all the different companies' schedules; read the fine print. (Call 77 71 24 03 for bus info.) Many people hitch easily from Roanne to Pouilly-sous-Charlieu, which is only 4km from Charlieu along D487.

Charlieu's squarish *centre ville* is bordered by a busy street that changes names seven times. The buses stop (usually, but not always) at pl. St-Philbert, where the **tourist office** (tel. 77 60 12 42 or 77 60 23 55) distributes a free map and a pamphlet describing the circuit of churches in the region. (Open March-Dec. Tues.-Sat. 10am-noon and 3-6pm.) The **post office,** 2, bd. Jacquard (tel. 77 69 06 53), is at the other end of rue Charles de Gaulle from the tourist office. (Open Mon.-Fri. 8am-noon and 2-6pm, Sat. 8am-noon.) The **postal code** is 42190. Rent **bikes** at B. Auroy, 6, rue André Farinet (tel. 77 60 25 20), off rue Charles de Gaulle. (25F per ½-day, 50F per day. Open Tues.-Sat. 8am-1pm and 2-8pm.)

Accommodations, Camping, and Food

There are few hotels in Charlieu; fortunately, demand is low. The **Hôtel Lion d'Or** (tel. 77 60 29 36), on pl. de la Porcherie down the street from the post office, has large rooms and luxurious bathrooms. (Singles and doubles 100-120F. Hall shower included. Extra bed 18F.) The **Hôtel du Champ de Foire,** pl. de la Bouverie (tel. 77 60 04 46), has large singles and doubles for 90F (showers 8F). The cozy restaurant downstairs serves a 55F *menu*. Rue Riottier takes you from the post office to the riverside **Camping Municipal** (tel. 77 69 01 70), with tennis courts and a swimming pool next door. (8.75F per person, 5.15F per tent. Hot showers included. English spoken. Swimming 9.30F per person. Office open April-Sept. daily 8am-10pm.) **Pizzeria l'Etna,** 31, rue Jean Morec, 1 block up from pl. St-Philibert, serves pizzas from 22F. (Open Tues.-Sat. noon-2pm and 7-10pm, Sun. 7-10pm.) **Le Sornin** at 6, pl. de la Bouverie, will feed you handsomely for 50-70F. (Open Tues.-Sun.) Fill your picnic basket at the **market** on Wednesday and Saturday morning in pl. St-Philibert before heading to the banks of the Sornin.

Sights

Three successive churches were built on the site of **Abbaye Benedictine,** the last of which was destroyed during the Revolution and subsequently auctioned off piece by piece. An informative 45-minute tour (text in English) takes you to a room above the Chapelle du Prieur, from which you can see traces of the foundations superimposed on one another. The southern portal is adorned with a typical tympanum sculpture of Christ wreathed in a mandorla (almond-shaped aureole), gracefully balanced by two angels and fantastic animals symbolizing the four evangelists. All the figures were guillotined by over-zealous revolutionaries.

To the left as you leave the abbey lies the Franciscan **Couvent des Cordeliers** named for the cords used to tie the monks' robes. Happily, the arched *cloître* was saved from adorning a Californian millionaire's tennis court when outraged locals had the French government declare it a national monument. Guides take small groups around pillar by pillar, explaining the animal and human iconography on each. (Convent tours every ½-hour, abbey tours every 45 min. Admission 10F, students 7F; to both 15F, students 12F, including a temporary exhibition near the abbey. Abbey and convent open June 15-Sept. 15 daily 9am-noon and 2-7pm; April-June 15 and Sept. 15-Sept. 30 Wed.-Mon. 9am-noon and 2-7pm; Oct.-Nov. and Feb.-March Thurs.-Mon. 9am-noon and 2-7pm.)

The **Circuit des Eglises Romanes** makes a good bike or car daytrip and is a great way to see the countryside. Ask at the tourist office for a map and description of the churches, the most important of which are Châteauneuf, Bois Ste-Marie, Paray-le-Monial, Anzy-le-Duc, Semur-en-Bois, and Iguerande.

Autun

In 10 BC, Emperor Augustus founded the city of Augustundum in the lush green valley that now cradles modern Autun. The prosperity of this trade center did not survive the decline of the Roman Empire. Thought to have been the home of Queen Brunhild and her Niebelung kin, whose intercinine struggles fill the medieval German epic *Niebelungenlied,* this beleaguered city eventually splintered into separate religious and economic settlements. In 1120, the ground-breaking for the cathedral and the arrival of the relics of St-Lazare drew pilgrims who ultimately brought in enough wealth to invigorate and reunite the two halves. Oblivious to the surrounding industrial zones, a fine theater, temple, and other remains of the largest Roman city in Gaul brighten this otherwise grey town of 16,000.

Orientation and Practical Information

The main street, **avenue Charles de Gaulle,** connects the train station to the central pl. du Champ de Mars. Rue St-Saulge and rue aux Cordiers both run from pl. du Champ de Mars into rue Chauchien, which changes name twice before reaching the cathedral in the heart of the old city.

Tourist Office: 3, av. Charles de Gaulle (tel. 85 52 20 34 or 85 86 30 00), off pl. du Champ de Mars. Helpful English-speaking staff. Map, brochure, and list of hotels and restaurants.

Currency exchange when banks are closed. Accommodations service 1F. In summer, daily guided tours at 10am and 3pm (16F, students 12F). Open Mon.-Sat. 9am-noon and 2-7pm, Sun. 10am-noon and 3-6pm; Oct.-April Mon.-Fri. 9am-noon and 2-6pm, Sat. 2-6pm.

Post Office: rue Pernette (tel. 85 52 05 85), up rue de la Grille from the train station. **Telephones.** Open Mon.-Fri. 8:30am-7pm, Sat. 8:30am-noon. **Postal code: 71400.**

Trains: pl. de la Gare (tel. 85 52 28 01), on av. de la République. TGV trains from Paris and Lyon stop at Le Creusot, whence Autun-bound buses depart daily (Mon.-Fri. 6 per day, Sat. 3, Sun. 1; 50 min.; 32F). A special SCNF bus runs from Chalon-sur-Saône, along the Dijon-Paris line (3 per day, 1 hr. 20 min.). If you really, *really* want to make the entire trip by train, you'll have to change 2-4 times in tiny towns with monstrous names (2½ hrs., 60F). The train station in Mâcon has a schedule explaining how to get to Autun; it looks like a final exam in Gaussian surfaces.

Buses: 13, av. de la République (tel. 85 52 30 02). The office is up the street to the left of the station, but buses leave from the station. To Dijon daily at 5:10pm (2 hr. 20 min., 55F).

Medical Emergency: Clinique du Parc, tel. 85 52 18 34.

Police: rue de la Jambe-de-Bois (tel. 85 52 18 01). Also 26 bis av. Charles de Gaulle. **Emergency,** tel. 17.

Accommodations and Camping

The cheapest lodgings are near the train station. Make reservations one week in advance during July and August.

Hôtel de France (tel. 85 52 14 00), on pl. de la Gare. Magnificent stairways bedizened with interesting photographs. Cheery, wallpapered rooms. Open Mon.-Sat. and Sun. after 5:30pm. Singles from 78F. Doubles from 84F, with shower 105F. Breakfast 20F.

Hôtel le Grand Café, 19, rue de Lattre de Tassigny (tel. 85 52 27 66), on pl. du Champ de Mars. One of the livelier spots in Autun. Central location. Quite luxurious rooms with showers. Singles and doubles from 120F. Breakfast 15F.

Tête Noire, 1-3 rue Arabesque (tel. 85 52 25 39), 1 block from pl. du Champs de Mars. Decent singles and doubles 95-110F. Extra bed 30% of original price. *Demi-pension* 172F.

Camping: Camping Municipal de la Porte d'Arroux (tel. 85 52 10 82), 1½km from town, past the bridge. A 3-star campground with swimming, fishing, and other water sports. Restaurant and grocery store nearby. 9F per person, 7F per tent. Open Easter-Nov.

Food

A **market** fills pl. du Champ de Mars Wednesday and Friday morning.

Restaurant Lardreau, 58, av. Charles de Gaulle. A small, cozy place with schizophrenic decor. 62F and 73F *menus. Fondue de volaille au porto* (chicken fondue with port) 51F. Open Jan.-Nov. daily noon-2pm and 7-9pm.

Auberge de la Bourgogne, 39, pl. du Champ de Mars. A family restaurant with adjoining bar. Frog legs *provençale* 53F. 55F and 90F *menus.* Open Tues.-Sat. noon-2pm and 7-9pm, Sun. noon-2pm.

Tête Noire, beneath the hotel. 70F "tourist" *menu* includes a horseburger. Those who have just decided they don't eat red meat will enjoy the excellent *menu pêcheur* (82F). Open April-Feb. Sun.-Fri.

Chalet Bleu, 3, rue Jeannin (tel. 85 86 21 30), near pl. du Champ de Mars. An ultra-spiffy place run by an award-winning chef. 75F, 120F, and 180F *menus.* Open July-May Wed.-Mon.

Sights and Entertainment

In its heyday, Autun was the largest city in Roman Gaul, and with a population of about 70,000, it was more than three times its present size. Furthermore, it was the only city to boast a circus, theater, and amphitheater. Today most of this splendor has faded into industrial sprawl. Standing 200m away is the huge brick **Temple de Janus.** Evidence suggests that it was actually dedicated to Demeter and built away from the city so that the decadence and sexual frivolity of the goddess's followers wouldn't shock the townspeople. Others believe it was a temple to the Gaulish god Esus (the equivalent of the Roman Mars). In any case, the ruin is a rare example of a temple built in Gaulish form using Roman construction techniques. A pleasant footpath off rue Faubourg d'Arroux passes the crumbling temple and returns to town via rue Faubourg St-Andoche. Two of the city's four Roman gates still stand: **Porte d'Arroux** on rue de Paris and **Porte de St-André** on rue Faubourg St-André. The **Théâtre Antique,** once capable of seating 30,000 enthralled spectators, now entertains picknickers. From here you can see the weird, conical **Pierre de Couhard,** 1km away on the hillside. No one knew what it was until excavations unearthed a plaque cursing anyone who dared disturb the eternal slumber of the man buried inside.

The intricately carved capitals in the outstanding **Cathédrale St-Lazare** recall those at the basilica in Vézelay, also constructed between 1120 and 1140. The magnificent tympanum of the Last Judgment over the central portal, a phantasmagoric vision in fresco, is the work of Autun native Gislebertus. Lightning destroyed the original lead-covered **beffroi** in 1469; the current stone one was built at the end of the 15th century. To combine aural and visual experience, make your ascent (3F) as the bells ring the hour. At 10pm on most summer nights, the cathedral and the Théâtre Antique host a majestic sound and light performance in French, "Autun aux Cent Visages" ("The Hundred Faces of Autun"). Large crowds flock to watch locals reenact their past lives. (Tickets from tourist office, 30F.)

On the same square as the cathedral, the **Musée Rolin** occupies a 15th-century hotel which belonged to Chancellor Nicolas Rolin. Even if you don't have time to inspect the well-orchestrated Gallo-Roman exhibit, examine the three delicate statues from the tomb of St-Lazare and Gislebertus's *Eve,* which poignantly captures the moment of the Fall. (Open daily 9:30am-noon and 2-6:30pm; Oct.-Nov. 15 10am-noon and 2-5pm; Nov. 16-March 15 10am-noon and 2-4pm. Admission 7F, students 3.50F.) Larger, less interesting Gallo-Roman architectural fragments occupy the **Musée Lapidaire,** 10, rue St-Nicolas. (Open daily 10am-noon and 2-6pm; Oct.-April 15 10am-noon and 2-4pm. Free.)

Every year in July, the festival **Musique en Morvan** brings an international sampling of young people's choirs to Autun. Throughout the summer, concerts take place at the Château of Arnay-le-Duc and at the Eglise Saulieu, two nearby sites accessible by car. Tickets are available from the tourist office.

Near Autun

Autun lies at the southeastern corner of the **Parc Naturel du Morvan,** a largely untamed forest that contains some sporting and camping facilities. Twenty-four km south of Autun, **Mont Beuvray** and **St-Léger-sous-Beuvray** are graced with magnificent scenery and the remains of a Roman military outpost. Public transport can't get you there, but many people hitch. Twenty-five km along D978, the unremarkable **Château de Couches** has little more than a manicured courtyard to show for itself. (50-min. tour July-Aug. daily 3-6pm. Admission 13F, students 6F.) Fifteen km northwest of Autun along the D326, **Château de Sully** was aptly dubbed the "Fontainebleau of Burgundy" by Paris socialite Mme de Sévigné. Birthplace of Marshall MacMahon, the Duke of Magenta and 19th-century president of France, this 16th-century palace now provides ample shelter to the current Duke. (No entry to interior. Gardens open Easter-Sept. 8am-6pm. Admission 5F.) At the center of the park and 40km from Autun, **Lac des Setton,** the largest of the Morvan lakes, entices visitors with almost every type of water sport possible, extensive camping, and adequate winter skiing. Nearby **Montsauche** has a modest tourist office (tel. 86 84 51 05) which sells a leaflet detailing six bicycle tours throughout the Morvan (10F). The cheapest bike rental is available at the station (50F per day, deposit 250F and ID).

Beaune

Of all the towns and vineyards which cultivate, hand-pick, and then crush the *pinot noir* grapes, only Beaune correctly claims to be the capital of Burgundy wine. The famous *Côtes de Beaune* vineyards encroach upon the town itself, where the finished product is sold on every street and stored beneath the 18th-century buildings in an extensive maze of *caves*. Beaune makes an excellent daytrip from Dijon, a mere 20 minutes away.

Orientation and Practical Information

The center of town is laid out roughly like a grid inside a large circle, with rue Carnot leading directly south from Dijon to the Hôtel Dieu on pl. Carnot. From the train station, follow av. du 8 Septembre, which becomes rue du Château. Turn left onto Rempart St-Jean, and cross rue d'Alsace onto Rempart Madeleine. Turn right onto rue de l'Hôtel-Dieu, which leads to the impressive **Hôtel de Dieu** and the tourist office.

Tourist Office: rue de l'Hôtel-Dieu (tel. 80 22 24 51). Well-equipped. Free maps. English spoken well. **Currency exchange** when banks are closed. Free accommodations service. Lists of *caves* in the region that offer tours. Free guided tours of the town (in French) July-Aug. daily at 3pm. Open daily 9am-midnight; March-May and Oct.-Nov. 9am-10pm; Dec.-Feb. 9am-7:15pm.

Post Office: rue de la Poste (tel. 80 22 22 32). **Telephones** and **currency exchange.** 1% commission. Open Mon.-Fri. 8am-7pm, Sat. 8am-noon. **Postal Code:** 21200.

Trains: av. du 8 Septembre (tel. 80 44 50 50). Beaune is on the Dijon-Lyon train line. To: Lyon (6 per day, 2½ hr., 93F); Dijon (12 per day, ½-hr., 32F); Nevers (4 per day, 2½ hr., 95F). The TGV to Paris stops in Beaune twice per day (2 hr., 173F plus 15F reservation fee).

Buses: Transco, tel. 80 71 40 34. Buses depart from rue Maufoux at bd. Bretonnière, opposite the Hôtel des Postes. To: Chalon-sur-Saône (2 per day, 45 min., 25F); Autun (1 per day, 1½ hr., 34F); Dijon (8 per day, 1 hr., 30F). Stops at all the important wine centers along the Côte d'Or. A schedule is available at the tourist office.

Car Rental: Loc Car, 6, av. du 8 Septembre (tel. 80 24 17 17). Also rents trucks and mountain bikes; one of the better deals in town. Open Mon.-Sat. 8am-noon, 2-6pm.

Bike Rental: At the station (tel. 80 22 80 56). 39F per ½-day, 50F per day, deposit 300F.

Laundromat: Next to the supermarket, off pl. Madeleine. Wash 15F, dry 15F, soap 5F. Open daily 7am-8pm. Also on the way to the campground at 24, rue du Faubourg St-Nicolas. Slower machines. Open daily 8am-8:30pm.

Hospital: Centre Hospitalier, av. Guigone de Salins (tel. 80 24 75 75).

Medical Emergency: tel. 80 26 60 46. **Ambulance,** tel. 80 22 23 09.

Police: av. du Général de Gaulle (tel. 80 24 64 00). **Emergency,** tel. 17.

Accommodations, Camping, and Food

Beaune teems from April through November. It's wise to make reservations far in advance, as most hotels fill by afternoon. You can always base yourself in Dijon or at the youth hostel in Chalon-sur-Saône, each only a 20-minute train ride away.

Hôtel Rousseau, 11, pl. Madeleine (tel. 80 22 13 59), in the far left-hand corner. From the station, follow the Celer Lyonnais and then turn right on rue Faubourg Madeleine. Beautiful wooden beds in clean rooms off a secluded courtyard. Strict 1am curfew, but Beaune shouldn't keep you out late. Singles from 90F. Doubles from 130F. Breakfast included.

Hôtel le Foch, 24, bd. Foch (tel. 80 22 04 29). Take av. de la République from the tourist office and turn right. Musty but cheap. Singles and doubles from 75F.

Hôtel de France, 35, av. du 8 Septembre (tel. 80 22 19 99), facing the train station and all its noise. Refreshingly tasteful and comfortable. May have a room when others don't. Singles and doubles 120F, with shower 140F, with toilet 180F. Extra bed 50F.

Auberge de la Gare, 11, av. des Lyonnais (tel. 80 22 11 13), 3 blocks left of the train station. Decent, no-frills hotel with a cheap restaurant. Singles and doubles 84F.

Camping: Les Cent-Vignes, 10, rue Dubois (tel. 80 22 03 91), 500m from the town center off rue du Faubourg-St-Nicolas. Head north on rue Lorraine from pl. Monge. Often overrun by trailers. Always has some space in the morning and always full by mid-afternoon in summer. 10F per person, 8F per tent, 5F per car. Hot showers included. Reservations accepted by mail before May 30. Open March 15-Oct. **Camping Municipal de la Grappe d'Or** (tel. 80 21 22 48), 10km south in Meursault. A 3-star site with swimming pool. Open April-Oct. 15.

Beaune's restaurants are predictably expensive. You'll probably find yourself at the **Supermarché Casino,** through the arches at 28, rue du Faubourg Madeleine (open Mon.-Sat. 8:30am-7:30pm), food or the large **market** that takes place Saturday mornings at pl. Carnot. The **Brasserie de la Gare,** 33, rue du 8 Septembre, next to the **Hôtel de France,** serves a 51F meal with wine included. (Open daily 11am-2pm and 7-10pm.) Elegant and airy **Brelinette,** 6, rue du Faubourg Madeleine, serves delicious regional dishes and *menus* for 58F, 78F, and 98F. (Open daily noon-2pm and 7-10pm; Sept.-June Thurs.-Tues. noon-2pm and 7-10pm.) Across the street at #7, **La Gouzotte** serves 58F, 78F, and 84F *menus,* as well as a delicious *coq au vin rouge* (50F)—a Beaune specialty. (Open daily noon-2pm and 7-10pm.)

Sights and Entertainment

A trip to Beaune would be incomplete without a descent into one of the numerous *caves.* The tourist office has information on all those open to public *dégustation,* with hours and fees. If you intend to visit more than one *cave,* stock up on bread (it slows alcohol absorption) and don't sample too many wines too quickly.

Patriarche, the largest company, owns many of these operations. The **Marché aux Vins,** rue Nicolas-Rolin (tel. 80 22 27 69), housed in a 15th-century church near the Hôtel Dieu, is the most prestigious of the *caves.* For 40F, you are given a glass and let loose on 37 open bottles of Burgundy's finest. (Open daily 9:30am-noon and 2:30-6:30pm; Nov.-March daily 9:30am-noon and 2:30-4:30pm.) Don't drink your limit too quickly—the best wines (*les grands crus*) always come near the end.

The oldest *caves* are the **Halle aux Vins,** 28, rue Sylvestre Chauvelot (tel. 80 22 18 34), in the 9th-century crypt of the former Eglise St-Martin. The 30F *dégustation* includes a slide show. (Open daily 10am-noon and 2-7pm; Oct.-March Mon.-Sat. 10am-noon and 2-6pm.) **Maison Calvet,** 6, bd. Perpreuil (tel. 80 22 06 32), ends its tour of the three cobwebbed kilometers of *caves* with tastings and a slide show. (Open Tues.-Sun. 9-11:30am and 2-5pm.) The **Caves des Cordeliers** (tel. 80 22 14 25), next to the Hôtel Dieu, features an inferior tour but satisfactory sampling *du tonneau* (from the keg). (Open daily 8am-noon and 2:30-7pm.) The schmaltzy tour offered by **Maison Patriarche Père et Fils,** 7, rue du Collège (tel. 80 22 23 20), leads past millions of dusty, aging bottles heaped along 9km of tunnels. Fortunately, the tour omits most of the tunnels and culminates in an energetic, though short, tasting session of Burgundy's most extensive collection of labels. (Open March 5-Dec. 18 9-11:30am and 2-5:30pm. Admission 30F, proceeds go to charity.) When you emerge from subterranean Beaune, rest your liver in beautiful **Parc de la Bouzaise** beyond the city ramparts or **place des Lions** just within the ramparts.

Nicholas Rolin, Chancellor of Burgundy and a most effective tax collector, founded the splendid **Hôtel Dieu** as a charity hospital in 1433. The colorful courtyard roof tiles and Roger Van der Weyden's panelled mural *The Last Judgment* both demonstrate the political and cultural ties this region once maintained with Flanders. The informative tour explains the daily operation of the infirmary, chapel, kitchen, and pharmacy. (Open daily 9am-6:45pm; Sept. 8-June 27 9-11:40am and

2-6pm. Admission 20F, ages 6-14 8F. 1-hr. tours every 15 min. in French only. Free pamphlet in English.)

The **Musée du Vin** lures oenophiles inside the **Hôtel des Ducs de Bourgogne,** in the picturesque pedestrian zone, and then maroons them in front of incomprehensible exhibits on winemaking and tapestry-weaving. Bring your dictionary. (Open daily 9am-noon and 1:30-7pm; Oct.-March Wed.-Mon. 10am-noon and 2-5:30pm. Admission 9F, students 6F. Free tours July and Aug. every hr.) The ticket also admits you to the **Musée des Beaux Arts** and the **Musée Etienne-Jules Marey,** both on rue de l'Hôtel de Ville next to the police station. The former has a mediocre collection of Gallo-Roman funerary monuments and paintings by Félix Ziem, a local 19th-century artist. The latter, though, is exceptional, especially if you're interested in the history of photography. Marey, also a *Beaunois,* invented a camera that supposedly took 2000 pictures per second and is considered the inventor of motion photography (chronophotography). (Open June 16-Sept. 15 daily 9am-noon and 2-6:30pm; Easter-April and Sept. 16-Nov. Wed.-Mon. 10am-noon and 2-5:30pm; May-June 15 Wed.-Mon. 9am-noon and 2-6:30pm.)

In the center of town, the **Basilique Collégiale Notre-Dame** merits a visit for its venerated 12th-century carved wooden Virgin and 15th-century Flemish tapestries depicting the life of the Virgin Mary. This is yet another church modeled after the abbey at Cluny. (Open 8am-noon, 2-5pm.)

Near Beaune: Chalon-sur-Saône

During the Roman campaigns in Gaul, Julius Caesar coveted Chalon-sur-Saône for its strategic position on the navigable Saône river. Today, the city is a strategic place to change trains and bed down in Chalon's youth hostel. The **Musée Nicéphore-Nièpce,** 28, quai des Messageries, honors the 18th-century *Chalonnais* credited with the invention of photography in 1822. The fascinating museum, housed in a large 18th-century *hôtel* overlooking the river, contains an exceptional collection of cameras, from the first ever made to the one used on the Apollo mission. (Open Wed.-Mon. 9:30am-noon and 2-5:30pm. Admission 10F, students 5F.) **Musée Denon,** on pl. de l'Hôtel de Ville, showcases Bronze Age implements, and the outstanding 18,000-year-old *Silex de Volgu,* and other archaeological finds. The highlight of the 19th-century exhibition halls is Gericault's *Tête de Nègre.* (Open Wed.-Mon. 9:30am-noon and 2-5:30pm. Admission 10F, students 5F.) The handsome 12th-century **Cathédrale St-Vincent** has interesting capitals and a 15th-century cloister. For a lovely view, cross pont St-Laurent to the small island in the middle of the Saône and climb the **Tour du Doyenné,** near the ancient hospital. (Open April-Sept. Mon.-Fri. 2-4:30pm.) Every year, Chalon hosts one of the most exuberant pre-Lenten festivals in France.

Finding a room in Chalon is not difficult. The basic **Auberge de Jeunesse,** rue d'Amsterdam (tel. 85 46 62 77), has a spacious kitchen and dining area, a river view, and a swimming pool and sailing club next door. You may have to share the place with a healthy population of mosquitos. (39F per person. Sheets 13F. Office open Jan. 15-Dec. 15 daily 7-10am and 5:30-10:30pm.) If you miss bus #11 from the train station, walk down av. Jean Jaurès and continue under the highway and past the tourist office as it changes to bd. de la République. Turn left on rue du Général Leclerc at pl. de l'Obélisque, go to the river, turn left, and continue along the river to the hostel (25 min.). Though the town's cheapest, **Hôtel Gloriette,** 27, rue Gloriette (tel. 85 48 23 35), is no slouch. (Singles from 60F. Doubles 85-90F. Showers 12F. Breakfast 17F. Closed Sun. noon-8pm.) **Camping Municipal de la Butte** (tel. 85 48 26 86) is a three-star riverside site in nearby St-Marcel. (10F per person, 13F per site.) Follow the directions to the hostel but cross the bridge when you come to it, continue straight across two islands, and turn left along the river on rue Julien Lenevu. **Fleurs d'Asie,** 20, av. Jean Jaurès (tel. 85 48 68 34), posts simple Vietnamese *menus* for 40F and up. (Open Thurs.-Tues.) There is a **Supermarché Casino** on av. Nicéphore-Nièpce, just off av. Jean Jaurès, 2 blocks from the train station. (Open Mon.-Sat. 8:30am-8pm.)

The **tourist office** (tel. 85 48 37 97) is in pl. Chabas on bd. de la République. (Open Mon.-Sat. 9am-12:30pm and 1:30-7pm.) The **post office** is on pl. de l'Obélisque at bd. de la République. (Open Mon.-Fri. 8:30am-7pm, Sat. 8:30am-noon.) The **postal code** is 71100.

Côte d'Or: The Wine Route

Ever since the Roman invasion brought wine-making to Burgundy, the Côte d'Or has produced some of the world's most notable wines, the *grands crus.* Charlemagne kept his personal vineyard at Aloxe-Cortone, and Louis XIV happily quaffed his Nuits-St-Georges on doctor's orders.

One of the four modern *départements* that make up Burgundy, this thin 60km strip running from Dijon to Beaune is more correctly called the **Côte de Nuits,** the region where Musigny, Clos de Vougeot, and Chambertin wines are produced. Montrachet whites and Corton and Pommard reds come from the **Côte de Beaune,** in the south.

While many *caves* offer free *dégustations,* a few gulps of wine are hardly worth the long, costly bus rides between *caves.* And while the bigger growers expect many tasters and few buyers, the smaller growers hope that tasters are at least seriously considering buying. Buy something you like and have it at lunch when the *caves* (and buses) are taking a break. All tourist offices should stock an outstanding series of free brochures designed to help you relax in the countryside. Ask for *Châteaux en Côte d'Or* (detailed information on all sites, not just castles), *Circuits en Côte d'Or* (suggested routes for drivers), and *Route des Forges et des Mines* (discussion of Burgundy's historical steel industry), as well as booklets on hotels and camping. Many of these brochures are available in English. For those still intent on wine tasting, consult the Dijon tourist office's colorful map *Le Vignoble de Bourgogne* (10F) or the Beaune office's even more useful (and free) *Liste des Viticulteurs et Négotiants-Eleveurs de la Côte d'Or et de l'Yonne.*

By car, take D122, the **Route des Grands Crus,** through the rolling hills covered with vines and punctuated by wine châteaux. The *route de vin* bus schedule reads like a wine list, with stops at all the major vineyards. One of the best wineries to visit is at the 10th-century **Château de Gevre-Chambertin,** just south of Dijon (tel. 80 34 36 13), which combines a modicum of history with a visit to its extensive *caves.* (Open Fri.-Wed. 10am-noon and 2-6pm, Sun. 11:30am-noon and 2-6pm. 30-min. tour, 20F.)

In nearby **Reulle-Vergy,** the municipal **Musée des Arts et Traditions des Hautes Côtes** has semi-interesting displays on the region's geology, geography, flora, fauna, archaeology, viticulture, agriculture, and history. (Open July-Sept. daily 2-7pm. Admission 9F.) More worthy of attention are the ruins of 9th-century **Monastère de St-Vivant** and the 15th-century polychromed wood reliquaries in 12th-century **Eglise St-Saturnin.** The **Château de Rochepot,** remarkable for its seductive hilltop setting and interiors, and a nearby 12th-century Roman church lie about 10km southwest of Beaune, accessible only by car. The paper *Eté 1990,* free at most Burgundy tourist offices, has up-to-date listings of events, museums, monuments, and other points of interest on the Côte d'Or.

Semur-en-Auxois

In 606 the monks of the Abbaye de Flavigny signed their charter in a village they called *Sene muros,* the "old walls." This is the earliest written record of Semur-en-Auxois although legend attributes its founding to Hercules. The exact age of the city is unknown. Today this tiny, provincial town of cobblestones and archways perches above a bend in the sluggish Armançon River. Venture downhill from the tourist office to find a towering church and fortifications 10 sizes too big for the rest of Semur. The *vieille ville* is illuminated on Saturday, Sunday, and holiday nights in July and August (about 10pm-midnight). The best seats for this free *lumière sans son* are on the pont Joly, pont Pinard, and quai d'Armançon.

Admirably fulfilling the Gothic ideals of height and light, graceful **Eglise de Notre Dame** outshines Semur's four hardy defense towers. The hilltop fortress is best approached by walking down to pont Pinard and following the Armançon River around the village to **pont Joly.** From here you can see above the huge granite **Tour de l'Orle d'Or,** the dungeon of the dismantled château, which, in spite of 5m thick walls, is cracked base to summit. (Open July-Aug. daily 10am-noon and 2-6pm. Guided tour in French, 30 min., 8F.) Along rue Buffon lie the oldest houses and the largest number of shops. Semur's eclectic **Musée Municipal,** rue J. J. Colenot, contains important manuscripts as well as rooms devoted to painting, archaeology, and natural history. (Open daily. Admission 10F. Students 5F.) Every May 31, Semur hosts the **Fête de la Bague,** France's oldest horse race. Circuses, outdoor concers, expositions, gallery exhibits and general good cheer raise Semur's spirits the week before and after the races.

Semur is not far from a train stop between Paris and Dijon; get off at Les Laumes and step onto the Semur-bound bus (3 per day, 30 min., 13F). The same bus company, **Transco** (tel. 80 43 58 97), runs buses throughout the entire Côte d'Or, connecting Semur directly with Dijon (2 per day, Sun. 1; 1½ hr.; 40.44F); Avallon (same frequency, 1 hr., about 20F); Saulieu (same frequency, 50 min., 12F). Semur's tourist office, pl. Gustave Gaveau (tel. 80 97 05 96), at the head of rue de la Liberté, posts bus schedules and imparts maps and a list of hotels. (Open daily 8:45am-noon and 2-6:30pm; Sept.-June Mon. 2-6:30pm, Tues.-Fri. 8:45am-noon and 2-6:30pm, Sat. 8:45am-noon, Sun. 3-6pm.)

The **Foyer des Jeunes Travailleurs,** 1, rue du Champ de Foire (tel. 80 97 10 22), is one short minute from the center of town at the end of rue de la Liberté. If there's no room at this comfortable inn, there will be at the annex. Ring the doorbell to enter after 10pm; reception is open all day. (Singles 36F. Breakfast 7F. Self-service lunch 34F and dinner 32F. Meals are served Sept.-July Mon.-Sat. Sheets 10.20F.) There are a few budget hotels in town, but plush rooms and a fulsome manager recommends **Hotel-Bar du Commerce,** 19, rue de la Liberté (tel. 80 97 00 18), in the center of town up the street from the tourist office. (Singles with shower 120F. Doubles with shower 180F. Huge breakfast 20F.) A **campground** lies 3km south of Semur on scenic Lac du Pont. (Open May-Sept. 7F per night.)

The cheapest decent meal in town is at **Sagittaire,** 15, rue de la Liberté (tel. 80 97 23 91). (Lunch *menu.* Pizzas from 15F. Open Tues.-Sun. noon-2pm and 7:15-10pm; mid-Sept. to April Tues.-Sat. only.) The tiny Semur **market,** also on rue de la Liberté, commodifies local farm products on Thursday and Saturday mornings.

Near Semur

Semur lies at the center of the **Route des Ducs de Bourgogne,** a historic tour tracing the châteaux and religious monuments built during the reign of the Burgundian dukes. Most of the sights are accessible only by car. Any of Burgundy's tourist offices can provide ample information on this popular, scenic route; the most useful brochure is **La Route des Ducs de Bourgogne** (free). The 12th-century Romanesque **Abbaye de Fontenay,** 23 km north of Semur, is one of France's most skilfully preserved Cistercian abbeys. (Open daily 9am-1pm, 2-6pm; Sept.-June 9am-noon and 2-6pm. Admission 25F.)

Perched on a hill at the edge of the Morvan, **Saulieu** is known for its 12th-century **Basilique St-Andoche,** which lies off pl. Docteur Rochore. A free brochure (in French) describes the delicately carved capitals. (Open daily 8:30am-6pm.) Next door, **Musée François Pompon** features the works of this popular turn-of-the-century sculptor from Saulieu in a reconstruction of a traditional Morvan home. (Open daily 10am-noon and 2-7pm. Admission 7F, students 5F.) The **tourist office** (tel. 80 64 09 22) in a kiosk on rue Argentine distributes information on trails and *gîtes ruraux.* Map #306, put out by the *Institute Geographique National* (36F), is the best map of the area.

Several inexpensive hotel-restaurants are scattered along the main road in town, rue Grillot and rue Argentine (1 road, 2 names). **Au Petit Marguery** at 4, rue Argentine (tel. 80 64 13 58), has singles for 80F, doubles or more from 130F. Breakfast is 17F. (Closed Jan. and Sun. nights.) Across the street at 1, rue Grillot, the larger **Hôtel de la Poste** (tel. 80 64 05 67), has singles from 100F and doubles from 150F. **Camping le Perron,** 500m north of town (tel. 80 64 16 19), is a three-star site. (Open March-Nov.) Several stores along rue de la Foire and pl. des Terreaux push picnic provisions.

Buses run to and from Dijon (1-2 per day, 2½ hr., 63F) and Semur (1-2 per day, 35 min., 21.20F). **Trains** run from Autun (3 per day, 1 hr., 36F) and Auxerre (13 per day, 2 hr., 52F).

Vézelay

On most autumn mornings, the hamlet of Vézelay (pop. 600) peeks through a layer of mist which covers fertile checkerboarded of a valley. Although the town itself is attractive, the view *of* Vézelay can't compare to the views *from* Vézelay. Before his first election, François Mitterand spent a weekend here reflecting amidst the medieval buildings which still see pilgrims pass on their way to St-Jacques de Compostelle in Northern Spain. Most moden visitors, pilgrims and tourists alike, head straight for 12th-century **Basilique de la Madeleine** and its crypt, still believed by some to contain the remnants of Mary Magdalen. THe flock is at its thickest on July 22, the official day of homage to *la Madeleine.* Carved in 1125 and subsequently restored, the **tympanum** above the narthex's main portal portrays a risen Christ welcoming worshippers to the inner nave of the church. Concentric crescents, each with its own array of bizarre characters, surround Jesus' halo. The capitals in the nave depict a mix of prosaic, biblical, and supernatural scenes. Tours (usually in French) are given daily according to a schedule on the south door. (Church open daily 7am-7pm, Sept.-June sunrise-sunset. Basilica illuminated Tues. and Fri. 9:30-10:30pm.)

A **museum** above the chapter room contains sculpture removed from the church and gives you a good idea of what Viollet-le-Duc's 19th-century restoration of the building must have involved. The tortuous, narrow staircase of Tour St. Michel (west end, in narthex) provides a vertiginous view of the entire town and surrounding hills. (Open July-Aug. Mon.-Fri. 10am-noon and 2:30-5:30pm, Sun. 2:30-5:20pm. Admission 5F.) It was here that St. Francis of Assisi decided to establish his first French brotherhood. The first Franciscan abbey in France, destroyed during the Revolution, has been rebuilt in its original place alongside the church.

Vézelay lies in the northwest corner of the national **Parc du Morvan,** which is sliced by the Grande Randonnée 13 and circled by another. The tourist's *Itinéraire Pédestre* (5F)map out short walks around the sights. If you're planning to explore the area, the 60F or so you pay for either GR guide is well worth it for the listings of emergency telephone numbers and varied rural accommodations which appear every 25km or so.

Vézelay's **tourist office,** rue St-Pierre (tel. 86 33 23 69), will **exchange currency.** (Open April-Oct. Mon.-Tues. and Thurs.-Sat. 10am-1pm and 2-6pm, Sun. 10:30am-6:30pm; Nov.-March closed to the public but will respond to mailed inquiries.) The **post office** is halfway up the hill on rue St-Etienne. (Open Mon.-Fri. 9am-noon and 2-5pm, Sat. 9am-noon.) **Trains** run from Auxerre to Sermizelles (5 per day, ¾-hr.); a bus then shuttles passengers to Vézelay once in the morning and once in the afternoon. **Cars de la Madeleine** (tel. 86 33 25 67) serves the route between Avallon and Vézelay. The schedule stays roughly the same: from Sept.-June a bus departs from Avallon's Café Europe (on pl. Vauban) at 8am, and then leaves Vézelay at about 5pm to return. (July-Aug. 2 trips per day, 15 min., 15-17F.) Many travelers find hitchhiking in the area easy; try to get a ride from tourists at the Basilica who are spending the night in Avallon.

Run by Pax Christi, a Catholic peace movement, the **Centre de Rencontres Internationales,** rue des Ecoles (tel. 86 33 26 73 or 86 33 21 69), provides central and inexpensive accommodations just below the Basilica. The facilities are simple, but the upper floors have fantastic views. (43F per person. IYHF card required. Breakfast included. Lunch and dinner 33F. Open July-Sept. 5. For reservations earlier in the year call 43 36 36 68 in Paris.) Located on a peaceful, rural site 700m from town, the **Auberge de Jeunesse (IYHF),** route de l'Etang (tel. 86 33 24 18 or 86 33 25 57), has slightly more luxurious accommodations with only four people per room. Follow the signs towards the *gendarmerie* from the base of the hill to the left. (Lockout 10am-6pm, but you can leave bags all day. 37F per person. IYHF card required. Extensive kitchen facilities. Open June-Sept.) Camping is available behind the hostel. (3F per tent or car. Showers, bathrooms and access to hostel kitchen facilities.)

Vézelay's restaurants are expensive, except for the very down-to-earth **A la Fortune du Pot,** below the parking lot on rue St-Etienne. (Lunch *menus* from 46F. Open Mon.-Fri. noon-2pm and 6-9pm, Sat. noon-2pm.) An appealing 62F *menu* with *coq au vin* is available at **Hôtel du Cheval Blanc,** pl. du Champ de Foire. (Open Sat.-Wed. noon-2pm and 7-9:30pm, Thurs. noon-2pm.) **Peyarot,** 39, rue St-Etienne, is a chic quiche and salad place. Try the homemade pastries. (49F *menu.* Open daily noon-5pm and 7:30pm-late.) The **Casino** near the bottom of the street is Vézelay's only supermarket. (Open Tues.-Sun. 8am-noon and 2:30-7pm.)

Avallon and the Morvan

During the past 50 years, industrialization has brought budget hotels and cheap restaurants to Avallon and workers have more than tripled the population of the surrounding area. Fortunately, this growth has not tarnished the *vieille ville* where the Avallon of Old, named *Aballo* (little apple) by the Druids, lurks just beneath the surface.

Anchored high on a granite mountain, the old city peaks above medieval ramparts. The two most prominent remnants of the town's ancient heritage stand adjacent to one another at the southern end of the *vieille ville.* Once the principal portal to the city, the **Tour de l'Horloge** now straddles rue Aristote and keeps the *Avallonois* running on schedule. Just down the street stands the **Eglise Collégiale St-Lazare,** which gained its present name in the year 1000 when the philanthropic Duke of Burgundy, Henry LeGrand, donated a part of St-Ladre's skull to the church.

The 11th-century origins of the **Eglise Collégiale St-Lazare** are most evident in its two Romanesque portals. The large one to the left is covered with zodiac signs, angels, vine leaves, and apocalyptic old men; the smaller one to the right must settle for carved flowers and plants. (Open Easter-Nov. daily 7:30am-7:30pm.) The **Musée de l'Avallonais,** housed in the 1653 Ancien Collège, contains a lovely Gallo-Roman mosaic, the *Mercure de Ste-Vertut,* and the well-known statuette of a god from Charancy. (We know it; don't you? Open June 15-Sept. 15 Wed.-Mon. 10am-noon and 3-7pm; in off-season only during school vacations. Admission 2F, students 1F.) **Promenade de la Petite Porte,** along the western ramparts, provides an excellent view of the Vallée du Cousin and several small châteaux. Featured on practially every Burgundy brochure is a small turret, **La Bastion de la Petite Porte;** resist the overpowering urge to take a picture. For a vista including both the valley and the city, cross the ravine to Parc des Chaumes, about 2km away; follow rue de Lyon to rue de la Goulotte to av. du Parc des Chaumes. A covered **market** fills pl. Général de Gaulle in the center of town on Saturday mornings. The tourist office distributes a complete map of the Morvan with plans for hikes (36F) as well as lists of hikes through the area's valleys, medieval sanctuaries, and fortresses. These take anywhere from a few hours to a few days; the longer tours include information on *gîtes d'étape.*

Situated at the north edge of the huge **Parc Naturel du Morvan,** Avallon is a good starting point for excursions into the region. For information on horseback riding, canoeing, sailing, and sightseeing in the park, contact the **Maison du Parc Naturel Régional du Morvan,** St-Brisson, 58230 Montesauche (tel. 86 78 70 16). The **tourist office,** 4, rue Bocquillot (tel. 86 34 14 19), is next to St-Lazare but a bit of a hike from the station. Head down av. du President Doumer, and take a right onto rue Carmot. At the large intersection make a left onto rue de Paris, which passes a large parking lot, becomes Grand Rue Aristotle Briand, passes through the Tour de l'Horloge, and lands you on the doorstep of the tourist office. The staff will help you find a hotel room (5F). (Open daily 9:30am-7:30pm; Oct.-Easter Tues.-Sat. 9:30am-12:30pm and 2-6:30pm; Easter to mid-June Mon.-Sat. 9:30am-12:30pm and 2-6:30pm.) When the tourist office is closed, call the **mairie,** 37-39, Grande Rue (tel. 86 34 13 50). **Bikes** can be rented only at the station (47F per day, ID and 300F deposit required). The region is very hilly; remember to check altitude points on a map before setting out. (For general hiking, the *Carte IGN* is recommended.) Vézelay is only 15km away, and except for a steep climb at the end, the route via Vallée du Cousin is relatively flat.

Mechanized transportation is not very efficient or prompt. Cars de la Madeleine (tel. 86 33 25 67) runs one daily **bus** to Vézelay on weekdays. Pick up a timetable at the tourist office. Six **trains** per day run like heck to Laroche-Migennes, where connections to Paris (45F) and Auxerre (1 hr., 40F) can be made. Three trains per day run to Autun (2 hr., 53F) and one train on Wednesday goes to Paris directly (3 hr., 118F). Transco **buses** (tel. 80 43 58 97) roll from the train station to Dijon (2 per day, 2½ hr., 70F), with a stop in Semur-en-Auxois (21F).

Languishing on the edge of town toward Vézelay, the **Foyer des Jeunes Travailleurs,** 10, av. de Victor Hugo (tel. 86 34 01 88), has singles in a modern high-rise. It is often full; call before you make the 40-minute trek. (Members 56F. Breakfast 11F. Lunch or dinner 33F.) **Au Bon Accueil,** 4, rue de l'Hôpital (tel. 86 34 09 33), is the most affordable hotel in town. (Reception open Mon.-Sat. Singles 75F. Doubles 85F, with shower 90F.) The popular restaurant below serves 40F and 69F *menus.* **Hôtel St-Vincent,** 3, rue de Paris (tel. 86 34 04 53), off pl. d'Odeberts, has friendly management—and clean rooms with sagging beds draped with fake fur blankets. (Singles and doubles 100F, with shower 120F. Open mid-Oct. to Sept.) Picturesque **Camping Municipal de Sous-Roche** (tel. 86 34 10 39) lies 2km away; walk along route de Lourmes and then climb back to the three-star riverside campground with fishing and a restaurant. (Open March 15-Oct. 15.) **Camping à la Ferme,** 3km down the route des Chatelaines south of town, is shady and pleasant but offers fewer amenities (10F per night). The restaurant at **Hôtel du Parc,** 3, pl. de la Gare, serves fantastic 47F, 66F, and 105F *menus.* Closer to town, try the cozy **Restaurant de la Tour** (tel. 86 34 24 84), at, you guessed it, the base of the clock tower. Watch the friendly staff twirl your 30-40F pizzas. (Pâtés for 25-30F. Open Mon.-Fri. 12:15-3pm and 7:15-10pm, Sat. 12:15-3pm.)

Auxerre

An important trade center since the Gauls dubbed it Autricum and the Romans polysyllabized it to Autessiodirum, Auxerre has spent the last half of this century tripling its population, modernizing its industries, and connecting itself by railroad to the rest of France. While wine production was Auxerre's chief livelihood for centuries, only one remaining vineyard contributes to its tourist-dependat economy. A superb location on the Yonne has made Auxerre a favorite stop for the fleets of leisure barges which tour Burgundy's canals. Auxerre provides those traveling by boat, car, or bicycle, or on foot with a central base from which to venture into northern Burgundy.

Orientation and Practical Information

Fifty-two km north of Vézalay and Avallon, and midway between Paris and Dijon, Auxerre is well connected to both major cities and obscure rural towns. The *vieille ville* and most of the action lie on the west bank of the river. From the train station, follow the signs for the *Centre Ville* and the Pont Bert along rue Ferry, hang a right onto av. Gambetta, and cross the river on Pont Bert. The tourist office is to the right, three blocks down quai de la République.

Tourist Office: 1-2, quai de la République (tel. 86 52 06 19), below the cathedral on the bank of the Yonne. Good city map. 7F accommodations service. Some English spoken. Open June 15-Sept. 15 daily 10am-12:30pm and 2-7pm; Sept. 16-June 14 Mon.-Sat. 9am-12:30pm and 2-6:30pm. Branch office at 16, pl. des Cordeliers (tel. 86 51 10 27), adjacent to the pedestrian streets. Open June 15-Sept. 15 Mon. 2:30-6:45pm, Tues.-Sat. 10am-12:30pm and 2:30-6:45pm.

Currency Exchange: Banque Populaire de L'Yonne (BPY), 18-22, pl. des Cordeliers (tel. 86 52 53 81). Accepts most types of traveler's checks. Commission 1%. Open Mon.-Fri. 8:30-11:55am and 1:35-5:30pm.

Post Office: (tel. 86 51 37 46) on pl. Charles-Surugue, in the town center. **Telephones.** Open Mon.-Fri. 8am-7pm, Sat. 8am-noon. **Postal code:** 89000.

Trains: (tel. 86 46 50 50), on Rue Paul Doumer, east of the Yonne. To: Paris (7 per day, 2½ hr., 100F); Lyon (7 per day, 4½ hr., 170F); Avallon (7 per day, 1¼ hr., 47F); Autun (7 per day, 3 hr. 20 min., 81F); Sermizelles (7 per day, 1¼ hr., 35F).

Buses: (tel. 86 46 90 66), on pl. Migraines just outside the northwest corner of the inner city. Infrequent connections to Avallon and the surrounding area.

Bike Rental: SNCF, at the train station (tel. 86 46 95 06). 50F per day, deposit 300F. You must show, but not leave, some ID.

Youth Information: Bureau d'Information Jeunesse de l'Yonne (BIJY), 70, rue du Pont (tel. 86 51 68 75), on the street off pont Paul Bert. Tons of information on travel, work (including archaeological digs), and sports. Open Mon.-Fri. 8:30-11:45am and 1:30-6pm.

Hospital: Hôpital Général, bd. de Verdun (tel. 86 48 48 48).

Medical Emergency: SMUR, tel. 86 46 45 67.

Police: bd. Vaulabelle (tel. 86 51 42 44). **Emergency,** tel. 17.

Accommodations, Camping, and Food

It should be no problem finding clean, inexpensive places to stay throughout the year. July and August weekends, however, can bring in crowds; reservations are advisable for a late Saturday arrival. The BIJY has a list of local farmers who welcome campers.

Foyer des Jeunes Travailleuses (IYHF), 16, bd. Vaulabelle (tel. 86 52 45 38). Follow the signs from the train station to *centre ville,* cross the bridge, and turn left; the first right is rue Vaulabelle. 5 min. from the *vieille ville,* the *foyer* is in an inconspicuous apartment building to the left, set back from the street and past a gas station. Singles 65F per night, 950F per month. Breakfast included. Meals 27-32F.

Foyer des Jeunes Travailleurs (IYHF), 16, av. de la Résistance (tel. 86 46 95 11). From the train station, walk south along the tracks to the end of the platform. After crossing the tracks on the little footbridge, continue straight to the signposted high-rise on the right (10 min.). 67F per person. IYHF card required. Meals 33F.

Hôtel de la Renomée, 27, rue d'Egleny (tel. 86 52 03 53), in the *vieille ville.* Open Mon.-Sat. Stately and quiet rooms 80F, with shower 100F. Hall showers included. Restaurant downstairs has *menus* from 50F. Closed first 3 weeks in Aug.

Hôtel de la Porte de Paris, 5, rue St-Germain (tel. 86 46 90 09), on the edge of the *vieille ville.* The owner, Jacques, runs a pleasant, clean hotel-bar. Almost always full by evening, but a very high turnover rate. One squive of a single 77F. Singles and doubles with shower 100F. Triple with shower 130F. Quad with shower 180F. Breakfast 17F.

Camping: (tel. 86 52 11 15), on route de Vaux, south of town on D163. A shady 3-star spot along the Yonne, with TV, laundry facilities, and a pool nearby. Dirt-cheap: 7.50F per person. Open April-Oct.

You should have no problem finding filling 50-70F *menus.* **Restaurant L'Ancien Chai,** 12, rue de la Fraternité (tel. 86 52 39 62) serves a delicious 40F lunch *menu* featuring roast duck. 58F fetches a lunch or dinner of steak, mussels, or chicken. (Open Mon.-Fri. noon-1:30pm and 7-9:30pm, Sat. noon-1:30pm.) The **Pony Express,** 113, rue de Paris (tel. 86 52 83 44), a few blocks off the pedestrian area, serves a 70F *menu,* but you can eat about the same quantity for less *à la carte* in this refurbished restaurant. Chili, lasagne, and *coq au vin* are all 40-70F. (Open daily noon-2pm and 7-9:30pm.) A **market** fills pl. de l'Arquelouse on Tuesday, Friday, and Saturday (9am-1pm). The Sunday market keeps the same hours in pl. Degas.

Sights and Entertainment

Thirteenth-century **Cathédrale St-Etienne** masks its elegant Gothic structure with a Flamboyant facade. Bas-reliefs on the portals depict biblical accounts of the Creation, the Garden of Eden, and Noah's Ark. Closer to eye level than those in many other churches, the magnificent 13th- and 16th-century windows narrate the stories of David and Saul and of St-Joseph. The small **treasury** contains enamel work, illuminated manuscripts, and 5th-century tunic of St-Germain. You'll find the ochre fresco *Christ on Horseback,* the only representation of its sort in existence, in the 11th-century **crypt.** (Open Mon.-Sat. 9am-noon and 2-6pm, Sun. 2-6pm. 8F.)

Closer to town, the **Abbaye St-Germain** attracted several medieval pilgrimages in honor of St-Germain, and still draws crowds to its exceptional Carolingian crypts. Unfortunately, intermittent construction on the abbey and the adjoining school may keep visitors out until 1992. (Open Wed.-Mon. Obligatory tours every ½-hr. 9-11:30am and 2-5:30pm. Admission 7.50F.) The ticket includes admission to the adjacent **Musée d'Art et d'Histoire,** a new museum with artifacts of four centuries of Roman occupation.

Stroll around the pedestrian zone near pl. des Cordeliers to see the old houses and **Tour de l'Horloge,** a two-faced 15th-century clocktower. **Musée Leblanc-Duvernoy,** 9bis, rue d'Egleny, in the west part of town, contains five 18th-century Beauvais tapestries, as well as a collection of porcelain. (Open May-Oct. Wed.-Mon. 10:30am-noon and 2-6pm; Nov. 15-April Wed.-Mon. 10:30am-noon and 2-5:30pm. Admission 6F, ages under 16 free.)

Sens

Sens first tasted power in the first century BC, when the eponymous Senoni tribe dominated the region. Ten centuries later, Sens became the ecclesiastical center of France, and its archbishops ordered around the mere bishops of Paris. In 1163, Pope Alexander III's residence made Sens the center of world Christianity for one brilliant year. The Wars of Religion, however, sent the town's fortunes tumbling, and Sens was traded between counties and provinces before finally landing in the laps of the Burgundian dukes.

Although **Cathédrale St-Etienne** is not, as some claim, France's first authentically Gothic cathedral (this honor goes to Paris's St-Denis), it was the model for England's reconstructed Canterbury Cathedral. Construction began in 1140, but changes and additions continued into the 16th century. Of particular interest are the four blue-toned stained-glass windows in the north ambulatory, the aisle by the chancel. The cathedral's treasury guards relics and liturgical vestments that belonged to two of Canterbury's renowned archbishops, St-Thomas (who spent six year in exile here) and Edward of Abingdon. In July, tours of the cathedral are given in French or English (1 hr., 10F). Unfortunate "heretics" were consigned to their gruesome fate in the downstairs courtroom ot the **Palais Synodal** next door. Ask the custodians to show you the 13th-century system of cells off the vaulted passageway, untouched since their construction. The cathedral treasury and mostly Gallo-Roman collections of the **Musée Municipal** are exhibited in the Henry II wing of the former archbishopric. (Open Wed.-Mon. 10am-noon and 2-6:30pm; Oct.-May Wed. and Sat.-Sun. 10am-noon and 2-6pm, Mon. and Thurs.-Fri. 2-6:30pm. Admission 10F.)

Before you leave Sens wander around the back streets in search of the Renaissance and neoclassical *hôtels particuliers,* whose beams and posts are sometimes adorned with decorative or religious figures. The tourist office's guide mentions almost all of them, including the notable **Maison d'Abraham,** on rue de la République at rue Jean Cousin. Its carved wood beams depict the Tree of Jesse.

Sens has many reasonably priced hotels but few affordable restaurants. A warm welcome and fluffy pillow awaits at the **Hôtel des Deux Ponts,** 22, av. Lucien-Cornet (tel. 86 65 26 81), on the main road into town from the train station, just over the first bridge. (Reception open Mon.-Sat. Decent singles 75F. Doubles 80-150F. Decent 57F *menu.*) The newly renovated **Hôtel Esplanade,** 2, bd. du Mail (tel. 86 65 20 95), off pl. Jean Jaurès, has well-decorated rooms with TVs. (Reception open Mon.-Sat. Singles and doubles 100-200F. Hall shower included.) The minute **Camping Municipal Entre-deux-Vannes** (tel. 86 65 64 71) is outside town on route de Lyon. (8F per night. Open June-Nov.) The cheapest meals in town are the enormous *couscous* platters (34F and up) at **Chez Said,** 89, rue du Général de Gaulle (tel. 86 65 40 46). There are adequate singles and doubles (85F, with shower 120F) upstairs, but you'll have to go by a St. Bernard the size of a cow to get to them.

Frequent service runs from Sens to Paris (1½ hr., 68F) and Dijon (2 hr., 110F). If you're headed for Champagne, **Trec** (tel. 25 82 23 43) sends two to four **buses** per day during the week from outside the train station and near the tourist office to Troyes for a train connection (2 hr., about 53F). The tourist office, pl. Jean Jaurès (tel. 86 65 19 49), has maps, historical commentaries, an accommodations service (5F), and a currency exchange in summer. (Open daily 9am-noon and 1-7:30pm; Sept.-June Mon.-Tues. and Thurs.-Sat. 9am-noon and 1-6pm.) From the station, walk down av. Vauban, cross the river, and follow the signs left on the curving road (20 min.). The cathedral looms two blocks away.

Franche-Comté

Franche-Comté ascends like an enormous stairway from the plains of central France to the mountains of Switzerland. In between, the flat-topped, wooded mountains of the Jura rise from the rolling Saône valley. Loosely translated, the province's name means "Free Country," a testimony to 700 years of struggle to maintain the region's independence. Grim military fortifications occupy the highest ground in most towns, where streets bear the names of generals and soldiers. First settled by the Celts in 58 BC, Franche-Comté came under German rule in 1032 but was ceded to Philippe le Bel of France in 1295. In 1447, the Hapsburgs annexed the region, only to lose it to the Spanish in 1556. Finally, in 1604, the French seized control of the war-torn area once and for all. When King Louis XIV annexed Franche-Comté, he sent the famous military architect Vauban to fortify the area with his ingenious constructions.

The region's beauty and history go underground as well. The sheer dimensions and strange, contorted beauty of the dozens of grottoes and caves often eclipse the memory of their functions as prehistoric shelters and war-time refuges. The Jura and Vosges mountain ranges provide abundant stomping ground for nature lovers. With over 5000km of rushing torrents, meandering streams, and placid lakes, Franche-Comté is a paradise for canoe and kayak enthusiasts.

Scientist Louis Pasteur, the great pasteurizer himself, was born in Dole and raised in Arbois. Today, just about everyone but the region's 300,000 milk cows seems bent on perpetuating Pasteurmania. The fresh, foamy country milk may as well be the local beer. It is also the main ingredient in most of the area's delicacies: 600 liters go into every 50kg of Comté, the regional big cheese. Fruity Arbois wines and cherry-flavored *kirsch* complement these mild flavors, as do the pungent smoked hams, sausages, and *eaux-de-vie* cheeses of Fougerolles. Trout are an easy catch in local rivers, and heaps of wild mushrooms fill townspeoples' baskets.

Trains run frequently between all cities in the region, and the Monts Jura bus company operates decent service to smaller towns and excursions into the mountains. Besançon is an excellent base for trips into the Jura or surrounding country, as most other towns are less than an hour away by train. As elsewhere in France, hitchhiking is not always safe or easy here.

Besançon

A horseshoe bend in the calm Doubs River cradles the old town of Besançon, a strategic military site and a cultural center since the 13th century. Expanding far beyond this original core, modern Besançon thrives as the prominent administrative capital of Franche-Comté and as home to a university and an international language school. Although the city is hidden in the mountainous terrain of the Jura region, the 200,000 *Bisontins* form an active, politically aware center of Franche-Comté.

Orientation and Practical Information

Besançon's *vieille ville, Citadelle,* and cultural centers all lie within the Doubs horseshoe, a 10 minute walk from the station. Follow av. Foch across the pont Denfert-Rochereau. To reach the tourist office from the train station, follow rue de Belfort, turn right on av. Carnot, and walk through the pl. Flore. Turn right and walk to the pont de la République. The tourist office is next to the bridge.

Tourist Office: 2, pl. de l'Armée Française (tel. 81 80 92 55). This friendly facility has information on regional excursions and festivals and will supply a list of hotels and restaurants or book a room for free. Some English spoken. Disabled access. **Currency exchange** when the banks are closed. Open June 16-Aug. Mon.-Fri. 9am-noon and 1:30-7pm, Sat. 9am-noon and 1:45-5pm, Sun. 9am-noon; Mar.-June 15 and Sept.-Oct. Mon.-Fri. 9am-noon and 1:30-6:30pm, Sat. 9am-noon and 1:45-5pm; Jan.-March Mon.-Fri. 9am-noon and 1:30-6pm, Sat.

9am-noon and 1:45-5pm. **Annex,** pl. du 8 Septembre, hall de l'Hôtel de Ville (tel. 81 61 51 41). Small supply of useful local brochures. Open June-Aug. Mon.-Fri. 2-6pm. **Centre d'Information et d'Acceuil Municipal:** 2, rue Megevand (tel. 81 83 08 24). Further information on sports, handicapped facilities, health care, lodging, etc. Open Mon.-Fri. 8am-noon and 1:30-6pm; Sept.-June Mon.-Fri. 8am-noon and 1:30-6pm, Sat. 9am-noon.

Post Office: 19, rue Proudhon (tel. 81 82 23 12), off rue de la République. **Telephones,** Poste Restante, and **currency exchange.** Open Mon.-Fri. 8am-7pm, Sat. 8am-noon. The **main office** 4, rue Demangel (tel. 81 53 81 12), is way out in the new town. **Postal Code:** 25000.

Trains: (tel. 81 53 50 50), on av. de la Paix. Besançon is about 4 hr. from Paris's Gare de Lyon via Dole and Dijon (6 direct per day, 6 via Dijon; 195F). Local connections run to: Lyon (6 per day, 2½ hr., 116F); Belfort (12 per day, 1 hr., 61F); Strasbourg (8 per day, 2¼ hr., 135F); Dijon (12 per day, 1 hr., 57F). Office open Mon.-Sat. 8:30am-6:30pm, Sun. 9:30am-12:30pm and 2-6:30pm.

Buses: Monts-Jura, 9, rue Proudhon (tel. 81 81 20 67). From the tourist office, turn left off rue de la République. To Pontarlier via Ornans (4 per day, 1½-2 hr., 33F) and Villers-le-Lac (leaves in the evening and returns the following afternoon, 41F). 3 buses per week to Salins-les-Bains in the foothills of the Jura (Mon., Wed., and Fri. at 6pm; 1 hr.; 33F), returning the following afternoon. Occasional summer excursions to Interlaken (155F), Zermatt (205F), and Mont Blanc (160F). Office open Mon.-Sat. 9am-noon and 2-6:30pm. **CTB,** 46, rue de Trey (tel. 81 50 28 55). Efficient city bus system. Tickets 5F per hr., *carnet* of 10 37.30F. "Bus-info" trailer in pl. 8 septembre most summer afternoons.

Taxi: tel. 81 80 17 76 or 81 88 80 80. 24 hrs.

Car Rental: Europcar, 7, av. Foch (tel. 81 80 33 39), 1 min. from train station. Small car with unlimited mileage 2500F per week. Open Mon.-Fri. 8am-noon and 2-7pm. **Avis,** 7, pl. Flore (tel. 81 80 91 08).

Bike Rental: At the train station. 40F per ½-day, 50F per day, deposit 500F.

Youth Information: Centre Information Jeunesse (CIJ), 27, rue de la République (tel. 81 83 20 40). Plan your life here. Complete library has regional, national and international information on lodging, travel, excursions, sports, concerts, tickets, employment. BIJ/Transalpino tickets. Ride board. Cartes Jeunes (60F). Open Mon. 2-7pm, Tues.-Fri. 10am-noon and 2-7pm, Sat. 2-6pm.

Laundromat: 54, rue Bersot, near the bus station. Wash 15F, dry 5F per 20 min. Soap 5F. Open 7am-8pm.

Gay Hotline: Collectif Homosexuel de Franche-Comté, tel. 81 83 58 50. A gay hotline (in French) for regional services, events, and advice.

Hiking Information: Club Alpin Français, 14, rue Luc Breton (tel. 81 81 02 77) in the *vieille ville.* Basic hiking information for the Jura mountains. **Topo-guides** 37F.

Hospital: Centre Hospitalier Régional, 2, pl. St-Jacques (tel. 81 52 33 22). From the tourist office, go down rue de la République, which becomes rue de l'Ormée de Chambres.

Medical Assistance: SAMU, tel. 81 52 15 15.

Ambulance: AUMB Urgence Médicale et Médecine de nuit, tel. 81 52 11 11.

Police: (tel. 81 82 03 67), on av. de la Gare d'Eau. **Emergency,** tel. 17.

Accommodations

Hotels in Besançon are generally pleasant but expensive. Fortunately, finding a room in one of the inexpensive *foyers* isn't tough, and the CROUS service can find you space in university buildings in summer.

University Housing: CROUS, Service d'Accueil d'Etudiants Etrangers, 38, av. Observatoire, bldg. B (tel. 81 50 26 88), is the administrative office. To get yourself a room July-Sept. go to the **Cité Universitaire.** From the tourist office, cross the bridge and take bus #7 (*direction:* "Campus") to the Université stop. Head to bldg. A-B, to the right of the Resto U. Mon.-Fri. 10-11:45am and 1-4:15pm go to the *secrétariat,* where you pay and get a room. At other times go directly to the concierge in the lobby of the same building. Ordinary dorm singles 60F, with student ID 40F, with Carte Jeune 50F. Call as far in advance as possible. CROUS offices can also arrange longer stays in university housing.

Centre International de Séjour, 19, rue Martin-du-Gard (tel. 81 50 07 54), near the university. Take bus #8 from the station to the Epitaphe stop. Approximates a youth hostel. Office sells *télécartes*. Office open 7am-1am. Singles 75F. Doubles with 2 beds 50F per person. Triples or quads 47F per person. Breakfast 15F. Meals 45F. Picnic lunch 27F. Rarely full. Reservations for up to 1-week stays accepted up to 1 week in advance.

Foyer des Jeunes Filles, 18, rue de la Cassotte (tel. 81 80 90 01). Women only. Friendly, quiet place maintained by nuns and long-term boarders. Prices depend on 1001 factors (length of stay, age, pension, etc.). Office open daily 8am-10pm. Singles about 60F. Showers and breakfast included. Sheets 20F. Meals 34F.

Hôtel le Levant, 9, rue des Boucheries (tel. 81 81 07 88), on pl. de la Révolution. Good location in the *vieille ville* near the river. Clean singles and doubles without windows 110F, with showers 120F. Triples 140F, with shower 150F. Breakfast 18F. Lively restaurant downstairs.

Hôtel Regina, 91, Grande Rue (tel. 81 81 50 22), smack in the middle of town. Large, clean, and comfortable rooms in a quiet alley. Reception open daily until 10pm. Singles and doubles 90-150F. Showers 10F. Breakfast 20F.

Hôtel Florel, 6, rue de la Viotte (tel. 81 80 41 08), 2 min. to the left of the train station. Nice 2-star place, but a bit expensive. Color TV 20F. Singles 100F. Doubles 120F. Triples 135F. Quads 145F. Breakfast 19F, in bed 25F.

Camping: Camping de la Plage (tel. 81 88 04 26), on route de Belfort in Chalezeule northeast of the city. Take bus #1 toward Palente and ask for the *camping*. A 4-star municipal campground. Access to nearby pool. One person and tent 15F, each additional person 6.50F; children 4.20F; 6.25F per car. Open Mar.-Oct.

Food

Plenty of eclectic, atmospheric restaurants cater to Besançon's cosmopolitan student population; look along rue des Boucheries and the rue Claude-Pouillet. **Pub de l'Etoile,** pl. de la Révolution, is often full of young *Bisontins*. Inexpensive pizzarias line rue Bersot. Tuesday through Saturday afternoon, visit the outdoor **market** in pl. de la Révolution. Comté cheese is abundant here; among the famous Arbois wines is expensive *vin jaune* (yellow wine), which tastes like sherry and goes well with Comté. Many excellent *charcuteries* along rue des Granges sell *jambon de Haut Doubs,* a regional smoked ham.

University Restaurants: The best food deals in Besançon. Mediocre but filling cafeteria meals 20F. Buy a ticket from a student in line (10F). *A la carte* options are slightly more expensive. **Restaurant Canot,** 73, quai Veil-Picard, entrance on rue A. Janvier, across the river from the old town. Open Mon.-Sat. 11:30am-1:15pm; Sept.-June Mon.-Sat. 11:30am-1:15pm and 6:30-7:50pm. **Restaurant La Bouluie,** at the *cité universitaire*. Open Mon.-Sat. 11:30am-1:15pm and 6:30-7:50pm. **Restaurant Megavand,** rue Megavanel, near rue de la Préfecture. Open 8:30-10:30am and 11:30am-1:15pm. Most stay open through July.

La Boîte à Sandwiches, 21, rue du Lycée, the next street to your right after Grande Rue, from rue de la République. A sandwich oasis in the desert of 3-course, sleep-inducing French lunches. Over 50 types of sandwiches, inclusing seaweed (14-40F). Salad selection includes an artichoke, hot sauce, and rice concoction (32F). Open Mon.-Fri. 11am-2pm and 5:30-10pm, Sat. 11am-2pm.

Le Levant, 9, rue des Boucheries. Shady place always crowded both inside and out. *Couscous* 36-64F. Good 43F *menu* and 65F regional *menu*. Open Sun.-Fri. noon-1:45pm and 7-9:45pm.

Le P'tit Loup, 9, rue du Lycée, down the street from La Boîte. Designer salads and a 35F *plat du jour* served inside stone walls. Try the *filet mignon au poivre vert* (45F). Open Mon.-Sat. noon-2pm and 7-10pm.

Kabouli, 9, rue Claude-Pouillet. A curious place with Syrian and Lebanese specialties. Full meals about 80F, main dihes about 40F. Middle Eastern music and neon pink decor. Open Mon.-Fri. noon-2pm and 7-11pm, Sat. 7-11pm.

El Latino, 23, rue Claude-Pouillet. Spicy chile con carne *à la Franche-Comtoise* 48F. 65F Peruvian *menu*.

Sights and Entertainment

Built in 1674 by Vauban on the site of an ancient Gallo-Roman acropolis, the **Citadelle** rises from sheer rock over the green mountains and the winding Doubs. Vauban's works, intended to thwart the Swiss, are described in the brochure *A la recherche de Vauban et de ses successeurs en Franche-Comté,* available from tourist offices. The series of buildings within the 20m thick walls house a variety of museums. The **Musée de la Résistance et de la Déportation** (tel. 81 83 37 14) displays a unique collection of sculpture and painting crafted by survivors of Nazi concentration camps. The period rooms of the **Musée Populaire Comtois** contain puppets, cheese makers, and bronze clocks. Endless rows of butterflies are pinned (but not wriggling) on the walls of the **Musée d'Histoire Naturelle;** the two rooms of African art, the zoo, and the aquarium are far more interesting. (Museums and Citadelle open March 26-Sept. 30 Wed.-Mon. 9:15am-6:15pm; Oct.-Mar. 9:45am-4:45pm. Admission Wed.-Mon. 22F, ages 10-18 15F, under 10 free. Admission to aquarium and zoo on Tues. 10F.) To reach the citadel, take the steep Grande Rue to rue des Fusilles. Non-decathaloners who think they can't might consider taking the hourly **Petit Train de Besançon** (tel. 81 81 45 05), which thinks it can, from the Parking Rivotte on the southeast corner of the old town. The train passes by the Musée des Beaux Arts, the Horloge Astronomique, the Musée Granvelle, and the tourist office. (June-Aug. 10am-6pm, April-May and Sept. 11am-6pm, 45 min., 20F, under 18 12F.)

At the foot of the citadel stands **Porte Noire,** a stern 2nd-century Roman triumphal arch, and the marvelously ornate 18th-century **Cathédrale St-Jean,** a double-apsed church with, shockingly enough, no main facade. Inside, the unique circular altar **Rose de St-Jean** and wooden Renaissance masterpiece *La Vierge aux Saints* are worth a look. (Tours July-Sept. Wed.-Mon. at 10:30am and 3:30pm, ½-hr., 9F.) In July and August, tours of all the church's treasures (27F, students 20F) leave from the tourist office Friday at 3pm. Behind the church ticks the locally crafted **Horloge Astronomique,** the sum of 30,000 parts. Daily at noon a puppet Christ leaps from his tomb as Hope blesses Faith and Charity, and two soldiers doze at their posts despite the ringing bells; another thrilling presentation occurs at 3pm, and less flamboyant mechanical theatrics occur every hour. Arrive 15 minutes before the hour. (Admission 15F, students 9F.)

Past Porte Noire and along Grande Rue, the elegant **Renaissance Palais Granvelle** now houses the **Musée Historique de Besançon Doubs** and its unremarkable 17th-century Bruges tapestry of scenes from the life of Charles V. (Open Wed.-Mon. 9:30am-noon and 2-6pm. Admission 10F, students 5F, Sun. free.) In summer free folk dance and classical music concerts are given in the courtyard; check the schedule in the tourist office, and show up early. Works by Tintoretto, David, Ingres, Constable, Courbet, Matisse, Picasso, and Renoir hang in the exceptional **Musée des Beaux Arts,** pl. de la Révolution (tel. 81 81 44 47; open Wed.-Mon. 9:30-11:50am, 2-5:50pm; admission 12F, students and Sundays free).

Les Vedettes Bisontines (tel. 81 68 13 25) runs daily *bateau-mouche* cruises on the Doubs and inside the citadel canals from Pont de la République, near the tourist office. (July-Sept. 14 Mon.-Fri. at 10:30am, 2:30pm, and 4:30pm, Sat.-Sun. at 10:30am, 2pm, 4pm, and 6pm; April-June and Sept. 15-Oct. 5 fewer runs; 1¼ hr.; 40F.) **Piscine du Sport Nautique Bisontine,** av. de Chardonnet (tel. 81 80 56 01), on the same side of the river as the tourist office near pont de Bregille, gives instruction in sculling, canoeing, and kayaking (introductory course 60F, students 40F; 265F per week; open May 15-Sept. 15 daily 10:30am-7pm). If you're already an experienced sculler, you can use a shell for free. They also have a pleasant outdoor swimming pool (same hours; admission 17F, students 12F).

The tourist office publishes a comprehensive list of all cultural events. The only remaining competition for young orchestra conductors in the world, the **Festival de Musique de Besançon** features world-famous classical musicians in the first two weeks of September. (Admission 40-200F, students 30-80F.) **Jazz en Franche-Comté** brings a flurry of free concerts in June and July. Most of Besançon's *boîtes de nuit* (nightclubs) have a 60F cover. **Pimm's Club,** 42, chemin de Mazagran, features French Top 40 in one room, and anything else (from the tango to Jacques Brel) in the other. **Excaliber,** 2, av. Droz, across from the tourist office, caters to a younger, new-wave crowd.

Near Besançon

Besançon is a good base for excursions into the **Jura.** The prehistoric glaciers of Franche-Comté have created a natural underground amusement park of grottoes and rivers. The closest (15km from Besançon), **Grotte d'Osselle,** is home to 3,000 cave-bear skeletons. To cool off, head 525m underground to the **Grotte de la Glacière,** the subterranean safe deposit box for a sparkling collection of minerals and crystals. Both are easily accessible by car on either N83 or D30, and Monts Jura runs several excursions (30-75F). Osselle is open June-Aug. 8am-7pm; April-May 9am-noon and 2-6pm; Sept. 9am-noon and 2-6pm; Oct. 9-11:30am and 2:30-5pm. Glacière is open June-Aug. 8am-7pm; March-May 9am-noon and 2-6pm; Sept.-Nov. 9am-noon and 2-5pm. Call the central Jura tourist office at 84 24 19 64, or pick up a copy of *Welcome to Jura,* which contains information on kayaking and hiking through the Jura massif.

A charming small town of stone buildings and windowboxes overflowing with begonias and geraniums, **Poligny** is accessible by train directly from Besançon (about 5 per day, 1 hr., 60F). To get to the main street, Grande Rue, take a right at the end of the road from the train station. Poligny has a beautiful church, **Eglise Collégiale Saint-Hippolyte,** with a vivid portrayal of the saint's martyrdom above the door and an enchanting polychrome statue of the Virgin and Child beneath it. Nearby is 15th-century **Couvent des Clarisses. Hôtel-Restaurant Les Charmilles,** route de Dole (tel. 84 37 24 51), is two minutes from the train station on your left. (Doubles 112F. Triples 132F. Breakfast 20F. Closed Dec. 20-Jan. 20 and first week in Sept.) A convenient place for a drink or a light meal is **Snack Bar Hôtel de Ville,** opposite its namesake on Grande Rue; their 52F *menu* is generous. The **tourist office** is down the street at #85 (tel. 84 37 24 21; open 9:30am-12:30pm and 2:30-6pm).

Pontarlier, near the border of Switzerland, produces a variety of liqueurs, chocolates, honey, and smoked hams in addition to proclaiming itself the capital of mountain *gruyère.* Eight footpaths take you away from the 17th- and 18th-century town center and into the forest. The first week in August, Pontarlier hosts a colorful international dance festival. In winter, locals ski at the nearby **Super-Pontarlier** on the Montagne du Larmont. In town, stay at the **Auberge de Jeunesse** on rue Marpaud (tel. 81 39 06 57), or try **Les Gentianes** (tel. 81 39 19 73), a three-star campground near the Paul Robbe municipal stadium. The **tourist office** is in the Hôtel de Ville (tel. 81 46 48 33). To get to Pontarlier, take a *Monts Jura* bus from the Besançon bus station (1¾ hr.) or a train from Mouchard. **Ornans,** accessible by the Pontarlier bus, is home to the **Musée Gustave Courbet,** Courbet's house, now filled with his works.

Belfort

First fortified in 1226, Belfort became a key defense city only after 1675, when military architect Vauban began enlarging and fortifying the château to resist attacks launched from the Vosges and Jura mountains to the east. Neither quaint nor graceful, this red-walled fortress still betrays its grim military function. Belfort's mascot, the 24m **Lion,** gazes fiercely toward the town from the northern face of the citadel. Sculpted from rock by Bartholdi (Mr. Statue of Liberty himself), the lion honors those who defended Belfort during the Franco-Prussian War. He is not related to Bruno Lion, current French undersecretary of rock and roll, who once muttered over the upturned collar of his $1000 leather jacket: "I don't know what French rock and roll is. I don't know what rock and roll is. I'm not even sure I know what a rock is." (Open daily 8am-6:45pm. Admission 3F.)

The pleasant old town, a roughly pentagonal area at the base of the château, contains most of the sights. Streets generally become trails that wind up the rock to the **Château de Belfort.** (Open daily 8am-noon and 2-7pm; Nov. 7-March Mon.-Fri. 10am-noon and 2-5pm, Sat.-Sun. 8am-noon and 2-5pm; April and Oct. Wed.-Mon. 8am-noon and 2-6pm.) The 10F charge admits you to ramparts and tunnels and to several small museums, one of which contains firearms, bayonets, and other weapons. The view of the Jura and the Vosges is worth the hike on a clear day. If you liked the first climb, you'll love scaling the hill across the valley to **La Tour de la Miotte,** a turret built on the ruins of Château de Montfort.

The sleek new **tourist office,** at pl. de la Commune (tel. 84 28 12 23), in the pedestrian zone, has a detailed map; be sure to ask for the indexed one. Pick up the student-published guide *Le Petit Geni* (free), a practical guide to Belfort's restaurants, lodgings, and sights. (Open June Mon.-Sat. 9am-12:15pm and 1:45-7pm; July-Aug. Mon.-Sat. 10am-7pm, Sun. 9am-noon; Sept.-May Mon.-Sat. 9am-12:15pm and 1:45-6pm.) A tourist office brochure, *Randonnées pèdestres autour de Belfort,* guides you through the forests on **la Colline de Salbert,** a hill outside of town, or on a two-hour walking tour around the fort and ramparts. The office also conducts guided tours of the old town (June-Aug. Thurs. at 3pm; 15F, students 8F). Belfort has a **train station** (tel. 84 28 50 50) and a **bus station** (pl. Corbis, tel. 84 28 59 02). The **police station** (tel. 84 21 40 34) is on rue du Manège; the **hospital** (Centre Hospitalier, tel 84 21 81 33) is at 14, rue de Mulhouse.

Accommodations, Camping, and Food

Belfort has plenty of cheap, clean rooms. University housing is only available during the school year; contact the CROUS office in Belfort (tel. 84 21 06 01) or Besançon (tel. 81 50 26 88). The attractive **Foyer des Jeunes Travailleurs,** 6, rue de Madrid (tel. 84 21 39 16), has singles, doubles, and triples for 45F per person. (Showers and sheets included. Breakfast 10F. Preference given to ages 18-25.) From the station, go left under the underground passage, continue up rue Parisot and av. LeClerc to rue de Madrid (10 min.). The **Hotel Vauban,** 4, rue du Magasin (tel. 84 21 59 37) has comfortable singles for 70-80F and doubles from 85F. (Extra bed 35F. Breakfast 20F.) The **Hôtel du Centre,** 11, rue du Magasin (tel. 84 28 67 80), across the street, lets some amazingly cheap rooms. (Singles and doubles from 50F, with shower 75F. Open Sept.-July Mon.-Sat.) The **Nouvel Hôtel,** 56, rue Faubourg de France (tel. 84 28 28 78), has simple clean rooms. (Singles 80F. Doubles 85F. Showers 10F.) The **Camping Municipal,** promenade d'Essert (tel. 84 21 03 30), before the *foyer,* occupies a grassy mound in a shady park. (4F per person, 4F per tent, 6F per car. Open May-Oct.)

The elegant **Restaurant Le Molière,** pl. de la Grande Fontaine, off rue de l'Etuve, serves a cold ham and asparagus platter (43F) and steaming *langoustines* (prawns) with green beans (45F). The simpler **L'Ancêtre,** 4, faubourg des Ancêtres, serves formidable pizzas (28-35F) in a plush, pink setting. Wednesday, Friday and Saturday morning, a **market** is held on rue Docteur Fréry on the old-town bank of the river; Tuesday, Thursday, and Sunday morning it moves to the Marché des Vosges, on av. Jean Jaurès, 20 minutes from *centre ville* (bus #1, direction "Valdoie," stop **Marché Vosges).**

Near Belfort

Twenty minutes from Belfort by train, tiny **Ronchamp** has only one real attraction for passersby: **Chapelle Notre-Dame du Haut** on the hill of Bourlémont. Known for its asymmetrical architecture by Le Corbusier and its curious history, the chapel will refresh the Gothic-weary traveler. Built in 1955, Notre-Dame du Haut is the most recent of three churches which have graced the hill; the first one, an 18th-century church, was struck down by lightning in 1913, and the second one was destroyed by Allied bombardments in 1944. (Open daily 9am-7pm. Admission 5F, ages 6-12 3F. For information, call 84 20 65 13.) The **Musée de la Mine** depicts Ronchamp's history as a mining town. (Open May-Sept. 15, daily 3-6pm.)

The tiny **tourist office** is on the first floor of the town hall. (Open Mon.-Fri. 8am-noon and 2-5pm.) It doesn't have many brochures or maps, but it might be able to help you with bus and train schedules, directions, and walks in the area. There is a **currency exchange** at Crédit Agricole, 10, rue Corbusier. (Open Mon.-Fri. 9am-noon and 2-6pm, Sat. 9am-noon and 2-4pm.) The **post office** is at 3, pl. Lagelée. (Open Mon.-Fri. 8:30am-noon and 2:30-5pm, Sat. 9am-noon.) The **postal code** is 70250. The town's pharmacy is across the bridge at 1, av. Pasteur. (Open Mon.-Sat. 9am-noon and 2-8pm.) There are no *télécarte* telephones in the town.

Rooms in Ronchamp run 60-90F. **La Pomme d'Or**, 19, rue le Corbusier (tel. 84 20 62 12), popular with the locals, has vibrating 80F singles and doubles—we're talkin' *close* to those train tracks. The cozy restaurant downstairs has a 46F *menu*. About 750m out of the town center on rue des Mineurs, **Le San Francisco** (tel. 84 20 63 88) has 60F singles and doubles (showers 5F) and a restaurant with a substantial 40F *menu*. Pick up picnic supplies at **Point Coops,** on rue Corbusier.

One train per day runs like heck from Belfort to Ronchamp at 6:30am (½-hr., 40F) and returns around 6pm. SNCF buses make a round-trip to Ronchamp (two per day, one way 18F), and CFIT buses run once a day to and from Ronchamp.

Arbois

Quiet Arbois (pop. 4000), home of the unique *vin jaune* (yellow wine), dozes at the heart of the *jurassien* vineyards. While the town itself may excite only diehard Louis Pasteur fans, the nearby *caves* provide an interesting alternative to the more crowded wineries in Burgundy.

Orientation and Practical Information

Less than 50km from Besançon, Arbois is served frequently by trains and buses. The central square, **place de la Liberté,** is one block up from the bus terminus and a good 15-minute walk from the train station. Everything in this compact town is near this square or on the narrow multi-named main street.

Tourist Office: 10, rue de l'Hôtel de Ville (tel. 84 66 07 45), in the Hôtel de Ville, off pl. de la Liberté. Dispenses train and bus schedules, a map, and a list of hotels and restaurants. The friendly staff will tell you (in French) which hotels probably have vacancies and which *caves* are open to the public. Ask for the leaflet on countryside tours. Open Mon.-Sat. 9am-6:30pm, Sun. 10am-noon; Sept.-June Mon.-Sat. 9:30am-noon and 2-6:30pm.

Currency Exchange: Banque Populaire, 13, rue de l'Hôtel de Ville. Open Mon.-Fri. 8:30am-noon and 1:45-6pm. **Crédit Agricole,** 58, Grande Rue. Open Tues.-Fri. 8:30am-noon and 1:30-6pm, Sat. 8:30am-noon and 1:30-4:30pm. No commissions.

Post Office: av. Général-Delort (tel. 84 66 01 21), off pl. de la Liberté. **Telephones.** Open Mon.-Fri. 8am-noon and 2:30-5:30pm, Sat. 8am-noon. **Postal Code:** 39600.

Trains: (tel. 84 47 50 50), on route de Dole. To: Dijon (4-5 per day, with transfers, 1 hr., 54F); Besançon (6 per day, ½-hr., 35F); Lyon (6 per day, 2 hr., 90F).

Buses: SNCF buses (free with railpasses) stop at pl. Notre-Dame across from the Hôtel des Messageries. To Monchaud (7 per day, 5 min., 10F). Schedules posted at the stops; ask at the train station or tourist office. For other destinations, call **Cars Monts-Jura** at 84 82 00 03.

Bike Rental: Patrick Aviet, 1, rue de Bourgogne (tel. 84 66 03 13). Decent 10-speeds 40F per ½-day, 60F per day. Open Mon.-Sat. 9am-noon and 2-5pm.

Police: 17, av. Général-Delort (tel. 84 66 14 25). **Emergency,** tel. 17.

Accommodations, Camping, and Food

Although tourists crowd Arbois in summer, you shouldn't have trouble finding a room.

Hôtel des Messageries, 2, rue de Courcelles or promenade Pasteur (tel. 84 66 15 45), 2 blocks from pl. de la Liberté. An exquisite old hotel with a bar and a *salon* upstairs. Attentive management. Wonderful hall shower. Singles and doubles from 100F. Breakfast 20F. Open March-Nov.

Hôtel le Memphisto, 33, pl. de Faramand (tel. 84 66 06 49), near the church. Comfortable, spacious rooms. No busts of Elvis. Singles 70F. Doubles 110F. Pizzeria below has a 40F *menu.*

La Poste, 71, Grande Rue (tel. 84 66 13 22), above a bar. Basic and clean with easygoing management. Singles 79F. Doubles 110F. Showers 10F. Breakfast 20F. The restaurant downstairs serves *steak-frites* for 35F.

Camping: Camping des Vignes (tel. 84 66 14 12), on av. Général-Leclerc, about 1km outside town next to an Olympic-size swimming pool. Follow the signs from pl. de la Liberté. A 3-star site. Open April-Sept.

A number of cafés around pl. de Faramand serve basic 40F *menus* (appetizer, *steak-frites,* and dessert). **La Finette, Taverne d'Arbois,** 22, av. Pasteur, serves a hearty 65F *menu* on tables made from wooden barrels. Their *mâchons* (snacks) can be a meal in themselves—try the *fondue des trois cantons* (30F). (Open daily 9am-midnight.) The **Restaurant des Arcades,** 22, Grande Rue, near pl. de la Liberté, serves substantial meals including an artichoke vinaigrette for 46F. (Open Tues.-Sat. noon-2pm.) A regional **market** fills pl. du Champs de Mars Tuesday and Friday until 1pm. A huge **market** takes place the first Tuesday of the month in the same place.

Sights and Entertainment

Come to Arbois to savor *jurassien* wines and learn about different winemaking techniques. **Henri Maire,** the biggest wine-producer in the region, shows an excellent free 20-minute film about wine cultivation in English and French. Daily guided tours of the vineyards are followed by a traditional *dégustation.* The visit takes you to *caves* where red, white, and the expensive yellow wines are produced. *Vin jaune* (yellow wine) takes six years to make; 20% of it turns to vinegar. The guides are generous with the wine. Consider bringing along some bread so that you can try them all. An *apéritif* is included: try *Montagnard,* a sweet rose-colored wine. Henri Maire also makes *vin de paille* (straw wine), a sweet white made by pressing grapes dried on straw. *Vin fou,* another local product, is Arbois's answer to champagne. (Usually open mid-June to Nov. Wed.-Mon. 10am-noon and 2-7pm, but check at Henri Maire's shop in the main square to be sure. Admission 7F, students 4F.) From July to mid-September, **Fruitière Vinicole d'Arbois,** 2, rue des Fosses, also gives frequent *cave* tours which include free tastings. Go only if you can't make a tour at Maire—these *caves* usually cater to bus tours. The tourist office distributes a list of smaller wine-making operations, but only the large businesses give tastings. At smaller houses, at least offer to pay for the tasting (*payer la dégustation*) if you don't buy a bottle.

Arbois was Louis Pasteur's childhood home and later his vacation retreat from the university where he taught. The ivy-covered **Maison Pasteur** still contains His original furniture and the laboratory where He did his experiments on fermentation. (Open for guided visits Wed.-Mon. 9am-noon and 2-6:30pm, Sun. 9am-noon and 2-5pm. Ring the bell to summon the guide. Admission 10F, students 5F.) Pasteur's small vineyard is now privately cultivated by Henri Maire; a film on Pasteur's life is shown several times per day in Henri Maire's shop.

For a view of Arbois sheltered amidst fields of grapes, climb to the top of the bell tower of the odd **Eglise St-Just** (visits 3 times per day at 11am, 4pm, and 5:30 or 6pm). A 15-minute *circuit pédestre* begins outside the church and passes an old waterwheel, a babbling brook, veggie gardens, and obscenely happy happy sheep.

The largest of Arbois' annual festivals is the **Grande Fête des Vins** (the last Sun. in July), when dancers and others in local garb proceed down the main street and wine flows freely. First prize in the raffle is the winner's weight in wine. The September and October harvests bring a flurry of smaller wine festivals.

About 5km from Arbois on CD107 and 250m underground are the **Grottes des Planches,** the eerie handiwork of a subterranean river. (45-min. tours June-Sept.

daily 9am-noon and 2-6:30pm; April and Oct. 10am-noon and 2-6pm. Admission 20F, ages under 12 10F.) You can't get to the caves by public transportation—walk or try to get a ride on one of the many tour buses passing through Arbois (they often have extra seats). Make the trip if 12°C sounds refreshing, but skip it if you think a stalagmite is just another hunk of crystal.

Dole

Like most of Franche-Comté, this red-roofed city on a hill has survived invasions by nearly every European power. Established as a monastic village in the 14th century, Dole soon became a quiet but important town with a thriving university. In 1479, it reached its cultural and political peak as the capital of the Comté de Bourgogne. However, the town's stubborn resistance to annexation by France spurred an enraged Louis XI to raze the town to its foundations. After two more centuries of resistance, Dole finally surrendered to Louis XIV in 1668, and several centuries later endured four years of Nazi occupation. Although the *Dolois* still possess an almost tangible spirit of resistance, this working-class town finds time to enjoy its small squares, beautiful canal, and hard-won calm.

Orientation and Practical Information

Dole lies along the Doubs River, halfway between Dijon and Besançon. **Place Grévy,** a few blocks north of the river, marks the center of town. From the train station, turn left and follow av. Aristide Briand to the second left, past the post office. Then take rue du Gouvernement to the tourist office.

Tourist Office: 6, pl. Grévy (tel. 84 72 11 22). Small office distributes a free map and list of hotels. Ask for a copy of *Jura été,* which lists cultural events. Open Tues.-Sat. 8:30am-noon and 2-7pm; Sept.-June Tues.-Fri. 8:30am-noon and 2-6pm, Sat. 8:30am-noon and 2-5pm.

Post Office: 3, av. Aristide Briand (tel. 84 82 15 71). **Telephones,** cash advances on Visa or MasterCard, and **currency exchange.** Wheelchair access. Open Mon.-Fri. 8am-6:30pm, Sat. 8am-noon. **Postal Code:** 39100.

Trains: (tel. 84 47 50 50), on pl. de la Gare, 5 min. from the center of town. To: Dijon (10 per day, 30 min., 40F); Besançon (10 per day, 30 min., 36F); Strasbourg (10 per day, 3½ hr., 55F); Belfort (5 per day, 1½ hr., 84F).

Car rental: Europcar, 61, bd. du Président Wilson, just past the first stop light, 5 min. from station. Open Mon.-Sat. 9am-noon and 2-6:30pm, Sun. 9am-noon and 2-7pm.

Taxis: tel. 84 82 13 70.

Buses: Monts Jura, 98, bd. du Président Wilson (tel. 84 82 00 03). Excursions to the Jura mountains.

Hospital: Centre Hospitalier, av. L. Jouhaux (tel. 84 72 81 21).

Police: Commissariat de Police, 1, rue du 21 Janvier (tel. 84 72 01 68). **Emergency,** tel. 17.

Accommodations and Camping

Comfortable student *foyers* open their doors to budget travelers throughout the year. Barring quirks of fate, Dole's several cheap hotels generally have space.

Foyer des Jeunes Travailleurs: Foyer St-Jean (IYHF) (tel. 84 82 36 74), on pl. Jean XXIII, a 15-min. walk from the station. Walk straight ahead, turn right on bd. du Président Wilson (the main street), turn left at the 3rd light (rue des Paters), right on rue Lachiche, and force yourself to head toward the hideous modern church St. Jean. The hostel is in a parking lot. You can also take bus #1 (direction Mesnils-Poiset, stop Les Paters). IYHF card required. Office open Mon.-Fri. 9am-6pm, Sat.-Sun. noon-1pm and 7-11pm. No curfew. Clean singles 45F. Croissants (2.50F) and coffee (3F) for breakfast. Lunch (noon-12:45pm) or dinner (7-7:45pm) 30F. Sheets included. You should have no problem getting a room here even July-Aug. **Washing machines** 20F, dry 10F. **Bike Rental** 15F per ½-day, 30F per day, 50F per weekend, deposit 500F.

Foyer Féminin Dolois, 8, rue Charles Sauria (tel. 84 82 15 21). From the train station, take av. Aristide Briand; take your 2nd right after the post office onto rue Lepine. The *foyer* is at the end. Men and women accepted. In an old convent with cavernous rooms. Office open daily 8am-7pm. Curfew midnight. No lockout. Singles 70F, ages over 25 75F. Showers, breakfast, and sheets included.

Hôtel Moderne, 40, av. Aristide Briand (tel. 84 72 27 04), across from the station. Singles and doubles 70F, with bath 120-160F. Breakfast 15F. Smoke-filled bar below.

Auberge du Grand Cerf, 6, rue Arney (tel. 84 72 11 68), off pl. Grévy. Lots of regulars stay here. Clean and comfortable. Singles 70F. Doubles 80F. Breakfast 15F. Open Sept.-July.

Camping: Camping du Pasquier (tel. 84 72 02 61), a 10-min. walk from pl. Grévy and on the river. One of the best views of the town and Eglise Notre-Dame. Hot showers. 10F per person, 15F per tent. Electricity 11.50F. Open March 15-Oct.

Food

Skip the expensive cafés and *salons de thé* around pl. Grévy and rue de Besançon. Put together your own meal in the nearby food shops and eat along the canals. Tuesday, Thursday, and Saturday mornings, the **market** in pl. du Marché, opposite the church, supplies generous portions of local specialties. There is an **Intermarché** supermarket on bd. du Président Wilson. (Open Mon.-Sat. 8am-noon and 2-7pm.)

Restaurant Associative, 8, rue Charles Sauria. Enter through the *foyer* and pay 34F at the desk. Go down the stairs and through a door marked "Sortie" for the best bargain in town. Five-course meals include wine. Popular with locals. Open daily noon-2pm and 7-7:30pm.

La Demi-Lune, 39, rue Pasteur, next to the Maison Pasteur. Particularly pleasant spot with a vaulted cellar. Some prime canal-side seats. Salads and *crêpes* 10-41F. Open March-Sept. and Nov.-Jan. Thurs.-Tues. noon-2pm and 7pm-midnight.

Buffet de la Gare, on pl. de la Gare. A fancy station restaurant that locals actually recommend. 54F *menu. A la carte* entrees come in larger portions and are garnished with fries. Open Fri.-Wed. 11:15am-2pm and 7-9pm, Thurs. 11:15am-2pm.

La Bucherie, 14, rue de la Sous-Préfecture. Eat a good variety of pizzas (25-40F) to a strange variety of music. Try the pizza *Franc-Comtoise* with artichokes, *escargot*, and bacon (40F) or the mushroom *pâté* (35F). Open Tues.-Sat. noon-2pm and 7-10pm, Sun. 7-10pm.

Sights

The 16th-century **Eglise Notre-Dame** dominates the downtown district with its 74m steeple. Interesting **Hôtel Terrier de Santans**, 44, rue de Besançon, preserves three staircases from the 16th, 17th, and 18th centuries. From rue de Besançon, take a right on rue de la Bière as you approach pl. Grévy. This narrow street leads down the hill to rue Pasteur: at #27 stands the **Collège des Orphelins Nobles de Broissia**, and at #43, the **Maison Natale de Louis Pasteur.** The town has made this a veritable shrine full of anything remotely associated with Pasteur, from old clothing to flasks of liquid used in his fermentation experiments. (Open April-Oct. Wed.-Mon. 9am-noon and 2-7pm, Sun. 2-6pm. Admission 10F, students 5F, disabled free.)

A small arch to the right of the house leads to the **Canal des Tanneurs**, where Pasteur's father cured hides (and perhaps tanned young Louis's). The **Musée Municipal**, 85, rue des Arènes, contains works by Vouet, Lebrun, Courbet, and others, as well as an archaeological section with Celtic, Gallo-Roman, and Merovingian displays. (Open Mon. and Wed.-Sat. 10am-noon and 2-6pm, Sun. 2-5pm. Tours of Dole (15F), the Basilica (10F), and the Hôtel-Dieu (10F) run from here July-Aug.)

Dole's most interesting "sights" are not found inside its churches and museums. Rather, look along the network of canals, paths, and gardens in the southern part of the *vieille ville.* Barges pass frequently through the locks; check out the slow process of changing water levels and opening gates. The particularly friendly *Dolois* often invite strangers to join the endless games of *boules* in the **Cours St-Marius**, across from the pl. Jules Grevy.

Alsace-Lorraine

Originally settled by Celtic peoples, these two provinces had their first taste of conquest when Roman legions marched through triumphantly in 58 and 52 BC. Since then, Alsace and Lorraine have been traded back and forth between France and Germany numerous times, most recently after the Franco-Prussian War of 1870-71 and during both World Wars. The result is an interesting mixture of Frankish and Germanic influences coupled with an often fervent loyalty to France. Yet these two provinces, however closely linked by geography and history, are separated by more than just the Vosges mountains.

Set in a carpet of vineyards and fields unrolling east from the forested Vosges, the well-preserved cities of Alsace welcome an international tourist crowd. Strasbourg, just a stone's throw across the Rhine from Germany, was the birthplace of both Gutenberg's printing press and of **La Marseillaise,** a Rhine Army marching song that became the French national anthem after revolutionaries from Marseille sang it in Paris. Come 1992, this international business center may be the seat of the European Parliment. Along the *route du vin,* a string of vineyards and picturesque villages that runs about 140km from Marlenheim to Thann; wine cellars distract hikers starting out on the long trails that wind up into the hills. Hundreds of kilometers of trails dotted with overnight refuges (*fermes auberges*) have been marked. Maps and guides are available from tourist offices and from Club Vosgien, 4, rue de la Douane, Strasbourg (tel. 88 32 57 96, open Mon.-Fri. 9am-noon and 2-5pm).

While Alsace may be glad to call itself French, its German heritage comes out strongly in its cuisine. Among the traditional dishes are *tarte à l'oignon, pâté de foie gras, choucroute garnie* (sauerkraut cooked in white wine sauce and topped with sausages and ham), *coq au Riesling* (chicken in a white wine sauce), and *baeckaoffe* (a casserole of marinated beef, pork, lamb, and potatoes that must sometimes be ordered a day in advance). *Tarte flambée,* another popular specialty, is a bacon tart traditionally cooked in a wood stove. Cheeses include the Germanic *Münster* and *Emmenthal.* The Alsatian vineyards produce six white wines and the dry rosé *Pinot Noir. Riesling,* dry but fruity, is the king of the local wines, while sweeter *Gewurtztraminer* is extraordinarily fragrant.

West of Alsace, Lorraine offers a less trumped-up view of French life. This alternately wooded and industrial region derives its name from the Frankish Emperor Lothair, who received the so-called "middle kingdom" between France and Germany when the 843 Treaty of Verdun divided Charlemagne's empire. It was annexed to France in 1766, when Duke Stanislas of Lorraine (a former king of Poland and father-in-law to Louis XV) burned to death in his own fireplace. Devastated by two world wars, Lorraine retains relatively little of its past. The rebuilt cities can seem solemn and graceless—still in mourning, it seems, for the millions of dead who covered their fields. Tiny Bar-le-Duc, former capital of the splendid and powerful duchy of Bar, was one of the few towns to escape destruction. Metz, a former fortress town and cultural center, boasts the luminous Cathédrale St-Etienne and Basilique St-Pierre-aux-Nonnais, one of the oldest churches in France. In chilling contrast, however, is Verdun. Reduced to rubble in WWI, the city and its surroundings are haunted by dozens of military cemeteries and echoing crypts.

What Lorraine's culinary specialties may lack in delicacy, they make up in heartiness: the bread is heavier than most, and potatoes or white cabbage are the usual accompaniment to meals. Bacon, butter, and cream are key ingredients in the artery-hardening dishes like many dishes, as in *quiche Lorraine,* the region's claim to gastronomic fame. In original versions of this much-maligned peasant dish, a hollowed-out loaf of stale bread was filled with egg custard and a few bits of meat. The hearty *pâtés* of Lorraine often contain marinated veal and beef. Sweets include *ramequin, madeleines* from Commercy, *macarons* from Nancy, and *dragées* from

Verdun. Don't forget to eat large quantities of chocolate-and-cherry *gâteau Forêt Noire* (Black Forest cake).

Trains are undoubtedly the best means of transport in both regions. Buses usually take twice as long as trains and cost nearly the same. Steep hills and frequent storms will discourage all but the most determined bikers. Many hitchers take advantage of the heavy industrial traffic, especially in Lorraine.

A word of caution: Perhaps (as the French claim) a result of German influence, a tendency to enforce regulations to an extent unthinkable elsewhere in France pervades the region. Expect regular and brusque examinations by *contrôleurs* (conductors) aboard buses and trains; losing your bus ticket before the end of the ride or forgetting to validate your train ticket on the platform could cost you 100F—no exceptions or excuses.

Strasbourg

Strasbourg impressed both Goethe and Rousseau—a feat probably not duplicated by any other city. Straddling the German-French border, Strasbourg seems to belong to both cultures. The covered bridges and overhanging half-timbered houses look German; the Gothic churches, wide boulevards, and spacious squares recall France. Part of the Holy Roman Empire in the Middle Ages, Strasbourg nonetheless had Gallic leanings. First attached to France in 1681, Strasbourg did not shift its allegiance during the more recent German presence in the city (1870-1918 and 1940-1944). As 1992 approaches, however,a more ecumenical mood prevails here. Strasbourg now serves as the seat of the 21-nation Council of Europe, an organization of European democratic parliaments and the oldest and largest of European political institutions. In adition, the city is currently locked in a passionate debate with Brussels over which city will become the permanent home to the European Parliament, the elected assembly for the European Community. A Rhine port, a large university town, the home of a considerable Chasidic Jewish community, and a cultural center, the city of over 400,000 handles its present duties with grace, combining modern and traditional elements to create a unique international environment. Hassle-free border crossings make daytrips to Germany convenient.

Orientation and Practical Information

Poised on the German border, Strasbourg lies 4½ hours by train from Paris and 2 hours from Zurich. The old city is virtually an island at the center of Strasbourg, bounded on all sides by a large canal. From the station, go straight on rue du Maire-Kuss and over the bridge to Grand'-rue, which leads directly to the cathedral via rue Gutenberg and rue Hallebardes. If you make a right after crossing the quay from the train station, you will arrive in **La Petite France**, a lovely neighborhood of old Alsatian houses, narrow canals, and restaurants.

Tourist Office: (tel. 88 32 51 49), a kiosk at pl. de la Gare opposite the train station. Almost as comprehensive as the one centrally located at 10, pl. Gutenberg (tel. 88 32 57 07), although the latter is more likely to have up-to-the-minute information on local events. Helpful 2F brochure, available in English, has an adequate map with a street index. Also stocks bus maps, festival brochures, the monthly brochure *Strasbourg actualités* (which covers various events, including the sessions of the European Parliament), and *Saison d'été à Strasbourg* (which lists summer events). Offices open 8am-7pm; April-May and Oct. Gutenberg open daily 9am-6pm, train station open 9am-12:30pm and 1:45-6pm; Nov.-March both open Mon.-Fri. 9am-12:30pm and 1:45-6pm (the Gutenberg office keeps these hours Sat. as well.)

Budget Travel: CROUS, 1, quai du Maire-Dietrich (tel. 88 36 16 91). Will try to set you up in a dorm for 50F per night (July-Aug. only; student ID required). Meal vouchers 10.50F. BIJ/Eurotrain tickets, Britrail passes, French railpasses, and ISICs. Lists hours and locations of student dining halls. Open Mon.-Fri. 9-11:30am and 1:30-4pm. **Centre d'Information Jeunesse d'Alsace,** 7, rue des Ecrivains (tel. 88 37 33 33). Mainly for locals but provides information on occasional organized junkets to the surrounding area. Open Mon.-Fri. 1-6pm.

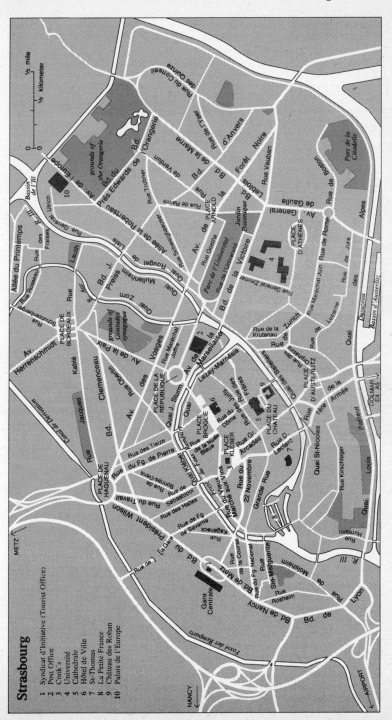

Strasbourg

1 Syndicat d'Initiative (Tourist Office)
2 Post Office
3 Cook's
4 Université
5 Cathédrale
6 Hôtel de Ville
7 St-Thomas
8 La Petite France
9 Château des Rohan
10 Palais de l'Europe

Consulates: U.S., 15, av. d'Alsace (tel. 88 35 31 04), next to pont John F. Kennedy. Open daily 9:30am-noon and 2-5pm. There is no official Canadian consulate, but citizens can seek aid at the office on rue de Ried (tel. 88 96 25 00).

Currency Exchange: Window at the train station open daily 9am-8pm. The best deal is at Change Cathédrale, 7, pl. du Marché-aux-Cochons-de-Lait (tel. 88 23 26 46), behind the cathedral. Decent rates with no commission. Open daily 9:15am-5:30pm.

Post Office: 5, av. de la Marseillaise. **Poste Restante** and **telephones.** Open Mon.-Fri. 8am-7pm, Sat. 8am-noon. Branches at the train station and pl. de la Cathédrale. **Postal code:** 67000.

Trains: pl. de la Gare (tel. 88 22 50 50). Strasbourg is a major European rail junction. To: Paris (every 2 hr., 4½ hr., 238F); Luxembourg (4 per day, 2½ hr., 121F); Frankfurt (every hr., 2½ hr., 181F); Zurich (frequent service, 3 hr., 166F); Vienna (2 per day, 11 hr., 672F); Rome (3 per day, 15 hr., 584F). Frequent connections to Colmar (30 min., 46F), Mulhouse (1 hr., 67F), Molsheim (30 min., 17F), and Obernai (45 min., 25F).

Buses: pl. des Halles (tel. 88 32 36 97). Office open daily 6am-7pm. Maps from tourist offices. Local buses are convenient. Purchase tickets (6.50F) from driver. A *carnet* of 5 (21.30F) available from the tourist office, banks, vending machines, and *tabacs* within sight of a bus stop. Buses go to a few larger towns along the *route du vin,* such as Obernai (frequent, 1 hr., 17F)

Bike Rental: At the train station. 12-speeds 40F per ½-day, 50F per day, deposit 500F. Check at *bagages consigne.* Open daily 6:30am-9:15pm.

Hitchhiking: If you chose to hitch to Paris, take bus #2, 12, or 22 to route des Romains. For Colmar, take bus #3, 13, or 23 to bd. de Lyon and then follow the signs for Colmar to the highway ramp. **Provoya** (tel. 16 1 47 70 02 01) in Paris can set you up with a driver for a small fee.

Bookstores: Librairie Internationale Kléber, 1, rue des Francs-Bourgeois (tel. 88 32 03 83) sells expensive new books in English, as well as those books of the gods, *Let's Go: France* and *Europe.* Open Mon.-Sat. 9am-noon and 2-7pm. **La Librocase,** 2, quai des Pêcheurs (tel. 88 25 50 31). Four shelves of cheap, used English paperbacks. Open Mon.-Fri. 9am-7pm.

Laundromat: 18, rue Edel; 3, rue des Tripiers; or 17, rue Jacques Peirotes. Wash 17F, dry 3F, soap 5F. Bring 10F and 2F coins. Open daily 7am-8pm.

Public Baths and Swimming Pool: 10, bd. de la Victoire (tel. 88 35 51 56). Laneless and lawless heated pool open Mon. noon-7pm, Tues. noon-2pm and 4-9:30pm, Wed.-Sat. 8:15am-7pm. Admission 10F, students 6F. Admission to the sauna or *bain-romain* 50F. Massage (8:15am-noon and 2-6:30pm) 90F. Call before you go, as times for each gender vary. To catch some rays, try the outdoor **Piscine du Wacken,** rue Pierre du Coubertin (tel. 88 31 49 10). 13F. Open June-Aug. daily 10am-8pm.

Pharmacy: Pharmacie de la Rose, 12, rue des Grandes Arcades (tel. 88 32 00 89), off pl. Kléber. English-speaking. Open Mon.-Sat. 9am-noon and 2-7pm.

Rape Crisis Line: SOS Femmes, 16, quai Kléber (tel. 88 75 10 79 or 88 35 25 69). Open 2-7pm.

Medical Assistance: SAMU, tel. 88 33 33 33.

Police: 11, rue de la Nuée-Bleue (tel. 88 32 99 08). **Emergency,** tel. 17.

Accommodations and Camping

Strasbourg is extremely popular. The city has its share of unpleasant budget hotels, and the good places fill quickly in summer. Student dormitories open their doors to travelers from June to September (singles 50F), but availability may be limited. Despite the presence of three hostels, phone reservations a day or two in advance are often necessary, especially on weekends. All the year-round hostels are immaculate and modern, though CIARUS claims by far the best location.

CIARUS (Centre International d'Accueil de Strasbourg), 7, rue Finkmatt (tel. 88 32 12 12). From the train station, take rue de Maire-Kuss to the canal, turn left, and take a left to rue Finkmatt (15 min.). A sparkling new hostel affiliated with the YMCA. Excellent facilities, concerned management, and central location. Curfew 1am. No lockout. Six- to 8-bed dorms 65F per person. 12-bed rooms 60F. Singles 140F. Mattress 50F. Fantastic breakfast included. Lunch or dinner 40F. No reservations accepted July-Aug.

Auberge de Jeunesse René Cassin (IYHF), 9, rue de l'Auberge de Jeunesse (tel. 88 30 26 46), 2km from station. Take bus #3, 13, or 23 from rue du Vieux-Marché-aux-Vins (6.50F, every 20 min.). To get to the bus stop from the train station, go up rue du Maire-Kuss, cross the canal, and take the 2nd left. Wait in the covered booth. An international meeting point. Game room. Reception open 7am-12:30pm and 2pm-midnight. Curfew 1am. Bar open until 1am. Dorm beds 50F. Singles 110F. Doubles, triples, and quads 72F per person. Breakfast included. Hearty lunch or dinner 38F. Camping 29F per person including breakfast.

Auberge de Jeunesse, Centre International de Rencontres du Parc du Rhin (tel. 88 60 10 20), on rue des Cavaliers on the Rhine across from Germany. Take bus #1, 11, or 21 from the train station to Pont-du-Rhin. Then turn left onto rue des Cavaliers and walk 5 min. Beautiful rooms, but inconvenient location and sky-high prices. Open daily 7am-1am. No lockout. Curfew 1am. Singles 150F. Doubles 95F per person. Triples 79F per person. Breakfast and sheets included. Lunch and dinner 45F.

Hôtel de l'Ill, 8, rue des Bateliers (tel. 88 36 20 01), near Eglise Ste-Madeleine. A pleasant two-star hotel next to the river. Singles from 110F. Doubles 155-220F. Bath or shower 10F. Breakfast 20F. Make reservations. Usually closed at some point in June and July.

Hôtel Patricia, 1a, rue du Puits (tel. 88 32 14 60), in the old town between rue de l'Ail and rue de Serruriers, behind Eglise St-Thomas. A bit hard to find, but tranquility and comfort at a reasonable price. Singles 85-100F. Doubles 100-180F. Breakfast 17F.

Hôtel du Jura, 5, rue du Marché (tel. 88 32 12 72), near the station inside the old city off rue du Vieux-Marché-aux-Vins. Clean and comfortable. Closed 11am-2pm. Curfew midnight. Singles and doubles 110-160F. Breakfast 19F.

Hôtel Michelet, 48, rue du Vieux-Marché-aux-Poissons (tel. 88 32 47 38). Excellent location 2 blocks from the cathedral, off pl. Gutenberg. Dark halls and stairways lead to cramped but clean rooms. Singles and doubles 95-195F. Showers 10F. Extra bed 20-25F. 15F breakfast obligatory with some rooms.

Hôtel Weber, 22, bd. de Nancy (tel. 88 32 36 47). Turn right out of the station and follow bd. de Metz as it becomes bd. de Nancy (5 min.). One of the more pleasant establishments near the station. Same management as Hôtel Patricia. Singles 90-150F, doubles 100-240F. Showers 12F. Breakfast 17F.

Camping: La Montagne Verte (tel. 88 30 25 46), on rue du Schnokeloch next to the René Cassin youth hostel. Take bus #3, 13, or 23 to Nid de Cigogne. Excellent facilities include showers, tennis courts, a bar, and restaurant (35F and 50F *menus*). Adults 9F, ages under 10 4.50F. 9F per tent. Electricity 6F. Open March-Oct. 7am-10pm. **Baggersee** (tel. 88 39 03 40), on route de Colmar on Lac du Baggersee. Take bus #13 or 23 (*direction* "Graffenstaden-Fegersheim") as far as Baggersee. Also excellent. Adults 10F, ages under 7 5F. 10F per tent. Electricity 8F. Open July to mid-Sept. 24 hrs.

Food

Restaurants around the cathedral and La Petite France are predictably expensive. If you're feeling profligate, dine in one of the *winstubs,* informal restaurants that were traditionally affiliated with an individual winery. Think twice about ordering the *choucroute garnie,* which often turns out to be multi-colored neon hot dogs in bland sauerkraut. Fast food places and several grocery stores cluster around pl. Kléber, but resist the call of the Big Mac and check out the Alsatian restaurants around rue de la Douane and pl. St-Etienne. Ask the tourist office about Strasbourg's numerous markets, held every day but Sunday. The largest fills pl. de Bordeaux with fruit and vegetables (Sat. 9am-1pm).

Au Pont St-Martin, 13-15, rue des Moulins. You can't miss this enormous tripledecker restaurant by the river in La Petite France. The volume of tourists and locals keeps their prices a little lower than the rest. Plates heaped higher than Brümhilde's wig. Three-course 40F lunch *menu* served Mon.-Fri. *A la carte* 38-72F. Open daily noon-3pm and 7-11pm.

La Plouzinette, 9, pl. St-Etienne, east of the cathedral. A small, pleasant *traiteur* with dozens of *crêpes* for under 30F and picnic tables facing the square. Kirsch and Grand-Marnier *flambées* 24F. A great place for lunch. Open Mon.-Sat. 11:30am-10:30pm.

L'Assiette du Chasseur, 16, rue des Tonneliers, off rue de la Douane. Small and homey. 38F *plat du jour* for lunch Mon.-Fri. *A la carte* is not so cheap, but offers a tasty *quiche Lorraine* for 35F. Open Tues.-Sun. noon-2pm and 7-11pm.

Royal Saigon, 8, rue de l'Ecurie, off rue de la Douane. Full of locals. Unusual Chinese and Vietnamese dishes 22-48F. Excellent, fiery specialties. If you call a day in advance, the chef will prepare exotic dishes such as Chinese mushrooms stuffed with shark's fin. Open Tues.-Sun. noon-2pm and 7-11pm.

Chez Faisan and **Chez Aldo 1 & 2,** 8, rue du Faisan. Even more popular with local youth than the New Kids. Large groups may have problems finding a table on weekend nights. Design your own pizzas and salads with unlimited toppings (36F). *Plat du jour* (39F) and Donnieburger (30F). Open daily noon-2pm and 6:30-11:30pm.

FEC, pl. St-Etienne. The best of the student restaurants. Tickets 19F, local students 9F. Other student restaurants are **Paul Appel,** 10, rue de Palerme (tel. 88 35 66 00); **Esplanade,** 32, bd. de la Victoire (tel. 88 61 32 57); **Gallia,** 1, pl. de l'Université; and **Le Minotaure,** next door. Only the first 2 are open in summer. CROUS knows what's open when.

Lait's Go, 27, rue des Frères, off pl. de la Cathédral. Pronounced just like the name of a premier travel guide, this popular place calls its menu *Le Guide du Lait's Go.* Everything from *café crèmes* to exotic cocktails (15F). Open Mon.-Sat. 7am-9pm. This is not a joke.

Sights

Constructed from rose-colored Vosges sandstone between the 11th and 15th centuries, the ornate Gothic **Cathédrale de Strasbourg** thrusts its single tower nearly high enough to puncture the ozone layer. Inside, the **Horloge Astronomique** demonstrates the technical wizardry of 16th-century Swiss clock makers. Each day at 12:30pm, the apostles parade out of the face and a cock crows to greet St. Peter. Get there at least a half-hour early in July and August to beat the crowds. (Admission 4F, tickets sold at the tourist office or cathedral.) While waiting to see the clock's display, examine the cathedral's central **Pilier des Anges** (Angels' Pillar), decorated by an anonymous 13th-century master from Chartres. The same artist also produced the statues flanking the south portal, which portray the church and the synagogue as two women. The cathedral's 142m tower made it the tallest monument in Christendom until the last century. If you climb for a view, you'll be following in the footsteps of Victor Hugo, who had particular affection for "perpendicular travel," as well as the young Goethe, who scaled the height regularly in hopes of curing his acute acrophobia. (Tower open June-Sept. 9am-7pm. Admission 7F.) The slightly corny yet eerie *son et lumière* presentation within gives a dramatic history of the city and cathedral. English presentations are scheduled to begin in 1991; ask the tourist office for times. (April 22-Sept. daily at 8:15pm (German) and 9:15pm (French). Admission 23F, students 14F. Cathedral open daily 7-11:40am and 12:45-7pm.)

The museums are all near the cathedral. The **Musée Alsacien,** 23, quai St-Nicolas, houses an interesting display of handicrafts, costumes, furniture, and regional art. A 14th- to 16th-century mansion opposite the cathedral, the **Maison de l'Oeuvre Notre-Dame** displays sculpture, stained glass, and other artifacts from the Romanesque, Gothic, and Renaissance periods. In the palatial **Château des Rohan,** a magnificent 18th-century building commissioned by the first Cardinal de Rohan-Soubise, a triumvirate of small, noteworthy museums that focus on archaeology, fine arts, and decorative arts. The excellent **Musée d'Art Moderne,** 5, pl. du Château, also across from the cathedral, has paintings and sculptures by Klimt, Chagall, Klee, and Arp (a *Strasbourgeois*) as well as Impressionist works. Many of the famous works are (rather prematurely) in storage while the museum prepares for their 1994 move into a larger building for which the ground hasn't even been broken. (All museums open Wed.-Mon. 10am-noon and 2-6pm; Oct.-March Mon. and Wed.-Sat. 2-6pm, Sun. 10am-noon and 2-6pm. Admission to Château des Rohan and its collections 15F, students 8F. All other museums 10F, students 5F.)

The **Palais de l'Europe,** composed of Vosges sandstone and oxidized aluminum, was opened by former French President Giscard d'Estaing in 1977 to house the Council of Europe and the European Parliament. When either organization is in session (at least one week every month), you may register at the desk for a look from the visitor's gallery, where headsets translating the debates into several languages are available. (Bring your passport. Guided visits in English Mon.-Fri. 10am and 4pm. Free.) Across the street lies peaceful **Parc de l'Orangerie,** designed in 1692 by Le Nôtre, architect of Versailles. Sadly, the animals in the small zoo aren't as well cared for as the flowers. (Always open.)

La Petite France, the old tanner's district, remains one of Strasbourg's prettiest and most visited neighborhoods. Tall Alsatian houses with steep roofs and carved wooden façades overlook narrow canals and locks. The streets here are full of budget-breaking cafés and tearooms.

Goethe, Napoleon, and Metternich all graduated from the **Université de Strasbourg,** established in the 17th century. Follow bd. de la Victoire or rue de Zurich out to the new university quarters at the esplanade. The seven faculties are located in the area known as Palais de l'Université, which extends across bd. de la Victoire to rue Goethe and rue de l'Université, where there are beautiful botanical gardens and parks.

Entertainment

For information on all kinds of free entertainment in summer, pick up *Saison d'été à Strasbourg* or the more complete *Strasbourg actualités* at the tourist office. Both are free. In the courtyard of **Château des Rohan,** a series of folk dancing demonstrations take place in June, July, and August (Sun. 10:30am and various evenings 8:30pm). From June through mid-September, free concerts are given on Thursday at 8:30pm in **Parc des Contades** and once per week in the **Pavilion Joséphine** in the Parc de l'Orangerie. June brings the celebrated **Festival International de Musique;** for information, contact the Société des Amis de la Musique, 24, rue de la Mésange (tel. 88 32 43 10). Last year's festival attracted the likes of Jessye Norman, Herbie Hancock, and Dizzie Gillespie. Some concerts are free, but most start at 150F. **Musica,** a contemporary music festival that takes place each September or October, has featured such novelties as music played underwater in the public swimming pool. Call 88 35 32 34 or 88 75 19 88 for schedules. From October through June, the **Orchestre Philharmonique de Strasbourg** performs at the Palais de la Musique et des Congrès, behind pl. de Bordeaux. Productions of the **Théâtre National de Strasbourg** are staged at their resident theater at 7, pl. de la République (tel. 88 35 63 60). (Admission to all plays 150F, students 50F.) The **Opéra du Rhin** brings opera, operetta, and ballet to the opera house at 19, pl. Broglie (tel. 88 36 43 41). (Admission 30-170F.) The annual **Festival Européen de Cinéma d'Art et d'Essai,** 32, rue du Vieux-Marché-aux-Vins (tel. 88 32 12 30) unreels each November and December.

Those without tuxedoes and spare cash may find themselves whiling summer evenings away in **place de la Cathédrale,** where musicians, mimes, comedians, and acrobats perform for huge crowds. In recent years, this area has been plagued by so-called "live mannequins," charlatans who try to make a buck by standing still for a few hours. Sports fans should check out the **water-jousting** competitions which occur Monday through Friday on the Ill river outside Palais de Rohan (July-Aug. 8:30pm).

Le Rock's Feller, rue du Jeu des Enfants (tel. 88 32 31 22) packs St. Vitus's dancers onto its American 1950s-style dance floor nightly. A slightly older and more *soigné* crowd gathers at **Le Charlie's,** 24, pl. des Halles (tel. 88 22 32 22) to writhe to the latest dance hits. **L'Appollo,** 1, rue du Miroir (tel. 88 32 63 74), is a popular gay and lesbian disco. All three clubs charge about a 60F cover and are open 11pm-late.

Near Strasbourg: The Route du Vin

The back roads connecting the many small towns and extensive vineyards, known as the *route du vin,* offer a rich sampling of Alsace's varied bouquets. The vineyards are peppered with medieval ruins and small villages, whose immense popularity hardly diminishes their charms. During the autumn grape harvests, the towns come alive with colorful bacchanalian festivals. Watch for vine wreaths hung outside establishments where *vin nouveau* is available. The vineyards are most easily visited by car. Hitchhiking is slow and many of the smaller towns are served either infrequently or not at all from Strasbourg. **Hertz,** 6, bd. de Metz (tel. 88 32 57 62), offers the cheapest car, a Ford Fiesta, for about 250F per day plus 3.99F per km. (Open Mon.-Fri. 8am-noon and 2-7pm; Sun. open until 6pm.) **Budget,** 31, bd. de Nancy (tel. 88 75 68 29), and **Avis,** pl. de la Gare (tel. 88 32 30 44), are worth a try. You'll want plenty of time to stop for *dégustations* in various *caves;* the tourist offices at Strasbourg (tel. 88 32 51 49) and Colmar (tel. 89 41 02 29) provide information on specific routes and *caves* and sponsor expensive weekly summer tours for around 80F.

Several of the larger towns are accessible by local trains. Located at the foot of the Vosges, **Molsheim** is the largest and quite popular. The town hall, the **Metzig,** has a tower, clock, and moondial from the 16th century. Pick up information near the center at small **Musée Regional,** which displays wine equipment and local curiosities. (Open Mon.-Fri. 2-6pm. Free.) There is no tourist office; call 88 38 76 95 for information on *cave* tours and wine tastings. Guided tours of the vineyards leave from the town hall (June-Aug., Mon. and Thurs. at 10am).

Riquewihr, 60km south of Strasbourg, widely considered the most beautiful town on the route, is unfortunately not connected by bus or train to Strasbourg. The 16th-century walled village lures thousands of tourists in summer, and prices for food and lodging are high. Built in 1291, the **Musée du Dolder** in the Tour du Dolder houses a collection of 15th-century firearms (open May-Oct. 5 daily 9am-noon and 1:30-6pm; admission 6F), while the beautiful **Tour des Voleurs** (Thieves' Tower) contains a bloodcurdling torture chamber with a collection of evil-looking devices to rival Donnie Wahlberg's curling iron. (Open Easter-Oct. daily 9am-noon and 1:30-6pm. Admission 6F). The **tourist office,** 2, rue de la 1ère Armée (tel. 89 47 80 80), distributes a list of rooms in private houses. Prices vary; the cheapest run from 85F. (Open July-Aug. daily 10am-7pm; June and Sept. 10am-noon and 2-7pm.) Otherwise, try the four-star **Camping International** (tel. 89 47 90 08), 1km from the town center. (12F per person, 6F per tent. Open April-Oct.)

A few kilometers south of Riquewihr at the entrance to the Weiss valley, the ancient, flower-filled village of **Kaysersberg** attracts fewer visitors than Riquewirh to its equally lovely streets. The 13th-century fortress is just a ruin, but some healthy 15th-century houses cluster around the 15th-century fortified bridge. The 13th-century **Eglise Ste-Croix** is home to Jean Bogartz's outstanding *retable,* completed in 1518. Located off a medieval courtyard at 62, rue du Général de Gaulle, the town's **musée** displays some excellent polychrome statues and a much prized 14th-century statue of the Virgin. (Open July-Aug. daily 10am-noon and 2-6pm; June and Sept.-Oct. Sat.-Sun. 10am-noon and 2-6pm.) Kaysersberg was also the birthplace of Nobel Prize-winning physician Albert Schweitzer; visit the **Centre Culturel Albert Schweitzer,** 126, rue du Général de Gaulle (open May-Oct. daily 9am-noon and 2-6pm; admission 7F). Farther along the street near the entrance to town, the **tourist office** (tel. 89 47 10 16), occupies the ground floor of the town hall. (Open Sat.-Thurs. 8am-noon and 2-6pm, Fri. 8am-noon and 2-5pm; in off-season Mon.-Thurs. 8am-noon and 1-5pm, Fri. 8am-noon and 1-4pm.) The four-star **municipal campground** outside of town on rue des Acacias (tel. 89 47 14 47) opens from April through September. (12F per person, 8.50F per tent.) Kaysersberg is only accessible by bus from Colmar (3 per day, 30 min., 19F).

Kintzheim, closer to Strasbourg and near Sélestat on the edge of the *route du vin,* possesses a remarkable library of priceless Merovingian documents. The **tourist office** on pl. de la Fontaine (tel. 88 82 09 90, in winter 88 82 09 88) has brochures of local sights. (Open in summer daily 10am-12:30pm and 2:30-6:30pm.) The ruined **Château de Kintzheim** (tel. 88 92 84 33) now holds Europe's best-known aviary of predatory birds; eagles, vultures, and falcons fly only a few meters above your head. (Open April-Sept. daily from 2pm; Oct.-Nov. 11 Wed. and Sat.-Sun. only.) At **La Montagne des Singes** (tel. 88 92 11 09), in the mountains fringing the town, 300 Moroccan macaques (otherwise known as Barbary Apes) cavort freely in 20 hectares of enclosed Vosgian forest. (Open April-Sept. Mon.-Sat. 10am-noon and 1:30-6pm, longer hours Sun. Admission, including a handful of popcorn to feed the macaques, 22F.) Ascend to the 755m peak of the mountain, where hundreds of tourists enjoy the view from the **Château du Haut Koenigsbourg.** Constructed in the 12th century and burned by the Swedish in 1618 during the Thirty Years' War, it was occupied and rebuilt by Emperor William II of Germany in the late 19th century. (Open March 16-Sept. daily 9am-noon and 1-6pm; Oct.-Jan. 5 and Feb. 5-March 15 9am-noon and 1-4pm. Admission 30F.) No accommodations exist at the top of the mountain, and those in the valley are expensive. The closest you can get by train to Kintzheim and its surrounding sights is charming St-Hippolyte; from there you'll have to walk the remaining distance (2 trains per day from Strasbourg, 1 hr., 37F).

If you're heading back to Strasbourg, try to go through **Obernai, Dambach-la-Ville,** and nearby **Scherwiller,** quaint villages hidden among vineyards. Several local *caves* offer *dégustations.*

Colmar

Surrounded by vineyards and the craggy Vosges mountains, Colmar (pop. 70,000) gets its name from the *colombes* (doves) Charlemagne kept at his estate along the Lauch river. Other illustrious past residents include sculptor Auguste Bartholdi, whose Statue of Liberty and other creations have provided birds all over the world with grandiose perches. Today, tourists flock here to wander the 15th- and 16th-century streets of scenic Petite Venise and wonder at Grünewald's magnificent Issenheim Altarpiece and Schongauer's *Virgin of the Rosebush.*

Orientation and Practical Information

Colmar lies 450km east of Paris, 375km north of Lyon, and 215km west of Stuttgart. To get to the tourist office from the station, turn left onto rue de la Gare and follow it as it becomes rue de Lattre de Tassigny and rue Roesselmann. Turn right onto rue des Interlinden; the tourist office will be on your left.

Tourist Office: 4, rue des Unterlinden (tel. 89 41 02 29), across from the Unterlinden Museum. A helpful city map. List of hotels, restaurants, campgrounds, and rooms in private homes (most available by the week or month only). English spoken. Organized tours to the villages of the region. Open mid-June to mid-Sept. daily 9am-12:30pm and 1:30-7pm; in winter Mon.-Fri. same hours, Sat. 9am-noon and 2-6pm, Sun. 9:30am-noon. 8am-12:30pm and 1:30-7pm, Sat. 9am-noon and 2-6pm, Sun. 9:30am-noon.

Post Office: 36-38, av. de la République, across from a park. Open Mon.-Fri. 8am-7pm, Sat. 8am-noon. **Postal code:** 68000.

Trains: (tel. 89 41 66 80), pl. de la Gare. To: Paris (6 per day, 5 hr., 264F); Basel (Bâle), Switzerland (15 per day, 1 hr., 51F); Nancy (3 per day, 2 hr., 123F); Lyon (4 per day, 4½ hr., 205F). Countless runs to Strasbourg (½-hr., 46F) and Mulhouse (½ hr., 33F). **Lockers** 5F. Information office open Mon. 8am-7:30pm, Tues.-Thurs. 7:40am-7:30pm, Fri.-Sat. 8am-10:30pm, Sun. 9:10am-8pm.

Buses: Several private companies run from the train station to Riquewihr, St-Hippolyte, Kaysersberg, Ribeauville, and Eguisheim on the *route du vin.* The tourist office's *Actualités de Colmar* lists schedules and destinations. **Voyages Pauli,** 55, rue des Clefs (tel. 89 41 66 80), offers organized tours of the region and beyond. To Fribourg, Germany, and the Black Forest, the Oberland Bernois (Switzerland) including Interlaken and Lucerne, and Lake Constance. Combined Rhine cruise and steam-train trip. Office open Mon. 2-6pm, Tues.-Fri. 8:30am-noon and 2-6pm, Sat. 8:30am-noon.

Bike Rental: (tel. 89 23 17 17), at the train station. 3-speeds 40F per ½-day (5am-1pm or 1-9pm), 50F per day. 10-speeds 50F per ½-day, 60F per day. Open daily 5:15am-9:15pm.

Laundromat: 8, rue Turenne, through La Petite Venise off the main canal. Wash 12-15F, dry 2F per 7½ min. Soap 4F. Bring 10F and 2F coins. Open daily 8am-9pm.

Pharmacy: Pharmacie du Lion, 4, rue Stanislas (tel. 89 41 22 85), off pl. Rapp. Open Mon. 1:45-6:45pm, Tues.-Sat. 8:15am-12:15pm and 1:45-6:45pm.

Medical Assistance: SAMU, tel. 15.

Police: 6, rue du Chasseur (tel. 89 41 08 00). **Emergency,** tel. 17.

Accommodations and Camping

No problem.

Maison des Jeunes (Centre International de Séjour), 17, rue Camille-Schlumberger (tel. 89 41 26 87), 3 blocks from the station in a pleasant residential neighborhood, 10 min. from the center of town. Walk straight out of the station and take the third right. Probably the best deal in Colmar. TV room, beer, and soda in the evening. Registration 8am-noon and 2-11pm. Curfew 11pm. 35F per person. Sheets 16F.

Auberge de Jeunesse (IYHF), 2, rue Pasteur (tel. 89 80 57 39). A 25-min. walk from the station along the tracks. Take the subterranean passage in the station to rue du Tir and follow it as it curves and becomes rue du Florimont. Cross pl. St-Joseph on your right, and take rue de la Bagatelle 1 block. Turn left onto route d'Ingersheim, then right on rue Pasteur. Fairly small but clean. Basic facilities. 37F per person; singles 52F. Breakfast 15F. Sheets 16F. Lockout 10am-5pm. Curfew midnight.

La Chaumière, 74, av. de la République (tel. 89 41 08 99), near the station. Most of the clean, simple rooms face a courtyard. Bar downstairs is a local hangout. Singles 130F. Doubles 150-180F. Showers 15F. Breakfast 25F.

Camping: A 3-star site (tel. 89 41 15 94) about ½km out of town. Take route de Neuf Brisach (RN415) out of town and across the Ill River. Alternately, take bus #1 (*direction* "Wihr") to plage d'Ill. 9.50F per person, 4.50F per tent. Open Feb.-Nov.

Food

Inexpensive restaurants are hard to come by in Colmar, so you may end up celebrating the Night of Cheese Sandwiches. Several concessions on rue des Clefs serve piping hot *tartes flambées* and pizza during the day. Fresh produce goes on sale in pl. du Marché-aux-Fruits (Thurs. 6am-6pm) and pl. de la Cathédrale (Thurs. 6am-6pm and Sat. noon-6pm).

La Taverne, 2, impasse de la Maison Rouge. An elegant place serving *salades composées* (39F), a 50F fixed lunch *menu*, and a 60F dinner *menu*. Try the sherbet. Open Tues.-Fri. noon-1:30pm and 7-10:30pm, Sat. 7-10:30pm.

Le Sereno, 12, rue des Marchands. Pizza from 34F. *Calzones* from 42F. Open noon-1:30pm and 6:45-11pm. Closed Thurs. and Sun. lunch.

Auberge de l'Ill, 8, rue de l'Ill (tel. 89 41 29 44). 2km northeast of town on route de Neuf Brisach (RN415) just 2 blocks beyond the canal, near the campground. Take bus #1 towards Horbourg and stop at Dornig. A real trek from the center, but definitely worth the trip. Where locals go for a special night out. Some of the largest portions you'll see in France. Main courses 40-80F. Salads and spaghetti from 38F. Open Wed.-Mon. noon-2pm and 7-10pm. Call ahead or be prepared to wait.

Cafétéria Flunch, 8, av. de la République, at pl. Rapp. An orgy of plastic self-service. Filling meals 30-50F. You will be charged for everything—bread, sauce, and air. Open daily 11am-9:30pm. **L'Ami Frit,** a busy take-out across the street in a parking lot, has hamburgers for under 15F. Eat in the park beyond the parking lot. Open daily 8am-midnight.

Sights and Entertainment

Colmar's restored half-timbered houses are excellent examples of regional architecture and of the local mania for painting plaster in various pastel shades. For the finest examples, visit the **Quartier des Tanneurs,** then follow rue des Tanneurs over a small canal to the delightful area called **La Petite Venise.** The multi-colored roof and amber-colored stone of **Collégiale St-Martin** stands out here. Set among the ancient homes around rue des Marchands, a beautiful 14th-century house with Gothic windows faces the church. Two blocks to the west on pl. des Dominicains,

Eglise des Dominicains, lit by mellifluous 14th-century stained-glass windows, displays Martin Schongauer's intricate *Virgin of the Rosebush* in its choir. (Altar open for viewing April-Oct. daily 10am-6pm. Admission 5F, students 3F.)

The extraordinary **Musée Unterlinden,** on pl. Unterlinden contains a large collection of medieval religious art in a former Dominican convent that retains its cloister and chapel. Famous for its primitive Alsatian masters, the collection has its true gem in Mathias Grünewald's *Issenheim Altarpiece,* a 16th-century blending of the realistic and the fantastic. Two rooms in the basement display modern art, including a tapestry rendition of Picasso's *Guernica.* (Open daily 9am-6pm; Nov.-March 9am-noon and 2-5pm. Admission 22F, students 11F.) At 30, rue des Marchands, across from the 16th-century Maison Pfister, the **Musée Bartholdi** displays Colmar memorabilia from the 11th through the 19th centuries as well as the sculptor's personal effects. (Open daily 10am-noon and 2-6pm; Nov.-March Sat.-Sun. 10am-noon and 2-5pm. Admission 10F, students 5F.)

Every Tuesday evening at 9pm from June to September, a folkart exhibition fills pl. de l'Ancienne-Douane. Eglise des Dominicains hosts evening concerts on Thursdays from June through August. (Tickets 45F, ages under 21 25F; the tourist office has a schedule.) The annual **Alsatian Wine Festival,** held in early August, means wine, beer, and agricultural equipment for all. From September 1 to 12, the overwhelmingly popular **Jours Choucroute** (Sauerkraut Days), bring feasting, dancing, roistering, and—you guessed it—*choucroute.*

Nancy

According to history books, Nancy (pop. 135,000) dates from the 11th century, when Gérard d'Alsace, founder of the hereditary duchy of Lorraine, built a fortified castle on a piece of land between two marshes of the Meurthe river. But according to the eyes, this fine Baroque city dates from the 17th century, when King Stanislas Lesczynski of Poland managed to erect gilded gates around pl. Stanislas and the intricate façades seen all over town before burning to death in his own fireplace. With a resident symphony, ballet, opera companies, and numerous museums, this rather aloof city claims to be the cultural hub of Lorraine. Fortunately, the 30,000 students support a number of interesting restaurants and bars and maintain Nancy's longtime passion for jazz.

Orientation and Practical Information

Nancy is 310km from Paris, 150km directly west of Strasbourg, and 130km from Luxembourg. Leaving the station to your left, take a right at the Hôtel Agora on rue Raymond-Poincaré, which turns into rue Stanislas, and opens onto the main square, pl. Stanislas. Although the town center lies close to the train station, Nancy's sights are scattered across a huge valley. Learn the bus system or wear sturdy shoes.

Tourist Office: 14, pl. Stanislas (tel. 83 35 22 41), to the right of the triumphal arch. The eager staff will find you a room free and load you up with dozens of brochures and maps. Tours of the city in French daily at 3pm (18F) and 9pm (20F), including the Hôtel de Ville and *son et lumière* (1½ hr., July-Sept. only). Open Mon.-Sat. 9am-7pm, Sun. 10am-1pm.

Post Office: rue Pierre-Fourier, behind the Hôtel de Ville, 1 block from pl. Stanislas. Open Mon.-Fri. 8am-7pm, Sat. 8am-noon. **Postal code:** 54000.

Trains: pl. Thiers (tel. 83 56 50 50). Frequent connections to Lunéville (30 min., 27F), Strasbourg (1½ hr., 90F), Metz (45 min., 40F), and Paris via Verdun (3 hr., 185F). Lockers 12-25F. Information office open Mon.-Sat. 5:30am-7:30pm, Sun. 6:30am-8:30pm.

Buses: Rapides de Lorraine, on pl. de la Cathédrale (tel. 83 32 34 20). To: Verdun (2 per day, 2½ hr., 60.70F); Epinal (2 per day, 2 hr., 46F); and Lunéville (1 per day, 1 hr., 24.50F). Information office open Mon.-Sat. 6am-8pm. Buy local bus tickets here (5.50F, *carnet* of 10 33F). Also **Transcars: Les Courriers Mosellans,** pl. Colonel-Driant (tel. 83 32 23 58).

Pharmacy: 4, pl. Thiers, across from the train station (tel. 83 36 53 58). Open Mon.-Sat. 9am-6pm.

Hospital: C.H.U. Brabois, on RN74 (tel. 83 55 81 20). **Emergency: SAMU,** tel. 83 32 85 79.

Police: Commissariat Central, 38, bd. Lobau (tel. 83 32 34 20). **Emergency,** tel. 17.

Accommodations, Camping, and Food

Finding a room here should be easy even in summer. Since the lcoation and early curfew of the *Centre d'Accueil* preclude painting the town even a faint pink, consider spending a few francs more for a hotel room in the *centre ville.*

Hôtel Pasteur, 47, rue Pasteur (tel. 83 40 29 85), on the other side of town from the train station. Turn left on either rue Patton or rue Kennedy behind the station, right on rue de Mon-Désert, and left on rue Graffigny to rue Pasteur. Attractive rooms in an upscale neighborhood. Singles and doubles 85-115F. Breakfast 18F. Sometimes closed on Sun.; call ahead.

Centre d'Accueil de Remicourt (tel. 83 27 73 67), 19, rue de Vandoeuvre, Villiers-lès-Nancy, 4km southwest of town in Château de Remicourt. Buy a bus ticket at the *consigne-baggages* desk in the train station. Take bus #4 from the station to Basch and walk left past 3 lights along the uphill bd. des Aiguillettes (25 min.). Bus #26 stops uphill from the hostel ("St-Fiacre" stop) but runs only Mon.-Sat. 7am-7:45pm. To your left, across a park, you will see the castle. Spectacularly inconvenient location. Extremely solicitous management. Bar and kitchen. Curfew 10pm. Singles with sheets 36F. Breakfast 9.50F. Dinner 34.50F.

Hôtel Le Jean Jaurès, 14, bd. Jean-Jaurès (tel. 83 27 74 14), on a continuation of rues Patton and Kennedy. A 2-star establishment with some cheaper rooms. Very reasonable prices for this caliber of hotel. Singles from 85F. Doubles from 95F. Breakfast 20F.

Hôtel Moderne, 73, rue Jeanne d'Arc (tel. 83 40 14 26). A kind, elderly proprietor manages the weary but decent rooms. Frayed carpets and peeling paint. Not a place where you would want to settle permanently, but incredibly cheap. Singles 44-67F, doubles 55-80F, triples 90F.

Camping: Camping de Brabrois (tel. 83 27 18 28), on RN74 towards Dijon. A 2-star site with telephones and showers. 9F per person, 4.40F per tent or car. Open April-Oct.

The art-nouveau **l'Excelsior,** 50, rue Henri Poincaré, across from the station, is an elegant (if extremely overpriced) place to sip coffee while waiting for train connections. The 65F *menu* at spiffy **Le Vaudemont,** 4, pl. Vaudemont, that includes a local dish and quiche. (Open daily 7pm-midnight.) For full meals with German flair, try **Taverne des Dominicains,** 45, rue des Dominicains (tel. 83 32 10 65), which serves authentic *choucroute* (42-60F) and presents live bands on Sunday nights in winter. (Open daily 8:30am-late.) **Le Téméraire,** 17, Grande Rue (tel. 83 37 46 91), presents live jazz and café-theater two nights weekly; call ahead for reservations. (65F *menu.* Open noon-2pm and 6pm-2am.) Just down the street at #31, **Le Taj-Mahal** serves Indian dishes spiced with cayenne peppers grown in Ben Lehrer's garden. (Lunch *menu* 65F, *entrees* 15-28F. Open daily noon-2pm and 7-10pm.) You can also buy food at the indoor/outdoor **market** held in front of Eglise St-Sébastien. (Open Mon.-Sat. 9am-noon and 2-5pm.)

Sights and Entertainment

Designed by 18th-century architect Emmanuel Héré, **place Stanislas** magnificently sets off the façades, balustrades, gilt-tipped wrought iron railings, and fountains of the 17th-century Hôtel de Ville. The square is most spectacular around 10pm, when the *son et lumière* arrive. The Bastille Day celebration here is fabulous, said to be rivaled only by the festivities in Paris.

The **Musée des Beaux-Arts,** 3, pl. Stanislas (tel. 83 37 65 01), has an impressive collection of 17th-century paintings and a good selection of modern works by Matisse, Modigliani, and Dufy. (Open Wed.-Sun. 10:30am-6pm. Admission 12F, students 8F, students free on Wed.) Pass under **Porte Royale,** the finest of Nancy's seven triumphal arches, and descend to **Parc de la Pépinière,** a blend of English and French garden styles and the site of frequent summer concerts. Peacocks strut about freely in the **zoo,** while tourists and *Nancéiens* pose in the outdoor café. To the left of the astounding rose garden, the **Palais Ducal** houses the **Musée Lorraine** (tel. 83 32 18 72), an eclectic collection of paintings, sculpture, Roman artifacts, costumes, tapestries from the ducal palace, and the standard of Henry II, reputedly the oldest French flag in existence. (Open Wed.-Mon. 10am-6pm, Sept. 15-April Wed.-Mon. 10am-noon and 2-7pm. Admission 15F, students 10F.)

A walk through the **Arc de Triomphe** from pl. Stanislas takes you to the 18th-century **place de la Carrière.** At the end of this courtyard, twisting streets lead to **Porte de la Craffe;** the impressive guard towers are all that remain of the 14th-century fortifications. On the periphery of the city, opposite the station, is the **Musée de l'Ecole de Nancy,** 36, rue du Sergent-Blandan (tel. 83 40 14 86), France's contribution to *art nouveau.* Walk 20 minutes from the town cente, or take bus #5 (5.50F) from *Point-Central.* It contains rooms with carved wood paneling, furniture, and glasswork, notably that of Emile Gallé. (Open Wed.-Mon. 10am-noon and 2-6pm; Oct.-March Wed.-Mon. 10am-noon and 2-5pm. Admission 12F, students 8F.) The **Musée des Arts et Traditions Populaires** in the Couvent des Cordeliers, 66, Grande Rue, depicts life in Lorraine before the industrial era. (Open Wed.-Mon. 10am-6pm; Sept. 15-April 10am-noon and 2-5pm. Admission 10F, students 7F.) Other museums include the **Musée des Sciences de la Terre** (geology), **Musée de Zoologie et Aquarium Tropical** (zoology), and the **Musée du Fer,** which traces the history of iron production through three millennia.

In mid-October, the **Festival de Jazz** showcases an international convoy of musicians who swing from dusk to dawn in a tent in Parc de la Pepinière. Call 83 35 40 86 for information. In winter, **La Comédie de Lorraine** produces excellent contemporary plays. Every two months, the tourist office puts out the free pamphlet *Spectacles à Nancy,* which has complete listings of expositions in progress and free concerts, theater productions, and movies. University crowds do the Desai until dawn at **La Scala,** 22, rue St-Dizier (tel. 83 32 83 42) and **Les Caves du Roy,** 9, pl. Stanislas (tel. 83 35 24 14). Both charge 60F cover and are open from 10pm-late.

Lunéville

In the first decade of the 18th century, Duke Leopold fled to this negligible town from French-occupied Nancy. Here, he and Duchess Elizabeth-Charlotte enjoyed peeled grapes at an elegant court, the so-called "Versailles of the last dukes of Lorraine and Bar." Leopold laid out wide boulevards and squares based on formal conceptions of 18th-century urban planning and began building Eglise St-Jacques. In 1766 Lunéville passed into the hands of the dethroned adventurer-king of Poland, Stanislas Leszczynski, who built the flamboyant pl. Stanislas in Nancy, completed Eglise St-Jacques in effusive Eastern European baroque style, and made his court into an important intellectual center, drawing Voltaire and other glowing literati. Upon Stanislas's accidental death by burning alive in his own fireplace, Lorraine became French. After a century of shuffling between German and French hands, Lunéville is today the peaceful home (and safe hearth) of 23,000. The town's marvelous château and gardens alone merit a daytrip from Nancy or Metz.

Orientation and Practical Information

Lunéville is 30km east of Nancy and 70km southeast of Metz. To reach the center of town from the station, walk straight ahead and bear left. Everything of interest is within a small radius of the old town.

Tourist Office: (tel. 83 74 06 55), on pl. de la 2*ème* D.C., in the château's left wing (to your right as you face the building). Maps and a charming homespun walking guide, *Un jour à Lunéville* (French only). *Lunéville programme* lists the month's events. The gregarious staff speaks very little English. Open daily 9am-noon and 2-6pm.

Post Office: (tel. 83 73 19 32), on rue de Sarrebourg. Open Mon.-Fri. 8am-7pm, Sat. 8am-noon. **Postal Code:** 54300.

Trains: 2, pl. Pierre Sémard (tel. 83 56 50 50 or 83 73 60 70). Frequent service to Paris (4 hr., 190F) and Strasbourg (1½ hr., 69F). Trains from Nancy (every 2 hr., 30 min., 26F). Information office open Mon.-Sat. 8am-7pm.

Buses: pl. Monseigneur Ruch in Nancy (tel. 83 32 34 20). Call for schedules of buses from Nancy and surrounding villages. Buses from Nancy cost slightly less than trians (24.50F) but take three times as long.

Hitchhiking: If you decide to hitchhike to Nancy and Paris, go along Faubourg de Nancy off pl. des Carmes, north of the center (RN4). For Baccarat and St-Dié along rue de la Libéra-tion, to the right of and behind the station (RN59).

Medical Assistance: Centre Hospitalier St-Jacques (tel. 83 73 17 49), on rue Level.

Police: 2, rue Caumont la Force (tel. 83 73 02 07). **Emergency,** tel. 17.

Accommodations, Camping, and Food

Reservations are often necessary when conventions invade this popular destina-tion. Avoid the overpriced hotels on rue d'Alsace.

Hôtel Saint-Nicolas, 1, rue Chanzy (tel. 83 73 20 12), across from the château in a beautiful location. A 15-min. walk from the train station, down rue de la République and across the canal. Pleasant owners. Some rooms with views. Singles and doubles 80-150F. Showers 15F. Breakfast 19F. Restaurant downstairs has *menus* from 50F. Open daily noon-2pm and 7-9pm.

Hôtel l'Evêché, 6, rue Carnot (tel. 83 73 00 50), straight down from the train station. Clean, pretty singles and doubles 90-140F. Breakfast 25F. Restaurant downstairs has 60-150F *menus.*

Hôtel de l'Agriculture, 14, pl. du Rempart (tel. 83 73 00 61), off rue de la République a few blocks from the château. The linoleum floors, 70s-style wallpaper, and velour bedspreads will make you feel as if you've just stepped onto the set of the Brady Bunch. Tiger and Fluffy lurk under your bed. Singles 70F, doubles 90-100F. Hall shower included. Decent 38F *menu* in the bar downstairs. Open Mon.-Sat.

Camping: Camping Municipal de Lunéville, 69, quai des Petits Bosquets (tel. 83 73 37 58), at the foot of the château's extensive parc des Bosquets. Reception open daily 8am-9pm. 4.40F per person, tent, or car. Open April-Oct.

Pack a picnic lunch and head for the château gardens on a sunny day. **Bravo Supermarket** at 41, rue Basset, off pl. Léopold, has everything you need. (Open Mon.-Sat. 8:30am-7pm.) Most of Lunéville's restaurants cluster near the château; rue de Lorraine is lined with *salons de thé, brasseries,* and a few ethnic restaurants. **Les Bosquets,** 2, rue des Bosquets, evokes rural manorial living and serves a week-day luncheon *menu* for 54F or 69F. The *à la carte* selections cost 75-135F. (Dinner *menus* from 69F. Open Mon.-Tues. and Thurs.-Sat. noon-2pm and 7-9:15pm, Wed. noon-2pm.) **Le Lunéville,** 43, rue de la République, has appetizing 50F and 60F *menus* featuring typical Lorraine specialties. Again, *a la carte* is expensive (45-107F). (Open Tues. and Thurs.-Sun. noon-3pm and 7pm-late, Wed. noon-3pm.)

Sights

French architect Boffrand designed the twin north and south wings, huge artifi-cial lakes, and pristine flower gardens of the **Château de Lunéville** with Versailles in mind. July, August and September bring *son et lumière* to the south gate. (Fri.-Sat. 9:30pm, Sept. 8:30pm; in off-season by appointment only. In bad weather and off-season held in the chapel.) The château houses the **Musée Municipal,** where you'll find an Egyptian mummy with shreds of skin and hair still clinging to it stranded among standard military exhibits. The museum also contains an interest-ing collection of Lunéville *faïences,* enameled ceramics which have been renowned since the 18th century for their floral patterns, rustic scenes, and *chinoiseries* (18th-century interpretations of Asian designs). (Open Wed.-Mon. 10am-noon and 2-6pm.

Admission 7.20F, students 3.40F.) Baroque-style **Eglise St-Jacques** was built according to the plans of Boffrand and Héré, designer of Nancy's pl. Stanislas.

In the courtyard at 45, rue de la République, you'll find a twisting 17th-century stairway and stone medallions. The **Maison du Marchand,** 15, rue de Lorraine, is a Baroque building in pink sandstone built during Stanislas's reign. Less fanciful architecture lines rue du Château.

Only 15km away in **Baccarat,** a **Musée de la Crystalline** (tel. 83 75 10 01) traces the history of the famous glassworks. Gawk at the Shah of Persia's candelabrum and a glass set specially commissioned in 1896 for the Czar of Russia, Nicholas II. (Admission 8F. Open June 15-July 15 daily 2-6:30pm; July 16-Sept. 15 10am-noon and 2-6:30pm; Sept. 16-June 14 Sat.-Sun. 2-6:30pm.) Contact the **tourist office,** Résidence Centre, rue Division-LeClerc (tel. 83 75 13 37), for details.

Metz

When the French army rolled out of Metz (pronounced MESS) at the end of World War I, it left behind denuded plots of land right in the center of town. City administrators voted to keep the area as parks, and Metz now boasts 25 square meters of green land for each of its 123,000 residents, making it one of France's three official "green cities." Metz is thought to be the oldest city in eastern France, with traces of a settlement dating from 1000 BC. Recognized as French by the Treaty of Westphalia, then German by the Treaty of Frankfurt, Metz was one of the principal strongholds of Germany's western front in World War II. Today this attractive capital of Lorraine has a lively pedestrian quarter and fascinating museum but none of nearby Nancy's congestion.

Orientation and Practical Information

Metz is 150km northwest of Strasbourg, 350km east of Paris, and 50km north of Nancy along the Moselle River, where it meets the Seille River. The train station is located in a fashionable neighborhood originally built by the Germans. From the train station, turn right and follow the contour of the gardens, making a left at rue Haute-Seille. Take another left at en Fourinirue and follow it to the cathedral and the tourist office (20 min.).

Tourist Office: on pl. d'Armes (tel. 87 75 65 21), across from the cathedral. More maps, calendars, maps, descriptions of monuments, and maps than you could ever want. Staff will book you a room for a deposit of half the night's fee. Two-hr. city tours leave here Mon.-Sat. at 10am and 2:30pm; call a day ahead to request an English-speaking guide (25F, in French 20F). Open Mon.-Fri. 9am-9pm, Sun. 10am-4pm. The **annex** (tel. 87 65 76 69) at the train station is convenient but extremely understaffed. It may be closed unexpectedly. Open—in your dreams—Mon.-Fri. 11am-1pm and 1:45-7:30pm.

Post Office: 1, pl. Général de Gaulle (tel. 87 63 13 55), across from the train station. **Telephones. Postal Code:** 57007. Open Mon.-Fri. 8am-7pm and Sat. 8am-noon.

Trains: (tel. 85 56 50 50; for reservations 87 63 50 50), on pl. Général de Gaulle. To: Nancy (every hr., 1 hr., 39F); Strasbourg (every 2 hr., 1½ hr., 89F); Luxembourg (every 2 hr., 1½ hr., 42F); Mulhouse (7 per day, 2½ hr., 143F); Lyon (6 per day, 5 hr., 218F); Verdun (1 per day, 1 hr., 52F). Open Mon.-Sat. 8am-7:30pm and Sun. 9:30am-noon and 2-6:30pm.

Buses: (tel. 87 75 73 73), on pl. Coislin. Mostly local routes. To Verdun (4 per day, 2 hr., 56.10F). Municipal buses and minibuses frequent and thorough. Route information at the tourist office. Local buses leave from pl. de la République.

Pharmacy: 2, av. Robert Schumann (tel. 87 75 02 32). Open Mon.-Sat. 8am-8pm.

Hospital: Hôpital Notre Dame-de-Bon-Secours, 1, pl. Phillipe de Vignuelles (tel. 87 55 31 31).

Medical Assistance: SAMU, tel. 87 62 27 11.

Police: 6, rue Belle Isle (tel. 87 37 91 11). **Emergency,** tel. 17.

Accommodations, Camping, and Food

Try to stay at the hostel. Metz's few reasonable hotels are far from the center of town.

Auberge de Jeunesse, allée de Metz Plage (tel. 87 30 44 02), on the far side of town from the train station. Take bus #3 or 11 from the station to Pontiffroy. On the Moselle River. A clean, simple hostel with jolly management and great facilities. Free bike rental. Game room and TV room. Give them your laundry the night before, and for 25F they'll return it clean and folded the next morning at breakfast. Lockout 9am-5pm. No curfew. Card not required. 50F per person, breakfast included. Call early in the day; fills fast.

Foyer Carrefour, 6, rue Marchant (tel. 87 75 07 26). Go right from the tourist office, turn right on rue St-Georges, then left on rue Marchant. A newer but dark and unfriendly hostel that doubles as a *foyer* for young French workers. A definite 2nd choice. Dorm beds 48F. Singles with cold shower 60F. Breakfast included. Lunch and dinner 29F. Sheets 16F.

Métropole, 5, pl. Général de Gaulle (tel. 87 66 26 22), across from the train station. Luxurious 2-star hotel with a few rooms for 90F, with shower 142F. Breakfast 20F.

Camping: Metz-Plage (tel. 87 32 05 58), a 4-star site in a beautiful tree-shaded spot next to the Moselle and the youth hostel. Telephones, showers, indoor swimming pool, and skating rink nearby. 8F per person with tent. 6F per extra person. Open June-Aug. only.

Do not come to Metz for its restaurants: there are few authentic French places and prices are high. Several unabashedly touristic restaurants line av. Robert Schumann off pl. de la République. Bright turquoise stucco walls, dioramas of Mexican village life, and Aztec masks make for an interesting evening at **Le Toucan,** 46, pl. St-Louis. Check out the *manchamanteles* (55F), a stir-fry of beef and fruit. (Open Tues.-Sat. 10am-2pm and 6-11pm.) **Cafétéria Flunch,** 17, rue des Clercs, serves decent food at reasonable prices (main dishes from 20F) and is open daily from 11am to 10:30pm. **Markets** fill pl. St-Jacques Tuesday and Thursday mornings and pl. du Marché and pl. de la Cathédraleon on Saturday mornings.

Sights and Entertainment

The tourist office's exhaustive guide, *Le Petit Futé,* is only of use to French speakers (37F). The cathedral and museum huddle near **place d'Armes,** an 18th-century square designed by Blondel, where a cloister and four churches once stood. Only the naves of St-Pierre in Beauvais and Nôtre-Dame in Amiens soar higher than that of **Cathédrale St-Etienne.** The 6500 square meters of stained-glass windows have earned it the moniker "Lantern to God." On the west side of the nave, opposite Chappelle du Sacré-Coeur, Hermann de Münster's monstrous 14th-century rose window sucks in enough light to bleach a priest's cassock. Chagall's colorful windows are on the left as you face the north transept and farther along the left where the ambulatory girdles the choir. (Open daily 7:30am-noon and 2-6pm).

Outside pl. d'Armes to the right of the Hôtel de Ville, the fascinating **Musée d'Art et d'Histoire** 2, rue du Haut-Poirier (tel. 87 75 10 18) contains a wealth of Gallo-Roman sculpture from Metz's days as a Roman frontier town. The section on domestic architecture exhibits wooden interiors of entire medieval and Renaissance homes. The art museum houses works by the school of Metz, the Italian school, Corot, Zurbarán, and others. Dramatically lit or mounted in order to re-create their original settings, the paintings are arranged in rooms dedicated to themes such as "daily life" and "religious architecture." (Open Wed.-Mon. 10am-noon and 2-6pm. Admission 14F, students 7F.) Rue des Clercs leads from pl. d'Armes to pl. de la République and the **esplanade,** a French garden with a balustrade overlooking the Moselle valley. To the left along the esplanade is **Basilique St-Pierre-aux-Nonnais,** the oldest church in France and currently under reconstruction. Built on 4th- and 7th-century foundations, it underwent alterations until the 15th century.

The tourist office puts out a monthly *Calendrier des manifestations* (Calendar of Events, free). Its slicker magazine, *Spectacles à Metz* (free), lists sports and cultural events. July 14 through August, there is a *son et lumière* show at 10pm on the esplanade. For three weeks in late June and early July, the **Festival Etonnante Musique** (tel. 87 36 16 70) brings different kinds of music and dance to town. The **Fête de la Mirabelle** on the last weekend in August and the first weekend in September features a hot-air balloon exhibition, fireworks, bands, and a parade led by the cherry-plum queen. (Katie Bunge, first winner of this laurel, went on to become a drum major and homecoming queen at Marginalia State University.) The local specialty, crusty mirabelle plum tarts, abounds. November brings a contemporary music festival, **Rencontres Internationales de Musique Contemporaine,** with many free events.

Verdun

The statues and war memorials scattered throughout town, 15,000 marble crosses in the National Cemetery, and the Trench of Bayonets where most of the 137th Infantry Regiment was buried alive in 1916 testify to the horror of the WWI battles fought around Verdun. Despite the long shadow cast by wartime devastation, Verdun (pop. 30,000) has slowly been rebuilt into an attractive, even pleasant city popular with conventions. Much of Verdun is modern and commercial, built to blend pleasantly with the remnants of the original town. The restored twin peaks of the cathedral suggest a less tumultuous past, and the frequent fishing boats and rowers cruising up and down the central Meuse river add a note of tranquility to the pedestrian district.

Orientation and Practical Information

Verdun is difficult to reach. Trains run infrequently from Nancy and Châlons-sur-Marne, and buses from Metz and Bar-le-Duc run only in the morning. The bus and train stations stare at each other from opposite ends of av. Garibaldi. The *centre ville* is to the west, tied up snugly in a loop of the Meuse.

Tourist Office: (tel. 29 86 14 18 or 29 84 18 85), on pl. de la Nation opposite Porte Chaussée. English spoken. Maps of Verdun and the battlefields nearby. Four-hr. bus tour to the principal sights (April-Sept. only; 131F includes museum entrace fees). Open Mon.-Sat. 8:30am-7pm, Sun. 10am-noon and 1:30-4:30pm; Oct.-May Mon.-Sat. 9am-noon and 2-5:30pm; hours vary slightly in winter.

Post Office: av. de la Victoire. Open Mon.-Fri. 8am-7pm, Sat. 8am-noon. **Postal Code:** 55100.

Trains: (tel. 29 86 25 65), on pl. Maurice Genevoix. To: Paris (change at Châlons-sur-Marne, 5 per day, 3 hr., 154F); Châlons-sur-Marne (5 per day, 1½ hr., 67F); Nancy (change at Conflans-Jarny, 2 per day, 2 hr., 70F); Metz (2 per day, 1½ hr., 55F). Information office open daily 6am-7pm.

Buses: (tel. 29 86 02 71), on pl. Vauban. To Metz (6 per day, 1¾ hr., 52F) and Bar-le-Duc (6 per day, 1 hr., 43.50F).

Bike Rental: At the train station. 50F, deposit 500F or major credit card. Battlefields less than 8km away. Only 4 bikes available, so call early to reserve. Open daily 6am-7pm.

Pharmacy: Pharmacie Principale, 8, pl. Foch (tel. 29 86 01 16). Open Mon.-Sat. 9am-noon and 2-7pm.

Hospital: Centre Hospitalier St-Nicholas, 2, rue Anthourd (tel. 29 83 84 65).

Police: 2, rue Chaussée (tel. 29 86 00 17). **Emergency,** tel. 17.

Accommodations and Food

Like much of the city, Verdun's hotels are overpriced and unmemorable. **Hôtel de la Porte Chaussée** (tel. 29 86 00 78), overlooking the river to the right of Porte Chaussée, claims the best location. Unfortunately, the availability of the lower-priced rooms depends on the whims of the manager, who only rarely summons the energy to climb to their location on the third floors to prepare them for visitors. (Singles and doubles 60-160F. Showers 10F. Breakfast 18F. The nearby **Hôtel de Metz,** 8, rue Edmond Robin (tel. 29 86 00 15), has musty, somewhat run-down rooms at great prices. (Singles 55-70F, doubles 70-130F. Breakfast 14F.) **Hôtel Verdunois,** 13, av. Garibaldi (tel. 29 86 17 45), has the cheapest rooms near the train station. (Singles and doubles 80-160F. Breakfast 17F.)

Cafés and fast food joints line quai de Londres by the Meuse. **Des Deux Gares,** 23, av. Garibaldi, is a *brasserie* serving a tasty *menu* for 46F. (Open daily 11:30am-2:30pm and 6:30-10pm.) An elegant seafood restaurant stranded in a bowling alley, **Bowling de Verdun,** rue de 8 Mai offers a filling 52F *menu, a la carte* dishes (40F), lanes of bowling (15-18F) and rental of those fasionable shoes (5F). Cross the river at pont Chaussée and follow rue de la Liberté; the restaurant is in the basement of the E. Leclerc supermarket. (Open 11am-2:30pm and 6:30pm-1am.) **Le Liberty's,** 40, rue Poincaré, specializes in Algerian cuisine. Try the delicious take-out *couscous* (40-55F) or devour 52F and 72F *menus* among colorful hanging gourds and stuffed iguanas. (Open daily noon-3pm and 6:30-11pm.) A year-round **market** is held Fridays 8am-noon on rue de Rû.

Sights

Verdun's chosen symbol, a dove floating above two hands clasped in peace, strives to counter the ample evidence of massive destruction caused by World War I and earlier conflicts. A bronze war statue by Rodin graces the **Porte Châtel** drawbridge on pl. St-Paul, which remains from the days when ramparts protected Verdun from northern invaders. Built in 1350, **Porte Chaussée,** on the quai des Londres, served as a prison and a guard tower before ultimately providing troops passage into the city during the Great War. Past the gateway stretches the **Monument à la Victoire,** a flight of 72 granite steps surmounted by a resolute warrior figure and cannons aimed at the German front. Its crypt encloses gravestones with war decorations. (Open 9am-noon and 2-6pm.) The nearby **Musée de la Princerie** is a 16th-century mansion filled with arms, armor, sculpture, and local archaeological finds.

The two choirs and transepts of **Cathédrale Notre Dame,** begun in 1048, rest on the highest point in the city. Once the most powerful in Lorraine, the cathedral's organ was warped during the drought of 1976. Vauban's **Citadelle Souterraine,** constructed on the site of the ancient Abbaye de St-Vanne, sheltered soldiers during WW I. The 7km of underground galleries were equipped with everything necessary to support an army, including nine large ovens that could cook almost 29,000 rations of bread in 24 hours. (Open daily 9am-12:30pm and 2-6:30pm; Sept.-June hours vary slightly.)

Battlefields encircle the city in an 8km radius, a swath encompassing entire villages annihilated in the war. Two of the most frequently visited forts are **Fort de Vaux** and **Fort de Douaumont.** (Both open 9am-6:30pm; Oct. to mid-March 10am-noon and 1:30-5pm. Admission 13F.) Other sights lie along the road to Douaumont. The **Mémorial-Musée de Fleury,** before Douaumont, displays models, uniforms, artillery, and reconstructed battlefields. (Open daily 9am-6pm; mid-Sept. to mid-March 9am-noon and 2-6pm. Admission 16F.) Near the fort, the rocket-shaped **Ossuaire de Douaumont** contains the bones of 100,000 soldiers. (Open daily 9am-6:30pm; Oct.-April 9am-noon and 2-5pm. Admission 14F.) The **Tranchée des Baïonnettes** nearby marks the spot where an entire platoon of infantry was buried alive in a trench on June 12, 1916. (Free. Always open.)

Bar-le-Duc

Capital of the ancient duchy of Bar, Bar-le-Duc's name derives from the barriers built by the Celts to repel invading Huns in the 5th century. The unscrupulous House of Bar inaugurated the region's golden age in the late 13th century, when its northern border extended to Luxembourg and its southern border to Burgundy. This era of flourishing court life ended with the ravages of plague and the Thirty Years' War. When Bar passed into French hands after Duke Stanislas died in 1766, only a fragment of the fortress-castle stood. Bar-le-Duc's most famous product, the widely-exported *confiture de groseilles épépinées* (seedless currant jam), has been locally produced since the beginning of the 15th century. On the eve of the Revolution, Bar-le-Duc was churning out 50,000 jars per year, most of which were given to visiting princes or dukes in return for protection. Although production has settled down considerably in these more peaceful days of apartheid and Saddam Hussein, the traditional method of hand-plucking the seeds out of currants with a goose feather persists.

During World War I, Bar was an important transport and relief base to the Verdun battlefields but escaped the heavy bombardments suffered by other cities. The steep cobblestone streets, the esplanade of the citadel, and the Renaissance façades on rue du Bourg all recall the former prominence of the town, which now wallows in its tranquil obscurity. There is not much excitement in Bar-le-Duc, but that's just what makes it attractive.

Orientation and Practical Information

The hilltop *ville haute* comprises the older part of the city, including what remains of the castle. The train station and commercial center are below in the *ville basse*. Walk straight out of the station onto rue de la Gare and cross the Ornain river; the second street on your right, bd. de la Rochelle, is the *ville basse's* main thoroughfare. To reach the *ville haute,* continue straight on rue Lapique, which becomes av. du Château as it winds its way through the old city. To reach the neighborhood behind the train station, where the pool, Hôtel Bertrand, and the Parc Varin Bernier are, make a left from the station onto rue de Sebastopol and make the next left onto rue St-Mihiel. You will have to climb the steep trestle to cross over the tracks.

Tourist Office: 5, rue Jeanne d'Arc (tel. 29 79 11 13), in the old hospital. Turn right onto rue Allende from the train station, and follow it as it becomes rue Jeanne d'Arc. Friendly and helpful staff do their best in English. Open Tues.-Sat. 9am-noon and 2-6pm.

Post Office: 32, bd. de la Rochelle (tel. 29 45 17 33). **Telephones.** Poste Restante at this office: 55013 Bar-le-Duc CEDEX. Open Mon.-Fri. 8am-7pm, Sat. 8am-noon. **Postal code:** 55000.

Trains: pl. de la République (tel. 29 45 50 50). To: Paris (13 per day, 2 hr., 144F); Strasbourg (5 per day, 3 hr., 144F); Nancy (7 per day, 1 hr., 62F). Information office open Mon.-Sat. 8am-12:15pm and 2-6:40pm; Sun. 9:30am-12:15pm and 2-6:40pm.

Buses: rue du Four (tel. 29 79 60 00), across from pl. Exelmans. To Verdun (4 per day, 1-1½ hr., 43.50F) and tiny towns in the region. Information office open Mon.-Sat. 7am-8pm.

Laundromat: 10, rue du Bourg. Wash 10F, soap 3F, dry 1F. Accepts 10F and 1F coins. Open 7am-8pm.

Pharmacy: 10, bd. de la Rochelle (tel. 29 76 20 56). Open Mon.-Sat. 9am-noon and 2-7pm; Sat. until 5pm.

Medical Assistance: SMUR, tel. 29 79 11 13.

Police: Gendarmerie, 19, rue Louis Joblot (tel. 29 79 02 80). **Emergency,** tel. 17.

Accommodations, Camping, and Food

Intimate Bar-le-Duc cannot accommodate many guests. Phone ahead or be prepared to move on to less idyllic towns such as Nancy. Most of the hotels and restaurants are in the *basse ville*. A small **Coop** grocery store is in the upper part of town at 27, rue des Ducs de Bar. (Open Tues.-Sun. morning 7am-12:30pm and 3-7:15pm). The enormous **Monoprix,** bd. de la Rochelle, dwarfs the neighboring *épiceries.* (Open Mon.-Sat. 8:30am-7:30pm.) On Tuesdays and Thursdays, a **market** takes over the area to the left of rue André Theuriet, up from pl. Exelmans (9am-noon).

Hôtel Exelmans, 5, rue du Gué (tel. 29 76 21 06). On a small street off bd. de la Rochelle in the center of town, on the far side of the Ornain river if you're coming from the station. A shipshape operation close to the city center. Singles and doubles 58-95F. Showers 13F. Breakfast 16F. Open mid-Jan. to Dec.

Hôtel Bertrand, 19, rue de l'Etoile (tel. 29 79 02 97). Turn right from rue St-Mihiel onto pl. de l'Etoile. Concerned management keeps the place well. Down comforters and spotless bathrooms. Singles and doubles 75-155F. Extra bed 40F. Breakfast 17.50F. Restaurant and bar downstairs.

Camping: Camping Municipal (tel. 29 79 17 33), behind the station in the Parc Varin Bernier. Spartan site in a beautiful lakeside setting. 4.15F per person, 1.80F per tent or car. Gates close 10pm. Open April-Sept.

Occupying an old guard tower in the *ville haute,* **Grill de la Tour,** 15, rue du Baile, has a crackling fire, low heavy beams, and 48F and 72F *menus.* (Open Mon.-Sat. noon-1:30pm and 7-8:30pm.) **Restaurant la Chaumière,** 44, rue St-Jean, resembles an Alpine ski lodge with its dark wood and cuckoo clock. The four-course *menu* costs 50F. (Open Mon. noon-1:15pm, Tues.-Sun. noon-1:15pm and 7:30-9pm.) The **student cafeteria,** at the Accueil des Jeunes, 2, pl. Exelmans, fills patrons with abundant if somewhat greasy food. Meal tickets cost 24F for students under 25, 31.50F for students over 25. (Ticket office open Mon.-Fri. 11:30am-12:30pm. Cafeteria open Mon.-Fri. 11:30am-1pm and 7-7:45pm, Sat. 11:30am-12:45pm.)

Sights

To reach the *ville haute,* take rue de l'Horloge left off av. du Château and slalom uphill. Alsatian timber houses stand alongside sophisticated buildings such as the 16th-century *hôtel* of the Florainville family, which bears French and *barrois* coats of arms. **Eglise St-Pierre,** Gothic in structure and Renaissance in proportion, dominates the square. The **Tombe de René de Chalon** in the transept contains *Le Sque- lette,* Ligier Richier's portrait of Chalon three years after his death. The triumphant pose of the gruesome figure symbolizes the Christian hope of resurrection. (Church and tomb open daily 9am-noon and 2-7pm.)

Between pl. St-Pierre and rue des Ducs lies **La Halle,** an ancient marketplace. In the other direction you'll find the entrance to what remains of the **château.** A map near where rue François de Guise forks off to the right shows the château's original plan. The only remaining structures are the **esplanade** (with an excellent view of the city), **Porte Romaine** (a relic of the original Roman settlement dating from the 1st century AD), and the 16th-century **Neufchâtel.** Neufchâtel now houses the **Musée de Bar-le-Duc's** exhibits on *barrois* archaeology, popular traditions, military history, and arts. Look for Julie Lorraine Gantz's portrait of Bob. (Open Mon. and Wed.-Fri. 2-6pm, Sat.-Sun. 3-6pm; Oct.-May Wed. 2-6pm and Sat.-Sun. 3-6pm. Admission 5F, students and everyone Wed. free.) Avenue du Château roughly traces the outline of the ancient fort. Once lined with shops, the rebuilt 14th-century **Pont Notre Dame** in the *ville basse* leads to the 13th-century **Eglise de Notre Dame.** Note the 18th-century façade. Notre Dame eclipsed St-Pierre when the nobility shifted the town's center from the *ville haute* to the *ville basse,* a displacement which allowed the preservation of the *ville haute.* Bar-le-Duc's most spectacular park, the **Clinique du Parc** on rue Lapique, hides a tiny zoo and lovely strams and gazebos. **Parc Varin Bernier,** off rue St-Mihiel behind the train station, lures picnickers with its fragrant flower beds and shaded benches.

Champagne

Brothers, brothers, come quickly!
I am drinking stars!

—Dom Perignon

Although grapevines have existed in the Champagne region since the Tertiary period, the Romans were the first to undertake a systematic program of wine production. The natural effervescence of champagne enchanted everyone who tasted it; the key to consistent production, however, remained a mystery. Not until the 17th century did a few individuals (among them the blind cellarer of the Benedictine abbey of Hautvillers, Dom Perignon) hit upon the idea of tying down the cork to keep in the sparkle. From that moment on, the wine's popularity expanded incredibly; Voltaire rhapsodized that "of this fresh wine the sparkling froth is the brilliant image of our French people."

The name "champagne" is jealously guarded by the region's vintners. If you have tasted the real stuff outside France, you (or your friends) have paid dearly for the privilege. According to French law, the name champagne can only be used without qualification for wines vinted from grapes of the region and produced according to the rigorous and time-honored *méthode champenoise,* which involves the blending of three different varieties of grape, two stages of fermentation, and frequent realignment of bottles by *remueurs* (highly trained bottle turners) to facilitate removal of sediment. If they are scrupulously faithful to the *méthode champenoise,* foreign impostors may use the word "champagne" with its place of origin (i.e., "California champagne") on their bottles. Sparkling wines made by a different process are called *"mousseux;" "crémant"* refers to a less effervescent variety. You can see the *méthode* in action at the region's numerous wine cellars (*caves*). As each manufacturer will remind you, it's the area's unique combination of altitude, climate, chalky soil, and cellars carved from limestone that makes champagne production possible. Originally carved by Roman chalk exporters, the fascinating *caves* all smell of penicillin mold, which thrives in the damp, cool air. Some *caves* have operated as wineries since Roman times. Epernay may be richer, but the most impressive of Champagne's 640km of *crayères* (chalk quarries turned *caves*) lie beneath Reims.

Economist John Maynard Keynes once confessed that his one regret in life was not having drunk enough champagne. To avoid this fate, enjoy a free tasting at the Mumm *caves* in Epernay, a *coupe de champagne* in any bar, or the non-sparkling variety in the sauces of regional specialities such as *volaille au champagne* (poultry) or *civet d'oie* (goose stew). Buying by the bottle can be expensive, even if you purchase directly from a *cave.* Monoprix supermarkets have the best deals.

There is much more to La Champagne than *le champagne.* French civilization is, so to speak, deeply rooted in the chalky soil of the *campagne* (country, from Latin *campus,* field). In 451 at the mysterious Champs Catalauniques, Romans, Visigoths, and Franks turned back the pillaging forces of Attila the Hun. Newly Christian Clovis received the first royal coronation in Reims in 498, inaugurating the city's special symbolic connection with the French monarchy. Every king from Henri I to Charles X (except Henri IV and Louis XVIII) was consecrated here. Charles VII helped turn the tide of the Hundred Years' War by receiving the *sacre* at the cathedral in 1429, at the insistence of Joan of Arc. Thousands died here during the Wars of Religion, the Franco-Prussian War, and the slaughter of WW I and WW II.

Champagne is a great place for excursions into the countryside by car, bike, or foot. If you are driving or hitchhiking, follow any of the *routes de champagne* through the Montagne de Reims, the Marne Valley, or the *côtes des blancs.* Tourist offices distribute route maps; ask for the free pamphlet *The Champagne Road.* You can wander off to visit the small villages and lakes dotting the region south and west of Epernay. Champagne's two national parks are ideal for hiking. The tourist office in Troyes has information on the Forêt d'Orient, while the tourist office in Reims sells a booklet of trails through the Parc Naturel de la Montagne de Reims (13F). Also of note are the Forêt de Verzy, a curious forest of twisted, umbrella-shaped dwarf beeches (*tortillards*), and the vast Forêt de Germaine. The camp-grounds here are often crowded. Frequent trains connect the major towns, but you will have to rely on slow and infrequent buses to reach the smaller villages off the tourist route.

Reims

The home of the Remes, a powerful Gallic tribe, during the first century BC, Reims (pronounced like "France" without the "f") later became the flourishing cap-ital of the Roman province of Belgica. Reims is perhaps best known for its long line of royal coronations, which began when St-Remi converted and baptized Clovis here in 498. The coronation of Charles VII, whom Joan of Arc led to Reims through the English lines in 1429, may be the most famous. In 1814, the city had the some-what dubious honor of being the site of Napoleon's last victory, causing General Marmont to declare Reims "the last smile of Fortune." Fortune frowned on another would-be conqueror of Europe on May 8, 1945, when the Germans surrendered in the small schoolroom Eisenhower used as his headquarters. You'll find the im-pressive *crayères* (chalk quarries turned *caves*) under Reims.

Orientation and Practical Information

Unlike many French cities its size (pop. 182,000), Reims was built on ancient trade routes rather than on a river. (The Marne flows 30km to the south.) Trains from Paris's Gare de l'Est roll a scenic 154km to Reims (1½ hr.). Because the city is on a secondary rail line, connections to other cities often involve changing trains. The tourist office and most of the sights are within easy walking distance east of the train station.

Tourist Office: 2, rue de Machault (tel. 26 47 25 69), next to the cathedral, in the ruins of the old charterhouse. From the station, head straight onto pl. Drouet d'Erlon (actually a road). After the church St-Jacques, hang a left onto rue Carnot and then a right after the theater. The tourist office is on the right. Efficient, English-speaking staff distributes the well-indexed town map (*Plan de l'office de tourisme*). The more detailed *Plan Blay* shows all bus routes (22F). Lists of *caves* and day hikes around Reims (*Promenades autour de Reims*). List of hotels and restaurants includes museum hours and local festival dates. Bad rates and a 20F commission at the **currency exchange.** Open Mon.-Sat. 9am-7:30pm, Sun. and holidays 9:30am-6:30pm; in winter Mon.-Sat. 10am-12:30pm and 1:30-5:30pm.

Post Office: (tel. 26 88 44 22), on rue Olivier-Métra and pl. de Boulingrin near the Porte Mars. **Poste Restante.** Branch office, 1, rue Cérès (pl. Royale), closer to the tourist office. Both open Mon.-Fri. Oct.-April 8am-7pm, Sat. 8:30am-noon. **Postal Code:** 51084.

Trains: (tel. 26 88 50 50), on bd. Joffre across the park from the town center and pl. Drouet d'Erlon. To: Laon (4 per day, 1 hr., 39F); Epernay (18 per day, ½-hr., 25F); Paris (12 per day, 1½ hr., 93F); Luxembourg (2 per day, 3 hr., 120F). Luggage storage open daily 5:45am-8:30pm. SNCF travel agency open Mon.-Fri. 9am-12:30pm and 2-6:30pm, Sat. 9:30am-12:30pm and 2:30-5:30pm. Information desk next to the ticket counter open Mon.-Fri. 8:30am-7:30pm, Sat. 9am-6:15pm. The booth marked *Accueil* provides information only about the station itself. Consult the huge city map outside the station.

Buses: Transport Urbains de Reims (**TUR**) buses stop in front of the train station. Tickets can be bought at the station, but the main information and ticket office is at the theater at 6, rue Chanzy (tel. 26 88 25 38). Local buses leave from here. 10F *carnet* available at bars or *tabacs*.

Taxis: Taxi de Reims, tel. 26 02 15 02. 24 hrs.

Bike Rental: Daniel Dubar, 26, av. de Paris-Tinquieux (tel. 26 08 53 12). Regular or mountain bikes 50F per day, 100F per weekend. **Boulanger,** 5, bd. Lundy (tel. 26 47 47 59), has the same prices.

Hitchhiking: If you decide to hitchhike to Paris, follow N31 via Soissons; take bus B or #2, *direction* "Tinquieux." For Luxembourg, try N380; take bus B, *direction* "Point de Witry," and get off at the terminus. To hitch a ride on a canal barge in the direction of Burgundy, go to the old port on bd. Paul-Doumer.

Lost Property: Objets Trouvés, tel. 26 09 21 04 or 26 87 18 82.

Women's Center: SOS Femmes, tel. 26 40 13 45. Provides moral support and abortion information.

Gay and Lesbian Services: Francine à Reims, tel. 26 88 40 01. **Oméga,** tel. 29 86 23 72. Anonymity guaranteed.

Laundromat: 24, rue de Cernay, and 32, rue Dr. Thomas. Wash 14F, dry 2F. Open daily 7am-9pm.

Medical Assistance: SAMU, 45, rue Cognacq Jay (tel. 26 06 07 08), or tel. 15.

Police: 3, rue Rockefeller (tel. 26 88 21 12). **Emergency,** tel. 17.

Accommodations and Camping

You must make reservations two or three days ahead in this popular city, even at the youth hostel. Inexpensive hotels cluster on **rue de Thillois** and **place Drouet d'Erlon.** The tourist office has information on Reims's numerous *foyers,* which are a good deal at about 60F per night but generally lie well outside the center.

Auberge de Jeunesse (IYHF)/Centre International de Séjour, 1, chaussée Bocquaine (tel. 26 40 52 60), across from Parc Leo Lagrange, beside Espace André Malraux. A 15-min. walk from the station. Continue straight from the train station, turn right at the far side of the gardens, follow bd. Général Leclerc, and cross the bridge. Take your first left on chaussée Bocquaine; the hostel is on the left. Expensive for a hostel, but excellent facilities: kitchen, book exchange, TV. Open 7am-11pm. Curfew 11pm, but you can get a key. No card required. Singles and doubles with breakfast 64-69F per person, without breakfast 64F and 59F.

Auberge de Jeunesse 31, rue du Bassin (tel. 26 97 90 10), at Verzy 20km south of Reims. Large dorm rooms. No public transportation. Open 7-10am and 5-10pm. 36F per person. Breakfast 13F.

University Housing: CROUS, 34, bd. Henry Vasnier (tel. 26 85 50 16). Take bus D at the train station to Yser (2-3km). 40F per person. May have room for travelers in July and Aug. Call ahead.

Hôtel d'Alsace, 6, rue Général Sarrail (tel. 26 47 44 08), near the station and not far from the sights. Proprietor offers brochures and helpful advice. Cheery hallways and large, simple rooms. TV and phones in most rooms. Relaxed bar downstairs. Singles and doubles 75-100F, with bathroom 145F. Showers 12F. Breakfast 20F.

Hôtel Linguet, 14, rue Linguet (tel. 26 47 31 89), on a quiet residential street. Clean rooms, some with fireplaces and stained-glass windows. Friendly management. Bonsai trees in the courtyard and fish tanks in the dining room. Recently renovated bathrooms. Closed Sun. 10am-8pm. Singles and doubles 70-120F. Showers 10F. Breakfast 17F.

Au Bon Accueil, 31, rue Thillois (tel. 26 88 55 74), only 10 min. from the station in the center of town. Reasonable prices, friendly management and large, clean rooms. Singles from 65F. Doubles from 85F. Showers 10F. Breakfast 16F.

Hôtel Thillois, 17, rue Thillois (tel. 26 40 65 65), down the street from Au Bon Accueil. Simple rooms. Singles from 60F. Doubles from 85F. Showers 10F. Breakfast 16F.

Camping: Camping-Airotel de Champagne (tel. 26 85 41 22), on av. Hoche, route de Châlons, 9km from downtown. Take bus #2 from the theater. Three-star site with 3-day max. stay. 18F per person. Children 8F, tent 15F, car 3F. Open Easter-Sept. 30. **Camping Ouignicourt-sur-Aisne** (tel. 23 79 74 58) stays open all year round but is 23km away from Reims (11F per person).

Food

Place Drouet-Erlon is lined with fast food places, overpriced cafés, and bars. Either look for a reasonably priced regional *menu*, or join the students who gather at pizzerias along rue Gambetta.

Shop around before you buy champagne. There are occasional sales on local brands at shops around the cathedral. Check first at **Monoprix**, one block south of the cathedral. If you miss the free taste that caps off the tour at Mumm, order a *coupe de champagne* in any bar (about 25-30F). The even smaller *coupette de Champagne* (15-20F) is barely worth the money but will at least give you a taste of the bubbly stuff.

Le Colibri and **Le Notre Dame**, 12, rue de Chanzy (tel. 26 47 50 67), facing the cathedral. Popular restaurant and bar. At night you can reserve a table with a view of the illuminated cathedral. *Menus* 60-150F. *Plat du jour* 30F. Filling take-out quiche and sandwiches 12-16F. Open daily 11am-10:30pm.

La Forêt Noire, 2, bd. Jules César, on the corner of the 2nd spoke off pl. de la République. Take a left from the station. Small place with wood ceiling beams and carved furniture. Host professes to speak all modern European languages fluently. Right. Dinner *menus* from 60F feature traditional *campagnard* dishes. Specialties include kidney *flambée* (30F). Open Tues.-Sun. noon-2:30pm and 7-10pm. Call for reservations.

Le Flamm' Steak, 17, rue Libergier, 2 blocks from the cathedral. A variety of delicious regional dishes and tasty *crêpes* cooked before your eyes. The candlelit setting upstairs is cozy, even at noon. The 45-130F *menus* are worth it just to sit here. Dinner *crêpes* 15-30F, dessert 10-30F, main dishes 30-60F. Try the *truite meunière*. Open Oct.-Aug. Mon.-Sat. 11:30am-1:30pm and 6:30-10:30pm, Sun. 10:30am-1:30pm.

La Boule d'Or, 39, rue Thiers. Excellent value, homelike atmosphere, fresh food. *Menus* 44F and 60F. Try the *pâté champenois* (10F) or *plat du jour* (30F). Open Tues.-Sun. 9am-10pm.

Cafétéria, in the Espace André Malraux beside the youth hostel, the 2nd building on your left after crossing the Pont de Vesle. Don't let the name deceive you; there is sit-down service and creative, tasty cuisine. *Menu* only 42F. Open Sept.-July Tues.-Sat. noon-2pm and 5-9pm.

La Coupole, 73, rue de Chativesle (tel. 26 47 86 21), off pl. Drouet d'Erlon. Well-cooked cafeteria fare. Great selection—they even have Jello. Open daily 11:30am-2pm and 6:30-10pm.

Les Brisants, 13, rue de Chativesle (tel. 26 40 60 41), off pl. Drouet d'Erlon. Sit inside the refreshing pastel green room or in the courtyard during summer. *Galettes* 27-55F, main dishes 40-75F, *menu* 65F. Open daily noon-2pm and 7-10:30pm. Reservations recommended on weekends.

Sights and Entertainment

Since the year 496, when the Frankish king Clovis was baptized here, coronation at Reims has been the *sine qua non* of legitimacy for French monarchs. Joan of Arc's mission was to deliver the indecisive Charles VII to Reims so the French could unite behind a strong monarch and drive "Les Goddams"—as the English were called because of their penchant for the expression—back across the channel.

A half-hour tour of Reims in a minitrain leaves from the tourist office (daily 9am-8pm every ½-hr., 20F), but you're better off walking the short circuit. Begin at **Cathédrale de Notre Dame**, visibly damaged during WWII but still splendid. The present cathedral, the third to occupy this site, is built of blocks of golden limestone quarried in the Champagne *caves* beginning in 1211. The west façade contains a spectacular rose window, with deep blue glass made from lapis lazuli. Be sure to examine the tapestries that portray scenes from the *Song of Songs* and Jesus' infancy (usually on display in summer). Chagall's windows in the apse depict the same events in modern style. (Open July-Aug. daily 9am-7pm.) For guided tours in English, ask at the tourist office or shell out 30F for the *Guide de Visite* in the cathedral.

Next to the cathedral stands the **Palais du Tau**, the former archbishop's palace, so named because the original floor plan resembled a "T." A museum here houses exquisite tapestries, statuary from the cathedral (including a Goliath-sized Goliath), and the extravagant gold and velvet coronation vestments of Charles X. The cathedral's dazzling treasure, housed in two exhibition halls, includes Charlemagne's 9th-century talisman and the 12th-century chalice from which 20 kings received communion. (Open daily 9:30am-6:30pm; Sept.-June 9:30am-noon and 2-6pm. Admission 23F, students 12F, children 5F.)

To the east lies the less-visited but equally interesting **Basilique St-Remi,** a Gothic renovation of a Carolingian Romanesque church reputed to contain the tombs of many of France's earliest kings. St-Remi's baptism of Clovis is credited with bringing the French people to Catholicism. His tomb, behind the altar, was grimthorped in 1847 with statues borrowed from an earlier monument. The interior of the basilica is 122m long but only 28m wide, giving it the air of a huge, dark vault. Adjacent to the church is the **Abbaye St-Remi,** 53, rue St-Simon, the city's archaeological museum. (Open Mon.-Fri. 2-6:30pm, Sat.-Sun. 2-7pm.) Admission to this and most city museums is 7F, though an 11F *billet commun* (valid for 1 month) allows you to visit all the museums except the Palais du Tau.

When walking around the cathedral near rues Colbert and Carnot, notice **Place Royale,** restored to look as it did during the reign of Louis XV. A Cartellier statue of the simpering monarch stands in the center. (The original *place* by Pigalle was destroyed during the Revolution.)

The **Salle de Reddition,** 12, rue Franklin Roosevelt, is the simple schoolroom where the Germans surrendered to the Allies on May 8, 1945. It has recently been modernized and features maps, period newspapers, photos, and an excellent film. (Open Wed.-Mon. 10am-noon and 2-6pm. Admission 8F, students with ID free.)

Formerly an abbey, the **Musée des Beaux-Arts,** 8, rue Chanzy, displays an eclectic collection of paintings and tapestries. The ground floor contains ceramics and enamel works. Upstairs, you'll find a set of portrait sketches by the Cranachs, elder and younger, as well as a fine collection of French art, including an extensive Corot cache and two rooms of Impressionist works. (Open Wed.-Fri. and Mon. 10:30am-noon and 2-6pm, Sat.-Sun. opens at 10am. Admission 8F, students free.)

For a glimpse of Reims's august Roman past, walk around the **Porte Mars,** by pl. de la République, a Corinthian-style triumphal arch erected in honor of Augustus two centuries after his death. The enormous three-arched monument still bears some bas-reliefs depicting Jupiter and Leda and Romulus and Remus.

Four hundred km of Roman chalk quarries, *les crayères,* wind underground through the countryside around Reims. Today, they house the bottles emblazoned with the great names of Champagne—Pommery, Piper Heidsieck, Mumm, Taittinger. Some of the smaller *caves* were built from chapels; others house illuminated shrines to St-Jean, patron saint of *cavistes.* (Dom Perignon, the blind cellarist who spent 50 years perfecting the *méthode champenoise,* was himself a monk.) The tourist office stocks a map with a list of the *caves* open to the public. Most organize free tours, but only **Mumm,** 34, rue Champ-de-Mars (tel. 26 40 22 73), still offers free samples. All of Reims's *caves* are usually open Monday through Saturday from 9 to 11am and 2 to 5pm, and sometimes on Sunday afternoons; schedules are listed on the map. Tours in French and English last a half-hour to an hour and leave every hour or so, depending on the inebriation of the guide and his flock.

Pommery at 5, pl. du Général Gouraud (tel. 26 05 71 61), probably gives the most elegant tour. **Taittinger,** 9, pl. St-Nicaise (tel. 26 85 45 35), in a former crypt, has some of the oldest and eeriest *caves;* their tour is a solid history lesson, beginning with a slide show. **Piper-Heidsieck,** 51, bd. Henry Vasnier (tel. 26 85 01 94), takes you around their cellars on a little electric train. **Veuve Clicquot-Ponsardin,** 1, pl. des Droits-de-l'Homme (tel. 26 85 24 08), leads mediocre tours, but screens a fine film (only on advance request) about Madame Clicquot, the grande dame of champagne history. (Open April-Oct. Mon.-Sat. 9-11am and 2-5pm.)

To see Reims's shocking attempt to mix driving with drinking, take a bus from the theater at 6, rue de Chanzy, to the **Musée de l'Automobile Française** (tel. 26 82 83 84), which displays French cars dating from 1891. (Open April-Nov. daily 10am-noon and 2-6pm, Dec.-March Sat.-Sun. 10am-noon and 2-5pm. Admission 30F, students 20F, under 10 free.)

Throughout July and August Reims hosts the fantastic **Flâneries Musicales d'Eté**, with almost-daily classical concerts, many of which are free. The best take place in front of the cathedral on Friday and Saturday nights before the immense **Nuit des Sacres Royaux** sound and light show. At 60F a pop you may be reduced to a *baguette* budget for the next few days, but this is one show that's worth the fee: it starts with a high-tech light performance in the Palais du Tau, progresses to a laser-beam reenactment of various coronations in the cathedral, and climaxes with yet another light show outside, tracing the construction of the cathedral and the ongoing restoration process. *Zut alors!* (July-Sept. Fri. and Sat. evenings. 60F, children 20F.)

A university town, Reims has more jazz clubs, wine bars, and discos than the average reveler would care to navigate in a month of Saturdays. At press time, the hot discos included **L'Echiquier**, 110, av. Jean-Jaurès (tel. 26 89 12 38; open Fri.-Sun.), and **Club St-Pierre**, 43, bd. Général Leclerc. **Le Palace**, 114, rue du Barbatre, features jazz bands in a luxurious bar decorated with works by local artists. Cover charges run 60-70F. Reims is justifiably proud of its **Théâtre de la Comédie**, 1, rue Eugene-Wiet (tel. 26 85 60 00).

Epernay

While Reims may be the official capital of Champagne, visitors will be hard-pressed to deny Epernay's position as the capital of champagne production. Miles of subterranean cellars contain 700 million bottles of "the king of wines." Each year, visitors guzzle more than 30,000 bottles—roughly one for every local citizen. Setting up shop at the crossroads of grape-growing, Epernay's grand old wineries extract their sparkling product from the light *Chardonnay* which grow to the south and from the dark *Pinot meunier* and *Pinot noir* which grow to the northwest and northeast respectively. These varieties fetch nearly four times as much on the open market as their Californian competitors. Moët & Chandon, Perrier-Jouet, Mercier, de Castellane—the palatial mansions on avenue de Champagne emblazoned with these and other names testify to the wealth that springs from the region's chalky soil.

Orientation and Practical Information

Epernay straddles the Marne in the heart of Champagne. By train it is a half-hour south of Reims and only one hour east of Paris's Gare de l'Est. From the station, cross the square to rue Gambetta and follow it to pl. de la République. The tourist office and the *caves* lie to the left on av. de Champagne (a 10-min. walk).

Tourist Office: 7, av. de Champagne (tel. 26 55 33 00). Information on Epernay's wine houses and maps for 3 different *routes de Champagne* to towns within 30km. Ask for the pamphet *Epernay et sa Région*. Earnest staff tries its hardest in English, but you may have to resort to sign language. (Imitations of various states of inebriation work well for directions to the *caves*.) Open Mon.-Sat. 9:30am-6:30pm, Sun. 11am-3pm; Nov.-Feb. Mon.-Sat. 10am-5:30pm.

Post Office: on pl. Hughes Plomb, (tel. 26 53 12 31). **Telephones** here. Open Mon.-Fri. 8am-7pm, Sat. 8am-noon. **Postal Code:** 51200.

Trains: tel. 26 88 50 50. Epernay is on the main rail line between Paris and the east. To: Paris (12 per day, 1¼ hr., 86F); Reims (frequent service, ½ hr., 25F); Strasbourg (4 per day, 3½ hr., 191F); Metz (2 per day, 2 hr., 123F); and Laon (transfer at Reims, 3 per day, 2 hr., 55F). Information office open Mon.-Sat. 9am-noon and 2-6pm.

Buses: on rue Rousseau, off pl. Notre-Dame (tel. 26 51 92 10). The information office is open infrequently and at random hours, but any bus driver can give you a schedule. To surrounding towns (2-3 per day) and Châlons-sur-Marne (4 per day, 1 hr., 25.50F).

Taxis: Taxi-Corbière (tel. 26 54 44 02), in front of the station. 24 hrs.

Car Rental: Avis, 70, rue de Champrot (tel. 26 54 11 92). **Europcar,** 16, rempart Perrier (tel. 26 51 58 68), in the Fina station.

Bike Rental: Claude Jeannel, 49, rue Cuissotte (tel. 26 55 22 90), off pl. de la République. 20F per ½-day, 40F per day. All-terrain bikes 80F per day. Deposit 500F.

Medical Assistance: Hôpital Auban-Moët, 137, rue de l'Hôpital (tel. 26 54 11 11).

Police: 7, rue Jean Chandon Moët, tel. 26 54 11 17. **Emergency,** tel. 17.

Accommodations and Food

Like many towns throughout the Champagne region, Epernay is invaded from June through September; book two to seven days ahead. As hotels are expensive, try to stay at the MJC Centre or make Epernay a daytrip from Reims or Paris.

MJC Centre International de Séjour, 8, rue de Reims (tel. 26 55 40 82), a 3-min. walk from the station. Bear left along the square and turn left onto rue de Reims. A pleasant if pricey hostel and *foyer.* Singles and dorm rooms 62F per person. Breakfast, sheets, lockers, and showers included. Laundry facilities. Cafeteria meals 36F. Call ahead, as rooms fill quickly in summer.

Hôtel St-Pierre, 1, rue Jeanne d'Arc (tel. 26 54 40 80), on a quiet street about 10 min. from the station. Elegant rooms and kind management. TV in all rooms. Singles and doubles from 84F, with shower 115F. Breakfast 20F.

Hôtel le Progrès, 6, rue des Berceaux (tel. 26 55 24 75). Comfortable, renovated singles and doubles 100-225F. Breakfast served in a pretty, skylit room (25F). Expensive but convenient. Check in at **Bar le Progrès,** a lively hangout on pl. de la République.

Hôtel du Nord, 50, rue Edouard Vaillant (tel. 26 51 52 65), in a shabby neighborhood 15 min. from the station and far from downtown. Clean, simple singles and doubles run a mere 67-85F. Breakfast 17F. Great 5-course, family-style meals 46.50F.

As in most French cities, restaurants around the train station and tourist attractions (i.e., on av. de Champagne) tend to be overpriced. Your cheapest option is the **MJC Cafeteria,** 8, rue de Reims, which serves complete cafeteria meals for 36F. (Open daily 11:30am-1:30pm and 6:45-8pm.) Across the square from the station, **Restaurant l'Hermite,** 3, pl. Thiers, offers a 56F *menu* on starched pink tablecloths. To celebrate Bart Simpson's timely demise, order their 89F *menu.* (Open Mon.-Fri. noon-2pm and 7-9:30pm, Sat. 7:30-10pm, closed Wed. evening.) **Restaurant l'Auberge d'Epernay,** 30, rue du Dr. Verron, to the left of Notre Dame, serves an extremely popular 49F Chinese *menu* and main dishes from 30F. Tippecanoe and take-out too. (Open Mon.-Sat. noon-2pm and 7-10:30pm.) Across the river from the train station, **La Terrasse,** 7, quai de Marne, is one of Epernay's more pleasant affordable restaurants; try the simple 60F *menu* or spiffier 110F and 155F *menus.* (Open Tues.-Sun. noon-2pm and 7-9:30pm; closed last 2 weeks in July.) Also across the river, **Mme Préjent,** 13, rue J.J. Rousseau, serves a 50F *menu* that includes drinks. (Open Mon.-Sat. afternoon; check ahead for exact hours.)

Sights and Entertainment

Epernay compensates for its lack of conventional historical monuments with the tastes and smells that emanate from sweeping **avenue de Champagne,** distinguished by its mansions, gardens, and monumental champagne firms. The best known is **Moët & Chandon,** 20, av. de Champagne (tel. 26 54 71 11), producers of the appallingly expensive Dom Perignon. The 45-minute tours (often in English) are informative and end with a free tasting. Napoleon was a great friend of Jean-Rémy-Moët and usually picked up a few thousand bottles of champagne on his way to the front. Unfortunately for the Emperor, Epernay was not on the way to Belgium in 1815; tour guides like to joke that the lack of Moët & Chandon champagne caused his crushing defeat at Waterloo. (Open Mon.-Sat. 9:30am-noon and 2-5pm, Sun. and holidays 9:30am-noon and 2-4pm; Nov.-March Mon.-Fri 9:30am-noon and 2-5pm. Free.) Moët also owns the beautiful private gardens across the street.

A 10-minute walk down the avenue at #73 is **Mercier** (tel. 26 54 75 26 or 26 51 71 11), whose tour features transport by electric train and a free sample. (Open April-Oct. Mon.-Sat. 9:30-11:30am and 2-5pm, Sun. and holidays 9am-5pm; Nov.

and Mar. daily 9:30-11:30am and 2-5pm; Dec.-Feb. Sat. and Sun. only 9:30-11:30am and 2-4pm.) The most informative champagne museum is at **de Castellane,** 57, rue de Verdun (tel. 26 55 15 33), across the street from Mercier. Tours in English culminate in free tastings. The **Jardin des Papillons,** between de Castellane and Mercier has a tropical greenhouse and gardens where 200 butterflies emerge from cocoons every week. (Open April-Oct. 10am-noon and 2-6pm. Admission 20F, students 15F.) The most concise overview of champagne and Epernay is a 20-minute slide show at 19, av. de Champagne (tel. 26 54 49 51). (Open 10:30am-6:30pm; shown in English, French, and German.) At the **Musée du Champagne et de Préhistoire,** 13, av. de Champagne (tel. 26 51 90 31), ascend to the top floor to view an exceptional collection of archaeological finds. (Open Wed.-Mon. 10am-noon and 2-5pm.)

Despite Epernay's somewhat abstruse preoccupation with things that go on in dark, moldy caves, conventional nightlife enjoys its own ferment here. Side by side at 12 and 14, rue Pierre Sémard, near the train station, are **Club St-Jean** (tel. 26 55 26 42) and the new-wave **Chintz Club** (tel. 26 51 89 07). Both charge a 60F cover, which includes the first drink, and cater to a hip, young crowd. **Le Tap-Too,** 5, rue des Près Dimanche (tel. 26 51 56 10), presents a bizarre new experiment in intergenerational disco: one half of the club blares Top 40 music for the college set and the other half spins slower jazz tunes for their parents. Groovy. (Open Thurs.-Sun. 10pm-4am).

Châlons-sur-Marne

Lacking the monumental majesty of Reims and the effervescence of Epernay, Châlons appears to be a *petit village* languishing in a post-inebriate stupor. As you wander along the ancient canals and explore the quiet residential districts, remind yourself that Châlons is a major transportation hub and home to more than 60,000 people. Although the town attracts far fewer visitors than its Champagne cousins, dazzling stained glass makes Châlons a great daytrip from either Reims or Epernay and an equally fine stopover for travelers heading farther east.

Orientation and Practical Information

As its full name implies, Châlons-sur-Marne lies on the Marne River. It is also on the main rail line between Paris's Gare de l'Est (1½ hr.) and Strasbourg (3 hr.). The center is a 15-min. walk east of the station; turn left out of the station, left again onto rue Jaurès, and continue down rue de la Marne. Buses A, D, and K follow the same route past the tourist office to the Hôtel de Ville.

Tourist Office: 3, quai des Arts (tel. 26 65 17 89), in the pedestrian zone just before the Hôtel de Ville. The free pamphlet *Le petit guide de Châlons* has a map, lists hotels and restaurants, and describes monuments. (Abridged version available in English.) Open Mon. and Sat. 2-6pm, Tues-Fri. 8:30am-12:30pm and 1:30-6:30pm, Sun. 10am-1pm; Sept.-June Mon.-Sat. only.

Post Office: 36, rue Jaurès, around the corner from the station. **Telephones** here. Open Mon.-Fri. 9am-noon and 2-6:30pm, Sat. 9am-noon. **Postal Code:** 51000.

Currency Exchange: The banks lining rue de la Marne are generally open Mon.-Fri. 9am-noon and 2-5:30pm, Sat. 9am-noon and 1:30-5pm.

Trains: pl. de la Gare (tel. 26 88 50 50). To: Reims via Epernay (7-8 per day, 35 min., 39F), Paris (frequent service, 1½ hr., 97F); and Metz (7-8 per day, 1½ hr., 102F). Information office open Mon.-Sat. 8am-noon and 2-7pm.

Buses: There is no *gare routière,* but **STDM** (tel. 26 65 17 07) runs ridiculously expensive buses that leave from the train station and pl. Tissier. To: Reims (3 per day, 2 hr., 79F) and Troyes (3 per day, 1¼ hr., 58F). Local buses leave from rue de Vaux (tel. 26 64 07 82).

Medical Assistance: tel. 26 64 91 91.

Police: pl. aux Chevaux (tel. 26 66 27 27). **Emergency,** tel. 17.

Accommodations, Camping, and Food

The possibilities don't dazzle. The **Auberge de Jeunesse (IYHF)**, rue Kellerman (tel. 26 68 13 56), is located on the other side of town from the train station on rue Chevalier as it runs through the park and through a gate on your right. Individuals are accepted in July and August only. (Reception open 6-10:30pm. 34F per person. Breakfast 12F.) A better deal may be the **Foyer de Jeune Travailleur Châlonnais,** 1, rue Faubourg St-Antoine (tel. 26 68 31 79), a 15-minute walk from the station into town. Alternately, take bus B to pl. aux Chevaux. Clean, well-located, and overwhelmingly friendly, this *foyer* serves filling three-course *menus* in its downstairs restaurant (26F). They are open year-round, but only to 18- to 25-year-olds. They *do* check. (No curfew or lockout. Singles 50F. Breakfast 5-10F.) Aptly named **Hôtel Jolly,** 12, rue de la Charrière (tel. 26 68 09 47), near the hostel, has singles and doubles with shower for 75-95F. (Breakfast 15F.) A friendly proprietor manages the convenient **Hôtel de Chemin de Fer** (tel. 26 68 21 25), on rue de la Gare across from the (surprise) train station. (Singles and doubles 90-130F, with toilet 112F. Breakfast 18F.) The restaurant's excellent cook prepares 50F and 85F *menus.* There's a four-star **campground** (tel. 26 68 38 00) just south of town on av. des Alliés. (12F per person. Open April-Oct.)

Traiteurs (like *charcuteries*) sell the cheapest lunches in town. **Machet,** 59, rue de la Marne, hands over quiche for 5.80F and yummy *allumette au jambon* (a ham pastry) for only 4F. Ask the chef to warm the cold specialties. (Open daily 7am-1:30pm and 2-9pm.) At 32, rue de Jaurès, near the station, **A Marion** has a tempting selection of salads: cucumber salad and various Greek and Moroccan dishes sell for 40-50F per kilogram. Young *Châlonnais* favor delicious if smallish pizzas (30-44F) at **Il Fluvio,** 18, rue Pasteur, a lively place decorated with plastic grapes and wagon wheels. (Open Mon.-Sat. noon-2pm and 7:30-11pm.) There is a fruit and meat **market** on Wednesday and Saturday mornings in pl. d'Art (open 8am-noon). After dark, sample a few of the 100 whiskeys at **La Cocktailerie,** 26, pl. de la République (tel. 26 65 10 27); their ice cream *coupes* are less potent but also good.

Sights

The tourist office's tour is a magnificent introduction to the city. Your 15F buys two to three hours of churches, parks, museums, *hôtels particuliers,* and many corners otherwise locked or obscure. (Tours from the tourist office July-Sept. Tues.-Sat. at 2:30pm. Call a week in advance to arrange a tour in English.) Boat tours of Châlons leave from in front of the Cathedral every Sunday June through Aug. (2-6pm, 8F.)

Stained glass fans will find Châlons second only to Chartres. In the center, facing one of the many ancient canals of Châlons, 12th-century **Eglise de Notre-Dame en Vaux** glows with the light filtered through 13th- and 16th-century rose windows set in the same pattern as those at Chartres. On Wednesday and Saturday the church's 56 bells supply the nearby market with a stirring soundtrack. (Open Mon.-Sat. 9am-noon and 2-6pm.) From the side street to the north, enter the **Musée du Cloître,** where medieval cathedral relics decapitated during the Revolution have been joyfully reunited with their heads. (Open Tues.-Sun. 10am-noon and 2-6pm. Admission 15F, students 9F, children 5F.) **Eglise St-Alpin,** off pl. Foch, features striking Renaissance windows in *grisaille,* grey and white glass with delicate yellows. To visit, call the tourist office—they will give you the key if you leave your passport.

Windows beyond description beckon you to 12th- to 16th-century **Cathédrale St-Etienne,** where St. Stephen's painful death by stoning is commemorated in glass and stone. Note the pervasive dark green tint—a hallmark of Châlons, just as blue is of Chartres. Renovations require you to enter at the southern side of the church. Châlons's deepest shade of green carpets **Le Petit Jard** and the adjacent **Grand Jard,** where pleasant canal-side walks lead past rare trees and a Henri IV-style turret a bridge. Enter the gardens at the corner of bd. Victor Hugo and av. du Leclerc. (Open

6:45am-11pm; Oct.-April 7:30am-6:30pm.) Châlons's municipal library, housed in the 17th-century **Hôtel des Dubois de Crancé,** jealously guards what is supposedly Marie Antoinette's prayerbook, in which she wrote at 4:30am on the day of her execution, "My God, have pity on me! My eyes no longer have tears to cry on you, my poor children, adieu, adieu! Marie-Antoinette." Call two to three days ahead to see the actual autograph; the attendants at the circulation counter can give you a booklet with photographs which argue (in French) for and against the document's authenticity. (Open Tues.-Sun. 9am-noon and 1:30-6pm.) The **Musée Municipal,** on pl. Godart by the library, displays a collection of statues representing Hindu deities, a reconstruction of a traditional *champenois* interior, local medieval sculptures, and a small collection of paintings. (Open Mon. and Wed.-Sat. 2-6pm, Sun. 2:30-6:30pm. Free.) The **Musée Garinet,** 13, rue Pasteur, preserves the atmosphere of a wealthy *châlonnais* townhouse of the 19th century, with period furniture and a typically 19th-century clutter of international art objects. (Open Wed.-Mon. 2-6pm. Free.) On Midsummer's Eve (June 21), Châlons holds an all-night **music festival** in various cafés and squares around the city.

Troyes

Troyes (pop. 65,000) belongs to the province of Champagne only because of a strategic move by the counts of Champagne, who acquired it in the 10th century. These vigorous and liberal princes built a city that fostered a large Jewish community and then, in the Renaissance, created its own school of sculpture. One of Troyes's prominent Jews may have been Chrétien de Troyes, the greatest of medieval *romanciers* (romance writers), who some claim took his name upon conversion to Christianity. The medieval *foires* (fairs) of Troyes, along with those of neighboring towns, made Champagne the hub of European commerce in the later Middle Ages. When the town was destroyed by fire for a third time in 1524, its artists designed the churches, gabled houses, tiny streets, and secret passages visible today. Although Tryoes has no *caves,* the downtown area is known as the *Bouchon de Champagne.* With its sweeping boulevards, beautifully restored St-Jean quartier (site of the *foires*), and tiny churches, Troyes provides a good introduction to aboveground Champagne.

Orientation and Practical Information

Troyes is about 130km south of Reims (2½ hr. by bus or car). If you're traveling by train, you'll have to go through Paris—and spend about four hours doing it. Fortunately, train connections between Paris-Est and Troyes are frequent.

The station at Troyes is only a block from the tourist office and two blocks from the rectangular old city, where almost all of the shops, restaurants, and hotels are located. From the station, cross over bd. Carnot and continue straight onto rue Général de Gaulle. The pedestrian district occupies the side streets on the right, just after Eglise Ste-Madeleine.

Tourist Office: 16, bd. Carnot (tel. 25 73 00 36), across from the train station and on the right. Not the most helpful, but they'll give you a city guide and accommodations list. From June to Sept. 15, guided walking tours of the city leave daily at 3pm from the front of St-Jean's church (in English by appointment, 2½ hr., 15F). Open Mon.-Sat. 9am-8:30pm, Sun. 10am-noon and 2:30-5:30pm; Sept. 16-May Mon.-Sat. 9am-12:30pm and 2-6:30pm. There is an annex at 24, quai Dampierre (tel. 25 73 36 88), in an old house opposite the Musée de la Pharmacie. Beware of currency exchange rates here. Open June-Sept. 16 Tues.-Sat. 9am-12:30pm and 2-6:30pm.

Post Office: (tel. 25 73 49 22), on rue Louis Ulbach, a street running south of the pedestrian zone in the Bouchon de Champagne. **Telephones** and **currency exchange.** Open Mon.-Fri. 8am-7pm, Sat. 8am-noon. **Postal Code:** 10000 (apocalyptically enough).

Trains: tel. 25 73 50 50. Ridiculously few destinations are directly linked to Troyes. Most involve a trip to Paris-Est (frequent service, 1½ hr., 94F). The main east line serves Chaumont, Belfort, Mulhouse, and Basel (Switzerland), with trains running daily every 1-2 hr. Information center open Mon.-Sat. 8:30am-noon and 2-6:45pm.

Buses: There is no information office, but buses depart next to the train station, which can help you with schedules but does not provide prices. Regional schedules are also available at the tourist office for 5F. To: Sens (7 per day, 1½ hr., 49F) and Châlons-sur-Marne (3 per day, 2 hr., 58F).

Taxis: Taxis Troyens (tel. 25 78 30 30), in the circle outside the station. Open Mon.-Thurs. 5am-2am, Fri.-Sun. 24 hrs. **Taxi Mestre,** 168, rue Général de Gaulle (tel. 25 73 07 40).

Car Rental: Europcar (tel. 25 73 27 66), **Hertz** (tel. 25 79 29 79), and **Budget** (tel. 25 73 27 37). At 2, 31, and 6 rue Voltaire, respectively.

Laundromat: Salon Lavoir GTI, 15, rue Turenne, in the pedestrian district. 20F wash, 6F for 15 min. dry, detergent 2F. 10 and 2F coins only. Open daily 8am-9pm.

Pharmacy: Pharmacie de la Madeleine, 116, rue Général de Gaulle (tel. 25 73 06 79). Open Mon.-Sat. 9am-noon and 2-7pm.

Medical Assistance: tel. 25 49 49 49. **Emergency: SAMU,** tel. 15.

Police: tel. 25 73 44 88. **Emergency,** tel. 17.

Accommodations and Camping

Troyes has many inexpensive hotels. There are several inexpensive *foyers,* but they only accept tourists on a one-day basis and often do not have room. Ask the tourist office for a complete list. Make reservations if your visit coincides with the annual Foire de Champagne, a champagne producers' convention (early June).

Auberge de Jeunesse (IYHF), 2, rue Jules Ferry (tel. 25 82 00 65), 5km from Troyes in Rosières. Take bus #6B (*direction* "Chartreux") from the tourist office to the last stop. From there, take bus #11 to the hostel, or walk 2.2km down a country road. Set in an old farmhouse complete with fireplace, garden, and gardener. Well worth the trek. Check-in from 6pm. 37F (card required). Breakfast 13F. Lunch and dinner 36F (groups only).

Hôtel du Théâtre, 35, rue Lebocey (tel. 25 73 18 47), on the northern limit of the Bouchon de Champagne. Warm and engaging proprietor. Better than average rooms. Singles 69F, with shower 113F. Doubles 88F, with shower 113F. Breakfast 15F. Open Sept.-July Tues.-Sun. evening. *Menus* starting at 52F downstairs. Restaurant open Tues.-Sun. noon-2pm and 7-9:30pm.

Hôtel de Paris, 54, rue Roger Salengro (tel. 25 73 11 70). A stylish 2-star hotel with a garden terrace. Built in a beautifully restored 12th-century building which once served as the mint for the counts of France. Singles 90-175F, doubles 105-190F. Breakfast 18F. Reservations recommended. Restaurant downstairs serves a 50F dinner *menu* and a 29F *plat du jour.* Open Mon.-Fri. 7-11pm.

Hôtel Thiers, 59, rue Général de Gaulle (tel. 25 73 40 66). Clean 2-star hotel with gregarious owner. Modern rooms with TV. Singles 90-160F. Doubles 110-190F. Breakfast 20F.

Hôtel Butat, 50, rue Turennes (tel. 25 73 77 39). Centrally located. Spacious rooms with Oriental rugs, perhaps a bit high toned for backpackers. Singles 90-165F. Doubles 110-185F. Breakfast 20F. Reservations recommended 1 week in advance.

Hôtel Le Marigny, 3, rue Charbonnet (tel. 25 73 10 67). A rickety, half-timbered hotel at the edge of the old town. Sagging floor needs plastic surgery. Singles 75-160F. Doubles 90-160F. Extra bed 30F. Breakfast 20F.

Camping: Camping Municipal (tel. 25 81 02 64), on RN60, 10150 Pont-Ste-Marie. A 2-star site with showers, shops, and a restaurant. 6.90F per person. 10.70 per tent. Open April-Oct. 15.

Food

The Quartier St-Jean is full of *crêperies* and inviting little restaurants, especially on rue Paillot de Montabert and rue Champeaux. **Les Halles,** near the Hôtel de Ville, brings together modern shops and traditional farmers from the Aube region. (Open Mon.-Thurs. 8am-12:45pm and 3:30-7pm, Fri.-Sat. 7am-7pm, Sun. 9am-

12:30pm.) For lunch, make yourself a picnic and take it to **place de la Libération,** a great park with fountains, flowers, and ice cream vendors. Try *andouillette à la mode de Troyes,* a small chitterling sausage served throughout France.

L'Accroche Coeur, 24, rue de la Trinité, off rue Emile Zola. Serves traditional dishes (including *andouillettes*) and a lip-smacking *steak au poivre* (42F). 49F *menus,* entrees 25-65F. Open Mon.-Sat. noon-3pm and 7-11pm.

Crêperie la Tourelle, 9, rue Champeaux, just east of Eglise St-Jean. Pocket-sized *crêperie* right in the middle of things. Tables trail out onto the sidewalk, and plates are passed through the windows. *Crêpes* 10-34F. Open Tues.-Sat. noon-midnight.

Le Café du Musée, 59, rue de la Cité, near the cathedral. Famous for its selection of beer—12 brands on tap, 60 in bottles. Open Mon.-Sat. 10am-3am. The rustic restaurant upstairs offers local fare of good quality. 4-course 60F *menu.*

Le Tricasse, 2, rue Charbonnet (tel. 25 73 14 80). Local musicians entertain the *Troyens* who frequent this popular bar. Beers from 10F. Standard café food, 12-18F. Open Mon.-Sat. 11am-3am.

Le Grand Café, 4, rue Champeaux (tel. 25 73 25 60), right in the pedestrian district. You pay for the central location. Sandwiches 15-25F. 54F *menu.* Try the *flan froid d'aubergines à la tomate fraiche* (cold eggplant soufflé with tomato sauce). Café open daily 7:30am-12:30am. Fancier restaurant upstairs open daily 12:30-2pm and 7-10pm.

Sights and Entertainment

If you haven't seen enough churches and museums yet, Troyes's collection alone may push you to the brink. The city center alone boasts eight interesting museums and nine churches, dating from the 12th to the 17th centuries. Perhaps the best way to explore Troyes is to wander through the streets around the handicraft museum. In contrast to the commercial Quartier St-Jean, this residential area's 16th-century buildings show Troyes's commitment to preservation and restoration.

The most impressive of the churches, **Cathédrale St-Pierre et St-Paul** was begun in the 13th century, expanded in the 16th, and like many others, never finished. Inside, 112 stained-glass windows light the airy nave and choir, one of the longest in France. (Open daily 8am-noon and 2-6pm; Sept. 16-June daily 9am-noon and 2-5pm.) The adjacent **trésorerie** contains the jewels of the counts of Champagne. (Open June-Aug. Tues.-Sun. 2-6pm. Admission 8F.) Built in 1150, **Ste-Madeleine,** the city's oldest church, is distinguished by its delicate stone lacework. **Eglise St-Urbain,** lit by 13th-century stained-glass windows, was founded by Pope Urbain IV in 1261. In **Eglise St-Jean,** Henry V married Catherine of France after signing the Treaty of Troyes in 1420, which opened the door to an English invasion. On July 9, 1429 Joan of Arc liberated the town from the English as she led Charles VII to be crowned in Reims. (Churches open daily 10am-noon and 3-6pm.) Troyes combines history and theater in **Cathédral de Lumière,** a sound and light show focusing on the stained-glass windows. (Shows June 29-Sept. 15. Admission 40F. Tickets available from the tourist office.)

Troyes's museums are expensive unless you buy the 20F pass, which admits you to all the museums except the Maison de l'Outil and the Musée Marguerite Bourgeoys. In the ancient Episcopal Palace next to the cathedral on pl. St-Pierre, the **Musée d'Art Moderne—Collection Pierre et Denise Levy** (tel. 25 80 57 30) leavens the city's heavy historical tone. One of France's finest collections of modern art, the Levys' cache includes 350 paintings and over 1300 drawings and sketches by the likes of Braque, Cézanne, Degas, Dufy, Matisse, Modigliani, and Picasso. (Open Wed.-Mon. 11am-6pm; guided tours Sat.-Sun. at 11am, 2:30pm, and 4pm. 15F.) On the other side of the cathedral at 21, rue Chrétien-de-Troyes, the eclectic **Musée St-Loup,** housed in the old Abbaye St-Loup, presents a fascinating if somewhat disorganized collection of Merovingian weaponry, Gallo-Roman statuettes, medieval sculpture, and 15th- through 20th-century painting. A locked glass door on the second floor allows you to admire from afar the largest library hall in France, once the dormitory of the abbey's monks in the 17th and 18th centuries. The room contains 90,000 volumes, with over 4000 precious manuscripts from the 7th through 18th centuries and 46,000 volumes from the 16th century alone. (Admission 15F, students free.) The **Musée Historique de Troyes,** housed in the 16th-century Hôtel de Vauluisant on rue de Vauluisant, exhibits religious articles, documents, and pieces of Renaissance *troyen* sculpture. In the same complex is France's only **Musée de la Bonneterie,** a collection of gloves, hats, and hosiery, for which Troyes is, amazingly, famous. The **Pharmacie de l'Hôtel-Dieu,** quai des Comtes de Champagne, houses a rare 16th-century apothecary with 320 painted wood boxes and 2140 *faïence* receptacles; the adjoining **Musée des Hôpitaux** contains old documents and a collection of ancient bust reliquaries. (Museums open Wed.-Mon. 10am-noon and 2-6pm. 15F each.)

The **Maison de l'Outil et de la Pensée Ouvrière,** 7, rue de la Trinité, is a marvelously restored 16th-century *hôtel* turned into a giant regional toolshed. Although the collection is poorly documented, the beautiful implements, artfully displayed, speak for themselves. (Open daily 9am-noon and 2-6pm. Admission 20F.) **Musée Marguerite Bourgeoys,** 8, rue de l'Isle, is worth a visit to those interested in hagiography. (You know who you are.) The displays trace the life and works of Marguerite Bourgeoys, a 17th-century *Troyenne* who founded the Congrégation Notre Dame in Montréal and was canonized by John Paul II in 1982. (Open in summer Mon.-Sat. 2-5pm. Free.)

Movie theaters jostle shops on rue Emile Zola, where only occasionally do the houses recall Troyes's heady days of yore. The best dancing is at **K'VO,** cour de la Gare (tel. 25 78 22 35), in the Grand Hôtel across from the station, where a thirty-something crowd in sophisticated yet puckish attire gathers nightly to mourn their lost idealism. (Cover 70F. Open 8pm-2am.)

The North

*This land here cost twenty lives a foot that summer.
. .see that little stream—we could walk to it in two
minutes. It took the British a month to walk to it—a
whole empire walking very slowly, dying in front and
pushing forward behind. And another empire walked
very slowly backwards a few inches a day, leaving the
dead like a million bloody rugs.*
— F. Scott Fitzgerald, Tender is the Night

Even after nearly fifty years of peace, the memory of two world wars is never far from the towns and villages of northern France. Nearly every town bears scars from the wanton bombing of World War II, and German-built concrete observation towers still survey the land. Regiments of tombstones stand as reminders of the massacres at Arras in Flanders, at the Somme in Picardie, and at Cambrai in Artois. Although thousands traveling to and from Britain pass through Calais, Boulogne, and Dunkerque every day, surprisingly few take the time to explore the ancient towns between the ports and Paris.

The best course for a tourist here is to bypass the overpriced major ports and make a pilgrimage to the great cathedrals, especially in Laon, Noyon, and Amiens, all built during the 12th and 13th centuries. If you're coming from Paris, the countryside will be a welcome change. In Picardie, undulating fields of wheat extend in all directions, dotted with the occasional clump of trees or wooden windmill. Along the rugged coast, chalk cliffs loom over the beaches, and cultivation gives way to cows and sheep that graze near collapsed bunkers and coils of rusty barbed wire.

Trains run infrequently, and many of the smaller towns are only directly accessible from the largest of cities. *Autoroutes* make for easy driving but somewhat tedious hitching. Cyclists will appreciate the mostly flat terrain although trucks and frequent rains can be a nuisance.

Once a possession of Flanders, the region has retained much of its Flemish influence. The architecture of many town halls (such as Dunkerque's, Calais's, and Lille's) is entirely Flemish, and Flemish cuisine remains the regional specialty. Mussels, prepared in a panoply of different cways, are especially popular, as are *pâté de canard* (duck pâté), *galettes* (salty *crêpes*), and *ficelle picarde* (a cheese, ham, and mushroom *crêpe*).

Calais

Ever since Richard the Lion Hearted and his crusaders arrived here in 1189 on their way to Jerusalem, hordes of travelers have made Calais the main link between England and the continental Europe. This year some 15 million voyagers will pass through Calais in as many as 160 daily channel crossings. When the celebrated Eurotunnel connecting the continent to Britain by rail is completed in 1993, Calais will be the last French stop on the line. Completely rebuilt after World War II, the town is full of flashing neon and chintzy shops. The only redeeming features are the interesting Hôtel de Ville, the famed Rodin sculpture *Burghers of Calais,* and the town's attractive, sandy beach.

Orientation and Practical Information

Calais is two and a half hours from Paris's Gare du Nord and has two train stations: **Gare Calais-Ville** and **Gare Calais-Maritime** (the latter near the ferry and hovercraft ports). Free buses connect the hoverport and ferry terminal with Gare

Calais-Ville, in the center of town. Taking a hovercraft is the fastest way to cross the channel for foot passengers (35 min. by hovercraft vs. 75 min. by ferry) and costs the same as or less than the ferry lines.

Tourist Office: 12, bd. Clemenceau (tel. 21 96 62 40), 1 block from the Calais-Ville station. Ferry information, free accommodations list, accommodations service (10F), and a perplexing city map with no street names. English spoken. Open Mon.-Sat. 9am-12:30pm and 2:30-6:30pm.

Currency Exchange: Open 24 hrs. at ferry terminal and hoverport, but the rates are *pourri* (i.e., they suck). In town, banks line **boulevard Jacquard** and **rue Royale.** Most open Mon.-Fri. 8:30am-noon and 2-5pm.

Post Office: 174, rue Mollien (tel. 21 96 55 30), on pl. d'Alsace. **Telephones.** Open Mon.-Fri. 8:30am-6:30pm, Sat. 8:30am-noon. **Postal Code:** 62100.

Trains: Gare Calais-Ville, bd. Jacquard (tel. 21 80 50 50). To: Paris (14 per day, 2½ hr., 158F); Lille (15 per day, 1½ hr., 64F); Boulogne (14 per day, 30 min., 32F); Dunkerque (4 per day, 50 min., 32F). Information office open Mon.-Sat. 9:30am-6:50pm. **Gare Calais Maritime,** Car Ferry Terminal. To Paris only in the afternoon. Open daily 8am-9pm. Helpful information office with free city maps. Lockers 5-10F. Open daily 9-10:45am and 2-7:40pm.

Ferries: Hoverspeed, Hoverport (tel. 21 96 67 10). To Dover (every ½-1 hr., 35 min., one way 200F, 60-hr. return 230F, 120-hr. return 300F). **Sealink,** Car Ferry Terminal (tel. 21 96 70 70). To Dover (every 2 hrs., 75 min., one way or 60-hr. return 190F, 120-hr. return 280F). Info. office open Mon.-Fri. 9am-5:45pm, Sat. 8:30am-noon. **P&O Ferries,** Car Ferry Terminal (tel. 21 97 21 21). To Dover (every 90 min., 75 min., one way 200F, 120-hr. return 300F). Bicycles cross for free on all 3 lines. Usually enough room, even in peak season.

Hitchhiking: If you decide to hitchhike to Paris, try bd. Gambetta (which leads to the N1) or bd. Victor Hugo (to the A26). For Lille, take bd. de l'Egalité to the A25. *Bonne chance.*

Laundromat: rue des Thermes at rue des Prêtres. 40F for 4kg dry cleaning, 12-18F wash and dry. 10F and 2F coins. Open 7am-10pm.

Pharmacy: Grande Pharmacie Richelieu, 29, rue Royale (tel. 21 34 55 62). Plenty of medication for *mal de mer*—seasickness. Open Mon. 2-7pm, Tues.-Sat. 9am-noon and 2-7pm.

Medical Assistance: SMUR (tel. 21 96 72 19). 24-hr. emergency service.

Police: (tel. 21 34 37 00), pl. de Lorraine. **Emergency,** tel. 17.

Accommodations and Food

Although you should have no problem finding a room, reserving one or two days in advance in July and August isn't a bad idea.

Point Accueil Jeunes/Maison Pour Tous, 81, bd. Jacquard (tel. 21 34 69 53), past the town hall away from the station. A large modern facility. Reception open 5-10pm. 35F per night. Open July-Aug. only.

Hôtel le Littoral, 71, rue Aristide Briand (tel. 21 34 47 28). Friendly owner. Huge, well-lit rooms with comfortable beds. Singles 85F. Doubles 95F, with shower 130F. Breakfast 15F. Showers 10F. In July and August reserve 1 month in advance. 55F *menu* in the restaurant downstairs.

Au Mouton Blanc, 44, rue du Vauxhall (tel. 21 34 71 52), two blocks away from bd. Jacquard. Predominantly senior clientele. Small but clean rooms with a sink and TV in each. Singles 86-114F. Doubles with shower and toilet 160F. Breakfast 14F.

Camping Municipale, 26, av. Raymond Poincaré (tel. 21 46 62 00), off rue Royale. A sardine tin with a beach view. 5F per adult, 2.80F per child, 7.70F per site. Showers 3.80F.

Dining in Calais is generally a (surprise!) unremarkable experience. Generic cafés with 55-80F *menus,* line **rue Royale** and **boulevard Jacquard.** Try **Taverne Kronenbourg,** 46, rue Royale, a large, friendly establishment with a three-course, 60F *menu.* (Open daily 9am-10pm.) At **Aux 3 Suisses,** 14, bd. Jacquard, an excruciatingly long wait culminates in a delicious, well-presented meal (59F *menu;* open daily 9am-9pm). Both the hoverport and the ferry terminal maintain mediocre, expensive self-service cafeterias. (Open 8:30am-3pm.)

Sights

If you have time between arrival and departure in Calais, check out the flamboyant **Hôtel de Ville,** a 20th-century reconstruction in Flemish Renaissance style. In front, Rodin's *Burghers of Calais* recalls a near-tragic moment in the final year of the Hundred Years' War. England's King Edward III had agreed to hang the mayor and several prominent citizens rather than slaughter all the city's inhabitants; the burghers' heroism prompted the impassioned and successful eleventh-hour intervention of Edward's French wife, Philippine. Calais remained British until François de Guise reclaimed it for the French in 1558. Pick up a copy of the tourist office's free booklet, *Calais and Its History,* much more interesting than the town proper.

Directly across from the town hall in **Parc St-Pierre** is a camouflaged bunker that served as the German navy's principal telephone exchange from 1941 to 1944. The building now houses the **War Museum,** a fine collection of military artillery and uniforms. (Open Mar.-Nov. daily 10am-5pm. Admission 10F, students 7F, children 5F.)

Boulogne

According to legend, in 636 a boat carrying only a statue of the Virgin Mary washed up on the beach of Boulogne, which subsequently became a famous pilgrimage site. Today, Boulogne (pop. 44,000) is no one's Mecca but plenty of peoples' stopover. Like Calais, Boulogne ushers thousands of passengers through its port every day, but unlike its northern counterpart, the city maintains an authentic French flavor. In this, the largest fishing port in France, French remains the first language in shop windows, and cafés still outnumber fast food joints. On the last Sunday in June, the medieval **Fête du Cygne** (Festival of the Swan) in the *vieille ville* features exhibitions of local artwork.

Orientation and Practical Information

Like Calais, Boulogne lies 2½ hours northwest of Paris and is served by two train stations: Gare Boulogne-Ville (from which most trains leave) and Gare Maritime. To reach central pl. Frédéric Sauvage from Gare Boulogne-Ville, cross bd. Voltaire and follow bd. Daunou to the canal. The post office, on your right, is at the southern end of the place, and the tourist office is at the northern. Pont Marquet, the bridge adjacent to the tourist office, leads to the ferry booking offices.

Tourist Office: pl. Frédéric Sauvage (tel. 21 31 68 38). English spoken. Crowded with ferry travelers. Free accommodations service, map, and ferry brochures. Open June-Sept. Sun.-Thurs 10am-7pm, Fri.-Sat. 10am-9pm; Oct.-May Tues.-Sat. 9am-noon and 2-6pm.

Currency Exchange: Banks open Mon.-Fri. 9am-noon and 2-5pm. Banks at Hoverport and Ferry Terminal open daily but offer gnasty rates.

Post Office: pl. Frédéric Sauvage (tel. 21 31 65 40), near the tourist office. **Telephones.** Open Mon.-Fri. 8:30am-5:30pm, Sat. 8:30am-noon. **Postal code:** 62200.

Trains: Gare Boulogne-Ville (tel. 21 80 50 50), bd. Voltaire. To: Paris (11 per day, 3 hr., 128F); Calais (19 per day, 45 min., 32F); Lille (13 per day, 1½ hr., 82F). Lockers 5-10F. Information office open Mon.-Sat. 9am-12:15pm and 1:45-6:45pm. **Gare Maritime,** Car Ferry Terminal. Less frequent service to Paris, connecting with ferry arrivals.

Ferries: Hoverspeed, booking office (tel. 21 30 27 26). To Dover (every 2 hr., one way 200F, 60 hr. return 230F, 120 hr. return 300F). **Sealink,** booking office (tel. 21 30 25 11). To Folkestone (every 3 hr., one way 190F, 60 hr. return 190F, 120 hr. return 280F). Information office open 24 hrs. **P&O Ferries,** booking office (tel. 21 31 78 00). To Dover (every 3 hr.; one way 200F, 120 hr. return 300F). Information office open daily 5:15am-midnight. All three lines are located on Pont Marquet and let bicycles sail for free.

Womens Center: Centre d'Information des Droits de la Femme, (tel. 21 30 45 41). Open Mon. and Tues.-Thurs. 3-6pm, Wed. 9am-noon, Fri. 3-5pm.

Laundromat: Lavomatique, 62, rue de Lille, across the street from the cathedral. Wash 14F, dry 2F per 5 min. Open 7am-10pm. 2F pieces only.

Pharmacy: Pharmacie Centrale, 41, Grande Rue (tel. 21 31 64 51). Stock up on seasickness remedies. Open Tues.-Sat. 9am-noon and 2-7pm, Mon. 2-7pm.

Police: rue Perrochel (tel. 21 83 12 34). **Emergency,** tel. 17.

Accommodations and Food

During the peak season Boulogne's hotels fill quickly, so make reservations 2-3 days in advance or show up early in the morning.

Auberge de Jeunesse (IYHF), 36, rue de la Port Gayole (tel. 21 31 48 22), just outside the *vieille ville* and a 10-min. walk from Gare-Ville. Take a right on bd. Voltaire, walk 1 block, turn right on bd. Beaucers to rue de Brequerecque, turn left, and go up the hill. Crowded but clean dormitories with 4 beds in each room. Kitchen facilities. Curfew 11pm. Office open 8-10am and 5-11pm. IYHF card required. 50F per night. Breakfast included. Sheets 13F. Camping out back 16F in your own tent. In July and August, make reservations 1 week in advance. Bike rental 29.50F per day, deposit 300F.

Hôtel Hamiot, 1, rue Faidherbe (tel. 21 31 44 20), facing the beach. Large, plain rooms. Cheerful owner also runs the fine restaurant downstairs (main courses 31-61F). Singles 93F. Doubles 106F. Bath 17F. Breakfast 17F. Often filled by tour groups, so reserve a month in advance in summer.

Hôtel au Sleeping, 20, bd. Daunou (tel. 21 80 62 79), down the street from Gare Boulogne-Ville. Small rooms on a noisy boulevard. Singles and doubles 83-163F. Breakfast 18F.

Hôtel le Mirador, 2, rue de la Lampe (tel. 21 31 38 08), off bd. Daunou. Attractive, well-kept rooms. Singles and doubles from 103F. Breakfast 18F.

Camping: Moulin Wibert, bd. Ste-Beuve (tel. 21 31 40 29), 2km west of the tourist office (quai Gambetta turns into bd. Ste-Beuve). 17.20F per adult, 9.80 per child, 7.30 per car. Hot showers and pool included. Open April-Oct. 15.

Restaurants in Boulogne are as unremarkable as the hotels. Though they do not cater to tourists as much as those in Calais, they all seem to offer the standard fare of seafood or steak. *Friteries,* simple cafés, and self-service cafeterias choke bd. Bambetta, along the canal. In the old city, *crêperies* and *brasseries* take over. On Wednesdays and Saturdays from 7:30am to 1:30 pm, pl. Dalton comes to life with an excellent open-air **market. Les Jardins de l'Europe,** 1, pl. Frédéric Sauvage, across from the tourist office, is an attractive cafeteria that offers filling dishes for 20-35F. (Open Mon.-Sat. 11:30am-2pm and 6:30-9:45pm, Sun. 11:30am-2:30pm and 6:30-9:45pm.) **Le Nabucco,** 78, bd. Gambetta, overlooking the port, serves excellent fish and grilled meat specialties. *Menus* are 57F and 95F; the *plat du jour* is 42F. (Open Mon.-Tues. and Thurs.-Sat. noon-2:30pm and 7-10pm, Sun. noon-2:30pm.) Across from the cathedral in the *vieille ville,* **Au Bon Accueil,** 55, rue de Lille, posts a fantastic, filling 45F *menu* (open Tues.-Sun. noon-2pm and 7-10pm).

Sights

Boulogne's *vieille ville* is built on the same hill which the Romans settled to watch over their city some two millennia ago. The maze of charming streets is surrounded by a thick wall, which you can scale for an excellent view of Boulogne's harbor. Like a goose guarding its golden egg, 19th-century **Basilique de Notre-Dame** sits atop the labyrinthine **crypts** of an earlier 12th-century edifice. One of the 14 chambers contains the vestiges of a 3rd-century Roman temple; another exhibits jeweled religious artifacts. (Crypt and treasury open Tues.-Sun. 2-5pm. Admission 10F, children 5F.) Next to the cathedral, the 13th-century **beffroi** (belfry), sends acrophobics into a swoon with its view of the port. (Open Mon.-Sat. 8am-noon and 2:30-6pm, Sat. 8am-noon. Free.) On Easter 1991, Boulogne is scheduled to open its **National Sea Center,** a huge aquarium with sharks and other members of the tropical finny tribe.

Dunkerque

Dunkerque (pop. 75.000) seems entirely oblivious to the foreign feet passing over its tiled sidewalks and sandy beach. A fishing village and small port in the 10th century, Dunkerque survived Flemish, Burgundian, Spanish, and English rule before becoming French in 1662, when Louis XIV wrote Charles II a bad check. The city's darkest hour came in June 1940, when battleships, private yachts, humble rowboats, and anything else British that could float gathered here to evacuate troops fleeing fierce German fire.

Orientation and Practical Information

Dunkerque lies on the RN1 between Calais (40km away) and the Belgian border (20km away), 274km from Paris. The city consists of two main sections: the town center, spreading east from the train station, and the area by the beach. To reach the tourist office from the station turn left on rue Nationale from av. Guynemer, which turns into rue Thiers and later rue du Sud, and continue to the belfry (3 blocks).

Tourist Office: pl. du Beffroi (tel. 28 66 79 21), on the ground floor of the belfry. English spoken. Cash only **currency exchange.** Provides excellent map, a free list of hotels and restaurants, and, only if you're desperate, a free accommodations service. Open Mon.-Sat. 9am-6:30pm; Sept.-June Mon.-Sat. 9am-noon and 2-6:30pm. **Dunkerque Informations** (tel. 28 66 46 90), across the street from the train station. Terrific maps of the city and hotel listings, but no information on the surrounding region. Open Mon.-Fri. 9am-noon and 2-6pm, Sat.-Sun. 9am-noon. If you arrive late, inquire next door at **Cotaxi** (tel. 28 66 73 00). Open 24 hrs.

Budget Travel: Transalpino, 3, rue Alfred Dumont (tel. 28 59 21 88). Ferry information and discount flights to points within Europe. Open Mon. 2-6:30pm, Tues.-Sat. 9am-noon and 2-6:30pm.

Currency Exchange: Banks along rue Clémenceau open Mon.-Fri. 8:45am-5pm. At other times, exchange at the tourist office.

Post Office: rue Pres. Poincaré, at pl. du Général de Gaulle. Open Mon.-Fri. 8:30am-6pm, Sat. 8:30am-noon.

Trains: pl. de la Gare (tel. 28 66 50 50). To: Paris (5 per day, 3 hr., 166F); Arras (7 per day, 1½ hr., 67F); Lille (9 per day, 1 hr., 54F). Last train (for Lille) leaves at 6:05pm. Information center open daily 8am-7pm.

Ferries: Sallyline, pl. Emile Bollaert (tel. 28 63 23 80). To Ramsgate (every 2 hr., 2 hr.; one way 180F, 60-hr. return 180F, 120-hr. return 260F). Information office open Mon.-Sat. 2-8pm.

Laundromat: 45, rue Terquem. 20F wash. 2F per 5 min. dry. 10F and 2F coins only. Open Mon.-Sat. 7am-7:30pm, Sun. 7am-1pm.

Pharmacy: 5, rue de l'Amiral Ronarc'h, across from the tourist office (tel. 28 66 89 86). Open Mon. 2:30-7pm, Tues.-Sat. 9:15am-12:15pm and 2:30-7pm.

Police: quai des Hollandais (tel. 28 66 30 05). Emergency, tel. 17.

Accommodations and Camping

Dunkerque is filled with inexpensive low-budget hotels, which should have room even in high season. Ask the tourist office for a comprehensive list.

Auberge de Jeunesse (IYHF), pl. Paul Asseman (tel. 28 63 36 34). Dorm rooms will make you feel like a packed sardine, albeit a clean one (hot shower included). No lockout. Curfew 10:30pm. 37F. Breakfast 13F. IYHF card required.

Hôtel le Moderne, 2, rue Nationale (tel. 28 66 80 24). Comfortable rooms above a lively café run by the same friendly owners. Singles from 90F. Doubles from 95F. Breakfast 20F.

Hôtel Terminus Nord, 2, pl. de la Gare (tel. 28 66 54 26), across from the station. Simple rooms are slightly worn and musty. Singles from 75F. Doubles from 95F. Shower 20F.

Hôtel du Tigre, 8 rue Clémenceau (tel. 28 66 75 17). Lovely 2-star hotel in great location. Large, comfortable rooms. Chatty owner actually *likes* Americans. Singles from 90F. Doubles from 120F. Breakfast 20F.

Camping: Dunkerque-Malo-les-bains (tel. 28 69 26 68), bd. de l'Europe. Take bus #3 (every 20 min.) to the Malo CES Camping stop or follow av. des Bains east for 4km. Comfortable campground with swimming pool. Open March-Nov.

Food

Inexpensive restaurants and cafés line the boulevard along the beach. The local specialty is mussels (*moules*), which come swathed in various white wine sauces.

Tête d'Ail, 26, rue Terquem (tel. 28 66 22 03). Intimate family-run restaurant serving meats and seafood. The 68F 3-course *menu* is *fantastique,* as is the 48F lunch *menu.* Open Mon.-Fri. noon-1:30pm and 7pm-2am, Sat. 7pm-2am, Sun. noon-1:30pm and 7-11pm.

L'Iguane, 15, digue des Alliés, overlooking the ocean. Huge but always crowded. Serves excellent mussels (45F) and other seafood (35-65F) under the envious gaze of large iguanas. Open daily 10am-10pm.

Pavois, 175, digue de Mer. Cavernous restaurant specializing in seafood at great prices. Always busy and always delicious. Open March-Oct. daily 11:30am-midnight.

La Torcia, 16, rue de Flandre, off digue des Alliés (tel. 28 59 15 08). Microscopically thin-crusted pizza (25-40F) baked before your eyes in a wood burning oven in this cozy, candlelit restaurant. Open daily 7pm-10:30pm.

Sights and Entertainment

The tourist office's free brochure will guide you through the city. Directly opposite the tourist office on rue Clemenceau, the 15th-century Eglise St-Eloi shelters Flemish paintings inside its impressive walls. The church's 500-year-old **belfry** is across the street; in July and August you can climb it for a great you-know-what. Continue along rue Clemenceau to reach the town's flamboyant **Hôtel de Ville,** a twin to Calais's Flemish city hall.

The **Musée des Beaux-Arts** (tel. 28 66 21 57), near the theater on pl. du Général de Gaulle, houses an impressive collection of 16th- to 18th-century paintings by important but relatively unknown French and Flemish artists whose names we can't reveal. (Open Wed.-Mon. 10am-noon and 2-6pm. Admission 6F, students 3F. Free on Sun.) The park across the bridge from the youth hostel trades typical French flowerbeds for rock gardens, modern sculptures, and concrete craters, all scattered among hills as round as Kojak's head and greener than year-old bread. Poised in the center of this chthonic Disneyland is the fantastic **Musée d'Art Contemporain,** rue des Bains (tel. 28 59 21 65), itself shaped like a folded paper sailor's hat. (Open Wed.-Mon. 10am-7pm. Admission 6F, students 3F.) The **Musée Aquariophile** (aquarium), 35, av. du Casino, instructs you not to feed their exotic fish. (Open Wed.-Mon. 10am-noon and 2-6pm. Admission 6F, students 3F).

Between the aquarium and the beach lies the picturesque neighborhood of **Malo-les-Bains.** Built in the late 19th century as an independant commune for the wealthy literary set, this commercial and residential district contains an eclectic mix of brick, tile, and half-timbered structures.

From May to September, the **Maison des Jeunes pour la Culture,** 43, rue Docteur Louis Lemaire (tel. 28 66 47 89), shows popular movies in English with French subtitles (23F). The Dunkerque **carnival** in February, the biggest festival in Northern France, unleashes a tide of drunken salaciousness that eludes psychohistorical explanation. Between July and September, the **Contemporary Art Festival** brings culture to the town's beach. In the first week of September, the **Fête des Moissons** (harvest celebration) spurs dancing, drinking, and good clean fun. Call the Mairie de Dunkerque (tel. 28 59 29 00) for details on these and other events.

Lille

Lille—the mere mention of that five-letter word causes most tourists to shudder with contempt for what is rumored to be a smog-drenched industrial behemoth. Indeed, Lille's location on the Pas-de-Calais trade route connecting Paris to the ports of Boulogne and Calais has brought enormous industrial and commercial success. A center for French textile production, Lille (pop. 200,000) has grown from an 11th-century transit station for boats passing on the river Deûle into the largest city in the north and the fifth largest in France.

Those who peer out over their upturned noses, however, will find an active, pleasant university city whose Flemish character extends beyond the aging townhouses lining rue Esquermoise.

Orientation and Practical Information

Lille is two hours by train from Paris's Gare du Nord and one hour from Calais. From the centrally located train station, head straight down rue Faidherbe to pl. de Gaulle; place Rihour is just a bit beyond to the south. Lille's residents are proud of their fully automated metro, which they claim is the most modern in the world. Though distances are short, it is worth taking at least one trip just to ride in a train without a conductor (the entire system is computerized) and see the stations, each designed in a contemporary style by a local architect. (Tickets 6.50F per ride, *carnet* of 10 50F.) Both the area around the train station and around the Wazemmes Market may be dangerous at night.

Tourist Office: pl. Rihour (tel. 20 30 81 00), in the remaining fragment of a 15th-century castle. Group tours Mon.-Sat. in English and French. Free accommodations service. Open Mon. 1-6pm, Tues.-Sat. 10am-6pm. The **information center** (tel. 20 06 40 65) at the train station can give you a list of accommodations and a map. They also perform a cash-changing service, although the rates verge on robbery. Open Mon.-Sat. 9am-12:45pm and 4-8:30pm. Diagonally across pl. Rihour is the **Comité Régional de Tourisme Nord-Pas de Calais**, 26, pl. Rihour (tel. 20 57 40 04). Maps and regional information. Open Mon. 2-6:45pm, Tues.-Sat 10am-6:30pm.

Budget Travel: Centre Régional d'Information de la Jeunesse, 2, rue Nicolas Leblanc (tel. 20 57 86 04), at pl. de la République next to the post office. Information on flights, temporary jobs, and housing. They match riders with drivers through a Paris-based network. Open Mon.-Tues. and Thurs.-Fri. 1-6pm, Wed. 10am-6pm and Sat. 10am-12:30pm.

Post Office: 7, pl. de la République (tel. 20 54 70 13). Poste Restante address: Bureau PTT, Lille R.P., 59000. **Currency exchange** and **telephones.** Open Mon.-Fri. 8am-7pm, Sat. 8am-noon. Branch office, behind the Vieille Bourse and pl. de Gaulle, on bd. Carnotard at pl. du Théâtre. Poste Restante address: Lille Bourse, 59001. Open Mon.-Fri. 8am-6:30pm, Sat. 8am-noon. **Postal Code:** 59000.

Flights: Aéroport de Lille-Lesquin (tel. 20 87 92 00). Fairly extensive service. Shuttles depart for the airport from the train station every 2-3 hrs. (25F). Contact the tourist office for schedules.

Trains: pl. de Gare (tel. 20 74 50 50). To: Paris (every 1-2 hr., 2-2½ hr., 144F); Calais and Boulogne (frequent service, 2½ hr., 67F and 86F respectively); Nice (3 per day, 10 hr., 547F); Lyon (3 per day, 5 hr., 356F). Information office open Mon.-Fri. 7:45am-8pm, Sat. 8:30am-7:30pm, Sun. and holidays 8am-8pm.

Buses: rue le Corbusier, next to the train station. **Metro Information Office,** pl. des Buisses, also next to the train station. Information for both, tel. 20 98 50 50.

Bookstore: Le Furet du Nord, pl. du Général de Gaulle (tel. 20 78 43 43). A 4-story monstrosity that claims to be the largest bookstore in Europe. Huge selection of travel guides, but none in English. Open Tues.-Sat. 10am-7pm, Mon. 2-7pm. **Book 'n Broc,** 17, rue Henri Kolb (tel. 20 40 10 02), off rue Léon Gambetta near pl. de la République. Gladly buys and sells English books.

Womens Center: Centre d'Information des Droits de la Femme, 17, quai du Wault (tel. 20 54 27 66). Sexual harrassment information. Open Mon.-Fri. 9am-12:30pm.

Laundromat: rue d'Arras at rue de Fontenoy. Open daily 6am-9pm. Another on rue Colbert. Open Mon.-Sat. 7:30am-8pm. A 3rd on rue Solferino. Open daily 7am-9pm. All charge around 20F per load.

Pharmacy: Grande Pharmacie de France, 3-5 rue Faidherbe (tel. 20 51 31 41). Open Mon.-Fri. 9am-7pm, Sat. 9am-12:30pm and 1:30-7pm.

Hospital: Cité Hospitalière (tel. 20 44 59 61), pl. de Verdun.

Police: 6bis, rue du Maréchal Vaillant (tel. 20 62 47 47). **Emergency,** tel. 17.

Accommodations

Decent hotels are expensive in Lille. Hotels cluster around the train station, but the area can be dangerous at night. Ask the tourist office or **CROUS,** 74, rue de Cambrai (tel. 20 56 93 40 or 20 52 84 00), about summer university housing, or about year-round *foyers.* (Open Mon.-Fri. 9am-noon and 2-4pm; Sept.-June Mon.-Fri. 9am-noon and 1-4pm.)

Auberge de Jeunesse (IYHF), 1, av. Julien Destrée (tel. 20 52 98 94), next to the Foire Internationale. Turn left down rue de Tournai from the train station. Take the pedestrian underpass beneath the highway, cross the parking lot, and go under the overpass. A newly renovated place with spacious, dormitory-type accommodations. Open daily 7-9am and 5-11pm. The 11pm curfew is strictly enforced. 50F, nonmembers 70F. Shower, sheets, and breakfast included. Camping in back 30F, nonmembers 40F.

Relais Européen de la Jeunesse (UCRIF), 40, rue de Thumesnil (tel. 20 52 69 75), in a shabby neighborhood 30 min. from the station. Large, comfortable, dormitory-style doubles. No curfew or lockout. Photo ID needed. 65F per person. Breakfast included. Bland, 3-course dinner 40F.

Hôtel Faidherbe, 42, pl. de la Gare (tel. 20 06 27 93). Immaculate but dimly lit. Sagging mattresses. Singles 85F, with shower 110F. Doubles 90F, with shower 120F. Breakfast 15F.

Hôtel Constantin, 5, rue des Fossés (tel. 20 54 32 26), near pl. Rihour. For a few more francs, you can escape from the station area into the agreeable pedestrian district. Most of the clean, spacious rooms overlook a flower-filled patio. Singles and doubles 80F, with shower 140F. Breakfast 17F.

Hôtel Chopin, 4, rue de Tournai (tel. 20 06 35 80). Small but comfortable. Affable proprietor. Singles 90F, with shower 110F. Doubles 100F, with shower 1130F.

Hôtel Paris-Nord, 14, rue du Molinel (tel. 20 06 27 54). Plain rooms on a side street near the station. Singles and doubles 70-120F, with shower 130F.

Camping: Les Ramiers (tel. 20 23 13 42), 52, rue César Loriden in Bondues. Take the bus from Lille to Bondues Centre. Open April-Oct. For more information about camping in the area, call **Camping Club de Lille,** 13, rue Baggio (tel. 20 53 77 40).

Food

Inexpensive restaurants and cafés cluster in the fashionable pedestrian area around **rue de Béthune,** a neighborhood also filled with *patisseries, boulangeries,* pizzerias, and ice cream stands. Most cafés are open from breakfast until 1am. Lille is known for its mussels, fish, cheese, and *genièvre* (juniper berry liqueur). Pick up edibles and wearables every Sunday at the **Marché de Wazemmes** (8am-1pm). **Supermarkets** are located on rue Léon Gambetta and on rue de Paris at av. Pres. Kennedy. (Open Tues.-Sat. 8:30am-12:30pm and 3-7pm, Mon. 3-7pm.)

Aux Moules, 34, rue de Béthune. *Lillois* come here to pack away mussels, mussels, and more mussels (31-47F). Open daily 11:30am-11:30pm.

Grillop's, 20, rue Anatole-France, behind the theater. Delicious pizza (35-47F) and pasta (35-44F) among marble statues and mirrored pipes. Open Mon.-Sat. noon-2:30pm and 7:30pm-midnight.

La Crêperie de Beaurepaire, 1, rue St-Etienne, in an alleylike street parallel to rue Nationale, 2 blocks from pl. de Gaulle. Sit in the cobblestone courtyard or join the students indoors.

Galettes 11-45F, dessert *crêpes* 11-30F, and delicious cider. Open Mon.-Sat. 11:45am-2pm and 7-10:45pm.

Bistro Romain, 20-22, pl. Rihour (tel. 20 54 53 69). Elegant restaurant featuring superb French *nouvelle cuisine*. 55F and 69F *menus*. Open daily 11:30am-3pm and 6:30pm-1am.

Café Leffe, 1, pl. Rihour. Two floors packed with that in crowd. Beers from around the world and typical café fare (9.50-28F). Open daily 7am-2am.

Sights and Entertainment

Generally considered one of France's finest museums, Lille's **Musée des Beaux Arts** gathers works by Rubens, Goya, el Greco, David, Delacroix, Renoir, and Picasso in a 19th-century building on pl. de la République. (Open Wed.-Mon. 9:30am-12:30pm and 2-6pm. Admission 10F.) The **Museum of Natural History and of Geology** features Egyptian mummies, two-headed **mutant cows,** and more conventional stuffed animals from around Europe. (Open Wed. and Sat. 10am-4pm, 5F.) Charles de Gaulle's birthplace at 9, rue Princesse has a vast collection of photographs and newspaper clippings on the leader of the *Résistance*. (Open Wed.-Sun. 10am-noon and 2-5pm. Admission 7F, children 2F.) Your ticket to the Musée des Beaux Arts also admits you to the **Musée de l'Hospice Comtesse,** 32, rue de la Monnaie, founded in 1237 by the Comtesse de Flandre and used as a hospital in the 15th century. The museum displays some old furniture and art works but is most notable for the beautiful Flemish tilework on its walls. (Open Wed.-Mon. 10am-12:30pm and 2-6pm; free Wed. and Sat. afternoon.) Just off rue de la Monnaie (entrance off rue du Cirque) **Cathédrale de Notre Dame de la Treille,** is an unfinished neo-Gothic church begun in the last century. Despite the unappealing brick of the west façade, the church contains some fine chapels and interesting choir masonry, and, in the crypt, the **Musée Diocésain d'Art Religieux.** (Open Sat. 4-5pm, 1st Sun. of each month 11am-noon. Free.)

The **Vieille Bourse** (Old Stock Exchange), on pl. de Gaulle between rue des Sept Acaches and rue Manneliers, is yet another Flemish Renaissance masterpiece. This courtyard, once the only stock exchange in France, now serves as a daily book and flower market. (Open Wed.-Tues.)

The ancient, star-shaped **citadelle** on the north side of Lille was restored in the 17th century by the Marquis de Vauban, as were many of the fortresses in this area. To enter this active army base, you must sign up for a group tour at the tourist office (Sun. 3-5pm only, 30F). Otherwise, settle for a view from the lovely **Jardin Vauban** across the street. The triumphal **Paris Gate** on bd. Louis XIV, used to lead to the main road connecting Lille to Paris. **Eglise St-Maurice,** a 14th-century blackened Gothic church near the station will initiate you into the mysteries of the Flemish *hallerkirk* style. (In case you didn't know, and we sneer if you didn't, that means five naves of equal height.)

Although the modern university lies several kilometers outside the city, most of its students live in Lille. At night you'll find a few specimens at **La Cave de Roi,** 97, rue Solferino (tel. 20 57 50 70), the only student disco that manages to stay popular year after year. The 30-50F cover includes your first drink. (Open daily 9am-late.) **Le Club 92,** 3, rue St-Etienne (tel. 20 57 08 34) also caters to a mainstream crowd. (Cover 25-50F. Open Mon.-Sat. 11pm-4am.) A slightly older group frequents **La Cave du Vieux Lille,** 55, rue Basse (tel. 20 06 61 31), a bar with weekend jazz concerts. 35F includes one cocktail. (Open daily 3pm-2am.)

The first weekend of September, Lille hosts "La Braderie," a terrific festival which clears the streets of cars and fills them with a city-wide flea market. *Lillois* peddle junk by day and blow their wad on mussels by night. For the past several years, Aux Moules (see Food) has captured the prestigious prize of being the city's most popular restaurant: its pyramid of empty mussel shells has outdone those of all other restaurants.

When Lille's excitement reaches apoplectic proportions, hop a frequent train to **St-Omer** (44F), 60km from Lille on the road to Calais and Dunkerque. Untouched by tourism, this town boasts 13th-century Basilique Notre-Dame, a ruined 15th-century abbey, a fine collection of Louis XV furniture and Delft ceramics, and even a few mussels.

Arras

Historians argue stodgily that the name Arras derives simply from *"arras,"* the hanging tapestries produced here during the 16th century. Legend, however, maintains that the name commemorates a guild of rats which overran the ill-fated city in the Middle Ages, pied pipers to the conquering king of France who came behind. Every year on Whit Sunday, the **Fête des Rats** pays homage *à rats* (to rats). Although badly damaged during the Revolution and again during the bitter trench warfare of 1914-1915, Arras retains many of its medieval buildings. Its finest Flemish treasures, Grande Place and Petite Place, display reconstructed Flemish façades identical to those on the Grande Place in Brussels. The thirty-odd war cemeteries in the surrounding area can be reached by train.

Orientation and Practical Information

Arras is on the main Paris-Lille line. To get to the tourist office and pl. des Héros from the train station, walk straight across pl. Foch, past the fountain, and onto rue Gambetta. Turn right onto rue Ronville (opposite the post office), and turn left to rue de la Housse, by the church of St-Jean Baptiste (5 min.). The tourist office is across the place, inside the left door of the Hôtel de Ville. The Grande Place is to the right, on the other side of the pl. des Héros.

Tourist Office: pl. des Héros (tel. 21 51 26 95), in the Hôtel de Ville. City map indicates accommodations. Regional and international information. Open Mon.-Fri. 9am-noon and 2-6pm, Sat. 9am-noon. and 2-5pm.

Post Office: rue Gambetta, 1 block from the train station. Open Mon.-Fri. 8am-6:30pm, Sat. 8am-noon. **Postal Code:** 62000.

Trains: pl. Maréchal Foch (tel. 21 71 00 42). Station open 24 hrs. Ticket office open daily 7:15am-7:15pm. Information hotline daily 7am-9pm (tel. 21 73 50 50). To: Paris (15 per day, 1½ hr., 115F); Lille via Douai (frequent service, 45 min., 41F); Dunkerque (10 per day, 1½ hr. 70F); Amiens (5 per day, 1 hr., 46F).

Buses: rue du Docteur Brassart (tel. 21 23 23 43), to the left of the train station. Inter-city buses only, with service to small towns in the Pas-de-Calais region as well as Lille (5 per day). Tourist office has schedule. **STCRA** runs city buses, all of which stop at the train station. Tickets 4.50F, *carnet* of 10 33F.

Laundromat: Superlav, pl. Vivani, near the tourist office. **Lavomatique,** rue Frédéric de Georges. About 22F per load. 10F and 1F coins only, but coin changers in laundromats. Both open daily 7am-8pm.

Hospital: 57, av. Winston Churchill (tel. 21 21 48 01). Take bus B, C, D, H, M, or Z from the station (every 10 min.).

Medical Emergency: SAMU, tel. 15.

Police: bd. de la Liberté (tel. 21 24 50 17). **Emergency,** tel. 17.

Accommodations, Camping, and Food

Cheap hotels are few and far between in Arras, and they fill up quickly during peak season.

Auberge de Jeunesse, 59, Grande Place (tel. 21 25 54 53). Sparkling clean and newly renovated, this centrally located hostel almost always has room. Excellent kitchen facilities. Open 7:30-10:30am and 5-11pm. Curfew 11pm. IYHF card required. 37F. Shower and sheets included.

Hôtel les Grandes Arcades, 12, Grande Place (tel. 21 23 30 89). Rundown rooms with sagging mattresses, but the location is ideal. Singles and doubles 82F and 95F. Triples 130F. Breakfast 21F. The restaurant downstairs is popular with local business people at lunch. 65 and 85F *menus.* Open Mon.-Sat. noon-2:30pm and 7-9:30pm.

Hôtel le Rallye, 9, rue Gambetta (tel. 21 51 44 96), close to the station. Small but clean rooms, all with TV. Noisy bar downstairs packed with young locals. Singles 100F and 125F. Doubles 125-165F. Renovations may raise prices.

Camping: 166 rue du Temple (tel. 21 71 55 06), at av. Fernand Lobbedez. From the train station, turn left on rue du Docteur Brassart, then left on av. du Maréchal Leclerc. Follow this street to the campground. Open April-Oct.

Inexpensive cafés line pl. des Héros; more elegant restaurants are found on the Grande Place. Genteel **Restaurant Montesilvano,** Grande Place, serves delicious salads (19-36F) and pizza topped with mussels and such (23-36F). (Open Sun.-Fri. noon-2pm and 7-11pm, Sat. 7-11pm.) **La Cave,** 50, Grande Place, is a popular place in—you guessed it—an old cellar. The 55F *menu* features a wide selection of dishes; more expensive house specialties include *choucroutes* (60F and 65F) and *maigret de canard* (duck, 90F). (Open Mon. noon-3pm, Tues.-Sat. noon-3pm and 7:30-11pm.) The **Grizzly Grill,** 36, bd. de Starbourg, vanquishes even the grizzliest appetite with its all-you-can-eat appetizers, salad bar, entrees, and bottomless glass of wine. At 79F per person this place ain't cheap, but locals swear on the stuffed Yogi by the door that it's worth it. (Open daily noon-3pm and 7-10:30pm.) The huge **Monoprix** supermarket on rue Gambetta across from the post office defies description. (Open Mon.-Sat. 9am-12:30pm and 1:45-7pm). Place des Héros and adjoining squares erupt in boisterous color every Wednesday and Saturday morning from 8am-1pm during Arras's open **market.**

Sights

The 15th-century **Hôtel de Ville** near the marketplace acquired a new façade in the early 16th century after a fire destroyed the original. Inside this purely French beauty, ask the concierge to take you upstairs to the municipal chamber, reception room, and marriage chamber, where all marriages officially take place. You can also ride the elevator to the top of the Hôtel's belfry. (Open same hours as tourist office. Admission 10F, students 4F, children 3F.) Serene **Grande Place** is surrounded by 155 homogeneous, 15th-century Flemish townhouses, whose first floors are collectively supported by 345 columns. This inspired Gothic composition was sliced down the middle by barbed wire during World War I when the French and Germans occupied opposite sides, yet it shows few battle scars. Boutiques, bars, and cafés line **place des Héros,** a block away.

Under the area around the town hall stretch Les Boves, 20km of interconnected subterranean **tunnels** built to house medieval chalk miners. They've served as refuges during different wars, most recently as a shelter and hospital for British soldiers during World War I. (Tours leave from the Hôtel de Ville Tues.-Sat. 10am-noon and 2-6pm, Sun. 10am-noon and 3-6:30pm; Oct.-April Tues.-Sat. 2-6pm, Sun. 10:30am-12:30pm and 3-6:30pm. ½-hr. tours 8F; 50-min. tours 17F, students 10F, children ½ price. Call 21 51 26 95 for information.)

After a thrilling day at Arras's dullish museums, recover at the **Oxford Bar,** below le Rallye hotel, which starts rocking around midnight with the help of hordes of college-age locals. Sample a meter of beer (10 glasses arranged on a meter-long board; the 11th is free) at the raucous **Café de la Plage,** 6, bd. Faidherbe. Disco fever stays alive at **Le Pago** in the Petite Place, where the cool crowd does the Bus-Stop until dawn. Cover 50F.

Near Arras

The site of heavy fighting during World War I, the area surrounding Arras is dotted with 30 war cemeteries and countless unmarked graves. The medieval town of **Douai** is also worth a stopover. Trains leave frequently from Arras to many small towns in the region, but groups traveling to more than one site may save time and money by renting a car or hiring a cab.

Eight km northeast of Arras along the RN25 is the **Vimy Memorial** (tel. 21 48 98 97), a monument to the 75,000 Canadians killed in World War I. Tours of the trenches, tunnels, and the memorial are given by extremely lively young Canadian guides brimming with information about the war as well as less weighty subjects such as nightlife in Arras. The 11,285 trees planted in the park represent the number of Canadian soldiers whose final resting place is unknown. (Open daily 10am-6pm; tours April-Nov. 15. Free.) Trains run infrequently to Vimy, and you still have to hike from the station to the memorial (22F round-trip). **Allo Taxi** (tel. 21 58 18 17) will either deliver you to the foot of the memorial or follow a more scenic route through the area's cemeteries, but they charge 70-80F each way.

Further west along the A26 lies **Neuville-St-Vaast,** the resting place of over 400,000 German soldiers. The rows of black crosses and civilian tombstones are as impressive as those of the D-Day beaches in Normandy, especially when one remembers that each cross represents four fallen soldiers. North of Neuville on the A25 is the French cemetery, basilica, and museum of **Notre Dame de Lorette.** 200,000 French soldiers of World War I rest here beneath rows of white crosses. (Open May-Sept. 8am-6pm, Dec.-Jan. 9am-4:30pm, Feb.-Mar. and Oct.-Nov. 8:30am-5pm. Entrance to the museum 10F, children 5F).

Twenty minutes from Arras by train is the sleepy town of **Douai** (pop. 45,000). Local excitement climaxes on Wednesday, when a cheese, fruit, and flower market fills pl. Carnot (8am-noon). The rest of the week, visitors will have to content themselves with Douai's modest permanent attractions.

A former convent, the **Chartreuse,** rue des Chartreux, now serves as the **Musée de Douai;** works by Van Dyck, Rubens, Corot, Renoir, and Rodin vie for attention. (Open Mon. and Wed.-Sat. 10am-noon and 2-5pm, Sun. and holidays 3-6pm. Admission 7.90F, students and children 3.95F.) Rising out of the Hôtel de Ville and topped by a sculpted lion, Douai's **beffroi** (belfry) contains Europe's largest single collection of bells. In addition to pealing every half hour, the *carillon* (bell collection) is rung in concert every Saturday (10:45-11:45am) and holidays (11am-noon). (Open Mon.-Fri. and Sun. 10am-noon and 2:30-5:30pm; Sept.-March Sun. 2:30-5:30pm; April-June Mon.-Fri. 10am-noon and 2:30-5:30pm, Sun. 2:30-5:30pm. Admission 7.90F, students 3.95F.) As late as the 15th century, Douai was entirely surrounded by a thick wall, broken only by gates leading to roads to nearby cities. Only the **Porte d'Arras,** and the more impressive **Porte de Valenciennes** remain. From July 1 to 7, the town more than doubles in size for the annual **Fêtes de Gayant** (Festivals of the Giant); a family of enormous mannequins parades through the streets before nightly concerts, exhibitions, and sporting events.

Trains run to Paris-Nord (every 2 hr., 2 hr., 128F), Arras (every hr., 20 min., 21F), and Lille (every hr., ½-hr., 26F). The **tourist office** (tel. 27 88 26 79) is in the Hôtel du Dauphin, 70, pl. d'Armes. (Open Mon. 10am-noon and 2-6pm, Tues.-Fri. 9am-noon and 2-6pm, Sat. 2-6pm.) To reach the tourist office from the train station, cross pl. de la Gare and turn left on av. du Maréchal Leclerc; follow this for several blocks. When you pass the **post office** on your right, turn right onto pl. d'Armes.

Amiens

" . . . Of Gothic, mind you!" exulted John Ruskin about the Amiens Cathedral, "Gothic clear of Roman tradition, and of Arabian taint; Gothic pure, authoritative, unsurpassable, and inaccessible." When the leaders of Amiens decided to rebuild their **Cathédrale de Notre Dame** in 1220, they sought to outdo the achievements at Paris and Laon. By cutting the classic Gothic cathedral design from four floors to three, they were able to incorporate taller arches, making the cathedral seem a leviathan even by French Gothic standards. Including the astoundingly complex west façade, the cathedral contains some 4000 figures tracing the episodes of the Old and New Testaments. (Open daily 7:30am-noon and 2-7pm.) (Treasury open Mon.-Sat. 10am-noon and 2-6pm. Admission 10F, children 5F.) *Son et lumière* transform the cathedral nightly from mid-April through mid-October. (Tues.-Sat. 45F. Shows available in English; check times in the information booth outside the cathedral.)

Aside from its cathedral, Amiens (pop. 150,000) is not an especially attractive or interesting city. The home of **Jules Verne**, at the corner of rue Charles Dubois and rue Jules Verne, is the brightest star in a rather dull firmament of museums. (Open Tues.-Sat. 9:30am-noon and 2-6pm.) This early science fiction writer lies .00046 leagues under in the **Cimetière de la Madeleine.** The **Quartier St-Leu** on the Somme and the *Hortillonages* (market gardens) northeast of the city may be worth a trip. The capital of the Picardie region, Amiens itself seems all but dead except on Saturday nights and during festivals.

Amiens hosts an international **Jazz Festival** during one week in May; trumpets bop and walking basses stroll in local clubs and public plazas. Also popular are the **Cinéma Festival** in November and the **Fête d'Amiens,** a great party the city throws for itself one weekend in June. Call the **Maison de la Culture** for dates and further information.

Orientation and Practical Information

Direct rail links connect Amiens to Rouen, Boulogne, Arras, and Paris. To reach the center of town from the train station at the east end of town, head down rue de Noyon. The street changes names several times, eventually becoming rue des Trois Cailloux when it runs into pl. Gambetta. The cathedral and one of the tourist offices are off to your right down rue des Sergents; rue de la République is to your left. Continue straight down rue Delambre, which turns into rue Gresset, and the main tourist office is in front of you on the right, in the Maison de la Culture. Keep in mind that literally every business establishment closes between noon and 2:00pm to accommodate the restaurants, which open for lunch at that time. At night, lone travelers should avoid the Cirque area.

Tourist Office: rue Jean Catelas (tel. 22 91 79 28), in the Maison de la Culture. English spoken. Open Mon.-Sat. 10am-12:15pm and 2-7pm. Branch office outside the cathedral, 20, pl. de Notre Dame. Open June to mid-Oct. daily 10am-12:15pm and 2-6pm. Also an office in the train station. Open Mon.-Sat. 9am-6pm, Sun. and holidays 9am-noon and 2-6pm. All can book hotel rooms. **CROUS,** 25, rue St-Leu (tel. 22 91 84 33). Be sure to call or visit if you're staying a while. Books cheap university housing, sells student meal tickets and BIJ/Transalpino tickets. Babysitting and job placement services too. Open Mon.-Fri. 9am-5pm.

Post Office: 7, rue des Vergeaux, 2 long blocks from the cathedral. **Telephones.** Open Mon.-Fri. 8am-7pm, Sat. 8am-noon. **Postal Code:** 80000.

Trains: Gare du Nord (tel. 22 92 50 50), pl. Alphonse Fiquet. To: Paris (frequent, 1½ hr., 81F); Calais via Boulogne (7 per day, 2¼ hr., 98F); Lille (12 per day, 1½ hr., 71F); Laon (5 per day, 1½ hr., 67F). Information office open Mon.-Sat. 8am-7:15pm, Sun. 9am-noon and 2-6:20pm.

Buses: Les Courriers Automobiles Picards, 6, rue de L'Oratoire (tel. 22 91 46 82). Buses leave to points in northern France from rue Jules Barni, to the left of the train station. **SEMTA** (tel. 22 43 84 00). All city buses stop at pl. Alphonse Fiquet, in front of the train station. **Pharmacy: Grande Pharmacie de Paris,** 4, pl. Gambetta (tel. 22 81 67 22). Open Mon. 1-7pm, Tues.-Sat. 9am-7pm.

Hospital: pl. Victor Pauchet (tel. 22 44 25 25).

Police: rue des Jacobins (tel. 22 92 06 43). **Emergency,** tel. 17.

Accommodations, Camping, and Food

Finding a room in Amiens should pose no problem; check out the large concentration of hotels located in the center of town. The tourist offices have a complete list. University singles are available July through September (42F). Check with CROUS.

Auberge de Jeunesse (IYHF) (tel. 22 44 54 21), on an unnamed street off bd. Beauville, 1km from the station. Turn right from the station onto bd. d'Alsace Lorraine and follow the signs for the campground. Turn left before the Elf station, at the sign reading *Accès Piétons.* The hostel is by a lake, in the middle of the campground. Spectacular view of the cathedral. Large, plain 20-bed dormitories. Hot water in morning only. Office open daily 7am-noon and 2-8pm.

No morning lockout. Curfew 10:30pm. IYHF card required. 37F per night. Sleep sacks included. Kitchen facilities but no breakfast. Open mid-March to mid-Dec.

Hôtel de la Renaissance, 8bis, rue André (tel. 22 91 70 23), on pl. de Notre Dame by the cathedral. Clean, small rooms in the center of town. Singles 80-100F, doubles 90-110F. Breakfast 15F.

Hôtel l'Unick, 45, rue Jules Barni (tel. 22 91 80 02), behind the train station. Sagging mattresses in tiny rooms, but the lowest price of the hotels near the station. Singles and doubles from 85-130F.

Camping: Municipal de l'Etang St-Pierre (tel. 22 44 54 21), by the youth hostel. Moderate site with a splendid view of the cathedral. 4.20F per person, 2.30F per site, 2.30F per car. Open year-round.

Local dishes include *pâté de canard* (duck *pâté*), *"tuiles amieénoises"* (chocolate and almond macaroons), and *ficelle picarde* (a stuffed *crêpe*). CROUS has information about university restaurants and sells meal tickets (15F). Intimate **Le Belu,** 63 rue Belu, in the Quartier St-Lou, serves regional specialities (37-55F) to students who gather at riverside tables. (Open daily noon-2pm and 6-10:30pm. Café open daily 10am-midnight.) The 40F *menu* at frenetic **Le Mangeoire,** 3 rue des Sergents, includes two *galettes,* a *crêpe,* and wine or cider.) Open Tues.-Sat. 11:30am-2:30pm and 5-11pm.) For cheap cafeteria fare (20-40F, pick up a tray at **Miami,** 44/50 rue des Trois Cailloux. (Open daily 11:30am-10pm.)

Laon

One of the little-known attractions of northern France, Laon (pop. 30,000) rests on a 100m hill in the midst of flat land, an unexpected butte crowned by a magnificent cathedral and humbler whitewashed stone buildings. To reach the *haute ville,* climb the steep public stairway straight ahead of the train station or hop on the brand-new POMA 2000 cable car system, which leaves frequently from the station. The capital of France under the Carolingian kings and the birthplace of Roland, Charlemagne's legendary companion, Laon witnessed the construction of France's great Gothic cathedral. Begun in 1160, **Cathédrale de Notre Dame** has an extraordinary west façade depicting the always cheering story of the Last Judgment. (Open daily 8am-7pm.) During guided tours, visitors may be allowed to climb the cathedral's towers. (25F, 20F students; consult the tourist office for times.) Less fanciful **Eglise St-Martin,** at the other end of the *haute ville,* is an example of primitive Gothic architecture from the 12th and 13th centuries. To visit the interior, ask at 4, av. de la République. Two blocks from Notre-Dame on rue Georges Hermant are the **Musée Municipale,** with its distinguished collection of Greek vases, and the charming 13th-century **Chapelle des Templiers.** Inside stand two statues of prophets that once supported the cathedral façade and the carved 14th-century "skeleton" of Guillaume de Harcigny, physician to Charles VI. (Both open Wed.-Mon. 10am-noon and 2-6pm; Oct.-March 10am-noon and 2-5pm. Admission 7F, students 3.50F.)

Hotels and restaurants in Laon tend to be expensive. The cheapest place in town is the **Maison des Jeunes,** 20, rue du Cloître (tel. 23 20 27 64). A *foyer* for students and young workers, this unattractive place features toilets that don't flush and a single pipe in the wall masquerading as a "shower." (No curfew. 65F per night. Breakfast and sheets included. Reserve 2-3 days in advance July-Aug.) While hotels in the *haute ville* run upwards of 120F per night, several budget establishments hold out along av. Carnot by the train station. **Le Vauclair,**16, av. Carnot (tel. 23 23 02 08), has modern singles (75-105F) and doubles (145F). **Les Chevaliers,** 3, rue Serrurier, serves excellent regional specialties for 40-60F. (Open Mon.-Fri. noon-2pm and 7-9pm.) The **Agora Crêperie** at rue des Cordeliers at rue de la Herse, features a 35F *menu,* and *crêpes* and *galettes* for 10-24F. (Open Mon.-Fri. 11:45am-2:30pm and 7pm-midnight, Sat. 7pm-midnight, Sun. 11:45am-2:30pm.)

Laon's **tourist office,** pl. du Parvis (tel. 23 20 28 62), next to the cathedral, distributes maps and gives guided tours by appointment only. The staff speaks some English. (Open Mon.-Sat. 9am-12:30pm and 2-6:30pm, Sun. 10am-noon and 2-6:30pm; Nov.-Feb. Mon.-Sat. 9am-noon and 2-6pm.) Direct trains run to Paris (frequent, 1½ hr., 82F), Reims (5 per day, 1 hr., 37F), and Amiens (6 per day, 1½ hr., 64F). Other destinations are only indirectly accessible. (Information office (tel. 23 23 23 35) open Mon.-Sat. 9am-noon and 2-6pm.)

Compiègne

Tranquil Compiègne (pop. 45,000) seems to have a knack for ending wars. The English captured Joan of Arc here in 1429, and the armistice ending World War I was signed on November 11, 1918 in a forest clearing about 6 km away. The town's luck, however, did not hold out for Hitler, who tried and failed to force the French to surrender at the same spot in 1940. Compiègne's 17th-century château, three unusual museums, and a web of hiking trails lure numerous daytrippers from nearby Paris. The center is sufficiently compact that wandering mapless among its winding, cobblestone streets may well be the best way to explore this historic town.

Orientation and Practical Information

Compiègne is an hour from Paris's Gare du Nord and easily accessible from Amiens or Laon. The train station is across the river from the center of town. To get to the center of town, cross pl. de la Gare in front of the station, turn right, and then turn left onto the bridge. Follow this road to the center and to the tourist office in the Hôtel de Ville. Free bus service runs throughout town from the train station, with most buses stopping at the Hôtel de Ville.

Tourist Office: pl. de l'Hôtel de Ville (tel. 44 40 01 00), in the Hôtel de Ville. Free pamphlet/map of hotels and restaurants. English spoken. List of sights with hours and prices. Simple map of the town is free, but shell out 5F for a detailed one if you plan to stay a while. Open Easter-Oct. Mon.-Tues. and Thurs.-Fri. 9am-noon and 1:45-6pm, Wed. and Sat. 9am-noon and 1:30-6pm, Sun. 9:30am-12:30pm and 2:30-5:30pm. **CROUS,** 6bis, rue Winston Churchill (tel. 44 20 36 28). Housing and meal tickets year round. Open Mon.-Fri. 8:30am-noon and 1:30-7pm.

Post Office: rue des Domeliers (tel. 44 40 13 88). Open Mon.-Fri. 8am-7pm, Sat. 8am-noon. **Postal Code:** 60200.

Trains: pl. de la Gare (tel. 44 21 50 50). To: Paris (frequent service, 1 hr., 55F); Amiens (mornings and early evenings only, 1-1½ hr., 51F); Laon (5-6 per day, 1½ hr., 49F); Lille (via Creil or Aulnoye, 5-6 per day, 3 hr., 126F); Noyon (5-6 per day, ½-hr., 21F). Information office open Mon.-Sat. 8:45am-12:30pm and 1-7:30pm, Sun. 8:30am-noon and 2:45-5pm.

Buses: Cars Acary, 10, rue d'Amiens (tel. 44 83 36 26). City and local buses leave from pl. de la Gare. Daily buses to Paris and Noyon slightly cheaper than the train. The tourist office has a complete schedule of intra-city stops, as well as those in surrounding areas. There are also 2 private bus companies in Compiègne: **Cars Charlot,** rue du Pont des Rets (tel. 44 40 21 09), in Choisy-au-Bac, with buses to and from Pierrefonds. Also **Cars STEPA,** 1, rue d'Amiens (tel. 44 83 38 75).

Bicycle Rental: Picardie Forets Verts, 10, pl. du Palais (tel. 44 40 22 65). Excellent bikes 100F per day, 480F per week. Mountain bikes 130F per day, 560F per week. ID card needed for deposit. Also provides maps and advice on good biking routes. Open daily 9:30am-7pm. Sat. afternoon and Sun. they move down the road to the *Carrefour Regional,* next to the campground.

Laundromat: Le Lavoir, 29, rue du Port à Bateaux. Wash 22F. Dryers 3F for 5 min. 10 and 2F coins only, but there is a coin changer. Detergent 1F. Open daily 7:30am-9pm. **Pharmacy: Pharmacie St-Jacques,** pl. St-Jacques (tel. 44 40 04 40). Open Tues.-Sat. 8:30am-12:15pm and 1:45-7pm.

Medical Emergency: Hôpital Général, 42, rue de Paris (tel. 44 20 99 20).

Police rue de la Surveillance (tel 44 40 13 80). **Police** tel. 17.

Accommodations and Camping

Compiègne has a shortage of cheap rooms. During the summer, start looking early in the morning or reserve a few days in advance.

Auberge de Jeunesse (IYHF), 6, rue Pasteur (tel. 44 40 72 64), at the end of rue des Cordeliers. From the train station, cross pl. de la Gare and turn right. Take a left onto the bridge, walk past the town hall, and turn right onto rue des Cordeliers. Simple hostel with 2 large dormitories, outdoor toilets and showers, and peeling paint. Reception open 7-10am and 5-10pm. 10pm curfew. Members only. 30F. Sheets 11F. Use of kitchen 8F.

Hôtel St-Antoine, 17, rue de Paris (tel. 44 23 22 27). Tiny but well-kept rooms in a quiet neighborhood. Managed by a kindly couple who also run the restaurant downstairs. Singles from 85F. Doubles from 110F. Breakfast 20F.

Le But Hôtel, 35, cours Guynemer (tel. 44 23 31 06), on the river. Decent rooms above a slightly raucous *brasserie*. Singles and doubles 65-75F. Breakfast 15F. Reservations recommended. Hotel and restaurant open Aug.-June Sat.-Thurs.

Camping: Camping Municipal (tel. 44 20 28 58), av. du Baron R. de Soultrait, in the Forêt de Compiègne. From Palais National, follow av. Royale southeast out of town for 2km. Beautifully situated on a 5km stretch of "Beaux Monts," the palace grounds designed by Napoleon in 1810 as a gift for his wife, Marie-Louisa. Clean but crowded. 6.50F per person, under 7 2.20F. 11F per site. Showers 5.70F. Open March 15-Nov. 15.

Food

Compiègne's few restaurants seem to all be pizzerias. **Les Halles du Grenier à Sel,** on rue de Lombard at rue de l'Etoile has a huge variety of fresh produce and cheese. (Open Mon.-Fri. 8:30am-12:30pm and 3-7pm, Sat. 7am-6pm.)

Le Phnom Penh, 13, rue des Lombards in the pedestrian zone. The three-course lunch *menu* (51F) is delicious but not quite filling. Cambodian dishes 38-58F. Open Sun. and Tues.-Fri. noon-2:30pm and 7-9:30pm, Sat. noon-2:30pm.

La Closeraie, 37, rue Solferino. Standard self-serve cafeteria with tasty dishes for 20-40F. Pitcher of wine 5.70F. Open Mon.-Fri. 11:30am-2pm and 6:30-9:30pm, Sat. 11:30am-2pm and 6:30-10pm.

La Galette de Marie, 14, rue des Patissiers, by the town hall. Crisp tablecloths and excellent prices. *Galettes* 7-35F, dessert *crêpes* 5.50-28F. Open Tues.-Thurs. 11:30am-9:30pm and Fri.-Sat. 11:30am-10:30pm.

Le Stromboli, 2, rue des Lombards. One of the better Italian restaurants in Compiègne. Eat pizza (30-49F) by candlelight. Open daily noon-2pm and 7-9:30pm.

Sights

Built for Louis XV as a summer "country cottage" and later serving as a second home for Napoleon, the **Palais National** contains 18th-century furniture and decorations and is surrounded by beautiful gardens. The palace also includes the **Musée du Second Empire** (tel. 44 40 02 02) and **Musée de la Voiture** (tel. 44 40 04 37), full of antique bicycles, tricycles for two, and carriages, including the ostentatiously painted vehicles in which Napoleon and Marie Antoinette used to go joyriding (not together, of course). (Ticket for all 3 museums 23F; students, seniors, and on Sun. and holidays 12F.) The only way you can visit the palace is to take a tour with a guide armed with an exhausting supply of anecdotes. (Tours every 15 min. Wed.-Mon. 9:30am-noon and 1:30-5pm. Last admission ½-hr. before closing.) The **Musée de la Figurine Historique,** in the annex of the Hôtel de Ville (tel. 44 40 72 55), contains a charming collection of toy kings, soldiers, and commoners reenacting highlights of French history. Its centerpiece is a fully staged Battle of Waterloo. (Open Tues.-Sun. 9am-noon and 2-6pm; Nov.-Feb. 9am-noon and 2-5pm. Admission 9F, students 5F. Wed. free for students.)

The château's beautifully maintained park makes an excellent picnic spot. Wander through the gilded gate to the edge of the gardens and you'll find yourself in the untamed **Forêt de Compiègne.** Long the hunting ground of kings, it's now ideal for strolling, biking, or horseback riding (inquire at the tourist office). Six km into the forest is the **Clairière de l'Armistice** (Armistice Clearing), where the treaty that ended World War I was signed in a railway carriage, now berthed in a small museum with a simple monument. (Open daily 8am-noon and 1:30-6:30pm; Nov.-March Wed.-Mon. 9am-noon and 2-5:30pm. Admission 3F.)

Twenty km from Compiègne along D973 sits the medieval **Château de Pierrefonds,** an imposing, turreted fortress entirely restored by Viollet-le-Duc under Napoleon III. (Open Wed.-Sat. and Mon. 9:30am-6pm, Sun. 9:30am-7pm; Oct.-March Wed.-Sun. 10am-noon and 2-4:30pm; last entry ½-hr. before closing. Admission 23F, ages 18-25 and seniors 12F, under 18 5F.) Several walking paths cross the forest around the town of **Pierrefonds.** Cars Charlot (tel. 44 40 21 09) sends three buses per day to Pierrefonds from quai #2 at the train station in Compiègne (Mon.-Sat.). The Compiègne tourist office has timetables. Pierrefond's **tourist office** (tel. 44 42 81 44) is on pl. de l'Hôtel de Ville. (Open April 15-Oct. 15 Wed.-Mon. 10am-noon and 2-6pm.)

Noyon

Noyon (pop. 15,000), the smallest of the great cathedral towns of the north, lies 24km northeast of Compiègne along the N32. Despite Norman and Spanish invasions and occupations during both World Wars, the *Noyonnais* can claim quite an illustrious past. Charlemagne was crowned King of Neustrie here in 768, and Hugh Capet's coronation as King of France took place in 987. John Calvin, renowned French Protestant, was born in this primarily Catholic town in 1509. His restored birthplace (tel. 44 44 03 59), on pl. Aristide Briand, contains pictures, engravings, and Calvin's original works on the Reformation. (Admission 8F. Open April-Oct. Wed.-Mon. 10am-noon and 2:30-5pm. Other times by appointment.) Although one of the earliest and purest Gothic cathedrals, Noyon's 12th-century **Cathédrale de Notre Dame** displays renegade Romanesque elements in its second-story arches. (Open daily 9am-noon and 2-6pm; mid-Oct. to mid-April 9am-noon and 2-4pm.) Flanking the cathedral, the 15th-century **bibliothèque** displays a 9th-century illuminated gospel and some 4000 other precious volumes. (Guided visits only; call the tourist office one week in advance.) *Noyonnais* gather every second Sunday of July for the bizarre **Marché aux Fruits Rouges,** a festival devoted entirely to trading recipes and selling cherries, strawberries, and currants. The highlight of the day is the question-and-answer session given by Nicolas le Jardinier (Nicholas the Gardener), who addresses individual problems with growing red fruits. (The inevitable questions about glowing Red fruits are redirected to Chernobyl scientists.)

Noyon's **tourist office,** pl. de l'Hôtel de Ville (tel. 44 44 02 97), passes out handsigned welcome cards from the mayor and suggests daytrips. (Open Mon.-Sat. 9:30am-noon and 2:30-6:30pm, Sun. 9:30am-noon; Oct.-May Tues.-Sat. 2-6pm.) Ask about excursions to the majestic **Abbaye Notre-Dame d'Ourscamp** (tel. 44 76 98 08), 15km toward Compiègne in tiny **Chiry-Ourscamp.** If you want to stay in Noyon, head for **Hôtel le Balto,** 18, pl de l'Hôtel de Ville (tel. 44 44 01 95), where the freshly painted rooms all have polished wood floors. (Singles and doubles 78-86F, triples 130F. Breakfast 17F.) **Camping "La Montagne,"** 3, rue de Chêne (tel. 44 76 98 29), is 3km away toward Ourscamp. (7F per adult, 2.10F per child, 2.50F per car. Shower 4F.) A small group of restaurants off bd. Mony post 45-55F *menus.* **La Galimafree Crêperie,** 27, rue J. Abel LeFranc, off pl. St-Martin, rolls tasty *crêpes* (7.50-37F) and offers a 36F *menu* and 20F children's *menu.* (Open Tues.-Sat. noon-2:30pm and 6-10pm, Sun. 5:30-10pm.)

Trains run to Noyon from Compiègne (3 per day, 15 min., 20F), Paris's Gare du Nord (11 per day, 1-1½ hr., 64F), and Laon (3 per day, change at Tergnier, 1 hr., 37F). **Trains** leave Noyon for Compiègne (5 per day), Paris (7 per day), and Laon (6 per day). The ticket office (tel. 44 21 50 50) at the station is open Monday through Friday 5am to 9:40pm, Saturday 5am to 6:30pm.

INDEX